ANTHONY TROLLOPE

Cartoon by Frederick Waddy for *Once a Week*, 1872. See p. 594.

Anthony Trollope

A Victorian in His World

Richard Mullen

Frederic C. Beil

Savannah

First published in 1990 by
Gerald Duckworth & Co., Ltd., London
First American edition published in 1992 by
Frederic C. Beil, Publisher
414 Tattnall Street
Savannah, Ga. 31401

ISBN 0-913720-77-1

Library of Congress Cataloging-in-Publication Data
Mullen, Richard.
    Anthony Trollope: A Victorian in his world/
    by Richard Mullen.
    p. cm.
    Includes bibliographical references and index.
    1. Trollope, Anthony, 1815–1882—Biography.
    2. Novelists, English—19th century—Biography.
    I. Title.
    PR5686.M84   1991
    823'.8—dc20   91-16912
    [B]   CIP

Printed in the United States of America

Contents

Plates between pages 400 and 401

Preface

One of the things that would most surprise Anthony Trollope about the late twentieth century is the tremendous popularity of his novels. Radio and television adaptations have made his name familiar to millions. Two elegant editions of his novels are being brought out in Britain with a third in the United States and almost all of his forty-seven novels are now available in paperback.

'The man of letters', Trollope wrote, 'is, in truth, writing his own biography. What there is in his mind, is being declared to the world at large by himself.' Few authors have declared their mind to the world so frequently as Anthony Trollope. The problem is that the world to which he declared it has changed and, in some cases, ceased to exist. When I first came to read Trollope, more than twenty years ago, I felt that his books offered the best, as well as the most enjoyable, introduction to the world of Victorian England. It was some time before I realised that he also offered the same insight to what he called 'the English World' – those countries and peoples who draw their language, literature and traditions from English soil.

My purpose in this biography is to place Trollope clearly in his world. His life and his forty-seven novels can only be appreciated by understanding the politics and issues of his time. In particular I was struck with the importance of religion to Trollope, something that had received surprisingly little attention. This was all the more amazing in the case of a writer who is best remembered for his portrayals of archdeacons, deans, bishops and bishops' wives. For many years I have been searching for those details that put Trollope in the perspective of his time as I have been at work on other great Victorians: from the Queen herself to Edward FitzGerald, who in his draughty Suffolk cottage listened to a village boy reading him novel after novel by Trollope.

In one of these novels, *Ralph the Heir*, Trollope depicts a character who is unable to complete a biography of Sir Francis Bacon: 'Days go by and weeks; and then months and years ... The dream of youth becomes the doubt of middle life ... '. At times I looked with dread at the conclusion of that sentence, 'and then the despair of age.' However, I then came across a letter Trollope wrote to an unknown correspondent when he was working on *Barchester Towers*: 'Pray know that when a man begins writing a book he never gives over. The evil with which he is beset is as inveterate as drinking – as exciting as gambling.' Anyone who attempts a biography of a man who wrote as much as Anthony Trollope would feel this, at least anyone not content 'to scrape together a few facts, to indulge in some fiction, to tell a few anecdotes, and then to call his book a biography'. Trollope, of course, told his own life in one of the greatest autobiographies in the language; yet, for all its radiant honesty, it did not, as he himself admits, tell the whole story.

The essence of Trollope's life, as I see it, was his desire to be respected as a serious writer. No matter how proud, justly proud, he was of his novels, he yearned to play an influential role in public life. He had, of course, already done so in his work as one of the main figures in that most extensive of all Victorian improvements, the Post Office. There is a monument to him as the originator of the pillar box in every village and town throughout the British Isles. Yet he wanted to have a more direct influence on his age and particularly on what he regarded as its greatest glory: the spread of English civilisation into every part of the world.

I soon came to the conclusion that Trollope's non-fiction, particularly those travel books describing his experiences in every English-speaking country, gives the best portrayal of his personality and the best insight into his mind. His articles, especially those on British and American politics, add to this picture of Trollope as a serious writer. I see his non-fiction as the key to his fiction. Naturally and rightly Trollope will survive as a novelist, but those wonderful novels can only be completely understood by seeing them in the light of his time. Nor do I think his novels can be fully appreciated without some understanding of the way in which Victorians wrote, published and read books, something I have discussed in Chapter Five.

As I proceeded with my research, I became convinced that there were two central figures in Trollope's life: his mother, who launched the family business of writing novels, and his wife, Rose, whom I have tried – I hope successfully – to rescue from the shadows. Without these two women I do not think the nineteenth, let alone the twentieth, century would have known the name and the genius of Anthony Trollope. To know Trollope is to gain an introduction not only into his world but also into that most complex of creations: the human personality.

I am happy to say, at the end of my labours, what Trollope said at the beginning of his biography of Cicero: 'I may say with truth that my book has sprung from love of the man, and from a heartfelt admiration of his virtues and his conduct as well as his gifts.'

19 August 1989   R.M.
Oxford

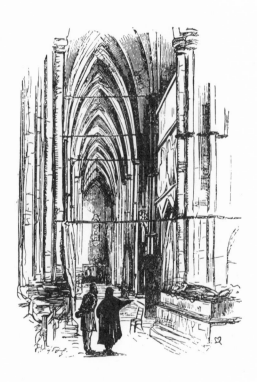

Acknowledgments

I would first wish to thank Her Majesty the Queen for gracious permission to consult and quote from manuscripts in the Royal Archives and to use material held under Crown copyright.

Anyone who embarks on a biography of Anthony Trollope is conscious of a debt to many other authors, most notably to Thomas Escott, his first biographer, who had the advantage of knowing his subject, and to Michael Sadleir both for his *Commentary* and perhaps even more for his *Bibliography*, an amazing piece of erudition. Two American scholars have also added greatly to our knowledge of Trollope by their editions of his letters: first, Bradford Booth and then, more recently, N. John Hall, responsible for the definitive edition of Trollope's correspondence. I have always been struck by both scholars' thoroughness when I read the same letters in manuscript. I have preferred to go to the manuscripts whenever possible because I have found that this is the only way a biographer can get the feel of his subject: to see the paper, the ink and, no matter how frustrating, the handwriting.

Having worked my way through more than fifty different manuscript collections, I am grateful for the courtesy and help of those who preserve these great holdings. The staff of the Bodleian Library, Oxford, particularly those in Duke Humfrey's Library, have provided me with numerous manuscripts, books and Victorian periodicals. The greatest amount of Trollope manuscript material is held in two large Collections at Princeton University named after their founders, Morris L. Parrish and Robert H. Taylor. It was my great good fortune to enjoy many meetings with the late Robert Taylor, who made his Collection of Trollope letters and manuscripts available for research, gave me permission to quote from them and willingly gave of his time and knowledge during several meetings, both in London and in Princeton, where he answered many questions about Trollope. Robert Taylor believed, and the Collection which survives him attests, that the first purpose of all literature is to add enjoyment to life. Without that, analysis, criticism and textual study are pointless.

My work in the Taylor Collection was made easier by the great help of its then Curator, Mrs Nancy Coffin, who will, I hope, forgive me for not sharing her complete admiration for Trollope's futuristic novel, *The Fixed Period*. Both Mr Taylor and Mrs Coffin provided me with much assistance for a BBC programme I made on the Collection under the guidance of that experienced producer, Mr John Knight. I would also like to thank Mr Alexander Wainwright, Mr Mark Farrell, the present Curator of the Taylor Collection and all the staff of the manuscript room at Princeton both for their help during my visits and for answering many requests for information.

I also wish to pay tribute to the late Alan Haydock, who did so much to preserve the highest traditions of the BBC and who asked me to write dramatised documentaries not only on Anthony Trollope, for the centenary of his death in 1982, but on his mother, Fanny Trollope. To hear Trollope's words and laughter come alive when spoken by such a talented actor as the late Paul Hardwick, gave me new insights into the story of the Trollopes.

I am also most grateful to the following libraries for permission to examine and quote from material in their keeping and to the people who work there: the National Library of Scotland, the British Library, the University of Illinois at Urbana-Champaign, especially Mr Gene K. Rinkel, Curator of Special Collections, the University of California at Los Angeles, the New York Public Library (in the Berg and Arents Collections), the Library of Congress in Washington, the Folger Shakespeare Memorial Library, also in Washington, the Beinecke Rare Book and Manuscript Library at Yale, especially Mr Christopher Carsten, the Houghton Library at Harvard, the Boston Public Library, the Pierpont Morgan Library, New York, and especially to Miss Inge Dupont, Head of Reader Services, the British Library Newspaper Library at Colindale, the Victoria and Albert Museum, the Public Record Office, the Royal Archives, Windsor, especially Mr Oliver Everett for the courtesy which one has come to expect from him and his staff, the Lilly Library at Indiana University, University College, London, Miss Alison Carpenter of the Bishopsgate Institute, London, the Greater London Record Office, Dr. Williams's Library, London, and Mr Richard Knight of the Local History Department, Holborn Library, London. I am particularly grateful to Miss Virginia Murray of the John Murray Archives for her help with the correspondence not only of Anthony Trollope but of his mother, and Mr Sidney Bowen and the staff at the Post Office Archives, who preserve not only the Victorian postal records but the Victorian belief in the speed of delivery.

I wish to thank the County Archivists and staffs of the Record Offices of Devon, Kent, Hertfordshire, Lincolnshire, Hereford and Worcestershire, Berkshire, Gloucestershire and West Sussex, who do so much to preserve English history, Mr Michael Boardman of Beverley Library, Yorkshire, the staff of Cheltenham Central Reference Library, the Controller, Mails and Operations, Department of Postal Administration, St Helier, Jersey, Miss Elizabeth Poyser at the Westminster Diocesan Archives for her help in tracing Father Bampfield, and Miss S.M. Shepard, Assistant Archivist, Central Library, Rotherham for her invaluable assistance in unravelling details about Rose Trollope's early life. I wish to place on record my indebtedness to Mrs Patricia Gill, West Sussex County Archivist and Mr Eeyan Hartley, the Keeper of Archives at Castle Howard, York, for their help in tracking down hitherto unpublished manuscript letters and records which shed new light on Anthony Trollope.

I am grateful to the Headmaster of Cheltenham College and Mr J.F.L. Bowes, Secretary of the Cheltonian Society, the Headmaster of Bradfield College and Mr F.E. Templer, Bradfield College Archivist, for his help in understanding the education of Trollope's sons, the Headmaster of Dean Close School, Cheltenham, Mr William Wallworth of San Jose, California for his genealogical research into the Heseltine family, to Mr Walter E. Anderton of Clearwater, Florida, Rose Trollope's great-great-nephew, the Rev. Canon C.H. Whiteman, the Rev. Stuart Brindley, Vicar of Rotherham, Professor Paul Thompson of the University of Essex, Professor J.C. Barnes of University College, Dublin and Mr Gavin Percy, General Manager of the Beverley Arms Hotel.

I am grateful to Mr and Mrs Peter J. Wild and Mr and Mrs William Macaluso for the gift of various books concerning Trollope. The late Eugene Wild and Mrs Vera Bradbury Munson gave me helpful guidance in understanding Trollope's attitudes both towards slavery and towards the war in America in the 1860s. My sister, Miss Nora Mullen, assisted me in working through the Parrish manuscripts at Princeton. My other sister, Mrs Anne Mary Evans, and my nephew Paul Evans, both then of Barnet, helped me in locating many of the sites connected with the Trollopes in Hadley, particularly the grave of Emily Trollope. Dr James Munson has contributed much towards this book, most of all his great knowledge of the Oxford Movement and the various meanings of the term 'High Church'. It was Mrs Cornelia Oddie who first pointed out to me the importance of Susan Grantly in understanding the Barset novels. Others of my friends including Miss Priscilla Tolkien, Mr Alexander Kerr, Mr Gerard Werckle, and Mr and Mrs Peter Gray of Kelvedon, have helped me in various ways. I am grateful to Mr Colin Haycraft, Mr Ray Davies and Miss Deborah Blake at Duckworth for their contribution to this book. My most important obligation is acknowledged in the dedication.

*

As there is no standard edition of Trollope's novels, references to them have been indicated by the chapter number which is placed in square brackets [ ]. Almost every edition has its own peculiarities of punctuation and spelling and there can also be differences between the serialised version and the text as published in book form. When the Trollope Society (9a North Street, London SW4 0HN) completes its edition of Trollope's novels in the year 2000 there will be for the first time a definitive text.

To

My Mother and Father

CHAPTER ONE

Some Small Fortune

It was close to midnight on Wednesday, 21 June 1815, when London society assembled at a mansion in St James's Square. As the portly Prince Regent began the quadrille, the music was drowned by shouts heard through the open windows. A major in a battered scarlet coat burst through the opulently dressed throng to fling two tattered French flags at the Prince's feet. From a green velvet bag he lifted the despatch reporting that Napoleon had been decisively defeated three days before at a small village called Waterloo. It did not take long for the momentous news to reach the sedate town houses of semi-fashionable Russell Square.

When Thackeray wrote *Vanity Fair* some thirty years later, he set much of his story in Russell Square at the time of Waterloo and wondered whether anything was going on in that 'little corner of the parish of Bloomsbury, London'. It is pleasantly ironic that at the very time of which Thackeray wrote – at the very time when Napoleon was hastening to his doom – a familiar enough excitement came to one family living in Keppel Street, just off Russell Square. On 24 April 1815 Mrs Thomas Anthony Trollope gave birth to her fourth son. A month later, on 18 May, the baby was carried to the parish church of St George, Bloomsbury and there, in the eighteenth-century splendour of Hawksmoor's architecture, was given the name of his father and his grandfather, Anthony. He would become one of the greatest and most popular novelists in the English language. To us Anthony Trollope is the writer who more than any other symbolised and chronicled the greatness and the glory that followed the triumphant news which spread through the streets of London when he was but a few weeks old.

*

Anthony Trollope was influenced even more than most children by his

1

parents. His father's struggles and his mother's successes determined both his character and his career. To understand Anthony Trollope we must know his parents. Thomas Anthony Trollope came from a long line of squires and country clergymen, the very types who were to people his son's novels. Anthony's elder brother started a family history with the not uncommon assertion that 'the family of Trollope is one of great antiquity'. The Trollopes originated in County Durham but in the mid-sixteenth century began to acquire land in Lincolnshire where they then settled. When Anthony and his brothers were sent to Harrow, a schoolfellow, Sidney Herbert, later a prominent Cabinet Minister, heard the family legend about the origin of their name. A name such as Trollope cried out for an explanation – the more romantic, the better – and the boys, with the customary kindness of the breed, forced frequent repetitions of the tale by 'sufficient punchings on the head'. According to this story, 'Tallyhosier the Norman came over to England with William the Conqueror, and being out hunting, with his Majesty in the New Forest, happened to kill three wolves, and "trois" being the French for "three", "loup" for wolves, he was called "troisloup", which with many changes during the countless centuries became "Trollope".'[1]

The family may have delighted in their supposed Norman origins, but they only really became prominent in the seventeenth century when the Trollope baronetcy was created by King Charles I. Anthony Trollope could almost claim, like a character in one of his novels, that his 'forefathers had been baronets since baronets were first created' [*The Prime Minister* XIII]. Trollope was proud of his father's family and of the right this gave him to qualify as a 'gentleman', and he marked this pride by using the baronet's coat of arms on his personal bookplate. The meaning and nature of the English gentleman would become the central theme in many of his novels. Baronets in Victorian fiction, standing as they did between the aristocracy proper and the commonalty, are normally either blundering buffoons or, more frequently, sinister villains who mislead winsome maidens. Trollope's baronets are a mixture of both good and bad, like Sir Alured Wharton in *The Prime Minister* [XIII]:

> Sir Alured was proud of his name, of his estate, and of his rank ... He was a melancholy, proud, ignorant man ... who thought the assertion of social equality on the part of men of lower rank to amount to the taking of personal liberty ... [he] read little or nothing, and thought that he knew the history of his country because he was aware that Charles I had had his head cut off, and that the Georges had come over from Hanover ... Sir Alured, with all his foibles and with all his faults, was a pure-minded,

simple gentleman, who could not tell a lie, who could not do a wrong, and who was earnest in his desire to make those who were dependent on him comfortable, and, if possible, happy. Once a year he came up to London for a week, to see his lawyers, and get measured for a coat, and go to the dentist.

Younger sons of the Trollope baronets could have no share in the estate's 6,000 acres which were entailed on the eldest son, and they therefore went forth with the aid of family influence to make their way in acceptable careers such as the Church, the Army or the Navy. In the eighteenth century two younger Trollopes became well-known admirals: one, Sir Henry, gained a knighthood and was notorious in the Royal Navy for that fierce temper which seems to have been a common trait among the men of the family. His zeal for fighting was so great that he is even said to have taken part in land battles such as Lexington and Bunker's Hill. In the 1770s, the younger son of Sir Thomas Trollope, the fourth baronet, took holy orders. Rather surprisingly the Rev. Anthony Trollope was also a barrister. In a successful clerical career he acquired two comfortable livings in Hertfordshire and the honorific title of 'Chaplain to the Duchess of Somerset'. He used his considerable income to advance the career of his only son, Thomas Anthony. The Rector, like many characters in his grandson's novels, made a good marriage with the local squire's daughter. Penelope Meetkerke was descended from a Dutch ambassador to Elizabeth I who had settled in England. Although the family had eventually acquired a large estate, the line was dying out by the end of the eighteenth century, and when Penelope's brother, Adolphus, became squire his only heir was his sister's son, Thomas Anthony Trollope. His education followed his uncle's: Winchester and Oxford. After attaining many University honours he went up to London to become a barrister but, unlike many aspirants to the bar, he faced no years of penury. His father died in 1806, 'leaving a son, in the Law' to whom he also left a comfortable income from wise investments in London property.[2] Thomas Anthony Trollope had, in addition to his inheritance, a Fellowship at New College, Oxford which burdened him with no other duties than remaining unmarried and accepting £200 a year. In itself this money would have been more than enough to support a young barrister.

At the same time that Trollope was settling into his house at No. 16, Keppel Street, another young man arrived with a similar background at No. 27. Henry Milton, like his neighbour, was a Wykehamist and the only son of a country clergyman. His salary as a War Office clerk was only £90 a year, but it was a start in the secure world of government service. His two sisters kept house for him, which allowed them not only to savour the delights of the metropolis but to escape from a vicarage increasingly ruled by their stepmother. Each girl enjoyed an annual allowance of £50 which helped the Milton household. It was not long before their neighbour, Thomas Anthony Trollope, was introduced to the younger sister, Frances, whom almost everyone called Fanny, a popular name in the early nineteenth century. Fanny's father, the Rev. William Milton, was yet another product of Winchester and New College although he did not spring from a family of such 'ancient antiquity' as the Trollopes. Most of the Miltons had been 'in trade' in Bristol, as had his father.[3] However, William Milton secured his status as a 'gentleman' by his education and ordination. His vicarages, first near Bristol where Fanny had been born in 1779 and then at Heckfield in Hampshire, a comfortable living in the gift of New College, were enlivened with the inventions of the vicar who was a skilled mathematician and a man of broad, if slightly eccentric, imagination. His plans to improve the Bristol docks received the official thanks of the Corporation but, unfortunately, nothing more tangible. He then turned his mind towards inventing a safer coach and wrote articles about his ideas for the *Gentleman's Magazine*, a periodical that lay on the mahogany tables of many of the clergy and squires of England. Heckfield vicarage saw that restrained elegance of a country parson's life, so familiar in the novels of Jane Austen, whose own father was a nearby clergyman. One grandson, writing at the end of the Victorian period, remembered his Grandfather Milton as a typical country vicar of the Georgian era:[4]

> He was an excellent parish priest after the fashion of his day; that is to say, he was kindly to all, liberal to the poor to the utmost extent of his means, and well beloved by his neighbours, high and low. He was a charming old man, markedly gentlemanlike and suave in his manner; very nice in his person; clever unquestionably in a queer, crotchety sort of way; and thoroughly minded to do his duty according to his lights in that state of life to which it had pleased God to call him. But he would have had no more idea of attempting anything of the nature of active parochial work or reform, as understood at the present day, than he would have had of scheming to pay the national debt.

His clerical income of approximately £400 a year, about half that enjoyed by the Rev. Anthony Trollope, made him comfortable but in no sense wealthy.[5] Although his father had been 'in trade', William Milton married into an old landed family called Gresley; his daughter, Fanny, would take great pride in this connection with the gentry. Anthony Trollope would remember his grandmother's name and use it for one of his best short stories, 'Mary Gresley'. The vicar had brought up his son, Henry, and his two daughters, Mary and Fanny, with a taste for comfort but without the means to satisfy that taste once they had left Heckfield.

Like many clergymen, William Milton gave his daughters a good education, particularly in literature and languages. In the midst of a book about Paris, published in 1836, Fanny paused to pursue a little digression on the important role of the English country clergy. Looking round her in Paris she noted the lack of an influential group who could say 'This may not be' to any outrageous behaviour. This great difference between England and the continent sprang from the civilising role of clerical families:[6]

> The clergy of England, their matronly wives and highly educated daughters, form a distinct caste, to which there is nothing that answers in the whole range of continental Europe. In this caste, however, are mingled a portion of every other ... While such men as these mingle freely in society, as they constantly do in England, and bring with them the females who form their families, there is little danger that notorious vice should choose to obtrude itself.

The social role of the country clergy is now preserved for posterity to read about and admire in the novels of her youngest son.

*

In the 1860s someone found a bundle of old love letters written by Anthony Trollope's parents and sent them anonymously to the famous novelist. He was never a great preserver of letters but fortunately he kept these: eventually they found their way to the library of one of America's greatest book collectors, Robert Taylor, at Princeton. Trollope was particularly struck with his mother's letters: 'so sweet, so graceful, and so well-expressed.' They carry us back to the tranquil world of Jane Austen, a world seemingly heedless of the battles that were shaking the continent. They reveal the contrasting characters of Fanny Milton and Thomas Anthony Trollope. As a well brought up young lady she was adept at folding her square pages into a neat packet, a much admired accomplishment in the age before envelopes. Her handwriting is clear and her spelling correct, whereas Thomas Anthony's educational achievements had not included either of these skills. These letters were eventually used by Anthony's sister-in-law in her biography of Fanny Trollope, where their contrasting appearance is well described: 'It is as if the stream of his mind, though clear in itself, were constantly fretted by little rocks and boulders in its course. Hers flow on more smoothly, with a cheerful ease.'[7] Here is a case where handwriting gives a clue not only to character but to fate.

When Fanny Milton and Thomas Anthony Trollope met in the summer of 1808, they enjoyed delightful conversations about literature, a subject about which each had strong views and of which each had considerable knowledge. Thomas sent her two of his Latin odes and included translations just in case. By September we find him writing from his chambers in Lincoln's Inn to 'My dear Madam', returning an umbrella that her brother had lent him when he was leaving No. 27 for No. 16. This allowed the formal lawyer to 'take the liberty of addressing this note expressing my best thanks for the loan of it'.[8] After another dinner at the Miltons, he walked the few steps to his own house carrying a novel given him by Fanny. It was *The Modern Griselda* by the well-known Anglo-Irish writer, Maria Edgeworth. Fanny had picked her book with care, for its theme was the nature of marriage. By the following morning Thomas writes from his chambers: 'When I had got home I could not persuade myself to throw it aside, intended as it was as a companion at my breakfast table this morning, without just peeping at a page or two; in consequence of this impatience I was led from chapter to chapter, tho' sitting without a fire after a walk home thro' the snow, till I had finished it.'[9]

It is a pleasant thought that a novel played some role in bringing about the engagement of Anthony Trollope's parents, for from that marriage would flow several hundred volumes of fiction. A few weeks later Thomas Anthony was ready to take the plunge. He wrote a letter beginning with a wordy preface asking if it were better to propose in person or in 'epistolary correspondence' which, he admitted, would save him 'the necessity of a more explicit avowal'. Having obviously chosen the latter, he announced that 'my chief delight has long since had its source in your society and conversation; and if, permit my vanity to indulge the hope, there has been the slightest degree of mutuality in this delight, then perhaps I confess I scarcely know what I was going to say'. Ironically he went on to write the perfect summary of what was to happen in their marriage:

I have had experience enough to teach me that happiness is not to be expected where the parties are no longer capable of enjoying those necessities and comforts of life to which they have been accustomed, and which are commonly incident to the rank and situation they hold in society.

He explained that while his present income was about £900 a year, £200 of that would vanish when he resigned his Fellowship. He ended his somewhat unromantic proposal to 'my dear Madam' by admitting that its manner 'was little adapted to its subject' but he had no time for the 'flippant nonsense' usual on such occasions. This was no passionate letter of a youthful lover but the cautious production of a middle-aged barrister.[10]

Fanny Milton waited only a few hours before answering. Although her reply was more romantic, it was also concerned with financial details: she had, she told him, £1,300 capital and an annual allowance of £50. She had no idea whether her father would provide a dowry to launch their married life with the comforts their position demanded. Such arrangements were important in any marriage between people of their social standing. Modern readers may be surprised that in almost every Trollope novel where marriage appears, and that is in almost every one, the principal subject seems to be what the young couple would 'marry on'. In this concern Trollope was reflecting the views not just of his parents but of his society. A girl's father was expected to provide capital, the interest from which would help the young couple meet their expenses.

For Fanny Milton the marriage seemed an excellent prospect as she was already in her late twenties. A rising barrister of good family who was also the heir to a large estate and already possessed of a comfortable private income was no bad catch. These were, no doubt, points she made when she went to Heckfield to talk about money. Her stepmother, 'Mrs Milton' as she calls her in a letter to her fiancé, implying no great affection, was responsible for arranging financial matters as the vicar was, presumably, preoccupied with his inventions. His obsession was already a private joke between the engaged couple who were amused that her 'fortune' would include a share in any profits from the 'patent cart'. The vicar offered his daughter £1,200 in stock plus £100 for clothes. These provisions were formalised by family solicitors with three trustees appointed to protect her income. Although married women were denied almost all property rights at the time, they could at least have the benefit of trustees who guarded their private income should a husband become a bankrupt. In addition, Thomas Anthony settled the large sum of £6,000 in investments on his new wife which would guarantee her about £200 a year in addition to her other income. These funds were likewise guarded by three trustees, one of whom was her brother, Henry.[11]

After his proposal had been accepted Thomas Anthony took the liberty of addressing his fiancée as 'My dear Fanny' and his love for her is present, however guarded. In his letters he permits himself few tender sentiments unless they be in French, at that time the language of the enemy but at all times the shield of the Anglo-Saxon when expressing the passions of love or when compiling menus: 'Adieu, aime moi toujours'; 'Adieu, amie de mon coeur'. Fanny replies in her franker, more robust way, 'Love you always? I believe I must, for I cannot help it, even though you do scold me when I don't deserve it.' He was well aware of his own reticence and ever anxious to justify it: 'I always feel afraid of raising doubts of my own sincerity by professing too much … Besides, if our professions are only consistent with our actions, where is the necessity for them?' There was only one small, black cloud on the horizon which, unbeknown to Fanny, heralded the storm that would almost wreck their marriage. On 10 February Thomas Anthony admitted that the day before he had been 'visited by one of my head-aches'.[12]

Through the mist of language we sense a heightening passion as the marriage drew near. It was to be at Heckfield on the bridegroom's thirty-fifth birthday, 23 May 1809. Fanny described her days to her fiancé: they included dutiful visits to labourers' cottages to admire their pigs, without which of course they would have had little if any meat, and days spent at home sewing, eating roast beef, reading the Bible and poring over Dante. In his last bachelor letter, Thomas Anthony informed his future wife of last-minute arrangements for the redecoration of the house: 'I have given orders for the blinds, for the grates to be put in – the cellar to be done.' Like many another man he came to grief when confronted with curtains: 'I found myself greatly at a loss – the first question the makers put to me *threw me on my back* and I was obliged to leave it entirely to himself.'[13] The couple were also encouraged by the gift of some silver forks from Sir John Trollope, the current baronet, and a most generous present from Thomas Anthony's childless uncle, Adolphus Meetkerke.

*

The marriage seemed ideal in its early years. Anthony Trollope later described his father as 'a man of some small fortune and of higher hopes'. Thomas Anthony Trollope prospered in his profession and gained recognition for a treatise on maritime law, an important topic in an age of overseas expansion. A large family began to populate the nursery at 16, Keppel Street: Thomas Adolphus, born in 1810; Henry, 1811; Arthur, 1812 and Anthony, 1815. A girl was born in 1813 but only survived one day. This was, of course, an age when about one in three London children died before their fifth birthday. The house which had seemed large when they first moved in six years before no longer appeared so after four sons had arrived. Thomas Anthony owned the Keppel Street house, which was rare in the nineteenth century when even quite wealthy people normally rented houses. It was a valuable property – he had once refused an offer of over £2,000 – but, even so, such houses often lacked elementary sanitation and comforts. The water-closet was placed under the stairs with neither ventilation nor light. There does, however, seem to have been running water, for Mrs Trollope boasted some years later: 'In London, up to the second floor, and often to the third, water is forced, which furnishes an almost unlimited supply of that luxurious article, to be obtained with no greater trouble to the servants than would be required to draw it from a tea-urn.'[14]

The expanding family made it difficult to maintain that appearance of gentility which was essential to the Trollopes. They became careful about the number of fires allowed in the house and found that they could light the drawing-room with only two tallow candles. Wax candles, at half-a-crown, were out of the question. Yet despite such economies they still had a footman resplendent in the livery of the Trollope baronetcy, even though there was a tax of £2 8s on male servants as well as a tax on the wig-powder used on their hair, measures introduced to pay for the war. However, a footman was necessary for the dignity of Thomas Anthony Trollope: in an age when every family with even the slightest pretension to be called middle-class had at least one maid, the sight of a man-servant gave a household an important distinction. A tall footman, particularly one with well-turned calves (newspaper advertisements often specified both height and good calves) proclaimed a family of some rank. Thomas Adolphus, the eldest Trollope son, later recalled: 'It never would have occurred to him or to my mother that they could get on without a man servant in livery.'[15] Perhaps Anthony Trollope was drawing on childhood memory when he asked with barbed wit in *The Last Chronicle of Barset* [XVIII]:

Who inquires why it is that a little greased flour rubbed in among the hair on a footman's head, – just one dab here and another there, – gives such a tone of high life to the family? And seeing that the thing is so easily done, why do not more people attempt it? The tax on hair-powder

is but thirteen shillings a year. It may, indeed, be that the slightest dab
... justifies the wearer in demanding hot meat three times a day, and
wine at any rate on Sundays.

The comforting presence of the footman in his livery and powdered
wig lent distinction to their parties. Mr Trollope, devoted to old ways,
insisted that the cloth should always be removed from the table after
the five-o'clock dinner, so that port and sherry decanters could be
placed on the gleaming mahogany table. Five o'clock was a late time for
dinner in the early nineteenth century, when lunch was not a normal
meal, but it allowed the conscientious barrister more time for work.
When friends dined, a magnum of his well-known vintage port was
placed on the table, sometimes supplemented with a decanter of
madeira. As he grew up, Anthony noted such customs and used them
and similar small details to enrich his novels for his contemporaries
and to reveal to later readers a vanished way of life.

The Trollopes' friends were drawn from leading figures in
professional, literary, theatrical, political and clerical circles, with a
sprinkling of gentry to provide ballast. To the Keppel Street house, and
later to their country residence in Harrow, came people like Lady
Milman, wife of a Royal Physician, the artist Sir George Hayter, who
once asked Thomas Anthony to pose as a lawyer for an historical
painting now at Woburn Abbey, and the writer Mary Russell Mitford.
She was one of Fanny's old friends who was living near Heckfield when
she wrote her famous sketches of rural life, *Our Village*. Miss Mitford –
she was almost always called 'Miss Mitford' – was also a playwright
and well-known letter writer with many literary connections. Mrs
Trollope's brother, Henry, was another guest: he had also blossomed
forth as a writer on art. His book, *Letters on the Fine Arts Written from
Paris during the Year 1815*, described the treasures in the Louvre that
Napoleon had looted from palaces all over Europe.

Among the Trollopes' distinguished clerical friends was the Rev.
George Nott, a prebendary of Winchester Cathedral, who could bring
news of royal events as he was the tutor to the heir to the throne,
Princess Charlotte. After her death in 1817 Nott inherited her books to
add to his own library which already had some 12,000 volumes. He was
a good example of the cultivated clergyman that the Trollopes liked, a
man devoted to civilised pleasure and to quiet devotion without any
hint of vulgar 'enthusiasm'. When he fell from the scaffolding while
supervising repairs to Winchester Cathedral, he solaced his recovery
with translating the Book of Common Prayer into Italian as he was
something of an Italian scholar. His translation was published in 1831

as *Il Libro delle preghiere Comuni.** Clergymen like Prebendary Nott, often distinguished by such quixotic pastimes, are frequently found in Anthony Trollope's novels.

Perhaps the most popular visitor was the strangest of all, General Guglielmo Pepe, the exiled Italian revolutionary. His popularity with the children came not from his radical politics, which made him welcome to the liberal and intellectual circles in which their parents moved, but from his arriving laden with presents of dried figs and mandarin oranges. The general retained the affection of a royalist brother who remained an officer in Naples, so exile did not deprive him, or his young friends, of Neapolitan luxuries. Politics were an important part of the Trollopes' life: they both were part of a liberal reaction to the conservative governments of the day, not just on the continent but in England, where the horrors of the French Revolution remained a living memory. The Tories dominated the years before and after Waterloo, years which saw great unrest and the famous Peterloo riot, when a radical mob in Manchester was dispersed by sabre-wielding cavalry. As a barrister, Mr Trollope's venom was reserved for the Lord Chancellor, Lord Eldon, who was seen as the very embodiment of reaction. When first appointed he showed a small sign of radicalism, asking George III if he could abandon his wig: 'I will have no innovations in my time,' replied the stalwart monarch. After this short murmur of unrest Eldon settled into a career of opposition to all change. On walks with his sons Thomas Anthony would point out Eldon's house and, while admiring the Lord Chancellor's legal acumen, warned: 'His mind was an instrument of admirable precision, but his soul the soul of a pedlar.' Teaching like this undoubtedly affected Anthony's later political views and writings.[16] In one novel, *He Knew He Was Right*, he portrays an elderly Tory spinster, modelled on one of his own cousins, weeping before her bust of Lord Eldon about all the dreadful innovations that were sweeping through Victorian England [VII]. She would not have found such a bust in Keppel Street.

*

The London into which Anthony Trollope was born was the largest city in the western world, with a population over 1,300,000. A real haymarket still flourished in the street which today only carries its name, open countryside stretched from the end of Oxford Street and as

---

*The Prebendary was not alone in his translating. Reading translations of the Prayer Book was a popular way to learn a new language. This was how the Duke of Wellington mastered Spanish.

late as 1828 one could still hunt in Regent's Park. On Mondays the cautious stayed indoors to avoid the rush of cattle and sheep being driven to Smithfield and at night the watchman with his blunderbuss, as often as not unloaded, kept the peace by walking his round and calling out the time and state of the weather. During the day the streets were thronged with knife-grinders, Italian boys with 'images to sell', chimney sweeps with their cries of 'Sweep, sweep', the Jewish pedlar, one hat stacked on top of the other, calling out 'Old clo's' and the organ-grinder with his ear-splitting hurdy-gurdy. Everywhere were signs of the city's growth which reflected the country's vast wealth and proclaimed its status as the capital of the world's most important nation. A Victorian historian, in a perfect example of contemporary pride, gave a telling instance:

> At the close of the great war only three bridges – London Bridge, Blackfriars, and Westminster – united the north and south banks of the Thames in London. It had taken five centuries to throw three bridges across the river. It hardly took five years to supplement these three bridges with three others, Waterloo, Vauxhall, and Southwark.

All this growth, however, only made the foul air worse. A visitor from America had commented a few years earlier:[17]

> It is difficult to form an idea ... of winter days in London; the smoke of fossil coal forms an atmosphere, perceivable for many miles, like a great round cloud attached to the earth ... when the weather is cloudy and foggy ... this smoke increases the general dingy hue, and terminates the length of every street with a fixed grey mist, receding as you advance ... the air ... is loaded with small flakes of smoke ... so light as to float without falling. This black snow sticks to your clothes and linen, or lights on your face. You just feel something on your nose, or your cheek – the finger is applied mechanically, and fixes it into a black patch!

This foul atmosphere was not good for someone like Fanny Trollope who had grown up in the country. She would return to her father's vicarage for fresh air and rest after her frequent pregnancies, and shortly after Anthony's birth she was pregnant yet again. Her husband decided that his family needed a home away from the crowded, noisy streets of London.

Anthony Trollope said that he was taken from Keppel Street 'while a baby', and it seems that the family moved within a year of his birth and let the house or at least part of it. It may be that they lived part of the time in London and part in the country as Keppel Street occurs frequently in his writings. In one of his short stories, which tended to be more autobiographical than his novels, the narrator gives his address as 'Keppel Street'.[18] One of his novels, written in his mid-fifties, has many scenes set in Keppel Street which, the author claims, 'cannot be called fashionable'. He recalled the 'genteel suite of drawing rooms – two rooms with folding-doors'. Upstairs were bedrooms and above them the garret for servants. The parlour, a 'dark gloomy chamber', obviously made a lasting impression for in an earlier novel he recalled 'the small dingy parlour in Keppel Street' [*Lady Anna* XX, XLXX; *Orley Farm* X].

Two years before Anthony's birth, in 1813, his father had rented a farm in Harrow from Lord Northwick. In those days the ten-mile journey from the centre of London to the village of Harrow-on-the-Hill passed through open countryside. The village was removed from the sooty atmosphere of London and yet close enough for Mr Trollope to go into 'Town'. In his gig, a small carriage with one horse, he could reach his chambers in about an hour. Gigs were convenient vehicles for clergymen or lawyers because they did not require a coachman. On longer journeys, the family footman, bereft of wig and livery, could become a groom and ride ahead to hire a fresh horse when required. Jane Austen wrote that 'the law was allowed to be genteel enough: many young men, who had chambers ... made a very good appearance in the first circles and drove about town in very knowing gigs'.[19] However, on dark winter evenings Fanny Trollope worried about her husband, particularly after a messenger riding to the French Ambassador's country house in Harrow was murdered on the road.

The farm Mr Trollope had rented had 160 acres which he hoped would provide not only food for his family but an increased income for himself. The existing farmhouse would not do, and his first expense was a new house which the lease allowed him to build. He now arranged a £3,000 mortgage to finance a new, four-storey mansion complete with fashionable columns and balconies. From one upper window there was a distant view of the towers of Westminster Abbey. Few things delighted Fanny Trollope more than setting up a new home, and she threw her enormous energies into the task. The new house was named 'Julians' after a local field and the Meetkerke estate in Hertfordshire that Thomas Anthony expected to inherit from his childless uncle. Fanny even asked Lord Northwick to drain 'a very ugly pond' at the bottom of the hill as it spoiled the view of 'our little valley'. The *Encyclopaedia Britannica* agreed that the 'best prospects of a rural kind' came from this hill and that 'the whole of the richly cultivated valley of Middlesex is comprehended in the view from it'.[20] This splendid sight of hay fields spreading towards the spires and towers of the greatest city in the world would have been one of the first views the young Anthony knew. Looking out from a hill over rich countryside towards a vast metropolis would be bound to affect the mind and outlook of any child, let alone an imaginative one. These earliest sights may well have imprinted indelible memories on his mind. Perhaps it is no accident that so many of Trollope's novels feature the connections and tensions between London and the countryside.

Biographers of Anthony Trollope have often depicted this move to Harrow as the first flash of unreasonableness, possibly verging on madness, in his father. With hindsight Trollope himself would write in later years: 'English farming ... for those who have not learned the work early, is an expensive amusement rather than a trade by which bread can be earned' [*John Caldigate* LXIV]. Anthony's father, however, had good reasons for his actions. Middlesex was famous for the high quality of its hay. It was a comparatively simple crop to grow; the county's farmers had perfected their own ways of production, and London provided a near and expanding market with its thousands of horses. Thomas Anthony was not totally without knowledge of agriculture as he had grown up in his father's rural parish and would have seen how his uncle, Adolphus Meetkerke, managed his land. As a 'gentleman farmer' he would, of course, have done little work on the farm: that was performed by labourers who would have been paid at the going rate of under ten shillings a week. Another of the sights Anthony would have seen as he grew up was hay-making, a delicate operation still done by hand. Great care had to be taken to preserve the newly cut hay's sweetness and colour: after it was cut by scythes it was broken up by hand-rakes to ensure that none of the valuable crop was lost.

As well as its clean air and proximity to London, Harrow had one other advantage. Thomas Trollope had the education of four sons to consider. Any qualified boy living in the parish could go to Harrow School for only ten guineas a term. Thomas Anthony was well aware of this as his friend, the Rev. Henry Drury, was one of the leading masters in the school. The father wanted his sons to follow him and countless other ancestors to Winchester, but Harrow would have to suffice, at least until a free place became available at his preferred school. The farm would also be a good preparation for the heir to the Meetkerke estate. The prospect of inheriting that estate was important for the whole family, especially as two daughters, Cecilia and Emily, were born after the move to Harrow: it would not only increase their wealth but raise their position in society, so that even a younger son, like Anthony, could eventually go forth with a small income. Thomas Anthony was anxious to please his Uncle Adolphus and had named his eldest son Thomas Adolphus. He even took the boy to Hertfordshire so that the tenants could behold their next two squires.

However, when Anthony was about two, disaster struck: Adolphus Meetkerke's wife had died, and within a short period he acquired a young wife and, worse, a son and heir. Some gossips claimed that the old man, a staunch Tory, resented his nephew's liberal views. The loss of this inheritance must have been among the earliest topics that Anthony would have heard in the house in Harrow. Years later he said it was a 'crushing blow'. Perhaps it is one reason why his novels are filled with plots about inheritances. In one of his last, *Mr. Scarborough's Family*, there is an elderly uncle with an estate located in the same part of Hertfordshire as Meetkerke's and the fictional uncle considers remarriage to disinherit a nephew whose liberal views had upset him. But as this was fiction, uncle and nephew are reconciled and the inheritance saved. Anthony's eldest brother, Tom, remembered visits to the estate and retained the amusing memory of Meetkerke's maiden sister who wandered about supervising the housework. She possessed only one book which she constantly carried with her, *Pride and Prejudice*, and when she had finished it she promptly started reading it all over again.

The 'crushing blow' was the beginning of the end for Thomas Anthony Trollope. The dream of becoming a country squire had vanished. Nor was his life as a gentleman farmer prospering. He had taken up farming just as British agriculture was plunged into one of its most difficult periods. 'Our wheat is good for nothing,' wrote Lord Eldon. 'As a farmer I am ruined. So much for peace and plenty.' For once Thomas Anthony would have agreed with the Lord Chancellor. Many farm labourers were forced out of work and had to be maintained, albeit at a miserable level, by taxes on land. In addition local landlords, who had appreciated the attraction of Harrow for tenants with young sons, had set their rents at a high level. It was a horrible time for the poor and not an easy time for landowners or gentlemen farmers, and the Trollopes, like almost everyone else, had to look for economies. Not surprisingly the collapse affected Mr Trollope's health: 'The continued ill state of my health has induced me with the advice of my medical friends,' he wrote to Lord Northwick, 'to return to my residence in town. I have it in contemplation therefore to let my house at Harrow, and to fit up the farm house for the summer vacation and other occasional visits to my farm.'[21] To what degree he carried out his plan is not known. This was not a mere excuse, as his health, like his finances, was in serious decline. Unfortunately he had taken the land not only at a high rent but on a long lease. Anthony later recalled that the children regarded their landlord as 'a cormorant who was eating us up'. Matters were not helped by the elder Trollope's temper, for his letters to Lord Northwick increasingly lacked those signs of deference that a peer expected. (Thomas Anthony Trollope, no doubt, knew that Lord Northwick's ancestry was not as distinguished as his own: the peer was only descended from a prosperous Flemish merchant who came to England when the Trollopes were already baronets.) Although he was unable to end his tenancy, he could save money by giving up their fashionable new residence. He moved his family back into the original farmhouse and found a tenant for the elegant new mansion.

This farmhouse, which was quite spacious, was really the earliest house that Anthony knew well. His parents called it Julian Hill, a courageous reminder both of their nearby mansion and of the lost Meetkerke estate. Forty years later Anthony used it as the model for 'Orley Farm' and arranged·for the distinguished artist, Millais, to draw the house. Trollope himself described the farmhouse:

> It consisted of three buildings of various heights, attached to each other ... surrounded by bakehouse, laundry, dairy, and servants' room ... The whole stood on one line fronting on to a large lawn which fell steeply away from the house into an orchard at the bottom ... it was irregular and straggling, but at the same time roomy and picturesque ... [with] the unmistakable appearance of an English gentleman's country-house [*Orley Farm* I].

*

Anthony Trollope tells us virtually nothing of his early childhood. His *Autobiography* jumps from his birth to his unhappy days at school. It is wrong, however, to see his boyhood as nothing but misery and ever-darkening gloom. He never mentions, to take but one example, the annual outing the children enjoyed to a Christmas pantomime. Another memory came back to him when visiting America, when he was shocked to see small children in hotels, eating steak and pickles and drinking iced water. He recalled that as a boy of three he would have been eating his bread and milk with 'a silver spoon of my own' and gobbling up 'my minced mutton mixed with potatoes and gravy' assisted by his nursemaid. This woman was known as Farmer and she relieved his mother of the drearier chores in looking after the young. Tom Trollope recalled that she 'inspired more awe than affection. She was an austere and somewhat grim sort of a body.' She was a Baptist and the children devised a little ditty:

Old Farmer is an Anabaptist!
When she is gone, she will not be missed!

The young Trollopes were not really fair, for she would remain faithful to the family through many difficulties yet unseen. However, at times the difference in religion between the servant and her charges could lead to difficulties. On one occasion Dr Nott was on a visit and the children were summoned to the drawing-room. The clergyman asked the conventional questions about their conduct. Tom, assuming the heavy responsibility of the eldest child, said that any little faults they had were due to the fact that their nurse was a Dissenter. Even as children the Trollopes were aware of the religious and social distinctions which surrounded them.

Fanny Trollope was not a woman to leave the more important aspects of child-rearing to a nurse. With a woman as imaginative and fun-loving as Fanny, no house could be constantly unhappy. As her eldest son wrote, she attracted 'what was pleasant around her as surely as a magnet draws iron'. She was also a clever woman who was anxious for her children's education. She had some small blocks, each of which had a different letter of the alphabet as decoration. She would scatter these 'bone counters' on the floor: the first child to find the right letter got a prize. Thus the little Trollopes soon learned their alphabet. Anthony acquired from her a love of reading that could not be destroyed, even by formal education, a love that never deserted him and that was to solace him in youth and in age. Few things are as characteristic of Fanny Trollope as using a game to teach her children to read. Equally characteristic was her husband's behaviour. He, too, was anxious that his sons follow him to Winchester and Oxford: to do so they must master Latin and Greek, and the earlier the better. 'From my early babyhood,' Anthony Trollope recalled, 'I had to take my place alongside of him as he shaved at six o'clock in the morning.' There the little boy had to repeat the rules of Latin grammar and the letters in the Greek alphabet. He had to incline his head towards his father so that if he made a mistake his stern parent could pull the child's hair without stopping the steady progress of his razor. At other times the father would sit with his arm over the back of the pupil's chair, ready to pull his son's hair though, to be fair, he never beat his children. Tom Trollope maintained that this hair-pulling method of education led to 'a nervous state of expectancy, not judiciously calculated to increase intellectual receptivity'. 'Lessons for us boys,' recalled Tom,[22]

> were never over and done with. It was sufficient for my father to see any one of us 'idling', i.e. not occupied with book-work to set us to work quite irrespectively of the previously assigned task of the day having been accomplished. And this we considered to be unjust.

Anthony often recalled in his writings the stress on 'elbow grease' in his home. The phrase has more the sound of his mother than his father, but both parents instilled in their children the belief that time was not something to waste: it was a gift from God for which they must some day give an account. Time should be spent in learning or in enjoyment, but never in idleness. Anthony remembered in the last year of his life that his father had found some consolation in the fact that the decline in his health and practice at least gave him 'more time to teach me and my brother Tom our classics'. The boys commenced their Latin studies with a standard guide dating from Tudor times, the *Eton Latin Grammar*. It was used, not just by boys at Eton, but throughout England by young people commencing the mysteries of Latin declensions and irregular conjugations. Indeed only a few years after Anthony started his early morning struggles with the *Eton Grammar*, the young Princess Victoria, four years his junior, was using it at Kensington Palace.[23] The elder Trollope also taught his sons when they were a bit older that great, and rare, art of précis-writing. He would give each boy a topic to summarise in clear and concise English. Perhaps of all the lessons that the brothers learned this was the most valuable for their future careers as writers. Both developed a staggering ability to dash off articles and books on a wide variety of subjects and to write English clearly. For this ability they could thank their unfortunate father.

There were, however, occasional breaks from these sombre paternal lessons. Fanny Trollope delighted in nature and frequently took her children on walks about the countryside, pointing out flowers and trees. Often she was accompanied by her Newfoundland dog 'Neptune'. Fanny later used Neptune in her novel, *Uncle Walter*, and Anthony did the same in *Dr. Wortle's School*, one of his last novels, where he has some children going on a walk with a Newfoundland called 'Neptune' [II]. Echoes of his mother's love of music also occur in his novels; she used to sing an old song, 'Miss Bailey's Ghost', about a girl who had been seduced by a 'Captain Bold of Halifax'. As Tom said, the children did not have 'the faintest notion of the nature of the evil which was inflicted on the poor girl and led to her suicide'.[24] But Anthony remembered it and later referred to one of his creations, an old rogue who tries to seduce the heroine, as a 'Captain Bold of Halifax' [*He Knew He Was Right* X]. The song, with its gruesome and rather explicit lyrics, demonstrates that Fanny Trollope was very much a creature of the eighteenth century. It is difficult to imagine a Victorian lady singing such a ballad to her young sons.

Travel and holidays seem to have played no role in Anthony's childhood. At least he does not say if he was ever taken on any trips by his parents. His eldest brother was, but his pleasure was lessened by his father's insistence that he study Virgil as they bounced along in the gig. However, Anthony must have been taken to see his grandfather, the Rev. William Milton, at Heckfield. Here the vicarage lawn usually boasted some strange mechanical device that the ingenious clergyman was working on in his mission to devise safer coaches. (He would no doubt be amused to see the offices of a computer firm now standing next to his church.) One model consisted of huge wheels joined by cross-bars which naturally invited a curious boy to jump on and push the contraption down the hill. 'Never,' said the elderly vicar to a bruised grandson, 'never put in motion forces which you are unable to control.' The children also delighted in watching the old gentleman at meals. Because he was unable to bear the occasional screech of a knife on a porcelain plate, he had silver pieces two inches in diameter fitted into the centre of specially made plates.[25] Surely the memory of the old vicar must have contributed much to his grandson's novels about the country clergy. Another delight for the children lay close to Heckfield: Stratfield Saye, the country house of England's greatest hero, the Duke of Wellington. Anthony Trollope would recall this countryside in a novel when fox-hunting brings one of his characters close to Heckfield Church:

> Perhaps in England there is no prettier district, no country in which moorland and woodland and pasture are more daintily thrown together to please the eye, in which there is sweeter air, or a more thorough seeming of English wealth and English beauty and English comfort. Those who know ... Heckfield and Stratfieldsaye will acknowledge it so. But then how few are the Englishmen who travel to see the beauties of their own country [*Ralph the Heir* XI].

The daily lessons during his father's shaving sessions were not just due to the demands of public schools. Thomas Anthony Trollope had the passion for classical education that marked the nineteenth century. What matter if a boy knew nothing else, provided he could

read Latin and construe Greek! The system could produce some
ludicrous results. In the 1840s a young peer, Lord Lyttelton, was
appointed Under Secretary at the Colonial Office. He was reputed one
of the cleverest men in the Government because he could write
splendid Greek poetry. Unfortunately, as one civil servant complained,
he could not find on the map most of the colonies for whose destinies he
had been made partly responsible. Years later, when Lord Lyttelton
committed suicide, his brother-in-law, William Gladstone, bemoaned
that the tragedy could have been avoided if only the poor man had been
encouraged to undertake a major translation of some Greek verse.
There were many, however, who criticised a system of education which
was interested in little but rote memorisation of Latin and Greek texts.
One anonymous poetaster wrote in *The Times* during Anthony
Trollope's boyhood.[26]

> Should you wish your hopeful Billy
> (Pride of *Pa*, and *Ma's* delight)
> Made a scholar, willy-nilly,
> Taught the classics, wrong or right:
> Should you wish him learn'd in Latin,
> While, in English, still a fool:
> All but useful knowledge pat in –
> Send him to a Public School.

Some knowledge of Latin and, to a lesser extent, Greek was an
essential part of every young gentleman's education, and to some, such
learning opened the doors to civilisations other than their own. One
relative wrote to a boy who started Harrow about the same time as
Trollope: 'If you are to be a literary man, which I hope you will (for be
assured old Cicero was right when he declared that learning was far
better than Empire) become a classical scholar – it is the first requisite
for a gentleman and a Divine.'[27] Young Henry Manning did study well,
and no doubt Latin did prove of great value to a cardinal. The real
question was not whether or not to teach the classics but how to do so.
In Trollope's youth, boys were rarely taught with any imagination or
idea of introducing them to the riches of Roman or Greek culture. All
too often the main importance of classical languages lay in their role as
a badge of the gentleman. The ability to recall a few vaguely
remembered lines of Latin demonstrated that the speaker or writer
was not as other men and had received the traditional education of the
upper orders. Representatives of the new England, the England of
factories and steam engines, men like Cobden and Bright, sneered at
the classics by saying that one issue of *The Times* had more of value

than all of Thucydides. The Duke of Wellington may have advised a new speaker never to use Greek in Parliament, but countless speeches were carefully sprinkled with classical allusions. The elder Trollope was only ensuring, albeit in his usual heavy-handed way, that his sons be prepared to assume a place in society befitting their rank as 'gentlemen'.

When Anthony Trollope was a boy there was no provision by the state for education. The first steps towards this were only taken in 1833 when grants were given to elementary schools. It was only in 1870 that government undertook to ensure that primary schools were available for all children, primarily in the expanding towns and cities of England. This was something in which Trollope strongly believed and which he advocated during his brief appearance as a politician. We have a good idea of the state of education in his boyhood because a Parliamentary committee collected statistics from every parish in England. From these we learn that 570,000 children were receiving some form of schooling, whereas over two million were receiving no formal education at all.[28] Most schools were part of an expanding Church of England network and in many parishes the parson's wife or daughters taught the basics of reading and the catechism. This centuries-old system survived well into Trollope's adulthood, and we see it in his Barset novels, where the wealthy wife of Archdeacon Grantly as well as the poor daughters of the Rev. Mr Crawley instruct the village children. Far above these schools, both in prestige and in achievement, were the grammar schools which provided the rising urban middle classes with an education. Farther yet, in prestige though often not in educational achievement, rose the public schools. For a family like the Trollopes with their position as an offshoot of the gentry to guard, there could be no question but that their sons must go to one of the ancient schools. In an article about public schools that Trollope wrote in the 1860s he described their central importance in Victorian England. They permitted 'the sons of those among our gentry who are rich, and of those who are comparatively poor, to be educated together, and thus to be welded into one whole, which is the backbone of English public and social life'.[29]

It is interesting to compare Anthony Trollope's education with that of some other Victorian novelists. Charles Dickens, who was three years older than Trollope, was sent to two private day schools in London when his father's chaotic finances permitted. William Thackeray, a year older than Dickens, went to Charterhouse and then on to Cambridge. Wilkie Collins's education was mostly private, as his father was an artist who spent much time in Italy. Benjamin Disraeli attended a minor private school and then became a solicitor's clerk: his education seemed little likely to enable a Jewish youth to become a well-known novelist and, eventually, Prime Minister. Girls were less commonly sent away to school although the two greatest women writers of the time went to minor boarding schools: Charlotte Brontë and George Eliot. Trollope, alone of those now seen as the principal novelists of the Victorian era, went to one of the great public schools where the aristocracy was educated. In fact, he went to two. Only Thackeray came close to that, but Charterhouse was not in the same league as Trollope's two schools.

Thomas Anthony Trollope's ambition for his four sons was well thought out. Thirty years later Anthony would write about a young clergyman's education: 'It was a great object with his father that he should get a scholarship at New College, to which, as all the world knows, his path lay through the college of Winchester' [*The Bertrams* I]. Both the College of St Mary of Winchester, to give New College its proper name, and Winchester College were founded by Bishop William of Wykeham in the late fourteenth century. If a boy did well at Winchester and happened to be there in a year when New College had vacant scholarships, he could proceed to Oxford with little expense to his parents. The next goal was to gain a Fellowship. As these did not require residence in college, they provided the perfect way to begin a career in the law. If, on the other hand, one of the Trollopes wished to become a clergyman, he could settle in college on the somnolent comforts of his Fellowship and wait, as their grandfather had done, until a well-endowed clerical living in the gift of the college became available. Even if he did not win a Fellowship a university education opened the door – the only door – both to the bar and to the Church.

*

Because Winchester boasted that it was the oldest public school, Thomas Anthony Trollope naturally looked down on Harrow, which was a mere two hundred years old, as 't'other school'. Under the will of its founder, John Lyon, Harrow was virtually free to boys from the parish so, until a free place became available 'on the foundation' at Winchester, the young Trollopes could be sent there with little expense. (Anthony remembered the phrase 't'other school' and used it in *Dr. Wortle's School* II.) Young Manning described the place at this time:[30]

> Harrow is a remarkably pretty place, situated on the top of a high hill.
> You are most literally aware that this place is celebrated as an abode of
> the Muses ... It bears no small resemblance to Parnassus ... Harrow is

distinguished by the peculiar salubrity of its atmosphere ... The town is remarkably clean.

Anthony began his career at Harrow in 1823, about the time of his eighth birthday. At first he had his elder brother Arthur as a companion for the daily trudge to and from school, but Arthur's health was weak and he had to be sent to his grandfather's vicarage at Heckfield where he died the next summer. (By the time he came to write his *Autobiography* Anthony Trollope appears to have forgotten that he had once had three brothers, as he only mentions Henry and Tom.) Young Anthony had to leave home early as school began at seven and lasted till five. This early departure did not aid his appearance, for he was a messy boy. Once he was stopped in the street by the Headmaster, Dr Butler, who still wore his hair powdered. He demanded to know if his school was 'disgraced by so disreputably dirty a little boy'. When Trollope came to write about this incident over half a century later he still had a sense of outrage: 'I do not doubt that I was dirty; but I think he was cruel. He must have known me ... for he was in the habit of flogging me constantly.' Then, in a typical sentence, Trollope disposes of his former Headmaster with bemused contempt: 'Perhaps he did not recognise me by my face.'[31]

Trollope's time at Harrow (he was to spend two separate periods there) was not happy. In his *Autobiography* he paints it in as dark a shade as possible and begins his second paragraph, 'My boyhood was as unhappy as that of a young gentleman could well be.' His account has many similarities with the autobiography of a much later Harrovian, Sir Winston Churchill. One must remember, however, that both Trollope and Churchill were skilled writers, anxious to present their early lives in as bleak a way as possible to enhance their own later achievements and happiness. It may be that as a boy Anthony felt neglected by his parents: of the four sons, the eldest, Tom, was closest to Fanny and the second, Henry, was his father's favourite. Because the third son, Arthur, two years older than Anthony, was sickly, Anthony may have felt neglected. In his most autobiographical novel, *The Three Clerks*, he refers to 'the not uncommon injustice of preferring the interests of the elder son' [I]. Some biographers have made too much of this: it was only a general reflection and such a feeling among children is not that unusual. Every child sees these things from his own perspective: Tom, when writing of the 'tender' love between his mother and his youngest brother, remembered 'in the old days of our youth we used to consider Anthony the Benjamin'. Trollope later admitted that part of the reason for his unhappiness was due to what he called his own lack of 'juvenile manhood'. In addition, when he went to Harrow the school was not in a particularly prosperous period. There were only about 200 boys enrolled. Almost all the lessons were taught in one large room with only one fire. Some boys even brought wax tapers so that they could see to read, but these provided more amusement than illumination. Years later, on a visit to South Africa, Trollope was to say that the native students had far better school facilities than he had known either at Harrow or at Winchester.[32]

About the time Anthony started his daily trek to school, Lord Byron's illegitimate daughter, Allegra, died at the age of five. These two seemingly unconnected events actually give us the most information about Harrow during Anthony's first time there. Byron asked that his daughter be buried in the churchyard of Harrow-on-the-Hill, as he had fond memories of sitting there as a boy. He wanted the burial service read not by the vicar, the Rev. J.W. Cunningham, but by his old tutor, the Rev. Henry Drury. Cunningham was a prominent Evangelical, well known for his book *The Velvet Cushion*, published anonymously in 1814. It claimed to be a history of the Church of England since the time of 'bloody Queen Mary' in a manuscript labelled 'My own history' and found by a Westmorland vicar in a pulpit cushion. Once the vicar's authorship was discovered his rather curious production gave rise to the nickname 'Velvet' Cunningham. The Trollopes and their circle regarded the Evangelical clergy, with their passion for preaching and constant moralising, their fundamentalist theology, obsession with 'conversions' and view that life was a 'vale of tears', their proximity to Methodists, and their low regard for the sacraments and teaching of the Church, as hypocritical, dangerous and vulgar. Tom Trollope later said he had understood that Evangelicalism was[33]

> a sort of thing that might be expected to be met with in tradesmen's back parlours, and 'academies', where the youths who came from such places were instructed in English grammar and arithmetic, but ... was utterly out of place, among gentlemen and in gentlemenlike places of education, where nothing of the kind was taught.

When the 'velvet vicar' received news of Byron's request he persuaded a meeting of church wardens and Harrow masters that it would set a bad example if the boys saw the illegitimate daughter of a notorious peer honoured in this way. So the poor little body was consigned to an unmarked grave. Fanny Trollope, a devoted admirer of Lord Byron, was outraged. She was even more furious when Drury reported, no doubt with glee, that Cunningham had asked him to convey to His Lordship the vicar's admiration of his poetry. To Mrs Trollope this was a perfect example of the Evangelicals' unctuous hypocrisy. She wrote a long poem satirising the vicar which then circulated in manuscript among her friends in Harrow. Henry Drury was so delighted with it that he presented her with the manuscript of one of Byron's poems. The whole Drury family, who dominated Harrow, hated Cunningham because he had once asked two daughters of the family to stop chattering during one of his polished sermons. Mrs Trollope's dislike of Cunningham was no doubt all the greater as it was he who had moved into the elegant new mansion the Trollopes could no longer maintain. They also looked down on him as the son of a London hatter, perhaps forgetting that the Rev. William Milton was himself the son of a Bristol tradesman. Mrs Trollope had heard that the velvet vicar was somewhat fond of giving a lingering Kiss of Peace to some of the young ladies in his parish, a habit Trollope would recall when he portrayed amorous Evangelical clergymen in his novels.

Some twelve years after his mother's poem was composed Anthony Trollope, by then in his late teens, made a careful study of it. His comments are among the earliest surviving writing in his hand and we are lucky that he went over the manuscript while his memories were still fresh. In the course of her over-long poem, Fanny Trollope mentioned the masters, all of whom were clergymen, and Anthony wrote marginal comments about them. He did not think much of the innumerable Drurys, except for 'old Harry' whose 'frankness is bearish, [he] is a good natured fellow though he has often nearly plagued my life out'. One of the other Drurys, the Rev. Mark, was a believer in strict discipline: 'Your clock,' he would tell the boys, 'requires to be wound every Monday morning' which was his oft-repeated description of his weekly floggings. (Fortunately his wife, 'Mother Mark', was a kindly woman and regularly lost the key to the cupboard where the birch was kept.) The Rev. Mark was so fat that he could no longer struggle up the hill to the school, so the boys came down to him. Of the Headmaster, that pompous soul who had berated him in the street, the young Trollope had no pleasant memories. 'As to Butler – I recollect very little except tho' he was very severe to little boys, he was a very inefficient master and the school went on declining till he resigned – he was altogether unable to keep the head boys in order, and rather feared them.' (Lord Byron had shared Trollope's contempt for Butler, whom he portrayed as 'Pomposus' in a poem he composed while still at the school.)*

---

*'On a Change of Masters at a Great Public School' was dated 'Harrow – July 1805'. Byron, along with other boys, had opposed Butler's election as Headmaster. Even after he took office some of the boys burnt his desk and there was a plot to blow up the school:

Fanny Trollope's strongest poetic venom, while perhaps not of Byronic quality, still had a virulence which was reserved for Cunningham. Imitating his most velvet-like tone, she portrays him addressing the church wardens:

> It is indeed a very shocking thing,
> That one who is so very great a man
> Should such disgrace upon our parish fling.
> ...
> But by my preaching I'll do all I can
> To counteract the influence of the bones
> Unhappily now laid beneath our stones.

Anthony's rereading of the poem stirred his own memories of Cunningham: the vicar had been well known to all the boys as he was in the habit of inviting them to dinner for earnest talks about religion. Trollope noted that the vicar 'was almost worshipped by the low church at Harrow, very unpopular with the gentry and much feared by the poor'. He recalled Cunningham's often speaking to him about religion but felt that he was a 'cringing hypocrite and a most confounded liar, who would give [his] eyes to be a bishop'. Surely here is the prototype of those scheming Evangelical clergymen whom Trollope depicted in such odious light in his novels. As in so much else, the man drew on the experience of the boy and the example of his mother.[34]

There was one other event connected with Byron which occurred while Anthony was first at Harrow. When word arrived in 1824 that the great poet had died in Greece, the boys of his old school went to the parish church where they heard the Headmaster preach on the abuse of 'natural gifts'. In time Trollope came to agree that Byron did have a bad influence, not so much in spreading immorality as in propagating the idea of the 'Byronic hero' who wraps his tragic fate lovingly about him like a great swirling cape. This was directly contrary to one of Trollope's basic beliefs, that manliness demanded that 'you should carry your outer self, that the eyes of those around you should see nothing of the sorrow within' [*The Vicar of Bullhampton* LXVIII]. In Trollope's novels a devotion to Byron is often the sign of a bad, or at least of a weak character. In this he came closer to the views of his old Headmaster than to those of his mother. Despite this he still retained a

---

cooler heads prevailed and the gunpowder was not ignited. In the seventh and eighth lines Byron referred to Butler: 'Of narrow brain, yet of a narrower soul,/Pomposus holds you in his harsh controul.'

grudging admiration for Byron's poetry till the end of his life.

His elder brothers had started at Harrow with the advantage of coming from the new brick mansion. Even so, they were still attacked as mere day-boys. For Anthony it was far worse: he trudged to school not from a new mansion but from an old farmhouse, enduring a 'daily purgatory' from the wealthy boarders. There were only seventeen 'home boarders' at Harrow and he may have suffered more than the other sixteen, if only because he was a particularly sensitive child. The misery he endured seethed below the surface throughout his life and frequently boiled over into his writings and actions, especially when confronted with rank injustice. In *Can You Forgive Her?*, for example, written when he was forty-nine and at the height of his success, he stops his novel to preach a little sermon:

> Boys have less of conscience than men, are more addicted to tyranny and when weak are less prone to feel the misery and disgrace of succumbing. Who has been to a large school and does not remember ... the tyrants and the slaves – those who domineered and those who submitted.

This was a topic that the adult Trollope would reflect on for a considerable time and, as so often when he had pondered, he said much worth remembering. He saw that it was not intellect, courage or even strength that gave the tyrants their predominance. 'I think,' he continued, 'the outward gait of the boy goes far towards obtaining for him the submission of his fellows.' After many years of thought, he was pleased to conclude, 'the tyrant boy does not become the tyrant man, or the slave boy the slave man, because the outward visage that has been noble or mean in the one, changes and becomes so often mean or noble in the other' [XVI]. Trollope's 'outward gait' was ungainly. While we know little about his physical appearance as a young boy, we do know that his clothes were often messy. As he made his way through the lanes, dusty in the heat of summer or muddy in the wet of winter, he occupied his mind with fantasies of great adventures in which he was, naturally, the hero, and gradually his plots became more intricate. Here, in these walks between the increasing tensions at home and the continuing misery at school, was born the future novelist. The long walk, as well as the lack of pocket money, gave the boy a tattered appearance and reputation. Many of the boarders came from aristocratic or, at least, wealthy families. Young Henry Manning's father, for example, was a Tory MP and a director of the Bank of England. He lavished an allowance of £250 a year on his son, who could afford to dazzle his schoolfellows with such luxuries as tassels on his boots. Years later these tassels were replaced by those on the red hat of a cardinal. In the 1820s, three Old Harrovians were distinguishing themselves as important politicians and would all eventually become Prime Minister: Sir Robert Peel, Lord Aberdeen and Lord Palmerston. Such examples made many Harrow boys acutely conscious of their position, and a messy boy like Anthony Trollope did not fit into that image. He was, therefore, marked down for persecution at worst, or loneliness at best.

There was another reason why he was unhappy. Five years before he was born some residents of the village brought suit against the school, alleging that the masters were violating the will of its founder, John Lyon. They claimed that the school should be for the benefit of the residents and not for the wealthy boarders, or indeed for the masters who did so well out of them. Even though the masters won the case, some of them still resented day boys such as Trollope. In the last year of his life he told his first biographer: 'The controversy had the effect of adding a fresh sting to my position as a day boy. The masters snubbed me more than ever because I was one of the class which had brought about legal interference with their vested right. The young aristocrats, who lived sumptuously in' the masters' houses treated me like a pariah.'[35] Years later he used a similar dispute as the plot for *The Warden*, the first of his novels to gain recognition.

There was one other aspect of life at Harrow which influenced his future career. Everywhere he looked he saw clergymen and the conflicts between them: the Drurys, who were friends of his parents, disliked the Headmaster, Butler, who had succeeded their father, Joseph Drury, as Head in 1805, and both Butler and the Drurys disliked the Vicar. Things came to a head in 1829: Henry Drury wrote to James Ingram, President of Trinity College, Oxford and a friend of the Trollopes, that 'the Head Mastership of Harrow is vacant ... The Evangelical Party will probably, under Cunningham marshalling it, be brought into play against me. I am anxious therefore if you can throw in anything about *"good parson."* ' By showing that he was a dedicated clergyman as well as a good schoolmaster he presumably hoped to lessen Evangelical opposition. There was one problem he did not have to worry about: 'Quadrouple [*sic*] postage is no object,' when gathering letters of support.[36] In the event Drury failed, and Charles Longley was elected, but the election was only another example of how clergymen pursued their centuries-old fondness for attacking one another with polite venom. The wrangling would not be lost on the young Trollope.

*

The masters' main function was not to teach but rather to hear translations from the Classics and to do little else. Although the school was conducted by clergymen there was little religious instruction as that would have smacked of 'enthusiasm', a vulgar Evangelical attribute. The boys were at least nominally Anglican, and the masters presumed that their parents had given them basic religious instruction. A large number of Trollope's schoolfellows did become well-known clergymen and few had anything good to say about the religious teaching at Harrow. The most prominent of them, Cardinal Manning, remembered that the only religious instruction was the reading of 'Waller's catechism for an hour every Sunday morning'. Another Harrovian, who became an Anglican bishop in Canada, wrote: 'As for *Religious Instruction*, there was none, or very little ... and that little was strictly confined to the sixth form, who on every Sunday read a few dry pages of Paley's "Evidences" with Dr. Butler. No pains were taken to make us either good Christians or intelligent Churchmen.'[37]

The public schools, as the young Queen Victoria complained to her first Prime Minister, Lord Melbourne, also made no attempt to teach boys French or any other living language. Indeed the schools viewed subjects like history, mathematics or modern languages, let alone English literature, with bemused contempt. Thirty years later another Harrovian, John Addington Symonds, who was to become a well-known historian of the Renaissance, was shocked as well as delighted at his schoolfellows' ignorance. His report also accurately described the school in Trollope's time:[38]

> I was so amused yesterday with hearing the answers of some of our Sixth Form to our History Paper ... One boy had the idea that 'the Tempest' was a political conspiracy ... Another declared that Rubens was a celebrated philosopher ... Another that Galileo was a remarkable divine ... I was talking the other day with a Sixth Form boy who had never heard of Chaucer, Cowley, Chatterton, Southey, Hood, Cervantes ... He had heard of Dryden, Sir J. Reynolds, Claude Lorrain, Wordsworth but was not sure whether they were celebrated for painting or poetry.

Unlike such boys, Trollope already knew a fair amount about history and literature. Sidney Herbert remembered that young Anthony was quite remarkable for his general knowledge and reading when he came to Harrow.[39]

Trollope's general knowledge was far from a common possession at the school, but he was growing up in a house where conversations about literature, the theatre, music and painting were frequent. Both parents, more especially Fanny, still shared fully in the cosmopolitan culture of London despite their living in Harrow. She made efforts to instruct her children in French and Italian and had them taught drawing by a professional artist. Her own writings are filled with references to French and Italian authors, particularly to Molière and Dante. Their family friend Prebendary Nott had brought out his own edition of Dante's *Divine Comedy*. As with her earlier lessons in the alphabet, she mixed learning with pleasure. The Trollope children's French was improved by their taking part in adaptations of scenes from Molière's plays which were performed for guests. This was Anthony's introduction to drama, something which was to be one of the great pleasures of his life. From it he drew not only his great skill in writing dialogue but plots for his own works. Likewise he would always retain an interest in Molière, an interest he passed on to his own son who was later to write a biography of the dramatist. Fanny Trollope often sprinkled her speech and her letters, and later her books with short French phrases, and Anthony would do the same in his early novels.

The Trollope children also acted little plays especially written by their mother. Her strong satirical side delighted in assaulting her enemies, particularly the Evangelicals. Copies were made in large copper-plate handwriting, perhaps by one of Anthony's sisters, and one can still see the faint pencilled lines to encourage good penmanship. The most amusing of the plays to have survived is called 'The Righteous Rout'. Unfortunately there is no indication which part young Anthony took, but echoes of the play's sentiments occur throughout his novels. Mrs Trollope portrays a tea party of 'the Saints' at the Rev. Mr Fripp's drawing-room, where various hypocrites sprinkle their every comment with pious platitudes such as 'He'll wash His own'. The gathering is mainly concerned with raising money for 'Sabbath Schools' which, it may be recalled, was an interest of Mrs Proudie in *Barchester Towers*. One character gives an account of the progress of the fund-raising so far:[40]

> Twopence a week paid by each private pew
> In doctor Cantwell's chapel makes one pound two; –
> Tracts on faith not said how many
> Sold by six beggars sixteen and a penny.
> From Starveall Workhouse by a farthing rate,
> Collected by myself, is one pound eight,
> Crumbs for the Lord from door to door
> Through Huntingdon nineteen pounds four.

Thomas Trollope did not neglect his children's cultural education, although his efforts were, characteristically, less enjoyable: he would read aloud from the works of the great eighteenth-century authors.

Perhaps it was from this source that Anthony acquired the habit of using older terms like 'fain', 'wax wroth' and 'fardel' that were beginning to go out of fashion when he wrote his novels. In this, as in many little habits, his father's influence took hold for, to quote an archaic phrase used in one of Trollope's own novels, he was 'the son of his loins'.

*

After two years it was becoming obvious that Anthony was making little progress at Harrow, where he was 'lag' of the School.[41] Even though no place was yet available at Winchester, Henry Drury recommended that he be removed from Harrow. Drury had another plan in mind, and although it would cost more it might help the boy prepare for his expected place at Winchester. There was a seemingly endless supply of ordained Drurys, and one of them, the Rev. Arthur, was a clergyman in Sunbury, then a quiet spot on the banks of the Thames. It was quite common for clergymen to take a few pupils to supplement their incomes and sometimes they established a small school where boys could be prepared either for public school or for Oxford or Cambridge. Trollope himself was to depict such an establishment in one of his best short novels, *Dr. Wortle's School*. Arthur Drury's school, however, was not of the same quality as Dr Wortle's. This Drury was not a very effective teacher: he was said to be the largest of that remarkably plump family and he also stuttered. Mr Trollope, economical as ever, forbade French lessons or anything that required an extra fee. Despite all this, Anthony was happier than he had been at Harrow and, although he still lacked pocket money and had few clothes, he was at least accepted by the other boys, among whom was Henry Drury's nephew, John Merivale, who remained one of Trollope's closest friends throughout life.

Yet even this happiness was not to last. One day he was accused of a 'nameless horror' which some commentators have asserted, with no evidence, to have been some mild form of 'schoolboy vice'. While homosexual behaviour is totally out of keeping with Trollope's later life, Harrow did have a reputation for it. When Arthur Drury accused Anthony and three other boys of the 'nameless horror' the ten-year-old furiously protested his innocence for the simple reason that he was not guilty. Drury, however, blamed Anthony more than the others because he was, after all, a public school boy and therefore should have known better. He now chose an annoying punishment: the boys were given sermons to copy out in their free time. As Anthony was given the longest, it took him most of his free time. Perhaps this is one reason he never would share the Victorian fascination with sermons. Lord Melbourne used to read them as a relief from politics, but this was before sermons became another form of politics. Trollope's novels contain only a few sermons and these are not very edifying. The four culprits were also singled out by being the last to be fed, which presumably meant they had little to eat. There was the added indignity that Mrs Drury would turn her head when one of the four malefactors approached her virtuous gaze.

A love of truth and justice was always regarded by Trollope as an essential attribute of the gentleman, and Drury had offended against both by not believing the truth when he heard it and not behaving justly when he punished Trollope for a crime he had never committed. Fifty years later, when writing about the incident, the memory welled up within him: 'It burns me now as though it were yesterday.' The other three boys were remembered as 'lily-livered curs' for not telling the truth about his innocence. The following term his innocence was finally established and Drury's pathetic attempt at an apology only made the unmerited punishment worse. Yet one cannot but think that this episode of school life played an important role in the formation of Trollope's attitudes towards truth, justice and manliness: all of which were to be central themes in his writing.

After two years at Sunbury Anthony received word that he had been elected to a free place at Winchester. Now he would not be at a small private school or even at Harrow but at the oldest public school in England. Sydney Smith, the wittiest clergyman of his time, perhaps of any time, had been at Winchester with Mr Trollope and described the thoughts that went through a father's mind when he sent his son to follow his footsteps:

> Have I been whipt for the substantives? whipt for the verbs? and whipt for and with the interjections? ... and shall my son be exempt from all this misery? ... Ay, ay, it's all mighty well; but I went through this myself, and I am determined my children shall do the same.[42]

*

In the spring of 1827, at the age of twelve, Trollope entered his third school. Presumably his father took his youngest son to Winchester, as he had taken his older ones, in his gig. Like many boys, Tom and Anthony could be easily embarrassed by their father's behaviour in public: in this case, his passion for saving money. When they arrived at

Winchester he would not stay at one of the fashionable inns but insisted on stopping at the Fleur de Lys, which was both older and cheaper. Anthony's brother Tom had been at the school for seven years and was a 'candle keeper', an exalted eminence in the hierarchy of that juvenile world, and, in addition, he had enjoyed the friendship of Prebendary Nott. In 1825 when he was planning on leaving Winchester to take up a living in Kent, Nott wrote to the Trollopes to tell them of a visit from Tom and Henry. Although the scene he describes occurred two years before Anthony arrived at the school, it does tell us a great deal about the way in which the Trollope boys had been raised. Prebendary Nott at first admitted that when the boys called for dinner he was 'vexed at having dined myself before they came' but he went on:[43]

I now rejoice at it ... they paid one in their good nature, and good manners twice the amount of the bill. As soon as dinner was over, and a little chat had passed, I took up my pen to finish a letter, and I begged they would amuse themselves till tea time with a Book. One chose Dryden's Prose Works, the other a vol. of Somers' Tracts. Bravo quoth I. The choice augurs well. But I doubt how far the body will keep pace with the Mind. Just as I thought, a warm fire, a good dinner, and a rare arm Chair were too much for their love of literature. In five minutes they were fast asleep and so comfortable did they seem, that I had not the heart to wake them till tea was quite ready, and there was no more than time to drink it before they were obliged to go into College. I again assure you that I was pleased highly with their manners and conversation, and not a little surprised at being asked by the eldest what I thought of Dante, and whether I did not consider the third, the finest book of the Inferno. Saucy fellow.

Tom obviously was thoroughly enjoying himself at Winchester and his memoirs recount, with loving detail, every time-encrusted custom that still prevailed, in contrast to Anthony's *Autobiography* which devotes only a few pages to his time there. (The other brother, Henry, ever idle, had been removed from the school as he had shown no aptitude for work.) Fanny Trollope wrote with maternal pride to her eldest son: 'Your father must certainly consider himself as very fortunate' in getting yet another son into Winchester. However, she added, 'it will not do us much good, unless we get some *dispers* of the New College loaves and fishes'. 'Dispers' was the school term for a portion of food, and Fanny was reminding her son that the struggle had only begun. The two brothers still had to gain places at Oxford by following the customary route to New College. She also reminded the seventeen-year-old Tom of his responsibility for his younger brother:

I dare say you will often find him idle and plaguing enough. But remember, dear Tom, that in a family like ours, *everything* gained by one is felt personally and individually by all. He is a good-hearted fellow, and clings to the idea of being Tom's pupil and sleeping in Tom's chamber, that I think you will find advice and remonstrance better taken by him than by poor Henry. Greatly comforted am I to know that Tony has a perfect brother.

She also urged Tom to be patient: he too had once been a new boy and she recalled, 'what I used to suffer at the idea of what my "little Tom" was enduring'. Unfortunately this maternal advice was quickly discarded: the big brother became the worst tyrant of all to young Anthony, who remembered that 'as a part of his daily exercise he thrashed me with a big stick'. Anthony reflected on this in his *Autobiography*: 'Since I began my manhood ... I and my brother ... have been fast friends. There have been hot words between us, for perfect friendship bears and allows hot words. Few brothers have had more of brotherhood. But in those school-days he was, of all my foes, the worst.'[44]

Young 'Tony' grew tired of Tom's favourite dictum: 'Hang a little boy for stealing apples and other little boys will not steal apples.' The tyranny was carried into lessons as well as other aspects of school life. The older boys acted as tutors to the younger and the pedantic Tom made Anthony's life a misery as his tutor. The great feat was to memorise 'as many lines of Latin and Greek as the memory could be made to carry'. 'Alas me, how easy it is to forget an "Aneid" and how hard to learn one' moaned the mature Trollope. Such forgetfulness and other faults met with a swift response: 'I have been flogged oftener than any human being alive. It was just possible to obtain five scourgings in one day at Winchester, and I have often boasted that I obtained them all.' The use of the word 'flogged' must have made his elder brother wince, for in his memoirs, written after Anthony's had been published, he lovingly recounts:[45]

The words 'flog' and 'flogging' ... were never heard among us ... We were 'scourged' ... Two boys ... stepped behind the form, turned the gown of a collegian or the coat-tails of a commoner over his shoulders, and unbuttoned his brace buttons, leaving bare at the part where the braces join the trousers a space equal to the diameter of a crown-piece – such was the traditional rule. And aiming at this with more or less exactitude the master inflicted three cuts ... It caused neither pain nor disgrace, and assuredly morally degraded nobody. I have been scourged five times in the day ... I had, say, come into chapel *'tarde'* i.e. after the service had commenced; I had omitted to send in duly my *'vulgus'*, I had been 'floored' in my Horace.

The boys may have studied Athenian authors but they lived under Spartan conditions. At Winchester there was no privacy and few comforts. There were no chairs at their desks and while preparing their work boys sat on the trunks containing their clothes. As at Harrow, all the masters were clergymen, the education was almost exclusively devoted to the Classics and the boys had to compose original Latin verses. In addition they were expected to have some small acquaintance with history after the fall of Rome. In *Questions for Junior Classes*, published at Winchester the year after Trollope's arrival, we catch a glimpse of the period, for every age best reveals its principles and its prejudices when it rearranges the past for its children. 'The Compiler's Caution to Young Readers' warns the boys: 'It is true, that a stock of learning, like a stock of wealth, is of little service, if you have not some by you for ready use; but let no boy think himself sufficiently rich, who has only a little of this small change in his pocket.' This 'small change' taught facts and views concerning scripture, chronology, history and geography in the form of a catechism:

Q. Who was Mahomet? A. The founder of a false religion prevailing in the East.
Q. What is the date of the Martyrdom of King Charles? A. 1649.
Q. What event put a final end to the usurpation of Napoleon Buonaparte?
A. The victory of Waterloo, near Brussels, in 1815.

Thus the rudiments of history were brought up to the year of Trollope's birth. The Tory atmosphere is seen not just in the reference to the 'Martyrdom of King Charles' but in the third question which preserved the Italian spelling of Napoleon's name. As Fanny Trollope said a few years later, 'all our great schools are Tory to the heart's core'.[46]

The boys' day began at 5.30 when they rose to attend chapel. Each chamber provided hard beds for about ten boys and each would hurry to the pillar on which were hung the surplices for chapel. As a junior boy, Anthony would place the washing basin on a table for his prefect, who was also his older brother. As an 'inferior', Anthony did not share Tom's privilege of washing inside the chamber. Like all the other 'inferiors', he had to wash in the open quadrangle whatever the weather. Looking back, Tom pronounced this custom particularly commendable: 'I say that it would have been difficult to find a healthier collection of boys.' Anthony remembered that since it was difficult to get hot water the boys rarely washed their feet: 'the very careful, once

a week, and by the very careless once a quarter.' He could never forget
the miserable duties of the younger boys:[47]

> To furnish some prefect with candlestick, snuffers, and extinguisher was
> the great trouble of my early years. How often have I wandered in my
> nightshirt, on a winter night, out under the buttresses of the chapel,
> looking for snuffers, where I might as well have looked for a crock of gold;
> have wandered searching where no finding was possible, have returned
> hopeless, snufferless, and suppliant, and have then been sent out again
> to wander, and again to search. It seems incredible that it should have
> been so; but the true wonder is that we, who have been so treated, should
> look back at it all with affection.

There were several hours of lessons before a breakfast of bread,
butter and beer at 10. 'Beer,' recalled Trollope, 'was the only beverage
provided, or indeed permitted, for breakfast, dinner, or supper.' The
old attitude that tea and coffee were not good for the young still
lingered at Winchester: tea was only permitted for boys who were ill. If
any tea pots were found in the chambers, a master would smash them
while remarking, 'What are these things, sir? William of Wykeham
knew nothing, I think, of tea.' Curiously the supplies of beer were
unrestricted: any boy could go to the college cellars and draw large jugs
from the huge hogsheads. Anthony, as a junior boy, must have made
many a trip to carry such jugs to his brother and other prefects. There
was little variety in the meals, which were served in the same hall
where they did all their schoolwork. The food was served on large
wooden trenchers but often the small boys had no fork or knife and
could use nothing but a wooden skewer. On Sundays there was a great
treat, roast beef, but at noon every other day the aroma of boiled beef
greeted them. About this there was an infuriating custom. Someone
had decreed that the boys should always give their beef to the
twenty-four women who weeded the quadrangle. How Trollope's sense
of justice must have joined his appetite in outrage at this! At least the
boys could eat the meat served at their evening meal: one night it
would be roast mutton, the next boiled mutton, and so on. Mutton was
cheap in the early nineteenth century and it was considered a good
meal for the young. Queen Victoria had had so much of it as a child
that she refused to eat it after she came to the throne. Mutton did not
have this effect on Trollope as he probably mentions a leg of mutton
more frequently in his novels than any other food. However, he did not
recall the Winchester mutton with any affection, for the pound 'lump'
given to the small boys was often nothing but fat. Occasionally a treat
would arrive when Farmer, the boys' old nurse, sent Tom a cake.

History does not record whether his little brother was given a piece.

Except on holidays, or during the two 'half-holidays' each week, only one hour each day was allowed for play or games. On these 'half holidays' the boys marched to St Catherine's Hill, about a mile from the College, where they played various games including badger-baiting and mouse-killing. Years later, Trollope would recall the badger hunts and use them as a description of his feelings when under intense questioning from a Parliamentary committee. He remembered too how the bull-dogs were taken to a badger hole and were encouraged by the boys' shouts of 'Draw him, bull dog! Bite him, badger!' while the two animals would maul one another for the amusement of the little brutes standing about [*The Three Clerks* XXXII]. Yet even then mediaeval tradition prevailed, and when it was time to return, Tom and the other prefects called out loudly, 'Domum! Domum!' Although Anthony was by now tall and physically strong, he appears to have had little aptitude for sport. Winchester was known as the best school for cricket, and Trollope played it because it was compulsory.[48] This meant that his mother and Farmer had to make and patch his cricket flannels as there was little money for a new pair. In one novel he recalled his youthful cricket by using its terms as a metaphor [*The Small House at Allington* XVIII]. He also would have done some regular swimming. It would be many years before Trollope found a sport he loved and that would be fox-hunting, which he would follow with a passion that more than made up for his youthful indifference.

When William of Wykeham founded Winchester College in 1382 he laid down strict rules for religious observances, and 450 years later the boys still followed his mediaeval routine. They went to chapel twice every day, except on Friday and Saturday, when they went three times. 'How sweet to me were those chapel chambers,' recalled the middle-aged Trollope, not so much for religious as for physical reasons: 'I could rest for half an hour with a certainty that no prefect would call for snuffers!' He also remembered one over-worked chaplain walking down the chapel nave muttering, 'I have read the Litany thrice this day; and I'm damned if I'll read it again.' On Sundays Trollope and the other boys could enjoy the splendours of Winchester Cathedral where, on one side, was the chantry chapel where William of Wykeham was buried in 1404, while almost opposite was the plain grave where Jane Austen had been buried just ten years before Anthony had come to the school. By the mid-1860s the moderately High Church Trollope looked back with 'something of a shudder' at the 'mode of those services'. His elder brother, writing at the end of the Victorian period, that age of remarkable religious feeling, observed the different attitude in his youth:[49]

We English were not a devout people in the days when George the Third was king, especially as regards all that portion of the world which held aloof from evangelicalism and dissent. We were not altogether without religious feeling in college, but it manifested itself chiefly in the form of a pronounced abhorrence for those two, as we considered them, ungentlemanlike propensities. For about three weeks, at Easter time, the lower classes in the school read the Greek Testament instead of the usual Greek authors, and the upper classes read Lowth's 'Praelections on the Sacred Poetry of the Hebrews', a book unimpeachable in point of Latinity and orthodoxy, for was not its author a Wykehamist?

*

The City of Winchester, which boasted that it was the ancient capital of England and even the possessor of King Arthur's round table, had become a sleepy place. Its life was dominated by the Cathedral and the College along with the clergy who served both. When a new bishop came to the rich and powerful see (he owed his appointment to the personal favour of King George IV) the year after young Anthony arrived, all the bells of the Cathedral, the College and every parish church rang out to greet him. Some fifty tradesmen rode out on horseback, accompanied by a band, to welcome their new 'Father in God'. The ways and customs of Winchester were not without value to the creator of Barchester. The school itself was full of old customs which were beginning to appear ridiculous to a utilitarian age. A messenger called 'Speedyman' still walked the fifty-three miles from Oxford to bring details of elections, deaths and marriages at New College. Although the news had long preceded him by coach, it was only deemed official when Speedyman limped into College. At a time when the world's first railways were starting in the north of England, Anthony Trollope could watch official news arriving by the oldest method known to man, a messenger on foot. There is something symbolic here: in his own life and writing there would always be a dichotomy between that part which looked back with veneration to the quiet ways of centuries past and that part which rejoiced in playing a role in an age of dazzling progress. The news brought by Speedyman was vital to that little world in which both Trollope boys lived, for any vacancy at New College could mean a place for them, and a place filled with 'dispers'.[50]

*

The 'dispers' were much needed because of the situation back in Harrow: Thomas Anthony Trollope's affairs were going from bad to worse. His health was declining as rapidly as his finances: he suffered from almost constant headaches which were so bad that he, who so hated 'idling', was forced to take to his couch. To try to cure these attacks, which could well have been due to a brain tumour, he took large doses of calomel, which only made his temper worse and may have caused an addiction. His wife disapproved of his dependence on the drug and in her first book attacked its prevalence in America. It was not only his family who suffered from his temper. He made little effort to be civil to solicitors and consequently his legal work was drying up. 'Your father,' an old acquaintance told one of his sons many years later,[51]

> never came into contact with a blockhead without insisting on irrefutably demonstrating to him that he was such. And the blockhead did not like it! He was a disputatious man; and he was almost invariably – at least on a point of law – right. But the world differed from him in the opinion that being so gave him the right of rolling his antagonist in the dust and executing an intellectual dance of triumph on his prostrate form.

In addition the 1820s were not the right time for a barrister to display such obtuse rudeness, for the ranks of barristers were fast filling up: when Thomas Anthony Trollope began his career there were under 600 barristers; now, twenty years later, there were over 800. Confronted by the irascible Trollope, solicitors simply took their briefs elsewhere and there was a decreasing need for Mr Trollope to don his wig.

Likewise, the farm would not prosper: English agriculture continued to suffer and by the late 1820s was in dreadful condition. Agriculturalists suffered because taxes fell so heavily on land. In his letter of proposal to Fanny Milton, Thomas Anthony had warned: 'Happiness is not to be expected where the parties are no longer capable of enjoying those necessities and comforts of life to which they have been accustomed.' Almost twenty years later that dreadful possibility had arrived. Mrs Trollope had to repair the children's clothes but she could at least joke about becoming a 'very good tailor'. She wrote constantly to her boys: most of her letters had large passages in French and Italian to encourage their familiarity with those languages. Letters also arrived from their father, filled with advice about getting a place at Oxford or with help on their lessons. If they wanted any Classical text he was happy to send it down to them from his well-stocked library. It was not often that the hard-pressed parents could send money. Occasionally their mother would find something: 'Half a crown from Papa, a proof at once of poverty and kindness. Without the former it would be more, without the latter it would be nothing.' She explained that 'all the world are as poor as Job, and rather poorer, for Job put none of his sons to public schools, and had no clients who did not pay him. Next year I fear we shall be poorer still.'[52] Yet, despite all her difficulties, Fanny went on to discuss the merits of the latest novel by Sir Walter Scott.

Anthony had only been at Winchester a few months when his mother described her plans for the summer holidays. All the family would gather at the farmhouse. 'Poor Henry' would return from Paris where he was attempting to become a banker. He sent word to his brothers that French food was not as bad or as oily as he had feared, but when he walked the streets he was often followed by little boys shouting 'Voici, le petit goddamn'. Even though it was only a dozen years since Waterloo the Parisian urchins were using a phrase which dated from the Middle Ages, when the sturdy soldiers from England were known as 'god-damns' because of their frequent devotion to that expression. Mrs Trollope was planning to combine the family reunion with a party to promote the romance of an old friend, Julia Garnett. She had invited Julia's fiancé, a German professor, to Harrow where the sight of happy family life, assuming Mr Trollope's temper was controlled, might nudge him toward matrimony. 'I have already been planning sundry "drolleries" to amuse us all,' she told her sons. Once again, the children would act scenes from Molière to keep up their French and to entertain their elders. In spite of financial worries there would still be treats: 'You will find some fruit left for you; at least the gooseberries, currants, peaches, nectarines and apricots, all promise largely.'[53]

It is worth pausing to note that among the tastes which Fanny Trollope passed on to Anthony was a fondness for fruit. Like his mother, he would take great pride in his garden and orchard, and both their books are filled with allusions to fruit which normally conclude that few foreign gardens equalled their own. Trollope, indeed, was to use fruit as a frequent metaphor in his writing. Many of his novels defend the superiority of young men who mature slowly, a subject understandably dear to the author's heart, and he almost invariably adds that the fruit that ripens slowly is the sweetest. Fruit is also often used as a metaphor for the good things in life. In *The Claverings* for example he compares the rich estate of a titled widow, who is anxious to marry again, to her apples:

> All her apples hitherto had turned to ashes between her teeth, because her fate had forced her to attempt the eating of them alone. But if she could give the fruit to him, – if she could make the apples over, so that

they should all be his, and not hers, then would there not come to her some of the sweetness of the juice of them [XXXVI].

Those enjoying the produce of Fanny Trollope's orchard in that summer of 1827 included the usual variety of people she liked to have round her. Her neighbour, Colonel Grant, had daughters of a similar age to Anthony and he formed friendships with them, friendships that would be 'life-enduring'. Perhaps it is of this period, a time when he enjoyed the last real happiness he was to know for several years, that he wrote half a century later as he watched children playing in South Africa:[54]

> After standing a while and gazing I perceived that the young people ... were playing kiss-in-the-ring. Oh – how long ago it was since I played kiss-in-the-ring, and how nice I used to think it! ... How the girls ran, and could always have escaped from the lads if they listed, but always were caught ... And how awkward the lads were in kissing, and how clever the girls in taking care that it should always come off at last.

Fanny's 'drolleries' were a great success. The amateur production of Molière's *Malade Imaginaire* went over well and Julia Garnett, who took a leading part, received the expected proposal from her German professor. When autumn arrived, Tom and Anthony returned to Winchester: Tom, no doubt, was pleased to return to his miniature kingdom. For his twelve-year-old brother the trip back would have been less happy for it was a return to a seemingly endless misery. The boys knew that their mother was planning a trip to Paris to try to sort out a future for 'poor Henry' while their father remained at home to supervise the hay harvest. Then, in November, they received the startling news that she, along with their brother, Henry, and their two sisters, Emily and Cecilia, had boarded a ship bound for New Orleans, accompanied by Mrs Trollope's protégé, a young French artist, two servants and the most notorious female radical in the English-speaking world, an apostle of women's rights and free love. Mr Trollope remained alone in the rambling farmhouse at Harrow with his hay and his excruciating headaches.

CHAPTER TWO

Perfectly Without Destination

In his *Autobiography* Anthony Trollope described his mother's character in a humorous and somewhat exaggerated passage:[1]

> She had loved society, affecting a somewhat liberal *rôle*, and professing an emotional dislike to tyrants, which sprung from the wrongs of would-be regicides and the poverty of patriot exiles. An Italian marquis who had escaped with only a second shirt from the clutches of some archduke whom he had wished to exterminate, or a French *prolétaire* with distant ideas of sacrificing himself to the cause of liberty, were always welcome to the modest hospitality of her house.

This delight in drawing-room revolutionaries led directly to her quixotic adventures in America and ultimately to Trollope's own career as an author.

Julia Garnett, whose romance had been assisted by the amateur production of Molière, was one of Mrs Trollope's oldest friends. She and her sisters had been taken to America by their father, a wealthy radical from Somerset. The family lived in New Jersey for many years and became close friends of a visiting young Scotswoman, Fanny Wright. Half a century later Trollope recalled 'a certain Miss Wright – who was, I think, the first of the American female lecturers'. In two novels, *He Knew He Was Right* and *Is He Popenjoy?* he caricatured several lady lecturers from the New World, but in his *Autobiography* he confessed that one had become 'a ray of light to me'.

Trollope's attitude towards these creations of his imagination as well as his later infatuation with Kate Field, was affected by his mother's friendship with Fanny Wright. In 1811, at the age of sixteen, this wealthy orphan stumbled across an Italian book, Carlo Botta's wildly inaccurate 'history' of the American Revolution. Contemporary attitudes towards female education are seen in the fact that while she could read Italian, she had never heard of America. It then became her 'fixed but secret determination' to visit 'a country consecrated to freedom', and eventually she eluded her guardian. After a three-year visit, she wrote an enthusiastic book, *Views of Society and Manners in America*. It delighted that ageing 'hero of two continents', the Marquis de Lafayette. Since his youthful participation in the American Revolution, Lafayette's career had led to a series of disasters both for himself and for France. This book reminded him of his own youth and his one success. Fanny Wright was soon in Paris with her friends, the Garnetts, some of whom were now living there. In time she was installed as Lafayette's 'adopted daughter' at his château and began helping him smuggle letters back and forth to London, especially to her friend Jeremy Bentham, the radical philosopher and constitution-maker. In 1822, she told Bentham to leave some English newspapers at Keppel Street with Mrs Trollope. Apparently these were English newspapers that Lafayette wanted smuggled into France past the police, who were watching most of his radical circle. 'She will find means of forwarding it.' (All this makes one assume that the Trollopes continued to use Keppel Street as some sort of *pied-à-terre* for their literary and political friendships in the capital.) Ten years later, in her book on America, Mrs Trollope claimed she had had. a leaning to 'sedition'. She was certainly never a revolutionary, but her family's financial setbacks during a long period of Tory domination no doubt increased her emotional attachment to various radicals. Trollope himself was to say, rather frequently, that he had sympathy for 'rebels'. Like so many aspects of his character, this came from his mother.[2]

In some ways the Garnetts in Paris were the connecting link in the early 1820s of a large Anglo-French network of radically-minded people which included Fanny Wright, Lafayette, Sir Francis Burdett, Joseph Hume, Sir Thomas and Lady Dyer, Mary Shelley and Thomas Campbell as well as the Trollopes. If anything, Anthony Trollope's assessment of his mother's drawing-room radicalism is an under-statement, and it is quite likely that the legend that Adolphus Meetkerke turned against his nephew Thomas Trollope for political reasons has some basis in fact. The Trollope circle included not merely English and French radicals but some Italian and Spanish exiles, the most famous of whom was General Pepe – surely the basis for Trollope's 'Italian marquis' – who was introduced to the Trollopes by Lady Dyer. In turn General Pepe was introduced to Lafayette by Fanny Wright whom Pepe had met at the Trollopes'. He soon got Lafayette involved in his Society of the Constitutionalists of Europe, and Fanny Wright began smuggling his letters to Lafayette. Pepe, part of the 'higher class of the Carbonari' or secret Italian revolutionary groups, worried about the amateurish attitudes of some of his new friends: 'It seems scarcely credible that a man like Lafayette should run after every petty conspiracy, so strong in him was the love of better institutions for his country.'[3]

In about 1823 Pepe arranged for some newspapers to publish a translation of an ode in honour of Lafayette written years before by the Italian poet Alfieri. Thomas Campbell, ironically best known for his war songs against the French, said the English version 'possessed much merit'. The translation had been done by Mrs Trollope at Pepe's request. He sent a copy of it to Lafayette himself. Soon afterwards the Garnetts invited Thomas Anthony and Fanny to visit them in Paris. The Trollopes, with such impeccable liberal credentials and, in Fanny's case, with such a good command of the French language and knowledge of French literature, moved happily not just in salons filled with French liberals but in those filled with literary celebrities such as Stendhal. It was Fanny who shone: when the American author Washington Irving met the Trollopes at one reception he described them as 'Mrs Trollop [*sic*] & husband': the once distinguished barrister was already an appendage to his wife.[4]

The trip's highlight was the invitation to Lafayette's château, La Grange. Not only had Fanny translated Alfieri's ode but she had assisted the plots against Louis XVIII by helping Fanny Wright as a postman. It was thrilling to hear the Marquis discourse on the great figures he had known: Washington, Franklin, Louis XVI, Marie Antoinette and Napoleon. Fanny Trollope had been an impressionable girl when accounts of revolutionary horrors had drifted across the Channel. Now, in a château in Brie, she could recline in the library with its parquet floor and its paintings of the apostles of liberty looking down from the walls and listen to one of the most celebrated actors from those early days of the Revolution. Here was the man who had persuaded the King and Queen to leave Versailles and accompany the mob of fishwives back to Paris. Yet three decades later Fanny Trollope could be delighted by his comment that Louis XVI was 'one of the best of kings' with a genuine devotion to liberty.

One day the Marquis took his guests to witness a dance by the peasants on his estate: 'Trollope', noted his wife in her journal, 'danced with them.' This is perhaps the only recorded instance of that morbid barrister abandoning himself to such pleasure, but then he was in France. At La Grange Mrs Trollope read Fanny Wright's American book and talked about it to Lafayette. It was gratifying to discuss equality with a Marquis while liveried footmen glided about refilling the wine glasses. 'The dear general' was quite impressed with the little lady from Harrow and told his 'adopted daughter', Fanny Wright, about her friend's 'agreeable and amiable qualities'. The following year, when Lafayette was aboard ship on his way to a triumphal tour of America, he wrote to Pepe and ended his letter asking him to offer his 'tendres amitiés a l'excellente Mme. Trollope, et a son mari'. His parents' French jaunt would considerably influence one of Anthony Trollope's early novels, *La Vendée*, set in revolutionary France. For this he could draw on his mother's recollections of her visit, the manuscript of which survives with a comment in Anthony's handwriting: 'My mother's Journal of a Visit to La Grange.'[5]

*

This visit had a more immediate effect on the Trollope family. Mrs Trollope became increasingly fascinated by Fanny Wright's ideas and enjoyed her company. Sometimes they would attend literary receptions such as one Hampstead party given for the exiled Italian poet Uno Foscolo. The host observed that 'Mrs. T. came in her deepest blue stockings' but that Foscolo seemed unimpressed with her 'Siddonian glances' and 'shrugged up his shoulders and observed that she was *very blue*'. It is also likely that she felt growing frustration with the parochial confines of her own life, a contrast made all the more obvious when the Scotswoman visited Harrow. Anthony retained only a distant memory of this exotic woman, but his elder brother never forgot her:[6]

> She was very handsome in a large and almost masculine style of beauty, with a most commanding presence, a superb figure, and stature fully masculine. Her features both in form and expression were really noble. There exists ... a large lithographed portrait ... She is represented standing, with her hand on the neck of a grey horse (the same old gig horse that had drawn my parents and myself ...) and if I remember rightly, in Turkish trousers.

Years later Trollope would poke fun at an Englishwoman in Turkish attire who 'seemed to think a good deal about her trousers' [*The Bertrams* IX] and one of his American characters, Olivia Q. Fleabody Ph.D., wears trousers while lecturing on womens' rights [*Is He Popenjoy?* XVII].

In 1824 Fanny Wright returned to America with a plan to eliminate the 'foul blot' of slavery which was the only thing that prevented the young Republic from being a utopia. Having bought land and slaves in Tennessee, she began to educate them for freedom; a successful experiment could be an example to enlightened planters who wanted gradual emancipation. In 1827 she was back in England looking for a lady companion. She failed to enlist Mary Shelley, the poet's widow and the creator of *Frankenstein*, who appears to have been visiting the Trollopes in Harrow. She also tried to recruit some of the Garnett sisters but failed again. She then withdrew to La Grange. That autumn Fanny Trollope visited Paris to see how 'poor Henry' was getting on. While there she was again invited to Lafayette's château where Fanny Wright asked her to come to America as 'a bosom intimate ... to lean upon in all the confidence of equality and friendship'. Mrs Trollope accepted, although the reasons why she did so cannot be completely explained, probably because she was not entirely clear herself. One reason certainly was her fervent admiration for Fanny Wright, as she confided to Harriet Garnett: 'Will it be possible to let this "angel" ... depart without vowing to follow her? I think not. I feel greatly inclined to say "where her country is, there shall be my country". The more I see of her ... the more I feel convinced that *all* her motives are right.'[7] Another reason was concern for Henry's prospects. Her visit to Paris had made her even more discouraged about his future. He seemed incapable of succeeding at anything, but he was however quite infatuated with Fanny Wright and her ideas. It might be possible to use these feelings to lead him towards a career in the prospering republic.

One final reason was Fanny Trollope's growing disenchantment with her husband. Anthony Trollope was to depict the anguish of the frustrated or bored wife in many novels, such as *Can You Forgive Her?* and *The Bertrams*. His mother had now reached such a stage after almost twenty years' experience of her husband's moods. 'He is a good, honourable man – but his temper is dreadful – every year increases his irritability – and also its lamentable effect upon the children,' she later confided to Harriet.[8] His temper was not helped by the continuing decline in his financial prospects. He told his wife on her return from La Grange that his earlier fears about their finances had been realised: they could no longer maintain their large rambling house, and would have to move to a much smaller and rather gloomy farmhouse in Harrow Weald, some three miles away. Anthony recalled the misery of this 'wretched tumble-down farmhouse ... one of those farmhouses which seem always to be in danger of falling into the neighbouring horse-pond.' From there the harassed man would attempt to supervise both his old farm (for he could not rid himself of his lease) and his new one at Harrow Weald.

The prospect of such a move was not an entrancing one for his wife.

She had been able to adjust to their earlier loss of the new mansion they had built when they came to Harrow, and her great skill at decoration had turned 'Orley Farm' into a comfortable house where she could entertain and hold amateur theatricals. Yet even she could do little to make the Harrow Weald farmhouse into anything respectable. The American adventure was a way out of her problems even though public controversy was now beginning to surround Fanny Wright and Nashoba, her Tennessee plantation. Emancipation of the slaves was only one of this busy woman's numerous causes; she also set herself up as a determined foe of religion and marriage. Soon gossip claimed that Nashoba was a veritable temple of free love. Mrs Trollope did not share these views on religion, or on free love, but she was annoyed at the fierce criticism swirling round her friend. 'Heaven knows,' wrote Mrs Trollope, this daughter and daughter-in-law of clergymen, 'I do not want to be talking radicalism – nor infidelity – but I should like to live among human beings who would not look upon reason as crime, nor on free discussion, as treason and blasphemy.'[9]

In the nineteenth century it was common procedure for a family like the Trollopes to 'retire abroad' when their income could no longer support their style of life. Thomas Trollope appears to have suggested this to his wife, although he probably had in mind a place like Brussels. However, Fanny Wright offered a far more thrilling and a far more distant refuge. Mrs Trollope could become her chosen companion in a great humanitarian work. She could take her two daughters as well as the purposeless Henry away from their father's temper and at the same time spare herself the disgrace of moving to a mere farmhouse. Fanny Trollope was approaching fifty. She was almost certainly conscious of her abilities, but these had been confined to amateur theatricals, the odd translation, entertaining friends and writing clever pieces of poetic spite circulated among her friends. Anthony later made a vague reference in his *Autobiography* to his mother's 'aspirations' as one factor in her decision. Younger women like Fanny Wright were travelling, writing books and influencing society while Mrs Trollope was confined at home with a husband who had an increasingly miserable temper and rapidly decreasing prosperity.

It took her some days to convince her husband that a lengthy visit to America was just the answer for their mounting problems. Within five days of a decision being taken Mrs Trollope was on the high seas. Her departure was both precipitate and shrouded in some mystery. One of Fanny Wright's party was the twenty-six-year-old Robert Dale Owen, son of the co-operative reformer and mill-owner Robert Owen. He had views on emancipation, socialism and education and was a disciple of Fanny Wright. The decision to leave from another port appears to have been dropped at the last minute in favour of a sailing from London, as he told a friend. 'Still,' he added, 'our party will be, as I before said, eight or ten.' Two days later Fanny Wright herself wrote to Bentham from on board the ship at Tower Stairs: she had been 'summoned at only a few hours warning'.[10] Whatever the reason for her hurried departure, her 'adopted father', the Marquis de Lafayette, was somewhat bemused when the news about Fanny Wright's companions reached his château: 'You will not be a little surprised to hear,' he wrote to a friend, 'that Mrs. Trollope, after a full explanation of the Nashoba experimental system has with the assent of her husband determined to become, with her daughters and son, members of the society and to give up the habits and comforts to which I thought her peculiarly attached.'[11]

It was many months before Anthony or Tom heard further news of their mother's bizarre adventure in America. Given the haphazard state of transatlantic communications, it is not surprising that nine of her letters to her husband went astray. (It is a pleasing reflection that it was Anthony Trollope who would help to organise a swift and secure transport of letters between Britain and America.) In addition, postage was quite expensive and Mrs Trollope eventually told Tom of the North and South American Coffee-House in London where he could make cheaper arrangements to send a letter to America by private means. Gradually word began to reach Winchester of the strange adventures befalling the four Trollopes in America.

The Trollopes had not left Harrow on their own. They were accompanied by a maid and a manservant as well as considerable amounts of furniture, for even in Utopia Fanny Trollope required some creature comforts. There was an even more incongruous member of the party: Auguste Hervieu, a young French artist who had lived for some time in the Trollope household where he instructed the children in the highly regarded accomplishment of drawing. Even rudimentary instruction in sketching buildings and people was one of the most formative influences among educated Victorians. What little talent Anthony may have possessed never seems to have advanced very far, but the lessons probably helped to develop that ability to observe characteristic details which became one of the strong points of his writing.

Mrs Trollope had tried to forward Hervieu's career by urging influential friends to see that his paintings were noticed in the press. She had written to her old friend Mary Mitford, about 'our protégé ... a being full of lofty aspirations ... yet dragged to earth by the pitiful necessity of earning his daily morsel'. Hervieu, the son of one of Napoleon's officers who had died in the disastrous Russian campaign, had also dabbled in revolution. He had fled to England after a farcical revolutionary attempt in Spain. Thus he was a ripe convert to the Wright crusade and he agreed to go to Tennessee to teach the slaves French and drawing. Of what use these two polite accomplishments would be seems not to have disturbed Fanny Trollope, Fanny Wright or Auguste Hervieu. It was such absurdities as this that no doubt stuck in the mind of Anthony Trollope, for in his last completed novel, *An Old Man's Love*, he has a young man considering some ridiculous things he could do to escape from an unhappy love affair. Among them is a proposal to 'join the colonists in Tennessee' [XVIII]. By the 1880s Tennessee contained neither colonists nor slaves, but Trollope could not forget the plantation that had cast such a shadow across his youth.[12]

The Wright plantation – the modern word 'commune' would be a better description – consisted of a few primitive log cabins in the midst of a vast and fever-ridden forest. Fanny Trollope observed that the pervading desolation did not disturb 'our philosophical friend' whose 'whole heart and soul were occupied by the hope of raising the African to the level of European intellect'. After ten restless nights under the leaking roof of a log hut Mrs Trollope decided to part company with her erstwhile 'angel'. The dream that had seemed so thrilling amid the chatter of a London drawing-room or the philosophical speculations of a French château had vanished amid the rain-soaked reality of a Tennessee forest. When Lafayette wrote to Mrs Trollope in November of the following year he admitted he had wondered 'at the determination of a London lady to make herself a forest pioneer'. Her departure did not surprise him, for he never 'thought that sort of forest-life could suit you', but he had been told by Fanny Wright that she bore Mrs Trollope no ill-will. Within a year, however, 'the angel' gave up the attempt at 'cultivating African negroes till they produced accomplished ladies and gentlemen' and was instead lecturing against Christianity. 'Wild and often mischievous, as her doctrines are,' Fanny Trollope wrote to Miss Mitford, 'she is a thing to wonder at, and you must see her if you can.'[13] Word eventually reached England that Mrs Trollope had rented a house in Cincinnati, Ohio, then a burgeoning town at the very crossroads of the frontier.

*

Meanwhile what of the twelve-year-old Anthony? He was at Winchester, where his life seemed more miserable than ever. Holidays would no longer be spent in Harrow, acting Molière or watching the hay-making but in the dreary surroundings of his father's chambers in Lincoln's Inn. Some said the rooms were haunted by a pupil of Mr Trollope who had committed suicide, a rumour Trollope would recall in his short story 'The Spotted Dog'. Young Anthony amused himself by wandering round the Inns of Court, observing details of the surroundings that would often feature in his novels when distressed country gentlemen and anxious clerics hurry up to London to see their lawyers, who are normally in Lincoln's Inn. In *Orley Farm* he recalled a set of rooms 'made oppressive by their general dinginess and by a smell of old leather which pervaded them'. These may well be based on his father's rooms, especially as the fictional barrister lived in Keppel Street. In this novel Anthony Trollope followed his usual habit of inserting his own opinions and recollections in the midst of describing the barrister's room: 'Of all the rooms in which I ever sat I think it was the most gloomy. There were heavy curtains to the windows, which had once been ruby but were now brown; and the ceiling was brown, and the thick carpet was brown, and the books which covered every portion of the wall were brown' [XII].

Among these books there was one that attracted his notice in the midst of this 'holiday'. It was a large bi-columned edition of Shakespeare. Trollope was to preserve this volume in his own library all his life. Shakespeare and the seventeenth-century dramatists were to be powerful influences on his writings as well as sources of pleasure throughout his life. Even before Shakespeare solaced his misery the young boy had been prepared to enjoy the plays not by the dreary pedants at his schools but by his mother who wanted her children to share her love of the theatre. She read Shakespeare with them, showing how characters like the nurse in *Romeo and Juliet* or the grave-digger in *Hamlet* heighten the drama.[14] This, of course, was excellent training for the future novelist. Ironically at just about the time that her lonely, youngest son was reading Shakespeare in London, Mrs Trollope was making a vain effort to defend him in Cincinnati, only to be told by a 'serious gentleman':[15]

> Shakspeare [*sic*], madam, is obscene, and thank God, we are sufficiently advanced to have found it out! If we must have the abomination of stage plays, let them at least be marked by the refinement of the age in which we live.

The young Trollope's other consolation was a diary which he began at about the age of twelve. Unfortunately in the last year of his life he destroyed it, although he did tell his first biographer that it 'was full of a heart-sick, friendless little chap's exaggerations of his woes'.[16] Diary-keeping, like drawing, was an important aspect in forming the Victorian mind. Learning to draw taught one to observe the details of places and people; keeping a diary taught one to examine his own actions and motives and to record what one did each day. Life was a serious matter, and in due course one would be held responsible for what he did with God-given time. Once again Trollope had stumbled on something that played an important role in preparing him for his future.

He was even more on his own when, in September 1828, his father went to America to see what his wife, who had been there for about nine months, now planned. He took Tom (who was preparing for Oxford) with him and thus the thirteen-year-old Anthony was the only member of his family left in England. One can only imagine the sense of isolation and rejection that a boy just entering into adolescence must have felt at this abandonment. Underneath the vibrant personality of his later years there always lurked the strains of this boyhood trauma. In a way he was lucky to be spared this introduction to travel. With his usual 'spartan contempt for comfort' (as Tom called it) Mr Trollope took two places in the steerage of a ship bound for New York. This, the lowest part of the ship, was teeming with poor emigrants who lived in common and cooked their own squalid meals. It was a horrible place for anyone, especially for educated gentlemen. The older Trollope took to his berth for the whole voyage, miserably ill from sea-sickness and headaches. The hearty Tom spent the thirty-eight nights of the crossing on the deck of the rolling ship, refusing to suffer the smells below except when he went down to help his father.

Mr Trollope made little provision for his youngest son; bills at Winchester were not paid and the local tradesmen refused him credit. He still had free board but all those little treats so dear to the schoolboy's heart were now things of the past. One day the master who was in charge of distributing the weekly shilling in pocket money or 'battels' informed Anthony that he would no longer receive his because his father was six months behind in forwarding the money and there was no more credit. That meant that he no longer had any money for the servants' tips. 'I never saw one of those servants,' he later recalled, 'without feeling that I had picked his pocket.' The thirteen-year-old boy probably spent his holidays with his uncle Henry Milton in Fulham.

Anthony's father and brother returned from America after an absence of some six months. Thomas Trollope now began to raise such capital as he could by selling land which he probably had bought with Fanny's inheritance from her father. At least here he made a profit: he needed the money so that his wife could begin what she later discreetly called a 'commercial speculation'. An incredible structure, soon called 'Trollope's Folly', rose in Cincinnati. Another English traveller described it as a 'large Graeco-Moresco-Gothic-Chinese looking building ... the effect of which is extremely grotesque', while Anthony, who saw it twenty-five years later, thought it 'showy'.[17] Mrs Trollope herself said it was loosely modelled on the Alhambra. Her plans for the building were as fantastic as its design. The bazaar would sell European luxury goods and provide cultural events, such as art exhibitions by the building's designer, Auguste Hervieu. The ridiculous venture was in many ways ahead of its time: it was in some ways the first American shopping centre and 'leisure complex'. However, it proved a complete disaster and the sheriff seized all her possessions.

Even before this news reached England Mr Trollope was making desperate attempts to economise. Since Tom had not gained a scholarship, his father had to find funds to support him at Oxford. One way to save money was to bring Anthony home from Winchester. In January 1831 Anthony was once again in Harrow, at 't'other school' as a parish boy. Ironically if Anthony had remained at Winchester he would have gained a free place at Oxford. Thus in his final desperation Thomas Anthony Trollope destroyed his great goal of seeing a son follow his footsteps from Winchester to New College.

*

Anthony now returned to the fourth home of his childhood, a run-down farmhouse at Harrow Weald where the 'mean and scanty' furniture reflected the deterioration of once bright hopes. Perhaps Trollope's *Autobiography* portrays this house and the events that occurred in it too darkly. This, at least, was what his brother maintained in his own memoirs: 'It certainly was no longer a very good house, but it was not tumble-down, as Anthony calls it, and ... [it] was indeed a much better house than merely a farmhouse.'[18] Of course Anthony was always inclined to portray his youth in sombre colours, just as Tom tended to see all his past through the serene glow of old age. Even the food seemed to share in the gloom hanging over the farmhouse, for it was neither good nor plentiful. Anthony could blame himself for some of this because he resisted his father's 'verbal incentives' to work in the kitchen garden. During holidays, however, he did help in cutting hay, the farm's principal crop.

Mr Trollope was never an indolent man but he was forced to spend much time in bed because of his awful headaches. His eldest son described them as 'bilious headaches' but the constant doses of calomel only caused more problems. 'I believe,' wrote Tom, who, unlike Anthony, inherited a propensity for these headaches, 'that it had the effect of shattering his nervous system in a deplorable manner. He became increasingly irritable ... that, unconsciously, we sought to avoid his presence, and to consider as hours of enjoyment only those that could be passed away from it ... I believe that he was destroyed mind and body by calomel, habitually used during long years.'[19]

When not supervising farm labourers or admonishing his son to join them, the desperate man was in his parlour 'shut up among big books' working on a great scholarly project, the *Encyclopaedia Ecclesiastica*. Its sub-title described his ambitious goal: 'A Complete History of the Church: Containing a Full and Compendious Explanation of all Ecclesiastical Rites and Ceremonies; a distinct and accurate account of all Denominations and of Christians from the Earliest Ages of Christianity to the Present Time; Together with a Definition of Terms usually occurring in Ecclesiastical Writers.' The first volume, numbering some 578 pages, began with Abaddon, who was defined as both the king of the locusts and the angel from the bottomless pit, and ended with an entry for Funeral Rites; and there were two addenda on Blasphemy and Burial. It was published by John Murray in 1834 and shows great research as well as skill in writing, which is all the more remarkable as he had little access to books outside his own library. (There is a characteristic remark in his introduction when he apologises for having recourse, in some instances, to previous encyclopaedias and for not doing original research in every instance.) He secured subscriptions from many old friends, several of whom were prominent clergymen. The nature of the project and the method of publication by subscription shows how essentially he remained a man of the eighteenth century. This absorption in the minutiae of ecclesiastical history and terminology no doubt helped to assuage the many miserable hours of a frustrated life. Undoubtedly he also saw it as a way to earn some much-needed money and, perhaps, restore some of that respectability that had slowly ebbed away from him.

When Anthony Trollope wrote his *Autobiography* he was about the same age his father had been during these miserable days: he looked back at the *Encyclopaedia Ecclesiastica* as another sad example of 'that huge pile of futile literature, the building up of which has broken so many hearts'. His father's fascination with 'monks and nuns' was yet another aspect of his parents' life that would affect his own writing. While his father's *Encyclopaedia* defined 'Archdeacons', 'Deans' and

'Bishops', Anthony's books provided the most memorable portraits in English literature of such dignitaries. In several novels Trollope illustrates the mild eccentricity of some characters by having them work on an erudite tome: the Warden in the novel of the same name is said to have published an obscure book on church music, while in *The Vicar of Bullhampton* Gregory Marrable, 'the projector of a new theory about Stonehenge', spends his time editing an 'unreadable' Anglo-Saxon text. These may well be echoes of that book-bestrewn parlour at Harrow Weald. Mr Trollope still had his passion for classical education. With Henry in America and Tom at Oxford, Anthony bore the burden of that passion. When his father came in from the fields or left his scholarly tomes, he would force Anthony to sit at a table with a Greek lexicon. His son's idleness was yet another misery for the poor man and once, in a rage, he picked up the folio Bible that he used for his research and knocked Anthony down.

Life was no easier for Anthony at school: his second time at Harrow was even more unhappy than his first, when he had at least come from a respectable home. Now he came from a tumble-down farmhouse and his mother's absence meant that his clothes were even messier than usual. Local gossip was well aware that his mother had left her husband and disappeared into the American backwoods with a young French artist and the notorious apostle of free love, Fanny Wright. Rumours of his father's financial difficulties were magnified by that mighty engine of imagination, the schoolboy mind: 'There was a story afloat,' recalled one Old Harrovian, 'that his father had been outlawed, and every boy believed it was the duty of a loyal subject of the crown to shoot or otherwise destroy "old Trollope" if possible. Fortunately, he never appeared among us.' Anthony took no part in games yet he 'longed for these things with an exceeding longing'. He was conscious of the feeling against him: 'What right had a wretched farmer's boy, reeking from a dunghill, to sit next to the sons of peers or much worse still, next to the sons of big tradesmen who had made their ten thousand a-year?' he recalled in his *Autobiography*. The use of 'dunghill' is a perfect example of how he could pile on misery when relating the story of his unhappy youth, but undoubtedly these years left a permanent psychological wound that could always be reopened when he felt inclined: 'As I look back it seems to me that all hands were turned against me, – those of masters as well as boys. I was allowed to join in no plays. Nor did I learn anything – for I was taught nothing.'[20]

Trollope gives a more detailed and a fairer account of his last few years of education in his article on public schools, written in 1865. At Harrow, the older boys, like Trollope, were put to work on the most difficult authors, such as Thucydides or Juvenal. The sixth-form boys were summoned into the presence of the Headmaster to display their learning. Dr Butler, who had once berated the eight-year-old Anthony about his messy appearance, had been replaced by Charles Longley. He, alone of Trollope's teachers, won any praise from the novelist in after life: 'Dr Butler only became Dean of Peterborough, but his successor lived to be Archbishop of Canterbury.' Yet Trollope recalled how his failures to construe the Greek text produced a 'look of irrepressible, unutterable misery' from the Headmaster. Trollope believed that Harrow, like Winchester, failed to provide basic teaching because there were not enough masters. In the 'pupil-rooms' that preceded the audience with Longley, the under-masters did little but hear the boys read, and naturally they were inclined to favour the best pupils:[21]

> To those who had much, much was given; and from those who had nothing, – or little, – was taken away even that which they had. A precocious boy, one who had at his command for the work in hand a man's desire for improvement and adult energy, – was pushed on and became, by his own merits, the glory of the school. But for the boys who were boys, there was no teaching.

At least, little money was needed for these final years of 'education'. His father's well-stocked library yielded up many of the classical texts his son needed and thus the boy in tattered clothes might walk to school carrying the 1575 Paris edition of Horace. Anthony's tutor kindly waived his right to the ten guinea fee but then boasted of his charity to the other boys, which hardly increased the young Trollope's reputation. In these days he was virtually friendless, yet when he was a man he made hosts of friends in many countries. One was Sir William Gregory, an Irish landowner, who had been at Harrow with the young Trollope. In the 1840s they became friends when Trollope lived in Ireland. Forty years later, when Sir William came to read Trollope's *Autobiography*, he remembered how the young Anthony had appeared to his school fellows:[22]

> He was a big boy, older than the rest of the form, and without exception the most slovenly and dirty boy I ever met. He was not only slovenly in person and in dress, but his work was equally dirty. His exercises were a mass of blots and smudges. These peculiarities created a great prejudice against him, and the poor fellow was generally avoided ... I had plenty of opportunities of judging Anthony, and I am bound to say, though my heart smites me sorely for my unkindness, that I did not like him. I avoided him, for he was rude and uncouth, but I thought him an honest,

brave fellow. He was no sneak. His faults were external; all the rest of
him was right enough. But the faults were of that character for which
school boys would never make allowances, and so poor Trollope was
tabooed, and had not ... a single friend ... He gave no sign of promise
whatsoever, was always in the lowest part of the form, and was regarded
by masters and by boys as an incorrigible dunce.

Trollope was not, of course, an 'incorrigible dunce', nor were 'all
hands' turned against him. During this period at Harrow the boys
prepared weekly English essays on set themes for which a prize was
given. One boy, Frederick Ponsonby, once took great pains with his
essay and was called to see Longley, who gave the prizes, not to be told
that he had won but that the prize had gone to Trollope. 'You did well,'
Longley told him, 'but, you see, Trollope writes better English than you
do, at present.' Ponsonby admitted that he 'was not satisfied then, but
acquiesced in the decision in after life'. For his part, when compiling
the *Autobiography* Trollope neither mentioned the prize nor a famous
schoolboy fight between himself and a boy named Lewis. The fight,
presumably held at the Milling Ground, the traditional spot for such
matches, must have gained him some recognition. One school-mate,
who went on to become a judge, remembered that it had lasted for
'nearly an hour' before Lewis limped away, defeated. Yet such
temporary triumphs could not end what Trollope called 'the worst
period of my life'.[23]

Friendless at school, the boy had at least one companion at home.
While his father toiled over his books in the parlour, fifteen-year-old
Anthony was in the kitchen flirting with the daughter of the bailiff who
managed his father's farms. Such flirtations would become a theme in
many of his novels, where callow young gentlemen enjoy mild
dalliances with girls from the 'lower orders'. Trollope also found the
soothing consolation that lonely adolescents find when they become
totally lost in a novel. Although his father liked eighteenth-century
fiction, the farmhouse only boasted one incomplete novel among the
numerous ecclesiastical and classical works: the first two volumes of
James Fenimore Cooper's *The Prairie*, published in 1827. They were
'the dishonest relic' of some circulating library: perhaps Mrs Trollope
forgot to return the books in her haste to visit those same prairies. The
exciting tale of Sioux Indians, wagon-trains, buffalo stampedes and the
aged frontiersman Natty Bumppo, so captivated the young Anthony
that he read it, he claims, dozens of times.

Ironically, his mother, separated from him by 4,000 miles, was
reading the same book. She too was deeply depressed and ill with the
deadly fever that stalked the American frontier. During her

convalescence she read all of Cooper's novels. So, like her son, Fanny Trollope never closed her eyes 'without seeing myriads of bloody scalps floating round me; long slender figures of Red Indians crept through my dreams with noiseless tread.' Cooper's novel introduced Trollope to the possibility of escape that a novel can give to the imaginative mind. Thirty years later he was still interested in Cooper and added a complete set of the American's novels to his library. Eventually Anthony read another novel, this time by Ann Radcliffe, who had died only a few years before. His reaction to her melodramatic work, recalled years later in a lecture on fiction, shows how sometimes fiction can be worse than reality:[24]

> I remember myself, to have been unable to leave my chair during the whole night when I was reading that awful book the *Mysteries of Udolpho* alone, amidst the gloom of a dark, flock-papered dining room. It was not that I could not put down the book ... but that I did not dare to stir from my chair, to turn my head, or to glare at the dark curtain behind which some horrible living ruffian, or more horrible departed hero, was at the moment so probably half-hidden, – half ready to come forth and freeze the marrow of my bones! So the unsnuffed candles burned themselves out; and I remained sleepless, – and at last sleeping in my chair.

Yet all was not fear and gloom at Harrow Weald. One day, when Tom was home from Oxford, the two brothers saw an advertisement for an extraordinary entertainment at Vauxhall, complete with grand illuminations and fireworks. Vauxhall Gardens, a relic of eighteenth-century pleasures, were renowned, among other things, for their spectacular illuminations, a fact that the homesick Mrs Trollope was recalling at about the same time her sons were visiting the pleasure grounds. For this special occasion the entrance fee was reduced to one shilling. The two brothers possessed exactly two shillings, so they set off and walked to Vauxhall, arriving about nine in the evening. Vauxhall was a boisterous and slightly disreputable spot. Thackeray described it in *Vanity Fair* as a place with a 'hundred thousand *extra* lamps, which were always lighted; the fiddlers in cocked hats, who played ravishing melodies ... the country dances, formed by bouncing cockneys and cockneyesses, and executed amidst jumping, thumping, and laughter.' Tom enjoyed the magnificent display of fireworks, while Anthony insisted on dancing until 1 a.m. After their evening's amusements the two brothers walked back to the farmhouse. They had not had any extra money for food or drink to sustain them on their thirty-mile return journey! This happy episode, which Anthony of course neglects in his *Autobiography*, although Tom remembered it in his, shows that the young Trollope was not always the miserable outcast he liked to portray.[25] The fact that Anthony was bold enough to ask girls to dance shows that already the vigorous man was struggling to break out of the restraints of the schoolboy.

As this escapade shows, both Trollope brothers were strong, but in spite of the five-year difference in age it was the younger who was the stronger. One day in 1830 Tom bought two sticks equipped with basket handles and challenged his brother to a fraternal fight. Perhaps Anthony saw this as a welcome revenge for all those beatings Tom had inflicted at Winchester. Tom noted in his diary (for he too kept one): 'Anthony much approves of them and this morning we had a bout with them. One of the sticks ... soon broke, and we supplied its place with a tremendous blackthorn.' With commendable fairness the elder brother concluded: 'Neither of us left the arena without a fair share of rather severe wales; but Anthony is far my superior in quickness and adroitness, and perhaps in bearing pain too.' He felt that his younger brother would always surpass him in 'quickness' and 'adroitness', which is a judgment certainly shared by anyone who has read novels by both men.[26]

*

On the night of 18 April 1830 the Harrow Weald farmhouse was disturbed at 12.30 a.m. by banging at the door. Within a few moments Anthony's brother Henry, now eighteen, was recounting his American adventures. In his early days there his mother had sent him to a 'progressive' school patronised by Fanny Wright. The school boasted of its devotion to liberty, but as is the way with such institutions it tottered between anarchy and tyranny. Henry was forced to spend his days toiling in the fields, and his health, never strong, broke under the strain. He then joined his mother in Cincinnati where an advertisement appeared in the press: 'Mr Henry Trollope, having received a completely classical education, at the royal college of Winchester, (England)' offered Latin lessons to gentlemen for fifty cents an hour.[27] Cincinnatian gentlemen, in spite of the name of their city, showed no interest in Latin. At last 'poor Henry' found a use, or rather a misuse, for his Latin and a smattering of his French when he hid behind a screen to provide the mystic voice for 'The Invisible Girl at the Western Museum', a curious pantomime that his mother produced in yet another exotic attempt to raise funds. Henry could also tell his father and brothers of the final disaster in Cincinnati when the sheriff seized all of Mrs Trollope's goods and even her house because of her debts to the builder of the bazaar. She and her dispossessed daughters then shared a bed at a friend's house while Henry and Hervieu made do with the kitchen floor.

This procession of disasters left Henry looking like a 'walking corpse', as his mother sadly noted.[28] The family in America had survived only because Hervieu gave art lessons and drew portraits of frontier worthies. Mrs Trollope scraped together enough money to send Henry to New York where a banker, Charles Wilkes, an old friend from the Trollopes' liberal circle, paid the boy's passage to Liverpool. Henry had just enough money for the coach to London, but then the ill and penniless lad had to walk the final sixteen miles to Harrow Weald. Surely in stories like these was laid the basis of Anthony Trollope's concern for money which was a constant preoccupation both in his life and in his books.

In the next year more news arrived from Mrs Trollope, who had left Cincinnati. Her life there had not been helped by the gossip about her friendship with Hervieu, although the relationship was an innocent one. With her daughters and Hervieu she made the lengthy journey to Washington in the vain hope that Congress might buy a vast painting of Lafayette that the young artist had exhibited at the bazaar. At least in a city full of politicians Hervieu could find enough men anxious to immortalise themselves on canvas. These portraits saved Mrs Trollope and her daughters from penury. One of the ubiquitous Garnett family lived near Washington and Mrs Trollope sought refuge with her. At one point her finances were so low that her girls were without shoes. Yet in the midst of all this misery, hope, ever Fanny Trollope's strongest virtue, came to her rescue, and while her friend played Mozart on a piano Mrs Trollope sat on a verandah overlooking the broad Potomac River and wrote her observations of American life. In May 1831 she told Mary Mitford: 'My book is gossiping and without pretension most faithfully true to the evidence of my senses.' She added, remembering that her old friend had been shocked by the American venture: 'I know your good father ... is a bit of a radical – so I was, too, once, but the United States offer a *radical* cure for this.'[29] She also wrote several letters to her husband asking for money to return to England. No money arrived, probably because he had so little available. In the end she only forced the money from him by threatening to write to his family.

On 5 August 1831 Mrs Trollope landed at Woolwich accompanied by her two daughters and the ever-faithful Hervieu. Anthony had not seen his mother for almost four years, since that summer in 1827 when she had been concerned to arrange some 'drolleries' for her boys. He had been twelve when she left and for four years his life, in some of its most sensitive years, had known little love or stability. More than any other member of the family Anthony had cause to feel abandoned, for at least Tom and Mr Trollope had visited America. Some biographers have imagined that there never was much affection between Fanny Trollope and her 'Tony'. This is not the case: she proved anxious to promote his career and survived to take great satisfaction in it. Nor had she forgotten him when she was in America. She wrote to Tom: 'My poor dear Anthony will have outgrown our recollection. Tell him not to outgrow his affection for us. No day passes, – hardly an hour – without our talking of you all.'[30] For his part Anthony took great pride in his 'Mammy' (as she was known in her family) and carefully preserved all her books throughout his life. Nevertheless this absence, which to the adolescent mind must have seemed a rejection, only added to the emotional scars that the young Trollope carried into his maturity and even partially to his grave.

The sudden return of his mother and sisters no doubt influenced the future novelist in another way. For the first time since he had gone to his private school at Sunbury Anthony lived in a house surrounded by feminine influences. His sisters, Cecilia, one year his junior, and Emily, three years younger, gave him his first real opportunity to observe the English girl, a subject on which he became the acknowledged master in English fiction. Because this influence had been so long absent, the young Trollope could contrast the effect of its sudden and happy reappearance in a house no longer dominated by his father's moods. His mother, who delighted in promoting gaiety among the young, strove to banish the hovering gloom from the house.

Fanny Trollope needed such distractions herself, for she had endured a great deal in America: her ridiculous utopian scheme had collapsed; she had almost died from illness; she had seen her 'commercial speculation' turn into a financial nightmare; she had watched a sheriff confiscate all her goods; and she had endured the insolence and ridicule of frontier hotel-keepers and fundamentalist preachers. These sufferings had changed her, at least physically. She told Tom she was an old woman now but her vibrant spirits remained.

In Harrow she found her husband's affairs even worse than she had dared to imagine. The previous year, 1830, had been a dreadful time for anyone dependent upon the land. A wave of riots had spread across the south of England supposedly led by a figment of lurid imagination called 'Captain Swing'. Desperate agricultural labourers burned the crops and new machinery of farmers and landlords. The Trollopes' landlord Lord Northwick received a roughly-printed note: 'Take warning or our emissaries shall and will do their work you have ground the labouring man too long. Swing.' Thomas Anthony Trollope was forced to increase wages. The economic gloom was made even worse by a catastrophic increase in the poor rate that landholders had to pay to keep the destitute from absolute starvation. For hay-farmers like Thomas Trollope the dreadful harvest of 1830 left them with even less resources to pay for increased demands. The political situation convinced many that England was heading towards revolution. After decades of Tory rule there was a new Whig government vaguely committed to reform. Across the channel in France a revolution had driven the last of the Bourbon kings from the throne and Mrs Trollope's erstwhile friend Lafayette installed the 'Citizen King' Louis-Philippe in his place.

Thomas Anthony Trollope had reacted to the economic upsets in predictable fashion. He drew up a petition for all of Lord Northwick's tenants asking for a reduction in rent. His lordship agreed to reduce the rents of all the tenants save Trollope because of the insulting language of the petition which had referred to Northwick's putting unearned 'large sums of money' into his 'own pocket'. Thomas Trollope's penchant for strong words also caused Tom trouble at Oxford. His father had detained him so that he returned to Oxford the day after the start of a new term. The Principal of Alban Hall insisted that Tom pay a small fine for his lateness. Thomas Anthony Trollope, summoning all the outraged dignity of a former Fellow of New College, unleashed a furious letter at the Principal who then dismissed Tom from the Hall. He was lucky to find another Hall prepared to take him. Such behaviour was likely to do little to find a place at Oxford for Anthony.

When Mrs Trollope returned home she found Anthony at Harrow and Henry at Cambridge 'perfectly without destination', which could not be said for her.[31] The American adventure may have begun in absurdity and ended in adversity but she planned to make good use of it. For years she had dabbled round the fringes of literature, entertaining authors, translating poetry, arranging private plays and circulating poems about Evangelical parsons. All this had been for the fun of it but now she desperately needed money. In Harrow she had had no subject she could make distinctively her own. In Cincinnati, however, she could observe a new society quite literally springing up around her, a society rich both in future potential and present-day peculiarities. For a woman gifted with a strong power of observation as well as a piquant, some would say sarcastic, style it was an ideal opportunity. She had the greatest luck a writer can have: she was at the right place at the right time. She began to write a book describing everyday life in the young republic. Her travels and her sufferings did not distract her from her task as she scribbled away, often using half-empty notebooks that her sons had used at Winchester. Nor did she allow any idleness during the weeks of her voyage back to England to go unused. Anthony would follow her practice of writing furiously while at sea and he would start and finish novels on the Atlantic, the Pacific and the Mediterranean.

Fanny Trollope was able to consult the letters she had sent to her sons to refresh her memory of certain episodes. She worked with frantic speed in a room her children called the 'sacred den of Harrow'. Scarcely a month after her return her book was ready and she turned to Mary Mitford for guidance; who replied that 'a first work must be given away to make a reputation – but then the reputation will afterwards bring money'. Fanny, desperate to earn as much as she could, had wanted to write articles but her friend warned against this: she should wait until the book was published and then she would have a name. Word soon began to percolate through the rather closed world of London publishing that a remarkable travel book was about to appear. It was about this time that Mr Trollope rose from his research and his headaches to make one of his now rare visits to town to see the publisher of the *Encyclopaedia Ecclesiastica*. In the midst of their discussions John Murray asked: 'By the bye! Trollope – who the devil is Mrs Trollope? Her book is the cleverest thing I ever read. I have read it through. So spirited! ... Why did she not bring it to me. But I will help it all I can.' He was true to his word and when *Domestic Manners of the Americans* appeared in March 1832 it was launched with a laudatory review of forty pages in Murray's *Quarterly Review*. The enthusiastic reviewer praised Mrs Trollope as 'an English lady of sense and acuteness' and compared the book to Captain Basil Hall's own fine work on America: 'We have now before us the story of a lady who also carried with her to the New World the most exaggerated notions of liberalism, and who seems to have returned, if possible, a stouter enemy of all such notions than the gallant Captain himself.' The anonymous reviewer was none other than 'the gallant Captain himself'.[32]

Fanny Trollope's book had the good fortune to be remarkably topical. For the last eighteen months the country had been convulsed by one of its greatest political crises. The Whig government of Lord Grey was pushing through the Reform Bill to widen the electorate as well as to remove the most glaring abuses of the old parliamentary system. The battle over reform raged from one end of the kingdom to the other: in Bristol the Bishop's palace was burnt by a radical mob, while in Nottingham the castle of the Duke of Newcastle was set alight. In Harrow itself the parish church had recently acquired a tablet to record the death of a judge, John Henry North, who, although only forty-four, had 'sunk beneath the efforts of a mind too great for his earthly frame, in opposing the revolutionary invasion of the Religion and Constitution of England'. Although Mrs Trollope avoided any detailed political discussions as being unseemly for a female writer, the main purpose of her book was to demonstrate how daily life was affected by the growing dominance of democratic theory and practice. If the Reform Bill should propel Britain towards a more democratic government, the experience of America was the best example of what would happen to British society. The young United States seemed the beacon or the whirlpool towards which the mother country was being drawn, and Mrs Trollope showed how democratic ideas affected religion, manners, art and, most upsetting of all, the availability of servants.

Domestic Manners of the Americans was a resounding success: 'I awoke one morning,' the author boasted with justifiable pride, 'and found myself famous.' Famous she was, particularly to Tory readers; to radicals and Americans she became infamous. She revelled in her new fame. The woman who a few months previously could not afford to buy shoes for her daughters was now a celebrated addition to aristocratic routs:[33]

> The Countess of Morley told me she was certain that if I drove through London proclaiming who I was, I should have the horses taken off and be drawn in triumph ... Lady Charlotte Lindsay *implored* me to go on writing – never was anything so delightful. Lady Louisa Stewart [*sic*] told me that I had quite put English out of fashion, and that every one was talking Yankee talk. In short I was *overpowered* ... How strange all this seems!

Perhaps even more gratifying was news from the Lake District that those two redoubtable Tories, Wordsworth and Southey, had enjoyed her book.

Domestic Manners of the Americans remains, along with Tocqueville's analytical study, published a few years later, one of the two most famous foreign accounts ever written on America. Fanny Trollope recorded her experiences, conversations and observations based on her life in Cincinnati and in her travels about America. Bold and outspoken, she was always ready to bestow praise but even more ready to fling censure. In her conclusion she summed up her basic impressions:[34]

> I suspect that what I have written will make it evident that I do not like America. Now, as it happens that I met with individuals there whom I love and admire ... [but] I speak not of my friends, nor of my friends' friends ... but of the population generally, as seen in town and country, among the rich and the poor ... I do not like them. I do not like their principles, I do not like their manners, I do not like their opinions.

American reviewers were eager to repay her dislike with a verbal bombardment, one of the many English inheritances they had retained. One reviewer, feigning false charity, concluded that her various mistakes sprang from her education 'which appears to have been French and flippant', which shows how thoroughly Anglo-Saxon Americans had remained. The *New England Magazine* saw no reason to disguise its venom: 'There is much in a name ... the name of Mrs Trollope, therefore, may be, at least, the shadow of a thing.' Timothy Flint, one of the few literary friends she made in Cincinnati, enlivened his review by describing her as 'a short, plump figure, with a ruddy, round, Saxon face of bright complexion ... singularly unladylike'. Nor indeed did that friendship with the French artist escape attention. Someone calling himself the 'editor' of the first American edition of *Domestic Manners* commented on the 'inscrutable mystery' of the author's travelling companion: 'she must, admitting her to be what she pretends, she must have had a protector.' Yet all this criticism only added to her growing fame in England, where a collection of these American reviews was published.[35]

In years to come many American writers came to accept that many of her observations on *frontier* society were accurate. Longfellow said he would forgive her strictures if she helped to eliminate the horror of tobacco-spitting which was her particular *bête noire*. For several decades it was quite common for Americans to cry 'Trollope! Trollope!' when they observed some ill-mannered behaviour in public. 'We were dreadfully angry at Mrs Trollope,' recalled a distinguished American journalist in the 1860s, 'but we read her book all the same ... and profited in no small degree by its lessons.' Perhaps the best tribute came fifty years after the book's publication when the greatest writer the American frontier produced, Mark Twain, carried her book with him when writing his classic *Life on the Mississippi*. Twain wrote: 'She knew her subject well, and she set it forth fairly and squarely without any weak ifs and ands and buts. She deserved gratitude but it is an error to suppose she got it.' Yet even he believed some garbled rumour about Hervieu, for at the end of his copy of Mrs Trollope's book he wrote 'Mrs T then married a French *valet*'.[36]

In the spring of 1832 Fanny Trollope's desire was neither for gratitude nor for fame. Her literary purpose was the sensible one commended by Dr Johnson: money. Her book soon went into four editions in English and was translated into French, German, Dutch and Spanish. It was an extraordinary achievement for an unknown writer, and Mrs Trollope made about £600, money that was desperately needed. For herself she bought little: a quarter pound of green tea and half a pound of unsalted butter, something she had missed in America. The bulk went into paying rent arrears and taxes and in buying candles, furniture, a decent bed and 'fixtures' to the extent of £70 for the Harrow Weald farmhouse, which apparently even lacked pillows. She also bought a cow, which eliminated the need to buy good butter, and paid for Henry's admission to the Middle Temple on 15 June. (He had been working with a London barrister since at least November 1831, after his short time at Cambridge had come to an end because of lack of money.) Within months of arriving back in England she knew what she wanted to do: in November 1831 she had written to her friend Julia Garnett, now Frau Professor Pertz and wife of the Royal Librarian and Archivist in Hanover:

> Shall I tell you of a bright vision which often floods before my eyes between sleeping and waking? I will. *If* my book should take, and if it should be favorably reviewed in the Quarterly (the Edinburgh, *if* it does any thing, must abuse it) I should offer the publisher to travel into Germany – to visit the watering places etc., and to write a volume of gossip of all I should see ... But observe, my dear friend, these thoughts are at present only moonshine – when one is rather in the dark however, even such borrowed light is worth something.

Fanny's 'bright vision' of 1831 was fast becoming a reality, and she asked her more experienced friend, Mary Mitford, about writing for magazines: 'What does one do to get business with the mags and annuals? Does one say, as at playing *ecarté*, "I propose", or must one wait to be asked? Remember, dear, that I have five children.'[37] She had no intention of waiting to be asked for she was already hard at work on her first novel, based on her recent, now celebrated, adventures in America.

*

What was the effect of all this upon Anthony? The most important result was that he, like Tom, became convinced that writing was an essential aspect of life. He saw his mother at her desk before dawn to earn enough to support the family. Yet, once that daily chore was completed, she was bursting with a sense of fun for the rest of the day. She communicated this rare combination of discipline and pleasure to her youngest son. From her he learned that writing could provide the means to enjoy life if the author were prepared to work at it. While still in his teens he acquired a knowledge of the business of writing and publishing, subjects that he, like his mother and brother, always treated with respect. Mrs Trollope would frequently employ her sons to go into London to see her publishers and thus Anthony was introduced at an impressionable age into the world of books. He never viewed authorship as some esoteric cult removed from the busy world of men, a fact that has annoyed some critics less well acquainted with the reality of literature.

Anthony studied his mother's famous book closely and in his *Autobiography*, written some forty years later, assessed it somewhat harshly: 'No observer was certainly ever less qualified to judge of the prospects or even the happiness of a young people … Whatever she saw she judged, as most women do, from her own standing point. If a thing were ugly to her eyes, it ought to be ugly to all eyes, – and if ugly, it must be bad.'[38] However, a close examination of *Domestic Mannners* will show many similarities to Anthony Trollope's own writings. Throughout both there is much lively writing, with the frequent use of small details to illustrate behaviour, most noticeably when either Trollope wished to turn the reader against a character. The mother could destroy a frontier fundamentalist preacher by observing that he spat filthy tobacco juice on the floor before commencing an interminable harangue. The son could perform a similar feat by noting the Reverend Mr Slope's sweaty palms as he moved about the cultivated drawing-rooms of Barchester. Both Trollopes had a gift for observing the nuances of conversation that so often reveal camouflaged aspects of a personality. Fanny Trollope indeed kept lists of peculiar expressions used in America and introduced them into her book. That is why Lady Louisa Stuart said that she had made 'Yankee talk' so fashionable. Anthony Trollope also was a great observer of similar nuances and used this knowledge to enrich dialogue throughout his novels, perhaps most notably in his Irish ones. He once said that he always read his dialogue aloud to himself to make sure it sounded accurate, and one suspects that his mother did the same.

Both mother and son were also remarkably honest writers: anyone who reads Anthony Trollope's *Autobiography* will attest to an impression of its fundamental truthfulness. A similar regard flows through most of Mrs Trollope's writings. She may be circumspect about why she went to America, but she presents her account of the life she saw there honestly if somewhat harshly. Nor is she ever above laughing at herself. In her book she freely admits that when she saw names carved into rocks at the Trenton Falls in New York she was about to denounce yet another example of American vulgarity. Suddenly some other visitor read aloud one of the carvings: 'Trollope, England.' Tom and his father had stopped there before her. For his part Anthony Trollope was prepared, particularly in his travel books, to portray himself in a somewhat ridiculous pose. He even admitted in his own book on America that he preferred to swim in the nude. This regard for truthfulness opened both the mother and the son to charges of 'vulgarity' – which to Victorians normally meant anything they disliked – and many reviewers delighted to lecture both Trollopes on their frequent departure from the narrow path of Victorian propriety.

The two concerns central to Mrs Trollope's American book were the role of women and the influence of religion on social behaviour, and these were to be dominant themes in many of her son's books. Neither had any use for feminist theories, but both believed that society was civilised by cultivated women. Nor was either particularly concerned with precise theological definitions, but each believed that religion could raise the moral tone of any society or plunge it into a morass of bigoted vulgarity. Anthony's inherited contempt for Evangelicalism, which began in Harrow, received confirmation from his mother's account of American fundamentalists who were in one of their earlier phases of being 'born again'. There is not a great distance from the mother's portrayal of a 'cottage apostle' in Cincinnati to the picture of Mr Slope in *Barchester Towers*, to take just one example. Fanny Trollope also showed in her first book a respect for Roman Catholicism, as well as a sympathy with Irish labourers on the American canals. She was to abandon both these views in her later works, but Anthony remained true to his mother's earlier opinions.

The mother and son were also alike regarding the business of authorship. Anthony would follow his mother's example and rise early to devote the time before breakfast to writing a predetermined number of words. Both had a stern determination to get their just rewards from their works and both kept up a lively correspondence with a succession of publishers. Perhaps more unusually, both were remarkable for delivering their work on time. Fanny Trollope was not interested in royalty payments; she preferred that publishers buy her books for an outright payment. Both Anthony and Tom tended to follow their mother's rule. She also believed that Hervieu's illustrations played a great part in the success of her first book. (They also made the book seem even harsher than it was.) Anthony inherited this belief in the value of illustrations and took great trouble with them in his novels. Finally, Mrs Trollope bequeathed to Anthony, and to a lesser extent Tom, the ability to unite the love of travel with the production of profitable books about the countries they visited. Following her example, her two sons were able to maintain an expensive way of life by the profit of their pens. Nor can one neglect that, for at least the next two decades of his life, Anthony was always seen as – to quote a newspaper announcement of his marriage – 'the son of the celebrated authoress'.

*

With the proceeds from her first book and hopes of profit from others, Fanny Trollope was able to move her family back to the comfortable house Anthony later called 'Orley Farm'. He recalled how she 'surrounded us again with moderate comforts'. Literary celebrities began to visit the house of a now famous author. Tom recalled an evening when the then scandalous poet Letitia Landon, better known as 'L.E.L.', was sat next to a clerical dignitary known more for his devotion to the good life on earth than for his speculation on what follows. Afterwards, when one of the young Trollopes asked L.E.L. what she had talked about, she replied: 'About eating to be sure. I always talk to everybody on their strong point. I told him that writing poetry was my trade, but that eating was my pleasure, and we were fast friends before the fish was finished.' Scenes like these provided good material for the future author of the Barsetshire novels. Like many literary families of that time (the Brontës are the obvious example), the Trollopes encouraged one another in their reading and their writing with a handwritten magazine *The Magpie* to which various members of the family and a few select neighbours made contributions. At first Anthony was not a frequent contributor, but soon little pieces of his prose and poetry began to appear. Even such a limited success must have given him some small sense of achievement.[39]

Anthony celebrated his seventeenth birthday only a few weeks after his mother's book was published. The return to 'Orley Farm' at least made his walk to Harrow School about three miles less each way. His father was increasingly concerned with Anthony's future education and hoped that he might get a Harrow exhibition to meet his expenses at Oxford. In his second time at Harrow Anthony had done much better. If he had left before with the discredit of being ' "lag" of the school' for three years, he was now on his way to becoming the seventh monitor. As we have seen, he won one of the English essay prizes and not long after her return from America, his mother told a friend that he had just got a prize, although this could have been the essay prize. Even so, like most of Mr Trollope's hopes, the exhibition failed to materialise. Anthony next tried for a scholarship at Trinity College, Oxford whose President, James Ingram, was a friend of his father. When Ingram was elected President in 1824 Mr Trollope heard the news from their mutual friend, William Drury, and wrote in typical vein, 'I am a bad hand at compliments particularly when a strong feeling of sincerity restrains me'. For the scholarship examination Anthony devoted a lot of time to studying Aristotle's *Ethics*. When John Henry Newman had gone up to Trinity a few years before, he was told that it was 'most gentlemanlike', but after getting there he came to a different conclusion: 'I really think if anyone should ask me what qualifications were necessary for Trinity College I should say there was only one – drink, drink, drink.' A few months later and he came to yet another opinion: 'If anyone wishes to study much, I believe there can be no college that will encourage him more than Trinity.' Trollope failed in his attempt to get the scholarship and so never experienced either the drink or the study that Newman had discovered.[40] Yet the memory of the attempt lingered and in one of his few novels with any university scenes, *The Bertrams*, Trollope portrays a Winchester boy who failed to get a place at New College but who managed to win a scholarship to Trinity. 'In those days,' wrote Trollope twenty-five years later, 'a lad of eighteen who could get a scholarship was considered to be nearly safe in his career' [I]. Neither he nor his family were to know such safety.

The Trollopes could not maintain Anthony at university without some help, so he next tried twice for a sizarship at Clare Hall, Cambridge. A sizarship would have been humiliating to one of Trollope's fierce pride: it had once involved waiting on other students and still carried a vague stigma of inferiority, something Trollope would allude to in *Barchester Towers*. His attempts at Cambridge were as unsuccessful as those at Oxford. Late in life he reflected that it was 'very fortunate ... that I did not succeed, for my career ... would have ended in debt and ignominy'. In his novels young gentlemen frequently emerge from one of the ancient universities deep in debt and hovering on the brink of disaster. In the Palliser novels his hero, Plantagenet Palliser, Duke of Omnium, has two sons. The elder, Lord Silverbridge, is sent down from Oxford for painting the Deanery red, while his younger brother, Lord Gerald, gets into trouble both with the head of his college and with debt collectors. However, Trollope normally makes little use of university life in his fiction. Only one novel, *John Caldigate*, is set in a university town – Cambridge – and we are scarcely aware of the university. When the novels do touch on university customs it is obvious that their creator is venturing onto thin ice. In his book on Thackeray Trollope dismissed the importance of Cambridge on his friend: 'It may be presumed ... that his studies there were not very serviceable to him.'[41] The fact that Thackeray left without a degree and with debts of £1,500 provides some – though not total – confirmation for Trollope's view, but whether he would have thought this in 1833 is another matter.

Certainly the young Trollope was involved in quite deep thought in that year, for the earliest known examples of any substantive writing by him are some marginalia, including a few words in Greek, which he made on a copy of Edmund Burke's *A Philosophical Enquiry into the Origins of Our Ideas of the Sublime and the Beautiful*, first published in 1756. A copy of an 1825 edition survives in which is written 'A Trollope – Harrow – Sep. 1833'. By this year Burke had come to occupy a lofty position in English thought: Tories looked upon him as the prophet who had seen the dangers of democracy, Whigs as the orator who lauded their contribution to liberty. For a youth of eighteen to conduct a private debate with a philosopher of Burke's stature shows that he lacked neither abilities nor confidence in those abilities. In his book Burke examined why certain objects give us aesthetic pleasure. Where he makes a comment on Virgil and Aristotle, Trollope, mindful of his recent reading for his Oxford scholarship, notes that the Roman poet provides 'pleasure' but understanding the Greek philosopher is 'hard work'. When Burke concludes that the human mind is normally in a state of indifference rather than of pain or pleasure, Trollope dissents: 'The question depends upon this – can a person be [in] a middle state, neither suffering pain or enjoying pleasure. If he can – they are entirely distinct – but if he cannot, (which I think is the case); as existence itself is a pleasure, when we are suffering no pain ... Moreover the mind is always at work, & must give us pleasant or unpleasure [*sic*] ideas.'

Although the youthful Trollope shows some skill at theoretical arguing and even some 'pleasure' in it, his later insistence on practical detail makes an appearance when he concludes: 'a man may eat jam whilst he has got the gout.' Nor was he content just to debate with the dead author. When Burke quotes Locke, Trollope checked the citation and found that Burke had been wrong. Although these marginalia show what a reflective and intelligent man Trollope already was, they also show that he was not an arrogant one. When Burke discusses the design of churches, Trollope notes: 'Not understanding architecture, I cannot follow this.' Few men, certainly not at eighteen, are ever so humble in marginalia! Yet another characteristic of the mature novelist emerges when at one point of disagreement he writes: 'I can find a much simpler reason in my own mind – & which in like cases – seems to actuate *me*.' Trollope always saw the world from his own perspective; it may not be remarkable to do so but he admitted it. Throughout his comments we see not only the knowledgeable youth but the early stages of the man who would show such a fascination with the way the unconscious mind governs different people. It is unfortunate, however, that Trollope's meaning in one marginal comment is not completely clear: 'The taste of sugar is not I think by all admitted to be ... palatable. What would my father say to this.'[42]

One of Trollope's comments on Burke's book soon seemed ironic: 'We talk of enjoying good health ... it is a pleasure & was meant by God as perhaps the greatest pleasure that we are capable of enjoying.' Within a few months of his writing this, an influenza epidemic spread across England. 'The season has been the most sickly ever known,' wrote one cynical observer. 'Everybody has had the influenza, as it is called, and though nobody, or very few indeed, have died of *it*, it seems to have disposed those who have it, to take the opportunity of dying of any other disease.' Mr Trollope, Henry and Anthony were all struck down, and Anthony was ill for ten days. As his mother told Julia Pertz, she was 'very seriously alarmed' although her youngest son, fortunately, did not avail himself of the 'opportunity of dying'.[43] His mother alternated between writing and nursing, for Hervieu had also been dangerously ill. Anthony was no sooner recovered than Henry, already weakened from his American adventures, showed alarming symptoms of consumption. He had recently accompanied his mother on a tour of Belgium and Germany where she gathered material for her second travel book. While in Belgium the ever-unlucky Henry had received a sword wound during an amateur production of a Goldsmith play.

These illnesses seemed to symbolise the end of that brief period of prosperity that had followed Mrs Trollope's sudden blossoming as a writer. Even her constant activity with her pen could do no more than stave off the impending financial collapse. The Trollopes, desperate to find any way of cutting their expenses, decided in the early months of 1834 to remove Anthony from Harrow. He would be nineteen in April and it was pointless to let him remain till the end of the summer term when there was no prospect of his going on to university. What did he take from his miserable time at the three schools he had attended – Harrow, Sunbury and Winchester?

First, he acquired an ability to do hard work. From early boyhood he had been accustomed to rising before the sun, and this in time would provide a key element in his amazing ability to produce so many books. Secondly, he acquired a deep familiarity with the liturgy of the Church of England, the beauties of the Prayer Book and the basic truths of Christianity. These are often quiet companions throughout his books, where we constantly encounter phrases and echoes of phrases from the Bible and the Book of Common Prayer. To take one example: it is almost impossible not to find some version of the quotation from the Psalms, 'his lines had fallen in pleasant places', in almost every novel.[44]

The third thing that he gained was a considerable grounding in the classics which was to give him an interest that lasted all his life. His attitude towards books, particularly the classical authors, is expressed by his hero Plantagenet Palliser when he is rebuking his two idle sons who, as mentioned earlier, had done badly at university:

> Cicero and Ovid have told us that to literature only could they look for consolation in their banishment. But then they speak of a remedy for sorrow, not of a source of joy. No young man should dare to neglect literature. At some period of his life he will surely need consolation. And he may be certain that should he live to be an old man, there will be none other; – except religion [*The Duke's Children* XXV].

Trollope's great love of Latin, particularly Caesar, Cicero and Horace, really began a few years after he ended his formal education. He would in time write a biography of Cicero and translate Caesar and his library would boast many classical texts and commentaries. It is true that Trollope gave his schools little credit for inculcating this devotion to the classics, but he did admit that they gave him 'that groundwork of the language which will in the process of years make its way slowly, even through the skin'.[45]

Trollope frequently makes classical allusions in his writings, as he naturally assumed that most of his readers could stumble through a familar Latin tag, though he often indicated the translation without insulting the reader. Sometimes he overdoes his classical references, as in *Framley Parsonage* where he got himself caught in a complicated comparison of Victorian politicians with the ancient gods and goddesses. He often uses the name of one of these deities to provide mild amusement, as in another novel, *The Bertrams*, where a somewhat cold though grand woman is frequently referred to as 'Juno'.

Latin quotations often appear when he wishes to summon ancient wisdom to buttress Victorian morality. Horace, his particular favourite, provides over half the Latin quotations in the novels and many in his travel books. Perhaps his favourite Latin quotation, which formed the theme of many of his novels and which he used many times, was the Virgilian 'Facilis descensus Averni', 'Easy is the descent to Hell'. Trollope also took from his study of the classics a grounding in basic English grammar. Tom Trollope recalled that he had never held a book of English grammar in his hand. It is easy enough for the armchair expert to find grammatical mistakes in the writings of Anthony or Tom Trollope, and contemporary reviewers were not loath to point them out. Nevertheless they both had an ability to write clearly and quickly, and usually correctly. In the end Anthony Trollope turned out the educated gentleman his father had wanted and never disgraced the family by ignorance or idleness.[46]

In spite of his own unhappy experiences at two of the great public schools, Anthony Trollope remained faithful to the basic principles upon which they were founded. He believed that they needed considerable reform in their methods of teaching but he saw them as essential to the task of producing the English gentleman. In an article he wrote about the reform of public schools, when this perennial topic was receiving one of its early airings in 1865, he gave his mature views:[47]

> We love our public schools, – loving even their faults dearly ... we are half unwilling to sacrifice the picturesque to the useful ... We remember chiefly, if not only, all that these schools have done for us ... There we learned to be honest, true, and brave. There we were trained to disregard the softness of luxury, and to love the hardihood and dangers of violent exercise. There we became men; and we became men after such a fashion that we are feared or loved, as may be, but always respected, – even though it be in spite of our ignorance.

*

The adage about the gentle slope to hell would almost certainly have occurred to that dedicated classicist Thomas Anthony Trollope, as he watched his youngest son in the spring of 1834. Yet before anything could be decided about Anthony's prospects a far greater crisis overtook the family.

The final tragedy in the long saga of the Harrow farm was at hand. Trollope's *Autobiography* presents the event in fairly simplistic terms: his is the account of an elderly man looking back on his father's collapse and, quite naturally, colouring it – with all his novelist's skill – in fairly stark shades. Fortunately the correspondence between Thomas Trollope, Lord Northwick and that peer's agent, George Quilton, has survived and gives a dramatic picture of a complex relationship. Northwick was not the 'cormorant' that the Trollope children liked to imagine. At times he was quite accommodating, as in allowing the elder Trollope to sub-let some land as a paddock to Anthony's new Headmaster, Dr Longley. Yet anyone looking at these letters – often lengthy exercises in self-justification – will at once see that all three men, tenant, agent and peer, were plagued by a variety of illnesses which did not aid their tempers. Thomas Trollope, in particular, was a man who always had to be in the right and was always prepared to prove it. By early April, Quilton informed Northwick: 'I fear Mr. T. is in a very bad situation & what is to be done with him I cannot conceive.' The elder Trollope said that for almost two decades the farm had caused him distress: 'I have given up almost all society, & the education of my children has been neglected.' Of course the Trollopes – and no doubt the agent – realised that with Anthony, the youngest son, coming to the end of his time at the school, there was no reason for them to struggle to pay a large rent for the right to free education that they no longer could use.

Quilton was keeping an eye on the eccentric household and informed the peer that 'Mr Trollope told me today that he was going to Cheltenham to recruit his health, but I understand from Coln Grant that he was gone to London in order to go a Broad.' Fanny Trollope had long wished to leave Harrow and its exorbitant rents behind her and she made little secret of this, although when she wrote to John Murray she presented it as her husband's desire: 'Mr Trollope having decided upon taking his family abroad for some time.' There was always a possibility that any of their creditors could apply for a warrant and then Anthony Trollope's father, like Dickens's father, could have been cast into debtor's prison where another of the peer's Harrow tenants was already languishing, but Lord Northwick was not anxious for anything like this.[48]

On Friday 25 April 1834 – the day after his nineteenth birthday – Anthony was called early in the morning and told to get the gig ready; the family still maintained that small carriage which had been used for Mr Trollope's trips to his chambers or to take his sons to Winchester. It was only after the morose man had settled himself in the gig that he told his son to take him to the London docks. Dickens would depict these docks in *Martin Chuzzlewit* as a busy and ugly place full of suspicious-looking passengers. Often the passengers had good reason for appearing suspicious because they were fleeing abroad to escape imprisonment. Thomas Anthony Trollope did not tell his youngest son that this is what he was doing. All the bright hopes of the former Fellow of New College were shattered as an ill, prematurely aged and broken man boarded a ship for Ostend. Personality and ill-luck had triumphed over ability and ambition.

As Anthony came driving back up the road to Julian Hill, a gardener who had once worked for the family ran out making strange signs and calling to him. The agent had got a distraint order against Thomas Anthony Trollope, which meant that all his goods could now be seized to satisfy the outstanding debts. Anthony thought quickly and drove the gig into Harrow and sold it to an ironmonger. The shopkeeper offered £17 for the gig, horse and harness, which delighted the young Trollope until he said that he would keep the £17 as that was exactly what the debt-ridden Trollopes owed him.

When Anthony got back to the house he found the bailiffs in possession. His sisters were sneaking some of their mother's favourite possessions to Colonel Grant's house. Cecilia and Emily, after all, were old hands at this as they had already experienced something similar in Cincinnati. Now the Grant girls joined in the fun and Anthony started to secrete some of his mother's favourite things ('pretty-pretties' he calls them in his *Autobiography*). Many years later the successful novelist pointed out to a friend the spot in the hedge through which the young smugglers carried their booty. A fair amount must have been saved by these devices as Anthony treasured some of the books all his life, including one on a subject far from his heart, *Sectionum Conicarum Elementa*, published in 1723. It was an obscure mathematical text bequeathed by his grandfather to Anthony's brother Arthur, who only survived the old man by a few days.

In his *Autobiography* Trollope neglects to mention that Lord North-wick's agent put a stop to what he regarded as robbery.* The auctioneer was forced to set a value on the purloined goods and Mrs Trollope paid £12 to retain these few relics of her once prosperous home.[49] A quarter of a century later Anthony Trollope described a similar scene in *Framley Parsonage*, the novel that started his great fame, when bailiffs invade a comfortable rectory. 'Oh ladies,' says Trollope, speaking directly and evidently from the heart to his readers: 'Oh ladies, who have drawing-

---

*Northwick appeared anxious that Mrs Trollope retain most of her possessions. He must have continued to take some interest in her writings, for I have in my own collection a copy of the first one-volume edition of her most famous novel, *Michael Armstrong*, published five years after this. Inside this copy is Lord Northwick's bookplate.

rooms in which the things are pretty, good, and dear to you, think of what it would be to have two bailiffs rummaging among them with pen and ink-horn, making a catalogue preparatory to a sheriff's auction' [XLIV]. Anthony Trollope required no imagination to depict that scene.

News of this disgrace was not sent to Tom lest it disturb his final term at Oxford. Mrs Trollope hurried down to Devonshire, to leave the still weak Henry with her cousin, Fanny Bent. Anthony, with one of his sisters, boarded a ship for the first of many Channel crossings. Mrs Trollope soon reunited her family in the mediaeval city of Bruges in the new Kingdom of Belgium.

'Antonius Trollopius: author of *The Last Chronicles of Cicero*' (Linley Sambourne, *Punch*, 1880).
See p. 579.

CHAPTER THREE

A Nobler Purpose

In Trollope's youth he learned some doggerel from a Frenchman, probably Hervieu: 'Are you go? Is you gone? And I left? Vera Vell!' [*The Three Clerks* XLIV]. Such was the mood of the Trollopes as they settled in Bruges in 1834. Mrs Trollope had visited there the year before when writing *Belgium and Western Germany*. She liked Bruges, the ancestral home of the Meetkeerke family: 'one of the most deeply Catholic cities left on the earth.' On a more material plane, she noted that its principal trades were 'beer and manure'. While Fanny Trollope was not too far from her publishers, her husband was just far enough away to avoid imprisonment for debt. She sent an optimistic account of their rented house, the Château d'Hondt, to a friend: 'Each of us have already learned to fix ourselves in some selected corner ... and believe ourselves at home. The old desks have found new tables to rest upon and the few favorite volumes ... are made to fill their narrow limits in orderly rows.' If she missed her room at Harrow, whence she could see Westminster Abbey, her new balcony provided a view of windmills in the surrounding countryside.[1]

With both Henry and Emily seriously ill she needed all her strength. As Anthony recalled, 'the horrid word, which of all words was, for some years after, the most dreadful to us, had been pronounced. It was no longer a delicate chest ... but consumption.' Poor old Mr Trollope was 'broken-hearted as well as ill', but between headaches he carried on his *Encyclopaedia Ecclesiastica*. His wife was working on yet another novel, for her writings allowed them to live in the style to which she had accustomed herself. The family was far from penniless because at last they were rid of 'the *pernicious* farm'. Since money went twice as far as in England, Fanny could, for example, afford two maids. Henry Milton had brought some order into his brother-in-law's tangled financial affairs and Fanny had the money settled on her at her marriage. She told her friend, Julia Garnett Pertz, in July 1834 that

her own money was 'sufficient to support us in perfect comfort here –
and if in addition to this, I continue able to gain money by my pen, we
shall be much richer than we have ever been'. Not surprisingly she
wrote: 'Oh! what a blessed thing is a settlement.'[2] Perhaps that is why
almost every novel by her son gives details of his characters' settled
income. At the most impressionable time in life, he had seen how
important it could be.

What the Trollopes lacked were settled futures for their sons in
situations becoming their rank as 'gentlemen'. Tom, at least, would
have his Oxford education, but Anthony appeared to have no goal and
no qualifications. Looking back at this period he felt that:

> I was an idle, desolate hanger-on, that most hopeless of human beings, a
> hobbledehoy of nineteen, without any idea of a career, a profession or a
> trade. As well as I can remember I was fairly happy, for there were pretty
> girls at Bruges with whom I could fancy that I was in love; and I had been
> removed from the real misery of school. But as to my future life I had not
> even an aspiration.

Thackeray, who visited Bruges a few years later, found it particularly
notable for 'uniformly gentle and pleasing' women. Yet even pretty
faces could not completely shut out the occasional pangs of guilt from
young Anthony, who knew he was idle while his mother laboured but
'we should probably have thought more of that had she not taken to
work as though it were the recognised condition of life for an old lady of
fifty-five'.[3]

Suddenly a rather exotic prospect appeared: Mrs Trollope obtained
the offer of a cavalry commission for Anthony in the Austrian army. It
is not certain where this originated, as she had made influential
friends in Belgium and was even invited to dine by King Leopold. A
more likely source for the commission is the Landgravine of
Hesse-Homburg, the widowed daughter of King George III, who sadly
missed her native land and kept in touch by reading the latest English
books. Mrs Trollope was anxious that a copy of her book on *Belgium
and Western Germany* be sent to the Landgravine. This was because
'our amiable Princess' was highly praised in the book, both for her
learning as well as for her hospitality. It was she who had guided the
Trollope party round her palace, taking evident pride in her library
and garden. Since Anthony had failed to get into Oxford or Cambridge
he could not follow numerous ancestors into the Church. The Austrian
position would give him a gentlemanly profession. We have some idea
of the requirements which applied in the 1830s, as the Landgravine
sent details to another English friend who desired an Austrian

commission. Anthony would have needed 'a good figure and good health', a baptismal certificate and the assurance that he belonged to no secret society of any type. In addition his parents would have to supplement his pay with a small allowance in gold.[4]

Anthony also would have needed some knowledge of French and German. For this his mother formed a plan with some old friends in Brussels, a city which Lord Palmerston, the Foreign Secretary, described in the 1830s as a place which 'swarms with rum English'. The Trollopes had not been the only Harrow family to flee from debt. Some of the Drurys, that clerical family who dominated Harrow, had also withdrawn abroad. Indeed, during all his troubles with the Trollopes, Lord Northwick's agent moaned that 'the Name of Drury was so notoriously known' that people refused to honour their 'bills' or extend them credit. 'Old Harry' had bankrupted himself by £30,000 mainly through his mania for book-collecting. The Rev. William Drury had established a private school in the Belgian capital and agreed to employ Anthony to help with his seventy pupils, mainly sons of the many other exiles from debt who congregated in Brussels.[5] This custom continued through much of the Victorian era and in one of his last novels Trollope describes Brussels as a place where Englishmen settle to find cheap education [*Mr Scarborough's Family* X].

Anthony taught classics at the school, where he was known by the old term of 'usher'. He was not paid but his mother would have one less mouth to feed. Many years later he commented: 'Who can say where the usher ends and the schoolmaster begins? He, perhaps, may properly be called an usher, who is hired by a private schoolmaster to assist himself in his private occupation' [*The Claverings* II]. He was, of course, not the first unsuccessful schoolboy to be 'forced by necessity into the stern bread-earning world'. He once used an image based on this event as an example of the way in which people adapt to changed circumstances: 'Yesterday he was taught, and fought, of course, against the schoolmaster. Today he teaches, and fights, as keenly for him' [*Doctor Thorne* XIV]. While teaching ancient languages he could practise modern ones. At least he was tall and powerfully built, so that he could overawe the thirty boys under his care. One of his duties was to take them for walks, but after the second excursion Mrs Drury announced that the boys' clothes could not stand any more expeditions with the energetic young usher.

*

In October 1834 Anthony's fate changed: his career as an Austrian

cavalry officer ended even before it had begun. A government position
had been found in London and he was sent to join Tom, who was doing
private tutoring there. Mrs Trollope wrote to Drury: 'Accept our best
thanks for your kindness to dear Anthony. The haste of his departure
was due to the fear of Sir Francis Freeling, who was himself doubtful if
he could keep the situation he had offered open for him till next week.'[6]
Anthony, like most Victorian liberals, would now be able to sneer,
whether on his travels or in his novels, at Austria's attempt to preserve
peace and stability in Europe [*Nina Balatka* I].

Sir Francis Freeling was the Secretary of the Post Office. Like Mrs
Trollope, he came from Bristol, where his memorial tablet in St Mary
Redcliffe praises his thirty-eight years of public service with his
'unwearied industry in the employment of great talents and by
unblemished Integrity, grounded upon Christian principles'. These
principles did not, of course, preclude filling the Post Office with his
family and friends. His elder son was Assistant Secretary, and a
younger, Clayton, was at the Stamp Office. Clayton's wife was one of
Mrs Trollope's 'dearest friends', who had much admired *Domestic
Manners*. When she heard of her troubles, she asked her father-in-law
for a position for the youngest Trollope boy. As so often in Anthony's
early life, the influence of the Drury family also appears to have been
at work: Freeling was an old friend of the Drurys and had franked all
of Henry Drury's letters soliciting help in his contest with Dr Butler for
the headmastership of Harrow. Fanny Trollope told her publisher
John Murray that her son had 'been appointed by my kind friends the
Freelings ... an appointment which under our present circumstances I
am very thankful for – but the present income from it is very small.'[7]
Freeling was a kind and generous man: in addition to helping Drury he
allowed Sir Walter Scott to have parcels sent care of the Post Office
and regularly sent money to the widow of the last postman hanged for
robbing the mails.

Anthony hastened to Bruges to take leave of his family. It was his
final farewell to Henry who, with that frantic strength of the dying
consumptive, had developed a passion for carpentry. The house was
constantly filled with the clatter of his hammer and saw. Another
sound was now heard, that horrifying warning that echoed through so
many nineteenth-century households: 'Who does not know that sound,'
asked Trollope in one short story, 'almost of two rusty bits of iron
scratching against each other, which comes from a suffering
windpipe?'[8] He saw the unmistakable signs of the family curse in
Emily. 'Of course she was doomed. I knew it of both of them, though I
had never heard the word spoken, or had spoken it to anyone.' As he

recalled forty years later, 'A sadder household never was held together. They were all dying, – except my mother, who would sit up night after night nursing the dying ones and writing novels the while, – so that there might be a decent roof for them to die under.' Henry died two days before Christmas, leaving behind him two memorials to a life of frustration: a recently published article on geology and his election to the Geological Society of London.

This hurried farewell to the dying Henry and the rest of his family was also a farewell to Anthony's childhood. At the age of nineteen he was leaving the direct control of those extraordinary parents who had so moulded his character and his personality. He was one of the many great figures of the Victorian era who experienced troubled childhoods. The Queen herself had grown up fatherless, under the dominance of an isolated and overprotective mother and in a household torn by fierce family feuds. Dickens was hurled into a blacking factory after his father had been imprisoned for debt. The five-year-old Thackeray was separated from his mother in India and sent to school in England. Tennyson's early life in a Lincolnshire rectory was darkened by a father far more ill than Thomas Anthony Trollope, and the sombre nature of that Yorkshire rectory of the Brontë sisters is unforgettable. Easy credit combined with primitive accounting could suddenly reduce a family from prosperous respectability to misery and disgrace: something known to both Manning and Newman. Thus Trollope's childhood was not unique. He had accepted the deaths of infants or of his brother Arthur without apparently any real psychological damage to himself. His wanderings among schools, while unhappy, were no worse than what many other boys endured.

Childhood however left two permanent marks on Anthony. The first was an appreciation of the joys of life and literature, acquired from his mother. Yet for many of his most formative years she was either absent from the house or, seemingly, giving greater love to the other children. This, combined with financial uncertainties and the strain of living with a father verging on mental collapse, left the second mark, a sense that prosperity and pleasure could end at any moment, as the contented person plunged into a bottomless pit of misery. For Trollope, this misery manifested itself in two ways: poverty and madness. Even when he became a rich and famous author he dreaded both. The fear of these two afflictions stayed in his mind and pervaded his novels. This dual legacy gave him the creative tension necessary for him to become a great writer, one possessed of a deep insight into the human mind and heart. As important as this tension is, we must be careful not to exaggerate it. 'My experience,' he wrote in his short story, 'A Ride

Across Palestine', 'tells me that early wounds are capable of cure.' It would take ten years before he was 'cured', but the scars always remained.

*

When Anthony reached London he went straight to Clayton Freeling, who took him to his elder brother, the Assistant Secretary. Since a clerk's main work was to copy records and correspondence it was important that he should be able to write legibly and correctly. This was a quarter of a century before competitive examinations guarded the portals of the Civil Service. The young Anthony was merely handed *The Times* and asked to copy a passage from the closely printed columns. His production was wretched, with ink blots from the quill pen and many misspelled words. 'That won't do, you know,' said the Assistant Secretary, but his brother pointed out that Trollope was nervous and needed more time. Freeling then asked if he was proficient in arithmetic. Trollope, conscious that he had never even learned the multiplication table, mumbled, 'I know a little.'

He was ordered to copy another passage at home and bring it back the next day, when he would be questioned on mathematics. In Tom's lodgings 'preparations for calligraphy were made on a great scale; a volume of Gibbon was taken down, new quill pens large and small, and steel pens by various makers were procured; cream-laid paper was provided, and ruled lines were put beneath it.' The next day he returned with his perfectly copied passage, but no one asked to see it, nor did the demon of mathematics appear. Instead he was shown to a desk to start his career as a clerk, at a salary of £90 a year. He drew on this experience for his most autobiographical novel, *The Three Clerks*, where Charley Tudor is modelled on the author. (One of the other clerks, Charley's cousin, returns from Brussels to take up his post: an apt illustration of how once Trollope recalled one aspect of his past, he would use others as well.) The novel depicts Charley's interview to become a clerk at £90 a year:

'Now,' said the great man, 'just copy the few first sentences of that leading article – either one will do,' ... To tell the truth, Charley did not know what a leading article was, and so he sat abashed, staring at the paper ... [when] Charley had half covered the half-sheet ... he unfortunately suffered a large blot of ink to fall on the paper ... 'That won't do, Mr Tudor, that won't do ... Oh dear! oh dear! this is very bad ... sympathy with an "i" sympathise with an "i", you must be very fond of "i's" down in Shropshire' [II].

On 4 November 1834 Sir Francis Freeling signed a warrant appointing 'Mr Anthony Trollope' a Junior Clerk in the Secretary's office. This was not only the centre of postal administration but a virtual staff college to train future leaders of this great engine of state. Sir Francis listed 'myself' as the person recommending the new clerk, who had to find two responsible persons to put up a bond of £200. Freeling noted in an official letter: 'Mr Trollope has been well educated and will be subject to the usual probation as to competency' of three months.[9] It was not a very grand position for a youth descended from baronets and educated at two ancient schools. The Post Office ranked low when compared with the Foreign Office, the Treasury, or even the War Office, where his uncle had begun his career thirty years before, although at the same salary of £90.

Some old-fashioned people, like one Tory lady in one of his novels, might even doubt whether a civil servant could be considered a 'gentleman' [*The Vicar of Bullhampton* IX]. Trollope himself never doubted that it was both a 'gentlemanly' and a 'manly' profession. A 'profession', Trollope was to write, 'signified a calling by which a gentleman, not born to the inheritance of a gentleman's allowance of good things, might ingeniously obtain the same by some exercise of his abilities' [*The Bertrams* VIII]. In a lecture to young postal clerks many years later he accepted that 'men do not go into the Civil Service with ambitious views ... The profession is generally chosen for them ... because an early income is desirable.' He always maintained that 'there is no profession by which a man can earn his bread in these realms, admitting of a brighter honesty, or a nobler purpose, or of an action more manly and independent'.[10] The Post Office proved, eventually, the perfect place for him, both as a man and as a writer. For the next thirty-three years it provided not only an income but the background to his life, and it is impossible to appreciate Trollope the writer without knowing Trollope the dedicated postal official.

The Post Office was already growing, as a result of the phenomenal expansion in population and commerce which marked the early nineteenth century. These increases demanded a better postal service which in turn brought about yet further expansion. The impressive new building at St Martin-le-Grand, built at a cost of £330,000, had opened five years before on 29 September 1829 when Sir Francis arrived with his staff of office and Secretary's chair. It covered two acres of part of what had been one of the worse sections of London, an area which before had contained no less than 142 houses with over 1,000 inhabitants. By Trollope's first year these had given way to 1,337 employees. Through the building's centre ran a vast hall lined with massive granite columns. Public opinion had forced the architect to make this a public thoroughfare to replace the old streets covered by the new building. At six each evening, hall constables would shout 'Stand back!' and 'Clear the way!' to make a path through the crowds to allow the mail to go out. Clerks with a few years' experience, like John Tilley, could tell the new recruit what their work was like before this move: Tilley had laboured in the disused kitchen of a City rectory. Sir Francis, a man of great abilities, had brought the Post Office to the verge of Victorian reforms from the chaos of earlier times.

Many aspects of the Post Office were still in the ferment of improvement. A French official visitor, who reported in the very year of Trollope's appointment, commented that while French mail-coaches averaged five miles an hour British ones reached almost ten, even allowing for frequent stops to change horses. A coach leaving London made the 203-mile trip to Liverpool in twenty hours and fifty minutes. The sight of these huge coaches – twenty-seven every night – thundering forth from the yard of the Bull and Mouth Inn, opposite the new Post Office building, would impress any young clerk with the importance of his work. At the back sat the guards, each heavily armed. Another of the great sights of London was the procession of all the Royal Mail coaches on the King's Birthday, with the men in livery and the postman's horns sounding above the roars of the admiring throng. An American poet saw it in Trollope's first year at the Post Office:[11]

> The drivers and guards in their bright red and gold uniforms; the admirable horses driven so beautifully; the neat harness; the exactness with which the room of each horse was calculated ... formed altogether one of the most interesting spectacles I had ever seen.

Yet the Royal Mail coaches were within a few years of their extinction by the railways. Many late Victorian memoirs contain lamentations for those colourful coaches, but Trollope had little sentimental regard for 'those awful vehicles of which we used to be so proud' [*Lady Anna* XX].

The increasing volume of the mail, which in 1838 was over 126,000,000 items, put an overwhelming strain on the coaches. Sacks were stuffed into every corner, and not just in the once sacred boot. Relief was already at hand because some mail was being hazarded to the infant railway. This was symbolic of one of the greatest decades of change in British history, when reform spread through government, church and society. In 1832 Parliament agreed to a reform of the House of Commons. Government, said *The Times* when it reflected on these changes, 'is laying aside the policeman, the gaoler, and the executioner, in exchange for the more kindly and dignified function of the father, the schoolmaster, and the friend'.[12] The new Liberal MPs, as some started to call themselves, began to look at other curious institutions to reform. The government of the cities was reorganised, the whole basis of relief to the poor was changed and faltering steps were taken in education and public health. Changes in the organisation and finances of the Church of England were started. The Post Office could not escape this reforming zeal, and 1834, the year Trollope became a clerk, saw the start of a campaign for its reform.

Outside Parliament there was much discussion of the question, for businessmen were increasingly aware that a more efficient post would help industry and commerce. In 1837 a Birmingham reformer, Rowland Hill, wrote a pamphlet, *Post Office Reform: its Importance and Practicability*. His advocacy of sweeping changes soon gathered powerful support. Every reform movement needed its own newspaper, and soon Hill had *The Post Office Circular* which contained cartoons by a young artist called William Makepeace Thackeray. A sceptical government were compelled to give Hill a temporary position at the Treasury to introduce an entirely new system, a uniform penny postage. Like many reformers Hill was not very tactful, and his campaign infuriated the postal establishment which, like any bureaucracy, disliked intruders.

When Trollope became a clerk there was no one single rate for postage. The cost, which was paid by the recipient, depended on how far a letter travelled. Hill had first become interested in postal reform when he saw his mother unable to pay this fee. The average cost was sixpence, but the variations were enormous. A letter from London to Glasgow cost 1s 1½d, but an additional twenty miles to Greenock cost almost half that amount. The most unjust aspect was that peers and MPs did not pay: their signatures, called franks, provided free postage. By the 1830s there were seven million franked letters each year, a heavy burden on the system. Peers and MPs were constantly asked to sign letters for acquaintances. Mrs Trollope, like many people, once moaned: 'I cannot get franks.' Thus the burden fell on businessmen and on the poor. Even Rowland Hill delayed his letters till he could persuade a friendly MP to provide a frank.[13]

Hill proposed several solutions for a cheaper and quicker post. If a slot could be cut in doors, a postman need not wait for an answer to his knock. Adamantine Tories like the Marquess of Londonderry growled that they would not damage their mahogany doors for a Mr Hill of Birmingham. The most radical proposal was for a uniform rate of one penny to be paid by the sender. 'The aristocracy are very furious at it,' wrote one Whig lady, the Hon. Caroline Fox, 'and think it beneath their dignity to understand anything about a *penny*, while I am *charmed* to have no longer the bore of asking for a frank.' The penny post came into effect on 10 January 1840: in its nearly universal effects it was one of the greatest reforms of the century. Another invention, the envelope, followed the introduction of postage stamps, and the basis of correspondence throughout the civilised world was established as other countries copied British ideas. As the *Standard Cyclopaedia* put it, 'Correspondence is the offspring of advanced civilisation.' We cannot understand Hill or Trollope without realising that they considered a better postal service not just an economic issue but a moral question. Indeed that veritable bible of Victorian Liberalism, G.R. Porter's *The Progress of the Nation*, listed postal reform under moral improvements. Yet Hill's opponents were correct in arguing that it would not be a financial success; in the first year profits fell by over half. No one, however, could deny its popularity: the volume of letters doubled in two years and continued to rise. This launched what Mrs Gaskell, in her story 'Cousin Phillis', called 'the never-ending stream of notes and letters which seem to flow in upon most households'. The change was so accepted that a quarter of a century later that same novelist felt it necessary to assure her readers that in the old days the recipient had to pay huge sums for letters.[14]

What was the effect of all this on Trollope? He was at the very centre of a great reform; yet, having quickly imbibed the conservative instincts beloved of any bureaucracy, he resented the theoretical outsider, Rowland Hill. On the other hand, his increasingly liberal political views caused him to feel passionately about 'the paramount importance' of spreading 'the blessing of letter writing', particularly among the poor. This divided attitude resembled his general ideas about Victorian society. On the Post Office, as on almost everything else, he united conservative instincts with liberal ideas of progress. He would later praise Hill's 'wise audacity', but he never really liked the man.[15] This undoubtedly influenced Trollope's portrayal of reformers in his novels, where so often we see them advocating a just cause but doing so in a repellent manner. He sometimes makes asides about Hill. In *Can You Forgive Her?* a character comments on the Victorian mania for letter-writing: 'Free communication with all the world is their motto, and Rowland Hill is the god they worship' [XXIII]. Trollope was content with the motto, but refused to offer his incense to that particular 'god'.

The most important result of Trollope's postal career was his discovery of a sense of belonging. For the first time he found happiness in an institution and in friendship with colleagues. This gave him the emotional stability to overcome the miserable uncertainties of his early life. Tom Trollope took pride in having been at an ancient public school; Anthony was proud of being part of a government department that was playing an important role in creating modern Britain. It was the only public service that was beginning to reach into every town and almost every village. His pride is seen in a remark, written after his retirement from his official career, praising the Post Office for 'that accuracy in the performance of its duties for which it is conspicuous' [*The Eustace Diamonds* XV]. The novels often contain comments, usually short and unconnected with the plot, on postal matters, as well as loving descriptions of a letter's route. The Post Office was at the centre of the Victorian achievement, and for almost thirty-five years it allowed Anthony Trollope to play a prominent role in that achievement.

There is another aspect of Trollope's work that played a part in his success as a novelist. The department placed great emphasis on well-composed documents. Freeling, in particular, was noted for the lucidity of his reports, and his example permeated to the most junior of clerks. By copying, summarising and writing official reports Trollope learned how to write quickly and clearly. His books constantly show the influence of this work. He has often been accused of having no 'style' or, at best, a commonplace one. Sometimes this charge came from more artistic novelists, such as George Meredith, but more frequently from critics with little appreciable experience of writing for a non-captive audience.

Two years after Trollope settled down to his desk, one of his favourite poets, Henry Taylor, himself a senior clerk at the Colonial Office, wrote a short book, *The Statesman*, which argued that a clear style was a pillar of good government:[16]

> Literary men, and the young still more than the old of this class, have commonly a good deal to rescind in their style in order to adapt it to business. But the young, if they be men of sound abilities, will soon learn what is not apt and discard it; which the old will not. The leading rule is to be content to be common-place – a rule which might be observed with advantage in other writings.

From his daily work Trollope learnt to be 'common-place', and he discovered how to use this skill 'with advantage in other writings'. Yet he well knew the difficulties of achieving such a style. In one novel he portrays a middle-aged doctor attempting a marriage proposal: 'He would use the simplest, plainest language, he said to himself over and over again; but it is not always easy to use simple, plain language, – by no means so easy as to mount on stilts, and to march along with sesquipedalian words, with pathos, spasms, and notes of interjection' [*Framley Parsonage* XXXIX]. Trollope's style was formed during his early experience of official life, much as Dickens's (which Trollope disliked) was shaped during his early years as a journalist. Trollope could never compose those elaborate prose poems, precariously balanced between exquisite beauty and boring repetition, that Dickens displays at the start of so many novels. Nor would Trollope ever agonise over Flaubert's 'le mot juste', for he believed that 'style to the writer [is] not the wares which he has to take to market, but the vehicle in which they may be carried' [*The Duke's Children* XXVI]. Even the homely metaphor shows the mark of the 'common-place' and sensible civil servant.

*

When he began work Trollope had to manage on his yearly salary of £90, which after three years rose to £110. As someone long given to dwelling in a world of fantasy, he liked to dream of fabulous incomes as he remembered almost half a century later: 'When the youth of nineteen enters an office, how far beyond want would he think himself should he ever reach the pecuniary paradise of £900 a year!' [*Ayala's Angel* II]. He worked with several other young clerks in a large room directly connected to the Secretary's office. Here he heard many office myths, some of which he would recall in his books, such as the story of a hapless clerk who had misdirected mail intended for the King. The poor lad was berated by his superior: 'Mis-sent the Monarch's pouch! Mis-sent the Monarch's pouch!' According to the story this so upset him that he needed six months' leave and a diet of asses' milk mixed with rum. When recounting this, Trollope inserted a reflection on his own early days:

> How well can I remember the terror created within me by the air of outraged dignity with which a certain fine old gentleman ... could rub his hands slowly, one on the other, and look up to the ceiling, slightly shaking his head, as though lost in the contemplation of my iniquities! I would become sick in my stomach, and feel as though my ankles had been broken. That upward turn of the eye unmanned me so completely that I was speechless [*The Small House at Allington* XXXVI].

He was required to be at work by ten and to stay till four, but he soon had a reputation not only for arriving late but for getting little done in the morning. When he started work there were six senior and seven junior clerks in the Secretary's office. An official order was eventually issued which the clerks had to counter-sign: this reminded them that the first hour of work was not for their breakfast but for copying and indexing documents in the huge office ledgers. Some nights Trollope was on duty, as one 'clerk in waiting' had to be in the building when it was closed, from 4 p.m. to ten the next morning. When doing this he had an apartment on an upper floor with a bedroom attached. This duty once brought him face to face with royalty. At about seven one evening word came that a visiting German queen wished to see one of the great spectacles of London: the Royal Mail coaches being despatched.[17] The twenty-one-year-old Trollope – a tall, gangling youth, no doubt blushing – conducted the Teutonic majesty round the building and, with proper courtly etiquette, walked backwards before royalty. After much consultation an equerry handed the disappointed youth a mere half-crown. We can almost hear Trollope's boisterous laughter as he recounted this in his *Autobiography*, adding: 'That also was a bad moment.'

The young man had many bad moments in these early years. The Freeling regime came to an end within two years of Trollope's appointment. The new Secretary, Lt. Col. William Maberly, who was only thirty-eight when appointed, had distinguished himself at Waterloo and had been an MP. On one occasion he introduced some military order among the clerks by issuing them with staffs and drilling them to combat any threatened Chartist uprising.[18] The tall, broad-shouldered military man soon developed a strong dislike for Trollope, who was extremely scathing about the Colonel in his *Autobiography*. Trollope's summation of Maberly as Sir Boreas Bodkin, the postal official in one novel, is more accurate: 'a violent and imperious martinet, but not in the main ill natured' [*Marion Fay* VII]. Maberly's wife was a fashionable lady novelist, and perhaps jealousy of Mrs Trollope was not absent.

His superiors grew increasingly annoyed with Trollope's frequent lateness and often reported his misdeeds to the Postmaster General. It may seem incredible that a government minister would take an interest in the disciplinary lapses of a young clerk, but the large ledgers still preserved in the Post Office Archives show that the 'P.M.G.' was informed about the smallest details of administration. 'It is my painful duty to bring to your Lordship's notice,' wrote the Assistant Secretary a few days before Christmas 1838 to the Earl of

Lichfield, 'the neglect of Mr Trollope, one of the Junior officers of the Secretary's Department.' As 'senior clerk in waiting' on the previous Saturday night he had failed to copy and despatch three important letters to railway companies and had postponed the task till Monday. 'I have observed with much regret,' continued the Assistant Secretary, 'an habitual carelessness on the part of this officer', and recommended suspension without pay for a week and a 'serious admonition' that 'if he does not see the necessity of manifesting a decided improvement and evince a desire to discharge his duties with care, accuracy and attention ... you will have no alternative but to resort to the painful step of removing him from the service'. Lord Lichfield replied: 'Let Mr Trollope be suspended from pay for one week and let him be most seriously warned.'[19] Rumours of his misdeeds reached his early patron, Mrs Clayton Freeling who sent for the errant youth and, with tears in her eyes, begged him to think of his mother.

The 'serious admonition' appears to have had little effect, as Trollope's troubles continued throughout the next year. Colonel Maberly wrote to the Postmaster General, Lord Lichfield, in May 1839 after the twenty-four-year-old clerk had returned late from weekend leave:[20]

> Mr Trollope has been cautioned so often that I am compelled to submit he be severely punished ... I recommend therefore that he be desired to remain two hours additional each day till his arrears is cleared off and that upon the first vacancy in the senior class he be passed over ... I regret to be compelled to make such a proposition but Mr Trollope is without excuse, as he has good abilities and as this neglect, which has undoubtedly brought the Dept. into discredit (for some of the Cases are most gross) is entirely produced by want of proper attention to his duty.

Lord Lichfield replied, 'I hope it may be a warning to him to be more attentive.'

On another occasion Trollope was summoned into the Colonel's office. Maberly said that Trollope had been the only one in the room when some money had disappeared from an opened letter. The Colonel turned his wrath on his young subordinate: 'The letter has been taken and by God! there has been nobody in the room but you and I.' Anthony had inherited his father's sense of justice, as well as his temper, and roared back: 'Then by God you have taken it.' His fist hit a desk, which propelled an open bottle of ink onto the Colonel's shirt and face. Maberly, in his rage, hit the poor Senior Clerk, who was only trying to mop up the mess. The incident ended in good farcical style when the

Colonel's private secretary appeared with the opened letter and its money.[21]

*

Perhaps one reason the Colonel had suspected Trollope of stealing the money was that everyone knew of his indebtedness, a not uncommon state among the clerks. Indeed one of them only escaped a persistent money-lender who had got into the Post Office by leaping onto a lift used for heavy mail sacks. Trollope's difficulties originated in a debt to a tailor for £12. By a circuitous route, familiar to readers of Victorian novels, this debt was taken over by a money-lender from Mecklenburgh Square who stalked the defaulter, even into his office. Trollope, anxious to get rid of the man, signed more 'bills' which extended the loan, but at exorbitant interest. The money-lender even advanced his victim a further £4. At the most unexpected moments he would slink into a room to announce: 'Now I wish you to be punctual.' Never one to forget such a colourful episode or telling phrase, Trollope used them in *The Three Clerks* and in *Phineas Finn*. Eventually he paid over £200 to settle this debt of £16. His frequent stories of young men in debt did not require much imagination.

Yet all was not gloom. He had friends with whom he could share his miseries, his joys and some of his dreams. He became increasingly close to another clerk, John Tilley, the son of a London merchant, who was two years older than Anthony. Trollope's oldest friend, John Merivale, a schoolmate from Harrow and Sunbury, also lived in London, where he was a rather idle barrister. His scholarly brother Charles was furious never to find him at home: 'With him life seem to be one continued breakfast.' Merivale's father assessed his son's personality, with probable reference to Anthony:[22]

> He is a dreamy imaginative sort of boy – exorbitantly attached to the reading of novels ... and excessively fond of his most intimate associates, whom he does not select from among those who are exemplary either for school learning or strict regard to discipline, but chiefly for some resemblance to himself in their rambling pursuits and propensities.

Together with another friend, whose later misfortune led Trollope to call 'W—— A——' in his *Autobiography* but whose name was Walter Awdry, they formed a club. Awdry, a shy but humorous man, had been at Winchester with Anthony and Tom, and was a friend of both. Unlike Merivale and Trollope, Awdry never reached what Trollope, in a

wonderful phrase, called that 'happy turning-point at which life first
loomed seriously on him, and then became prosperous'. 'The Tramp
Society' was the first of those clubs that were to play such a large role
in Trollope's life and writings. One of the three was elected temporary
ruler and enforced his absolute authority by imposing fines on the
others. The three were great walkers and they wandered on foot over
the Home Counties, even going as far as eighty miles to Southampton.
Their rambles were in tune with literary fashion: *The Pickwick Papers*
began their extraordinary success in April 1836. The idea of a group of
wandering friends was therefore hardly unique. As 'The Tramp
Society's' rule restricted daily expenses to five shillings they sometimes
slept in hay-lofts and on one occasion a farmer's lad was terrified when
his pitchfork awoke the three young men. With youthful delight in
tricks they once pretended that Awdry was a madman with Trollope
and Merivale as his keepers. They continued the charade to the very
door of the lunatic asylum. Trollope's detailed knowledge of the south
of England, the scene of so many of his novels, owed much to these
youthful rambles.

Trollope also appears to have started his fondness for glee-singing
while a young clerk. He and other young men would make up silly
words and rhymes for their own amusement, often with recourse to
Latin to add ribald humour. This was a fairly common pleasure among
government clerks, even in the aristocratic Foreign Office.[23] Trollope's
own group called themselves 'The Goose and Glee Club', and Trollope
introduced them into what many call his best novel, *The Last
Chronicle of Barset* [XLII], as well as into his worst one, *The Struggles of
Brown, Jones, and Robinson* [XIII].

*

During these London years Trollope lived mainly in lodgings. His
earliest were in Little Marlborough Street, which he shared with Tom,
who was giving private tuition in the classics for ten shillings an hour.
The house was kept by a tailor and his mother, who made the young
men 'comfortable' but imposed a 'despotic rule'. The brothers were not
long here as Tom spent much of the early months of 1835 in Bruges
helping his mother in the immediate aftermath of Henry's death. He
was then offered a mastership in King Edward's Grammar School in
Birmingham. The salary of £200 a year must have seemed a princely
sum to his younger brother. Anthony spent more time at 22,
Northumberland Street (now Luxborough Street), near Regent's Park.
For an active walker that was but a short distance to the Post Office.

The lodgings overlooked Marylebone Workhouse, an insight into the darker aspects of his time. A few years later Prince Albert discovered that of the 1,506 adults in that workhouse 1,032 had been in service. This was in an age when seventy per cent of servants, one of the largest groups of workers in the country, ended their days seeking public assistance.[24] In the late 1860s Trollope made a rare reference to life in a workhouse, and it is set in this neighbourhood of his youth. A foreign aristocrat sneers: 'You see that black building, – the workhouse. I call it Little England. It is just the same. The naked, hungry, poor wretches lie at the door, and the great fat beadles swell about like turkey-cocks inside' [*The Claverings* XLVI]. In spite of a daily view of such misery at the most impressionable time in his life, Trollope made little attempt to follow his mother in using fiction to attack the treatment of the poor. He did use the location of his lodgings in *Orley Farm*, however, when a character recalls living in Keppel Street (Trollope's birthplace) and in 'dirty lodgings ... somewhere near the Marylebone workhouse' [XLIX]. It was a dreary place, but Trollope could hardly ask for better as he was frequently unable to pay his landlady. In the days of his prosperity he had great sympathy for women who kept lodgings: 'Few positions in life', he wrote, 'could be harder to bear' [*The Small House at Allington* LI].

Ninety pounds a year did not allow many luxuries. As Trollope wrote of one fictional clerk, '£90 per annum will hardly suffice to afford an ample allowance of gin-and-water and ... tobacco, over and above the other wants of a man's life' [*The Three Clerks* II]. However, one must set the figure in the context of his time. When Sir Robert Peel started his police force a few years before, he found that a guinea a week attracted numerous recruits, often men with families. There was a minor industry in compiling budgets for those on lower incomes and one claimed that a policeman could support a family of five on his weekly guinea, even managing to save a few shillings.[25] Trollope's income was almost double that of the policeman and he had no family but he did have to maintain his appearance as a 'gentleman'. Since his salary was paid quarterly, it was not easy to attempt a budget. His novels show a familiarity with the plight of young gentlemen trying to make do on a small income. In one of his last novels, *Marion Fay*, he actually portrayed a postal clerk. However, his portraits of Johnnie Eames in *The Small House at Allington* and Charley Tudor in *The Three Clerks* are the most autobiographical. Eames resembles Trollope in many ways: he had a brief period as an usher at a school and he liked to day-dream during long walks. His father was 'a man of many misfortunes, having begun the world almost with affluence, and having ended it in poverty ... having at one time ... lost much money in experimental farming' [*The Small House at Allington* IV]. Trollope did not have to look far to sketch that portrait!

Johnnie Eames, like many similar characters, is called, in one of Trollope's favourite terms, a 'hobbledehoy': an unhappy being suspended between boyhood and manhood.* 'Social meetings are periods of penance to them, and any appearance in public will unnerve them. They go much about alone, and blush when women speak to them' [*The Small House at Allington* IV]. Perhaps no other Victorian novelist gave as much attention to 'hobbledehoys' as Trollope, and this was not an inconsiderable factor in his success since 'hobbledehoys' and 'hobbledehoyas' tend to be great readers of novels. It was Thackeray, however, rather than Trollope who provided the best description of them:[26]

> A gawky lad, at that uncomfortable age when the voice varies between an unearthly treble and a preternatural bass; when the face not uncommonly blooms out with appearances ... when boys are seen to shave furtively with their sisters' scissors, and the sight of other young women produces intolerable sensations of terror; when the great hands and ankles protrude a long way from garments which have grown too tight for them; when their presence after dinner is at once frightful to the ladies ... and inexpressibly odious to the gentlemen ...

Trollope knew from his own life that some young men mature slowly: 'Some lads will be men at twenty, others are little more than children.' The novels frequently contain one of his favourite aphorisms: 'The fruit that ripens the soonest is seldom the best' [*The Duke's Children* LXI]. Young Trollope's 'fear of ridicule' and 'inability of speech' sprang from the 'general pervading sense of inferiority' which he believed to be the fate of almost all young Englishmen [*The Prime Minister* XV]. This made him reluctant to venture outside the restricted orbit of a clerk's life. The possibilities of civilised society were not, however, completely outside his ken. He was a welcome guest in the artistic world of his uncle's house in Fulham. John Forster, the friend and eventual biographer of Dickens, made several unsuccessful attempts to invite the young man. So, too, did Henry Taylor, the poet he so admired who was just then famous for his verse play, *Philip van Artevelde*, published in 1834. Trollope never appeared at either house. Nor did he

---

*The term 'hobbledehoy' dates from the sixteenth century and was first used by John Palsgrave in his 1540 translation of Fullonius Acolastus: 'Theyr hobbledehoye tyme ... the yeres that one is neyther a man nor a boye'. [I.1]. Steele used it in 1723 in his play, *The Conscious Lovers*, as did Swift in 1738 in his *Polite and Ingenious Conversation*.

respond to invitations and offers of influence from the head of his own family, Sir John Trollope.

Undoubtedly the worrying news of his family in Bruges did little to make him happier. Mrs Trollope had little time to mourn Henry for, as she told her publisher, 'I … may not indulge, as persons differently situated might do, in writing books only to beguile their idle hours, while enjoying the blessing of indifference as to the time and manner of their publication.'[27] Soon she paid an extended visit to Paris to write another colourful travel book and to let French doctors examine her increasingly ill husband. When, in October 1835, she despatched *Paris and the Parisians* to her publisher she excused her bad handwriting by the continual strain under which she worked.

The next day, 23 October 1835, at 3.30 in the afternoon, Thomas Anthony Trollope died at the age of sixty-two; his Paris doctors had assumed he was over eighty. For his wife this was a 'melancholy and unexpected event'. The once bright prospects of the brilliant Oxford scholar ended in a rented house in Belgium, supported by the pen of a valiant wife. Even the obituary in the *Gentleman's Magazine* commented more on his family than on him: the magazine noted that he was 'cousin to Sir John Trollope, Bart.' and, secondly, that 'His widow is the celebrated Mrs Trollope whose clever novels and travelling sketches have attained so high a popularity.'[28] Thirty years later Anthony Trollope paused in the middle of a novel to reflect on marriage. The fact that his reflections were written in the last months of his mother's life and published in the same month as her death indicates that he was thinking of his own parents:

A wife does not cease to love her husband because he gets into trouble. She does not turn against him because others have quarrelled with him. She does not separate her lot from his because he is in debt! Those are the times when a wife, a true wife, sticks closest to her husband, and strives the hardest to lighten the weight of his cares by the tenderness of her love! [*Rachel Ray* XX].

In one of her courtship letters a quarter of a century before Fanny Milton had assured her suitor: 'Love you always? I believe I must, for I cannot help it.' Through many tribulations she had remained faithful to that pledge.

The body of Thomas Anthony Trollope was borne to the Protestant section of the cemetery and laid next to Henry, where a Latin inscription composed by Tom disguises the sorrow that was buried within. On his table lay the notes for the unfinished *Encyclopaedia Ecclesiastica*; the only published volume ended with an entry on funeral rites. The dead man would at least have been gratified to know that the English translation of his death certificate described him as 'Gentleman'. Years later Anthony Trollope admitted that he still looked back on his father's life, 'meditating for hours together, on his adverse fate'. He went on in his *Autobiography* to analyse his father's character: 'He was a man, finely educated, of great parts, with immense capacity for work, physically strong ... addicted to no vices, carried off by no pleasures, affectionate by nature, most anxious for the welfare of his children.' But, his son recalled, 'everything went wrong with him' and he was cursed with a 'temper so irritable that even those whom he loved the best could not endure it. We were all estranged from him, and yet I believe that he would have given his heart's blood for any of us. His life as I knew it was one long tragedy.'[29]

His widowed mother soon joined Anthony in Northumberland Street. Within a few months she settled in the Hertfordshire village of Hadley, just outside Barnet, some twelve miles from London where, even today, old houses look out onto a quiet common. She hoped that her native climate might save the rapidly declining Emily, a delightful girl of eighteen. When, in telling friends of her children's activities, she came to Emily she said her youngest child was 'as usual about 24 inches from my elbow'. Tom long recalled a picture showing her with 'flowing flaxen curls and wide china blue eyes sitting with a brown holland pinafore' blowing a soap bubble, while on her desk was a copy-book on which was written 'study with determined zeal'. In Hadley there was always a bedroom for Anthony when he could come out. With Tom in Birmingham, Anthony became for the first time his mother's confidant. When, two decades later, he recalled the horror in hearing the word 'consumption' – 'the name of which has broken so many mothers' hearts' – he knew whereof he spoke [*The Three Clerks* XXXI]. On 12 February 1836 he wrote to Tom:[30]

> It is all over. Poor Emily breathed her last this morning. She died without any pain, and without a struggle. Her little strength had been gradually declining and her breath left her without the slightest convulsion, or making any change in her features or face. Were it not for the ashy colour, I should think she was sleeping. I never saw anything more beautifully placid and composed ... It is much better that it is now, than her life should have been prolonged only to undergo the agonies which Henry suffered.

The next day Anthony went to Pinner to tell Cecilia of her sister's death; she had been at that same house when Tom brought her similar news of Henry's death. In little over a year Fanny Trollope had lost a son, a husband and a daughter. Anthony and his mother selected a spot behind the east end of Hadley's grey church for Emily's grave, which can still be located. In *The Bertrams*, when Trollope is describing the bells of Hadley church ringing for a wedding, he suddenly emerges from his normal calm narration to speak directly to the reader: 'I know full well the tone in which they toll when the soul is ushered to its last long rest. I have stood in that green churchyard when earth has been laid to earth, ashes to ashes, dust to dust – the ashes and the dust that were loved so well' [XXX].

*

Fanny Trollope was bowed by her latest tragedy but, as Tom said, she could no more be permanently crushed than grass can be by a great storm. Her writing now provided a solace as well as an income. Anthony was often her messenger and negotiator with publishers, most of whose offices were near St Martin-le-Grand. In 1840 her publisher Richard Bentley was informed that 'Mr Trollope called this morning to say that owing to the lowering state of political affairs his mamma will not go to Italy before the spring.' There had obviously been some disagreement over the title of her latest novel and Anthony had been instructed to say that 'She wishes her book, if you don't like the title of the Cousins to be called The Ward of Thorpe Combe', which was agreed.[31] On another occasion he was sent to ask for more money for one of her books. Although he failed, the mission was undoubtedly valuable training for a future writer. These negotiations, and the literary people he had met through his mother, gave him an introduction to the real world of writing and, to re-use his favourite analogy, this fruit would mature slowly. 'When young people begin their world of reading there is nothing so pleasant to them,' the mature Trollope reflected, 'as knowing the little secrets of literature; who wrote this and that, of which folk are then talking; – who manages this periodical, and puts the salt and pepper into those reviews' [*Orley Farm* LVIII].

His mother increasingly viewed writing as the family business and wanted her two sons to take up their pens, although she insisted that they also have the security of a steady income. Tom, who was already finding the schoolmaster's scheduled life burdensome, was despatched to Brittany, with Anthony's friend Awdry, to spend a summer gathering material to manufacture into a travel book. When it was published, the celebrated name of Mrs Trollope appeared on the title page as 'editor' and thus she squeezed 300 guineas from a publisher:

this must have seemed a fortune to young Anthony. Mrs Trollope, who was producing one three-volume novel in November and another in May, for each of which she garnered £700, expected Tom to take Holy Orders and settle into a comfortable clerical income.

Mrs Trollope also sought literary work for Anthony and on at least two occasions asked John Murray, who had published her travel book on Belgium, for some proof-reading or similar work. 'He is a good scholar,' she wrote with maternal pride, 'and, as I believe your friend Henry Drury will allow, has very good abilities.' It is not known whether Murray obliged, although Trollope later depicted the work of a proof-reader and indexer with great sympathy in a short story, 'The Spotted Dog'. His mother also had a scheme to edit a magazine, which might bring family and friends into the brightness of literary fame. She would write a series of poetical lampoons on reformers, while Hervieu would draw anti-Whig cartoons. This scheme came to nothing and it was Anthony who many years later started a literary magazine with frequent contributions from the family's stable of authors. He yearned to see himself in print. One Sunday in May 1835 – just six months after he became a clerk – he wrote to his mother's publisher, Richard Bentley. After discussing his mother's proof-sheets, he turned to his own hopes: 'Is it in your power to lend me any assistance in procuring the insertion of lucubrations of my own in any of the numerous periodical magazines etc. which come out in such monthly swarm ... My object of course is that of turning my time to any account that I am able.'[32] As far as is known, this cumbersome and evidently over-polished letter produced no result. Yet it does show how anxious he was to emulate his mother's literary success.

Over thirty years later Trollope wrote a story, 'The Panjandrum', which gives a good portrait of a dreamy youth. In this rather inferior tale, set in the 1830s, a group of idealistic young friends plan to establish a magazine to promote their liberal views. There are good grounds for asserting that Trollope dreamed about editing the perfect newspaper, but like most such dreams it never materialised.[33] In this story the narrator recalls how he wanted to write 'short political essays which should be terse, argumentative, and convincing, and at the same time full of wit and frolic. I never quite succeeded in pleasing even myself in any such composition.' After several boring discussions common to idealistic youth the friends part company 'under the walls of Marylebone Workhouse'. Here is another example of how Trollope's mind would disgorge tiny details from his past. Yet the most fascinating aspect of this story is that it provides the best account of his habit of 'castle-building'.

It may be recalled how Anthony solaced his walks to school by creating a fantasy world with himself as the inevitable hero. As a clerk he continued this while walking to work and, one fears, sometimes at his desk. In 'The Panjandrum' the narrator, who is also an avid 'castle-builder', recalls how such a world was fashioned. The young man is walking about Regent's Park thinking, as young men are apt to do, of unleashing some earth-shattering article about social injustice, when he sudddenly sees a servant leading a girl. The narrator's interest in the child increases when he overhears a snippet of conversation: 'Oh, Anne, I do so wonder what he's like!' 'You'll see, Miss,' replies the servant. From such prosaic material the young man is inspired into a new dream world:

> Gradually, as the unforced imagination came to play upon the matter, a little picture fashioned itself in my mind. The girl was my own sister, – a sister whom I had never seen till she was thus brought to me for protection and love; but she was older, just budding into womanhood.

As the fantasy evolves, he eventually sees the dream sister marry his best friend and thus the exclusive delight of his new love is lost to him. There are obvious parallels with Trollope's real sisters: Emily had been lost to him by death and Cecilia had married his close friend John Tilley in 1838 and left London for Penrith where Tilley was to be Post Office Surveyor for the district. These parallels reveal how the unconsious mind can suddenly thrust facts into dreams or even into day-dreams. One cannot, as the narrator in 'The Panjandrum' testifies, command the mind to produce a 'wondrous castle in the air':

> It is when they come uncalled for that they stand erect and strong before the mind's eye, with every mullioned window perfect, the rounded wall there ... the drawbridge down ... I had sat with this girl by my side, calling her the sweetest names ... I had seen her blush when my friend came near ... I ... took the girl to church, gave her away ... and came back and sobbed and sputtered out my speech.

The plot sounds like a summary of several Trollope novels about virtuous young maidens who, at last, marry eligible young men. Here we gain an insight into the mind of the novelist: an example of how another person can plant the germ of a whole story. (One is reminded of how Arnold Bennett was inspired to write *The Old Wives' Tale* after watching two women in a Parisian restaurant.) In his *Autobiography* Trollope claimed that, if he had not perfected this habit of castle building, it was unlikely 'I should ever have written a novel'. The young Anthony was not wasting his time by his day-dreams: the fruit would ripen in due course.

*

A superficial reading of Trollope's *Autobiography* can easily give the impression that he was sunk in idleness and unnamed dissipation in his days as a clerk. He actually used his time to do a vast amount of study. A neglected aspect of Trollope is his wide and deep reading. Throughout life, in spite of the strain of maintaining two careers, he managed to read widely in literature, history and the classics. Perhaps only George Eliot, among the other great Victorian novelists, equalled him as a reader. He undoubtedly used these early years to lay up a store of reading. As an elderly author, he gave an address when handing out prizes at the City and Spitalfields School of Art and told the students of the drawbacks involved:[34]

> An old relative of his – a dear old lady – wrote him a letter recommending him, when he left his office ... to be sure and go home to tea and read a good book. That was all very well in its way but it did not bring him a sufficient idea of the life he had to lead.

This advice probably came from his aunt, Henry Milton's wife, and it appears in many of his books. 'When it is found that a young man is neglecting his duties ... the usual prescription of his friends is that he should lock himself up in his own dingy room, drink tea, and spend his hours in reading good books,' he says in one novel [*The Vicar of Bullhampton* LI]. Another novel contains a reply to this remedy: 'Who should expect that any young man will do so? ... yet mothers, and aunts, and anxious friends do expect it – very much in vain' [*The Three Clerks* XI]. Nevertheless young Trollope must have spent many evenings reading, writing down his impressions and possibly even drinking tea. As a successful novelist, however, he was always careful to see that his Aunt Milton received an autographed copy of his latest book.

Trollope's reflections when he reread his mother's poem about the Vicar of Harrow have already been quoted. They were written during his early days as a clerk. He devoted much of his reading to poetry and commented on what he read. His strong devotion to Milton, a love he shared with his mother, caused him to fling Johnson's *Lives of the Poets* from his window into Northumberland Street when he found the sneering references to *Lycidas*. He disliked 'the unmeaning pomposity' of Johnson's style and probably resented the magisterial dismissal of Milton: 'The diction is harsh, the rhymes uncertain ... there is no truth; there is no art.'[35] Trollope's devotion to Milton remained throughout his life, as shown in his novels where that poet is more quoted than any other writer except Shakespeare. He once offered £5 to any of his nieces who would memorise *Lycidas*. Ten years after Anthony's death Tom liked to recall how his younger brother delighted in reciting his favourite lines from the poem:[36]

Fame is the spur that the clear spirit doth raise
(That last infirmity of noble mind)
To scorn delights, and live laborious days.

He wanted to be a poet himself and considered writing a long dramatic poem about Richard II and Henry IV, although he realised the dangers of a subject 'so perfectly handled by Shakespere [*sic*]'. Long poems on historical subjects delighted him, particularly those by Henry Taylor which appeared during these years. Perhaps he was drawn to a civil servant, who set some of his verses in Bruges. Years later he wrote of Taylor's poems: 'I have loved them so long and so well.'[37] Much time was also spent in devouring volumes of Byron, another taste inherited from his mother. In time he came to believe that Byron was a dangerous addiction, particularly for the young. Warnings about 'Byronic weakness' and 'poetry in bedrooms' are found in several novels, including *Rachel Ray* [IV] and *The Eustace Diamonds*, where he illustrated the absurdity of Lady Eustace through her devotion to Byron. Trollope himself always enjoyed Byron's poetry, but even in his youth he saw that the poet's attitudes were rather facile because he never thought 'out his thoughts to their conclusion'. The young man in Northumberland Street was trying to do just that.

In his late forties, while depicting John Eames, he realised the role his own adolescent reflections had played in his later life:

Very young men, – men so young that it may be almost a question whether or no they have as yet reached their manhood, – are more inclined to be earnest and thoughtful ... I fancy that, as we grow old ourselves, we are apt to forget it was so with us ... We constantly talk of the thoughtlessness of youth. I do not know whether we might not more appropriately speak of its thoughtfulness. It is, however, no doubt true that thought will not at once produce wisdom. It may almost be a question whether such wisdom as many of us have in our mature years has not come from the dying out of the power of temptation, rather than as the results of thought and resolution [*The Small House at Allington* XIV].

Seen in this light, these years as a clerk in London set the ground for
Trollope's popularity in his own time and his continuing importance as
a writer.

His mother gave him some wise advice which he later repeated to his
first biographer:[38]

> You left school sooner than you ought to have done, or than we once
> expected there would be any need for you to do. Make good the dropped
> stitches of your own education before you take upon yourself to teach or
> amuse others in print. Remember the time for reading is now. Reading
> you must have, not so much because of what it will tell you as because it
> will teach you how to observe, and supply you with mental pegs on which
> to hang what you pick up about traits and motives of your
> fellow-creatures.

These wise words are typical of Fanny Trollope in their mixture of
literature and homely allusions. Trollope himself felt that reading was
a habit that had to be acquired early in life: 'If a man have not acquired
the habit of reading till he be old, he shall sooner in his old age learn to
make shoes than learn the adequate use of a book … Let those who are
not old, – who are still young ponder this well' [*The Claverings* XLV].

Trollope also realised that reading without a purpose would never
provide the education he had missed, so, in August 1835, after he had
been in London for nine months, he started a 'commonplace book' –
carefully marked 'private' – in which he noted facts, sources and
opinions about authors who included not just British writers but
French, Italian and Spanish, surely reflecting his mother's influence.
Under 'm' comes Malaspina and Metatasio; under 'p', Pope's *Essay on
Man*, under 'h' his idea for a 'dramatic poem' on Henry IV and Richard
II, under 'a', Alfieri whose ode on Lafayette his mother had translated
and under 'l', 'Lope de Vega (Lope Felix de Vego Carpio) born at Madrid
1562, died 1635. Said to have written 2,200!! dramatic pieces.' At other
times Trollope analysed contemporary fiction and decided that one of
Georges Sand's novels was moral because it made 'vice ugly and virtue
beautiful'.[39] This was surely apt training for a novelist who would
write during an era when the sending of moral messages became a
principal aim of fiction.

About 1840, perhaps remembering his father's grand vision for his
Encyclopaedia Ecclesiastica, and thinking to make use of his reading
over the last five years, Trollope thought of writing nothing less than a
'history of literature' which would cover the civilised world. He first
devised an outline for the plan for disciplined reading including Dr
Johnson on the poets, Hallam, Tooke, Coleridge, Sismondi's history of

the literature of Southern Europe and 'Hermes' Harris on philology. In this plan, he pondered how to approach his *magnum opus* which would naturally demand several volumes and would cover such topics as history, poetry, periodical literature, biography, criticism, fine arts, theology and 'romance'. In his commonplace book, in the entry for 'Order-Method', he had already noted the one great failing which could undermine such a project:

> I am myself in all the pursuits (God help them) and practices of my life most disorderly and the injury which this failing has occasioned is so near ... to utter ruin that I can but set myself as an example to others ... The first impression which a parent should fix on the mind of a child is I think love of order.

He reached a conclusion that sounds remarkably like his mature writing: '[Order] is the reins by which all virtues are kept in their proper places and the vices, with whom the virtues run in one team, are controlled.' Here we have two major themes of his novels: the human personality is a curious mixture of both good and bad; secondly, a useful and happy life can only be achieved through discipline. He listed five areas where he had a 'vital' need for order: religion, studies, personal finance, diet and cleanliness. His superiors at the Post Office, had they peered into this 'private' commonplace book, might have noted that he did not include work or punctuality![40]

Trollope's reading included English as well as continental authors. He read and reread English novels and cherished strong opinions: *Pride and Prejudice* was the greatest novel in the language, though he wavered when he reread *Ivanhoe*. The task of keeping up with his mother's novels would have taken some time, for she produced ten, all in the standard three-volume format, during his time in London. Trollope read other popular authors of his youth and devoured Dickens's earliest work, *Sketches by Boz*, as it came out during 1836. Likewise he enjoyed *The Pickwick Papers* which his uncle Henry Milton brought with him when he walked out to visit Fanny at Hadley.[41]

He frequently left the novels of Bulwer Lytton unfinished, but the young Trollope's analysis of why he did this shows critical discernment. He put the florid volumes down 'not from the fault of the author but from my own – I can get up no interest in the characters'. He admitted that Bulwer had put thought into his novels, but 'how false his philosophy is'. The fashionable novelist:

affects a contempt for the frivolities of the pursuits of men ... [and] the power of ambition ... He has no human nature in any thing he ever wrote ... The man is the same whether he be a murderer – a successful Democrat – an English nobleman ... all damned gentlemanlike ... As to women, Bulwer has attempted but little to draw their character, and in that little he is equally unnatural.

Already, the young 'hobbledehoy' has seen, in reverse, all those strengths that would mark his own novels, which would be praised for their subtlety of characterisation, their depiction of the 'frivolities' of life, their portrayal of ambition, their unfolding of the intricacies of human nature and their understanding of the female character. One wonders whether the young clerk could ever imagine that Bulwer Lytton would become an admirer of Trollope's novels in years to come.[42]

These youthful comments show his serious nature, perhaps nowhere more than in his reflections on Pope's *Essay on Man*. When he reread it in August 1836 the twenty-one-year-old Trollope wrote: 'I read this some three years ago and fancied I understood it – perhaps I did but I can hardly do so now – Since that time by idleness – dissipation – and riot of my mind I have lost in a measure the power of thinking and reflecting.' Having enjoyed castigating himself, he proceeded to analyse Pope's ideas. While rereading this poem, Trollope, like most intellectual adolescents (and he was still in essence an adolescent) was grappling with the concept of God. He accepted, as a youth and throughout his whole life, that 'God made the world', an assertion which 'of course must be a datum'. Trollope would never treasure, let alone spread, religious doubt. He disliked those who used God as an excuse to sneer at 'the pursuits of men', or Calvinists who – like their latter-day Marxist counterparts – proclaimed that man was nothing but 'a puppet not only of his passions (which is true enough) but of the workings of a system'. Here we have another theme that flows through his novels: life and its pleasures are divine gifts meant to be enjoyed, but that enjoyment is enhanced by making the correct moral choice.[43]

Among the pleasures he enjoyed during these years were frequent visits to the first home of the National Gallery, the 'small dingy house on the South side of Pall Mall'. For him it was a 'spot ... which I shall always regard with warm affection, for there I conceived my first ideas of the nature of a picture'. His early visits were probably guided by his uncle, Henry Milton, who was a writer on art as well as a civil servant. Trollope never claimed to be a learned critic, but visiting galleries became one of the great delights of his life and travels. During these years of private study the young Trollope also delighted in feuding with dead authors. 'I love to disagree – to cavil – to oppose – to attack – to condemn – countermine – and argue – but have never store of argument to carry on the battle.' He had already, as we have seen, been drawn to the writings of Edmund Burke, particularly his influential *Philosophical Enquiry into the Sublime and Beautiful.* In that book Burke, who almost a century before had also had a period of intense private reading in London, wrote words that could well be applied to the Anthony Trollope of the 1830s:[44]

Imitation is one of the great instruments used by providence in bringing our nature towards its perfection ... God has planted in man a sense of ambition, and a satisfaction arising from the contemplation of his excelling his fellows in something deemed valuable among them.

*

The many hours spent in reading did not allow Trollope much time for 'dissipation'. Like some of his fictional clerks he enjoyed flirting with barmaids in the taverns where he had his dinner, something he was to portray in *The Three Clerks.* In *The Bertrams* he gave a good idea of what he meant by 'a life of dissipation' when he describes one young man in early Victorian London: 'I do not intend that it should be understood that he utterly gave himself up to pleasures disgraceful in themselves ... and allowed himself to live such a life as is passed by some young men in London. His tastes and appetites were too high for this ... He did not become filthy and vicious.' Bertram's 'vice' is like the young Trollope's: he lacked order and, therefore, gave the appearance of idleness because he 'was not preparing himself in any way to live as a man should live by the sweat of his brow' [XVIII]. Like Trollope, Bertram indulged in that favourite pastime of youth: self-pity because his efforts produced no immediate results. When discussing Bulwer Lytton's novels Trollope wrote:[45]

I can't warm myself to excitement. I feel a want when reading novels of something which will more occupy my heart or mind. When I read anything more abstruse or which takes any labor or thought, I get fatigued and leave it ... When reading, I long to be writing and attempting to write, I become weary of the labor, & do nothing; I am not contented with mediocrity – want the perseverance to accomplish superiority, and therefore fall into utter inferiority.

Another reason for not paying too much heed to Trollope's denunciations of his own 'dissipations' is that he spent some of his years as a postal clerk living with his mother. He lived with her at Hadley for some time, although she feared that the daily coach trips took up too much time: commuting back and fourth consumed four hours each day. (Barnet, next to Hadley, was normally the last place where coaches changed horses before London, which made it a good spot to get a coach into town.) Like any good mother, Fanny worried and, sometimes, she had cause. 'Anthony was on the river,' she wrote to Tom, 'and fell into the water as he got out of the boat ... in the middle of the night after which he had to walk dripping wet from top to toe from Westminster Bridge.' It is hardly surprising that he then suffered a severe attack of rheumatism. 'I think,' his mother added with a mixture of pride and concern, 'it would have killed most people.' Trollope's autobiographical hero, Charley Tudor, tumbled into the Thames to rescue a girl. Whether Anthony adapted the details of his own adventure for his mother or for his novel will probably never be known. At Hadley Mrs Trollope delighted in having young people round her, such as the rector's family. In his book on Thackeray Trollope remembered a distant cousin of his fellow novelist, 'a Rev. Mr. Thackeray of Hadley, [whom] I knew well as rector of Hadley'. The rector's family included several girls whom the young postal clerk also knew well. Once, in 1838, his mother advised him not to come to Hadley on a Sunday 'because all the Thackeray family will be [away] from town'.[46]

There had long been a flirtatious side to Trollope. Even in his most miserable period at the Harrow Weald farmhouse he had spent happy hours in the kitchen dallying with the bailiff's daughter. Now that he was emerging from his hobbledehoyhood, he increasingly enjoyed female company and the mild endearments that his era permitted. *The Bertrams* is set in Hadley and recalls not only the sad scene of Emily Trollope's burial but happier days as well. In the novel an engaged couple set out on a walk from Hadley churchyard, and this leads the author into one of the most personal recollections in all his fiction:

> Oh, those lovers' rambles! A man as he grows old can perhaps teach himself to regret but few of the sweets he is compelled to leave behind him ... The polka and the waltz were once joyous; but he sees now that the work was warm, and that one was often compelled to perform it in company for which one did not care. Those picnics too were nice ... But, ah! those lovers' walks, those loving lovers' rambles ... 'Twas then, between sweet hedgerows, under green oaks, with our feet rustling on the crisp leaves, that the world's cold reserve was first thrown off, and we

found that those we loved were not goddesses ... but human beings like ourselves, with blood in their veins, and hearts in their bosoms [XXVIII].

Trollope, scribbling away in the deserts of the Middle East while on a postal mission, asked: 'I wonder whether wickets are ever standing there now on summer afternoons!' It would delight him to know that they still do, and perhaps Hadley remains closer to what Anthony Trollope knew than almost any other place about which he wrote.

Because so little is known about Trollope's private life in this period some biographers have kindly invented various vices for him for which there is no evidence. Unlike his friend 'W. A.', Trollope did not flee from 'the rustle of a lady's dress' nor the swish of a barmaid's apron. The type of mild flirtation he enjoyed is seen in one of his few surviving letters from this period. This was to a Miss Dancers, to whom he sent pink and white gloves. He also enclosed playful messages for two other girls, one of whom was told: 'she should never allow grief for anyone to prey upon her spirits so long. It is very bad for the complexion.' He thanked another of her friends for the 'flowers blooming on my desk the envy of all the clerks in the office'.[47]

On another occasion, after a girl in the country proposed marriage to him, he fled from her house, even forgoing dinner, although he had been too frightened to give her a decided refusal. The girl assailed him with letters, to which he made no reply. She was determined to marry him: 'a very foolish young woman she must have been to entertain such a wish,' recalled the elderly author, who admitted that his hair still stood on end when writing about the incident after forty years. One day while Trollope and the other clerks were working at the Post Office a commotion was heard outside. A woman wearing a large hat and carrying a big basket forced her way into the room demanding in a loud voice: 'Anthony Trollope, when are you going to marry my daughter?' Unfortunately we do not know his reply. However, when Charley Tudor suffers the same ordeal in *The Three Clerks*, where even the details of the basket and hat are included, Charley persuades the weeping mother to leave after assuring her that he would visit her daughter in a few days [XXVII]. 'We have all had our worst moments,' concludes Trollope in his *Autobiography*, 'and that was one of my worst.'

*

Mrs Trollope could not long remain content spending all the year in England. In 1836 she negotiated contracts for two novels and two travel books, one on Austria and the other on Italy. For these she received almost £2,000, which must have increased Anthony's longings to have his 'lucubrations' published. Within a short while she reached another agreement to produce two three-volume novels each year. This income provided an elegant home for Anthony, who certainly lived in better style when she was in England. Food and wine were far more plentiful than in lodgings, when he dined on a chop and half pint of sherry for 1s 6d. His mother, who liked to entertain, ordered large quantities of wine, some from a wine-merchant in Oxford, while another tradesman in Soho had to await payment for four dozen bottles of Marsala. Fortunately the wine-merchants of that civilised era were used to waiting for payment.

At the end of 1837 – the first year of Queen Victoria's reign – Mrs Trollope moved from Hadley to a house in York Street, Portman Square. She wished to make life easier for her son: 'four hours out of every day is too much for Anthony to pass in, or on, a coach, which is what he does now.' She was also anxious to 'be among clever literary people'. Her recent novel *The Vicar of Wrexhill* was a vitriolic attack upon the Evangelical clergy and it convinced many people that she was far too clever. Just as Anthony would, she attracted considerable criticism for churning out novels in quantity. Once at a dinner party she was seated next to Samuel Rogers, a rich and pompous poet now only remembered for his literary 'breakfasts'. Not recognising her, he said: 'They told me Mrs Trollope was to be here. She has written a great deal of rubbish, hasn't she?' 'Well,' replied the indomitable little lady, 'she has made it answer!'[48]

At Christmas 1838 the busy mother rejoiced in gathering 'my trio' round her to celebrate with roast beef and plum pudding though she warned a guest: 'I send my servants to enjoy the ... holiday with their friends and we are literally to wait upon ourselves during the evening but you shall have tea and coffee and cold sandwiches and punch at six o'clock.'[49] With her increased income it is likely that she gave Anthony an allowance to supplement his postal salary, something which was quite normal for clerks from 'good families'. She did help him with some of his debts but, like Charley Tudor, he was ashamed to admit all to his mother [*The Three Clerks* XXIII]. From time to time the sheriff's officers would serve 'uncanny documents' on him and twice they held him prisoner until his mother or a friend came to his rescue. She probably remained ignorant of the bothersome money-lender from Mecklenburgh Square.

*

Anthony paid several visits to Paris with his mother during the 1830s. At least one may have included official work because decades later he recalled escorting the mail from Paris to London one winter. He was in a diligence, a particularly French carriage that he liked: 'those dear old continental coaches ... which did not deserve death as fully as did our abominable vehicles. The coupé of a diligence, or better still the banquette, was a luxurious mode of travelling' [*He Knew He Was Right* XXXVIII]. On this occasion it got caught in a snow drift: Trollope had the best horse unharnessed and, with mail sacks both before and behind, rode through the storm to Calais, just managing to catch the boat. Mrs Trollope's book on Paris, which Anthony considered her most successful, gave her an entrée to literary salons.[50] She introduced him to these circles, and although he says nothing of them in his *Autobiography* he discussed them with his first biographer. Two characters in his novels have similarities to ladies who presided over salons in the late 1830s. In *The Claverings* he portrays, without total success, Madame Sophie Gordeloup, who is thought to be a Russian spy known for her reports to St Petersburg. She bears some resemblance to the famous Princess Lieven, wife of the Russian Ambassador in London until Lord Palmerston forced her to leave for Paris. Throughout her long diplomatic career – where she specialised in affairs with Prime Ministers – she was well-known for her letters to the Tsar, keeping him informed about life in the more interesting parts of western Europe. In Trollope's Palliser novels one of the central characters is Madame Max Goesler, who has similarities to Madame Mohl, a noted Parisian hostess who as Miss Clarke had known the Trollopes in the 1820s and was a close friend of his mother.

Trollope did not accompany his mother to the Tuileries when she was presented to King Louis Philippe. The King, perhaps a trifle maliciously, asked whether she had any desire to revisit America, a country where he had spent some time as an exile. According to Trollope family legend, she replied by asking him the same thing, knowing, as everyone else did, that his throne was none too secure. Louis Philippe was one of the few continental monarchs whose abdication aroused regret in a Liberal like Anthony Trollope.[51] Perhaps he intended a compliment of sorts by naming a character in *Doctor Thorne* after the unlucky 'Citizen King'.

Trips to Paris in the 1830s only stimulated the interest the young Trollope already had in politics. It would have been difficult to avoid them in that decade of constant reform. He could not vote because, even after the 1832 Reform Bill, only householders had the franchise. In any case postal clerks, being government officials, were ineligible to vote. Trollope's father had raised his sons to dislike the Toryism of the years after Waterloo. Mrs Trollope, of course, had abandoned her liberalism after her American experiences. Her books on France and Austria proclaimed her devotion to the strong conservatism that she admired in people like the Austrian Chancellor, Prince Metternich, who became her friend in Vienna. It seems that Anthony never adopted his mother's Toryism. In a letter to Tom in 1836 he refers to the Conservatives as 'her own party', and it is clear that they were not his.[52] He paid considerable attention to the political battles of the 1830s: novels, such as *Lady Anna*, and short stories, such as 'The Panjandrum', contain allusions to the controversies of that period.

Trollope had a mild interest in the fashionable topic of 'Political Oeconomy' – 'perhaps the most useful of all studies' – which was as much a fad then as sociology is today. As noted before, he liked to dream of editing a newspaper which would be 'political without party passion ... right and just without pride ... not conscious of its omniscience'. These are the perfect dreams of a young man anxious for fame and influence. The more mature Trollope concluded that 'humanity is not capable of any work so divine'. In the 1830s the literary and political worlds had close links and many young men sought fame and money in writing as a springboard to politics. When the Prime Minister, Lord Melbourne, encountered the young novelist, Disraeli, he was only mildly amused that the exotic youth proclaimed he too planned to be Prime Minister. Thus for Anthony Trollope to tell his uncle that he planned to become an MP was not all that far-fetched. His mother had a hope that both of her surviving sons might eventually go into Parliament.[53]

*

In the spring of 1840 Anthony returned from a holiday in Paris with his mother. A few months later he was struck down with a mysterious and nearly fatal illness. His mother, fearful of losing yet another child, wrote to Rosina Bulwer Lytton, the estranged wife of the novelist:[54]

My poor darling lies in a state that defies the views of his physician as effectually as it puzzles my ignorance. It is asthma from which he chiefly suffers now; but they say this can only be a symptom, and not the disease. He is frightfully reduced in size and strength ... you would not find even a distant resemblance to the being who, exactly three months ago, left us in all the pride of youth, health, and strength. Day by day I lose hope, and so ... do his physicians.

In her despair she turned to her own doctor, John Elliotson (the first man to use the stethoscope). Elliotson should live in the gratitude of novel readers, for he was physician to Dickens and to Thackeray, who dedicated *Pendennis* to him. Like Mrs Trollope, however, Elliotson had a fascination with spiritualism. His public demonstrations of mesmerism featured the Okey sisters, who claimed to know when someone was dying because they 'saw Jack' by the patient's side. They paid frequent visits to Anthony's sickbed, where they 'saw Jack by his side, but only up to his knee', which implied that Anthony had some hope of recovery. Within a few weeks, his mother wrote: 'Anthony goes on decidedly improving, but so slowly as to make every morning's inquiry one of fear and trembling.' Anthony later made fun of 'those spirit-rapping people' in *The Claverings* [XXXIX]. By the time he wrote that novel a daughter of one of the Okey sisters was installed in his own elegant country home – as a maid![55]

Perhaps Fanny Trollope was correct in her diagnosis, if not in her remedy, when she wrote that Anthony's illness had more than physical causes. He was suffering from asthma, which can have a psychological origin. The twenty-five-year-old clerk's problems at St Martin's had not abated: in February 1840 there had been another dispute with Maberly over 'carelessness'. He was acutely conscious of abilities for which he could find no outlet and was undoubtedly frustrated. All his family were busy at books – all save Anthony. Even his uncle, Henry Milton, had blossomed as a novelist, and Tom was attempting his own travel book about America. Mrs Trollope drew on her younger son's frustration for a new novel which began to appear in the month of Anthony's illness. Her story centred on a youth who 'panted' for 'fame, renown, applause ... such as he had heard of ... achieved by ... Sir Walter Scott ... and ... Lord Byron ... These were the sort of people ... whose fame in his heart of hearts he hoped to realise.'[56]

When Anthony recovered, his mother gave up housekeeping in London. 'The fact is,' she explained to Tom, 'potatoes have been quite exceptionally dear.' She decided to move to the Lake District and to build a new home for herself and Tom near Cecilia. She also started to make plans for her projected trip to Italy, and while she did so, Trollope resumed his work at the Post Office, where conditions were no better. In the November after his return the Secretary circulated a Minute among the clerks. He was concerned about increased expenditure caused by 'neglect'. Of the eight clerks, the Minute pointed out, seven had one case against their name; one had three. This was Trollope. The Secretary therefore ordered that 'the gentlemen in the Secretary's Office, especially Mr Trollope' must sign the Minute.[57]

These years after 1834 were a compound of bad moments: outraged debt collectors, weeping mothers, official reprimands, lost pay and an ink-stained Colonel Maberly. Mixed with them were happy ones: flowers from young ladies, walking expeditions with other dreamy youths and quiet evenings devoted to books and tea. In these London years Anthony Trollope had learned much about life: his later descriptions of lodging houses with their curious inhabitants, taverns with their cockney serving-girls, and youths with their large debts and far larger dreams all derive from this period. He walked; he read; he thought; and as he dreamt he 'built castles'. He formed bitter-sweet reflections on the past and the future. In one novel set in this period he uses a comparison which is almost certainly autobiographical: 'some hard-toiling youth who, while roaming listlessly among the houses of the wealthy, hears, as he lingers on the pavement of a summer night, the melodies which float upon the air from the open balconies above him' [*Lady Anna* XI]. Wandering between Post Office and tawdry lodging houses, Anthony Trollope must often have wondered whether he would always be condemned to listen to life's melodies from the public pavement.

Despite the hostility of Colonel Maberly and his own scapegrace reputation he had slowly attained some respect at St Martin-le-Grand, where he had advanced to senior clerk. His salary likewise had grown, and by 1841 he was earning £140. Surely he was like his hero, John Eames: 'In truth his hobbledehoyhood was dropping off from him, as its old skin drops from a snake. Much of the feeling and something of the knowledge of manhood was coming on him, and he was beginning to recognize to himself that the future manner of his life must be to him a matter of very serious concern' [*The Small House at Allington* LI]. In 1841 there came an opportunity: a vacancy for a Surveyor's Deputy in Ireland, that country that proved the graveyard of many an Englishman's reputation. For Anthony Trollope it would open up the balcony doors to a contented life.

CHAPTER FOUR

Married: Hurrah!

On the fifteenth day of September 1841 a ferry boat came in sight of the Irish coast and made for the port of Kingstown near Dublin. From the deck, the twenty-six-year-old Anthony Trollope gazed on a land about which he knew virtually nothing, a country in many ways more alien than France or Belgium. Before leaving London he had only consulted an old cousin, the family lawyer, who, having lent him £200 to settle his debts, looked 'with pitying eyes' at the idea of going to Ireland. While his mother and Tom were in Italy and could offer no advice, his friends and fellow clerks reacted in the same way. Anthony himself was not sure that he had done the right thing in applying for the post but at least he would escape from Colonel Maberly.

Throughout Trollope's boyhood, Ireland had been a central issue in British politics: 'that fruitful source of constantly recurring and painful discussion' was how Sir Robert Peel would later describe her.[1] In 1829 the Duke of Wellington's government enacted legislation allowing Catholics to sit in Parliament after an extraordinary campaign by Daniel O'Connell. Most Irishmen regretted O'Connell's failure to regain a separate Parliament. However, many Englishmen resented the time 'their' Parliament spent on Irish issues. A dilemma was created which was not resolved till decades after Trollope's death: the Irish had to remain within the British Parliament but were criticised if they exploited parliamentary time, tactics and tricks to promote Irish causes.

The constitutional position did not change during Trollope's lifetime: Ireland was part of the United Kingdom and sent 105 MPs to Westminster, about one sixth of the total. Irish peers elected twenty-eight of their number to the House of Lords, where there were also four Church of Ireland bishops until the 1860s. There was little real sentiment, at least during most of Trollope's lifetime, for a complete break with Britain: the Union allowed Irishmen to play their part in the expanding Empire. O'Connell indeed could be quite fervent about the 'dear little Queen'.

Trollope's writings present examples of the types of men who dominated Irish public life. Irish MPs turn up throughout his work: at the centre of two Palliser novels is the young Irish Catholic Phineas Finn, an honourable politician. Trollope also portrayed the more conventional Irish MP in the Hon. Laurence Fitzgibbon, anxious to pluck every plum of office. The novelist knew the complexity of Irish life, where the vehemence of political and religious ranting could mask friendship based on a common Irishness. Thus in *Phineas Finn* the hero's father is a Catholic doctor married to a Protestant. Phineas is brought up a Catholic while the daughters follow their mother's religion. Dr Finn is friendly with a local peer, who sets aside his usual Orange views to support the son of his old Catholic friend. Trollope's acute powers of observation, united with his kindly feelings, allowed him to understand Ireland in a way few Englishmen of his time – or indeed of any time – ever have. One reviewer in the Catholic publication, the *Dublin Review*, discussed Trollope in 1872 as 'the leading novelist of the day' and wrote:[2]

> This Englishman, keenly observant, painstaking, absolutely sincere and unprejudiced, with a lynx-like clearness of vision ... writes a story as true to the realities of Irish life, as racy of the soil, as rich with peculiar humour, the moral features, the social oddities, the subtle individuality of the far west of Ireland ... Mr Trollope has throughly imbibed its spirit, and mastered its forms more completely than any other writer who ever studied them.

Anthony Trollope's parents had not been innately hostile to the Irish. His mother, in her American book, showed concern for the Irish poor, unlike most English travellers. However, during the 1830s she, like many Englishmen, became more alarmist about Ireland. Her books on Paris and Vienna contained frequent and quite violent digressions about O'Connell, although by this point Anthony was not much influenced by her political views. So, unlike most English officials, the young Trollope arrived in Ireland without an established collection of prejudices against the country.

*

At about the same time as this junior official in Her Majesty's Post Office took his first steps on Irish soil the Queen's Viceroy, Lord de Grey, was arriving as part of the new Conservative government. What did these two officials find? They found an island of some 8,200,000 people with the fastest-growing population in Europe: this was one of the prime reasons for its acute economic problems. The country lacked currency and among the poor barter was still common; there was little capital for investment as rent often went to absentee landlords. The census taken in the year of Trollope's arrival showed that almost half the rural population, in a country that was overwhelmingly rural, lived in 'houses' which were no more than one-room, windowless, mud cabins. While some landlords were trying to build decent houses, the bulk of the people lived in 'dreadful cabins, worse than one's worst pigstyes' as an English traveller noted.[3] Trollope, describing Irish hovels in his first novel, wondered whether many of them could be 'the habitation of any of the human race?' [*The Macdermots of Ballycloran* IX]. Potatoes were often the only food the poor could grow on their small plots, a situation made worse each time the plots were sub-divided. The peasants often could not pay the rent and were forced off their land. As Trollope put it: 'Driven from their cabins and little holdings, their crops and cattle taken from them, they were everywhere around desperate with poverty, and discontented equally with their own landlords and the restraints put upon them by government' [*The Macdermots* VII].

Well over 6,500,000 of the population were Catholic, but wealth and power were concentrated in Protestant hands, although the government was making notable attempts to give important offices to Catholics. From London the Prime Minister asked the Viceroy to '*look out* for respectable Catholics for office'. Yet tradition did not make this easy; one can still see letters in the Postmaster General's correspondence urging that a particular man be given the post of a letter carrier in Dublin because he was a good Protestant. There were some signs of hope as more Catholics advanced into the prosperous ranks of the middle classes, particularly in the larger cities. In the countryside, however, many Catholics were refusing to pay tithe to what they regarded as an alien church, a church which claimed the allegiance of less than one Irishman in fourteen.[4]

Almost every visitor, whether friendly like Sir Walter Scott or critical like Thackeray, agreed that one continually encountered poverty, dirt, indolence and beggars. J.G. Lockhart, who accompanied Scott, wrote:[5]

As we moved deeper into the country, there was a melancholy in his countenance ... The constant passings and repassings of bands of mounted policemen, armed to the teeth ... the rueful squalid poverty that crawled by every way-side, and blocked up every village where we had to change horses ... the contrast between these naked clamourous beggars ... and boundless luxury and merriment surrounding the thinly scattered magnates who condescended to inhabit their ancestral seats ... could at so advanced a period of European civilisation, sicken the heart of a stranger by such wide-spread manifestations of the wanton and reckless profligacy of human mismanagement, the withering curses of feuds and factions, and tyrannous selfishness of absenteeism.

In the fifteen years between Scott's tour and Trollope's arrival, things improved somewhat and the political and religious tensions seemed less because of 'Catholic Emancipation'. Yet no one could know that this was but the lull before the storm. Five years after Trollope's arrival, he would witness the greatest peacetime disaster in modern European history: the Irish potato famine.

*

These aspects of Irish society were far from Trollope's mind as he made his way through the Georgian glories of Dublin to a 'very dirty' hotel. Though he had the usual prejudice against the architecture of the previous century, he came in time to admire Dublin's classical buildings. Concerning the Bank of Ireland he later wrote: 'It may almost be said that in no capital in Europe is there a finer specimen of Grecian architecture.'[6] Yet on his first evening his thoughts were of more mundane matters. As he pictured Ireland as a 'land flowing with fun and whisky, in which irregularity was the rule of life', he ordered whisky punch with dinner. This cheered him, but then he brooded about being 'in a country in which there was not a single individual whom I had ever spoken to or ever seen'. The next day he went to the General Post Office where the Secretary, Augustus Godby, told him that Colonel Maberly had sent a very bad report on the 'worthless' Trollope. Godby dismissed this by saying: 'I shall judge you by your own merits.'

Trollope had been appointed to Banagher on the river Shannon, in King's County in the centre of Ireland. It was a town with a population of just over 4,000 and boasted a church which proclaimed 'built in the year of God 474'.[7] He probably took a boat from Dublin, and arrived in the midst of Banagher Fair with its collection of sheep, horses and colourful characters from all over the Irish Midlands. Perhaps the boisterous humour echoed his mood as he walked up to the Post Office to meet his new master, James Drought, the Surveyor for the West of Ireland. The boy who had been miserable at Winchester and Harrow, and frustrated in Brussels and London, was to achieve happiness in an obscure Irish town. As he put it: 'From the day on which I set my foot in Ireland all these evils went away from me. Since that time who has had a happier life than mine?'

Trollope's principal duty, as head clerk to the Surveyor, was to inspect post offices and postmasters. He was, in effect, Deputy Surveyor and his tasks were particularly extensive in such a large district. Among Ireland's many ills was poor transport, and this hardly helped postal deliveries. The west, the poorest part of the island, had the worst roads. Fortunately Trollope was a competent, if not elegant, rider, for which he could thank Tom, who had forced him to ride bareback round the farm. The perils of travel which he now faced were well described by an English lady who had visited the island five years before:[8]

> The horses we got here realised all one has read and heard of Irish posting ... One poor horse refused to stir the moment the ground rose in the least – no wonder! for his whole shoulders were one deep, dreadful sore. The men were obliged to turn the wheels and push him on; by degrees he was coaxed into a gallop, and then the men mounted as they could. The road was hilly, the stage long, the miseries may be imagined.

Trollope himself was later to write during a visit in South Africa: 'I know so well the way in which a poor weary brute may be spirited up for five minutes; not, alas, without the lash.' Undoubtedly his nearly twenty years' experience of Ireland must have occurred to him. Most of his Irish travels were on horseback, but at other times he endured the miseries of coaches – 'jingles' and 'covered cars' – which he described in *Castle Richmond* [XII]:

> The sitter sits sideways, between a cracked window on one side and a cracked doorway on the other; and as a draught is always going in at the ear near the window, and out at the ear next the door, it is about as cold and comfortless a vehicle for winter as may well be imagined.

There was, however, one great improvement in transport. This was a remarkable network of coaches set up by Charles Bianconi which carried both passengers and mail. Bianconi came to Ireland from Italy in 1815 and Trollope paid him considerable tribute in a history of the Irish Post Office he prepared for a Parliamentary committee: 'It may, perhaps, be said that no living man has worked more than he has for

the benefit of the sister kingdom.' Bianconi gave him valuable advice
on ways to make mail delivery faster and cheaper. Years later
Trollope's elder son wrote Bianconi's biography. Bad transport meant
that Irish postal costs were much greater than English: it cost four
times as much, for example, to maintain a coach in Ireland. By the
time Trollope finished his Irish work postal costs were less than in
England or Scotland. In that improvement no man had had a more
important share than Anthony Trollope.[9]

*

Even before he set foot in Ireland Trollope had begun to reform what
he considered his greatest weakness: a lack of order. A developing
sense of order can be seen in the careful accounts he began to keep of
his official travels, beginning on 15 September, the very date of his
arrival. In a series of six manuscript books, now preserved at Princeton
University Library, we can follow his various travels, first in Ireland
and eventually round the world. These records were important as they
formed the basis of much of his income. His salary of £100 a year was
supplemented by a payment of fifteen shillings for every day of travel,
plus sixpence a mile. He evidently set to work at once, for by 5 October
he calculated that he had travelled sixteen days, covering 316 Irish
miles. (The Irish mile was about one and a quarter English miles.)
These first few weeks produced a profit of £13 11s 1½d after deducting
expenses for transport and hotels, which came to just over six
guineas. Because his allowance was based on English, rather than
Irish, costs he was able, quite honestly, to realise a tidy profit. By the
end of his first three months he saw his quarterly income rise from £25
to over £91, so that instead of making £100 a year he was actually
earning over £300. Of course there was always the possibility that
some of his expenses could be questioned: the Post Office refused, for
example, to refund his travel expenses to Dublin.[10]

It was not only primitive roads that made journeys difficult. The
weary traveller could rarely relax in anything resembling the snug
comforts of an English inn.[11] At the end of two decades in Ireland
Trollope described a typical Irish hotel. As in all of his Irish writings,
criticism was tinctured with genuine love for the people. Before
describing how primitive the hotels were, he first offers a tribute:

> I have travelled all over Ireland, closely as few other men can have done,
> and have never had my portmanteau robbed or my pocket picked. At
> hotels I have seldom locked up my belongings, and my carelessness has

never been punished. I doubt whether as much can be said for English inns [*Castle Richmond* I].

Irish hotels may have been bastions of honesty but they were far from clean, and cleanliness was a virtue Trollope rated highly. 'In dear old Ireland they have some foibles', such as calling ramshackle places 'hotels'. Their corridors usually boasted no floor-covering but 'damp, dirty straw', and the 'coffee room' emitted a 'strong smell of hot whisky and water' [*Castle Richmond* VI].

One of Trollope's best short stories, 'Father Giles of Ballymoy', was based on a stay in such a 'hotel'. In this autobiographical tale a young English official, 'Mr Green' – a name Trollope frequently used for himself as narrator in his short stories – arrives in a town on the shores of Lough Corrib, Ireland's second largest lake. A long journey by canal boat and jaunting car in pelting rain did nothing to dampen the fierce temper that Trollope had inherited from his father. He found a hotel, where the landlady refused to light a fire in his bedroom 'because the wind blew so mortial sthrong down the chimney since the pot had blown off'; still, she boasted that her room was 'as clane as clane and as dhry as dhry'. Before sleeping, Green compared this room with his birthplace, 'Keppel Street, Russell Square', and the contrast between the gentility of the English room and the exotic atmosphere of the Irish chamber amused him. He was suddenly awakened when a man began to climb into his bed, but Green jumped up and threw him down the stairs.

The Englishman's victory quickly turned sour when the landlady's screams revealed that the injured stranger was none other than the local Catholic priest. She had not mentioned that he had allowed the English official to share his room. As the news of the priest's injuries spread, outraged villagers threatened violence and the young Englishman was hustled off to the safety of the gaol. Once the priest recovered the use of his voice he saved Green from the mob's fury. A friendship then sprang up between the Englishman and the Irishman. One suspects that the story's conclusion is based on fact: that the priest came over frequently to visit Green once he had returned permanently to England. Trollope says, in his *Autobiography*, that the 'main purport' of the story is true, even if a few details were added. We get an idea of how he developed a plot by comparing the published account with the version he told an Irish friend. According to the latter, for example, there were two beds in the hotel room, but obviously Trollope knew the story would be more dramatic if there were only one.[12]

As 'Fr Giles' demonstrates, Trollope had the capacity to make friends among the Irish, even in unpromising circumstances. He was one of the few prominent Englishmen of his time to like the Irish: 'I soon found them to be good-humoured, clever – the working classes very much more intelligent than those of England – oeconomical, and hospitable.' This is not to say that he was any more blind to their faults than he was to those of any nation or group. 'They are,' he wrote, 'perverse, irrational and but little bound by the love of truth.' There is much accuracy in his first biographer's assertion that he was 'a sounder authority on most Irish subjects than nine-tenths of the statesmen legislating for them at Westminster'. It is unfortunate that his contribution to Anglo-Irish relations was limited to postal communications. 'It has been my fate,' he wrote in America, 'to have so close an intimacy with Ireland, that when I meet an Irishman abroad, I always recognise in him more of a kinsman than in an Englishman.'[13]

Trollope frequently came across the disregard for 'truth' when inspecting postmasters' accounts. When he arrived in Ireland he knew little of the Post Office's methods of accounting. His education had avoided 'arithmatic', for as his brother said it was a subject 'utterly out of place among gentlemen and in gentlemanlike places of education, where nothing of the kind was taught'. Within two weeks of his arrival he persuaded a Galway postmaster to demonstrate how accounts were kept. The pupil proved too adept, and quickly discovered that his teacher was defrauding the government: the postmaster was dismissed. Trollope evidently believed that bluster, which was natural to him, was needed to deal with the Irish. On one occasion he observed a postmaster carefully locking his desk after Trollope entered the office. A few days later the Surveyor announced that some money was missing from the post. Trollope at once hired a horse and reached the suspicious postmaster's house after midnight. He walked straight into the office and demanded that the locked desk be opened. The man claimed he had lost the key. One kick from the powerful Trollope smashed open the drawer to reveal the stolen letter. This is a good illustration of what a careful student of behaviour he already was: apt training for a novelist, particularly one whose strongest point became the delineation of character. His bluster was not always successful. Once – and this is a story not mentioned in his *Autobiography* – he arrived in a small town on a Sunday and demanded to inspect the postal records. The postmaster refused to desecrate the Sabbath. Trollope raged, and 'declared he would sit where he was until the books were brought. "Then, sir," said the postmaster, "you'll just sit there till you die." Exit Mr. Trollope.'[14]

Another duty was to call on anyone who complained about the service. He enjoyed this work as it took him about the countryside and allowed him to increase his profits from travel. On one visit he drove up in his jaunting car through a snow-storm to a squire's house in County Cavan. The man had written several irate letters complaining of bad postal service. When the postal official appeared the Irishman turned on all his charm and sent his butler for brandy and hot water. Then he insisted that his guest must dine and spend the night. It was only after breakfast the next morning that the squire agreed to discuss business and admitted that he had no real complaint. He amused himself in his lonely abode by writing outraged letters to various government departments.

*

Yet it was not only on such quixotic missions that Trollope encountered the Anglo-Irish gentry with that eccentric charm which has endeared them to so many writers. In Ireland he discovered a sport which would become the most demanding of his pleasures. The Surveyor kept a pack of hounds and soon his new deputy bought a hunter. Trollope's tall, ungainly figure was now seen in company with the gentry, leaping over fences and hedges, in pursuit of foxes all over the Irish Midlands. The early nineteenth century was the classic age of fox-hunting. In England, and even more in Ireland, hunting became a way of life. A whole literature sprang up round it, with the hunting novels of R.S. Surtees at the centre. Riding to hounds quickly became the enduring passion of Trollope's life and he followed it with unremitting ardour for almost forty years. It influenced his writing considerably: one reason he wrote so much was to get money to hunt. Hunting often forms the subject of several chapters in his novels. Fox-hunters often argue that he is one of the best delineators of the sport. Readers who do not ride to hounds, however, often wearily agree with his own admission about fox-hunting: 'I have dragged it into many novels, – into too many no doubt.' Its language also drifted in and many characters are compared to the poor fox whom the hunter both pities and pursues.

Trollope later became a fervent defender of fox-hunting against attacks by 'philanimalists' – 'self-anxious people who think they possess among them all the bowels of the world' [*The American Senator* LXXIII]. With as much fervour as he pursued the fox he chased its defenders by writing articles about his favourite, indeed his only, sport. The great Anglo-Irish historian W.E.H. Lecky, observing these arguments, commented that fox-hunting was essential because it was the only pastime that kept landowners in Ireland. As 'the chief animating principle of Irish country life' it also provided a focus for all classes and religions in the countryside. Fox-hunting gave Trollope more than pleasure: it gave him social acceptance. As he recalled in a short story, 'The O'Conors of Castle Conor', some hunting men may have looked a little askance at their English recruit, but he soon demonstrated his ability.[15] Nothing better illustrates the change from the sullen youth to the happy man than his frequent visits to Coole Park, the Galway home of William Gregory, a rising Tory politician. At Harrow he had avoided that 'dirty boy' – Trollope – but in Ireland they became hunting companions and close friends.* Undoubtedly some hunters must have been surprised when the two Old Harrovians took to quoting Virgil and Horace, a proof incidentally that Trollope had learned more than he liked to let on.

He not only came to relish the excitement of the chase and the joy of the capture, but also the panoply of hunting. He resented the increasing sobriety, not to say boredom, of the dress Victorian society prescribed for gentleman. In his youth men still retained some of the rakish elegance of the eighteenth century, but just as he was becoming successful fashion increasingly ordained that a gentleman must conform to a colourless uniformity. He conformed, but he always disliked this drabness. Hunting allowed him to array himself in vibrant colours. In one Irish novel, *Castle Richmond*, he elaborated on this:

> We have come to be so dingy ... so careless of any of the laws of beauty in the folds and lines and hues of our dress ... it is not permitted to the ordinary English gentleman to be anything else but ugly. Chimney-pot hats, swallow-tailed coats, and pantaloons that fit nothing, came creeping in upon us ... it has come to this, that if a man go in handsome attire he is a popinjay and a vain fool ... But an Englishman may still make himself brave when he goes forth into the hunting field. Custom there allows him colour, and garments that fit his limbs ... In my mind men, like churches and books, and women too, should be brave, not mean, in their outward attire [XXIII].

Trollope, however, who had little vanity about his appearance, was even more concerned to be well mounted: 'the fit of the saddle is of more moment than the fit of a pair of breeches' [*Ralph the Heir* XXXI].

His increasing enjoyment of Irish life was not based solely on hunting, for he observed closely all aspects of society which, with its

---

*Decades later, after Trollope's death, Coole Park, under Sir William's young widow, Lady Gregory, became the centre of the Irish literary revival led by W.B. Yeats.

confusing mixture of similarities to and differences from England, provided good training for a future novelist. In Ireland he saw an exaggerated form of the social distinctions that marked English life. He visited the peasant in his one-room mud hut, which he shared with the family pig, as well as the lord in his Georgian mansion with his servants, his silver and his crystal. One Irish lady recalled that Trollope's close study of all aspects of daily life reminded her of a woman examining the material of a new dress.[16] Perhaps she did not realise that, as in so many other things, Anthony was his mother's son.

*

One pleasant feature of the Victorian Civil Service was the long annual holiday. Trollope was to use these throughout his official life to travel widely. In his first holiday from Ireland, for which he got his leave extended by a month, he appears to have gone to his mother's new house in the Lake District. Fanny Trollope had been moved as much by her maternal desire to be close to her surviving daughter as by her Romantic passion to settle amidst scenery made famous by Wordsworth. She was pleased with her son-in-law, the postal Surveyor for the district, who was providing 'all the minor matters of income, house and so forth' for Cecilia, as Mrs Trollope somewhat grandly put it. She bought a few acres overlooking the ruins of Brougham Castle and had a large house built for herself and Tom who set to work planting hundreds of trees for 'a cloistered walk ... from which to enjoy the splendid prospects'.[17] Anthony would eventually use this view in a short story, 'The Mistletoe Bough'.

Both brothers shared a passion for long walks, which Anthony recalled in one novel, *Can You Forgive Her?*, by contrasting his own experience with that of a rather despicable MP:

> Wearily and wretchedly he plodded on. A man may be very weary in such a walk as that, and yet be by no means wretched. Tired, hungry, cold, wet, and nearly penniless, I have sat me down and slept among those mountain tracks, – have slept because nature refused to allow longer wakefulness. But my heart has been as light as my purse, and there has been something in the air of the hills that made me buoyant and happy in the midst of my weariness ... What are five miles of a walk to a young man, even though the rain be falling and the ways be dirty? what, though they may come after some other ten that he has already traversed on his feet? [LVII].

In addition, the ever-observant Trollope used the Lake District as a setting for two other novels, *Sir Harry Hotspur of Humblethwaite* and

Lady Anna.[18] It provided the perfect background for the old-fashioned Tory gentry, who hold fast to feudal traditions far into the era of Victorian reforms. As a Liberal, Trollope reluctantly shook off many of these old attitudes, at least on a rational level, but deep within him remained the Romantic streak inherited from his mother. The consciousness of his descent from the gentry also led him to portray squires with respect, particularly those who seemed to preserve older codes of honesty, honour and loyalty.

His holiday gave Trollope a chance to hear about his mother's Italian jaunt, about which she was writing her fifth, and dullest, travel book. Her writing was not improved by the fact that she had to cut short her stay: when she heard that Cecilia was expecting her first child, she and Tom made a hurried trip from Rome to the Lake District. A severe winter forced them to cross the Alps on a sledge pushed by twelve sturdy peasants. Once back in England, she resumed her frantic schedule of writing before dawn shone through the windows of her new house. She had embarked on a new tack by writing novels of social protest. Her Toryism led her, as it did Disraeli, to use the novel to expose the social ills that seemed to go hand in hand with industrialism and political reform. In *Michael Armstrong*, the only one of her novels to survive in public favour, she depicted with considerable skill the sufferings of children employed in factories. This was one of the earliest novels of factory life, and for it the formidable old lady made a tour of factories in the North. In her preface she made clear her aim 'to drag into the light of day, and place before the eyes of Englishmen, the hideous mass of injustice and suffering'. Although she had become one of the best paid novelists of her time, she never lost either her kindness or her passion for justice.[19] She also wrote *Jessie Phillips* to attack the Poor Law enacted by the Liberal Government she so detested.

*

In the autumn of 1842 Tom accompanied his brother to Ireland to see the sister kingdom. Because Tom had seen that Anthony was 'already a very different man from what he had been in London', he was all the more anxious to explore his brother's new home. In Banagher he was somewhat taken aback when the door of the Surveyor's house was opened by a barefoot and dirty servant girl, but he was soon pleased to discover that Drought and his wife were extremely hospitable and particularly fond of his younger brother. Tom had a simple explanation for Anthony's success: 'My brother stood high in [Drought's] good graces by virtue of simply having taken the whole work and affairs of the postal district on his shoulders.' He concluded with genuine fraternal pride: 'The rejected of St Martin-le-Grand was already a very valuable and capable officer.'[20]

Anthony arranged a tour of Killarney for Tom and then joined up with him for a lengthy walk. They had a memorable time in the mountains, for after all they were children of the generation that had come to revel in the grandiose splendour of mountain scenery. Both the Trollopes long remembered the sights: 'the truly grand spectacular changes from dark, thick enveloping cloud to brilliant sunshine, suddenly revealing all the mountains and the wonderful colouring of the intertwining sea beneath them.' The two men, by now wet through, returned to their inn and sat, wrapped in blankets 'like Roman senators', to dine on roast goose and whisky punch. For the next forty years this became a frequent topic of conversation between the two brothers, and when Tom recalled it in his own memoirs, written several years after Anthony's death, he exclaimed: 'Alas that we shall never more talk over that day again.'[21]

It was not only the natural beauty that Tom saw in his brother's new home. With Anthony to guide him, he enjoyed many encounters with the people. Once they went to an election meeting: in the 1840s Irish elections were particularly exuberant affairs because political passions had been stirred as O'Connell's crusade for a separate Parliament reached its climax. Tom found the whole scene 'one seething mass of senseless but good-humored hustling and confusion'. An excited crowd gathered on a huge platform to listen to political harangues. An ominous crack was heard and the platform crashed to the ground causing many serious injuries. The two Trollopes stumbled to their feet and began to rescue the injured. Each grabbed hold of an arm of a little man, who was crushed under the weight of several people. When they dragged him out they discovered he was a priest. 'Tell me your names that I'll pray for ye!' he shouted. The two Englishman laughed and said it would be no use for they were 'heretics'. 'Tell me your names', the priest shouted once again, 'that I'll pray for ye all the more.'[22]

*

A country like Ireland, so rich in eccentric characters, beautiful scenery, colourful speech, ancient feuds and violent passions was an ideal place for a budding novelist. Anthony Trollope had for a long time been preparing, at first unconsciously, for this career. When he was a boy he had lightened his miseries and loneliness by weaving little tales

in his head as he trudged the muddy lanes of Harrow. He continued
this practice as a clerk, while walking through the teeming streets of
London. By then, like most young men of a literary turn, he 'thought it
possible that [he] might write a novel'. For years he did nothing, 'yet no
day was passed without thoughts of attempting, and a mental
acknowledgement of the disgrace of postponing it'.

Most modern novelists – certainly any with a background as exotic
as Trollope's – would make their first novel autobiographical. This was
not the Victorian convention, and it certainly did not appeal to
Trollope. Many years later he told his friend George Eliot how furious
he had been at Dickens's parody of his own father as Mr Micawber in
David Copperfield. Such behaviour was a 'disgrace' to any writer. For
Trollope, to have attempted an autobiographical novel would have
reopened wounds, and most likely have exposed his father to ridicule,
and this during his mother's lifetime. Trollope could use, sometimes
unconsciously, some of his father's traits but he never parodied that
tragic man in fiction. Only late in life did he deal, sympathetically,
with both his parents in his *Autobiography*.

There is another reason why he did not consider an autobiographical
novel, and it is one that separates the nineteenth-century mind from
the twentieth. Trollope saw himself, as Victorians tended to do, as part
of a continuity or, to use Burke's phrase, 'a partnership not only
between those who are living, but between those who are dead, or those
who are to be born'. To write a novel of his early life was to dissolve
that partnership. The liberated and lonely soul would then stand
naked before the world. Severed from his ancestors, he could advance
by the light of his reason and his emotions. That was not Trollope's
way. The powerful emotions that seethed inside him needed something
other than his own past to begin a novel. Like his mother, he needed a
setting to force him to put pen to paper.

Ireland now provided that setting. In the early decades of the
nineteenth century there had been a considerable vogue for Irish
novels. Writers such as Charles Lever, whom Trollope read, portrayed
the rollicking humour of the 'land of punch, priests and potatoes' in
Harry Lorrequer. After William Gregory introduced the two men, a
friendship began between them. It was always warm on Trollope's
side, even though Lever eventually resented the younger writer's
greater success. Trollope was also familiar with the works of other
novelists such as Maria Edgeworth, who had depicted the grim reality
of Irish life in books such as *Castle Rackrent*. He had good cause to be
interested in her works: it was, after all, one of her books that had
helped promote the romance between Fanny Milton and Thomas

Anthony Trollope. However, seven years before Anthony Trollope first set foot on Irish soil Maria Edgeworth had decided that the time had passed when one could write such novels:[23]

> It is impossible to draw Ireland as she now is in the book of fiction – realities are too strong, party passions too violent to see, or care to look at their faces in a looking glass. The people would only break the glass, and curse the fool who held the mirror up to nature – distorted nature.

Other Irish novelists had also despaired of any improvement in their native land and gradually moved away from fiction, leaving the field fairly vacant for a well-informed outsider.

The spirit of place often played a large part in inspiring Trollope's writing. In the next decade the evocative sight of the spire of Salisbury Cathedral soaring up into the moonlight gave him the inspiration to start his Barchester novels, and in the late 1860s a visit to the oldest synagogue in Europe prompted him to write a love story between a Jewish man and a Christian girl in Prague. His first novel also sprang from a sudden view of a building when he was showing his oldest friend, John Merivale, round the West of Ireland in 1843. He could combine postal work with the pleasant task of acting as guide. His duties called him to County Leitrim, where yet another postmaster had come to 'sorrow' over his accounts, and he took his friend with him. In his *Autobiography* he remembered that it was on his postal mission to the villages of Drumsna and Mohill in September 1843, that he discovered the place and the plot for his first book. *The Macdermots of Ballycloran* informs the reader of its origins in the opening words of the first chapter:[24]

> In the autumn, 184-, business took me into the West of Ireland, and, amongst other places, to the quiet little village of Drumsna, which is in the province of Connaught, County of Leitrim, about 72 miles W.N.W. of Dublin, on the Mail Coach Road to Sligo. I reached the little inn there in the morning by the said mail; my purpose being to leave it late in the evening by the day coach, as my business was but of short duration, I was left, after an early dinner, to amuse myself. Now, in such a situation, to take a walk is all the brightest man can do, and the dullest always does the same.

These sentences would be the despair of any 'Professor of Creative Writing'; yet they launched the career of one of the most successful and enduring of novelists. Although, mercifully, he did not continue this Ordnance Survey style, several of his later characteristics are present. There is the matter-of-fact tone, the refusal to give the exact year, and the little joke at the end. The walk took him and Merivale to the ruins of a manor house and his Romanticism was called forth by the melancholy scene. The sight stirred a man who was himself descended from a landed family yet one whose parents had been driven from a variety of homes and eventually forced into self-imposed exile. He sat down on a fallen ash tree, lit a cigar and 'meditated on this characteristic specimen of Irish life'. The setting sun behind the ruin gave it 'a still stronger appearance of death and decay, and brought into my mind thoughts of the wrong, oppression, misery, and despair, to which some one had been subjected by what I saw before me'. His description is so accurate that it is still possible to discover the real place. Ironically some local people now believe that the ruins were originally called Ballycloran and that the family were the Macdermots. Fiction and fact, as so often in the mists of Ireland, have blended into one.

By the time Merivale left, Trollope had already evolved a plot and written the opening chapters. This, in itself, shows that even at the start of his career, his discipline – that 'order' he had longed for in London – allowed him to complete several chapters in the midst of official work and a visit by his oldest friend. Yet it would be four years before it was published. *The Macdermots of Ballycloran* is not a pleasant book, for it portrays a country on the verge of the greatest tragedy in an already tragic history. In it the violence and the poverty of pre-famine Ireland are memorably etched. By making the main characters Catholics rather than Anglo-Irish Protestants, Trollope made a startling change from most earlier writers about Ireland. The novel is the story of an impoverished family of Catholic gentry in which the son, Thady Macdermot, murders his sister's seducer. Trollope undoubtedly drew upon painful recollections when portraying Thady's mad father, Larry, who collapses under the strain of a huge debt owed to the builder of his house, just as the elder Trollope was driven to distraction by the large rent for his farm in Harrow and the loss of his wife's money in America. The most moving part of the book is the friendship between Thady and a Catholic priest, Father John McGrath. Trollope was careful not to caricature the priest – *The Times* often referred to them as 'cultivated ruffians' – for Father John is a bibliophile unable to afford shelves for his books.[25] Although the priest is not devoid of the Irish humour Trollope so relished, it was 'unceasing charity' that 'made the great beauty of Father John's character' [XIV]. It is somewhat ironic that the best-known depicter of Anglican clergy began his clerical gallery – as he ended it – with a sketch of an Irish Catholic priest.

Trollope used his superb gift for observing minor details of language and custom. In portraying a wedding, he includes a phrase used only in Irish Catholic services: 'When I come', Father John says, 'to *"salute nostrâ"* – those are the last words – you're to kiss the bride' [XII]. His interest in Irish dialect is present throughout: Father John addresses all sorts of characters as 'my darling' and there are phrases like 'It's little heart I have' [V]. The book is over-written in parts and the dialogue, with its phonetic spellings, demands too much of the reader, especially as it is used to tell almost all the tale. There is little sense, so apparent in later novels, of the avuncular story-teller guiding readers through the novel and offering reflections about life. Yet, almost a century and a half after publication, it remains a powerful story and a good introduction to the still difficult relations between England and Ireland. To take one example: a recurring theme in Anglo-Irish relations has been the use of paid informers – 'supergrasses' in twentieth-century jargon – to help the authorities combat terrorism. This presents a difficult moral problem; but Trollope, English official though he was, was in no doubt that it was wrong:

> It is true, that by paid spies and informers, real criminals may not unfrequently be brought to justice; but those who have observed the working of the system must admit that the treachery which it creates – the feeling of suspicion which it generates – but, above all, the villanies to which it gives and has given rise, in allowing informers, by the prospect of blood-money, to give false informations, and to entrap the unwary into crimes – are by no means atoned for by the occasional detection and punishment of a criminal [XI].

Even in this first novel Trollope was anxious to make serious points.

*

Trollope took a long time to write the book, not just because he was a novice, but because his postal work absorbed so much of his time. Also, he was about to take the most important step in his private life which, like his book, sprang from one of his Irish journeys. He enjoyed visiting Kingstown, the port where he had first set foot on Irish soil. He was there for much of July 1842. He was fond of sea bathing, and in future years was always happy to take off all his clothes and plunge into water. This may well have begun in Ireland, for he does not mention bathing at the English seaside in his youth and his mother admitted she was 'no sea-bather myself'. In fact late in life he wrote that Kingstown was a better place for swimming than any seaside town in England. He also claimed that seaside holidays were far more popular at this time among the Irish than among the English.[26]

Kingstown was only a short journey from Dublin by Ireland's first, and at that time, only railway. It offered lovely views of the Bay of Dublin, which enthusiastic Irishmen, with only a small amount of blarney, compared to that of Naples. Nineteenth-century travel writers spent much time debating the relative merits of the Bays of Naples, New York and Dublin, though Trollope eventually decided that Sydney surpassed them all. Thackeray, who rattled through Ireland in 1842 gathering material for a spiteful travel book, described Kingstown as a 'town irregularly built, with many handsome terraces, some churches and showy-looking hotels ... a hideous obelisk, stuck on four fat balls and surmounted with a crown on a cushion (... no bad emblems perhaps of the monarch in whose honour they were raised)'. The obelisk, and indeed the new name of the town commemorated George IV's visit some twenty years before. He was the first English king to visit the island in peacetime. Other Englishmen followed his example and Kingstown became a place where the middle classes could have a cheap holiday – a room in one of the best hotels was only 2s 6d – in a strange land without the annoyance of having to attempt a foreign language.[27]

Among the visitors during that summer of 1842 was the family of a Yorkshire banker, Edward Heseltine. He was a widower, whose wife had died two years before in one of those railway accidents that were so common in the first decades of rail travel. Ironically Heseltine was also a director of a Yorkshire railway company and was able to use some of his money to dabble in his hobby of collecting armour. In his eighteenth-century dress he was a well known figure in Rotherham, 'a chevalier of the old days' in a blue coat with gilt buttons, 'sunning himself daily on fine days'. Rose was his fourth daughter, a girl in her early twenties. In Rotherham, Rose and two of her sisters were known as 'The Three Graces'. Evidently Trollope agreed for by the end of the summer he was engaged to Rose Heseltine.

Rose Trollope's true importance in the life of her husband has not been recognised in previous biographies. Instead of trying to understand the woman who played the most important role in Trollope's life, biographers have been preoccupied with the novelist's friendship for a young American, Kate Field. One cause of this neglect is that so little has been known about Rose and her background. Even her birthdate was unknown. Fortunately much more information is now available and this proves rather surprising. Rose Heseltine was born on 13 December 1820, the daughter of Edward Heseltine who was born in 1779 or 1780, the son of a merchant clerk. His wife, Martha, was also born a Heseltine, which suggests theirs was one of those frequent nineteenth-century marriages between cousins, so often used in the novels of the time. Edward had been baptised in St Mary's Church, Hull, in 1780 where he started work as a bank clerk. After his first two daughters were born he moved to Rotherham where he became a bank manager. By the time of Rose's birth, he was attending Hollis Unitarian Chapel in Rotherham although he did not come from a Dissenting background and had had his first two daughters, born in Hull, baptised in the Church of England. It was in Hollis Chapel that Rose was baptised on 5 July 1821, almost seven months after her birth. Thus the wife of the greatest portrayer of the Anglican clergy was born a Dissenter and not only a Dissenter but a member of the smallest and most unorthodox of all nonconformist sects at the time, the Unitarians. They not only rejected two-thirds of what other Christians believed about the Trinity but tended to see themselves as something of an intellectual and social elite amongst Dissenters. Their eighteenth-century rationalist heritage hung round them well into the nineteenth century. Indeed, they were inclined to take as much pride in their intellects as Victorian Quakers did in their humility.

Rose's family lived in the bank building exactly as did one of the 'Two Heroines of Plumplington' in Trollope's last short story, which is about a bank manager's daughter. The fictional bank in Barset was evidently a better place than the real one in Yorkshire. A few years after Rose's marriage, her father gave evidence for a report on drainage in Rotherham which shows the dreadful conditions that even prominent and reasonably well-off people endured, particularly in the manufacturing cities. 'For want of drainage,' he said, 'I am obliged to have my cellar pumped, I should say six or seven times a day.' On rainy days there would often be four feet of water in the cellar, but this was not just rain water: 'The contents of half the water-closets in High-street remain now at the bottom of the street ... Mrs Heseltine has suffered several times from the effluvia arising from the cellars.' He said that some servants had been forced to leave after they contracted fevers, his children had often been struck down by these same fevers and he frequently had to send them away in the summer. His neighbour, a surgeon, had the same problem and claimed that the fevers were often a form of typhoid. Little wonder that Heseltine concluded 'If I were not obliged I would not live in the house.'[28]

Thus Rose Heseltine's visit to Kingstown may have come about for the entirely un-romantic purpose of escaping the filthy drains of her father's house. If so the visit ended on a much more romantic note, with a proposal from Anthony Trollope. It is quite likely that he was thinking of his own experience when he wrote a quarter of a century later: 'It takes years to make a friendship; but a marriage may be settled in a week, – in an hour ... The young people meet each other in their holiday dresses, on holiday occasions, amidst holiday pleasures, – and the thing is arranged. Such matches may be said to be heaven-made' [*Ralph the Heir* LVI].

Few men have made as many proposals of marriage as Anthony Trollope. Many years later he came down to breakfast and startled his hosts by saying 'I have just been making my twenty-seventh proposal of marriage.'[29] Of course these were in his novels. In real life, as far as is known, he made only one, the memory of which he drew on to make the following revealing interjection in *Doctor Thorne* after Frank Gresham has asked Mary Thorne to marry him: 'A man cannot well describe that which he has never seen nor heard; but the absolute words and acts of one such scene did once come to the author's knowledge.' This is a strong indication that the little story within the novel was based on his own proposal to Rose. Other details strengthen this assumption: the location at the seaside, the straightforward language without any hint of poetic exuberance, the description of the pair as 'by no means plebian ... [and] sufficiently given to mental pursuits' and the fact that this was written when Trollope was about to embark on his first lengthy absence from his wife. Indeed he had so arranged it that Rose would be copying out these passages as he was on his way to Egypt for the Post Office in 1858. This is typical of his behaviour: to leave an expression of strong love behind him once he could not be embarrassed by it. This 'passionate scene was [on] the seashore, on which they were walking' and his anonymous 'gentleman' proposes in the following manner:

> Gentleman. 'Well, Miss ——, the long and the short of it is this: here I am; you can take me or leave me.'
> Lady – scratching a gutter on the sand with her parasol, so as to allow a little salt water to run out of one hole into another. 'Of course, I know that's all nonsense.'
> Gentleman. 'Nonsense! By Jove, it isn't nonsense at all: come, Jane; here I am: come, at any rate you can say something.'
> Lady. 'Yes, I suppose I can say something.'
> Gentleman. 'Well, which is it to be; take me or leave me?'
> Lady – very slowly ... 'Well, I don't exactly want to leave you.'

Trollope then concludes this interruption of his plot with a rather emotional passage:

> And so the matter was settled: settled with much propriety and satisfaction; and both the lady and the gentleman would have thought, had they ever thought about the matter at all, that this, the sweetest

moment of their lives, had been graced by all the poetry by which such
moments ought to be hallowed [VII].

It would be fascinating to know what Rose Trollope thought as she
copied out those passages in her fair copy for the publisher.

Marriage is a central preoccupation of almost every Trollope novel;
indeed he even maintained that marriage was the 'proper ending' of a
novel [*Ayala's Angel* LXIV]. Again and again there is a young girl
debating whether she should marry, or whom she will marry. Quite
often some poor maiden – sometimes there are several in one novel –
takes three volumes to decide both questions. These problems are not
restricted to women, for almost as often young men contemplate the
possibility of marrying and then do battle to acquire their beloved. It is
therefore essential to have some idea of Trollope's own view of
marriage and his general attitude towards women, for these provide
not only an important aspect of his own life but a crucial element in his
writing.

*

By all rules laid down by psychology for our guidance, Trollope should
have had a jaded view not only of married life but of women. As a child
he had felt the increasing tensions between his parents, as their
prosperity and their marriage tumbled from one misfortune to
another. While his father's health broke under the strain the young
Anthony must have heard numerous arguments about the family's
fight to maintain the status befitting gentle birth. Just as the he was
entering adolescence, with all its moody doubts, his mother left her
husband's house and disappeared into the backwoods of America
under the guidance of a fanatic female. Deprived not only of his
mother's loving influence but also of his two sisters, the young Trollope
existed for several years without any relief from the all-male
atmosphere of his schools. When his mother returned, he witnessed
the strange spectacle – to early-nineteenth-century eyes – of a
gentleman's family being supported by the wife's work. He also
witnessed – on several occasions – the misery that parents endure by
the death of children. Finally, he must have noted that his mother
enjoyed a new lease of life when his father's mournful existence ended
in exile. As a perceptive reader of her novels he must have noted how
frequently she presented married life in an unhappy light.

Yet none of this seemed to make much difference to Trollope's
attitudes towards women or marriage. Unlike many young men of his

era, he showed an interest in girls from a fairly early age. He delighted in flirting with the daughters of a neighbouring family at Harrow. When the Trollope brothers walked the fourteen miles to Vauxhall it was Anthony who had danced with the girls while Tom looked on shyly.

Trollope's *Autobiography*, unlike most Victorian memoirs, does not contain rhapsodies about the male friendships that were so common in that period and were so gloriously celebrated by *In Memoriam*. Tennyson was not the only man who had been infatuated with his brilliant friend Henry Hallam. Even before the moody poet met Hallam at Cambridge, that earnest youth William Gladstone had been devoted to him at Eton. Half a century later Prime Minister and Poet Laureate had a violent political disgreement; yet guests at a country house were amazed to see them arm in arm and almost in tears: they were talking about their beloved friend who had been dead for half a century. Trollope knew no such passions, though he could occasionally depict deep friendship between young men in novels such as *The Bertrams*.

Irish girls delighted him as he danced to 'those provocative Irish tunes, which ... compel the hearers to dance whether they wish it or no' [*The Macdermots of Ballycloran* XIII]. 'Where,' he asked in his short story, 'The O'Conors of Castle Conor', 'does one find girls so pretty, so easy, so sweet, so talkative as the Irish girls?' Yet he was anxious to defend their honour: 'And then with all their talking, and all their ease, who ever hears of their misbehaving. They certainly love flirting, as they also love dancing. But they flirt without mischief and without malice.' 'No girls,' he asserted in *The Macdermots*, 'know better how to dress themselves than Irish girls, or can do it with less ... expense'; but his new found devotion to hard work had affected his attitude: 'they are too much given to morning dishevelment' [VIII]. With all these experiences and opinions Trollope was no bashful youth who endured misery in the company of girls his own age.

Yet if there had been any serious romance before he met Rose Heseltine it does not appear in his remarkably frank *Autobiography*. It is observable that the only genuine love in *The Macdermots* is that of a brother for his sister, which is also the principal emotion in the short story he set in the time of his youth, 'The Panjandrum'. Nor is there evidence that he indulged in that secret sexual world that lay under so much of Victorian respectability. In some marginalia in a copy of Bacon's *Essays* he commented, with words he never imagined would be seen by others: 'Lust is ever bad, and love is ever good. That I take to be a truth as arranged by God.'[30]

*

Yet if Trollope disapproved of 'lust' he certainly always had a ready eye for beauty. His novels are full of descriptions of young girls, so much so that in one novel – written not even half way through his career – he moaned: 'For once I will venture to have a heroine without describing her. Let each reader make what he will of her' (*The Bertrams* IV). This, however, is a most unusual occurrence and from the myriad descriptions he gave we gain some idea of what type of woman he admired. He seems to have had a fascination with noses, and while it would be possible to list hundreds of descriptions it is amusing to recall a few. While his most popular heroine, Lily Dale, has a nose that is too broad [*The Small House at Allington* VI], his most wicked woman, Lady Eustace, possesses a nose that is described as 'exquisite', 'eloquent' and 'graceful' [*The Eustace Diamonds* II]. One may wonder what an 'eloquent' nose is, but he was still using the adjective many novels later, in describing an American girl who is to become a Duchess: 'Her nose spread at the base a little, so that it was not purely Grecian. But who has ever seen a nose to be eloquent and expressive, which did not spread' [*The Duke's Children* XXVIII]. It helps to come of ancient lineage: what we might call Trollope's first nose belongs to Feemy Macdermot, who, we are assured, had 'a well-formed nose, as all coming of old families have' [*The Macdermots* II]. Noses often indicate character: the 'aquiline nose' of one French girl makes people hesitate to contradict her [*The Golden Lion of Granpère* I]. Most of Trollope's characters, male as well as female, seem to have some minor flaw in the structure of their noses. However, Clarissa Underwood, in *Ralph the Heir* [II], is fortunate: 'Her nose was perfect; – not Grecian, nor Roman, nor Egyptian, – but simply English.'

As for complexion, he admitted while describing a girl with a somewhat darker hue than Victorian beauty prescribed: 'For myself I am not sure that I love a clear complexion. Pink and white alone will not give that hue which seems best to denote light and life, and to tell of a mind that thinks and a heart that feels.' Lips could send Trollope the novelist into near ecstasy, and at times his earthy comments must have upset more prudish readers. Nor was this confined to novels, for in his Australian travel book he refuses to criticise any woman's views if they come from 'ruby lips'.[31] Trollope adhered to the traditional view that thin lips characterised untrustworthy people, like Lady Eustace, who lacked that 'expression of eager-speaking truthfulness which full lips often convey' [*The Eustace Diamonds* II], although occasionally a heroine, like Mary Thorne, can have thin lips. He admitted a sensual reason for this in his last completed novel, written in his sixties: 'Her lips, alas! were too thin for true female beauty, and lacked that round and luscious fulness which seems in many a girl's face to declare the purpose for which they were made' [*An Old Man's Love* III]. He was not one of that 'class of critics to whom it is a necessity to cavil rather than to kiss', and his novels, like *Ralph the Heir* [II], abound with phrases about the joys of kissing. He allows young men to kiss a woman's hand while courting, but 'a good honest kiss, mouth to mouth' is normally reserved either for the rapture that follows the acceptance of a proposal or for after the wedding [*Miss Mackenzie* XIII].

Yet for Trollope true beauty manifested itself in the way a woman moved. In an age when ladies delighted in appearing in elegant attire, this could add so much to that sense of presence that Victorians admired. Perhaps he acquired this attitude from his mother, one of whose strictures against American women was that 'they do not walk well, nor in fact, do they ever appear to advantage when in movement'.[32] Trollope thought Irish girls remarkable for the dignity of their walk and in his first novel Feemy Macdermot was described as a 'tall, dark girl, with that bold, upright, well-poised figure, which is so peculiarly Irish. She walked as if all the blood of the old Irish Princes was in her veins' [*The Macdermots of Ballycloran* II]. As he travelled through more countries, he was pleased to add to his list of mobile beauty: Spanish women impressed him greatly during a quick visit in the late 1850s. 'Alas!' he moans, 'how few women can walk! ... They scuffle, they trip, they trot, they amble, they waddle, they crawl ... but, except in Spain, they rarely walk' [*The Bertrams* IX]. When visiting the Middle East he was not impressed with 'the female followers of the Prophet' with their faces partially hidden by a veil: 'No one could behold them without wishing that the eclipse had been total.' However, to Jewish women he had a different reaction: 'The Mahomedans were ape-like; but the Jewesses were glorious specimens of feminine creation.' He much enjoyed the sight of 'their naked shoulders and bosoms nearly bare' [*The Bertrams* IX]. He was, however, fortunate that while his eyes could admire foreign beauty, as a true Victorian he preferred Englishwomen:

> I have seen in Italy and in America women perhaps as beautiful as any that I have seen in England, but in neither country does it seem that such beauty is intended for domestic use. In Italy the beauty is soft, and of the flesh. In America it is hard, and of the mind. Here it is of the heart [*Rachel Ray* VII].

Essential in Trollope's idea of female beauty was a certain softness: in his short story, 'Ophelia Gledd', he called it 'personal charms', which ultimately made a woman attractive – charms 'which men love most, –

sweet changing colour, soft flowing lines of grace, and womanly gentleness in every movement'.

Henry James, in his essay on Trollope, believed that the older writer's 'genius' as a novelist lay principally in his depiction of the English girl:[33]

> Trollope settled down steadily to the English girl; he took possession of her ... He never made her the subject of heartless satire ... He is evidently always more or less in love with her ... But, as I have said, if he was a lover, he was a paternal lover; as competent as a father who has had fifty daughters. He has presented the British maiden under innumerable names, in every station and in every emergency in life ... Trollope's heroines have a strong family likeness, but it is a wonder how finely he discriminates between them. One feels, as one reads him, like a man with 'sets' of female cousins ... Trollope's girls, for that matter, would make delightful cousins.

Anthony Trollope retained all his life that romantic view that led him as a young clerk to imagine the joys of rescuing some young girl from danger. 'Chivalry' was a real concept to Trollope and he praised it in his books and practised it in his life. To him it was a 'spirit [that] has taught men to endure in order that women may be at their ease; and has generally taught women to accept the ease bestowed on them with grace and thankfulness'. Twenty-five years before Trollope's birth Edmund Burke had proclaimed that 'the age of chivalry is gone. That of sophisters, economists, and calculators, has succeeded; and the glory of Europe is extinguished for ever.'[34] The Victorian age was pre-eminently an age of economists, and indeed of sophisters; yet many gentlemen struggled to maintain into its last decades the older ideals that Burke so praised. For Trollope this meant what Burke called 'a generous loyalty to rank and sex'. In his summation of Lily Dale and her sister Trollope spoke for the Victorian gentleman when he described the two as possessing 'that sense of security which women should receive from an unconscious dependence on their own mingled purity and weakness' [*The Small House at Allington* VI].

Trollope's views are, of course, not fashionable today, and some may argue that he held them in order to have a sense of psychological dominance. This is wrong. He held these views because, at the very base of his being, he was a strong traditionalist, who felt that what he regarded as a God-given arrangement in society provided protection for women against men. Towards the end of his life, while on a visit to Australia, he set out his concept of 'chivalry' in detail:[35]

Women, all the world over, are entitled to everything that chivalry can give them. They should sit while men stand. They should be served while men wait. Men should be silent when they speak. They should be praised, – even without dessert ... All this chivalry should do for women ... But there is a reason for this deference ... A man will serve a woman, will suffer for her, – and if it come to that will die for her, – because she is weaker than he and needs protection. Let her show herself to be as strong, let her prove by her prowess and hardihood that the old idea of comparative weakness has been an error ... and the very idea of chivalry, though it may live for awhile by the strength of custom, must perish and die out of men's hearts.

*

All of these quotations from Trollope's writings originate after his marriage because he published nothing before it. However it is fairly likely that most of these attitudes and interests were present when he met his future wife at Kingstown. It was only in 1842 – the year he met Rose – that he could begin to think of marrying. Several of his novels cope with the difficulties of marrying in the 'middling' ranks of society. For a rich man or the poor man 'with no pretension to rank, or standing', as he explains in *The Eustace Diamonds*, money was not a prime factor in taking the decision.

But between these there is a middle class of men, who, by reason of their education, are peculiarly susceptible to the charms of womanhood, but who literally cannot marry for love, because their earnings will do no more than support themselves [LXXVI].

In his years as a clerk Trollope had been in that unhappy position, but in Ireland he had virtually trebled his income. By the end of the summer in which he met Rose he calculated that he had received a total of £406 8s 1d since coming to Ireland. Once he had subtracted the actual costs of his travels, he was left with £313 4s 2d, which was an excellent income for a young man, particularly in Ireland. When Sir Robert Peel introduced Income Tax that same year he wanted to make sure that it would only apply to those who were comfortably middle-class, so he set the threshold at £400 a year. (For complicated reasons Income Tax did not apply to Ireland, so Trollope was spared this burden.) When thinking about marriage he had to plan for a home not only for his wife and himself but, eventually, for a large family of the type that the Queen and Prince Albert were starting to make fashionable. Money would be needed for the education of any sons, while daughters should be sent forth into the world with a dowry. Of course a Trollope household would require servants. Their wages, particularly in Ireland, might be comparatively small, but board and lodging had also to be provided. He had also to consider that as so many men died young he would have to have life insurance.

Throughout much of his early life Trollope had been forced to make economies. He had accepted this as an unmarried man but, as one of his characters comments, it was another thing to contemplate a threadbare marriage:

> I don't think I should have much enjoyment with a cheap wife. I like cold mutton and candle-ends myself very well, but I do not love feminine economies. Family washing-bills kept at the lowest, a maid-of-all-work ... and a dark morning-gown for household work, would not, if I know myself, add fuel to the ardour of my conjugal affection. I love women dearly; I like them to be near me; but then I like them to be nice. When a woman is nasty, she is very nasty [*The Bertrams* XIV].

However, as with most important questions, Trollope was never totally on one side. Some contemporary critics pointed out that his novels seemed to endorse both caution and carelessness, when considering the prospect of marrying without sufficient security. Though he often shows the disasters that follow too hasty a marriage, particularly when an educated man marries greatly beneath his rank, Trollope most frequently argues that young couples should begin their new life with economies in the early years. One reviewer attacked him for sacrificing *The Small House at Allington* to 'his favourite hobby of the advisableness of young people marrying without being too careful as to their future income'.[36] Yet he believed:

> There was something noble in this courage, in this lack of prudence. It may be a question whether men, in marrying, do not become too prudent. A single man may risk anything, says the world; but a man with a wife should be sure of his means. Why so? A man and his wife are but two units. A man and a woman with ten children are but twelve units. It is sad to see a man starving – sad to see a woman starving – very sad to see children starving. But how often does it come to pass that the man who will work is seen begging his bread? We may almost say never unless, indeed, he be a clergyman. Let the idle man be sure of his wife's bread before he marries her; but the working man, one would say, may generally trust to God's goodness without fear [*The Three Clerks* XXXI].

Trollope always maintained that men and women approached marriage differently. He was, of course, aware that in early Victorian society women had few chances to make decisions about their lives. In one novel from the late 1850s a young gentleman asks a young lady about her 'future'. She replies, with some bitterness: 'It is useless for a woman to think of her future; she can do so little towards planning it, or bringing about her plans' [*The Bertrams* X]. For Trollope, as for most Victorians, women had been designed by a beneficent Providence and a benevolent society for one purpose: marriage. As he told Kate Field, an American feminist to whom he was devoted: 'Go and marry a husband.'[37] In the 1860s, probably stimulated by his long stay in America where there was increasing talk about careers for women, Trollope inserted sermons into most of his books, both fiction and non-fiction, advising girls that marriage

> is a woman's one career – let women rebel against the edict as they may ... women learn the truth early in their lives. And women know it later in life when they think of their girls; and men know it, too when they have to deal with their daughters ... Nature prompts the desire, the world acknowledges its ubiquity, circumstances show that it is reasonable, the whole theory of creation requires it [*The Vicar of Bullhampton* XXXVII].

This is not to say that he was without sympathy for unmarried women. Some of his most memorable creations are genial spinsters, such as Miss Thorne in *Barchester Towers* or the card-playing Miss Todd in *The Bertrams*. In his story, 'The Journey to Panama', he shows an exceptional understanding of the plight of an Irish governess sent out to Panama to marry a virtual stranger. This, like so many of his short stories, was based on fact: he had made friends with just such a young woman on his trip to the West Indies.

One of the main reasons why he urged women to marry was simply because there seemed little else for them to do. Although he normally supported improved education for girls, he disapproved of women's working. Naturally this did not apply to the largest class of women workers: the vast army of servants whose labours made possible the comforts of Victorian society that Trollope enjoyed in his life and celebrated in his writing. He accepted that a lady could, without any disgrace, be a painter or writer, professions which it would have been difficult for Fanny Trollope's son to attack. 'Fortunately for us and for the world at large,' he announces in one story, 'Mrs. Brumby', 'the port of literature is open to women.' It was 'the only really desirable harbour to which a female captain can steer her vessel'. What he objected to was women taking up 'men's work', work which required physical strength. Economic necessity could force a woman to work, such as one Irishwoman who undertook the demanding chores of an ostler – saddling and unharnessing horses at an inn. She was excused because she had no choice but to take over her husband's work when he fell ill. Nevertheless Trollope maintained that 'the sight was disagreeable, and seemed, as far as it went, to degrade the sex'.[38]

This was Trollope's theoretical position and it was characteristic of Victorian thought. Yet in practice he often helped women who had to work. As an editor he gave particular consideration to women writers. He was also a supporter of efforts to improve the conditions of shop girls and of the notable attempt by Emily Faithful to establish a firm of women printers. He even contributed some of his work free to raise money for her cause and, when visiting America, distributed business cards advertising her work. However, he always saw such women as exceptions. He wrote for and about young women whose natural career was to marry.

While Trollope believed that it it was natural for all women, or at least those 'healthy in mind and body', to marry, he disliked the Victorian convention that girls should 'never wish to be wooed' [*The Vicar of Bullhampton* XXXVII]. They should try to attract young men, although it was the man's role to propose marriage. When Trollope attempted to emulate Thackeray by creating a bad woman – Lady Eustace – one of the many wicked things he allowed her to do was to ask a man to marry her. Perhaps this is a distant echo of the country girl's proposal to the young postal clerk? For him this was an inversion of the natural order, and of social custom, and indicated a scheming woman who would set both aside to achieve her goal.

Trollope constantly preached that it was almost as important for most men to marry as it was for women. His novels often feature a young man who needs only a good wife – preferably with a good fortune – to set him on his way to comfortable Victorian prosperity. Bachelors are usually portrayed as wild with money or as living in such disorder that only a wife can introduce moderation and decency into their lives. A bachelor normally is one who has 'no fixed hour for his meals, no fixed place for his books, no fixed wardrobe for his clothes' [*Doctor Thorne* III]. Trollope had felt that his own life needed greater order in those days when he had drawn up plans not only for literary projects but for his own reformation. In Ireland he conducted his business affairs with order but saw that marriage would keep him on that track and allow him to live in a home rather than in the hotel in Banagher where he had stayed since 1841. Marriage would also provide an insight into the world of women that would be essential to a novelist, whose greatness would lie in the depiction of normal life. In *Doctor Thorne* he announces why a country doctor should marry and the words could just as easily apply to a novelist:

Another misfortune was, that he was a bachelor. Ladies think, and I, for
one, think that ladies are quite right in so thinking that doctors should
be married men. All the world feels that a man when he marries acquires
some of the attributes of an old woman – he becomes, to a certain extent,
a motherly sort of being; he acquires a conversance with women's ways
and women's wants, and loses the wilder and offensive sparks of his
virility [III].

Often Trollope used his novels to poke fun at 'rights of women'
advocates: sometimes they were real people such as John Stuart Mill
and sometimes fictional creations such as Baroness Banmann, the
feminist lecturer in *Is He Popenjoy?*, whose ideas spout forth from a
mouth adorned with a 'considerable moustache'. Yet he was never an
admirer of unrestrained male dominance. His novels show how women
exercise power through their husbands: this can be done subtly by the
Duchess of Omnium on her husband, the Prime Minister, or by Mrs
Grantly's admonishing the Archdeacon in the privacy of their bed-
chamber. To Trollope this is good, and in fact almost every admirable
male character is considerably under the influence of some woman.
The social fabric is only endangered if a woman attempts the open
domination of her husband. Trollope created perhaps the most famous
example of this in English literature: the immortal Mrs Proudie who
rules the diocese of Barchester through her weak-willed spouse.
Throughout his writings Trollope makes it clear that the unrestricted
rule of either woman or man in marriage can lead to disaster. In his
last complete novel, written after almost forty years of a happy
marriage, he describes an elderly housekeeper addressing her old
master, who is contemplating marriage with his ward. Mrs Baggett,
herself the victim of a miserable drunken husband, advises her
employer to force his will on the girl: 'If a man is master, he should be
master ... I never knew no good come of one of them soft-going fellows
who is minded to give up whenever a woman wants anything. What's a
woman? It ain't natural that she should have her way; and she don't
like a man a bit better in the long-run because he lets her.' Having
listened to this homely sermon, Mr Whittlestaff (a character who
resembles Trollope in many ways) takes a volume of Horace and
wanders off to muse on these notions. He arrives, quite characteristically, at a moderate view blending classical wisdom with Christian
truth:

After all, was not Mrs Baggett's teaching a damnable philosophy? Let the
man be the master, and let him get everything he can for himself ... he
told himself that no teaching was more damnable. Of course it was the

teaching by which the world was kept going in its present course ... Did
the lessons of Mrs Baggett run smoothly with those of Jesus Christ? [*An
Old Man's Love* XVI].

Marriage was to Trollope a partnership with each partner having
specified rights and duties. 'Fear acknowledges a superior,' he
maintained, whereas 'love desires an equal' [*The Duke's Children* XXI].
Yet he admitted there had to be a leader: 'the stronger ... takes the
lead, whether clothed in petticoats, or in a coat, waistcoat, and
trousers' [*The Belton Estate* XI]. It was unrestricted dominance – like
any other unrestrained power – that was the evil. Dominance, to
Trollope, was often united with jealousy, and some of his most
powerful novels portray the danger of what can happen to a marriage
when one partner begins to entertain petty jealousy of the other.
Sometimes it is merely annoying, as in *Orley Farm* when Mrs Furnival
supects that her husband's devotion to the interests of a beautiful
titled client surpasses that normally expected of a barrister. In other
novels, such as *Phineas Finn, Phineas Redux* and *He Knew He Was
Right*, Trollope portrays powerfully how two men sink into insanity
through jealousy of their wives. Indeed jealousy, particularly in its
most virulent forms, is normally a male vice – at least in the world of
Trollope's novels.

*

It is relatively easy to discover Trollope's views about women or
marriage, for when he held a view he inserted it into his books. It is
virtually impossible, however, to discover much about the woman he
married. At times an invisible censor seems to hover over every effort.
In the 1920s, for example, a minor figure from the Victorian literary
world gave some manuscripts to the Bodleian Library, even including
two of Trollope's cancelled cheques. The donor told Bodley's Librarian
that Rose Trollope 'was a dear friend of mine, and I have a packet of
her letters ... but hers would not find a place in a collection of course'.[39]
Few letters from Rose have survived in other collections and relatively
few even of Anthony's letters to her. The fact that Rose's widowhood
was so long – she survived her husband by well over thirty years – may
well have prevented contemporary writers, such as Trollope's first
biographer, from making any comment about her.
    A close examination of Trollope's surviving letters, his non-fictional
writings and what few reminiscences there are, allows a portrait of
Rose Heseltine Trollope to emerge from the shadows. We may assume

that it was her womanly charms and not her physical beauty which won Trollope's heart. Although little is known of her appearance as a girl, the few later photographs do not reveal a woman of outstanding beauty. A granddaughter remembered her as being relatively short; someone else recalled that her 'beautiful feet made a great impression on me'.[40] One suspects – or at least hopes – that she had green eyes, for her husband writes in one novel: 'How few there are among women, few perhaps among men, who know that the softest, tenderest, truest eyes which a woman can carry in her head are green in colour!' [*The Eustace Diamonds* II].

Rose seems to have had a flair for dressing well and took great delight in clothes and in shopping. When her husband's income became quite substantial she indulged in some luxuries, such as a special Eau de Cologne from Paris. This is not to imply that she became a spendthrift, for she appears to have been an excellent housekeeper and a thrifty one, doing such things as saving reusable envelopes. Rose had a great talent for sewing and one of her embroideries won a prize at the Great Exhibition in 1851. She was an omnivorous reader; even in her nineties she got through several books a week. She had a considerable interest in contemporary literature and, fortunately, shared some of her husband's opinions about books: both had a fierce devotion to Thackeray and considered *Henry Esmond* the greatest novel in the language. Indeed her only known annoying trait – at least to Trollope's biographers – is that she liked to cut off the signatures of famous figures, such as Thackeray or Longfellow, at the bottom of letters which, no doubt, led to the loss of many letters that could have shown more about the Trollopes. Another taste she shared with her husband was gardening, which went well with her concern for good food. Her gardens were devoted to vegetables and fruit as much as to flowers – she was particularly fond of roses. Food was important, for her husband had strong views on it as on most other things. When she was entertained by a publisher, her main concern was to get a recipe. She, in her turn, was a good hostess when prosperity allowed the Trollopes to fill their house with guests.

Rose evidently had considerable physical strength: any wife of Anthony Trollope would have required that. She was no Victorian invalid confined to her couch. She accompanied him on many of his travels, including one in the 1870s when they went round the world. Like her husband, she enjoyed riding and she certainly did not resent, at least unduly, his addiction to fox-hunting. When she was over forty she climbed a mountain in America, probably impelled to do so after being told that it could only be done by a young woman. She enjoyed accompanying Trollope on numerous European visits, though she insisted on sleeping for at least one night out of every four in a bed. She did not protest when postal duties called her husband away on long trips and sometimes travelled with her own friends while he remained in England or went off on travels of his own.

Like Anthony, Rose appears to have been moderately religious (having conformed to the Church of England) and was certainly kindly. When one of Rose's sisters died the Trollopes adopted one child who in time became a virtual daughter. They also gave a home to two of Anthony's nieces in times of family distress. Rose seems to have been an excellent mother and wife. She did not have that vice that Trollope so detested, jealousy, and she did not mind his friendship with young women such as Kate Field. Trollope was deeply devoted to Rose and there can be no doubt that his salutation to her in letters, 'Dearest Love', represented his true feelings. He respected her domain and was careful to obey her rules: he confined his cigars to the garden and did not do his writing in the drawing-room. As he believed that such domestic order came from marriage, he was happy to obey its dictates. In one novel he describes the rooms of an unmarried clergyman, who 'had fallen into that terrible habit which prevails among bachelors, of allowing his work to remain ever open, never finished, always confused, – with papers above books, and books above papers, – looking as though no useful product could ever be made to come forth from such chaotic elements' [*The Claverings* XXXIV].

The domestic order that Rose embodied allowed her husband to produce novels at incredible speed. Part of this order was based on the Victorian concept that even in a close and happy marriage both parties were entitled to privacy, to their own 'space'. Trollope makes a revealing correction in a passage in his book on America: 'There is no spot on the earth's surface so dear to me as my own drawing-room, or rather my wife's drawing-room at home.' This was even the case in less public rooms. When Archdeacon Grantly and his wife are dressing or undressing, he is in his dressing-room adjoining their bedroom but his wife has the privacy of that room for herself. This appears to have been the case in the Trollope household: when reading a poem by the Earl of Lytton, Trollope added a marginal note which he assumed would never see the light of day. The poem describes a lady undressing after a ball. Trollope disagreed with Lytton and noted: 'I rather think,' which by his use of language is more an admission of ignorance than an opinion – 'that my wife takes off her diamond stars before she takes off her dress'.[41] Once the Trollopes were prosperous – and quite prosperous they were if Rose could adorn herself with diamond stars – Victorian

convention allowed each to have private friends and even to go to
dinner parties separately. Trollope eventually became a devoted
clubman, where of course Rose could not go. She tried a woman's club
but found it rather pointless. She preferred to entertain her friends
and family at home or by paying the carefully regulated 'calls' that
were governed by complicated social rules.

*

Most of Trollope's attitudes towards women and marriage, crucial as
they are to any understanding of his works, were refined over the next
four decades. In 1842 Anthony and Rose were concerned with deciding
when to marry: in the event it would be 1844 before they could do so.
The two years allowed him to save money as well as to pay off debts,
such as the money he had borrowed to buy a good horse for hunting.
One cause of the delay may have been that Rose's father was about to
marry again. Two marriages in succession in the Heseltine family
might have given rise to too much expense. It is unlikely that Rose's
father was able to do much to help the young couple; all that Trollope
says in his *Autobiography* is that Rose 'had no fortune'. It was not, in
many ways, a 'good match' for a young gentleman who numbered
baronets and clergymen among his ancestors. In 'The Two Heroines of
Plumplington' the rather feeble plot centres on the marriage of a
provincial bank manager's daughter. 'To be manager of the Bank,'
thinks the heroine, 'was not very much in the eyes of the world.'
However, Trollope concludes in his narration: 'The one great line of
demarcation in the world was that which separated gentlemen from
non-gentlemen. Mr Greenmantle [the bank manager] assured himself
that he was a gentleman ... There could be no doubt that he was on the
right side of the line of demarcation.' Heseltine's right to be a
gentleman was recognised in the published report of his evidence
about drainage and sanitation in Rotherham: other witnesses such as
the surgeon and surveyor are listed as 'Mr,' but the bank manager is
'Edward John Heseltine, Esq.' If a man can maintain his status when
describing the sewage floating in his cellar, he must indeed have been
a 'gentleman'. Anthony Trollope could, at least, maintain that his
father-in-law was one, although in a few years he would be revealed to
be an embezzler!

By the spring of 1844 Trollope was ready to marry. At twenty-nine
he was three years over the average age at which men married as
shown in the 1851 Census. The three extra years did not bother him as
much as the difficulty of getting extra leave. When, several decades

later, he wrote in a short story of a young girl asking for time off to get married, he must have recalled his own experience. Hers, says Trollope, was 'a plea against which the official rigour cannot prevail. I remember once when a young man applied to a saturnine pundit ... for leave of absence for a month to get married. "To get married! ... Poor fellow! But you must have the leave".' Armed with his leave, Trollope took the ferry and made his way to Rotherham, part of that industrial England which is virtually ignored in his writing. A handbook for travellers, published about the time of Rose's birth, noted that Rotherham 'is by no means a handsome town, but contains a spacious and rather elegant parish church, of Gothic architecture'. It was in that parish church of All Saints that Anthony Trollope and Rose Heseltine were married on 11 June 1844. 'Perhaps,' Trollope said, 'I ought to name that happy day as the commencement of my better life.' The *Sheffield and Rotherham Independent* listed their wedding along with eighteen others that week and gave the occupation or rank of fifteen: nail-maker, shoe-maker, cutler, coachman, woodman, file-smith, merchant, farmer, fishmonger and gentleman. Trollope's position in the Post Office is not mentioned. Instead the announcement reads: 'On Tuesday last, at the Parish Church, Rotherham, Mr Anthony Trollope, son of the celebrated authoress, Mrs Trollope, to Rose, fourth daughter of Mr Heseltine, one of the Managers of Sheffield and Rotherham Bank.' Trollope's view, present in almost all of his novels, that marriage is more important for a woman than for a man, is nicely illustrated by the fact that while he scrawled the one word 'Married' across a page of his Travelling Journals, Rose later wrote in her chronology which she prepared to assist him with his *Autobiography*: 'Married 11th June (Hurrah.)' Yet whatever he might say in his novels, his own life shows that marriage is of equal importance to man and woman. As *The Times* commented three-quarters of a century later, when Rose died, 'The marriage, it can truly be said, had an important effect on English letters.'[42] In one novel, written when Trollope was on his first long absence from Rose, a young couple agree to be married on 11 June. The novelist adds, in what surely was a private message for his wife: 'Let us trust that the day may always be regarded as propitious' [*The Bertrams* XLIV]. For him it was 'propitious'. 'No social question has been so important to us as that of the great bond of matrimony,' he said in a lecture on English novels. 'And why? Because every most wholesome joy and most precious duty of our existence depends upon our inner family relations.' Some might say that such public sentiments mean nothing. They may think so; Trollope did not. After the lecture he inscribed a copy for his wife: 'Rose Trollope from her obedient slave, The Lecturer.'[43]

It was a formidable experience for the new Mrs Anthony Trollope to spend much of the honeymoon with her mother-in-law. The name of 'the celebrated authoress' must have been long familiar to such a determined reader as Rose. The house must have seemed like one of the Lake District's first writers' conferences. Her mother-in-law was hard at work on yet another novel, having already completed seventeen in the dozen years since her first great literary success. Rose's sister-in-law, Cecilia Tilley, was working on her High Church novel; Tom was full of new plans for books and her husband had managed to complete one volume of his first novel, *The Macdermots*.

Almost fifty years later, when all these Trollopes were dead, Rose recalled the visit in reminiscences she contributed to a biography of her mother-in-law:[44]

> There was no one more eager to suggest, and carry out the suggestion, as to mountain excursions, picnics, and so forth. And she was always the life and soul of the party with her cheerful conversation and her wit. She rose very early and made her own tea, the fire having been prepared over night – (on one occasion I remember her bringing me a cup of tea to my room, because she thought I had caught cold during a wet walk in the mountains) – then sat at her writing-table until the allotted task of so many pages was completed; and was usually on the lawn before the family breakfast-bell rang, having filled her basket with cuttings from the rose-bushes for the table and drawing-room decorations.

This experience was a useful one for the young wife: within a few years, she would see her husband following the same ways. Rose evidently got on well with her mother-in-law. Fanny Trollope was pleased that her son had found a wife who read so much, and one of her main concerns was that Rose take back a 'a good package' of library books 'to comfort you in your retreat' in Ireland. Within a few weeks Fanny Trollope was signing her letters to her first daughter-in-law, 'Your affectionate friend and mother'.[45]

*

When Trollope's leave ended, he took his new wife back to Banagher. Her arrival was somewhat marred when the driver of their cart drove them into the river Shannon, an event Rose remembered years later when helping Anthony in writing his *Autobiography*. Before his marriage he had requested transfer to the Northern District. One reason may have been that some local friends apparently felt he had 'behaved badly' to Ireland by not marrying an Irish girl. It is also likely that he was frustrated after three years in the same post. Because his Surveyor was not an active man, Trollope was carrying almost all the duties of the district but not receiving adequate recognition. He would have felt this all the more after seeing his brother-in-law, John Tilley, although only a few years his senior in the Post Office, had a Surveyor's salary well over twice his own. Fanny Trollope sympathised with her new daughter-in-law's dilemma: 'This delay is *very* vexatious and must be very vexatious to you – for suspense is always more tormenting than any certainty.' His original request was turned down when someone with seniority was appointed. However, within a few weeks news arrived that Anthony had been appointed Head Clerk or Assistant Surveyor in the Southern District.[46]

He took up his appointment in Cork in September 1844, but it was March, a few weeks before his thirtieth birthday, before he and Rose could rent part of a house in Clonmel in County Tipperary. The house, located on the High Street, was historic, as Cromwell had stopped in it after capturing Clonmel in 1650: luckily the town had been spared the butchery that often followed that godly tyrant. In *The Bertrams* – the novel in which Trollope revealed so much of his thoughts about marriage – he draws on his own experience to offer advice to his younger readers:

> To neither man nor woman does the world fairly begin till seated together in their first mutual home they bethink themselves that the excitement of their honeymoon is over. It would seem the full meaning of the word marriage can never be known by those who, at their first outspring into life, are surrounded by all that money can give. It requires the single sitting-room, the single fire, the necessary little efforts of self-devotion, the inward declaration that some struggle shall be made for that other one ... Ah, my friends, do not count too exactly your three hundreds a year – your four hundreds [XXX].

It is interesting that Trollope should chose his own income at the time he set up his first house. In his *Autobiography* he wrote that many might think that he and Rose 'were two fools to encounter such poverty together' but 'since that day I have never been without money in my pocket'. Trollope's 'poverty' should be contrasted with that of rural letter-carriers in Ireland who had five shillings a week; but then poverty, like so many things, is in the imagination of the beholder.

*

During these years at Clonmel Trollope became the father of two sons. On 13 March 1846 Rose gave birth to a boy, whose health may well have been delicate, as he was baptised privately, eleven days afer his birth, as Henry Merivale. His godparents were his grandmother, Fanny, his uncle, Tom, and John Merivale. In their choice of names the parents paid a tribute to this old friend, as well as to Anthony's dead brother, Henry. A year and a half later, on 27 September 1847, a second son, Frederic James Anthony, was born. He was baptised at the Church of Ireland parish church of St Mary on 17 November 1847. His godparents were Rose's sister, Isabella, and Anthony's brother-in-law, John Tilley. The third was James Kendrick, the District Surveyor and Trollope's immediate superior, which indicates that once again Anthony was making a good impression. Almost half a century later Henry told his Uncle Tom that his parents took the opportunity of Fred's baptism to have Henry publicly 'received into the Church' which Tom thought somewhat odd. It is a clear indication of how seriously Rose and Anthony Trollope took their religion.[47]

Of Trollope's early years of fatherhood little is known. Babies and children occupy scant space in his novels. He occasionally poked mild fun at 'Baby Worship', as a pleasure mainly confined to women (*Barchester Towers* XVI). Yet undoubtedly he gathered information of use to a novelist: 'The baby was really delightful; he took his food with a will, stuck out his toes merrily whenever his legs were uncovered, and did not have fits. These are supposed to be the strongest points of baby perfection' [*Barchester Towers* II]. As with any parent, there were crises that must have been upsetting for a man who had seen so many of his brothers and sisters die. Young Harry had a serious illness in March 1848 but recovered. Trollope endorsed the Victorian dictum that children should not dominate their parents' lives. When he followed his mother's example in writing a book of American travels one of his relatively few criticisms was the unrestricted freedom children had there. As one of those men who are uneasy with the 'uncontrolled energy' of the small child, he was disturbed that American children had 'full dominion over all hours and over all places' and were never 'banished, snubbed, and kept in the background as children are kept with us'. He believed that children were much happier when their early lives were carefully ordered: being in bed by six and being fed on a wholesome diet of bread and milk. To us, Victorian family life seems, either for good or ill, to have been a highly regulated existence. Yet for Victorians of Trollope's generation, who naturally looked back on their own childhood, it appeared the opposite. In a lecture he gave as he was approaching fifty, he said: 'It has become a fashion in these days, – a very pleasant fashion it is – to banish from our houses altogether a certain sternness of demeanour, a certain parental severity, both of manner and of action, which even half a century ago used to prevail in our families.'[48]

Trollope enjoyed a close and affectionate relationship with his sons, something he had never known with his own austere father. As they grew up, he was anxious not only that they be well educated and well read but that they learn to ride and to follow the hounds with his own enthusiasm. He made considerable financial sacrifices to establish both sons in some profitable way of life. Trollope never followed the practice of favouring 'Harry', as the elder son, over 'Fred'. He had criticised this practice in novels and probably had resented it in the days of his youth at Harrow. Some have claimed that Trollope's family had little influence on his writing. The opposite is the case. His travel book and several novels on Australia grew directly out of the fact that his younger son settled there. If we take a relatively minor novel, *Sir Harry Hotspur of Humblethwaite*, written in the late 1860s, we can see how family events worked their way into his fiction. In this novel he shows familiarity with the way a young man purchased a cavalry commission. This is hardly surprising, because his elder son had recently become a cornet in a regiment of mounted yeomanry. Towards the end of the novel there is a discourse on how the love of children for their parents does not equal that of parents for their children:

> The hold of a child upon the father is so much stronger than that of the father on the child! Our eyes are set in our face, and are always turned forward. The glances that we cast back are but occasional [XVI].

When he wrote this his younger son had just returned from Australia to tell his parents that he planned to settle permanently in New South Wales. Again, one cannot help but think that Rose Trollope, who was so adept with the needle, did not inspire this simile used in connection with a young girl who is contemplating the character of her roguish lover: 'Poor Emily Hotspur had not yet learned the housewife's trick of passing the web through her fingers, and of finding by the touch whether the fabric were of fine wool, or of shoddy made up with craft to look like wool of the finest' [II].

It was not only in remarks about sewing that Rose Trollope inspired her husband's novels. From her he learned to understand women and marriage. In his first book the female characters are rather lifeless, and no major character enters into marriage: a rare lack in Trollope's forty-seven novels. It is no accident that his ability to write novels at such an amazing rate begins with his marriage. He had only finished the first volume of *The Macdermots* at the time of his wedding; it took him less than a year after his return from his honeymoon to complete it. That was in the midst of moving to a new position and searching for a house. For almost forty years Rose Trollope provided the most important support in his life as a writer. It was Rose who often wrote a clear copy of his manuscripts for publishers. When he was travelling abroad on postal business she was given permission to change words in his writings. Nor was she ever loath to criticise. He told one publisher, when sending him a story, that Rose had found it 'ill-natured'. Often she found fault with his penchant for silly names. When he later edited a magazine she sometimes assisted him by reading manuscripts and even deciding whether to accept or reject them. Years later he advised Henry, who was working on a book, to seek his mother's opinion. 'I should take mamma's advice ... for she is never mistaken about a book being good or bad.' Trollope frequently inserted little private jokes into his novels for Rose's amusement: his most celebrated comic episode in *Barchester Towers*, as will be seen, contains a private joke about a piece of jewellery belonging to his wife. Those who enjoy his novels have good cause to be grateful to Rose Trollope: as Julian Hawthorne, the son of the famous American novelist, said after meeting the two Trollopes: 'His wife was his books.'[49]

By the mid-1840s Anthony Trollope, seated in his house at Clonmel, had reason to be content. When he had landed in Ireland in 1841 he had been a lonely and unsuccessful clerk. Within a few years he had achieved the respect of his superiors and was recognised as one of the best civil servants in the Post Office. In exercising authority over Irish postmasters he had at last gained self-respect and the discipline necessary to fulfil his literary dreams. In the green fields of Ireland he had found excitement and social acceptance by discovering his passionate devotion to fox-hunting. In Rose Heseltine he had found a perfect companion and wife, and in his two young sons he had found a secure family life. All he now needed was to find a publisher for his first book, so that he could enter the fascinating world of Victorian fiction.

CHAPTER FIVE

A Novel-reading People

'This is the golden age for popular writers,' proclaimed one of the numerous literary journals of the Victorian era. By 'popular writers' the *Literary Gazette* meant the novelists, whose works were spreading to all corners of 'the English world'. By the late 1850s the *Saturday Review* was castigating Victorians for their pursuit of novels for 'mere amusement': 'We are all of us drowned in business on the one hand, and in amusement on the other ... We take more trouble about idling than most nations do about working.' Novels did much more than amuse Victorians: they helped them to fashion their image of their world. Since then, they have had an even greater effect in fashioning the views of later generations about that splendid era, whose shadow still lies across our own. Just as it is impossible to think of Elizabethan England without drawing on Shakespeare, so it is impossible to imagine Victorian England without recalling some novel of the period. The Victorians knew that novels played an important role in their culture. 'We have become a novel-reading people,' Trollope claimed in a lecture in 1870, 'from the Prime Minister down to the last-appointed scullery-maid ... Poetry also we read and history, biography and the social and political news of the day. But all our other reading put together hardly amounts to what we read in novels.'[1] The seemingly endless stream of fiction – novels alone were selling over a million copies a year by the late 1850s – was designed to meet the taste and demands of the age. The procedures that governed the production of novels were almost all in place when Trollope completed his first book. He eventually became a 'popular writer' because he understood the desires of readers as well as the business of publishing. Although he did not reach this happy state until he had written several books, anyone interested in his life needs to know how the Victorians wrote, published, obtained and read fiction. Before we can follow Trollope the novelist we need to know the world of the Victorian novel.

'A remarkable novel is a great event for English society,' declared the *Quarterly Review* when *Vanity Fair* and *Jane Eyre* first appeared. These two classics came forth within a few months of Trollope's first novel, *The Macdermots of Ballycloran*. The *Quarterly* argued that a popular novel filled a deep-seated need in the English character:

> It is a kind of common friend, about whom people can speak the truth without fear of being compromised, and confess their emotions without fear of being ashamed. We are a particularly shy and reserved people, and set about nothing so awkwardly as the simple art of getting really acquainted with each other ... For this purpose a host of devices have been contrived by which all forms of friendship may be gone through, without committing ourselves to one spark of the spirit ... Our various fashionable manias, for charity one season, for science the next, are only so many clever contrivances for keeping our neighbour at arm's length. But there are ways and means of lifting the veil which equally favour our national idiosyncrasy; and a new and remarkable novel is one of them – especially the nearer it comes to real life ... We simply discuss Becky Sharp, or Jane Eyre, and our object is answered at once.

Within a few years Trollope would be adding characters whose names became as well known as the two immortal governesses Jane Eyre and Becky Sharp. As he later admitted to his friend and publisher, John Blackwood, as a novelist he depended 'more on character than on incident for his interest'.[2] His success would be based on the ability to fill that need in the collective unconscious of his countrymen.

Trollope spent almost forty years, from 1843 to 1882, writing forty-seven novels. Naturally they changed as his life and times changed; yet there are certain aspects of fiction writing that pertained throughout. It is helpful to know why and how authors wrote before looking at how Trollope managed to produce so many books in the course of a full and varied life.

*

It was hardly a profound understanding of the Englishman's psychological need for fiction to promote conversation that drove authors to their desks. Trollope, in his book on Thackeray, explained why so many Victorians turned to writing: 'It is a business which has its allurements. It requires no capital, no special education, no training and may be taken up at any time without a moment's delay. If a man can command a table, a chair, pen, paper, and ink, he can commence his trade as a literary man. It is thus that aspirants generally do commence it.' To admit such a 'business' motive is a ghastly fault in the eyes of some critics. Yet he was only revealing the reason which drove many Victorian men, and even more frequently women, to write fiction. As Mrs Oliphant wrote to the husband of another woman novelist, Mrs Craik: 'Men have such a huge advantage over us, that they have generally something besides their writing to fall back upon for mere bread and butter.'[3] Trollope's mother was a good example of a woman who earned her bread and butter or at least her Florentine villa from writing. Others, such as the Brontës, were driven by a desire to hint in fiction at feelings that their society and their isolation did not allow them to express in reality. There were, of course, many Victorian writers who wrote novels as propaganda. Some used their fiction to support a particular religious goal: Trollope's sister Cecilia wrote her novel *Chollerton* to propagate High Church ideals. Generally speaking the great Victorian novels – those that have survived their own time and its particular *mores* and are thus acclaimed as classics – were written by authors who were motivated to a considerable extent by the desire for money. None may have proclaimed this as vociferously as Anthony Trollope, but Charles Dickens, William Thackeray and George Eliot agreed with him.

Yet most authors accepted that the novel had a moral purpose as well. Novelists were well aware that young people were one of the largest segments of their audience. Trollope, in particular, emphasised this:[4]

> The bulk of the young people in the upper and middle classes receive their moral teaching chiefly from the novels they read ... The novelist creeps in closer than the schoolmaster, closer than the father, closer almost than the mother. He is the chosen guide, the tutor whom the young pupil choses for herself. She retires with him, suspecting no lesson, safe against rebuke, throwing herself head and heart into the narration ... and there she is taught, – how she shall learn to love ... It is the same with the young man, though he would be more prone even than she to reject the suspicion of such tutorship.

Trollope did not confine such remarks to articles or lectures about the novel. He frequently informs readers of his novels that his story is conveying a moral message. In *Ralph the Heir*, he tells them in the last few pages that:

> The reader of a novel, – who has doubtless taken the volume up simply for amusement, and who would probably lay it down did he suspect that instruction, like a snake in the grass, like physic beneath the sugar, was to be imposed upon him, – requires from his author chiefly this, that he shall be amused by a narrative in which elevated sentiment prevails, and

gratified by being made to feel that the elevated sentiments described
are exactly his own ... It is the test of a novel writer's art that he conceals
his snake-in-the-grass; but the reader may be sure that it is always
there. No man or woman with a conscience, – no man or woman with
intellect sufficient to produce amusement, can go on from year to year
spinning stories without the desire of teaching; with no ambition of
influencing readers for their good. Gentle readers, the physic is always
beneath the sugar, hidden or unhidden. In writing novels we novelists
preach to you from our pulpits ... [LVI].

He frequently drew a parallel between the sermon and the novel, and
for Trollope both were meant to make people good. Within every one of
his forty-seven novels there is a moral message and normally quite a
few lurk beneath the sugar-coating of this master confectioner.[5]

*

It was the use of the novel as a sugar-coated messenger service that
lifted it into the ranks of respectable literature. In the year of
Trollope's birth, Sir Walter Scott said that few people admitted to
reading 'these frivolous studies'. 'A novel', he added, 'is frequently
"bread eaten in secret".' Sixty years later Trollope paid tribute to
Scott's own role in changing attitudes:

> I could well remember that, in my own young days, they had not taken
> that undisputed possession of drawing-rooms which they now hold ...
> When George IV was king ... the families in which an unrestricted
> permission was given for the reading of novels were very few, and from
> many they were altogether banished. The high poetic genius and correct
> morality of Walter Scott had not altogether succeeded in making men
> and women understand that lessons which were good in poetry could not
> be bad in prose.

Despite the popularity of fiction in Victorian England there lurked
many narrow-minded puritans anxious, as ever, to suppress what they
could neither understand nor enjoy. When Charles Kingsley began to
combine the role of priest and novelist an outraged friend was horrified
at a clergyman's writing 'decorated lies'.[6]

One of the young Victoria's early acts on becoming Queen was to
read Scott's *The Bride of Lammermoor*.[7] Under the strict supervision
of her mother she had been shielded, like many young people, from the
beguiling excitements of fiction. For the rest of her reign she and her
subjects enjoyed the works of an extraordinary generation of superb
novelists. Charles Dickens, born three years before Trollope, gained

enormous success with his first novel, *The Pickwick Papers*, which began to appear in parts in 1836, when he was twenty-four. W.M. Thackeray, born in 1811, did not achieve fame until the 1840s. Charlotte Brontë was a year younger than Trollope, as she was born in 1816. Another great woman writer – Trollope would have said the greatest of all – George Eliot, was born in 1819: her celebrity as a novelist dated from the late 1850s. When Trollope's name was heard in that same decade, he was seen as a valued addition to this gathering. Among the other acclaimed novelists of the time – Benjamin Disraeli, Mrs Gaskell, Wilkie Collins, George Meredith, Mrs Oliphant and Charles Kingsley – all, except for Disraeli (born in 1804), had been born between 1810 and 1828.

These writers succeeded because they knew the type of readers they needed for success and because they mastered the skills required to reach them. They have endured beyond their own time because they managed, each in a different way, to say something of universal interest. Trollope and his contemporaries came to exert such influence on their age that the politician Spencer Walpole wrote in his *History of England*:

> It might be said of the present age that the power of controlling thought is passing ... to the novel-writer. Political speeches are studied by some; sermons are avoided by many; history has only a few students; but every one reads novels. The novel influences for good or for evil the thoughts of its readers: the thoughts of its readers may ultimately determine the government of the world.

Like the Queen, whose era they embodied, novelists could only succeed if they too approached their work with the vow: 'I will be good.'[8]

*

Trollope needed no external pressures to make him see the novel in this moralistic light. Yet if he was tempted to wander outside fictional rectitude there were two powerful buttresses which reinforced the walls of Victorian morality. The first was the widespread popularity of reading aloud. The nineteenth century saw a tremendous increase in the population combined with a remarkable distribution of the new prosperity among the expanding middle classes. In addition there was a continual growth in leisure time, as well as such material improvements as better lighting, which extended the hours when people could see beyond the time when they had to work. For respectable families who would never frequent public houses or could not move 'in Society', entertainment was provided in the home. These hours were increasingly filled by reading aloud.

Countless generations had listened to someone reading, but in the past the emphasis had been on religious books. The Victorians certainly did not abandon religious reading; many households heard a sermon read aloud every Sunday and more books were published on religion than on any other topic. The *London Catalogue* shows that of the 45,000 books published from 1816 to 1851 – that is, in the first half of Trollope's life – 10,300 were on religious topics and 3,500 were works of fiction. The growth in the size and number of newspapers provided yet more print to be read aloud. Florence Nightingale has left a delightful account of her reactions to her father's daily practice of reading the entire issue of *The Times* to his two daughters: 'To be read aloud to is the most miserable exercise of the human intellect ... It is like lying on one's back, with one's hands tied, and having liquid poured down one's throat.'[9]

As in so many other things, Florence Nightingale was the exception to the rule of Victorian ladies. For the most part they saw it as their duty to listen to Papa's readings or, as the years wore on, to read to the dear *paterfamilias*. Throughout the country families gathered by their coal fires to listen as someone read aloud. There could sometimes be mild difficulties: thus even the saintly John Keble, who read novels to the ladies at his vicarage, was suspected of secretly reading ahead to discover the outcome before his listeners. Reading aloud could cause embarrassment, as one teenage girl recorded in her diary, after reading to her eighty-four-year-old grandfather. Things had gone quite well as the elderly gentleman slumbered through four volumes of an edifying history recounting how a Quaker banking family went about the godly business of amassing a fortune. Then the grand-daughter, looking for something lighter, picked up John Evelyn's diary of life in Restoration England:[10]

> It is very awkward sometimes in the middle of a sentence, or description, to stop short, stammer, leave off and go on in quite another place ... Old books always are improper. People were coarse then and therefore what they wrote was too. Horrid people ... that is is not a fit book for us to read.

Fortunately this young lady and so many other Victorians had the perfect solution to avoid the boredom of newspapers or the shock of books from racier times. There was a seemingly unending stream of novels from Anthony Trollope and his contemporaries to cheer one through lengthy evenings. In every type of Victorian household includ-ing the Queen's – she read *Barchester Towers* to Prince Albert – the latest novel resounded among the antimacassars of drawing-rooms and the Staffordshire pottery dogs of cottage firesides. For the last time in England there was a common contemporary literature that appealed to all sorts of people.

Trollope himself had known family evenings spent listening to his father reading from eighteenth-century novels. His brother remem-bered Hervieu drawing an amusing caricature, while dreary old Mr Trollope droned on.[11] Half a century later Rose Trollope – no doubt with some form of embroidery in her skilful hands – sat with her niece, listening to the elderly novelist as he read aloud in their comfortable London town house. Yet Trollope also enjoyed listening to someone else reading novels aloud. Indeed it was after a convivial dinner in 1882 while someone was reading from a humorous novel that he suffered his fatal stroke.

Because Victorian novelists were conscious that their works were read aloud in mixed company they were wary of using incidents or words that could bring a blush to innocent maidens of either sex. Trollope read his dialogue aloud – at least to himself and, one suspects, to Rose – and this no doubt helped his superb accuracy in catching the nuances of speech. He would also have known that in an age when many people delighted in amateaur theatricals, good dialogue allowed a skilful reader to portray the different characters. Reading aloud enabled the listener, at least those who were awake, to enter into the story, as it unfolded in all its leisurely complications and sub-plots. The characters came alive as the sympathetic listener unconsciously became a parti-cipant. One of the best descriptions of this effect comes from one of Trollope's greatest admirers, the poet Edward FitzGerald. He had abandoned that fashionable world which Trollope drew so well, and in his draughty Suffolk cottage forgot the intricacies of Omar Khayyam's verse to listen to a local boy whom he paid to read to him:[12]

This is Sunday night: 10PM. And what is the Evening Service which I have been listening to? The 'Eustace Diamonds' ... I really give the best proof I can of the interest I take in Trollope's Novels, by constantly breaking out into Argument with the Reader (who never replies) about what is said and done by People in the several Novels. I say 'No, no! She must have known she was lying!'

*

The other buttress shoring up the sensibilities of the reading public was the power of subscription libraries, the most famous of which was established by Charles Mudie in 1842. The Victorian ditty,

> As children must have Punch and Judy,
> So I can't do without my Mudie

summed up its position without exaggeration. Although it is a comparison that would have annoyed Trollope, Mudie has rightly been called 'literature's Rowland Hill'. Subscription libraries were not a Victorian invention, as Sheridan's gentle jibe at one in *The Rivals* shows. The Fenimore Cooper novel that the young Trollope read over and over again in the 1820s was 'a dishonest relic' from a subscription library, which allowed his mother to keep up with the latest fiction. It was the Victorian achievement, in this as in so many things, to extend these libraries throughout the expanding reading public. A French journalist who visited England in the last years of Trollope's life saw this widespread distribution of literature as the key to British predominance. For him the circulating library was 'the great pumping engine' of this restless advance:

> There is nothing more curious and characteristic than the spectacle ... about four or five o'clock in the afternoon, at Mudie's Library in Oxford Street – the principal market for the books whereon everyone is nourished. Not only do we see young and pretty girls, and ladies of all ages, but ... servants of all degrees, arriving or leaving with packets of books under their arms. Horses are champing their bits and rattling their harness; carriages and broughams are filled with visitors ... Entering into a vast hall we perceive a row of extensive counters ... The order is given through a tube, and in two or three minutes the desired volumes arrive from the depths of underground cellars ... The subscription is relatively dear ... but this sum figures regularly in the family budget; it is the intellectual tax, the voluntary contribution paid by the head of the family, that his household may participate in the literary life of the country.

The Frenchman particularly stressed how Mudie ensured that the novel remained pure as it was ' "reading for all" – the great sermons of the century, as the (late) eminent writer, Anthony Trollope, defined it'. Mudie was a devout Nonconformist and his 'Select Library' would not give space to a book that offended the moral code of the age. As a religious man Mudie might not have liked Julian Hawthorne's quip about Trollope, 'He was afraid of nobody except God and Mudie', but it aptly stated the situation.[13]

It is impossible to understand the Victorian novel without realising that the circulating libraries dictated its size, its subjects and, to a degree, its language. All successful novelists – and swarms of unsuccessful ones – bowed to the demands of Mudie and his fellow literary despots. Publishers also obeyed and eventually several of them actually became large shareholders in Mudie's business. The person who wished to read a new novel had three choices: he could buy the book, borrow it from a friend or take it out of his subscription library. Not until the end of Trollope's life was there any system of free public libraries. Indeed when he visited America he was greatly impressed by such a system in Boston and returned to England as a firm supporter of them.

The high cost of quality fiction naturally led to private borrowing and, if that failed, to Mudie. When George Eliot wrote to her publisher that she had heard of 'one paper-covered American copy of *Felix Holt* being brought to Europe, and serving for so many readers that it was in danger of being worn away', she was expressing a common and continuing grievance of writers. Five years later – just after the publication of *Middlemarch* – she was bemoaning the public's 'indisposition ... to buy books by comparison with other wares, and especially to buy novels at a high price'. When the *Athenaeum* was launched as a new journal to encourage the arts, it knew that 'no Englishman in the middle class of life *buys* a book'.[14] Certainly very few Victorians bought first editions of novels.

The most popular way to read the latest fiction was to borrow it from circulating libraries. Even publishers advertised that their new works were available in these libraries. A review of Trollope's first novel concluded: 'We advise our readers to get it into every circulating library in which they may have any voice; and by so doing they will oblige others as well as themselves.'[15] Mudie charged his subscribers a guinea a year, which entitled them to borrow one volume at a time. Those who could afford more and had heartier literary appetites could pay a higher fee for more volumes. Mudie had demonstrated a superb example of the great driving principle of the Victorian economy: to realise a large profit, undersell your rivals and provide a cheaper service to more people. His subscription was low enough to allow the middle classes to enjoy the run of his ever-expanding collection: by 1850 he advertised that he was increasing his collection by 12,000 volumes a year.

A guinea a year certainly brought books and journals within the ambit of young clerks on £90 a year, such as Trollope had once been. Nor did one have to live in London, for Mudie's own vans were soon carrying books to nearby towns. Eventually it was possible to receive deliveries all over the kingdom (smaller provincial libraries often had their own subscription to Mudie's) and eventually to parts of the Empire. Any of Mudie's subscribers who had paid at least two guineas and lived within a twenty-mile radius of London (this would include Trollope in the 1860s and 1870s) had only to post a letter and, thanks to the superb service of the Victorian Post Office, Mudie's van would arrive with a copy of the latest novel that same day. It is a pleasing reflection to know that by the 1860s many novel readers were sending for Trollope's novels by putting a letter into his other creation, the pillar box.

Mudie appealed to almost every level of society above the working classes, which also had smaller circulating libraries in many places. Even the Queen had a subscription, so she could keep up to date on what her subjects were reading. Fanny Trollope, it may be recalled, was delighted to hear that her new daughter-in-law, Rose, had a paid-up library subscription as well as 'a good package' of books to take to Ireland. Rose made much use of her Mudie subscription as one of her many wifely duties was keeping her husband aware of contemporary novels and other books. Escott noted that Trollope 'always had a regular supply of books from Mudies. These, if he did not look into them, he expected his wife, his niece or some other member of his home circle to read and to talk about to him.' He ensured that his two sons became members of an Irish subscription library and once wrote from Paris telling Rose he would repay young Henry's five shilling fee.[16]

*

Trollope eventually became one of the most popular authors on Mudie's shelves. As early as 1859 – when only three of the Barset novels had appeared – *The Times* pronounced: 'If Mudie were asked who is the greatest of living men, he would without one moment's hesitation say – Mr Anthony Trollope; and Mudie's opinion is worth much.'[17] Mudie's prosperity depended upon novels, which were about one third of his total stocks and, one suspects, an even higher proportion of borrowings.

Probably no other novelist of the era made so many references in his works to Mudie as Trollope. He knew that many readers would have a warm glow of familarity when they were suddenly united to a fictional character who also used Mudie's. In *Orley Farm* a barrister's wife calls at her husband's chambers in Lincoln's Inn. Her real purpose is to spy on him, but she justifies her visit by announcing: 'I happened to be in Holborn – at Mudie's for some books' [XIII]. Trollope even uses Mudie's to illustrate how one girl suffers when she is sent to live with an economical aunt 'who did not subscribe to Mudie's'. The distressed girl recalls from her earlier life 'that Mudie's unnumbered volumes should come into the house as they were wanted had almost been as much a provision of nature as water, gas, and hot rolls for breakfast' [*Ayala's Angel* I, II]. Mudie himself is even quoted in another novel as ordering 2,000 copies of a theological work [*The Bertrams* XVIII].

There was one disadvantage of the system which those who were reading Trollope in such a volume might well know: the yellow label, 'Mr Mudie's suspicious ticket', could reveal that the book was nothing but a novel. This happens to one pompous barrister in *The Prime Minister* [III]. Later in the same novel a tyrannical husband suspends his wife's subscription to Mudie's to force her to ask her wealthy father, the same barrister, for more money [XLVII]. Trollope permits criticism of the literary dictator in one novel, when a Scottish countess informs her new companion: 'I don't subscribe to Mudie's, because when I asked for "Adam Bede" they always sent me the "Bandit Chief" ' [*The Eustace Diamonds* XXXIV]. He saw how this spread of books was affecting society, particularly women. In *He Knew He Was Right* he has a young girl in Devon whose previous sources of information had been limited to books lent by a clergyman and to a weekly newspaper borrowed from a publican for a penny a week. She begins to think for herself once she subscribes for 'a box of books from Exeter, and a daily paper from London' [XIV].

Mudie was not without rivals either in London or in the rest of the country. 'Morrow's Library', known as 'the Mudie of Dublin', gave rise to a popular joke attributed to Archbishop Whately of Dublin referring to a popular Irish preacher called Day: 'How inconsistent is the piety of certain ladies here. They go to *Day* for a sermon and to *Morrow* for a novel!' There were smaller libraries in Irish provincial towns. In Trollope's first novel Feemy Macdermot 'was addicted to novels when she could get them from the dirty little circulating library at Mohill' [*The Macdermots of Ballycloran* II]. In England Mudie's most important rival was W.H. Smith who, in addition to his subscription library, started a series of railway bookstalls in 1848. Trollope introduced these into a novel, *The Small House at Allington*, when Johnnie Eames encounters his foe, Adolphus Crosbie, at Paddington Station. The combative Johnnie seizes the 'confounded scoundrel' by the throat and knocks him into 'Mr Smith's book-stall, and there Eames laid his foe prostrate ... falling himself into the yellow shilling-novel depot' [XXXIV]. Yet even

before this fictional affray, Trollope saw how the railways had created
a new demand for books:

> We are a locomotive people, and during these last twenty years in no way
> has the national taste for literature been so developed as in the
> arrangements for facilitating railway reading. Railways have done much
> for the world; but in no respect have they more essentially benefited the
> constant traveller than in allowing him to save from loss the hours spent
> on the road. A man's seat in a railway carriage is now, or may be his
> study; and to men obliged so to pass a considerable portion of their
> existence such a facility as this is a vital benefit.

Trollope as a 'constant traveller' himself used railways as a place to
read and write novels. His first biographer encountered him in the
1870s at Euston Station and noticed that he slept for the first half of a
long journey and spent the second writing several chapters of a
serialised novel.[18]

Trollope had good reason to be fascinated with the importance of
railway bookstalls. As one unfriendly critic noted in the 1890s:
'Trollope was in his lifetime more popular than any of his
contemporaries. Twenty years ago it would hardly have been an
exaggeration to say that half the novels on railway bookstalls were
his.' Here again he was following family tradition: for many years his
mother was one of the most popular authors in railway bookstalls. The
Victorians, ever an inventive people concerned with their own comfort,
thought of many things to make rail travel easier and more productive.
One guidebook, published in 1862, urged travellers to take a special oil
lamp to help them read the fine print and offered advice on how to
'dispose' the arms so as to impart 'elasticity and *aplomb* to the volume'.
Incidentally this guide also shows that books could have a social – or
rather an un-social – purpose:[19]

> Always ... provide one's self with a book ... you know you possess it, and
> can at any time fly to it by way of relief. It also forms an excellent weapon
> of defence against bores, that impertinent, intrusive, and inquisitive
> race, who can only be silenced by levelling a volume or a journal at their
> heads.

Victorian novelists were therefore lucky in their generation and in
their nationality. Whether readers took up their books to provide a
topic for conversation, as the *Quarterly Review* claimed, or used them

as a weapon to avoid it, they could bask secure and prosperous in the regard of their increasingly literate countrymen.

*

To understand how Mudie and his rivals affected the Victorian novel it is necessary to see how publishers went about their business. Today's system of a fixed percentage royalty was by no means the rule in Victorian England. Many authors preferred outright payment, or at least payment for the first edition, believing, as Trollope told the publisher of his second novel: 'It is, and must be, much more the publisher's interest to push a work when it is his own property.' As one distinguished scholar concludes: 'None of the Trollope family believed in the royalty system.' From her first success, Fanny Trollope always preferred to negotiate a fixed sum for her books because she was often in need of money. Her son Tom maintained that the royalty system was 'an essentially bad one ... it places the interests of the publisher and author necessarily in opposition to each other'.[20]

If publishers paid lump sums they were anxious to have books that would bring in immediate returns. In 1876, Trollope estimated that a publisher spent about £200 for a first edition of 600 copies of a three-volume novel. Such an edition could make just over £400, leaving the publisher just over £200 to pay an author and for his own profit. Publishers were often loath to bring out a large first edition. In 1858 one told Trollope that he had sold about 700 copies of the third Barset novel, *Doctor Thorne*: 'I might print 250 more, [and] if I can sell these I will be satisfied.'[21]

The basic problem was that first editions of quality fiction were too expensive. Even novels at the lowest end of the scale which sold for a shilling had to have enormous sales of over 20,000. For this they depended on 'external decorations' on the outside and 'absolutely worthless rubbish' inside. Novels of substance did not follow the general trend of most other items and drift downwards in price as industrialisation made production cheaper. Indeed the price increased after the eighteenth century. It became accepted that the price of any three-volume novel was 31s 6d or one-and-a-half guineas. At such a huge price – almost the equivalent of a week's salary for a postal clerk – it was a rare person who bought a first edition. Book-buyers waited until the cheaper one-volume editions appeared or, if they were canny, thronged to pick up bargains when Mudie sold off surplus copies. These sales became major events, where distinguished bargain-hunters, such as Gladstone, could be seen acquiring novels and other books at a fraction of their initial cost. Thus in 1860 Trollope's *Castle Richmond*, originally published at the sacred price of 31s 6d, was on sale for 9s within a few months of publication.[22]

The publishers could only recoup their initial costs if the libraries ordered many copies. In 1857 Longmans printed 750 copies of the first edition of *Barchester Towers*, of which 200 copies went to Mudie. He was adept at forcing publishers to sell copies at a bargain price: he paid less than half the normal price for *Barchester Towers*. At a hearing of a Royal Commission which enquired into publishing John Blackwood replied to a question from Trollope, who was serving on the Commission, that 'as Mr Trollope well knows' publishers did not receive the guinea-and-a-half price from the libraries. Often they had to be content with half that. Blackwood added: 'I am no lover of circulating libraries.'[23] Yet, like all major publishers of fiction, he was locked into the system.

*

The circulating libraries supported the system of three-volume novels for one simple reason: it encouraged subscribers to opt for the larger fee. If a reader paid only his yearly guinea, he was only entitled to one volume at a time. He would therefore be left in suspense about Mrs Proudie's machinations or Lily Dale's romance until he borrowed the next volume. Subscribers who paid two guineas could have all three volumes at once. Pressure from the libraries, in particular from Mudie's, encouraged publishers and authors to produce the 'three-deckers' which also appealed to Victorian taste. While many Victorian novels were not published in three volumes, this format was the standard to which all novelists looked. Trollope, the most business-like of the great novelists, accepted the status quo in his early days and said that each volume should contain about 66,000 words and the whole work just under 200,000 words. Just over one-third of his novels – seventeen out of the forty-seven – were in three volumes. One, *The Prime Minister*, ran to four volumes, but it was published in parts. Many of his two-volume novels, such as *Orley Farm*, *The Small House at Allington* and *The Last Chronicle of Barset*, were really as long as some of the three-volume ones, but because they had first appeared in serial format they were published as two volumes. Trollope eventually felt that the three-decker was forcing fiction into an unnatural mould. By the late 1860s, he was convinced that its day was passing, but he did not know what would take its place. A good example of how the three-volume rule affected authors occurred in Trollope's family, when his sister-in-law accepted her publisher's request to increase one of her novels from two to three volumes. She commented:

> The only thing to be done, is to endeavor to lay out one's story so as honestly to fill a bigger canvas, without too much mere talkee talkee. People who have only struck ink and not oil, must consider the profit question ... So it is evident that both publishers and writers must for the present stick to the three volumes.

The Victorian attitude was summarised by Trollope's nephew: 'When Mr. Mudie sends us home a one-volume novel, we look upon it with contempt.'[24]

In 1894, twelve years after Trollope's death, Mudie and W.H. Smith issued a joint edict banning three-volume novels as changes in prices meant they were no longer profitable. Within a few years the three-decker ceased to exist. That made Lady Bracknell's comment, in the last act of *The Importance of Being Earnest*, so topical in 1895, when her ladyship told poor Miss Prism that her famous lost 'hand-bag' had contained nothing but 'the manuscript of a three-volume novel of more than usually revolting sentimentality'. As Oscar Wilde's audiences laughed they knew that the fictional form that dominated their early lives had already sunk. Even before the death of the old Queen the Victorian age had ended at least in fiction. An anonymous poet – actually it was Rudyard Kipling – mourned the passing of the age of the three-deckers:[25]

> Full thirty foot she towered from waterline to rail.
> It cost a watch to steer her, and a week to shorten sail;
> But, spite of all modern notions, I found her first and best –
> The only certain packet for the islands of the Blest.
>
> We asked no social questions – we pumped no hidden shame –
> We never talked obstetrics when the Little Stranger came:
> We left the Lord in Heaven, we left the fiends in Hell.

Some modern readers, who find all the attributes Kipling listed excellent reasons to seek out Trollope and the other great Victorians, complain about the size of their books. Complaints about the length of novels were heard in Victorian times as well. As early as 1858 one critic praised *Doctor Thorne* but said it would have been better in two volumes: 'Few tales are strong enough to hold out for three volumes without showing symptoms of distress.' Henry James, who in years to come would suffer similar criticism, accused Trollope in a review in

1865 of being prone 'to swell his book into the prescribed dimensions'. Unlike James, Trollope preferred to answer critics not in prefaces to novels or in essays but in his asides to his readers. Thus in the opening paragraph of one novel from the late 1870s he says: 'We novelists are constantly twitted with being too long; and to gentlemen who condescend to review us, and who take up our volumes with a view to business rather than pleasure, we must be infinite in length and tedium' [*Is He Popenjoy?* I]. Many readers preferred lengthy novels. Cardinal Newman, who had written two novels himself, wrote to a lady friend, yet another novelist, that her recent work was too short, which made incidents seem too exciting. 'This is the reason, I think, why skilful novelists like Trollope have underplots. Such a contrivance obliges events to go more slowly – also it gives opportunity for variety and repose.' Some critics of the period defended Trollope's lengthy novels and complained, like the Cardinal, if he gave them a shorter work. When *Miss Mackenzie* appeared in 1865, one perceptive reviewer commented:[26]

> Mr Trollope is a novelist who requires space to bring out his conceptions to their full perfection; his longest novels are as a rule his best ... *Miss Mackenzie* loses by being a tale in two volumes, and two short volumes, instead of being spread in his usual leisurely way over his usual long perspectives.

'The usual leisurely way' allowed – indeed forced – Trollope to introduce into almost every novel a variety of plots and sub-plots. When he needed a bit of 'padding' he could always insert a few letters from one character to another. This had been fashionable in the early days of fiction, and Trollope argued that it gave 'more natural truth than any other' writing in a novel [*Doctor Thorne* XXXVIII]. It is ironic that Trollope, whose own letters, written early in the morning in a great rush, tend to be direct, short and often dull, could produce some of the best letters in fiction. His novels have numerous examples: 'I fear to introduce another epistle,' he noted in one novel. 'It is such an easy mode of writing and facility is always dangerous' [*Doctor Thorne* XXXVIII]. Letters also fitted nicely into his daily schedule of writing, as he could more easily produce his quota of words. If he felt there were too many letters he could summon up a recent experience or give a chapter or two about a fox-hunt. As lengthy letters and fox-hunting scenes could not in themselves stretch out a book to three volumes, sub-plots became essential even if he once wrote that his aim was 'straightforward, simple, plain storytelling' [*Doctor Thorne* II].

Sometimes these had little to do with the main story, like the tiresome tale about a London painter, which is clearly 'padding', in *The Last Chronicle of Barset*. A fourth device was the well-worn convention of contrasting his plots of 'high life' with similar scenes of 'low life'. Here he was increasingly influenced by his extensive reading of the old dramatists. Long novels brought their own problems: characters sometimes achieve an importance early in the story and are then lost sight of until the end: one reviewer of *The American Senator* complained of 'the Senator disappearing occasionally even for a volume at a time'.[27]

Trollope, as a reader, enjoyed long novels himself. Late in life he commenced an ambitious programme of rereading novels for a history of fiction he planned but never completed. When he read Scott's *Old Mortality* he noted in his copy: 'I hold it to be a convincing sign of a good novel that it takes long in the reading – that the reader finds that with due attention to the story he can hardly skip.' Yet he was not without criticism about length: while he admired Thackeray's 'delightful digressions', he admitted that some times his friend's novels were too long. Certainly the same criticism is true of Trollope. Indeed it is difficult, most of the time, to avoid agreeing with the opinion of the foremost authority on Victorian publishing that the three-volume novel itself was 'overlong, overpriced and almost from the first overdue for extinction'.[28]

*

Victorian publishing was dominated not just by the circulating libraries and the three-decker but by several remarkable men, many of Scottish origin, who impressed their forceful personalities on their firms. The houses tended to be controlled by one man or his family, though occasionally new partners would be added. Thus Trollope bought a large share of Chapman and Hall, who published most of his books. Some of the older publishing houses avoided fiction, notably John Murray. Others made a happy mixture of fiction and non-fiction, such as Smith and Elder. Many fiction publishers also found it profitable to own a magazine. This was often useful to authors, for their novels could appear in serial form before being brought out in the stately grandeur of three volumes. Such a connection with a magazine also allowed an author to place short stories or articles which could bring in extra money. Trollope established close friendships with several of his publishers, such as George Smith, who published Thackeray and Charlotte Brontë as well as owning the *Cornhill*.

Trollope was also a friend of the Blackwood family, the publishers of George Eliot and owners of the venerable *Blackwood's Magazine*. In the course of his career as a novelist Trollope dealt with fourteen publishers and with almost all of them – with the significant exception of the first – he remained on good terms.

Publishing was less organised than it has since become. Literary agents did not exist until the end of Trollope's career although friends sometimes took on some of their functions: Trollope's brother-in-law, John Tilley, arranged the details for the publication of *Barchester Towers*. As we have already seen, in his days as a postal clerk the young Anthony had often acted as his mother's agent in dealing with publishers. Both Trollope brothers assisted one another, but since Tom spent most of his life abroad Anthony undoubtedly did more. As a famous novelist, he was often asked to help young writers. Knowing all too well the misery of unfulfilled ambition, he would recommend publishers and advise on terms. Thomas Hardy is only the most famous of the many young writers he helped.

Writers like Hardy appealed to Trollope not only because he was successful but because he had the justified reputation of taking the business of writing seriously. Although not one to save letters, he took considerable care of his business papers, many of which are preserved in the Bodleian Library. No other Victorian novelist paid as much attention to the vexed question of copyright, which is why he was asked to serve on the Royal Commission investigating that subject in 1876-7. For the present it is sufficient to say that throughout his working life copyright lasted for 42 years from the date of publication, or for the life of the author plus seven years. The author, or his heirs, were entitled to their rights for whichever of those two periods proved the longer. 'Seven years is rather short,' said Trollope to the witness who summarised the complicated law.[29] Again, a successful writer often received nothing if his works were popular in America, where the law allowed publishers to help themselves to any foreign book. Trollope felt strongly about this injustice and played a large role in the campaign to remedy it.

Trollope had a considerable interest in what he once called 'the paraphernalia of authorship'. For example, one characteristic that differentiated Victorian novels from most modern ones was the use of illustrations. These greatly fascinated Trollope. He must have known that his mother attributed much of her American book's success to the illustrations by Hervieu, who provided drawings for several of her early works. In his book on Thackeray Trollope maintained that his friend often gave a wrong impression of characters by illustrating so many of his own works, yet he admitted: 'How often have I wished that characters of my own creating might be sketched as faultily.'[30] Trollope's early novels did not enjoy the luxury of illustrations. Once he was established, many of his books were illustrated, although sometimes by only a frontispiece. A large work such as *Orley Farm* contained forty engravings by John Millais, who became a close friend. Indeed Trollope believed that these drawings were the finest of any produced for a Victorian novel. He had taken some care to show Millais one of his boyhood homes as a model for *Orley Farm* itself. In *Orley Farm* Millais paid a sly tribute to their happy partnership in his drawing of Sir Peregrine Orme's visit to a London solicitor's office. Behind the baronet and the solicitor is a tall bookcase with the black metal boxes used by lawyers. The names on the boxes associate the author with a character in the novel and with his Queen. They read: 'A. Trollope', 'I. Mason' and 'V R'.

Trollope usually selected the scenes that were to be portrayed and made comments on the back of the original drawings. He never again found an illustrator to equal Millais. He was particularly unhappy with H.K. Browne, who as 'Phiz' is well remembered for his illustrations of Dickens. (Browne also illustrated a novel by Fanny Trollope.) His drawings in Trollope's *Can You Forgive Her?* are quite insipid.[31] One of Trollope's illustrators was a woman, and it is interesting to note that Matilda Edward's drawings for *The Claverings* portray the men as less 'manly' and not so hidden by beards as those of Trollope's male artists.

Trollope also took an interest in other practical aspects of book production. He was familiar with various methods of printing and, at times, visited printers to observe his works coming forth. He observed in his short story, 'The Panjandrum', that the quality of paper was deteriorating from the days of his youth: 'Paper was paper then.' The vast expansion of publishing in his lifetime led to a decline in the rag-content of paper, a fact that causes misery to librarians in the late twentieth century as they see the works of Trollope's contemporaries falling out of crumbling periodicals. He took less interest in the advertising of books. Indeed he viewed the whole subject of advertising with disdain and came to regard it as a mark of decreasing honesty in English society. His worst novel, an absurd attempt at comedy, *The Struggles of Brown, Jones, and Robinson*, was an attack upon advertising. In the 1860s when writing 'The Panjandrum', he looked back to his early days when 'literary advertising, such as is now common to us, was unknown'. He felt that its main effect was to promote the works of bad authors.[32] Fortunately for Trollope and his publishers, much of the advertising for his books was done by that ever useful person Charles Mudie, who regularly informed his subscribers that yet another novel by Mr Trollope was available.

*

How did Trollope's novels actually look? Because first editions have become such collector's items few readers will ever own or even see one. It is of interest, therefore, to describe one novel. *Barchester Towers*, published by Longmans in 1857, was in the classic three-volume form, each volume measuring 4¾ by 7¾ inches and containing about 300 pages of text. The binding was in pale brown cloth to match *The Warden* which had been published by the same firm two years before. The price was, of course, the standard 31s 6d. In 1858 'A People's Edition', which compressed the whole text into one volume, was sold for five shillings, and even cheaper editions eventually appeared. Many of Trollope's novels travelled this familar route from the luxury of the three-volume edition to the austerity of the 'cheap edition', where minute print was crowded onto wretched paper. Often these cheaper editions were known as 'yellowbacks' from the colour of the cover. As the century wore on, and the author's fame grew, yet cheaper editions followed, so that within a few years of Trollope's death a one-shilling version appeared. These cheap editions could bring in handsome rewards to a publisher: W.H. Smith calculated that it cost him 9d to produce the yellowback novels that his railway bookstalls sold for 2s.[33]

There was also a 'Tauchnitz' edition of *Barchester Towers* in two volumes available in 1859. Baron Tauchnitz played an important role in the spread of Victorian culture. Working from Leipzig, he began a 'Collection of British and American Authors' which produced compact editions of famous English-language books. They became popular not only with foreigners but with English travellers and residents on the continent, who needed some novels in order to relax amidst the hectic life of the cultural tourist. Tauchnitz was not a pirate, but paid small amounts either to the original publisher or to the author if he had retained European rights. Many of Trollope's novels and all his travel books were available in this form. In 1872 he told Tauchnitz: 'I am so fond of your series that I regret to have a work of mine omitted from it.' Subsequently he included clauses in his contracts giving Tauchnitz the right to republish his books on the continent. It was illegal to import these continental editions into England, and Trollope said they were 'kept out of England like rinderpest'. Anyone coming into England might be forced to pay duty on books. When he was returning from Bruges in the 1830s Tom Trollope had to pay 4s 7d duty on two or three books. Many people must have sympathised with Douglas Jerrold's Mrs Caudle in the famous *Punch* serial when that fearsome lady returned from an overnight trip to Boulogne. The alert customs officers saw that she was smuggling a French copy of a 'beautiful English novel'. They 'chopped it to bits like so much dog's meat ... And when I so seldom buy a book! ... If you can buy the same book in France for four shillings that people here have the impudence to ask more than a guinea for – well, if they *do* steal it, that's their affair, not ours. As if there was anything in a book to steal!'[34]

*

There were two other ways readers encountered the novels of Trollope and his contemporaries. These were by serialisation in magazines or by part issues. Both methods were used by most of the great novelists. Trollope's first nine novels, from 1847 to 1860, appeared as completed books. With these he became a well-known writer, but it was the serialisation of *Framley Parsonage* in *Cornhill* that established his reputation as one of most successful novelists of his age and greatly increased his income. After that almost all his novels appeared first either in magazine serialisations or in part issues: twenty-six novels from 1860 to 1882 were serialised in periodicals. Eight others, beginning with *Orley Farm* in March 1861, appeared in part issues. Virtually all his novels after 1860 were written to enable readers to read a few chapters at a time. Of the four post-1860 novels published first in book form two had been intended for serialisation, and only editorial problems frustrated his intentions. (*Rachel Ray* was intended for *Good Words*, but Trollope withdrew it after the editor feared it might offend that periodical's readers. *Ayala's Angel* was sold to a Press Agency in 1880 which seems not to have found anyone to serialise it.) *An Old Man's Love* was published as a book after the author's death. Thus *Miss Mackenzie* was the only novel published after 1860 with which Trollope did not attempt some form of serialisation. Ironically he did not enjoy reading serialised novels but he did like the extra income his own produced.

Dickens had made part issues famous with the publication of *The Pickwick Papers* in twenty instalments, and Thackeray had found it a successful method for *Vanity Fair*. The danger was that buyers would tire of characters or plots that took twenty months to reach fruition, one part per month. It is noticeable that the eight novels which

Trollope published in part issues have all stood the test of time and have seen frequent reprinting in our own century. These eight are: *Orley Farm, Can You Forgive Her?, The Last Chronicle of Barset, He Knew He Was Right, The Vicar of Bullhampton, Ralph the Heir, The Way We Live Now* and *The Prime Minister.* All are distinguished by strong plots and memorable characters. Trollope thought *The Last Chronicle of Barset* his best book. Many modern critics have awarded the palm to *The Way We Live Now.*

The novels serialised in magazines vary in quality. While they include some good novels and some very popular ones, there are also several that are forgettable or, quite frankly, bad. The worst is *The Struggles of Brown, Jones, and Robinson*, serialised in the *Cornhill* because the publisher was anxious not to lose his valuable new contributor. Other magazines that serialised Trollope include *Blackwood's, Macmillan's, Good Words*, the *Fortnightly*, the *Graphic* and *St Pauls.* Several of these were owned by publishers who bought the rights to publish the novel first as a serial and then as a book in several volumes.

One day in January 1861 a clever undergraduate, John Addington Symonds, described how he passed his days at Oxford. In addition to riding his white pony and attending a sermon by Bishop Wilberforce denouncing the 'Neglect of Revelation', he strolled from Balliol to the Oxford Union, where 'I do read for amusement. I am carrying on 4 periodical novels – *Tom Brown* [*at Oxford*], *Framley Parsonage, Great Expectations*, and Thackeray's new tale [*The Adventures of Philip*].'[35] At least the Dickens and the Trollope books remain classics, and certainly Thackeray's last completed novel and the continuation of the famous Tom Brown story by Thomas Hughes are still well worth reading.

We may wonder how the Victorian novel was affected by serialisation. It was, first of all, a powerful prop to Victorian prudery. Magazine editors were often more concerned about the sensibilities of their subscribers than publishers were about the readers of their books. Trollope, like many other authors, had sad experience of this. One of his novels, *Rachel Ray*, was rejected by a magazine appealing to religious readers because it might offend them. Sometimes editors wielded the censor's pencil before allowing a novel to appear. The younger Charles Dickens, who carried on his father's *All the Year Round*, made several changes in Trollope's novel *Is He Popenjoy?* in the late 1870s. The word 'improper' was removed from 'improper affection'. Nor were readers to be horrified by such a sentence as: 'The dimples on her cheek are so alluring that I would give my commission to touch them once with my finger.' Dickens also removed many passages about the young Marchioness's plans to nurse her baby. Out went a comment that porter is good for nursing mothers. In the previous decade Trollope had been annoyed when Thackeray rejected his short story, 'Mrs. General Talboys', for its references to illegitimate children and to 'a woman not as pure as she should be'. Yet he agreed that 'an impartial Editor must do his duty. Pure morals must be supplied.'[36] Magazine editors ensured that their serialised novels did not cause even the slightest ripple in the Victorian stream of 'pure morals'.

A far worse effect was that novels had to expand to the length demanded for the serialisation. This reinforced the pressure from the circulating libraries to produce long novels. It also made novelists structure their stories so that each instalment left the reader wondering what would happen next. Novelists tried to include most of the important characters and sub-plots in each episode, so that the periodical reader did not forget which virtuous maiden was agonising over which winsome youth. (We see this today when these same novels are adapted for radio or television.)

There was one great boon from this system, as the *Athenaeum* observed when Trollope brought the story of Barchester to a finish with *The Last Chronicle of Barset* in 1867: 'There is one advantage in writing a story as a serial – the individual portions have an elaboration and finish which a novel written in the piece does not always obtain at the hands of the author.' Actually this comment did not apply as much to Trollope as to some other novelists, for he had usually completed the whole novel before serialisation began. 'It was my theory,' he wrote,

> and ... has been my practice, – to see the end of my work before the public should see the commencement ... [Thackeray] by no means held to my theory ... But neither did Dickens, or Mrs Gaskell, both of whom died with stories not completed, which, when they died, were in the course of publication. All the evidence goes against the necessity of such precaution. Nevertheless, were I giving advice to a tiro in novel writing, I should recommend it.[37]

Trollope suffered the usual fate of those who give advice: he died leaving an uncompleted novel, *The Landleaguers*, in the course of publication.

*

There were, of course, many types of fiction. Scott had established the historical novel, but this was passing away when Trollope began his career. His one historical novel, *La Vendée*, was not a success. Towards the end of his life he did set the odd novel, such as *Lady Anna*, and some short stories, in the times of his youth. The historical novel declined in popularity after the 1840s and tended to be the preserve of minor writers like Harrison Ainsworth and G.P.R. James. At the same time as this was happening, a new type of fiction arose: the novel of social protest. Mrs Trollope had been an early pioneer, using her books to attack the factory system (*Michael Armstrong*), the new Poor Law (*Jessie Phillips*) and American slavery (*Jonathan Jefferson Whitlaw*). Disraeli used his fiction to attack many of the abuses of the rising industrialism, as well as to present a rather obscure amalgam of ideas called 'Young England'.

Trollope's fiction is not usually concerned with social reform although he took a great interest in political and social questions. He used his travel books more than his novels to expound his views, particularly on education which he increasingly saw as vital to national progress. His Irish novels are, of course, full of that country's desperate state. Many of his short stories deal with topical questions, whether it be the extreme distress in Lancashire during the 'cotton famine' ('The Widow's Mite') or the plight of single women adrift in a world that had little place for them ('The Journey to Panama'). While some novels deal with 'social problems' – *The Vicar of Bullhampton* has a sympathetic treatment of a 'fallen woman' – most are less concerned with the immediate questions of the day than with exploring the human personality and those difficulties all people face, whatever their century. Trollope's best novels have a perennial appeal precisely because they uncover permanent aspects of human nature and are not enmeshed in social problems that have long since passed away.

Trollope's *forte* is the depiction of the life he saw about him. From his mother he inherited an interest in 'domestic manners'. His own reading reinforced this. Jane Austen, whom Trollope once described as 'my chief favourite among novelists', greatly influenced him. She excelled in portraying the life about her, however limited it may appear to later generations. Trollope likewise was fascinated by the myriad ways human beings manipulate and affect one another. To this he added an unrivalled knowledge of his own time. In a review of Jane Austen, Sir Walter Scott had foreseen a great danger for novelists who deal with contemporary life: 'He who paints a scene of common occurrence, places his composition within that extensive range of criticism which general experience offers to every reader.'[38] In the event, contemporaries found few mistakes in Trollope's portrayal of their own age. Time and again they used that new invention, the 'photograph', as a metaphor for his novels. This accuracy came from his postal work, which took him throughout the British Isles. Because he was a tireless traveller he visited most European countries, as well as every part of the English-speaking world. These trips gave him the perspective to see his own society in relation to that wider world in which it played such a dominant role.

*

One of Trollope's great contributions to English fiction was to establish the idea of a series of novels. Thackeray had re-employed some characters from one book in another, such as having *The Newcomes* narrated by the hero of an earlier work, Arthur Pendennis. The most conspicuous contemporary example of novels in a series was, of course, Balzac; but Trollope seems to have been little influenced by him. (He only had three volumes of Balzac in his library.) At a dinner of the Royal Literary Society in 1867 – just as the final numbers of *The Last Chronicle of Barset* were appearing – the distinguished historian Earl Stanhope praised Trollope for his use of reappearing characters in a series of novels, an 'invention ... of which ... the original merit belongs to M de Balzac'. Trollope, in his reply, commented:[39]

> I should be happy ... to drink long life to M de Balzac. I am told he was the man who invented that style of fiction in which I have attempted to work. I assure any young man around me who may be desirous of following the same steps that they cannot find any style easier. The carrying on of a character from one book to another is very pleasant to the author; but I am not sure that all readers will participate in that pleasure.

Of course Balzac had been dead for seventeen years. If Trollope had required an example of how a prolific novelist could make writing easier by re-using characters, he need have looked no further than his mother, who frequently employed this device. Perhaps her most popular novels were the three concerned with the adventures of the Widow Barnaby.

It was Trollope's achievement to have created a whole world – the English *Comédie Humaine* – in his Barchester Chronicles, beginning with *The Warden* in 1855 and ending twelve years later with *The Last Chronicle of Barset*. These six novels portray the world of the gentry and clergy in unforgettable detail, and they have always remained central to the author's reputation. When they came to an end thousands mourned that they would hear no more of long-familiar friends. Professional critics have often sought to place some of his other novels above them, but readers have ignored these opinions. His other series, the Palliser or political novels, deal with a mixture of politics and society. Some of its scenes take place in Barsetshire and have fleeting glimpses of old friends. He considered yet another series tracing the fortunes of a tailor and his titled wife in Australia, but he only wrote the first instalment, *Lady Anna*. In addition to serialised novels, he had many characters who turn up in different books, the most notable of whom is the barrister Chaffanbrass.

In both series, and in the many single works, we can see his concept of the novel being realised:[40]

> A novel should give a picture of common life enlivened by humour and sweetened by pathos. To make that picture worthy of attention, the canvas should be crowded with real portraits, not of individuals known to the world or to the author, but of created personages impregnated with traits of character which are known. To my thinking, the plot is but the vehicle for all this; and when you have the vehicle without the passengers, a story of mystery in which the agents never spring to life, you have but a wooden show. There must, however, be a story. You must provide a vehicle of some sort.

*

How did Trollope set about providing and peopling his vehicle? It is helpful to have some idea of how he went about this before resuming the story of his life. Although Trollope is not normally regarded as a novelist remarkable for plots, his contemporaries often thought otherwise. The *Athenaeum* in its obituary of Trollope maintained that he 'often excelled' Dickens and Thackeray 'in the technicalities of plot-making'. His long habit of 'castle building' was of great use in the fabrication of plots. Once at a dinner party in Berkeley Square a young man asked the by then elderly novelist: 'They tell me, Mr Trollope, that before sitting down to write your – may I say? – delightful novels, you always make a prefatory sketch.' 'Never did such a thing in my life, sir, and never shall.' He was not being completely honest, but his aim was probably to avoid a discussion about the theory of writing. He did sometimes make a list of principal characters and he put much thought into his work:[41]

> When we were young we used to be told, in our house at home, that 'elbow grease' was the one essential necessary to getting a tough piece of work well done ... Fore-thought is the elbow grease which a novelist ... requires. It is not only his plot that has to be turned and re-turned in his mind, not his plot chiefly, but he has to make himself sure of his

situations, of his characters, of his effects, so that when the time comes
for hitting the nail he may know where to hit it on the head.

He felt that the most frequent cause of bad novels was the avoidance
of this forethought and believed that thinking – by which he meant
disciplined thought – is 'the hardest work which a man is called upon
to do' [*Castle Richmond* XII]. He told one editor who had asked for a
Christmas story: 'The labour is in arranging a plot, rather than in
writing the tale.' The best description of how he fashioned his plots
comes in an essay he wrote in 1879, almost forty years after he first
took up his pen. 'A Walk in a Wood' shows how the elderly novelist
used long walks to build his plots just as the young Anthony toyed with
them in the muddy lanes of Harrow. Great forests, whether in
England, Germany, New Zealand or California, provided the best place
to think, for there he found the quiet he needed:[42]

> Gradually as I walk, or stop, as I seat myself on a bank, or lean against a
> tree, perhaps as I hurry on waving my stick above my head till with my
> quick motion the sweat-drops come out upon my brow, the scene forms
> itself for me. I see or fancy that I see, what will be fitting, what will be
> true, how far virtue may be made to go without walking upon stilts, what
> wickedness may do without breaking the link which binds it to
> humanity, how low ignorance may grovel, how high knowledge may soar,
> what the writer may teach without repelling by severity, how he may
> amuse without descending to buffoonery; and then the limits of pathos
> are searched, and words are weighed which shall suit, but do more than
> suit, the greatness or the smallness of the occasion.

This, and not his dinner-table retort, is the most important passage for
anyone anxious to grasp Trollope's genius as a novelist. Here he sets
out not only how he formed his plots but how he portrayed his
characters. Undoubtedly this is a subtle criticism of Dickens, whose
greatness was much compromised, according to Trollope, by inflated
language and excessive sentimentality. This passage has the Victorian
insistence upon the need to teach 'virtue', but that can only be done if
the virtuous are believable characters – not 'walking on stilts' to use
one of his favourite metaphors. Nor can the wicked be exposed unless
their wickedness be seen as human rather than unrelieved satanic
evil. As he once said at a Royal Literary Fund dinner, the novelist's
moral duty is to 'teach ladies to be women and men to be gentlemen'.[43]

Trollope was not, however, a novelist who needed a complete plan of a novel's development before writing:[44]

> To construct a plot so as to know, before the story is begun, how it is to end, has always been a labour of Hercules beyond my reach. I have to confess that my incidents are fabricated to fit my story as it goes on, and not my story to fit my incidents.

Here he gives two examples: in *Orley Farm* he did not decide whether or not Lady Mason had forged a will until he reached the chapter before she confesses. In *The Eustace Diamonds* he did not decide who had stolen the jewels until he reached the page where he tells the reader.

*

One plot that was standard in almost every Victorian novel was the love plot. In a lecture on novels Trollope developed his idea that this was essential. Novels, he argued, 'not only contain love stories, but they are written for the sake of the love stories. They have other attractions, and deal with every phase of life; but the other attractions hang round and depend on the love story as the planets depend upon the sun.' He claims, not entirely accurately, that he attempted one novel, *Miss Mackenzie*, without a love plot, though he decided to introduce one before the end. Many of his larger novels contain several love plots and the last chapters seem full of happy marriages. As Trollope himself said: 'Novels deal mainly with one subject, – that, namely, of love; and [it is] equally certain that love is a matter in handling which for the instruction or delectation of the young there is much danger.' Here Trollope, like every other novelist of his time, ran up against the standards of his era or what a later generation has called Victorian prudery. Prudery there was certainly and it was capable of the most absurd prohibitions: the publisher of *Barchester Towers* insisted that 'fat stomach' be changed to 'deep chest'. Probably Trollope had to be more circumspect than many novelists because so many of his characters were clergymen and their wives.* Early in his career he had

---

*A dramatist had to be even more careful when dealing with the clergy. When Trollope was asked by a theatre manager to make a play out of *The Last Chronicle of Barset*, he defrocked all his clergymen. Mr Crawley appears as a schoolmaster, while Bishop and Mrs Proudie lose their joint mitre and appear as a magistrate and his wife. It is fortunate that this travesty, called *Did He Steal It?*, was never put on the stage.

a 'terrible and killing correspondence ... with W. Longman because I would make a clergyman kiss a lady whom he proposed to marry'.[45]

One does not get the sense that Trollope was being constantly constrained by Victorian conventions, such as one senses when reading Thackeray.[46] Nevertheless there were times when he was forced to suppress a phrase, an incident, or even − as mentioned earlier − a whole story, that was thought to reveal too much about the immorality that lurked within the edifice of respectability. Every age imposes an internal censorship upon its writers and the Victorians were no different: they preferred not to be reminded about the conflict between their public devotion to sexual morality and the flagrant private disregard for it just as succeeding generations prefer to ignore other dark aspects of national life.

The immorality of the times was visible to every perceptive man though well hidden from many women or, rather, ladies. William Glenn, an American friend of Trollope's, found this the most noteworthy aspect of his visit to England in the 1860s:[47]

> What most surprised me perhaps was the state of Morals among the humbler classes of society in and around London, which was a perfect hotbed of vice. There were a great many anecdotes told me by fast men of the loose life in the upper classes − and several cases of *crim con* were made public during my stay in England.* But I speak not of those who shop in carriages, as all ladies do. I refer to those who walk. Of them, I think it fair to say, that there is scarcely one whom a clever, well looking man cannot with a little address join & enter into conversation with and from whom he cannot obtain a promise to meet him again.

Trollope normally deals with this aspect of Victorian life by the same type of 'hints' he accused Thackeray of using in *Vanity Fair*. He knew that women were the largest part of his audience and he hesitated to offend them. As he admitted, with some humour, in a lecture, he was 'absolutely dependent in a great measure on the laziness of ladies for my daily bread'. In *Can You Forgive Her?* Burgo Fitzgerald, a dissipated young man of stunning beauty (this in itself made him an untrustworthy character to his creator) wanders about London two days before Christmas. As he saunters into Oxford Street he is accosted by 'a poor wretched girl' who asks for money, even a penny to buy a glass of gin. Though Trollope refrains from actually saying so, the girl was one of that vast army of prostitutes which swarmed through Victorian London. The normally despicable Burgo takes pity

---

*'Crim-con' or criminal conversation was a polite term for adultery when indulged in by the aristocracy. There was even a scandal sheet called *Crim-Con Gazette*, 'reporting' the latest rumours.

on her and invites her into a public house, where he sees that she is properly fed. He then gives her money for a bed and for breakfast. This could be read aloud by any virtuous maiden of the time, who could see it as an example of drunkenness and of Christian charity from someone least expected to extend it. Trollope knew that his male readers understood his hints, but he was coming to believe that many women could and should do so as well.[48]

In this same episode Burgo utters an astonishing line to the girl. He has just failed in his hopes to run away with the rich and recently married Lady Glencora Palliser. 'We are alike then,' says the ruined roué, who had hoped to live off his beloved's wealth. This scene also is a good example of Trollope's belief that a villain – and Burgo most certainly is a villain – must sometimes exhibit a trace of human feeling. It is an interesting coincidence that William Glenn was invited to spend Christmas 1863 with Trollope. The two friends shared a taste for cigars just as Burgo and a friend do in the earlier part of the chapter about Burgo's encounter with the prostitute. It is likely that amidst their cigars Glenn discussed his astonishment at the immorality of London with his host who was in the process of writing this novel.

Trollope returned to the subject of prostitution a few years later in *The Vicar of Bullhampton*. He was conscious that he was treading on potentially dangerous ground for he included his only preface, despite his view that 'the writing of prefaces is, for the most part, work thrown away; and the writing of a preface to a novel is almost always a vain thing'. The reason he had violated his rule was because he was

defending myself against a charge which may possibly be made against me by the critics ... I have introduced ... a girl whom I will call, – for want of a truer word that shall not in its truth be offensive, – a castaway. I have endeavoured to endow her with qualities that may create sympathy, and I have brought her back at last from degradation at least to decency ... There arises of course, the question of whether a novelist, who professes to write for the amusement of the young of both sexes, should allow himself to bring upon his stage such a character ... It is not long since, – it is well within the memory of the author, – that the very existence of such a condition of life ... was supposed to be unknown to our sisters and daughters, and was, in truth, unknown to many of them. Whether that ignorance was good may be questioned; but that it exists no longer is beyond question ... It may also at last be felt that this misery is worthy of alleviation, as is every misery to which humanity is subject.

This was his greatest challenge to the Victorian code of silence. Trollope had judged the changing mood well, for the critics on the whole accepted his defence.

Perhaps emboldened by this he was much more open in a novel begun a few months later, *Sir Harry Hotspur of Humblethwaite*, where one of the main characters has a mistress. Although the word is avoided (even in Trollope's private working list of characters she is referred to as 'the woman with whom [the baronet's heir] ... is entangled – ill-used'), it is quite obvious what she is. Even more remarkably she is shown to be a sympathetic woman.[49] The novel's virtuous heiress – so Victorian that she even dies from a broken heart – attempts to defend her cousin and fiancé from her father's attacks on his immorality: 'Papa, I have often thought that in our rank of life society is responsible for the kind of things young men do ... he is what he is, because other young men are allowed to be the same' [XIII].

In allowing a young lady to make vague reference to such practices, Trollope reveals how 'Victorianism' was starting to fade. In 1870 *The Times* accepted this: 'It used to be printed on some French novels, "*La mère en défendra la lecture à sa fille*," and the same might be said of parts of *Sir Harry Hotspur*. But the reading world is not entirely composed of young ladies. This book may do good to many of both sexes more advanced in life.'*[50] In earlier novels, such as *The Bertrams*, Trollope had only hinted at such goings-on: the old roué Sir Lionel Bertram has, in addition to his own rooms, 'another smaller establishment in a secluded quiet street' [XXI].

*

It was not only sex that caused novelists to pause before they described an incident. They also had to watch their language. Trollope is said to have had a fairly colourful vocabulary – particularly when his explosive temper was ignited. One publishing firm long preserved a legend of his swearing 'like a sergeant-major' when he stormed into the office clad in hunting costume and carrying a riding crop![51] This aspect of his personality rarely surfaces in his writing. In his novels there are about a dozen usages of such terms as 'damn', 'devil' and 'hell'. 'Damn' is normally given with sufficient dashes to alert the frightened reader to skip over the term. This profanity, if such it can be called, almost always occurs in the speech of male characters. The reaction of many Victorian ladies is well described in one book, where a nobleman is annoyed when his wife advises him to consult their chaplain:

*In Trollope's books a fondness for French novels is often a sign of moral weakness: in *Sir Harry Hotspur* [XII] we see the young reprobate returning from a visit to royalty, obviously the Prince of Wales at Sandringham. Young George Hotspur is engrossed in a French novel while his servant reads an 'English sensational' one.

'D—— Mr Greenwood!' said the Marquis. He certainly did say the word at full length, as far as it can be said to have length ... Her ladyship heard the word very plainly, and at once stalked out of the room, thereby showing her feminine feelings had received a wrench which made it impossible for her any longer to endure the presence of such a foul-mouthed monster [*Marion Fay* XVIII].

Although Trollope tried to avoid terms like 'pregnant' in his books and was even sparing of such euphemisms as 'family way', 'interesting event', or perhaps best of all 'an occurrence to which married ladies are liable' [*Ayala's Angel* LVII], nevertheless he was frequently chastised for being 'vulgar'.[52] As seen in the previous chapter, he not only alluded to bosoms and lips but introduced quite explicit terms into the sanctity of the Victorian drawing-room. Sometimes this comes from his preference for slightly archaic meanings for words such as 'bowels'. Not all of his readers in his own time, let alone now, would have understood his meaning in such a curious sentence as 'Her bowels yearned towards her child, and she longed to give her relief with an excessive longing' [*Rachel Ray* XXIII]. In another novel a character explodes in anger after hearing a denunciation of fox-hunting:

'The fact is, I hate with my whole heart ... [the] small knot of self-anxious people who think that they possess among them all the bowels of the world.'
'Possess all the what, Reginald?' [a shocked lady replies.]
'I said bowels, – using an ordinary but very ill-expressed metaphor' [*The American Senator* LXXIII].

*

The need to avoid, or at least obscure, such words as 'damn' was only a minor matter of style which pales beside the larger criticism that Trollope had no real 'style' at all. He had neither the temperament nor the time to spend hours searching for '*le mot juste*' like Flaubert. He approached style, like most things, with an eminently practical outlook. 'Style to the writer [is] not the wares which he has to take to the market, but the vehicle in which they may be carried. Of what avail to you is it to have filled granaries with corn if you cannot get your corn to the consumer?' [*The Duke's Children* XXVI]. He evidently liked this metaphor for, in another book published in the same year, he comments when discussing Thackeray's work that:[53]

manner and style are but the natural wrappings in which the goods have been prepared for the market. Of these goods it is no doubt true that unless the wrappings be in some degree meritorious the article will not be accepted at all; but it is the kernel which we seek, which, if it be not of itself sweet and digestible, cannot be made serviceable by any shell however pretty.

'Trollope's normal style,' according to one expert, 'is remarkably uniform, from beginning to end; uniformly easy, flowing, clear, plain, unlaboured, unaffected, unmannered, and above all businesslike. It is also remarkably "Modern".' He wrote too much and too quickly to maintain an elegant style such as contemporaries acclaimed in Cardinal Newman or Matthew Arnold. Trollope distrusted prose he found too elegant or considered affected, such as Disraeli's, which had 'a smell of hair-oil'. Writing that was too flowery or ornate carried more than a hint of France and that was no recommendation to Trollope. 'Now among us,' he wrote in 1865, 'plain English, a plain narrative, whether in verse or prose, is everything.'[54]

Trollope was, however, influenced, as all writers are, by what he read. Although he had studied Burke as a young man and revered Gibbon throughout his life, he was not devoted to those long rolling Georgian sentences such as Thackeray makes fun of in the first chapter of *Vanity Fair*, and Mrs Gaskell ridicules through Miss Deborah Jenkyns, in *Cranford*. He was impressed with Macaulay's style, and had a type of 'love-hate relationship' with Carlyle's. There is no writing so ridiculously bad in all of Trollope as that in which he attempts to write like Carlyle, addressing the reader as 'Brother'.

Normally Trollope wrote in relatively short, declarative sentences, which he varied by longer, more involved ones. He frequently uses conjunctions such as 'and', 'but' and 'then'. As a boy he had listened to the majestic cadences of the Book of Common Prayer in several services each day, and it is well known that much of its beauty comes from frequent repetition of conjunctions. To be elevated into this world of sublime language would have had a lasting effect upon his style. (It is, of course, no accident that, since the ruling clergymen of today have decreed that the beauty of holiness should be crushed beneath a craven devotion to the commonplace, the English language itself should fall victim to the guitar culture of modern liturgy.) Trollope, in particular, made deft use of the word 'but' which allowed him to engage in his favourite device of revealing those strange blends of goodness and naughtiness that exist in all people. It encouraged him to reuse one word from a previous clause to unite the sentence in a flowing and enjoyable whole. His sentences move with a relaxed cadence similar to a contented hunter returning from a good day's run. Like all Victorians he was fonder of the comma and the dash than is currently fashionable. Perhaps the fact that most people now read Trollope in editions with tiny print obscures the subtle pleasures of his prose. His style was also greatly influenced by his official work, just as Dickens's superb gift of painting word pictures came from his journalistic background. Throughout his postal career, which lasted almost thirty-five years, Trollope was responsible for writing numerous reports and 'minutes'. These, as well as the many non-fiction books he wrote, helped to keep his prose clear.[55]

The constant study of classics at his schools, and those more enjoyable years when he read them for amusement, also had an effect upon his writing. He constantly drew on classical allusions, and some are fairly obvious: doctors are usually referred to as 'Galen', while imposing ladies resemble 'Juno'. Sometimes he works in a translation for the benefit of Victorian lady readers, which now is of use to those who have drunk only from the arid wells of modern education. One of Trollope's annoying habits is his over-use of these allusions as a private joke, like a schoolboy parading new knowledge. Thus in *Framley Parsonage* there are too many comparisons between ancient gods and Victorian Cabinet ministers. It may be mildly amusing to despatch Mercury to the Post Office and rather obvious to appoint Mars to the War Office but why Juno should preside as Lord President or Apollo rule over the India Board must have appeared a mystery to most readers of the *Cornhill*. Even in a short novel like *The Warden* there are frequent references to the ancient world, including Croesus, Agamemnon, Iphigenia, Jupiter, Mount Olympus, nectar, Themis, Bacchus, the Paphian goddess, the Muses and Priam. These terms are almost always used to add a final touch of irony or humour, but in such a way that ignorance of the words does not prove a barrier to understanding the story.

Trollope, like every prolific writer, has certain phrases which he uses again and again. These, to his devoted readers, soon take on the appearance of old friends. When he made a curious attempt to publish an anonymous novel, his most perceptive critic, R.H. Hutton of the *Spectator*, spotted the author by the phrase 'made his way' which occurs constantly in his novels. Most Trollopeans will have their own favourites, but perhaps the most frequent, as we have noted, is the reference to a man whose 'lines have fallen in pleasant places'. This comes from Psalm 16 in the Authorised Version but is different from the Coverdale translation in the Book of Common Prayer that Trollope would have known from church. It is usually men who find their lines so falling. However, Mrs Dale tries to persuade herself that 'her lines had been set for her in pleasant places' in *The Small House at Allington* [III]. The careful manner in which Trollope observed Victorian society and the subtlety he used in describing it can be seen in the way that 'the lines' of wealthy young men 'fall', while a woman's fate is 'set' and the impoverished man's is 'cast'. Occasionally Trollope turns the phrase round, as when the embattled curate, Josiah Crawley, prays 'My God, what have I done against thee, that my lines should be cast in such terrible places?' [*The Last Chronicle of Barset* VIII]. 'You cannot touch pitch and avoid being defiled' is another Biblical maxim frequently met with in Trollope. It is taken from Ecclesiasticus 13:1 ('He that toucheth pitch shall be defiled therewith'). The fact that Shakespeare used it would have increased its familiarity. In Trollope it often heralds the approach of moral danger for a young man, and he is sure to cap the man's ruin by reminding us either in English or in Latin how easy is the slope to hell.

Trollope's large vocabulary was continually supplemented by travel and extensive reading. Long residence in Ireland gave his ear that heightened awareness of how the English language can be used by the different peoples who speak it. Travel introduced him to new words, including such Americanisms as 'institution' or 'buncombe'. In one novel from 1875 a young lady tells her rejected lover: 'I don't want to talk buncum' [*The Prime Minister* XVII]. He also had a devotion to old words, such as 'fain', 'ruth' (whose opposite, 'ruthless', survives) or 'exigent', words that were already antiquated to many Victorians. In one manuscript his publisher struck out 'exigent' and replaced it with 'urgent'. Occasionally he used new words like 'pundit', from the Hindu pandit or legal expert. He always tried to avoid using the same word too frequently in a chapter and on one occasion wrote to Rose from Paris asking her to 'alter any words which seem to be too often repeated' in the fair copy she was preparing of *Doctor Thorne*.[56]

*

One aspect of Trollope's style that must be considered is his use of grammar. The only sure way to avoid grammatical error is to write nothing. Trollope could not be accused of that! The speed at which he turned out such an astonishing number of books was, no doubt, a cause of his mistakes, as critics were quick to observe:

> Capable as he is of writing pure, racy, and pleasant English, nothing but overhaste can account for the lapses into slovenly and ungrammatical language, of which he is habitually guilty. Such phrases as 'whether or

no,' 'those sorts of things,' 'to do other than,' are of frequent occurrence in all his novels.

Nor were such comments restricted to reviewers. Lady Waldegrave noted when reading *Orley Farm*: 'I never read Trollope without longing to make him write better English. He is always making mistakes.' Her ladyship had either slid into a large amount of exaggeration or was operating on the venerable principle that correct English is that favoured by the critic's immediate circle and endorsed by herself. Writing at the speed he did was, in a sense, part of his 'style'. As he told a correspondent in 1874, 'It has been my metier to write "currente calamo" ', and, he added, 'a man at my age cannot change his line'. Trollope certainly wandered into various errors, but considering the amount he wrote his record is surprisingly good. Grammar had not reached its brief period of prosperity in Trollope's youth. His brother, writing in the late 1880s, boasted: 'I had never – have never, I may rather say – had any English grammar in my hand from my cradle to the present hour.'[57] There is no reason to think that Anthony's education differed from Tom's on this point.

We should also be careful not to assume that all Trollope's grammatical 'mistakes' would have been seen as such by educated contemporaries. One of his strangest 'mistakes', to modern eyes, is his inconsistent use of comparatives, about which it is difficult to discern his rule. He will often use the comparative for more than two. In one short story, 'The O'Conors of Castle Conor', there are three sisters but one is called 'the younger' while one of two brothers is called 'the eldest'. His mother could write a phrase such as 'the elder of our three boatmen', her son surpassed this by writing 'the elder ... [of] all the four daughters'. The use was an old one, dating at least to the seventeenth century, before modern grammatical rules had been formulated. Also, one wonders whether the high mortality rate among Victorian children caused confusion about whether one remembered dead siblings when talking of 'elder' and 'eldest'? Many Victorians appear to have done the same as Trollope. It can even be called 'Queen's English', as Victoria herself used phrases such as 'tallest of the two' when comparing one of her children to one of Gladstone's sons.[58] Trollope, like Jane Austen, continued using past tenses which were dying out in England such as 'gotten', which many volunteer guardians of the language declare was invented by misbegotten Americans. In the event it was America which remained true to the old and England which opted for the new, as she did when changing from the 'or' to the 'our' spelling in 'honour' and so on.

Trollope's grammatical mistakes did not spring from any contempt for rules. He insisted that grammar was important and inadvertently illustrated the difficulty anyone faces when pronouncing on it when he insisted that 'without correctness he [a writer] can be neither agreeable or [*sic*] intelligible'. For those who criticised him, he had an effective weapon. He agreed:[59]

> Rapid writing no doubt will give rise to inaccuracy, – chiefly because the ear, quick and true as may generally be its operation, will occasionally break down under pressure ... A singular nominative will be disgraced by a plural verb, because other pluralities have ... tempted the ear into plural tendencies ... A rapid writer will hardly avoid these errors altogether. Speaking of myself, I am ready to declare that, with much training I have been unable to avoid them.

Trollope's emphasis on the 'ear' gives an indication of how he wrote. He read his dialogue aloud: one suspects he read everything aloud. Because he heard his own words with his 'ear' and knew that many would read the novels aloud, his writing conveys that sense of listening to an elderly gentleman who, in spite of seeing much of the world, retains a pleasing blend of good will toward his fellows coupled with an amused acceptance of their foibles. It was Trollope's practice to read everything he wrote at least three times in manuscript and at least once in proof. The system of proof-readers and sub-editors was not highly developed, and once he was an established novelist Trollope's publishers – with the exception of John Blackwood – do not appear to have gone over his work with great thoroughness. His handwriting deteriorated as constant use of his hand took its toll. In his old age 'writer's cramp' made it painful for him to hold a pen, but he was at least spared the fate of his equally busy contemporary Mrs Oliphant, who actually wore a hole into her hand after years of churning out three-volume novels.[60] While his handwriting lacked the easy precision of Thackeray's, it never reached the flowing confusion of Queen Victoria's, whose later letters were passed from one perplexed minister to another for deciphering.

We can but marvel at the achievement of the printers who were able to interpret the handwriting of so many eminent Victorians. Trollope at least acknowledged: 'I am indebted to them.' There were times when they could not make out some of his writing. Thus the third chapter of *The American Senator* opens with the Masters family having tea at 'six o'clock one November morning', which may lead one to think that the author transferred his own early habits to his characters. In fact he had scrawled 'one November evening', but the printer misread his writing. A far worse mistake, at least to Trollope and his fellow hunters, came from another misreading of the same manuscript. In the book a farmer, who is too fat to ride, delights in the fact that he always has 'a fox in the springs at the bottom of his big meadows'. Trollope had written 'in the spinnies', but presumably the printer was so busy leaping the hedgerows of the author's handwriting that he slipped into topographical error.[61]

*

For a writer who wrote so much fiction the selecting of names for characters was a constant problem. Sometimes he decided to change the names while writing. The main family in *Sir Harry Hotspur* was originally called 'Brandon', but he changed it to Hotspur. In *The American Senator* he made many changes: the Masters – that family whom the printer roused for tea at six in the morning – had two daughters, Dolly and Molly, but after describing the latter as 'jolly', Trollope finally rechristened her Kate.[62] Even more absurd was the original name for Lawrence Twentyman, perhaps Trollope's best portrait of a gentleman-farmer. The farmer objects when others call him 'Larry' because 'a man should not have his Christian name used by every Tom and Dick', but his original name 'Launcelot' would have been even worse [I].

It is impossible to say where Trollope got most of his names. He does not seem, like some novelists, to have kept a list of useful names. We can see where some came from and guess at others. Some were borrowed from his family: 'Mary Gresley', the title of a story, was his grandmother's name, and 'Garrow', used in another story, 'The Mistletoe Bough' was his sister-in-law's. Sometimes he borrowed names from fellow novelists, as he acknowledged with 'Lord Cinquebars' who had been invented by Thackeray [*Can You Forgive Her?* XVI]. Trollope acknowledges this 'little theft' in a footnote paying tribute to his recently deceased friend. Dickens's immortal Mrs Gamp makes an appearance in *The Three Clerks* [XXII]. Trollope's repulsive clergyman Obadiah Slope, we are told, is a descendant of Dr Slop from Sterne's *Tristram Shandy*, but the family had added an 'e' 'for the sake of euphony' [*Barchester Towers* IV]. Trollope detested Disraeli, so when he wished to introduce him into a novel, he lifted a name from one of the politician's own novels, 'Sidonia'. He had used it once before for a Jewish moneylender in *Barchester Towers* [IX].

He had to be careful not to give offence by using real names. 'Mrs. General Talboys', the story about a married woman's love affair which

Thackeray rejected, also caused its author upsets because of the name he had chosen. He was forced to ask a publisher: 'I hope & trust that there is not & never has been any real General of that name.' (There had in fact been several mediaeval military commanders of that name.) Sometimes he changed one letter of a real name: thus when he wrote *Dr Wortle's School* at the Northamptonshire rectory of Lowick, he set the novel there but called it Bowick. This novel has a Lady Margaret Momson living in Lincolnshire. The author, himself the descendant of Lincolnshire baronets, surely would have known of another distinguished family of barons in that county, the Monsons. Trollope drew on his ancestral connections for the 'Rufford and Ufford' hunt which appears in many of his novels. He would have known that his cousin, Sir John Trollope, owned a country house at Ufford.[63]

At other times his travels seemed to present him with names. Thus after his stay in America in 1861-2 the names of several people prominent in Washington politics and society turn up in novels. Trollope met Senator John Crittenden at a dinner and borrowed his name to use in one novel and the story of his two sons, who fought as generals on opposite sides, for a short story, 'The Two Generals'.[64] The Eames family were leading society hosts in Washington and Trollope records meeting at least one of them. When he returned to England he began work on *The Small House at Allington*, in which Johnnie Eames is a main character. Finally the widow, Mrs Greenow, became the amusing heroine of a sub-plot in *Can You Forgive Her?* a few years after Trollope had stayed in Washington, where there was much discussion of the courageous Southern spy Rose Greenhow. (In this novel he calls an American girl Lucinda Roanoke, the name of a river in Virginia and of a city in the same state that was prominent in military campaigns during his stay.) Whether these names had been absorbed into Trollope's subconscious must remain speculation, but there do seem to be many coincidences.

One aspect of his choice of names has been found annoying. This is his penchant for silly names: Legg and Loosefit for a firm of hosiery dealers in *The Struggles of Brown, Jones, and Robinson*; Slow and Bideawhile, the solicitors who appear in at least six novels; Dry and Stickatit who are also solicitors in *The Bertrams*; and the Tappitt family, brewers, in *Rachel Ray*. This habit expanded as he wrote more. His first novel has only one, the barrister Mr Allewinde. Fifteen years later *The Three Clerks* has: a clergyman, the Rev. Mr Everscreech; a retired seaman, Captain Cuttwater; and an incompetent bureaucrat, Major Fiasco; as well as Sir Warwick Deepdene, a thin disguise for Sir Stafford Northcote. Sometimes these names destroy the flow of the story. This novel has a superb example of Victorian 'pathos', where a young wife is kneeling before her ruined husband, who is about to admit that he had taken a bribe. The mood is destroyed when the servant announces the lawyer Mr Gitemthruet [XXXIX]. This excessive use of silly names has been one reason why certain critics have not condescended to take Trollope seriously.

*

Another trick employed to excess by Trollope throughout his fiction was his continually popping up to address the reader with comments and reflections. This was common in Victorian fiction: Thackeray, in particular, was well known for it. The *Saturday Review*, which often sniped at Trollope, found this an annoying habit and criticised him for belonging to 'the "conversational" school, who address their readers from first to last in a tone of raillery'. The most telling attack comes from Henry James:[65]

> He took a suicidal satisfaction in reminding the reader that the story he was telling was only, after all, a make-believe. He habitually referred to the work in hand (in the course of that work) as a novel, and to himself as a novelist, and was fond of letting the reader know that this novelist could direct the course of events according to his pleasure ... We are startled and shocked in quite the same way as if Macaulay or Motley were to drop the historic mask and intimate that William of Orange was a myth.

Without pausing to consider how much Macaulay's William of Orange *was* a myth, we can only reply that Trollope would have insisted that the novel is not history and that anyone who assumes it is does not know where the border between fact and fiction lies.

Sometimes Trollope addresses only a part of his audience. Here he usually dons his favourite guise of a wise uncle talking to his 'gentle readers' – that is, young ladies, who were such an important segment of his readership. In one story, 'The Journey to Panama', two men on a transatlantic crossing talk about a woman passenger and conclude that she is ugly. 'Dear young ladies,' announces the author, 'it is thus that men always speak of you when they first see you on board ship!' Usually interjections occur when he decides that it is time to tell the reader how he is going about his writing. He began this in his first novel [*The Macdermots of Ballycloran* XXV] and it is difficult to think of any subsequent novel in which it does not occur. He often complains that it is difficult to begin a novel, which usually leads to a little chat with his readers. In *Doctor Thorne* [II] he explains: 'I quite feel that an apology is due for beginning a novel with two long dull chapters full of description.' He justifies it by the need to introduce the background: 'This is unartistic on my part, and shows want of imagination as well as want of skill. Whether or not I can atone for these faults by straightforward, simple, plain story telling – that, indeed, is very doubtful.'

The worst interjections are those in which he gives away the plot. Trollope often boasted that he did not like to keep 'secrets' from readers, but some of his interjections destroy the element of suspense that so many readers like. A well-known example occurs in *Barchester Towers*, where Eleanor Bold is subjected to a series of proposals from men who know of her fortune. Trollope has been painting amusing accounts of the wooing of Eleanor when he suddenly interrupts:

> But let the gentle-hearted reader be under no apprehension whatsoever. It is not destined that Eleanor shall marry Mr Slope or Bertie Stanhope. And here, perhaps, it may be allowed to the novelist to explain his views on a very important point in the art of telling tales. He ventures to reprobate that system which goes so far as to violate all proper confidence between the author and his readers by maintaining nearly to the end of the third volume a mystery as to the fate of their favourite personage ... Our doctrine is that the author and the reader should move along together in full confidence with each other [XV].

The worst example of this 'confidence' occurs not in a novel but in a short story, 'Aaron Trow', where an escaped convict attacks a woman in an isolated cottage in Bermuda. It is difficult to think of any other page in Trollope's fiction so filled with suspense. Then, right in the midst of the woman's desperate struggle, Trollope pops up to discuss her later reflections. The suspense is ruined: we know that she survived. However, there is one advantage of this annoying habit: one can reread the novels with little fear that memory will ruin the story. Indeed we can argue that except when he gives away the plot his interjections are not a fault but rather a reflection of his view that the novel is a partnership between author and reader, with the writer as a storyteller who interrupts not to ruin the flow but to maintain the confidence. This was particularly the case when novels were so frequently read aloud, especially when *paterfamilias* was the domestic narrator. Again, as with his rapid writing, we are talking to some degree about his 'style'. Perhaps the best test of the difference between someone who enjoys Trollope and the true Trollopean is that the latter looks forward to 'authorial intrusions', knowing that an old friend is approaching with some reflection that blends humour and wisdom. A good example occurs in *The Small House at Allington* [XXXI]: 'If you, my reader,' Trollope asks, 'ever chanced to slip into the gutter on a very wet day, did you not find that the sympathy of the bystanders, was by far the severest part of your misfortune?'

*

Anthony Trollope's outstanding strength as a writer and his claim to be taken as a great novelist lie in his ability to draw unforgettable characters. This came from his own fascination with observing humanity in all its varieties and vagaries. Towards the end of his life, on a visit to South Africa, he was invited to go to the famous Observatory. 'Do you care for stars?' the director asked politely. Trollope replied with customary bluntness: 'I care only for men and women.' This attitude was present when he read the works of other authors. After finishing Marlowe's *Edward II*, he noted in his copy: 'Not a single character which can excite sympathy.' His aim throughout his writing was to excite sympathy for his characters by allowing the reader to understand their complex make-up. Yet he was conscious how difficult it is to understand another person. 'Why be discomforted because you cannot learn the mysteries of Italian life,' he wrote in some newspaper sketches about travelling, 'seeing that in all probability you know nothing of the inner life of the man who lives next door to you at home.' His characters did become real and well-known to his contemporaries – particularly when they read about them in serial form. A reviewer of *Ralph the Heir* saw how Trollope had surpassed the social purpose of the novel, quoted at the beginning of this chapter. Not only had he given a shy race something to talk about, but he had enabled them to reach a better understanding of themselves:

> Which of us can say that we know even our own circle of friends ... half as well as we have learned within the last twelvemonth to know Sir Thomas Underwood and his daughters and niece, his ward Ralph, and his ward's cousins; ... To the mass of men, such a novel as *Ralph the Heir* brings not only a very large increase in their experience of men, but a very much larger increase than their own personal contact with the prototypes.

The *Dublin Review* of October 1872 contrasted Trollope's creations with Dickens's 'bright, fantastic fancies' and concluded, 'Mr. Trollope has given life, and speech, and motion to scores of portraits, has sent them to walk abroad and continue, and to have their names on men's lips when the actual everyday affairs and incidents of life are talked of '.[66]

*

This ability to endow characters with such believable behaviour flowed from Trollope's deep insight into human nature. For him almost every person is a complicated amalgam of good and bad. It was, of course, easier in his century to believe that there was no such thing as unmitigated evil. He rejected 'that worst of all diseases, – a low idea of humanity' [*The Eustace Diamonds* XXVIII]. Yet he also scorned that 'perfect faith in mankind which is the surest evidence of a simple mind' [*Mr. Scarborough's Family* XXXII]. With such a balanced view he could reject what he regarded as the baneful pessimism of Carlyle or the sentimental optimism of Dickens:

> We are perhaps accustomed in judging for ourselves and of others to draw the lines too sharply, and to say that on this side lie vice, folly, heartlessness, and greed, – and on the other honour, love, truth, and wisdom ... But the good and the bad mix themselves so thoroughly in our thoughts, even in our aspirations, that we must look for excellence rather in overcoming evil than in freeing ourselves from its influence [*He Knew He Was Right* LX].

If we were to be so rash as to select one basic theme of his writing, this acceptance that everyone is a mixture of good and bad would take us close to it. Throughout his work runs the need to make a choice. That choice is never an easy one, because there are always attractions to each side as well as the constant pressure of society upon each person. Whether it is an elderly clergyman contemplating resignation from a comfortable sinecure, a young maiden weighing the pros and cons of marriage, a powerful Duke considering his resignation as Prime Minister, or a civil servant toying with a subtle bribe, there is always choice, always the possibility to exercise, no matter with how much difficulty, the God-given responsibility of free will. With this concept of free will and the moral choice facing each individual Trollope saw that his century had placed a powerful weapon in the hands of those who influenced so many minds, the novelists. A novelist could only exercise this power properly if he refused to depict people as better or worse than they are, for only then could he preach that essentially Victorian sermon of self-improvement:

To make ... ourselves somewhat better, – and not by one spring heavenwards to perfection, because we cannot so use our legs, – but by slow climbing, is ... the object of all teachers, leaders, legislators, spiritual pastors and masters. He who writes tales ... probably also has, very humbly, some such object distantly before him ... The true picture of life as it is, if it could be adequately painted, would show men what they are, and how they might rise, not, indeed, to perfection, but one step first, and then another on the ladder [*The Eustace Diamonds* XXXV].

In his novels Trollope embodied those characteristic Victorian ideals expressed by Cardinal Newman in the words of his prayer, 'One step enough for me', as well as by Tennyson:[67]

> To mingle with the human race,
> And part by part to men reveal'd
> The fulness of her face –
> ...
> Turning to scorn with lips divine
> The falsehood of extremes!

Trollope's greatness lies in his ability to express the spirit of his century and yet still to speak to those who have come after it. His understanding of human nature and human behaviour has few rivals. We close most of his novels, as we leave a Shakespeare play, having seen into the minds and hearts of people who have ceased to be strangers. New lives have been revealed through a superb blend of pathos and humour. Trollope has concealed his message beneath his sugar-coating and delivered wisdom hidden in pleasure: 'Works of imagination' he told his audience at the Liverpool Institute on 13 November 1873, 'are the sermons of the present day. They are at any rate the sermons which are listened to with the most rapt attention.' As a minor Victorian poet said: 'He has helped to ameliorate the asperities of our middle-class existence.' Anthony Trollope put it somewhat better when in Liverpool: 'I am simply known to you as being one who has helped by his writings to amuse the age in which he lives.'[68]

CHAPTER SIX

Famine and Fiction

Anthony Trollope knew only some of the practical considerations about publishing when he completed his first novel in the early summer of 1845 in his new home at Clonmel. Shortly after finishing *The Macdermots of Ballycloran*, he and Rose took the ferry to England and went to a family reunion at Carlton Hill, which the Tilleys had taken over from Fanny Trollope. She had returned from Italy to visit her daughter and had paused in London to reach yet another agreement with her publisher, Henry Colburn, to produce two novels and a two-volume travel book for the next year. Eight volumes in one year was a remarkable achievement for a writer in her mid-sixties, but she had to continue that output if she was also to maintain her way of life. Only Rose Trollope had read her husband's manuscript when he asked his mother's help to find a publisher. She told him that, while she would be glad to assist, it would be better if she did not not read the novel first. Trollope's account of this in his *Autobiography* is somewhat defensive:[1]

> I knew that she did not give me the credit for the sort of cleverness necessary for such work. I could see in the faces and hear in the voices ... around me at the house in Cumberland – my mother, my sister, my brother-in-law, and, I think, my brother – that they had not expected me to come out as one of the family authors. There were three or four in the field before me, and it seemed to be almost absurd that another should wish to add himself to the number ... I could perceive that this attempt of mine was felt to be an unfortunate aggravation of the disease.

This does not really stand up to careful examination; it is one of the final flings of Anthony Trollope, the self-pitying youth. Undoubtedly his family had an hereditary inclination to write, but the only Trollope known to the literary world at this time was his mother. He even mentions that his father had been an author but that unfortunate man

197

had only brought forth two books, a legal tome and an incomplete reference work on ecclesiastical terms which no one remembered. His sister's sole novel was still in manuscript and Tom's two travel books on France had hardly brought him fame. So for all practical purposes the only author bearing the name 'Trollope' was his mother. As her standard prescription for depression was to encourage the sufferer to write a book, she would hardly deprive her son of the pleasure of seeing his name in print. She had tried to get him work with publishers when he had been a miserable clerk in London, and the theme of one of her novels at that time had been the frustrations of a young man aspiring to the life of an author.

Her real fear almost certainly was that Anthony would abandon a profession in which he was beginning to succeed. This is clear from her letter to Rose of the previous year: 'I rejoice to hear that Anthony's MS. is found, and I trust he will lose no *idle* time, but give all he can, without breaking in upon his professional labours, to finish it.'[2] While she would hardly encourage her son to write a novel just to amuse himself or to improve his handwriting, she did not want him to damage his career by dabbling at literature. She understood what financial difficulties could do to a marriage and she knew what was involved in the constant struggle required to support a family on the uncertain rewards of writing. It is likely that the motherless Rose had confided the news of her pregnancy to her mother-in-law, thereby increasing her concern. Maternal caution rather than parental jealousy was the explanation for any lack of enthusiasm that Fanny Trollope may have shown to her youngest son's hopes. Anthony, always morbidly sensitive to any apparent slight from his family, may well have magnified this in his diary upon which he drew when writing his *Autobiography*.

Trollope did admit that 'my mother ... did the best she could for me'. Unfortunately her 'best' was not very good. Perhaps her normal publishers, Colburn or Bentley, were not interested in a new author. She took the novel to Thomas Newby, a minor publisher with a disreputable history. That remarkably kind woman Mrs Gaskell said of Newby in her *Life* of Charlotte Brontë: 'I understand that truth is considered a libel in speaking of such people.' At least in Trollope's case Newby was quick with his verdict: he would publish the novel on a half-profits basis. His costs would be covered if half the 400 copies were sold, leaving publisher and author to split the profits on the remaining copies, which meant that Trollope might make about £100. This was not spectacular, but it was not many years since that was his annual salary.[3]

After copying, signing and returning the contract in September 1845, Trollope heard nothing. Almost a year later, when Mrs Trollope revisited England, she tried to force Newby to live up to his agreement. (Newby was also delaying the publication of another new novel, *Wuthering Heights*.) She reported on her efforts to Cecilia. 'I have seen Newby about Anthony's book. He, like everybody else, gives a most wretched account of the novel-market. He has offered to print the book at half-profits, but declares that he has no hope that there will be anything above expenses. He says that he thinks it very cleverly written, but that Irish stories are very unpopular.'[4] *The Macdermots of Ballycloran* finally appeared in the spring of 1847, a year when England was distracted by problems: a famine in Ireland, one of the worst financial crises of the century, and a general election. It was nevertheless a superb year for fiction: *Jane Eyre* and *Wuthering Heights* appeared and Thackeray began to publish *Vanity Fair*. Another 'Trollope novel' would need advertising to attract attention. Newby, in a characteristically shady trick, actually listed 'Mrs Trollope' as the author in some newspaper advertisements. (We have seen that her name as 'editor' had also been used to promote Tom's first book.) *The Observer* was annoyed that the title page lacked the author's Christian name: 'Many readers will take them up under the impression that they are from the pen of Mrs Trollope though only the production of an unknown Mr Trollope.'[5]

This deception was not frequently repeated, for the simple reason that Newby placed few advertisements. As the leading authority on Victorian publishing says, 'early advertisements of *The Macdermots* are almost as rare as that collector's dream, a first edition'. The reason first editions are almost unknown – there are said to be only three perfect copies – is that Newby did not distribute the 400 copies specified in the contract. He kept some back and issued them as a spurious second edition in 1848. The book is one of the three rarest first editions of Victorian novels, rivalled only by Hardy's and Gissing's first fiction.[6] Trollope thought about fifty copies were sold, but he bore no ill-will towards Newby: Miss Mitford's warning about a first book bringing no money, while not true of Fanny's, was true of her son's.

Trollope later claimed that no one paid any attention to his first novel: 'If there was any notice taken of it by any critic of the day, I did not see it.' In fact it received several reviews, many of them very favourable. It was, of course, a depressing book with its stories of madness, mutilation and murder all enacted against the stark background of Ireland and, unlike the three famous novels of the same year, it lacked a strong female character. The *Spectator*, which was ever to be his most perceptive critic, immediately spotted Trollope's greatest skill: 'The characters are natural, without much of book exaggeration: they are human in their vices, not mere abstractions of unalloyed folly, villany, weakness, or virtue.' Trollope told his first biographer that he drew upon a surprising source for this insight into human behaviour – Aristotle's *Ethics*, which 'at least helped me here, though they had not done so in the Oxford scholarship examination for which I read them'.[7]

Another comment that would apply to most of his fiction came from the ultra Tory *John Bull*, which praised the novel even though the descriptions of Irish life were at odds with its own editorial stance: 'The reader lays down the work at the end with the impression that he has visited Ireland, [and] conversed with the individuals who are introduced.' It recognised a 'dramatic power akin to that which we find in Sir Walter Scott's novels': high praise indeed for a novice! An obscure magazine called the *Critic* lived up to its name by complaining of 'slovenly writing' and announced: 'Whether Mr Trollope be boy or man, we know not ... Years will ... bring both discretion and improvement ... But if he have already reached maturity of years, his case is hopeless.' *Howitt's Journal*, edited by that ever-busy husband-and-wife team, William and Mary Howitt, alluded to literary gossip about 'Mr. A. Trollope': 'If this work be, as is said, by the son of Mrs. Trollope, then the son assuredly inherits a considerable portion of the mother's talent.' However, the *Athenaeum*, the most important literary journal, gave two pieces of advice to the new novelist: change his name to avoid confusion with his mother and develop his evident sense of humour to produce more enjoyable stories.[8]

In his *Autobiography* Trollope exaggerated the failure of *The Macdermots*: 'I can with truth declare that I expected nothing. And I got nothing. Nor did I expect fame, or even acknowledgement. I was sure that the book would fail, and it did fail most absolutely. I never heard of a person reading it in those days.' Yet it was well enough known in Ireland that within a few years a barrister would taunt the author about it when he appeared as principal witness in a postal case. Once Trollope established a reputation in the late 1850s another publisher brought out several cheap one-volume editions, but the novel never won a widespread audience. This is unfortunate because it would have given readers a sympathetic understanding of Irish life. A quarter of a century later the *Dublin Review*, the leading exponent of Irish Catholicism, examined Trollope's novels as a tribute to the man they proclaimed the greatest living novelist. It singled out *The Macdermots*: 'If an Irishman had written [it] ... the achievement would have been less surprising, but we cannot imagine any Irishman bringing to the task such unsoftened candour, such an entire impartiality.' The magazine knew why the book had failed: ' "The Macdermots of Balycloran" is one of the most melancholy books that ever was written.' As Trollope himself commented in an article on eighteenth-century fiction: 'Maintained misery may please through a short story; but the world of readers is averse to be steeped in wretchedness through a long series of volumes.'[9] By 1847 readers had had more than enough wretchedness from Ireland in fact to seek any more in fiction.

*

During the summer of 1845, when Trollope was completing *The Macdermots of Ballycloran*, his postal inspections in Cork and Tipperary gave him ample opportunity to study the countryside. Having grown up on a farm, he was well aware of the dangers of a wet summer. That summer farmers and politicians throughout the British Isles were keeping a closer watch on the weather than normal. In August the Prime Minister, Sir Robert Peel, who had already received warnings of problems in Ireland, wrote from his own estate in Staffordshire: 'We are looking here with surprise and pleasure at the novelty of the Sun – its first appearance on the stage this summer.' Incessant, chilling rain had spread over Ireland. As summer turned into autumn, it became clear that a ruined potato crop had left Ireland on the brink of disaster. Trollope was now to witness the greatest peacetime horror to strike Europe since the Black Death five hundred years before. Two years later, at the height of the famine, Lord Brougham proclaimed that the Irish Famine was worse than anything 'to be found in the pages of Josephus, or on the canvas of Poussin, or in the dismal chant of Dante'.[10]

Although the Irish peasantry's dependence on the potato produced a monotonous diet, it was a relatively wholesome one. It allowed an enormous population – over half that of England and Wales – to farm small plots of land, often of very poor quality. Trollope said these were usually less than an acre and the mud walls dividing one holding from another frequently took up a quarter of the land [*Castle Richmond* XXXIII]. Peel did not spend much time contemplating the weather but sent a Commission to Ireland. In October, as one of the Commissioners read their report to the Cabinet, the Home Secretary interrupted: 'I believe that Ireland will be decimated by the famine.' He was too optimistic: in 1845 the Irish population stood at 8,250,000. Six years

later the census recorded 6,552,385 people in Ireland: the loss was not
one in ten but two.[11]

Trollope's reactions to the Famine were complex. He was, beneath
his external bluffness, a kindly man and, unlike many English
officials, he had a genuine liking for the Irish. He rejected the idea that
the Famine was a divine judgment upon a wicked people. This view
was being propagated by a fanatical Evangelical clergyman, the Rev.
Alexander Dallas, who believed himself divinely appointed to rescue
the Irish from the 'trammels of Rome'. Trollope's God was one of mercy,
not wrath. Trollope did maintain, however, in his later writings, that
the Famine ultimately brought benefit as it began 'the cure of the evils'
that beset Ireland.[12] Like almost all his contemporaries he accepted
that the Irish population had grown too large. He also argued that
Ireland lacked an energetic middle class. This, more than religion,
distinguished her from England and Scotland: 'The fault had been the
lowness of education and consequent want of principle among the
middle classes; and this fault had been found as strongly marked
among the Protestants as it had been among the Roman Catholics.
Young men were brought up to do nothing. Property was regarded as
having no duties attached to it' [*Castle Richmond* VII]. The idea that
property had no duties was pernicious to Trollope. Most of his English
novels stress the close connection between the great landlord and all
who lived on his estates. As one clergyman says to a landlord: 'To every
man living on your land you owe ... a debt' [*The Vicar of Bullhampton*
LXVIII].

Trollope's 'Travelling Journals' for the summer of 1846 – as the
Famine's full horrors were being realised – show that he rarely spent a
night in his own house. This meant that his travels brought him past
many horrific sights. As a humane man he was made deeply unhappy
by what he saw. In *Castle Richmond*, which was published in 1860, he
wrote: 'Those who saw its course, and watched its victims, will not
readily forget what they saw' [VII]. He remembered little violence or
theft and saw only one shop, a baker's, being looted. The impression
this made on him was so strong that he recalled the event in a letter to
Rose written during a return visit to Ireland in the last months of his
life.[13] Unlike most Victorian novelists, Trollope tended to avoid long,
pathetic passages describing human misery. Extended death-bed
scenes are rare in his books: a bankrupt scoundrel may fling himself in
front of a train, or a tyrannical priestess may have a sudden heart
attack, but the Dickensian set-piece, such as the death of Little Nell,
was avoided.

However, recollections of the Famine caused him to write perhaps the most pathetic passage in his fiction. In *Castle Richmond* Herbert Fitzgerald, a young gentleman, rides into an isolated cabin in County Cork. Trollope explains that, while no one would do this to an English cottage, it is 'no uncommon' thing to see horses brought into an Irish cabin for refuge a..ong the people and pigs already there. 'People,' he says, 'are more intimate with each other, and take greater liberties in Ireland.'

> 'I have come in out of the rain for shelter,' said he.
> 'Out o'the rain, is it?' said she. 'Yer honour's welcome thin.'
> 'You seem to be very poorly off here,' said Herbert ... 'Have you no chair, and no bed to lie on?'
> 'Deed, no.'
> 'And no fire?' said he, for the damp and chill of the place struck through to his bones.
> 'Deed, no,' ... but she made no wail as to her wants.
> 'And are you living here by yourself, without furniture or utensils of any kind?'

After his eyes adjust to the darkness, he sees a dead, naked child and a baby dying in the mother's arms. 'In those days,' Trollope tells his readers,

> there was a form of face which came upon the sufferers when their state of misery was far advanced, and which was a sure sign that their last stage of misery was nearly run. The mouth would fall and seem to hang, the lips at the two ends of the mouth would be dragged down, and the lower parts of the cheeks would fall ... There were no signs of acute agony ... none of the horrid symptoms of gnawing hunger by which one generally supposes that famine is accompanied. The look is one of apathy, desolation, and death.

The woman tells him that the dead child was 'my own little Kittie' who 'guv' over moaning' but a few hours before. 'At first,' Trollope admits, the visitor

> did not like to touch the small, naked, dwindled remains of humanity from which life had fled; but gradually he overcame his disgust, and kneeling down, he straightened the limbs and closed the eyes, and folded the handkerchief round the slender body. The mother looked on him the while, shaking her head slowly, as though asking him with all the voice that was left to her, whether it were not piteous; but of words she still uttered none [XXXIII].

Fitzgerald gives the woman some money and rides off to summon what little help is available. This moving scene has a realism about it and corresponds to first-hand accounts of the period. Nothing is exaggerated, nothing is imagined: the reader is in the presence of absolute desolation. That is because the writer had seen it all.

Trollope's attitude towards the Irish, an attitude so at odds with that of most of his readers who never knew famine and the forced break-up of families, found expression when he described a railway station filled with emigrants for America. 'O, my reader,' he asks, 'have you ever seen a railway train taking its departure from an Irish station, with a freight of Irish emigrants? If so, you know how the hair is torn, and how the hands are clapped, and how the low moanings gradually swell into notes of loud lamentation.' To his English readers, who might say 'It means nothing', Trollope replies:

> It means much; it means this: that those who are separated, not only love each other, but are anxious to tell each other that they so love. We have all heard of demonstrative people. A demonstrative person, I take it, is he who is desirous of speaking out what is in his heart. For myself I am inclined to think that such speaking out has its good ends ... What is in a man, let it come out and be known to those around him; if it be bad it will find correction; if it be good it will spread and be beneficent [XXXII].

Trollope also saw the other side, the difficulties faced by those in Ireland who made such valiant efforts to help. This ability to look sympathetically on different characters, so apparent in his novels, was also present in his description of the Famine:

> The hardest burden which had to be borne by those who exerted themselves ... was the ingratitude of the poor ... or rather I should say thanklessness. To call them ungrateful would imply too deeply a reproach, for their convictions were that they were being ill used by the upper classes. When they received bad meal which they could not cook, and even in their extreme hunger could hardly eat half-cooked; when they were desired to leave their cabins and gardens, and flock to the wretched barracks which were prepared for them; when they saw their children wasting away ... it would have been unreasonable to expect that they should have been grateful. Grateful for what? Had they not at any rate a right to claim life ... But not the less was it a hard task for delicate women to work hard, and to feel that all their work was unappreciated [VIII].

He recalled the wife of a Church of Ireland rector who showed him her larder with two loaves of bread and a pan of porridge, all she had to feed her family and to help the starving. It is scarcely to be wondered that she did not long survive [XXXVII].

The Famine, whose effects continued into 1850, brought in its wake epidemics and pervasive despair. Government and private charities made valiant efforts to cope but had little success: when food did arrive the worse-off could not afford to buy it; when money was voted for public works the men were too weak to work and the pay was too small to buy what food there was. It should also be remembered that the crop failure made food in short supply throughout the British Isles and in much of Europe. Things appeared worse when people saw food being exported, but farmers were desperate to get some currency, always in short supply in Ireland, to pay their rents and to buy seed. The south-east of Ireland, where Trollope lived, had some of the worst suffering and any export was understandably resented. Cork, south-west of Tipperary, had perhaps the worst time of all: in Skibbereen, near the coast, almost 11,000 people perished from hunger or disease. On one occasion a man cried out, 'Ah, me! Your honour, there'll never be a bit and a sup again in the County Cork! The life of the world is fairly gone!' [XXXI].

It may well be asked what Anthony Trollope did to help the victims. It is impossible to answer this question as he rarely wrote about his own kindnesses or charities. When he became famous, others noted his charitable acts. In 1867 Dickens wrote to him after hearing that he was raising money for a widow, 'I knew she could have no stauncher or truer friend.' In the 1870s, when living in London, he visited his club every day. On his way there he would stop to deliver a pheasant, some delicacies or fruit to an ailing friend forced to live in lodgings. On another occasion he rescued an old Irishman from a slum and paid to keep him in comfort till he died, simply because he had slightly known the man in Mallow and because of his love for the Irish. Even when not travelling round Ireland Trollope was unable to escape the Famine: another English official reported that the hated barges which took Irish produce to the ports 'leave Clonmel once a week with the export supplies under convoy which, last Tuesday, consisted of 2 guns, 50 cavalry and 80 infantry'.[14] It can only be assumed that he must have taken part, as did so many others, in private efforts to alleviate distress.

Trollope did not share the fashionable English view, which Scott had held twenty years earlier, that Ireland's greatest curse was the absentee landlords who used Irish rents to finance extravagances in London or Naples. Such landlords are not as prominent in his novels as in many other fictional accounts of Ireland, although *The Kellys and the O'Kellys* does feature Viscount Ballindine, whose entire life was spent 'hovering about the fringes of the English Court'. Trollope makes him farcical by giving him a post as custodian of the Queen Dowager's lace [II].[15] To Trollope, both in his novels and in his factual articles, the problem was not the great absent landlords but the small ones who were all too present: 'The scourge of Ireland was the existence of a class who looked to be gentlemen living on their property, but who should have earned their bread by the work of their brow. There were men to be found in shoals through the country speaking of their properties and boasting of their places, but who owned no properties.' He was to present several characters from this group in his first two Irish novels, the most notable being Larry Macdermot. Such men were principal factors in creating 'a state of things ... which discouraged labour, which discouraged improvements in farming, which discouraged any produce from the land except the potato crop; which maintained one class of men in what they considered to be the gentility of idleness, and another class, the people of the country, in the abjectness of poverty' [*Castle Richmond* VII].

In most of his writing, particularly his travel books, Anthony Trollope stressed the sacredness of work. He would not have known the phrase 'Protestant work-ethic' but he both preached and practised it. It was in Ireland that he first discovered his boundless capacity for hard work as well as an increasing dislike for those who did not share this passion. He could be quite intolerant of anyone, be they Irish peasants, ex-slaves in the West Indies, conquered Zulu warriors or idle young dandies in Mayfair, who did not follow the gospel of work. Tom Trollope, writing after his younger brother's death, saw in Anthony's attitude a fundamental difference between them. By then Tom had almost rivalled Anthony in numbers of printed words: 'Yet,' he admitted, 'I have a very pretty turn for idleness too ... Anthony had no such turn. Work to him was a necessity and a satisfaction. He used often to say he envied me the capacity for being idle.'[16] This devotion to work led Trollope to over-emphasise the effect that idleness by all classes had on the Famine. For him one did not alleviate the consequences of Famine, let alone avoid another, by romanticising the victims.

Almost a decade later he returned to his favourite sermon on work. The Famine had had the good effect, he argued, of raising not only the Irishman's regard for labour but also the general respect accorded to a man who worked: 'Seven short years ago how were the workmen of the soil treated? They were called scum of the earth, the dregs of humanity ... Irishmen could not realise to themselves then that not only the wealth of a country, but its honour also, all its dignity among nations, must depend upon its labour. They are beginning to learn the lesson, now that their labourers have gone from them.'[17] The popular notion that Trollope's writings depict the pleasantries of Victorian life among the idle is based on selected recollections of the Barset novels. If we stray outside the comfortable borders of Barsetshire, we see that Trollope was a fierce exponent of the Victorian gospel of work. He delivered that message with a forcefulness worthy of Samuel Smiles or Carlyle. In a 1879 lecture on the Zulus in South Africa he told his audience: 'The natural, I may say, the only happy condition of a man is to work for his living.'[18] Old Mr Trollope's frequent denunciations of 'idleness' had obviously had a lasting effect on his youngest son.

The Famine made the work of the Post Office more difficult as emigration both to Britain and America increased the volume of post just when it became difficult to obtain feed for the horses. Yet, by carrying on its service in the midst of this unparalleled catastrophe, the Post Office played a crucial role in aiding relief efforts, such as those whereby English parishes 'adopted' Irish parishes and regularly sent sums of money through the post. A reliable and cheap postal service allowed scattered families to maintain at least some contact. An efficient Post Office also helped to maintain those commercial links that were vital to Irish recovery.

*

Throughout Trollope's life he had a strong interest in public affairs and a desire to influence events. Because he is known as a novelist, the 'public man' is forgotten. As we have already seen and as he admitted in his autobiographical short story 'The Panjandrum', he had dreamed of editing a political magazine or newspaper in his hobbledehoy days. Once he was famous, he not only stood for Parliament but started journals with a strong political flavour. All his travel books were used to influence political opinions, and in some public lectures his Liberal beliefs were obvious. So it is hardly surprising that such an horrific spectacle as the Famine should have turned his thoughts towards the press.

In 1848 he revisited Lincoln's Inn, twenty years after his miserable school holiday there, when he read Shakespeare in his father's chambers. He called on John Forster, best remembered today as the biographer of Dickens but then editor of the *Examiner*, a leading Liberal publication with sales of 6,000 a week, a large circulation for the period. The editor was also, in spite of his politics, a friend of Fanny Trollope. The *Examiner* had a distinguished literary pedigree, from the days when its editor, Leigh Hunt, went to prison for libelling the Prince Regent. As the American novelist Fenimore Cooper stated, 'for vigour, consistency, truth, and distinctiveness of thought ... this journal stands at the very head of this species of literature'. To Trollope, Forster was the best editor of a weekly newspaper in England.[19]

Trollope offered to write on the Irish situation. As a faithful reader of *The Times*, he had been infuriated by articles by 'S.G.O.', written after a tour of Ireland. The initials concealed, though not very effectively, the Rev. and Hon. (later Lord) Sidney Godolphin Osborne. Trollope did not question much of S.G.O.'s descriptions of Poor Houses filled with beds containing the dead, the dying and the barely alive. His fury arose from Osborne's assertion that the government had done virtually nothing. Trollope always took a strong pride in the work of government officials. Few things enraged him more than clever jibes from men like Osborne whom he regarded as dilettantes making off-hand criticisms of complicated subjects. This distinguished Trollope from Dickens or his own mother, whose novels attacked corruption or incompetence and promoted social reforms. Throughout his life, Trollope often attacked 'philanthropists' which to him meant woolly-minded apostles of theoretical progress. 'S.G.O.' was just the first: he would later attack American abolitionists and opponents of British colonisation in New Zealand.

Forster agreed to publish Trollope's articles as 'letters', signed only 'A.T.' The first appeared in August 1849 and contrasted his experiences with Osborne's: 'I have been eight years in the country, and have passed those years in continual journeys through its southern, western, and midland portions ... I have been thrown much among Irishmen of every class ... I have observed, I will not say as an alien or a foreigner, but still as a stranger.' After this first article 'A.T.' sent five more the next year as the Famine was ending. His main argument was that Osborne and other critics of government action had ignored the difficulties faced as well as the achievements made. He defended the Liberal Prime Minister, Lord John Russell: 'No minister of Great Britain had ever such a job of work set before him.' Indeed posterity has not been fair to the efforts made by British officials to cope with this unparalleled disaster. Trollope knew most of the difficulties: poor communications and transport, lack of confidence in local officials, religious bigotry on all sides and general apathy. He dismissed the idea that the dead had been left unburied: 'The whole period was spent by me in passing from one place to another in the south and west of Ireland. I visited at the worst periods those places which were most afflicted; and if corpses lying exposed, unheeded, and in heaps, were to be seen, no man's eye would have been oftener offended in that way than mine.'

He praised the attempts to get food to the starving. This was the first major famine where government, private charities and even international help attempted to meet a virtually insoluble problem. He pointed out how difficult it was to organise food or work for three million people by remarking that there were said to be only three men in England capable of manoeuvring 50,000 soldiers out of Hyde Park. The late twentieth century has seen how difficult it is to cope with famines even with modern transport, communications and well-organised charities. The British government bought large supplies of maize from America and distributed vast quantities of it, though many Irishmen refused to eat a grain they considered unfit for human beings.[20]

Gradually the Government determined that the only way to assist present need and ensure future prosperity was to provide public works so that men could earn money as continual distribution of free food would destroy any hope of salvaging Irish agriculture. Trollope endorsed these 'wise and good rules' although years later he expressed his sympathy with the 'unfortunates' who were forced from their small plots into regular work: 'They were wretched-looking creatures, half-clad, discontented, with hungry eyes, each having at heart's core a deep sense of injustice done personally upon him They hated this work of cutting hills ... hated it, though it was to bring them wages and save them and theirs from actual famine and death' [*Castle Richmond* XVIII]. His main concern in the *Examiner* articles, particularly the later ones, was not to rake over old controversies or even to defend civil servants. It was to assess the future possibilities for Ireland, where he saw grounds for hope: the spring planting reached a new record and the decline in the number of small farms promised agricultural improvement. As always he stressed facts: he had discovered how much the Irish estates of the Duke of Devonshire had prospered since the rent for tenant farmers had been cut. Trollope was well aware, from his father's bitter experience, of the struggle to reconcile a high rent with bad harvests. He therefore praised those landlords who had helped their tenants, a fact often neglected in folk memory or nationalist harangues. Many years later he recalled how his political hero Lord Palmerston aided his Irish tenants. Trollope believed that the best thing for Ireland would be for industrious men to take up farming. To some extent this happened and did improve the Irish economy in the mid-Victorian period. He paid much attention to the complicated issue of selling estates, for the relations between landlord and tenant were always important to Trollope. He would return to this theme in his last novel, *The Landleaguers*. In his final *Examiner* article Trollope argued that despair was the greatest danger:[21]

> To combat this feeling should be the effort of every friend of Ireland; to encourage the industry, the hitherto feeble industry of the country; to do battle with the habitual sloth, and almost habitual despair; to awake a manly feeling of inward confidence and a reliance on the justice of Heaven, should now be the work of Government, of Parliament, and of every individual who has an interest in the country.

It might be thought odd that a civil servant should write a series of controversial articles. There were however several precedents, including that of Sir Charles Trevelyan, one of the most important officials of his time. In 1843 Trevelyan had toured Ireland and written some articles in the *Morning Chronicle* under the pseudonym 'Philalethes'. The Prime Minister and the Home Secretary were not pleased; Peel called him 'a consummate fool' for revealing an official trip to the public, but Trevelyan's career was not damaged. The Lord Lieutenent of Ireland, Lord Clarendon, was in regular communication with the owner of the *Economist*, 'leaking' much official information.[22] Even if there were others, Trollope was taking a risk that someone in the Post Office might find him a 'consummate fool'. Perhaps to avoid this, 'A.T.' claimed that he had no connection 'with any of the officers or measures of the Government'. As a postal official, Trollope may not have been involved with government policy, but he always had a strong sense of his own identity as a public servant. He did not even receive any payment for the articles to compensate for the time or risk he ran.

The *Examiner* 'letters' show that Trollope lacked the concise style needed for effective journalism. As in much of his later non-fiction, he could not resist inventing a character, 'John Armstrong of Castle Armstrong', as an example of a landlord. The articles had no real impact and have largely been forgotten, but at least Trollope had the satisfaction, as he later wrote, of giving his views albeit 'with a voice that was not very audible'[23] [*Castle Richmond* VII]. They remain an impressive, if wordy, account of the Famine, even to an age used to seeing famines on television screens, and are still worth reading because of the Famine's bitter legacy to Anglo-Irish relations. The historian or politician anxious to understand the troubles in Northern

Ireland could well examine them with some profit, though with little pleasure.

*

Neither the Famine nor journalism kept Trollope from his real literary work: writing novels. The failure of *The Macdermots* might have discouraged most novelists, or at least forced them onto a new subject. Trollope remained faithful to the novel and to Ireland. Much of his second novel appears to have been finished before the first one reached its delayed publication. The second, at least, had a better publisher, Henry Colburn, who had already produced thirteen of Fanny Trollope's novels. Trollope had originally approached her other publisher, Richard Bentley, but told him: 'I will *not part with the Mss. on any other terms than that of payment for it. I mean, that I will not publish it myself – or have it published on half profits – or have the payment for it conditional on the sale. It is & must be, much more the publisher's interest to push a work when it is his own property.'* After reading the novel Bentley had rejected it – at least on Trollope's terms. The author finally accepted a half-profits arrangement from Colburn, negotiated by one of the Merivales. Colburn felt that the topical Irish subject demanded that 'it should appear as soon as it could be printed'.[24]

The Kellys and the O'Kellys is set before the Famine. It is the story of two families, distant cousins, the one Protestant aristocrats and the other Catholic tenant farmers. The plot follows the son of each family until he marries an heiress, devices which would become standard fare in many of Trollope's later novels. The story drew widely on the author's experience of Irish life, particularly on his travels and knowledge of inns, such as that kept by Mrs Kelly. He continued his fictional portrayal of mental instability: one character, 'Anty' Lynch, is regarded as not quite right in the head. With her, Trollope first reveals his great sympathy for the lone woman:

> She was never pretty; but, in all Ireland, there was not a more single-hearted, simple-minded young woman. I do not use the word simple as foolish; for, though uneducated, she was not foolish. But she was unaffected, honest, humble, and true, entertaining a very lowly idea of her own value ... She had been so little thought of all her life by others, that she had never learned to think much of herself; she had had but few acquaintances, and no friends, and had spent her life, hitherto, so quietly and silently, that her apparent apathy was attributed rather to want of subjects of excitement, than to any sluggishness of disposition [IV].

So many of his strong points are evident in this passage: the careful use of language in distinguishing between 'simple' and 'foolish', the attempt to present a real character and not a Dickensian caricature, and a description which in its gentleness matches the woman being described. He also gives the precise details of her fortune: £400 a year. Her brother is a great villain, a man driven nearly insane by greed for his sister's fortune, even to contemplating murder. In his first two books Trollope showed a fascination with psychological obsession and madness: themes that were to be repeated in novel after novel. The dreadful brother ended up like most of Trollope's villains: an exile on the continent.

The Kellys and the O'Kellys introduced other features of his novels: the first fox-hunting scene, referring to a doctor as 'the Galen' of his town and using some variant of 'Richard' as a name for a servant [XXIII, XXIX]. One suspects that Trollope was enjoying another private joke with Rose about her sewing when he refers to a wife spending her time among 'wool and the worsted, and the knitting-needles, the unfinished vallances and interminable yards of fringe' [XXIX]. Most later critics have agreed Trollope's own verdict: while the plot is not as good as in his first novel, the story is better told. His mastery of dialogue is seen by his more effective use of Irish dialect. In the first novel there was so much dialect that it made some chapters rather tedious. One of the main love plots in *The Kellys* is not very well handled as the couple, who have been driven apart before the novel begins, are only allowed to meet again in the penultimate chapter.

The novel does show that Trollope had established his ability to bring characters alive, perhaps the most important difference between the mere storyteller and the great novelist. This was not apparent in *The Macdermots*. In the second novel we are introduced to the Earl of Cashel in the same way in which the author must have encountered similar local potentates who had complained about the postal service. First the reader sees the old castle, 'now a cow shed', and then the modern mansion which is 'like the grounds, large, commodious, and uninteresting'. Then the narration takes us to the book room, where sits the Earl himself:

Lord Cashel was a man about sixty-three, with considerable external dignity of appearance ... He had been an earl, with a large income for thirty years; and in that time he had learned to look collected, even when his ideas were confused; to keep his eye steady, and to make a few words go a long way. He had never been intemperate, and was, therefore, strong and hale for his years, – he had not done many glaringly foolish things, and therefore had a character for wisdom and judgment. He had run away with no man's wife, and since his marriage, had seduced no man's daughter; he was, therefore, considered a moral man [XI].

This is really as fine and funny as many descriptions in the later novels.

Once again, as in *The Macdermots*, a great part of the story concerns clergymen. It is evident from *The Kellys* that Trollope had spent much time observing the nuances in bigotry between Ireland's churches. Only a few days after his arrival in the country he had been much criticised by a Protestant acquaintance for going to dinner at a Catholic's house and was told he must choose one side or the other. He never did, but instead became an observer of both. Trollope shows that the complex nature of Irish society was not merely a case of native Catholics oppressed by alien Protestants, something rarely grasped by visiting journalists, resident preachers or 'jet-set' politicians of the present day. In *The Kellys* Trollope is particularly concerned with attitudes within his own church, the Church of Ireland, which was not mentioned in his first book.* He knew the Anglican clergy in Ireland well, not only from his own attendance at church but from his official travels, which brought him into frequent contact with parsons, often the only gentleman in a parish. In years to come he would say many harsh, and some inaccurate, things about the Church of Ireland; yet one of the strong points in this novel is its insight into different views within his own Church.[25]

In a later novel, *Castle Richmond*, Trollope depicts the strained relations between a Catholic priest and an Anglican parson brought together on a Famine Relief Committee. The priest was convinced that the rector was practising 'souperism', that is offering soup to the poor if they converted to Protestantism. Trollope shows how the two men had come to 'hate each other'. At this point he interjects his own recollection: 'I do not wish it to be understood that this sort of feeling always prevailed in Irish parishes between the priest and the parson even before the days of the famine. I myself have met a priest at a parson's table, and have known more than one parish in which Protestant and Roman Catholic clergymen lived together on amicable terms.' After showing how the two rivals come to a grudging respect for one another in a time of calamity, Trollope asks: 'How often does it not

---

*After the Act of Union in 1801 Ireland was fully incorporated into a new United Kingdom of Great Britain and Ireland. Under the Act the established Church of Ireland was joined to the Church of England to create the United Church of England and Ireland. The United Church continued until the Irish Disestablishment Act of 1869 dissolved it as of 1 January 1871. Trollope was therefore automatically a member of the Irish Church when he arrived in Ireland.

happen that when we come across those we have hated and avoided all our lives, we find they are not quite so bad as we had thought?' [X, XIII]. By a skilful use of dialogue he presents a variety of religious convictions and prejudices revealed by priests, parsons, servants and the bigoted wife of the parson – a woman quite similar to Mrs Proudie. In *The Kellys and the O'Kellys* two rectors discuss their Catholic neighbours. One clergyman is a fanatic who rants about 'the scarlet woman'. Here Trollope is depicting the type of Evangelical clergyman who was of increasing importance in the Church of Ireland. (Trollope, almost certainly, is enjoying another little joke in calling this bigot Mr O'Joscelyn, as Lord Jocelyn was a leading fanatic who spent his time uncovering new horrors perpetrated by the 'Scarlet Woman'.) The other fictional rector goes away from the conversation with what was surely the novelist's own opinion: 'I'd sooner by half be a Roman myself, than think so badly of my neighbours' [XXXVIII]. This rector could ask the local priest to loan him some parishioners should he want a large congregation to impress a visiting superior: it was a trick actually played in Ireland.[26]

Throughout *The Kellys* Trollope drew on his great knowledge of Irish life. It is obvious, for example, how well he knew Dublin. Although many of his comments about Ireland are tinged with fondness – 'Kates, particularly Irish Kates, are pretty by prescription' – he attacked aspects of life that irritated him. Trollope was increasingly a man who hated to waste time. All of life should be occupied in purposeful activity: seeing that letters arrived on breakfast tables, chasing dishonest postmasters, leaping ditches in pursuit of a fox, scribbling words on paper, working up schoolboy Latin, or seeking out some historical spot. In this, as in so many things, he was the true Victorian. The slower – he would say idler – ways of Irish travel infuriated him not so much because of the discomfort as because of the immoral waste of time. Therefore in *The Kellys* he fired a broadside, similar to his mother's attack on American steamboats, at the Ballinasloe canal boats which he regarded as 'floating prisons':

Reading is out of the question. I have tried it myself, and seen others try it, but in vain. The sense of motion ... the noises above you; the smells around you ... the fumes of punch; the snores of the man under the table ... the loud complaints of the old lady near the door, who cannot obtain the gratuitous kindness of a glass of water; and the baby-soothing lullabies of the young one, who is suckling her infant under your elbow. These things alike prevent one from reading, sleeping, or thinking. All one can do is to wait till the long night gradually wears itself away.

When writing such a passage, he obviously dredged his memory for every detail.[27] Having relived on paper many miserable trips, his mind naturally recalled the food on these boats: 'the eternal half-boiled leg of mutton, floating in a bloody sea of grease and gravy'. We come close to Trollope's vibrant personality when he concludes: 'I believe the misery of the canal-boat chiefly consists in a pre-conceived and erroneous idea of its capabilities. One prepares oneself for occupation – an attempt is made to achieve actual comfort – and both end in disappointment; the limbs become weary with endeavouring to fix themselves in a position of repose, and the mind is fatigued more by the search after, than the want of, occupation' [VIII]. This passage reveals that curious combination of restlessness and the need for comfort that drove him to write over sixty books.

The Kellys opens with an actual event, the trial in Dublin of Daniel O'Connell for conspiracy in 1843. Trollope's comment is not without continuing relevance: 'Nothing ever so strengthened the love of the Irish for ... O'Connell, as his imprisonment; nothing ever so weakened his power over them as his unexpected enfranchisement' [I]. Trollope must have attended many sessions and heard much of the oratory that rang round the courtroom. The case against the Irish MP aroused great interest in England. W.H. Russell, later to become a friend of Trollope, launched his career as the most famous reporter of the age by covering the trial for *The Times*. That paper was so keen to be the first with the verdict that a special steamer waited at Kingstown for Russell to begin his dash to London. It was all in vain, as Russell mistakenly revealed his exclusive news to a rival journalist whose paper scooped *The Times*. (In no other novel did Trollope refer to so many living characters: there were references to the great 'Apostle of Temperance', Father Mathew, and even to royal personages such as the Dowager Queen Adelaide and the young Princess Royal.) If Trollope thought use of the famous trial as an overture would commend the book to English audiences he was again disappointed.

The Kellys did not receive as much praise from the reviewers as *The Macdermots*. One review, however, remained in Trollope's mind and thirty years later he recalled its substance. A friend got *The Times* to review the book. Although the paper misspelled the book's title it praised the humour, even if it was described as 'coarse', a criticism frequently made about his mother's books. The second novel, like the first, was a failure: only 140 of the 375 copies printed were sold. 'I changed my publisher,' Trollope recalled years later, 'but did not change my fortune.' Colburn, whose losses came to £63 10s 1½d, told Trollope that 'it is evident that readers do not like novels on Irish subjects so well as on others'. The publisher advised him: 'It is impossible for me to give any encouragement to you to proceed in novel writing.'[28] Like *The Macdermots, The Kellys* was eventually reprinted; but only after Trollope had become a known author.

*

In the autumn of 1848 Anthony and Rose Trollope with their two young sons, Henry and Fred, moved from Clonmel to Mallow, an old spa town on the river Blackwater in County Cork. Here he rented a tall Georgian house on the High Street. This was the first home of their own; in Clonmel they had only rented part of a house. Mallow was more central for his postal duties, and it was at the centre of one of the most celebrated hunts in Ireland. It was close to Killarney, whose beauties delighted Trollope and his many visitors. Mallow offered other advantages: there was, for instance, a regular delivery of fish, including that favourite Victorian delicacy, turbot, brought round by a man on his donkey, an event Trollope fondly recalled in *Castle Richmond* [XXXVII]. Nor did he mind the large amount of rain: he told Tom that while it was frequently 'sloppy' there was little snow or frost.[29] Years later he set *Castle Richmond* in the countryside round Mallow.

By 1848 the worst ravages of the Famine were ending. That year also saw a attempt by an Irish MP, Smith O'Brien, to raise a rebellion. Trollope laughed at his fellow Harrovian's attempt, which ended in a cabbage garden where the few revolutionaries surrendered. He recalled all this decades later when he visited the reprieved O'Brien's house in Australia. In his last novel, *The Landleaguers*, Trollope declared that O'Brien 'achieved little beyond his own exile – but his words acting upon his followers, produced Fenianism' [XLI]. Though Trollope regarded the whole episode as a farce, his mother, writing from Italy, itself in revolutionary turmoil, was worried. Reports had appeared in *The Times* that Clonmel was one of the towns where 'the insurrection' would occur and that the struggle would commence 'on the line stretching from Cork to Tipperary'. It was only natural that Fanny Trollope should worry that her son would be caught up in any fighting as he carried out his official duties. He blamed *The Times* for exaggerating the disturbances: 'everybody now magnifies the rows at a distance from him.' In his *Examiner* articles he referred to 'these accounts ... published in the "Times" describing the movements of rebels in towns, of which the inhabitants of those towns had heard nothing'. It was, he added, 'frequently only on the receipt of that paper that ladies learnt that they had been moving about in the midst of an armed insurrection!' He also assured his mother that there was no possibility of a revolution in England after the working-class Chartist demonstration had proved another farce, because 'there is too much intelligence in England for any large body of men to look for sudden improvement; and not enough intelligence in Ireland for any body of men at all to conceive the possibility of social improvement'.[30]

However much revolutionary attempts proved damp squibs in England or Ireland, they were more successful across Europe in 1848. In the Austrian Empire, Italy, Germany and France dynasties fell or were shaken to their foundations. To Anthony Trollope the mobs' victims were literally household names. Prince Metternich, the veteran statesman who fled from Vienna to an elegant mansion in Brighton, had been a great friend of his mother: 'Coming to Vienna and admiring Prince Metternich is one and the same thing,' she had written ten years before. The Grand Duke of Tuscany, whose weekly receptions had been much frequented by Fanny and Tom Trollope, temporarily left Florence. Louis Philippe, who also stumbled ashore onto English soil disguised as 'Mr Smith', had once received Mrs Trollope in the Tuileries. 'Few kings have fallen in my day in whose fate I have not rejoiced,' Trollope wrote almost fifteen years later, 'except that poor citizen King of the French.'[31] The 1848 revolutions undoubtedly turned Trollope's mind towards that greater Revolution, the final act of which ended at Waterloo in the year of his birth.

His first two novels had drawn upon his intimate knowledge of Ireland. Now he changed tack completely and, following the example of Sir Walter Scott, wrote an historical novel, *La Vendée*, about the heroic resistance of the royalists in western France, where the wholesale slaughter of nobles, priests and peasants had become notorious, even by the standards of revolutionary murder. He began his novel of the French Revolution in 1848, almost a decade before Dickens began *A Tale of Two Cities*. Dickens drew upon Carlyle's *French Revolution* which had appeared in 1837, but Trollope placed his reliance – too great a reliance – upon French memoirs. Nor did Trollope have any great familiarity with the country he was writing about as his visits to France appear to have been confined to Parisian jaunts. Tom, however, had written two books about western France, the heartland of the royalist cause.* In addition Fanny Trollope had gathered some anecdotes during her visit to Lafayette. No doubt Trollope's Irish

*In the first of these, *A Summer in Brittany*, Tom introduced a new word into English usage: when referring to an architectural style he used the French term for revival or renewal and said it dated from 'the renaissance' period. Anthony's first use of the word

experiences helped him understand the passionate devotion to Catholicism which played such a large role in that other Celtic outpost, Brittany. Whereas Tom depicted the French priests as 'blind leaders of the blind', Anthony was much more sympathetic to the religious feelings that inspired the peasantry. Father Jerome, one of the main characters in this novel, is depicted as an intelligent, devout and energetic man but one who never hestitated to use 'superstition to forward his own views' [III]. *La Vendée* also contains the longest sermons in any of Trollope's fiction.

The novel opens with the fall of the French Monarchy in August 1792 and ends, in the year of the author's birth, with the entrance of the allied armies into Paris after Waterloo. Most of the book follows the military campaigns of the peasant armies of western France in their attempt to restore the Bourbons. The novel is strongly royalist in tone and the denunciations of revolutionaries remind one of Edmund Burke. However, it also shows Trollope's habit of sympathising with the point of view of his principal characters: he is telling the story of the royalist uprising and therefore tells it from their point of view. In addition his novel draws most of its facts from the royalist *Memoirs of the Marquise de La Rochejaquelin*, which he even cites in a footnote. From it he got most of his details, like the peasants' devotion to a captured cannon nicknamed 'Marie Jeanne', now at the Musée des Invalides. This book, which had been translated by Sir Walter Scott in 1816, quickly became one of the most popular accounts of the Revolution, and a copy was said to have been found in Napoleon's carriage at Waterloo. The author was still alive at the time Trollope wrote. In the novel she is Madame de Lescure; it was only after the Vendean wars that her second marriage gave her the name that dominates Trollope's book, Rochejaquelin. Trollope based the novel on the Rochejaquelin family: he used the historical novelist's privilege of inventing a new daughter for the family so that he could introduce a love story. Her brother Henri's exploits were well remembered at the time Trollope was writing. Tom Trollope had highly praised the royalist leader as 'the noble-hearted Larochejaquelin'. Tom, however, had tried to see the background to the uprising more objectively than his younger brother.[32]

Trollope also acknowledged a debt to Lamartine's recent history, *The Girondists*. Only a few years before Trollope wrote *La Vendée*

appears to be in his *The West Indies and the Spanish Main* where he refers to a cathedral in Panama as being in a style 'so generally odious to an Englishman's eye and ear, under the title of Renaissance' by which he meant what we call Baroque.

Archibald Alison's massive history of the French Revolution had appeared. While Disraeli made fun of Alison as 'Mr Wordy', his history, which still decorates the shelves of many second-hand book shops, is a vast collection of day-by-day accounts, which Trollope appears to have used or, rather, over-used in his novel, although he later said he found Alison 'unreadable' if reliable.

He exaggerates the role of Jacques Cathelineau as the inspirer of the uprising and portrays him as an heroic figure who realises that his love for Rochejaquelin's aristocratic sister is an impossible one. Ironically the cause for which he fights itself prevents his love's being fulfilled. Trollope's fiction provides a perfect romantic death for the peasant hero by allowing Agatha de La Rochejaquelin to reach him before his firal hour. Although the real Cathelineau was a carter, Trollope makes him a postillion. Perhaps that was the only example of an ordinary Frenchman that Trollope had yet had time to observe on hurried trips to Paris. *La Vendée* is an early example of what would become a trend in Trollope's non-English novels: giving important roles to characters from the lower social classes. This is often not obvious in *La Vendée* because of the novel's greatest fault: the dialogue makes no distinctions and all the characters, whether noblemen or peasants, speak the same.

Trollope was aware that Robespierre was a hated figure although he predicted, quite accurately, that 'some quaint historian' would some day attempt to vindicate him. The novelist in no sense does this, but does grapple with the contradictions in the man's character. He shows his good points but concludes that the popular condemnation is accurate:

> He believed in nothing but himself, and the reasoning faculty with which he felt himself to be endowed. He thought himself perfect in his own human nature, and wishing to make others perfect as he was, he fell into the lowest abyss of crime and misery in which a poor human creature ever wallowed. He seems almost to have been sent into the world to prove the inefficacy of human reason to effect human happiness [XXII].

This offers an important insight not so much into Robespierre as into Anthony Trollope: it shows not only his constant attempt to see contrasting sides of a character but his distrust of both absolute power and absolute reason. He had inherited enough of his mother's Romanticism and read enough of Burke to know that reason rarely is the sole driving force of humanity but, when it pretends to be, misery follows in its wake. *La Vendée* is important for any understanding of Trollope's outlook for it shows the strong layer of romantic conservatism that underlay his Victorian liberalism. The Vendean cause had a perfect appeal for him: it allowed him to sympathise with rebels against Utopian tyrants. Trollope concludes his novel with a reference to the 1848 Revolution and the hope that 'France will congratulate herself on another restoration'. Napoleon III and yet another French republic occurred before this novel was brought out in a cheap one-volume form allowing Trollope to add in a footnote in the 1870s: 'France must again wait till the legitimate heir of the old family shall be willing to reign as a constitutional sovereign.'

When Henry Colburn reported the sad news about the sales of *The Kellys* in November 1848 he added: 'As however I understand you have nearly finished the novel of La Vendée, perhaps you will favor me with a sight of it when convenient.' Trollope cannot have been as far advanced as Colburn had assumed, for he did not send the manuscript until February 1850, when it was accepted. Tom acted on his brother's behalf and managed to get £20 as an advance: it was the first money Anthony Trollope made from writing. *La Vendée* was published in June 1850 and was a complete failure. In the 1920s Hugh Walpole, himself a distinguished historical novelist, praised the 'true strain of human sympathy running through the book'. He maintained that Trollope wrote a better historical novel than Bulwer Lytton or Harrison Ainsworth, the two most popular exponents of the genre. Walpole was particularly impressed with Trollope's depiction of Adolphe Denot, a coward who betrays the royalists. As Walpole so rightly said, such a figure would have been most unattractive to Trollope. 'Had Denot been the work of a modern novelist,' wrote Walpole as a 'modern novelist' in 1928, 'he would have been compelled to yield to a very drastic course of psycho-analysis', but Trollope allows this contemptible figure to reveal himself in his own actions and words.[33]

Ironically Balzac, with whom Trollope has so much in common, had launched his own career with a novel on the Vendean uprising, *Les Chouans*, though on a later phase; it is far superior to Trollope's. Both writers had been influenced by Scott, Fenimore Cooper and Maria Edgeworth. *La Vendée* attracted less notice than Trollope's first two novels and even the *Examiner* had to strive to find something good to say about its recent contributor, 'A.T.': 'Apart from an ultra-royalist bias (real or affected) Mr. Trollope has good sense, candour, and some power of analysing character.'[34] When Trollope looked back on his historical novel he agreed it was 'inferior' to his two Irish ones because 'I ... knew ... nothing of life in the La Vendée country'. He had violated one of the basic canons of the successful novelist: to write only about what one knows.

Trollope's first three novels shared two fates: they were a failure at the time and have been, for the most part, neglected ever since. Yet for anyone interested in Trollope they reveal much about his character. All three show his ability to observe alien societies with a combination of detachment and sympathy. They show how strong a well-spring of Romanticism existed beneath his gruff Victorian realism. Those two most characteristic causes of Romantic feeling, the ruined manor house and a devotion to fallen greatness, stirred him to write. These books also show two aspects that are normally neglected by most of his devoted readers: an interest in violence and a fascination with madness. They teem with violence – murder, executions, seduction and revolution – and the violence is often connected with the effect of madness or obsession on a family. He did not need to imagine this: he had only to recall the Harrow farmhouse after his father's temper drove most of the family to America, leaving the young Anthony alone with that increasingly demented parent. The three novels also share a theme of vanished grandeur, be it Irish Catholics dreaming of the glories of past centuries or French aristocrats driven from their châteaux. This too had an obvious appeal to a man always conscious of his status as a 'gentleman' yet one who had witnessed the gradual decline of his family.

Anthony Trollope could not know that the failures of his earliest novels would soon be followed by success and fame. Those blessings would help to dilute the the bitterness that underlay his childhood and the frustrations that bedevilled his youth. Yet underneath most of his later novels, books that often glow with the depiction of security and wealth, lay themes of madness, dispossession and violence. There was the ever-present fear that one could so easily be flung from the comfort of a rectory or the luxury of a country house into the swirling world of misery and poverty that lurked round them.

*

Anthony Trollope was thirty-five when *La Vendée* was published. Despite its failure he persevered in trying to find some type of writing that would bring money and a sense of achievement. He was buoyed up by his common sense: 'The idea that I was the unfortunate owner of an unappreciated genius never troubled me.' He tried book reviewing when Charles Merivale, the elder brother of Trollope's closest friend, produced the first volumes of his *History of the Romans under the Empire*. Trollope read them carefully and sent a review to the *Dublin University Magazine*. Though he was unknown to the editors, they published his article in June 1851. He paid considerable attention to the author's style of writing. In spite of Trollope's criticism that the *History* was too much a biography of Caesar, Merivale pronounced it the best review of his book, a comment Anthony proudly retailed to Tom when he forwarded a copy of the journal to Florence.[35] Trollope, like many men of his century, was fascinated with Caesar, whose career had close parallels with Napoleon's and indeed with Napoleon's nephew, who was himself currently in the process of terminating another French republic. In years to come both Trollope and Napoleon III would write books about Caesar. Trollope's article at least gave him some recognition in the literary world of Ireland. Trollope never liked to be thought of as just a civil servant, or even as just a novelist. He always yearned to be regarded as a thoughtful and well-read man. Not only did this review give him a real interest in Latin literature, it led to a continued study of Caesar's character and ambitions, a not unuseful pursuit for a novelist.

Trollope, unlike many Victorian civil servants, was not content to rely on the odd review to maintain his status as a man of letters. He decided to try his hand at a play. Most well-known Victorian novelists attempted to write for the theatre. A successful play could bring in more money than a successful book, and there was no Mudie to stand between the author and his profits. Dickens, Thackeray, Bulwer Lytton, Wilkie Collins, Charles Reade and Henry James all tried to use their reputations as novelists as springboards to the stage. The Trollope children had grown up in a somewhat theatrical household: the theatre had always delighted Fanny Trollope and she had numbered playwrights and, somewhat shockingly, actors and actresses among her friends. She had shared this love with her children by asking them to analyse scenes and characters in Shakespeare and by writing plays for them to act. She had also adapted scenes from Molière to improve the children's French, and to increase their interest in French literature. The theatre, therefore, held a familiar attraction for Anthony Trollope. As he was, perhaps, already conscious that he had failed with *La Vendée* by setting it in a place he did now know, he now chose a city he had lived in, albeit for only a short time: Bruges. It was also the place where some of his Meetkerke ancestors had been involved in the turbulent politics of the Reformation.

La Vendée had not ended Trollope's interest in the French Revolution and he set his play in the period when the Low Countries were the main battleground between revolutionary and conservative forces. Here he was much influenced by Henry Taylor's blank verse drama *Philip van Artevelde*, which had been set in Bruges. The plot of

Trollope's play, *The Noble Jilt*, centred on a girl's rejecting her lover out of boredom with his perfection. When the play was finished, he recalled, 'it pleased me much'. He sent it to George Bartley, one of his mother's theatrical friends. After starting a career under Sheridan, Bartley had become stage manager at Covent Garden. Trollope read his reply 'a score of times' and reproduced part of it in his *Autobiography*. It was a kind, though decisive, rejection: 'There is not one character, serious or comic, to challenge the sympathy of the audience; and without that all the good writing in the world will not ensure success upon the stage.' Bartley admitted he might be wrong, but his 'regard and respect for your excellent and highly gifted mother and all her family' compelled him to say that he could not recommend the play for production. Anyone who more than glances at *The Noble Jilt* (it has finally been printed in this century as a minor curiosity) will agree with Bartley's view, and ultimately Trollope himself came to share it.[36]

Nevertheless it was not a wasted effort. Thirteen years later Trollope adapted the plot to a contemporary English setting for *Can You Forgive Her?* Even in this novel the plot threatens to become tedious as one of Trollope's most forgettable young women, Alice Vavasor, agonises over accepting her perfect young man. Trollope had a laugh at his theatrical aspirations by alluding to a play in another novel, *The Eustace Diamonds*, where some ladies go to the Haymarket Theatre to see a new work by 'a very eminent author'. It is none other than *The Noble Jilt*. 'The play, as a play,' Trollope announces in the novel, 'was a failure ... The critics, on the next morning, were somewhat divided – not only in judgment but as to facts' [LII]. This is a perfect example of how he inserted private jokes into his novels. No one except Rose would have known that the unpublished play lay in their house, a relic of those years of frustrated efforts. Perhaps it is not imagining too much to see husband and wife laughing in their elegant country house when Anthony inserted that little joke into the manuscript of *The Eustace Diamonds* in 1870.

About the same time as he wrote his play Trollope made an attempt at yet another type of writing, one very much in the family tradition. On a visit to London he met John Murray, who had published Mrs Trollope's second travel book and her husband's ecclesiastical dictionary. Trollope suggested an Irish book for Murray's famous guidebooks, then the virtual Bible of travellers. There was no subject he knew better, and Murray agreed to read a sample. His timing was at least good, for Murray, at Peel's suggestion, had begun to publish guides about Britain.[37] Trollope soon sent off chapters on Dublin and the lakes of Killarney. Murray had promised a decision within two weeks and when the author heard nothing after nine months he wrote a furious letter. The manuscript was returned and it was obvious that it had never been read. Ill luck continued to plague the manuscript, and it has disappeared.

*

The failure of the guidebook is perhaps no great loss to literature, but it is a misfortune for those interested in Irish history, because few people travelled about Ireland as much as Trollope did. He later claimed that he had been in every parish in the island. Most of his travels were on postal business, but he frequently acted as a guide to family and friends, among whom was his mother, perhaps the most celebrated traveller of the age. She visited her youngest son in July 1849, when people were once again visiting Ireland for pleasure. Only a few weeks later Queen Victoria paid the first of her four trips to the country. For Fanny Trollope this was her only visit to Ireland, and indeed the only time she ever stayed in Anthony's home. In later years Rose wrote her memories of the visit for a biography of Fanny and, fortunately, these also tell us a great deal about Rose herself. They show her kind nature as she tried to make the old lady's stay as happy as possible. Fanny Trollope enjoyed her two grandsons and the 'hospitable domicile' of her youngest son. She also liked the food at Rose's table and singled out the 'new-laid eggs, salmon curry, Irish potatoes ... bread and butter, together with a little honey and a little coffee, and a little porter from the same green land'.[38] It may seem odd to mention butter as a treat, but, it may be recalled, one of her many objections to America had been its lack of decent butter and she had celebrated the publication of her first book by buying in addition to some tea, a pound of good butter. Anthony shared his mother's view that foreign butter was normally bad and he was adamant that one never got good butter in Italy.

From Mallow, Fanny Trollope reported to a friend: 'Anthony and his excellent little wife are as happy as possible.' Naturally she was anxious to see everything she could, and poor John Tilley, who accompanied her to Ireland, must have been in misery for he did not share the general Trollopean passion for scenery. Her family even persuaded her, after much argument, to try one of the Bianconi cars that carried both passengers and mail. The old lady was frightened at the rather 'ramshackle-looking machine', but after a dozen blessings of 'Niver fear, yer honour!' from Mick the driver she set off and returned almost convinced that she had found the best way to see Ireland. Not everything went as well. Rose recalled another expedition when Fanny 'was tired with her journey; the tea was rubbish; the food detestable; the bedrooms pokey; turf fires disagreeable'. When Rose wrote about this in the 1890s she agreed with all the complaints and admitted: 'I should vote it – nasty.'[39]

Like her son, Fanny could exhibit a rough exterior, but like him she had a kind heart. One day she saw a man breaking stones for the road. She 'pattered downstairs' – as Rose recalled – and gave the old man sixpence. Anthony employed a faithful servant called Barney Fitzpatrick who had two essential tasks: he looked after his master's horses and he saw that Trollope was awake every morning before dawn to start his writing. Barney was delighted with Mrs Trollope's kindness to the stone-breaker and soon he had informed all of Mallow: 'Sure, her honour gave the ould man a shilling every day for a month.' Eventually Barney produced a new edition of his tale by magnifying the sixpence into half-a-crown! Fanny Trollope, amused at her expanding charity, laughed: 'Ah, that shows on what slight threads hangs the report of our good deeds – and our evil ones!' The highlight of her trip, as it was of most visitors, was the Lakes of Killarney. Here she amazed Anthony and Rose by climbing 'as if she had been twenty-nine instead of sixty-nine'. One evening she exhibited the normal Anglo-Saxon trepidation when a bag-piper enters a room. Yet, when Rose next looked at her, the old lady was in tears – 'from the pathos of the music'. It recalled the scene earlier that day when she heard the strains of a bugle played by the piper's son echoing round the romantic scenery of Killarney.[40] Only a few months before Alfred Tennyson had heard those sounds at the same spot and conjured up the scene in his poem, 'Blow, bugle, blow':

> The splendour falls on castle walls
> And snowy summits old in story:
> The long light shakes across the lakes,
> And the wild cataract leaps in glory.
> Blow, bugle, blow, set the wild echoes flying,
> Blow, bugle: answer, echoes, dying, dying, dying.

*

No doubt another reason for Fanny Trollope's tears at Killarney was recent grief at yet another family tragedy. The occasion for her visit was to provide solace after the death of her last daughter, Cecilia Tilley. Cecilia's husband, John, had risen even higher in the Post Office in September 1848 when he was appointed Assistant Secretary. His selection was a further indication that the Victorian idea of merit was replacing the eighteenth-century idea of a 'job' for someone with powerful patrons. Among the defeated candidates was none other than Thackeray who longed for a comfortable salary, in this case £800 a year, to provide security for his writing. This, no doubt, accounts for the ferocity with which Trollope wrote of his fellow novelist's candidacy. He probably was right in saying that Thackeray lacked the temperament for official life. The idea of such an appointment infuriated Trollope because it implied that civil servants were paid 'a generous salary, and have nothing to do'. It offended his belief that appointments should go to those who had earned them: 'Men who have been serving in an office many years do not like to see even a man of genius put over their heads.' If the appointment was an advancement for Tilley, it was a tragedy for Cecilia: the move from the pure air of the Lake District to the fetid atmosphere of Victorian London proved fatal.[41]

Cecilia, who was one year younger than Anthony, had long shown signs of that weakness of the lungs that had caused the death of her brothers, Arthur and Henry and her sister Emily. In one of her earliest letters to Rose, Fanny Trollope wrote: 'Cecilia is but so, so, she cannot walk without suffering so much from fatigue.' Nor did that scourge of so many Victorian wives, frequent pregnancies, help her fragile health. In February 1849 Trollope hurried to Kensington for a final farewell. Mrs Trollope made an equally hurried dash from Italy. The Tilley household was a sad sight: the devoted husband and the aged mother, who knew all too well the horrid signs of the consuming disease, shared the duties of watching by the dying Cecilia's bedside while in another room her eldest child, Fanny, was also mortally ill with consumption. Mrs Trollope resumed her old routine of leaving a death bed to write amusing novels. Cecilia was a devout High Church Anglican for whom the 'beauty of holiness' was a living reality. In Victorian life and literature the sight of a pious death strengthened the faith of a sorrowing family, as Fanny Trollope admitted when writing to Rose:[42]

> Sad as the scene was, I almost wish you could have witnessed her departure. She was like an angel falling asleep in happy certainty of awakening in Heaven. I am very *very* glad my dear Anthony saw her on her death bed – The impression left on his mind, however painful at the moment of receiving it, will remain with him forever, more as a consolation, than sorrow.

Anthony had returned to Ireland before his sister's death, but when he left her house he knew he had had his last sight of her on earth. In one of his novels, *The Three Clerks*, the dying consumptive girl makes a recovery at the end of the book, but that is the difference between fiction and fact. Trollope could not afford another trip to London for the funeral. His letter of condolence to John Tilley reveals much of his character. A 'manly' Victorian normally concealed deep emotion. 'You should so carry your outer self,' says one of Trollope's clergymen to a friend, 'that the eyes of those around you should see nothing of the sorrow within' [*The Vicar of Bullhampton* LXVIII]. Trollope therefore tried to assure Tilley that it was all for the best because her suffering was ended. He stressed 'manly' duty: 'You are not the man to give way to sorrow.' He avoided the endless pietistic platitudes that often occupied pages of such letters, but at the end his emotion broke through: 'God bless you my dear John – I sometimes feel that I led you into more sorrow than happiness in taking you to Hadley.'[43]

Anthony and Rose feared the effect of Cecilia's death on Mrs Trollope, who admitted that 'the last month has been the most suffering period of my existence'. At the same time Mrs Trollope's brother, Henry Milton, was also dying: it had been at his house almost half a century before that Fanny Milton had first met Thomas Anthony Trollope. Now of their seven children only two remained. Cecilia Tilley left several small children, most of whom were already showing signs of weak lungs. Anthony and Rose took one child, Edith, to live with them, which led Mrs Trollope to write to Rose: 'God bless you for all your kindness to her, my dear daughter! We shall none of us ever forget it.'[44] Edith was the first of three nieces who lived in Trollope's house. All three undoubtedly contributed to his understanding of the English girl. He could observe a niece with more detachment than he could have watched the daughters he never had. Edith stayed for about one year and returned to her father after his remarriage to Cecilia's cousin. Trollope retained a fondness for Edith throughout his life and when he suffered his fatal stroke in 1882 she was at his side.

On her Irish visit Mrs Trollope at least had one happy subject to discuss: Tom had at last found a wife. Theodosia Garrow came from a somewhat exotic background: she was one quarter Scottish, one quarter Indian and half Jewish.[45] 'Theo' was yet another Victorian lady with delicate health, which confirmed Tom in his decision to live in Italy. She was a talented poet and an old friend of Elizabeth Browning. Fanny Trollope was delighted with Tom's new wife and all three of them, joined by Theodosia's father, pooled their resources and found an elegant mansion in Florence. In his memoirs Tom informs readers that his wife brought only £1,000 with her, exactly as Anthony would write of so many fictional brides. Tom now settled down to writing Italian history, eventually varied with novels, often to pay for his hereditary addiction to travel. He also wrote an enormous number of articles on Italian politics and art. Theodosia became a zealot for the cause of Italian unity and a fanatical anti-clerical writer (perhaps spurred by her brother's becoming a Roman Catholic priest).

The two surviving Trollope brothers had now put behind them any legacy of bitterness from their schooldays. For the rest of their lives – Tom survived Anthony by ten years – they remained close friends who wrote numerous letters to one another. Their correspondence benefited from the improvements in the post which reduced cost and time: it took only 50 hours and 10 minutes – as Tilley proudly informed a Parliamentary committee – for a letter to go from London to Florence. The only difficulty was that the postage to Florence was expensive and cost more than a letter to America; Fanny Trollope solved the difficulty in characteristic manner by persuading the Minister to send the manuscripts of her novels in the diplomatic bag![46] It is unfortunate that so many of the Trollope brothers' letters have been lost or mutilated: this probably happened when Tom's second wife wrote her biography of Fanny Trollope. Yet enough survive to show how the brothers assisted one another. Once Anthony had become a recognised figure in the London literary establishment in the 1860s, he was able to help Tom and his wife find publishers. Tom's famed hospitality in Florence was extended to many of Anthony's literary acquaintances and therefore reflected well on the younger brother.

Sometimes their correspondence reveals the numerous interests they shared. In 1850 Anthony asked Tom, his wife and his mother to take part in a game he had invented by compiling lists of the people who had most influenced history. There were six categories, such as 'great captains' and 'great rebels'; each category had to include thirteen names. When the lists arrived from Florence Anthony chided his brother for ignoring women, as well as figures from the Ancient World – a comment that may well have annoyed Tom who was a far better classicist than Anthony. He also chastised Theodosia for including Jacques Cathelineau, the Vendean leader, as a 'rebel', for as Trollope correctly pointed out 'he took up arms for his king'. Theodosia would wait several years for her last word on this subject. This, of course, reflects Trollope's recent novel, *La Vendée*. Only six men were on all lists: Shakespeare, Mahomet, Napoleon, Pitt and, rather surprisingly, two Cardinals – Richelieu and Wolsey. Anthony was convinced that

Caesar was the greatest man of all time. There was only one woman on all the lists: Joan of Arc.[47]

*

During these years of literary frustration the Post Office remained the centre of Trollope's life. As a Surveyor's deputy he was constantly inspecting the postal service throughout southern Ireland. In 1849 his salary, after a modest quarterly increase of fifty shillings, reached £130 a year. His real income still came from the daily allowance and generous travelling expenses of eightpence a mile which he was legitimately allowed. Thus in the last three quarters of 1849 he records his total net income as £301 5s 9d, or just over two-and-a-quarter times his official stipend.[48] With a total annual income, therefore, averaging over £500, he was reasonably comfortable, particularly as prices tended to be lower in Ireland and Irish incomes were still not taxed. Nevertheless with two sons and a niece he had little room for extravagance, save his devotion to fox-hunting. Authorship still beckoned as a means of gaining more money to spend on luxuries.

One of Trollope's duties, as indeed of all surveyors and deputy surveyors, was to see that no money was stolen from the mails. In Ireland there was an added reason for this as emigrants who had fled the Famine often sent pounds or dollars to relatives at home. For a long time the Post Office had urged people to cut bank notes in two and send each half in separate envelopes. For Trollope, as for other dedicated officials, thefts from the post were a serious matter which called into question the reliability of the largest government service. It may have annoyed him all the more since he maintained that the Irish were a particularly honest people, more so than the English. When the Surveyor, James Kendrick, received a complaint that coins were disappearing from envelopes, he and his deputy were anxious to find the culprit. Trollope put a small mark on a sovereign – a small scratch on Queen Victoria's neck – and sent the coin through the post. At each town where the mail cart halted, he suddenly galloped up, demanded the envelope, examined his seal and felt if the coin was still inside. When he arrived at one village, Ardfert, and the letter did not, he rushed to Tralee, a distribution centre about which there had been complaints. Here he had the bags opened to find the letter missing. He then got a constable and they searched the house of the postmistress, Mary O'Reilly, where they found the coin in her purse. She was committed for trial. Because she was a popular figure, friends raised money to import a celebrated barrister from Dublin, Isaac Butt QC, who had achieved fame after a debate with O'Connell. At this point Butt was a prominent Tory whose career was being forwarded by Sir Robert Peel, but eventually he became O'Connell's successor as leader of the Irish Party. Butt was also a man of letters and a founder of the *Dublin University Magazine*. He has been dismissed as 'agreeable, convivial and largely ineffectual' as a political leader, but as a barrister he was formidable.[49] In late July 1849 the case came before Judge Ball at the Kerry Summer Assizes. Trollope was naturally called as a witness and the contest between him and Isaac Butt bears some similarity to the celebrated encounter between another writer and an Irish barrister, Oscar Wilde and Edward Carson, although Butt had none of Carson's vicious vulgarity. The spectators naturally sympathised with the pretty Irish postmistress rather than the English official, but Trollope raised many laughs by his humour. Perhaps Trollope was thinking of this when he later alluded to an Irish court scene with its 'substratum ... of Irish fun which showed to everybody that it was not all quite in earnest' [*Castle Richmond* XXXV]. There was a great deal of sparring when Butt wanted details about the spot on the Queen's head where Trollope had made his mark:

> Butt: On the head under the neck!
> Trollope: I did not say that. You are making more mistakes than I am.
> Butt: I ask you, was it on the head?
> Trollope: I marked it under the neck on the head (great laughter).
> Butt: You marked it under the neck on the head! You are acquainted
>   with the English language, writing it occasionally?
> Trollope: Occasionally.
> Butt: And yet you cannot give an intelligible answer on this head.
> Trollope: You had better give it up.

Butt made great play of the fact that Trollope had to use his glasses to find the mark. Years later Trollope told his biographer that at one point he had begun to hesitate under Butt's skilful attack. Then he recalled a Commons debate where a Scottish MP had called the Irish members 'talking potatoes' and this description seemed to apply to Butt's face. The exchanges continued:

> Butt: What was the name of your Correspondent?
> Trollope: Miss Jemima Cotton.
> Butt: She had no existence except in your fine imagination?
> Trollope: It was purely a fictitious name ...
> Butt: You seem to deal in fictitious characters.
> Trollope: In another way.
> Butt: Do you know *The Macdermots of Ballycloran?* (laughter)

Trollope: I know a book of that name.
Butt: Do you remember the barrister of the name of Allwind? (laughter)
Trollope: I do.
Butt: And another named O'Napper.
Trollope: Yes.
Butt: I believe in drawing that character, it was your intention to favour
    the world with the beau ideal of a good cross-examiner?
Trollope: Yes. I dreamed of you (loud laughter).

Butt read a passage from the novel in which Trollope had wondered what the red cloth over the judge's chair would say, if it could speak, about 'the consciences of judges, and the veracity of lawyers'. Butt – perhaps the first critic to use Trollope's 'authorial intrusions' against him – hoped that the novelist no longer thought that. To tremendous laughter, Trollope replied, 'I'm rather strengthened in my opinion.' Butt then asked, 'Had you the mark of the money under the neck on the head when you dreamed of me?' Trollope admitted, 'Not that mark exactly.' Butt replied, 'Fine imagination.' The witness, not to be out-done, retorted, 'Admirable cross-examiner.' Trollope maintained his composure and his wit under Butt's questions and they parted with mutual salutes: 'Good morning, triumphant Post Office Inspector' was met with 'Good morning, triumphant cross-examiner.' Although Mary O'Reilly was dismissed from the Post Office she walked out of court a free woman as the jury was unable to reach a verdict. Justin McCarthy, who, like Butt, would become a prominent Home Rule politician and a mediocre historian, was present as a journalist. He recalled that 'neither combatant for a moment lost his temper or his self-control, and the spectators ... were filled with intense delight ... Butt himself felt, I think, that he had not had quite the better of it.'[50] The questions and the laughter about *The Macdermots of Ballycloran* indicate that some at least knew that the postal official was also a writer.

The encounter was undoubtedly a useful experience for a novelist who was to depict so many barristers. Though Trollope appears to have enjoyed the contest, it actually strengthened his distaste for barristers' methods. His frequent attacks upon the honesty of the legal profession were in part an echo of that case in Kerry. In *Phineas Redux* he even has a novelist as a witness when Phineas Finn is tried for murder [LXI]. One of the barristers is called Serjeant Birdbott, and it is amusing to note that Phineas Finn had first been elected to represent Loughshane, the name of another person in the O'Reilly case. In the midst of another of Trollope's fierce attacks upon lawyers he drew on one more Irish experience to describe his most famous barrister, Mr

Chaffanbrass: 'I knew an assassin in Ireland who professed that during twelve years of practice in Tipperary he had never failed when he had once engaged himself. For truth and honesty to their customers – which are great virtues – I would bracket that man and Mr. Chaffanbrass together' [*Orley Farm* LXXV].

*

By 1851 Trollope was becoming manifestly frustrated both in his postal career and in his literary aspirations. After ten years in Ireland, where he had shown himself to be an efficient official, he had still not advanced beyond the rank he held when he arrived: Surveyor's Clerk. While his salary and his income had increased along with the respect in which he was held, his ambitions to be a Surveyor showed no signs of fulfilment. He remained in a part of the Post Office's expanding empire which was not highly rated in London where Hill worried about the 'neglect and blundering' by Irish Surveyors.[51] Yet in this decade Trollope had achieved much: he had found agreeable work, he had discovered his favourite delight of fox-hunting, he had discarded his self-image as a miserable failure, he had learned to write novels and, above all, he had found a wife who provided the love and security he needed to go further.

1851 was the year of the Great Exhibition: an event that recorded and symbolised the unparalleled progress made by Britain. It celebrated those inventions that had done so much to revolutionise the world since Trollope's childhood. When he first heard of it, he shared the prevalent scepticism. The fact that it was seen as the creation of Prince Albert and Sir Robert Peel would not have endeared it to Trollope, who did not admire these great men. Nor would an Exhibition to celebrate progress appeal to a man who felt he had made little. He wrote with unusual bitterness to his mother after the failure of his third novel: 'I mean to put three or four works into the Exhibition. They will, at any rate, give me as much encouragement as Colburn does.'[52] Perhaps his views began to change under the influence of Tilley, who was involved in planning the Exhibition.

Many people, such as the aged Duke of Wellington, were concerned about hordes of foreigners descending upon London: they might, after all, be dangerous revolutionaries. Trollope made fun of this fear when he wrote to his brother: 'We intend going to see the *furriners* in June. I think it will be great fun seeing such a crowd. As for the Exhibition itself, I would not give a straw for it, – except the building itself, and my wife's piece of work which is in it.' Rose had made a large embroidery for a triptych screen, the main feature of which was a knight holding the Trollope family arms. This shows how much she shared not only the fashionable mediaevalism of the age but Trollope family pride in their ancestry. Her embroidery was evidently of high quality, for she was awarded a bronze medal by the Commissioners and the screen became a treasured heirloom in the family. Perhaps because of this, Rose acquired an interest in Exhibitions and when she drew up a chronology to help her husband with his *Autobiography*, she listed several other Exhibitions they had visited.[53]

Trollope unfortunately wrote little of his impressions of the Great Exhibition. However, within a week of the opening and almost a month before his own visit he urged Tom to come from Florence: 'I am sure it is a thing a man ought to see.' He went on to say that Tilley was full of enthusiasm: 'I think he is right. It is a great thing to get a new pleasure.' Although Trollope only alludes in passing to the Exhibition in his novels, he would have been a most unusual Victorian if he had not been moved by the sight [*The Three Clerks* VII]. With their passion for statistics, Victorian commentators recorded that 6,009,948 people visited the Exhibition (almost equal to the population of Ireland) and, among other things, consumed over two million buns. What they saw was how the world about them was being changed by the driving force of steam. All sorts of hitherto irksome tasks were being done by machinery and new wonders were continually appearing. Britain had taken the lead in almost all these improvements and inventions. Perhaps even more than showing British power, the Exhibition emphasised British stability. As the worries about the 'furriners' proved groundless, the press at home and abroad re-echoed astonishment that vast crowds could congregate without crime, riot or revolution. History held no example of this, and the Victorians exulted, in the words of Trollope's favourite journalist, 'Jacob Omnium' in *The Times*: 'I overheard a German and a Frenchman disputing about English loyalty. "It is a principle," said the one. "No it is a passion," screamed the other ... while in truth, it is both.'[54]

In Trollope's youth speeches and diaries resounded with fears about the unruly masses. Many a Tory luminary had savoured his port while meditating on the approaching tumbrils. The farm labourers of the 1830s had alarmed the farmers of Harrow, and Mrs Trollope had denounced the dangers of vulgar democrats. Colonel Maberly had ensured that Post Office clerks such as Trollope were armed with stout clubs to suppress the expected uprisings of the 1830s and 1840s. Now the Exhibition of 1851, coming in the mid-point of Trollope's life, demonstrated that Britain had reconciled progress with stability. That was an even greater discovery than steam power. With it the Victorian world, at least that increasingly large and comfortable class in the middle, sailed into the long sun-lit afternoon of prosperous security of which Anthony Trollope would be the greatest chronicler. His novels would reflect a world that was only possible because of reform combined with stability, what he called 'that exquisite combination of conservatism and progress which is her [England's] present strength and best security for the future' [*Can You Forgive Her?* XXIV]. Only a few years later Trollope summed up the confidence of his fellow countrymen, a confidence justified by the Great Exhibition of 1851:[55]

It is impossible for an Englishman to be hopeless of his country. Industry and genius belong to him, indomitable industry and undying genius.

Fox-hunting scene from *Orley Farm* (J.E. Millais).

CHAPTER SEVEN

The Purlieus of the Cathedral

Within weeks of Trollope's visit to the Great Exhibition he had an opportunity to see England at closer range than almost any man of his time. The Post Office had been impressed by his improvement of the Irish rural service. Rowland Hill had always been anxious to extend rural deliveries in England and he assigned Trollope to do this in the Western District. As deputy to the District Surveyor, G.H. Creswell, Trollope set out to inspect and reorganise rural post. The summer of 1851 was an appropriate time to start this work. It was also the first year in which postal revenues returned to the level of 1840, when the penny postage had begun. The 1851 census showed that most of the population lived in towns: the first time this had occurred in any country. By the early 1850s the main railway trunk lines were completed. These brought great changes throughout the country, perhaps most of all to agricultural regions, changes which are reflected in Trollope's novels. In 1849 the first express train ran from *the* Paddington Station (Trollope always uses the definite article for London stations) to Exeter. It was now possible to make hurried trips to London, as Mr Harding did in *The Warden*. This spread of fast travel caused a great change in the way Victorians looked at their world: the time-table and the clock, not the sun, ruled the day. The pressure of that time-table soon made London time standard throughout the country. But the agreement in the clocks only illustrated the differences between the quickening pace of town life and the more traditional life of the countryside. This tension is often seen in Trollope's novels: busy Londoners whose sudden appearances cause upset to those in the country – people who follow 'the well-bred ceremonies of life, so many of which went out of fashion when railroads came in' [*The Vicar of Bullhampton* XXIV]. In an essay written within days of Trollope's death his most perceptive critic said: 'In Miss Austen's world, how little you see of London ... In Mr Trollope's novels

235

... nothing can be done without London.'[1]

The railways also affected provincial towns. If they acquired a rail link they prospered: Torquay grew from less than 6,000 in 1841 to almost 22,000 by 1871, whereas older resorts like Exmouth and Lyme Regis, beloved of Jane Austen, declined.[2] Such towns were the victims of Victorian progress and Trollope found them deeply depressing:

> To me, had I lived there, the incipient growth of grass through some of the stones ... would have been altogether unendurable. There is no sign of coming decay which is so melancholy to the eye as any which tells of a decrease in the throng of men ... That street had formed part of the main line of road from Salisbury to Taunton, and coaches, wagons, and posting-carriages had been frequent on it: but now, alas! it was deserted [*The Belton Estate* VII].

For Trollope the postal official the main effect of the railways was that they brought the mail quickly to provincial towns: he would make it his 'mission' to get these letters to breakfast tables in the countryside.

The penny post had not guaranteed delivery to a house. The Post Office did employ some rural letter-carriers, who were often miserably paid and inefficient. Some years before Trollope went to the Western District *The Times* carried a story of 'Post Office liberality' when Marian Adams died in Ashburton in Devon, aged 74: her meagre stipend of 2s a week for two daily deliveries of letters and one of newspapers had not given her many possessions save 'poor Betsey, her far famed donkey', her bridle, side-saddle and 'plated spurs' which brought 3s 6d at auction. For many years postal service was supplemented by all sorts of private arrangements. In some rural areas post was left at turnpike gates where it might lie for a week until someone agreed to take it to an isolated village. It is possible to follow the reform of rural delivery through one Devon family: the Torrs had a small estate near the village of Lustleigh, about five miles from Chagford. In 1843 the squire described how the postal bag was delivered to a town several miles away. People in Lustleigh paid a woman sixpence a week to deliver and pick up their mail every day including Sunday. By 1852, after the railway reached Newton Abbott, Torr wrote: 'We have now a government appointed letter-carrier here ... this man delivers free, and carries free.' As with all progress, there was a victim: 'The old woman, greatly to her discomfort, is out a berth.' This improvement, for all except the poor old woman, was directly due to Anthony Trollope, and it was a process repeated wherever he went.[3]

Trollope later wrote of this work as 'two of the happiest years of my life'. He began in Devon, where he had many family connections. His novels and stories frequently attest to his conviction that Devonshire was the most beautiful of English counties and he chastised Englishmen who devoted all their travels to more exotic spots for not knowing the beauty of their own country.[4] 'The prettiest scenery in all England,' he wrote in one short story, 'The Parson's Daughter of Oxney Colne',

> and if I am contradicted in that assertion, I will say in all Europe – is in Devonshire, on the southern and south-eastern skirts of Dartmoor, where the rivers Dart, and Avon, and Teign form themselves, and where the broken moor is half cultivated ... In making this assertion I am often met with much doubt ... Men and women talk to me on the matter, who have travelled down the railway from Exeter to Plymouth, who have spent a fortnight at Torquay ... But who knows the glories of Chagford? Who has walked through the parish of Manaton? Who is conversant with Lustleigh Cleeves ... Gentle reader, believe me that you will be rash in contradicting me, unless you have done these things.

He knew all these places from laying out postal routes and arranging free delivery for people like the Torrs of Lustleigh.

The Post Office had complicated rules for rural routes because they knew that the Treasury kept a sharp eye on expense. Trollope's main task was to make each 'walk' by a postman pay its own way. Generally speaking, half of each penny stamp was expended on local delivery. He had to measure the length of each walk and the number of letters carried. A few years later he advised an ambitious postal clerk: 'Do not lose any opportunity when you are at country offices of getting up the rural posts. Make a point of walking them all with the men whether you are employed to do so, or no.' Because no postman could be required to walk more than sixteen miles a day, Trollope became adept at finding short cuts across fields. He had the advantage on the postman because he could measure out the walks from his horse. He rode on average forty miles a day and, in addition, measured some 'walks' on foot.[5] By being 'sanguine in his figures' he could add yet another village to the spreading network of free delivery. Often this meant more work for the postmen, and Trollope admitted in later life: 'Perhaps I was sometimes a little unjust to them.' Even so, the work was much sought after as it provided a steady income and sometimes a pension and more benefits than almost any other work open to ordinary men.

In testimony Trollope later gave to a parliamentary committee he agreed that the 'best distance' an English postman could do was sixteen miles, which he called 'a full day's work'. The postmen normally received 10s 6d a week, but revision of the rural post often raised this to 12s and it was possible to get as much as 14s. Most Victorian postmen delivered other people's opinions rather than their own, but one exception occurred in the area where Trollope was at work. Edward Capern, the 'letter carrier poet' of Bideford, had one particular grievance, Sunday post:[6]

> O! the postman's is as blessed a life
> As any one's I trow,
> If leaping the stile o'er many a mile.
> Can blessedness bestow.
>
> If toiling away through a weary week
> (No six days work but seven)
> Without one holy hour to seek
> A resting place in heaven.

For his journeys Trollope had brought his two hunters from Ireland and he would sometimes hire another horse, all looked after by his faithful groom Barney. Trollope often travelled in hunting clothes and many local postal officials were startled when suddenly confronted by a fox-hunter demanding to know all the details of their work. In particular he asked questions about the illegal habit by which postmen forced villagers to pay an extra penny for delivering and picking up letters. Some people were not anxious to discuss this, either from a genuine concern for the postmen or from a fear that their correspondence would suffer. In his novels Trollope frequently introduces postmen as minor characters. They are almost invariably late with the post and have a tendency to spend too much time chatting with servants in country houses. In one novel, *He Knew He Was Right*, a one-legged postman delivers his letters on his donkey.

The easiest way to see how Trollope went about his postal work is to examine one area. One of his first reports was on the Channel Islands, which were part of the Western District. A self-contained island like Jersey is the best place to see what he achieved. His report on his work there during three weeks in November 1851 led to the most extensive change to the British landscape that any novelist ever produced. In 1851 Jersey, with a population of about 60,000, suffered from bad communications both within the island and with the mainland. Boats arrived and departed three times a week carrying the mail, but collection and distribution within the island were so slow that local merchants followed the common Victorian practice of complaining to the GPO.

The Post Office responded by despatching Trollope. He carefully observed the work of the postmaster and clerks in the St Helier Post Office and recommended ways in which the sorting could be made more efficient. Armed with a formidable array of maps, he explored the island, before preparing a long report and completing a printed form – in the 1850s government departments were making increasing use of printed forms – about every postal route. Ten rural 'messengers' carried the post throughout the island. Unlike most houses on the mainland, every house in Jersey was already entitled to free delivery, but this was only on three days a week. Trollope wanted to abolish 'the blank days'. The work of the postmen was often hampered because their bags grew heavier from picking up letters as they went about their routes. Trollope solved this problem by selecting central locations where a 'horse post' could pick up the mail. He gathered estimates from men who could provide the horses. Once the 'horse post' was working the number of rural messengers could be cut from ten to eight. One of the surplus men could be transferred to other duties but the other should be dismissed: 'He is a habitual drunkard, insubordinate in his conduct.' Trollope had heard complaints about him from many people along the route.

This is a good example of Trollope's attitude: the Post Office should try to provide for the decent man but the incompetent drunkard had no claim for consideration. Trollope was not without sympathy for postmen: he noted that several had to walk as much as five miles before setting off on their sixteen-mile 'walk'. For this they received 9s a week. Throughout his career Trollope tended to favour increasing the wages of postmen. Rowland Hill, always concerned with reducing costs, actually wanted to lower their wages. In Bristol, for example, he urged a reduction to as little as as 6s a week. The Post Office could not neglect political considerations when dealing with postmen. These appointments were often sought after by MPs as rewards for the servants of influential constituents. To take just one example, the MP for Banbury – one of the areas where Trollope reformed rural routes – made at least eight requests for such minor appointments. Neither the Postmaster General, nor even a political schemer like Hill, could ignore such people.[7]

What Trollope realised in Jersey was that, while much attention was being given to postal delivery, little thought had been given to collection. His solution would change not only the daily lives of millions of people but the appearance of every town and village in the British Isles. He advised the Post Office to erect special iron boxes in the shape of pillars to receive the mail. He had seen ornate versions of this in

France – presumably on one of his trips with his mother in the 1830s. If there were permanent pillar boxes there would be no need for the fees paid to local people to act as receivers of post. The Post Office accepted the idea and a local founder, John Vaudin, made four pillars for St Helier at a cost of £7 each. The Jersey Postmaster advertised that 'Roadside Letter Boxes' would begin service on 23 November 1852. The first pillar boxes were about four feet high, with the royal arms on three of their six sides. For those who imagine that vandalism is a modern invention it is worth noting that one of the first pillar boxes was deliberately damaged twice in the first three weeks of its existence. The pillar boxes proved an immediate success, as the local postmaster reported to the GPO: 'I feel assured that their introduction into England would be followed by most beneficial results.'[8]

Within a few years the idea was adopted on the mainland. In 1855 six pillar boxes were erected in London, and Trollope has Lady Eustace use the one erected outside the Temple. Throughout his time at the Post Office there were many modifications to the design, mainly to make them more secure. While the earliest were painted red, green became more common on the mainland. In the 1870s the Post Office went back to red. The pillar box was the most important contribution of Trollope's official career. It is appropriate that when two newly designed pillar boxes were opened in front of St Paul's Cathedral in 1968 the Postmaster General posted the first letter to a descendant of Anthony Trollope.[9]

Trollope took considerable pride in his creation. He often has characters drop their letters in the pillar box, and he poked mild fun at the opponents of the new device. There is an old lady (based on his cousin) of the most adamantine Tory views in one novel who already 'regarded penny postage as one of the strongest evidences of the coming ruin' [*He Knew He Was Right* VII]. She is even more horrified when the next innovation reaches Exeter:

> As for the iron pillarboxes which had been erected of late years ... one of which, – a most hateful thing to her, – stood almost close to her own hall door, she had not the faintest belief that any letter put into one of them would ever reach its destination. She could not understand why people should not walk to a respectable post-office instead of chucking them into an iron stump – as she called it, – out in the middle of the street with nobody to look after it [VIII].

Throughout 1852 and 1853 Trollope continued his revision of postal routes in Cornwall, Somerset, Dorset, Oxfordshire, Worcestershire, Herefordshire, Wiltshire and Gloucestershire. He was also asked to extend his work into South Wales. 'I had an opportunity of seeing a considerable portion of Great Britain, with a minuteness few have enjoyed.' Many of his novels would be set in these counties for it was here that he could observe the clergy and gentry whom he met in their natural habitat. Some of them used influence to gain free delivery. That eccentric clergyman and poet, Hawker of Morwenstow, had persuaded the Postmaster General to give him free delivery as 'a special compassion to my loneliness' in his isolated village in north Cornwall.[10]

On his travels Trollope could sometimes draw on connections from Harrow or Winchester. One Devonshire clergyman's son recalled his arrival at the rectory in Budleigh Salterton to have lunch with a fellow Wykehamist. Young Thomas Escott remembered a large man whose massive overcoat gave him the appearance of a sea captain. He seemed in a great hurry, when he shouted 'Boy, help me on with my coat' before he mounted his horse. Decades later the boy became Trollope's first biographer. Improvements in the post held a particular importance for the clergy, who usually had family and friends throughout the country. As Hawker of Morwenstow said, only the post kept him 'fastened to the far world'. It also aided the ever-increasing circulation of religious periodicals and the creation of organisations and 'movements' impossible in the past. There was one occasion at least when it was a disadvantage: many clergymen were furious when the Government said that 'the great facilities' of the penny post and railways meant that there was no reason for a new bishopric for Cornwall.[11] Thus the postal achievements of Anthony Trollope might have undermined the hopes for a mitre of some ambitious cleric!

*

For Trollope the novelist these postal travels were of crucial importance. He gained a vast knowledge of the 'domestic manners' – of dress, dialect, countryside, buildings, food and customs – of his country which no other writer of his time, perhaps of any time, could rival. His insatiable curiosity led him to peer into the country houses, the vicarages, the cottages and even the hovels of those along his routes. His ready ear for dialogue was always listening, always recording, the peculiarities of speech. He absorbed all the nuances of provincial life that had taken centuries to build. His novels record the customs that were on the verge of being crushed by the centralising forces of rapid communication, forces which his own postal work was doing so much to forward.

To take but one example: he would often use country inns to add colour to his novels, as he had used Irish hotels in earlier books. It was his rule to stay at the best hotel in a provincial town, but often he had no choice in villages. In time the prosperous Trollope would book a bedroom, dressing-room and private sitting-room, but he could not do this in the 1850s. He depicts one country inn which boasted 'two clean bedrooms' and a landlady who 'could cook a leg of Dartmoor mutton and make an apple pie against any woman in Devonshire'. Such people had little patience for the 'exacting traveller'. 'Cock you up with dainties!' she tells one guest, probably the author himself. 'If you can't eat your victuals without fish, you must go to Exeter. And then you'll get it stinking mayhap' [*He Knew He Was Right* XIV]. To serve fish before a meat dish was a sign of regard, and in some provincial hotels the landlord himself made a point of setting the fish before a noteworthy guest, as in *The Warden* [XVI]. When John Eames returns to his mother's house after he has achieved rank in the Civil Service, she shows her pride by providing 'a little bit of fish' before his leg of mutton [*The Last Chronicle of Barset* XXVII]. In one of his last novels he drew on a lifetime's experience to pronounce that roast fowl was 'the safest dinner at an English inn' [*An Old Man's Love* IX]. The novels also provide details of long-lost customs: it was the duty of the 'boots', for example, to provide a gentleman with a pair of slippers as well as with his candle [*Last Chronicle* XLIII]. Sometimes Trollope names real hotels: 'I beg to assure any travelling readers that they might have drunk tea in a much worse place' than the Bedford Hotel in Tavistock, a rather odd statement as he mentions that the tea is made with lukewarm water [*The Three Clerks* VII]! Some years later, while travelling in America, he recalled one West Country hotel where he found a desolate Frenchman. The tired traveller had called at the hotel and, in broken English, had asked for a place to sit, whereupon he was given a gloomy private sitting-room dark with mahogany and horsehair furniture. Here he had sat in lonely misery till Trollope found him.[12]

While the isolated Frenchman was no doubt relieved to see Trollope, even with his rudimentary command of the language, postal officials were not always so happy when he burst in upon them. Undoubtedly a sudden appearance by the Deputy Surveyor could be disconcerting. One man at Falmouth, an important port for colonial post, remembered his 'stalking into the office, booted and spurred, much to the consternation of the maiden lady in charge'. Not unnaturally he seemed 'the very incarnation of the martinet, though I have since heard that he was a very kind-hearted man'. One Falmouth postman, whose route was to be measured, met a sticky situation. The terrified man was taking £1 worth of penny stamps to a sub-office along his route. He put the 240 stamps, which at the time were not perforated, under his hat for safe-keeping, only to discover that the heat had made them stick to his head. Trollope roared with laughter and took him to a barber to free the stamps. It is pleasant to record that he occasionally met his match. The postmistress in Penzance was so furious when he stormed in that she ordered him out and told him he was 'no gentleman'. Since he always had a grudging respect for those who withstood his bluster, they soon became friends.[13]

Cornwall presented its own particular problems due to its geography, poor communications and isolation: the railway stopped at Plymouth. Wilkie Collins visited Cornwall about the same time as Trollope, and the title of his travel book shows how rapidly the Victorians had adjusted to new ways: *Rambles Beyond Railways*. Trollope cannot have enjoyed his Cornish experiences for he did not draw upon the county for many of his novels. When he did, it was usually for a distant spot where uncomfortable things occur: shares in a tin mine are used to bribe a civil servant (*The Three Clerks*), or a particularly uncomfortable election takes place (*The Duke's Children*). He did write one story with a Cornish setting, however. 'Malachi's Cove' gives a good feeling both of isolation and of the struggle by the poor to eke out a living from the sea.[14]

Trollope experienced another Cornish defeat in the fishing village of Mousehole, where the sub-postmistress, Betsy Trembath, a Quaker, was not awed by her visitor. A version of their conversation lingered among postal legends:

> Trollope: 'I am an Inspector from the General Post Office, and I wish to make some enquiries about the posts in this neighbourhood.'
> Miss Trembath: 'From the General Post Office, arta? I'm bra glad to see thee sure 'nuf. Wusta ha' a dish o'tay?'
> Trollope: 'I say I wish to make some enquiries. Can you tell me where –'
> Miss Trembath: 'Lor' bless the man. Doantee be in such a pore. I can't tellee noathin' if thee'st stand glazing at me like a chucked pig, as thee art now.'
> Trollope (losing his temper): 'Don't thee and thou me, my good woman, but answer my questions. I will report you.'
> Miss Trembath: 'Good woman, am I? Report me, wusta? And I be'n so civil toee, too. Thees't better report my tuppence farden a day.'

This conversation resurfaces a decade later in *The Small House at Allington*, where the postmistress's bad temper is excused by Trollope because she only receives 'tuppence farden a day', an amount which would not keep her in shoes [XXI]. At the end of the novel Miss Trembath, transformed into Mrs Crump, tells Lily Dale of a visit from a postal official:

> Drat them for letters. I wish there weren't no sich things. There was a man here yesterday with his imperence ... down from Lun'on, I b'leeve: and this was wrong, and that was wrong, and everything was wrong; and then he said he'd have me discharged the sarvice ... Discharged the sarvice ... Tuppence farden a day. So I told 'un to discharge hisself, and take all the old bundles and things away upon his shoulders [LX].

Meetings like this with village postmistresses were among the many ways Trollope's work gave him a wider view of Victorian society and a deeper insight into its people than were possessed by most novelists. Although the higher offices in the Post Office were a male preserve, many villages and small towns had a postmistress who found the income a useful addition to her shop-keeping. (One is reminded here of the postmistress Miss Dorcas Lane in Flora Thompson's *Candleford Green* who enjoyed the 'supervision of her neighbours' affairs and the study and analysis of their motives'.) No other novelist of his time would have come in contact with so many working women of independent mind.[15]

Trollope undoubtedly presented an imperious front to postmistresses or letter-carriers but he was a man with a mission and he was not prepared to allow anything to stand in his way. The Post Office was, after all, the only government service reaching into all parts of the country and touching all classes. His task was to extend its benefits as far as possible into almost every village. This was the ethos of the Victorian Post Office, and men who were successful in it, be they Rowland Hill, John Tilley or Anthony Trollope, did not get on by undue worrying about the sensitivity of their subordinates. This spirit permeated the Post Office and made its remarkable achievements possible. It was only by discipline from the centre that inefficiency, dishonesty and petty graft could be eliminated. In one novel Trollope has a mother trying to retrieve a letter her daughter had written rejecting a suitor. At first the postmaster accepts her lie that a wrong letter had been posted, but at the crucial moment this 'servant of the public' remembers that he 'had been throughly grounded in his duties by one of those trusty guardians of our correspondence who inspect and survey our provincial post offices' [*The American Senator* XXXIV]. Thus the girl's letter is safe from her mother's interference. To Trollope this was a fictional portrayal of what he had made a fact: that only a sense of discipline, and even fear, could mould the postal service into a trustworthy 'servant of the public'.

*

Rose and the children accompanied Trollope on many of his West Country travels. These must have been difficult years for her as they moved from one set of lodgings to another: in 1852 and 1853 they lived in Exeter, Bristol, Carmarthen, Cheltenham and Worcester. The boys were sent to school in Cheltenham. 'Harry and Freddy, ... are very nice boys,' he told their grandmother in Florence, 'very different in disposition, but neither with anything I could wish altered.' When he heard that his brother Tom was about to become a father, he wrote:

> I am glad you are to have a child. One wants some one to exercise unlimited authority over, as one gets old and cross. If one blows up one's servants too much, they turn round, give warning, and repay one with interest. One's wife may be too much for one, and is not always a safe recipient for one's wrath. But one's children can be blown up to any amount without damage, – at any rate, for a considerable number of years.

He obviously relished the role of counselling his elder brother, and, 'joking apart' concluded: 'I ... assure you that, to my way of thinking, nothing that could happen to you would be so likely to add to your happiness as this.'[16] This letter offers us a rare glimpse of the pleasure Trollope took in his two sons. Some biographers have assumed that because he was as reticent about the joy his children gave him as he was about the happiness of his marriage, he lacked parental feeling. Nothing could be further from the truth.

Two of the towns he came to know in the early fifties especially influenced his writing. Exeter would figure in many of his novels. It is likely that he knew it in his early days as his mother often sent her children on visits to her cousin, Fanny Bent. In *He Knew He Was Right* Trollope used her as the basis for Jemima Stanbury, one of his best portrayals of a provincial lady, whose life was regulated by precise rules of social position and obligations. In the second town, Cheltenham, Trollope used the location of his family's lodgings, the Paragon Buildings, in several novels, where the town is often disguised as 'Littlebath'. In *Miss Mackenzie* the heroine takes lodgings there. 'Now it is known to all the world' – this phrase usually means it is known to Trollope from experience – 'that the Paragon is the nucleus of all that is pleasant and fashionable at Littlebath.' She is told that rooms will cost £2 10s a week or nine guineas a month (a saving of 11s) which included fuel for the kitchen fire. One suspects that Rose had heard a similar patter because the landlady announces that 'the price ... never alters' [II]. In *Can You Forgive Her?* Alice Vavasor stays with her relative, Lady Macleod, at No. 3, Paramount Crescent, Trollope's name for the Paragon: the Trollopes had lived at No. 5. Perhaps their rooms had overlooked the yard like Lady Macleod's and Trollope too had had to inhale 'the effluvia of the stables' [XV]. This may have been one reason why he did not remember the site with affection.[17]

Cheltenham provided a vital stimulus for much of his clerical writing. The spa town, then and even today, was known as a centre of Evangelical Anglicanism which drew support from the many comfortable widows, spinsters and jaundiced veterans of the East India Company who found it a comfortable and godly abode. Years later, in *The American Senator*, one character complains of another's 'somewhat illiterate language' which the novelist attributes to his education at Cheltenham College, where he was made miserable by the Evangelical Rector of the town [I]. The real Rector was Francis Close, who was in Cheltenham from 1826 to 1856 when he became Dean of Carlisle. According to *The Times*, he was 'the Pope of Cheltenham,' whose 'social decrees were accepted without a thought of the possibility of opposition'. He had preached a famous sermon, 'The Restoration of Churches is the Restoration of Popery', and such a view would not have endeared him to Trollope. It is noticeable that virtually every novel that has scenes in Cheltenham also has fierce attacks upon the Evangelicals. Although there were people who enjoyed dancing and cards, the town's social life was dominated by the 'pious set' who 'live on the fat of the land. They are a strong, unctuous, moral, uncharitable people. The men never cease making money for themselves, nor the women making slippers for their clergymen' [*The Bertrams* XIII]. This was a direct attack upon Close, who was said to have received 1,500 pairs of slippers from his devoted flock.[18] Trollope's comment in *The Bertrams* about 'hecatombs of needlework' being made for Dr Snort and his curate was hardly exaggerated [XXII].

On the whole Trollope enjoyed his English travels, but he was less pleased with Wales. Perhaps it is impossible for an Englishman to give his heart to more than one Celtic nation, and he had already pledged his to Ireland. His temper was not helped by the heavy rains and flooding that occurred in the autumn of 1852: 'I have very frequently had to swim for it – The people here are mostly swimming ... those at least who are not sinking.' However, even floods could not dampen his incredible energy. He burst into one country post office where his 'giant foot-fall' caused some consternation: 'I have walked up from Cardiff,' he announced, a distance of twenty-four miles. He then asked to be directed to the best hotel and 'marched out, still at a 6-mile-an-hour stride'. As he left, he announced: 'Back soon, going to have a raw beef steak.' 'He left me,' recalled one postal worker, 'pondering over his powerful build, his physical go and his reference to the "underdone".'[19]

Perhaps a Welsh hotel had overcooked his steak on the day he wrote to his friend Thomas Walton, the Postmaster of Bristol: 'You are not my enemy but if you were, & if I could not bring myself to wish you well in a charitable Christian manner, but were excited by the Devil to wish you all evil, I could wish you nothing worse than a residence in South Wales for the rest of your life.' It was only in the last years of his life that he set a novel, *Cousin Henry*, in Wales, and the book is not remarkable for any spirit of place. Trollope's work in rearranging the Welsh post was so successful that within a few years travellers were complaining that letters moved much faster than people. When a friend of Thackeray asked about this he was told: 'Because you can't put a penny stamp on yourself and be sorted into a little letter bag, and be caught off a pole at midnight by a train going 40 miles an hour, and then be delivered by a letter carrier two or three *hours before you are up*.'[20]

*

If Wales failed to inspire a spirit of place in Trollope, one of his other travels did so, with happy results for English literature. In May 1852 his duties took him to Salisbury and there, while meditating on its soaring spire, he discovered a world that would bring him fame: 'Whilst wandering there on a midsummer evening round the purlieus of the cathedral I conceived the story of *The Warden*, – from whence came that series of novels of which Barchester, with its bishops, deans, and archdeacon, was the central site.' Immediately after this oft-quoted remark he gives the most misleading statement in his *Autobiography*, when he says he knew little of the ways of clergymen, having never lived in any cathedral city but London. This has led many to assume that Trollope knew little about the Church of England and that he had few firm religious opinions. Both these views are absurd.

During the early 1850s he had little time for writing fiction. Travel occupied most of his days, while official reports demanded most of his evenings. The fact that his first three novels had been failures, as had his play and his articles, may have lessened his desire to write. Nevertheless lengthy rides provided an opportunity for his old habit of 'castle building'. He had spent an hour on the bridge at Salisbury imagining the scenes of a novel about the clerical society of a cathedral city. His travels brought him to other cathedrals such as 'the sweet close at Hereford' which increased this interest. On 29 July 1853 he began writing *The Warden* in the small spa town of Tenbury on the Worcestershire-Shropshire border. He did not finish it until October 1854, when he was in Belfast on postal duties. Never again would he take so long over the planning and writing of a short novel: perhaps that is one reason why it has so many beautiful passages. It is ironic that this novel, a classic portrayal of the Anglican clergy, was completed in Presbyterian Belfast.

The Warden is the first of six volumes in what became known as the Barsetshire novels. Trollope had not planned a series set in this imaginary county, although it was these stories that brought him fame in his time and still are the favourites of most of his readers. The six are: *The Warden* (1855); *Barchester Towers* (1857); *Doctor Thorne* (1858); *Framley Parsonage* (1861); *The Small House at Allington* (1864); and *The Last Chronicle of Barset* (1867). Although clergymen occupy relatively little space in two of the novels – *Doctor Thorne* and *Small House* – the Barset series gave Trollope in his own time, and even more since, the reputation of being the premier novelist of clerical society. A great many clerical and semi-clerical disputes have centred on which cathedral city Trollope took for his model. He never provides much description of Barchester cathedral.[21] Many have assumed that it is based on Salisbury because that is where he conceived the idea. Yet in the last weeks of his life Trollope was assisted up a hill overlooking Wells by the historian E.A. Freeman. He told his friend that while Somerset was the inspiration for Barsetshire the city of Barchester was based on Winchester.

The Barset novels allowed Trollope to invent many colourful characters, but they also provided an opportunity to depict the English character itself. He firmly believed that the progress of the world was made in cities but that 'the English character, with its faults and virtues, its prejudices and steadfastness, can be better studied in … country houses, in parsonages, in farms and small meaningless towns, than in great cities'.[22] In the opening of the third Barset novel he described the county he had invented:

> There is a county in the west of England not so full of life, indeed, nor so widely spoken of as some of its manufacturing leviathan brethren in the north, but which is, nevertheless, very dear to those who know it well. Its green pastures, its waving wheat, its deep and shady and, – let us add, –

dirty lanes, its paths and stiles, its tawny-coloured, well-built rural churches, its avenues of beeches, and frequent Tudor mansions, its constant county hunt, its social graces ... has made it to its own inhabitants a favoured land of Goshen. It is purely agricultural ... There are towns in it, of course; depots from whence are brought seeds and groceries, ribbons and fire shovels; in which markets are held and county balls are carried on ... from whence emanate the country postmen [*Doctor Thorne* I].

Today this glows with nostalgia. Yet in many ways Trollope was describing a world that was already passing beyond the ken of many of his readers, the majority of whom, like the majority of the population, lived in cities some of which were the 'manufacturing leviathans' that he detested. The Barset novels, even when written, were part of that long tradition of an idealised countryside. Fanny Trollope's friend Mary Mitford had gained her greatest fame with her essays about rural life. The Victorians increasingly liked books about rural bliss, especially if soaked in piety: *Ministering Children*, a saccharine novel about a devout squire by Maria Louisa Charlesworth, was published only a few months before *The Warden*. It sold 276,000 copies before sinking into well-deserved oblivion fifty years later. Barset is an accurate portrayal of part of Victorian England: it is the quiet part, the one without the driving force of industrialism, the disturbing power of Nonconformity or the festering horrors of the slums. This is not to say that its creator hides its blemishes: the miserable poverty of the brickworkers at Hogglestock, for example, is painted with sympathy. Yet most readers for well over a century have picked up, and put down, the Barset novels with a desire to dwell in the snug rectories and mellowed Tudor mansions that Trollope loved and described so well.

Critics of recent decades have maintained that some of Trollope's other novels, such as *The Way We Live Now*, are superior to the Barset series. Yet Trollope will always be known first and foremost as the portrayer of Anglican clergymen moving about their natural habitat of cathedral close and vicarage drawing-room. Trollope's clergy were not confined, of course, to the Barset series, for he soon learned that the public expected his novels to contain at least one interesting clergyman. Thus the religious views of Anthony Trollope are important for any understanding of him as a novelist. They are even more important if one is to arrive at any comprehension of the inner man, for, as with so many Victorians, religion lay at the centre of his being.

*

In discussing Trollope's religious views we must remember his own *caveat*: 'It is very hard to come at the actual belief of any man. Indeed how should we hope to do so when we find it so very hard to come at our own?'[23] We can, however, distinguish those sources which made up his religious heritage and fashioned his beliefs: the early influence of his family and his later reflections. Both his grandfathers were country clergymen, as were several other relatives. Both parents wrote about religious topics: in *Domestic Manners* his mother blasted the American fundamentalists. In novels such as *The Vicar of Wrexhill* she extended her cannonade towards the Evangelicals, while some of her later fiction, such as *Father Eustace*, warned about Catholic plots. Her husband had, of course, devoted his declining years to his encylopaedia of ecclesiastical terms. Discussions about religion, or rather about the Church, played an important role in Trollope's childhood homes. His mother wrote plays ridiculing Evangelicals for her children to act. Henry Milman, who became Dean of St Paul's in 1849, was a family acquaintance of his youth. High Church clergymen, like Prebendary Nott of Winchester, frequented Fanny Trollope's parties. At almost every turning-point in the young Anthony's life we detect the influence of that important clerical family the Drurys: they advised the Trollopes to move to Harrow and where to send their sons to school; one Drury was his master at Harrow and another ran the private school at Sunbury, while yet another employed Anthony at his school in Belgium.

Winchester was, of course, a cathedral city and the College was remarkably like a cathedral close, full of clerical intrigues and gossip, much as Harrow had been. The boys had spent many hours engaged in that favourite clerical pursuit of speculating about places at Oxford. Anglican clergymen had guided Trollope's entire education, an education whose main aim was to produce more clergy. There is some ground for thinking that he, as well as Tom, was intended to follow many of his ancestors 'into the Church'. In one essay, when discussing if a clergyman may hunt, he said: 'Had my pastors and masters, my father and mother, together with the other outward circumstances of my early life, made a clergyman of me ... .'[24] From his schools he acquired a familiarity with scripture and with Anglican liturgy, echoes of which occur time and again in his writing. He admitted in his *Autobiography* that when he got his postal clerkship he knew nothing of arithmetic but could name every bishop in the Church of England. He often drew on the Old and New Testaments to enrich his stories: almost every literate Victorian understood the allusion to Joseph and Potiphar's wife in *The Last Chronicle of Barset* or the reference to the land flowing with milk and honey in *Barchester Towers*. Many modern readers are as unaware of the Bible as the silly daughter of Lady Pomona Longstaffe in *The Way We Live Now*. Lady Pomona, distraught over her daughter's engagement to a Jew, moans: 'It's unnatural ... I'm sure there's something in the Bible about it. You never would read your Bible, or you wouldn't be going to do this' [LXXVIII].

Trollope's religious outlook may be summarised as follows: he was a convinced Christian and a reasonably devout member of the Church of England inclining towards a moderate acceptance of the High Church position. He half jokingly referred to himself in 1874 as 'a good son of the Church' which was, in essence, true. He believed in the 'ancient constitution of Church and State' but saw no reason to argue about it: 'For myself, I love the name of State and Church, and believe that much of our English well-being has depended on it. I have made up my mind to think that union good, and not to be turned away from that conviction. Nevertheless I am not prepared to argue the matter. One does not carry one's proof at one's finger-ends.' George Eliot, who was as knowledgeable about what she did not believe as Trollope was about what he did, said that while Tom Trollope had become a free-thinker her close friend Anthony 'is a Church of England man, clinging to whatever is, *on the whole*, and without fine distinctions, honest, lovely and of good report'. His convictions were always tempered by his common sense and his liberalism. Dogmas were not particularly important to him, although he followed, with some interest, the theological debates that went on during his lifetime. In *The Last Chronicle* he criticises the near-mad clergyman Josiah Crawley as being too interested in the 'mystery' of religion and not enough in its 'comforts' [I]. Trollope's position was the opposite of Mr Crawley's, as the 'comforts' or consolation offered by Christianity are frequently mentioned in his writing about religion.[25]

The first principle in his religious make-up was an absolute conviction of the existence of God. When he was twenty-one, as we have seen already, he set down his thoughts on the theological aspects of Pope's poetry. He insisted that the idea that God made the world 'of course must be a datum'. This conviction remained with him through life, and forty years later he accepted as a 'fact' that the 'intercourse of man with man demanded' God's existence. For Trollope belief in God was essential if the individual and society were to be preserved from that whirlpool of temptations that threatens so many of his characters. His God was a merciful one who did not expect from anyone, and certainly not from a Victorian gentleman, any unseemly clap-trap of false humility. Not surprisingly he did not like too much prattle about

God: 'I must say,' he wrote to a friend in Australia, 'I judge a man by his actions with men, much more than by his declarations Godwards.' Beliefs unrelated to practice were as nonsensical to him as were ideas unrelated to individuals. In his *Life of Cicero* he discusses doctrines by relating them immediately to men: 'The two doctrines which seem to mark most clearly the difference between the men whom we regard, the one as a pagan and the other as a Christian, are the belief in a future life and the duty of doing well by our neighbours.'[26] His characters tend to have an instinctive belief in a God-given order for the universe, and when one departs from this his creator treats him fiercely: three men who appear without any semblance of religion are driven to suicide in *The Bertrams, The Prime Minister* and the short story 'The Spotted Dog'. The materialist view of life receives one of the strongest outbursts in all his writing: in *Orley Farm* Moulder, a commercial traveller for 'Messrs. Hubbles and Grease, tea and coffee merchants', is celebrating Christmas and in the midst of the festivities makes a sneering reference to church-going and Providence. Trollope comments: 'Such is the modern philosophy of the Moulders, pigs out of the sty of Epicurus' [XXIV].

Always conscious of his own morbid side, Trollope argued that belief was of particular importance for the ordinary man who should strive for 'that Sunday-keeping, church-going, domestic, decent life' [*Ralph The Heir* LI]. This became even more important as one grew older and more prone to thinking 'that everything is vanity'. 'It is the presence of thoughts such as these,' Trollope continued, 'that needs the assurance of a heaven to save the thinker from madness or from suicide. It is when the feeling of this pervading vanity is strongest on him, that he who doubts of heaven most regrets his incapacity for belief. If there be nothing better than this on to the grave, – and nothing worse beyond the grave, why should I bear such fardels.' Arrogant thinkers, who put their own intellects above the received wisdom of the ages, might well end their days 'stranded in the mud of personal condemnation'.

He was as equally convinced there was a hell – or at least a devil – as well as a heaven. In one novel a young civil servant is led into corruption. For the novelist this is a good instance of 'that awful mystery, the fall of man ... we cannot hear the devil plead, and resist the charm of his eloquence. "To listen is to be lost." "Lead us not into temptation, but deliver us from evil!" Let that petition come forth from a man's heart, a true and earnest prayer, and he will be so led that he shall not hear the charmer, let him charm ever so wisely' [*The Three Clerks* IX]. He was, however, influenced by the growing theological liberalism of his age. 'Creeping doubts', as he called them, had become common among Anglicans by the end of his life. 'I am inclined,' he wrote, 'to welcome such doubts rather than repudiate them (not being a clergyman) and to think, whether I share them or not, that they are doing good.' By 'creeping doubts' he meant the repudiation of a rigid orthodoxy, particularly the literal interpretation of all Biblical texts, views which were advanced by the 'Higher Criticism' originating in Germany. The controversy dated back to his boyhood at Harrow when a 'Cunningham mouthpiece' denounced old Harry Drury's reading of Milman's *History of the Jews* to his pupils as 'an attempt to introduce German scepticism'.[27]

Liberal theological and scriptural views were popularised in England through the books of men such as the Bishop of Natal, J.W. Colenso, who was deposed and excommunicated by his superior, the Bishop of Cape Town, for his rejection of Biblical inerrancy and other traditional church teaching. Colenso appealed to the Privy Council, had the deposition overturned and retained possession of his see. In England he was a Liberal hero, and Trollope was one of his admirers: he called on Colenso in 1877 when visiting Africa. Another *cause célèbre* of Victorian England was the publication in 1860 of *Essays and Reviews*, a volume of articles, some of which were written by leading Liberal Churchmen like Mark Pattison and Benjamin Jowett. It was condemned by the Church of England in 1864 for its 'minimising spirit', its rejection of eternal punishment and its dismissal of the Genesis story as a literal account: it was among the few theological works in Trollope's library. Yet he rarely allowed such reading to appear – at least openly – in his fiction. Once the Lord Lieutenant of Ireland asked him what would be the effect of *Essays and Reviews* 'upon Barchester Society'. Trollope replied: 'I do not know how the Essays and Reviews may be handled by our hyper protestant pastors and masters in Ireland, but I am afraid that they will be almost too much for the Society of Barchester.' Trollope also read Sir John Seeley's *Ecce Homo*, published anonymously in 1865. This was a popular attempt in the minimising tradition at creating an 'historic Jesus' without considering His divine nature. The Evangelical leader Lord Shaftesbury with characteristic moderation denounced it as 'the most pestilential book ever vomited from the jaws of hell'. While Trollope might read Seeley, he never adopted the minimising tendency: in his study of Cicero he comments in an aside, 'Christ came to us, and we do not need another teacher.' In his fifties he astounded the agnostic writer John Morley, whom he was interviewing for the editorship of a journal, by roaring out: 'Do you believe in the divinity of our blessed Lord and Saviour Jesus Christ?'[28]

Trollope's liberal views are best shown by his own doubts as to whether the punishment of the damned was eternal. In one short story of 1870, 'The Spotted Dog', a clergyman hurries to a sordid public house where the manuscript of his life-long work of Greek scholarship has been destroyed by a drunken proof-reader before he committed suicide. 'The mercy of God is infinite,' says the cleric, to which Trollope adds, in a comment on eternal damnation: 'To threaten while the life is in the man is human. To believe in the execution of those threats when the life has passed away is almost beyond the power of humanity.' Here he was expressing his own views on eternal punishment only six years after the church had condemned *Essays and Reviews* for advocating the same view. For himself, however, he had a straightforward conviction of eternal salvation: 'I own I feel that it is impossible that the Lord should damn me ... I expect ... eternal bliss as the reward of my life here on earth.'[29]

As to religious practice, all evidence points to his being a regular church-goer. As a youth of twenty-one he had argued in his commonplace book that 'salutary religion' could only come from regular worship and prayer. He adhered to this throughout his life and it evidently gave him 'comfort': one Sunday, while on a visit to South Africa, he was unable to get to church in the morning but later managed at least to hear a hymn while standing outside the church under an oak tree. He found it 'the longest hymn I ever heard; but I thought it was very sweet; and as it was all that I heard that Sunday of sacred service, I did not begrudge its length.' The rector of the Sussex village where he spent his last years described him as 'an alert and reverent and audible worshipper, and a steady communicant'. Private prayer seems to have been particularly important to Trollope, though he frequently alludes to how difficult it was to keep the mind concentrated on spiritual topics.[30]

Linked with his idea of God was his idea of man, and without some understanding of this the Barset novels, as well as his other writings, cannot be understood. He was convinced that man was by nature self-centred and that this was the basis of society: 'Every man to himself is the centre of the whole world; the axle on which all turns. All knowledge is but his own perception of the things around him' [*Can You Forgive Her?* XXIX]. In addition people were a complex compound of good and bad; hardly anyone is without this mixture. Human behaviour was rarely either white or black but, rather, 'that sombre, uninviting shade of ordinary brown' [*The Bertrams* XIX]. That is why he disliked Dickensian characters, who tended to be either saints or monsters. 'Men as I see them,' countered Trollope, 'are not often heroic'

[*The Claverings* XXXVIII]. This was the case not only when he reflected on the behaviour of his characters but when he contemplated mankind in general: 'Man is never strong enough to take unmixed delight in good, so we may presume also that he cannot be quite so weak as to find perfect satisfaction in evil' [*The Eustace Diamonds* I]. In this Trollope is only expressing a traditional Christian view of the nature of man.

For those who rejected this view and preached that humanity was either good or bad, Trollope had perfect contempt. 'Perfect faith in mankind ... is the surest evidence of a simple mind' [*Mr. Scarborough's Family* XXXII]. However, he had far greater distaste for depictions of man as inherently evil. This was 'that worst of all diseases, – a low idea of humanity' [*The Eustace Diamonds* XXVIII]. He saw overemphasis on man's evil motives as essentially un-Christian and even criticised his literary hero Thackeray for seeing in all human actions 'the seed of something base'. Baseness was due at least partly to the quality of a person's life, and here education was the key: 'The tendencies and influences which send children to school, send them and their parents to church also', a view borne out by the low church attendances among the uneducated rural poor. (Of course, one sometimes paid a price: education among 'the most favoured classes' did produce 'a tendency in the man's mind to think that he can best suffice to himself as his own priest'.) To Trollope the importance of religion was that it made it easier for a person to develop the nobler aspects of humanity and to do right towards others. At a protest meeting in 1876 he appealed to the basic 'difference between good and evil' as something that had distinguished all Christian churches from 'the Turk'. He saw the unique achievement of Christianity: 'Looking back to history I find that in spite of blots which have stained [it] ... the Xtian religion has carried with it humanity & softness and hatred of cruelty wherever it has gone.' Because Trollope's God was a merciful one he frequently repeated the proverb that God tempers the wind to the shorn lamb:[31]

> No lesson is truer than that which teaches us to believe that God does temper the wind to the shorn lamb. To how many has it not seemed, at some one period of their lives, that all was over for them, and that to them in their afflictions there was nothing left but to die! And yet they have lived to laugh again, to feel that the air was warm and the earth fair, and that God in giving them ever-springing hope had given everything [*Orley Farm* LXXIX].

In his own role as a creator Trollope normally lessened the winds of wrath. Few sinful characters, even after their justified punishment has been inflicted, are sent off without some small income, some welcome gift or some mysterious pension to temper their shorn existence, even if it be at some unseemly spot on the continent.

*

Trollope avoided the common error of confusing 'religion' with the 'Church'. He stressed the difference between 'things ecclesiastical ... things theological ... [and] things religious' [*The Last Chronicle of Barset* XXXIV]. His fiction rarely touches 'things religious' and only once touches 'things theological', in *The Bertrams*, but the novels often deal with 'things ecclesiastical'. His attitude towards the Church, particularly towards his own Church of England, is traceable throughout his novels. Because religion was seen as a serious matter, people, or at least the middle classes, took it seriously. 'In my days,' wrote Trollope in the 1870s, 'I have written something about clergymen but never a word about religion.'[32] 'Never a word' is a slight exaggeration, but this is only apparent if one knows how to peer behind some of Trollope's comments. To do so is to see how concerned he was about the most frequently discussed topic of his time. Most of the great intellectual debates of the age were centred on the position of the Church which affected almost every political topic from Reform Bills, Corn Laws and education to the appointment of magistrates, the selection of parliamentary candidates and the conduct of elections. The American Unitarian, Emerson described its importance just when the first Barset novels were appearing:[33]

> The national temperament deeply enjoys the unbroken order and tradition of its church; the liturgy, ceremony, architecture; the sober grace, the good company, the connection with the throne, and with history, which adorn it ... the stability of the English nation is passionately enlisted to its support, from its inextricable connection with the cause of public order, with politics and with the funds.

This perfectly describes Trollope's attitude towards his Church.

The seriousness with which Victorians viewed the Church did not stop at such weighty topics as salvation or hell-fire. To take one good example from the very area where Trollope was at work on rural postal delivery: Lady Charlotte Guest was a highly accomplished translator of Welsh poetry and an active manager of the largest iron foundry in the world. Yet her diary is much taken up with religious matters, mainly worries about 'Puseyism'. For several days she refused to stir from her bedroom lest she meet a Catholic bishop who was visiting a Spanish relative. At her country home in Dorset she was so upset at seeing a print of the crucifixion in the parish church that she hurried up to London to complain to the Archbishop of Canterbury and to seek comfort from that venerable and 'velvet' Evangelical, the Rev. Mr Cunningham at Harrow.[34]

*

It is obvious to anyone who reads Trollope that he despised Evangelicals. It is not easy to say exactly what he meant by the term, but he was aiming at those enthusiastic and extreme Low Churchmen who stressed 'hatred of Rome, strict observance of the Sabbath; and abhorrence of worldly wealth, pleasure, and sensual appetites'. Some of this was a legacy of childhood, for his mother had a fierce hatred of them even before encountering Cunningham. Neither she nor her sons took account of the good work Evangelicals had done in alleviating the condition of the poor at home or of the slaves abroad. She taught her children that ' "evangelicalism" ... was a note of vulgarity – a sort of thing that might be expected to be met with in tradesmen's back parlours ... but ... utterly out of place among gentlemen'. Trollope told a young writer that he had 'inherited some of my good mother's antipathies towards a certain clerical school'. Faithful to this teaching, his novels present a procession of Evangelical clergymen, some of whom are sinister, most of whom are unattractive and almost all of whom lack that nebulous quality of gentility. Mr Slope is Trollope's most memorable portrait of a sinister clergyman. In *Rachel Ray* Trollope readily acknowledges that the Evangelical clergyman Samuel Prong was a 'devout, good man; not self-indulgent; perhaps not more self-ambitious than it becomes a man to be; sincere, hard-working, sufficiently intelligent, true in most things to the instincts of his calling'. He was, however,

> deficient in one vital qualification for a clergyman of the Church of England; he was not a gentleman. I do not mean to say that he was a thief or a liar; nor do I mean hereby to complain that he picked his teeth with his fork and misplaced his 'h's.' I am by no means prepared to define what I do mean, – thinking however that most men and most women will understand me. [VI]

It was not absolutely necessary for a 'gentleman' to be 'gently born', and a few of Trollope's clergy, such as the Dean of Brotherton, spring from 'humble' circumstances [*Is He Popenjoy?* I]. Trollope even criticises that fictional Dean for not taking pride in the fact that he rose by his own abilities. Yet the novelist normally preferred his good clergymen to have some vague claim to gentility, which was not difficult in an age when almost all clergy were assumed to be Oxford or Cambridge men. Trollope's view was a widely held one; when the Liberal Prime Minister, Lord John Russell, was looking for a new Archbishop of York he told Lord Lansdowne about one candidate: 'You know more of him than I do – I fear he is timid, and shabby – but a gentleman ... '[35]

For Trollope dislike of Evangelicals was not based solely on inherited prejudice or snobbery. He disliked their opinions, particularly their oft-expressed view that life on earth was 'a vale of tears'. Gladstone, who had grown up as an Evangelical, saw this attitude towards amusement as 'rigid and superficial'.[36] Trollope believed that life was a divine gift to be enjoyed, and this belief grew as his prosperity brought more luxuries. His Evangelicals are either hypocrites or people whose sense of enjoyment had been crushed out of them. Thus in *Rachel Ray* the heroine's mother 'taught herself to believe that cheerfulness was a sin, and that the more she became morose, the nearer would she be to ... future happiness' [I]. She is at least capable of savouring such worldly delights as hot buttered toast (a particular favourite of Trollope's after a hunt), not to mention such an enormity as clotted cream. However, she is careful to hide the relics of these sins from Rachel's elder sister, who is under the domination of Prong, the Evangelical clergyman. Trollope was perceptive in seeing how the 'godly' derive pleasure from mortification. Rachel's sister 'was approaching that stage of discipline at which ashes become pleasant eating and sackcloth is grateful to the skin. The self-indulgences of the saints in this respect often exceed anything that is done by the sinners' [V]. To Trollope, writing in *The Belton Estate* [VII], this was a heresy, a rejection of the world God had made: 'Why has the world been made so pleasant? Why is the fruit of the earth so sweet; and the trees, – why are they so green; and the mountains so full of glory? Why are women so lovely? and why is it that the activity of man's mind is the only sure forerunner of man's progress?'

Trollope liked to show the way Evangelical clergy could manipulate women. Almost all his religious fanatics are either Evangelical clergymen or women who inflict a stern regime upon any girl committed to their care. To such women 'the acerbities of religion are intended altogether for their own sex' [*Linda Tressel* I]. With them 'superstition' was as powerful as with 'any self-flagellated nun' [*John Caldigate* XIX]. A second powerful reason for Trollope's dislike was his belief that the Evangelicals had a contempt for women's minds. In his satirical essay 'The Zulu in London' he portrays a meeting of

Evangelicals devoted to the conversion of the Jews. This was in Exeter Hall, the 'cathedral' of Evangelicalism, erected in the 1830s in the Strand. Here were held what became known as the 'May Meetings', annual rallies of various Evangelical, Nonconformist and reforming bodies which sometimes lasted up to a week and were an important part of London life. They were roughly equivalent to the modern annual political assemblies. Trollope was asked to write a series about them but found that one visit was enough and gave up the idea. He chose to write the article in the somewhat unlikely guise of a Zulu as a way to support Bishop Colenso, whose appeal to the Privy Council against his deposition as Bishop of Natal had been upheld in March.* One clergyman, whom Trollope adds is 'beautiful to the eyes' – a sure sign that he was not to be trusted – patronises his largely female audience. He turns his back on them to tell fellow clergy on the platform about keeping any doubts they might have to themselves: 'Then he waved his white hand gracefully over the heads of the ladies, and again as he did so repeated his prayer – "Let not these poor ignorant ones be vexed with vain doubts." Now, Mr. Editor, let me tell you that Zulu women would not stand such a treatment as that. In what we believe and what we don't believe our women go along with us.'[37] This was the only time when Trollope failed to complete a literary agreement; his son Henry, who accompanied him, took the sensible course and slept through the ranting.

*

The 'saints' had committed two other unforgivable sins by attacking both of Trollope's vocations: the Post Office and the novel. In their continual crusade for Sabbatarianism anathemas were pronounced against Sunday trains, and even fiercer attacks were levelled against the Post Office for Sunday deliveries. After postal clerks refused to work on Sundays a rally of Evangelicals at Exeter Hall went so far as to hiss at the mention of Rowland Hill's name. A sudden parliamentary vote stopped Sunday deliveries for three weeks in 1850, much to the fury of postal officials, as well as of Queen Victoria, who thought it 'a

---

*In his book *The Pentateuch and the Book of Joshua Critically Examined*, published in parts between 1862 and 1879, Colenso described how one of his Zulu converts who was helping him translate the Bible asked if he really believed in the story of Noah and the ark. The convert was also appalled at the law in Exodus 21:20-21, that if an owner accidentally killed his servant he should be punished. On the other hand, if the servant 'continue a day or two, he shall not be punished: for he [the servant] is his money' (I.vii.9). In the arguments Trollope gives his visiting Zulu he shows a familiarity with Colenso's writing.

very *false* notion of obeying God's will'. Even after the Post Office resumed Sunday delivery it was possible for an area to request no Sabbath post: such exceptions, about one in every two hundred households, caused havoc to the orderly methods of Surveyors. In one Trollope novel the heroine, who lives in the Evangelical bastion of Cheltenham, does not receive word about a dying brother until it is almost too late because the clergy had arranged that the doors of the faithful would not be disturbed by a postman's knock on the Sabbath. Close, the real rector, had tried to do this [*Miss Mackenzie* XIV]. When some 'special friends of the postmen' suggested to Archdeacon Grantly that his village could do without Sunday post that sturdy High Churchman told them they were 'numskulls' [*The Last Chronicle of Barset* LXXIII]. Sunday post provided Trollope with another chance to portray Sabbatarians as hypocrites; when Bishop Proudie writes to a clergyman on a Sunday night he takes care to date his letter Monday morning [*Last Chronicle* XVII]. In rejecting Sabbatarianism Trollope stressed his old watchword 'comfort': 'Whatever our Sundays be, let them be a comfort to us ... Unless our day of worship be a comfort, our worship will avail us but little.'[38]

If Evangelicals thundered against Sunday post, they thought novels wicked on every day. Many of them looked upon them as 'a kind of Devil's Bible'. By the end of Trollope's life this attitude was fading: 'The ordinary old homily against the novel, inveighing against the frivolities, the falsehood, and perhaps the licentiousness ... is still familiar to our ears.' Nonconformists, whose attitudes in this as on most social questions, were virtually indistinguishable from Evangelicals, also had a distrust of fiction, partly due to a dislike of novels inherited from the last century and partly based on the view that 'untrue' stories distracted people from the seriousness of real life as a preparation for eternity. All, however, could not resist temptation. One Methodist schoolmaster remembered that 'Anthony Trollope was found too worldly for the columns of *Good Words*: but, for all his hatred of Dissent, he made his way into the most pious households.'[39] As the century wore on, these attitudes first weakened and then disappeared as Nonconformity produced its own novelists, few of whom are remembered today.

Another Evangelical trait despised by Trollope was the penchant for scattering religious phrases into everyday chatter. As a child he had taken part in his mother's play about an Evangelical tea party, 'The Righteous Rout', and he imbibed its hatred of using sacred language to attain one's own ends. He would have agreed with his mother's rule: 'I rarely converse much on the subject of religion; it is a theme in my estimation more belonging to the heart than the tongue.' In one novel he uses his favourite device of allowing people to reveal themselves through dialogue. At a Cheltenham tea party the heroine is astonished at the 'special freedom' of a clergyman's talk, 'how he spoke of St Paul as Paul ... and how he named even a holier name ... with infinite ease and an accustomed familiarity' [*Miss Mackenzie* IV]. (This tea party has a strong resemblance to 'The Righteous Rout' which Fanny Trollope had written for her children to perform. Trollope may have included this holy gathering in his novel as a tribute to his mother who had died a few months before.) Trollope saw how some of 'the godly' dangled religious phrases to manipulate people: Mr Slope is always talking of the 'Sabbath', and Mrs Proudie invokes the 'souls of the people' to browbeat her husband.* Trollope himself was not one to scatter divine blessings on all sides. In his correspondence he normally reserves 'God bless you' for his wife, mother and sons, and occasionally for extremely close friends at moments of crisis. In the novels there are frequent references to 'God' and 'Providence', but normally Christ is called 'our Saviour'.[40]

*

For non-Evangelical clergy Trollope had respect but not veneration. This attitude is best encapsulated in his portrayal of Archdeacon Grantly, of whom he grew fonder as he wrote. That venerable clergyman is 'a man to be furthered and supported, though perhaps also to be controlled' [*The Warden* XX]. Priests should witness to the truth but not cut themselves off from mankind. In *The Claverings* the curate, Samuel Saul, is criticised by his rector for his excessive other-worldliness: 'It is not that he mortifies his flesh, but that he has no flesh to mortify. He is unconscious of the flavour of venison, or the scent of roses, or the beauty of women' [II]. The clergy were meant to conduct the public worship of God in a dignified manner and, if possible, amid beautiful surroundings. A clergyman should always remember his position but should not dedicate himself to reminding others of it [*An Old Man's Love* XVII]. It is not surprising that he disliked the new 'seminary priests' produced by the theological colleges in the second half of the century. While the clergy could be called upon to help and advise 'the lower orders', Trollope sensibly insisted that

---

*Trollope's mother made these same points in her *Domestic Manners of the Americans*, where she describes how she listened to a 'rant of miserable, low, familiar jargon' in the form of a prayer in all churches excepting the Episcopalian and Catholic (p. 105). She, too, was appalled at the influence held by ministers which 'approaches very nearly to what we read of in Spain, or in other strict Roman Catholic countries' (p. 60).

'the ordinary life of gentlefolk in England does not admit of direct clerical interference' [*John Caldigate* XXXII]. The notion that the clergy should guide the national political conscience through ad hoc committees or abstruse reports would have struck someone of Trollope's common sense as an absurd fantasy. His ideal priests, be they Catholics in Ireland or Anglicans in Barset, are men who go about their duties, usually in the countryside, doing good, mainly to the poor, and exuding in their own lives the 'beauty of holiness'. This was the type of clergyman he describes walking about his churchyard on a starlit night:

> His lines had been laid for him in very pleasant places ... Things outside were dark, – at least, so said the squires and parsons around him ... But to our parson it had always seemed that there was still a fresh running stream of water for him who would care to drink from a fresh stream. He had heard much of unbelief, and of the professors of unbelief, both within and without the great Church; – but in that little church with which he was personally concerned there were more worshippers now than there had ever been before. And he had heard, too, how certain well-esteemed preachers and prophets of the day talked loudly of the sins of the people ... but to him it seemed that the people of his village were more honest, less given to drink, and certainly better educated than their fathers. In all which thoughts he found matter for hope and encouragement in his daily life [*Ralph the Heir* XIV].

To many Victorians this portrait of a vicar, ignoring a pamphlet from Carlyle or another sermon from the latest doubting bishop, would call to mind John Keble. That great prophet and saint of the Oxford Movement had retired to his 'little church' at Hursley when he tired of battles about 'the great Church'. As someone drawn to the old High Church tradition, Trollope was naturally sympathetic to men like Keble and to those early Tractarians who carried on the work he had inspired by his 1833 Assize Sermon. According to Escott, a man knowledgeable in church politics, Trollope's 'sympathies were ... inclined towards the moderate, lettered, and generally accomplished members of the High Church party'. He had heard Newman preach at St Mary's in the 1830s and he certainly always spoke of the Cardinal, who is mentioned in several of the novels, with respect. It is appropriate that Newman's favourite novelist was Trollope who was delighted to receive, only days before his fatal stroke, a warm letter from Newman praising his novels. Trollope even spoke with kindness of 'poor Froude' whose *Remains*, published after his early death and edited by Newman, so disturbed earnest Protestants with its attacks on the Reformation. Trollope was friendly with the Sewells, a family who played a prominent role in High Church activities in Oxford. In *The New Zealander* he highly praised the beauty of the new church in Margaret Street. All Saints, at the time this was written, was the very symbol of the most catholic element within the Church of England. To praise the church without criticising the ritual and teaching that went on within was a sign of his inclinations. If Trollope had any dislike of Tractarianism, he would have denounced this church; on the other hand, if he were inclining towards ritualism, he would have used the church's ornamentation as a way to promote those views. He also appears to have followed the practice of abstaining from meat on Ash Wednesday, something ordered in the Prayer Book.[41] Perhaps most convincingly, he selected a High Church school, Bradfield, for his two sons.

The highly theological speculations on the priesthood, the church and the Eucharist that came to dominate the *Tracts for the Times* would have had little appeal to Trollope. Likewise he did not think, as did the High Tory Keble, that the Church should dominate life and guide the state. For Trollope, results rather than theories were what mattered, and here he paid tribute to the Tractarian Movement:[42]

> Dr Newman has gone to Rome, and Dr Pusey has perhaps helped to send many thither; but these men, and their brethren of the Tracts, stirred up throughout the country so strong a feeling of religion, gave rise by their works to so much thought on a matter which had been allowed for years to go on almost without any thought, that it may be said ... that they made episcopal idleness impossible and clerical idleness rare. Of course, it will be said ... that no school of clergymen has so run after wiggeries and vestments and empty symbols as have the ... men whom I have named. But the wiggeries ... have been simply the dross which has come from their fused gold. If you will make water really boil, some will commonly boil over.

Nor did he regard religious controversies as bad. Victorians really did believe in the Church Militant and in doing battle for what they thought right. To Trollope disputes, provided they did not become too vicious, strengthened the Church:

> We are much too apt to look at schism in our church as an unmitigated evil. Moderate schism, if there be any such thing ... calls attention to the subject, draws in supporters ... and teaches men to think upon religion. How great an amount of good of this description has followed that movement in the Church of England which commenced with the publication of Froude's Remains! [*Barchester Towers* XX].

Throughout the 1850s – the years in which he wrote the first three Barset novels – Trollope introduced religious comments, particularly praise of the Tractarians, into almost every book. When he was in the West Indies, at the end of this decade, the unadorned churches reminded him of the dreary ones of his youth: 'The church itself, with its rickety pews, and creaking doors, and wretched seats made purposely so as to render genuflexion impossible, and the sleeping, droning, somnolent service, are exactly what was so common in England twenty years since; but which are common no longer, thanks to certain much-abused clerical gentlemen. Not but that it may still be found in England if diligently sought for.' Trollope's casual reference to 'genuflexion' shows his sympathies with the Tractarian revival of older ritual practices which outraged many Anglicans. This may well be what his rector was referring to in the 1880s when he spoke of Trollope's 'reverent' attitude during Communion.[43]

Trollope was, therefore, from inheritance and inclination, a High Churchman as the name was used in his early days. High Churchmen took the Church of England seriously as a sacramental body, as opposed to those who saw it as part of the established political and social order, whose beliefs could be framed by Parliament. They remained 'Protestant' because they still protested against the Pope's claim to a universal primacy; they remained 'Catholic' because they claimed to be part of the universal church. Another legacy from the previous century, evident in figures like Archdeacon Grantly and Mr Harding, was a reticence in expressing dogmatic teaching and a fear of 'enthusiasm' which inevitably produced an imbalance.[44]

This was Trollope's inheritance as a High Churchmen. He had a friendly feeling for Catholics though he had no desire to 'pervert' to Rome. To him the faults of Catholicism could be corrected 'by the force of the human nature of its adherents' unlike extreme Protestantism, where 'the austerity of self-punishment' was at war with human nature [*Linda Tressel* XIV]. He was always happier when visiting Catholic countries, though he believed that Protestantism embodied the progress of his age. He adhered to the sacramental aspect of religion – as his Sussex rector said, he was 'a steady communicant' – but he had little regard for preaching, which Low Churchmen and Evangelicals emphasised. While his aesthetic sense and feeling for old buildings gave him a sympathy for Catholicism, his liberalism pulled the other way. Nor can one ignore the fact that the Church of Ireland, whose services he attended for almost two decades, was marked by an old-fashioned, pre-Tractarian High Church ethos.[45] His Irish experiences also coloured his attitude towards attacks on 'Puseyism' as he tired of hearing fearsome denunciations of 'the wicked infamous Pusey' from Protestant ladies [*Castle Richmond* V].

As the nineteenth century wore on, the Tractarian Movement became more concerned with ritual approximating Roman Catholic usages. In the last pages of *Barchester Towers*, Trollope cleverly portrays this by contrasting the views of Eleanor Bold, after her marriage to Dean Arabin, with those of her sister, Susan Grantly, wife of the Archdeacon. Eleanor 'assumes a smile of gentle ridicule when the Archbishop of Canterbury is mentioned': a practice quite common among the very High Church for well over a century. With her 'inkling' towards a Catholic view of the Eucharist, she sends a donation towards 'legal expenses ... incurred in Bath' which Trollope's contemporary readers would have known to be the trial of Archdeacon Denison for his sermon on the 'real presence'. Eleanor's sister, Susan Grantly, remains true to the older High Church views and finds her younger sister's views amusing but not really dangerous: an approach the novelist explicitly endorses.* Several times he distinguished between the old High Church 'which is now scandalously called the high-and-dry church' from the innovations 'which are somewhat too loosely called Puseyite practices' [*Barchester Towers* VI]. While he belonged to the high-and-dry-school he had accepted some aims of the younger men including, for example, a desire for more dignified services. He depicted his position in a non-fictional work, *The New Zealander*, by inventing two clergymen who represented the extremes between which he was caught: the Evangelical, Mr Everscreech, devoted to destroying the 'comfort' of religion, and Dr Middleage, addicted to the fashionable craze for medievalism and the restoring of old rituals. There is also a zealous young girl, who dates her letters by saints' days. Trollope was, no doubt, thinking of his dead sister Cecilia who had done the same. Mrs Proudie regarded this practice as a mark of 'the scarlet woman'. Macaulay, with a little more restraint, hoped 'these follies should sink amidst a storm of laughter'.[46] Trollope did not want a storm of laughter: he preferred to dismiss them with a gentle mockery. There appears to be only one example of Trollope's dating a letter by a saint's day: in 1875 he wrote to Rose from the Persian Gulf on 'St Patrick's Day', but this springs from his love of Ireland rather than from any sudden conversion to pious affectation.

---

*This is a good example of the way printing errors could distort Trollope's meaning. The well-known 'Oxford World's Classic' edition reads 'Mr. Arabin's church is two degrees higher than that of Mrs. Grantly' (p. 505). Trollope actually wrote: 'Mrs. Arabin', as confirmed by the text of the collected edition of *The Chronicles of Barsetshire* prepared by him (II.387).

While Trollope accepted that the excessive practices of later generations of the High Church Movement appeared 'sincere', they had one fault, 'the huge evil of unreality'. For the growing devotion to celibacy he had bemused contempt. In his novels he dealt with it easily: Tractarian clergymen, like Francis Arabin and Caleb Oriel, soon abandon romantic notions of celibacy when they leave Oxford, enter the real world and meet ladies doubly blessed with beauty and dowries. While Sydney Smith believed that nothing settled a clergyman so much as a good living, Anthony Trollope believed that a good wife was an even more settling experience. He was not much concerned with battles about clerical dress: in his youth he would have seen clergymen in the pulpit wearing the black Geneva gown; the surplice and black stole were only put on to celebrate Communion. As the century wore on, the surplice became the standard dress throughout services. Trollope admitted to being 'mainly indifferent to the vestment in which our clergyman preaches to us, so long as it be seemly, sober, and clerical'. Interestingly enough, this was similar to the view of the noted High Churchman, Gladstone. In the late 1870s when Trollope described some South African clergy as 'High Church' he added: 'It might be supposed that I was accusing them of a passion for ribbons.' On that visit he was mildly annoyed at seeing a priest in a green 'ribbon', by which he meant a stole in the ecclesiastical colour for the season of Trinity. From various comments he made it seems that Trollope was quite satisfied with the state Anglican worship reached in the 1860s, when the Tractarians had restored a sense of beauty and decorum within the limits inherited from the previous century and without copying Roman Catholic worship. In 1862 he wrote after visiting churches in Holland: 'It has been hard to steer between idolatry and irreverence, between too much ceremony and too little. We, with our much maligned church in England, may perhaps boast we have done so.'[47]

In theory Trollope believed that all Christians should respect one another's beliefs and practices. In Australia he was pleased by a sermon advocating friendly feelings towards other denominations: 'Who then shall attempt to exclude from the Church of Christ,' he asked, 'those who are but professing believers?' Yet his novels hardly glow with that charitable virtue. It is going too far to say that he 'hated' Dissent. He had, after all, married a Unitarian, and he was certainly far less scathing than Dickens or Thackeray in his treatment of Nonconformists. While he thought their red-brick chapels were ugly and spoiled English villages and found their ministers rude and uneducated he also showed a certain sympathy which was not flattering to the Church of England. In *The Vicar of Bullhampton* he introduced the Rev. Mr Puddleham, a Primitive Methodist minister. He 'is an earnest man, who, in spite of the intensity of his ignorance, is efficacious among the poor' – here Trollope again shows his understanding of rural life, because the Primitive Methodists were the most working-class and rural of the leading Nonconformist bodies. Later on he describes the new chapel: 'It was acknowledged that it was ugly, misplaced, uncomfortable, detestable to the eye, and ear, and general feeling', except, he adds with a sting, 'in so far as it might suit the wants of people who were not sufficiently educated to enjoy the higher tone, and more elaborate language of the Church of England services' [I, LX]. Perhaps, like one of his clergyman – a man of 'kindly, gentlemanlike, amiable prejudices' – he 'thought that Dissenters were, – a great mistake'.

In most novels they do not occur, and when, as in *The Vicar of Bullhampton*, they do, his lack of interest is seen when a builder who is a Baptist in Chapter XXXVI is called a Wesleyan Methodist in Chapter LV. His view was more a social attitude based on Nonconformity's position within English society than a theological belief. What he disliked were those traits they shared with Anglican Evangelicals and their growing obsession with politics during the 1840s, especially their raucous cries for the disestablishment of the Church, something he always opposed. The Quakers were the one body he particularly disliked, although one of his last heroines, Marion Fay, was a Quakeress.[48] It is noticeable that he is always more neutral towards Dissent in those stories set outside England or in his travel books, but of course outside England they ceased to be Nonconformists and became simply Protestant denominations. Basically Trollope was simply not interested in Nonconformity. It was not really part of his world.

His attitude towards the Catholic Church was quite different, as we have noted. Because of his friendly feelings, Catholic priests are almost always treated with respect and even with affection. 'I have lived much with clergymen of your Church,' he told one Catholic lady, 'and have endeavoured to draw them in their colours as I saw them. But, because they were the priests of a church which was not my church, I have never drawn one as bad, or hypocritical, or unfaithful.' Unlike his brother Tom, whose Italian novels express a detestation of priests, Anthony portrayed continental priests quite favourably in *La Vendée* and *Nina Balatka*. An Irish priest was, after all, the hero of his first novel.[49] In *The Way We Live Now* he did portray a fanatical priest, but only in his last novel did he describe a wicked priest, one who helps an Irish terrorist by making a boy take an oath not to reveal information.

*

To what extent were Trollope's portrayals of clergymen accurate? Many of his contemporaries testified to his acumen: 'They are photographic portraits of men his readers know: nature clothed with the form of art: and from their exquisite truthfulness they derive their interest.' Anyone who examines the private letters between bishops and politicians will see how accurately Trollope captured the spirit of his age. It may be recalled how frequently his clergymen discuss their ecclesiastical battles over port, another subject on which they seem to have strong views. It is likely that Trollope would have heard a story told to his friend William Frith, the artist, by Bishop Sumner who was still Bishop of Winchester in 1863 although he first came to that Cathedral when Trollope was but a young boy at the College. Frith wondered how the Bishop had stayed so well: 'I have eaten of whatever good things were put before me, and I have drunk a bottle of port wine every day since I was a boy. The only precaution I have taken has been in the quality of the wine; for unless it was old and good, I would have none of it.'

To those who have not studied the Victorian Church the ambitions and cultivated intrigues of Barchester clergymen may seem exaggerated. In fact the manuscript collections of Prime Ministers teem with letters from ambitious clerics and their friends. There is a good example in the enormous correspondence of William Gladstone. No Prime Minister had a deeper care for the best interests of the Church; yet he well knew that bishops are rarely selected from the most spiritual of men. Only a few years after *The Last Chronicle of Barset* the Rev. Lord Arthur Hervey wrote to remind his fellow Etonian of his desire for a mitre. Hervey even adapted one of Trollope's favourite quotations from the Psalms: 'My lines have fallen in more quiet perhaps more pleasant places' than those of his ever-busy school-fellow. Gladstone had two dioceses available for his old friend. He thought Carlisle would be the better choice, but Lord Arthur preferred Bath and Wells because the palace was more comfortable for his wife and because that diocese was a better place for his daughters to find husbands. Lady Arthur sounds remarkably like Mrs Proudie. Several years after settling behind the moat of that delightful palace, Bishop Hervey wrote again to his old friend that the Dean was in a 'very precarious state of health and might be called away almost at any moment'. He asked that the Prime Minister should not recommend too 'high' a clergyman, as such a Dean could disturb his peace. This sounds remarkably close to the clerical machinations that went on round the deathbed of Dean Trefoil of Barchester! Trollope not only knew the ways of Victorian England but understood human nature, even when it was camouflaged by 'the cloth'. After *The Barchester Chronicles* appeared on television a layman asked the Bishop of Peterborough whether the portrayal of the weak-willed Bishop Proudie was accurate. 'Yes,' replied the real prelate. 'He's just like most of the present Bench of Bishops.'[50]

Many have argued that Trollope's novels do not show the Anglican clergy as spiritual men. 'It never really occurs to us,' sneered G.K. Chesterton, 'to think of them as the priests of a religion.' This is not true. Several are shown, albeit briefly, going about spiritual duties with a seemly English reserve. Almost every appearance of the aged Septimus Harding is tinged with a quiet spirituality, essentially English and essentially genteel. One must remember that Victorian country clergy had less strenuous duties than their modern counterparts and much of the 'charitable' work was undertaken by their wives or daughters. Nor did Trollope wish to scatter piety throughout his books; he was writing novels, not tracts. The prayers or pious advice of the laity, as well as the clergy, are usually only hinted at, because the novelist did not believe that fiction was the proper place for them. When Mrs Orme and Lady Mason discuss the moral implication of Lady Mason's forgery, Trollope comments: 'I will not attempt to report the words that passed between them ... for they concerned a matter which I may not dare to handle too closely in such pages as these' [*Orley Farm* LX]. Trollope never saw his novels as means of religious propaganda. By the 1850s the 'religious novel' was well established. In the early days these stories, whose religious purpose often was the excuse for bad writing, centred on the Oxford Movement. Some writers, like Newman or Trollope's sister Cecilia, praised it; others, like J.A. Froude, brother of Hurrell, condemned it. The tradition continued throughout the century but produced very few memorable novels.[51]

Trollope did not have the common Victorian love of the sermon, which he regarded as boring collections of 'platitudes, truisms and untruisms'. The most memorable of the few sermons in the novels is Mr Slope's rant against dignified services in Barchester Cathedral [*Barchester Towers* VI]. Trollope was fortunate to live in an age when sermons did not provide a ready excuse for scattering political nostrums. He endured a bout of this in America, where the political sermon in its modern format was invented, and concluded: 'One hardly knows where the affairs of this world end, or where those of the next

begin.' He was among the first to wonder whether 'the holy men [are]
... doing stage-work or church-work?'[52] His exclusion of religious
propaganda from his novels is a legacy of the old High Church
reticence in talking about things spiritual:

> It would not be becoming were I to travestie a sermon, or even to repeat
> the language of it in ... a novel. In endeavouring to depict the characters
> ... I am forced to speak of sacred things. I trust, however, that I shall not
> be thought to scoff at the pulpit, though some may imagine that I do not
> feel all the reverence that is due to the cloth. I may question the
> infallibility of the teachers, but I hope that I shall not therefore be
> accused of doubt as to the thing taught [*Barchester Towers* VI].

In concluding this discussion of the religious ideas behind the Barset
novels, it should be said that the best summary of Trollope's view of the
'comfort' of Christianity is found, most appropriately, in a toast his
saintly Warden Harding gives as he takes leave of the bedesmen: 'I
hope you may live contented, and die trusting in the Lord Jesus Christ,
and thankful to Almighty God for the good things he has given you'
[*The Warden* XX].

*

The first three novels had failed because Trollope misjudged his subjects, his settings and, most of all, the public mood. However, with the
first Barset novel, he picked the right time and subject. The decade
before *The Warden* was published had seen a continuous series of
ecclesiastical stories of great public interest. In spite of Newman's
'secession' in 1845, the Oxford Movement's influence grew, as did the
controversies surrounding it. Most of these took place in the dioceses
where Trollope's postal work was centred. In the vicarages where he
stopped he must have heard many discussions about local church affairs
which had become national news. In Exeter there were riots when a
clergyman attempted to wear a surplice. A few years later the Bishop of
Exeter caused another national debate by banning a Low Churchman
for 'heretical' views about Baptism. When the Privy Council overruled
the Bishop, several prominent churchmen, including Trollope's old
schoolfellow Archdeacon Manning, became Roman Catholics. (Two
other schoolfellows, F.W. Faber and W.G. Ward, had already done so.)
Trollope's district included the dioceses of the three most
controversial bishops: the ever-combative High Churchman Henry
Phillpotts of Exeter; 'Soapy Sam' Wilberforce of Oxford, who was
wrongly suspected of Tractarian intrigues; and Hereford's 'liberal

heretic' Renn Hampden, whose appointment caused fury among other bishops. These three stirred passions, particularly among their opponents. The West Country had a large share of other controversial clerics. In Somerset G.A. Denison, Archdeacon of Taunton, was making the title 'Archdeacon' familiar to newspaper readers. From his days at Oriel, when he had spent ten minutes rebuking a chef for the social outrage of sending up a hot rhubarb tart rather than a cold one, Denison made a battle of every cause. Now his High Church teaching on the Eucharist led to a prolonged trial which stirred fierce passions and a multitude of pamphlets: in *Barchester Towers* Eleanor Arabin sends money for his trial at Bath. In Frome W.J. Bennett, whose ritualistic practices led to his being driven from a London church, had sought refuge under the protection of the Marchioness of Bath. In neighbouring Dorset, the well-known clerical journalist 'S.G.O.', who had aroused Trollope's anger before his *Examiner* letters, continued to write controversial articles.[53] Men like these fill the Barset novels, and indeed both Bishop Phillpotts and Bishop Wilberforce were parodied in *The Warden*.

In addition the Pope's re-establishment of the Roman Catholic hierarchy led to an outburst of anti-Catholic riots and pamphlets which even affected the Post Office when the Headmaster of Rugby petitioned the Postmaster General to dismiss a Catholic postman! The nature of Oxford and Cambridge was under assault from advocates of educational reform as well as from those who wanted to open the ancient universities to non-Anglicans: university reform was debated not only by Bishop Proudie and the Archdeacon at Mrs Proudie's reception but even by young Bertie Stanhope [*Barchester Towers* XI]. The quiet world of Barchester close was further threatened by the results of the first, and only, 'religious census' in English history – that of 1851 – which showed that Anglicanism was losing the expanding towns and cities of the new urbanised, industrialised England. Even more alarming was that on Census Sunday just under two-thirds of all Englishmen did not attend any church at all.[54]

For years radicals had been attacking the many abuses, often mediaeval survivals, in the Church of England. The right to nominate a clergyman to a vacant 'living' could still be bought as an investment through newspaper advertisements. Pluralism still existed: Sir Robert Peel's brother-in-law, the Rev. Francis Dawson, not only had a cathedral prebendary's stall, worth £1,500 a year, but four livings. His total annual income was £3,000, and all he had to find out of this was perhaps £280 a year to provide a pittance of, say, £70 a year to each of the four curates who looked after the four parishes. He could, if he had wanted, have paid less.[55] Trollope thought pluralism wrong, and he portrays its ill effects through the Rev. Dr Vesey Stanhope who leaves his three parishes in the hands of curates while he spends a dozen years seeking a cure for his sore throat in Italy. There was still nepotism on a grand scale: Bishop Hampden may have been a liberal in theology, but he happily ordained his sixty-year-old son-in-law and conferred three livings worth almost £1,800 on the reverend recruit. Bishops were notorious for feathering not only their own nests but those of their families: Bishop Sparke of Ely had bestowed so many rich rectories on his family that it was said anyone could cross the Fens on a dark night by the light from the Sparkes on both sides of the road.

Radicals constantly assaulted the large incomes enjoyed by a few clerical dignitaries. A step towards reforming episcopal, if not parochial, incomes had been taken in the 1830s when the new Ecclesiastical Commissioners decided that most new bishops should have an annual salary of £5,000, on which they could still live comfortably, plus whatever the Commissioners would pay for palace maintenance and even gamekeepers' fees. (Trollope took an interest in clerical stipends and obtained figures showing that a French bishop received 12,000 francs, or £480, a year.) When Bishop Proudie and his wife make their first appearance in the second Barset novel, they are unhappy because the huge income earned by old Bishop Grantly has been reduced. The mediaeval order was passing away and new men were taking over: the battle between the Grantlys and the Proudies symbolised this. The Barset novels show these changes: 'Bishops,' Trollope wrote in an essay on 'English Bishops, Old and New', 'may be now seen, – as bishops never were seen of yore, – sitting in cabs ... and walking home after an ordination. These ears have heard,' Trollope admitted, 'and these eyes have seen a modern bishop hallooing from the top of his provincial High-street to a groom ... brandishing his episcopal arms the while with an energy which might have been spared.' Bishop Grantly, as one of the 'great priest lords', would never have been seen 'hallooing', but one could imagine Bishop Proudie doing so. Despite the nostalgic longing for bishops as 'wealthy ecclesiastical barons' Trollope admitted that, 'looking back for many years, a churchman of the Church of England cannot boast of the clerical doings of its bishops'. 'In seeking for the useful, we are compelled to abandon the picturesque. Our lanes and hedgerows and green commons are all going; and the graceful dignity of the old bishop is a thing of the past.' The division between the 'graceful dignity' of Bishop Grantly, an example of those bishops who 'wore their wigs with decorum and lived the lives of gentlemen' and Bishop Proudie, a man 'selected in order that he may work', is a central theme running through the Barset novels. Trollope was nowhere more prophetic than in his description of the modern bishop, like Proudie, who rose through his aptitude for committee work.[56]

With uncharacteristic brevity Henry James summarised the theme of *The Warden*: 'It is simply the history of an old man's conscience.' As we have seen, it is much more than this. It is a profound insight into the changes that were remaking the Church of England. If the sight of the serene beauties of Salisbury inspired Trollope with the idea for a clerical novel, contemporary political battles and church reforms gave him the background for his tale. More specifically, in the early 1850s reformers were busy with the complicated subject of charitable institutions. Throughout the country there were numerous almshouses, schools and charities established by pious founders which had had grown wealthy as a result of the increasing value of land. Winchester's Hospital of St Cross had been founded in 1136 by Bishop Henry de Blois. The young Anthony Trollope would have seen this ancient almshouse every time the Winchester boys were marched to St Catherine Hill. We can well imagine what thoughts the sight may have inspired in the mind of an adolescent boy whose own family was careering towards financial ruin. The Victorian Master of St Cross was a veritable godsend to radical pamphleteers. As both an earl and a wealthy cleric, Lord Guilford seemed a supreme example of a rich priest growing fat on the money intended for the poor. It was usually forgotten that he had increased the stipends of his bedesmen, an example followed by Trollope's Warden. Rochester had another clerical scandal: the battle between the Cathedral Chapter and the Rev. Robert Whiston, headmaster of the Cathedral Grammar School. This dispute about the location of a stove grew, in time-honoured clerical fashion, into legal cases about the rights of cathedral chapters. A somewhat similar controversy was taking place at Dulwich College about the ownership of its founder's valuable art collection.[57] All three struggles are mentioned in *The Warden* and were immediately recognised by informed readers. We are told that Archdeacon Grantly sent letters to the press about 'that turbulent Dr Whiston' and wrote a pamphlet signed 'Sacerdos' to defend Lord Guilford. In his own youth Trollope had suffered because of a legal dispute between Harrow School and local residents anxious to reassert the founder's intentions. In that pre-Reform age, the clergy had won, but day-boys, like Anthony, had still felt the sting of their wrath.

There are many similarities between the Rochester dispute and the fictional one at Barchester. Both the actual and fictional Archdeacons owed their lucrative positions to their father, the Bishop, who also acted as official visitor to the two controversial charities. In *The Warden* Trollope alludes to the Radical MP Sir Benjamin Hall. On 30 June 1851 this wind-bag had launched a violent assault upon the cathedral clergy at Rochester by announcing that the Dean was suffering from 'moral leprosy'. Another Radical MP, Edward Horsman, is also mentioned by Trollope: he had provoked lengthy debates by reading in the Commons an anonymous letter from a 'professor' who had been forced to overhear, solely as a result of the flimsy walls in German inns, a conversation by a High Church priest who kept talking about 'Rome'.[58]

All these events were well covered in *The Times*, Trollope's main source of news. In his last years he told his first biographer that much of the impetus for *The Warden* came from letters in that paper, where a lengthy battle was under way about clergymen who enjoyed rich livings and employed ill-paid curates to do the work. In the months after Trollope stood on the bridge in Salisbury gazing on its spire, *The Times* was full of stories and letters about ecclesiastical 'abuses'. For example, 'Memor' – no doubt a cleric in disguise – provided a detailed account of the income of two prosperous clergymen in the diocese of Canterbury. The Archdeacon of Canterbury enjoyed an income that may well have inspired that bestowed on the Archdeacon of Barchester. The real Archdeacon had £1,391 10s 10½d from just one living and a further £1,000 from his canonry at the Cathedral. A few days later 'Amicus Ecclesiae' gave a vivid portrayal of the other end of the clerical spectrum by describing a poor clergyman trying to support a wife and three children on £75 a year. *The Times* even printed official documents including a long report from the Chapter Clerk of Rochester to his Bishop, something no doubt useful to a novelist about to depict the Barchester clergy working with lay officials like Mr Chadwick in *The Warden*. Trollope told Escott that after reading these letters he tried to imagine the lives of those clergymen who wrote them and who were depicted in them. The Barchester novels are thus the result of Trollope's detailed knowledge of people's ways of life gained on his postal travels and of his 'castle building' stirred by a real controversy. Perhaps we too can engage in some 'castle building' by trying to imagine him, riding about Somerset in his hunting garb and meditating on a clergyman's outraged letter in that morning's *Times* when suddenly he arrives at the door of a vine-clad rectory to ask if their letters had arrived on that morning's breakfast table.

Trollope's knowledge of clerical abuses and controversies did not, however, come only from newspapers. His library had many radical pamphlets regarding church reform issued in the 1830s and early 1840s, although these could have been acquired later. His reaction to attacks upon the Church is characteristic of his divided attitude towards most political questions. Years later he argued that it was essentially English to have 'a loving tenderness with which admitted abuses are endured and palliated'. 'With us,' he reflected, 'regret is almost stronger than hope. We venerate old things because they are old.' In the same year in which he wrote this he also wrote his *Pall Mall Gazette* essays on clergymen in the Church of England. Here he said simply, 'We hate an evil, and we hate a change.' To Trollope this internal warfare between conservative and liberal was not some unique possession: 'In almost every bosom there sits a parliament in which a conservative party is ever combating to maintain things old, while the liberal side of the house is always conquering, but its adversary is never conquered.' Not for him the simplistic view that a house divided against itself cannot stand! The fact that his novel was finished in Belfast perhaps made him less sympathetic to the reformers by the end of the book: Trollope was always most favourable to English institutions when he was away from England.[59]

The great strength of Trollope's fourth novel lies in his characters. Septimus Harding, who gives the novel its name, is the closest Trollope ever came to portraying a saint. The Warden and his combative son-in-law Archdeacon Grantly stand for the old-fashioned High Church, with which Trollope felt most comfortable. As the Barset series progresses, the Archdeacon becomes more likeable. He shares with his creator one trait: a temper so fierce that in his case it undermines any chance of victory. Yet it is difficult not to agree with George Saintsbury's view: 'There are few *men* in fiction I *like* better, and should more like to have known, than Archdeacon Grantly.'[60] With the Warden's daughter, Eleanor, Trollope created the first of those English girls who were so much admired in his time. The great failure of the book is the radical reformer, John Bold, who launches a public attack upon the large income which was intended for the bedesmen but was instead enjoyed by his friend, the Warden. Bold never comes alive as a person; by the beginning of the second Barset novel Trollope has killed him off, much to the author's relief and to that of most readers. Trollope had great sympathy for church reform but little for reformers. In portraying this tactless agitator he almost certainly drew on his experiences of Rowland Hill.

The Warden has often been slighted by critics who do not consider it one of Trollope's best books. Yet it is one of the most important, not only because it begins the series that made the author famous but because it shows his strengths and weaknesses as well as his attitudes towards the world in which he moved. Unlike most of his novels, or indeed most Victorian novels, it is neither dominated by a long sentimental love tale nor complicated by numerous sub-plots. The one flaw lies in the author's giving way to his ever-present temptation to sarcasm. This was yet another inherited characteristic: it had ruined his father's legal career and marred his mother's books. In *The Warden* Trollope turned his guns on three of the great potentates of Victorian England: Charles Dickens, Thomas Carlyle and *The Times*. Dickens is portrayed as 'Mr Popular Sentiment', a powerful novelist who brings out a tale, *The Almshouse*, about the battle in Barchester. Trollope parodies Dickens's style, which he disliked, with some skill, but the overall impression of this insertion is unpleasant: it has all the appearance of an unsuccessful novelist jealous of the fame and fortune of the most notable writer of the day.

Trollope's attitude towards Carlyle was complex. He used 'to swear by' some of the sage's earlier works, but a few years before he started *The Warden* he bought the *Latter Day Pamphlets* and, as he wrote to his mother, he felt he had wasted his eight shillings: 'The grain of sense is so smothered up in a sack of the sheerest trash, that the former is valueless ... I look on him as a man who was always in danger of going mad in literature, and who has now done so.' The memory of those lost shillings seems to have rankled and he portrays Carlyle as Dr Pessimist Anticant, a Scot addicted to German thought. He also parodied Carlyle's style. It would have been better if he had forgotten Carlyle after that, but the 'Sage of Chelsea' always had an attraction for him. That attraction would lead Trollope to attempt one book in 'anti-cant' tone and several silly efforts at addressing 'my brothers' in his novels. Apparently he eventually got over the loss of the eight shillings, for by the 1870s his library had fifty-four volumes of Carlyle's works. For his part Carlyle had little use for Trollope's fiction: he regarded his novels as 'alum', but then he also dismissed Jane Austen's books as mere 'dish-washings'.[61] It would have surprised the novelist to know that in the twentieth century few bother with Carlyle while thousands read Trollope (and Jane Austen).

Trollope also exercised his ire against *The Times*. Here his satire is better than in his attacks on Dickens or Carlyle. His timing was perfect. He was finishing his novel in the midst of the Crimean War, when many were terrified at the paper's dominance. There was a popular joke going the rounds within weeks of *The Warden*'s publication: 'What is the difference between the Tsar and the *Times*? The one is the type of despotism and the other the despotism of type.'

Archdeacon Grantly comments: 'What the Tsar is in Russia, or the mob in America, that the *Jupiter* is in England.' Trollope denied that with Tom Towers he attempted a portrait of the famous editor of *The Times*, J.T. Delane. At that time they were unacquainted, though they later became friends.[62] In attacking 'The Jupiter' Trollope did not forget his old fury at S.G.O.'s investigations of 'the cabins of Connaught' [XIV]. His dislike of *The Times* – 'the Vatican of England' – lay in its pose of infallibility. The fictional editor is depicted as 'studiously striving to look like a god, but knowing within his breast that he was a god' [XIV]. Trollope also attempted a rather clumsy portrayal of three prominent bishops by giving their Christian names and their well-known public characters to the Archdeacon's sons. Henry (Phillpotts of Exeter) is quarrelsome; Samuel (Wilberforce of Oxford) appears friendly but is deceitful; Charles James (Blomfield of London) is dignified and moderate [XII].

*

The Drury-Merivale connection once again played a crucial role in Trollope's life. Through John Merivale he met William Longman, head of London's oldest firm of publishers. Longman agreed to look at his manuscript but advised him to change his original title, *The Precentor*. It would be interesting to know what the author thought of the report by Longmans' reader, who said that the satire would make the book 'acceptable to all Low Churchmen and dissenters'. Longmans offered no better terms than Trollope had yet had and published the book early in 1855.[63] They printed 1000 copies and by the end of the first six months had sold 388. This hardly sounds like success. As its author said, it 'never reached the essential honour of a second edition'. At least it brought him some small amount of money: £9 8s 8d. As Trollope ironically said, 'stone-breaking would have done better'. Yet in its way it was a success, because its author felt it to be. 'The novel-reading world did not go mad ... but I soon felt that it had not failed as the the others had failed.'

Despite Trollope's later recollections, both publisher and reviewers were complimentary, and the book was praised in most of the main literary journals, although there was the persistent criticism that it was uncertain whether the author was on the side of reform or not. Although the *Spectator* welcomed the 'keen observation of public affairs ... pungent closeness of style, and great cleverness', it wondered whether 'the object of the writer is not clear, nor would it seem he had reached any conclusion himself'. By the time this appeared he was in

the midst of writing a sequel, *Barchester Towers*. Longman meanwhile
had asked a clergyman, who wrote books on cricket, for his opinion of
The Warden. The Rev. James Pycroft replied:[64]

> Here at least you are breaking new ground. Novels of adventure, of naval
> or military life ... must be at a discount. But the domestic economy of the
> Church, as it is sketched here, is absolutely virgin soil. Let your new
> author stick to that; so will he add to your wealth and, if he have staying
> power, build up his own fame.

Mr Harding leaves Barchester Cathedral observed by
Adolphus Crosbie, from *The Small House at Allington*
(J.E. Millais). See p. 454.

CHAPTER EIGHT

The Charms of Reputation

In the summer of 1854 Fanny Trollope was enjoying the cooling breezes at the Baths of Lucca when she received a letter from Tom enclosing one from Anthony. She was distressed by Tom's comment: 'You will not only sympathize in his vexation, but ... feel as I do most bitterly the indignation which such treatment calls forth. How can we trust to any promises ... made by such people. It is *too* shameful!' When she wrote about this to her son in Ireland, she ended with evident pride: 'God bless you and yours – Bear your plagues, as you have always done – *philosophically*.' Trollope's frustration was caused by his lack of promotion. This was not the first time she had heard this, for two years before he had written from Wales: 'The more I see the way in which the post-office work is done, the more aggrieved I feel at not receiving the promotion I have a right to expect.' Yet he did not wish her to think he was totally down-hearted or that he had lost his 'philosophical' attitude: 'I can't fancy any one being much happier than I am, or having less in the world to complain of. It often strikes me how wonderfully well I have fallen on my feet.' That same year he admitted to Tom: 'But somehow, the months and years so jostle one another, that I seem to be living away at a perpetual gallop.'[1]

By 1852 Trollope's success in improving the rural post had won his superiors' respect. Despite this, his rank remained what it had been for the last dozen years. There were only two possible avenues of advance: he could become either a Surveyor or a departmental head on the staff in London. In November 1852, while still in England, he heard from John Tilley that a new Superintendent of Mail Coaches was to be appointed. He wrote to the Postmaster General, Lord Hardwicke, on 25 November to solicit the appointment, 'I believe I may confidently refer your Lordship to any of the officers under whom I have served', and he added somewhat ironically, 'especially to Col. Maberly, as to my fitness for the situation.' There was obviously a coordinated campaign: on the evening before Trollope wrote, Tilley called on the PMG to press his brother-in-law's case. On the following day Hardwicke received a formal letter of support from Tilley who stressed that 'his competency is beyond dispute'. Finally, there was a letter from Trollope's cousin, Sir John Trollope MP, President of the Poor Law Board, who wrote to his colleague in support of 'this kinsman of mine' and recalled a conversation about his cousin several months before. Hardwicke and Sir John were members of what was known as the 'Who? Who? Government'. Lord Derby's first administration got this unflattering name because the old Duke of Wellington, who had grown deaf, had not recognised the names of the Ministers when they were announced and had called out 'Who? Who?'. Thirty years later Trollope wrote: 'No weaker Government ... was ever formed in England.' Perhaps he had forgotten his cousin's involvement when he added: 'We hardly knew who they were.'[2]

The Earl of Hardwicke, although he was Postmaster General only from March 1852 to January 1853, quickly gained a reputation at the GPO as 'Old Blowhard' from his naval career. He ordered that when the Clerk-in-Waiting took command at 4 p.m. he was to be greeted with 'All's Well!' and when he turned over his authority the following morning at ten he was to say, 'All's well!' Hardwicke had better luck with the clerks than with the Secretary, and after a 'show-down' he joined the list of PMGs whom Hill 'avoided' if at all possible. In this case he had no choice but to consult him. Although Hill believed that Trollope 'deserves promotion' and would 'I doubt not, fill the office well', he would not support the application. He had his own reasons: 'I intend to advise that the appointment be given to one of the Surveyors.' He wanted to allow 'two others to retire, so as to admit of the adoption (immediate though partial) of a more efficient and economical arrangement'. Ironically the suggestion for this had come ten days before in an unofficial proposal from Trollope himself. 'My views, if adopted,' Hill wrote, 'will also benefit ... Trollope.'[3] It was hardly surprising, at least to Hill, that an official with more years of service than Trollope's eighteen received the appointment. For Trollope this was a lucky escape. If he had joined the staff he would have been largely confined to London where he would have been enmeshed in the intrigues of the GPO with far less time for writing.

Less than a year later the Surveyor of the Northern District of Ireland was taken ill: this time Trollope got the appointment. At the end of August 1853 he arrived in Belfast as Acting Surveyor. He still had to wait another year before he knew that this would become a permanent position. About three one morning he sat down to write to his 'Dearest Mother' to tell her the news. His income, which was about £600, might increase to £650, the equivalent of £750 in England. Perhaps because he was elated and also because it was so early in the morning, he ended the letter with an unusual expression of deep emotion: 'God bless you, dearest mother. Ever your own little boy, A.T.'[4]

To his brother, Trollope was more explicit: 'I trust my state of vassalage is over.' However, there were still a few months of worry because the GPO was in the midst of its greatest power struggle yet. For some years Maberly and Hill had uneasily exercised joint authority while Hill schemed with various Radical MPs to get the Colonel removed. At last a seat at the Board of Audit was found for Maberly, and from 24 April 1854 Hill reigned supreme as sole Secretary. At last his nose-bleeds, if not his neurotic suspicions, stopped. Whenever he took a respite from his own plots, Hill saw others plotting against him. In November, when Tilley showed him Trollope's informal suggestions for reform, he had feared there was some scheme by Tilley and Trollope – 'the brothers' as he called them – to ensure that Maberly would be succeeded by Tilley. Also, was it not sinister that Tilley would sometimes wait a day before showing him Trollope's letters? Again, why had 'the brothers' used the code name 'Brown' for Maberly in their correspondence?[5] It would be interesting to know if they had a codeword for Hill!

The Ireland to which Trollope returned in 1853 was a very different place from the country to which he had come in 1841. For a start, the population had declined by over 1,600,000 because of famine and emigration. The 1850s were relatively peaceful and prosperous years particularly in the Northern District, the wealthiest part. Prosperity had its price, however: four months before Trollope's return Gladstone announced that improved conditions justified the extension of income tax to the Irish. Trollope would now have to pay 7d in the pound on his income.

The Surveyors were 'the eyes of the Department'. In many ways their duties resembled those of bishops. Ten years after he resigned from the Post Office Trollope described the Surveyors as 'those trusty guardians of our correspondence' [*The American Senator* XXIV]. That was always his concept of the office, and his aim was to ensure an efficient and economical service. Surveyors had to make an official visit to each post office in their district, examine the accounts, hear complaints and try to correct them. They also had considerable control over appointments though there was much political interference and, in Trollope's district, many attempts to exert influence by powerful clergymen. The Surveyors were assisted by several clerks. The senior clerk was in effect Deputy Surveyor, and could deputise on inspections to minor post offices. This of course was the rank Trollope had held for thirteen years. He was not happy with one of his clerks, ironically one of the Maberly family. Once the Colonel was safely out of the GPO, Tilley and Trollope demoted his relative!

To be a clerk in the provincial service was not as impressive as in London; indeed the salary of £60 was one-third less than Trollope and other clerks had received at St Martin-le-Grand. R.S. Smyth, who began his work in Trollope's Northern District, remembered that the Surveyor 'was held out to the juniors in the service as a terror'. Yet, said Smyth, 'he was brusque in manner, certainly, but he had a kind heart'. He recalled one time in 1857 when Trollope was inspecting the work at the new post office in Queen's Square, Belfast. One important duty was to record the time each postman returned from his round. Trollope, having noted that there were several mistakes in the record, spoke 'sharply' to Smyth, who told him that the new building did not have a clock. When he learned that Smyth did not have his own watch, he ordered: 'Then you must get one at once.' 'Certainly, at once, as you so instruct me, but —' 'But what?' demanded Trollope. 'I would prefer to wait till I can pay cash for it,' replied the clerk, who knew that it would cost him a month's salary. From the Surveyor came only a 'growl'. A few days later the Belfast Postmaster told Smyth that the Surveyor had ordered a clock for the office and had told him to tell Smyth that it was to save him the expense of a watch. 'I thought this very considerate. It caused me to form a more favourable opinion of him, which subsequent experience only tended to increase.' Several years later he gave Smyth some advice 'in a very friendly, almost fatherly way'. Smyth had become dissatisfied with his prospects and consulted Trollope about whether he should leave the service. Trollope advised him to remain but told him it was a good sign that he was dissatisfied because such a condition is natural 'with men of energy'. Trollope seems to have been particularly helpful to clerks who were 'men of energy' and anxious to succeed. In at least one case he appears to have provided the money for the bond which the Post Office required of those holding certain offices.[6]

The Surveyor was responsible for the honesty and efficiency of his district. Many monthly reports, on how many postage stamps were held by each post office, for example, had to be sent to the GPO which had the Victorian passion for statistics. The Surveyor had to be alert for suspicious behaviour by postmasters or letter-carriers. One young postman was surprised to see a large man stick his head out of a carriage window demanding to look inside his mail bag. The boy refused and started to run through the fields pursued by the man. After grabbing the boy the breathless Trollope demanded: 'You young rascal, why didn't you give me the bag in the first place?' When the boy answered, 'Because I didn't know who you were', Trollope was delighted and had him commended for his stewardship of the post. A Surveyor also had the responsibility of protecting money sent through the mails and had to deal with letters that could not be delivered. The Irish had the most problems with dead letters, and the addresses on envelopes could be rather eccentric: 'To my sister Bridget, or else to my brother Tim Burke, in care of the Praste [*sic*], who lives in the parish of Balcombury in Cork, or if not to *some dacent neighbour in Ireland.*' Irish letters were also often full of money 'illustrating', according to a contemporary, 'both the careless and affectionate nature of the people'.[7]

The Northern District had a particular problem because of the political and religious tensions in Ulster. The Surveyor had to enforce the sensible rule that no postmaster could belong to a secret society or to one committed to extreme political or religious views. Thus no supporter of the Repeal Movement, a cause virtually moribund after O'Connell's death in 1847, or of the Orange Order, the fanatical Protestant movement committed to bigotry in the name of liberty, could be a postmaster. The Surveyor also issued strict instructions reminding postmasters that as public officials they could not vote in any parliamentary election; if they did so, they suffered both the loss of their position and a £100 fine. Village postmasters must obey complicated rules about the time when slides should be drawn across a pillar box, a question of paternal interest to Trollope. The village post office must be kept open every day, even on Sunday when it was closed only during religious services. Postmasters also had to be on the look-out for anyone trying to cheat the Post Office by enclosing a letter within a newspaper. If such a letter was discovered the whole parcel was weighed and charged at three times the weight.[8]

Shortly after Trollope's appointment Surveyors' salaries were increased to £700 a year plus 20s a day when they were away from their headquarters. They could also claim 'the actual expenses of locomotion'. As mentioned earlier, Hill (who had a salary of £2,000 a year) believed that the Surveyors were too liberal about their expenses, and he ordered stricter controls. Trollope felt this severity when he submitted a claim for hotel expenses after illness forced him to extend his stay in one of the towns in his district. He was told that he could only claim for days when he was actually at work. Since

Surveyors normally used their homes as their offices, they could also claim a rent of £30 a year for the space occupied by themselves and their officials.[9]

*

With his comfortable income Trollope was now able to indulge his hereditary appetite for travel. In the 1850s he and Rose made four European trips. Rose evidently enjoyed these and years later made a list of places they had visited as a help for her husband when he was writing his *Autobiography*. The goal of most of these trips was Florence, where Anthony could visit his mother and brother, who had been settled there since 1843. Trollope once wrote that travellers were divided into Cookites and Hookites: those who allowed Thomas Cook to arrange everything for them and those who did it on their own hook [*The Prime Minister* LXVII]. His many travels were on his own hook, but he did have a ready-made travel expert in his brother, who liked nothing better than planning holidays, although he did expect his relatives to follow a fairly arduous schedule, as Tilley once complained: 'Tom is a tyrant – to hear is to obey.'[10]

John Tilley, who after Cecilia's death had married a cousin of Trollope's, accompanied Anthony and Rose on many of these trips. At times it must have been difficult for him as he did not share Anthony's or Rose's passion for scenery. The Victorians, unlike earlier travellers, thought of scenery as something to be enjoyed, not something to be endured on the way to a foreign court. Trollope noted this when reading, and dismissing, Bacon's essay on travel: 'We find no mention here of scenery, of pictures, of architecture, or even of the manners of the people; and we think how the tastes of men have altered in three centuries. Who now travels that he may attend courts of Law or look after Arsenals or armouries? We travel rather to delight our eyes than to instruct our minds.'[11] He did not look on a holiday as a time to put his feet up: 'All holiday-making is hard work, but holiday-making with nothing to do is the hardest work of all' [*The Small House at Allington* XLVI]. He once listed the 'traveller's first main questions. When is the table d'hôte? Where is the cathedral? At what hour does the train start to-morrow morning?' [*The Bertrams* VI].

The first of these trips to Italy began in April 1853 when Rose, Anthony and Tilley left by night train for Paris; in those days a first-class London-Paris return fare cost twenty-four shillings. They must have encountered some difficulties when entering France since Rose's account notes: 'Three custom house officers.'[12] Before the

Commercial Treaty of 1860 between England and France there were often extensive searches of baggage, which is probably the explanation for Rose's terse comment. In addition they would have required passports, which perhaps led to Trollope's reference in one novel to a 'French passport officer' as being particularly skilled at minute description [*The Three Clerks* XVII]. The journey southward still had many of the miseries of the Grand Tour of the eighteenth century, for only part of their way was by rail. Next they transferred to a canal boat, which made Tilley ill, and then to a diligence, a rather cumbersome coach, to cross the Alps at Mount Cenis. While Alpine crossings were still difficult and somewhat frightening, Trollope revelled in them; once the railways had made the journey safer, but also more boring, he looked back with regret to the older method:

> A seat up above, on the banquette of a diligence passing over the Alps, with room for the feet, and support for the back, with plenty of rugs and plenty of tobacco, used to be on the Mount Cenis ... a very comfortable mode of seeing a mountain route. For those desirous of occupying the coupé, or the front three seats ... difficulties frequently arose ... There would be two or three of those enormous vehicles preparing to start ... twelve or fifteen passengers had come down from Paris armed with tickets assuring them that this preferable mode of travelling should be theirs ... It would generally be the case that some middle-aged Englishman who could not speak French would go to the wall, together with his wife. Middle-aged Englishmen with their wives, who can't speak French, can nevertheless be very angry, and threaten loudly, when they suppose themselves to be ill-treated ... when he finds himself with his unfortunate partner in a roundabout place behind with two priests, a dirty man who looks like a brigand, a sick maid-servant, and three agricultural labourers [*He Knew He Was Right* XXXVII].

The passionate nature of this outburst makes it almost certain that the 'middle-aged Englishman and his unfortunate partner' were none other than Anthony and his wife. For her part Rose was a hearty traveller and in later years told her granddaughter that she had been four times over the St Gothard pass: by diligence, by sleigh, by train and on foot. On some of their travels there were quarrels with other travellers. Trollope could, of course, read French and could, at least in calmer moments, almost make himself understood by a patient Frenchman. Yet at times they must have found it difficult to be patient with him! He did not always share Tom's absolute loathing for the French, but did view their country with suspicion, which was not helped by his detestation of Napoleon III. One one journey the two Trollope brothers returned to the diligence after a quick scramble up an Alp to find that two Frenchman had taken their reserved seats. Tom, assuming the authority of the elder brother, ordered: 'Stand below, Anthony, and I will hand them down!' Anglo-French relations suffered a double blow as the two astonished Frenchmen were passed from Tom to Anthony and then deposited on the ground.[13]

They had a night's rest in Turin which Trollope described tersely as 'parallelogrammatic as an American town ... as dull and uninteresting as though it were German or English' [*He Knew He Was Right* XXXVIII]. However, when travelling Rose did insist that she be allowed to spend one night in four in a hotel bed! Her husband had mild fun with this in *The Last Chronicle of Barset*, when John Eames escorts the Dean's wife home from Italy. She also insists on a hotel in Turin, 'not finding herself able to accomplish such marvels in the way of travelling as her companion' [LXX]. Like Eames they probably put up at Trompetta's Hotel, where Trollope could catch up on the latest English news, such as the current debate in the House of Lords on admitting Jews into Parliament, from *Galignani's Messenger*, a newspaper which kept travelling Englishmen in touch with all the events at home. It was in that same newspaper at Trompetta's that Eames read the news of Mrs Proudie's death.

The Trollopes and Tilley pushed on by rail and omnibus. 'Tom meets us at Genoa,' recalled Rose, '[and] scolds us because [we are] four hours behind time.' One feels rather sorry for some poor coachman in Pisa after reading Rose's cryptic note: 'Row with the driver when we start.' To encounter both the Trollope brothers and the somewhat less imposing Tilley must have tried the good will of many a continental servant. After their first view of Florence there was the almost equally stunning sight of the Villino Trollope. This was a far cry from the dreary lodgings on Northumberland Street, which Anthony had shared with Tom. The large house in the Piazza Maria Antonia had become the centre of English literary and social life in Florence. The Brownings were frequent guests, for Elizabeth was an old friend of her fellow poet Theodosia Garrow, now Mrs Thomas Adolphus Trollope. The exotic Theodosia, as we have noted, was a fanatical supporter of Italian unification.* Inside the house Anthony and Rose met their niece with the suitably Florentine name of Beatrice, who was only a few weeks old. (There was chatter in the gossip-laden circles of the English colony that 'Bice' was not really Tom's daughter.) The elegant life of the villa was maintained by the busy pens of Tom, his wife and Fanny Trollope, who

*A plaque on the house in the renamed Piazza dell'Indipendenza pays tribute to Theodosia Trollope as the English poet with the Italian heart.

turned out eight three-volume novels in the 1850s. The mansion was somewhat enthusiastically described by a young American visitor, Kate Field:

> Ah, this Villino Trollope is quaintly fascinating with its marble pillars, its grim men in armour ... its majolica, its old bridal chests ... and carved furniture, its beautiful terracotta of the Virgin and the Child by Orgagna, its hundred *oggetti* of the Cinque cento. The bibliophile grows silently ecstatic as he sinks quietly into a medieval chair and feasts his eyes on a model library, bubbling over with five thousand rare books.

If one wished to retire outside, the Villino Trollope boasted the city's largest garden of orange and lemon trees, where Anthony or Rose could sit sipping the lemonade that was famous throughout the English colony.[14]

Tom was the ideal guide to Florence and the Tuscan countryside, as he was writing a history of the city. Anthony and Rose must have enjoyed several picnics, a particular delight of Tom and his mother. The favourite spot was the Pratolino, a park belonging to the Habsburg Grand Duke, about seven miles from the city. After the carriages had reached the park the guests had a view over the whole Val d'Arno with 'its thousand villas, and Florence, with its circle of surrounding hills'.[15] Anthony had also inherited the family love of picnics about which he had firm views: 'A picnic should be held among green things. Green turf is absolutely an essential. There should be trees, broken ground, small paths, thickets and hidden recesses. There should, if possible, be rocks, old timber, moss, and brambles. There should certainly be hills and dales ... and, above all, there should be running water' [*Can You Forgive Her?* VIII]. Tom's picnics provided almost all of these and not only running water but a helpful gardener who would hurry out with a boiling kettle when the 'milords' needed their tea. Wine must have flowed with ready abandon, for as Tom Trollope wistfully recalled, a large flask of the best chianti, holding more than three normal bottles, cost less than sixpence. Some of the 'picnics' could go on for two or three days when Tom took his guests farther afield, for example, to distant monasteries.

The Trollopes were among the best-known residents of the city. Tom had founded and edited a short-lived newspaper for English residents, *The Tuscan Athenaeum*, and Fanny held weekly 'reunions' for visitors and resident Englishmen. Here she would, if she could find enough players, indulge one of her great loves, whist. At the Pitti Palace they attended the weekly balls given by the Grand Duke for all foreign residents and visitors, or at least those who appeared respectable. The

Grand Duke's own subjects were more concerned with doing their shopping and frequently brought newspapers to wrap the hams and chickens they grabbed from the well-stocked tables. English visitors tended to content themselves with looting the Grand Ducal *bonbons*.[16] Whether Anthony or Rose helped themselves to these is not known!

Fanny Trollope showed Rose all the sights of the city and delighted her with the gift of an Italian silk dress. She also gave Rose a valuable brooch made from a Roman mosaic featuring a cherub. Mrs Trollope's friend Princess Metternich had presented it to her in Vienna. This jewel would soon appear in the funniest scene Trollope ever wrote. Rose thought her mother-in-law 'the most charming old lady who ever existed ... nothing conventional about her, and yet ... worlds asunder from ... the "Emancipated Female" School'. However, the Irish novelist Charles Lever when visiting Florence refused to sit opposite her at her whist table as he found her so formidable and feared he would turn up in one of her novels. If he had, he might not have recognised himself. 'Of course, I draw from life,' admitted the elderly lady. 'But I always pulp my acquaintances before serving them up. You would never recognise a pig in a sausage.' She had an increasing fascination for spiritualism, which especially annoyed Anthony. At one of these silly gatherings the table began moving towards the door. 'Damn it, let it go,' shouted Fanny Trollope. 'That was rather hard upon the spirit concerned,' said Robert Browning who was present.[17]

Certainly Trollope did enjoy the sights and was soon convinced that the tower of the Duomo was the greatest work of man. Many happy hours were passed in galleries that were still royal residences. He did not claim vast knowledge of 'high art,' nor did he see it as providing some sort of moral platform from which to lecture the world. Such was the posture of Ruskin, whom Trollope thoroughly despised: 'That such a man should write on Art may be very well, but that he should preach to us either on morals or political economy is hardly to be borne.' The enjoyment of art did not demand theories: 'God has given us eyes, and we must use them, as we do upon a landscape. But we must use them with patience.'[18]

Providence, however, had not bestowed particularly strong eyes on him and so he stared long at favourite paintings. In Florence he asked an attendant to bring him a chair; by the time he reached Bologna he was carrying one about with him from room to room. In Munich they appeared not to have heard of chairs, which 'made the work of seeing the pictures ... terrible,' but he soon found a simple solution: 'I used to lie along on the dirty floor; but there are many picture seekers who would not like that.' Needless to say, whether seated or lying on a dirty floor, he had strong views: he did not share the Victorian veneration for Raphael, believing that he and Michaelangelo had led art away from truth. In paintings, as well as in novels, he liked the realistic touch. He revered Titian and made a visit to his birthplace. Here was another taste shared with his mother, who regarded Titian's paintings as 'Heaven's own workmanship'; indeed in one of her novels she recommended all English tourists to stop and visit his birthplace. Trollope was equally explicit about his dislikes, and Guercino was dismissed as 'that vilest of painters'. Pursuing art with his customary energy, Trollope shared many of the attributes of 'The Art Tourist' he described in one essay: a man noted for 'that laborious perseverance which distinguishes the true Briton as much in his amusement as in his work'.[19]

While Trollope was most assuredly a 'true Briton', he was not the stereotyped English tourist who was becoming so heartily disliked by continentals. His mother had written a novel making fun of these travellers, and her son shared her contempt. His compatriots, he maintained, had a unique 'mixture of fun, honest independence, and bad taste'. One such figure, who interrupts High Mass to view a fresco, was inserted into *The Bertrams*:[20]

> Look at that man standing on the very altar-step while the priest is saying his mass; look at his grey shooting-coat, his thick shoes, his wide-awake hat stuck under one arm, and his stick under the other, while he holds his opera-glass to his eyes. How he shuffles about to get the best point of sight, quite indifferent as to clergy or laity! All that bell-ringing, incense-flinging, and breast-striking is nothing to him: he has paid dearly to be brought thither ... All men of all nations know that that ugly grey shooting-coat must contain an Englishman ... If any one upsets him, he can do much towards righting himself; and if more be wanted has he not Lord Malmesbury or Lord Clarendon at his back? But what would this Englishman say if his place of worship were disturbed by some wandering Italian? [IX].

This is an interesting passage for anyone concerned with Trollope or his times. He could certainly be a bluff traveller himself, but only if his fury were aroused by others' interference with his rights or by servants' not doing their duty. Otherwise he was a courteous and sensitive man, who tried to respect the feelings of others and show some regard for their culture. Although he was in so many ways a typical Victorian, his wide travels made him less chauvinistic than many. Encounters with obtuse compatriots gave him that disconcerting feeling that flows from such meetings, but sometimes they left a good anecdote in their wake. On one visit to the Pitti he was tapped on

the back by a confused Englishman: 'Where is it that they keep the
Medical Venus?' This found its way into several books including his
Autobiography.[21]

In the course of these travels in the 1850s the Trollopes noticed how
improved communication was beginning to change Italy, as it had
already changed England. Sometimes this could cause upset, as when
Trollope used the newly installed telegraph line to reserve rooms at the
famous Due Torre hotel in Verona, where a few years earlier Ruskin
had spent part of his unexciting honeymoon. The choice of this hotel,
still Verona's finest, shows that Trollope always liked the best. As the
train pulled into the station a great cry was heard for 'Signor Trollopi'.
The landlord had arrived with six servants and three carriages to
welcome the first guest to reserve a room by telegraph. He could not
believe that Signor Trollopi was not a great figure with a numerous
suite: he and his flunkies spent much time vainly searching for the
Signor's 'people'.

Although Florence remained the pivot of their trips, they liked to
spend about nine days in travelling to and from the city. In 1855
Anthony and Rose met his mother in Venice before Tilley and Trollope
went off to climb an Alpine peak. The two ladies made their way
towards Innsbruck, but Mrs Trollope began to feel weak due to her age
and need for some food. When they stopped at a Tyrolean inn, they
were given only soup and fish because it was a fast day. A young man
saw how tired she looked and came over: 'Madam, I am an Austrian
soldier on sick leave and as such I am exempted from fasting ... You
are my mother; pray share my portion! You are old and fatigued with
travelling.' It was indeed one of her last travels as she was on her way
for a final look at her native land. Rose was so moved that she wanted
to kiss the man's hand, but he turned to her and said, 'You are young
and look strong. I shall order you some coffee.' Ironically Fanny
Trollope might have become the mother of an Austrian officer if the
Post Office had not intervened. The Trollopes only stayed in Innsbruck
long enough for Anthony to conclude: 'Perhaps no town in Europe can
boast a site more exquisitely picturesque' [*The Bertrams* XII]. Their
visit introduced them to the Tyrol, a part of Austria that he and Rose
revisited several times and where Rose would return after his death.
Trollope had told his brother that he and Rose wanted to spend as
much time as possible near the Alps. In this they were, as so often,
people of their age and Anthony, at least, knew where the impulse
came from: Sir Walter Scott had 'imbued us,' he wrote, 'with a love of
lakes and mountains'.[22]

As all of Trollope's non-European trips were made into travel books their effects on him are clear. Yet what were the effects of his continental rambles on his fiction? He was convinced that the era of the 'travel novel' was over as he saw the middle classes venturing 'abroad'. Travel no longer had any real place in novels: 'I should consider myself dishonest,' he wrote, 'if I attempted to palm off such matters on the public in the pages of a novel' [*Can You Forgive Her?* V]. While in many of his novels characters do travel round Europe, he makes little attempt to describe the conventional sights of Notre Dame, the Colosseum, or even his beloved Giotto Tower in Florence. He did however draw on his travels to give some specific detail that strengthens the realism of the book: the name of a hotel in Innsbruck or the quality of the food at Bologna Station. A good example of this occurs in *Can You Forgive Her?* when the casino in Baden-Baden provides the exotic setting for Lady Glencora Palliser and her husband to encounter the man who once attempted to seduce her. Trollope does not give an extended description of Baden, such as his mother gave in her travel book *Belgium and Western Germany*. However, having been there a few months before writing this novel, he picks out a few details so that the reader can see the room and its unhappy inhabitants. When Palliser follows the ruined Burgo Fitzgerald, the novelist gives precise descriptions of the gendarme in his cocked hat and the doors leading from the gambling salon [LXXV]. This episode is also an example of how he used the continent as a refuge for ruined characters. Here he is drawing not only on Victorian prejudice but on the memory of his father and father-in-law, who both had to flee abroad.

However, his European travels came to dominate two areas of his fiction. As will be seen, he attempted in the 1860s to establish a second career as a novelist by writing anonymous novels about continental life. In addition most of his short stories have foreign settings which came directly from his travels. Many of these occur in inns and hotels, such as 'Why Frau Frohmann Raised Her Prices', an amusing story set in the Tyrol, or 'La Mère Bauche', a tragic tale set in the French Pyrenees. Such an inveterate 'castle builder' could not resist imagining the lives of those whom he saw: even amidst the pleasures of the Volksgarten in Vienna he had to invent a love story for an elderly violinist playing the haunting melodies of Johann Strauss. It may seem odd that so few of his stories have an Italian setting, but that would have been poaching on his elder brother's territory. The experiences of this first and of later Italian trips were evident when he wrote his next novel, *Barchester Towers*, in the creation of one of his most memorable and exotic women, the Signora Madeline Vesey Neroni, the Italianised Englishwoman.

*

The Trollopes' first Italian trip had lasted from 19 April to 31 May 1853, but they were not able to make a return visit for two years. On 29 July he began writing *The Warden*, and at the end of August the family settled in Belfast where he finished it. Indeed he sent that delightful book to the publisher on 8 October, the day before his official appointment as Surveyor. He did not really like Belfast and asked permission to move to Dublin. 'I should prefer,' he wrote to his old friend, the Postmaster of Bristol, 'the South to the North of Ireland, preferring on the whole papistical to presbyterian tendencies.' He could justify his request by pointing out that Dublin produced four times as much postage revenue as Belfast. What is more likely the case is that London realised that Trollope could be of greater use if he were in Dublin. Indeed by the autumn he was acting as a representative of the Irish Post Office regarding an increase in postmen's wages.[23]

On 2 May 1855, therefore, the Trollopes were able, as Rose said, 'to leave Belfast for good'. They rented a large Georgian brick house on Seaview Terrace in Donnybrook, about two miles from the centre of Dublin. It was a good time to move to Donnybrook as this year saw the abolition of its famous but unsavoury fair, established in 1204. Dublin was their home for four and a half years and Trollope appears to have been reasonably content. Yet one senses that Ireland no longer held the attraction it once did. Unlike his other Irish posts, the Dublin years had little effect on his fiction. The Irish capital offered some literary society as well as many impressive public buildings, and its Anglican cathedral was famous for having one of the best choirs in the British Isles: perhaps of some interest to a novelist who was writing about cathedrals and their choirs. Yet he grew increasingly anxious to obtain a surveyorship in England when one became available.[24]

By the end of the year Rose's father had finally resigned from the Sheffield and Rotherham Bank and retired with his second wife and remaining family to the West of England. By the standards of the mid-nineteenth century he had reached the amazing age of seventy-three. If anyone had wondered why he had stayed so long at his post they were to find out in the new year, 1854, when bank officials began examining the books. An audit discovered that at least £4,000 had disappeared and it seemed fairly obvious that the slightly eccentric Mr Heseltine, famous for his armour, his Unitarianism and his eighteenth-century dress, had been embezzling since 1836. The bank was anxious to avoid a public scandal if at all possible as even rumours of misappropriations could bring a disastrous 'run'. Rose's step-mother dealt with all the correspondence by claiming that her husband was too ill to return to Rotherham to face his questioners.

When the bank's letters became too pressing and legal proceedings seemed inevitable, Heseltine suddenly fled to France, where he died in Le Havre on 15 September 1855. It is not known how much, if any, of this sad tale was known to Rose or her husband. It seems unlikely that they could have remained entirely ignorant of the reasons for her father's sudden departure for France, particularly as Rose's brother-in-law, Joseph Bland, was head clerk at the Bank.* If Trollope did know, his knowledge may well have been a factor behind his growing absorption in the one topic that dominated almost all his writing in the next decade: dishonesty.[25]

The Warden was published by Longmans in January 1855 when Trollope was still living in Belfast. He could not have known that he had begun the series that would bring him lasting fame. He had intended to write a sequel to *The Warden* and appears to have started work in January. Like the rest of the country, he soon turned his attention eastward. In March 1854 Britain and France had gone to war with Russia. This was the only European war that Britain fought in his lifetime, save for those first few weeks of his life when Napoleon's fate was being sealed. The first effect of the war on Trollope, as on anyone who was comfortably off, was a sudden doubling of his income tax to 1s 2d in the pound. By December 1854 he could read Russell's famous articles in *The Times* recounting the sufferings of the British army in the Crimea – sufferings due more to incompetent military administration than to the Russian army.

Although he was a faithful reader of *The Times*, Trollope believed that its virtual monopoly was a growing menace to effective government and freedom itself. He had already attacked the paper as 'The Jupiter' in *The Warden*, where it exercises a baneful influence over the events of the day. Trollope did not accept the common clamour against government for the failures of supplies to the army. Here he differed from Dickens who became, in effect, the leader of the Administrative Reform Association, which also had the support of Thackeray. As a dedicated civil servant, Trollope always resented attacks upon government by outsiders. In his fiction he was quite prepared to recount the absurdities of office life, as in *The Small House at Allington* [XLVI], but he also defended his profession. As we shall see, in *The Three Clerks*, published in 1858, he would take his stand

*In 1982, the bank granted a form of pardon to its former manager, when Williams and Glynn's Bank (the successor to the Sheffield and Rotherham Bank) held an exhibit in connection with the BBC Television adaptation of the first two Barsetshire novels during the centenary tributes to Trollope. Edward Heseltine's embezzlements were now seen, according to the *Sheffield Morning Telegraph* (17 December 1982), as 'in the best tradition of Barchester scandal'.

against Dickens. His essential fairness is shown by his support for the beleaguered Duke of Newcastle who bore the brunt of the attacks. Newcastle had been a strong supporter of Sir Robert Peel, whom Trollope disliked, but he praised the Duke as a hard-working official, a man with many similarities to his later creation Plantagenet Palliser, Duke of Omnium. He believed that when press criticism had disappeared into 'the wind', 'the voice of history' would share his opinion, which has to some degree been the case.[26]

The dispiriting war news may well have been a contributing factor in the disappointing sales of *The Warden*. Trollope wrote to Longmans in February to see if *The Warden* was 'taking', but the reply was disappointing. Trollope decided to turn his hand to a serious examination of British life in keeping with the national mood of self-examination and fear that the era of British predominance was coming to an end. He decided to call his book *The New Zealander* and took the title from Macaulay's comment that some day a 'traveller from New Zealand shall, in the midst of a vast solitude, take his stand on a broken arch of London Bridge to sketch the ruins of St Paul's'. Although the book was motivated by the national mood of doubt, there are other factors in his attempt to portray British society. Trollope had long had a penchant for a sweeping view of a large topic from the days when he planned his history of world literature. He had tried something similar on Ireland in his *Examiner* articles. His recent postal work gave him an almost unrivalled knowledge of rural and provincial life. (The book would have been much better if he had concentrated on these aspects.) His first visit to Italy allowed him to see a different society as well as the ruins of another great Empire that had perished when it turned from its old virtues. Finally, when he settled in Ireland in 1853, he felt a strong desire to return to England. No longer did Irish life offer a joyous escape for a sullen youth. Instead a serious official, now middle-aged, wanted to return to what his brother rightly called 'the centre of the civilized world's system'.[27] At least, by reflecting on the condition and prospects of his native land, he could feel part of it. Most important, a work of non-fiction gave him an opportunity to appear as a serious writer rather than just as a novelist.

Trollope wrote during February and March 1855, a period he later recalled: 'We still remember how "red tape" and "routine" were in all our mouths. Mail after mail brought home news of increased suffering … England was miserable with the sense of failure.' An historian, who has carefully examined those same months, confirms Trollope's remembrance: 'For the first six months of 1855 at almost every articulate level ... the war represented an inescapable challenge which stripped away the shams and compromises and time-honoured habits which gave British society its stability and cohesion.' Exposing 'shams and compromises and time-honoured habits' was precisely what Trollope set out to do in his book. Several well-informed foreign observers were amazed at the sudden change in public opinion in those months as more and more people questioned whether 'the System' and the aristocracy who administered it could carry on a war. The novelist Nathaniel Hawthorne, American consul at Liverpool, felt that aristocratic dominance had been shaken more in one year than in fifty ordinary ones, while across the Channel Tocqueville watched 'the terrible clamour against the aristocracy' which reminded him of the days before the French Revolution.[28] It was increasingly believed on the continent that England's hour had passed: reactionaries rejoiced that liberal institutions were being exposed as failures, while revolutionaries enjoyed another burst of hope that the proudest aristocracy in the world would now be brought low.

The New Zealander examined the Monarchy, Parliament, the Church and the military, as well as topics like the growing power of the press, literature, art and the role of professions such as medicine and the law. Trollope worked quickly – far too quickly – on this book, often drawing upon recent issues of *The Times* for his facts. He submitted it to Longmans, whose reader dismissed it with unqualified scorn: 'If you had not told me that this work was by the author of *The Warden* I could not have believed it. Such a contrast between two works by the same pen was hardly ever before witnessed ... All the good points ... have already been treated of by Mr Carlyle, of whose *Latter-Day* pamphlets this work, *both in style and matter*, is a most feeble imitation.'[29]

Although the version of *The New Zealander* seen by Longmans' reader has not survived, it is difficult not to agree with his harsh verdict. (The manuscript, much reworked by Trollope, was only published in a scholarly edition in 1972.) To see how weak much of the book is, we need only examine one chapter, that on 'The Crown'. Trollope had, of course, no real knowledge of the workings of the Monarchy. Probably the closest he had come to royalty was walking backwards before a German royal visitor to St Martin-le-Grand. Nor is it likely that he knew anyone close to royal circles: even Rowland Hill was not presented at Court until 9 June 1854 after his triumphant victory over Maberly.[30] Trollope's main information came from *The Times*, a newspaper particularly hostile to Prince Albert's work in reforming the Monarchy in order to make it an efficient force in the conduct of government. It was only two decades later, when reading

Theodore Martin's *Life of the Prince Consort*, that Trollope discovered how powerful the royal couple had been in the 1850s.

At the time he was writing the Monarchy was temporarily unpopular because many people believed that Albert's intrigues had caused the war. It was rumoured that the Prince, and in some versions even the Queen herself, was on his way to the Tower of London, and crowds actually gathered outside to await their arrival! Trollope always approached the Monarchy from an eighteenth-century, or at the most an early-nineteenth-century, point of view. He had none of the sentimental attitude that grew during Victoria's long reign. (It is significant that he places greatest reliance on an eighteenth-century study of the Constitution by Jean Louis de Lolme.) He starts from the premise that the Monarchy is 'the most popular' of 'all our institutions' and is regarded as 'all but sacred', though he firmly dismisses any lingering vestiges of divine right.

While his theories about royal powers are little more than rehashed Whiggery, his few attempts at facts prove ludicrous. A good example comes in his assertion: 'All the world knows that the Queen does not make the bishops.' As is so often the case, what 'all the world' knows is wrong; those in government during Victoria's long reign knew otherwise. Soon after coming to the throne she insisted on appointing her old tutor, Dr Davys, to the see of Peterborough, and throughout her reign she played an important role in the choice of bishops. It was on her urging, to her later regret, that Samuel Wilberforce was made Bishop of Oxford. Undoubtedly she often gave way when a persistent government insisted, but she won many victories in the appointment of bishops and archbishops. In 1868 she cleverly 'outmanoeuvred' Disraeli to make Archibald Tait Archbishop of Canterbury. As Disraeli's biographer tersely puts it: 'She got her own way on some of the most important decisions.'[31]

To say, as Trollope does, that if the Queen had her choice she would probably never change her ministers is again a misstatement of fact: she was not sorry to get rid of the Tory government in 1852, nor of the Liberal government in 1858. Indeed if we look at royal involvement in government merely in the two months Trollope devoted to writing *The New Zealander* we can see what a vital role it played. Far from being a decorative though delightful feature, like the spire of Salisbury Cathedral – a favourite metaphor of Trollope's for the Monarchy – it was a vital part of the structure itself. The Queen began February 1855 with politics in a state of crisis. She spent days trying to encourage party leaders to form a new coalition government. Some of the problems flowed from the fact that she had virtually dismissed Lord

Palmerston from the Foreign Office in 1851. She intervened with the government to have decent hospitals built for wounded soldiers, while on 19 March she refused to approve the sending of a fleet to the Baltic until she had received a complete list of the ships.[32]

Trollope's chapter on the Monarchy is, therefore, virtually useless. It reminds one of a clever undergraduate essay: a desperate concoction of opinion and rhetoric, with a few facts, and those few wrong, thrown in for ballast. The chapter on the House of Lords is little better and is also filled with errors. This is not to say that the book is without interest. It shows the author's strengths as well as his weaknesses, and for anyone concerned with his opinions it offers many insights. Trollope is at his strongest when he draws on his own experiences, particularly on his recent travels. As a young man he had berated himself for his failure to understand 'more abstruse' arguments.[33] This was something he never achieved, which is fortunate, as the lover of the abstruse normally calls only to his fellows and it is only they who can understand his call. Trollope could not comprehend the theory of the House of Lords, but in the next decades his novels would provide superb portraits of individual peers going about their work.

In *The New Zealander* Trollope launched an outspoken attack on the treatment of the poor, particularly those he had seen on his postal missions:

> No Englishman can be proud of the state of the men labouring ... Let him who would see and know penetrate into those strange and monstrous villages ... on the hill-sides of Glamorganshire, and talk awhile to the dusky denizens who work beneath the soil ... Or go into the quiet cornfields of heavy Wiltshire, and talk awhile with the clod pulling rustic ... You can almost doubt within yourself whether or not this man has really a living soul within him ... Nothing hitherto has been done towards civilizing him ... it is the fact that in most of those countries which we delight to look on as lagging behind ourselves in the march of intellect, the state of the labourer of the soil is less debased than it is with us.

Here is Trollope at his best: he has seen something and he tells others what he has seen. Although he believed that no empire could escape eclipse, he also felt that there was hope for England to postpone this fate, provided 'we are or can make ourselves an honest people'. Both at the beginning and at the end of the book there were sermons on the intertwined themes of national decay and dishonesty. Trollope saw dishonesty all round him, in advertising, the law, medicine, food manufacturing and even literary criticism, and he repeats over and over again a line from a Scottish song: 'It's gude to be honest and true.'[34] Fortunately the book was not published in his lifetime, for it could well have endangered his position within the Post Office and, far more disastrously, it could have encouraged him in his attempt to set himself up as another Carlyle. One such gloomy prophet is more than enough for any century!

*

Despite the rejection, Trollope must have thought highly of his work, because he devoted a considerable amount of time in 1855 and 1856 in revising the manuscript. It eventually proved useful as a quarry, and he lifted various stones from its bed when he wanted to make some serious point in a novel. In the summer of 1855 he and Rose were able to pay their second visit to Italy, and on their return they moved to Dublin. In March 1856 the Treaty of Paris formally ended the Crimean War; with peace most of the unrest faded away. On 12 May Trollope at last returned to the joys of Barset and resumed work on *Barchester Towers*. We know the date because he started to make work sheets or calendars when he began a novel. He would fold a sheet of paper and keep a record of how many pages he wrote each day. Thus on 12 May he managed eight pages. This novel has always been among his most popular books, and it is perhaps the best remembered. It was certainly the longest in preparation: from January 1855 to November 1856. Never again would he labour so long on any novel. The main reasons were not just the time he took to write *The New Zealander* but his involvement in other activities, not least in learning his new district, which involved considerable travel. Post Office business often called him to London and at other times there were meetings with other Surveyors, such as one to improve deliveries between Ireland and Scotland. If he was to complete this novel he had to find himself more time: one solution was to write while travelling. Most of his travels were now by rail rather than on horseback and he was soon able to write, in pencil, in railway carriages and even on the 'knifeboard' of an omnibus. At first he felt a bit conspicuous, as it was unusual for Victorians to work in a railway carriage, but he soon got over this. He carried on this practice into his last years and in the 1870s asked a young journalist who was a fellow passenger if he wrote on trains. When told 'no', he replied 'I always do', pulled out a pencil and tablet and wrote 'without a break'.[35]

When he brought his latest chapters back to Donnybrook, Rose would make a fair copy in ink. It was at this stage that she must have had a considerable influence, for he greatly respected her judgment. It is certainly noticeable in *Barchester Towers* how frequently ladies' costumes and hairstyles were described, and Rose took a considerable interest in both topics.[36] There is one telling detail in *Barchester Towers* [X] that shows how husband and wife enjoyed little jokes. When La Signora Vesey Neroni arrives at Mrs Proudie's first reception in Barchester, her extraordinary costume includes a red velvet hair-band decorated with a mosaic brooch featuring a cupid. This is none other than Princess Metternich's Roman mosaic jewel, which Fanny Trollope had given to Rose on her first trip to Italy.

Longmans' reader was not particularly impressed with the novel. He found it 'inferior to *The Warden*' although not 'uninteresting'. He disliked the Signora, whom he called 'a great blot on the work'. Regarding the Proudies he had little to say: 'Such a bishop and his wife ... have not appeared in our time.' He also claimed that there was no plot but then contradicted himself by saying that it turned on who would fill the position of Warden. He thought that the book should be shortened and seemed to suggest that one could get rid of Mrs Proudie's reception at the Palace. Fortunately Longman paid little attention to such an absurd opinion. Trollope, who was in Dublin, asked Tilley to conduct the negotiations. He was not pleased with the report that William Longman objected to paying the author an advance: 'It appears to me that you think £100 too high a sum to pay in advance for the book. It seems to me that if a three vol. novel be worth anything it must be worth that.' There were still difficulties even after an advance had been agreed. Trollope refused to cut the work as much as the reader had suggested and would not change the title. He did give way to the excesses of Victorian propriety: 'At page 93 by all means put out "foulbreathing" and page 97 alter "fat stomach" to "deep chest".' Perhaps he agreed because he was in a rush: 'I write in a great hurry in boots and breeches, just as I am going to hunt.'[37] Some poor Irish fox had to bear the brunt of his frustration that day!

*

It is worth looking at *Barchester Towers* in some detail to see how skilled a writer Trollope had become. Since it was so much larger than *The Warden* he was able to introduce a host of characters, who add richness to his mosaic of life. This is nowhere better shown than when he draws upon his recent Italian trips to bring the Stanhope family back to Barchester from their long residence on the shores of Lake Como. Chapter IX, where he introduces this family, shows that his

genius at characterisation had now reached its maturity. He has long
been admired for this; he is less often thought of as a writer of pithy
and epigrammatic prose, yet his ability to combine characterisation
with such prose is evident in this chapter.

There are five members of the family of the Hon. and Rev. Dr Vesey
Stanhope. The reverend gentleman himself had gone to Italy seeking a
cure for his sore throat and stayed for a dozen years before being
summoned home by the new Bishop, in whose diocese he holds several
well-endowed livings. Although 'heartlessness' is the chief characteristic of the family, all the members appear, at first, good-natured. 'The
Stanhopes would visit you in your sickness, – provided it were not
contagious, – would bring you oranges, French novels, and the last new
bit of scandal, and then hear of your death or your recovery with an
equally indifferent composure.' Although Dr Stanhope had some vague
religious convictions, 'he rarely intruded them, even on his children'.
There was only one fault he held against his family: 'inattention to his
dinner.' Mrs Stanhope, who plays little part in the novel, is one to
whom 'the *far niente* of her Italian life had entered into her very soul'.
Her principal, indeed her only, activity is dressing, and she does look
impressive when she appears some time after three in the afternoon.
We are told that 'in early life she had undergone great trials with
reference to the doctor's dinners'. In this couple Trollope has portrayed
the worst aspects of upper-class life. Both Stanhopes took pride in the
fact that their brothers were peers and did little else in life. They were
lazy but not vicious.

The three children are far worse, for each violates that highest of
Trollopean virtues: honesty. The eldest, Charlotte, dominates the
family, and although at first she may appear the least interesting, a
careful following of her activities reveals a skilful portrait of someone
who manipulates family and friends to preserve power. 'She prided
herself on her freedom from English prejudice.' This did not endear her
to her creator, who cherished so many of his own. She delighted in
trying to shake what remained of her father's religion, 'but the idea of
his abandoning his preferment in the church had never once presented
itself to her mind'.

Dr Stanhope's only son, Bertie, had one 'great fault' which was 'an
entire absence of that principle which should have induced him, as the
son of a man without fortune, to earn his own bread'. He was not
without talent, but he frittered his energies away: converting to
Catholicism for a while and then becoming a Jew in Palestine. He had
changed from being a painter to a sculptor, though Trollope adds that
Carrara was no place for an Englishman to settle. This reflects his

acquaintance in Florence with an American sculptor Hiram Powers, an old friend of his mother. Bertie is superficially charming, but he is a man 'above, or rather below, all prejudices' and quite heartless. Bertie is everything that his creator despised: a talented man who wastes his life away through laziness, and one who does not know what honesty is. Yet his creator treats him with a fairness that at times verges on sympathy. Henry James says of this: 'There could not be a better example of Trollope's manner of attaching himself to character than the whole picture of Bertie Stanhope.'[38] Indeed there could not be a better description of Trollope's greatest gift than Henry James's phrase 'attaching himself to character'. (One wonders how much the Stanhopes may have inspired the Baroness and her artistic brother who create such havoc among their quiet New England cousins in *The Europeans*.)

The most fascinating member of the family is Madeline, who after many adventures had made an unfortunate marriage to a penniless Italian. She returns to her father's villa after some mysterious injury, probably at the hands of her husband, and takes on the title of La Signora Madeline Vesey Neroni. She spends her life on a couch from which she constructs plots and conducts flirtations. She wrote 'a kind of poetry' and carried on an extensive correspondence and, adds Trollope, 'her letters were worth the postage'.

All these details are observed with such precision that the whole family excite our interest and almost arouse our sympathy. It is only as they weave their cosmopolitan wiles among the unsophisticated clergy of Barchester that the real heartlessness of the family emerges. Trollope saw many Italianised Englishmen sipping lemonade at his mother's whist tables. Like her, he may well have borrowed a trait from one and a habit from another to produce his own 'sausage'. He has an interesting remark on this when praising the details Thackeray used in depicting a hypocrite, Barnes Newcome, in *The Newcomes*: 'Thackeray had lately seen some Barnes Newcome when he wrote that.'[39] One feels certain that Trollope had seen some Berties and some Signoras before he wrote about them!

It is not only in handling a small group like the Stanhopes that he demonstrates his abilities. He is also able to get almost all the world of Barchester to Miss Thorne's *fête champêtre*. For a novelist, as for a painter or a director, few things are more difficult to handle than a large crowd scene. In his first novel Trollope had tried it with a horse race but he was too inexperienced to make it succeed. A decade later he achieved it effortlessly. This must be one of the longest parties in literary history, as it goes on for eight chapters. In these he introduces a cross-section of rural society excluding only the agricultural labourers. Miss Thorne, like the novelist, is faced with a problem over who will sit on the lawn with 'the quality' to eat 'breakfast' and who will be beyond the 'ha-ha' in the paddock, where the 'non-quality' partake of a 'dinner'. It is easy enough to order 'the bishop and such like within the ha-ha'. Yet, as Trollope says, 'who shall define these such-likes? It is in such definitions that the whole difficulty of society consists.'

As always in his novels, the good and the bad of each class appear: the upper orders are represented by the family of Countess de Courcy, always scheming and usually hypocritical, as well as by the Thornes, who, while they may be antiquated, are nevertheless noble in their old English honesty. By contrasting these two families, Trollope has a little sport with the fashionable Norman *versus* Anglo-Saxon battles that interested so many contemporary historians. The 'vain proud countess with a frenchified name' represents all that is false about a hierarchical society, while Miss Thorne, with her delight in her pure Anglo-Saxon descent, is often silly but never false. All types of clergymen are present, from the saintly Mr Harding to the odious Slope, 'more than ordinarily greasy'. There are two types of tenant farmers: the honest Greenacre family and the Lookalofts, who try to move among the gentry after renaming Barleystubb Farm 'Rosebank'. This sub-plot allows the novelist to employ two favourite devices: observing the absurdity of upper-class behaviour by parodying it in 'low life', and using women to point out the fine distinctions that govern social behaviour. A discussion among the tenant farmers' wives, the 'dames', shows how carefully the novelist had listened to the subtle gradations of speech during his postal travels in Somerset, the origin of the fictional Barset.[40]

His postal work also gave him the idea for the setting, for Ullathorne is modelled on Montacute 'which I had chiefly in my mind's eye when I described Mr Thorne's house'. Trollope saw this famous Somerset mansion long before Lord Curzon and the National Trust restored it to its old splendour. Ullathorne is depicted as a centre of hospitality, a trait for which the real mansion had a cherished reputation: even Archdeacon Denison was somewhat taken aback when he heard the Squire of Montacute say, 'John step down and bring up four hundred bottles of port wine.' Trollope was an early devotee of the English country house in the days when they received little attention: 'Men who know Florence and Rome ... and who rave of the extensive effects of French designs, have never visited Somersetshire and Dorsetshire, and know nothing of the quiet gems which are embosomed among the finest trees of Europe, the productions of all but unknown English names in the sixteenth century.'[41] He always loved Tudor and Jacobean architecture, which he saw as essentially English. He also revelled in the 'that delicious tawny hue which no stone can give, unless it has on it the vegetable richness of centuries' [*Barchester Towers* XXII].

Ullathorne is a perfect setting for Wilfrid Thorne, one of the novelist's best portrayals of a Tory squire. Trollope, as a Liberal, did not agree with their political views or their social attitudes, but he admired those who remained loyal to old verities. Thorne, for instance, looks to 'those fifty-three Trojans, who as Mr. Dod tells us, censured free trade in November, 1852, as the only patriots left among the public men in England'. The Trojans admired by Mr Thorne were those fifty-three Tories who remained loyal to the idea of agricultural protection as enshrined in the old Corn Laws abolished some six years before. Among them was none other than Sir John Trollope MP, who was in that very month writing letters to help his Liberal cousin, Anthony! The novelist resists the conventional idea that a Tory squire must be illiterate: Wilfrid Thorne 'knew more perhaps than any other man in his own county, and the next to it, of the English essayists of the two last centuries'. When he has finished his portrayal of the Thornes of Ullathorne, he concludes: 'Such, we believe, are the inhabitants of many an English country home. May it be long before their number diminishes' [*Barchester Towers* XXII].

Barchester Towers saw the appearance of one of Trollope's most famous characters, Mrs Proudie, the domineering wife of the new bishop. The Victorians delighted in laughing at a marriage where a husband was the victim of a domestic tyrant: *Punch* achieved its great popularity when it published Douglas Jerrold's *Mrs. Caudle's Curtain Lectures* in 1845. (Trollope used this directly in the last two Barchester novels, where a clerk nicknamed 'Caudle' eventually marries a bossy woman.) In *Barchester Towers* men are constantly being guided by strong women: Mrs Quiverful fights for her weak husband; Mrs Grantly acts as a sensible restraint on the Archdeacon; and Miss Thorne is a good guide for her brother, Wilfrid. The importance of women is seen throughout the Stanhope saga: the two sisters each dominate men and both toy with them. Mrs Proudie's great crime in her creator's eyes is not that she is powerful, or even that she leads her husband, but that she does it in public and glorifies in it. The novel is as much a study of the role of powerful women in Victorian society as it is a comedy of manners in a clerical society. Mrs Proudie is a far better creation than Mrs Caudle: some indeed feel her to be Trollope's greatest character. Writing six years after his death, Henry James commented: 'Mrs Proudie has become classical; of all Trollope's characters she is the most referred to.' Many Victorians became fascinated by the search for the original of Mrs Proudie, and many a bishop's wife must have been closely watched for the slightest sign of tyranny. When John Addington Symonds was asked to dine with the Bishop of Bangor, this thought was in his mind: 'Trollope must have been here before he wrote *Barchester Towers*. Dr C [Bishop Campbell of Bangor] is quiet small suave conciliating – not to say pusillanimous. Mrs C is large and & *maniéry*, a regular Mrs Proudie. Her little remarks upon Society religion novels etc were all in the worldly pious vein.' Even if Trollope's postal work had taken him to North Wales, Bishop Campbell was not consecrated until two years after the publication of *Barchester Towers*. One church newspaper was surely correct in asserting that the Proudies were 'not taken direct from any specimen of clerical human nature'.[42]

The greatness in the creation of Mrs Proudie flows from one simple fact: she was real. She was not real in having a progenitor in some episcopal palace, but real in her creator's mind: 'the Bishop and Mrs. Proudie were very real to me,' he wrote in his *Autobiography*. The years of 'castle building' had paid off: he had lived with Mrs Proudie in his mind. Decades later his elder son would say that one could find Mrs Proudies in most households, a view as frightening as it is absurd. However, Trollope did believe that the increase in the number of bishops would lead to an increase in the numbers of ladies trying to wear the mitre in their family. As he told one clergyman:[43]

> Before you put her down as a freak of fancy, let me ask you one question. Review the spiritual lords and their better halves such as you have known, and tell me whether it is the bishop or the bishop's wife who always takes the lead in magnifying the episcopal office.

*

Barchester Towers made Trollope's reputation. In the *Athenaeum*, the main literary periodical and the only one regularly read by Trollope, the reviewer noted that 'we are by no means strangers in Barchester'. He felt that the book was a marked improvement on its predecessor: 'It is certainly more dramatic in its construction; the characters are more varied; an infusion of romance gives lightness and brightness to the ecclesiastical picture.' In the *Westminster Review* George Meredith saw what was to be a strong point of the author's appeal: 'without resorting to politics, or setting out as a social reformer, [Trollope has] given us a novel that men can enjoy.' Admiration was not confined to those favourable to clerical society. A year later, in a long essay devoted to Trollope, the Unitarian *National Review* said: '*Barchester Towers* is undeniably one of the cleverest and best-written novels ... of late years.'[44]

How did individual readers react to the book? John Henry Newman spent one evening reading the first volume and, as he wrote to a friend, 'after I was in bed ... I am ashamed to say, I burst out laughing, and, when I woke in the middle of the night I began laughing again.' In later years Trollope felt that the book became 'one of those novels which do not die quite at once, which live and are read for perhaps a quarter of a century; but if that be so, its life has been so far prolonged by the vitality of some of its younger brothers' in the Barset series. Yet not all contemporaries, let alone succeeding generations, accepted his judgment. In 1865, when all but the youngest of its brothers had appeared, a young man in London, who had not yet begun his own first novel, sent his sister a copy of *Barchester Towers* saying 'you are probably acquainted with Eleanor Bold, etc. This novel is considered the best of Trollope's.' Thomas Hardy added, with all the authority of an architect, 'I think Wells is the place intended.'[45]

It is possible to see how the novel appeared to different members of one family. The Royal Family had a better chance than almost any other of knowing bishops, and that perhaps gave some colour to their views. In December 1858 Queen Victoria ended a letter to her eldest daughter, the Crown Princess of Prussia, giving advice about a woman's first 'confinement': 'There is a very amusing book called *Barchester Towers* by A. Trollope.' A few months later (the birth of the future Kaiser Wilhelm II intervening) the serious young Princess replied: 'I like "Barchester Towers", it makes one laugh till one cries, it is so very true; but I think it is very mischievous and rather wicked, everyone is bad in it almost, and it is illustrated* to make one dislike everyone.' Others in the Royal Family had different views. Prince Albert read the novel in December 1858 and apparently enjoyed it because of his interest in 'novels of character'. By March the Queen told her daughter: 'I have not read Barchester Towers all through, but I am told it is not meant to be so ill-natured. But I didn't like reading it aloud to Papa as there was not enough romance in it. The people I could not interest myself in.' This is hardly surprising as the Queen, who had been frightened as a child by

---

*By 'illustrated' the Princess did not mean that it had drawings, for it had none, but that examples of characters' bad points were given to make their personalities clear to the reader.

bewigged bishops in aprons, had little sympathy with prelates in reality or fiction; as an old woman she was reported as startling one lady-in-waiting by announcing: 'I do not like bishops.'[46]

The Queen had a half-sister to whom she was devoted. Princess Feodora had left England to marry into her native Germany, but she deeply missed the country where she had spent so much of her youth and kept in contact by reading English books. When she had received a copy of *Barchester Towers* from the Queen, 'her devoted thankful sister' Feodora replied that it 'amuses me much. It is very clever and well written and the characters admirably drawn after life. I read it slowly – *pour fair durer la plaisir!*' Just as George Meredith's comment illustrates one aspect of Trollope's enduring popularity – his appeal to male readers – so does that of Princess Feodora. The Barchester novels would have a particular appeal to Englishmen who had gone abroad and to those who looked upon England as a spiritual home. A good example of this is Bishop Colenso, a prelate against whose views both Mrs Proudie and the Archdeacon could have united; he found great delight in reading the novels in Zululand.[47]

*

By the time Longmans published *Barchester Towers* in May 1857 Trollope had already spent three months on his sixth and most autobiographical novel, *The Three Clerks*. His new habit of writing on trains and following a daily schedule was evidently working well as it only took him six months to complete this three-volume work. Although he set it in the late 1840s and early 1850s – there is a reference to the 1851 Exhibition – he based it on his own experiences in the 1830s. *The Three Clerks* is the story of three friends who are beginning their careers in the Civil Service. Charley Tudor, as has already been mentioned, resembles Trollope himself in his hobblede-hoy days. The scene of Charley's interview to join the Board of Weights and Measures is a direct copy of the novelist's own debut at the Post Office. He also drew on his past for the love plots. Katie Woodward, who recovers from consumption to marry Charley, bears some resemblance to Trollope's own sisters, especially Emily. Perhaps that is why he admitted in his *Autobiography* that tears still came to his eyes when he re-read the scene where Katie, thinking she is dying, takes leave of Charley; for Emily Trollope, as we have seen, there had been no such miraculous recovery. Among the many aspects of his own youth which the author inserted is the enjoyment he had had in flirting with barmaids. There are other echoes of Trollope's own life, many of which have already been mentioned: a reference to his birthplace, Keppel Street; teaching at a school in Brussels; and the advice to Charley and other young men to drink strong tea and read good books. Finally there are the standard attacks upon the Evangelicals.

Trollope's sixth novel is really the first to show any strong signs of 'padding'. There are two chapters which have little to do with the plot but much to do with the author's continuing desire to be seen as a serious critic of his age. Chapter XXII, 'Crinoline and Macassar; or, My Aunt's Will', is the text of a novel that Charley Tudor has written. This is a satire by Trollope on some of the more revoltingly sentimental fiction of his day. Today it may be safely avoided by any reader other than students of early-nineteenth-century fiction. Another chapter, an extended essay on the Civil Service, was mercifully removed after the first edition.

The Three Clerks is much more than a recollection of the author's early life. As in his other novels, Trollope used his story as a means of commenting on current issues and satirising current figures. Like many Englishmen, he detested Napoleon III's military 'despotism'. This detestation finds its way into *The Three Clerks*, where the French fortune-hunter Victoire Jaquêtanàpe embodies many of those characteristics that Trollope found loathsome in Imperial France: 'The happy Victoire was dressed up to his eyes. That, perhaps, is not saying much, for he was only a few feet high ... he did not carry his finery like a hog in armour, as an Englishman so often does when an Englishman stoops to be fine.' On a jaunt to Chiswick Gardens, he is joined by various English friends and two more Frenchmen whom Trollope depicts as products of that 'mould' by which Parisians make themselves resemble the Emperor. It is a characteristic of his writing that once he embarks on an attack he warms to his description:

> The cut of the beard, the long prickly-ended, clotted moustache, which looks as though it were being continually rolled up in saliva, the sallow, half-bronzed, apparently unwashed colour ... But how it has come to pass that every Parisian has been able to obtain for himself a pair of the Emperor's long, hard, bony, cruel-looking cheeks, no Englishman has yet been able to guess ... Can it be that a political phase, when stamped on a people with an iron hand ... will leave its impress on the outward body as well as on the inward soul? [XXV].

However, the novel's main political attack is devoted to the debate over reforms in the Civil Service. Trollope had been infuriated by Dickens's attack on civil servants in *Little Dorrit* which began publication in monthly parts in December 1855 and ended in June

1857. This meant that Dickens's portrayal of the Circumlocution Office had delighted the public in February 1856, exactly a year before Trollope began writing *The Three Clerks*. Comments such as 'It is true that How not to do it was the great study and object of all public departments and professional politicians all round the Circumlocution Office' were not likely to win favour with a man who had recently spent months riding all round the country devoting himself to discovering 'how to do it'. Trollope wrote an article criticising Dickens within days of the Office's debut. Of all magazines, he chose to send the manuscript to the *Athenaeum*, which never published it. By sending it to a journal whose editor was not only sympathetic to Dickens but had contributed to his periodical *Household Words*, Trollope showed how far removed he was from the London literary world. The two novelists eventually became friends, but neither could comprehend the other's attitude towards politics and government. By the time of Dickens's death Trollope's anger had cooled, but even in a generous essay written then, he could not refrain from saying that the older novelist regarded public servants as 'almost beyond the pale of sincerity'. By surviving Dickens, Trollope was able to have the last word over the Circumlocution Office, the sting of which he had never forgotten. In his novel *John Caldigate*, published twenty-three years after *Little Dorrit*, he referred to the 'popular novelist' who roused the public to think that 'the normal Government clerk is quite indifferent to his work'. 'No greater mistake was ever made,' he insisted, 'or one showing less observation of human nature. It is the nature of man to appreciate his own work' [XLVII].[48]

Underlying Trollope's attack on Dickens's sneers was his fury at the Report on the Civil Service drawn up by Sir Stafford Northcote and Sir Charles Trevelyan for Gladstone, the Chancellor of the Exchequer. Northcote was a good example of the best type of Victorian politician: honourable, hard-working, and more than a trifle dull. He began his political life as Gladstone's secretary and ended it as Tory Leader of the Commons. Trevelyan was a more intellectual figure and strengthened this reputation by marrying Macaulay's sister. Yet Macaulay, for all his regard for his brother-in-law, depicts him as having many of the qualities of Rowland Hill: efficient, clever but tactless. To their official report, *Organization of the Permanent Civil Service*, published on 23 November 1853, was added a long letter by one of the most prominent tutors at Oxford, the Rev. Benjamin Jowett. He had gained recognition for his support of university reform and was a fervent believer in the 'stimulus of examinations'.[49] The report's main conclusion was the need to introduce competitive examinations for new recruits to the service.

Trollope was deeply upset by this enquiry partly because he was still waiting for his permanent appointment as Surveyor of the Northern Division. He must have felt vulnerable: had he not received his post through the private patronage of the Freeling family? He also knew that John Tilley owed his appointment to his mother's friendship with Freeling. If Trollope's 'examination' had been farcical, so had Tilley's: he had been summoned to the Freeling house and interviewed by Sir Francis and his daughters. Yet, in spite of these curious beginnings, were not both hard working and valuable public servants? Rowland Hill was another example of an important official brought in through private patronage and, in his case, outside pressure largely guided by himself. It seemed that, just as Trollope was about to settle into a comfortable berth, his profession was being challenged and ridiculed. Much of the debate centred on the way young men were recruited, and while this would make Trollope's account of Charley Tudor's interview topical it would also give useful ammunition to the reformers. This was not his aim, which was to show that, of the three clerks, two turn out to be good public servants while the third, the most promising of all and the one who does best in examinations, takes bribes and is eventually imprisoned. Yet Trollope continued in many of his novels to portray bumptious civil servants, such as Major Fiasco and Sir Raffle Buffle. The casual reader would hardly emerge from his novels with anything approaching the high view the author himself had of government officials. In his treatment of the Civil Service, as of every thing else, Trollope's 'divided mind' towards reform is always present.

In *The Three Clerks* Trollope attacked 'the three kings' connected with the Report: Jowett is transferred from Oxford to Cambridge and becomes the Rev. Mr Jobbles who

> had for many years been examining undergraduates for little goes and great goes, and had passed his life in putting posing questions, in detecting ignorance by *vivâ voce* scrutiny, and eliciting learning by printed papers. He, by a stupendous effort of his mathematical mind, had divided the adult British male world into classes and sub-classes ... Every man should, he thought, be made to pass through some 'go'. The greengrocer's boy should not carry out cabbages unless his fitness for cabbage-carrying had been ascertained [XI].

Thus did Trollope dismiss the scholar who can claim to be among the first academics to be summoned into public life as an 'expert'. Sir Stafford Northcote appears under 'the feebly facetious name' (as Trollope later admitted) of Sir Warwick Westend, 'a man born to grace, if not his country, at any rate his county'. The most memorable of the

'kings' is Sir Gregory Hardlines, 'something of a Civil Service Pharisee
... forced to acknowledge to himself that he was born to a great destiny'
[VI]. So effective was this portrayal that years later Lady Trevelyan
told its author that her husband was always called 'Sir Gregory
Hardlines' in his own family. By then Trollope and Trevelyan had
become friends.[50]

One reformer had told Gladstone in the 1850s that the 'existing
corps of civil servants' opposed the proposed reforms because they
would force them 'to bestir themselves, and because they cannot hope
to get their own ill-educated sons appointed under the new system'.
For his part Trollope was not afraid to bestir himself, and as his sons
would not reach their maturity until the late 1860s he did not yet have
to worry about getting them places. He was concerned, however, to
defend the Civil Service and for the next few years did so in articles,
lectures and comments in his novels. He admitted there were many
faults with the old system, particularly the increasing power of party
patronage; yet however much he might support reforms he still
disliked the theoretical proponents of sweeping change. It was also
annoying that those departments which did need reform were used to
discredit the whole service, including those departments, like the Post
Office, which were efficient and well run. Yet, by 1865, he was frank
enough to admit that many of his fears had been excessive, although he
still wondered about some of the questions asked of young men
applying for the Civil Service in India, which was the first branch to
feel the reforms. Why should a young man being sent there be asked to
discuss the 'earlier dramatists from whom Shakespeare borrowed'?
Nevertheless he was prepared to accept that the system did produce
good officials. He wondered, however, if any scheme, however good,
should be extended to absolutely everyone working for the
government. He was amused to point out that the new system was not
totally fair: in the mid-1860s one young man got a clerkship at the
GPO with lower marks than two who were rejected the day before. The
luck of the calendar had replaced the advantage of knowing the
Freeling family.[51]

*

Trollope finished *The Three Clerks* on 18 August 1857: he had been
working at it since 15 February. His working calendar, the second he
kept, shows that some weeks he worked extremely well: between 5 and
11 April he wrote 170 pages, an average of just over 24 pages a day; the
following week, 12-18 April, he did even better, writing 191 pages, an

average of over 27 pages a day. In March, however, he had done hardly any writing and scrawled aross the column reserved for figures, 'Bad Foot'. Work was interrupted by business trips, such as one to Manchester from 7 to 13 June. On 18 August he finished and wrote: 'Finis coronavit opus griam [?] cito' (The end has crowned the work quickly). Three days later he offered it to William Longman but insisted that he wanted twice the amount paid for *Barchester Towers*. He then heard that the sales of his second Barset novel appeared to be bad and wondered if Longman was interested. Longman offered £100, which Trollope refused, although he took the point that if his sixth novel were also unsuccessful financially it would be worth under £100. 'And it may very likely be that I cannot write a successful novel, but if I cannot obtain moderate success I will give over, and leave the business alone. I certainly will not willingly go on working at such a rate of pay.' The obvious answer was to go elsewhere, and Longman tried to dissuade him by asking 'whether our names on your title-page are not worth more to you than the increased payment'. To this Trollope answered: 'I did think much of Messrs. Longman's name, but I liked it best at the bottom of a cheque.'[52]

In September he took the manuscript with him when he and Rose paused in London on their way to Florence. He called at Hurst and Blackett, the firm that had succeeded Colburn, who had published his second and third novels. When the publisher was late for the appointment, the foreman tried to persuade Trollope to leave the manuscript, but he would not do so without a definite offer for the book. The foreman, remembering no doubt the failure of *La Vendée*, offered some advice: 'I hope it's not historical, Mr Trollope? Whatever you do, don't be historical; your historical novel is not worth a damn.' He hurried from their office at Great Marlborough Street to New Burlington Street to see Richard Bentley, where he had called on his mother's behalf over twenty years before. Trollope left the manuscript and hurried off on his third trip to Florence. Perhaps his trips round publishers had left him a bit ruffled, as Rose remembered that 'the conductor takes us for discharged prisoners'.[53]

In one sense Trollope was like a 'discharged prisoner', standing somewhere between two contrasting states of existence. On the one hand he could not get what he demanded from Longman; on the other he did not have to take what Longman offered. He had enough standing as a writer to approach another publisher who might well give him better terms. When he reached Florence he found his mother in decline: it was the first year since 1831 that she was not working on a book, but she told her son that she was delighted that he should be taking up where she left off. She had written this to him the year before:

> I am in truth grown most woefully idle, and, worse, still, most woefully *lazy* ... But the degree of activity of which I have been wont to boast, and on which I have so often been complimented might have been accounted in my very best days as positive *idleness* when compared to what you manifest. Tom and I agree in thinking that you exceed in this respect any individual that we have ever known or heard of – and I am proud of being your mother – as well for this reason as for sundry others.

From Florence Trollope wrote to Bentley to tell him when he would be back in London briefly en route for Dublin: would he either send the manuscript to Trollope's hotel, showing he did not want it, or agree to meet. Bentley then offered £250 for the copyright. Four days later, on 17 October, they met to confirm the arrangement, and the following day Rose and Anthony were back in Dublin. Two days after this he started on his third Barset novel, *Doctor Thorne*.[54]

It was only a few weeks after Anthony and Rose left Florence that *The Three Clerks* arrived at the Villino Trollope. Theodosia lent it to her old friend Elizabeth Browning, who wrote: 'I was wrung to tears by the third volume.' Understandably the story of a young invalid's recovery aided by the power of love would stir her tears, but she went on to say 'What a thoroughly *man's* book it is!' As a proof of this she said that her husband 'who can seldom get a novel to hold him' was delighted with it. Her only objection was the inclusion of that awful tale written by Charley Tudor. Tom Trollope agreed with this criticism, and indeed it is hard to think of anyone who disagreed then or later. Trollope himself believed that *The Three Clerks* was his best novel so far, an opinion few would share today. The reviews were, on the whole, favourable. The *Literary Gazette*, while praising him as 'no inconsiderable master of irony', hoped that 'he has not withdrawn altogether from the domain of our cathedral establishments'. The position he had now reached is shown by a very favourable article in the *Saturday Review*, a journal of avowed High Church sympathies. It thought that *Barchester Towers* had already 'raised him into a very considerable position among the novelists of the present day'. With the publication of *The Three Clerks* they saw signs that 'if Mr Trollope will but do himself justice, he may delineate characters that will almost rival' Thackeray. There were two criticisms, both justified, that would reappear throughout his career: he wrote too rapidly, and he was liable to mistakes when dealing with legal questions. (This novel marks the first appearance of his most celebrated lawyer, Chaffanbrass.) The article concluded that if he could curb these flaws 'he has the path clear before him – he can make himself such a name as will not easily be forgotten'.[55]

*

There is a change in tone perceptible in *The Three Clerks*. In his earlier novels Trollope had been mainly content with telling a story. Sometimes, most noticeably in *The Warden*, he inserted homilies or denunciations. However, beginning with this sixth novel, he begins to assume more and more the mantle of a moralist. Fortunately it was usually a light mantle and he was the type of preacher who not only kept his sermons short but made them pleasing to the ear. This moralising trend reflects two aspects of the author: his desire to be regarded as a serious writer, and his increasing belief that society was becoming less honest and more open to the forces of organised corruption. Many people assume that this was something that preoccupied him late in life, most noticeably from the publication of *The Way We Live Now* in 1874-5. This view is incorrect: from the 1850s he was convinced that serious dangers threatened Victorian society. Naturally, none of his readers knew of the rejected manuscript of *The New Zealander* that lay among his papers, but the drive that led him to write it began to surface in his novels: it was his need to be seen as a serious commentator on his age.

The most frequent and the most inaccurate portrayal of Anthony Trollope is as a talented and amusing novelist who reached the status of the nearly-great by a series of entertaining novels which have continued to delight thousands of readers even though his books are unfortunately bereft of those deep psychological insights bestowed on those who hold this patronising view. There is a grain – a small grain – of truth in this. Yet the only way to understand Trollope as well as to appreciate the force of his writing, is to see him as he saw himself: an honest man trying to express serious thoughts not only on contemporary issues but on the nuances of human nature for the benefit as well as the amusement of his countrymen. He admits that he always had 'before my eyes the charms of reputation' as well as the wish, the laudable wish, to make money:[56]

Over and above the money ... I wished from the beginning to be something more than a clerk in the Post Office. To be known as somebody, – to be Anthony Trollope if it be no more, – is to me much. The feeling is a very general one, and I think beneficent. It is that which has

been called the 'last infirmity of noble mind.' The infirmity is so human
that the man who lacks it is either above or below humanity. I own to
that infirmity.

For him, almost all the threats facing his society could be summed
up in one fault: dishonesty. From his earliest novel, it runs as a theme
providing an underlying message and often forcing on the plot. In his
first novel it is the dishonest bailiff who leads Thady Macdermot to the
gallows; in *La Vendée* it is Adolphe Denot who betrays his royalist
friends. Yet these are individual acts by men blinded by greed or
jealousy. Beginning with *The Three Clerks*, the dishonesty no longer
arises in individuals' weaknesses but begins to flow from forces outside
them, from behaviour inherent in the world they inhabit. Increasingly
we are faced with a dishonest society with honest people in it, not an
honest society with dishonest people.

Trollope's mind was essentially an untheoretical one. He tended to
focus on a specific instance of a problem rather than analyse the
problem itself. This is seen, for example, in his repeated attacks upon
adulterated food, particularly coffee, which was a prominent topic of
the 1850s. The *Lancet*, in that decade a radical medical journal, began
the campaign in January 1851 with a fierce assault on those who
adulterated coffee by adding things like potatoes, burnt sugar,
sawdust, beans and mangel-wurzels. The paper also attacked
merchants who added chicory, but not everyone was agreed that this
was illegal, especially as much of the chicory used was grown on the
estates of the Whig Chancellor of the Exchequer. The crusade was
taken up by *The Times*, so that Trollope was kept well informed. It
became a political issue when the Tory government added chicory to
the list of banned items only to have this reversed by the succeeding
coalition government.[57]

References to this topic are found in many of Trollope's writings,
particularly in the late 1850s and early 1860s. 'It is the fashion now of
all trades to sell false articles in lieu of true; – chicoree [*sic*], for
instance, instead of coffee, and horses' liver instead of chicoree.'[58]
'Englishmen,' announces one character in *The Bertrams*, 'have a
partiality for chicory, but none at all for coffee' [VIII], while in a novel
written a few years later Trollope comments while dismissing the
power of eloquence: 'No living orator would convince a grocer that
coffee should be sold without chicory' [*Orley Farm* XVII]. As so often, he
appears particularly excited when his own tastes can be united with
his passion for honesty and justice. It always annoyed him that he
could rarely have a decent cup of coffee in England and that he had to

go to France for one. (By the 1880s his brother Tom, with that delight of the elderly in bemoaning the present, upstaged his younger brother and held that even the French could no longer make coffee!) The curt order of one character in a Trollope novel has all the hallmarks of a remembered comment by the author himself: 'Waiter ... Ask them from me whether they know how to make coffee. It does not consist of an unlimited supply of luke-warm water poured over an infinitesimal proportion of chicory. That process, time-honoured in the hotel line, will not produce the beverage called coffee' [*Orley Farm* XVIII].

To some, coffee may appear a trivial subject, but to Trollope it was symptomatic. He was equally furious at a political example of 'dishonesty' in his time. Few Prime Ministers have enjoyed such a uniformly high reputation from contemporaries and historians as Sir Robert Peel, who had died in 1850. Yet Trollope detested Peel and inserted diatribes against him in several novels. There is no question but that he was unfair to Peel. Trollope always had a strong belief that the function of Tories was to act as a brake on the coach of progress whose natural drivers were Liberals. This was a convenient attitude for a Liberal like Trollope. In *The Three Clerks*, having alluded to some petty politicians whose careers had ended in disgrace, he suddenly turns on Peel:

> Who has given so great a blow to political honesty ... as Sir Robert Peel? ... He has taught us as a great lesson, that a man who has before him a mighty object may dispense with those old-fashioned rules of truth to his neighbours and honesty to his own principles, which should guide us in ordinary life ... How prone we are, each of us, to look on our own object as great, how ready to make excuses for receiving such a lesson for our guide [XXIX].

This was the heart of Trollope's annoyance with Peel. He approved Peel's sudden conversions, most notably to free trade in 1845, but he felt that an honest statesman had no right to change his principles because it was 'expedient' and stay in office. Peel should have resigned and let his opponents carry out the repeal of the Corn Laws in 1845-46. In fact Peel tried to do so but his opponents were too weak and too crafty to accept what Disraeli called 'the poisoned chalice'. Trollope may well have been affected by the fact that his cousin, Sir John, was one of 'the hard knot of revengeful Tory members' who destroyed Peel.[59] In spite of the fact that Trollope is wrong about Peel, his underlying message still has validity: public men by their actions guide private morality. His belief in the connection between the lives of public men and the state of private morals underlies Trollope's insistence on moral values in politics and society.

Perhaps another reason for the increasing number of comments about politics is that Trollope's postal work was bringing him into contact with more politicians. In the 1850s many Irish MPs were trying to promote better postal service between England and Ireland and there were many questions put regarding the speed of trains to Holyhead and of steamers to Kingstown which only experts like Trollope could answer. He was frequently called to London to attend meetings at the GPO and to testify before Parliamentary Committees. As we have noted before, he may well have been allowed to live in Dublin in order to enable him to act as virtual spokesman for the Irish Post Office. He spent over a month in London in 1855, much of it dealing with a Parliamentary Committee investigating postal deliveries in the south of Ireland. This Committee called seventeen witnesses and asked 4,014 questions of which Trollope answered 1,671, far more than any other witness. Rowland Hill was also called but only answered some 200 questions. Hill and Trollope presented a united front with that air of mildly condescending omniscience that the knowledgeable official assumes in the presence of enquiring politicians, among whom was Sir Stafford Northcote. Trollope told them: 'I have local knowledge over the whole of Ireland ... by chance it has happened that I have been through the whole of the country.' On his third day of questioning – Lunae, 16 Julii, 1855, for the days were still listed in Latin – he described the work of Irish postmen. They were expected to walk 20½ English miles each day, almost five more than their English counterparts, but as there was less mail in Ireland their bag was not as heavy. Trollope testified: 'I do not think the rate of pay of the rural messengers in Ireland is high enough, and ... I am about to bring the question forward, with the object of increasing the pay to some extent.' As we have already seen, he returned to London in October to press his argument on Hill and achieved some success.

Most of his testimony was a calm recital of facts about the Irish post, but occasionally sessions got over-heated. One of the issues being debated was whether to have special overnight mail trains instead of the scheduled day trains: Trollope and Hill opposed this because of the extra expense and because it was unnecessary, and Trollope's evidence probably decided the Committee to reject the proposal. When the chairman, Thomas Meagher, MP for Waterford, asked about the possibility of deputations concerning the poor service, Trollope demurred. Meagher insisted that he was entitled to use the term 'poor' even if only two people complained about one letter – the one who posted it and the one who received it. At this Trollope flared up because he suspected ulterior motives. He agreed that there might indeed be deputations 'if a company in which they [the sender and the receiver] were interested were to receive £6,000 for that letter'. The Committee resented his implication that many of the complaints about the service in the area under discussion were only for the 'benefit of the railway'. There were two calls for him to withdraw his remark but he refused, and his reason contains an interesting sentence which did little to placate the Irish MPs on the Committee: 'I think it very natural that men should have a bias in their minds ... and that they should be led to wish for one object, when the reason for wishing it is connected with another object.' Anyone who reads his novels will see many developments of that belief being worked out in the lives of his characters.

His time before the Committee obviously made an impression: in *The Three Clerks* he referred to railway corruption in Ireland and discussed the work of a Parliamentary Committee pursuing 'their animated inquiries ... all through the sultry month of July' [XXXIV]. He more than implies that the committee's enquiries are an example of 'sharp' practice to trick the Commons into voting for an unnecessary bridge in order to benefit interested parties. The fictional committee has an aggressive Irish MP, 'The M'Carthy Desmond', who with another MP assault one poor witness who will not play their game with 'no less than 2,250 questions' over three days. Finally, much of the wording of the official recommendation of this fictional committee was identical to that of 1855. Not surprisingly, Trollope wrote that the hearings reminded him of the brutal sport of badger-baiting he had known as a boy at Winchester [XXXII].[60]

*

On 15 July, just over a month before he finished *The Three Clerks*, Trollope wrote to William Longman to see if he was interested in a shorter novel to be called *The Struggles of Brown, Jones, and Robinson; by One of the Firm*. It would be a 'hit at the present system of advertising ... in the guise of a tale'. He was careful to add that 'Publisher's advertisements are not reflected on'. After *The Three Clerks* was completed on 18 August 1857 Trollope gave himself six days off before starting work on the new novel which was an extended satire on the bankruptcy of a firm of haberdashers. It was meant as another instalment of his campaign against dishonesty in public life which he saw reflected in the growing practice of advertising. This was becoming 'the bane of the nineteenth century' and the main 'cause in sapping the strength of our empire'. Through it 'men are taught to believe that lies and honest industry are compatible'. By the 1850s London seemed awash in advertising, much of it remarkably tasteless. A seven-foot hat was mounted on wheels and pulled through the street by an old nag, much to the fury of Carlyle. Hoardings sprang up everywhere, even on the cliffs of Dover. Paintings of the Queen were used as a common advertising illustration, implying some sort of royal favour. 'Sandwich men' (a term invented by Dickens) paraded the streets, advertising all sorts of miracle cures or other dubious products.[61]

Trollope had only worked on his manuscript for two weeks before he and Rose left for their third visit to Florence on 7 September. It would have been better if he had taken the manuscript with him and dropped it in the Channel. The novel, to which he did not return until 1861, is generally and rightly thought his worst. He and Rose were back in Dublin by 18 October, having stopped in London to see the Crystal Palace, which had been moved from Hyde Park to Sydenham after the Great Exhibition of 1851. While in Florence, Trollope had been 'cudgelling [his] brain for a new plot'. Finally he asked his brother Tom, who had not yet written a novel, to sketch one for him. He did so and produced the story of *Doctor Thorne*, which was to become the third Barset novel. However it was not centred on the clerical society of the Cathedral partially because, as Trollope later admitted, he did not think a continuation of the series would be successful. 'I hardly dared to do more than allude to a few of my characters.' Two days after his return to Dublin he began writing. It was the only time Trollope ever consciously took a plot from someone else, and Tom's outline is uniquely Victorian: a girl suddenly inherits a large fortune which allows her to marry her beloved, the heir to an old estate in difficulties. His work on the novel was delayed by postal trips when he could do no writing, although he tried to make up for this by writing six pages on Christmas Day 1857. Then, on 12 January, he left for London, this time on his own, for a new mission. His work sheet has the explanatory note opposite the dates for 12-31 January, 'Preparing for Egypt in London'. He was to go to Egypt to negotiate a new postal treaty.[62]

In the days before the International Postal Convention, countries made individual agreements about the costs and methods of postal deliveries. Egypt, which was only nominally under Turkish sovereignty, was vital for the all-important mails to India. The need for swift communication had become obvious the year before when the Indian Mutiny sent a thrill of horror throughout England as both government and people waited for the latest news. A telegraph line from Alexandria to Aden had been financed by British capital and the government took great interest in improving mail deliveries to India. That Trollope combined the roles of postal official and diplomat shows how high he now stood in the eyes of his superiors at St Martin-le-Grand.[63]

Because he had to be in London for his instructions, Trollope had time to see Bentley, who agreed to his demand for £400 for the yet unfinished *Doctor Thorne*. However, the next day Bentley came to St Martin's and told Trollope that he could only afford £300. Just as earlier Trollope had refused Longman's terms for *The Three Clerks*, so now he refused Bentley's reduced offer and, with only an hour's free time, hurried to Piccadilly to Chapman and Hall, the firm which had become famous as Dickens's publishers. He 'rushed to Chapman and Hall ... and said what I had to say ... in quick torrent of words'. Edward Chapman looked at the author 'as he might have done at a highway robber who had stopped him on Hounslow Heath'. He agreed to buy the novel for £400, but 'he held the poker in his hand all the time I was with him'. This is the story Trollope bequeathed to posterity in his *Autobiography*. However, in the Bodleian Library there is a letter from Bentley written on 25 January telling Trollope that he cannot afford £400: this is four days before Trollope signed the agreement with Chapman to deliver volumes one and two by the middle of March and volume three by the middle of April. In Trollope's memory, and perhaps in his desire to make a good story better, a letter became a visit and the four days between 25 and 29 January became one hour. What is more likely is that on 25 January, the day he heard from Bentley, Trollope did have only an hour's free time, presumably for lunch. Annoyed with Bentley and anxious to get the money he felt he deserved, he arrived at Chapman's offices in Piccadilly in a flushed state. Part of his condition could have been due to the difficulty in getting there: 25 January was the day on which Queen Victoria's eldest daughter, the Princess Royal, was married to the heir to the Prussian throne in the Chapel Royal, St James's Palace. The streets were thronged with spectators. He might well have been very hard pressed to get from St Martin's to Piccadilly to negotiate the terms of an agreement and to get back to work, all within an hour, assuming that the 'hour' is itself not an exaggeration. An agreement was then drawn up and Trollope made a second trip on 29 January, the day before he took the boat train for Paris, to sign the document. Two days and two visits became one in his recollection.[64]

The quickest route to Egypt was overland to Marseilles via Paris. Travellers to France had to procure a passport from the French

Embassy, which cost ten francs plus another two francs for an internal passport. Trollope, as a faithful reader of *The Times*, would have known how this outraged English visitors, particularly those who were only travelling through France on their way to India. After a rough crossing, he met his brother in Paris on 30 January. Tom was there with two Italians: the ones, as Anthony told Rose, 'who used to be hanging about when they were selling their pots & pans'. It is likely that Tom was using his knowledge of Tuscan art to engage in the business of selling artifacts; a tradition has survived that he made some money by such deals.[65] In any case the Trollopes were lucky not to be taken up by the French police. On 14 January bombs had been thrown at the carriage of Napoleon III and Empress Eugénie, killing several bystanders. It soon became known that this was the work of Italian terrorists operating from England, and a wave of anti-English sabre-rattling swept through the French army. For two large, loud and not very self-effacing Englishmen to rendezvous in Paris and associate with two Italians with parcels of 'pots and pans' was somewhat indiscreet, to say the least.

Even during this brief interval in Paris Trollope, now with a deadline to meet, kept on with his writing of *Doctor Thorne*. Fortunately his absence provides a welcome but all too brief glimpse of Rose's contribution to his writing. She was busy in Dublin making a 'fair' copy of the chapters he had written before leaving Ireland. He sent her chapter titles, as well as the text of Chapter XII: 'This I think will be good for 18 of your pages. You will of course let me know – The slips are long. I think I have made it intelligible how it goes – You must of course be careful about the reading, and also alter any words which seem to be too often repeated.' This was the first long absence from Rose in almost fifteen years of marriage and they were both upset: 'Do not be dismal if you can help it – I feel a little that way inclined, but hard work will I know keep it off.' Rose, for her part, had her sister Isabella to keep her company at Donnybrook. Trollope's schedule of five pages a day kept him from visiting the Louvre, but he could not resist a hurried trip to Chartres with Tom to see the stained glass: 'the finest in the world ... magnificent.' He promised to take Rose to see it, which he did in September of the following year.[66]

He was soon on his way to Marseilles, where he took ship for Alexandria. The Mediterranean was rough in February, and he often had to interrupt his writing because of sea sickness; nevertheless he stuck to the system he devised for *Barchester Towers*. When he started a new book he made a diary, allotting a set number of pages for each day, 'so that if at any time I have slipped into idleness for a day or two, the record of that idleness has been there, staring me in the face'. He allowed 250 words per page and then set a quota of pages for each week, depending on his other business. The average number of pages was about forty, but there would be weeks when he reached as high as 112. He met his daily quota by rising with the sun and doing his literary work before attending to his postal duties. As one newspaper said of him after his death: 'His multitudinous volumes were chiefly written at a time of day when most literary ladies and gentlemen are snug between the sheets.'[67] His father's attacks on 'idleness' and his mother's example of writing at dawn had borne fruit which was at last ripe! It was only this disciplined schedule that allowed Trollope to write so many books as well as to carry on his work for the Post Office.

He arrived in Alexandria on 10 February and must have been amazed, as Thackeray had been some years earlier, that all the donkey-boys who met the ship shouted for potential customers in good English.[68] Trollope recorded his impressions of Egypt in a short story 'An Unprotected Female at the Pyramids': he was delighted to learn 'with some little pride' that English-speakers were treated better than other foreigners. His reactions to Alexandria were typically Victorian. He knew its reputation from classical times as 'the favoured seat of the earth's learning', but he soon decided that it was 'the most detestable of cities ... it has all the filth of the East, without any of that picturesque beauty with which the East abounds'. Fortunately it was not hopeless: 'Fate and circumstance must Anglicize it in spite of the huge French consulate, in spite of legions of greedy Greeks, in spite even of sand, mosquitos, bugs, and dirt, of winds from India, and of thieves from Cyprus' [*The Bertrams* XXXVIII]. Here we have the Victorian creed: hatred of dirt, a love of progress which was inevitable, and the conviction that it would come through English influence. It all seems rather simple now, but it was, on the whole, true. Even the caustic reference to the 'huge French consulate' is characteristic: its size had also annoyed Thackeray.

Trollope spent almost two months in Egypt, most of it in negotiating with Nurbar Bey, an Armenian Christian in Egyptian service. Faithful to his rule, he was staying at Cairo's best hotel, Shepheard's, where the Armenian made frequent calls, accompanied by servants bearing pipes and coffee. Trollope had prepared for the pipes by smoking numerous cigars in Paris, or at least that is what he told Rose. The British terms regarding money were quickly accepted, but for weeks they battled as to whether the mail could be carried from Alexandria to the Red Sea in twenty-four or forty-eight hours. Trollope, needless to say, insisted on the shorter time, while the Armenian said that if he agreed it would lead to his resignation and much bloodshed. This did not disturb Trollope: 'I smoked my pipe, or rather his, and drank his coffee, with oriental quiescence but British firmness.' He was secretly convinced that some officials of the P & O line did not want the quicker time for their own reasons. He was also sure that Nurbar Bey's constant talk about the need for 'tranquillity' in transport was because P & O did not want the mail to go any faster than the merchandise they were already transporting. Trollope busied himself in measuring the average speed of camels as well as in deciding whether the mail bags would be safe from Arab attempts to cut them open. Like Palmerston and almost all British officials, Trollope did not believe that there was any chance of building a Suez Canal, so the need was to provide overland transport across Egypt which was as quick and secure as possible.[69]

In the late 1880s Escott asked Nurbar Bey, who was three times to serve as Prime Minister under the Khediv, Tawfiq, if he remembered the novelist. He recalled that Trollope had been pleasant but peremptory: 'His manner of negotiating had about it less of the diplomatist than of the author who might have meditated scolding his publisher if he did not come round to his terms, and of carrying his literary wares elsewhere.' One wonders if Nurbar Bey had not been reading the *Autobiography*.[70]

*

Trollope had written, probably on his way to Egypt: 'When one is impatient, five minutes is as a duration of all time, and a quarter of an hour is eternity' [*Doctor Thorne* XII]. He never, at any time, had much patience: everything he did, he did at the gallop. Perhaps that is why fox-hunting delighted him. Sitting in 'Grand Cairo' and puffing on a *nargileh* had little appeal. He was anxious to complete his official duties so that he could have a hurried tour of the Holy Land. He managed to see the Pyramids and found them less impressive than he had expected. Nevertheless, once there, he had to get inside, as he admitted in *The Bertrams* [XXXVIII]:

A man who goes to Cairo *must* see the Pyramids ... but I must enter a loud, a screeching protest against the Arab brutes ... who have these monuments in their hands. Their numbers, the filthiness of their dress ... their stench, their obscene indecency, their clattering noise, their rapacity ... their abuse, as in this wise: 'Very bad English-man; dam bad; dam, dam, dam! Him want to take all him money to the grave' ... This, be it remembered, from a ferocious, almost blackened Arab, with his face within an inch of your own.

He advises readers, when he recounts his adventures, that no lady should climb the Pyramids, while a gentleman should, of course, go armed with a stout stick and 'mercilessly belabour any Arab who attempts either to bully or to wheedle' [XXXVIII]. He found the climb up the outside and the descent down the inside of a Pyramid a waste of time. However, the approach to Jerusalem was different: 'There is something enticing to an Englishman in the idea of riding through the desert with a pistol ... There is a *soupçon* of danger in the journey just sufficient to give it excitement; and then it is so un-English, oriental and inconvenient; so opposed to the ordinary haste and comfort of a railway' [VI].

He had wanted to enter the Holy City with devout feelings 'but what piety can withstand the wear and tear of twelve hours in a Turkish saddle?' Contempt, rather than devotion, was his mood at the Church of the Holy Sepulchre, where the differing branches of Christianity fought to erect altars closest to the spot of Christ's tomb. At such a crowded time – the week before Easter – it was difficult to squeeze his bulky figure through the four-foot-high door and, even worse, to back out of it through surging crowds of Orthodox peasants, 'cut-throat-looking wretches, with close shaven heads, dirty beards ... cloaks, filthy, foul, alive with vermin, reeking with garlic, – abominable to an Englishman'. Yet, in spite of his revulsion, he admired their simple devotion: 'Christ to them was an actual living truth, though they knew how to worship him no better than by thus kissing a stone.' Aided by his dragoman, as well as by his unshakeable self-confidence, he pushed his way through surging crowds throughout the city: 'How is it that Englishmen can push themselves anywhere?' he later asked in his story 'A Ride Across Palestine'. 'I doubt, after all, whether a ferocious eye and a strong smell of dirt are so efficacious in creating awe and obedience in others, as an open brow and traces of soap and water.'

It was not only fellow Christians who came under his critical gaze. He was pleased, as we have noted, that 'the female followers of the Prophet' covered their faces with veils – 'no one could behold them without wishing that the eclipse had been total' – and was full of admiration for the Jewish women he saw in their ancestral land:

The Mahomedans were ape-like; but the Jewesses were glorious specimens of feminine creation. They were somewhat too bold, perhaps; there was too much daring in their eyes, as, with their naked shoulders and bosoms nearly bare, they met the eyes of men that were looking at them. But there was nothing immodest in their audacity; it was defiant rather, and scornful [*The Bertrams* IX].

His deepest religious experience came not in a crowded church but in the open air: 'If there be one place told of in holy writ, the name of which gives rise to more sacred feelings than any other, it is that of the Mount of Olives; and if there be a spot in that land of wondrous memories which does bring home to the believer in Christ some individualized remembrance of his Saviour's earthly pilgrimage, that certainly is it' [*The Bertrams* VII].

*

Trollope left Egypt on 4 April 1858 after a stay of some seven weeks. On his way home he had to inspect the post offices in Malta and Gibraltar. His report on Malta, where he spent a week, gives a good idea of his thoroughness and fairness as a postal official. Though he accepted that the heat meant that men could not work as hard as in England, he still found that the office was over-manned and needed one less clerk. Rather than dismiss one man, he decided that the next vacancy should not be filled and that this salary should then be distributed among the other clerks. He also advocated that the men be given two free afternoons each week when the pressure of incoming mail allowed. He even made some plans to extend free delivery throughout the capital. Money could be saved by cutting down on government forms which 'create unnecessary labour', an idea he discussed with the Accountant-General when he returned to London. He also advocated that the Maltese postmaster should follow the Surveyors' practice and send monthly reports on the number of postage stamps in their charge. All these proposals were approved by Lord Colchester, who had become Postmaster General in Lord Derby's new government during Trollope's absence.[71]

From Malta he sailed for Gibraltar, and on leaving the colony his ship called at Cadiz, which allowed him a few days to see some of Spain and to admire the walk of Andalusian women. It also gave him time to travel from Cadiz up the Guadalquivir River to Seville. On board ship Trollope and a companion had a farcical encounter with a Spaniard whom they mistook for a bull-fighter, whose 'gold ornaments' they toyed with and who, naturally, they assumed spoke no English. It turned out that he was not a bull-fighter but a Duke who spoke English: 'How gracious he was to us, and yet how thoroughly he covered us with ridicule,' Trollope admitted in his *Autobiography*.

Never one to throw away a good story, he adapted it for one of his most amusing short stories, 'John Bull on the Guadalquivir', where the Spaniard becomes a Marquis.

When Trollope returned to England he could look with some satisfaction on the position he had now reached. In the midst of all his travelling and despite his official work, he had finished *Doctor Thorne* on 31 March 1858. The very next day he had begun a new novel, *The Bertrams*, and that first day had written seven pages. By the end of the week the total had risen to forty. His system was evidently working well: he had never before started a new novel before the ink was barely dry on the previous one, and by finishing his writing a fortnight before the deadline he had ensured that, even with Rose's copying the final chapters, *Doctor Thorne* should be in on time.[72] In his new novel he was showing that he could make good use of his experiences while abroad. In addition, maybe because of his absence from home and friends, he was far more reflective and outspoken than hitherto. Also, perhaps his experiences in Jerusalem had made him more aware of religious topics, and he skilfully introduced that developing Victorian obsession, the loss of faith, into two chapters [XVIII and XXVI].

The Bertrams opens with the friendship between two young men, Arthur Wilkinson, a vicar's son, and George Bertram, the nephew of a rich miser. Bertram, headstrong and clever, has religious doubts. A third young man, Henry Harcourt, begins a rapid rise as a Tory politician and lawyer, and wins the hand of Bertram's fiancée after her engagement is broken off. Their marriage is a disaster, and Harcourt's brilliant career ends in suicide. Eventually the widow and Bertram are married. Like *The Three Clerks*, this novel explores the different ways in which success and ambition affect the honesty of the three friends.

The book interested two of the greatest minds of his time. John Henry Newman was reading it at an hotel in Dover: 'It is decidedly the most powerful thing of his that I have read – tragic, instructive, humiliating – but there is a touch of scepticism which I have never seen in him before. I fear it is one of his last, if so he is progressing uncomfortably.' By the time Newman got to the third volume he had moved on to Deal and was, quite rightly, less happy with the final volume: 'The third volume of the Bertrams was a dreadful fall off. The truth is few people can end ... It is like the *facilis descensus* etc. It is deplorably bad, that third volume.' It is rather ironic that Trollope's favourite Latin tag was turned against him. However, not everyone agreed. Thousands of miles east of Deal, on his estate at Yasnaya Polyana, Tolstoy turned from his manuscript of *War and Peace* in 1865, the year it began appearing, to read *The Bertrams*. At first he was critical and noted in his diary, 'Read Trollope. If only there was not diffuseness. Excellent.' Three days later he wrote: 'Trollope captivates me with his mastery. I console myself that he has his and I have mine. To know one's self, or rather, that which is *not one's own self*, that is the greatest skill. As for me, I must work like a pianist [i.e. practise].'[73]

The story does indeed have flaws apart from the 'diffuseness' which annoyed Tolstoy, the greatest of which is a series of weak female characters with the exception of some delightful spinsters. Trollope himself did not think highly of the plot, but it is on the whole sound, although possessing two great faults: Trollope evidently tired of one main character, Arthur Wilkinson, and dropped him. He did not bring him back until the latter part of the book. Secondly, he did not develop some of the minor characters, who could have enriched the book. The rich uncle's clerk is greatly devoted to young Bertram, and while Dickens would have made much of such a character Trollope never allows us to see any details of the man's life. Again, the scheming Harcourt is spied on by a footman, a subject that Thackeray would have developed but which Trollope only recounts. The author himself rightly says that many of the love scenes are weak, as star-crossed lovers meet only to part. Finally, the novel suffered from two aspects of Trollope's work: the first was his amazing speed at writing. If he had been prepared to work on it as long as he had on *The Warden*, it could well have been a very great novel. The second aspect was the extraordinarily peripatetic history behind its writing. At the top of his work sheet Trollope wrote: 'The Bertrams begun in Egypt, and written on the Mediterranean – in Malta, Gibraltar, England, Ireland, Scotland and finished in the West Indies.'

Rose was waiting in London when he returned in the second week of May: he had been gone for almost four months. Perhaps his long absence allowed him to reflect how important she had been, both to his happiness and to his increasing success. Certainly the novel on which he was currently working had two references to amuse her, both of which have already been mentioned: he referred to the delights of walking with a wife, and he used their wedding date, 11 June, for a marriage in his story: 'Let us trust that the day may always be regarded as propitious,' he had written. For him it had been [XXVIII, XLIV].

They now set off for a holiday in Sherwood Forest and on 27 May travelled on to Scotland. Trollope had been ordered to Glasgow to revise deliveries. Rose stayed with him until 9 June, when she left; he stayed on for another seven days but was unable to do any writing. This was not surprising because he was required to climb to the top of the tenements with the letter carriers to measure the time they took. 'It was midsummer,' he later wrote, 'and wearier work I never performed.' The postmen grumbled, but Trollope grumbled louder and wondered 'how it would be with them if they had to go home afterwards and write a love-scene'. On his return to Dublin he carried on with the new work, although he had set-backs: four times in August and September he confided to the work sheet that no writing had been done, and beside each admission were the words 'Ah me!'[74] His writing was to be interrupted once more by a postal mission, this time to sort out deliveries in the West Indies, and he left London on 16 November 1858, this time to be gone for over seven months. When he returned in July 1859, he would be half way through the single most important year in his life.

Phineas Finn and Lady Laura Kennedy from *Phineas Finn* (J.E. Millais).

CHAPTER NINE

The Age of Success

When *The Bertrams* was published in March 1859 Trollope was in the West Indies. Readers must have been somewhat puzzled by the lengthy lecture that prefaced it. This sermon on society's attitudes towards success is one way in which the frustrated author of *The New Zealander* could use his critical faculties. Far more important, he was now in his mid-forties and beginning to reflect on his past and his future. Certainly by 1859 he could consider himself successful. In his personal life he had a happy marriage and two healthy sons. He had obtained a Surveyorship in the most prestigious district in Ireland and the Post Office was increasingly using him for important work at home and abroad, work which gave promise of future advancement to yet higher rank. His writing was also successful: he was able to produce more than one novel a year, which meant that his earnings from books were equal to about three-quarters of his generous (though he would have bridled at that word) salary. He was, particularly by Irish standards, well-off. The Victorians did not use terms like 'mid-life crisis': they had already invented enough silly language of their own and had to leave something for their descendants. Even if they had, the term would not have applied. Trollope was certainly not in any 'crisis' but, rather, on what might be called a 'mid-life plateau' from whence he could look to what might lie ahead. To us it seems absurd that he had anything of which to complain. Yet he was ever a restless man, anxious to succeed and then to press on to even greater success and, most of all, to recognition. To him this was a natural and 'manly' trait. 'Success,' as one reviewer wrote in commenting about *The Bertrams*, 'is a great incentive to exertion in literature as well as in other matters.'[1]

Yet success was often bought at the price of expediency, particularly in public life. That was his charge, his inaccurate charge, against Peel which he repeated in *The Bertrams*. This struggle between honesty and success forms an underlying theme in most of the novels from the time the Warden decided that the comforts of his large clerical income were not worth an uneasy conscience. However, the Warden is a virtual saint and, as such, unique in Trollope's writing. Other men, normal men, men like Trollope himself, face the daily question of how much principle can be swept aside as one strides ahead. In his novels the active man who suddenly says that he will go no further if it requires dishonesty is the character he wishes us to admire. In *Barchester Towers* the loathsome Slope has no scruples about thrusting himself forward, but in the same novel an equally ambitious but thoroughly honourable gentleman, Archdeacon Grantly, is confronted by a moral dilemma. He stands by the bedside of his dying father the Bishop. If the old man breathes his last before the fall of the Tory government the son will succeed him. He 'dared to ask himself whether he really longed for his father's death'. Almost immediately 'the proud, wishful, worldly man' is on his knees praying for his father only to be interrupted by the 'velvet step' of Septimus Harding coming into the room. The saint has appeared in time to see the normal man's victory in resisting temptation. Yet this is Trollope the realist, not a religious tale by Charlotte Yonge, and no sooner does the old Bishop depart with a blessing on his lips than the Archdeacon is thinking of the telegram to Downing Street. It is the Archdeacon's behaviour that Trollope thinks most people are capable of, and it is the aim of his novels to help them towards such sensible virtue.

The meaning of 'success' is the text of Trollope's sermon in *The Bertrams*. His first sentence declares that 'this is undoubtedly the age of humanity – as far, at least, as England is concerned'. More concern for the poor, the decline in capital punishment (a postman had been hanged for stealing from the post only two years before Trollope became a clerk) and the use of chloroform in operations showed a developing respect for the physical existence of life. He did not mean to be contemptuous by seeing these as 'comparatively low', but for him it was always a truism that 'the body [is] lower than the mind':

> But in the inner feelings of men to men, and of one man's mind to another man's mind, is it not an age of extremest cruelty? There is sympathy for the hungry man; but there is no sympathy for the unsuccessful man who is not hungry ... Success is the god we worship.

His concern was with the 'cruelty of spirit that is thus engendered'. This is not the Trollope of popular repute but the serious and thoughtful figure questioning the values of his time, looking back regretfully to older ways while himself forging ahead with energetic determination. Undoubtedly his starting the book while in Egypt is an important factor: his loneliness, his stay in a non-Christian country and the effects of his pilgrimage to Jerusalem had caused him to reflect. His absence from home and, presumably, from much normal conversation had forced him to reveal more of his thoughts than in any of his previous novels, and he had fallen into that sceptical vein regarding the values and goals of his society which Newman had detected.

As we have seen, Trollope always had a serious side to his character and a desire to be treated with respect as a writer; occasionally this manifested itself in a gloominess, as now, when he felt his writing career was not a great success. Even if the income from his novels could almost equal his salary, it was still only half what his mother had earned at one time. Living as he did in Dublin, he was unknown in the world of London literary society. The decisive, though deserved, rejection of *The New Zealander* seemed to symbolise that his attempt to be seen as more than a moderately successful writer of pleasant novels would always be frustrated. In 1859 David Masson, Professor of English Literature at University College London wrote: 'There is no debate more common, wherever literary talk goes on, than the debate as to the respective merits of Dickens and Thackeray.'[2] Trollope was not even mentioned. Success, Trollope was discovering, if moderate, could have its price as much as failure.

*

Trollope, had he but known it, was on the verge of fame. In May 1859, while he was still out of the country but two months after publication of *The Bertrams*, an article occupying two and a half columns appeared in *The Times*. The anonymous article – still among the finest assessments of Trollope – was written by E.S. Dallas, one of the best Victorian reviewers, who analysed Trollope's achievements. How the opening sentence must have gratified him when he read it, probably on his return to Donnybrook:[3]

> If Mudie were asked who is the greatest of living men, he would without one moment's hesitation say – Mr. Anthony Trollope; and Mudie's opinion is worth much ... This majestic personage, whom authors worship, and whom readers court, knows that at the present moment one writer in England is paramount above all others, and his name is Trollope. He is at the top of the tree; he stands alone; there is nobody to be compared with him. He writes faster than we can read, and the more that the pensive public reads the more does it desire to read. Mr.

Anthony Trollope is, in fact, the most fertile, the most popular, the most successful author ...

What a delightful welcome-home article for a writer! It is true that Dallas added a qualification at the end of the quote: 'the most popular, the most successful author – that is to say, of the circulating library sort.' This was not meant as a sneer. Dallas's summation of Trollope's novels – that is, those since *The Warden*, as he appears unaware of the first three books – is similar to the normal judgment in surveys of English literature: 'He is always clever, often amusing, sometimes even great, or very near being great, but his predominating faculty is good sense.' What Trollope himself would have most enjoyed are the final lines, that he was 'a practised writer, a thoughtful man, and a kindly satirist'. The man who had spent much of the decade berating 'The Jupiter' now had good reason to be grateful for its Olympian power.

*

A thoughtful man! Trollope was at last to demonstrate this in his next book: his first published work of non-fiction which grew directly out of his assignment to the Caribbean. The GPO was anxious that the colonial post come under local control and, as part of this policy, Trollope was sent to examine ways of improving postal services between Britain and the islands. The West Indian postal services were the most costly to the Post Office. Although the islands no longer played a crucial role in the British economy, their geographic position was useful. They were close to the Americas and were particularly valuable as a stopping place for ships leaving the Gulf of Mexico. Boats carrying the mail used their many ports before making the two-week voyage to England. Trollope's work was to 'cleanse the Augean stables': dealing with an incompetent postmistress in Grenada and prodding a postmaster in Demerara who was slow in remitting money to London.

More important, he was to negotiate with the Spanish colonial authorities in Cuba and to reach agreement with the Republic of New Grenada (now Colombia) about ways to speed the post across the isthmus of Panama, then controlled by the Colombians. The fact that he did not speak Spanish did not trouble him or the GPO. The California 'Gold Rush' in the previous decade had led to improved transport across the isthmus and this opened up the possibility of quicker deliveries to Australia. There were also commercial pressures demanding improved postal services. British exports to South and

Central America had quadrupled from £2,531,000 in the year of Trollope's birth to £10,100,000 in the year he left on this trip. Finally there were diplomatic reasons for better communication because of tensions with the United States, who were intervening in the affairs of Latin America. There was also the prospect that Imperial France might follow this example.[4] All these factors made Trollope's trip a necessity and ensured that any book would be topical, to say the least.

John Tilley, who always seems to have watched his brother-in-law's energy with bemused affection, noted that Trollope set off 'in great force' for Southampton on 16 November 1858, after two weeks in London for briefing on the postal affairs of the West Indies.[5] The official correspondence about West Indian postmasters, all carefully recorded in the vast record books kept by the young clerks, was available for him to study. Trollope, in his turn, had to brief Tilley about a task he had accepted: Chapman would be sending the proofs of *The Bertrams*, when it was finished, to him for correction. He had already undertaken this thankless task with *Barchester Towers* and, with Rose Trollope, deserves some credit for his brother-in-law's success as a novelist.

The voyage on the *Atrato* out of Southampton took about two weeks. Trollope was not bored, in spite of bad weather, because he had the final chapters of *The Bertrams* to finish and because he could use the time for his favourite card game of whist, though he was annoyed that the captain did not permit games to go on beyond 11 p.m. There were other minor annoyances: the claret was bad and the walnuts were rotten, and no doubt from time to time Trollope must have thought of the foxhounds racing across the Irish countryside. On 2 December the ship reached St Thomas in the Virgin Islands, the Danish colony which, somewhat surprisingly, was the main port for British ships. Trollope was quite enchanted when a woman, 'as black as my boot', came aboard to do the washing and handed him a rose, saying, 'That's for love, dear.' His first assignment was in Jamaica, but he found the work difficult as the temperature reached the 80s even in December. He grew increasingly restless as he realised his work would keep him away from home far longer than he had thought. He was not, however, the typical tourist, for he was annoyed that the miserable inns insisted that he must eat English food – roast beef and beer – when he wanted to try avocados and yams. While he disliked Kingston, he found the countryside delightful. Anxious for the celebrated view of the sunrise, he climbed, stick in hand, to the top of Blue Mountain, some 8,000 feet above sea level, pausing occasionally to refresh himself with brandy and water. His efforts were in vain: he spent a miserable, damp night on the mountain and could not even see the sun.

As much as he revelled in scenery, Trollope was even more interested in West Indian society, and one of his encounters became a cherished anecdote in literary circles: anxious for a bath and frustrated at the delay in getting it, he called out to a servant in his hotel, 'Halloo, old fellow! how about that bath?' When a second request met with no reply, he roared: 'Put down those boots, sir, and go and do as I bid you.' 'Who you call fellor? You speak to a gen'lman gen'lmanly, and den he fill de bath.' 'James,' said the mildly chastened Trollope with a bow, 'might I trouble you to leave those boots, and see the bath filled for me?' Just as with a West Country postmistress or an Irish letter carrier, anyone who stood up to his bluster gained his respect. Slavery had been abolished only twenty-five years before and there was still a considerable debate in England as to whether this had been successful. Trollope had inherited from his mother a detestation of slavery, but he was not sure that emancipation produced immediate gains for the former slaves. To him work was not only the greatest of personal delights, but the appetite for it indicated a superior civilisation. For 'idleness' he had his father's contempt: 'These people are a servile race, fitted by nature for the hardest physical work ... He *is* a man; and if you will, a brother; but he is the very idlest brother with which a hardworking workman was ever cursed.' Here he is poking fun at the emblem of the Abolitionists, used by Wedgwood in his famous plaque, showing a kneeling slave asking 'Am I not a man and a brother?' Trollope did not take enough account of the fact that the West Indies, particularly Jamaica, had suffered greatly as a result of Britain's adoption of free trade, which ruined the colonial sugar and coffee trade. The islands had exported twenty million pounds of coffee to Britain in 1831, but in the year of his arrival this had fallen to under three.[6]

He was particularly interested in the 'coloureds', those of mixed race, as he felt they would come to dominate the island. As a good Victorian believer in 'progress', he saw it as inevitable that the whites would be ousted by the coloureds. This would be, on the whole, a good thing because Britain would then have fulfilled her mission of establishing 'civilization, commerce, and education'. It might be that a British governor would still be sent decades hence by 'Queen Victoria's great-grandchild's grandchild', but for Trollope this was of little importance. 'We Britishers have a noble mission,' he wrote, and that was to spread civilisation, something which could not be measured by counting spots of red on the map.[7] In some ways this was like his own 'mission': once he had reorganised the postal service, it could be run efficiently under local control. In this he was very much an early

Victorian, uninfluenced by the Imperialism of the 1870s. He was not concerned so much with temporary power as with permanent influence. This is why he believed that 'Great Britain should surely be more proud of the United States than of any of her colonies'.

On 20 December *The Bertrams* was finally finished and, following the pattern he established in Egypt, Trollope wanted to begin a new book immediately. By this time he had mastered the art of composing a straightforward letter to a publisher. 'As I always have a prudent eye to the future', he told Edward Chapman about his idea for a new book when sending him the news that the final chapters of *The Bertrams* were on their way:

> I shall be glad to know whether you will think well of a volume of travels on these parts ... My idea is about 450 pages of the Dr. Thorne size ... to be put into one goodly volume ... to come out before Xmas. Mss – to be with you by 31 October – (most probably a good deal earlier.) Price £250 for three years. Whether this would suit you – or whether no – be kind enough to let me have an answer. Send it to Mr Tilley.

Perhaps he felt that a little flourish should end this telegraphic prose: 'Ah – I wish Providence had made me a publisher.' When Providence did so, it would not prove an entirely happy experience! Turning his mind to his first travel book naturally led him to think of the founder of the family firm: 'Brig *Linwood*. Dearest Mother ... Tom will be in England, I presume, when this reaches you, looking after the family literature. John Tilley says that he has done all that he can. His house is now quite full, and he *cannot* stow away any more Trollope books.' Poor Tilley! There were still over one hundred volumes to come! Trollope's knowledge of the 'family literature' is shown by the fact that he warned his mother that two dubious publishers were adding new titles to some of her earlier novels and re-issuing them as if they were new books. He knew her thirty-five novels well enough to spot a rogue title even when he was far from home. Apparently he also remembered her early teaching, for he excused himself: 'Do not be angry at the bad writing, for the ship tosses.' Tom, indeed, was in London negotiating with Chapman for a book by himself. This allowed him to sign an agreement on Anthony's behalf on 9 April for a West Indian book 'about 450 pages similar to Dr. Thorne'.[8]

Fanny Trollope had written some of her first travel book aboard ship and now, almost twenty-eight years later, her youngest son began *The West Indies and the Spanish Main* on a ship bound for Cuba. Writing provided solace for a miserable journey and a monotonous diet of salt pork, biscuits, bad coffee and yams. As he normally travelled with some of his own food, he had a small ham as well, and a friend had stuck a tin of sardines into his pocket. Yet the ship rolled so much 'in a nauseous manner, disturbing the two sardines which I have economically eaten, till I began to fear that my friend's generosity will become altogether futile'. As on all his travels, Trollope was well-armed with brandy and cigars. He even risked the danger from sharks by swimming from the side of the ship. One small shark was spotted, captured and then eaten: 'In spite of the popular prejudice', Trollope admitted, 'I have to declare it was delicious.'

Trollope was not pleased with his hotel in Havana, as he was forced to share a room with a stranger. When he complained to an American fellow guest, he found out he was comparatively lucky: 'One companion! why I have three; one walks about all night in a bed-gown, a second snores, and the other is dying.' However he found the Spanish colonial authorities delightful: they instantly won his regard by a gift of fine cigars, something for which he had a passion. For the rest of his life he would order prodigious quantities of Havana cigars to the delight of many of his friends though apparently not to Rose's. He was even permitted to see a sugar plantation with its slave labour, whose appalling conditions were normally kept from visitors. Yet, in spite of the kindness he met from the Spanish, he was convinced that Cuba must soon fall under the rule of the United States, which seemed highly likely as most Americans agreed with a Manifesto by their diplomats that 'by every law human and divine' they had the right to that island.[9] Here again we meet his devotion to the inevitability of 'progress', because Spain 'as a matter of course ... will go to the wall'. After Cuba he visited other islands and thought the importation of Chinese workers (altogether almost 200,000 Asians had been brought to the West Indies in the decade preceding his visit) would improve the economy by forcing the ex-slaves to work harder.

Trollope felt that travel books should be written on the spot: 'The descriptions and opinions came hot on to the paper from their causes. I will not say that this is the best way of writing ... But it is the best way of producing to the eye of the reader, and to his ear, that which the eye of the writer has seen and his ear heard.'[10] Therefore we can see his attitudes changing as he journeyed: in Jamaica he had said that a limited black franchise could work well. By the time he reached Central America, he had revised this opinion: 'As far as I am able to judge, a negro has not generally those gifts of God which enable one man to exercise rule and masterdom over his fellow-men. I myself should object strongly to be represented, say in the City of London, by any black man that I ever saw.'

He had not expected the trip to be so long, and he grew annoyed with official delays and with the ever-present heat which 'made me uncomfortable ... I lost all pleasure in eating, and indeed in everything else ... [I] was always glad when my watch would allow me to go to bed.' He was also beginning to suffer from travel fatigue caused by moving from island to island: 'In travelling these are the things which really occupy the mind. Where shall I sleep? Is there anything to eat? Can I have my clothes washed?' He was almost always frustrated in achieving a satisfactory answer to these perennial questions. Yet still he pressed on, accomplishing what he had been sent to do, examining accounts and measuring distances. As he often had to wait for replies, he had time for private travel in Central America, where his expansive energy helped restore his spirits. When he reached the isthmus of Panama he had to pay £2 10s to have his luggage transported from the Atlantic coast to the Pacific even though he only had 'the ordinary kit of a travelling Englishman ... a portmanteau, bag, desk, and hat box'. It must have been a large portmanteau as it kept sliding off the mule's back. 'No muleteer could ever make anything of it,' he recalled, 'it has been condemned in [the] Holy Land, in Jamaica, in Costa Rica, whenever it had to be fixed upon any animal's back.' In almost all of his future journeys, he would have difficulties about his luggage, but he could rarely bring himself to abandon the accoutrements that announced the arrival of the Victorian gentleman. In spite of the expense of land transport across the isthmus, Trollope was as pessimistic about the possibility of building a Panama Canal as he had been the previous year about one at Suez. (The failed attempt at a Panamanian canal had provided much of the Scatcherd fortune in *Doctor Thorne*.) He feared that even if engineering and climatic conditions could be overcome, it would still be a valuable resource in the hands of an incompetent and corrupt regime in Panama. He wondered: 'Who can tell what government will prevail.' Indeed, he had little regard for officials throughout Central America. Customs officers were even worse that those in Europe as they appeared to have no idea what they were searching for in Trollope's mounds of luggage. As he later wrote in his short story 'The Journey to Panama', they 'look at the trunks just as monkeys might do'.

Perhaps the officials were puzzled by Trollope's appearance: he was clad in a short canvas jacket and wore a straw hat from which hung a piece of white calico which only partially hid his large beard! It is hardly surprising that he and two companions mounted on mules were suspected of being 'filibusters' or American adventurers anxious to seize power. He had entered Costa Rica in this garb because he was anxious to make a long trek to see a volcano. His lazy guide tried to discourage him by announcing that people often failed to reach the mountain. 'But we won't be such people,' roared Trollope, 'Andiamos; Vamos.' Recounting this, he advised his readers: 'The first word which an Englishman learns in any language is that which signifies a determination to proceed.' Once at the volcano, he insisted upon going down into the crater – before breakfast. 'You'll surely kill yourself, Mr Trollope; you surely will,' warned a companion. Yet he knew that a new friend of his, the diplomat Sir William Ouseley, had recently made the descent. 'Sir William got as far as this. We will do better than Sir William. We will go down into that hole where we see the sulphur ... Look at the huge column of white smoke; how it comes all in this direction!' Down he plunged with customary impulsiveness until he reached a spot beyond Ouseley's achievement. 'What a triumph we will have over Sir William!' He now faced the more difficult task of getting back up as mist and sulphurous smoke nearly choked and blinded him. 'Going down hill,' the forty-four-year-old Trollope added, 'suits me better than going up. Years and obesity tell upon the wind sooner than they do on the legs – so, at least it is with me.' With great effort he hauled himself the final few yards out of the crater and fell exhausted onto the mountainside, where he slept despite the pouring rain.

Trollope's passion for new sights forced him onto a mule to ride from the Atlantic coast to the Pacific. The beasts made slow progress as they frequently sank in the mud. Finally his party reached the Serapiqui River, by means of which they could get to the great lake of Nicaragua. The canoe at least was more comfortable than the back of a mule:

> Here, for the first time in my life, I found my bulk and size to be of advantage to me ... having a seat to myself, being too weighty to share a bench with a neighbour. I therefore could lean back among the luggage; and with a cigar in my mouth, with a little ... weak brandy and water beside me, I found that the position had its charms.

Thus, relatively comfortable, while natives paddled his canoe, Trollope spent two days drifting down the river, watching macaws flying overhead and hearing monkeys chattering in the trees.

As in Egypt, Trollope was distrustful of the figures given him both by the Post Office and by private shipping interests. In one spot he was told that it took three days for a man to carry the mail on his horse across rough terrain. He was convinced that it could be done in two. Of course he was told that he knew nothing of the primitive roads. He announced: 'I will ask you to do nothing that I ... cannot do myself.' At

dawn the next morning he set out with the local courier. A particularly
bad horse and a miserably uncomfortable saddle (presumably the
'Western' type he would not have known) were provided. Nevertheless
he pressed on and resisted all the courier's pleas for a rest. By the time
he dismounted at night he was in a dreadful state and almost thought
he must concede defeat. Then he had an idea: at the inn he ordered two
bottles of brandy, poured them into a basin and sat in it! Tom, who
recounts this tale, said 'His description of the agonising result was
graphic!' Unfortunately Victorian restraint has denied it to us.
Knowing Trollope's temper and colourful language, it can be imagined.
Nevertheless the cure worked and the next day he was in his saddle
without pain, able to complete the journey in the two days he had
vowed.[11]

Trollope arrived in Bermuda in time for the celebration of Queen
Victoria's fortieth birthday on 24 May 1859. He saw enough of a local
prison to recall it later in a short story, 'Aaron Trow', where an escaped
convict attacks a woman in a lonely cottage. In one of his novels he
remembered speaking to convicts, including one murderer who
maintained that life imprisonment was wrong: he should have been
hanged or set free [*John Caldigate* LIV]. Trollope later recalled that the
island was beautiful, but 'triste', as the people appeared content to
accept their poverty. Nothing outraged him, or any other good
Victorian, more than this.[12]

> One cannot teach oneself not to be desirous of progress. One cannot but
> feel it sad to see people neglecting the good things which are under their
> feet ... There seemed to be no energy among the natives, no idea of going
> a-head, none of that principle of constant motion which is found so
> strongly developed among their great neighbours in the United States.

In Bermuda he finished his postal work and now could sail for home.
First, there was a long-planned diversion, a quick visit to the country
which had inspired the 'family literature'. There were no direct
sailings from Bermuda to England, so 'in company with a rather large
assortment of potatoes and onions' he sailed for New York. He had
originally hoped that Rose could meet him there, but this did not prove
possible. While he did not have time for a long stay he visited the
American publishing house of Harper and Brothers and talked about
writing stories for their magazine as well as about the republication of
his novels.[13] Mrs Trollope, like most European travellers, had praised
the still exquisite scenery of the Hudson valley, and so her son followed
some of her route though he regretted not visiting the Trenton Falls in

upstate New York. It had been the scene of the amusing incident we have noted: Mrs Trollope was about to make a scathing comment on Americans who carved their names on the rocks when suddenly she saw the words 'Trollope, England'.

However, he did reach his goal, the far grander Niagara Falls. In that farmhouse in Harrow, he must have heard stories from his mother and his two sisters of the mighty roaring waters, which to the nineteenth century symbolised the height of nature's power. When he reached the Falls he made his way to a lonely spot at the bottom and stood gazing at the awesome spectacle. This led him to erupt in *The West Indies and the Spanish Main* into one of those Carlyle-like interjections that disfigured his writing in the 1850s: 'Oh, my friend, let there be no one there to speak to thee then; no, not even a heart's brother. As you stand then speak only to the waters.' With Trollope, as with so many Victorian realists, the Romantic occasionally burst forth from beneath the sombre frock coat. After a short trip into Canada he returned to New York, where he boarded the *Africa* bound for Liverpool.

From Liverpool, which he reached on 3 July, Trollope made a hurried dash across to Dublin as he had been absent from his family for seven months. Indeed he had spent just under half of the last two years – two fox-hunting seasons no less – travelling on Post Office business, work that had nothing to do with his duties as Surveyor. He was soon on his way to London to make his official report, which pleased Rowland Hill. Hill was especially delighted that Trollope came back with a list of modifications to the existing packet service, which had been based on an Admiralty contract which Hill had disliked. Trollope's main recommendation was that Jamaica replace the Danish colony of St Thomas as the main centre for mail shipments. Ironically Jamaica, which Trollope disliked, benefited most by his visit. When his recommendations were adopted, they saved both time and money, the Post Office's abiding obsessions. This work received public recognition in the Postmaster General's next annual report:

> Mr. Anthony Trollope, as mentioned in the last report ... ably discharged a similar duty in the Mediterranean and in Egypt, and performed the new work assigned to him with even greater success. Not only did Mr. Trollope devise many improvements in the details of the service, and effect a considerable saving, but, although a landsman, was able to propose a scheme of routes for the mail packets.

The Hydrographer at the Admiralty admitted that Trollope's plans for shipping routes were better than those drawn up by the Admiralty: high praise for Trollope and welcome ammunition for Rowland Hill in his warfare with other departments.[14]

The West Indies and the Spanish Main was published on 1 November 1859, just under four months after the author's return. By his standards it is a short book, under 400 pages, and it is certainly a lively and colourful account. Years later in his *Autobiography* he felt it was 'on the whole ... the best book that has come from my pen'. It is easy to see why he thought so, for it is an intensely personal account and the elderly Trollope must have relived his adventures in climbing up a mountain and down a volcano when he reread it. No one today would accept his verdict. The book certainly has its merits, particularly the attempts, perhaps not always successful, to paint a picture of the places and people he saw. Throughout the book he was at war with the 'philanthropists', those people who were trying to mobilise English opinion on questions such as slavery. Trollope always thought it both morally and economically wrong, but he felt that many of 'the philanthropists' did not understand the complexities of slavery or indeed of emancipation. Many of Trollope's conclusions and much of his language could now be dismissed as 'racist', but it is important to set his views in the context of his time.

There had been a tremendous increase in anti-slavery feeling following the unparalleled success of Harriet Beecher Stowe's *Uncle Tom's Cabin*, which was even more popular in Britain than in America. Trollope detested Stowe as a writer: she was 'falsely sensational and therefore abominable'. (He seems not to have been influenced by the American's calling on his mother in Florence to pay her respects to the first novelist to use fiction in the war against slavery.) It is likely that Trollope, like most professional writers, resented the vast success of the Stowe book, although he must have learnt that she got no royalties for her non-American sales. The attacks throughout *The West Indies* on a 'Duchess' are aimed at the Duchess of Sutherland, who was Mrs Stowe's greatest fan and lionised her during her 1853 tour of Britain. Trollope's dislike of 'philanthropists' was far from unique: Dickens and Thackeray fully agreed. Dickens had depicted the archetypal busybody in Mrs Jellaby, while Thackeray had used his scathing wit in *Vanity Fair* [XXXIII] by inventing a Lady Emily Sheepshanks: 'A mature spinster, and having but faint ideas of marriage, her love for the blacks occupied almost all her feelings.' She was, Thackeray said, famous for her poem:

> Lead us to some sunny isle,
> Yonder in the western deep;
> Where the skies for ever smile,
> And the blacks for ever weep.

All three novelists resented the 'philanthropists' because they often appeared to think slavery the only moral question facing society, to the exclusion of evils closer to home which they did not wish to see. The most famous exponent of this view was Thomas Carlyle. In no sense was the inventor of 'Dr Pessimist Anticant' a disciple of Carlyle. Yet if we look at that name it embodies Trollope's conflicting views of the Scottish thinker: he disliked his pessimism, but he admired his attacks on cant. The book's conclusions naturally pleased Carlyle. (Indeed a modern West Indian politician and historian has denounced Trollope's book as an echo, 'merely an expurgated version of Carlyle's *Nigger Question* of some ten years before'.) Almost two years later George Eliot took Trollope to tea at Carlyle's house. G.H. Lewes, who was present, wrote to Tom Trollope: 'Carlyle had read and *agreed* with the West Indian book, and the two got on very well together.'[15]

The book also pleased *The Times*, which devoted three articles to fulsome praise of it. Significantly the paper placed them as news items and not as book reviews. Trollope later met the author of these articles but did not give his name in the *Autobiography*. They were almost certainly inspired, if not written, by Mowbray Morris, the Manager of *The Times* and the brother-in-law of the editor, John Delane. As the son of a West Indian planter, Morris would have relished Trollope's favourable remarks about a group usually vilified in the English press. Using language far sharper than Trollope's, 'The Jupiter' could not say enough in praise of its erstwhile satirist:

> We looked for amusement from Mr Trollope and we are inveigled into instruction ... Floods of pathetic eloquence and long years of Parliamentary struggling have taught us to imagine that the world was made for Sambo ... The negro is, no doubt, a very amusing and a very amiable fellow, and we ought to wish him well; but he is also a lazy animal, without any foresight, and therefore requiring to be led and compelled ... [this book is] the most useful, if not the most brilliant, volume which he has yet published.

Trollope was delighted with these articles because they 'made the fortune of the book'. They also meant that, as Trollope himself wrote, 'I was much raised in my position as an author'. So much so that when he went to Chapman and Hall in that same summer of 1859 to negotiate his next contract he was able to demand a sizeable increase.[16]

Two months before this Trollope had been given an equally warm reception from *The Times*'s great enemy, the *Saturday Review*, a publication devoted to Tory and High Church interests:

It is a great thing that the author of a book should be clever. It is a great thing for the reader ... Mr Trollope seems to us to be more accurately described by the word 'clever' than perhaps any other living English writer ... To most English readers this volume will be like a new discovery of the West Indies. Hitherto, they have been mere names of hot places peopled with the ghosts of ruined planters and lazy niggers ... Mr Trollope gives us exactly what we want and he gives it us in a shape which we cannot praise too highly.

Like *The Times*, the *Saturday Review* devoted more than one issue to praising the book. The *Spectator* agreed that this was an 'important blue-book in the disguise of a popular work from Mudie's'. With *The West Indies and the Spanish Main* Anthony Trollope achieved his desire: he was now someone to notice, to study and to quote in serious discussion. By 1869 the book had gone into six editions. The year after publication in London it was republished in New York. In the United States, where political controversy about slavery was approaching a climax, the book's appearance was topical, to say the least. A work by the son of one of the first outspoken foes of slavery which described the ill effects of emancipation was welcomed by defenders of the 'peculiar institution'. One of the most fanatical was Edmund Ruffin, a Virginian who had achieved eminence in scientific studies about soil conservation as a way to preserve the economy of the southern states. He finished the book on 1 October 1860 and was delighted. To him Trollope had furnished 'plenty of facts to show, and admits the manifest conclusions, that the improvement of the negroes is hopeless'. He did criticise Trollope for being so 'foolish as to rely upon the future amalgamation of the white and black races to produce a mixed breed capable of self-support and industry'. Ruffin was annoyed that Trollope 'is also an advocate (rather cold indeed) of the act of emancipation – though his book is full of evidence of its ruinous effects'. Within six months Ruffin was given the 'honour' of firing the first shot of the war that would end slavery. When the Confederacy was defeated he committed suicide.[17]

*

Trollope did not read any of these reviews in his house at Donnybrook. For, on 2 August 1859, when in London on postal business, he sat down in a remarkably jovial mood and wrote:[18]

To ye. ladie of Waltham House in ye. Countie of Herts.
These –
Deareste Madame

Havinge withe infinite trouble & pain inspected & surveyed and pokèd manie and diverse holes in ye aforesaid mansion, I have at ye laste hirèd and taken it for yr. moste excellente ladieship – to have and to hold from ye term of St Michaels mass next comynge. The whiche Waltham House is now the property of one Mistress Wilkins, who has let it to your lovynge lord & husband for 7-14-or 21 yeares, with manie and diverse clauses which shall hereafter as time may serve be explained to your excellente ladieship –

In ye. mean time I am with all true love and affection your ladieships devoted servant and husband

Anthony Trollope
The second daye of this monthe of Auguste in the yeare of our Lord 1859.

Rose must have been as delighted with the style as with the contents of this letter, as it is among the relatively few from her husband that she preserved.

At long last his dream had come: he had been given an English surveyorship over the Eastern District. As early as 1852 Rowland Hill wrote that he 'deserves promotion'.[19] Since then he had only enhanced his standing by his work in Ireland, by his special assignments in England and Scotland and by his missions to Egypt and the West Indies. His new area included Essex, Suffolk, Norfolk, Cambridgeshire and Huntingdonshire, as well as parts of Bedfordshire and Hertfordshire. For Trollope it was an excellent location: it was close to the literary and social delights of London and it boasted many fox-hunts.

*

Soon Trollope would become a familiar figure as he leapt across the ditches of Essex in pursuit of a fox. 'Bulky' and 'bearded' are the two adjectives most frequently used to describe his appearance in middle age. One art historian has seen him as the personification of the Victorian look with 'the wiry entanglement of whisker and spectacle behind which Trollope's face was almost invisible under the bald crown'. Yet this is the look of the mature Trollope, the successful author and clubman. It is regrettable that we know so little about how he looked in the first half of his life. Of his youthful appearance, especially, little is known. He was tall, strong and powerfully built, but he thought he was 'ugly'. Tom describes himself as a child 'sturdily built, with flaxen hair, rosy cheeks, and blue eyes; broad of hand and foot; strong as a little pony – a veritable Saxon in type'. Given the close physical resemblance between the brothers in later life, it is likely that Anthony shared at least some of those characteristics.[20]

The best description Trollope gave of himself as a mature man was in *The West Indies*. It occurred during that particularly reflective period when his boat lay becalmed off Jamaica. He studied the passport the Spanish consul had given him to go to Cuba. Perhaps thinking of those French passport officers he had so resented, he was pleased that the Spaniard had found him tall; he had also been tactful about his weight. 'Never before this have I obtained in a passport any more dignified description of my body than robust.' The consul had peered through Trollope's spectacles and decided that his eyes were blue: for some curious reason observers never agreed on the colour of his eyes. The official decided that his hair was chestnut, but it was not this that had offended Trollope:

> Now any but a Spaniard would have declared that as to hair, I was bald ... If I have any personal vanity, it is wrapped up in my beard. It is a fine, manly article of dandyism, that wears well in all climates, and does not cost much, even when new. Well, what has the Don said of my beard? It is *poblada*. I would give five shillings for the loan of a Spanish dictionary at this moment. *Poblada*!

Trollope had probably acquired his thick (*poblada*) beard a few years before, when a curious mania for beards swept over British manhood. Who can ever explain such sudden mass conversions? It is as impossible to understand why millions of men in the mid-nineteenth century suddenly sprouted beards as it is to explain why one hundred years later millions of men stuffed themselves into blue-jeans to express their individuality. It is often thought that soldiers returning from the Crimea set the fashion: the *Manchester Guardian* noted that when the Queen's cousin, the Duke of Cambridge, returned in 1855 'he was bearded "like the pard" – lip, cheek and chin being alike innocent of the razor ... our young men at home, who can ring for their shaving water ... are cultivating a beard in addition to a luxuriant moustache and whisker.' Before this a beard was regarded as the sign of a 'communist', according to a Tory Foreign Secretary, while his Liberal opponent, Palmerston, in a letter quoted by Trollope in his book about that politician, referred to the 1848 Chartists as 'whiskered and bearded rioters'. Whatever the cause, the new fashion spread rapidly: by 1874, only two MPs out of a total of 658 were said to be beardless.[21]

After the Crimean War beards increasingly became the sign of 'manly' appearance.

It is likely that Trollope's beard made its debut about the time of the Crimean War, for none of the comments about his postal work in the West of England describe him as bearded, when it would still have been unusual. Elizabeth Browning was somewhat surprised by it in 1860: 'Anthony has an extraordinary beard to be grown in England,' she wrote to her brother.[22] Although the Spanish consul described it as 'chestnut' most later witnesses called it black and, in due course, white. Since Trollope refers to his beard as 'a manly article of dandyism', it is likely that he saw it, as he had seen fox-hunting attire, as a way to escape from the increasingly drab uniform of the Victorian gentleman. Up to the late 1850s he seems to have resisted the idea that complete black was the only choice for a man, as one of the earliest photographs shows him in checked trousers, but in time he conformed. The beard, spectacles and virtual black uniform often made it difficult to distinguish one man from another, and two years after Trollope's death people seeing Edward Lear often thought they had seen Trollope.

Naturally beards began to sprout in his fiction as well as on his face. When young Frank Gresham returns to Barsetshire in the mid-1850s from a trip to Egypt he sports a long beard whose 'silken sheen' captivates the young ladies. Even his old-fashioned father is proud of 'this patriarchal adornment' though he wonders how his son can eat soup. Apparently this was a difficulty, for Trollope has Frank 'covering it with every spoonful, as men with beards always do' [*Doctor Thorne* XXXIII, XXXV]. In real life one young officer on a visit to Waltham House was fascinated by Trollope's 'long thick beard, which it was difficult to keep one's eyes off, as it had a singular attraction for fragments of cigar ash'.[23] Increasingly Trollope enjoyed depicting his male creations with beards. Beards, according to Trollope, gave 'character' to the face [*Can You Forgive Her?* XXII]. Good men, like John Eames, have beards which they are proud of, while unprincipled scoundrels like Burgo Fitzgerald – 'a man whom neither man nor woman could help regarding as a thing beautiful to behold' – refuses to disguise 'his almost godlike face' with a beard [*Can You Forgive Her?* XXIX]. Within a decade the beard had become the badge not only of respectability but of manliness.

Other than his beard the most noticeable thing about Trollope was his size. Both surviving Trollope sons inherited their height from their father, and Anthony was not much under six foot. With the passing years he put on weight, somewhat surprisingly considering his constant activity. His reference to his 'bulk' in the canoe in *The West Indies* implies that he had been a large man, in all senses, for some time. In the same book, however, he actually gives his weight: fifteen stone. Trollope did not have strong sight and this often caused him to stare through his small spectacles. One difficulty in describing his appearance is his habit of exaggerating any feature to make it appear worse. Thus his fifteen stone become his 'bulk', and his eyes are not weak – he is, rather, 'blind'. Trollope had no illusions that he was a handsome man, though he did take considerable care to dress well and he had a veritable passion for cleanliness. He did not like the mid-Victorian mania for photographic *cartes de visite* for one simple reason: 'I do not like photographs, and dislike my own worse than all others.'[24]

*

When in New York Trollope had paid a brief visit to Harper Brothers and had agreed to supply them with two 'tales' or short stories at £20 or $100 each. They were to be based on his foreign trips, with each story set in a different country, and were to be published in *Harper's New Monthly Magazine*, then in its ninth year. This was a breakthrough for Trollope: by publishing in America he would be reaching a new market, and even if it was smaller than that of the United Kingdom it was still profitable. More important, he was venturing into a new field: short stories. Although the form was relatively weak in England, it was well established in America through writers like Washington Irving, Poe and Hawthorne. Even if English writers of short stories never reached the artistic achievements of Americans or Frenchmen in Trollope's lifetime, they were still able to establish the genre in England. (To some degree the serialisation of novels may have lessened the attraction of short stories.) Once back in Dublin Trollope began work and by August he had posted the first two, 'The Courtship of Susan Bell', set in America, and 'Relics of General Chassé', set in Antwerp.

Exhaustive travels, the daily work of a Surveyor, the demands of a new position, the taking of a new house, the requirements of editors or the deadlines of publishers could not keep Trollope from his annual holiday in 1859. Once again he would combine business with pleasure. On 1 September he wrote to the New York publisher to thank him for the £40 and to suggest a new project: a series of stories which would 'run to from 24 to 28 in number, & would average in length 10 of your monthly magazine pages'. The series would include the two already sent. He would keep the right to republish the stories in two collections to be called 'Tales of all Countries'. Indeed he began work on his stories the same day he wrote to New York. At some date, presumably at the end of October, he noted in his work-sheet for his current novel beside the dates 1 September to 29 October, 'Pyrenees Five Tales'.[25]

The Pyrenees were a favourite holiday spot for Victorians, who liked the bracing air and the opportunity for walks in the mountains. Of the stories Trollope wrote on holiday the most notable was 'La Mère Bauche', set in a Pyrenees village. It is the touching story of an orphan girl who is adopted by an ambitious innkeeper, La Mère Bauche. The girl becomes a chambermaid and falls in love with her employer's son. Their love is frustrated and she is forced to marry an older man. In despair she throws herself off a cliff. If we contrast this French tale with his historical novel, *La Vendée*, written a dozen years before, we see not only how far Trollope had developed his skills as a writer but how far he made use of the setting of his story. In 'La Mère Bauche' he uses small details of hotel life that he most likely had observed: no one can have any meal outside the prescribed hours and the *patronne*, Mère Bauche, indicates the current level of her regard by the amount of cognac she spoons into a guest's coffee. As in so many of his short stories, this tale is remarkable for the sympathy he shows for the poor, a sentiment less observable in his novels. This tragic tale often reads more like Balzac than Trollope. In the event, while Harper Brothers paid for the story they refused to publish it, perhaps because of the suicide.

For the 1859 trip the Trollopes, including Tom and Tilley, no longer needed passports to enter France, as Napoleon III had recently freed British subjects from that annoyance. Yet even if Trollope felt gratitude to the Emperor, which is unlikely, he soon lost it and replaced it with a personal grievance. Rose remembered tersely: 'Emperor nearly drives over us in Bayonne.' The Trollopes spent part of their autumn tour at Biarritz, where Napoleon III and Empress Eugénie had a holiday villa. The Emperor was not only relaxing after his recent war in Italy but was trying to keep the Empress from learning about his new mistress. So perhaps 'the Imperial Sphinx' had much on his mind when his coach nearly ran down the Trollopes. In any case Elizabeth Browning was delighted to find Trollope, just a year later, 'Anti-Napoleonist'. Since the sixteenth century, the political attitudes of many English writers have been greatly affected by the current continental 'tyrant'. The Victorians were lucky to have the comparatively mild and slightly comical figure of Napoleon III. Nevertheless Trollope asserted, a decade after the exiled Emperor's death, that even the memory of the man was detestable to him.[26]

*

In addition to having reached his first agreement with an American publisher Trollope had also signed an agreement with Chapman and Hall on 2 August for a new novel, *Castle Richmond*, which he began writing two days later and which he set aside for his 'tales'. Fortified by the accolades in *The Times* and his agreement with Harper Brothers, he demanded and got £600 from his publishers, an increase of £200 over *The Bertrams*. *Castle Richmond*, which would not be published until 10 May 1860, was a farewell to Ireland, the country where he had lived for almost two decades: 'I am now leaving the Green Isle and my old friends, and would fain say a word of them as I do so.' The novel is set at the time of the Famine and some of its harrowing descriptions have been quoted in an earlier chapter. The Famine forms a stark background to a rather complicated plot about the legitimate heir to an estate in County Cork, not that far from Mallow, where the Trollopes had lived. Bigamy, illegitimacy and blackmail all play a part in the story. Trollope began the novel with a curious apology:

> I wonder whether the novel-reading world ... will be offended if I lay the plot of this story in Ireland! That there is a strong feeling against things Irish it is impossible to deny. Irish servants need not apply; Irish acquaintances are treated with limited confidence; Irish cousins are regarded as being decidedly dangerous; and Irish stories are not popular with the booksellers.

'I do strongly protest,' announced the novelist, 'against the injustice of the above conclusions', and he continued: 'Irish cousins I have none. Irish acquaintances I have by dozens; and Irish friends ... whom I can love and cherish – almost as well, perhaps, as though they had been born in Middlesex. Irish servants I have had some in my house for years, and never had one that was faithless, dishonest, or intemperate.'

In the 'Conclusion' of the novel Trollope was pleased to observe how much conditions had improved in Ireland in the last dozen years. He attributed the changes to hard work and Providence for 'His mercy endureth for ever.' He accepted that much remained to be done and that many of the improvements were not yet fully established but, employing one of his favourite Shakespearian allusions: 'The cakes and ale are there; – and the ginger, too, very hot in the mouth.'

As he stood on the deck of the ferry in November 1859 and saw the disappearing view of the beautiful bay of Dublin and the resort of Kingstown with its hotels and its obelisk of George IV, his mood must have been markedly different from that of eighteen years before when, as a clerk of twenty-six, he had first seen Ireland. Now, at the age of forty-four, he was returning permanently to England with a wife he had met in Kingstown, an important position in the Post Office and a growing reputation as one of the most popular novelists of his time. Ireland, in many ways, had been good to him, and he also to Ireland, for no one had worked harder to give her an efficient, speedy and honest postal service, which aided the spread of commerce and solaced the cottages of the lonely.

In *Castle Richmond* Trollope's genuine sadness at leaving Ireland comes through, particularly when describing another family's departure for England in a chapter significantly entitled 'Preparations for Going', written within weeks of his own departure. For a man in his mid-forties there was a pang in leaving his house and his garden in the land where he had discovered how to be happy [XXXII]:

> Let all who have houses ... think how considerable a part of their life's pleasures consists in their interest in the things around them ... When will the seakale be fit to cut, and when will the crocuses come up? will the violets be sweeter than ever? and the geranium cuttings, are they thriving? we have dug, and manured, and sown, and we look forward to the reaping ... The very furniture which ministers to our daily use, is loved and petted; and in decorating our rooms we educate ourselves in design.

Yet it was not only the pleasures of house and garden that Trollope loved and knew he would miss. There were deeper emotions as well:

> The place in church which has been our own for years, – is not that dear to us, and the voice that has told us of God's tidings – even though the drone become more evident as it waxes in years, and though it grows feeble and indolent? And the faces of those who have lived around us, do we not love them too, the servants who have worked for us, and the children who have first toddled beneath our eyes and prattled in our ears, and now run their strong races, screaming loudly, splashing us as they pass ... Do they not all contribute to the great sum of our enjoyment? All men love such things, more or less, even though they know it not. And women love them even more than men.

There are few other passages in his writings which so summon up the personality of Anthony Trollope, moving among the things he held dear. This is the quiet, domestic, kindly man, not the boisterous and exuberant celebrity he was about to become. This deep affection for objects and the investment of them with an almost spiritual significance is characteristic of his age. Did not Cardinal Newman always kiss his bed when he was leaving a place he had held dear, and did not the Queen herself ensure that every possession of Prince Albert should become a relic? Trollope's farewell passage also shows his attachment to the regular, what then seemed timeless, flow of life, a life measured by the return of spring and crocuses, not a world where instant communication and lightning transport almost abolish the seasons and threaten nature itself. And then there is that very Victorian reserve even in the midst of an emotional passage. As the sentences reveal the deepest emotions, it is necessary to add a small hint of humour: the drone of the clergyman and the prattle of the infant. These almost constitute an embarrassed cough in print, lest the rich warm heart of the writer become too apparent.

*

On 21 November 1859 Trollope took up his new duties as Surveyor of the Eastern District and settled into his new home at Waltham Cross. Orders had to be given to make the house comfortable: 'perhaps ten ton' of coal was needed just for the larger coal hole. 'I hope he will give me the best household coal; otherwise of course I cannot get more from him', something which may seem petty to those who have never had bad coal. Trollope, at least, was prepared to pay ready money, a rare event for Victorian tradesmen. Moving entailed not only a sentimental farewell to Ireland but much hard work, most of which must have fallen on Rose: 'Who does not know how terrible are those preparations for house-moving; – how infinite in number are the articles which must be packed, how inexpressibly uncomfortable is the period of packing, and how poor and tawdry is the aspect of one's belongings while they are thus in a state of dislocation?' People who 'understand the world and have money commensurate with their understanding' hire professional removers and take themselves off 'for a fortnight to Brighton' [*The Small House at Allington* XLIX].

Waltham House was located on the borders of Essex, Middlesex and Hertfordshire, a county which had been the residence both of his grandfather, the Rev. Anthony Trollope, and his rich great-uncle Meetkerke. Trollope followed the usual Victorian custom of 'taking' the house on a lease; later, and somewhat unusually, he bought the freehold. Waltham Cross took its name and fame from the great memorial cross erected by Edward I in 1294 to the memory of his Queen, Eleanor. As with all 'Eleanor Crosses' it marked the spot where the Queen's body rested on its final journey to Westminster. There was an even earlier historical association, as the great Norman Abbey contained the remains of the last Anglo-Saxon King, Harold, which had been carried there after his death at Hastings. Waltham House was a solid, early-eighteenth-century brick house of four stories with an elegant door crowned by a fanlight. There were buildings on either side forming a courtyard into which visitors' carriages could enter. One wing was given over to horses, while the other became offices for the clerks who assisted the Surveyor in his postal work.

One great benefit of Trollope's position was that he could do much of his work at home. In the post office wing, for which he received rent, the clerks answered letters complaining of postal irregularities or delays. Much time was taken up with compiling statistics for the GPO. Every postmaster in the district had printed instructions from Trollope requiring him to complete a form for every error in delivery, giving such details as the time of the letter's arrival. The age of government forms was well under way, for postmasters were reminded that there was a different form for 'Registered Letter Irregularities' and the 'Failure of Letter Bills'. The Surveyor had to make certain that the letter-carriers in his district obeyed the increasing number of regulations, such as one prohibiting them from receiving Christmas 'boxes'. He also had to decide some quite ludicrous cases: in 1862, a letter-carrier was taking a letter to a butcher in the pleasant town of Kelvedon in Essex, which Trollope knew well from his fox-hunting. Suddenly a crow swooped down, grabbed the letter and, by the time the distressed postman reached the field where the crow had landed, the impudent bird had ripped a cheque for £30 in pieces! Trollope himself spent much time inspecting the post offices in his particularly extensive district as well as visiting people who made complaints. Of course all this travel allowed him to claim his travelling allowance. Because of his closeness to London, he was frequently asked to attend committee meetings at the GPO. Although he could be very combative at such gatherings, his gentle side came to the fore when he saw someone in distress. In particular, he tried to help young men who were anxious to get on as he had once been. We have seen how he had helped J.B. Blake, who had been his stationery clerk, even to the extent of standing surety for the bond required for certain postal positions. The news that Blake, 'a very deserving young man', had died of consumption and left a widowed mother, must have struck some bitter memories in Trollope's mind. He wrote to the Postmaster General to see if a clerkship could be found for Blake's younger brother so that the family would not be left without support.[27]

*

When *Castle Richmond* was published in the spring of 1860 it added little to Trollope's reputation. It cannot have proved in great demand at

Mudie's, and within a few months it was being sold off by the great literary despot at nine shillings, less than a third its original price. Apparently 'the novel reading world' had no desire to roam amid the sombre scenes of the Irish Famine when they had a comforting tale of the rectories and country houses of Barsetshire to absorb them. To a large extent he was becoming a victim of his own success: by the time *Castle Richmond* was published, another book, his first serialised novel, would be a literary sensation. As the *Saturday Review* cleverly put it: 'Mr. Trollope is in the position of a man who, after becoming the father of an enormous family in a very short time, takes at last to having twins.'[28]

Trollope had chosen – or rather the fortunes of the Post Office had picked – just the right moment for his return to England. That same year, 1859, saw the publication of books that are still seen as embodying Victorian England: George Eliot's *Adam Bede*, Darwin's *Origin of Species*, Dickens's *A Tale of Two Cities*, John Stuart Mill's *On Liberty* and Tennyson's *Idylls of the King*. Within the next two years would appear *The Mill on the Floss*, *Great Expectations*, *The Woman in White*, not to mention *Essays and Reviews*, that collection of essays by prominent clergymen – 'the seven against Christ' – which began to make 'doubt' as fashionable as crinoline.[29] (It is indicative of the vast difference between French and English literature at the time that the 1850s in France had seen the publication of Flaubert's *Madame Bovary* and Baudelaire's *Fleurs du Mal*, works far from the close at Barchester!) Millais was busy with his painting, the lions were being placed in Trafalgar Square, Palmerston was breakfasting on mutton chops in Downing Street, the Queen and Prince Albert's ninth child was in the nursery at Balmoral, reform was once again moving forward slowly, India passed under direct Imperial control and Italy was slowly being unified. God seemed in His heaven, in spite of *Essays and Reviews*, and all seemed right with the world – at least to those who could afford a Mudie's subscription.

In the autumn of 1859 – shortly before Trollope left Ireland – this busy literary world was full of rumours about a new magazine to start in January 1860. After much debate Thackeray had exercised his privilege as editor-designate and christened it the *Cornhill Magazine*, after the location of the offices of the publisher, George Smith. Trollope may well have heard the news from Chapman, who may also have mentioned that Thackeray had told him how much he admired Trollope's novels. Thackeray had for some time been his literary hero but they had never met, even though Trollope had known some of his cousins at Hadley. Both Mrs Trollope and Tom had known Thackeray in France in the 1830s, and indeed Thackeray had been nearly killed in an accident while on one of Mrs Trollope's beloved picnics near Paris. However, Trollope took no advantage of such distant memories when, only two days after his return from holiday in the Pyrenees, he began a letter to Thackeray as 'Dear Sir'. He offered to write some stories for Thackeray's magazine. With characteristic honesty he had explained his agreement with *Harper's* which also let Thackeray know his rate of pay.[30]

This new sideline in short stories seemed a sensible way to make use of his travels as well as to bring in extra revenue. He had also undertaken to provide another publication with stories: this was *Cassell's Illustrated Family Newspaper*, a weekly periodical established by John Cassell, a well-known teetotal and radical publisher, earlier in the 1850s. Cassell paid him £40 for each 'tale', a sum which has to be seen in context: even London letter-carriers, the 'pedestrian post-trotters' as *The Times* called them, received at the most £1 3s 8d a week, while rural carriers in Trollope's new district received far less than that. Thus the five short stories which Trollope had written, mainly while on holiday, brought him £200 or almost four times the annual wage of a postman who walked fifteen miles every day and had no holidays.[31]

It may be that Trollope had heard of Thackeray's leisurely ways because in a postscript to his letter he asked for a reply 'as soon as may be convenient'. Within three days he had one, but not from Thackeray. It came from the new magazine's publisher, George Smith, who wrote that they would accept the short stories at the rate Trollope had suggested. Smith went on: 'We should however much prefer a continuous story ... equivalent to the bulk of an ordinary three volume novel, and for the entire copyright of which we should be happy to pay you One Thousand pounds.' This must have made pleasing reading at Trollope's breakfast table – one assumes that the Surveyor's letters were in time for his breakfast! For the first time, his earnings from a book would exceed his official salary; for the first time they would surpass his mother's fees, and for the first time he would enter the highest rank of authorship, the serialised novel.[32]

George Smith was one of the greatest figures in that golden age of publishing. Trollope later said he never 'let anything worth doing slip through his fingers, rated a manuscript's value too high or too low, or ever misjudged the humour of the hour and the taste of the public'. (Actually Smith made one conspicuous mistake only a few months later when he allowed Wilkie Collins's *The Woman in White* to slip through his fingers.) Smith was a good example of the self-made man of wealth driven by a restless energy and a genuine desire to do good.

Like many great publishers, Smith was Scottish by descent. After an apprenticeship in his father's bookselling and stationery business he expanded the firm into the lucrative trade with India and dealt in all types of goods. He was a superb entrepreneur: on his honeymoon he heard about the discovery of gold in Australia and immediately despatched a supply of revolvers, believing, correctly, that violence followed gold. Smith used his vast wealth to promote many of the great literary institutions of Victorian England: in addition to the *Cornhill*, he later founded the *Pall Mall Gazette* and at the end of his life, the *Dictionary of National Biography*. He explained what a publisher required: 'An expert knowledge of all forms of business but a taste for speculation and a high degree of courage in taking risks. Many able and cultured men fail just at this point.' Yet his greatest contribution to English literature had occurred in his early twenties. He later described the event to Trollope. He had found a manuscript in his office which he began reading at nine in the morning and continued till evening, 'absorbed in the small, clear calligraphy enshrining such strange, strong thought'. He was, therefore, the first reader outside the Yorkshire vicarage to be enthralled by *Jane Eyre*. Charlotte Brontë found her patron 'very pleasant' and '*practical*', views echoed by Trollope.[33] Smith believed that good writing was fostered by liberal payments and he used his fortune to pay writers well: this proved a good investment for him and a boon for readers.

Smith's letter was soon followed by a charming one from the new editor, making it plain that he wanted far more than just one novel: 'Whatever a man knows about life and its doings that let us hear about. You must have tossed a deal about the world, and have countless sketches in your memory ... Please to think if you can furbish up any of these besides the novel. When events occur on wh. you can have a good lively talk, bear us in mind.' Trollope was delighted that Thackeray wanted him to write something other than fiction. His literary hero saw him as a serious writer with something more than a talent for amusing tales. 'One of our chief objects in this magazine,' continued Thackeray, 'is the getting out of novel spinning, and back into the world.' This also would have pleased Trollope unless it were meant to imply that one wrote novels only for money. Thackeray immediately laid this doubt to rest in a manner guaranteed to delight Trollope:

Don't understand me to disparage our craft, especially *your* wares. I often say I am like the pastry cook, and don't care for tarts, but prefer bread and cheese – but the public loves the tarts (luckily for us), and we must bake & sell them. There was quite an excitement in my family one evening when Paterfamilias (who goes to sleep over a novel almost always when he tries it after dinner) came up stairs to the Drawing Room wide awake and called for the second volume of The Three Clerks.

This letter made such an impression on the Trollopes that Anthony included it in his *Autobiography*, while Rose cut off the signature for the autograph, a common and infuriating Victorian custom.[34]

It is of course quite extraordinary that an author should have been asked to have the opening chapters of a novel ready to launch a magazine only some two months before it was scheduled to appear and all due to a chance letter. Trollope himself explained the circumstances years later, although he characteristically underestimated the high regard which his hero had for his work:

> I was astonished that work should be required in such haste, knowing that much preparation had been made, and that the service of almost any English novelist might have been obtained if asked for in due time. It was my readiness that was needed, rather than any other gift! The riddle was read to me after a time. Thackeray had himself intended to begin with one of his own great novels, but had put it off till it was too late. *Lovel the Widower* was commenced at the same time with my own story, but ... was not substantial enough to appear as the principal joint at the banquet. Though your guests will undoubtedly dine off the little delicacies ... there must be a heavy saddle of mutton ... I was the saddle of mutton, Thackeray having omitted to get his joint down to the fire in time enough. My fitness lay in my capacity for quick roasting.

Trollope hurried over to England and arrived in London on Thursday morning, 3 November and left the next day. (This is one of the rare times in the *Autobiography* when he gives days of the week.) Faced with the prospect of having a novel organised and the first part written in time for a January publication, Trollope thought the obvious solution was to offer the half-completed *Castle Richmond*. Chapman and Hall generously agreed, but George Smith did not. 'I demurred,' he later recalled. 'An Irish novel would not suit my public. His genius shone in delineating clerical life and character and I wanted a clerical novel.' Trollope later recalled, 'The details were so interesting that had a couple of archbishops been demanded, I should have produced them.'[35]

Trollope wasted no time. On that Friday evening in November, as his train sped through the West Country – through that mythical Barsetshire – towards the Irish ferry-boat, his pencil began to write the opening sentences of his tenth novel, which he set in the area he was passing through: 'When young Mark Robarts was leaving college, his

father might well declare that all men began to say all good things to
him, and to extol his fortune in that he had a son blessed with so
excellent a disposition. This father was a physician living at Exeter.'
Because of his friendship with a fellow Harrovian, Mark eventually
finds himself with a comfortable clerical living, a beautiful wife who is
naturally endowed with a few thousand pounds and a delightful house
that gives the novel its name: *Framley Parsonage*.

Even by Trollope's standards the speed with which he wrote was
astonishing. It had always been his practice to have a large part of a
novel completed before approaching a publisher. Yet, in the midst of
moving house and taking up a new position, he wrote the first
instalment and handed it to Smith when he arrived in London on 22
November. By the end of the month he had completed over 200 pages.
It would be impossible to better his own summary of *Framley
Parsonage*:[36]

> I had got into my head an idea of what I meant to write, – a morsel of the
> biography of an English clergyman who should not be a bad man, but one
> led into temptation by his own youth and by the unclerical accidents of
> the life of those around him. The love of his sister for the young lord was
> an adjunct necessary, because there must be love in a novel. And then by
> placing Framley Parsonage near Barchester, I was able to fall back upon
> my old friends Mrs. Proudie and the archdeacon. Out of these slight
> elements I fabricated a hodge-podge ... The story was thoroughly
> English. There was a little fox-hunting and a little tuft-hunting, some
> Christian virtue and some Christian cant. There was no heroism and no
> villainy. There was much Church, but more love-making.

Underneath his typically off-hand summary can be found those
subjects that had been present in his writing throughout the decade.
Robarts achieves his success by his charm and by good luck, but he is
almost corrupted by success just as another clergyman, who makes his
appearance in this book, Josiah Crawley, is nearly crushed by poverty
and failure.

When the *Cornhill* appeared on 1 January 1860 *Framley Parsonage*
was given pride of place – first violin, as Thackeray said – and it made
the future of both the author and the periodical. The magazine had a
wide appeal because of its judicious mix of fiction and serious articles.
The printers had to work overtime as 120,000 copies were needed to
satisfy public demand. These contained the first three chapters of the
novel, which introduced readers to the new characters, Mark Robarts
and his patron, Lady Lufton and her son, as well as to old favourites,
such as Bishop and Mrs Proudie. Thackeray paid it a charming

compliment in the first 'Roundabout Paper', published in that opening number, by mentioning the custom on transatlantic steamers when the first night's dinner featured great moulded jellies decorated with British and American flags. In the same way the new magazine featured the first chapters of Trollope's novel as well as those of the shorter Thackeray story, *Lovel the Widower*: 'Two novels under two flags, the one that ancient ensign which has hung before the well-known booth of *Vanity Fair*; the other that fresh and handsome standard which has lately been hoisted on *Barchester Towers*. Pray, sir, or madam, to which dish will you be helped.'

Within a few months Thackeray himself acknowledged, with no bitterness, that the readers clearly preferred the 'fresh standard'. If one considers the likely readership of the 120,000 copies, given both the size of Victorian families and the fact that the magazine could be borrowed from some circulating libraries, Trollope's readership was not far from a million. Mrs Gaskell told her publisher, Smith: 'I wish Mr Trollope would go on writing Framley Parsonage for ever. I don't see any reason why it should ever come to an end, and everyone I know is always dreading the *last* number. I hope he will make the jilting of Griselda [Grantly, the Archdeacon's daughter] a long while a-doing.'[37]

Mrs Gaskell, by nature a generous woman, was not at all annoyed that another writer was dominating the most successful literary periodical. Others, however, were not so pleased with Trollope's expanding fame. Starting with *Framley Parsonage*, a tone of carping criticism against him appeared almost constantly in the *Saturday Review* which was annoyed that the *Cornhill* had lured away some of its writers and perhaps some of its readers. Nevertheless it recognised Trollope's popularity:[38]

> The author ... is a writer who is born to make the fortune of circulating libraries. At the beginning of every month the new number of his book has ranked almost as one of the delicacies of the season; and no London belle dared to pretend to consider herself literary, who did not know the very latest intelligence about the state of Lucy Robarts' heart, and of Griselda Grantley's [sic] flounces ... It [the novel] has been an inmate of the drawing-room – it has travelled with us in the train – it has lain on the breakfast-table. We feel as if we had met Lady Lufton at a country house, admired Lord Dumbello at a ball, and seen Mrs. Proudie at an episcopal evening party.

Even before 1860 there had been complaints, not entirely unjustified, that Trollope wrote too quickly and too much. After the success of *Framley Parsonage* such complaints only increased but were ignored by those who demanded his latest novel at Mudie's or bought the periodical that contained yet another instalment.* Nor was his popularity confined to his native land. The *Cornhill* became very popular in America, and with it the name of Mrs Trollope's son. Mary Chesnut, a Senator's wife, complained when the December 1860 issue had too much about the romance between Doctor Thorne and Miss Dunstable: 'I wanted to see how the young lovers were getting on.' Trollope was quite pleased when a long article praising him appeared in the highly influential *Revue des Deux Mondes*. In Florence, Elizabeth Barrett Browning noted: 'How good this "Cornhill Magazine" is! Anthony Trollope is really superb.' Her husband, who had been critical of *The West Indies* – it 'exceeds in slovenliness any clever man's production within my experience' – found few mistakes.[39]

This may lead one to wonder how the *Cornhill* was viewed in another Florentine house, the Villino Trollope. Perhaps they never heard the rumour, in one literary periodical, that *Framley Parsonage* was really written by 'our old acquaintance, Mrs. Trollope'. We do not know for sure whether 'our old acquaintance' actually managed to read either it or the small tribute Thackeray had paid her in the first issue by asking: 'Does the author of the *Vicar of Wrexhill* laugh over *The Warden* and *The Three Clerks*?' (Perhaps he intended some small apology for his vicious review of her novel years before.) In spite of her ill health, she probably did manage to get through a few numbers because Tom complained – mildly, for he was a loving and dutiful son – that she kept *Castle Richmond* on her table for several weeks. Since that novel was published in May 1860 (Chapman apparently hurried its publication to take advantage of the author's fame), Fanny Trollope should have seen several issues of the *Cornhill* before her son's Irish novel arrived. The old lady's memory was failing and she spent long hours simply sitting in her chair or in the garden amid the lemon trees. As Tom wrote with tender feeling, 'the bright lamp began to grow dim and gradually sink into the socket'. Yet some time before the twilight encircled her completely she managed a final, short letter to her youngest son:[40]

My dear Anthony,
    You asked me to write – I and my pen have been so long divorced that I hardly know how to set about it – But you ask me to write and therefore write I will – though I have no news to tell you more fresh than that I love

---

*Between the publication of *Barchester Towers* in 1857 and *Framley Parsonage* in book form in April 1861, Trollope published four novels and one travel book. Thackeray produced only one major novel, *The Virginians*, and *Lovel the Widower*. Dickens, apart from finishing the final numbers of *Little Dorrit*, wrote two novels: *A Tale of Two Cities* and *Great Expectations*.

you dearly – I should like to see you again, but can hardly hope it! God bless you my dear dear Son!

Your loving mother
Frances Trollope.

Happily, she would see him again, for on 24 September Anthony and Rose set out on another Italian journey. With his new position as an English Surveyor and his literary fame, we can only assume that their travels were more lavish than in the past. One item gave him a rather grand look and his description of how he acquired it comes in one of his best letters, which also provides a charming glimpse of Anthony and Rose in their new house at Waltham Cross. In the letter to George Smith he told how they were examining a fresh – he calls it 'damp' – copy of the *Cornhill* when a large parcel arrived. Trollope decided not to send it down to the 'butler's pantry' but to open it himself. He unwrapped, one assumes with his customary lack of patience, 'fold after fold of packing paper – varying from the strongest brown to a delicate tissue of silver'. Inside he found a large travelling bag. Then came this dialogue:

Anthony (angrily): I never ordered it.
Rose: It's a present.
Anthony: Gammon – It's a commission to take ... for some dandy and I'll be ——

Rose apparently hoped it might be for her, but inside they discovered 'a brandy flask and a case of razors'. Trollope had as much use for the first as he had little use for the second! Rose then said: 'It's [from] the lady who said she wrote your book intending to make some amends.' (There was a deluded girl who had caused Trollope considerable annoyance by spreading rumours that she was the real author of *Framley Parsonage*. Her father, who believed her, even stormed into Smith's office only to discover the truth.) The bag was full of those little luxuries that seem to sum up the Victorian way of life: silver soap dishes, gold pins, and cut-glass containers for colognes. They soon discovered it was a present from the ever-generous Smith. Trollope was delighted and in his letter of thanks said it was really he who owed the publisher a present, 'seeing that you have brought me in contact with readers ... counted by hundreds of thousands, instead of hundreds'. Trollope signified his pleasure by dropping the formal 'Mr Smith'; hereafter he wrote to 'My dear Smith'.[41]

*

The Trollopes, along with the new bag, were soon on their way to Florence. Since their last visit, much had changed. In April 1859 Tom had watched Grand Duke Leopoldo lead a procession of his carriages out of the city as Tuscany was invaded by the King of Sardinia, anxious to create a new united Italian kingdom for himself. 'We have made at Florence a revolution with rosewater,' boasted Theodosia Trollope, 'a dynasty has been not overturned but calmly put aside.' One of the first visible signs that Anthony and Rose would have noted as they drew up in front of the Villino Trollope was that the square had been renamed the Piazza dell'Indipendenza. Instead of Grand Ducal receptions at the Pitti Palace with its plates of tempting bonbons, there was the prospect of listening to endless harangues by Theodosia about the glories of Garibaldi and the enormities of 'priestly tyrants'. It may be recalled that Trollope and Theodosia had clashed years before over the royalist hero of *La Vendée*, and it is amusing to note that in one of her magazine articles written in the last weeks of Anthony's stay she inserts an attack upon the soldiers from La Vendée, referring to 'good blood spilt recklessly in a rotten cause'. Perhaps there had been another little disagreement between Anthony and Theodosia.[42]

Trollope supported the cause of Italian unification, but preferred the more constitutional wiles of Cavour to the revolutionary violence of Garibaldi, who was, 'to my thinking, a little too much of a rebel'. All this would naturally have been topical in Florence, and even more so when Anthony made his first visit to Rome, then in its last years under Papal rule. The fascination that Englishmen felt for the *Risorgimento* was of great benefit for Tom Trollope, who wrote many articles on Italian politics. The Trollope brothers were always anxious to help one another with publishers, and within a few months of the appearance of the *Cornhill* Tom was able to say he was 'one of you' by arranging, with some help from Anthony, to write on Italy for the new publication. The government of Victor Emmanuel II, who would proclaim himself King of Italy on 17 March 1861, took this quite seriously and offered to supply him with secret information. Trollope wrote to Smith that 'we' by which he meant 'I – and the travelling bag ... with my brother' were on their way to Rome and Naples. Smith replied, 'I hope you do not intend to do any fighting at Naples.' The Garibaldian armies prevented a trip south of Rome, and after two weeks in examining ancient ruins and modern politicians the brothers returned to Florence.[43]

The two weeks had also sufficed for Anthony to gather enough background for another tale, 'Mrs. General Talboys', set in Rome. It was about this time that Tom Trollope took up writing novels: his first was set in contemporary Italy. Eventually he wrote both historical novels and some with an English setting. 'I often tell my brother, who knows more than any man I know,' Trollope later wrote to a friend, 'that he is too didactic, too anxious to teach to write a good novel.' This was one reason why Tom's novels have not survived. The other was that he lacked the ability to portray character, a talent that had passed from his mother to his younger brother. 'Mr T.A. Trollope', said one literary journal, 'occupies a position among writers of fiction, which, if it were not for an unfortunate contrast with his highly gifted brother would be more respectable.' Anthony was a 'full-blooded claret' while Tom was a 'very drinkable *vin ordinaire*'. It says much for Tom Trollope that he never appeared to feel any jealousy of his younger brother's pre-eminence. Another celebrated Anglo-Florentine was soon enrolled among the *Cornhill*'s writers: Elizabeth Barrett Browning. She was delighted that her friend Tom brought Anthony to see her: 'Yesterday we had a visit from Anthony Trollope, the clever novelist ... I like both brothers – The novelist is surpassingly clever as a writer ... And he has a very kind feeling for me.' The Trollopes returned for another visit a few weeks later: 'I agree with you in adhering to Anthony Trollope – & indeed Robert & I both consider him first-rate as a novelist – *Framley Parsonage* is perfect it seems to me.'[44]

*

It was on this visit that Trollope met Kate Field. Before discussing his 'love' for her, it is helpful to have her describe the two Trollope brothers in the Florence of 1860:

> Here is Anthony Trollope, and it is no ordinary pleasure to enjoy simultaneously the philosophical reasoning of Thomas Trollope – looking half Socrates and half Galileo – whom Mrs Browning called 'Aristides the Just', and the almost boyish enthusiasm and impulsive argumentation of Anthony Trollope, who is an admirable specimen of a frank and loyal Englishman.

Trollope spoke of her in his *Autobiography*, published the year after his death. There has been much speculation about the following passage:[45]

> There is an American woman, of whom not to speak in a work purporting to [be] a memoir of my own life would be to omit all allusion to one of the chief pleasures which has graced my later years. In the last fifteen years she has been, out of my own family, my most chosen friend. She is a ray

of light to me, from which I can always strike a spark by thinking of her. I do not know that I should please her or do good to any one by naming her. But not to allude to her in these pages would amount almost to a falsehood. I could not write truly of myself without saying that such a friend has been vouchsafed to me. I trust she may live to read the words I have now written, and to wipe away a tear as she thinks of my feeling while I write them.

Kate Field's name was not mentioned. When Trollope's son, Henry, prepared the manuscript for publication, he omitted the words 'an American' in the first line. This has led to some of the exaggerated importance given to the friendship. The paragraph follows immediately after an extended analysis of the American character. Trollope had been very critical in the preceding pages about the dishonesty of some American publishers who pirated English books. From that he went on to discuss his liking for Americans and concluded with the paragraph quoted above. Indeed the darkness of ink on 'American' in the original manuscript implies that Trollope was stressing that, in spite of his criticisms about publishers in America, he had an *American* friend. Thus the Kate Field saga, which has been so distorted, flows largely from taking the passage out of its context. It also comes from a misunderstanding of Trollope's use of language. He does not say that he 'loved' Kate Field, though he does say in the *Autobiography* that he 'loved' Sir Charles Taylor, a well-known member of the Garrick Club. On hearing of the death of the writer Robert Bell, Trollope wrote: 'He was a very manly fellow. I loved him well.' In another letter he said of George Eliot: 'You perhaps know how I love and admire her.' Trollope, therefore, was happy to use the word 'love' to describe his feelings for men and for women other than his wife. When he wrote of Kate Field, however, he said she was 'in the last fifteen years ... out of my own family, my most chosen friend'. Thirty years later another American woman – the elderly widow of a famous Southern general – quoted Trollope's words about 'a ray of light from which I can always strike a spark' and said 'he expressed the feeling that most people had in meeting her ... There was in her radiant personality a glow that flashed a lasting light into the lives that came near her own.'[46]

Kate Field, the twenty-two-year-old daughter of a well-known American actor, was then residing in Florence and regarded the Villino Trollope as her 'second home'. In those autumn days Trollope enjoyed numerous discussions about Renaissance art, American politics and literature with her. Naturally a middle-aged man like Trollope (particularly when his fame was new to him) would enjoy long literary discussions with a beautiful and vivacious girl who realised she was in the presence of a famous figure. She informed a friend: 'Anthony

Trollope is a very delightful companion. I see a great deal of him. He has promised to send me a copy of the "Arabian Nights" ... in which he intends to write "Kate Field from the Author".' Once he was back in England the book was sent but, as he did not know her address, it went in a large box containing a saddle for his niece, 'Bice'. With it came a letter: as with almost every letter he would write to her, this first one contained advice. She should read the book slowly and not in a furious burst; she must be careful 'not to throw away time that is precious' but to use it to study the great art that was all round her.[47] In years to come his letters would tease her about her 'feminism', and even more, about her lecturing on it. He liked to think that most female lecturers, something regarded as particularly American at that time, were rather ugly. It perplexed and annoyed him that Kate Field, who was undoubtedly beautiful, should take up such a cause. Perhaps he was thinking of her when he wrote about a woman planning to lecture 'in one of those large Western Halls, full of gas and intelligence' [*Kept in the Dark* XXII].

Rose Trollope never resented her husband's friendship with a girl almost twenty-five years younger than he. Rose also became her friend, entertaining her when she visited England and exchanging letters at other times. If Rose had resented the *Autobiography's* allusion to Kate Field, Henry Trollope (who was living with his mother while editing the book) undoubtedly would have struck it out, just as he struck out some passages about other writers. Perhaps Trollope's best description of his feelings occurs in 'Mary Gresley', a short story about an editor's attempt to help a girl who wants to be a writer. Trollope wrote this when he was himself editing a magazine:

> In love with Mary Gresley, after the common sense of the word, we never were, nor would it have become us to be so ... We were married and old; she was very young ... She looked upon us ... as a subsidiary old uncle. Nevertheless we were in love with her, and we think such a state of love to be a wholesome and natural condition ... We forgave all her faults. We exaggerated her virtues.

In the story the editor invites the girl and her mother for Christmas dinner. This is done at the suggestion of his wife, after 'we had made a clean breast of it at home with regard to our heart-flutterings'. That indeed is the best description of Trollope's feelings for Kate Field: 'heart flutterings.' For the next two decades his heart fluttered when he saw her, and he evidently enjoyed writing long letters of advice, usually urging her to marry, as well as warning that her many talents would come to naught without discipline. He had learned that lesson himself in Ireland, but it was one she never mastered. She wandered about the world, dabbling at writing, at acting, at lecturing. It is characteristic of Trollope that, while he would send stern letters about a woman's duty to marry, he would then take great trouble trying to advance her career as a writer. She was what the Victorians called a 'lion hunter': she enjoyed the company of the famous. She fascinated both women and men, and she certainly enjoyed the friendship of famous writers like Walter Savage Landor and Robert Browning and politicians like Charles Dilke. She even earned a footnote in royal history when, in 1878, she took part in the first telephone call to a royal residence by singing 'Kathleen Mavourneen' and the 'Cuckoo Song' to Queen Victoria at Osborne.[48]

Although there never was an 'affair' between Trollope and Kate Field, there was always a mildly flirtatious side to his friendship. He ended one letter in 1868, when he was miserable and lonely in a hot July in Washington:[49]

> Give my kindest love to your mother. The same to yourself dear Kate – if I do not see you again, – with a kiss that shall be semi-paternal – one third-brotherly, and as regards the small remainder, as loving as you please.

She undoubtedly filled certain emotional needs for Trollope. The vibrant young American girl added sparkle to his life: she reminded him of his youth and of those walks with girls at Hadley. He was also fascinated at the difference between English and American girls, who were allowed more freedom than their more restricted English sisters. He introduced this contrast into numerous stories and novels and discussed it particularly in *Mr. Scarborough's Family* [XLVII]. For almost all these American girls he drew upon small aspects of Kate Field, but she is never any one character. Trollope's friendship – indeed his love – for Kate Field can only be understood if one first realises that Rose Trollope always remained what he called her in his letters, 'Dearest Love'.

*

When Trollope returned from this autumn trip in November 1860, he was one of the best-known writers in the country. He had also become, within weeks of the serialisation of *Framley Parsonage*, an important figure in London literary society. To celebrate the success of his magazine, George Smith commenced the pleasant custom of monthly '*Cornhill* dinners' for the contributors. Trollope always remembered the first 'memorable banquet' where he met 'many men who afterwards became my most intimate associates. It can rarely happen that one such occasion can be the first starting-point of so many friendships!' Fellow guests were men like W.H. Russell of *The Times*, John Millais, and the well-known writer on philosophy and science G.H. Lewes, who is now unfairly only remembered as the 'husband' of George Eliot. Yet Smith, Russell, Millais and Lewes were only a prelude to the moment Trollope had been waiting for: his introduction to the man whom he regarded as the greatest living novelist. The genial host led him up to Thackeray and presented him. 'How do?' replied Thackeray and turned away. Smith long remembered 'the expression on Trollope's face ... and no one who knew Trollope will doubt that he *could* look furious on an adequate – and sometimes on an inadequate – occasion!' The morning after the banquet Trollope hurried round to Smith in 'a very wrathful mood' to announce that he had vowed never to speak to Thackeray again. The explanation for the *contretemps* was a simple though tragic one. Thackeray was in poor health and at times suffered moments of great pain. A spasm had come on him just at the moment of introduction. Trollope also discovered later that Thackeray was not particularly comfortable at large parties, preferring small groups, where his genius and wit could sparkle. Fortunately all the ill-will of the first meeting faded as Trollope soon found Thackeray to be a delightful companion. In a book he wrote about the older novelist Trollope recalled his appearance at the time of their first meetings: 'He was then forty-eight years old, very gray, with much of age upon him, which had come from suffering ... speaking as though the world were all behind him instead of before; but still with a stalwart outward bearing, very erect in his gait and a countenance peculiarly expressive.'[50]

The two novelists had shared several similar experiences: a difficult youth, a frustrating early career, and travels through Ireland and in Egypt. There were, however, fundamental differences, which Trollope later analysed. The greatest was Thackeray's indolence: 'He was always idle and only on some occasions, when the spirit moved him thoroughly, did he do his best.' Trollope always liked to portray idleness as leading to unhappiness, even in a friend: 'To find on Monday morning an excuse why he should not on Monday do Monday's work was ... an inexpressible relief to him, but had become a deep regret, – almost a remorse, – before the Monday was over.' His own work was so highly disciplined that he could not see that some people can only work in fits. Thackeray, unlike Trollope, lacked self-assurance: 'Though he was aware of his own power, he always, to the last, was afraid that his own deficiencies should be too strong against him ... To such a one it was not given to believe in himself with that sturdy rock-bound foundation which we see to have belonged to some men from the earliest struggles of their career.' Trollope thought – although it was an opinion few others shared except Rose – that Thackeray's *Henry Esmond* was the greatest novel in the language. When he told this to his new friend, Thackeray replied: 'They don't read it.' In addition Thackeray, unlike Trollope, lacked a wife to provide stability for him. After a few years of happy marriage, his wife went mad and had to be confined for the rest of her long life.[51]

This cherished friendship almost came to a sudden end when Trollope was caught up in one of the silliest episodes in literary history. It grew out of an article in the *New York Times* by Edmund Yates, a minor novelist and journalist who was also a rival of Trollope's at the Post Office. His claim to fame, if it be such, is as the inventor of the 'gossip-column' which he wrote under a name that would prove ominous for him, 'The Lounger at the Clubs'. As such he perhaps deserves the name that Thackeray bestowed on him: 'Tom Garbage.' Although Trollope made an effort to maintain friendly relations, Yates grew increasingly jealous of his success. Victorian writers tended to enlist either behind Thackeray's banner or Dickens's, not just when discussing questions of style but even when forming friendships. Just as Trollope saw himself as a follower of Thackeray – a 'gentleman writing for gentlemen' – so did Yates, a 'Bohemian' in his fiction and his friends, enlist behind Dickens, who was said to write for the masses. Some years before, Yates had been expelled from the Garrick Club at Thackeray's insistence for reporting private conversations he overheard. This soon became a battle between the partisans of Dickens and Thackeray. (Behind some of the animosity was gossip about why Dickens had left his wife.) Outraged at the treatment of Yates, Dickens led his friends out of the Garrick. All this had happened while Trollope was still in Dublin. However, the affair rumbled on for several years and Thackeray had even inserted into *The Virginians*, the last monthly instalment of which only appeared in October 1859, a recognisable portrayal of Yates as 'Young Grubstreet who corresponds with three penny papers and describes the persons and conversations of gentlemen whom he meets at his "clubs"'.[52]

Yates's *New York Times* article revived the feud, for it recounted an event at the first *Cornhill* dinner which portrayed George Smith as ignorant of literary history, which was certainly not the case. The article said that Thackeray, who was in the chair, compared the gathering to a party given by Edward Cave, the eighteenth-century printer and publisher. The story which Thackeray told would have been known to any well-read person: Cave had given a party for his authors, one of whom was Samuel Johnson, who was so ashamed of his shabby coat that he ate his dinner behind a screen. When he had finished telling the famous story Thackeray, according to Yates, called out to George Smith: 'I hope you've not got Johnson there behind that screen?' Smith was said to have replied: 'Johnson? God bless my soul, my dear Mr. Thackeray, there's no person of the name of Johnson here, nor anyone behind the screen.'

The *Saturday Review*, anxious to attack its rival the *Cornhill*, took the opportunity, while deploring the publication of such gossip, to recount all the details. No one knew where Yates had got the embarrassing story from until Trollope went round to see Smith and confessed that he had told it to Yates, who no doubt had then touched it up. 'I told the story not against you, but against Thackeray.' Smith was quite understandably angry, but he recalled that Trollope took his rebuke 'very meekly' and said, 'I know I have done wrong, and you may say anything you like to me.' This does show another side of Trollope: though he could bluster, he could also admit a fault when he knew he had been in the wrong. Smith was not a man to hold a grudge. For Trollope it was a valuable lesson. He was entering, rather late, the dangerous waters of the London literary world, where some of the man-eating fish would have frightened even Rowland Hill. Convivial dinners with world-famous names were delightful but care was needed lest one be dragged into old feuds. Discretion must be the most important element in the code of a literary gentleman in London. Yates was no gentleman, and Trollope should not have treated him as if he were. He was lucky that his foolish mistake in trusting such a gossip-writer did not end his friendship either with Thackeray or with Smith.[53]

Trollope certainly appeared at home at one *Cornhill* dinner according to another well-known journalist of the time:[54]

> Anthony Trollope was very much to the fore, contradicting everybody; afterwards saying kind things to everybody, and occasionally going to sleep on sofas and chairs; or leaning against sideboards, and even somnolent while standing erect on the hearthrug. I never knew a man who could take so many spells of 'forty winks' at unexpected moments, and then turn up quite wakeful, alert, and pugnacious ... [he] had nothing of the bear but his skin.

Behind all this gossip and dining Smith and Trollope were thinking about another book: an account of life in India, a subject much in the news after the mutiny by native troops in 1857. The dreadful violence

of the Indian mutineers had sent a shiver of horror through the British
public and convinced the government that the administration of the
most important Imperial possession must be controlled from London.
Trollope was mildly interested: 'I should certainly like to do the India
book, but will not break my heart if the plan falls to the ground. *Per se*
going to India is a bore – but it would suit me professionally.' He asked
£3,000 for a two-volume book, which shows how much his reputation
had grown. Perhaps he was hoping that he could combine his two
professions as postal official and writer. Direct control from London
would require improved communication. As the man who had
arranged better transportation of British post through Egypt, he would
have been an obvious choice in any mission to improve the Indian mail.
However, his Asian venture never came off and the closest he got to
India, the only important part of the 'English world' he did not see, was
a visit to Ceylon twenty years later. Given the rather hostile portrayal
in *The Bertrams* of colonial types returning from India, it was perhaps
lucky for Trollope's popularity that the Indian book never materialised. However, the idea for such a book does show his continued
hankering to produce 'serious' works. Tom Trollope (perhaps more
interested, because of his wife's Indian background) saw such a project
as an important step for his younger brother: 'I am sorry for the Indian
scheme; I feel confident that the book would have improved your
literary position, and given you a standing among government men,
and such like, which the most successful novel-writing will not do.'[55]

*

The failure of the Indian project did not mean that Trollope's relations
with Smith came to an end. In some five weeks in the summer of 1861
he finished *The Struggles of Brown, Jones, and Robinson* which he had
abandoned four years before. He managed to persuade Smith to give
him £600 – 'the hardest bargain I ever sold to a publisher'. This truly
appalling tale, as we have noted before, is Trollope's attempt at an
extended satire on advertising and it is the only one of the novels in
which there is virtually nothing of interest, except to biographers of
Trollope or historians of advertising. It was serialised in the *Cornhill*,
where its unpopular reception led to a rumour that Smith had cut it
short. Newspapers and magazines often commented on individual
parts of a novel as they appeared in another journal. The *Illustrated
News of the World* refused to believe the rumour about the anonymous
story's authorship: 'The tale – let us hope not by Mr Trollope … is
detestable, low, and untrue as ever.' Smith did not even bother

bringing it out as a one-volume novel for almost another decade. Luckily this unfortunate serial did little harm to the author's reputation, because by the time it appeared readers were already absorbed in his latest novel, *Orley Farm*, which began monthly publication in parts in March, the month before the last instalment of *Framley Parsonage* appeared. For his latest book he returned to his old publishers, Chapman and Hall, who gave him £2,500, a far cry from the £600 they had given for *Castle Richmond* in 1859. The large sum, plus the fact that the contract dealt with foreign rights, demonstrated his new popularity. This was the first of his novels to appear in part issue, where each of the twenty parts sold for one shilling. This was the method that had made Dickens famous with *Pickwick Papers*, which had also been published by Chapman and Hall. It was a more risky method by the 1860s, as the rise of magazines like the *Cornhill* and its imitators, where for the same price a reader could get several chapters of two novels plus other articles, made part issues seem old fashioned. Nevertheless the novel proved a great success, giving, as one reviewer commented, 'almost always a shilling's worth of story for our money'.[56]

Orley Farm has one of Trollope's best plots, only marred, as he himself agreed, by his giving away the heroine's 'secret' when there are still thirty-five chapters to come. He admitted in his essay 'A Walk in a Wood' that he had only decided whether or not the central character was guilty of a crime when he was writing the chapter before she confesses. The story centres on whether a widow, Lady Mason, has forged a will so that her son will inherit 'Orley Farm'. The sub-plots add greatly to the novel, allowing Trollope to portray life at different levels of the upper and 'middling' classes. This strengthened his claim as the greatest portrayer of contemporary family life. The *Saturday Review*, never one to overpraise Trollope, said: 'He does the family life of England to perfection. No one has drawn English families better – without exaggeration, and without any attempt at false comedy. His gentlemen and ladies are exactly like real gentlemen and ladies, except, perhaps, they are a trifle more entertaining.' For one sub-plot he drew on his frequent travels to present the world of the Victorian commercial traveller, particularly the rules and practices of commercial rooms in provincial inns. He does this through the eyes of a London solicitor, who stops at an inn in Leeds and is somewhat horrified at its habitués. This is a part of society rarely met with in Trollope. The subject and his treatment of it remind one of Dickens. Throughout the book Trollope attacks lawyers, and many reviewers, often briefless barristers, found fault with his mistakes on legal language and peculiarities. It is odd that Trollope, the son of a barrister, appears so frequently hostile to the Bar. Part of it comes from his old obsession: honesty. He could not understand how a barrister could defend someone he thought guilty. Trollope was not alone in this view: at about the time he expressed it in *Orley Farm* Queen Victoria was saying virtually the same thing to Mr Gladstone at Balmoral.[57] In *Castle Richmond* [XLIII] Trollope had already answered lawyers who complained about errors in his earlier novels:

> Had it perchance fallen to thy lot, O my forensic friend, heavy laden with the wisdom of the law, to write tales such as this of mine, how charmingly might not thy characters have come forth upon the canvas – how much more charmingly than I can limn them! While, on the other hand, ignorant as thou now tellest me that I am of the very alphabet of the courts, had thy wig been allotted to me, I might have gathered guineas thick as daisies in the summer ... It is all in our destiny.

In his *Autobiography* Trollope records that most of his friends thought *Orley Farm* his best book. Although he looked back on it with pride he could not regard it as his finest because 'the highest merit which a novel can have consists in perfect delineation of character' and he did not think the characters here were his best, which indeed they are not. One aspect of publication gave him tremendous pleasure: the illustrations by John Millais which were 'the best I have seen in any novel in the language'. Smith had brought Millais in to do illustrations for *Framley Parsonage* after the first few instalments. 'Should I live to see my story illustrated by Millais,' the novelist told George Smith, 'no body would be able to hold me.' As has already been mentioned, 'Orley Farmhouse' was based on that rambling house where Trollope had spent so much of his youth. He was anxious that the drawing reproduce it accurately and suggested that a photograph be made or that Millais go to see the house. In years to come Trollope liked to take friends to Harrow to see the farmhouse. The daughter of another artist, William Frith, remembered one visit with Anthony and Rose when he pointed 'with many chuckles' to the hedge through which he and his sisters had smuggled some of his mother's 'pretty pretties' when the bailiffs were taking possession of the house.[58] Using the farmhouse in a novel (and one composed soon after he had written an account of the bailiffs in possession of the Robarts's house in *Framley Parsonage*) was undoubtedly a way of proving to himself that the frustrations and miseries which he and his family had endured there were now over. These events had left behind scars that could never heal, but they had also given him the inner drive to succeed, as well as a deep compassion for the miseries of human life itself.

It is certainly significant that, immediately after the discussion of *Orley Farm* in the *Autobiography*, he writes:

> I now felt that I had gained my object ... I had achieved that which I had contemplated when I went to London in 1834 ... I had created for myself a position among literary men, and had secured to myself an income on which I might live in ease and comfort, – which ease and comfort have been made to include many luxuries.

By 1861 he and his family were settled in an elegant mansion. He associated with some of the greatest names in English letters. That year saw one novel's serialisation end and another's begin. It saw the first part-issue of one of his novels and the publication of his first collection of short stories. Finally, it saw him earning as much from one book, *Orley Farm*, as he had earned from his first ten. Yet Trollopes were a restless breed, ever-anxious to travel and to see new things. Even among the comforts and luxuries of Waltham House, Anthony Trollope, like his mother in the real 'Orley Farm' more than thirty years before, was looking westward – where the land was no longer bright.

CHAPTER TEN

To Realise Niagara

One of America's greatest diarists, Mary Chesnut, was a devoted follower of Trollope's novels. During February 1861 in Montgomery, Alabama, while her husband, the Senator from that state, was involved in the establishment of the Confederate States of America, she solaced herself by reading an episode of *Framley Parsonage* in the *Cornhill* and commented, 'How much I owe of the pleasures of my life to these much reviled writers of fiction.' Yet it was only in the last days of 1863, more than twenty months after English readers had learned of the marriage of Lucy Robarts to Lord Lufton, that this Southern lady could finish the novel. Even so, she felt herself lucky because a friend had managed to smuggle through a naval blockade 'the last number of the *Cornhill*. He knew how much I was interested in Trollope's story.'* Mrs Chesnut had been deprived of her favourite pleasure and many other pleasures by the War Between the States, the greatest war of Trollope's lifetime. Just as the Alabama lady yearned to read Trollope, so did he yearn to see her now dis-united land.[1]

Trollope's visit to America, which lasted from August 1861 to March 1862, came not only at a crucial point in history but at a decisive moment in his own life. The trip offered him an opportunity not only to observe American society but to reflect, away from the pressures of postal work and novel writing, on his own recent achievements and future ambitions. For that reason this American visit is the single most important episode in his mature life. His remaining two decades were all heavily influenced by the conclusions he reached while there: some years later, in an article about the War and its consequences, he wrote, 'We will acknowledge that, to us, no political subject is more interesting.'[2] This trip, and the controversy surrounding it, marked a

---

*In addition to *Framley Parsonage*, Mrs Chesnut was able during the war to read *Castle Richmond*, *Rachel Ray*, *The Small House at Allington* and *Doctor Thorne*, which she read twice. As she noted, 'Anything from Trollope is very welcome.'

divide in his life between the postal official who wrote novels and the man of letters who happened to work for the Post Office. In addition the detailed account of his comings and goings which he included in the book that describes his trip, *North America*, gives us the best single portrait of himself and, also, of his wife.

If any man in England had ample grounds for disliking the United States it was Trollope. As a boy of twelve he had seen his mother, one brother and two sisters disappear into the enveloping mists of the American frontier. It was several years before they returned, leaving behind them the wreck of the family's hopes and wealth. His mother soon became a hated figure to Americans: derided in magazines, pulpits and theatres throughout the Union. His brother and his two sisters eventually died of consumption, a disease not helped by the privations they endured in America. Furthermore Trollope, like all British authors, had to endure the sight of American 'pirates' reprinting his books without royalty payments. Yet, in spite of all this, he had already developed a fascination, a friendly fascination, for the American republic. His early knowledge had come from people like Fanny Wright and Julia Garnett who brought optimistic stories about the young country to the farmhouse in Harrow. From his brother Henry, and later from his mother, Anthony heard different accounts, sinister stories about the darker side of American life: slavery and intolerance. Of course he read his mother's famous *Domestic Manners of the Americans* and the novels she later wrote about America.

The young Anthony had balanced his mother's unfavourable account with other books. As a boy he had been enthralled by a Fenimore Cooper novel which he read and reread. Like so many Englishmen, he admired Washington Irving and Edgar Allan Poe. He also read Tocqueville's influential *Democracy in America*, published only a few years after Fanny Trollope's work. In the 1850s Trollope read of the growing sectional conflict in America as *The Times* gave considerable attention to American news. In *Barchester Towers*, published in 1857, he poked fun at the amount of American news in 'The Jupiter' (*The Times*): 'Those caterers for our morning repast, the staff of the Jupiter, had been sorely put to it for the last month to find a sufficiency of proper pabulum. Just then there was no talk of a new American president. No wonderful tragedies had occurred on railway trains in Georgia or elsewhere' [XLIII].

One of the consistent themes in English coverage of America was the intolerance of American public opinion, particularly when stirred by a rabble-rousing press. Dickens, for example, made great play of this in *Martin Chuzzlewit*, a novel Trollope had read. In some of his earliest comments about America, Trollope did the same. In *The New Zealander*, when discussing the English press he added a reflection on America:[3]

> For a man who has ever loved the idea of liberty how sad it is to see that the very landmarks of freedom which have been longed for in one age, become, in the next, when acquired, the very strongest holds of tyranny! Look to the American States where every man is equal; from which all dominion of ascendant classes has been banished; where political power rests solely with the people, and there you will see such tyranny as is not compassed even at St. Petersburg. Who there can dare to advocate opinions contrary to those prevalent with the mob?

*

In May 1859 Trollope had visited America at the end of his postal mission to the West Indies, and arranged to write some stories for *Harper's New Monthly Magazine*. One of the first, 'The Courtship of Susan Bell', had an American setting, Saratoga Springs, New York, a resort he had visited on his brief trip. He knew how to write for American readers: when a character reads poetry aloud, Longfellow is included along with Byron and Shakespeare. A Baptist minister appears as a minor character in a not altogether unpleasing light, whereas in his novels 'dissenting ministers' are rare and, when they do occur, are usually less than attractive. In this story Trollope avoids the word 'chapel' when mentioning the Baptist 'meeting house' as he knew American Protestants might well see 'chapel' as a sneer. The dialogue is well done, with no attempt at parody, although he overdoes the use of 'I guess', which Englishmen saw as the most characteristic Americanism, conveniently forgetting how fond Chaucer had been of the phrase. For a man who had spent only a few hectic days in America at the end of a long and exhausting business trip, 'Susan Bell' is a considerable achievement. Trollope was evidently pleased with it: he not only included it in his first collection of short stories, *Tales of All Countries*, but took the plot and gave it an English setting for a novel called *Rachel Ray*, published in 1863.

Tales of All Countries included another story, 'An Unprotected Female at the Pyramids', featuring an American character. The friendly attitude towards Americans evident in the story was no mere pose to curry favour in America. Throughout this tale Jefferson Ingram, 'who was comprising all countries and all nations in one grand tour, as American gentlemen so often do', emerges as an admirable man. It was a convention of English fiction to have American characters lecture on the glories of their Constitution. Trollope, with his usual passion for accuracy and fairness, does have Ingram holding forth on the benefits of his own country, but he also has to endure listening 'by the half-hour as to the virtue of the British Constitution' from an English fellow-traveller. Ingram eventually marries the English heroine: Trollope, in fact, was to make a minor speciality of transatlantic marriages in his fiction long before Henry James patented the idea.

At the end of his book about the West Indies, which Trollope wrote on the ship taking him from New York to Liverpool, he informed his readers: 'On the United States I should like to write a volume, seeing that the government and social life of the people there – of that people who are our children – afford the most interesting phenomenon which we find as to the new world – the best means of prophesying what the world will next be, and what men will next do.'[4] The tone is already more that of the analytical Tocqueville than of the sardonic Fanny Trollope.

*

The next two years had allowed him no time to fulfil this ambition. From 1859 to 1861 Trollope was remarkably busy even by his standards, completing four novels, his West Indian book, and several short stories. Yet, in spite of his writing, his new house and his new postal district, America was never far from his mind. When he was in Florence in the autumn of 1860, and first met Kate Field, talk about American politics must have interrupted contemplation of Giotto's Tower. In those months the long-simmering American political crisis was culminating in Lincoln's election as President. In the deep South of America Mrs Chesnut recorded sadly 'our fate sealed' when she saw men waving the 'Palmetto flag' of South Carolina. At Waltham House Trollope also thought of this when writing 'The Journey to Panama'. He recalled the many flags he had seen in the Caribbean: 'There are citizens of the stars and stripes, who find their way everywhere – alas! perhaps, now also citizens of the new Southern flag, with the palmetto leaf.'[5] This story, which is based on fact, is one of Trollope's finest and tells of an Irish governess sent out to South America to make an arranged marriage. He contributed it free to *Victoria Regia*, a luxurious collection of works by authors such as Thackeray, Tennyson, Monckton Milnes, Tom Trollope and his wife and issued to support Emily Faithfull's 'Victoria Press for the Employment of Women'. In the early weeks of 1861 almost every issue of the *The Times* carried news of the secession of more Southern states. The news was followed closely in a country whose manufacturing industry was so largely dependent on their cotton. Trollope saw that this was the right time for a book on America: the developing crisis would make it both topical and profitable. The book would enhance his claim to be seen as a serious writer. There was, however, one difficulty: the Post Office.

*

The Post Office was in a difficult state. For some months in the summer of 1860 it had lacked an effective head as Lord Elgin, the Postmaster General, had been sent to force a treaty on 'John Chinaman', as the Prime Minister, Lord Palmerston, called the Emperor of China. Eventually Lord Stanley of Alderley was made Postmaster General as there was 'much wants doing at the P.O.'. The recent lack of a political head had given increased importance to Rowland Hill. One consequence of Trollope's becoming an English Surveyor was that Hill, ever on the look-out for plots and rivals, increasingly began to suspect him, particularly as he became outspoken about the Civil Service. Trollope had always been anxious to help young men who were eager to advance and educate themselves. Even before moving to England he had played a large role in establishing a library for London clerks, speaking at its inauguration and donating copies of his novels and many books by Carlyle. He had spoken and written about the Civil Service, always stressing its honourable status, its independence, its freedom from the corruption which had marked it in the past and its professional status. He also warned against too slavish a devotion to competitive examinations. In 1860 he promoted a series of lectures for the clerks at St Martin's and persuaded other literary men, including his brother Tom and G.H. Lewes, to participate.[6]

On 4 January 1861 Trollope gave the first lecture. His subject was 'The Civil Service as a Profession'. He summarised his efforts in this lecture: 'My chief object ... indeed I may say my only object, – has been to raise our profession to the level of other professions.' Remembering perhaps his own youth, he recalled in one of his articles that 'many a lad placed in London, with six hours' work to be done in the day, and with no amusements provided for his evenings, has gone to shivers on the rocks of the Metropolis'. He wanted promotion 'by merit' abolished as it led to favouritism. He also urged that civil servants be given the right to vote. Hill was furious when Trollope arranged for an abridged version of his lecture to be published in the *Cornhill*. He told Tilley (knowing that he would inform Trollope) that this was 'unwise and indiscreet'. Trollope's reaction was to have the whole lecture printed privately so that he could give copies to friends.[7]

It was, therefore, hardly surprising that Hill was not pleased when Trollope applied for nine months' leave to visit America in order to advance his literary career. There was 'no precedent for such an application' Hill told the PMG, although he did accept 'that on two occasions viz. when he visited first Egypt, and afterwards, the West Indies, – Mr. Trollope performed services valued in themselves, and beyond the range of his ordinary duties'. For his part Trollope believed that the Post Office owed him some recompense for all the extra time he had spent on these exhausting trips. He now took his request directly to the Postmaster General, a man he much admired. Nine months was long even by the generous standards of the Victorian Civil Service. The jovial peer asked: 'Is it on the plea of ill-health?' The novelist replied that he enjoyed excellent health but that he needed the time to write a book about America. He justified this somewhat extraordinary request by citing his extra work. The PMG, anxious for compromise, suggested that Trollope could combine his visit with postal business. The worsening crisis could upset postal arrangements between Britain and America, particularly if the Washington government suspended service to the South. Hill found this idea 'in many respects objectionable' but would condone it if Trollope agreed that the leave would be a final settlement for his extra work. While such a suggestion infuriated Trollope, who was always touchy about his extra work, Hill could not defeat the combined forces of Trollope and the PMG.[8]

Trollope's desire to travel must have perplexed that peer, who was a perfect specimen of the self-satisfied Victorian who looked with bemused pity and contempt on the rest of the world. As his daughter wrote, 'Papa does so hate being abroad, he says the barbarians offend every one of his senses and that he hates them, but the English abroad still more'.[9] Lord Stanley of Alderley seems like a character from one of Trollope's political novels. In society he was known as 'Ben' because his caustic wit reminded people of Sir Benjamin Backbite in Sheridan's *School for Scandal*. He had three eccentric sons: one, the heir, became a Mohammedan and made a strange marriage abroad which sounds rather similar to those depicted by Trollope in *Is He Popenjoy?* and *Mr. Scarborough's Family*; another became a Roman Catholic bishop, and a third, an agnostic! The PMG, who kept up with contemporary fiction, was well aware of Trollope's increasing importance as a writer. Although a close friend of Thackeray's, he had forbidden his daughters to read his novels because they contained too accurate a portrayal of London Society. His wife, for good measure, added Dickens's *Dombey and Son* to their private Index of Forbidden Books. Trollope, however, had made sure that his writing did not upset his political master by taking the wise precaution of showing a proof copy of his lecture on the Civil Service to Lord Stanley before the abridged version appeared in the *Cornhill*.

Perhaps all these factors explain why the PMG was so blunt in his reply to Hill:[10]

> I consider that the valuable services rendered by Mr. Trollope to the Department, justified me in granting the leave requested, though somewhat out of the ordinary course. I never thought that Mr. Trollope made any claim for compensation, nor did I intend that the Leave now granted should be considered as such. Mr. Trollope's services discharged with zeal, diligence, and ability will always give him that claim to consideration which the exhibition of such qualities must entitle any officer to expect from the P.M.G., and the Leave now granted can in no respect be considered as diminishing such claims on the part of Mr. Trollope.

Such a firm rebuke is not likely to have increased Hill's regard for the troublesome Surveyor! Trollope was granted his leave without any need to undertake postal work in America.

Trollope wanted a contract for his American book before he left England. At this time he was dividing his cascade of publications between Chapman and Hall, who had brought out most of his books since 1858, and George Smith of the *Cornhill*. Chapman had paid £250 for his first travel book, *The West Indies*, but since then Trollope had become famous and could demand more for a two-volume book on such a topical subject. Chapman agreed to pay £1,250 for the right to print 2,500 copies of 'a work on America'. This time Trollope retained greater control over the copyright: his publishers were given a two-year copyright, after which they would have to pay a further £750 for a half-share in any further edition. Realising that the book would have considerable appeal in the United States and knowing full well the lack of any international copyright, Trollope reserved the American rights for himself, to negotiate while he was there.[11]

*

Copyright was just one of the issues that affected the attitude of English writers towards America. Nothing prevented a publisher on either side of the Atlantic from reprinting any book originating on the other side without paying a royalty, although occasionally a publisher might agree to pay an author from the other country a sum for his work.* English books were far more popular in America than vice versa, so English authors suffered more than American. Since so many novels first appeared either in part issues or in magazines it was easy to reprint English books only weeks after they appeared as a bound volume in London. The cheapness of these pirated books was an important factor in what many Americans, such as Emerson, believed was the continuing cultural imperialism of the mother country.

The copyright abuse gave America a reputation for dishonesty, and that reputation formed part of the intellectual baggage of any visiting Englishman. There were other items as well: in the 1840s several American states had suspended payment of interest on their debts. Britons made up the overwhelming bulk of foreign investors in America. Sydney Smith, the witty clergyman and essayist, whose Whig views had always inclined him to look with favour upon the young republic, had put some money into Pennsylvania bonds. When that state announced it was suspending payment, Smith wrote: 'I loved and admired honest America when she respected the laws of pounds, shillings, and pence; and I thought the United States the most magnificent picture of human happiness: I meddle now in these matters because I hate fraud – because I pity the misery it has occasioned – because I mourn over the hatred it has excited against free institutions.' This was his last literary effort and Trollope recalled it twenty years later when he visited Pennsylvania:[12]

> I confess that I have never felt any regard for Pennsylvania. It has always had in my estimation a low character for commercial honesty, and a certain flavour of pretentious hypocrisy. This probably has been much owing to the acerbity and pungency of Sydney Smith's witty denunciations against the drab-coloured State ... Nevertheless, Pennsylvania is rich and prosperous. Indeed it bears all those marks which Quakers generally leave behind them.

Trollope did not intend the last sentence as a compliment, as he normally regarded Quakers with considerable distaste. Perhaps he should have remembered that Philadelphia publishers had the best reputation for treating English authors fairly!

America's image in England was based almost totally on the printed word. Occasionally other methods of communication would influence

---

*American publishers sometimes gave token payment for 'early sheets' of a book. Escott was given a list of payments by J. Henry Harper which his firm claimed to have made to Trollope from 1859 until two years after his death. These amounted to £3,080.

attitudes. There was for example a shared tradition of popular music. It comes as something of a surprise to read in Lord Malmesbury's diary that 'Gladstone, who was always fond of music, is now quite enthusiastic about negro melodies, singing them with the greatest spirit and enjoyment, never leaving out a verse, and evidently preferring such as "Camp Down [*sic*] Races".' Stephen Foster's music illustrates that common Anglo-American culture that writers like Trollope were able to exploit. In 1846, the *Daily News*, a new and radical newspaper edited by Dickens, published the poem 'A Good Time Coming' by Charles Mackay which celebrated the repeal of the Corn Laws as a symbol of peace and progress. The poem soon crossed the Atlantic where the young Foster used it for one of his first songs. Perhaps no words better express that vision of progress – and it was an almost religious vision – that Victorians on both sides of the Atlantic shared, be they Trollope, Gladstone or Stephen Foster. Trollope was familiar with the poem and was to use the phrase 'Good time coming' in numerous novels including *The Three Clerks, Framley Parsonage, Phineas Finn, The Eustace Diamonds, Ralph the Heir* and *The Belton Estate*. In his book on Australia he uses it to describe the hoped-for gains from a gold mine he visited, and in *The Prime Minister* it even provides a euphemism for pregnancy. Apparently his mother also developed a fondness for the poem and her old friends, the Garnetts, believed that this demonstrated Fanny Trollope's return to the liberal attitudes they had once shared.[13] This common transatlantic faith in progress is perfectly expressed in some of the stanzas of Mackay's poem:

> There's a good time coming, boys,
> A good time coming:
> We may not live to see the day,
> But earth shall glisten in the ray,
> Of the good time coming
> Cannon balls may aid the truth,
> But thought's a weapon stronger;
> We will win our battle by its aid;–
> Wait a little longer.
>
> There's a good time coming, boys,
> A good time coming:
> Little children shall not toil
> Under or above the soil,
> In the good time coming.
> Religion shall be shorne of pride,
> And flourish all the stronger;

And Charity shall trim her lamp;–
Wait a little longer.

This shared vision of inevitable improvement, based on a common heritage of liberty, made Englishmen and Americans anxious to live together in peace. The enthusiastic reception given to the Prince of Wales when he visited America in 1860 symbolised the joint desire of both governments and peoples to have friendly relations. The thought of a war between them was increasingly referred to as a 'civil war' and therefore 'an impossibility' in the nineteenth century. Yet in 1861 America found herself involved in another 'civil war' – within her own borders.

*

The American war stirred passions about slavery, a topic about which English visitors had held determined opinions for over half a century. Trollope was solidly in the tradition of almost every English traveller in having strong anti-slavery views.[14] Conservatives like Mrs Trollope saw the 'peculiar institution' as an example of hypocrisy: Americans preached liberty and practised slavery. Radicals like Dickens saw it as a foul blot on noble ideals. *Uncle Tom's Cabin*, perhaps the most influential novel in history, had a great impact on opinion outside America, especially in England where most copies were sold. Yet, surprisingly, this opposition to slavery did not determine attitudes towards the war. Once the fighting started sympathy for the South grew, particularly as Lincoln repeatedly declared that he had no intention of liberating the slaves. That outspoken Scotsman, Thomas Carlyle, had long maintained that Englishmen who ranted about the evils of slavery while ignoring the 'white slaves' in their own factories were as hypocritical as Americans who defended slavery while shouting about freedom. Carlyle spoke for those who did not see the war as a moral question: 'There they are cutting each other's throats, because one half of them prefer hiring their servants for life, and the other by the hour.'

It is often said that 'Society' supported the South while 'working people' defended the North, despite the suffering caused by the virtual disappearance of American cotton, but this is far too simple. Some liberals in all classes favoured the Southern cause because they saw it as similar to Italian or Polish nationalism: a valiant people struggling to be free. Other Englishmen admired the South because they felt a vague kinship with its traditions or disliked the emerging power of the North.

Englishmen were interested in the war because they knew that their great economic prosperity was largely built on cotton. In 1861 452,000 people were employed in the cotton mills, including 22,000 boys and 18,000 girls under thirteen. A blockade that threatened this trade could prove disastrous to British prosperity. Trollope saw the need for an accurate account because he knew that behind all English interest there was an enormous expanse of ignorance. Leslie Stephen, now better known for fathering Virginia Woolf than for his own writing, began his literary career with a survey of the attitude of *The Times* during the American War. He would write in 1865: 'The name of America five years ago, called up to the ordinary English mind nothing but a vague cluster of associations compounded of Mrs. Trollope, *Martin Chuzzlewit*, and *Uncle Tom's Cabin.*' This ignorance could be quite astounding. One MP told a visiting American clergyman in the midst of the war:

> Why, there are you Northerners ... placed in North America all by yourselves! Then, there comes the isthmus – see, Panama, or whatever it is. Then, separated from you by this narrow bit of land, are the Southerners down there in South America. Now, my dear sir, I think you must admit, it is perfectly obvious that nature never meant you to be a Union.

Ignorance was fed by stereotypes which, as so often, were half-true. Americans were portrayed (in the cartoons of *Punch* to give a well known example) as loud and boastful. This, of course, was exactly the picture presented by Mrs Trollope and Dickens. Anthony Trollope agreed that the Americans were boastful, but he had seen the underlying reason, as he wrote in his book on the West Indies:[15]

> And are the Americans the first bumptious people on record? Has no other nation assumed itself to be in advance of the world, to be the apostle of progress, the fountain of liberty, the rock-spring of manly work? If the Americans were not bumptious, how unlike would they be to the parent that bore them! It is a proud reflection that we alone, of all people, have such children; a proud reflection and a joyous one; though the weaning of the baby will always be in some respects painful to the mother.

*

These, then, were some of the factors influencing writers like Trollope and their English readers when they thought about America. Naturally a similar mix of factors affected Americans when they met a famous English author come among them. It was not only American readers, like Mary Chesnut, who were beginning to notice Trollope: American writers had spotted a new star in the dazzling firmament of Victorian novelists. In February 1860 Nathaniel Hawthorne, coming to the end of his term as American consul in Liverpool, wrote to the Boston publisher James T. Fields:

> Have you ever read the novels of Anthony Trollope? They precisely suit my taste; solid and substantial, written on the strength of beef and through the inspiration of ale, and just as real as if some giant had hewn a great lump out of the earth and put it under a glass case, with all its inhabitants going about their daily business and not suspecting that they were made a show of. And these books are just as English as a beefstake [*sic*].

When Fields repeated this to him a few months later at a dinner in London Trollope was so delighted that he wrote it down and carried it about with him. (It still survives in his handwriting in the Taylor Collection at Princeton.) He much admired the American novelist. It is difficult to think of a better description of Trollope's novels. Their author, who normally paid little attention to reviews, evidently agreed and later wrote in his *Autobiography* that 'it certainly is true in its nature'. It is characteristic of him to record his agreement with this tribute as he saw no reason to parade a grandiloquent show of false modesty. It is equally characteristic to place himself behind many other writers, particularly those with greater powers of imagination. Thus he refers to Hawthorne as 'a brother novelist very much greater than myself'. Trollope greatly admired Hawthorne's fiction and almost twenty years later wrote an excellent essay about it. He felt that Hawthorne exemplified the tendency to 'speculation' common in American literature. 'On our side of the water we deal more with beef and ale and less with dreams.'[16]

Because of his long residence in England, Hawthorne did not know whether Trollope's novels had been republished on the other side of the Atlantic. 'Have they been tried in America?' he asked Fields. 'It needs an English residence to make them thoroughly comprehensible, but still I should think that human nature would give them success anywhere.' By the time of Trollope's visit several of his novels had been published there: *Barchester Towers, The Three Clerks, Doctor Thorne, The Bertrams, Castle Richmond* and *Framley Parsonage*. His earliest novels on Ireland had not been republished. His West Indies book had been brought out and, as we have seen, attracted considerable interest for its portrait of a society coping with the problem of emancipated slaves. American reviewers had also begun to notice Trollope. Of course he had the mixed blessing of his name, one that was still known and not liked by many Americans. *Harper's New Monthly Magazine*, in its review of *Doctor Thorne* in September 1858, alluded to his inheritance: 'The vein of caustic satire which has given a certain bad eminence to the name which this author inherits has become mollified in his case into a sub-acid, piquant humour, which he brings to bear effectually on the weak and ludicrous points of English society.'[17] It is ironic that Trollope is now regarded as the writer who best chronicled the comfortable ways of Victorian England but, in his own time, he was often seen as a critic of that society.

Americans were particularly anxious to learn the nuances of life in what Hawthorne called 'our old home'. The American poet and traveller Nathaniel Willis had seen how important this was for the popularity of English novelists in America:

> The Atlantic is to us a century. We picture to ourselves England and Victoria as we picture to ourselves England and Elizabeth ... The immense ocean between us is like the distance of time; and while all that is minute and bewildering is lost to us, the greater lights of the age and prominent features of society stand out apart, and we judge of them like posterity.

With his unrivalled knowledge of English country life, Trollope described all those customs that nineteenth-century American readers (and now twentieth-century English readers) wished to understand – the type of carriage driven by a vicar, the mode of dining and the social gradations among physicians in county society. In the 1860s a fondness for Trollope seemed to be one of the few tastes that bridged the 'Dis-United States'. In Richmond, Virginia, the Confederate capital, one Southern lady in 1864 advised her readers in the *Southern Illustrated News* to read *Orley Farm*, while only a few miles from her desk, three-quarters of the thousand Northern officers held in Richmond's Libby Prison were said to be 'beguiling the tedium of their imprisonment' with the 'ingenious stories of ... Anthony Trollope'.[18]

Well-known English writers could be sure of a good reception in America where they were treated as visiting dignitaries: Dickens had been received with all the hysteria we mistakenly assume was invented for transient 'pop stars'. Thackeray had gone twice to lecture. In her diary Mrs Chesnut mentions a friend who spent seven hours reading Thackeray so that he could converse in 'the Queen's English' with the visiting journalist W.H. Russell. Russell himself recalled an American taking a seat next to him in a small boat carrying passengers out to a transatlantic ship. He was astonished that the man's sole reason for climbing into the rolling boat was to speak with Russell because 'I shall know for the rest of my life that I have spoken to one who has conversed with Thackeray'. Robert Garnett did not have long to enjoy his meeting with Russell, for shortly afterwards as a Confederate general he became the first high-ranking officer to be killed in the war. Trollope had no intention of giving lectures or readings from his works. If he had done so, he could have made a considerable sum, particularly if he had chosen to speak about England and the war. However, he did not like lecturing and was not very good at it. If he had been nothing but a money-grubber, as some still maintain, he would have followed the precedent of many other English writers and mounted the lecturer's podium.

Despite the adulation given to British authors, Americans still feared that their 'cousins' might view them with bemused condescension. No other prominent author who visited America better understood these mixed attitudes towards the mother country than Trollope. The American heroine in his short story 'Miss Ophelia Gledd' tells her English suitor: 'You English people are certainly wanting in intelligence, or you would read in the anxiety of all we say about England how much we all think of you. What will England say of us? what will England do in this or that matter as it concerns us? that is our first thought as to every matter that is of importance to us.' It was this 'anxiety' which led Mary Chesnut to write: 'All Britons come here to make a book armed with three things "pen, paper, and prejudices".' Anthony Trollope had undoubtedly packed his pen and his paper but he had tried to leave his prejudices behind.[19]

*

The Trollopes left Liverpool on 24 August 1861 on the Cunard mail packet *Arabia*. Just three years before, this steamer had been the subject of the first substantial transatlantic cable message. When the *Arabia* collided with another ship a cable was sent to England. The next day the English reply arrived, saying that all were safe: the messages had taken less than two-and-a-half hours to cross and re-cross the Atlantic. 'This (though by no means so quick as it will be) seems the acme of all that is wonderful,' exulted one diarist in London.[20] Unfortunately the cable broke shortly afterwards and rapid communication was not restored until after the war. (It is interesting to speculate whether rapid communication would have made the task of British and American diplomats easier or harder during those difficult years!) The Trollopes' crossing went not only safely but quickly, taking only twelve days. It had taken his mother almost eight weeks in 1827.

The *Arabia* stopped briefly at Nova Scotia to take on fresh water. When ships called in there, any urgent diplomatic messages could be telegraphed to Washington or equally pressing financial ones to New York. London newspapers were flung overboard in a special floating case so that the telegraph wires could start humming with English news and prices even before the ship docked. Perhaps nothing illustrates better the close links between the economies of Britain and America. Strangely Trollope, who was usually fascinated by all aspects of communication, did not mention this. His seven hours in Halifax allowed him time to find his land legs. In his book he poked gentle fun at the hurried research of travel writers including himself. These seven hours, he wrote, were 'not quite sufficient to justify me at this critical age in writing a chapter of travels in Nova Scotia, but enough perhaps to warrant a paragraph'.[21] As his cousin was in command of the Halifax garrison, Anthony and Rose were well entertained.

When the *Arabia* sailed into Boston harbour at 7 a.m. on Thursday, 5 September 1861, Trollope thought not of the scenery 'but of the tea that had been sunk there' almost ninety years before. Yet he also had 'much nervous anxiety' about more immediate concerns. How would a visiting Englishman be received? In America, particularly in Boston, there was considerable hostility to Britain because the British and French governments had granted belligerent status to the Confederacy. One of the city's great literary figures and one of Trollope's recent acquaintances, James Fields, who had shown him Hawthorne's letter, even disliked referring to the 'English' language. 'Don't let us talk or write any longer,' he told Longfellow, 'of the vernacular spoken in treacherous Great Britain. I speak only American henceforward.' Trollope himself was more concerned about how he would use that 'vernacular'. Like a good general, he had planned his strategy:

> I knew what the feeling there was ... and I knew also how impossible it is for an Englishman to hold his tongue and submit to dispraise of England. As for going among a people whose whole minds were filled with affairs of the war, and saying nothing about the war, I knew that no resolution to such an effect could be carried out. If one could not trust oneself to speak, one should have stayed at home in England ... I always did speak out openly what I thought and felt ... I encountered very strong – sometimes almost fierce – opposition, [but] I never was subjected to anything that was personally disagreeable to me.

It was Rose who was subjected to something disagreeable, or rather comical, as she came ashore. An American in the customs shed noticed the name on her luggage and was convinced that it was the infamous Mrs Trollope returning for another look at the embattled Republic. Nothing could convince this person that Rose had been only eleven when *Domestic Manners of the Americans* burst upon the literary world of 1832 or that Fanny Trollope was now a feeble lady of eighty-two, gently sleeping her life away in a Florentine villa. 'I guess you wrote that book' appeared to be the final judgment.[22]

Trollope arrived armed with letters of introduction. A sensible traveller always secured such letters from any acquaintance who knew people, particularly influential people, in the country he was planning to visit. These letters were often left unsealed so that the bearer could read the nice things said about him. Various unprepared hosts would then be startled by the sudden appearance of the visitor's card accompanied by the unsealed letter. It was an accepted convention that one owed some hospitality to anyone who followed these rules.[23] Trollope's best source for such letters was Richard Monckton Milnes MP (later Lord Houghton) a witty and charming man well known as the biographer of Keats and, to a more select circle, as the owner of Britain's largest collection of pornography. He had recently put forward Trollope's name for the Cosmopolitan Club in London, and it is probable that Milnes wrote letters for him. Such an introduction would open doors in Boston. Milnes's counterpart in America was Senator Charles Sumner of Massachusetts, and it is therefore no surprise to find Trollope meeting him only one day after his arrival. Even before that, in fact within hours of his walking down the gangway, Trollope was visiting Quincy, near Boston, the well-known seat of generations of the Adams family. One of the family, probably the young Charles Francis Adams, entertained the Trollopes to dinner a few nights later. Within a few months young Adams was off to the war, where he eventually commanded a regiment of ex-slaves. His father, the American Minister in London, was anxious to encourage British support for the Union, and Milnes, his most important ally, may well have mentioned Trollope's planned book.

Trollope also made contact with important figures in the Boston literary world, such as John Gorham Palfrey, the owner of the *North American Review*. (Years later Trollope would write articles on Hawthorne and Longfellow for the *Review*.) Palfrey, like many of the leading lights of the Bostonian firmament, had commenced his career as a Unitarian Minister. On the first Sunday of this trip Trollope even carried his research to church. He decided to go to the Unitarian

Church, not out of any regard for its doctrines but because of its importance in Bostonian life.

*

The Trollopes did not stay long in Boston, being 'driven out of it by the mosquitos' after only four days. They made for Newport, Rhode Island, the most fashionable of the sea-side watering places. 'Have you rooms?' Trollope asked a clerk at the Ocean Hotel. 'Rooms enough. We have only fifty here,' was the reply. The vast hotel with 600 rooms and only fifty guests had an abandoned and melancholy air.* Newport, once the summer resort of wealthy Southern planters, was now empty because of the war. A few Northern families still found it a comfortable retreat. Among them was the James family, but we do not know if the eighteen-year-old Henry encountered Trollope as the callow youth and the bearded novelist each walked about the streets. Their formal introduction would come many years later on a transatlantic voyage.[24] The Trollopes did not enjoy their week at the resort. It was worse for Rose, whom Anthony confesses he 'basely deserted' to the gloom of the nearly empty lounge. She relieved the tedium by an occasional ride.

It was probably at Newport that a man asked Rose: 'You like our institutions, ma'am?' 'Yes, indeed,' she replied, though, as Anthony remarks, 'not with all that eagerness of assent which the occasion perhaps required'. Such half-hearted enthusiasm only encouraged her inquisitor: 'Ah, I never yet met the down-trodden subject of a despot who did not hug his chains.' Trollope well knew that English visitors were always asked about 'our institutions'. As the United States then had more political prisoners and opposition journalists in its fortresses than almost any 'despotism', the question about 'our institutions' was not well timed. The word itself, which covered all aspects of public life, was regarded in England as a particularly absurd Americanism. Mrs Trollope – Mrs Fanny Trollope, that is – had made great sport of American boasts of 'our divine political institutions'. Yet, as always, such usages made their way into England, and within a few years Trollope's friend George Eliot was using it in one of her novels. Only a few months after his return from America Trollope himself was

---

*The modern hotel was an American invention. While the word was used as early as the Revolutionary era the vast, elegant structures which Trollope described are normally said to have begun with the Tremont House in Boston, where he would enjoy an elegant dinner in November. It was opened in 1829. Soon the American hotel featured water-closets, bathrooms and central heating on all floors: luxuries unheard of in England. In 1859 the first practical passenger lift appeared when the Fifth Avenue Hotel in New York installed its first 'elevator'.

proclaimed 'a national institution' by one English magazine. However, it was Trollope who gave the term its ultimate seal of approval when he said in a political speech about education seven years later, 'I do not desire to Americanise our English institutions.' While he did not mind questions about 'our institutions' he was amused when one person asked him whether 'lords' ever spoke to men who were not 'lords'.[25]

Perhaps this question was asked in the hotel bar where Trollope spent considerable time 'liquoring up' while talking about the war, smoking a cigar or devouring the newspapers. The recollection of such rooms was to be hauled out of his memory and used in *Dr. Wortle's School* where he describes 'the large hall, in which, as is usual in American hotels, men sit and loafe and smoke and read the newspapers' [VI]. The word 'loafe' was as repugnant to him as the act. His father's war on 'idling' had formed Trollope's attitude to work, and even his holidays had to be justified with frantic activity. Yet, by his standards, he was to some degree 'loafing' for he did no writing when at Newport and did not begin *North America* until 16 September, eleven days after his arrival. He only managed three pages that day and just thirty that week.[26] He tried swimming in the ocean to relieve his boredom but disliked mixed bathing because it forced him into a cumbersome costume. He preferred, as he informed his readers, to swim in the nude: this admission was one of the reasons why some considered that, like his mother, he had a 'vulgar' streak.

After a week of 'loafing' he was no doubt delighted to embark on a whirlwind tour of New England. In Maine he was annoyed by the state's celebrated teetotal laws which forbade drinking in public. These laws were much admired by zealots in England, although the Prince of Wales on his recent visit had laughingly persuaded the Governor to drink a glass of wine on HMS *Hero* as the royal party was about to sail from Portland harbour. Trollope, who detested the two extremes of drunkenness and prohibition, was at least partially mollified when the hotel-keeper quietly set a bottle of ale at his place but, to comply with the absurd law, made no charge. 'But they advertise beer in the shop-windows,' Trollope later protested to his driver: 'A man can get drunk on it.' 'Wa'al, yes,' was the jovial reply, 'if he goes to work hard, and drinks a bucketful.'[27]

*

The Trollopes then crossed the border: a Canadian visit always indicated the underlying outlook of British travellers. The radical, like Fanny Wright, denounced Canada as a backward land under the double horror of Church and Crown, while her erstwhile friend Fanny Trollope was delighted to cross from the vulgar republic into a kingdom where children saluted her with curtsies. When her son arrived he, characteristically, had mixed feelings. 'We – the refined gentlemen and ladies of England ... are very apt to prefer the hat-touchers to those who are not hat-touchers.' Yet he did not allow his personal treatment to dominate his conclusion that 'that which is good and pleasant to us, is often not good and pleasant altogether'. Although he saw people and places he liked, he argued that Canadian growth was lagging behind that of its republican neighbour. Quebec was a 'very picturesque town, – from its natural advantages almost as much so as any town I know', but it did not appear to be moving ahead. Statistics showed that Canadian cities had not grown as fast as American ones: the centuries-old Quebec had a population of 60,000, while the new city of Chicago was more than double that already. Trollope is usually seen as a novelist of peaceful rural life; yet he saw the dynamic force that was shaping life on both sides of the Atlantic:

> It is through great cities that the civilisation of the world has progressed ... Man in his rudest state begins in the country, and in his most finished state may retire there. But the battle of the world has to be fought in the cities; and the country that shows the greatest city population is ever the one that is going most ahead in the world's history.

Trollope was convinced that it was both inevitable and good that Canada would, in time, separate completely from Britain. He thought it would be wise for one of Queen Victoria's younger sons to succeed to a Canadian throne to preserve a tie with Britain. This was not such a strange view. Prince Albert was considering a similar plan, in which some of his younger sons would rule the most important colonies. In fact his two eldest sons had both recently visited Canada. Trollope encountered a familiar problem in Canada, one he had known in Ireland: the tension of two communities divided by religion. That tension had increased when some Orangemen tried to turn a visit to Toronto by the Prince of Wales into an anti-papist display. The Prince, even then anxious to be a peacemaker, agreed that his barge would not stop at the city. Trollope thought the French Canadians were being increasingly assimilated into an English-dominated society. He accepted 'as a fact that a Roman Catholic population can never hold its ground against one that is Protestant'. Here he is a good Victorian, fully in accord with the spirit of his age and in company with other writers like Dickens and Macaulay, but he had a sense of fairness and a romanticism that they both lacked. 'And yet,' he muses, 'I love their religion. There is something beautiful and almost divine in the faith and obedience of a true son of the Holy Mother. I sometimes fancy that I would fain be a Roman Catholic, – if I could; as also I would often wish to be still a child, if that were possible.' The Trollopes saw many of the cities and much of the scenery in the few weeks they were there. Trollope was invited to dinner by Sir Edmund Head, the Governor General, who had been at Winchester a few years before him. He repaid this hospitality by heaping praise on Sir Edmund whenever possible in his book.

At Owl's Head Mountain on the border with Vermont the ever-active Anthony scorned the idea of spending a day fishing. As in Central America or the Pyrenees, a mountain presented a challenge that had to be met. Here we get one of our best glimpses of Rose and can see how she shared her husband's love of adventure. (Those writers who delight in asserting that she did not fill some deep, though unspecified, need in her husband's 'psyche' would be well advised to read his proud account of their adventures on the mountain.) Rose was no vapid Victorian lady designed for a life on a couch surrounded by servants. Someone warned her that a two-mile climb was too much for a middle-aged lady, although 'young women' managed it 'at times'. Such words were too much for Rose at forty-one! 'After that,' recalled the proud husband, 'my wife resolved that she would see the top of Owl's Head, or die in the attempt.' They reached the top after the steepest climb of his life and sat surveying the two countries spread out below, each alive with the vivid reds and golds of the autumn maple leaves which can only be seen in North America. The exquisite beauty enthralled them too long, and as they started down the heavily wooded mountain a blinding darkness descended and a heavy rain storm made the ground so soft that they sank up to their knees in the mud. Luckily they spotted the flickering lights of lanterns held by men searching for them. 'In spite of which misadventure,' the indomitable Trollope added, 'I advise all travellers in Lower Canada to go up the Owl's Head.'

*

On this trip Trollope the traveller and writer did not entirely efface Trollope the postal surveyor. He was always observing how the mail was handled. The Canadians won his praise for spending half as much as the English to transport a coachload of mail, even though they used two horses whereas the English used only one. He was not impressed, however, with the Canadian indifference to speedy and regular delivery, a subject close to his heart. Things were even worse in the United States where the government delivered the mail only to the local post office. Anyone who wanted delivery to their house had to pay for a private service. It may be remembered that Trollope had seen it as his official mission to get the post to Englishmen's breakfast tables. In Vermont, he had a conversation with a mail driver:

> Trollope: 'Are you going this morning? I thought you always started in the evening?'
> Mail-Driver: 'Wa'll; I guess I do. But it rained some last night, so I jist stayed at home.'

Trollope's reaction is predictable: 'I do not know that I ever felt more shocked in my life, and I could hardly keep my tongue off the man.' Yet he realised he was powerless in Vermont. 'I was obliged to walk away crestfallen.'

As an experienced traveller, he was anxious to take his wife to the greatest 'lion' in America, Niagara Falls. He, of course, had already seen it on his hurried trip in 1859 and held it in great awe: 'Of all the sights on this earth ... I know no other one thing so beautiful, so glorious, and so powerful.' Unlike modern tourists who merely gape, Trollope hurried about seeing the Falls from every angle on both the American and Canadian sides. Clad in cumbersome oil-skins, he struggled down steep and slippery rocks to get close to the thundering roar and spray. While he scurried about, he was perplexed that Americans, even then, preferred carriages to walking. He eventually found a cause of this vice: overheated rooms. In *North America* he gives sensible advice about which angles a tourist should select for the awe-inspiring sight. His favourite spot was a wooden bridge:

> Seat yourself on the rail, and there sit till all the outer world is lost to you ... To realize Niagara you must sit there till you see nothing else ... hear nothing else and think of nothing else ... You will fall as the bright waters fall, rushing down into your new world with no hesitation and with no dismay; and you will rise again as the spray rises, bright, beautiful and pure. Then you will flow away in your course to the uncompassed, distant and eternal ocean.

Trollope was more than a realistic novelist: in him had survived, somewhat subdued under his Victorian reserve and broad-cloth, a large part of his mother's romanticism.[28]

*

After two days at the Falls the Trollopes turned westward and began an amazingly energetic tour, mainly by steamboat and train. Thirty years before his mother had warned: 'Let no one ... commence their travels in a Mississippi steam boat ... I declare I would infinitely prefer sharing the apartment of a party of well-conditioned pigs.'[29] Her son generally found the steamboats comfortable and clean but complained that, like almost everything else, they were over-heated. 'But as the boats are made for Americans, and as Americans like hot air, I do not put it forward with any idea that a change ought to be effected.'* Another feature of American travel that disturbed him was the large number of children. He shared to the full the Victorian view that children belonged in the nursery for the simple reason that 'the uncontrolled energies of twenty children round one's legs do not convey comfort or happiness'.

That British invention, the railway, had proved of greater importance to the development of America than any other discovery in the thirty years that had elapsed since Fanny Trollope's visit. While she had bounced her way across frontier roads, squeezed into a springless coach, her son sat back in comfort while the train carried him hundreds of miles every day. A railway guide published in England during Trollope's visit praised American railways: They 'present the acme of comfort and convenience. You can buy your railway ticket in the carriage; and there you can have every convenience of a moving hostelry ... You can purchase a newspaper or a book to while away the time ... you can have a bed at night; in short, you might literally lodge in the train.'[30]

Trollope was delighted with that 'thoroughly American institution of sleeping-cars': to be able to sleep while moving ahead was too attractive an idea for him to ignore. At this time British trains did not have such facilities except on the royal train, which carried the Queen from Windsor to Scotland. Trollope explained how the American sleeping-cars were organised:

> The travellers may have a whole bed, or half a bed ... I confess I have always taken a delight in seeing these beds made up ... The work is usually done by negroes or coloured men; and the domestic negroes of America are always light-handed and adroit ... for every four seats in the railway car he builds up four beds ... Mattresses slip out from one nook and pillows from another. Blankets are added, and the bed is ready.

To him this was not just an amusing spectacle but an essential attribute of the American character:

---

*Trollope's frequent comments about the American penchant for over-heating led one friendly critic in the *North American Review* to call it 'his hobby which he rides through the book most amusingly'.

> The great glory of the Americans is in their wondrous contrivances, – in
> their patent remedies for the usually troublous operations of life. In their
> huge hotels ... one fire heats every room, passage, hall, and cupboard ...
> Men and women go up and down stairs without motive power of their
> own. Hot and cold water are laid on to all the chambers; – though it
> sometimes happens that the water from both taps is boiling ... [but] of all
> their wonderful contrivances that of their railroad beds is by no means
> the least.

At La Crosse in Wisconsin the Trollopes boarded a river-boat to take
them along the Mississippi. In spite of the heat of the cabins, which
Trollope found 'almost unbearable', and the noise of the children, he
revelled in the rich autumn scenery of the Upper Mississippi as it
twisted its way south between the states of Wisconsin and Minnesota,
Iowa and Illinois. Yet, as much as he loved to look at scenery, people
were always more important. When his steam boat's wheel broke, he
turned the lost time to good account. He clambered up the 'bluff' and
walked till he found two lonely cabins belonging to families who
survived by cutting fire-wood for the boats. Perhaps he recalled
Hervieu's illustration in his mother's book of the woodcutters, and her
statement that 'I never witnessed human nature reduced so low, as it
appeared to be in the woodcutters on the unwholesome banks of the
Mississippi.'[31] While she had only gazed from the boat, her son went to
investigate.

Wherever he travelled, whether in England or Ireland or now in
America, Trollope was as interested in what went on in cottages as in
vicarages or mansions. The unscheduled breakdown allowed him time
to inspect the two cabins, and he was impressed that they contained
books. The woodcutters told him they earned half a dollar a day
chopping down trees to appease the voracious appetite of the steam
boats' boilers. He sat in one cabin and chatted for an hour about
English politics and how they might affect the war in America. All the
while the wife continued cooking, the woodcutter played with his
children, the grandfather bounced a child on his knee, and the
grandmother knitted, 'as old women always do'. This little episode
gives us the key to Trollope's greatness as a novelist. The reason he
was able to depict human behaviour in all its myriad forms and
subtleties was that he used every opportunity he had to observe people
in their daily lives.

The only thing that annoyed him about this interlude was that he
was the only passenger who used the delay to visit and talk to the
isolated dwellers. Other passengers remained on the boat in a sullen
mood. He had already remarked that Americans did almost all their

travelling in stony silence. He rejected the adage that 'Two Englishmen meeting in the desert would not speak unless they were introduced'. 'The further I travel,' he wrote, 'the less true do I find this of Englishmen, and the more true of other people.' Certainly no one, in any of the six continents Trollope was to visit, could ever accuse him of being a quiet traveller!

Trollope finished his rapid tour of the Upper Mississippi impressed with the vast agricultural production of America. As always, he went wherever he could to observe activity and gather facts. When he saw that new invention, the grain elevator, he had to climb it – twice. In Chicago he hurried to the Post Office to exchange statistics with the Postmaster. In another building in the city he was not welcomed when he tried to watch people depositing their voting papers in a ballot box. This was a novel experience as Englishmen still called out their vote in public. He was turned out of the election place with 'some slight tumult' apparently because the officials were worried about the huge amount of corruption already prevalent in Chicago elections. Comedy, however, proved more enjoyable than politics: 'I never laughed more heartily in my life,' he wrote, than at the theatre in Chicago. Perhaps the reason Trollope laughed so much was that the programme was made up of *The Yankee in England* and *The Post Office Mistake*.[32]

*

Trollope reached New York on the last day of October. Unlike his mother, who had warmly praised 'this fair city', he was not particularly comfortable there. The city was already the third largest in the world – at least by Trollope's reckoning, for he loftily dismissed any oriental rivals as those 'Chinese congregations of unwinged ants'. New York was too manifestly given over to unrestrained materialism to appeal to him. 'I have never walked down Fifth Avenue alone without thinking of money.'* One writer, Henry Tuckerman, was sitting in his library when,

> in response to his 'Come in', the door flew open, a stout, hairy-faced, ruddy-complexioned Englishman burst in upon his solitude like a rough shaggy Newfoundland dog about to leap upon him in the exuberance of

---

*Trollope was evidently affected by his stay in America when he refers to 'Fifth Avenue' without the definite article. Normally he follows the Victorian English usage – 'The Fifth Avenue' – just as he said *'the* Paddington Station'. In one of his last novels, *The Duke's Children*, he uses 'the' in the narrative while the American heroine does not do so but speaks of 'Fifth Avenue'. This is a small example of how careful he was with the nuances of speech.

animal spirits. 'My name is Anthony Trollope!' exclaimed the visitor in brusque voice, 'and I've brought you a letter of introduction from a mutual friend in England.' In physique, manner and speech he might have been taken for a dragoon in mufti, or a sportsman fresh from an invigorating run in the fields; certainly not for a novelist whose forte lay in depicting the salient traits of English clergymen, the delicate shades of character among English maidens, and in composing those inimitable love-letters which so plentifully bestrew the pages of his lifelike romances.

Henry Tuckerman's was a common reaction, in England as well as in America: how could such a rough figure produce such delightfully subtle novels? It is rather amusing for an American writer to think Trollope looked like a fox-hunter and almost as ironical to compare him to a Newfoundland dog, since that was a favourite simile of his own. This description ends with the fascinating comment about the novelist's spectacles 'through which he seemed to inspect men and things with a quiet scrutiny, as if making perpetual mental memoranda for future use'. That is precisely what he was doing. On 6 November he compiled another memorandum when he went with Tuckerman to hear the celebrated diplomat and historian George Bancroft lecture at the New York Historical Society. Trollope studied the lecturer carefully and in the midst of some applause leaned over and whispered, 'Do you suppose he himself believes what he is saying?' Nevertheless Trollope became friendly with the historian and added his seven-volume *History of the United States*, the last volume of which appeared that year, to the burgeoning library at Waltham House.[33]

Although he complained about the difficulties of getting about, Trollope did agree that 'New York is a most interesting city'. He managed to see most of 'our great institootions'. He may have thought the word silly, but he was most impressed with the achievements it was used to describe: 'The country in this respect boasts, but it has done that which justifies a boast.' Like almost all other English visitors he was taken to admire the new reservoir (a massive Egyptian-style fortress on the site of what is now the New York Public Library), the largest store in the world, Central Park, and schools for the deaf and dumb. Charles Dickens had made visits to special schools almost obligatory after he gave such praise to the way in which the handicapped were taught in America. However, Trollope had also inherited this interest from his mother. She even visited mental asylums in her travels; this could be a most upsetting experience in the nineteenth century. In her book on Paris she calls this 'my usual love for the terrible'. Her son pronounced the New York mental asylum 'perfect' in spite of a tour by the physician who introduced patients to him in the following manner: 'An English lady, Mr Trollope. I'll introduce you. Quite a hopeless case. Two old women. They've been here fifty years. They're English. Another gentleman from England, Mr Trollope. A very interesting case! Confirmed inebriety.' However, one incident he did not mention in his book occurred at the New York Hospital when he 'was so overcome by one of the sights that he grew faint by the side of the superintendent as he was taking him around the wards'.[34]

Of all the 'institutions' none impressed Trollope so much as the state schools. He was becoming increasingly concerned about education for all children, something in which he believed that literary men and women should take an interest. Having visited free or 'charity' schools in London, he compared the statistics and frankly admitted that New York was far ahead: America had proved that a state system of free schools did not have to have the social stigma attached to 'free' schools in England, aimed at the children of the poor. With his firm belief that 'seeing and hearing are always more effective than figures' he included an account of his visit to a girls' school:

> The female pupil at a free school in London is, as a rule, either a ragged pauper, or a charity girl ... We Englishmen know well the type of each ... We see the result afterwards when the same girls become our servants, and the wives of our grooms and porters. The female pupil at a free school in New York is neither a pauper nor a charity girl. She is dressed with the utmost decency. She is perfectly clean. In speaking to her, you cannot in any degree guess whether her father has a dollar a day, or three thousand dollars a year ... As regards her own manner to you, it is always the same as though her father were in all respects your equal. As to the amount of knowledge, I fairly confess that it is terrific.

One girl was asked to explain the properties of an hypotenuse to the famous English writer. Trollope, whose own youth had left him blissfully ignorant of the miseries of geometry, was quite puzzled. In the next class the topic was one to which his own unhappy youthful education had been dedicated: the Classics. 'Why did the Romans run away with the Sabine women?' asked the schoolmistress. 'Because they were pretty,' replied a perceptive girl. Trollope concluded that these schools were 'leagues beyond that terrible repetition of A B C' which marked the free schools of London. Unlike many English visitors, he did not take the view that learning about the past was a privilege fit only for gentlemen. A civilisation's culture should be enjoyed by all classes of men and women: in thinking of this, his thoughts flashed back to that hard-working woman, the wife of the woodcutter, whose cabin he had visited. Trollope was sure that her education had made it easier for her to withstand the hardships of her life. His examination of American schools made a profound impression on him, as he said in his speeches when he stood for Parliament and advocated better education for all the people of England.[35]

*

In spite of his admiration for New York schools, Trollope was delighted to return to Boston on 12 November. He already had met many people there, and soon the old Puritan capital had become one of his favourite cities. His acquaintances soon ripened into friendships, as he spent a total of three separate periods there. He became quite lyrical when writing of it: 'There were houses to which I could have gone with my eyes blindfold; doors of which the latches were familiar to my hands; faces which I knew so well.' One reason for his delight in Boston was the ready reception given him by the city's literary men. Some English writers and society figures liked to laugh at the presumptuousness of the 'Western Athens', as the popular quote attributed to a Bostonian visiting England testified: 'There aren't twelve men even in Boston who could have written as well as Shakespeare!'

Trollope, however, admired the achievements of the city's great writers. In London 'serious' writers such as Carlyle or Tennyson paid scant regard to the works of a novelist such as Trollope, but Emerson and Longfellow made him welcome in Boston, where he was entertained at many literary dinners. He had not forgotten Hawthorne's praise, and he returned the compliment in *Can You Forgive Her?* in 1864, referring to 'our excellent American friend and critic, Mr. Hawthorne' [XXXIII]. The publisher of the *Atlantic Monthly*, James T. Fields, who had first told Trollope of the older novelist's comments, brought them together at a dinner on the afternoon before the Trollopes started their New England tour. Fields later wrote to Hawthorne, 'Trollope fell in love with you at first sight and went off moaning that he could not see you again. He swears you are the handsomest Yankee that ever walked this planet.' One of the best descriptions of Trollope in conversation comes from James Russell Lowell, who met him at a dinner, apparently the same one to which Fields had invited Hawthorne and Emerson. Lowell was a poet as well as a Professor at Harvard, and a fervent abolitionist. He was in a passion against Britain, refusing to write to any of his English friends until the war had ended. Decades later, at the end of Trollope's life, Lowell would be a popular Minister to England. The poet scrutinised the novelist and found him 'a big, red-faced, rather underbred Englishman of the bald-with-spectacles type. A good roaring positive fellow who deafened me (sitting on his right).' This comment shows Americans were as capable as Englishmen of firing off snobbish remarks about one another![36]

Trollope proceeded to one of his favourite dinner-party gambits by describing his schedule of producing a set number of words every day and, as so often, compared his work to that of 'a shoemaker on a shoe, only taking care to make honest stitches'. Among the guests was Oliver Wendell Holmes, whose *Autocrat of the Breakfast Table* was one of the most popular books of the day on both sides of the Atlantic. If there was an 'Autocrat' who ruled the Bostonian Republic of Letters it was undoubtedly the genial Holmes. He and Trollope soon were settled into a most enjoyable argument about wine. As he grew prosperous, Trollope, quite naturally, became more interested in wine and with that interest came, again quite naturally, fiercely held opinions. Many Americans still preserved the eighteenth-century devotion to madeira, and argued that the long voyage to America improved the wine. In England it was increasingly dismissed as a wine for invalids. It may be recalled that old Bishop Grantly in *Barchester Towers* was given a 'modicum of madeira' as he lay dying. Lowell compares Holmes's arguments on this weighty topic to 'pelting a rhinoceros with seed-pearl'. Holmes flung the first pellet:

> 'You don't know what madeira is in England?'
> Trollope: 'I'm not so sure it's worth knowing.'
> Holmes: 'Connoisseurship in it with us is a fine art. There are men who will tell you a dozen kinds.'
> Trollope: 'They might be better employed.'
> Holmes: 'But you may be assured ... '
> Trollope: 'No, but I mayn't be *asshorred*. I won't be *asshorred*. I don't intend to be *asshorred*' (roaring louder).

Lowell was amused but also, perhaps, slightly embarrassed. Years before he had refused to attend a public dinner in honour of Dickens because wine would be served; he had been afraid of offending his wife, a fanatical teetotaller. He ended his account of the dinner for Trollope: 'And so they went it. It was very funny. Trollope wouldn't give him any chance. Meanwhile, Emerson and I, who sat between them, couched down out of range and had some good talk, with the shot hurtling overhead.' Lowell records his own 'one little passage at arms with T. apropos of English peaches'. As we have seen, Trollope had inherited his mother's patriotic devotion to English fruit and he ended this battle by saying, 'England was the only country where such a thing as a peach or a grape was known.' Lowell then 'appealed to Hawthorne who sat opposite. His face mantled and trembled for a moment with some droll fancy ... and then he said, "I asked an Englishman once who was praising their peaches ... exactly what he meant by a peach, and he described something very like a cucumber." ' Trollope's recollection of this badinage was that he tried to praise the superiority of English peas while Hawthorne defended American vegetables 'almost with violence'. Despite all these oral cannonades, it might surprise some modern readers that Lowell concluded, 'I rather liked Trollope.' Trollope and he, like most Victorians on both sides of the Atlantic, held and expressed their views with a vigour that is now often thought intolerant.[37] Fifteen years later Trollope would use Holmes's words in *The American Senator* when Senator Gotobed boasts to his English host, 'In the matter of wine, I don't think I have happened to come across anything so good in this country as our old Madeiras' [XLII].

It was not only living American authors who occupied Trollope's time. He still admired James Fenimore Cooper, who had died in 1851. It may be recalled that the lonely young Anthony read and reread two stray volumes of *The Prairie*, when most of his family were on the edge of that same wilderness which Cooper had made known to the world. Now the highly successful Trollope casually asked a Boston bookshop to send him all thirty-two volumes of Cooper's works for his expanding library. With shopping, dining, attending lectures, travelling and meeting other writers it is not surprising that Trollope was falling behind in his writing by the time he left Boston. He visited Concord to see Emerson and Hawthorne and Cambridge to see Longfellow; he had his big dinner at the Tremont Hotel on 26 October and on the following day met Wendell Phillips, the Boston abolitionist lecturer; on 2 December he went to see Lowell, Massachusetts, the 'model industrial village', leaving the next day for New York.

*

While in Boston, Trollope was able to see Kate Field: to meet her again was an added delight to the American excursion, though certainly in no sense the reason for it. She was surprised that Rose planned to return to England several months before Anthony. He assumed that air of mock outrage which delighted Rose as well as Kate, and told her: 'You write ... as tho' she were as free from impediments in the world as your happy self. She has a house, and children and cows and horses and dogs and pigs – and all the stern necessities of an English home.'

Frances Trollope from a drawing in the *New Monthly Magazine* of 1839 which was used four years later as a frontispiece for her novel, *Jessie Phillips*, an attack upon the treatment of the poor.

'Orley Farm' from a drawing by Millais for Trollope's novel of that name. It is based on the second house the Trollopes occupied in Harrow.

A rural letter-carrier about the time of Trollope's retirement from the Post Office. (Post Office Archives)

The 'wretched tumble-down farmhouse' at Harrow Weald, where the young Anthony spent the most miserable part of his youth with his father, while his mother was in America. From *The Bookman*, 1903.

An illustration from Trollope's *He Knew He Was Right* drawn by Marcus Stone. The lady in black, Jemima Stanhope, was based on Trollope's cousin, Fanny Bent. Her devotion to old ways is indicated by the bust, which may well be that of her hero, Lord Eldon.

One of the earliest pillar-boxes. This one was in Guernsey. Trollope first recommended their use in Jersey. This is the same design, the hexagonal 'Vaudin' named after the maker. Trollope always took a paternal interest in these, his most important contribution to the postal service. (Post Office Archives)

"The Village Postman" engraved for the *Illustrated London News* from a painting by J.M. Carrick. Trollope spent much of the 1850s improving the delivery of the post in rural areas. (Post Office Archives)

Sir Francis Freeling, who
appointed Trollope to a clerkship
in 1834. (Post Office Archives)

Sir Rowland Hill, the originator of
the 'Penny Post'. There was little
sympathy between him and
Trollope. (Post Office Archives)

Four Secretaries of
the Post Office

Colonel William Maberly — a
youthful picture, probably
painted about the time when he
fought at Waterloo. (Post Office
Archives)

Sir John Tilley, one of Trollope's
closest friends, who married his
sister, Cecilia. (Post Office
Archives)

Thomas Adolphus Trollope and Anthony Trollope. A photograph taken in Florence. In sending this to a relative in 1864 Trollope wrote, 'You will perceive that my brother is pitching into me. He always did.' (Bodleian Library)

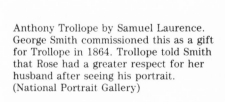

Anthony Trollope by Samuel Laurence. George Smith commissioned this as a gift for Trollope in 1864. Trollope told Smith that Rose had a greater respect for her husband after seeing his portrait. (National Portrait Gallery)

Rose Trollope in one of only two known photographs. She seems to have shared her husband's dislike of posing for photographs. (Boston Public Library, Massachusetts)

Kate Field, the young American girl whom Trollope met in Florence and with whom he carried on a long friendship and correspondence. From LaSalle (Corbell) Pickett, *Across My Path: memories of people I have known*, 1916.

George Smith by G.F. Watts. It was Smith's *Cornhill Magazine* that gave Trollope his great fame in 1860. He published several of Trollope's best novels. From *Dictionary of National Biography*, vol. XXII, 1909.

John Blackwood, the publisher of several of Trollope's novels. Trollope gave him the copyright of one book free as a 'birthday present'. Blackwood was an enthusiastic golfer, hence his cap. From Mrs Gerald Porter, *John Blackwood*, 1908.

Richard Monckton Milnes, Lord Houghton. A minor politician and poet but a major figure in London literary society. He arranged for Trollope to join the Cosmopolitan Club. A *Vanity Fair* caricature by 'Spy' (Leslie Ward).

William Makepeace Thackeray, Trollope's literary hero: he thought Thackeray's *Henry Esmond* the greatest of English novels. They became friends in 1860. Engraved for the *Eclectic Magazine*.

Trollope with three friends playing whist: Abraham Hayward,
the best informed political journalist of the time; W.E.
Forster, M.P. best remembered for the Education Act of 1870;
Sir George Jessel, M.P., Solicitor-General and Master of the
Rolls. From M.L. Irwin, *Anthony Trollope: a bibliography*,
1926.

Waltham House, Waltham Cross, Herts, where Trollope lived from 1859 to 1871.
(Cheshunt Library, Herts)

Election poster, Beverley 1868.
(Beverley Public Library)

ELECTORS OF BEVERLEY
BE NOT DECEIVED.

Sir H. Edwards did vote to take one Member from Beverley.

Mr. Sykes declared at the Norwood Rooms that the last vote he gave in the House was to preserve Two Members for Beverley.

Sir H. Edwards voted the very opposite to Mr. Sykes. If the proposal Sir H. Edwards' voted for had been carried we should now only have one Member to elect.

Mr. Sykes and Admiral Duncombe voted for a motion which preserved our representation as it is now.

Sir H. Edwards and Lord Hotham voted with the Tory Government to take one member from us.

Facts are stubborn things. The names of those who vote in the House of Commons are preserved.

Sir Henry Edwards sat on the Government wall ;
Sir Henry Edwards obeyed the Government call ;
Sir Henry Edwards will have a great fall,
And all Sir Henry's shufflings, and all his Men,
Can't lift Sir Henry on the wall again.

ELECTORS! Vote for
Maxwell and Trollope,
WHO WON'T DECEIVE YOU.

Anthony Trollope in his mid-sixties, taken from *Men of Mark: contemporary portraits of distinguished men, third series*, 1878. Photograph by Lock and Whitfield.

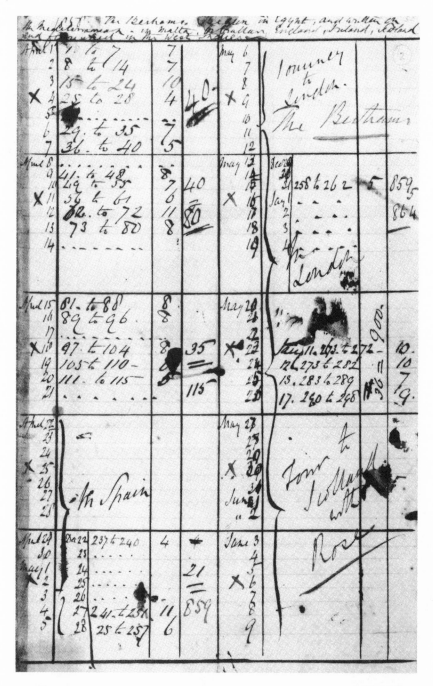

Trollope's worksheet for *The Bertrams*, 1858. The note at the top records its being written in Egypt, the Mediterranean, Malta, Gibraltar, England, Ireland, Scotland and the West Indies. The first column gives the date; the second the pages written that day; the third the daily total and the fourth the weekly total. He also records events that kept him from work, such as 'tour to Scotland with Rose'. As this was a holiday, he did no writing. (MS Bodley Don c 9 — Trollope Business Papers.)

The worksheet for *Ralph the Heir*, 1869. At the top is Trollope's estimate of words. On 15 April he breaks off to write a political article, 'Mr Disraeli and the Mint'. Later in April he stops work to accompany his younger son, Fred, to Plymouth on his way to Australia. Trollope was spending heavily, establishing his two sons, hence his note at the bottom on how much he was receiving for each page! (MS Bodley Don c 9 — Trollope Business Papers.)

Trollope's book on Australia and New Zealand was also sold in 4 volumes to make it affordable to potential emigrants. The hunter on top might be intended for the author himself. From the cover of the 1875 2s 'yellowback' edition.

Kate sought the guidance and influence of her famous friend to promote or, as the Victorians said, to 'puff' her writing. His constant advice was that she should settle down to the hard work of writing, as he had done, and stop wasting her time:

> I fear you are idle: – that you spend your time in running after false gods … seeking the excitement of ultra ideas and theoretical progress, while you begrudge the work of your brain, and the harder work of your fingers and backbone. Those lectures are but an intellectual idleness, an apology for sitting without a book to read or a skirt to hem or a shirt to fell instead of with them. You want to go ahead of other folk, – you know you do; but you wish to do it lazily; – or rather you are lazy in your mode of wishing it. You would whistle for a storm like a witch; but storms now a days will not come for whistling. You must sit down with a trumpet and blow at it till your cheeks would split. If you'll do that, something of a puff of wind will come at last. Now I hope you will find yourself well rated, & will send me your story off hand.

To Trollope there was one unfailing cure for Kate's idleness and scatterbrained ways. A few months later he wrote from the banks of the Mississippi recalling a talk with the Reverend W.G. Eliot, a Unitarian minister, founder of Washington University in St Louis and, more notably, the grandfather of T.S. Eliot: ' "Let her marry a husband," said he. "It is the best career for a woman." I agreed with him – and therefore bid you in his name as well as my own, to go & marry a husband.'[38]

As the prime portrayer of the nuances of English 'domestic manners', Trollope took an avid interest in how these same manners had evolved in America. In his fiction there are well over thirty American characters. Henry James's comment that 'his American portraits … are always friendly' is somewhat exaggerated: as with every other type of character, he presented both the good and the bad side.[39] One of the ways in which American 'manners' had diverged from the English was in the role of young ladies of the middle and upper classes. It was Kate Field who gave Anthony Trollope a unique opportunity to understand the American girl, and such girls pass through stories like 'The Courtship of Susan Bell' or novels like *He Knew He Was Right*. As we have seen, he has a strong claim to be one of the first to introduce the transatlantic marriage into English fiction. Trollope made it a main feature of many of his novels, including *He Knew He Was Right, Dr Wortle's School, The Duke's Children* and his incomplete, final work, *The Landleaguers*. Such marriages almost occur in *The Eustace Diamonds* and *The Way We Live Now* and frequently take place in short stories such as 'An Unprotected Female at the Pyramids' and 'The Widow's Mite'.

Trollope's best depiction of such a match is in the story 'Miss Ophelia Gledd', which sprang directly out of his stay in Boston. When he wrote it about a year later many details were still vivid in his memory. He admitted: 'There have crept into American society so many little social ways at variance with our social ways ... that the words, and habits, and social carriage, of an American woman, of the best class, too often offend the taste of an Englishman....' Yet, Trollope adds with his characteristic balance, 'as do, quite as strongly, those of the Englishwoman offend the American'. Ophelia Gledd is a Boston girl who after much discussion marries a visiting Englishman, the younger brother of a baronet. Her main worry is the reaction of her titled in-laws. Trollope, as usual, was absolutely accurate in depicting the fears of a girl faced with entering a strange world that knew little of her background. He may well have been aware of the marriage a few years earlier of Ellen Dwight, like Ophelia the daughter of a prosperous Boston merchant, to the Hon. Edward Twisleton, the younger brother of Lord Saye and Sele. They had become well-known figures in London literary society, but she was amused when a maid at the ancestral castle in Oxfordshire assumed that her bracelet was a 'badge' of her Indian tribe. She used to say that she gained acceptance when her English acquaintances heard that her family in Boston used Crown Derby china.[40] Ophelia Gledd is not Kate Field, but the heroine clearly shares some characteristics with Trollope's young friend: she goes to 'lectures ... to political debates, and wherever her enterprising heart and inquiring head chose to carry her'. The story also features a sleighing accident and Trollope himself had been involved in such an accident on 8 March 1862 when his horses bolted as he was taking a lady out for a ride. Both Trollope and the character in the story managed to regain control, and the latter concluded, 'sleighing was excellent fun'.

Late in November Trollope saw Rose safely aboard ship for her return trip to England. They had agreed months before that she would not spend the winter in America. Not surprisingly at that time of year she had a rough and miserable crossing before reaching home in time to celebrate Christmas with Harry and Fred. For this rough crossing she got scant sympathy from Anthony, who told Kate Field: 'I presume you will have heard from Rose. She was very unhappy on her voyage, having resolved that she would be so – But now is at peace with her cows and pigs. Write to her.'[41]

It was an unhappy Trollope who left for Washington to investigate the war which raged only a few miles from the beleaguered capital. It is ironic that somewhere within the battle lines that stretched from Virginia to Texas was his own nephew. Rose's eldest sister, Eliza, had married an Irishman named Samuel Anderton. Their son, Walter, had emigrated to America and settled in Baltimore from where he had joined the Sixth Infantry Regiment of Connecticut Volunteers. Apparently Trollope was ignorant of his family's involvement in the war he had come, in part, to observe. His immediate problem was his writing: his many jaunts had delayed his work, and by 4 December he writes on his work sheet for *North America*, 'Two weeks short', and instructs himself to improve, using the old word, 'vie vie'. Improvement was immediate, and the next day he completed his first volume, three months after he had arrived in the country. He no longer had his wife as a travelling companion, and was leaving Kate Field as well as other friends in Boston. His book contains an emotional tribute to the city: 'Farewell to thee, thou Western Athens! When I have forgotten thee my right hand shall have forgotten its cunning, and my heart forgotten its pulses.' Listing the names of his friends such as Longfellow, Lowell, Emerson, Holmes and Hawthorne, he asked: 'Who is there among us in England who has not been the better for these men? Who does not owe to some of them a debt of gratitude? In whose ears is not their names familiar? ... What city has done better than this? ... What other town of the same size has done as well in the same short space of time?' Times had indeed changed since Fanny Trollope had sneered at the 'insect authors' of America, and her son now concluded: 'I am thankful that my steps have wandered thither at such a period.'[42]

*

If Trollope liked Boston he positively loathed Washington. He thought the United States had made a great error in building a new capital rather than in remaining in one of the older cities like Philadelphia. Here he disagreed with his mother, who liked Washington because it was free from 'all sights, sounds or smells of commerce'. Once again we see his divided outlook towards so many aspects of life: he criticised Quebec because it was not forging ahead but criticised the people of Cincinnati because in forging ahead they had produced a town that was 'dingy and uninteresting'. He had found New York uncomfortable because it was too 'commercial'; yet he disliked Washington because it was an artifical creation with no business but government. Of New York he said that 'every man worships the dollar, and is down before his shrine from morning to night'; yet he himself rose early to finish his writing in order to earn enough to maintain a very comfortable life and to spend a small fortune on fox-hunting. He carefully compiled a detailed list of every penny he earned from his writing, and included the list in his *Autobiography* for the world to read. Writing was a craft he had mastered and he was proud of his mastery, much as the cobbler would have been of his well-stitched boots.

He arrived in the beleaguered capital about ten days before Christmas 1861. Undoubtedly his homesickness and Rose's absence did not put him in a good humour. He was also in considerable pain from a succession of carbuncles on the small of his back – 'if ', he wrote to Kate Field, 'my back has a small'. Then a large boil, or anthrax, erupted on his forehead. He was confined to his lodgings kept by 'Wormley, a coloured man, in I Street, to whose attention I can recommend any Englishman'. The anthrax had to be cut across, cauterised and bandaged with a huge linseed poultice. 'I was hardly out of the doctor's hands while I was there.' He even attempted a sketch of his forehead for Kate Field, which shows how little he had learnt about drawing from Hervieu.[43] Trollope was also depressed because Britain and the United States were on the verge of war.

The crisis had begun about a month before when a Northern naval captain, Charles Wilkes, stopped a Royal Mail packet, the *Trent*, and removed two Confederate diplomats on their way to England and France. When the news reached Boston the whole city rejoiced; as Trollope's first host, Charles Francis Adams Jnr., recalled, joy was 'universally expressed'. Trollope was outraged at this insult to Britain and open violation of international law. It was also an assault on the Post Office and on a ship on which Trollope himself had travelled when he was in the Caribbean.* The diplomats were on their way to St Thomas and he knew the area near the island where the incident had occurred. Stories appeared in the British press recounting how the daughter of one of the diplomats slapped the Yankee officer crying, 'Back, Back, you – cowardly Poltroon.' Trollope fumed to Kate Field: 'There will be war if those two horrid men are not given up. I wish Wilkes with his whole cargo had gone to the bottom.'[44] Wilkes himself formed yet another link with Trollope as he was of the family of the New York banker who had paid for Henry Trollope's return to England

---

*During his Central American travels, Trollope had been a guest on another ship destined to play an historic role in the war. The USS *Merrimac* had enjoyed a double conversion: it had become a Confederate warship (the CSS *Virginia*) and was iron-plated. Its fight with the USS *Monitor*, during the last week of Trollope's American visit, marked the doom of wooden warships. Trollope saw some of the significance of this in his 'Conclusion' to *North America*.

some thirty years before. Trollope actually met Wilkes during his trip and later recalled that he was the sole American who continued to abuse England once he had realised Trollope's nationality. War seemed imminent: the Grenadier Guards were ordered to Canada, and every post brought further news of preparations for battle. British residents in Washington gathered at the Embassy and beguiled themselves with amateur theatricals led by *The Times*'s war correspondent William Howard Russell, known in America as 'Bull Run Russell' because of his caustic account of that great defeat for the Northern armies.

On the night of 27 December Trollope was invited to dinner by William Seward, the Secretary of State. Seward, known to his cabinet colleagues as 'Billy Bowlegs', had made his career by a series of rabble-rousing speeches in which he pulled the tail of the 'British lion'; once in office, he had tried to pursue a more conciliatory tone. The dinner did not begin on a happy note: Trollope went in knowing that the next day was the deadline set by London and that unless Lincoln yielded, war would be declared. Seward's seventeen-year-old daughter, who had remained loyal to her father's earlier style, found Trollope 'a great homely, red, stupid-faced Englishman, with a disgusting beard of iron grey'. Trollope, despite the international crisis, was seated on Seward's right as guest of honour. Another guest, a Congressman, recalled that Trollope's very presence 'was ... a surprise, if not a satire on the occasion', especially as he found his fellow guest the incarnation of 'burly English heartiness'. For a diplomat it must not have appeared a very diplomatic choice, but Seward, unlike his guests, knew a secret. As Trollope left the dining room he was told the crisis had ended: the Federal government had accepted British demands. The captured Confederate diplomats would be released. 'The plastic forms of soft diplomacy' (as the bombastic Senate chaplain put it) had prevailed, 'for the moment'. The news reached London with almost record speed and was known at St Martin-le-Grand in nine days. Palmerston rejoiced: 'If we had not shewn that we were ready to fight, that low minded fellow Seward would not have hit the deck.' 'Billy Bowlegs' was only able to remain on the deck because Prince Albert had softened the tone of Palmerston's original despatch enough for Seward and Lincoln to accept it. The price of that revision may well have been the life of the Prince Consort who, already ill, wore himself out in his effort to prevent war. Trollope, like almost every Englishman, was distressed when word of Prince Albert's death reached Washington: 'I am greatly shocked at the Prince's death. The effect on the Queen will be terrible.'[45]

Even after these hectic days, Trollope was not happy in Washington. The vast but uncompleted Capitol dome seemed to symbolise the ruined Union. One day he was galloping along one of the broad and muddy boulevards on his 'nimble trotter' only to be stopped by cavalrymen 'rattling their trappings': civilians were forbidden to ride quickly in the wartime city. Trollope hated to do anything slowly, from novel writing to riding, but even more he resented arbitrary authority, particularly military authority. 'I hate military belongings,' he wrote, expressing the usual Victorian contempt for the soldier. He also detested the corruption that percolated through a city overflowing with military speculators and tawdry politicians. Washington even lacked that great Victorian comfort, the pillar box. Trollope noted with paternal pride that they had appeared in several large cities in the United States, but not in Washington. Despite his difficulties he gathered information for his book. He was frequently entertained by the British Minister, Lord Lyons, one of the best diplomats of the century. He visited Congress, talked with the Secretary of the Treasury, had more talks with Seward, and, of course, enquired into the workings of the Post Office. He met the prominent Kentucky politician John Crittenden, whose whole career had been a struggle for a compromise to avoid conflict. Although Trollope thought his final proposals 'moonshine', he borrowed the story of Crittenden's two sons who fought on opposite sides for his short story 'The Two Generals' in 1863.

Trollope was anxious to get close to the seat of war. He had already made a hurried foray across the Potomac to Mount Vernon to pay his respects at the tomb of George Washington and to see a more recent historical spot in Alexandria, where Lincoln's friend Colonel Ellsworth had pulled down a Southern flag and was immediately shot by a local innkeeper, who was in turn killed by Ellsworth's troops. Some claimed that these men were the first two to die in the conflict. (There is still a plaque in Alexandria to mark the spot where the gallant innkeeper, James Jackson, was killed.) On the first day of 1862 Trollope clambered across a bridge into northern Virginia, which was now occupied by the Federal army. Trollope spent four days in their camps, without washing, where the cold at least froze his hated foe, the mud. At night, however, he suffered: 'I ... managed to keep my body warm by an enormous overstructure of blankets and coats; but I could not keep my head warm. Throughout the night, I had to go down, like a fish beneath the water, for protection, and come up for air at intervals, half-smothered.' He admitted to Kate Field that he 'had quite enough of it'.[46]

He had 'a vague hope, – a hope which I hardly hoped to realise' to visit the South. He made several visits to Baltimore, a city he placed second only to Boston in his admiration, but the sight of the military rule imposed upon the pro-Southern city was somewhat disturbing. Despite its military occupation he liked Baltimore so much that he returned in February after his trip to the west. His stay in Baltimore, in the border state of Maryland, was the only occasion on his American trip where he heard the views of Confederate sympathisers. Apparently through Russell, he met William Watkins Glenn, who arranged for prominent English visitors, such as the Marquess of Hartington, to be smuggled into the Confederacy. Glenn, who was quite wealthy, had started a newspaper to oppose the policies of the Lincoln government, and was quickly imprisoned, along with many Maryland legislators, in a Federal fort where he was told by an officer, 'You will have no comforts and you will be treated like a dog.' Yet, as is so often the case, money soon tempered despotism and Glenn was not treated too harshly. Eventually he was released.[47] Trollope appears to have met Glenn on his second Baltimore visit, although he obviously could not mention him by name in *North America* lest he again be imprisoned without trial.

Glenn records in his diary that Trollope was 'exceeding Republican [i.e. pro-Lincoln] and believed in the great history of Democratic institutions'. The two men became friendly in spite of their differing views. Glenn found Russell an example of 'the toadyism of middle class Englishmen' towards people of rank, but Trollope was the opposite: 'without being conceited [he] put a proper estimate upon himself. He was always willing to yield to others the place that the accidents of society entitled them to, but he was never subservient.' This is one of the best descriptions of Trollope's social attitudes. Through Glenn, he met two other prominent figures. Andrew Low was an English banker, who had extensive investments in the South. When he, too, had been hauled off to a Federal fortress, his close friend Thackeray wrote about the incident in the *Cornhill*. (Thackeray's fury at 'Lincoln and his hirelings' only increased when he learned that Federal authorities would not allow medicine through their blockade, thereby causing the death of Sally Baxter, the American girl whom he had used as the basis of 'Ethel Newcome'.) Glenn and Trollope joked with Low about Thackeray's nickname for the heavy-set banker: 'dear old Buffa-lo.' Glenn also introduced Trollope to the Northern Congressman Clement Vallandigham, a leader of the 'peace Democrats'. Eventually he became too outspoken and the government ordered him deported![48]

Glenn wanted to send important Englishmen south in the hope that they would return home supporting the Confederacy. With Dickens already hostile to the war and Thackeray outspoken in his defence of the Confederacy, a pro-Southern account by another famous novelist could be valuable, but he had no luck with Trollope, who explained his unusual timidity: while he 'was anxious to go South' he was not prepared to do so if he had to abandon most of his luggage; he was also afraid that if caught by Federal authorities he would be plunged into prison in a land where habeas corpus and other elementary rights had been suppressed. He was already indignant about passport restrictions put on visiting Englishmen by his erstwhile host, Seward. Trollope did not forget Glenn, and when the Baltimore man had to flee abroad a few years later he found a ready welcome at Waltham House.

In spite of his visit to Confederate sympathisers Trollope retained his belief in the Northern cause. However, meeting men who had suffered persecution may have influenced his section in *North America* on the misuse of habeas corpus. The greatest weakness in Trollope's book is that it presents a picture of a nation in the midst of a civil war, but only from the point of view of one side. Even a friendly critic like *Fraser's Magazine* observed, 'Nothing throughout the book impresses us so constantly as the consciousness how little Mr. Trollope knows about the South, and how ill qualified he is to write disquisitions about their struggle for independence.'[49]

*

If Trollope was ill-informed about the South he was perceptive about the rising power of the West, by which he meant the states bordering the Mississippi, or what today is known as the Middle West. He had toured the upper Mississippi valley with Rose in October 1861 and on 14 January 1862 he left Washington for the West, partly to visit Kentucky and Missouri, two slave states, some of whose men were fighting on opposite sides. Trollope noticed the importance of German immigrants in St Louis, Missouri. He also saw that the war would be won not on the historic fields of Virginia but in the West, in the battle to control the Mississippi. (Only a week after he left the area Northern forces achieved the first of a series of victories which soon gained control of the Mississippi and split the Confederacy in two.) However, Trollope no more cared for the 'western' states than his mother had: 'I was always happy and comfortable,' he wrote, 'in the eastern cities, and generally unhappy and uncomfortable in the West.' He was thoroughly miserable in Cairo, Illinois, which Dickens had pilloried as 'Eden' in *Martin Chuzzlewit*. The city held some perverse attraction to

English novelists; Thackeray, who had visited it in 1856, found it 'dreary', though he did predict that 'it will be a great city in five years'. Even with a year's grace Trollope found that Thackeray's prediction had not come true. Ten years later while visiting Australia he would still recall his miserable time there.[50]

Trollope also went on a private pilgrimage to Cincinnati and made his way to that fantastic structure which his mother had erected some thirty years before. 'Trollope's Folly' was now a 'Physico-Medical Institute' divided between 'a quack doctor on one side, and ... a college of rights-of-women female medical professors on the other'. The current owner of this absurd building told the son of its builder, 'I believe, sir, no man or woman ever yet made a dollar in that building; and as for rent, I don't even expect it.' His mother was remembered even further west. When he reached Rolla, Missouri, a newspaper reporter asked, 'Air [*sic*] you a son of the Mrs. Trollope?' When Anthony admitted he was, he was told, 'Then, sir, you are an accession to Rolla', and was invited to 'loaf about'. Trollope, of course, never had time to 'loaf about', whether in Rolla or anywhere else.

Part of the reason why he disliked the West was the absence of that essential of civilised Victorian travel, the helpful porter. Any guest arriving at Waltham Station was advised to have a porter carry even a small bag to the near-by Waltham House. Yet on 30 January 1862 the master of that house and a friend were walking to a hotel in Rolla. Trollope was carrying his huge trunk, presumably the one that kept falling off the mule some years before in Costa Rica:

> I shall never forget that walk ... up hill and down hill, with an occasional half-frozen stream across it. My friend was impeded with an enormous cloak lined with fur ... Our guide ... carried an umbrella and a small dressing-bag, but we ourselves manfully shouldered our portmanteaux ... I could tell at great length how I fell on my face in the icy snow, how my friend stuck in the frozen mud when he essayed to jump the stream ... Why is it that a stout Englishman bordering on fifty finds himself in such a predicament as that? No Frenchman, no Italian, no German, would so place himself, unless under the stress of insurmountable circumstances ... As I slipped about on the ice and groaned with that terrible fardle on my back, burdened with a dozen shirts, and a suit of dress clothes, and three pair of boots, and four or five thick volumes, and a set of maps, and a box of cigars, and a washing-tub, I confessed to myself that I was a fool ... No American of my age and weight will ever go through what I went through ... if I go to Rolla again during the war, I will at any rate leave the books behind me.

Trollope always travelled with a mound of luggage, including a hat box, although he sometimes looked askance at Rose's bonnet box! Most of the eastern hotels were products of the great American boom in hotel-building and as such had baths in the rooms, but Trollope, who was particular about cleanliness, was not prepared to risk the loss of his daily bath, so 'I always carry my own and have never failed in getting water'. He had at least rid himself of his writing-desk, that is to say, an American railway porter had broken it by dropping it on the platform. To add insult to injury, the porter and the bystanders had only stood by laughing and told the indignant Trollope, 'Guess you'd better get it glued.' Curiously, Charles Dickens had come to similar grief with his travelling desk while in America.

*

Trollope's attitude towards the destruction of his desk illustrates one of the two main themes in *North America*. After initial outrage he reflected on the porter's lack of 'civility' and, through this, reminded his fellow Englishmen about an essential aspect of the American character. The porter and the bystanders, he wrote, 'are arguing in their minds that civility to you will be taken by you for subservience, or for an acknowledgement of superiority; and looking at your habits of life, – yours and mine together, – I am not quite sure that they are altogether wrong.' To Trollope – and here he was in agreement with Dickens – the greatest of America's achievements was that 'education has made life for the million in the Northern States better than life for the million is with us'. The main result of his travels would be his desire to enter politics to improve the lot of ordinary people.

The other main theme was, of course, the war. His attitude towards it was not a simple one, and to understand it we must look at what he said on the subject in articles, short stories and a lecture he gave in England. He consistently supported the North, although he accepted that 'romantic fervour' could inspire an Englishman to be 'led away by a false feeling of chivalry' to support the Confederacy. This was particularly the case in the last days of fighting when 'as might have been expected of them from their blood, they [the Confederate armies] have fought with the tenacity of bull-dogs': they were, after all, English by race. These words, written towards the end of the war, indicate that residual sympathy with 'rebellion' discussed earlier. Trollope liked to think himself a 'rebel', a sentimental link, no doubt, with his miserable days at school when he felt an outsider and with his hobbledehoy days in London when he stood on the pavement listening to the music floating through the open windows. When he reviewed Goldwin Smith's *The Civil War in America* in 1866 he wrote that rebellion was 'the highest duty of man', but it is difficult to name any rebellion, other than Garibaldi's landing in Sicily, which he supported. Underneath all the talk about 'rebellion' was the man who, at last, had risen quite high and had done so by hard work within an established structure. He had no desire to see that structure overturned and his talk of rebellion was a middle-aged man's *cri de coeur* harking back to the days of his youth and, as such, not to be taken seriously.[51]

Although he admitted that the South had more 'pluck' and fought better, he correctly predicted that the overwhelming might of the North would prevail. While he did not think military victory could force the whole South back into the Union it could bring back border states like Virginia. He also thought that eventually some of the western states would form a separate nation. In his 'futuristic' novel *The Fixed Period*, which he set in the 1980s, the western states have done just this. While his support for the North came from his dislike of slavery he was anxious to avoid the charge that he was a radical: 'I am no abolitionist ... I do not wish to have dealings with the African negro either as a free man or as a slave ... believing that his employment by me, in either capacity, would lead to my own degradation ... he impedes the civilisation and progress of the white man.' As one pro-Southern review rightly said, this view is 'revolting'.*[52] Attending an abolitionist lecture in Boston had only increased his loathing for those who advocated immediate emancipation: 'There is no being so venomous, so bloodthirsty as a professed philanthropist ... when the philanthropist's ardour lies negro-wards, it then assumes the deepest die of venom and bloodthirstiness.' The abolitionists to Trollope were just another version of the Utopian and theoretical radicals he detested in England.

His dislike of slavery was based on his concern for the white man, not on moral outrage at the treatment of the black. 'It is the degradation of the white master which moves me rather than the hardship of the African' was how he put it to an English audience when he lectured in support of the North. He repeated what he had felt in the West Indies, that slavery undermined the moral character of the master more than it hurt the slave, a view shared by many Southerners including General Robert E. Lee. Trollope came to feel, as he expressed it in his short story 'The Two Generals', published in

---

*We should remember that if Trollope's attitude appears harsh today it was, before and during the war, the view held by the majority of Northern Americans. While disliking slavery as an institution and the South as a region, they equally disliked having Negroes in their own states. This was the foundation for the 'free soil' movement which gave rise to Lincoln's Republican party in the 1850s. To have a soil free of slavery also meant to have a soil free of Negroes.

December 1863, that many Southerners would have 'thrown off the plague chain of slavery if the prurient virtue of New England would have allowed ... But virtuous New England was too proud of her own virtue to be content that the work of abolition should thus pass from her hands.' A year after the war had ended, however, he argued that 'the bloodshed and misery have been as nothing to the good they have done' in ending slavery.[53]

Trollope, looking beyond the temporary horrors of the fighting, stressed the vast spaces and great resources of America: 'We must remember that we live in a tea-cup, and they in a washing-tub.' The country may have appeared even larger than it was because he did not proceed round it in a well-organised fashion: he shuttled back and forth along the east coast like a modern executive. From his travels he had begun to see an essential difference between English and American minds:

> The American, though he dresses like an Englishman, and eats roast beef with a silver fork, – or sometimes with a steel knife, – ... is not like an Englishman in his mind, in his aspirations, in his tastes, or in his politics. In his mind he is quicker, more universally intelligent, more ambitious of general knowledge, less indulgent of stupidity ... but he is more brittle, less enduring, less malleable, and I think less capable of impressions. The mind of the Englishman has more imagination, but that of the American more incision.

Yet throughout the book and in all his articles on America, the predominant attitude is his great pride in 'those wondrous children' of English civilisation.[54] He was to repeat in many of his travel books his view that America was England's greatest achievement:

> These people speak our language, use our prayers, read our books, are ruled by our laws, dress themselves in our image, are warm with our blood. They have all our virtues; and their vices are our own too ... They are our sons and our daughters, the source of our greatest pride, and as we grow old they should be the staff of our age.

*

After a final hurried trip to Boston to take leave of friends Trollope returned to New York, and on Wednesday 12 March he boarded another Cunard steamer. Like his mother before him, he used the voyage to work on his book. One word, 'Alas!', in his work-sheet testifies that he had been so busy in these last nine days that he had not written a thing.[55] When the ship called into Cork for coal, Trollope had a few hours in 'the dear old place ... happy to know that I was once more in Ireland' although he felt ashamed when he saw the swarm of beggars: 'What would those Americans think of them ... and of the country which produced them?' By Tuesday 25 March he was at Liverpool and the next day, at Waltham Cross. He handed Rose a cherished present, one of Longfellow's poems in the poet's own hand, and, no doubt, looked for early signs of spring in the garden he had so missed during his seven-month trip.

On 27 April he completed the final seventeen pages, which made the book somewhat longer than intended. He came to feel that he had written with too great a haste; he would like to have softened his criticism of certain aspects of American life, yet he remained loyal to his conviction that a travel book should reflect the immediate reactions of the author even if those are caused by petty annoyances. Making use of his free postal facilities, he sent that part of the manuscript dealing with constitutional questions to Richard Henry Dana, whom he had met in Boston. Trollope, perhaps remembering the rough treatment of his friends in Baltimore, maintained that Lincoln's suspension of habeas corpus was 'a breach of the constitution'. Although Dana is now best remembered for his exciting book *Two Years Before the Mast*, he was also a distinguished legal scholar. Trollope had already followed his earlier advice about showing these sections to an English lawyer, but he wanted an authoritative American opinion on such a complex topic. He was afraid that his book would annoy Americans who were still notoriously sensitive about criticism from Englishmen, let alone one named Trollope. Adopting his ridiculous pose of writing like Carlyle, he cried: 'O, my friends with thin skin, ye whom I call my cousins and love as brethren, will ye not forgive me the harsh words that I have spoken? They have been spoken in love, – with a true love, a brotherly love.' Ironically Dana himself had given evidence of thin skin when he first met Trollope on 9 January. He confided to his diary that Trollope was 'intolerable, no manners, but means well, & would do a good deal to serve you, but says the most offensive things – not a gentleman'. Fortunately they later became good friends, but the American's initial response is interesting because it shows the way in which not a few people reacted to Trollope on first meeting him. (Lowell had first referred to him as 'a rather underbred Englishman'.) Those who were fortunate persisted and discovered that his boisterousness was a way to counteract his basic shyness and a means to control sensitive feelings. If he said offensive things he expected the offended party to correct him on the spot, not to confide his pain to a diary.[56]

Trollope need not have worried about the American response to his book because it received a favourable press, at least in the North, where his obvious desire to praise excused his criticisms. (Many of these were of the west and of the lack of honesty in public dealings he had found there: the reviews, were on the whole, written in the north-east.) His first sentence invited a favourable response: 'It has been the ambition of my literary life to write a book about the United States, and I had made up my mind to visit the country with this object before the intestine troubles of the United States Government had commenced.' American critics saw that he had found faults but that, unlike his mother, he never sneered or patronised. Even his criticisms were tempered by his genuine good will. The *North American Review* praised the book, particularly admiring the emphasis on education. Their only real criticism was that he failed to see 'the true moral significance' of the war. *Harper's Magazine* was even more fulsome about the best book 'that has been produced by a foreigner upon us, saving always the philosophical work of De Tocqueville'. They were amazed that 'he even breaks into rather un-English enthusiasm'. Most of his friends in New England were pleased with his attitude towards the war. They would also have liked the fact that he swallowed their absurd view that the war had been caused by a 'conspiracy' between Southern politicians and Northern traitors. Longfellow spoke for many of Trollope's personal friends when he wrote to thank him for a complimentary copy:[57]

> As yet I have not had time to read it, but have brought it with me to the seaside. I come, therefore, only to thank Caesar, not to praise him. But, like me, like my book! and as I do like you, the other will not fail. I am sure to find it frank, outspoken, and friendly; and you are sure in return, to find in me a friendly reader, and not a captious critic ...

One American friend was not entirely pleased: Kate Field wrote, 'blowing me up' because she had not received a free copy. Trollope was not the first or the last author to explain 'I had to buy all the copies I gave.' 'One gives presentation copies to old fogies & such like' was his excuse. He told his young friend, who had apparently felt that the book was not as analytical or as radical as she had hoped:

> Your criticisms are in part just – in part unjust, – in great part biassed by your personal (– may I say love?) for the author. The book is vague. But remember, I had to write a book of travels, not a book of political essays – and yet I was anxious to ... introduce, on the sly, my political opinions.

The attempt has not been altogether successful. The book is regarded as readable, and that is saying as much for it, as I can say honestly.

He ended with a curious comment which shows the impact of the visit. He wrote that 'nature intended me for an American rather than an Englishman. I think I should have made a better American. Yet I hold it higher to be a bad Englishman, as I am, than a good American.'[58]

*

American interest in the book was so strong that Harper Brothers rushed out a pirated edition four days before Lippincott of Philadelphia, with whom Trollope had negotiated an American edition, could bring out their version. The Harper brothers ignored the 'ordinary courtesy' that existed among American firms when it was known that one publisher had arranged to publish a British author's book. When Lippincott delayed bringing out the book to 'await semiannual settlements' the Harpers rushed in and sold their version at about the cost of printing. Their cheap pirated copy sold at 60 cents or just under 2s 6d, while in England the two-volume edition cost 34s. It meant that Lippincott would probably end up as '*positive losers* in the enterprise'. Trollope was understandably furious and wrote a long letter – one of the longest he ever wrote – denouncing this 'literary piracy'. Although addressed to James Russell Lowell in Boston, Trollope sent it as an open letter to the *Athenaeum*:

> To you and me, and to men, who, like us, earn our bread by writing, the question is, of course, one of pounds, shillings and pence, or of dollars and cents; although there are those who affect to think that an author should disregard such matters, and that he should work for fame alone. For myself, I profess that I regard my profession as I see other men regard theirs; I wish to earn by it what I may honestly earn, – so doing my work that I may give fair and full measure for what remuneration I may receive ... I am pleading here for the honest payment for goods supplied by me to your countrymen; but I am pleading also for the honest payment of goods supplied by you to my countrymen.

Some years later he was calculating his earnings from books and when he reached *North America*, he stopped, dipped a pen in red ink and wrote one word: 'Cheated.'[59]

Trollope's *Athenaeum* letter had no more effect on settling the issue of international copyright than Carlyle's 'Petition'. Where it did have an effect, and one he had not foreseen, was with Rowland Hill, who had not forgotten his defeat over the special leave to visit America. He read the letter on the day of publication and decided that anyone who boasted of earning his 'bread by writing' must be 'neglecting his official duties to attend to his literary labours ... the Cornhill magazine ... numerous novels ... as though literature was his profession'. Gossip about Trollope's activities had already reached Hill from America. A friend of his, Pliny Miles (the name sounds like one of Trollope's sillier characters), claimed that Trollope had belittled the penny post when he was in Washington. Miles wrote a letter to the *New York Herald* attacking Trollope as 'an English writer of fiction of moderate reputation, now sojourning in this country'. It was typical of the neurotic Hill that he should not only write lengthy entries in his Journal and prepare statements for the Postmaster General but that he should drag in one of his brothers to investigate. He was always looking for anyone who criticised him, so in his 1862 Journal he added, 'see subjoined extract from my old journal – May 27 & 28, 1847 – as to similar misrepresentations in France by Mons Dunon'. Ironically, when Trollope's book appeared in May 1862, the chapter on the American Post Office praised Hill's 'wise audacity'. However, Hill became increasingly convinced that Trollope, while 'undoubtedly clever ... is dishonest – E. Page to whom I mentioned the circumstance in confidence assures me, also in confidence, that T. has recently spoken of me in his presence, in a manner quite inconsistent with his present professions.' One wonders how much Hill 'neglected' his 'duties' scurrying about St Martin-le-Grand, gathering gossip, analysing it, cross-referencing the latest story with one fifteen years before and then entering the whole in his Journal![60]

*

Trollope was quite wrong when he claimed in his *Autobiography* that his book was 'well received' by the critics, at least if he meant British critics. The day before he finished it, the *Literary Gazette* had alerted its readers to such a topical book: 'As Mr Trollope, in his West Indies ... exhibited the true characteristics of an intelligent traveller, his work will be expected with considerable interest.' Many leading periodicals, like *Blackwood's* and the *Saturday Review*, were strong supporters of the South and they naturally disliked the book. *Blackwood's* sent the book to one of its favourite reviewers, Colonel Edward Hamley, a military historian and novelist. Hamley told his friend John Blackwood: 'I wish to do justice to Trollope's general cleverness as a writer disputing only his merits as an advocate of the North.' He had a high regard for Trollope's novels, 'some of which I like extremely'. In his review Hamley praised the author as 'a man who deserves respect as well as liking', but he damned his book: 'Not only the style but the thought is often slipshod.' He rightly attacked the resort to fictional characters to explain a complex situation (a frequent weakness of Trollope, which he had first used in *The New Zealander*). The comparison of the break-up of the Union to a divorce in the Jones family does seem simplistic. Hamley urged him to return to his 'native heath' of Barset: 'We like his plots better than his travels ... Mrs Proudie ... is even a more interesting old woman than the President [Lincoln] himself. Mr Harding surpasses the entire Federal Cabinet, and five minutes with Eleanor Bold is better than a whole sitting of Congress.' The *Saturday Review* called the book as 'thin-spun, tedious, mooning a journal of travel' as had been published for many years. Trollope's friend G.H. Lewes, who was 'immensely pleased' with the first volume, took exception to this 'nasty notice' and arranged to write a review in the *Cornhill*. By the time this appeared he had altered his view and was somewhat critical of the book, saving his main attack on the ethics of the *Saturday Review*.[61]

Whereas Trollope was seen as an erring friend by *Blackwood's*, he was given a far nastier review in *The Index*, a newspaper set up in England as an organ of Confederate propaganda. They knew just where to hit the author at his weakest: his attempt to forsake 'his natural line of business – literary genteel comedy' to try 'the part of a political sage'. They laughed at his habit of referring to his other travels, although these did add some perspective, as in his interesting comparisons of hotels in different countries. *The Index* attacked his 'revolting' attitude towards Negroes as typical of that of hypocritical Northerners such as Lincoln. Even so, the paper admitted, 'Mr Anthony Trollope is not to be confounded with the herd of bookmakers who gather knowledge in the British Museum and vegetate in suburban lodgings'.[62]

The book did find some influential readers: the important Whig politician Lord Clarendon wrote to one duchess: 'Have you read Trollope's North American [*sic*]? I have been reading it aloud here in the Eveng: & we have liked it. It's rather long but he tells very pleasantly all the things one does not know & that one ought to know about those legions who call themselves Americans.' Ironically it would be Clarendon, as Foreign Secretary, who would have to negotiate with 'those legions' over the various claims for damage caused by British-built Confederate war ships. The book was known in even higher circles, for in 1870, when the Queen's youngest son, Prince Arthur, visited Washington, his 'minder' wrote back to Windsor: 'I was certainly disappointed with Washington. Trollope describes it exactly: 2 or 3 splendid buildings separated by a wilderness of mud.'[63]

North America is undoubtedly a book with many faults. It is one-sided, badly organised, too long and too diffuse. It is full of lengthy digressions on topics like the constitution of New York State – something which held a mysterious fascination for British visitors of the period. It certainly lacks the sparkle and pungency of his mother's book. Yet, with all its faults, it is still an important work for anyone interested in Anthony Trollope. It illustrates so many aspects of his character: his energy, his love of travel, his passionate concern for politics, his never-ending desire to be regarded as a serious writer and his peculiar blend of liberalism and conservatism. His time in America would influence his writing for the rest of his life. The friendships he made and the experiences he had had would affect his character and he returned to England determined to make his mark on his age as had those American writers he had met: Emerson, Longfellow, Lowell and Holmes. *North America* is far from being the best portrait of its subject, but there is no better portrayal of its author.

CHAPTER ELEVEN

Domestic and Worldly Happiness

On Wednesday 26 March 1862 Anthony Trollope turned into the courtyard of Waltham House. He had been away for over seven months and had many tasks awaiting him. In addition to finishing his American book and returning to novel writing, he had to resume his postal work. Yet his adherence to his schedule allowed him enough free time to take an increasing part in social life without neglecting his two careers. With a large income and a growing fame, he could settle into the comfortable role he had made for himself in his Hertfordshire home. Here he could give dinner parties or set out for a fox-hunt or go up to London to his clubs.

Within weeks of his return he was dining with the Alpine Club, where he sat next to the Vice-President, none other than William Longman, who had published *The Warden* and *Barchester Towers* and rejected *The New Zealander*. Another member noted that Trollope 'is a good fellow, modelled on Silenus, with a large black beard'. Such a convivial figure naturally responded to the demand for a speech by recalling a recent occasion in Washington, where an official had asked if the English passion for clubs included one which met on top of the Alps. 'In my anxiety to support the credit of my country, I may have transgressed the strict limits of veracity, but I told him what he heard was quite true.' He concluded by saying he wished he could join the Alpine Club but 'time and flesh' were against him, even though he was only forty-seven.[1] He remembered the Alpine Club well enough to mention it in many novels, including *Can You Forgive Her?*, written about a year after the dinner, and *Ayala's Angel*, published in 1881, as well as making the 'Alpine Club Man' one of his *Travelling Sketches*.

'Time and flesh' did not, however, prevent him from joining less active clubs. A month after his return he was elected to the Garrick, having been proposed by Robert Bell, a well-known man of letters, and seconded by Thackeray, who dominated the club. Here he quickly felt at home: one day, as Thackeray was about to enter the Club, he may have wondered about his new recruit when he heard the loud voices of Trollope and another novelist, Charles Reade, booming out into the street from an upper storey. As Thackeray listened to the roars of the two men, both in their late forties, he wondered, 'What must they have been at eighteen?'[2] Even before he had left for America, Trollope was elected to another club, the Cosmopolitan, and in 1864 he would become a member of the most influential of all, the Athenaeum. These three clubs were to play important roles in his life, providing background and information for many of his novels.

Clubs, like so many other 'institutions', had grown enormously in the early Victorian period. They had, of course, existed in the eighteenth century and had ranged from the political and gambling sets of Charles James Fox to the more edifying dining 'Club' immortalised through Dr Johnson. Both provided patterns for Victorian clubs: the formalised institutions with elegant buildings and the informal groups of friends sharing a common taste, such as the one the young Trollope had joined for glee singing. The political clubs – the Carlton for Tories and the Reform for Liberals – developed into party headquarters, and even the Radicals formed a Free Trade Club in 1846. Yet social clubs grew even faster due to the increasing number of 'gentlemen' and the improvement in transportation. When the Warden hurried up to London to consult his lawyer in the early 1850s, he had nowhere to relax except a 'cigar divan' in the Strand [*The Warden* XVI]. Later, clergymen could make use of a club especially formed for clerical tastes.[3] A club provided the Victorian gentleman with a place to read, to eat, to drink, to slumber, to meet friends, to talk, to hear the latest gossip, to play cards and, sometimes, to smoke – and all this away from the reproving glances of wives or mothers. Clubs sprang up for every profession and interest, such as the Civil Service Club of which Trollope was a founder. He joined clubs that appealed to his tastes, such as the Arts Club, though he left when he realised that he had not entered its doors for several years.

Trollope's three main clubs reflected that 'easy, relaxed, self-confident culture that had come into existence in London in the 1850s and 1860s'. Both the Garrick and the Athenaeum continue, but the Cosmopolitan is gone, taking with it the Victorian world of cultivated conversation and assured gentility. Insofar as there was a Victorian Establishment, its headquarters was the Cosmopolitan, and Trollope's ready admission shows how prepared members were to accept that the author of *Framley Parsonage* 'had arrived'. It was the most important of Trollope's clubs as an influence on his writing. Founded in the early

1850s, it had no elegant building and provided no meals: it only existed for talk. The 'Cos' rented two rooms in a painter's studio on Charles Street, Berkeley Square. The rooms were only open twice a week, on Wednesday and Sunday evenings. Wednesday was selected as the Commons rose at six especially to allow members to scatter to their great political dinners. The 'Cos', which was open from ten until after midnight, offered only tea, brandy and water. It allowed smoking, but even the haze from dozens of cigars could not hide the huge fresco by Watts of a naked maiden fleeing various furies as recounted by Boccaccio. This vast canvas caused Milnes to remark: 'You have heard of Watts' *Hymns*, now come and see Watts' *Hers*.' The male atmosphere was evident as soon as a member or guest entered as another 'work of art' guarded the portal: this was a large Chinese screen depicting every form of torture. The Club made an effort to extend membership to a wide variety of distinguished names in politics, literature and art: at the beginning of each London Season a list of candidates was circulated and each member could approve by underscoring as many names as there were vacancies. Browning and Tennyson were both members, though Tennyson appears to have pleaded his usual excuse of poverty to avoid paying the annual membership fee of two guineas. Thackeray was somewhat cynical about his fellow-members:

> Everybody is or is supposed to be a celebrity; nobody ever says anything worth hearing; and every one goes there with his white choker at midnight, to appear as if he had just been dining with the aristocracy. I have no doubt ... that half of us put on the white cravat after a solitary dinner at home ... and so go down among the Cosmopolitans.

Perhaps Sir Algernon West, like Trollope an important civil servant, was right when he said that Thackeray 'never took in the spirit of the place'.[4]

The Cosmopolitan allowed literary men to meet politicians and exchange gossip about their respective worlds. Thus when John Blackwood, who later published many of Trollope's books, visited London, he found the club fascinating. 'I had a capital night at the Cosmopolitan,' he wrote in 1864, 'Kinglake came in and sat down ... Then young Lytton, who fresh from Copenhagen, is a great lion; so we became the centre of the room, which was full of celebrities of one kind or another. It is the best gathering in London. Kinglake and other Whig members expected our party to make a set at the Government tonight.' A.W. Kinglake had achieved fame with his huge history of the Crimean War and his exquisite travel book, *Eothen*, and he was then an MP, while Edward Lytton, son of Bulwer Lytton, was both a poet and a diplomat. His arrival from Denmark, where he was Secretary of the British Legation, gave members the latest news of the German attack on that country. Thus a literary figure like Blackwood could gain the latest political and international news by one visit to the club. On the other hand a politician like Lord Stanley – son of the Tory Prime Minister – recorded a long talk at the Cosmopolitan with Thackeray who was in one of his depressed moods. He told Stanley that 'the public had got tired of him ... that the world wanted not descriptions of life and manner, but startling incidents, adventures, and so forth'. He complained that while George Eliot had got £7,000 for *Romola*, *Esmond* had only brought him £1,500. Stanley also noted that 'he spoke of his colleagues in literature: praised Trollope highly'.[5]

Writers from other countries were often brought to the club. Within a few weeks of his arrival in London, John Lothrop Motley, the American diplomat and historian, was taken there by a member. 'The object of the club', he assured his wife, 'seems to be to collect noted people and smoke bad cigars.' He did not mention the nude painting to the good lady in New England. He talked with such well-known figures in the worlds of literature, learning and politics as Richard Monckton Milnes MP, A.H. Layard, known for his excavations at Nineveh and also an MP, and Matthew Higgins, 'a gigantic individual who writes in *The Times* under the name of "Jacob Omnium" '. All three were friends of Trollope: Milnes was behind his membership of the 'Cos', Layard would write articles for the magazine Trollope later edited and Higgins was regarded by the novelist as the greatest journalist of the age. Motley – who became Trollope's close friend – gives an insight into the club's shared sense of talent:[6]

> They all said civil things to me ... It is not considered good taste here, as you know, to throw a man's writings very hard in his face. The formula is 'we know you very well in England,' 'Your name is very familiar to us,' 'Your fame has preceded you' or words to that effect. It is however a convenience to observe that one's name is more or less known, whether they read a word of you or not, because as Tristram Shandy observes, a man is always puzzled if asked to say who he is.

This was the perfect atmosphere for Trollope. He genuinely hated excessive praise, which he likened to having melted butter poured down his back, but he did crave acceptance and respect and, as we have seen, could be embarrassingly off-hand in public about his own work.[7] It was a 'convenience' for him to observe that his name was now known to the other Cosmopolitan lions, and no doubt his trip to America made him the focus of many conversations. The importance of this club for Trollope, the writer, was that it gave him an opportunity to talk with and study the important politicians he would soon start to portray in his political novels. He had been able to observe the gentry and the clergy in his postal work, but it was only in a club like the Cosmopolitan that he could make the careful studies which he needed for his later fiction. That is the difference between the naive Trollope, who wrote *The New Zealander* in the 1850s, and the sophisticated clubman who wrote the political novels in the following decades. Before he frequented the Cosmopolitan, politicians were people he read about in *The Times* or annoying men who occasionally fired semi-ignorant questions at him at a parliamentary committee. Now they were equals who, as Trollope said in his *Autobiography*, would 'whisper the secrets of Parliament with free tongues'.

It is appropriate that he portrayed the Cosmopolitan, mildly disguised as 'The Universe', in one of his Palliser novels: 'domiciled in one simple and somewhat mean apartment ... open ... only on two nights ... Its attractions were not numerous, consisting chiefly of tobacco and tea ... But the thing had been a success and men liked to be members' [*Phineas Redux* XXXIV]. A later chapter depicts the members and includes a man 'devoted to literary pursuits' as well as 'a foreign minister, a member of the Cabinet, two ex-members of the Cabinet, a great poet, an exceedingly able editor, two earls, two members of the Royal Academy'. 'Royalty might come in at any minute, speak a few benign words, and blow a few clouds of smoke' [XLVI]. Among the members of the 'Cos' was the Prince of Wales who delighted in the club as a place to meet his future subjects (though few of them lived that long) and to smoke, free from his mother's prohibition. Trollope uses the club as the place where Phineas Finn and Mr Bonteen have their quarrel. Bonteen leaves only to be murdered in Lansdowne Passage.[8]

Trollope's two other clubs were also important to him. The Garrick became a favourite spot to indulge his passion for whist, particularly in the 1870s. Within two years of his joining he was one of the key members on the Committee, having been elected to fill Thackeray's vacant chair. At the Athenaeum the library provided a place to read as well as to write. Some chapters of his novels were written there and it was there, he claims, that he took the dreadful decision to kill Mrs Proudie. The French author Taine, who became a temporary member about this time, was delighted with the club: 'The servants in livery are numerous, attentive, quiet. The library contains 40,000 volumes; the reading room is splendid, containing all the reviews, in all languages;

every new publication; easy-chairs, as comfortable in summer as in winter ... Every want is provided for; all the senses are soothed.'[9] It also provided a place to observe bishops, for it was a well-known haunt of the Victorian episcopate in their gaiters, aprons and frock coats. 'Soapy Sam' Wilberforce, Bishop of Oxford – who had been caricatured in *The Warden* – was a celebrated member although not popular with many because of his annoying habit of grabbing several newspapers and sitting on them till he had time to read them.

By 1862, therefore, one review of *North America* could accurately describe its author as a 'club man'. Only five years before Trollope had referred with the wistfulness of the outsider to 'the comforts of a first-rate club' [*The Three Clerks* VIII]. For him these comforts were now real, but it was not so much the deep armchairs or the well-filled tumblers of brandy that delighted him as the sense of acceptance and friendship. For more than four decades he had felt himself an outsider: the miserable dayboy at a wealthy school, the one member of his family abandoned when the others crossed a vast ocean, the clerk without prospects and, even as a successful novelist, a writer marooned in Ireland. Now, suddenly, he walked into rooms where the Poet Laureate might be chatting with the Prime Minister or the Foreign Secretary with the Prince of Wales. 'I think that I became popular among those with whom I associated,' wrote Trollope about his life as a clubman:[10]

> I have long been aware of a certain weakness in my own character, which I may call a craving for love. I have ever had a wish to be liked by those around me, – a wish that during the first half of my life was never gratified. In my school-days no small part of my misery came from the envy with which I regarded the popularity of popular boys ... It was not till we had settled ourselves at Waltham that I really began to live much with others. The Garrick Club was the first assemblage of men at which I felt myself to be popular.

Trollope was truly popular with his friends because beneath his bluffness there was always a warm heart whose 'craving for love' reached out to help others. One of his many objections to Bacon's essay, 'On Friendship' was: 'Is there a word of the delight of serving your friend?' For his part Trollope delighted in serving his friends: in the 1860s he came to the aid of one he had met in somewhat unpromising circumstances in Costa Rica. When he called on a British diplomat, he heard the man say: 'Oh, tell Mr. Trollope to go to the devil. It's much too hot to see anyone.' Nevertheless Trollope was soon spending happy days lying in William Synge's hammock. Synge's case was a good example of the danger a Victorian could face if he married without an adequate income; he had married an American woman, partly on the advice of his friend Thackeray. Soon their large family began to impose a strain on Synge's income. Back in England in the early 1860s he encountered Trollope and told him of his desperate need for a loan of almost £2,000. This was a large sum – equal to about three years of Trollope's salary. Shortly after hearing this sad tale Trollope was walking through Whitehall pondering on it, when he suddenly spotted the tall figure of Thackeray. Standing between 'the two mounted heroes at Horse Guards' the novelists discussed their friend's plight. Thackeray exploded: 'Do you mean to say I am to find the two thousand pounds?' He agreed, however, to find £900. Trollope, who tells the story in his book on Thackeray, does not add that he put up another £900. After the Whitehall meeting Thackeray wrote to Synge: 'I have just met a Trojan of the name of Trollope in the street ... and the upshot is that we will do what you want between us.'[11]

*

Trollope did not restrict his friendship with Synge to arranging a large loan. When Synge was abroad his children spent their holidays at Waltham House, and once Trollope, who had inherited his mother's fondness for placing fruit before schoolboys, was much amused when Bob Synge refused a banana by saying: 'At school that's the cheapest grub we can buy!' The Synge children were among the many who enjoyed the wide hospitality of Waltham House. This must have been difficult, in many ways, for Rose Trollope who would have had little experience of entertaining or of managing a large house in her childhood home above the bank. There were five servants living at Waltham House, three of whom, including Barney the groom, were from Ireland. Trollope, it may be recalled, had paid tribute to his Irish servants at the beginning of *Castle Richmond*. In addition there were two English servants: a cook and a twelve-year-old girl as undercook. Although on his large income he could easily have afforded a butler to do justice to the butler's pantry – in 1863 his total income would come to £3,496 17s 7d – the memory of the liveried footman moving amid his parents' debt-ridden rooms may have been too strong. There must have been additional help to cope with the large grounds as well as the chickens, cows, horses and pigs.[12]

Trollope did some garden work himself: George Smith was amused to see his well-known novelist dragging about a lawn roller at a 'canter' on one non-hunting morning, but the lawn had to be kept smooth for the new, fashionable game of croquet. For Trollope the game had two recommendations: it had been introduced into England by an Irish lady and the first game was said to have been played on the lawn of the Postmaster General. It may be recalled that Lily Dale was devoted to croquet which had 'become quite an institution' [*The Small House at Allington* II]. Trollope was also fond of the game, and one friend remembered him sticking his head out of the library window at Waltham and shouting to the croquet players, 'I'll join you in twenty minutes; I have three more pages of manuscript to fill.' Both Trollopes took an interest in their fruit and vegetables: they were lucky because the soil round Waltham Cross was notable for producing good crops. The number of nurseries in the district today still testifies to this fact. Trollope shared his mother's and brother's interest in designing gardens. He disliked 'a square prim garden, arranged in parallelo-grams, tree answering to tree at every corner' [*The Belton Estate* VII]. No doubt such contrived rationality savoured of France. At Waltham House, the garden was remarkable for its old English roses, so much so that when William Paul 'the Rose King' acquired the house after the Trollopes gave it up he retained all the old bushes as they were 'inimitable'. One lady who stayed at Waltham found its grounds rather formal: 'The handsome stiff garden of the Queen Anne style, with a square pond at one end of it and a smooth grass lawn at the other. We walked round and round this garden many times, Anthony Trollope smoking and talking all the way.' One reason why Trollope spent so much time in the garden is revealed by his American friend William Glenn who had entertained the novelist in Baltimore. Glenn's pro-Southern sympathies had finally forced him to flee Maryland lest the Lincoln government imprison him yet again for his beliefs. Trollope did everything to make his erstwhile host a contented guest, even arranging temporary membership of the Garrick. Trollope also invited him to spend Christmas 1863 at Waltham, where Glenn found that 'even Anthony Trollope in his snug little house only smoked in an outhouse, beyond the kitchen ... In fact the only place in an English house where one is permitted to smoke is *outside* of it.'[13]

Another guest was impressed with the 'old-fashioned red-brick house of about William the Third's time, with a good staircase and some large rooms in it, and standing in equally old-fashioned grounds'. Trollope spent about £1,000 on adapting Waltham House and eventually bought the freehold. His taste in architecture had always been for the Jacobean and Tudor styles, which were not only older than his house but more 'English', whatever that means. In one novel he portrays a brick house from 1701 as 'not the best period for English architecture as regards beauty, but one in which walls and roofs, ceilings and buttresses, were built more substantially than they are to-day' [*The American Senator* I]. Inside the house each Trollope had a separate sphere and Anthony's was his library, where he could write and have long chats with visiting men. They could see his growing number of books, which by 1867 reached to more than 5,000 volumes. This room was decorated with portraits of literary friends and heroes: the centrepiece of the collection was a portrait of Thackeray by Samuel Laurence, which came as a gift from George Smith in 1864 though Trollope clearly regarded it as a present to Rose as well as to himself. Smith soon presented the Trollopes with another Laurence portrait: one of Trollope himself, which is now in the National Portrait Gallery. Trollope told the generous publisher: 'my wife liked the portrait *very much indeed*. She seemed to have a fuller respect for me when she had seen it than ever before.' He may also have hung in his library some paintings of Irish scenes including one of an old bridge.[14]

Another sign of Trollope's growing prosperity was seen on his desk: sheets of expensive notepaper at first only embossed with the address in red, 'Waltham House, Waltham Cross', but by 1866 boasting the leaping stag, the crest of the Trollope baronetcy. When family deaths occasioned it, Trollope, who disliked the wilder excesses of Victorian mourning, used the prescribed paper with its black bands and the address embossed in black. Before acquiring this he was content to write on any sheet of paper that lay about. Like his other writing, he preferred to do his letters in the morning: 'at evening I am tired and hate the sight of a pen.' He also had some GPO stationery for his postal work which went on, for the most part, in one wing of the house. Trollope was normally scrupulously honest about using official notepaper only for Post Office business. When he travelled he took supplies of both official and private paper with him. Many Victorians placed great emphasis on such things: Gladstone, for example, was very precise in distinguishing between 'public' and 'private' coal at No. 10 Downing Street, although Queen Victoria was once amused to see that a private letter from Mrs Gladstone had been sent in an official envelope – an event she noted. Young Henry Trollope had also sinned by using a GPO envelope to preserve a letter sent him by his grandmother in Florence. It was only when Trollope had left the Post Office that he used up his remaining sheets of official paper to write part of *Phineas Finn*. Trollope liked good quality and was prepared to pay for it; he also believed it only natural that any 'workman' took a natural interest in the tools of his trade. When he met an English riding-master in America whose conversation centred on horses he reflected that his own concern was 'pens, ink, and paper of good quality'. His desk would also have had a supply of pen wipes, one of which is preserved in the parish church of his last country home, Harting. His letters, whatever one may say about the handwriting, were almost always written on good quality, heavy paper with good pens and ink, which is more than one can say of many Victorians including, alas, his sister-in-law, Frances Eleanor Trollope.[15]

It was most likely in the library that Trollope kept his carefully preserved and ever expanding collection of contracts and business records. He was not one to save many social letters and some would have been grabbed by Rose for her autograph collection. However, he did take great care of his business papers and these have become the single most important collection of Victorian literary contracts, not only because of his fame but because of his wide dealing with so many different publishers. He followed the normal Victorian practice of folding letters lengthways and 'docketing' the sender's name and sometimes the subject on the back. Occasionally, if he were writing a particularly important letter, he would first make a draft copy, which would give him a record. All these contracts were kept in such a way that should he ever suffer a fatal fall when out hunting Rose would know exactly what her rights were.

A young writer who was a weekend guest in 1868 described the most noticeable feature of the library: 'One wall ... was entirely hidden by small cupboards or bins, each with a separate glass door, and filled with cigars ... to allow free circulation of air. On wet days the doors were all kept closed, in dry weather they were open.' A small stud was moved every time a bin was empty so that Trollope knew to select a cigar from the next oldest batch. These must have been kept well stocked as Trollope wrote to George Smith in 1865 saying he had just received a consignment of 12,000 cigars, some of which he offered to Smith and other friends. Trollope apparently had made arrangements for this supply when he visted Cuba. (Winston Churchill did the same thing half a century later.) For another batch of 6,000 cigars in 1866 he paid £31 7s 9d.[16]

Of the other rooms at Waltham House less is known. Trollope once wrote: 'If you want to ascertain the inner ways or habits of life of any man, woman, or child, see ... his or her bedroom. You will learn more by a minute's glance round that holy of holies, than by any conversation.' However, he offers us no glimpse into his own holy of holies except when he told one American lady that 'our bed room' contains pictures of 'people whom we love well'. Naturally the bedroom would have had a dressing-room, a luxury which appeared to be unknown in America as Trollope discovered: 'What do you mean by a dressing-room and why do you want one?' asked various hotel clerks when Anthony and Rose appeared. They needed one because it was not common for ladies or gentlemen to dress or undress together as can be seen from those scenes in which Archdeacon Grantly is in his dressing-room while his wife is undressing in the bedroom. Trollope admitted that he could be rather messy in leaving keys and money lying about, so the dressing-room could also have provided space for his clutter. Rose would also have needed room for her large wardrobe as well as for the quantity of a special eau de cologne she bought from a shop in the rue St Honoré, a luxury she may have acquired from her mother-in-law. She found the French perfume improved if stored for two years.[17]

Trollope, of course, recognised the drawing-room as his wife's special domain, where she would receive callers on those afternoons when she was 'At Home'. 'There is no spot on the earth's surface so dear to me,' Trollope wrote in a passage cited earlier, 'as my own drawing-room, or rather my wife's drawing-room at home.' Here husband and wife would sit on those evenings when he was not at one of his clubs. It is to be hoped that this room was 'pretty as it is the bounded duty of all drawing-rooms to be' [*Can You Forgive Her?* II]. For a room to be 'pretty' Trollope liked it to have some shape other than a square and he liked bright colours, as most of the sombre scenes of his childhood seemed to have occurred, at least in his memory, in dark rooms. One suspects that Rose's prize-wining fire-screen with the Trollope coat of arms of leaping stags was in this room. It is likely that the furniture would have been good solid English pieces, for Trollope as 'a stout Englishman' (in many senses) had little use for what he regarded as flimsy French chairs. (Rowland Hill's family had been afraid that one of their 'slightly built' chairs would collapse under Trollope's 'large vigorous frame' when he was invited to their Hampstead home.)[18] Yet the most important aspect of the drawing-room, as indeed of the whole house, was the mood within it. In the first novel he started at Waltham House he wrote: 'For those who have managed that things shall run smoothly over the domestic rug there is no happier time of life than these long candlelight hours of home and silence. No spoken content or uttered satisfaction is necessary. The fact that it is felt is enough for peace' [*Orley Farm* XXI]. Because Trollope knew such 'long candlelight hours' of domestic peace – almost alone among the great Victorian novelists – he could portray the joys of home life to an era which placed such importance on the family.

*

One important family consideration when Trollope moved to England in

1859 was finding a school for Henry, who was thirteen, and Fred, who was twelve. Both boys had attended a variety of schools in Ireland and England and the evidence, as well as the boys' behaviour in later years, indicates that while Trollope and his sons got on remarkably well, their education was even more peripatetic than his. Worried that they were acquiring too strong a brogue from attending school in Cork, in 1855 he sent the boys to a school near Chester kept by a clergyman, presumably to prepare them for public school. Then they were sent to St Columba's in Dublin where one of them got into trouble, which was made all the worse because he lied about it. Perhaps this reminded Trollope of the time he was unjustly punished at Sunbury. The family's move to England, along with the vast increase in his literary income, now gave him an opportunity to find an English school.[19]

Trollope selected a new school, St Andrew's College at Bradfield near Reading, founded ten years before by the village rector in his manor house. Thomas Stevens was an example of that essentially Victorian species, the wealthy rector who bestowed his wealth on his parish. As both squire and rector, he ruled as absolute monarch of all he surveyed: 'rector, squire, priest and king' a contemporary called him. Trollope saw Stevens in early December 1859 and the headmaster wrote to the Warden of St Columba's: 'Mr Trollope has informed me that his son has been in disgrace with you and has been sent away for a breach of discipline and for lying to conceal his fault.' Stevens, however, was a sensible man, and said that if this fault did not come from 'habits of low tone ... it would seem to be unkind to shut him out from the chance of making good.' A week later Stevens wrote to Trollope: 'I did sympathise very keenly with you in your distress about your boy ... I was ready to sympathise very strongly too with my brother school-master who betrayed no signs of selfishness but earnest devotion in working for right ends with, as I *thought*, a *very foggy* view of the way that would lead to them.' To a relative, Stevens was more explicit: 'The two Trollope boys are to come after Xmas – that Irish Warden is only fit to be employed in Ireland – an awful muff!! A sort of donkey that would be likely to make hypocrites of honest boys ... I hope the boys will do well here. I have no fears about them.'

The boys entered Bradfield in January 1860, and Trollope seems to have been pleased with it, although in the winter of that year he did ask G.H. Lewes to enquire about a school in Geneva for both boys; Lewes's son had just returned from a Swiss school. (He may have been thinking of further education in languages but decided the boys were too immature for such a venture.) It cost Trollope £130 a year for each boy at Bradfield or a total for the two of just five per cent of his annual income which, in the sixties, averaged about £4,500. The choice of Bradfield confirms Trollope's sympathy with the Oxford Movement. The school had been founded as a 'kind of happy thought, a fortunate accident in the course of a quaint and original career' of a Rector anxious for a good parish choir. Set in the centre of its beautiful village, the school was soon recognised as a product of the Oxford Movement. It was dominated by a strong High Church ethos and produced many clergymen of pronounced Tractarian views. There was another reason for his choice. He believed that the ancient schools still did not provide enough teaching: 'What we require is not better masters at our schools ... but more masters.' In discussing this in an article written a few months after Fred completed his education, Trollope specifically pointed to Bradfield as a place that the older schools should emulate, for Stevens ensured there was one master for every fourteen boys.[20]

Henry Trollope was clever but seemed to lack the energy and determination that drove his father. He perhaps shared some of the traits of that tragic uncle whose name he bore. He developed an interest in stamp-collecting, a hobby his father, to whom stamps were the stuff of business, thought odd, but fortunately his uncle in Florence could supply him with many foreign stamps. Fred was less intellectual but more active, playing both cricket and football for the school. Both must have had traces of an Irish accent as they were called 'Paddy Major' and 'Paddy Minor'. Fred became a 'popular hero' of a 'great historic fight' (to quote the school history) when he defended an invalid boy who was being bullied. The bully was much bigger but in the end young Trollope triumphed. However, Fred could not go home on his holidays for several days as he was so 'knocked about'. The younger Trollope was also known as 'an excellent story teller'. Henry remained at Bradfield until July 1863, and Fred until April 1865.[21]

*

The assured prosperity of Waltham House was, of course, in stark contrast to what Trollope had known as a boy; something only emphasised when he and Henry arrived in Florence in September 1863. Fanny Trollope, at eighty-four, was in sad decline, and it must have been painful for Anthony to see her. In the last few months she lost all her once glittering mental faculties. Tom thought that she was suffering the ill effects of those wretched days at Bruges where, after nursing her dying husband and son, she sustained herself through nights of novel-writing on a diet of green tea and laudanum. Even Anthony, who had inherited so many of her traits, could not watch by a deathbed and then write a novel. Indeed his work sheet shows he wrote nothing on his current book, *Can You Forgive Her?* in those weeks at Florence. She lingered on, and Anthony had to return to his postal duties. As he left the Villino, he knew that it was the last time he would see his mother alive. Fanny Trollope, who had taught him to read by scattering bone counters on the floor of 'Orley Farm' almost fifty years before and had shown him how to be a writer by disappearing into the 'sacred den of Harrow', died on 6 October 1863, about a week after he returned home. At the end her memory had that final flicker of an exhausted candle and her thoughts turned towards the last of all those children who had accompanied her in her travels and had died of the family curse. 'Poor Cecilia' were her last words. Tom honoured a gruesome promise by persuading a doctor to open a vein in her arm after she died, for her imaginative mind had had a horror of being buried alive. Tom composed a Latin inscription for her grave at the English Cemetery in Florence as he had done for his father's in Bruges. It informs the reader: 'In Agro Somerset, Anglorum, A.D. 1780 nata, Florentiae Tusculum A.D. 1863 nacta est.' There was a mistake here which Fanny would have enjoyed: she was actually born in 1779. Perhaps Anthony's tribute was better: 'Her career offers great encouragement to those who have not begun early in life, but are still ambitious to do something before they depart ... of all people I have known she was the most joyous, or, at any rate, the most capable of joy.'[22]

Rose, the boys and probably the maids would have gone into some form of mourning and the notepaper with black borders soon appeared at Waltham House, although Trollope had inherited from his mother a commonsense attitude towards mourning. He frequently denounced the view that one must mourn even if one did not genuinely feel grief, as well as the complicated rules that prevailed until the end of the century. His special venom was saved for the idea that widows should hide themselves away in a form of English *suttee*. In spite of all the bereavements she had suffered, Fanny Trollope had never taken permanently to widow's weeds. There was little for Anthony to inherit as far as money went, although he received some shares she had held in a London bank.[23] He did provide some basic facts to ensure that she had an obituary in the *Athenaeum*. For Tom there was an even worse blow not much more than a year later, when he had to make another trip to the cemetery, this time to bury his wife Theodosia. Again, Trollope made a hurried dash to Florence to be with his brother, and a few days after his fiftieth birthday Trollope returned to Waltham bringing his niece Beatrice with him.

When Beatrice eventually returned to Florence the question of a governess arose: several years before, Fanny Trollope had met Frances Eleanor Ternan who was in Florence studying singing. Her lessons were due to the generosity of Dickens, who had made her younger sister Ellen his mistress. Anthony and Rose, who had entertained Frances Eleanor at Waltham, thought she would be an excellent governess for Beatrice at Tom's new villa near Florence. They also thought she might soon be advanced to another role in the villa, for when Tom informed his brother that he had asked the governess to be his wife, Anthony replied, 'Yes, of course! I knew you would.' In October 1866 Anthony and Rose went to the British Embassy chapel in Paris to see Tom married to Frances Eleanor. Even before becoming a Trollope she had started to write. Now the new 'Fanny' Trollope naturally took up 'the family literature' and produced eleven novels, as well as much other writing. In 1895 she published a biography of her mother-in-law with considerable help from Rose.

There was another death that much affected Trollope. On Christmas Day 1863 he was 'stopped' by the news that Thackeray had been found dead in his bed on Christmas Eve. Trollope had last seen him about ten days before and had found him in a better mood about his health. Trollope's American friend Glenn had seen Thackeray at the Garrick only three days before his death, when W.H. Russell urged him to have a certain operation. He insisted that there was little danger and that only one in every hundred died of it. At first 'Thack' replied, 'Ah! I would be that one', but then brightened and added: 'I feel I have twenty years of life in me yet and I will do something better than I have ever done before.' Trollope was one of the large crowd of mourners who stood round Thackeray's grave at Kensal Green. He wrote a tribute to his friend for the *Cornhill* – the magazine to which he owed his own great popularity, thanks to Thackeray's encouragement. At first he refused any payment, but then asked Smith for a particular edition of *Henry Esmond* for Rose, as her copy had become worn out with reading and lending to friends. Throughout the rest of his life Trollope held Thackeray's memory in high honour and befriended his daughters. Nothing could ever shake his conviction that Thackeray had been the greatest novelist of his time. He could never have imagined that his own novels would be more widely read and cherished than those of his literary idol. Years later Trollope was at a London dinner party which had reached that stage where the ladies had swept into the drawing-room, leaving the men to their port, cigars and chatter – on this occasion, about the nature of the 'after-life'. Perhaps the conversation became too metaphysical for Trollope, who disliked theoretical talk as much as glib repartee about matters so close to his heart. Whatever the reason, he suddenly announced, 'If I thought I should never see dear old Thackeray again, I should be a very unhappy man.'[24]

*

When Trollope brought Beatrice to Waltham House there was already another niece living there. Rose had been quite devoted to her sister Isabella, who had often stayed with her when Anthony was absent on long trips like those to Egypt or the West Indies. Isabella had married Joseph Bland, the head clerk of the Rotherham Bank, where Rose's father had been the manager. By 1863 both the Blands had died leaving several children. Just as Anthony and Rose had given a home to young Edith Tilley for a year after Cecilia's death, so now they gave a home to one of Isabella's daughters, Florence. As Trollope wrote in a novel a few years later: 'When a girl has a mother, her aunt may be little or nothing to her. But when the mother is gone, if there be an aunt unimpeded with other family duties, then the family duties of the aunt begin – and are sometimes assumed with great vigour' [*The Belton Estate* I]. Florence Nightingale Bland was eight when she came to live with her aunt and uncle at Waltham House in 1863 and was one of that generation of girls named in honour of the heroine of the Crimean War. For young Florence it must have been a startling change from industrial Rotherham, in a house with only one maid, to a country house with several servants, a large garden and a stable full of horses.[25]

Florence became the daughter Trollope never had. He had always delighted in the company of girls, which was part of Kate Field's attraction. 'Flo' was not treated as the unfortunate orphan but as the daughter of the house, and much love and money were lavished upon her. Trollope delighted in her accomplishments: he once offered to give each of his three nieces £5 if they could memorise his favourite poem, Milton's *Lycidas*; Florence and Edith Tilley claimed their reward, but the headstrong Beatrice did not. Eventually Florence was sent to Aix-la-Chapelle for her education. Trollope believed that girls should have a good education; indeed he later gave Florence an autographed copy of a lecture he delivered 'On the Higher Education of Women'. In his *Autobiography* he jokingly calls Florence 'the young tyrant of my household'. In the last decade of his life she became his secretary and, as Trollope's sister-in-law noted, 'she adored him'.[26]

Trollope liked to have children in the house, particularly at holiday times. One of his nephews later said that all he had to do was to read the 'Christmas at Noningsby' chapter in *Orley Farm* to be reminded of his holidays at Waltham. One suspects that Millais is having a small joke with one of the illustrations and that the large bald man blindfolded and playing children's games under the mistletoe is none other than 'Uncle Tony' himself, while the lady who appears to be the hostess could well be Rose Trollope. Waltham House must have had mistletoe at Christmas, for in one short story, 'The Mistletoe Bough', Trollope claimed that some people – presumably of an Evangelical cast – had begun turning against this old custom because 'kissing, I fear, is less innocent now than it used to be'. According to Trollope's nephew, 'Uncle Tony' joined in all the children's games – snapdragon, blindman's buff and 'commerce', where he used various tricks to make sure the children got the right cards. Food, of course, was also important, as his idea of Christmas ordained 'a fine old English dinner at three o'clock – a sirloin of beef a foot and a half broad, a turkey as big as an ostrich, a plum pudding bigger than the turkey, and two or three dozen mince-pies'.[27]

*

Food was important to Trollope, not just at Christmas but throughout the year. He was not one of those men who took no interest in food until it arrived at his table. He liked the best quality and would pay for it, not being in any way like Mrs Proudie who chose 'bad tea from a low-church grocer' [*Last Chronicle of Barset* LXVII]. Mrs Proudie's patronage of a Low Churchman was not unusual: it was quite common for Victorians to chose their shops by the shopkeeper's religious or political loyalties, as these were often public knowledge. Trollope evidently knew a considerable amount about buying food, and almost all his travel books, following his mother's example, discuss the way people buy and prepare food and what they pay for basic items. 'Did you ever buy your own meat?' he asked George Smith when the publisher suggested large cuts in a story. 'That cutting down of 30 pages to 20, is what you proposed to the butcher when you asked him to take off the bony bit at this end and the skinny bit at the other.' In a series of articles he wrote for the *Pall Mall Gazette* late in life Trollope surveyed the world of tradesmen including greengrocers, butchers, fishmongers and wine merchants. In the article on butchers he recalled his visits to their shops and the comments he made on the joints offered him.[28] Trollope was good at estimating how far each joint would go, a necessary skill given the Victorian appetite for meat. In one novel a girl goes to the market with her parsimonious aunt to buy a twelve-pound shoulder of mutton. Trollope says that this would be enough for two days for the family of three and their two servants. He adds that 'there was always a more lavish consumption in the kitchen than in the parlour' [*Ayala's Angel* IV]. Even the Crawleys, Trollope's best example of a poor clergyman's family struggling to survive, have three pounds of meat a day at ninepence a pound [*Last Chronicle* IV]. From a variety of sources we know that Trollope liked his beef rare and his mutton well done and, above all, not greasy, that he had a fondness for soup (Rose would even take her own cook to Australia, partially to ensure he got the soup he liked) and that he had a devotion to fresh fish, large cups of tea and good coffee, a delight he found difficult to obtain in England.

Vegetables played a large role in his diet. 'My objection to your country, sir,' said one American to him, 'is that you have got no vegetables.' After an initial explosion at this nugget of wisdom, Trollope began to meditate on his garden at Waltham: 'Out of my little patches at home I have enough for all domestic purposes of peas, beans, broccoli, cauliflower, celery, beet-root, onions, carrots, parsnips, turnips, seakale, asparagus, French beans, artichokes, vegetable marrow, cucumber, tomatoes, endive, lettuce, as well as herbs of many kinds, cabbages throughout the year, and potatoes.'[29] Asparagus seems to have been a particular favourite as one of his questions to Rose in the last few months of his life was about the progress of their asparagus beds. Trollope was also lucky in having a good stomach. It may be the case, as his contemporary Bagehot once said, that the foundation of Toryism is a sound stomach. If so, this was only one of many conservative traits shared by the Liberal Trollope. As one foreign count says in *The Claverings*:

> What a blessing is digestion! ... It is to be in paradise. Adam and Eve were in paradise. Why? their digestion was good. Ah! then they took liberties, ate bad fruit ... ruined their constitutions, destroyed their gastric juices and ... were expelled ... Milton had a bad digestion, because he is always so cross; and your Carlyle must have had the worst digestion in the world, because he never says any good of anything. Ah, to digest is to be happy! [XIX].

Trollope, like his parents, had a good palate for wine and, as soon as he could afford to do so, began to lay down a cellar: 'I like wine ... it seems to me that my dinner goes down better with a glass of sherry than without it.' It was quite common for Victorians to drink sherry, normally a medium one, during a meal, particularly when dining alone. Only a few months after settling at Waltham House, he asked George Smith: 'Who sells good champagne? could you get a dozen sent down to my address here ... If I liked it I would get more. I care as much as anybody about price, but I care almost more about quality – It is very impertinent in me to ask you to do this, but you kept me so long today I had not time to go anywhere.' Nor did he neglect his older publisher, Chapman, who was asked to obtain some German wines. It may seem odd for an author to ask publishers to order wine, but they often undertook practical tasks, particularly for writers who were not in London. Smith, for example, arranged a 22½ per cent discount for Mrs Gaskell on china and glass for her house and may have done the same for the Trollopes. Through his trade connections Smith may have been able to get a discount on champagne. Trollope's favourite wine was a claret, Château Leoville, particularly the 1864 vintage 'which I regard as the most divine of nectars' [*Ayala's Angel* V]. This was not just an opinion inserted in a novel, for late in life he laid down a prodigious quantity – twenty-four dozen bottles at seventy-two shillings a case on one occasion – mainly as a present for Henry. He was not fond of the lighter, and cheaper, clarets, which were known as 'Gladstones' after the statesman who lowered the duty on certain table wines in an effort to curb drunkenness which often flowed from heavy wines like port.[30]

The Victorians, fortunate in so many things, lived in an age when the price of good wine fell. At the time Fanny Trollope was ordering wine for her house in York Street, in the late 1830s, a bottle of St Julien cost three shillings; by 1867 it had dropped to half that: it is no wonder that Trollope was furious when American hotels charged him $2 or eight shillings a bottle, some six times the London retail price.[31] With his strong views on wine, as on almost everything else, he resented being served bad wine by friends (his oldest friend, John Merivale, was notorious for his bad wine), and he always served the best, even to those who did not appreciate it:

> What service do you do to anyone in pouring your best claret down his throat, when he knows no difference between that and a much more humble vintage ... And yet the hospitable hero who would fain treat his friends as he would be treated himself can hardly arrange his dinners according to the palates of his different guests ... I, – I who write this – have myself seen an honoured guest deluge with the pump my, ah! so hardly earned, most scarce and most peculiar vintage! [*The American Senator* XLII].

One of the reasons he disliked the fashionable, newer method of dining was that it doomed the old custom of removing the cloth so that gentlemen could pass the port round a gleaming magohany table –

such as his father had done with the magnums of vintage port at Keppel Street.

*

In many of Trollope's novels there are attacks, some open and some covert, on this new fashionable mode of dining, the *service à la Russe*, that was becoming increasingly popular in the mid-Victorian era. Although Trollope was in the West Indies when *The Times* devoted its letter columns to an extensive correspondence over whether or not people in the upper middle class should adopt the new fashion, he read the letters. 'The *service* à la Russe,' wrote Trollope's club friend Abraham Hayward, 'divides the opinions of the best judges.'[32] Trollope had no doubt where he stood on this question, and his frequent references to it in his novels show both how he used topical issues and how he saw 'domestic manners' as the best insight into the state of society. The traditional 'English' method, familiar to any reader of eighteenth-century diaries such as Parson Woodforde's, was for a staggering variety of dishes to be placed on a table in a few courses and for the host and guests to help one another, with some assistance from servants. *Service à la Russe* was a more formal and involved procedure where courses were brought in and handed round by servants in a carefully prescribed order. This left the centre of the table free for massive displays of silver, flowers or decorations. No longer did the host carve at his own table, but instead a footman pared thin slices on a sideboard (mindful no doubt that servants could gorge themselves on what was left). It also led to more elaborate dishes, usually of French origin or at least disguised by a French name. No one other than the aristocracy could afford to maintain the large kitchen staff and the well-trained chefs to produce elaborate dishes to such a complicated time-table. This led to the growth of caterers, like the famous Gunters, who prepared grandiose concoctions so that the upper middle classes could ape aristocratic fashion. Trollope had no time for such pretence:

> It may be a doubt whether such tradesmen as Messrs. Stewam and Sugarscraps do ever produce good food ... It is certain I think that the humblest mutton chop is better eating than any 'Supreme of chicken after martial manner,' – as I have seen the dish named in a French bill of fare, translated by a French pastrycook for the benefit of his English customers ... But the outside look of things was handsome, and there were many dishes, and enough of servants to hand them and the wines, if not good, were various [*The Prime Minister* XLVIII].

His dislike of the new style was not just a conservative resistance to foreign notions, though an element of this was always present. It was not that Trollope disliked 'foreign' food: he had after all poked fun at Englishmen in the West Indies who insisted upon eating roast beef in the tropics while resisting native food such as avocadoes and yams. Unlike Thackeray who had seen the new style as yet another form of snobbery, Trollope saw it as an example of something even worse: that dishonesty which threatened English society.[33] Normally his fictional characters who adopt such fashionable ways are somewhat disreputable people who are trying to use artifice to hide deceit, men like Ferdinand Lopez in *The Prime Minister*, while those who adhere to old ways are likely to prove reliable. Thus it is an early sign of Mr Toogood's honesty in *The Last Chronicle of Barset* that he warns his nephew, John Eames, that if people 'wanted to be regaled à la Russe they must not come to number 75, Tavistock square'. This honest solicitor offers 'a leg of mutton and trimmings ... and a glass of port such as you don't get every day of your life' [XL].

For Trollope *service à la Russe* basically showed how dishonesty could spread through different layers of society as the middle classes began to present pretentious concoctions to their friends. Pretensions were essentially a form of dishonesty, and it was but a brief step towards cheating customers to get more money to pay for such nonsense. Of course, nothing appears more trivial to later generations than the battles over fashion fought by their ancestors. Yet it is important to see that Trollope's views were a reflection of his consistent belief that English society should uphold those traditional values and practices which were both founded in history and responsible for the nation's greatness. He believed that the new practice 'has become a vulgar and an intolerable nuisance among us second-class gentry with our eight hundred a year – there or thereabouts' [*Framley Parsonage* XVII]. Of course Trollope was aware that anyone could have consulted a parliamentary report to discover that £800 was close to his own salary! However, the 'thereabouts' of his income was soon over five times that, thanks to his writing.

While his attacks on this 'intolerable nuisance' had a serious purpose, he also knew it provided a superb subject for ridiculing the pompous, something that both Dickens and Thackeray had long done. Trollope's best description of the new fashion occurs in *Miss Mackenzie*, at a dinner given by the heroine's brother, a partner in an oil-cloth business:

The construction of the dinner was no doubt à la Russe; and why should
it not have been so, as Tom Mackenzie either had or was supposed to
have as much as eight hundred a year? ... in the centre there was a green
arrangment of little boughs with artificial flowers ... there were figs and
raisins, and little dishes with dabs of preserve on them, all round the
green arrangement.

The soup, brought in from a pastrycook's, is cold. Only the hired
footman, Grandairs, can serve the wine and his main duty is to make
one bottle of champagne do duty for the whole company. The little
dishes 'could hardly have been intended by Christian cooks as food for
men' and even the meats were ruined. Grandairs takes so long to serve
the potatoes that the saddle of mutton becomes cold and greasy, the
depth of misery to Trollope. Cold greasy mutton, whether from his days
at Winchester when lumps of it were plopped on to wooden trenchers,
or served half raw on Irish canal boats, struck some deep unhappy
chord within him. It is hardly surprising that the purpose of this
dinner is to extort some of her inheritance from Miss Mackenzie [VIII].
Trollope also disliked the new method for the simple but not
unimportant reason that he did not get enough to eat.

The new method marked the death-knell of that pleasant old custom
where one guest saluted another by a private toast:

Seeing a lady the other day ... I ventured to ask her to drink wine with
me. But when I bowed my head at her, she looked at me ... struck with
amazement. Had I suggested that she should join me in a wild Indian
war-dance, with nothing on but my paint, her face could not have shown
greater astonishment. And yet I should have thought she might have
remembered the days when Christian men and women used to drink
wine with each other. God be with the good old days when I could
hob-nob with my friend over the table as often as I was inclined to lift my
glass to my lips, and make a long arm for a hot potato whenever the
exigencies of my plate required it [*Framley Parsonage* XVII].

We may be sure that this foreign fashion did not invade Waltham
House. No hired footman like Grandairs flitted about with little dishes
or carefully measured out bad wine. Instead the master of the house
sat at the head of his table and carved from a 'good leg of mutton, how
noble a thing it is ... juicy, sweet, and high-flavoured' in a room
boasting 'those appearances of plenteous hospitality which a dining
room should have' [*Can You Forgive Her?* II]. Trollope was not the type
of man to display his wealth in mountains of plate, though no doubt he
did take pride in the one piece he bought at the auction of Thackeray's
goods in 1864.

The location of Waltham House made it fairly accessible as it was about a dozen miles from London. The house was less than half a mile from Waltham station, a walk which Trollope claimed took five minutes. Guests were advised to take the 5.10 train from Shoreditch station, a train much used by Trollope himself when returning from postal business in London. Anyone arriving with luggage was told to have a porter carry it from the station. The porters must have been quite busy, as guests were often invited to spend the night: 'We have lots of beds,' Trollope informed a cousin from Exeter. All sorts of people were invited, from Thackeray and Millais, to 'that female Caxton of the Age E. Faithfull' whose work for women printers had received Trollope's active support.[34]

Dinner at the Trollopes was normally at six. In the nineteenth century the dinner hour moved steadily later. It may be recalled that Tom Trollope mentioned that his parents, in the early decades of the century, dined very late, by which he meant five. By the 1870s Anthony and Rose, by then living in London, were dining about seven. Since Trollope did not bother much with any form of mid-day meal, which he felt ruined one for afternoon work, he would not have wanted a dinner much later than six. (He once laughed at George Smith for eating pork pies in his office.) If guests left London at 5.10, they must not have had much time for dressing, especially as Trollope did not like lingering in the drawing-room before the march into dinner: 'Almost every man can talk for fifteen minutes, standing in a drawing room, before dinner, but where is the man who can do it for an hour?' [*Miss Mackenzie* VIII]. He preferred his talk at the dinner table and afterwards, although he liked to be in bed by ten. One clergyman recalled such evenings:[35]

At Waltham House among his cows and rows of strawberries Trollope delighted to welcome at his dinner table some half-dozen intimate friends. Those who were occasionally guests there remember how in the warm summer evenings the party would adjourn after dinner to the lawn where wine and fruits were laid out under the fine old cedar tree, and good stories were told, while the tobacco smoke went curling up into the twilight.

Trollope, like most prosperous Victorians, accepted that meals were governed by rules about dress and by other customs, most of which appear in his novels. To understand Trollope the man, we must remember that he saw such customs as a sign of a healthy society with everyone playing their assigned role. He lived his life according to the motto of Winchester: 'Manners Makyth Man.' His attitude towards such rules shows his fundamental conservatism as well as the way in which most of his views were ultimately grounded in religious principles:

> Conventions are apt to go very quickly, one after another, when the first had been thrown aside. The man who ceases to dress for dinner soon finds it to be a trouble to wash his hands. A house is a bore. Calling is a bore. Church is a great bore. A family is a bore. A wife is an unendurable bore. All laws are bores, except those by which inferiors can be constrained to do their work.

Of course all this entertaining did have one bad result, as Trollope told the Alpine Club when bemoaning 'time and flesh'. He already weighed fifteen stone before moving to Waltham, which the wine on the lawn with his own strawberries and cream did not help. He went on a diet following one of the first of that never-ending succession of panaceas. 'Banting's Diet' was devised by William Banting, remembered in Trollope's strangest novel as 'the great Banting who has preserved us all so completely from the horrors of obesity' [*The Fixed Period* IX]. The diet was based on avoiding sugar, so even carrots and parsnips were banned. For breakfast Trollope was allowed six ounces of any meat except pork or veal and a large cup of unflavoured tea or coffee. He did not normally eat a mid-day meal but at night was restricted to three to four ounces of meat or fish. With this he could have a glass or two of claret or sherry but no champagne or port. A nightcap 'if required' could consist of a glass of claret or a 'tumbler of grog'. In desperation he could turn to dried toast or a rusk dipped in spirits. He must have stuck to Banting's regime for some months because George Eliot noticed in December 1864 that 'Mr A. Trollope is thinner ... and is otherwise better for the self-denial'. Yet, as so often, it was only a temporary victory for Trollope continued to complain, particularly when speaking of fox-hunting, that he rode heavy, and a friend recalled that he was between sixteen and seventeen stone in the saddle.[36]

His concern for his 'flesh' only increased after a tour of Holland he made with John Tilley in September 1862. Trollope had inherited Dutch blood from his Meetkerke ancestors and, in addition, greatly admired Dutch art. 'If you care for Dutch pictures,' he advised readers, go to Holland, although he did complain of the lack of fresh air in the galleries and the sparse light available to study such masterpieces as Rembrandt's 'Night Watchman'. He rejected the English prejudice that the Dutch were fat; they had, he insisted, 'pleasant English features'. There was only one thing wrong with them: they wore French hats. But he had an obvious solution: 'Put on his head a hat made in

England and you will take him for an Englishman a little under-sized.'
Trollope himself was not 'under-sized' as he found when he went
bathing at Scheveningen. 'For myself,' he announced in the *Cornhill*, 'I
do not love machines, and prefer bathing *au naturel*.' French phrases,
unlike French hats, apparently were useful when one wished to avoid
too great a shock to genteel readers. His problem was that he could not
fit into the costume he had rented, so, having left the bathing machine,
he began to swim about quite happily. Without his spectacles he could
just make out distant figures on the shore pointing at him, and he
began to think he would be arrested for his nakedness. Actually, the
spectators thought he was drowning.[37]

*

Trollope was not only busy as a host, for he and, to a lesser extent, Rose
frequently dined out with private friends. Sometimes he would attend
those vast public dinners in which the Victorians revelled and where
he might be called upon to reply to a toast to 'Our Literature'. He was
often a guest of that hospitable publisher, George Smith, whose
daughter remembered well into this century how the Smith children
liked to peer over the rail to watch Trollope perform his curious ritual
of ruffling what remained of his hair before striding into the
drawing-room. A daughter of the artist William Frith remembered
that at one dinner party, where a fellow guest was Matthew Arnold –
'quite the ugliest man I ever saw in my life' – Anthony and Rose were
very quiet and spoke only to their immediate neighbours. It makes one
wonder whether Anthony was not quite so boisterous when Rose was
present. Perhaps Arnold's whispery tones made him fearful of being
reduced to the ranks of the 'philistines'. Certainly he was not normally
cowed by intellectuals. In April 1867 he was one of the two honoured
guests at a 'little dinner' given by Lord Amberley, the heir to Earl
Russell. The other guest was the philosopher T.H. Huxley. Their
hostess, Lady Amberley, was rather annoyed: 'A [Lord Amberley] and I
thought T's voice too loud, he rather drowned Huxley's pleasant quiet
voice which was certainly better worth hearing.' She made up for this
after dinner by discussing with Huxley a superior way in which to
bring up children. One lady at another dinner, noticing that Trollope
helped himself to large portions of everything that was offered, said,
'You seem to have a very good appetite, Mr. Trollope.' 'Not at all,
madam,' he replied, 'but, thank God, I am very greedy.'[38]

Before his move to England Trollope had little opportunity to enjoy
the activity he so often depicted in his novels: country house visiting.

However, he made up for it in the 1860s when his increasing fame and expanding circle of friends brought him invitations. His personality was designed for larger houses, and when he stayed in a smaller house he could be a much remembered guest, at least according to the daughter of a fellow Surveyor: 'No more repose was left in the house when he awoke in the morning. Doors slammed, footsteps resounded, and a general whirlwind arose, as he ... returned from his bath, or walked out in the garden, and from that time until nightfall, he was as busy as a man could be.' He often stayed with his cousin, Sir John Trollope, at Casewick, the family's ancestral seat in Lincolnshire. When Lord Houghton invited him to stay at his well-known house, Fryston in Yorkshire, he knew his guest's ways well enough to add: 'You can write (?) here in the composition of a chapter and when here you can have all your time to yourself when not eating or talking.' (It is a good example of the efficiency of the Victorian Post Office that Houghton could write on Christmas Day from Scotland and Trollope could reply the next day from Hertfordshire!) Among the other guests during the Trollopes' four-day stay were the Low Church Bishop of Ripon and another literary civil servant, James Spedding, as well as Lady Rose Fane, the daughter of the Earl of Westmorland. She felt 'rather *lost*' among all the 'literary society here; they talk an amount of literary shop', and Lord Houghton read the proof sheets of a new life of Charles Lamb at breakfast. She had the same reaction to Trollope as several people in America: the novelist was not at all like his books. She wrote to her mother the day after the Trollopes arrived:

> I wish I had never seen Mr. Trollope. I think he is detestable – vulgar, noisy, & domineering – a mixture of Dickens vulgarity & Mr. Burtons selfsufficiency – *as unlike* his books as possible – Mrs. Trollope seems a quiet sort of woman & wd. be well enough only she has perfectly white hair which is *coiffé en cheveux* in the most fashionable way with (last night) a white rose stuck in it wh. looks *most absurd*.

Perhaps Rose was paying tribute to her native Yorkshire by appearing with a white rose. One suspects that some of Trollope's noise arose from arguments with the Bishop, who had once led an extreme Evangelical group which tried to convert the Irish.[39]

Trollope's increasing fame also brought with it invitations to speak, which he preferred to avoid if at all possible. In 1864 he addressed a meeting, chaired by Dickens, to establish the Shakespeare Foundation Schools for the Royal Dramatic College. He also joined a host of other celebrities, including Disraeli, Froude, Tennyson, Charles Reade and the popular rhymster Martin Tupper, as a Vice-President of the

Newspaper Press Fund. On another occasion, in 1867, he was at a great dinner where 450 men met to honour Dickens before he set off on his second tour of America. The hall was decorated with crossed British and American flags above the word 'Pickwick'. Trollope, in replying to one toast, took the occasion to defend fiction from the latest sneer by Carlyle about the 'cousinship it has with lying'. 'We who write fiction,' Trollope proclaimed, 'have taught purity of life, nobility of action, and self-denial, and have taught those lessons with allurements to both the old and the young which no other teacher of the present day can reach, and which no prophet can teach.' At this type of public dinner a curious old custom prevailed that the ladies sat in the gallery and peered down on the proceedings. Though they may have been denied the celebrated turtle soup, they could enjoy a cold 'collation' and then retire to a drawing-room till the gentlemen swarmed in, searching for coffee and tea. One young girl watched as Wilkie Collins, Matthew Arnold and Edwin Landseer entered. Then a 'very pleasant old gentleman ... bowing with old-fashioned politeness said, 'Can I get you anything, dear ladies?', only to be interrupted by Dickens himself asking the girl whether she still read *The Old Curiosity Shop*. She was amazed that he had remembered a conversation they had had years before about 'Little Nell'. The old gentleman told her after Dickens had left, 'Authors never forget those who admire their works.' The 'old gentleman' – he was only fifty-two – was Anthony Trollope.[40]

*

Much of the Trollopes' own entertaining was done during the winter fox-hunting season, when his house was often full of people 'more or less in the boot and breeches line'. To him 'the real campaign' began in November and carried on until spring. He avoided 'cub' hunting, 'of all sports ... the sorriest', which began in October [*Ralph the Heir* XXVII, XXXI]. He had originally wanted to ride to hounds three days a week but by 1862 accepted that this was simply not possible, as he told George Smith: 'I have been trying to hunt three days a week. I find it must be only two. Mortal man cannot write novels, do the Post Office and go out three days.' He described himself in his short story 'The O'Conors of Castle Conor' as 'an erratic fox-hunter', by which he did not mean one who followed the sport occasionally but someone who wandered 'from one pack of hounds to another'. Since first taking up hunting in the early 1840s in Ireland he had devoted increasing time and money to it. One of the debts he incurred in Ireland was buying his first hunter. By the time he reappeared in England to revise the rural posts he had two hunters, which he brought with him. A decade after that he cheerfully informed one friend, 'I am full of horses', and he always seemed to have enough to provide mounts for visitors. By the 1870s he startled one young man, a nephew of the Foreign Secretary and a scion of one of the wealthiest ducal families, by arriving at a Northamptonshire rectory which he was using as a hunting base with a string of seven horses for his hunting.[41]

'If you go to stay at a gentleman's house you understand,' Trollope wrote in *The Last Chronicle of Barset*, 'you will be provided with meat and drink. Some hosts furnish you also with cigars. A small number give you stabling and forage for your horse; and a very select few mount you on hunting days' [LII]. Trollope was among those 'very select few'. Buying horses – a good hunter could cost as much as 500 guineas, although Trollope was known for not being a very good buyer of horses – paying for a man to look after both, providing feed and stabling and paying the tax on horses was very expensive. Trollope estimated that it cost him at least £5 for each horse for every day he hunted and this did not include his expenses for his sons or his guests [*Phineas Redux* XVI]. If we assume that he normally had four horses and used two on the two days he rode each week, his annual bill would have come to about £500 a year, over two-thirds of his Post Office salary. The five pounds alone would have amounted to some seven weeks' wages for a letter-carrier.

The horses were looked after by Barney (there is much disagreement on his last name), Trollope's faithful old groom who had been with him since Banagher – thus knowing his ways even longer than Rose. He also knew Trollope's views on horses: if fed on good oats throughout the year they required little preparation for hunting save special exercises in September and October [*Ralph the Heir* XXXI]. It was Barney who appeared before dawn with a cup of coffee in his hand to ensure that Trollope was at his desk. For this task he received an extra five pounds a year. On those rare days when Trollope refused to get up, he paid Barney another five shillings, both as a fine on himself and as an incentive to get up. On a racing morning the master's first question was 'Is it freezing now?' Barney would often ride an extra horse to a long meet so that Trollope could change mounts. At other times he would take the horses to the station where Trollope would have written in advance for a horse-box.

The Irishman had a mind of his own, which no doubt endeared him to Trollope. Once when Thackeray, on a visit to Waltham House, came into the stables, the 'curious old groom' said, 'I hear you have written a book upon Ireland, and are always making fun of the Irish. You don't like us.' 'God help me,' replied Thackeray, bursting into tears and turning his head away, 'all that I have loved best in the world is Irish.' Barney, of course, could not have known that Thackeray's wife, who spent most of her life in a private mental asylum, was from County Cork. Although it was said that Barney could neither read nor write, he kept accounts of the stable expenses which were never a penny out during his long service with Trollope. It was he who put young Harry and Fred on horseback before they could walk and when, some years later, Harry was somewhat frightened when his small horse, 'Miss Vesey', was prancing on her hind legs, Barney announced: 'Shure, Master Harry, she's as quiet as a lamb.' All the Trollopes were devoted to him, and when an old aunt gave 'Bice', Tom's daughter, a gift of ten guineas, 'Uncle Tony' told her she should seek advice on how to spend it from Aunt Rose, Barney 'and all the other wise people'. It says much about Anthony Trollope that two of his Irish servants remained with him for over thirty years. In his *Autobiography* he paid tribute to his 'old groom' who was never once late with the coffee: 'I owe more to him than to any one else for the success I have had. By beginning at that hour I could complete my literary work before I dressed for breakfast.' 'Fancy getting up at five,' exclaimed one minor novelist, 'and sitting down in a cold room with grubby hands after lighting your own fire, and then writing about pretty girls and love.' As one of the obituaries said, Trollope achieved his fame by working 'at a time of day when most literary ladies and gentlemen are snug between the sheets'. Anyone who enjoys Trollope's novels ought to spare a thought for the old Irishman, virtually illiterate, who made his way up the stairs at dawn bearing that cup of coffee.[42]

We get an idea of what Trollope was like on a hunt from the diary of his American friend, William Glenn, whom he invited to 'see so thoroughly British an institution as a fox hunt'. Trollope was able not only to mount Glenn but to lend him some of Fred's 'toggery' so that he would appear well dressed. The exile paid several visits to Waltham for hunting in that winter of 1863 and 1864 and was surprised that out of some 200 riders only about twenty were still left in the field after a run. He saw that the experienced riders, like Trollope, knew when to leap a fence and when to go through a gate but he was surprised that there was so much 'heartlessness' in the rivalry. As he and his host raced across the Essex countryside, a difficult barrier appeared: a wide ditch, surmounted by a raised bank topped with a railed fence. They slowed down to steady their horses for a leap when suddenly 'a Londoner', anxious to show off, spurred on his horse to take the fence at full tilt. The

horse hit the top rail, tossing rider and horse into the field. The loss of
the top rail made the jump much easier for Trollope and his guest. The
American visitor thought they would stop and help the man catch his
horse, but not so Trollope, who shouted: 'Halloa. We are much obliged
to you. A damned good thing you did for us. I don't know what we
should have done without you.'[43]

Trollope recalled some of this in an episode of *Can You Forgive Her?*,
written within days of this very hunt, when one rider knocks the top
bar off a fence and is thrown from his horse. Among the other riders at
this fictional hunt is a 'sporting literary gentleman ... [who] weighed
without his boots, fifteen stone!' Recounting this, Trollope does
comment that 'a man with a wife and a family is justified in avoiding'
such formidable barriers. Perhaps he had discussed Glenn's shock at
the fierce rivalry, for he explains that hunting men approaching gates
are 'hating each other with a bitterness of hatred which is, I think,
known nowhere else' [XVII]. Years after he had given up hunting he
explained his basic rule: ' "Always to excel and to go ahead of
everybody" should, the present writer thinks, be in the heart of every
man who rides to hounds' [*Ayala's Angel* XXIV]. Episodes from hunts
turn up in many novels because Trollope, as a 'sporting literary
gentleman', always carried a small notebook when hunting to jot down
events and characters. For example, the 1869 season began badly for
the Essex Hunt when three hounds were lost as a result of eating
poisoned herrings. Trollope remembered this incident and used it as a
sub-plot in *The American Senator* written six years later. Because his
descriptions of hunts were accurate he wanted any illustration to be
the same, and in 1865 he criticised one drawing for a novel because the
artist made the usual mistake of supposing that a horse goes at a fence
in the full stride of his gallop. He told George Smith that someone who
rushed at a fence would go right through it – much like the unfortunate
'Londoner'. For Trollope, the novelist of Victorian country life, hunting
was essential, for it allowed one 'gradually, but unconsciously, [to]
discover the secrets and the manners of rural life in England'. Indeed,
he added, 'the best half of hunting is in the social intercourse which it
gives'.[44]

Although Trollope lived in Hertfordshire, he was so close to Essex
that he normally followed the Essex hounds, in a county notorious for
its deep ditches. One huntswoman remembered him and his two huge
horses, 'Banker', a dark chestnut, and 'Buff', a blue roan. She thought
they looked 'more like coach horses ... but his huge squat bulk required
weight carriers'. As so often, Trollope enjoyed a private joke by
inserting 'Banker' and 'Buff' into a novel, making them two of the four

horses owned by a character in *Ralph the Heir* [XXVII]. He frequently stayed with friends near Kelvedon when hunting in Essex. The granddaughter of one lady novelist and fellow hunter long recalled how other guests used to be amused as Trollope wandered in and out of other men's rooms for a talk and a laugh while he was dressing. He was always a forgetful man: losing umbrellas and wallets as easily as he would forget minor details in novels. He was no better with his hunting garb, and so he wandered about his room talking to his missing garments. 'Oh, Mrs Sock, where have you got to? Not under there?' 'Why, I do declare, there you are hiding near the curtain. I've got you, Ha! ha! ha!' 'Now Mr. Top Boot, where is your twin?' 'A fine thing to run away on a hunting morning.' In the midst of this would comes bursts of song 'in a guttural voice, always horribly out of tune'. 'A hunting we will go, ho! ho!' he sang, invariably giving an extra burst to the final 'ho'. Then he would stomp down to breakfast reminding all the impatient children who were longing to be off that: 'No one can't go hunting who don't eat a good breakfast.' This anecdote may well give us a glimpse into his method of writing and his mastery of dialogue, as it is likely that he acted out some of the scenes as he wrote them.[45]

No doubt the lost garments also explain what he meant when he told George Smith that 'a good wife always does head groom' on hunting days. In one of Rose's few surviving letters she told Kate Field that he 'has gone to hunt and on such days I always write heaps of letters because I dont like to be out of the way never knowing at what hour he may be in'. Undoubtedly one of her many duties must have been to ensure that an ample supply of hot toast and tea was ready for his return, for he liked nothing better when he stormed into the house after a meet. During the hunt he sustained himself from his flask of sherry and a packet of sandwiches. Nothing, however, was allowed to stop his literary schedule, for as the Marquess of Huntley noticed, he did not come down after a hunt if he had not finished his daily quota of words.[46]

Trollope's rather weak eyesight made it difficult for him to see where he and his horse were going, and so he often landed in a ditch: indeed he once claimed to have landed in every ditch in Essex. According to a book on the Essex Hunt, it was 'good betting' whether Trollope or his son Henry landed in the ditch first. It was remarkable, given his poor sight and his reckless determination, that he was not seriously injured, let alone killed from a fall, as was his fellow novelist George Whyte-Melville in 1878. On one occasion he did suffer a very serious fall and while on the ground saw his horse about to trample on his head. His mount, however, rather than kill his master, pulled back despite intense pain. Afterwards the horse was not sold but put out to grass in an honourable retirement under the care of the faithful Barney. Trollope did not believe hunting to be particularly dangerous, and he pointed out that while Sir Robert Peel and Bishop Wilberforce did die because of falls from horses, neither was hunting.[47]

He drew on the Essex countryside for names in his fiction, such as Ongar, which is used in *The Claverings*, while the Clavering family take their name from an Essex village. The hunting club in *Can You Forgive Her?* was drawn from The Sun and Whalebone Inn near Harlow. The Master of Fox Hounds, when Trollope came into the Essex country, was a colourful character, the Rev. Joseph Arkwright, who was about seventy, and the grandson of the Richard Arkwright whose inventions helped to launch the Industrial Revolution. This may well be why Trollope often considered that vexed question of whether clergymen should hunt. For his part he always found hunting clergymen the most pleasant of companions, yet he knew that opinion, particularly episcopal opinion, had been turning against the sport. Samuel Wilberforce spoke for many other bishops when in 1854 he refused to license a priest in his diocese because he hunted, and added: 'A sporting clergyman is a great evil in a parish.' This debate is portrayed in *The Claverings* when Bishop Proudie orders Mr Clavering to give up following the hounds [II]. Trollope reluctantly concluded in 1879 that the time had arrived for clergymen to give up hunting, 'yet for the life of me, I cannot see the reason against it'.[48]

As an 'erratic' hunter, Trollope rode with hunts other than the Essex. He enjoyed the hospitality of the Rothschilds when he galloped with 'the Baron'. At other times, like some of his characters, he came into Oxfordshire to follow the Bicester hounds. He did not care for the hallowed fields round Melton Mowbray 'where sportsmen ride in brilliant boots and breeches, but with their noses turned supernaturally into the air' [*Mr. Scarborough's Family* XVIII]. Although he liked to dress in good attire, he had little use for dandies. He had even less time for women who dressed up 'like a box of painted sugar-plums'. He greatly admired women riders, whom he noted had far fewer falls than men, or at least laymen, for the clergy had wonderful ways of keeping in the saddle. Much of this was, of course, due to the saddle: 'The fit of the saddle is of more moment than the fit of a pair of breeches,' he wrote [*Ralph the Heir* XXXI]. In one of his last novels, written after he had sadly laid aside his hunting, he wrote, 'I hold that nothing is so likely to be permanently prejudicial to ... hunting ... as a certain flavour of tip top fashion ... There is a pretence of grandeur ... which is, to my way of thinking, destructive of all sport itself' [*Marion Fay* XIII].

This is a crucial point for any understanding of why Trollope was, in his own words, 'a slave to hunting'. To him it was a 'sport' that brought pleasure and allowed him, as Glenn saw, to release the fierce passions and competitive spirit inside him. He fully accepted that it was 'that most anomalous, most irrational, most exciting, most delightful, and most beneficent sport', but then he was not one of those to whom all of life was meant to be rational. For Trollope the writer it provided the same opportunity as clubs and dinner tables: a place to observe his countrymen and women as they leapt about with 'that mingled look of business and amusement which is so peculiar to our national sports' [*Phineas Redux* XVI].[49]

*

Fox-hunting, club life, country week-ends, dining and entertaining must not obscure the fact that Trollope had to maintain two careers to provide the money to pay for it all. 'What with the post office and what with publishers,' he told a cousin, 'I find it very difficult to call any time my own.'[50] While he was wandering round North America his eleventh novel, *Orley Farm*, had been appearing in twenty monthly parts at a shilling each. This was the first time he had ever had a book brought out in this form, and he was paid £2,500. The series ended in October 1862, after which it was published as a two-volume novel. Within a few months of his return he started work on what would prove one of his most popular novels, *The Small House at Allington*, for which he received £3,500.

In the next five years, which were his final years at the Post Office, he completed an amazing number of novels. After *The Small House at Allington*, the Barset series was brought to an end with the sixth and greatest, *The Last Chronicle of Barset*, begun in 1866. Yet even before ending this series he embarked on the Palliser or Parliamentary series, by starting *Can You Forgive Her?* in 1863, followed by *Phineas Finn* in 1866. There were two shorter novels, each focusing on women who were weighed down by the pressures of their society: *Rachel Ray* and *Miss Mackenzie*. Each had sub-plots employing his old theme of commercial dishonesty. There were also two novels on the perennial Trollopean problem of finding a suitable spouse amidst the background of country life: *The Claverings* and *The Belton Estate*. He embarked on a totally new field with anonymous novels set on the continent: *Nina Balatka, Linda Tressel* and *The Golden Lion of Granpère* (though the last was not published till 1872). Nor did he neglect short stories as two more collections appeared: the second series of *Tales of All Countries* in

1863 and *Lotta Schmidt and Other Stories* in 1867. Of the eighteen stories in these two collections sixteen had already appeared in periodicals. *Lotta Schmidt* had stories drawing on his time in Ireland, his travels in the West of England, his holidays in Italy and Austria, and his sleighing jaunt in Boston. Two stories, 'The Two Generals' and 'The Widow's Mite', were set against the tragedy of the American Civil War, showing in the first how it split one Kentucky family and in the second how it affected the cotton workers of Lancashire.

  The Small House at Allington first appeared in twenty instalments in the *Cornhill* between September 1862 and April 1864 with illustrations by Millais. It was published as a two-volume book at £1 6s in March 1864. Trollope did not consider it part of the Barset series as the main characters, the Dale family, live in the next county. However, popular opinion has always felt that the book belongs to Barchester, and Trollope was compelled to include it in the collected edition of *The Chronicles of Barsetshire* which he arranged in his last years. He also came to dissent from the public idolatry of the book's heroine, Lily Dale, and in his *Autobiography* admitted: 'In the love with which she has been greeted I have hardly joined with much enthusiasm, feeling that she is somewhat of a female prig.' However, the public was only following his own advice in the first episode: 'Lilian Dale, dear Lily Dale – for my reader must know that she is to be very dear, and that my story will be nothing to him if he do not love Lily Dale' [II]. Likewise one writer recalled telling Trollope how much he had admired Lily, to be told, 'You can have no idea how pleased I am to hear you say that: I am so fond of her myself.' Perhaps by the time he wrote the *Autobiography* he had tired of similar compliments. She was so popular that, as one diligent scholar has discovered, she had two ships, one English and one Canadian, named after her.[51]

  Lily Dale was a perfect Victorian heroine, particularly to men: everything about her is subdued. She is mildly isolated, moderately comfortable, and only half-tragic. Her life is painted not in the vivid colours of a Byronic tale or in the dark hues of a modern 'psychological' investigation but, appropriately, in the subtle shades of a Victorian water-colour. Her situation poses one of Trollope's favourite questions: can anyone, particularly a woman, love more than once? When she is jilted by Adolphus Crosbie, a fairly important civil servant, she cannot erase his image from her heart to allow her to accept the true love of John Eames, a young government clerk, just emerging from his hobbledehoy days. Eames, of course, is modelled closely on the young Trollope.

  Many modern readers may well agree with Trollope that 'dear Lily' is a bit of a 'prig'. In many ways, Crosbie is the most interesting character and Trollope's treatment of him illustrates the author's genius. Crosbie best embodies Trollope's belief that the human character is a mixture of good and bad. All that is good in Crosbie draws him to Lily Dale, but no sooner has he won her love than he jilts her to make what he thinks is a better match with Lady Alexandrina de Courcy.* Trollope does not depict Crosbie as a melodramatic villain. His cruel act does not result in a searing catastrophe as a similar act would in a later novel, *An Eye For An Eye*. Instead Trollope provides a more exquisite punishment for Crosbie by making him the victim of the scheming de Courcy family, the details of whose various machinations rival those of the Stanhopes in *Barchester Towers*. *The Small House at Allington* is also remarkable for the way in which the author moves between the quiet life of the countryside and the bustling world of London. The near-Arcadian bliss of the 'Small House', with Mrs Dale picking peas in her sprawling garden and the old squire 'thin and meagre in his mental attributes ... but yet worthy of regard in that he had realised a path of duty and did endeavour to walk therein', is contrasted to the sordid world of London lodging houses where Eames flirts with the landlady's daughter.

The reviewers were almost unanimous in their praise. As with *Framley Parsonage*, serial publication heightened public interest. 'There has been as much speculation whether Lily Dale would marry Johnny Eames as about any "marriage on the *tapis*" (as the *Morning Post* phrases it) in any town and village in Great Britain.' The *Athenaeum*, in this review, gives an idea how the Victorians absorbed their fiction: 'Those who have taken it in monthly fractions will go over the ground again with something of regret, recognising the old landmarks where the story broke off, leaving them hungry and impatient at the month's pause ... [Many] would have rashly offered to forfeit three weeks ... if they might thus have learnt the progress of the story a little further ahead.' The *Reader* – an excellent literary journal which, like so many of that calibre, was short-lived – provides a good summary of Trollope's position at the height of his fame: 'For the last year Crosbie has been as much a public character as Lord Palmerston' – a remarkable statement given the Prime Minister's vast popularity.

---

*Trollope shows his ear for language in choosing her ladyship's name. By the time she appears in Chapter XVII the name Alexandra was on everyone's lips in expectation of the Prince of Wales's forthcoming marriage to Princess Alexandra of Denmark. Trollope, however, knew that his character would have been born in the early 1840s. Then she would have been named after the Queen, so he chose Alexandrina, Queen Victoria's first name.

'Mr Trollope's pages have been perused rather as news than as fiction.'
The journal also predicted how future generations would see him:
'Each of his novels is an epitome of contemporary English life; nor is
there any other novelist from whom posterity will, on the whole, derive
so true and vivid a conception of the actual condition of our society.'
The *Spectator* noted one episode which showed how the novelist's
choice of words reflected his subtle understanding of humanity. It is
the scene in which Earl de Guest, a lonely but kindly old peer, finds
Eames asleep. He had known the young man's father, who, like the
novelist's father, had come to grief by taking up farming. 'What touch
could be better,' asks the *Spectator*,[52]

> than his first question ... 'Have you got into trouble? You look as though
> you were in trouble. *Your poor father used to be in trouble.*' – which
> expresses with curious subtlety the rough sort of logic of an earl used to
> breed cattle, and evidently grounded on his deep belief in the hereditary
> character ... which he has learned from his breeding and ... which he
> accepts as a part of his aristocratic creed.

Several characters from the earlier Barset novels reappear, perhaps
most movingly when Crosbie pauses at Barchester Cathedral on his
way to Courcy Castle. The verger recounts how Septimus Harding
gave up the Wardenship. Trollope's description of this aged priest as he
walked out of the transept after Holy Communion shows how he
painted a scene that moved him personally [XVI]:

> He was a little, withered, shambling old man, with bent shoulders,
> dressed in knee-breeches and long black gaiters, which hung rather
> loosely about his poor old legs, – rubbing his hands one over the other as
> he went. And yet he walked quickly; not tottering as he walked, but with
> an uncertain, doubtful step. The verger, as Mr. Harding passed, put his
> hand to his head, and Crosbie also raised his hat. Whereupon Mr.
> Harding raised his, and bowed, and turned round as though he were
> about to speak. Crosbie felt that he had never seen a face on which traits
> of human kindness were more plainly written. But the old man did not
> speak. He turned his body half round, and then shambled back, as
> though ashamed of his intention, and passed on.
>   'He is of that sort that they make angels of,' said the verger. 'But they
> can't make many if they want them all as good as he is.'

Much of Trollope's greatness as a writer lies in this passage, especially
in his ability to use a carefully layered arrangement of details to depict
an emotional, indeed a spiritual, moment. Although the emotions are
stirred, they are restrained by a seemly reserve. He does not lecture, he
does not preach; he only observes and allows his readers to see and to

contrast that which is of the angels and that which is of fallen man. Having lifted his readers up, Trollope must let them down into reality quickly though not brutally. The very next words come from the verger: ' "I'm much obliged to you, sir." And he pocketed the half-crown which Crosbie gave him.' One is clearly back on earth.

*

The *Athenaeum* concluded its review by saying: 'we demand of Mr Trollope that he tells us the further fortunes of characters in *The Small House at Allington*.' Perhaps it is best to accede to this demand in a period in which Trollope was so productive and conclude the discussion of the Barset series. It was almost three years from the time Trollope finished *The Small House at Allington* until he started *The Last Chronicle of Barset*, and in those thirty-five months he wrote seven other novels. *The Last Chronicle* came out between December 1866 and July 1867, this time in weekly numbers of twenty-four pages at sixpence a number. George Smith paid the author £3,000. The plot centres on a sorely tried curate, the Rev. Josiah Crawley, who is accused of stealing a cheque for twenty pounds. Because he is such a strange man, no one, not even Crawley himself, can be sure he did not commit the crime. Once again, serial publication added to the suspense, particularly as Trollope did not follow his usual course of giving the plot away. Indeed one prominent clergyman was said to be so caught up in the unfolding drama that he included 'Josiah Crawley' in the prayer for 'all those who are any ways afflicted, or distressed, in mind, body, or estate'.[53]

The Rev. Josiah Crawley, the Perpetual Curate of Hogglestock who barely survives on £130 a year, is one of Trollope's greatest achievements.* It is much harder to create a character who is neither a veritable saint, like the Warden, nor a complete hypocrite, like Slope. It is often said that Crawley is actually Thomas Anthony Trollope transported from his Harrow farm and set down amid the squalor of Hogglestock. Trollope, as has been mentioned, normally disapproved of portraying real people in his fiction. He thought Dickens's use of his father as the basis for Mr Micawber contemptible. When he read the

---

*It is not insignificant that Trollope symbolised Crawley's situation by making him a 'perpetual curate' and not a rector or vicar. Although in time perpetual curates were addressed as 'vicars' their status was popularly seen as inferior. It was only in 1838 that their 'perpetual licence' was deemed in Church law to be a 'living'. Perpetual curates, for example, were not inducted by the Bishop but only licensed. The choice shows the depth of Trollope's knowledge of the Church.

first volume of Forster's biography he told G.H. Lewes and George Eliot that the book 'is distasteful to me ... Dickens was no hero ... very ignorant, and thick-skinned, who had taught himself to be his own God ... Forster tells of him things which should disgrace him, – as the picture he drew of his own father ... .' Yet Trollope's study of the process by which pride and ill-luck lead a gifted man like Crawley to the edge of madness must have been deeply affected by recollections of his own father, who had been dead for thirty years. In Crawley's fierce determination to give his daughter some of his own love for the classics and, by so doing, to preserve a shred of pride and sanity, there is much of Trollope's father. It may be remembered that he found consolation in his decline by the increasing free time it gave him to teach his sons Latin and Greek. As one critic said almost twenty years later, Trollope's attitude had none of Dickens's rancour towards his father and if there is anything of Thomas Anthony Trollope in Crawley it is 'a sympathising picture, and not a lampoon'.[54] There is also an echo of Fanny Trollope's statement that her husband was a good man but one whose fierce temper was ruining the family in Mrs Crawley's description of her husband. One does wonder whether Anthony Trollope had yet received the anonymous gift of his parents' old courtship letters, the reading of which is so bitter-sweet to anyone who knows the misery and tragedy that were to come.

Trollope's analysis of Mrs Crawley's attitude towards her husband shows how deeply he had thought about his own mother's attitude towards her husband and how, through their marriage, he had pondered the tragedies of life [XLI]:

> I think that ... nobody saw clearly the working of his mind, – not even his wife, who studied it very closely, who gave him credit for all his high qualities, and who had gradually learned to acknowledge to herself that she must distrust his judgment in many things. She knew that he was good and yet weak, that he was afflicted by false pride and supported by true pride, that his intellect was still very bright, yet so dismally obscured on many sides as almost to justify people in saying that he was mad. She knew that he was almost a saint, and yet almost a castaway through vanity and hatred of those above him. But she did not know that he knew all of this himself.

'I sometimes look back, meditating for hours together, on his adverse fate,' Anthony Trollope would write of his father in his *Autobiography*. That unforgettable character, Josiah Crawley, was the fruit of this meditation. His deep passion for classical scholarship, his penchant for triumphing over all with whom he came in contact, especially those who tried to help him, his determination to wear his poverty about him like a cloak, his arrogant contempt for all those whom luck or connections had placed above him – all of these unlovely aspects of his father were used in creating Mr Crawley. There is however a crucial difference between Dickens's Micawber and Trollope's Crawley. One never laughs at Crawley: his tragedy is never a subject for humour, and he is never held up to ridicule. It is interesting that we never see Crawley with his son in *The Last Chronicle*. 'Young Bob' remains at Marlborough, thanks to the generosity of Dean Arabin, and thus Trollope was spared the task of showing the tragic scholar with his son, something which might have made the portrayal too autobiographical.

Archdeacon Grantly is also of biographical interest. When we first meet him in *The Warden*, he seems merely an embodiment of clerical arrogance and power; yet as the series goes on he develops both in the depth of his character and in the nobility of his acts. It is, of course, always dangerous to say any fictional character 'is the author'. Theophilus Grantly is not Anthony Trollope, but they share so many traits that anyone who wishes to know the novelist must also know the Archdeacon. Both the creator and his creation saw themselves as powerful officers of great institutions; both were contemptuous of anyone in those institutions who did not come up to their high standards; both had fierce tempers which more often than not harmed themselves more than others; both were determined to establish their sons and neither could resist the sight of a charming girl in distress. To an extent Trollope's portrayal of the Archdeacon's character is a perceptive analysis of his own strengths and weaknesses. One also suspects there is some resemblance between Susan Grantly and Rose Trollope, for each was the only real critic whose strictures their proud husbands would accept. For at the heart of each man, the fictional churchman and the real author, was what the latter called 'the real kindness of the archdeacon's nature' [LXIII]. This is exactly what countless contemporaries said of Trollope himself: that beneath the outspoken, gruff, bear-like exterior beat a warm and generous heart, one that compelled him to act, if not always to speak, with kindness and with justice.

In addition to the Archdeacon, Trollope brings back in this final volume most major characters from the five earlier Barset books: Mr Harding, Eleanor Bold, Dean Arabin, Henry Grantly, whose love for Grace Crawley provides the major love plot, Bishop and Mrs Proudie, Lady Lufton, Mark Robarts, Adolphus Crosbie, Dr Thorne and his wife, the former Miss Dunstable with her fortune from patent medicine. Lily Dale is an important figure in the story and we are led to believe that she is on the verge of accepting poor John Eames only for her to refuse him once again. Of the earlier major characters in the vast saga only the Stanhopes, presumably intriguing once again on the shores of Lake Como, and the loathsome Mr Slope are missing. The novel is also memorable for two deaths: of Mr Harding and Mrs Proudie. The first dies the peaceful and pious death of the saint: ' "There is nothing left for me to wish, my dears; – nothing." He never spoke again above his breath; but ever and anon his daughters, who watched him, could see that he was praying' [XXXVIII]. The death of the fierce, unnatural lady-bishop is not the quiet passing away of the saint, and there is as much struggle in her dying as there has been in her living. She has failed in her final battle for 'righteousness' which she has been waging against her husband, her constant though contemptible victim. Her aim has been to drive poor Crawley from his parish even before his case could be brought to trial. In the end the worm – if it is not too disrespectful a term for a bishop, even a fictional one – turns and tells his wife that she has destroyed him as a bishop and almost as a man. As her world collapses round her, her distress finds voice and she calls her husband 'Tom' and not 'Bishop'. The 'would-be priestess' then withdraws to her bedroom where, in her self-inflicted desolation, she collapses with a fatal heart attack.

*

'It was with many misgivings that I killed my old friend,' Trollope wrote in his *Autobiography* when explaining his decision:[55]

> I was sitting one morning at work upon the novel at the end of the long drawing-room of the Athenaeum Club ... two clergymen, each with a magazine in his hand, seated themselves ... They soon began to abuse what they were reading, and each was reading some part of some novel of mine. The gravamen of their complaint lay in the fact that I reintroduced the same characters so often! 'Here,' said one, 'is that archdeacon whom we have had in every novel he has ever written.' 'And here,' said the other, 'is the old duke whom he has talked about till everybody is tired of him. If I could not invent new characters, I would not write novels at all.' Then one of them fell foul of Mrs Proudie. It was impossible for me not to hear their words ... I got up, and standing between them, I acknowledged myself to be the culprit. 'As to Mrs Proudie,' I said, 'I will go home and kill her before the week is over.' And so I did.

This murder has become part of the literary heritage of the English-speaking, and English-reading, world. The incident behind it soon became one of those stories on which Trollope frequently 'dined out'. As so often happens, various versions began to appear. When he told the story to his cousin, Cecilia Meetkerke, he said the two clergymen were not reading 'a magazine' but part-issues of *Last Chronicle* which, of course, made the story even better because it meant that Trollope had to change the plot after the book had begun appearing. This would date the Athenaeum conversation after the appearance of Mrs Proudie in the second number, which occurred before Christmas 1866, in what is now Chapter V. It does not hold water because Trollope's almost invariable practice was to finish a novel before any instalment had appeared. In this case he began writing the book on 21 January 1866 and completed it on 15 September that same year. The first weekly number was issued two-and-a-half months later on 1 December and Mrs Proudie does not die until Chapter LXVI which appeared in the twenty-sixth part, in the summer of 1867.[56]

An examination of the surviving letters from Trollope to George Smith shows no letter asking for such a change, something he could easily have done because he was sent the proofs for correction. In August 1866, for example, he asked Smith to make a change in the proofs of *The Claverings*, then in serial publication, but there is no evidence that either wanted any change other than in Trollope's original title for *The Last Chronicle*. An even more important letter, written to an unidentified correspondent who had criticised his handling of Mr Crawley, has survived in the Ogden Papers in University College London. In his reply, written on 15 June 1867, three weeks before the end of the series, Trollope wrote:[57]

Many thanks for your kind letter, which, alas, is all too late, as the entire work was written & printed, before the first number came out. I have never been able to correct such errors as those pointed out ... because I always complete my story before the first printing is published, & the printer, taking advantage of this, prints in advance.

In other words Trollope had adhered to his normal practice and completed the story to enable the printers to set it before the first number appeared in December 1866. One suspects that his cousin, herself a writer, got carried away with her recollections and decided to enhance the story in a Trollopean fashion.

The benefit of the other versions is that they allow us to see how Trollope presented his own work to others. The review of *The Last Chronicle* in *Blackwood's* was by Mrs Oliphant, herself the creator of the seven-part clerical series 'The Chronicles of Carlingford'. In her review she said that she felt Trollope had been wrong to kill Mrs Proudie and that he must have done the deed in 'some fit of weariness of passion'. In one way her intuition was correct: the overheard conversation, whenever it occurred, was the straw that broke the camel's back, especially as Trollope so liked his 'would be priestess' – 'so great was my delight in writing about Mrs. Proudie'. In another version Trollope traced the conversation not to two clergymen but to 'an unknown critic', and indeed it was the critics' complaints of his reusing old characters that had sounded the real death-knell for Mrs Proudie. In at least four separate articles in the *Saturday Review*, the *Dublin University Magazine* and the *London Review* he had been taken to task for this supposed fault. This makes sense of the version Augustus Hare's friend was told, in which the overheard complaint and Trollope's impulsive promise that 'Mrs. Proudie shall die in the very next book I write' make sense. The decision both to end the series and to despatch Mrs Proudie within its last volume was part of the same reaction. He had taken the criticisms to heart because they were directed at his professionalism as a writer, something in which he took great pride. The incident in the Athenaeum was seized on and remembered because it could serve as the excuse for his action, because it was a good story, because it accorded with his own quick temper, and because it allowed him to maintain his off-hand way of discussing his own writing: his decision to get rid of Mrs Proudie, like his decision to wind up the Barset series, was based on a careful appreciation of the criticisms that had been made, but his actual doing of the wicked deed was triggered by some conversation he overheard. He admitted in his *Autobiography*, however, that 'I have never dissevered myself from Mrs. Proudie, and still live much in company with her ghost', as do his readers.[58]

*

The Barset novels end as they begin with questions of conscience and justice predominating. How does a man confront a grave charge against himself, particularly when he is unsure in his own mind whether the charge is true or not? Both the Warden and Josiah Crawley have to come to terms with this. Trollope was fascinated with unravelling the complexities of human nature as a respected figure is nearly crushed by a sudden and intolerable burden. How does society itself react to an individual's dilemma and the decision he finally reaches? These are the questions Trollope poses in *The Warden* and in *The Last Chronicle of Barset*, the two most serious books in the Barset series. In the sense that they deal with a deep underlying moral question, both have not only a moral purpose but a religious one. Reviewers and other critics were and are sometimes perplexed as to why a series which appears to be dominated by clergymen has so little about 'religion'. Anthony Trollope was not his sister Cecilia or Charlotte Yonge or Silas K. Hocking: he did not write novels to promote religious propaganda. He is not concerned with the number of candles on an altar or whether the wicked Anglo-Catholic curate will pervert the innocent young Methodist maiden, but with the inner light that guides a man in a time of misery, some of it self-inflicted. It is never quite clear how the critics thought Trollope should inject 'religion' into his novels: was Mr Crawley to discuss the Athanasian Creed with the brickmakers of Hogglestock, or the Warden to warn the bedesmen of Hiram's Hospital about the dangers of the Pelagian heresy?

Trollope was to say throughout his *Life of Cicero* that two basic principles distinguished Christianity from paganism: a belief in an after-life and a conviction that you should do unto others as you would have them do unto you. Both of these are present throughout the whole Barset series. For example, Trollope naturally makes no attempt to portray eternity, but in all death-bed scenes there is an implicit belief in the soul's survival. One had to be quite a radical Victorian to discard this, and when Anthony died his brother Tom, who was something of a free-thinker, was convinced that they would meet again. In the Barset novels we see constant acts of kindness motivated by Christian feelings: Lady Lufton's sending food to the Crawleys or Mr Toogood's taking on Crawley's case even though he knows there will be no fee. One character, whom the novelist clearly likes, Lady Julia de Guest, expresses Trollope's basic views when she writes to tell her old foe Squire Dale that Crosbie has betrayed his niece: 'I do to you as I would wish that others should do unto me' [*The Small House at Allington* XXVI]. To Trollope as to most Englishmen, Christianity had over the centuries become so commingled with the principles of decent behaviour that religion had become a matter of what one did, not of what one said or even thought, let alone of what others said or thought.

On Saturday 15 September 1866 Trollope sat down – presumably before dawn had lighted the gardens at Waltham House – to write the final twelve pages of the last Barchester novel. It was over fourteen years since that midsummer evening when he had wandered round 'the purlieus of the cathedral' at Salisbury gathering the inspiration for *The Warden*. That morning was also exactly a quarter of a century, to the very day, since he had arrived in Dublin. On this Saturday morning in 1866 he dipped his pen in his ink-well to complete the final paragraphs of *The Last Chronicle of Barset* and to answer those who had attacked his portrayal of the clergy: 'My object has been to paint the social and not the professional lives of clergymen ... as no men affect more strongly, by their own character, the society of those around than do country clergymen.' Once again he reflects his mother's teaching in a passage quoted earlier: while 'the clergy of England, their matronly wives and highly-educated daughters ... mingle freely in society ... there is little danger ... [of] notorious vice'. The son would not have put it in quite so didactic a manner, but the message is the same. Trollope believed that 'I, as a novelist, may feel myself entitled to write of clergymen out of their pulpits ... [but] I have no such liberty to write of them in their pulpits.' Having answered those who criticised him for not being 'religious' enough, he turned to pay an emotional farewell to his county and his friends:

> If the reader will allow me to seize him affectionately by the arm, we will together take our last farewell of Barset and of the towers of Barchester ... to me Barset has been a real county, and its city a real city, and the spires and towers have been before my eyes, and the voices of the people are known to my ears ... To them all I now say farewell. That I have been induced to wander among them too long by my love of old friendships, and by the sweetness of old faces, is a fault for which I may perhaps be more readily forgiven, when I repeat ... the promise made in my title, that this shall be the last chronicle of Barset.

At the bottom of his work sheet he wrote one word 'End' and drew four lines under it. The Chronicles of Barsetshire were finished.[59]

*

'The general effect of this announcement,' said the *Spectator*, was disconcerting. Its reviewer found 'the loneliness very oppressive' since he could no longer meet 'almost the best known and most typical ... fellow-countrymen again'. A friend had declared, 'What am I to do without ever meeting Archdeacon Grantly? He was one of my best and most intimate friends ... Life has lost one of its principal alleviations. Mr Trollope has no right to break old ties in this cruel and reckless way.' Other reviewers hoped that 'he will *not* keep his word' and that he would return to Barset.[60] Sad to say, Trollope did keep his word and did not return. Occasionally old characters made appearances in other novels, but the familiar world of rectories and cathedral close had vanished.* He resisted numerous appeals urging him to allow John Eames to marry Lily Dale. It was virtually impossible for him to resume the series once the two principal foils, Mr Harding and Mrs Proudie, were dead: he needed the contrast to frame his picture. Furthermore the Barsetshire Chronicles are derived from Trollope's vast knowledge of the West of England based on his postal work in the early 1850s. By the 1870s things were changing: an agricultural depression began to undermine rural society, and depopulation of the countryside was gathering momentum. The Church of England was also changing: the cultivated, restrained world of High Church gentlemen like Archdeacon Grantly was giving way to a harsher world where Ritualists and zealots bred up in the new clerical seminaries (something Trollope much disliked) did battle for the Church and fought both Roman Catholics and Low Churchmen. For all their good points, they were less interested in living at peace with their neighbours than in enforcing their own nostrums on them. They also seemed less concerned with the 'comfort' of religion and were as intolerant and severe as the old Evangelicals. Trollope could no longer write about Barset in the 1870s because it had ceased to exist.

*

This did not mean that Trollope stopped portraying clergymen or country life but that he no longer 'lived' with them as he had done in Barset. Both *The Belton Estate* and *The Claverings*, the novels immediately preceding and following publication of *The Last Chronicle*, have great similarities with the Barset series. *The Belton Estate*, for example, is set in those 'rich Somersetshire pastures' [VI] that were the inspiration for Barsetshire and features a fanatically religious woman who has some similarity with Mrs Proudie. *The Claverings* has a superb portrait of a lazy clergyman who is forced to give up fox-hunting by none other than Bishop Proudie. However, from the biographical point of view, the main interest of these two novels is the circumstances in which they were written. Even though *The Claverings* was published after *The Belton Estate*, it had been written in the previous year, 1864. *The Claverings* shows how fast Trollope could write: he started his manuscript on 24 August and completed it on the last day of that year. The year had not been an easy one: between April and July he was caught up in a rather nasty exchange of

---

*He made one feeble attempt at a short story set in Barset, 'The Two Heroines of Plumplington', which he wrote during the last months of his life. It was published after his death in the Christmas issue of *Good Words*.

letters with officials at St Martin-le-Grand, including his brother-in-law, over an increase in salary which surveyors felt they were owed. Although the correspondence ended officially in April, Trollope kept it alive with furious letters to both Tilley and the Postmaster General. In addition he had taken Henry, who had left Bradfield in 1863, to Florence, where he studied privately from the autumn until May 1864.

In spite of battles with the Post Office, his own work as surveyor and his hunting, he had managed in 1864 to complete *Can You Forgive Her?* in April, *Miss Mackenzie* in August and *The Claverings* in December: three novels in twelve months. For the last, *The Claverings*, he received one of his highest payments, £3,000, for the right to publish it in the *Cornhill* and as a two-volume book. (It may be recalled that books that had appeared in parts or in magazine serialisation often appeared in two, rather than three, volumes.) Here, too, he was facing problems: he was beginning to over-produce. After Thackeray's death in 1863, there were only two novelists who were normally ranked ahead of Trollope, both in critical regard and in payment by publishers: Dickens and George Eliot, each of whom only produced two novels between 1863 and 1870. Trollope, however, produced more than twice as many as his two nearest rivals put together in the same period. Furthermore most of his novels appeared, particularly to those who had only read some of them, to have a similar setting and theme. Nor was he the only Trollope writing novels. As he put it in 1866, 'there are so many Trollopes who male & female all write books'. Tom had begun to produce them to supplement his income from journalism and historical writing and his second wife blossomed forth as a novelist, although for a while she appeared anonymously as 'a new writer'.[61]

These factors made Trollope's incredible outpouring seem even greater than it was. There had already been complaints by the late 1850s, often good-natured ones, that he wrote too much and that his quality and his permanent fame would be bettered if he took more time with his work. It is difficult to disagree with this, yet it is a criticism which does not take his nature into consideration. Trollope genuinely liked to write; indeed he had to write. Like hunting and pulling rollers about the croquet lawn, it was a way in which he released the extraordinary powers that were at work within him. Perhaps no one spoke more often, and certainly no one spoke more openly, about the money an author should make from his writing. Yet it is often forgotten that he also said many times that he would write even if no one would buy or publish his work, and this was before he became famous. It was no idle boast: on one occasion he was prepared to give the manuscript of a book to a publisher as a birthday present!

Trollope's creative genius was of the type that had to produce its work quickly if it was to produce it at all. This is not unique: both Mozart and Haydn were the same, and yet no one would say their glorious creations are less enduring than those produced by some modern composers who agonise for years to produce a 'meaningful' cacophony.

Trollope needed to write for financial and emotional reasons, and he wrote a lot. By so doing he had created a position for himself by the 1860s as the most popular novelist of the circulating libraries. On the whole his books dealt with the country life of the landed gentry and their clerical cousins. His readers liked this and expected an unending supply. Yet, when he provided a good stock for Mudie's shelves there were complaints, not from readers but from critics, that he overdid it. Conscious of the danger, he made two notable attempts to diversify. In the mid-sixties he produced two relatively short novels, both concerned with women whose lives are more restricted than his Barset ladies: *Rachel Ray* and *Miss Mackenzie*. The first grew out of a request from yet another magazine, *Good Words*, which had begun in the same year as the *Cornhill* but cost only sixpence, half what Smith charged. Its appeal, therefore, was to the lower reaches of the middle classes. It was owned by a Scottish publisher, Alexander Strahan, and edited by Norman Macleod. Macleod, like his father before him, was a minister in the Church of Scotland. Both were leading figures in the religious life of Scotland, both were appointed as Chaplains to Queen Victoria, and both became royal confidants. The younger Macleod sometimes recited Burns to the Queen while she plied her spinning wheel, and sometimes he was assigned the more thankless task of delivering rebukes to wayward royal sons.

Macleod was anxious not to produce yet another pious journal and wanted to attract first-rate novelists. He wrote to Trollope in terms to please any author: 'As the Editor of a humble sixpenny monthly ... I approach you with the respect & reverence becoming a beggar seeking crumbs from a rich man's table ... name your price to Strahan ... you & Kingsley are the only two men whom I should like to have a story from ... I think you could let out the best side of your soul in Good Words – better far than even in Cornhill.' (Kingsley's *Hereward the Wake* appeared in 1865.) The humorous tone of the letter, with no trace of sanctimoniousness or any indication that it was from the same man who had helped to establish the Evangelical Alliance, no doubt encouraged Trollope to see the publisher. Strahan agreed to pay him £600 for a one-volume novel. Some months later they agreed to raise the fee by £400 and to double the length. Trollope had warned the editor that he was a 'worldly' writer, but Macleod persisted. Trollope delayed writing the promised book until 1863 in order to complete *The Small House at Allington*. He also took time off to write a short story for Macleod's Christmas issue, for which he received £100. 'The Widow's Mite' recounts how a girl gives the money she had saved for her trousseau to help the suffering workers in Lancashire who had lost their jobs because of the cotton famine caused by the war in America. He did not begin the novel, *Rachel Ray*, until March 1863 and finished it on 29 June.[62]

In *La Vendée* Trollope had neglected one of the first rules of writing: write of what you know. Now, highly experienced though he was, he broke another rule: know your audience. The great success of *Good Words* was due to the fact that the readership, made up principally of Evangelicals, Scottish Presbyterians and English Nonconformists, trusted Macleod to bridge the gap between 'improving' and 'entertaining' literature. This publication had been the only general magazine to receive the praise of the Society for Purity in Literature. The manuscript of *Rachel Ray* read as if Trollope wished to have it rejected, because he used the book to mount one of his fiercest attacks on Evangelicals. The plot is basically the same as 'The Courtship of Susan Bell', the short story set in America and published there in *Harper's*. The American story had certainly contained occasional 'hits' at religious fanaticism, but *Rachel Ray* seems dominated by it. Rachel Ray lives with her widowed mother, a lady 'in reduced circumstances', in a small Devon town. Both are subject to the dictates of her fierce sister, who is guided by an Evangelical clergyman, the Rev. Samuel Prong. Though Trollope's picture of religious tyranny on the domestic level was superbly done, it was neither politic nor likely to please *Good Words*, and Macleod, not surprisingly, refused to publish it. He was perhaps all the more sensitive since the *Record*, a particularly nasty Low Church newspaper, had mounted several assaults on its rival for planning to publish 'Mr. Anthony Trollope, this year's chief sensation writer'.[63]

Trollope was, understandably enough, furious at Macleod's rejection and wrote one of the few quasi-legal letters in his correspondence. The settlement he suggested, which was adopted, gives us a good insight into Trollope's honourable nature. After first asserting his 'undoubted right' to the full £1,000 he suggested that, as he was sure to place the book elsewhere, Strahan should pay him £500 which, when added to what he would get from the other publisher, would mean that he would not be out of pocket and that Strahan would be out £500 and not £1,000. Should the other arrangement fall through, however, he would demand the second £500. Many writers, then and now, would have demanded the full amount and then placed the manuscript elsewhere. On the same day on which he wrote to Strahan he reached the expected agreement with Chapman, so that he got altogether £1,500 for the novel. Macleod sent a letter 'full of wailing and repentance', and he and Trollope remained friends. Indeed some years later an elderly gentleman staying at a Highland inn complained to the inn-keeper about the laughter and loud talking coming from the bedroom below his own and lasting far into the night. The landlord assured him that the occupants of the room, the Rev. Norman Macleod, Anthony Trollope and the chairman of the Cunard Line, had had nothing stronger than tea and fresh herrings. 'Bless me, if that is so, *what would they have been after dinner?*'[64] In years to come, Trollope wrote several stories for *Good Words* as well as his important essay 'A Walk in a Wood'. His novel, *Kept in the Dark*, was appearing in that magazine at the time of his death.

Perhaps the difficulties over *Rachel Ray* influenced the decision not to have another novel about a woman, *Miss Mackenzie*, serialised. As mentioned earlier, almost all his novels published after 1860 appeared first either in magazines or in part issues. *Miss Mackenzie* is also unusual because Trollope tried to produce a novel without a love story, but he did not proceed far before he had to introduce one. *Miss Mackenzie*, which was written in just under twelve weeks, is a moving portrayal of a lone woman in Victorian society trying to fend off men determined to control her and her comfortable income. The story also allowed the author to continue his war on the narrow-minded Evangelicals as well as the world of commercial dishonesty. Some of the characters from the 'Littlebath' (Cheltenham) episodes of *The Bertrams* made another appearance. Shortly after it was published in 1865 Trollope received a letter from Sir Edward Bulwer Lytton. Thirty years before, the young clerk had analysed the famous author's novels, not altogether approvingly. Now Lytton told Trollope that he had long wanted to write to praise his books, but had feared such 'praise to an author so successful might be considered rather an *impertinence* than a compliment'. Trollope assured the older novelist of his delight at receiving a tribute 'from the author of *Pelham*'.[65]

Bulwer Lytton hoped that he would have a chance to meet Trollope, and they were brought together on one rather odd occasion. One day Mr and Mrs Edward Ward, both well-known artists, were staying with Bulwer Lytton at his exotic house, Knebworth in Hertfordshire, a Tudor mansion he had rebuilt in the 'Gothick' style. Lord Lytton – for such he had become in 1866 – was driving the Wards through the grounds of Panshanger, the nearby Hertfordshire estate of the Cowpers:[66]

We saw to our intense amusement Anthony Trollope about to have a fight with a broad-shouldered rubicund tradesman. Anthony had divested himself of his coat and was shaking his fists in his opponent's face, as he danced round him. Though we never heard which gladiator won, the betting was all on Anthony, who had gained a reputation for never risking defeat when he made a challenge.

*

Because Trollope was sensitive to the criticism that he wrote too much, he undertook one of the most curious experiments ever attempted by a highly successful novelist. He was fascinated by the question of whether his books succeeded because of their intrinsic merit or because of the author's name on the title page. He therefore decided to write novels anonymously. This was not new: some years before, Mrs Gore, the queen of the 'silver-fork' novelists, had produced many anonymous books simply because she too wrote so quickly. There were two other factors behind Trollope's experiment with anonymous fiction. The public and the publishers more or less demanded that his novels contain clergymen and English country life. He enjoyed writing those, but he wanted other settings as well and knew he could produce them. His love of travel gave him many possibilities for novels with a continental flavour, but if he used his name he might intrude into his brother's territory. Finally, at some point, though it is not clear when, Trollope came increasingly to think that Henry could be trained to be a novelist in order to carry 'the family literature' into a third generation. It may well have occurred to him that Henry, who had shown a taste for continental life during various stays in Florence, might eventually be brought into the writing of these anonymous novels.[67]

Trollope wrote three such novels in the later 1860s, and again all three centred on women, in this case on women who suffered because of opposition to the men they had chosen for husbands. As with *Rachel Ray* and *Miss Mackenzie*, all were short books, allowing him the luxury of foregoing the complicated sub-plots required by three-deckers. All three drew on his holiday jaunts in the mid-sixties. *Nina Balatka* is about a Christian girl in Prague who is in love with a Jewish merchant. *Linda Tressel* concerns a girl who lives in Nuremberg under the domination of that sturdy Trollopean standby, the fanatically religious aunt, who finally drives Linda to death by opposing her romance with a young radical. Ironically the young man is shown to be something of a scoundrel. *The Golden Lion of Granpère* is set in Alsace-Lorraine and concerns the love of Marie Bromar for the son of an innkeeper. The boy's father opposes the match, hoping for a better marriage, much as

La Mère Bauche had opposed her son's marriage in the short story of that name. The last of these novels, though written in 1867, was not published until 1872 in *Good Words*, which only agreed to publish on the understanding that Trollope's name should appear. He also had to make some changes in the beginning of the story because between the time of writing and publishing Alsace-Lorraine had been been incorporated in the new German Empire.

Nina Balatka is the most interesting of these novels, for it shows the breadth of vision which Trollope could, at times, employ. On his 1865 visit to Prague he had been fascinated by the old quarter, particularly the Synagogue, said to be the oldest in Europe. Just as the sight of the ruined manor house in Ireland had inspired his sympathetic portrayal of Irish society, this visit gave him the idea of portraying the tensions between Christians and Jews in Central Europe. This seems a most un-Trollopean theme, at least to those who imagine that Trollope could write of nothing but bishops, fox-hunts and indecisive maidens. To those who know only some of his writings, it may also appear surprising that he could approach a Jewish character, and one who ultimately marries a Christian girl, with such understanding. Most assume that Melmotte, the sinister financier in *The Way We Live Now*, written eight years later, in 1873, shows Trollope to be conventionally anti-Semitic. The truth is far more complex than that and goes to the heart of the manner in which Trollope approached any group.

Trollope's attitude towards groups was the same as his attitude towards individuals: they are a mixture of good and bad. Thus it is possible to draw up whole categories of characters and show that he has presented contrasting specimens of every group. His novels portray good and bad dukes, admirable and vicious clergyman, noble wives and scheming viragos, lazy and hard-working civil servants, deceitful lawyers and others with a passion for justice, stupid fox-hunters and virtuous people who take it up for well-merited relaxation. Thus the fact that Melmotte appears to be Jewish and is clearly a contemptible character does not mean that Trollope meant to attack Jews, any more than the fact that Slope is detestable meant that he hated the clergy of his own Church. In the same book which features Melmotte, Trollope has a banker who is definitely Jewish and who is one of the few honest people in the story.

He began *Nina Balatka* on 3 November 1865 and finished it on the last day of the year. As usual he had set out his writing schedule when he began, and on top of the page he had written '300 pages at 230 words – 10 weeks at 30 pages a week.' It is a relief to see that sometimes even he could not keep to a schedule: on Christmas morning he only managed to do three pages, and he wrote none at all between 29 December and 2 January. Perhaps the demands of fox-hunting drew him away from the streets of Prague. Trollope was lucky in one thing: the book appeared when both the location and the Jewish theme made it topical. Prague was much in the news as Prussian armies swept across Bohemia in their attack upon the Austrian Empire. Although the novel began to appear in *Blackwood's* after that short war had ended, it oddly contains no hint of it and little idea that Bohemia was part of the Empire. The Jewish theme was topical because 1867, the year in which it was published as a book, was the year in which all civil restrictions on Jews ended in the Austrian Empire. In the following year new marriage laws made inter-faith unions, like that between Nina Balatka and Anton Trendellsohn, easier.[68] The central plot is the love between the Catholic girl and the Jewish merchant, who owns her bankrupt father's house, but round it Trollope places some of his standard characters dressed in Bohemian costumes. Under Nina's fanatical aunt, Sophie Zamenoy, can be recognised a Czech Catholic version of our old friend Mrs Proudie. As so often in his books, there is that curious combination of conservatism and liberalism: the Catholic priest is treated with respect, as is the one Jewish girl who dislikes this mixed marriage, but, while Trollope makes the standard Liberal references to Austrian 'barracks', all his romantic pity is stirred by the idea of the former Habsburg Emperor, who abdicated in 1848, living out his days in the Haradschin castle. There is even an appeal to Victorian pride: Nina's family conclude they cannot shove her into a convent because 'the English people would hear of it' [II].

Anton Trendellsohn is the most interesting character in the book. Trollope, as so often, enjoys a little joke by having him sign a letter as the author often did: 'A.T.' This portrayal of the Jewish merchant is an early indication that Jews were beginning to be seen in fiction, not as caricatures, like the criminal Fagin in *Oliver Twist*, or as all-wise prophets, like Disraeli's Sidonia, but as ordinary people. (It is interesting that Trollope tackled this issue nine years before the appearance of George Eliot's *Daniel Deronda*.) Trollope's approach struck one of the reviewers: 'In the character of Anton Trendellsohn, the author seeks to vindicate the Hebrew ... He is a human being, neither very good nor very bad; possessed of middle qualities that neither exalt nor degrade – that neither awaken admiration nor excite contempt.'[69]

In March 1866 Trollope sent the manuscript to Smith offering it to the *Cornhill* for £300 or £500 if Smith also wanted the right to publish it as a book. The comparatively low figure (he had received £1,200 for

Miss Mackenzie) shows how much Trollope's name was worth, but he had known that an anonymous work would bring less. Smith did not want the story: perhaps he feared it would be a failure, like the dreadful *Struggles of Brown, Jones, and Robinson*. Joseph Langford, a friend from both the Cosmopolitan and Garrick, acted as head of the London branch of Blackwoods and agreed to mention the story to the head of the firm in Edinburgh. *Blackwood's Magazine* was, of course, much older than the *Cornhill*, having started in 1817. Its strong Tory line made it particularly popular with military and colonial readers. John Blackwood was puzzled by the novel but concluded: 'The great merit ... seems to me the clearness with which it stands out. There is an individuality about it which will make any one who reads it remember it. Whether this is sufficient to make it really popular & stand out ... as the work of an anonymous author is a doubtful point.'[70] As a summary of the book's fate, this cannot be bettered. Blackwood agreed to pay £450 to publish it first in his magazine and then as a book.

The anonymous story attracted attention but little else. As Blackwood moaned: 'The anxiety about the authorship shows that the book is telling although not selling.' Literary circles were intrigued to know the author's name and some suggested it was Tom Trollope. One of Blackwood's authors, Laurence Oliphant, wrote to the publisher: 'I am much questioned as to the authorship of "Nina Balatka"; is it Trollope?' Blackwood replied that, while it was a secret, he might hint that it was by Disraeli. R.H. Hutton was actually dining at the Athenaeum with the last instalment of the tale in *Blackwood's* as his companion, when he publically announced: 'The "great unknown" of the *Blackwood* story is Anthony Trollope.' This was done loudly enough to see if he could get a rise from Laurence Oliphant at a nearby table, but that author, anxious not to offend his publisher, gave a Delphic answer: 'I believe they are satisfied with its reception.' In his *Spectator* review Hutton was puzzled why Trollope would not use his name which 'is worth a great deal in mere money value'. 'Still,' he went on,

> no one who knows his style at all can read three pages of this tale without detecting him as plainly as if he were present in the flesh. Indeed, the present writer ... said to himself, 'If it is written by Mr. Trollope, I shall soon meet with the phrase "made his way," as applied to walking where there is no physical difficulty ... but only a certain moral hesitation' ... and behold within a page ... came the very phrase.

There are indeed many tell-tale signs, such as calling the doctor a 'son of Galen', as well as giving away the outcome before it happens. Meanwhile another Blackwood author, the novelist Mrs Oliphant (who was not related to Laurence Oliphant though she later wrote his biography), had guessed the secret. She wrote to her publisher while on a short visit to Prague, where she was 'going to look for Nina Balatka's bridge etc – a pilgrimage which Mr Trollope (I beg your pardon, I forgot he was anonymous) should take as a compliment from a veteran novel-reader like myself '.[71]

John Blackwood had ended his first letter: 'Hoping that the correspondence we have now entered into may prove a pleasant and advantageous one to us both.' It was to prove so in spite of the fact that neither *Nina Balatka* nor its anonymous successor, *Linda Tressel*, was profitable to the publisher. Blackwoods became one of Trollope's principal publishers along with George Smith and Chapman and Hall. In addition to publishing several of his novels they brought out his *Autobiography*. Both Anthony and Rose became friends with Blackwood and his wife. Although Scotland plays little role in Trollope's fiction, the Blackwoods came to play an important part in his and Rose's life. She so enjoyed one visit with them that she wrote 'a romantic ballad' about a goose, which referred to some humorous episode the Trollopes and the Blackwoods had shared. The Trollopes enjoyed several visits to Blackwood's house, Strathtyrum, only a mile from the 'Golfer's Paradise' of St Andrews, when Trollope liked to tease Blackwood on his strong Tory views. Blackwood's daughter recalled one such visit during August 1878:[72]

> Mr and Mrs Anthony Trollope's was one of these never-to-be-forgotten visits. The echo of Mr Trollope's laugh seems to come back to me as I strive to recall his genial presence ... the walk, the games of golf he insisted on playing on the Ladies' Links, pretending to faint when he made a bad shot, his immense weight causing a sort of earthquake on the sandy ground.

*

Trollope had also become friendly with Blackwood's greatest novelist six years before the publication of *Nina Balatka*. 'Last Tuesday', wrote George Eliot in her journal in November 1860, 'Anthony Trollope dined with us, and made us like him very much by his straightforward, wholesome *Wesen* [personality].' Thus commenced one of the most surprising and yet one of the most treasured of Trollope's friendships. It would be difficult – at least at first – to imagine a greater contrast than Anthony Trollope and George Eliot: the boisterous fox-hunter and the introverted free-thinker. However, both writers have been caricatured, often by their own most fervent admirers, who project some vision of themselves onto their hero and heroine. For twenty years Trollope was a frequent visitor at George Eliot's home, particularly her celebrated Sunday afternoon receptions where many from the Victorian literary world gathered. Some people would not call on her because they knew she was not really married to the man whom she called her husband: George Henry Lewes. Trollope knew of these rumours and probably knew that Lewes could not marry because he was unable to obtain a divorce from his wife. After both Lewes and Eliot were dead Kate Field wanted to write an article about the great novelist and asked Trollope for private information. Trollope was rather coy in what he told her and gave a mild warning which has been quoted earlier but deserves to be mentioned again: 'In truth she was one whose private life should be left in privacy, – as may be said of all who have achieved fame by literary merits.'[73]

Trollope had become friendly with Lewes in 1860 and, when he asked for information about getting his son a post office clerkship, Trollope obliged and wrote directly to the Postmaster General for a nomination, which the Duke of Argyll gave. Of course the young Lewes still had to sit the examination, which luckily he passed, to join the clerks in the Secretary's office at St Martin's as Trollope had done almost thirty years before. Trollope regarded Lewes as one of his closest friends: 'There never was a man so pleasant as he with whom to sit and talk vague literary gossip over a cup of coffee and a cigar.' The cigar often came from Trollope's annual supply from Cuba. He and Lewes also shared an interest in drama and the classic French actors, and Trollope encouraged him to publish some essays on this topic. However, he made no effort to understand Lewes's writings on philosophy or science, two subjects that held no appeal to Trollope. 'To me personally,' wrote Trollope in an obituary tribute, 'Lewes was a great philosopher only because I was told so.'[74]

George Eliot was deeply moved by Trollope's friendship with her 'husband', and both she and Lewes were deeply touched by Trollope's acceptance of their situation: he frequently referred to them as 'Mr and Mrs Lewes' and, in writing to him, would refer to her as 'your wife'. In her letters to Trollope (and to Tom as well) George Eliot – or Mary Ann Evans, to use her proper name – signed herself 'M.E. Lewes'. In addition the two novelists greatly admired one another's work, although Trollope always insisted that his 'stuff' could never equal her carefully thought-out fiction. They exchanged new books as well as useful advice on characters, and no doubt on financial matters, for both were equally insistent that they be well paid for their work. 'No expression of satisfaction is so agreeable as that which is conveyed in the eloquence of cheques': these were the words not of the 'mercenary' Trollope but of the 'intellectual' George Eliot. (Trollope's words used when reflecting on some protracted negotiations with William Longman about the value of his name were, as already quoted: 'I liked it best at the bottom of a cheque.') She once told another novelist: 'I am not at all sure, that, but for Anthony Trollope, I should ever have planned my studies on so extensive a scale for *Middlemarch*, or that I should ... have persevered with it to the close.' After her warm praise for *Rachel Ray*, with its 'subtleties of art which can hardly be appreciated except by those who have striven after the same result with conscious failure', George Eliot went on to make a general comment on Trollope's books, which expresses what many of his readers still feel:[75]

> But there is something else I care yet more about, which has impressed me very happily in all those writings of yours that I know – it is that people are breathing good bracing air in reading them – it is that they, the books are filled with belief in goodness without the slightest tinge of maudlin. They are like pleasant public gardens, where people go for amusement, & whether they think of it or not, get health as well.

George Eliot watched with an amazement almost tinged with envy the speed with which her friend turned out novel after novel. Once, at a dinner party at her house, they discussed their different methods of writing. Trollope told her, 'I sit down every morning at 5:30 with my watch on my desk, and for three hours I regularly produce 250 words every quarter of an hour.' Another author who was present said that George Eliot 'positively quivered with horror' and then moaned, 'There are days and days together when I cannot write a line.' 'Yes,' boomed Trollope, 'with imaginative work like yours that is quite natural; but with my mechanical stuff it's a sheer matter of industry. It's not the head that does it – it's the cobbler's wax on the seat, and the sticking to my chair.' This is a typical Trollopean way of paying a compliment to a cherished friend and of making light of his own achievement and his inventive genius that made such 'mechanical' writing possible. The 'cobbler's wax on the chair' was one of his favourite expressions and many dinner tables heard it in differing versions, particularly the exact time at which he set to work.[76]

It was indeed the 'cobbler's wax' and the 'sticking to my chair' that allowed Trollope to write novels that are as amazing for their quality as for their quantity. It gave him the means to enjoy other seats as well, whether on horseback as he chased foxes across the fields of Essex, in the leather armchairs at his clubs as he gossiped and made contacts, or in the mahogany carvers of his own dining-room with his wife and family round him. It was to Lewes that he had written at the beginning of the 1860s, the decade that brought him fame and fulfilment:

> As to myself personally, I have daily to wonder at the continued run of domestic & worldly happiness which has been granted me; – to wonder at it as well as to be thankful for it. I do so, fearing that my day, also of misery must come ... But no pain or misery has as yet come to me since the day I was married; if any man should speak well of the married state, I should do so.

Yet, even with all his achievements and all his domestic happiness, there was always that longing to write of serious things and to influence public life. In his book on America he had said that English society was a staircase while American society was a platform. He had mounted quite high on that staircase, but he longed, more than ever, to reach the top so that he could influence the public life of his countrymen.[77]

Christmas at Noningsby, from *Orley Farm* (J.E. Millais). See p. 435

CHAPTER TWELVE

To Build Things New

'In almost every bosom,' wrote Trollope in 1865, 'there sits a parliament in which a conservative party is ever combating to maintain things old, while the liberal side ... is striving to build things new.' 'In this parliament, as in the other,' he continued, 'the liberal side is always conquering, but its adversary is never conquered.' This is not only a good description of his times but an apt summary of his attitude towards politics. Although Anthony Trollope supported the Liberal Party, there was always a strong conservative side to his nature. One of his close friends, a Tory clergyman, claimed: 'On some theoretical points his Liberalism was of the most advanced type ... The truth was this, that all his instincts and feelings were Conservative.' Indeed anyone reading nothing but the Barset novels could well imagine that he was a Tory, because these books celebrate that longing for old customs and old certainties that Trollope believed lay not only in his own 'bosom' but in the permanent character of his countrymen. This longing for the past is beautifully depicted by him in a newspaper article about clergymen who supported, as did the novelist himself, Bishop Colenso's right to challenge traditional interpretations of the Bible:[1]

> If one could stay, if one could only have a choice in the matter, if one could really believe that the old shore is best, who would leave it? Who would not wish to be secure if he knew where security lay? ... With hands outstretched towards the old places, with sorrowing hearts, – with hearts which still love the old teachings which the mind will no longer accept, – we, too, cut our ropes, and go out in our little boats, and search for a land that will be new to us, though how far new, – new in how many things, we do not know. Who would not stay behind if it were possible to him?

In his *Autobiography* Trollope described himself as 'an advanced conservative liberal', a description that is quoted in almost every book about him but rarely put into context. After the passage of the Reform

476

Bill of 1832 party names, like so much else, were buried in what Trollope called the 'avalanche' of reform. Many still preferred to call themselves by the old terms of Whig or Tory but others preferred more ideological names such as Conservative, Liberal or Radical. Yet even these did not satisfy some, whose involved labels caused confusion to their contemporaries and untold misery to later historians. This was particularly the case after the break-up of the Conservative party following Peel's controversial repeal of the Corn Laws in 1846. Many of his followers took the name 'Liberal Conservative'. Gladstone, the most talented of them, was still described as a Liberal-Conservative as late as 1870 in *Dod's Parliamentary Companion* – 'the cautious Dod', as Trollope describes that book – and this was two years after Gladstone became the Liberal Prime Minister. There were others: two who crossed Trollope's path were Isaac Butt, the Irish barrister, and W.H. Smith who emerged from his circulating library to enter politics in 1865. Lord Derby, the Tory Prime Minister, once defined this term as one in which 'the black was not to be very black, nor the white so very white'. The public never shared the politicians' fascination with complex party names and it had become a joke by the time the Queen of the Fairies in *Iolanthe* decided that her son, Tory from the waist up but an owner of radical legs, was nothing but 'a Liberal-Conservative'. Yet for Trollope to call himself an 'advanced conservative liberal' was not an amusing quip, but an attempt, shared by many Victorians, to hold on to what was good while advancing to what might be better.[2]

Throughout his life Trollope had taken a considerable interest in public affairs, and as he approached fifty in 1865 this interest became much stronger. The next few years would see him heavily involved in politics: he started two periodicals, stood for Parliament, went on a diplomatic mission to Washington and became deeply interested in colonial topics. His novels also became increasingly intertwined with political and social questions. Perhaps the best way to see the evolution of his views is to see where he stood on the main questions of his age. It will be remembered that his father was anti-Tory and that his mother was involved with a set of drawing-room radicals, some of whom did more than just talk. Her American trip changed her views, but Anthony remained loyal to his parents' liberal outlook. In his *Autobiography*, he would say that 'my political feelings and convictions have never undergone any change'. In one of his earliest surviving letters he had referred to his mother's 'party' – after she had returned from America – and made it clear that it was not his own. By the time he became a clerk the 'avalanche' of reform was beginning to lose its force. If, as seems likely, the narrator in the short story, 'The Panjandrum', represents the author in the 1830s (and many clues point to it) he was fairly radical. This young man, who dreams of writing trenchant political essays, says: 'I was ready to "go in" for anything that was undoubtedly liberal and radical.' 'I was regarded as a democrat,' he recalls, 'because I was loud against the Corn Laws; and was accused of infidelity when I spoke against the Irish Church Endowments.' Although the young man did not support universal manhood suffrage, he accepted one of the favourite points of the Chartists, annual elections to Parliament. What certainly sounds like a recollection of Trollope's own views is the narrator's comment that he had little use for the conservative Whig Prime Minister Lord Melbourne: 'Lord John was just then our pet minister.' Lord John Russell always remained a 'pet minister' to Trollope and in the last year of his life he wrote that Russell was probably the greatest statesman of his time, with the possible exception of Palmerston, something few historians would accept.[3]

From Trollope's book, *Lord Palmerston*, his political essays in periodicals and various other sources it is possible to give his opinion on most public questions when the radicalism of youth had slid away. He approved of the repeal of the Corn Laws but very much disliked the way Peel 'betrayed' his followers. To Trollope this was an example of dishonesty against which he inveighed in most of his books. He believed that Russell's government, which succeeded Peel's, had done the best possible job in coping with the Irish Famine. The 1848 revolutions evoked a strongly hostile response, if his sympathy with the royalists of *La Vendée* is any indication of its author's views about the 'tribe of Republicans'. He supported the Crimean War and resented attacks by Dickens on the officials who conducted it. He wanted Italian unification but disliked the revolutionary violence of Garibaldi. He increasingly distrusted Napoleon III's France but late in his life came to wonder about the dominance of Bismarck's Germany. His liberal views are perhaps best seen in his support for the North in the American Civil War. Yet he was never an extreme Liberal as is evident from his dislike of Cobden and Bright, particularly for their attacks upon a strong foreign policy.

He favoured moderate reforms to increase the size of the electorate but vehemently opposed the secret ballot, thinking that honest Englishmen should never be afraid to show how they voted. Although he supported improvements in the social and legal status of women, he did not think they should be allowed to vote. He advocated economic reforms for Ireland and the disestablishment of the Church of Ireland but he opposed Home Rule, believing that Ireland benefited from the Union. Although he was a committed supporter of his own Church of England and opposed to its disestablishment, he was in favour of most moves towards religious freedom. Although deeply interested in the spread of English civilisation and the welfare of the colonies, he scorned Victorian Imperialism. He had a high opinion of civil servants but did not think they were competent to administer the economy. It may be said that 'but' played as large a role in Trollope's politics as in his style. Actually, his general political views were remarkably similar to many other Liberals, including Gladstone himself.

Essential to all Trollope's political views was his conviction that something had to be done to alleviate the 'terrible inequalities' of Victorian society. This is something that may come as a shock to casual readers of his novels, which can seem exclusively concerned with the life of the comfortable. Yet Trollope, who had looked into the miserable dwellings of the poor in Ireland and in the West of England, and even investigated the tenements of Glasgow, did feel passionately that something must be done to lessen not only the immediate suffering but some of the distinctions between the well-off and the poor. He accepted that social distinctions were of 'divine origin' and would always exist, and he knew full well that if those of his day were abolished new ones would arise. Therefore he rejected 'any sudden disruption of society in quest of some Utopian blessedness'. What he wanted was to promote a 'tendency towards equality', which was the ultimate reason why he was a Liberal.[4]

For Trollope there was one way to do this: education. This subject is central to almost all his non-fiction and can be found in many of his novels as well. In his first book, *The Macdermots of Ballycloran*, he depicts one hard landlord, Jonas Brown, who was 'actuated by the most superlative contempt for the poor, from whom he drew his whole income'. Brown realises that 'the only means of keeping the peasantry in their present utterly helpless and dependent state, was to deny them education' [XXV]. It is not at all fanciful to regard Trollope as a man determined to bring them that education. He was, in the truest sense, an educator. Even when old and ill he took time to play his part on his village school's management committee. He was deeply committed to 'the gradual improvement of the minds and intellects of the people themselves, a work on which all men and women concerned in literature should be more intent than any other'.* Writing in the

---

*This is but one example of a change in Trollope's writing noticeable in the 1860s and 70s. He often refers to 'men and women', whereas before he tended to refer simply to 'men'.

Liverpool Mercury in 1875, he spoke quite passionately: 'With a full stomach,' he argued, it is easy to 'revel in the memories of Blenheim, Trafalgar, and Waterloo; but unless a country can feed its people, and educate them, and so treat them that life shall be a source of enjoyment and not of pain, such memories are of but small moment.' In this concern for education he often recalled his visits to New York schools, which he had continued to praise as 'the most perfect system of general tuition that the world has ever produced'.[5] His later visits to Australia and New Zealand only increased his conviction that the mother country could learn much about education from these new lands. In these attitudes and convictions he very much reflected the Liberal view as it developed through the century.

*

When in the 1860s and 70s politics assumed an increasing role in Trollope's writing, he used his novels, especially his Palliser series, 'as safety-valves by which to deliver my soul', places where he could unseat ministries, produce electoral victories, resolve Cabinet crises and hand out seals of office. As we have seen, before he had finished his Barset novels, he began a second series on whose name there has never been agreement: Parliamentary, Political or Palliser. In many ways the last is the most accurate, for the figures of Plantagenet Palliser and his wife, Lady Glencora, unite the novels, even though they do not dominate every book. When in the twilight of his long life, Sir Winston Churchill – born in the same year that *The Prime Minister* was written – came to read that book, he was asked by his doctor what was the great difference between the politics of Trollope's time and that of the mid-twentieth century. 'They mixed up society and politics' replied the real Prime Minister. This mixture between politics and Society – the Society of 'the Upper Ten Thousand of this our English world' as the first sentence in the series defines it – is the theme that underlies all the Palliser books. Like the Barchester Chronicles, there are six novels: *Can You Forgive Her?* (1864), *Phineas Finn* (1867), *The Eustace Diamonds* (1871), *Phineas Redux* (1873), *The Prime Minister* (1875) and *The Duke's Children* (1879). (These dates are those of their first appearance in any form.) The six books occupy about 3,500 pages, which well justifies one critic's comment that 'no English novelist has worked on so colossal a scale'.[6] Indeed the best comparisons are to be made with series across the Channel, with Balzac and Proust.

Plantagenet Palliser, nephew and heir to the powerful Duke of

Omnium, made his first appearance in *The Small House at Allington*, when he was enamoured of the Archdeacon's daughter. In *Can You Forgive Her?* he reappears to marry a wealthy heiress, Lady Glencora MacCluskie, and the tensions in their marriage are one of the major themes in the novels. Lady Glencora, unlike her husband, has a nature so passionate that it leads her to consider abandoning both respectability and her husband by running off with a fascinating but worthless lover. In the second novel the Pallisers are less important, and the dominant figure is a young Irishman, Phineas Finn, who by good luck obtains a seat in the Commons and by good looks fascinates several aristocratic ladies. Many contemporaries were not drawn to an Irish hero, and Trollope himself later thought he had made a mistake in having an Irishman as the central character. He claims he only did so because he happened to be on a visit to Ireland when thinking of the plot. Yet this accident gives the novel much force and also makes it a superb introduction to the world of Victorian Society and politics for modern readers, who can follow Finn into a world that is even stranger to us than it was to him. At the end of this book Finn returns to his native island and marries a good, though boring, colleen. Just as Trollope had to kill off John Bold to proceed from *The Warden* to *Barchester Towers*, so he had to despatch young Mrs Finn before the fourth novel, the appallingly named *Phineas Redux*, can see the 'restored' Irishman return to London political life. Eventually, after he is proved innocent of murdering a member of the Cabinet, he marries the fascinating and wealthy Madame Max Goesler, one of those convenient heiresses whom Trollope normally had to hand.

The last two books concentrate on Palliser himself, first as Prime Minister and then as head of a great family, whose children make marriages outside the ranks of the 'Upper Ten Thousand' with whom the series began. Indeed the marriage of Palliser's heir, Lord Silverbridge, to a rich American is strikingly similar to that between Lord Randolph Churchill, a younger son of the sixth Duke of Marlborough, and the beautiful American, Jenny Jerome. They were married after a stormy engagement during which each fought a determined battle against a reluctant father. The suddenness of their engagement, let alone the underlying fears on the Duke's part about his proposed daughter-in-law's ability to fill her new position, were tackled by Lord Randolph when he broke the news. His letters, along with their story, show how accurately Trollope knew not only his subjects but their ways of thinking and speaking. This is Lord Randolph, not Lord Silverbridge, writing to his father:

I know, of course, that you will be very much surprised, and find it difficult to understand how an attachment so strong could have arisen in so short a space of time ... I now write to tell you of it all, and to ask you whether you will be able to increase my allowance ... to put me in the position to ask Mrs. Jerome to let me become her daughter's future husband ... Mr. Jerome is a gentleman who is obliged to live in New York to look after his business. I do not know what it is. He is reputed to be very well off, and his daughters, I believe, have very good fortunes, but I do not know anything for certain.

In the end both fathers had to give way, although negotiations were interrupted while Lord Randolph was returned as MP for the family borough of Woodstock, much as Lord Silverbridge was for Silverbridge. The final hurdle was Mr Jerome's objections over his daughter's settlement. These were cleared when the couple threatened to marry without money and live on what he earned. This was too much, and the New Yorker capitulated. They were married on 15 April 1874, and it was their first son who would find Trollope's political novels so diverting in his last years.[7]

This brief summary has neglected the third book, *The Eustace Diamonds*, mainly because Trollope did not see it as part of the Palliser series, any more than he saw *The Small House at Allington* as part of Barset. Although the main story concerns the rather wicked Lady Eustace (an attempt to imitate Thackeray's Becky Sharp) and the theft of her jewels, many characters from the Palliser novels are in the background and the series is incomplete without it. To give just one example, the man who murders the Cabinet Minister in *Phineas Redux* first appears as Lady Eustace's second husband.[8]

Some Victorian politicians believed that the actual political events in the Palliser novels suffered because Trollope was never in the House of Commons, and some critics found the political episodes 'absurd' because 'they depended on the story instead of the story depending on them'. Ironically this is the very reason why many modern readers like them and prefer them to Disraeli's political novels. Yet a biography has to answer the more important question: were the political episodes realistic to Trollope's Victorian readers? In the entire series no one episode seems more 'absurd' than that in *Phineas Redux* in which the Tories seek to disestablish the Church of England. One is at first inclined to attribute this to nothing more than Trollope's detestation of Disraeli and his view that Tories never hold a belief but to give it up in due course. They had opposed reform and then passed the 1867 Reform Bill. Could they not turn round on the question of the Establishment? Trollope was not alone in thinking this a real possibility and was drawing on current views: another novelist, Charles Lever, Consul at Trieste and Fanny Trollope's erstwhile whist partner, thought Disraeli would deal with 'parsons' exactly as he had dealt with the 1867 Reform Bill. A better informed man, Bishop Magee of Peterborough, who owed his appointment to Disraeli, had no doubts that 'the Church will never weigh with an English *politician* like Disraeli, against the interests of his party'. Finally Lord Salisbury, who would succeed Disraeli as Tory leader, wrote in 1867 (admittedly when disillusioned with his party): 'they are lukewarm about the Church, and would no doubt give it up, as they have given up other things, for the sake of office.' Trollope's account, no matter how startling it first appears, is far from absurd.[9]

In recent years many critics have preferred the Palliser books to the Barchester series, although the reading public has refused to follow them. One reason for this preference is that the Palliser books are more technically interesting because of the way in which the author handles multiple plots and his use of narrative art. Trollope's enthusiasm for Palliser himself was almost limitless: 'such a one as justifies ... the seeming anomaly of an hereditary peerage.' In the last pages of his *Autobiography* Trollope defended his portrayal of Palliser, who by that time had succeeded to his uncle's title: 'I think that Plantagenet Palliser, Duke of Omnium, is a perfect gentleman. If he be not, then I am unable to describe a gentleman.' Trollope never expected his works to survive, but if they should, he thought his fame would rest on Palliser, Lady Glencora and the Rev. Josiah Crawley. Yet many of those who have maintained the novelist's greatness in this century do not 'like' Plantagenet Palliser. Some devoted Trollopeans would agree with Sir Winston Churchill's comment to his doctor after reading *The Duke's Children* that his Grace of Omnium is 'a poop'. In this they mistake Trollope's aim: he was not concerned that readers should like this 'perfect gentleman' but that they should respect him for his disinterested devotion to the public good and his code of honour. It is only in the last book that the Duke, bereft of his Duchess and in conflict with his children, becomes a likeable figure in his own right.

*

There has been much debate about the origin of characters in the series and whether or not they are based on real people. When Disraeli's novels appeared it was easy for anyone 'in the know' to identify the model for a character. The difference between the two writers is that Disraeli, with his admittedly greater knowledge of politics and politicians, had more opportunity to draw upon real people and was often anxious to settle scores. The danger of using what appeared to be obvious models for characters had been well described by Monckton Milnes in a review of one of Disraeli's novels in 1847:

> The moment a character is known to represent Lord —— or Mr. ——, it loses all power as a work of art ... the fidelity of the likeness is the only object of attention, not the moral fitness, the entireness, the beauty or the grandeur of the character. The great poet or novelist should mould his men and women out of the large masses of humanity, out of the strivers and losers, and actors and sufferers; and surely he degrades his function when he condescends to draw miniatures of individuals.

Trollope, who detested Disraeli both as a novelist and as a politician, would have agreed. He told one friend how he had fashioned Arabella Trefoil in *The American Senator*: 'I swear I have known the woman, – not one special woman, not one Mary Jones or Sarah Smith, – but all the traits.'[10] One remembers Fanny Trollope's wonderful comment that, while she took aspects of people she knew to form her characters, no one could recognise the pig in the sausage.

There were times in his fiction when Trollope did draw portraits of living people. In *The Warden* he had done this not only by his satire on Dickens and Carlyle but by using the Archdeacon's sons to represent three prominent bishops; in *The Three Clerks* he satirised the men behind the Civil Service reforms. In his short stories in particular he made use not only of characters he had observed but of incidents in his own life. In the Palliser novels it has often been maintained that Mildmay is Lord John Russell, Gresham is Gladstone and Daubeny is Disraeli, and that there are aspects of the three real Prime Ministers in them. Daubeny possesses 'that enduring courage which was his peculiar characteristic' [*Phineas Redux* XXXIX] and it is true that Gladstone singled out Disraeli's 'great parliamentary courage' in his speech of tribute to his dead rival.[11] Yet Trollope wrote his description of Daubeny ten years before Gladstone's tribute.*

Escott is responsible for much of the game of 'spot the originals', and he even made the ludicrous suggestion that Lord Chiltern, the

---

*When Trollope drew on a real figure as the source for a character, he often used some word or phrase identified with the real person. It may well be that this was an unconscious act. A good example occurs in *Orley Farm* [XVII]. He has previously depicted Lord Boanarges, a busy and loquacious legal reformer devoted to statistics and to attending conferences. Victorians would have immediately thought of Lord Brougham. Trollope then goes on to quote the Latin tag *Vox et praeterea nihil* and to add, 'To practical Englishmen most of these international congresses seem to arrive at nothing else.' Brougham's full title was Baron Brougham and Vaux and it was a frequent, though unfair, joke to say he was *Vox et praeterea nihil*.

hot-headed fox-hunter, was based on Lord Hartington. Other than that both were titled and bearded, it is difficult to see many similarities between the fictional character who settles down in rural bliss with his wife and his hounds and the real Marquess who divided his time between an active political career and his long-standing mistress, the Duchess of Manchester. The idea that a minor Irish politician, Sir John Pope Hennessy, is the original of Phineas Finn – an idea endorsed by his grandson with commendable ancestral loyalty – has no validity, because descriptions of the real politician show a man totally different from the fictional one. Are we to assume that after two decades in Ireland, Trollope could not invent a handsome and ambitious Irish MP?[12]

Trollope himself insisted that his politicians were 'more or less portraits, not of living men, but of living political characters'. Often the minor characters, or at least those occupying minor roles in the political sphere, seem closer to real people. Thus Mr Emilius, the Jewish convert and successful preacher, shows considerable similiarity to Ridley Hershell and Joseph Wolff, two Central European converts who achieved prominence in Evangelical circles. Both died a few years before Trollope began the Palliser series. A great part of this game of finding real fathers for fictional sons seems to be based on the idea that Trollope was incapable of creating a character without a model, as if he were a sculptor. He was quite annoyed when the *Daily Telegraph* accused him of transferring real politicians into his fiction. 'Is it gentlemanlike,' asked the paper, 'for any novelist to put into a novel of the day malignant little touches professing to lift the veil of private life and to depict a public man as he appears in private society?' In particular, it claimed that John Bright had been caricatured as Turnbull in *Phineas Finn*. Trollope wrote a letter to the editor:

> Certainly it is neither gentlemanlike or right to do these things ... I cannot imagine how any likeness justifying such a charge against me can be found. The character I have drawn has no resemblance to [Bright] ... It was my object to depict a turbulent demagogue; – but it was also my object so to draw the character that no likeness should be found in our own political circles ... I intended neither portrait or caricature, and most assuredly I have produced neither.

There were, indeed, many parallels, mainly in political attitudes, between Bright and Turnbull. Bright was always turbulent and could be demagogic, but he was not a demagogue. It is easy to assume the real radical from Rochdale, and the fictional one from Stalybridge are the same. There is, however, one crucial difference: 'It could hardly be said,' Trollope wrote, 'that he [Turnbull] was a great orator.' Bright, however, was a superb orator, if he was little else, with a staggering ability to marshal simple words in a magnificent manner, and Trollope's readers would have known this.[13]

What Trollope was portraying in Turnbull was not John Bright but an enduring type in politics: the utopian windbag. This, after all, was a type Trollope had long disliked, whether as Civil Service reformers or American abolitionists. If one looks at the description of Turnbull, it is easy to find candidates to fill the bill in every generation, although, like Trollope's old game of selecting the greatest people in history, each list will necessarily be different. Trollope defined him thus:

> Having nothing to construct, he could always deal with generalities. Being free from responsibility, he was not called upon either to study details or to master even great facts. It was his business to inveigh against existing evils, and perhaps there is no easier business when once the privilege of an audience has been attained. It was his work to cut down forest-trees, and he had nothing to do with subsequent cultivation of the land [*Phineas Finn* XVIII].

*

Another important question to ask about Trollope's Palliser series, and one which also applies to his other 'political' novels, is the source and quality of his information. How accurate was it? As has been mentioned earlier, Trollope had long been a devoted reader of *The Times*, which gave an enormous amount of space to Parliamentary speeches. Yet nothing could take the place of actually hearing a debate: when, therefore, Trollope was in the midst of the Palliser novels, he obtained a pass from the Speaker to attend the House. He had already had the experience of being a witness before various committees, and even if he had not enjoyed the experience he had been given a good vantage point to observe MPs and peers. He had also frequently met politicians socially, at dinner parties and at country houses. Yet newspaper reports, the to-and-fro of a Commons' debate, committee sittings and social gatherings could never provide the type of first-hand information Trollope required to write his novels. His single greatest source of information and gossip was the Cosmopolitan Club and the men he met through it. Once he became an active clubman he made a number of friends from whom he gained insights into political life in the relaxed atmosphere of a club which encouraged confidential talk. He was acquainted with many members of the Cabinet, mainly in Liberal governments.

Much of his information seems to have come from those people who stood on the edge of the political shore, observing every tide and picking up the flotsam and jetsam of political life left behind. According to Escott, Trollope received valuable advice from Alfred Montgomery, a shadowy figure who turns up in many Victorian diaries. He was reputed to be the illegitimate son of the Marquess Wellesley and therefore a nephew of the first Duke of Wellington. In his turn he became the grandfather of Lord Alfred Douglas, thus linking the scandals of the 'Upper Ten Thousand' from one end of the century to the other. A 'place' had been found for Montgomery at the Board of Inland Revenue (where John Eames wound up) and he was one of the best-known characters in Society, a repository of anecdotes and secrets. Montgomery had been a protégé of Lord Brougham, the former Lord Chancellor, of whom it was said, quite unfairly, that if he had known a little law, he would have known a little of everything. There are many similarities to Brougham in Trollope's portrait of 'the all wise' Lord Boanarges who teaches Miss Dunstable 'to blow soap bubbles on scientific principles' [*Framley Parsonage* VIII]. After Brougham's death in 1868. Trollope helped that peer's brother to bring some order into the diffuse and inaccurate Memoirs he left behind him. This also provided useful information about the background to his own times.

Richard Monckton Milnes, who had introduced Trollope into various clubs, was one of the central figures in Society: 'the Perpetual President of the Heaven and Hell Amalgamation Society', as he specialised in bringing diverse people together. Milnes sat in the Commons until he was created Lord Houghton, and while never an effective politician he was a repository of political gossip, some of which Trollope must have imbibed on visits to his country house in Yorkshire. The Hon. Frederick Leveson Gower, younger brother of Earl Granville, Gladstone's confidant and Foreign Secretary, was a close friend of Trollope, and they shared a similar distrust both of Tories and of the developing Imperialist fervour. Trollope's passion for whist brought him into contact with politicians like Henry James, who held legal offices in several of Gladstone's governments, and W.E. Forster, who played a prominent role in putting through the Education Act of 1870. A print was made showing Trollope playing whist with James, Forster and Abraham Hayward. Hayward played a crucial role in the unguarded border between journalism and politics. A man of letters known for his translations and his book on *The Art of Dining*, he also acted as Lady Palmerston's principal aide in selecting guests for her famous Saturday night receptions, something Lady Glencora imitates.

After Palmerston's death in 1865 Hayward became a prime source of information to Gladstone about opinion in the literary world. Among the information he passed on was an assurance that Trollope remained true to Liberalism. Hayward's hatred for Disraeli was legendary: while some gossips said that this was because both were Jewish, others remembered that it was he who had exposed Disraeli's elaborate panegyric on the Duke of Wellington as a plagiarism from a French *éloge*. Disraeli returned the hatred by branding Hayward a 'louse on Literature'. It seems certain that Trollope's long-standing distaste for Disraeli received powerful ammunition from Hayward. It was from men like Montgomery, Leveson Gower, Milnes and Hayward that Trollope gathered the fine details needed to create the world of the Pallisers.[14]

*

Nevertheless Trollope could still make curious mistakes. To take just one example: for centuries peers could vote either in person or by proxy in the House of Lords. Careful readers of *The Small House at Allington* may recall that John Eames's patron, Earl de Guest, that bucolic peer who preferred breeding cattle to listening to politicians, made certain that his 'proxy was always in the hand of the leader of his party' [XII]. The Earl could do this in the early 1860s, but by the next decade it was no longer possible. Yet Trollope carries on using proxy votes not only in the Palliser novels but even in *The American Senator*, where the bumptious Senator Gotobed denounces the procedure as allowing 'do nothing legislators' to influence national affairs [XXIX]. This was published almost a decade after the Lords had ended the use of proxies. The reason for Trollope's mistake may be that he was leaving for his third trip to America when the Lords 'discontinued' the system. Of course Trollope's biases could lead him into curious statements. Although a firm supporter of constitutional monarchy, he never had that fervent devotion to the Queen as a person that became so prevalent in the last years of the century. To say, as he does in *Phineas Finn* [IX], that in the midst of a Cabinet crisis the Queen 'telegraphed to Germany for advice' is, frankly, absurd.[15]

The key to Trollope's political message, if such it may be called, is found in the first Palliser novel when he describes Palliser as 'one of those politicians in possessing whom England has perhaps more reason to be proud than of any other of her resources, and who, as a body, give to her that exquisite combination of conservatism and progress which is her present strength and best security for the future'

[*Can You Forgive Her?* XXIV]. His importance does not come from great intellect, for 'he was not a brilliant man', from great charm, for 'he rather prided himself on being dull', from eloquence, as he believed 'that oratory, as oratory, was a sin against that honesty in politics by which he strove to guide himself'. Palliser's greatness comes from his 'honesty' and his 'industry', the two greatest Trollopean virtues. Palliser was a natural product of those childhood sermons warning the Trollope boys against 'idling' and falsehood, from the concern over public honesty expressed in *The New Zealander* and repeated, however badly, in *The Struggles of Brown, Jones, and Robinson*.[16] Palliser is Trollope's answer to the question he had posed in *The New Zealander*: how can a great Empire hold back inevitable decline? The answer was: by hard work and integrity. It says much about Trollope's politics that his political hero was neither a middle-class gentleman nor a working-class craftsman but a duke.

The 'exquisite combination of conservatism and progress' required each political party to fulfil its role. Trollope possessed that persistent trait in British politics whereby a member of one party kindly interests himself in the current state of his opponents and bemoans their failure to live up to their own traditions, suitably defined by himself. Few things annoyed him more consistently than the failure of the Conservative party to conserve. Most of the great political changes of his lifetime – Catholic Emancipation, the repeal of the Corn Laws, and the Second Reform Bill of 1867 – had been carried by Tories who had spent years opposing these very measures. This infuriated Trollope who wanted the Tories to oppose change: to be the brake on the Liberal coach of progress. 'Indeed, unless the coach goes on running, no journey will be made. But let us have the drag on both the hind wheels. And we must remember that coaches running down hill without drags are apt to come to serious misfortune' [*Phineas Finn* XXXV]. The Tories were ever to be the brake and therefore usually in opposition, while the Liberals would drive the coach. When Tories were in government they should govern on the basis of past Liberal victories: as he wrote in his short story 'Why Frau Frohmann Raised Her Prices', 'Let the Toryism of the Tory be ever so strong, it is his destiny to carry out the purposes of his opponents.' Trollope had a genuine fondness for old-fashioned Tory squires and his novels teem with them. He avoids the conventional caricature of John Stuart Mill, that they are stupid:

He who said that all Conservatives are stupid did not know them. Stupid Conservatives there may be, – and there certainly are very stupid Radicals. The well-educated, widely-read Conservative, who is well assured that all good things are gradually being brought to an end by the voice of the people, is generally the pleasantest man to be met [*The Eustace Diamonds* IV].

Yet to Trollope such men, 'genuinely English' though they may be, are doomed as the age of progress moves ahead [*Lady Anna* XLVIII]. What he hated was the Tory politician who embraced liberal measures to stay in office. As with every other human being, principles always went hand in hand with prejudice, and when denouncing the two brief Tory governments of the 1850s the facts that Trollope was a Liberal, hated Disraeli and had not been given the position of Mail Coach Superintendent by the Derby-Disraeli government are not absent from his memory:

> No reform, no innovation ... stinks so foully in the nostrils of an English Tory politician as to be absolutely irreconcilable to him. When taken in the refreshing waters of office any such pill can be swallowed ... Let the people want what they will, Jew senators,* cheap corn, vote by ballot, no property qualification, or anything else, the Tories will carry it for them, if the Whigs cannot [*The Bertrams* XVI].

This passage comes from the late 1850s and shows the cynical and sarcastic tone that Trollope, still only moderately successful, took when viewing public life. This is also evident in *The Warden* when that saintly figure Septimus Harding visits the House of Commons to consult his lawyer, the Tory Attorney General. The Warden receives, as do the readers through him, the impression that he is looking upon disreputable people. This was the general tone of Trollope's treatment of politicians throughout the 1850s. Then there is a change, seen in an eloquent passage in the first of the Palliser novels, in which Trollope depicts a new MP walking through the Members' Door between a 'pair of gilded lamps'. This passage has become a favourite, not just among MPs, but wherever Trollope's political ambitions are discussed:

> Ah, my male friend and reader ... hast thou never stood there and longed, – hast thou never confessed, when standing there, that Fate has been unkind to thee in denying thee the one thing that thou hast wanted? I have done so; and as my slow steps have led me up that more than royal staircase, to those passages and halls ... I have told myself, in anger and in grief, that to die and not to have won that right of way ... is to die and not to have done that which it most becomes an Englishman to have achieved [*Can You Forgive Her?* XLV].

*After a long battle N.M. Rothschild was allowed to take his seat as an MP in July 1858 when the Commons altered the Oath to remove the words 'on the faith of a Christian'. This happened while Trollope was writing *The Bertrams*. Although the change occurred under a Tory government, it was as much due to the efforts of Lord John Russell as to Disraeli or any other Conservative.

It is not often noted that four years before he had another man standing at the same 'privileged door between the lamps' watching with envy as men saunter through the entrance denied to him [*Castle Richmond* XLI]. This testifies to the same desire, to achieve 'the highest and most legitimate pride of an Englishman to have the letters M.P. written after his name' [*Can You Forgive Her?* XLV]. The change in tone between the cynical Trollope of the 1850s and the politically ambitious Trollope of the 1860s is not just the middle-aged man's abandonment of the idealism of youth. It also flows from the fact that by 1860 his literary earnings were enough for him to envisage a career in politics in an age when MPs were not paid.

*

One great road-block lay athwart his ambitions: the Post Office. By law its officials could not hold a seat in the Commons, or even vote for those who did. This restriction had been brought in in 1782, to prevent office holders from influencing constituencies with small electorates. Thus when Colonel Maberly was appointed to a public office he had to give up his seat as Member for Chatham. As a Surveyor, Trollope was reminded of his own disenfranchisement every time he had to notify postmasters of the dangers of losing their positions and incurring a £100 fine should they attempt to vote. As the years passed he grew increasingly resentful of this injustice, which was made all the worse as it did not apply throughout the Civil Service but only in departments with large staffs such as the Post Office. In the small and aristocratic Foreign Office officials could vote. Trollope recalled that he had 'once urged upon a Cabinet Minister that this was a stigma on the service, – and, though he was a Whig, he laughed at me. He could not conceive that men would care about voting. But men do care; – and those who do not, ought to be made to care.' He was no more ready to forget someone's laughing at him than he was to accept a slight upon his profession.* In his lecture to the GPO clerks in 1861 he spoke of his personal campaign: 'I consider such a barrier to citzenship as that to be a stigma on the profession.' He told them – and this must especially have annoyed Hill – that he had been to see Lord Elgin, the PMG, about this and had even gone to Lord John Russell to ask him 'to

---

*Ironically postal officials received the right to vote shortly after Trollope left the Post Office. The bill was passed after a long campaign by the Liberal MP, Charles James Monk. This is well described in his privately printed *Reminiscences*. One wonders whether this had any effect upon Trollope's naming 'the most advanced Liberal' MP 'Joshua Monk' in *Phineas Finn*.

liberate us from our bondage'. To Trollope this exclusion denied his profession not only their rights as gentlemen but their duties as men:[17]

> I do not much mind what a man's politics are, so that he has got politics. So that he will concern himself with the public welfare of his country and of his race, and give his mind up to the matter ... But I don't love a man with whom I can neither agree nor disagree; who will say that politics are nothing to him. Such a one seems to me to shirk the first of man's duties.

When Trollope took up his duties as Surveyor of the Eastern District in 1859, it was almost exactly a quarter of a century since he had first sat at his clerk's desk. Once he became an English Surveyor his postal career seems to have become less interesting, while his other career as a novelist expanded. Part of the reason was that he was no longer sent on foreign missions. His duties were mainly routine, though he had the freedom to set his hours, provided the District ran smoothly. Since the Post Office expected six hours' work a day from clerks, it was relatively easy for Trollope, getting up so early and working at home, to perform his duties while turning out novels, stories and articles and, during the winter months, while hunting. One of his tasks was to arrange schedules in his district that happened to have the largest number, sixty-six, of post-towns in England. There was also an increasing amount of paper-work: as the Post Office grew, its bureaucracy, as is normal, expanded at an even greater rate. London was also continually bringing in new rules both enlightened, such as those helping employees to purchase life insurance, and silly, such as those requiring all letter-carriers to report details of their Christmas 'box'.

Much of the Surveyor's time was taken up in dealing with complaints by important people or, far worse, by people who considered themselves important. In their letters they normally moaned about their village's suffering because a neighbouring village received better service, something Trollope recalled in *The Vicar of Bullhampton* [XXII]. One moaner was the Rev. Charles Merivale who was unhappy with the service to his rich living at Lawford in Essex. Merivale was not only the elder brother of Trollope's friend but the Roman historian whose book he had reviewed in his Irish days. For his jovial reply he borrowed a metaphor found in his novels: 'You remember how the friendly bear drove away the flies from his friend's face – & the injury he did. Whenever we try, in the post office, to do a good and beneficent turn ... we always turn out to be bears.' Before answering Merivale's complaint, he examined the figures, which one of his clerks would have carefully prepared. These showed that Lawford had less letters than its neighbours, sending only twenty-two letters each week. Therefore he could not rearrange the post so that Merivale could get his letters somewhat earlier, let alone provide a second delivery. In this case Trollope attempted to add humour to an official letter:[18]

> I have just got back from Rome, where I learned that the Pope has but one delivery daily – his letters reaching the Vatican at 11 – all too early and all too often as he thinks. So it is whispered among the Cardinals. The archbishop at Rheims does not get his letters till near ten. The bishop of St. Davids has but one delivery a day. (!!!) The bishop of Jerusalem has none at all. And the letters of the canons of Seville are read before they get them.

*

To what degree Trollope still enjoyed his postal work cannot be said but what was obvious after he had returned from America in 1862 was that it provided only a small part of his income. Since his earnings from writing were averaging £4,500 a year, his salary did not even come to a fifth of that: in 1869, for example, his total income soared to £6,994 18s 1d and the previous year his income from dividends alone came to £605 10s whereas his Post Office income was £735 3s 10d. His was now an odd position. To a degree he and Rose lived virtually as landed gentry in Essex. When in London, Trollope mingled with some of the most famous names in literature and politics, at his clubs or at George Eliot's Sunday gatherings. Yet when he returned to Waltham he was once again a Post Office employee with little hope of advancement, a man whose official life was increasingly nothing but routine work. Nor did all this help his attitude towards Sir Rowland Hill as he knew that his superior's salary was less than half his literary income. Where Hill was mistaken was in his view that Trollope was 'neglecting' his postal duties. His literary tasks were normally finished by breakfast and his hunting never stopped his official work. Yet Hill must not have been the only man in the Post Office to wonder. A man as exuberant as Trollope made enemies, and even some friendly colleagues must have wondered at his prosperity and his half-year in America. A fellow Surveyor sent him a newspaper cutting which claimed that Trollope had been offered £2,000 a year to become nominal editor of a magazine, *Temple Bar*. In fact Trollope had rejected an offer of £1,000 for the use of his name with the understanding that Edmund Yates, ironically his jealous foe at the Post Office, would do the actual work.[19]

Trollope and Hill had a long-standing history of arguments, but after 1862 Hill was convinced that Trollope was 'dishonest' and plotting against him. Once, some years before, they had clashed when Trollope criticised the wording of a document. Hill replied slowly – 'enunciating the letter "r" in each word with Midland distinctness' according to another official – 'You must be aware, Mr. Trollope, that a phrase is not always intended to bear a literal construction. For instance … I end my letter with the words, "I am, Sir, your obedient servant," whereas you know I am nothing of the sort.' According to Yates, admittedly never to be trusted where Trollope is concerned, the 'calm and freezing' Hill gave his views on another occasion only to be answered by the 'spluttering' Trollope: 'I differ from you entirely! What was it you said?' In 1864 Hill retired with his £2,000 salary guaranteed for life and a £20,000 grant from Parliament. Trollope sent him a warm letter of congratulation and praised his great achievement, the penny post. Hill recorded: 'Among the numerous letters of congratulation are several from P.O. officials. Some even come from men whom I have had too much reason to believe unfriendly. There is an excellent letter, among others, from Trollope.' John Tilley succeeded Hill as Secretary to the Post Office and soon Hill was recording in his Journals that Tilley, who had always hedged his bets between the reigning PMG and Hill, was proving himself 'disloyal' to Hill's legacy.[20]

Perhaps Trollope thought that now that his brother-in-law was in charge all would go well. Yet he soon had disagreements with Tilley, whose promotion opened the post of Assistant Secretary. Trollope applied, only to see it go to Frank Scudamore, his junior in seniority and yet another of those writers who seemed to flourish in the GPO. Trollope was furious as he, and Tilley, had long argued for the importance of seniority, provided the senior candidate was competent. 'I for one will never press for the promotion of men by simple seniority,' he had told the postal clerks three years before, 'but I do maintain that if a man be fit to perform the duties of a class to which he has risen by length of service, he is entitled to the promotion by all equity.'[21] Since it would be difficult to argue that Trollope was not fit to be a Surveyor, the rejection of him for a higher post in favour of his junior cast a slur upon his work. Nor could there be any idea that Trollope was ineligible because Tilley and he were brothers-in-law, since Hill's brother, Frederic, had been an Assistant Secretary and a nephew also held office at St Martin's.

Trollope provided one good reason for his failure, when discussing the difference between Daubeny and Gresham in the Palliser novels:

There is nothing so prejudicial to a cause as a temper. This man is declared to be unfit for any position of note, because he always shows temper. Anything can be done with another man, – he can be made to fit almost any hole, – because he has his temper under command ... the calm and tranquil man is preferred for public services. We want practical results rather than truth [*Phineas Redux* IX].

A fierce temper ran in the Trollope family: it was said that it lead one relative, an Admiral, to ruin his career and eventually to commit suicide.[22] Thomas Anthony's temper had not only blighted his work and his life, but had almost driven his wife and family from him. Anthony's temper never reached those heights. No doubt it was fortunate that once again he escaped a staff position in London, for it would have led him into many feuds, and would have given him less time to write and hunt. While a place at St Martin's would have helped his biographers and critics by reducing his novel-writing, it would have deprived many more people of the pleasure of those thirty novels yet to be written.

One of Trollope's friends later said that he 'could be bitter when he thought himself in any way ill-used'. At first this hardly seems the case, for in his comments on Scudamore in the *Autobiography* he wrote: 'He no doubt was possessed of gifts which I did not possess. He understood the manipulation of money and the use of figures and was a great accountant.' Actually this is one of the nastiest barbs in his book for, in May 1873, Scudamore was at the centre of what one Cabinet minister called the 'Post Office scandals'. In promoting his pet project, acquiring the private telegraphic services for the Post Office empire, he had used his skill as a 'great accountant' to move almost one million pounds from postal savings banks and Post Office receipts to make up the purchase price. Thus what one historian rightly calls 'the first measure of nationalization' was carried out by somewhat shady means.[23] Scudamore was not in any sense involved in private fraud but in manipulating official funds without informing the PMG, Trollope's old friend Monsell. Trollope, who surely learned many of the details from Tilley, inserted another private joke into a novel he was writing at the time of the scandal, *The Way We Live Now*. Here a character bemoans the effect of telegraphs and 'would certainly have gladly hanged Mr. Scudamore' [L]. With this Trollope assuaged his bitterness at being passed over for higher office in the Post Office.

In the same year that Scudamore was appointed, 1864, Trollope acted in a manner remarkably similar to his father's; his action was based on a combination of Trollopean anger and a fierce Anglo-Saxon devotion to what is 'right'. In April the Surveyors met in Bedford to discuss their grievances over pay and the old problem of allowances; they also appointed a chairman, William Godby, to write to Tilley asking him to recommend an increase in the scale of pay. Godby's letter reflected the long-standing tension between the Surveyors, whose work was increasing, and the London staff, whose salaries were increasing. Tilley replied saying in effect that there was no point in discussing the matter. Trollope was always convinced that the Surveyors' pay, the highest level of which was £700 plus a complicated system of allowances, was not high enough, and even after he had left the Post Office he resented any popular demand to lower it.[24] Tilley's reply infuriated him and, like his father with Lord Northwick, he now felt that a principle was at stake. Trollope was the only one to protest and, naturally, he did so loudly. For him it was not the money – he could have £100 for a few days' work on a short story – but his oft-cited principle that the workman was worth his hire. When his anger was aroused he could not restrain himself and was like one of his own characters: 'Neither in argument nor in contest would he ever allow himself to be wrong; never at least to anyone but to himself' [*Doctor Thorne* III]. He fired off a long letter to Tilley on 8 July.

In his letter Trollope wrote 'to remonstrate': he would have done so sooner but admitted in effect that his efforts to rally the other Surveyors to carry on the fight had been a failure. He repeated the demands and arguments. He reminded Tilley that he had never before 'either separately or jointly with others, requested a reconsideration of my Salary; – and I am aggrieved that I should now have received such an answer.' He rather tactlessly told Tilley that when he had been Hill's assistant, he could never claim to have done 'any special services' such as various Surveyors had claimed. He recalled his own work in the Post Office and ended:

> I think that as an old, and I believe I may say meritorious, officer of the Crown, I have a right to ask the Postmaster General to reconsider ... and to readjust the Salaries of the Surveyors in accordance with the amounts actually paid to other officers. And I also think that I am justified in asking his Lordship to recommend the newly appointed Secretary [Tilley] to be more considerate of the feelings of those officers among whom he passed his official life, till he received his promotion.

Tilley forwarded – unofficially – a copy of 'this most intemperate letter' to the Postmaster General. If Tilley had married into the Trollope family in time to have known his father-in-law, he would have understood the extraordinary fury that 'Tony' evinced in such matters. For his part the PMG, Lord Stanley of Alderley, was annoyed and had

Tilley reply, referring to Trollope's 'numerous inaccuracies'. Not at all daunted, Trollope fired off yet another strong letter, this time directly to Lord Stanley, buttressing the Surveyors' demand by a fictional parallel: 'It was exactly the way in which Oliver was treated when he came forward on behalf of the Charity boys to ask for more; – and I own that I thought Mr Tilley was very like Bumble in the style of the answer he gave us.'[25]

One wonders what Tilley thought when he saw his brother-in-law using Dickens as a weapon! News of these quarrels enlivened Hill's retirement: 'I must own that I am not very sorry to hear that the conspirators against me are now quarrelling as to division of the spoil. There has, I learn, been a fearful passage of arms between Trollope and Tilley – Trollope, of course, being the aggressor.' Tilley did not want to quarrel with his old friend and tried to mollify him by tempting offers: another postal mission abroad or the Surveyorship of London. Even though Trollope rejected both offers, the breach was soon healed and they were once again on 'My dear John' and 'My dear Tony' terms. Trollope did agree to act as temporary Surveyor for North and West London in 1866. Working from the Post Office on Vere Street, he supervised the rearrangement of postal deliveries in London. It was his last major official service. One man who served under him remembered his working 'at a stand-up desk, with his handkerchief stuffed into his mouth, and his hair on end, as though he could barely contain himself'. When another official worried whether he could take on new responsibilities, Trollope turned on him: 'Why don't you pay an old woman sixpence a week to fret for you?' Comments made in the heat of demanding work to fretting subordinates must not hide the fact that Trollope continued to show a concern for those working under him: he asked St Martin's to spend £40 to move the lavatories away from the staff kitchen. The days of the dreadful drainage that his father-in-law had complained about were slowly being ended.[26] As so often, Trollope enjoyed a small joke by using one of the post offices he was reorganising, that on the Edgware Road, in *The Last Chronicle of Barset* which he was writing at the time [LIX].

His two battles in 1864 made him increasingly anxious to leave the Post Office, where there was now virtually no chance of promotion. In addition the work was increasing when he needed time for other activities, some of which gave greater pleasure and some, far greater income. This was even more the case as he was now going into London two to three days a week during 'the season', rushing off trains before they had stopped and throwing himself into the nearest cab en route to one of his clubs, a publisher or a dinner. His exuberance for life was as great as ever, but there was simply not enough time and he told one correspondent that 'I feel myself beginning to neglect the office'. He 'had determined some years previously,' he later wrote, 'after due consideration with my wife, to abandon the Post Office when I had put by an income equal to the pension to which I should be entitled if I remained in the department till I was sixty.' By 1867 he had reached his goal and had put by enough to guarantee an annual income of about £500 which he would have had from the Post Office. (As we have seen, his annual dividends alone exceeded that amount.) On 3 October, a day that was miserable to him, he resigned from the Post Office. Appropriately two of the last acts of his career were stopping attempts to deprive one town of an early delivery and to cut letter-carriers' wages. Always sensitive to any suggestion that he had been forced to resign because of 'neglecting' his duties for writing, he included in his *Autobiography* a letter from Tilley praising him as 'among the most conspicuous servants of the Post Office'. There is no reason not to accept Trollope's assertion, 'I did not allow my literary enterprises to interfere with my official work. A man who takes public money without earning it is to me so odious that I can find no pardon for him in my heart.'[27]

On Thursday 31 October, the day of the actual retirement, a dinner was held at the Albion Tavern in Aldersgate Street where some 100 friends gathered to honour Trollope. The Moray Minstrels, a group of singers, of which Trollope himself was a member, entertained the guests with songs, some of which must have been the old, slightly vulgar, glees beloved of the Goose and Glee Club of his days as a clerk. He had never lost his delight in glee-singing and amid all his other activities had found time to join the Minstrels when they sang, normally in rooms above a fruit shop in Jermyn Street. Many of the other members were well-known artists such as Millais, Holman Hunt and Leighton as well as a fashionable tailor. As so often on these occasions, the dinner had its little touch of hypocrisy: the successful rival, Scudamore, was in the chair with Yates as vice-chairman. Among the guests was Henry Trollope, perhaps amused at the spectacle of men in their fifties recalling the boisterous songs of their youth. This was a favourite Victorian male pastime: only a few weeks before the members of the Tory Cabinet had regaled one another with political glees about 'dishing the Whigs' at their traditional whitebait dinner at Greenwich.[28] By the time Trollope walked from the Albion Tavern, so close to where as a boy of nineteen he had taken his desk in Sir Francis Freeling's room, his life as a civil servant was over. For thirty-three years he had played a large role in the most important government service of his time. More than any other aspect of government, the Post Office had symbolised the age of progress. Trollope had made a considerable contribution to this progress in an improved service in Ireland, England, Wales and Scotland, in better conditions of employment for letter-carriers, in a more efficient international post and in those pillar boxes which were fast becoming a British 'institution'. 'Possibly there is no Government department,' declared *The Times* in February 1868, 'which so clearly shows the increasing vitality of this Empire as that of the General Post Office.' For three decades Trollope had been part of that vitality: his remaining years would be concentrated on the politics of 'this Empire'.

*

In his *Autobiography* Trollope said that the years 1867 and 1868 were 'the busiest in my life'. In that book, he had difficulty arranging his numerous activities during the late 1860s and anyone who attempts to tell the story of his life runs into the same problem. In addition to resigning from the Post Office, negotiating a treaty in Washington and standing for Parliament, he completed the second Palliser novel, *Phineas Finn*, as well as two of his shorter continental novels, *Linda Tressel* and *The Golden Lion of Granpère*, founded one magazine and edited another. While in Washington he worked on a large novel, *He Knew He Was Right*, and then began *The Vicar of Bullhampton* which he completed in the month of his electoral battle when he began *Sir Harry Hotspur of Humblethwaite*.

In addition to a frenetic involvement in politics, whether on the hustings or in the novel, Trollope wrote a host of articles, mainly on topical subjects. He recognised that periodicals were a key element in Victorian culture: 'How little do they know, who talk of the padding of our periodicals, how much of the best thought the nation produces is given to ... ephemeral literature.' They fulfilled 'the universal craving of the day for light literature, and especially for literature that shall be short'. It is virtually impossible to pick up a stray issue of the leading Victorian journals – weeklies, monthlies and the imposing quarterlies – without being staggered not only at the wide coverage but at the serious depth of the articles. Newman paid 'ephemeral literature' a back-handed compliment in his lectures on university education when he said:[29]

> Every quarter of a year, every month, every day, there must be a supply, for the gratification of the public, of new and luminous theories on the subjects of religion, foreign politics, home politics, civil economy, finance,

trade, agriculture, emigration, and the colonies. Slavery, the gold-fields,
German philosophy, the French Empire ... Ireland, must all be practised
on, day after day, by what are called original thinkers.

Most of Trollope's novels of the early 1860s show less interest in
politics than either his earlier or his later ones. In this, as in so much
else, he reflected the general mood. As he wrote in a short story 'The
Widow's Mite' after his return from America, 'political feeling in
England had become extinct' during these final years of Palmerston's
rule. 'Pam' carried his party to victory in July 1865 only to die a few
months later. 'He held a great bundle of sticks together,' wrote Lord
Clarendon to Lord Granville. 'They are now unloosed, and there is
nobody to tie them up again.' The *Pall Mall Gazette* predicted that with
Palmerston gone 'the politicians of the salon' would be ousted by 'the
politicians of a creed': this epigram could serve as a summary of much
of the political tension in the Palliser books.[30] One consequence of all
those 'sticks' being unloosed was a sudden increase in public interest in
politics. The degree to which Trollope shared this renewed interest is
seen in the increasing amount of magazine writing he undertook over
the next two years.

His involvement with three new periodicals illustrates how public
issues had come to dominate his mind. In 1865 George Smith
established an evening newspaper, the *Pall Mall Gazette*, which took
its name from the fictional paper in Thackeray's *Pendennis*, 'written by
gentlemen for gentlemen'. Smith drew on many of the original
contributors to the *Cornhill* to write for him. Trollope appeared in the
first issue with an article on the American war and was a frequent
contributor over the next few years. In that first year, 1865, his records
show that he was paid £234 17s 6d, writing on a wide variety of
subjects. As well as political articles, he wrote a series of short essays
in the *Pall Mall* during 1865 and 1866 which were then made into books:
Hunting Sketches, Travelling Sketches and *Clergymen of the Church of
England*. (His final series, *London Tradesmen*, was not published until
1880, and was not gathered into a book until 1927.) The essays about
different types of English travellers, ranging from the 'Art Tourist' to
the 'Alpine Club' men, are the most entertaining. By 1868, however,
his contributions had fallen greatly and his *Pall Mall* income was only
£7 17s 6d.[31]

The essays on clergymen unleashed the greatest criticism including
what Trollope called 'the most ill-natured review that was ever written
upon any work of mine'. Henry Alford, Dean of Canterbury, launched a
violent tirade in the *Contemporary Review*, of which he was the first

editor, proclaiming that Trollope was 'almost entirely ignorant' of clergymen and possessed a 'hair-dresser's estimate of mankind'. As a Greek scholar of some standing, he attacked any allusion by the novelist to what Trollope later called 'that pride-producing language'. No doubt he was annoyed that many of Trollope's barbs were aimed at places connected with the Dean, such as Trinity College, Cambridge. He would not have relished Trollope's comment in that article devoted to 'Deans' that 'A Dean has been described as a church dignitary who ... has little to do and a good deal to get.' Within a few years, however, Alford himself was writing to the Archbishop of Canterbury that deans were 'practically useless ... almost without employment, and absolutely without power'. The Dean also attacked Trollope's grammar. This reflected another hobby-horse of the under-worked Dean. His recent *Plea for the Queen's English* assaulted 'Americanisms', something which provoked the delightfully named George Washington Moon to write *The Dean's English* in order to point out the numerous mistakes in the very reverend gentleman's grammar. Trollope was probably having a little joke at Alford's expense when, in his *Autobiography*, he alluded to the 'metropolitan moon' in his reference to the attack upon him by a 'great dean of that period'.[32]

However, a far more enlightening discussion of one of the main points of Trollope's essays took place when they were published as a book in 1866. The *Guardian*, perhaps the best of all Church newspapers, disliked the book and took him to task for his comments on the low income of some curates: it was 'unworthy of Mr. Trollope' to 'endorse a popular error'. The best excuse for the essays, it concluded, was that they were caricatures and 'with this understanding, we may afford to laugh over them'. Trollope, however, did not laugh: his concern over the plight of underpaid curates was neither new nor erroneous. He had alluded to it in the Barset novels as well as in *The Claverings*, which was appearing in the *Cornhill* at the time of the controversy. Here he introduced another poor curate, the Rev. Samuel Saul, who does almost all the work of the parish for a rich but idle rector. Several curates wrote to the newspaper citing their own cases and others in support of Trollope's strictures. 'A Curate' wrote about one incumbent with a living worth £1,600 a year who gave his curate, who actually did the work, only £120 and a house. How, he asked, was such a priest 'who has to hold the position of a gentleman' to do so on such a meagre stipend? Trollope told Smith that he was 'very keen' about this topic and returned to the attack in the *Pall Mall Gazette*. His sense of justice was outraged when men who did the work were denied their just rewards. Once again we see the degree to which serious questions often underlay the plots he created in his novels.[33]

*

In 1864 Trollope had been the leader of a group of prominent literary figures and intellectuals in establishing the *Fortnightly Review*, which to some extent was based on the *Revue des Deux Mondes*. Although open to all opinions, it was in effect a Liberal journal. Each of the founders put up £1,250. Trollope became Chairman of the Board and persuaded G.H. Lewes to become editor. Trollope also took the lead in insisting that articles be signed, which was not done in the august quarterlies and many other periodicals. 'The critic ... should dare to make himself known.' He accepted that it might lead to fewer critics 'but we should probably have more of real criticism'. Advertisements claimed that the new magazine's aim was 'to remove all restrictions of party and of editorial "consistency" '.[34]

In the next two years the *Fortnightly* provided Trollope with space for articles on favourite topics like America, the Irish Church and the Civil Service, as well as a platform to attack Ruskin when reviewing *Sesame and Lilies*. Ironically Trollope had been alone among the founders in opposing the idea of having a serialised novel in the *Fortnightly* as he felt it would distract from its serious purpose. Yet his colleagues knew that a novel, particularly one by their chairman, would gain readers. Consequently the first instalment of *The Belton Estate* appeared in May 1865 after the opening segments of Walter Bagehot's *English Constitution*. Trollope's own summary of his novel in the *Autobiography* cannot be bettered: 'It is readable, and contains scenes which are true to life; but it has no peculiar merits, and will add nothing to my reputation as a novelist.' *The Eustace Diamonds* and *Lady Anna* also appeared in the same journal, as did five novels by George Meredith.

As one well-informed late Victorian writer said, 'the contributors included some of the ablest men in England ... It took at once a foremost place among English periodicals. But the manangement of its finances was in the hands of authors exclusively. So the thousands of pounds subscribed by Anthony Trollope and his friends melted away.' In November 1866 the periodical became a monthly while retaining its title and in due course it was taken over by its publisher, Chapman and Hall. The *Fortnightly*, like the Cosmopolitan Club, played an important role in introducing Trollope to politicians, particularly those in the rising school of radical and 'intellectual' men like John Morley, who succeeded Lewes as editor after a gruelling interview with Trollope, and Frederick Harrison. These were proponents of the new politics of 'creed' about whom the *Pall Mall Gazette* had spoken. Trollope, in general, did not share their views but was prepared to listen as well as to reply.[35]

Trollope had one of his most celebrated literary duels in the *Fortnightly* when the historian E.A. Freeman attacked fox-hunting in the issue of 1 October 1869. Freeman's plan was, as he told a friend, 'to deal with the fox-hunters as they deal with the foxes, give them no peace and rout them out of every corner'. He knew Trollope would reply: 'I shall wait for what he says, as he will doubtless be better worth answering than the smaller fry.' Nothing annoyed Trollope more than Freeman's citing Cicero's amazement that a cultivated man could pursue brutish amusement. After Trollope's reply Freeman wrote a rejoinder which Trollope wanted to answer, but Morley persuaded him to let the argument rest. Perhaps Trollope was still angry with Freeman in November when his Travelling Journal records that between 10 and 27 November he followed the hounds on 10, 13, 15, 17, 19, 23, 26 and 27 November. Trollope carried on intermittent hostilities, either with barbs in novels such as *The American Senator* or with footnotes in his *Life of Cicero* which accuse Freeman of misconstruing Cicero's Latin. Trollope was also vastly amused when he saw Frederick Harrison at a fox-hunt in Essex. Harrison claimed that he had come only to escort a young lady, but abandoned his positivist philosophy long enough to gallop after the hounds. Trollope always had great sport with Harrison's 'desertion' whenever he saw him at the Cosmopolitan.[36]

*

The third journal in which Trollope was involved fulfilled one of his oldest desires: to edit his own publication. James Virtue, the art printer, suggested that Trollope edit a new monthly magazine, similar to the *Cornhill*. While Trollope warned Virtue of the risks, he knew that the salary of £1,000 would more than replace his postal income. Indeed it was the prospect of this editorship which convinced him in 1867 that he could risk resigning without a pension. He also saw the new magazine as another place to express his political views. If he managed to secure a seat in the Commons, the possession of a political journal as well as a celebrated name would immediately lift him above the ranks of ordinary backbenchers. He pushed Virtue towards the idea that the magazine should have a strong political flavour, expressing the editor's own brand of Liberalism despite the effect this would have on some potential readers. The first difficulty for editor and publisher was just what it had been for Thackeray and Smith when planning the *Cornhill*: a name. Virtue suggested 'Trollope's Monthly', but the editor objected that would mean nothing if he left the magazine.[37] Trying to stress its political commitment, he proposed 'The Monthly Westminster' or 'The Monthly Liberal'. By September 1867, with only a month to go before publication, they had still not agreed a name: this absurdity was made public by advertisements for 'ANTHONY TROLLOPE'S New Magazine ... devoted to Fiction, and to Subjects Artistic, Literary, Social, and Political, edited by ANTHONY TROLLOPE'.

At last Virtue and Trollope followed the examples of the *Cornhill*, *Temple Bar, St. James's* and other periodicals which took London topography for their name and chose *Saint Pauls*.* The first number appeared in October 1867, the month of its editor's resignation from the Post Office. It opened with a rather apologetic statement from the editor expressing his 'liberal-conservative' creed: 'To declare one's self to be a Reformer at the moment in which household suffrage has been just carried ... would indeed be to say nothing ... And who is there also that does not feel himself to be a conservative while the perils hang over us of our untried household suffrage.' Nevertheless 'we ... in this new enterprise think that the good old Liberal cause still needs support'. The main ingredient of *Saint Pauls* would be politics, 'of all studies to which men and women can attach themselves ... the first and foremost'. Yet the editor accepted that such a periodical could only succeed by having novels 'to regale its friends from month to month' for 'the preaching of the day is done by the novelist, and the lessons which he teaches are those to which men and women will listen.' 'It is not probable,' Trollope went on,

> that the present Editor should feel himself called upon to quarrel with the public taste in this respect. It has been his humble, but not unpleasant task, as a man of letters, to sing, in prose, long love-ditties for his readers, and he has sung them till the singing of them has become second nature to him.

The *Spectator*'s judgment on the first issue could apply to the entire history of *Saint Pauls*. It found 'a certain obvious want of ardour ... [but it is] a readable magazine, a cultivated magazine'. The first issue began the second Palliser novel, *Phineas Finn*, which continued until May 1869. This, incidentally, provides a telling example of how periodicals would comment on individual episodes in another journal. When the novel had been running for over a year the *Illustrated*

---

*There is a great disagreement among scholars about the Pauline apostrophe. I have followed the magazine's title page and rejected *Saint Paul's* for *Saint Pauls*.

London News remarked: 'At present Phineas is very low down; but we expect to see him up again next month.'[38] Trollope contributed two articles on hunting for a series on sports which in 1868 he edited as *British Sports and Pastimes.* He also wrote a series of short stories for the magazine, which were later published as *An Editor's Tales.* These are among the most interesting of his 'tales'. All deal with people who fail to establish themselves as writers, and several show his developing fascination with disturbed minds. From his own early struggles, and even more from his father's crushing failure, Trollope had a deep sympathy for unsuccessful writers. *An Editor's Tales* is one of the best places to meet examples of that legion of the frustrated who yearned to join the famous and fortunate ranks of established Victorian authors.

Sympathy is not an editorial virtue and Trollope admits that he occasionally published articles 'not for the sake of the readers, but for that of the writer'. As he wrote when discussing Thackeray's editorship of the *Cornhill,* 'Of a magazine editor it is required that he should be patient, scrupulous, judicious, but above all things hard-hearted.' Trollope was not hard-hearted, but at least this led him to encourage young writers. He took particular pride in bringing Austin Dobson's poetry to public notice, thus launching the career of another writing civil servant, who is still remembered as the author of charming essays on the byways of eighteenth-century life. In his turn, Dobson dedicated his first book of poems to Trollope.[39]

Saint Pauls was financially no more a success than the *Fortnightly:* Virtue had estimated that he needed 25,000 subscribers and the most he got was 10,000. The problem was that the periodical never equalled the *Cornhill*'s ability to attract famous writers. Novelists, other than Trollope himself, who appeared in it included Mrs Oliphant, Tom's wife Frances Eleanor Trollope, and Madame Blaze de Bury, whose name well indicates her style. As the *Illustrated London News* commented, there were some political papers of 'considerable merit', particularly on foreign affairs, such as Adam Gielgud's on Poland and Russia and Henry Brackenbury's on 'The Military Armaments of the Five Great Powers'. Immediately following Brackenbury's piece was an article called 'A Sheffield Workman's Week Excursion to Paris and Back for Seventy Shillings'. In this piece Jehoida Rhodes describes how after a 'conference ... between self and wife' he visited Napoleon III's Paris to see the 1861 Exhibition, something Trollope and his wife did as well. Rhodes was able to get a thirty-four-shilling special workman's ticket for the return journey from Sheffield to Paris. He enjoyed his 'coffee, bread and butter, a "bifteck", and a small glass of brandy, for elevenpence'. He added, as many Englishmen have over the years, 'I don't say the steak was not horse; I don't know.' For his part, Rhodes, unlike one of his companions, did not hurry off on Sunday to an English dissenting chapel near the Madeleine to sing hymns but returned to his lodgings to recuperate from the journey. Since Rhodes's trip cost him a total of £3 10s and Trollope paid him £7 10s, his expenses were less than half what he got for his travel article, something few modern writers could ever hope to achieve. The Rhodes article not only puts into some perspective the six guineas a page Trollope charged for his stories, but shows his attempt to encourage self-educated working men. It may also reflect his acceptance that the readers of *Saint Pauls* were 'not among the highest class of men & women'. To later generations it is to Trollope's credit that he accepted this piece, but at the time it would have done nothing to raise the magazine's standing in literary circles.[40]

Trollope was only able to carry on his editorial work because he paid about one-quarter of his salary to an assistant editor. In addition Rose was sometimes enlisted to read articles and decide whether they should be accepted, yet another indication of her essential role in his literary career. He was also helped by his disciplined habits. The Rev. Edward Bradley – better known as 'Cuthbert Bede', author of that most delightful of Oxford novels, *The Adventures of Mr Verdant Green* – met Trollope at a country house in the first months of his editorship. Bradley had seen him playing whist till past eleven one night and then found him the next morning editing an article for *Saint Pauls*. Dressed in hunting attire, he announced that he had been working since five: 'Since then I have earned twenty pounds by my pen.' When he opened the morning post and found the proofs for the February 1868 issue he asked Bradley's help in cutting one article. 'I was much struck with the rapidity he showed in getting through this business, and also in keeping up a running conversation with those present, at the same time that he was reading proofs and writing letters.' After a 'hearty breakfast' the editor was off to a day of hunting. That same night Bradley found him at another country house for dinner 'fresh as ever, full of conversation' and ready for more whist. Perhaps Trollope should have paid a little more attention to the proofs, for one article in that February issue spoke of Lord Brougham's villa at Caen – it was in fact at Cannes, a not unimportant geographical distinction because it was Brougham's example which had led to the English devotion to the South of France. Bradley enjoyed this meeting so much that when he noticed a photograph of Trollope in a shop window in Birmingham he bought it. This was partly because of his amusement at seeing the shop label it 'Martin Tupper', the popular poet whose *Proverbial Philosophy*, a collection of didactic ditties, was dismissed by Trollope and other real writers.[41]

Trollope explained to Virtue in December 1868 that he did not want to start a new serialised novel immediately after *Phineas Finn* would come to an end in May 1869. He would still be able to provide enough fiction to carry them over till the beginning of 1870 when they would need a new novel. He was prepared to offer one (*Ralph the Heir*) which would run for eighteen months and cost Virtue £2,520 which was, he added, £280 cheaper than he had charged another magazine for a similar novel. Instead he could ask George Eliot for a novel, but she would charge 'double': Virtue chose Trollope's offer but was clearly having doubts about the magazine's future. In May, disappointed at the failure of *Saint Pauls* to reach his goal of 25,000 readers and to find a niche in the highly competitive and overcrowded magazine world, Virtue transferred control to Alexander Strahan of *Good Words*. The following January Virtue wrote unofficially to let Trollope know that Messrs. Strahan intended 'to try the Editorship for themselves by way of economy'. Trollope readily acceded and seems to have shed no tears at handing over editorial control in June 1870. The magazine struggled on until 1874 when it ceased altogether. Trollope never really had his heart in his editorial work – his absence of almost four months within the first year of publication would be evidence of this – and he concluded: 'I think, upon the whole, that publishers themselves have been the best editors of magazines.'[42] Undoubtedly the fact that the editor was preoccupied with other aspects of his life did not help matters.

*

When Trollope retired from the Post Office in October 1867 he had the time and the money to do what he wished. Tilley, on holiday in Scotland, wrote to another civil servant on holiday, John Merivale: 'I poor creature have to go back in three weeks. After all what is your 10 weeks to Anthony's 52.'[43] The choice of October 1867 was not just because of the launching of *Saint Pauls* but because Trollope knew an election was imminent. Since he was already fifty-two and elections could be as much as seven years apart, he had to make his debut as a politician at the next contest if he was to have any chance of strutting through the members' door at Westminster.

That makes his acceptance of an offer by Tilley in January 1868 to go on another postal mission one of the most puzzling episodes of his career. He certainly did not need the five guineas *per diem* that the

Post Office would pay him. Perhaps he saw this American mission as a 'compliment' or public statement that he had not been forced to resign because of devoting too much time to his novels. Nor can one neglect his hereditary appetite for travel and his great affection for America. If he was looking for reasons he soon found another by arranging with the Foreign Office to empower him to try to reach an agreement with the American government to recognise English copyright and thus to end the pirating of books. Since his battle with Harpers over their edition of *North America*, Trollope was increasingly outspoken and informed on this topic. In 1866 the National Association for the Promotion of Social Science asked him for a paper on international copyright for their annual meeting. He agreed but was unable to attend as the conference conflicted with a visit to Italy to see Tom; his paper was read in his absence.[44] If Trollope had been successful in helping to resolve this vexed question, he would have removed a major irritant between the two countries, earned the gratitude of his fellow authors and greatly increased his own income. Trollope therefore went to America representing two government departments.

The end of the war had led to a great increase in transatlantic trade and, with it, complaints about the time it took for letters to cross. Some interests in the City were calling for the postal subsidy to be removed from Cunard and given to one of the German companies, who claimed to cross the ocean in shorter time. Tilley must have been reading the letters of complaint in *The Times* for he had written to the Duke of Montrose, PMG in the Tory Government:

> If the Americans signify their willingness to make a new convention, as they no doubt will, they require no little smoothing down and management. It will be necessary to send a strong man and I think of proposing to you to ask Mr Trollope ... as we shall get the benefit not only of his ability but of his personal popularity with the Americans. I know no one else who would do this work so well.

The Duke soon informed his American opposite number that he was appointing 'Mr Anthony Trollope, who was for many years, and until his recent retirement from the public service, one of the principal officers of this department'. Trollope was given 'full power to settle by negotiation the terms of a Convention, better calculated than the present to afford satisfaction to the people of the two countries'.[45]

Since Trollope would be acting in a diplomatic capacity he first had to be presented at Court and, as a man, he would attend a Levee – Drawing Rooms were for ladies. Anyone holding high office under the Crown had to be presented and, at least in theory, no Englishman could be presented at a foreign court before making a bow to his own Sovereign. It is rather ironic that Trollope had poked fun at this ceremony in the first issue of *Saint Pauls Magazine*. Like many others, he had become increasingly annoyed by Queen Victoria's withdrawal from ceremonial duties after Prince Albert's death. With Gladstone and many others he believed this weakened the Monarchy. Most people, Trollope wrote, having seen the Queen, became 'by the very fact of that seeing, a friend to the Sovereign', even though he accepted that 'doubtless it may be wearisome to sit for many hours ... receiving strings of maidens with lace trains, files of gentlemen somewhat awkward with their swords'.[46] Yet within a few months he asked to be one of the awkward gentlemen. It was appropriate for a man who loved Ireland that he was presented on St Patrick's Day, a day when all the knights appeared 'in their collars'. The Prince of Wales himself had just been made a Knight of St Patrick by his mother and stood in for her at the Levee as presentations to him counted as presentations to the Sovereign.

For Trollope a formal presentation was a superb opportunity to observe the world of the Pallisers at work, although he may not have seen a great deal, as the curious eighteenth-century convention that spectacles were not worn at Court still prevailed. Since there were no ladies present Trollope could wear trousers and did not have to force himself into knee breeches with their notorious propensity for splitting just as one bowed. The Levee began about two, when the Prince of Wales arrived at St James's Palace accompanied by several other Princes. Trollope already had been introduced to the young Prince, when he took the chair at the Royal Literary Fund dinner at which Trollope had replied to the toast to 'Literature' in May 1864, but this did not count as a formal 'presentation'. Among the 800 gentlemen in the Palace were men from every aspect of 'the Upper Ten Thousand' portrayed in the Palliser novels: twenty-six peers, bishops, politicians, generals, Privy Councillors, royal dukes and numerous diplomats attended by their suites. An Irish bishop presented a new archbishop, and Disraeli, who had become Prime Minister three weeks earlier, presented a new Dean of Exeter. Gentlemen were marshalled in alphabetical order. 'Mr Anthony Trollope', having been announced by the Lord Chamberlain, took his place in the file processing before the royal presence and was presented by his friend, Earl Stanhope, President of the Royal Literary Fund. The novelist made his bow to the Prince and moved on. All this was done with tremendous speed: a young friend of Trollope's, George Leveson Gower, who was later a court official, calculated that men were presented at the rate of sixteen to the minute. If Trollope glanced towards the 'General Circle' made up of the most important men there outside the royal party, he might have seen Stafford Northcote, whom he had portrayed in *The Three Clerks*, talking with Disraeli, whom he had had in mind when creating the moneylender Sidonia in *Barchester Towers*. He might have noticed that Disraeli was looking rather tired as he had been up to two that morning to write to the Queen about Gladstone's announced intention to disestablish the Church of Ireland, a topic that would dominate the election Trollope hoped to contest.[47]

*

Trollope arrived in New York just as Charles Dickens was finishing his triumphant second tour. When Trollope heard that he was leaving on the *Russia*, he hurried out to the ship. Dickens's manager, who was busy fending off American tax agents anxious to grab a share of Dickens's earnings, recalled the older novelist's 'delight and amazement' at Trollope's unheralded, enthusiastic and typical gesture: he had come to shake his hand and to wish him God speed. Trollope later recalled: 'I found him with one of his feet bound up, and he told me, with that pleasant smile that was so common to him, that he lectured himself off his legs.' Indeed Dickens never really recovered from this tour. Trollope's recollection of this meeting, when England's two greatest living male novelists met in New York Harbour, appeared in his memorial tribute to Dickens.[48]

It is unlikely that Dickens told Trollope much about the chaos in Washington, but by the time he arrived there on 24 April – his fifty-third birthday – President Andrew Johnson had been impeached by the lower house and was awaiting trial by the Senate. The American Postmaster General, Alexander Randall, an ardent defender of Johnson, told Trollope that it was virtually impossible to negotiate treaties as the entire government could be forced to resign if the President were convicted. Furthermore Randall refused Trollope's plan for a treaty to last for at least three years as he said American law would not permit him to make one for more than two years. Trollope also demanded to know why the existing treaty meant that a letter to America was charged at the rate of 24 cents per ounce while one to England was only 15 cents. Two days after his arrival he sent a memorandum to the GPO which they claimed to have lost when a curious MP asked to see it. This eventually provoked a furious debate in the House of Commons. Trollope was forced to wait weeks in Washington, a city he grew to dislike even more than on his last visit, as all about him was the corruption that had accompanied the North's victory. Delay never made him reasonable, and he came to dislike Randall even though they did share one habit: the American politician, who had begun life as a village postmaster, was 'a consistent and orderly worker, he rose very early and performed the day's drudgery before office hours. That method provided leisure for conferences, visits, and joviality of which he was exceptionally fond.' The delay allowed Trollope time to visit friends in Boston, including Kate Field, to see Richmond, the former Confederate capital, and to gather information for articles on American politics. In these he protested against the 'tyranny' of the Reconstruction governments in the Southern states and noted the hypocrisy of enforcing black voting in the South but not in the North. He felt the military coercion of the South would lead to 'infinite suffering for poor Sambo'.[49]

His misery increased when Rose decided not to join him. He complained to Kate Field that if he had told Rose not to come 'woman-like she would have been here by the first boat'. Quite characteristically he added: 'However, she is quite right, as Washington wd. kill her.' He composed an epitaph for himself, making a pun on the name of his old host, Senator Sumner, who had flung all his venom into the campaign against the President:

> Washington has slain this man,
> By politics and heat together.
> Sumner alone he might have stood,
> But not the Summer weather.

Next to the third line Trollope wrote two words, 'very doubtful'. It was not just the sultry weather but the mosquitos which kept him awake all night. When he tried to burn them with his candle he only succeeded in setting the mosquito netting alight. He was amused at a Boston newspaper which Kate Field sent him describing this 'strange looking person, Anthony Trollope':

> His head is shaped like a minnie ball, with the point rounded down a little ... It is small, almost sharp at the top, and bald, increasing in size until it reaches his neck. His complexion and general bearing are much like Dickens's. His body is large and well preserved. He dresses like a gentleman and not like a fop, but he squeezes his small, well-shaped hand into a very small pair of colored kids. He 'wears a cane' as all Englishmen do.

'If I saw the writer,' Trollope told Kate, 'I should be apt to go off and let him know that I never wear gloves. What fools people are.'[50] One suspects that after an initial explosion they could well have become friends! Perhaps Trollope was thinking of this description when some months later he wrote: 'there is a baldness that is handsome and noble, and a baldness that is peculiarly mean and despicable' [*Ralph the Heir* XXII].

He was also unhappy at the cost of this prolonged stay of almost four months and was anxious both for repayment of his expenses and instructions from London. Tilley implored the Treasury to 'take pity on Trollope' and asked the Chancellor of the Exchequer, none other than the Stafford Northcote of *The Three Clerks*, to reach a decision about the terms finally proposed by the Americans: 'Trollope went out to please me at some inconvenience to himself, and he is most anxious to get back.' By the beginning of July, Tilley 'the wiseacre who controls the British Postal department' (according to a Washington newspaper that Trollope sent him) could cable: 'Make Treaty on the best terms you can.' The final terms were not what Tilley and Trollope had wanted. Mail would be delivered from Southampton to New York in 288 hours or twelve days, except for the winter months, when 312 hours or thirteen days were allowed. (More than a century of 'progress' means that sea mail now takes between three and four times the time agreed by Trollope, while air mail is frequently not much quicker than the ships of the 1860s!) Postage on a single international letter, weighing fifteen grammes on the metric scale, would not exceed twelve cents in the United States or sixpence in Britain. Within a week of his return to England Trollope was at work on *Saint Pauls* and wrote to Bulwer Lytton asking him to write a Christmas story for the magazine. He added, 'I have just returned from Washington where I have spent a most odious summer.'[51]

Although Trollope hardly had the temperament of a diplomat, he had done his best and was warmly praised by Montrose and Tilley. His attempt to reach an agreement on international copyright led to nothing. Englishmen who had attempted this before were usually told that the only way to secure an agreement was to employ a lobbyist to bribe Senators. This was the case before the War and was even more so in the years following 1865. The American State Department, only just recovering from the impeachment crisis, was preoccupied by a far more important dispute: the attempt to reach an agreement whereby Britain would pay for the damages caused to Northern shipping by the British-built Confederate raiders. Disraeli was not alone in feeling that the Americans wanted to see how the elections went in England before finally committing themselves. Although Trollope never lost his deep affection for America, his unhappy diplomatic mission in the heat and corruption of Washington gave him a more suspicious attitude towards the American government, then at its nadir. In his article on Gladstone's new Liberal cabinet, published early in 1869, he discussed the complacent nature of foreign policy since the death of Palmerston and specifically mentioned the need to take a strong line with Washington.[52]

*

One consequence of Trollope's unexpectedly long stay in America was that by the time he returned preparations for the election were well under way and the Liberals had already selected candidates for the best seats. There had been talk of his standing for an Essex seat. Although he lived just across the border in Hertfordshire, his hunting had been mainly in Essex, where he had many friends including Charles Buxton, whose brother had sat for the county until 1857. Apparently the Liberals had agreed that Trollope would stand for the predominantly urban Southern District. While he was away, the party, anxious to conciliate the growing power of the Nonconformists, especially in traditionally strong Dissenting areas like Essex, selected a candidiate who was sure of their support. This was a hard setback, for the two Liberal candidates were returned unopposed although, as Trollope points out in his *Autobiography*, they only lasted one Parliament.

'Anthony's ambition,' wrote Dickens to Tom Trollope 'is inscrutable to me. Still, it is the ambition of many men; and the honester the man who entertains it, the better for the rest of us, I suppose.' Fanny Trollope had once hoped that her sons might some day get into Parliament, but Anthony's uncle had laughed when the young boy told him that that was his ultimate ambition. In spite of Dickens's bemusement – based on his jaundiced view of politicians – it was a common goal of many literary men. Thackeray had stood for Oxford in 1857 and Samuel Warrèn, then a celebrated novelist, sat for Midhurst. In the 1868 election, called by Disraeli, himself a novelist, thirty-one Liberals, described as 'men of letters' became MPs. Walter Bagehot had no doubt that novelists ranked below MPs when he wrote about the advantages of becoming a Member of Parliament: 'It is far more comprehensible to most people than eminence in science or literature. A common person, who reads little, has but very little notion what the books of the day are about ... But no one can help thinking of

Parliament ... a distinction much more intelligible to most people than to have written a book.' Bagehot himself had tried to get into the Commons for the borough of Bridgewater, but his supporters were shown to have made 'corrupt payments'.[53]

When Trollope asked what seats were still available, he would have been told that there was a rush for seats as everyone expected a Liberal landslide. The problem, as one of the Whips told Gladstone, was that 'We still want candidates for counties, & have too many for the boroughs', where Liberals felt safest. For such unpromising seats as were left Liberal leaders had a new source of information, but one with which they were rather embarrassed. The 1867 Reform Act had increased the electorate by about 82 per cent, but no one was quite certain about the intentions of the new working-class voters. The Reform League sent workmen to report on Tory seats. These reports were much valued by Liberal leaders, but they were fearful lest anyone find out they were in communication with radical workmen. Trollope was offered the East Riding borough of Beverley. Fortunately the League's report on this constituency has survived and provides the best account of the task facing Trollope. It might be mentioned, before quoting it, that one peer suggested during the Reform Bill debates that the suffrage should be confined to those who could write legibly: had this been the case, Thomas Sanders, the working man who compiled this excellent report in a magnificent copperplate hand, would have been far more likely to have got the vote than that other newly enfrancised elector, Anthony Trollope. Sanders reported:[54]

> In Beverley the Political position is one of a very peculiar character, nearly the whole of the adult population being in the possession of the Franchise, but the sitting member Sir H. Edwards having carried on such a system of Bribery the Borough has become so thoroughly corrupt, that the Working Classes look upon the privilege of the vote only as a means to obtain money ... There are no Liberal candidates in the field ... We found it impossible to form a Working-Men's Committee in the Town, so few of them having Political Honesty. The number of Electors on the old register was 1,474, the probable on the new, will be 2,114.

When Trollope arrived on the five o'clock train from York on 30 October, he, like the modern rail traveller, saw the inspiring sight of Beverley Minster rising above the flat countryside. He had no connection with the town, although once it had suited his fiction to pretend it had a bishop [*The Warden* V]. The only Yorkshire connection he could claim was Rose's descent from the Heseltines of neighbouring Hull, but it behooved him to be silent about his father-in-law. Trollope did not approach party politics with that evident fairness with which he approached so many other topics. A year after this election and still smarting from its wounds, he wrote: 'We are among those who desire the ascendancy of our party for sheer party purposes. We own to a feeling of canine pugnacity and we thirst, politically, for the blood of our adversaries. We delight to tear their ears with our political teeth and to send them howling into corners, maimed, bloody, and with drooping tails.' He was only in the town for a few hours before he mounted a temporary balcony, at a tailor's house, to make 'one of the ablest and most fluent addresses ever heard in Beverley', according to the Liberal newspaper, the *Beverley Recorder*. Putting aside his thirst for blood, he told his listeners that he could see some virtue in the opposing side. He borrowed a favourite metaphor from his political novels:[55]

> It is not natural in a town like this, that you, the electors should be Tories ... It never astonishes me to find a Conservative farmer or Conservative landlords and tenants ... Contact with the soil creates that feeling, which, mind you, is necessary. It is useful to us because we should not like to go along without a drag upon the wheel. We should soon come to a mighty smash.

A Liberal politician had warned Trollope: 'You won't get in. I don't suppose you really expect it. But there is a fine career open to you. You will spend £1,000, and lose the election. Then you will petition, and spend another £1,000. You will throw out the elected members. There will be a commission, and the borough will be disenfranchised. For a beginner such as you are, that will be a great success.' The prediction was exaggerated only with reference to money: the election cost Trollope some £400. Parliament was an expensive pastime for a Victorian gentleman: not only was he unpaid, but he had to pay much of the expenses of his election, including the fees of the returning officer.[56]

Trollope found making speeches easier than he had thought, and his addresses are far better than he claimed, but he was utterly miserable when canvassing. One would have thought that a man used to peering into houses on postal missions and travels and possessed of such a rigorous bonhomie might have enjoyed the work. He did not object to the people he met but to those who led him about: it was 'a bitter tyranny from grinding vulgar tyrants'. The worst tryant was a local publican, which should not have surprised a novelist who only a few years before had portrayed their crucial role in elections. Trollope must have reflected how accurate he had been in *Can You Forgive Her?*

where a publican describes how he made candidates spend as much money as possible: 'It's the game I looks to. If the game dies away, it'll never be got up again; – never. Who'll care about elections then?' [XII]. In the last of his Palliser novels, *The Duke's Children*, he would devote a chapter to an election, describing in detail the torture of the candidate and obviously drawing on his own experiences:

> Perhaps nothing more disagreeable, more squalid, more revolting to the senses, more opposed to personal dignity, can be conceived. The same words have to be repeated over and over again in the cottages, hovels, and lodgings of poor men and women who only understand that the time has come round in which they are to be flattered instead of being the flatterers ... Some guide, philosopher, and friend, who accompanies him ... has calculated on his behalf that he ought to make twenty such visitations an hour, and to call on two hundred constituents in the course of a day. As he is always falling behind in his number, he is always being driven on ... till he comes to hate the poor creatures to whom he is forced to address himself, with a most cordial hatred [LV].

In another novel a candidate grumbles: 'men when they are canvassing never dine; – and not often after they're elected' [*Ralph the Heir* XXIII]. Trollope never forgot the misery, and even in his *Life of Cicero*, written ten years later, he referred to 'the dirty arts of canvassing with which we English have been so familiar'. In Beverley, a two-member constituency, it was the Tories who were flagrantly dishonest though the Liberals were as bad in some other boroughs. The main Tory candidate, Sir Henry Edwards, had also become the town's principal employer, 'partly to promote the prosperity of the place and partly to secure for the Conservative Party, the votes of the Majority of the Workmen', as he frankly admitted to Disraeli. Since there were municipal elections taking place shortly before polling day, many voters in Beverley were anxious to get as high a price as possible for their support.[57]

It was universally accepted that the election was about one issue: the disestablishment of the Church of Ireland. In his Election Address Trollope assured the Beverley electors that:

> for many years I have been one of those who denounced the gross injustice and the absurd uselessness of the Irish Church Establishment. The Protestant church ... established in Ireland means the ascendancy of the rich over the poor ... It has none of those attributes which should grace a church. It does not open its bosom to the poor. It lacks charity. It assumes the virtue of the Pharisee.

In his electoral enthusiasm he had evidently forgotten his portrait in *Castle Richmond* of the dying wife of an Irish rector who showed him her meagre supply of porridge with which she struggled to feed her family and help the poor. The Address contained two other points: a pledge of personal loyalty to Gladstone and a commitment to 'the Education of the People'. 'I am of the opinion that every poor man should have brought within his reach the means of educating his children, and that those means should be provided by the State.' He stressed this in a speech to the Liberal Working Men's Association: 'The education of the people of this country is not equal to the education of the people of America, where every adult can read and write. I do not desire to Americanise our English institutions; but I do want to see a system of education established by which every man, woman, and child, and the poorest of the land, may be benefited by it.' He avoided details, because he knew that the topic always raised the old Dissenting bugbear about the role of the Church of England in a 'state school'. Religious tensions were already roused to considerable heights by the debate over the Irish Church. Yet *The Times* reported that both Liberal candidates in Beverley had 'met with a very good reception'.[58]

The election throws light on the religious tensions that lay beneath the England described in Trollope's novels. Beverley's strong Dissenting interest had 'considerably increased during the last half century'. Most Dissenters saw the disestablishment of the Irish Church as a matter of justice, a convenient platform from which to attack establishment in general and, therefore, a precedent for an attack on the Church of England. However some, particularly the Methodists, were worried about too close an association with Radical Dissenters and with attacking fellow-Protestants thereby appearing to support Catholicism. Trollope was fortunate in having the local Baptist minister, the Rev. William Carey Upton, as his most stalwart supporter.[59]

Trollope was rather annoyed when Canon Birtwhistle, the Vicar of the Minster, turned a non-political breakfast for the new mayor into an attack upon the Liberal candidates as 'the foes of the Church'. Trollope offered the excellent advice that 'speakers on such occasions are expected to be merry, to be complimentary, to be dull, but, above all things, not to be political'. The Tories enjoyed the support of most Anglicans, particularly those influenced by the noted preacher William Burton Crickmer, Perpetual Curate of the Minster, who was a powerful force in the borough. His normal Sunday congregation could reach 700, with people even crowding onto the altar steps and with

Anthony Trollope

'rows of the female sex perched up above the reredos'. Crickmer was one of those preachers who treat captive audiences to a recital of political prejudices dressed up as religious principles. His tirades were particularly aimed at the dangers of Popery. As 'the driving force' of the 'Royal Alfred Lodge of Loyal Orangemen of Beverley' he had militant opinions about the Irish Church. Trollope was quite furious when he was advised by his agent that a Liberal candidate was not welcome at the Minster even though he was a Churchman. He should have been grateful to be spared a harangue by the Perpetual Curate. He greeted with equal fury the suggestion by the tyrannical publican that he forego a day's relaxation with the hounds.

Crickmer's Orange fantasies seemed nearly realised when the name of the other Liberal candidate was announced: the Hon. Marmaduke Maxwell, son of a local Roman Catholic peer. The religious issue now reached its height, or depth, when Sir Henry Edwards decided not to attack the religion of Maxwell but that of his chief. He announced in a speech not remarkable for internal consistency: 'I don't say Mr. Gladstone is a Roman Catholic, but he looks deuced like it ... Gentlemen, I tell you plainly and frankly that I believe Mr. Gladstone is a thorough Roman Catholic, and of the worst description, because he is a Jesuit.' This ingenious discovery by Sir Henry received national attention which refused to die down, and a month after the election he was still trying to persuade Disraeli to rescue him from the tumult. Behind the scenes, some local politicians were searching for one of those traditional agreements in two-member constituencies. The Tories offered to withdraw Captain Kennard, their second candidate, if the Liberals would withdraw Trollope, thus allowing each party a seat. Sir Henry clearly regarded Maxwell as his main opponent and never mentioned Trollope in his correspondence with Disraeli. The Liberal working men, impressed with Trollope's speeches on education, would not hear of his withdrawal.[60]

Some of the national papers found it amusing that the 'well known novelist' as *The Times* always called him, was standing for Parliament at the same time as his second 'political' novel, *Phineas Finn*, was appearing. The *Illustrated London News* thought 'some personal experience in the ways of the House of Commons will be useful for the correction of a second edition of his biography of the Irish member'. The local Tories picked up this theme in their 'Electoral Tip for Beverley' which gives a flavour of the contest:[61]

> 'Tis said that our worthy friend Anthony Trollope
> Would like to be Member for Beverley Town.
> Oh! do not elect him, 'twould be such a pity.

For really with work he is getting quite thin;
Just fancy him stuck on a Draining Committee,
Or bored like his own Mr Phineas Finn!
Say no to him sweetly without any fighting,

...

Friend Anthony Trollope is wanted for writing.

On 16 November the four candidates mounted the hustings in the Market Square. After formal nominations were made, each man made a speech and the mayor called for a show of hands and then declared that the two Liberal candidates were elected. For a moment it may have seemed to Trollope, standing there in the rain, that he had achieved his ambition, that all the hand-shaking had been worth it and that he would soon be walking between those gilded lamps to take his seat. The Tories, knowing that many of the hands belonged to non-electors, asked for a poll to take place on the next day. A large crowd of about 5,000 gathered on the seventeenth: for the first two hours the Liberals kept in the lead, but about eleven the Tories began to pull ahead. Then the Mayor stepped forward to loud cries of 'bribery' and 'they haven't won fairly' to announce the result:

Edwards	1132
Kennard	986
Maxwell	895
Trollope	740

The Liberals, convinced that the Tories had been bribing voters since mid-morning, raided the Tory Committee rooms and seized a bag of money. Beverley and bribery were synonymous: as *The Times* put it, 'in 1854 there really was a pure election, but it was quite an accident'. In this case not only were hundreds of voters bribed, but the Tories also paid for the support of many of those useful publicans. One person in Beverley long remembered watching the Tory agent at the 1868 election. The agent, appalled when someone presented a bill for his services, said, 'Go home and double it', something the man had already done. Yet when he returned with the bill the second time, the agent said it was still the lowest bill he had – which he did not mean as a compliment.[62]

Trollope could at least rejoice that, except for a few places in the North, the Liberals were swept to victory. He took his own defeat in good heart and, before leaving, told his supporters that he might return for another contest. He did return to Beverley, but not for another election. The Liberals now organised a petition against the return of the two Tories, alleging many instances of bribery. Such petitions were quite common, and at the same time in Westminster supporters of John Stuart Mill were organising one against his successful opponent, W.H. Smith, arguing that he had spent £9,000 hiring cabs to bring voters to the poll and had laid on a large number of somewhat intimidating newspaper vendors. Beverley, however, was one of three English constituencies whose behaviour was so notorious that a Royal Commission was eventually appointed to investigate. When the petition was tried, evidence showed that Tory managers had given bribes for the municipal election so that the money would have been paid before the parliamentary candidates appeared. An auctioneer called Watson had sat at the well-named 'Golden Ball' with a bag of gold coins and a book to record the names of those he bribed. 'No secrecy was observed and batches of three or four went up at a time,' said the presiding judge, Sir Samuel Martin. The traditional bribe for municipal elections had been 5s, but in 1868 it reached as high as £1, though the normal price was 17s 6d. The judge decided that 'more than 800 Parliamentary electors were bribed'.[63]

Trollope was summoned to give evidence, and he explained how he had paid his election expenses when he first arrived: 'To my knowledge none of the money was used to corrupt the electors, either by money or by beer.' The Commission was satisfied with his behaviour and exonerated both Liberal candidates of being 'parties directly or indirectly to the bribery'. The corruption of Beverley was so vast that it was one of the two boroughs disenfranchised. Trollope took some satisfaction in this:

> Beverley's privileges as a borough and my Parliamentary ambition were brought to an end at the same time ... I had done some good ... Nothing could be worse, nothing more unpatriotic, nothing more absolutely opposed to the system of representative government, than the time-honoured practices of the borough of Beverley ... To have assisted in putting an end to this, even in one town, was to a certain extent a satisfaction.

The Minster's Perpetual Curate also found consolation in a new topic for a sermon: 'It is against God that we have offended; it is His laws which we have broken ... why have these troubles come as the Judgment of God upon the sins of this community.'[64] For once Trollope would have agreed with this real-life Mr Slope.

CHAPTER THIRTEEN

To the Antipodes

'There are men who love work ... who attack it daily with renewed energy ... who go to it almost as the drunkard goes to his bottle, or the gambler to his gaming-table' wrote Trollope a few months after his defeat at Beverley [*Ralph the Heir* LI]. However, it had been several weeks after that defeat before even he had enough 'renewed energy' to resume his writing. When he retired from the Post Office, George Eliot wrote to their mutual friend and publisher John Blackwood, 'I cannot help being rather sorry ... it seems to me a thing greatly to be dreaded for a man that he should be in any way led to excessive writing.'[1] Trollope certainly was led into 'excessive writing', a principal reason for which was his need for money to establish his sons, the same motive that had prompted so many of his mother's books. He also needed to write because of that restless energy which found relief in disciplined work. Yet there was another motive: he felt an increasing desire to help his countrymen come to a new understanding of themselves, both in the working of their minds and in their changing social attitudes. Finally, he wanted them to understand the world that one of his sons and the sons of thousands of other Englishmen were creating on the other side of the globe. In search of all these goals Trollope would follow his fictional characters 'to the Antipodes'.

He began his twenty-sixth novel, *Ralph the Heir*, in April 1869, and made effective use of his Beverley experiences. The main plot is a rather confusing story about two men, each named Ralph Newton. The first is the legal heir to his uncle Gregory Newton of Newton Priory; the other is Gregory Newton's illegitimate son whom he prefers. One sub-plot concerns the unsuccessful adventures of Sir Thomas Underwood while standing for election at 'Percycross', the name chosen for Beverley. (During his stay there Trollope must have paid a surreptitious visit to Beverley Minster to see the magnificent late-fourteenth-century canopied tomb of Lady Percy.) The novel draws on many of the author's recent experiences, even quoting the same advice that a politician gave him about losing his money only to see the borough disenfranchised [XX]. Sir Thomas is a Conservative, but many of his attitudes are the same as Trollope's, such as his acceptance that 'men such as I am do not have seats offered to them without a contest'. A Reform League candidate appears, as Trollope no doubt knew of the League's report on Beverley quoted earlier.

There are numerous similarities between the real and fictional boroughs. Percycross has just managed to keep its two seats in spite of 'the great reformer of the age', an ironic reference to Disraeli. There is talk that the Liberals and Conservatives should make a deal so that each could have one member. The Nonconformist vote is important, but Sir Thomas resents the need to be polite to a Methodist minister, who spoke in 'a voice made up of pretence, politeness and saliva'. Percycross, like its model, is a quagmire of corruption: there is even a man paying bribes and writing the names in his book. Sir Thomas, like Trollope, was found innocent of any connection with bribery when the petition was tried. Like Trollope he happily shook off 'the dust of that most iniquitous borough' [XLIV]. The novel began appearing in January 1870 in *Saint Pauls*. Given the £2,500 Trollope received, his election expenses had borne a good return. Money was never far from Trollope's mind in writing this novel, for he noted on the bottom of his working calendar: '£3.3s.7½d. per page.'[2]

*

Strahan, the new owner of *Saint Pauls*, was already involved in publishing one of Trollope's most ambitious novels, *He Knew He Was Right*, which appeared in thirty-two sixpenny weekly numbers starting in October 1868 and ending in May 1869. 'The practice of publishing fiction in weekly numbers,' commented one journal about the time of the fifth part, 'whatever exception may be taken to it on some accounts, is favourable to Mr. Trollope. It has the effect of putting him on his mettle.'[3] He had started this novel about two weeks after his retirement but had written most of it while in Washington, which accounts for the introduction of so many American characters. No doubt his description of one 'tall, thin, clever Republican of the North, – very fond of hearing himself talk, and somewhat apt to take advantage of the courtesies of conversation for the purpose of making unpardonable speeches' was based on several of his own experiences [LXXXVII]. As always, the current phrases of the day appear in his novels: thus when dealing with one of his favourite topics – whether young people should marry without an adequate income – he uses the phrase 'leap in the dark' which had been made famous only a few months before by Lord Derby in his final speech on the Reform Bill [XXXIII]. The novel moves from London to Exeter, providing a contrast between the provincial conservatism of the Cathedral city Trollope knew so well and the world of radical journalism in London, a world he had first introduced in the obnoxious person of Mr Quintus Slide in *Phineas Finn*. The action then shifts to Florence, allowing Trollope to make use of his many visits to see Tom.

The theme of the novel is a man gradually being driven mad by jealousy. There are frequent overtones of Othello, most appropriately in the Venetian scenes. The original trouble springs from a particularly Victorian cause: an old roué begins to call the young wife of Louis Trevelyan by her Christian name, Emily. Madness had interested Trollope from his first novel, with the demented Larry Macdermot, to his recent success with Josiah Crawley in *The Last Chronicle of Barset*. Two of his stories for *Saint Pauls*, 'The Turkish Bath' and 'The Spotted Dog', also show the tragedy of demented minds. His interest in the slow descent towards madness came not only from his boyhood experiences of his father but from tours of mental asylums, a standard feature of his travels. Some of this interest may have come from deep within himself, for he had a fear that as he aged he might lose his own mental faculties as his mother had. All of this gave him a fascination with madness and, with this, a capacity to portray mental instability remarkable in a pre-Freudian writer [XXXVIII]:

There is perhaps no great social question so imperfectly understood among us at the present day as that which refers to the line which divides sanity from insanity. That this man is sane and that other unfortunately mad we do know well enough; and we know also that one man may be subject to various hallucinations, – may fancy himself to be a teapot, or what not, – and may yet be in such a condition of mind as to call for no intervention either on behalf of his friends, or of the law ... We know that the sane man is responsible for what he does, and that the insane man is irresponsible; but we do not know, – we only guess wildly, at the state of mind of those, who now and again act like madmen, though no court or council of experts has declared them to be mad.

He insisted that 'Trevelyan was, in truth, mad on the subject of his wife's alleged infidelity'. Although Trevelyan continually prayed that his suspicions would prove groundless, he still studied the newspapers every day looking for stories of women who had been unfaithful. Trollope reveals in one sentence how close, how superb, a student of human behaviour he was: 'They who do not understand that a man may be brought to hope that which of all things is the most grievous to him, have not observed with sufficient closeness the perversity of the human mind' [XXXVIII].

For the modern reader, few novels show the power of Trollope's writing and the subtlety of his understanding of the human mind – with its ever-shifting 'Antipodes' of emotion – better than *He Knew He Was Right*. It also contains one of his few 'sensational' scenes – the kidnapping of the child by agents of the estranged father – a scene reminiscent of Wilkie Collins. His portrayal of the detective, Bozzle, 'his Iago figure', reads more like Dickens, and he has given him some wonderful lines: 'I don't see as parsons are better than other folk when they has to do with a lady as likes her fancy-man.' This novel also provides a good example of Trollope's acceptance of the public desire for 'parsons' in his books. While a minor canon at Exeter is entirely forgettable, in Mr Outhouse the author made an attempt, not entirely successful, to present a new type of clergyman, at least new to his writing, the hard-working slum-priest. Trollope was not pleased with this book, but it stands as one of his most impressive achievements in its scope, in its handling of a large number of sub-plots and, above all, in its picture of a mind collapsing under the corrosive power of jealousy. Contemporaries were much divided on the book: *The Times* found it 'a mere piece of realism', while Mrs Oliphant wrote to tell Trollope of the 'hot discussions' going on in her circle at Windsor as to Trevelyan's fate. Another incisive contemporary, Edward FitzGerald, correctly commented that the book was damaged by its author's tendency to 'longueur'.[4] *He Knew He Was Right* is one of the best examples of Trollope's drawing on his own experiences and travels to provide the rich texture for his novels. He recalled childhood songs about 'Captain Bold of Halifax', and used recollections of his cousin, Fanny Bent, for the Devonshire scenes centred on the stalwart old Tory, Jemima Stanbury, with her hatred of innovations like afternoon tea and pillar boxes. He drew upon his and Rose's many trips to France and Italy to describe how the journey across the Alps had become much easier, though less exciting, after the opening of the tunnel.[5] While writing of the Alps he did not forget to include his friends of the Alpine Club. Incidentally, one reflection made while describing the French breakfast on the trip through the tunnel shows how so much of Trollope's writing is still relevant:

We are often told in our newspapers that England is disgraced by this and by that; by the unreadiness of our army, by the unfitness of our navy, by the irrationality of our laws, by the immobility of our prejudices, and what not; but the real disgrace of England is the railway sandwich, – that whited sepulchre, fair enough outside, but so meagre, poor, and spiritless within, such a thing of shreds and parings, such a dab of food [XXXVII].

There are some scenes at his mother's favourite retreat, the Baths of Lucca. Nor, one suspects, was his recent battle with the Dean of Canterbury forgotten in his depiction of a journalist writing 'stinging articles' about the Church [XLIII]. In the colonial governor Sir Marmaduke Rowley and his family can be found recollections of Trollope's West Indian tour, while his American experiences are always present.

Kate Field thought that she was the original of Wallachia Petrie, 'the Republican Browning', a feminist poet who is always spouting about American 'institutions' and the 'rights of women'. 'I never said you were like W. Petrie,' Trollope replied. 'I said that young woman did not entertain a single opinion on public matters which you could repudiate.' What is interesting in his letter to Kate Field is his next comment about these opinions: 'She was only absurd in her method of expressing them.'[6] Although Trollope is scathing about feminist lecturers – as he always is about any 'utopian' or fanatic – he is at the same time increasingly sympathetic to unmarried women in an era when, as one character says, they could easily be defined as a 'nobody ... [who] isn't wanted anywhere' [LI].

The treatment of Americans rubbing against the older ways of Europe in *He Knew He Was Right* reminds one more of Henry James than any other of Trollope's books. Appropriately, James placed it high among Trollope's novels:[7]

> He often achieved a conspicuous intensity of the tragical. The long, slow process of the conjugal wreck of Louis Trevelyan and his wife ... arrives at last at an impressive completeness of misery ... Touch is added to touch, one small, stupid, fatal aggravation to another; and as we gaze into the widening breach we wonder at the vulgar materials of which tragedy sometimes composes itself. I have always remembered ... [the] powerful picture of the insanity of stiff-neckedness. Louis Trevelyan, separated from his wife, alone, haggard, suspicious, unshaven ... is a picture worthy of Balzac. Here and in several other places Trollope has dared to be thoroughly logical; he has not sacrificed to conventional optimism; he has not been afraid of a misery which should be too much like life.

*

Only three days after finishing *He Knew He Was Right* Trollope began a new novel in which once again he was 'not afraid of misery'. *The Vicar of Bullhampton* was begun in Washington on 15 June 1868 and finished on 1 November, during the first few days of the Beverley campaign, an apt illustration of how Trollope allowed nothing to stand in the way of writing. The title must have seemed to many who saw it advertised to vouchsafe a welcome return by Mr Trollope to those clerical pastures beloved by his readers. *The Times*'s review of *He Knew He Was Right* had complained that the Barset novels were 'so perfect in themselves, that we wish for nothing else than they give us'. His latest novels 'are pleasant reading for leisure hours, but are not such imperative claimants on the busiest lives as *Barchester Towers*'. It is often said that *The Vicar of Bullhampton* is a novel about prostitution. It is not: the story of the 'fallen woman' is only one of the sub-plots, if the most memorable. Nevertheless Trollope knew that by including it he was touching one of the most delicate topics in Victorian England. It has already been observed how he had alluded to prostitution in *Can You Forgive Her?* His increased political awareness included an interest in social problems other than education. Thus an early issue of *Saint Pauls* had an essay by him on 'The Uncontrolled Ruffianism of London' in which he refused to panic and concluded: 'We decline to recognise any necessity for altering our usual mode of living.'[8] The violence of London was also introduced into an episode of *Phineas Finn*, where the hero rescues a Cabinet Minister from garroting, a subject much in the news [XXX].

Prostitution had become a topic that could be discussed 'in front of the ladies' once Josephine Butler had begun her campaign against the Contagious Diseases Act. This act allowed state inspection of 'prostitutes' in specified towns, normally those in which sailors and soldiers congregated, in order to control the spread of venereal diseases. To many it was a virtual acceptance of prostitution, and there was a public outcry. Trollope was quite outspoken when a West End play discussed the topic. Dion Boucicault's *Formosa* opened at Drury Lane, and Trollope later wrote that 'the whole Formosa business was to my thinking detestably false'. Trollope attacked the play not because 'fallen women' were once again on the stage but because 'the character is utterly false, false to human nature, false to London life'. Where he had been discreet in *Can You Forgive Her?* a few years before, he was ready to assert in *Saint Pauls* in 1869: 'We do not think that any attempt should be made to conceal the existence of such a class of women from our wives and daughters.' He was convinced, as was Josephine Butler, that knowledge would lead to reform: 'Let the truth of the evil be told, and the truth will always deter, – deter from vice.'[9] Even so, he still felt it necessary to add a preface to *The Vicar of Bullhampton*, the only time he did so, to justify his inclusion of this 'castaway'. His own view was expressed by the Vicar's comment to the girl's father: 'How small is the sin, and how terrible is the punishment!' [XXVII]. The Vicar – the most pastoral of Trollope's clergymen – is indignant, as the narrator says, 'at the hardness of the world ... the world that knows so much better how to treat an erring sinner than did Our Saviour when on earth' [XLI].

This novel also dealt with another major theme in Victorian life: the rivalry between Church and Chapel. Bullhampton is convulsed when the Primitive Methodists, the most rural and uneducated of the main Nonconformist denominations, get land to build a 'staring brick Methodist chapel, with the word Salem inserted in large letters over the door' directly opposite the vicarage gate [XXXIV]. Usually Trollope avoided this contentious subject but, like all Liberals, he was being made uncomfortably aware of the increasing power of Nonconformity in his party. When he began the book he probably already knew that he had lost the prospect of a safe seat because the Liberals wanted to please the Dissenting interest in Essex, and his time in Beverley did not lessen his dislike for Nonconformity. Even so, his presentation is an extremely balanced one and he shows a remarkable sympathy for the Primitive Methodist minister, Mr Puddleham, an uneducated and combative man who, 'in spite of the intensity of his ignorance, is efficacious among the poor'. Nevertheless it is the Vicar, Frank Fenwick, who rejects Mr Puddleham's gossip about the village's fallen woman. It is he, and not the minister, who identifies himself with the prostitute: 'Are we not in a bad way, – unless we believe and repent? Have we not all so sinned as to deserve eternal punishment? ... But you and I, as Christian ministers, should never allow ourselves to speak so thoughtlessly of sinners' [I, XVII].

Ironically there was little controversy about the inclusion of a 'fallen woman' in the novel. There was, however, a great controversy between the novelist and the magazine editor who had commissioned it. E.S. Dallas was one of the leading Victorian critics: it was he who had been the author of the long article in *The Times* of May 1859 which had proclaimed Trollope the greatest novelist of the circulating libraries. Almost exactly ten years later, in March 1869, Dallas, as editor of *Once a Week*, had to ask whether Trollope would allow its publishers, Bradbury and Evans, to bring out *The Vicar of Bullhampton* in another of their journals. The reason was that they had bought the rights to Victor Hugo's novel *L'Homme Qui Rit*. The Paris publication had been delayed 'through the incessant corrections of the author' and they could not bring out their translation until the French publication had appeared. If they started Trollope's novel as agreed they would then have two novels in each issue and there was not enough room. Dallas therefore proposed publishing *The Vicar of Bullhampton* on the date agreed but in the *Gentleman's Magazine* and not in *Once a Week*. 'Do, like a good fellow, say that you agree.' Trollope was furious that 'the Frenchman's grinning hero' would take precedence over 'my clergyman'. He disliked the 'pretentious and untrue to nature' fiction of 'this sententious French Radical'. It was not just personal pique 'that I should be asked to give way to a Frenchman' but a matter of principle for an author who prided himself on turning his work in on time. His disciplined system of a set number of pages each day was arranged to ensure this. He would not be a 'good fellow' and allow his novel to be put into another magazine. Bradbury and Evans then issued it in eleven monthly parts between July 1869 and May 1870. Trollope was still fuming seven years later when writing of it in his *Autobiography*: 'The industrious must feed the idle. The honest and simple will always be the prey of the cunning and fraudulent.' He comforted himself in thinking that he, like all 'earthly sufferers', was moving 'heavenwards', while Hugo was going 'elsewards'.[10] For once Trollope was in agreement with Napoleon III!

*

In the 1870s Trollope devoted much time to the Colonies and spent about a third of the decade visiting and writing about Australia, New Zealand and South Africa. There was a personal reason for some of this. In 1865 his younger son Fred had left for Australia near his eighteenth birthday.[11] The Trollopes had only agreed to his going if he promised to return before taking any definite decision about his future. When Fred did so in December 1868 he informed his parents that he wished to settle permanently in Australia. For the last time Trollope could see both his sons gathered round his table at Waltham House and well mounted in the hunting fields of Essex. In the early months of 1869 the four Trollopes had a 'council' to decide the two boys' futures. 'His mind was always on the subject' was how Trollope described a fictional father's thinking about his son's inheritance, and as so often, whenever the novelist's own mind was working on a subject, it appeared in his novels. Often it was heralded by a sudden burst of eloquence as in this passage from early 1869 in *Ralph the Heir* [XI]:

> His mind was always on the subject, though it was not often that he said
> a word about it to the son ... His thoughts were always dwelling on it ...
> As the sun is falling in the heavens and the evening lights come on, this

world's wealth and prosperity afford no pleasure equal to this. It is this delight that enables a man to feel, up to the last moment, that the goods of the world are good.

A few pages earlier he had referred to another problem that was on his mind. The defeated candidate at 'Percycross' was thinking about his adopted niece: 'If a man have no children of his own ... he can give all ... But a man feels that he owes his property to his children ... Had she been in truth his daughter, he would have felt that there was enough for three; but she was not his daughter, and yet he was telling her that she should be to him the same as a child of his house!' [VII]. What to do for Florence Bland would perplex Trollope for twelve more years and the answer to that worry would also be announced in a novel. These passages open a new insight into his mind. Critics have long recognised his great skill at showing through dialogue and, even more, through his characters' thoughts, their unconscious minds. Yet these passages, written at the time of the family 'council', show how his own mind, consciously and unconsciously, emerged in his writings.

Trollope's novels of the 1850s had shown a great interest in the way young men were established in a profession. These reflected his own experiences. In 'settling' his sons Trollope was helped by the fact that by the mid-1860s the number of professions was increasing: in *The Claverings*, which began appearing in February 1866, a young man of 'good family' becomes an engineer and marries his employer's daughter. Fred Trollope, however, seemed to show no desire to follow any profession in England, whether old or new, while his elder and cleverer brother, Harry, had the opposite problem: he could not make up his mind what he wanted to do. At first it seemed he would emulate his grandfather and become a barrister. Then he was attracted to military life and got a cornet's commission in the Mounted Yeomanry at about the time Trollope retired from the Post Office. There was also some idea that he might take up a career in the Foreign Office as he had already acquired a knowledge of French, and presumably Italian, during long stays with his uncle in Florence. Just as G.H. Lewes had asked Trollope to help him get his son a place at the Post Office, so Trollope now called on his friends to help him obtain a coveted nomination to the Foreign Office. These, however, were still an aristocratic preserve, although apparently one old peer tried to help for a rather curious reason: he said he could remember dancing with Harry's grandmother, Fanny Milton, more than half a century before and had never forgotten her delicate ankles! In spite of such gallant support Harry did not get into the Foreign Office. There was yet another possibility, for Trollope had long had the notion of bringing up a son as a novelist.[12] In all this the Trollopes were part of their time. Two of Dickens's sons went to Australia and one tried to get into the Foreign Office. There also was an increasing tendency for writing to become a family occupation. Many novelists like Thackeray and Mrs Oliphant were able to use their connections with magazines to introduce their children to the joys and perils of authorship.

At last Trollope decided that the best way for Henry to have a profession and to carry on the 'family literature' was to establish him as a publisher. He invested £10,000, a very large sum, in his principal publishers, Chapman and Hall: this provided Henry with a partnership as well as one-third ownership of the firm. He was fortunate in having advice from Joseph Langford, who, as manager of Blackwood's London branch, was one of the best-informed men in the publishing world. Langford, a bachelor, was a frequent guest at Waltham House and was very fond of Trollope, whom he saw almost every week either at the Cosmopolitan or at the Garrick. On 30 August 1869 Trollope signed Henry's articles of partnership. 'I am quite certain that Trollope has taken no step in the dark,' Langford informed John Blackwood, who had asked him to help Trollope. 'He is thoroughly right-minded.' Trollope had no intention of committing thousands of pounds to the care of an inexperienced son, or of Chapman, who had not proved the best of businessmen. 'Practically,' continued Langford, 'the business will be carried on under the inspection of Trollope and Harding – Chapman's father-in-law, who is one of the first businessmen in the city.'[13]

Ten years before, when Trollope was in the West Indies, he had joked with Chapman: 'Ah – I wish Providence had made me a publisher.' Chapman replied in the same spirit: 'Providence has too good a regard for you to make you a publisher, it was a very fine business some 20 years ago but authors are too knowing now-a-days.' In the years to come Trollope would bitterly regret his direct involvement in publishing and perhaps wonder if he had not been wrong in contradicting Providence. Henry only remained at Chapman and Hall for about three years and then left 'with more pecuniary success than might have been expected from the short period of his labours', according to his father. He then decided to become a writer, aided presumably by interest from the capital his father had settled on him from Chapman and Hall. His knowledge of French gave him some work as a translator and he wrote some articles and books on French literature. Trollope concluded his discussion of Henry's life in the *Autobiography*: 'Whether he will work at it so hard as his father, and write as many books, may be doubted.' Since Henry edited that book, he must not have objected to this statement. Henry's correspondence regarding the publication of his father's *Autobiography* shows how deeply he loved him. It also shows Henry to be a rather fussy man who could write numerous letters about one sentence.[14]

It may be recalled that Trollope alluded to some of these family events in a short novel he wrote at this time, *Sir Harry Hotspur of Humblethwaite*, where he accepts it as natural that a father's love for his children is stronger than theirs for him [XVI]. The novel contrasts the solid, old-fashioned virtues of a Tory squire and his daughter in the Lake District with the flashy and dishonest world of the squire's nephew and heir in London. The behaviour of young George Hotspur allowed Trollope to make discreet hints about a matter of growing public interest, the rumours about the fast set gathered round the Prince of Wales. The Squire's daughter, the heir to the family fortune, loves her cousin George, the heir to the baronetcy. When she finally accepts that her cousin is irredeemable, she dies of a broken heart. Although George Eliot had not read her friend's book she knew its basic plot when she wryly commented: 'Men are fond of that sort of dog-like attachment.'[15] The old squire's attempt to reconcile his duty about the inheritance with his regard for his descendants was to find an echo in many of Trollope's final novels and was no doubt influenced by his desire to provide for his two sons as well as for his niece. On 24 April 1869 Trollope celebrated his fifty-fourth birthday and two days later accompanied Fred to Plymouth for his return to Australia. It was no doubt a sad moment for him when the ship sailed on its two-month voyage. Two of Trollope's deepest emotions, his love of travel and his love for his son, induced him to consider what would be his longest trip yet. Less than a year after Fred sailed out of Plymouth, Trollope was telling Kate Field that he and Rose were planning a voyage round the world to see Fred and his sheep in Australia.

*

At the end of April 1871 Anthony and Rose spent their last night at Waltham House. The preceding weeks had been hectic with all the tasks associated with closing up a large house, such as ensuring that his library was well packed and safely stored. There had also been a fruitless search for a tenant to take the house. As so often, his publishers helped in practical ways: Edward Chapman agreed to look after some of Trollope's horses till he returned and decided whether his hunting days were over. His mood was not helped by the fact that the winter of 1870-71 had been the worst season the Essex Hunt had ever known. There were several hurried farewells to friends such as George Eliot, who introduced him to Turgenev. The two novelists got on well and Trollope arranged temporary privileges at the Athenaeum for him. Although Trollope was so busy that he even turned down a request for a short story from his American friend James Fields, he was not going round the world without any literary luggage. In January he agreed terms with Chapman, an easy task now that he was virtually a partner, for a two-volume book on Australia and New Zealand. He was to receive £1,250, the same sum he had had for *North America*.* Seeing no reason why he could not make some more money, he arranged to supply the *Daily Telegraph* with a series of articles on the colonies. When a friend joked, 'You will write a novel on the voyage?' Trollope replied: 'I have two finished and one half finished, which I shall complete and I shall do another besides.'[16]

Trollope later described these long voyages to Australia, 'the peculiar life ... governed by its own rules and having its own roughness and amenities'. For two months 'no work is required from any one. The lawyer does not go to his court, nor the merchant to his desk' [*John Caldigate* v]. Work, however, was required from one man who went daily 'to his desk'. On this voyage, as on every other he made, Trollope had arranged for the ship's carpenter to fix up a desk in his cabin. He busied himself with the novel he had said he would write, *Lady Anna*. On the eight-week voyage he produced sixty-six pages of manuscript each week, making each page hold 250 words. At the top of his work sheet he made his calculations: '9 pages a day for 59 days = 531 pages.' 'Women have often been hardly used by men,' he wrote as he began his task on 25 May, the day after the *Great Britain* sailed from Liverpool. He managed six pages that day, but by the next he was in his stride and was producing ten pages. He worked regularly at his task: the least he managed was six pages, the most, twelve. He worked every day of the voyage, except 6 July when he wrote one word 'Ill' in his work sheet. By 19 July, eight days before the ship arrived in Melbourne, he could write at the bottom of his sheet: 'Finished at sea in 8 weeks.' He had finished his thirtieth novel on schedule and could then relax for the final few days of the trip.[17] This is a perfect example of how Trollope's

---

*The first edition, complete with eight maps, was published in 1873, at 36s. Trollope wrote that 2,000 copies were sold and it was reprinted, although he later wrote that the pages 'drag'. In 1874 the publishers reissued the book in four parts at 3s each: these would have been suitable for an emigrant, who had already selected his destination. In 1876 the book was reissued in two volumes. It also appeared in six parts in Australia in 1873. These extra editions only brought Trollope an additional £50.

self-discipline worked in channelling his energy and making use of his enormous creativity.

To most writers the idea of producing a two-volume novel in eight weeks at sea sounds both absurd and depressing. Yet once Trollope had built his 'castle in the air' he set to work constructing his specified number of turrets and walls each day. When viewed in this light, the work is not all that much. He was able to do one of his pages in about fifteen minutes, so even on his maximum days that was only 3 hours of work, which left the rest of the day free for any other work he had to do or any pleasure he wanted to enjoy. For these eight weeks of work he received £1,200, one-third more than his annual salary as a Surveyor. Since he had done all the hard work of thinking out his plot and characters, the physical act of writing was not difficult for him. Before leaving he had asked one old friend to correct the proofs of a short novel, *The Golden Lion of Granpère*, which was published while he was away. This friend was amazed that the manuscript was 'entirely free from alterations'. 'It seemed to have flowed from his pen like clear liquor from a tap.'[18]

Before starting *Lady Anna* Trollope had asked a lawyer about the law of bigamy, as that provides the background to the novel. He had grown more sensitive to attacks about his mistakes on points of law, and he had already been careful to ask a lawyer friend to write the chapter about the decision on the ownership of the jewels in *The Eustace Diamonds*, the novel that began to appear in the *Fortnightly* in the last weeks of his Australian trip. *Lady Anna*, which dealt with the tensions between romantic love and the demands of rank, annoyed his contemporaries. They seemed more prepared to accept the story of the 'fallen woman' in *The Vicar of Bullhampton* than the idea that an Earl's daughter would marry a tailor, as in *Lady Anna*. (When Michael Sadleir was building his great collection of Victorian fiction in the 1920s, he noticed that copies of *Lady Anna* were in a much fresher condition than other Trollopean survivors of Mudie's Library, which implies that this novel spent more time on the shelf.) Trollope's answer to Lady Wood, a hunting friend and fellow novelist, who was reading the story in the *Fortnightly* and wondering whether the heroine would indeed marry beneath her, led Trollope to provide some insight into the origin of his novels:[19]

Of course the girl has to marry the tailor. It is very dreadful, but there was no other way. The story was originated in my mind by an idea I had as to the doubt which would, (or might) exist in a girl's mind as to whether she ought to be true to her troth, or true to her lineage ... and I determined that in such case she ought to be true all through. To make the discrepancy as great as possible I made the girl an Earl's daughter, and the betrothed a tailor.

This was always the basis of Trollope's best novels: how human beings coped with a set condition. The Barchester series had come not only from the sight of Salisbury Cathedral in the moonlight but from the author's speculations about the homes and lives of the clerical dignitaries who lived in its shadow and who wrote those indignant letters to *The Times*. This fascination with human nature had never left him.

Lady Anna was one of Trollope's novels which fall into the category noted earlier in which there is a struggle between inheritance and status on the one hand and the demands of love on the other. The status is not that of a Lord Fawn, a titled office-holder in the world of the Pallisers, but of a great family whose history was intertwined with that of England: the very name of Lovel conjures up stories of bold mediaeval Earls, of families with Shakespearian associations and Romantic legends of Minster Lovel on the banks of the swift-flowing Windrush in Oxfordshire where Richard III's last follower was said to have come home to die. In the novel Trollope also drew on his own past and his wide knowledge of English scenery. Much of the story is set in his birthplace, Keppel Street, with its 'dark gloomy parlour' [XLII]. The elder tailor, father of the one who falls in love with the Earl's daughter, is active in radical politics and seems to owe something to the famous Francis Place, the 'Radical tailor of Charing Cross' who lived not all that far from Trollope's youthful lodgings on Northumberland Street.* Like *Sir Harry Hotspur*, some of the novel is set in the Lake District and there are also scenes in Yorkshire reflecting Trollope's recent stay in the awe-inspiring Wharfdale countryside near Bolton Bridge. For once Trollope deserted his usual devotion to Devonshire and proclaimed: 'No more luxuriant pasture, no richer foliage, no brighter water, no more picturesque arrangement of the freaks of nature, aided by the art and taste of man, is to be found,

---

*Tailors move in and out of Trollope's life and works: his debut at Beverley had been from the balcony of a Liberal tailor. A fashionable tailor was a member of Trollope's singing club, the Moray Minstrels, and his first London landlady had been the wife of a tailor. The President whose impeachment had so delayed Trollope in Washington, Andrew Johnson, started life as a tailor. Victorian gentlemen, particularly those of expanding prosperity like Trollope, would naturally and frequently come into more intimate contact with tailors than with any other tradesman. A fashionable tailor had occupied a prominent role in *Ralph the Heir*, and the preacher Mr Emilius in *Phineas Finn* had lodgings with a tailor in Northumberland Street. Tailors had long had a reputation for being active in radical politics.

perhaps, in England' than the countryside round the ruins of Bolton Abbey [XV]. Exactly one year before beginning *Lady Anna* Trollope had written to a friend from the Yorkshire Dales that 'this is the prettiest spot in England'.[20]

Trollope wrote this novel at the same time as George Eliot was writing *Middlemarch*. Each was set in the 1830s, when both authors were young and when, as George Eliot said, reform was easier to support. She also told another woman novelist that she would never have completed *Middlemarch* except for Trollope's encouragement.[21] *Middlemarch* is much the greater novel, but Trollope clearly saw *Lady Anna* as the start of a third series. At the end, the newly married couple decide to go 'to the Antipodes' as a place where titled ladies and radical tailors could dwell in democratic bliss. 'Of the further doings of Mr. Daniel Thwaite and his wife Lady Anna, – of how they travelled and saw many things; and how he became perhaps a wiser man, – the present writer may, he hopes, live to tell.' If he had persevered in this projected series, Trollope would have become the pioneer of that feature of modern times, the Australian family saga!

*

'Mr Anthony Trollope', commented the *Spectator*, 'apparently aspires not merely to write as many novels as Alexandre Dumas, and (it is whispered) to surpass the mightiness of Nimrod in hunting but will also essay to be a greater traveller than Marco Polo.' As with *North America*, Trollope had picked a good time to write about another part of 'the English world'. There was surprisingly little interest in the colonies in the first three decades of the Victorian era, the time when Lady Anna left for the 'Antipodes'. Naturally those who had business or family links took an interest, but the general public showed little sustained concern. This began to change just about the time Trollope went to Australia. A united Germany in Europe and the reunified Republic in America began to cast ominous shadows across that British predominance which had been born in the same year as Trollope. In 1868 Charles Dilke published his *Greater Britain* which argued the importance of the Empire. In the same year the Queen's second son visited Australia, where an attempted assassination by an Irish terrorist only increased the enthusiasm with which he was received and the attention his visit got at home. It is noticeable in that excellent record of contemporary interest, the *Times Annual Summaries*, that in the late sixties and early seventies there were increasing references to colonial topics or what in 1868 it called somewhat grandly 'the prosperous monotony of the Colonies'. In 1872 Disraeli, in a speech at the Crystal Palace, brought the Empire directly into British politics by proclaiming: 'The people of England, and especially the working classes of England, are proud of ... belonging to an imperial country, and are resolved to maintain, if they can, their empire.'[22]

Imperial education had not kept pace with imperial enthusiasm, especially with regard to Australia, and in the 1870s general ignorance was even greater than it would be two decades later when a character in *Lady Windermere's Fan* proclaimed: 'Dear Agatha and I are so much interested in Australia. It must be so pretty with all the dear little kangaroos flying about. Agatha has found it on the map.' There had been occasional flurries of interest, as when gold was discovered in the 1850s. Trollope had written then about 'men with soft hands and unused muscles, who could quote a line or two of Virgil' hurrying out in search of gold. Devoted novel readers could read of those adventures in Henry Kingsley's *Geoffrey Hamlyn*, which recounted his own experiences. Australia had been of other use to novelists: Mrs Trollope found it a good origin for a character who suddenly appears in *Uncle Walter*, while Trollope himself occasionally mentioned it as a place where characters could be sent. Ten years before Fred left for Australia his father had asked in one book: 'But who would not sooner look forward to seeing his son a shoemaker at Melbourne, if as such he could be educated as becomes a gentleman?' He continued, 'We wish our children to be pious and happy', and therefore one should be grateful 'if they can be pious and happy on some foreign shore'. Addressing a mythical farm labourer, he asked if his son might not prosper by emigrating 'to tend his sheep' far from home. Fifteen years later Trollope was on his way to see his own son doing just that.[23]

Trollope's aim in writing his book – other than his laudable one of making money – was to eliminate the ignorance of people like 'dear Agatha' and to illustrate his own view of 'imperial' expansion. He had begun his researches even before leaving. This included paying sixpence a pound for some tinned Australian meat, which was just beginning to be imported into Britain. 'It was sweet and by no means unpalatable, but was utterly tasteless as meat.' His servants refused to eat it 'because, no doubt, they could get better'. This is something about which 'dear Agatha's' mother would complain as well when confronted with tinned beef: 'I fancy it is something the servants always refuse to eat.'* In a lecture about the American war Trollope had proclaimed: 'I

*According to R.H. Horne in his review of Trollope's book in the *Contemporary Review*,

believe that every hearty Englishman looks upon it as England's mission to Anglicize the whole world. I confess that that is my own theory.' Yet he sought an even higher authority than his own opinion or that of his audience. 'Emigration,' he wrote five years later, 'and especially emigration from England has been God's ordained means of populating the world.' Such statements seem to indicate that Trollope was just what he looked like: a typical John Bull Englishman determined to see as much of the map take on as pink a hue as his face. Yet he was far from that. All his views on Australia, New Zealand and later South Africa were coloured by his understanding of America and its history. All his colonial writings make constant references to the American example of independence and prosperity.[24]

His reading of history had already convinced him that all Empires have their day: a virtually inevitable conclusion for one whose first breath was contemporary with Waterloo and whose early education had consisted of little save the study of Greece and Rome. The aim of his unpublished book, *The New Zealander*, had been to show how England could retard the inevitable day when Macaulay's legendary New Zealander would wander among the ruins of London, brooding on the fate of the mother country. As we know, Trollope's basic remedy, as good for any ill as a Victorian patent medicine, was honesty. One aspect of that honesty was to recognise that colonies, like children, could not forever be ruled from home. In *The West Indies*, written at the end of the 1850s, he spoke of looking forward to the 'inevitable, happily inevitable day' when Australia would follow the United States to independence. Trollope is often accused of being 'insensitive to ideas'. Yet his views on Imperialism show that he neither wholly accepted nor wholly rejected the ideas of his time, but examined them critically and came to his own conclusions. As R.W. Chapman wrote while editing some of Trollope's novels in the middle of the Second World War, 'I cannot agree that T. was "insensitive to ideas". He was a pachydermatous Englishman in many ways; yet he was able to admit the idea that the British Empire was doomed to decline and fall.' To Trollope structures like Empires were of secondary importance. He had a noble vision which he described in *Australia and New Zealand*:[25]

We may probably take the language spoken as the truest indication of the influence of nationality and the justest source of national pride. From our little island we have sent forth a people speaking English who are

---

British servants declined to eat Australian tinned meat because 'they fancy it will be a saving to their master, and that by these means their wages are indirectly lowered'.

spreading themselves over all the world. It is a much greater boast than that of ruling dependencies on which the sun never sets. Though none of the English-speaking nations ... should any longer acknowledge themselves to be dependent on England, it would matter nothing to the happiness of the race, and nothing to the true glory of the nationality, – so long as the numbers increased, and the material prosperity of those numbers.

It is a pleasant reflection that Trollope's novels are now one of the bonds that keep that spirit alive throughout the whole English-speaking world.

Although Trollope had little previous knowledge of Australia, he was not one of those travellers who go about a country revelling in their ignorance of its history. Early in his stay, he read a new work on Australian history, a pamphlet on the early days of Port Philip. He had an added reason to enjoy the work: it was dedicated to him by a new friend he made in Australia, G.W. Rusden, Clerk of the Legislative Council. He had been born in Surrey but had lived in Australia for many years. He had many contacts in England, and Dickens had asked him to look after one of his sons when he arrived in the colony. If that dangerous source, the obituary, can ever be trusted, that of Rusden explains why Trollope soon considered him a close friend: 'We don't know any Australian resident so distinctively English ... What a delicious bundle of prejudices was Rusden! ... And honest as the day.' In spite of their friendship, Trollope disagreed with Rusden, who was an able representative of those Australians who were increasingly stressing the link with the Mother Country. Rusden, said Trollope, 'seems to regard the colonies as an element in England's future glory ... I ... who am an Englishman, look upon the colonies as an element, and a very material element, in the future happiness of Englishmen, – or of men and women of English origin, thinking that England's glory should be left altogether out of the question in any consideration of the matter.' He told Rusden of his disagreement on this point and said he looked forward to 'an argument in which I shall delight, – and shall listen'. Trollope's views on the inevitability of independence were by no means unique to him: while he was enjoying his debates about Australia's future, the man responsible in large part for that future, the Colonial Secretary, the Earl of Kimberley, wrote in his diary: 'I have no doubt that in due time Canada and the Australian colonies will become independent.'[26]

An unfortunate result of Trollope's reading of Rusden was that he fell into the trap that accompanies new knowledge: the urge to inflict it on others. Thus a large part of his large book – 1,049 pages in two volumes – is occupied with the history of each separate colony, detailing its exploration and early settlement. He knew that when he casually alluded to the tea in Boston harbour in *North America*, his English readers would know what he meant, but he could not make the same assumption in this travel book. The emphasis on historical background is just one factor that makes this a much less enjoyable work than his two preceding travel books. In both of those, one could always see Fanny Trollope's bonnet peeking out from under Anthony's top hat. *Australia and New Zealand* impresses one as a much fairer book, but fairness is not necessarily a virtue in a travel writer. Trollope was always conscious that his son had chosen to live in Australia and it would not do for the father to leave a host of enemies behind him. Therefore there are few of those wonderful vignettes of people that enlivened the American and West Indian books. Instead of people, we get statistics. Normally Trollope looked on the Victorian devotion to statistics with disfavour:

> I utterly disbelieve in statistics as a science and am never myself guided by any long-winded statement of figures from a Chancellor of the Exchequer or such like big-wig ... Figures, when they go beyond six in number, represent to me not facts, but dreams, or sometimes worse than dreams.

Yet at times the Australian sections of the book read more like a Surveyor's report to the GPO than a travel book. Trollope had been given statistical information by Australian officials and he may have felt obliged to include it. His younger son's example perhaps made him remember those who were thinking of emigrating – and their parents as well – and he used the book to inform people about where to go and what to expect if they followed Fred's footsteps. That is why he gave the history and current conditions of each of the Australian colonies, paying particular attention to the acquisition of land. Finally there was present that same yearning to be treated as a 'serious' writer which had first emerged in book form with *The New Zealander* and can be traced in part to his earliest Irish novels which dealt with religious rivalry and madness. *Australia and New Zealand* was Trollope's most 'serious' book, but it is not his most enjoyable, nor does it give as good an insight into his life as *North America*.[27]

What does emerge in the book is a pervading spirit of friendliness and pride: pride in a continent that had been civilised almost completely in his own lifetime. He discovered that the Australians, like the Americans, revelled in praise and resented criticism, particularly from 'home'. He saw this 'blowing' with resignation and humour:

> I suppose that a young people falls naturally into the fault of self-adulation ... The wonders performed in the way of riding, driving, fighting, walking, working, drinking, love-making, and speech-making, which men and women in Australia told me of themselves, would have been worth recording in a separate volume had they been related by any but the heroes and heroines themselves.

Trollope, fortunately, found plenty to commend without need of exaggeration. Melbourne, a city whose population had already reached 200,000, had excellent gardens and public buildings.[28] He followed his tradition of visiting the mental asylums, particularly praising that of Adelaide. In every large city he visited the post offices where again he singled out Adelaide. This gave him a welcome chance to criticise recent architectural changes at St Martin-le-Grand. He was always anxious to provide information about the condition of ordinary people and the treatment of the poor. For potential emigrants he gave prices of meat and flour and then summarised what they could expect: 'Work is more plentiful. Wages are higher. Food is cheaper.' A cook could get from £35 to £45 a year, whereas in Barsetshire a parson paid his cook £16 a year – although an Earl paid as much as £60 [*The Small House at Allington* LIII]. In Melbourne an artisan could earn as much as ten shillings a day, more than many English farm labourers got in a week. Trollope concluded that 'the artisan with £3 a week, paying 4d. a pound for his meat and 7d. for a 4lb. loaf may live very plentifully' but must expect to work hard. He made continual pleas that young 'gentlemen' should not come out seeking sudden fortunes from gold, a plea strengthened when he met one of Fred's schoolmates, a boy who had been frequently entertained at Waltham House, but who was now living a miserable life hunting gold at Gympie.

At Ballarat Trollope descended into a gold mine, and later in his trip he went down a copper mine, 'finding it always to be a duty to go down a shaft on visiting any mining locality'. Yet after the copper mine he came up so exhausted that he swore he would never go down another. He had not left all his prejudices behind, for when noting the colourful names of the mines, including the delightfully named 'Who Can Tell Mine' he was pleased to see half a dozen boasting the name of Gladstone. 'To be fair, I must add that there is a Disraeli Company', but he added with evident delight, 'I do not, however, find it quoted among those that are paying dividends'. He was also impressed with some of the newspapers and Australian books, calling particular attention to Marcus Clarke, who was so pleased that he later sent Trollope an advance copy of the most famous Australian novel of the century, *For the Term of his Natural Life*, a graphic account of convict life. (Trollope probably first encountered it in serialised form in the *Australian Journal*, where it had been running for over a year before his arrival.) He was obviously greatly taken with the success of Australian publishers, especially Robertsons in Melbourne whom he must have met to talk about their bringing out his forthcoming book in Australia and from whom he probably got his information about Australian publishing. He later told a Royal Commission on Copyright that Melbourne probably had more books published per capita than any other city.[29] There was a strong appetite for novels: 3,000 people in Melbourne would attend Trollope's December lecture 'On English Prose Fiction as a Rational Amusement' in which he defended novels against the sneers of their detractors.

He also tried several varieties of Australian wine. While he found the wines of South Australia too 'heady', the table wine of Victoria was 'certainly superior both in flavour and body to the ordinary wine drunk by Parisians'. He did not like the 'fine' wines because they were not allowed to age long enough. (In his own cellar fine clarets were allowed ten years to reach their maturity.) It annoyed him to see working men preferring wretched spirits to a half-pint of 'the best vin-ordinaire that I ever drank' costing only threepence a glass. His earlier disappointment with tinned meat did not prevent him from investigating the methods of preservation. Although the first experiment to send refrigerated meat to England failed in 1873, the same year his book was published, Trollope saw hope for the future: 'Great commercial feats are always heralded by failures.'

As he sailed into Sydney his life-long quest for the world's most beautiful harbour ended. Sydney's surpassed New York, Cork and even Dublin, of which he had such fond memories from his courtship days. 'Sydney is one of those places which, when a man leaves it knowing that he will never return, he cannot leave without a pang and a tear. Such is its loveliness.' Small wonder that his book received a warm welcome when it appeared: the *Sydney Morning Herald* said, 'he sees among us nothing but beauty everywhere'. The *Sydney Punch* even gave the unique description of Trollope as 'noiseless':[30]

As noiselessly as the creatures of your own delightful fancy that have stolen into our hearts for years and made their home there, you have come amongst us, the brave master, the kindly magician, the eloquent teacher. The very city seems nobler when we think you are walking its streets, and that its citizens may look upon one who has given so much happiness to millions.

It is rather amusing, given this extravagant praise, that it was not unusual for Trollope to be introduced as 'the son of the famous novelist, Mrs Trollope', even though her last novel had been published sixteen years earlier and his own fame was far greater than hers had ever been.

He was particularly struck with the public gardens, which he was to recall in a later novel, *John Caldigate*, which was partially set in Australia, as 'that loveliest of all places, the public gardens at Sydney' [XII]. The public garden in Adelaide was second only to Sydney, but Melbourne's were too scientific, like 'a long sermon from a great divine, – whose theology is unanswerable, but his language tedious'. He was surprised to see many old-looking buildings, remembering that 'in his father's lifetime the place was covered by gum-trees and peopled by savages'. One old church, 'pewed round with high dark panels ... like an English comfortless church of the last century' provoked the same criticism as that provoked by a similar West Indian church twenty-five years before: an apt illustration of the consistency of his views. The Cathedral, however, won his praise, and not just for its appearance: 'I heard an excellent sermon there, in which I was told that it was the practice of St Paul to teach his own religion rather than to abuse that of others, – a lesson which is much needed at home.' Any stray Evangelical reading this passage may have uttered a hearty if ironical 'Amen'.

As always on his travels, he was interested in the state of religion, which he saw as closely connected with education. He found religious sentiment stronger in the Australian colonies than in England and attributed this, as with almost all other improvements, to better education for the mass of people:

The tendencies and influences which send children to school, send them and their parents to church also, – even though the schools be in all respects secular. Teaching produces prosperity; prosperity achieves decent garments, – and decent garments are highly conducive to church-going. Among us in England that portion of our rural population which never goes to church, and which is utterly ignorant of all religious observances, consists of the unfortunates upon whom the kindly dew of instruction has never fallen, and who have been left in brute-like ignorance.

*

Yet the Trollopes had not come half way round the world to admire gardens and report on schools. Shortly after their arrival in July, Rose had gone to stay with Fred at his sheep station near Grenfell in New South Wales, about 250 miles west of Sydney. Trollope arrived there at the end of October 1871 and wrote to Rusden: 'I find my son all that I could wish, – steady, hardworking, skilful & determined.'[31] Fred's life at Mortray Station is portrayed in the chapter 'Country Life in the Bush', in his father's book, where the son is mildly disguised as a 'friend'. Trollope was evidently proud of what Fred had achieved by hard work, work which included erecting forty miles of fencing round his paddocks to hold about 16,000 sheep. Trollope watched all the operations of sheep raising and shearing, although he admits the smell of sheds where this was done could be overwhelming.* Occasionally, however, Trollope's pride, so evident in the book, seems overtaken by boredom, monotony and loneliness in a life where the visit of the postman was 'a great blessing'. The retired Surveyor noted how the 'mailman' did favours for all along his enormous route and, in return, received hospitality.

Life at the station was a far cry from the elegant comforts of Waltham House. Fred's home consisted of a sitting-room with a bedroom on each side, but Trollope found his greatest pleasure on the verandah, where he liked to sit at night with his cigar. Sitting there would have been more pleasant if his efforts at promoting whist had been more successful: 'Whist is a jealous mistress, – and so is a sheep-station.' This was also the busiest time of the year for Fred and his workers: 'the sheep were always being washed, and always being shorn.' Riding offered some relief from the monotony:

> The melancholy note of the magpie was almost the only sound that was heard. Occasionally kangaroos would be seen ... When approached they would move, – always in a line, and with apparent leisure till pursued ... One seems to ride for ever and to come to nothing, and to relinquish at last the very idea of an object. Nevertheless, it was very pleasant. Of all places that I was ever in this place seemed to be the fittest for contemplation.

According to a family legend passed down by his grandson, Trollope

---

*R.H. Horne's comment in his *Contemporary Review* article is worth quoting: 'As for the management of sheep in general, and in detail, I am not aware of any book of travels ... that gives so much information. It is amusing, in fact, quite delightful in its way, to find an English novelist telling you how a sheep is born, washed, and shorn.'

would sit under a tree in the garden and do his allotted pages of writing before breakfast, as he followed his usual custom of writing his travel book as he went along. This grandson also claimed that Rose 'hated the country and said many unkind things about it'. If so, we can only assume that she must have been annoyed at having come half way round the world from a comfortable country house to see her younger son living in a three-room bungalow! Sometimes Trollope liked to listen to Susan Farrand, to whom Fred was engaged, sing the songs of the day, and he presented her with the sheet-music of many ballads.[32]

Four or five meals a day, some prepared by Fred's Chinese cook, provided the other main distraction. Rose had also brought her own cook from England to ensure that her husband had soup and salad to vary the endless diet of mutton. At times it must have seemed like his schooldays at Winchester with mutton appearing daily. Rose's cook also acted as a lady's maid in helping her mistress to arrange her hair. While she was at the station, she met a man of some substance who asked her to marry him. Six months later, when Trollope returned after some more roaming about, he found their former cook 'quite the lady'. He admired her for this, particularly as she had kept her appetite for hard work. To him this incident – just like that of the broken desk in America – had a moral: 'When I think of her, I feel that no woman of that kind ought ... to stay in England if she can take herself or get herself taken to the colonies.'

Towards the end of the book he thought of the farm labourers he had seen in his last postal district, those of Essex, Suffolk and Cambridgeshire:

> I need hardly say that at home in England there are still among us millions of half-starved people ... What must it be to the working man ... [who sees] some advertisement to emigrants ... He goes to the parson, or to the squire ... and is recommended to remain. The adviser ... is probably impregnated with the patriotic idea that there is no place for an Englishman like England. For members of parliament, and men with £5,000 a year, or with prosperous shops in Cheapside ... England is a very comfortable home. No land can beat it. But for Englishmen in general, that is, for the bulk of the working population of the country, it is by no means the best place. A large proportion of our labouring classes cannot even get enough to eat. A still larger proportion are doomed so to work that they can think of nothing but a sufficiency of food.

Always behind Trollope's thoughts on emigration was the fear of a someone who had lived through the Irish Famine and who knew the horrors the poor could suffer if agriculture failed on an overcrowded island. This was a point that also struck the man who wrote the best

review of *Australia and New Zealand*. The poet Richard Hengist Horne
had only recently returned from seventeen years in Australia where he
had done an amazing variety of things, from being a commissioner of
Crown lands and commanding the gold escort from Ballarat to
teaching gymnastics. Although he had written *Australian Facts and
Prospects*, he generously praised Trollope's volumes as 'the best that
have appeared on these most extensive and important of the British
colonies'. 'They are calculated,' he continued, 'to do great and extensive
good':

> Every library of any pretensions should have these volumes, down to the
> smallest mechanics institute; and the close attention of the working
> classes of the United Kingdom – and indeed, the working classes of every
> over-populated country – should be expressly directed to ... them.

Yet the new country, with all its potential, could also witness
complete ruin for men who had invested money and labour in
sheep-farming. This concern may have been at the back of Trollope's
mind when he wrote to the Prime Minister of New South Wales. A
friend, who also sat in the colony's legislature, had put forward Fred's
name as a possible Justice of the Peace. Trollope wrote that he would
be 'much obliged to you if you assist him in this way to enter the
position which I should be glad to see him occupy. I feel sure that he
will not disgrace the bench.' The following September Fred was
appointed a magistrate in the Forbes district.[33]

Despite his evident admiration for much that he saw round him,
Trollope knew that with his temperament and his prosperity England
was the only place for him, and his thoughts often turned there,
particularly when he received letters from friends like George Eliot
and G.H. Lewes:

> I am beginning to find myself too old to be 18 months from home. Not
> that I am fatigued bodily; – but mentally I cannot be at ease with all the
> new people and new things, and I find myself asking myself that terrible
> question of cui bono every morning. I am struggling to make a good book,
> but I feel that it will not be good. It will be desultory and inaccurate; –
> perhaps dull & where shall I be then?

To his old publisher, George Smith, he admitted that he was 'heartily
homesick', particularly as he thought of his favourite pastime: 'I seem
to regret greatly last year's hunting, – feeling that there can be but few
more years of hunting left to me & that I should lose none of it.'
Trollope's frustration can be felt in his *Australia and New Zealand*.

The *Spectator* commented that he must have been 'bored'. This usually friendly journal felt that his 'weariness' came through in his writing and the author, whose 'style usually flows in such a clear, swift stream' produced a book full of 'obscurity and confusion'.[34]

The Trollopes left the station on 13 December, the day before Fred married Susan Farrand, the daughter of a police magistrate, at Forbes which was not too far from the station. It seems rather odd that the Trollopes had come half way round the world only to leave the day before their son's wedding! Actually they had delayed their departure by over a month. In addition Trollope had agreed to give evidence to a New South Wales parliamentary committee in Sydney about the Civil Service (where he would recommend they adopt competitive examinations), to give a lecture in Melbourne on 18 December and afterwards to attend a public dinner in his honour. Perhaps, too, they felt that they would be an encumbrance in the three-roomed home of a newly married couple.

Anthony and Rose returned there a few months later, after a visit to Tasmania, which he found the 'prettiest' of the Australian colonies. The island was already known for its fervent loyalty to the Crown and to English customs: it was 'almost English-mad' according to Trollope. He was amused at their devotion to 'that ancient and most uncomfortable English' mail coach with the guard dressed in red 'because red has been from time immemorial the royal livery of England'. Throughout Australia Trollope was amazed – and a little annoyed – that he met no one who thought there would ever be any need for Australia to break completely from Britain. However, he was not so tolerant about the Australian desire to break from the Victorian worship of free trade. Although he shared to the full the Liberal devotion to this economic policy, which had been raised into a secular religion, it was one of the few topics he tended to be fairly quiet about in his writings. However, in the Tasmanian section of his Australian book he made his most outspoken commitment to it.

Although penal transportation had been stopped a few years before Trollope went to Australia, he noted that there were still 1,985 convicts there – an example of the statistical precision which runs through the book. He thought it was still too early for 'the English world' to decide whether transportation had been a good system. Naturally he had to investigate not only the convicts' living conditions but those of aboriginal criminals on Rottnest Island. The Governor took him round to meet them and then arranged a 'corroboree' or tribal dance where they 'go through various antics with smeared faces and bodies, with spears and sticks, howling and moving their bodies in time'. Trollope was utterly bored, but the Aborigines were delighted when he left five shillings' worth of tobacco as a present. While, in general, he had little sympathy for the Aborigines, he thought it wrong that the white prisoners got tobacco as a right while the black ones had to dance for theirs. Before Trollope left Western Australia he was given the required certificate by a policeman:

I hereby certify that the bearer, A. Trollope ... is not and never has been a prisoner of the Crown in Western Australia.

Signed —— Resident Magistrate.

*

On 29 July 1872 Anthony and Rose left Australia, having spent a year and two days there. They sailed out of Melbourne on their way to New Zealand. A surviving fragment of his diary tells us that he 'worked' and 'smoked' on the voyage. The New Zealand section of his book was a return to his happier and lighter mode of travel-writing. When he first landed he felt it much stranger to be there than in Australia because 'New Zealand had come up in my own days'. Robert Godley, 'my old schoolfellow', who had been captain of cricket during Trollope's second time at Harrow, played a large role in its settlement. Coming from a landed family in County Leitrim, where Trollope had set his first novel, Godley had been horrified by the Irish Famine and, like many Victorians, believed it urgent to establish colonies for the surplus population. He had been part of that group organised by Lord Lyttelton who saw their work as a religious mission.[35] Godley was a Tractarian, whose recently published correspondence had much moved Trollope's own High Church sympathies. Yet it was not only pious thoughts that occurred to Trollope, for he remembered hearing of Sydney Smith's famous remark to Bishop Selwyn, hoping that this missionary would disagree with any cannibal who might eat him!

By the time Trollope reached his inn and had his bath he felt he was back in England. With his comfort restored, he immediately began firing questions about 'the price of tea and sugar and the amount of wages'. The longer he stayed, the more he felt at home: 'In New Zealand everything is English.' Where he saw some scenery that did not remind him of England, it recalled the coast of County Cork. By the end of his visit he had reached a conclusion similar to that of many modern travellers: 'The New Zealander among John Bulls is the most John-Bullish. He admits the supremacy of England to every place in the world, only he is more English than any Englishman at home.'

He had arrived in the New Zealand winter and hospitable people continually told him he had come at the wrong time. As an experienced traveller, he was used to people telling him that he had come at the wrong time to see some great sight. On his way to Dunedin he settled in bed one night in a rather primitive inn, constructed of corrugated iron and thin walls which allowed every sound to be heard. As the landlady was arranging her hair in her bedroom, Trollope could overhear her husband ask, 'So this is Mr. Anthony Trollope?' When she said yes the man announced, 'Well, he must be a —— fool to come travelling in this country in such weather as this.' Trollope, at that point, was in full agreeement.

It was said to be the worst winter in living memory, and several feet of snow covered the roads. The fifth day of this coach trip was the worst, and Trollope and another male passenger walked for twelve miles to relieve the burden on the horses. The driver wanted to turn back, but Trollope would not hear of it, no more than he would fifteen years before when he resisted a similar request from a guide taking him to a volcano in Costa Rica. 'I hate going back, and I made up my mind that if the mud and snow were no worse than British mud or British snow, we would make our way through.' The coach was suddenly halted by huge drifts, and the horses were only got out after two hours of shovelling by the driver and Trollope. They were no sooner back inside than the horses slipped and Trollope was out shovelling again. The driver later remembered that he and Trollope had to take the place of the horses and pull the coach downhill. At one point Trollope remarked that he was 'more at ease with a pen than a shovel'. Eventually Rose had to get out to trudge through the snow, which caused her petticoats to become 'balled up with the soft snow'. The driver recalled that 'she was an enormous size and a wonderful sight to behold'. Whether he meant that she was naturally large or that the snow made her appear as such is not clear.[36] It was hours before they reached an inn where Rose warmed herself in front of a fire while the landlady 'comforted her with dry stockings'. One wonders whether it was then that Rose decided that her colonial travels had come to an end. Trollope sat nearby, having already had his dinner along with some brandy and water.

Everywhere in New Zealand, as in Australia, there was a desire to see the celebrated writer, and the colony's government went out of their way to treat him as an honoured guest. Just then New Zealand needed some encouraging publicity to increase immigration: the Maori Wars had dragged on throughout the 1860s and the colony's debt had risen to extraordinary heights. The Trollopes were the guests of the

Governor at Government House in Wellington, and at the final banquet honouring him the Chief Justice took the chair. In 1937 one old lady remembered her excitement when an opportunity presented itself to see the novelist in her own town, Invercargill. She had first encountered his works two years before as a little girl of ten when she had read *Framley Parsonage* in some old issues of the *Cornhill*. She hurried to the church and watched 'the stalwart man of letters, whose tread shook the church' as he was guided to his seat by the parish priest. She recalled:[37]

> If he was not actually six feet in height, he succeeded in looking much more. A burly, upstanding man with a massive head, made more leonine by the whiskers and beard of old Victorian days; these, with his hair greying, an English complexion as of one living much in the open, and kindly blue-grey eyes to match. Such was Anthony Trollope as I saw him those brief moments. And I can imagine his voice, hearty and genial to match his aspect.

As always on his travels, he wanted to know what people read. If his coach paused in any town he hurried to the library, and he was pleased to see many books 'well-thumbed'. He rarely mentioned how excited readers were at the arrival of a man whose novels gave them the best depiction of 'home'. When he visited Dunedin the local subscription library placed a special advertisement: that 'ANTHONY TROLLOPE'S NOVELS may be had at WISE'S LIBRARY Subscription 21/- New books and magazines by every Suez Mail.' In Auckland a bookseller sent a letter to the newspaper announcing that he had large supplies of most of Trollope's novels, even *The Macdermots of Ballycloran*. At a banquet given in his honour before leaving the colony he spoke of his pleasure at finding books, including some of his own works, in almost every house he had visited. Trollope had high hopes for the future of New Zealand and said so both in his books and in his articles. Only two things troubled him: the staggering size of the colonial debt and the dangerous tendency to rely on government. With the authority of a man who had played a key role in managing the largest public service of his time, he declared:

> Government cannot get the same work out of its workmen that is got by private employers. It cannot build a ship, or manage an estate, or erect a palace with that economy which a private master can ensure ... A profuse expenditure of government money in any community will taint the whole of it with the pervading sin.

It has taken a century for Trollope to be proved right on this, as on so much else. In spite of his optimism he resisted the temptation to write a novel about New Zealand, although a few years later he would set one short story, 'Catherine Carmichael', there, as well as using some aspects of the islands in his strangest novel, *The Fixed Period*. When he had been in Melbourne Sir George Bowen, the new Governor of Victoria, fresh from his work in New Zealand, had urged him to write a novel on the recent war with the Maoris, but Trollope declined, saying: 'It was a good suggestion', but his 'forte was observation and not imagination.'[38] He did think the fate of the Maoris could be the subject for a poem, but 'such an attempt is not my way'. The *Spectator* also thought that he would have put his visit to better purpose had he written Australian novels rather than a huge travel book.

Perhaps no aspect of Trollope's opinions is more opposite, or indeed repugnant, to those of most modern readers than his attitude towards the 'native races' he encountered in his travels. Although he professed himself 'ignorant of Darwin' he was as affected by his teachings as modern people are by Freud's. He accepted it as a fact that 'natural-selection' would mean that the native races would disappear before the restless advance of English civilisation. At home he also accepted it is as inevitable that groups he respected, such as old-fashioned Tory squires, would meet a similar fate. At times he was troubled about the fate of what he saw as 'savages', but he saw no way it could be stopped. In New Zealand he 'had the pleasure of meeting' one of the Maori chiefs and was told that this convert to Christianity embodied a step in the civilising process: his grandfather had killed men and eaten them and then been eaten himself; his father had killed men and eaten them, but the convert had only killed men. Trollope found the Maori 'more highly gifted than other savage nations I have seen', yet he was certain that they would 'melt' away before the irresistible march of Anglo-Saxon civilisation. 'I encountered nothing but Maori friendship; – but at the same time I encountered no Maori progress.' In all his colonial travels his concern was for the future prosperity of colonial settlers – ordinary Britons who could find their way there. He wrote to one New Zealander declining to give a lecture because 'my attention is almost more than fully occupied with my endeavours to learn something of the British settlements'.[39] His breadth of vision was in many ways great and was not limited by personal inconvenience, whether it was a rude American porter breaking his desk or a cook leaving him to better herself in Australia. Yet all vision, however broad, is still partial, and his focused on the fate of his own people.

However, before leaving New Zealand for San Francisco, Trollope had an interesting experience with some Maoris when he went on a lengthy expedition on horseback to the famous geysers at Lakes Tarawera and Rotomahana, south of Auckland. This required a ride of several days, but he had been given an excellent guide and two orderlies by the authorities, anxious for him to find as much to praise as possible. The guide was Captain Gilbert Mair, a hero of the recent Maori wars. Six constables rowed them across the twenty-odd miles of Lake Taupo on North Island, with Trollope apparently refreshing himself with several nips from a flask, presumably of brandy, that he always carried on his journeys. One of the rowing constables told a later traveller that he 'had read every word the fellow ever wrote' – a far greater feat of endurance than rowing twenty miles – but was furious that Trollope did not give him any money and decided, 'writing pretty is one thing and acting like a gentleman is another'. If the anecdote is true, Trollope's uncharacteristic meanness may have come from several earlier experiences in his first days in New Zealand, when attempts by either of the Trollopes to give some money to servants or others who helped them were met with great resentment.[40]

One night Trollope and Captain Mair decided to bathe in one of the hot pools behind their inn. When the two men reached the pool they found 'three Maori damsels' enjoying the water. Drawing sustenance from the Garter motto, *Honi soit qui mal y pense*, Trollope slipped into the pool and spent a pleasant half-hour in the hot water. In his book he says the damsels encouraged his enjoyment by patting him on the back. Half a century later, Captain Mair reported one detail Trollope had left out:[41]

After we had been in the water some time the old chap said 'I wish I had something to lean against,' and so I whispered to a fine young woman of splendid proportions, popularly known as 'the Duchess,' who immediately set her capacious back against him, whereat he exclaimed 'Well, Mair, this is very delightful, don't you know, but I think I did wise in leaving Mrs. Trollope in Auckland.'

CHAPTER FOURTEEN

The Man among his Books

The Trollopes arrived in San Francisco in early November 1872, having changed ships in Honolulu. Then they had a 3,000-mile journey across America by train, pausing in Salt Lake City, where Trollope called on 'the great polygamist' Brigham Young, second leader or President of the Church of the 'Latter Day Saints'. Years before, in *Doctor Thorne*, Trollope had had a laugh at 'the religious observances as regards women, of a Brigham Young' [XXXII]. The President, not even doing Trollope the courtesy of inviting him into his sanctum, met him at the front door and asked whether he was a miner. When told his guest was not, the desert patriarch demanded: 'Then how do you earn your bread?' Trollope's reply, that he was a writer, was spurned. 'I'm sure you're a miner.' The audience was over. This must have given added amusement to a man who had recently decided to give up his 'duty' of descending mines on his travels. As so often, Trollope turned the joke on himself: 'I was properly punished, as I had been vain enough to conceive that he would have heard my name.' Young's ignorance must be excused not only by his semi-illiterate background but by the constant duties of a man who had fathered fifty-six children and had had somewhere between nineteen and twenty-seven wives (Latter Day Saint ecclesiologists are in some dispute on this point) which left him little time to read of Lily Dale or Archdeacon Grantly.

When the Trollopes reached London shortly before Christmas, they had been away for over a year and a half. They did not even have a home to return to as they had given up Waltham House before leaving and had sold most of their furniture, saving only a few treasured possessions such as Rose's prize-winning firescreen with its embroidery of the Trollope arms. The house had originally been taken because it was in his postal district. It had come to mean a great deal to Trollope, as there he could play a minor version of his favourite role, the English country gentleman. Without his salary and minus the large amounts of capital he had bestowed on his two sons, Waltham House threatened to become a burden. He had hoped to find a tenant but had failed, and the house stood empty for almost two years before he was forced to sell it at a loss. He had written in *The Eustace Diamonds*, which had been appearing in the *Fortnightly Review* while he was away, 'Let nobody dream that he can be somebody without having to pay for that honour; – unless, indeed, he be a clergyman ... In some insidious unforeseen manner, – in a way that can only be understood after much experience, – these luxuries of fashion do make a heavy pull on a modest income' [XXXII].

Trollope's income had hardly been modest by any standard: for about ten years, from 1862 to 1871, it had averaged £4,500 a year and occasionally soared well above this: in 1869 it had reached £6,994 18s 1d. This is put into some perspective by figures given by an Essex squire, John Bateman, who compiled a statistical survey called *The Great Landowners of Great Britain and Ireland* in the 1870s. In order to explain the meaning of the statistics, Bateman invented a typical squire with 3,500 acres producing an income of £5,000. Almost a third of this disappeared immediately into pensions settled upon his mother and other relations. After the inevitable expenses involved in keeping up a landed estate, the squire was left with a net income of £1,032 to pay for his and his immediate family's necessities and pleasures. This might be set against the £1,200 Trollope received for *Lady Anna*, to which he devoted eight weeks of writing at sea on his way to Australia. It shows how well-off Trollope was although, like so many people thus favoured, he liked to claim he was not, just as he liked to say that his poor sight was 'blindness'. People who take their own cook to Australia are not wanting for money!

Trollope's income, like his blood, put him clearly in the lower ranks of the gentry without most of the obligations that fell on the owner of an estate big enough to produce a net income as large as his. A landed aristocrat like Lord Stanley may have found Trollope 'middle-class', but from the less lofty perspective of most other Englishmen Trollope was by income and inclinations on the outer fringes of those 'Upper Ten Thousand' who fill the pages of his Palliser novels. It is true that most of the aristocracy had far greater incomes than Trollope: a great magnate like the Duke of Devonshire had £180,750 from his estates alone and Trollope's cousin, Sir John, recently ennobled as Lord Kesteven, had £10,856 a year from land. Yet many other ennobled politicians, as well as several dozen peers created for legal and military reasons, had incomes far under Trollope's. A few weeks before the Trollopes returned to England the *Spectator* claimed that only 60,000

British families out of 4,600,000 were in the wealthiest or 'comfortable' class which required about £800 a year. Trollope enjoyed at least five times that amount.[1]

While Trollope had inherited his mother's taste for the 'luxuries of fashion', he had always saved one-third of what he made. This must have provided some of the money to set Henry up in publishing and to provide Fred with thousands of sheep. Having disposed of so much capital and at the same time being faced with the need to acquire and furnish a house, Trollope occasionally exercised his novelist's imagination to convince himself he was 'poor'. He wrote on 20 December that he was giving up cigars for a pipe because at over eightpence each they had become too expensive: he would be forced to live on tea and toast at his club since that was only sixpence. Neither resolution was followed, although from time to time he made an effort to cut down on his smoking. Of course, he was increasingly aware that his prosperity depended upon his pen and that he would have to provide for the pension he had lost because of early retirement. Upon their return the Trollopes took rooms in Holles Street off Cavendish Square until they bought a house in Montagu Square, using the money from *The Eustace Diamonds* to meet some of the payments until they had money from the sale of Waltham House. The new house had to be papered and painted before they could move in, but Trollope was there in time for his fifty-eighth birthday on 24 April 1873. Soon they were entertaining old friends such as Robert Browning, Wilkie Collins and Kate Field to dinner.[2]

Trollope had been so involved in moving and hunting that he had almost neglected his writing. His first literary task upon his return was, of course, to complete *Australia and New Zealand*, which he did on 15 January 1873. High praise of the colonies was not just confined to his book, for he told a friend that he had seen 'a very much better life than we have here ... The horror of this country is that let men work as they will there is not and cannot be enough for them all.'[3] The following June he broke off from the major novel on which he was now working to devote the month to a short novel, really a novella, about a young Englishman's struggles on his Australian sheep station. For *Harry Heathcote of Gangoil* Trollope drew on Fred's experiences and his own recent trip. The short work – it is under 40,000 words – was done for the Christmas number of the *Graphic* and Trollope received £450. For many readers, its main interest was the account of how English Christmas customs and food were kept alive in the heat of an Australian December; to Trollope it served as another, personal tribute to the colonies and to his own son's efforts.

*

The major novel whose writing Trollope had interrupted to write his Christmas number was *The Way We Live Now*. On 1 April Trollope signed the contract with Chapman and Hall. April was devoted to settling into the new London home, and he began the novel on 1 May when he wrote twelve pages. Three days before Christmas he wrote: 'Completed in 34 weeks (instead of 32) – but five weeks occupied on Harry Heathcote and therefore this novel, *The Way We Live Now* has been done in 29 weeks.'[4] (In addition to the time devoted to his Australian story he and Rose had a fortnight's holiday in Killarney in August.) This book, which annoyed so many of his devoted readers in his time, has become one of his most admired novels today. It is a story of the dishonesty and corruption which have spread throughout society – whether it be the novelist, Lady Carbury, scheming to secure favourable reviews, or old families desperate to gain ill-gotten wealth through marriage or by fawning on speculators. The novel reflects both his long-standing obsession with dishonesty and his own immediate mood, which was gloomy and disoriented. The fact that he had lost money in selling one house and was spending more on a second made him acutely conscious of money, particularly now that he had no salary and, even worse, no pension. Complaining to Rusden, his friend in Australia, about the cost of furniture, he recalled that once a house could be furnished for £200 but now it required £1,500 plus another £500 for 'prettiness'. These figures reflect more the taste Trollope had acquired for the 'luxuries of fashion' than any tremendous increase in the cost of furniture. He was hearing a similar tale from his brother, who was selling his villa in Florence. Tom had planned to return to England but then was appointed the *Standard*'s correspondent in Rome. He lost £10,000 on the sale of his villa because the price of Florentine property fell after the Italian capital was moved to Rome.[5] Such news was not likely to have increased Anthony's regard for speculators.

Everywhere he looked he seemed to see dishonesty and corruption. His travels had brought him back through America, where sordid scandals continued to rack the Grant administration. It is significant that one of the speculators in *The Way We Live Now* 'had sprung out of some Californian gully ... perhaps ignorant of his own father and mother' [XXXV]. As Trollope settled down to his novel the Scudamore scandal about Post Office officials' shifting funds to buy private telegraph companies not only forced the resignation of two old schoolmates, Robert Lowe, as Chancellor of the Exchequer, and William Monsell, as Postmaster General, but almost brought down Gladstone's government. Trollope took some pleasure in the fact that his successful rivals, Scudamore and Yates, were behind this malpractice but he still had a great pride in his old department whose reputation had been sullied, something he would allude to in this novel [L].

Nor could Trollope look to his family for comfort, for he had discovered a domestic scandal brewing. In *The Last Chronicle of Barset*, the Archdeacon, furious that his son Henry is planning a 'bad' marriage, laments that it was as horrible as 'if he took her out of the streets' [LVI]. Trollope arrived home from Australia to find that his own son Henry was proposing to do exactly that – to marry a girl 'from the streets'. The story survives because Joseph Langford interrupted his usual Christmas Eve letter of greetings to tell his employer, John Blackwood, 'You will be surprised to hear that Harry Trollope has gone on a visit to Australia ... It will be attributed to a business quarrel but the cause is one which has troubled our sex from the earliest periods and the young man has shown himself amenable to reason and obedient to parental authority. Trollope has behaved with his usual promptness.' 'Promptness' is something of an understatement – Trollope had only been home for a few days! He had discussed the crisis with a few close friends from the Garrick Club like Sir Charles Taylor and Henry O'Neil, the artist. He may also have wanted the advice of someone whose own life had been tinged with scandal, for G.H. Lewes noted in his diary on New Year's Day, 1873: 'Trollope came to lunch. Told me of his trouble with Harry wanting to marry a woman of the town.'[6]

There is another factor worth mentioning as an influence on the novelist's disillusion at this time. About two years before, his view that an Empire hastened its fall by corruption received powerful support when Napoleon III's Imperial edifice toppled after his defeat by Prussia. Like most Englishmen, Trollope had supported the Prussians, not realising, in the words of one diplomat, that Europe had exchanged a mistress for a master. Trollope's attitude towards this catastrophe is revealed by an unusual word in his fiction. In his novels he normally avoided words like 'prostitute', although he used it in serious articles. However, in the opening chapter of one short novel which he had begun in 1870, *An Eye For An Eye*, we are told how an heir to an earldom is ruined by a 'French prostitute'. Trollope began writing that novel on 13 September, the day before *The Times* published details of the safe arrival in England of Empress Eugénie and her son, the Prince Imperial.[7] When Trollope started *The Way We Live Now* in May 1873 the memory of Napoleon III's France would have been again in his mind because the ex-Emperor had died four months earlier and *The Times* had had numerous articles about him.

Trollope was not alone in worrying about the general trend of English society. Queen Victoria, who had had her own share of troubles with her sons, had been worried for some time that the aristocracy was becoming increasingly debased because the young men were 'ignorant, luxurious and self-indulgent' while the young women were 'fast, frivolous and imprudent'. She, too, attributed much of the decline to the French example. This was one subject on which she and Gladstone agreed, and they discussed it only two weeks before Trollope signed the contract for his novel. Gladstone, for his part, said in that same year that 'Ploutocracy' produces 'a bastard aristocracy and aristocracy shows too much disposition, in Parliament especially, to join hands with this bastard.' He believed that the increasing desire for great wealth was causing corruption 'in the Clubs and in the Army'. This sounds like a summary of *The Way We Live Now*.[8]

Of course, some of this was the natural reaction of people beginning to feel themselves old and shaking their greying heads at the antics of the young. Yet there was a perceptible change occurring in English society. *The Times* was becoming particularly outspoken in its criticism of the growth of commercial dishonesty and 'banking speculation'; like Trollope, it saw a connection between this and the 'all pervading financial delinquencies in the United States'. In America Mark Twain and C.D. Warner were at work on their novel *The Gilded Age*, depicting financial and political corruption there, at the same time as Trollope was writing *The Way We Live Now*. Trollope almost certainly knew much about the involvement of Colonel John Stanley, son of the former Postmaster General, as a director of the Emma silver mine in America. This corrupt company, promoted by the American Minister in London, destroyed the fortunes of many credulous Englishmen. Indeed Trollope may have visited Col. Stanley on his way through Salt Lake City, and it is no surprise to find the American speculators in the novel referring to that place quite frequently. Several decades later a perceptive observer looking back on the 1870s remembered that two things happened: the increasing importance of Americans in Society and the fact that 'the Stock Exchange began to make itself felt as a social power outside the City ... Before that time hardly anyone in the West End of London understood anything about stocks and shares.' Trollope himself had become involved with City financiers in his 1869 negotiations to make Henry a partner in Chapman and Hall. The older attitude towards 'speculation' was often recalled by John Tilley in his anecdote about a country gentleman bemoaning that his daughter was marrying a 'pawnbroker'. When told it was a 'stockbroker' the old squire asked, 'What, pray, is the difference?' Nor were novel readers kept in ignorance of the dangers of corruption as Bulwer Lytton's last novel, *The Parisians*, recounting how France had been humiliated, began to appear in *Blackwood's* only two months before Trollope's return from New Zealand.[9] Once again Trollope had sensed – just as he had with *The Warden* – a topic of public concern.

The Way We Live Now revolves round Augustus Melmotte, who appears out of nowhere to play a crucial role in English commercial and political life. Trollope's notes show how he thought out details of his characters: 'Melmotte's house south side of the square' and 'Melmotte has been in prison at Hamburg'. Many parallels for Melmotte have been sought but one cannot do better than the career of Albert Gottheimer, the first man to realise how a fortune could be made by using the protection of limited liability. He raised the enormous sum of about £24,000,000 in capital, mainly from widows, clergymen and other small investors and then lost £20,000,000 of it. Like Melmotte, he became an MP, changed his name to Grant and in 1873 began to build himself a huge house next to Kensington Palace. In that same year he purchased Leicester Square. Like Grant, Melmotte was involved in speculation about mines. Just as Grant's grand house was used for only one occasion, a famous Society ball, Melmotte's was used only once, for the visit of the Emperor of China. For this Trollope drew on Society's kow-towing to another eastern despot, the Shah of Persia, who visited Britain six weeks after Trollope began his novel. Grant, unlike Melmotte, was made a Baron by the new King of Italy (himself a man of little morality). A popular ditty contained, as so often, sound sense:[10]

> Honours a King can give, honour he can't:
> And Grant without honour is a Baron Grant

Trollope's notes for what he called the 'Carbury novel' reveal that by beginning and ending his story with the lady novelist, he hoped to show that in the end decency can reassert itself. Yet this optimistic message is obscured by the figure of Melmotte. To the first readers of the novel this seemed even more the case as the cover of the part issues showed scenes from Melmotte's life observed by a miserable Father Time. To many *The Way We Live Now* has a strong element of anti-semitism because Melmotte, the mysterious alien widely thought to be Jewish, comes to dominate, although that was not the author's original intention. Melmotte seemed to take over the novelist as well as everything he encountered. Actually it is never clearly stated that Melmotte, 'the great French swindler', is Jewish although it is clearly stated that Madame Melmotte is. His evil has nothing to do with religion or race. He is an 'alien': someone who appears from nowhere and who has no role in an ordered society but usurps every place he can find. Yet Trollope's outrage is not directed so much at creatures like Melmotte as at the reactions of 'Society' towards him. In the novel one of the few pleasant characters is Roger Carbury, a Tory squire who expresses the novelist's own view as to Melmotte's significance:

> A hollow vulgar fraud from beginning to end, – too insignificant for you and me to talk of, were it not that his position is a sign of the degeneracy of the age ... They who do set the example go to his feasts ... What follows as a natural consequence? Men reconcile themselves to swindling. Though they themselves mean to be honest, dishonesty of itself is no longer odious to them ... the existence of a Melmotte is not compatible with a wholesome state of things in general [LV].

Trollope may have come across financiers with some of Melmotte's traits when he was hunting, because in 1873 he transferred his main base from Essex to Buckinghamshire, to hunt with the hounds of Baron Ferdinand de Rothschild there and in Bedfordshire. Melmotte is certainly not a portrait either of Baron Ferdinand or of another acquaintance of Trollope's, Baron Meyer de Rothschild, as he liked both men. Indeed he was among the first to be asked to write in Ferdinand de Rothschild's guest book, the *Livre d'Or*, when visiting the Baron at Leighton Buzzard:[11]

> You want me to indite something elegant and terse,
> I never writ a poem and I seldom made a verse.
> A novel in three volumes you would think a little long –
> A sermon or an essay would be coming out too strong.
> An anagram or rebus is quite beyond my power;
> Or a satyre, short in twenty words, ill-natured sharp and sour.
> Pretty little witty things have never been my game.
> So I'll just write, as I always write, my own ill written name.
>
> Anthony Trollope
March 10 – 1873

Trollope's attitude towards Jews in *The Way We Live Now* seems at first sight strikingly different from the sympathetic portrayal in *Nina Balatka*. Behind his picture of Melmotte's circle stands Trollope's hatred of Disraeli, which at times became quite irrational. He was not even mollified by Disraeli's kind comment to him at a dinner at Lord Stanhope's: 'I have long known, Mr. Trollope, your churchmen and churchwomen; may I congratulate you on the same happy lightness of touch in the portrait of your new adventuress.' Since Disraeli was speaking of *The Eustace Diamonds*, this was not all that long before *The Way We Live Now* began appearing. Trollope has the leader of the Conservative Party assisting Melmotte into the House of Commons and, lest contemporary readers needed any extra help to recognise 'Dizzy', Trollope reminds them: 'Melmotte was not the first vulgar man whom the Conservatives had taken by the hand, and patted on the back, and told that he was a god.' As so often, Trollope provides another character from the same group or profession to present opposite qualities. Thus Georgiana Longstaffe nearly marries Ezekiel Breghert, a Jewish banker. 'He was,' Trollope tells us, 'an honest man', and as such a rare creature in this novel! [LXXIX]. As one critic well says, it is the Christian girl Georgiana, daughter of an old gentry family, 'who has the traditional attributes of greed and craftiness so often a part of the Jewish stereotype'.[12] It is dangerous to try to understand Trollope's attitude towards any group by looking at only one character or even one novel.

Trollope's notes for *The Way We Live Now* survive among his business papers and show that he still sometimes drew on real people for minor roles. Thus the bishop in the novel is based on 'Old Longley', Trollope's last headmaster at Harrow and a man whom he admired. He had become Archbishop of Canterbury in 1862, only to die six years later. The office of one of the newspapers in the novel is based on the *Pall Mall* offices, and one character, Paul Montague, is given the name of Trollope's new London address. The most important minor character based on a real person is Father Barham, the convert Roman Catholic priest who spends his time attacking the religious beliefs of any Anglican who befriends him. In him we see a different view of a Catholic priest. It is difficult to think of any other group who did so well in Trollope's earlier books. A priest had been the hero of his first novel: 'in the character of Father John there I have drawn as thoroughly good and fine a man as I know how to depict.' A French *curé* is an admirable character in *La Vendée*, and in 'Father Giles of Ballycloran' the priest is not only likeable but worthy of respect. In *The Way We Live Now* Trollope was settling a personal grievance, something he seldom did in his writing. He explained this to a Catholic lady, Mary Holmes, the former governess to Thackeray's daughters. He corresponded with her for many years and wrote about his works with an intensity few others saw:[13]

The parish priest I knew myself, & loved, & opened my house to him, and fed him when he was fearfully, horribly, hungry from sheer want, – and he was a gentleman at all points; but I could not go on with him, not because he was intent on converting me, for which I did not care; but because he would say nasty things of my religion which could only be answered by nasty things as to his, which I could not say to any guest, or to any sincere Christian. But yet he was a man who will certainly go to heaven, if a mortal may presume to say so much of any man.

The priest – called in his notes, the 'Waltham priest' – was the Rev. George Bampfield who was known for 'controversial writing' and for building new churches, something which his fictional counterpart, Father Barham, does – even bursting in on Melmotte to obtain a donation for the new St Fabricius Church. Trollope's objection was not to Catholic priests but, as he says in the novel, to 'fervent Romanists' which some of the converts became. Many of them, particularly the minor ones, abandoned all concepts of courtesy in their crusade for their new Church. Like Barham, Bampfield was an Oxford man who 'went over to Rome' in 1855, ten years after Newman. He set up a Roman Catholic chapel in Eleanor Road, Waltham Cross in about 1861 and remained there till about 1864 when he left for Barnet, which means that Trollope's memory had long festered before it was lanced in his general assault upon dishonesty. '[I] opened my house to him in full friendship. He was a thoroughly conscientious man ... what we call a pervert and you a convert,' wrote Trollope to Mary Holmes, but the priest's fanaticism meant that 'I was obliged to drop him. He made himself absolutely unbearable.'[14] In referring to 'St Fabricius' Trollope is having a joke at Bampfield's expense, one based on Roman history: Gaius Fabricius Luscinus was a consul renowned for his opposition to the growing luxuries of Rome. Although Barham is himself a good and honest man, he has a place in the novel because 'fervent Romanists' – and 'fervent' is the key word – employ 'dishonest' means to achieve their ends. Trollope's own view, his civilised and 'ecumenical' view, appears in this novel in almost the same words he would use in his *Life of Cicero*: 'I suppose men will go to heaven ... by doing as they would be done by' [LV].

The first of the novel's twenty parts, which sold at a shilling each, began appearing in February 1874 and ended in September of the next year. Trollope later admitted that by taking 'the whip of the satirist' he gave the book the fault common to satire: 'The accusations are exaggerated. The vices implied are coloured so as to make effect rather than to represent truth ... The spirit which produces the satire is honest enough, but the very desire which moves the satirist to do his work energetically makes him dishonest.' As he had said concerning 'satyre' when writing in Ferdinand de Rothschild's book, the novel leaves an 'ill-natured sharp and sour' taste. Ironically the corruption he had set out to attack ended up turning him from his normal view that characters must present an honest balance of good and bad. That is why *The Way We Live Now*, while a very good, perhaps a great, novel, is not a good 'Trollopean' novel. As Tom Trollope wrote to one publisher, '*[The] Way We Live Now* was a charming book to us exiles ... so very consolatory! Upon my life you must have become a delightful set of people ... at least if there is truth in Anthony's picture.' There was 'truth in Anthony's picture', but it was an Impressionist painting with too many dark colours. He cautioned a friend who objected to some of the portrayal in the novel, 'you must remember that no satirist can take the exact state of things and represent it ... The man whom he sees stealing a shilling he must accuse of stealing two shillings, – or a sovereign – It is the proclivity and not the depth of the sin which he handles.'[15]

Reviewers on the whole were not impressed and shared Trollope's later view that the satire was overdone: the *Spectator* said: 'The author has made a mistake, which he made once before in the disagreeable story called *Brown, Jones, and Robinson*, and has surrounded his characters with an atmosphere of sordid baseness which prevents enjoyment like an effluvium ... There is no relief, no pleasantness, the subordinate comic characters even being disagreeable.' The *Saturday Review*, while referring to Trollope's 'extraordinary fertility and resource', also commented on his 'indiscriminate onslaught'. The *Examiner* missed 'the agreeable play of kindly humour which in Thackeray, Mr. Trollope's great predecessor in depicting the illusions of Vanity Fair, tones down the harsh judgment'. Almost alone in praising the book was *The Times*, which said that the book was 'a likeness of the face which society wears to-day'. It did not find the satire too heavy-handed and referred to the author's 'extreme fairness'. This reviewer did not find Melmotte a villain but a man who 'compels a certain sort of grudging admiration ... by his audacity, his courage, his resources, and – his success'. It was, in short, 'one of Mr. Trollope's very best stories', and the reviewer concluded: 'It should make us look into our own lives and habits of thought, and see how ugly and mean and sordid they appear, when Truth, the policeman, turns his dark lantern suddenly upon them, and finds such a pen as Mr. Trollope's to write a report of what he sees.'[16]

*

'Montagu Square and Bryanston Square are twin deformities' put up by 'economical modern builders' to 'dispose of with profit to those who wish to live near the great'. This was the scathing assessment of one later Victorian writer on London. 'The mansions in Montagu Square are constructed after the most approved Brighton fashion, each with its little bulging protuberance to admit of a peep into the neighbours' parlour.'[17] Some of those passing by the house must have wished to peer into the window – in a suitably discreet manner – to see something of one of the most famous writers of their age. Yet as Kate Field had once been told, Trollope, like all prominent Victorians, was dedicated to keeping out the peering glances not only of passing strangers but of prying biographers.

To an old hunting friend Trollope described the Square as 'not a gorgeous neighbourhood, but one which will suit my declining years and modest resources'. Since it was 'north of the Park', the price was reasonable. The square featured tall white town houses looking onto a central garden suitably fenced with iron railings. It provided elegant homes for those on the borderland between the gentry and the upper middle classes, people like Trollope's old friends, the Pollocks: Sir Frederick was an important barrister, the Queen's Remembrancer and a man who engaged in that popular Victorian pastime of translating Dante, while his wife was a minor author. They had been frequent visitors to Waltham House and the Trollopes had stayed at their house, 59 Montagu Square. For Trollope the move to 39 Montagu Square meant that he would have to write in the middle of a bustling and noisy city, 'the capital of the human race' as a new Londoner, Henry James, called it. No longer did Trollope have the peace of Waltham House where the echo of a croquet ball might provide the only noise coming through the library windows. London was increasingly bothered with German bands and Italian organ-grinders, the latter unmindful, as the *Illustrated London News* noted, of 'the anguish he inflicts upon sensitive nerves'. The fact that Montagu Square belied its name and was more of a rectangle than a square could have made the noise worse. However, Trollope, in an essay at the end of the decade, was thankful that it was spared at least some of the clamour:

> Here, in our quiet square, the beneficent police have done wonders for our tranquillity, – not, however, without creating for me personally a separate trouble in having to encounter the stern reproaches of the middle-aged leader of the band when he asks me in mingled German and English accents whether I do not think that he too as well as I ... [as] he points to the nine stalwart, well-cropped, silent and sorrowing Teutons

around him, – whether he and they should not be allowed to earn their bread as well as I.

As always, after his initial fury, Trollope struggled to understand another person's point of view. He accepted that the 'comparative peace within the heart of a huge city is purchased at the cost of many tears'. His next comment seems to summon up much of the disparity of Victorian London that he observed on walks to and from his clubs: 'I see in some small crowded street the ill-shod feet of little children spinning round in perfect rhythm of a dance, two little tots each holding the other by their ragged duds, while an Italian boy grinds at his big box ... I say to myself that a novelist's schemes ... may be purchased too dearly by the silencing of the music of the poor.'[18] There are few better portraits of Trollope's trying to fathom 'the way we live now' than of the wealthy novelist looking at bare-footed urchins and concluding that they had as much right to pleasure as he had to peace.

*

If during the 1870s we had strolled into the tranquillity of Montagu Square, climbed the three steps and walked through the door under the half-circle fan-light, what would we have found? The house was not as large as that at Waltham but it was still a reasonably sized town house, certainly for a family of four which included Rose's niece, Florence Bland, and sometimes Henry or at least his books. A new cook saw to the meals in the basement kitchen. There were several maids and one manservant, who was inclined to sneak out to join his friends for too many drinks. The servants would have had small rooms on the top floor. Visiting ladies were usually asked not to bring their own maids as Rose's lady's maid could see to their clothes and arrange their hair. A new visitor would hand the maid his card and she might disappear upstairs with it. The statement that the master was in his library might cause such a visitor to say he did not want to disturb the writer and hurry off, as one American acquaintance did. When Trollope met him at dinner a few days later he was annoyed that this American diplomat had been fearful of disturbing a novelist because he might be in the midst of writing a tender love scene. 'What if I was?' roared Trollope.[19]

If we had been more persistent, we would have been ushered into the room where he was at work. His library of books was too large to be fitted into one room so he had his study on the ground floor, behind the dining-room – with its 'bulging protuberant' windows. More of his books were in the room above as he had confiscated 'one part of the large double drawing-room, the largest rooms in the house'. (Some years later John Murray's son, Hallam, was able to arrange art lectures in his drawing-room at Montagu Square for at least thirty Edwardian ladies in full fig and all could fit into the room.) Trollope normally received literary friends and visitors in this upstairs library. The first sight when the door opened would be the bulky figure of the novelist seated at his desk writing with his straight pen. He would jump up, hurry to the mantle, where lay 'a whole army of spectacles for the exact pair which should enable him to read the face of his guest'. That done, he would seat himself in his armchair 'not however occupying it for long, but jumping up violently, and taking up his usual position on the hearthrug, too impetuous even for the appearance of ease'. The hearthrug was a sort of throne to Victorians from which they could orate *ex cathedra*. In his days of prosperity Adolphus Crosbie, in *The Small House at Allington*, always occupied the hearthrug at his club, pontificating to his friends. This distinction was also made at the highest level: at Windsor Castle only the Royal Family stood on the hearthrug and when the novelist Bulwer Lytton made his first appearance there he wandered round the room so casually that the Queen whispered in some agitation, 'If you don't do something to attract his attention, in another minute he'll be – on the rug!' So Trollope, in this as in almost everything the quintessential Victorian, would stand on his hearthrug speaking about his friends, offering help, quoting Horace or denouncing Disraeli. There was one great change since the Waltham House days: as Trollope no longer had a garden, he was permitted to smoke his cigars in his library. In this Rose was moving, however reluctantly, with the times as tobacco consumption had doubled in the last thirty years.[20]

Perhaps the visitor was a young writer come to ask advice or to solicit influence. Such was Cecilia Meetkerke, who had married one of those sons that Adolphus Meetkerke had fathered in old age to deny Thomas Anthony Trollope his expected inheritance. She has come to ask his help in getting an article into the *Fortnightly*. Normally he is a polite gentleman with ladies but in his library, on his hearthrug, discussing literature it is different, as he explains to her. 'I like a good contradictory conversation in which for the moment the usual subserviency of coat and trousers to ... skirts and petticoats, may be – well – not forgotten – but for the moment put to one side.' Will Cousin Anthony write a letter of introduction to John Morley, that rationalist intellectual who had taken over as editor? Cecilia Meetkerke long remembered how his face took on that look that Wilkie Collins described: 'To me, he was an incarnate gale of wind. He blew off my hat, he turned my umbrella inside out ... [but he was] as good and staunch a friend as ever lived.' 'But why the *Fortnightly*?' he asks his cousin: 'The learned editor is so indefatigable, that every word you write down will be weighed to the last pronoun. Perhaps you wish to be so weighed – but you are ignorant! ignorant! *not of what you ought to know – but of what you ought not to know!*' And what is that? The gale, having raged round the room, subsides. He explains what a new writer seldom does know: the characteristics of different magazines and editors. Having said all this he then picks up his young cousin's article, reads it, and writes the letter to Morley.[21]

If, while the gale was blowing, Cecilia Meetkerke chanced to look round the room, she would have passed over the view from the window which, Austin Dobson recalled, looked out onto 'nothing'. Inside the room she would have seen, as at Waltham, that the library was decorated with portraits and photographs of literary figures who were his friends. Thackeray still dominated in the large painting by Samuel Laurence. There was also a small statue by Edgar Boehm showing the great novelist strutting about with his hands in his pockets. A much cherished bust of Milton testified to Trollope's lifelong love of his poetry. Yet the main adornment were thousands of books. 'Let a room be ever so long or broad you can only put books on the outside, round the walls,' said Trollope of his library where 'there was much wall space every inch of which was utilized'. The books were well but not expensively bound. Twice a year, he and his niece, Florence, dusted each one for, as one American friend noted, 'London, with its fogs and soot-laden air, is not a place where valuable books can be exposed with impunity.'[22]

*

One admiring obituary of Trollope would note that he 'failed to impress you with the persuasion that he cared about the recreations of the library'. Whether he succeeded or failed in 'impressing' people was to him beside the point in this as in other things. The fact was that he cared passionately for books and reading as he had done throughout his life. His library became the chief joy of his final decade. It also played an increasingly important part in his writing. In the later novels not only are characters depicted by their literary tastes, such as Mr Whittlestaff who reveres Horace in *An Old Man's Love*, but scenes take place in libraries where the books seem to sit in judgment on an idle man, as in *Mr. Scarborough's Family*, or on a deceitful one, as in *Cousin Henry*. In the 1870s he was frequently asked to distribute prizes at the growing number of educational institutions that promoted that essentially Victorian passion for self-improvement. At one of these events in 1876 he spoke on 'the art of reading'. He told the audience that they should mix light reading with more serious books, but that if they had to choose only one type it would be better that they never read another novel. Reading was 'a never-failing source of enjoyment, but only to be obtained by practice'.[23]

To Trollope reading was a habit that had to be acquired, as his had been, in youth: 'If a man have not acquired the habit of reading till he be old, he shall sooner in his old age learn to make shoes than learn the adequate use of a book' [*The Claverings* XLV]. For his own part, he could seldom read for above an hour and a half at one sitting and not much more than three hours a day. 'I cannot sit down to the reading of any work like a gentleman at ease,' he told his biographer. 'I read only by scraps, and take the marrow and pith of my time for my daily work.' In April 1880 he wrote to his son Henry and, after carefully noting that it was his sixty-fifth birthday, passed on to some volumes about Renan's agnostic account of Christianity: 'I have read them as far as I seemed to want them. I have not time for merely promiscuous reading. I am getting old and I prefer going to bed.'[24]

Yet still he went on reading and on many evenings he read to Rose and Florence. When he had been involved in writing novels throughout the day, the books he chose to read aloud were normally poetry, which he always rated higher than prose. He kept a list of this reading from 1876 until the last year of his life, 1882. If we look at 1878, for example, we see that he read the *Iliad* and the *Odyssey* in Pope's translation as well as three works, including the 'seraphic excellence' of *Hiawatha* and *Evangeline*, by his friend Longfellow, of whom Rose was particularly fond, 'various Tennyson' and three poems by Goldsmith. Looking through the entire list, one sees a judicious mix of poets of his own century – Byron, Wordsworth, Shelley, the Brownings and Thackeray's ballads – with works from the past, including Spenser's *Faerie Queene*, some of the *Canterbury Tales* and *Paradise Lost*, which alone occupied most of the winter of 1881.[25]

Some of his reading was done at his clubs while yet other books arrived from Mudie's, but books which Trollope wished to study were bought. This was a family tradition: his father had attempted his work of scholarship from his own library. Tom built up an extremely valuable collection of 14,000 volumes on Italian history which he housed in a fifty-foot-long room at his villa outside Florence. Even after a turn in his fortunes compelled him to sell most of his library, his passion for books never slackened, something he shared with his wife who wrote: 'We shall continue to collect books as long as we have money to spend ... We quite agree about that. I would much rather go shabby than have no books ... I would rather *eat* shabby than read shabby!' Tom never lost his love of reading and many of his surviving letters to Henry in the 1880s, after Anthony's death, include requests for his nephew to find him some desired volume.[26]

Although Anthony's collection did not rival his brother's, either in magnitude or in rarity, he took immense pride in it. We know much about it for a curious reason that throws some light on his character. He spent much time in his first year at Montagu Square arranging his books, which had been stored before he left for Australia, and in preparing a catalogue. Part of the motivation was Trollope's increasing love of 'making lists'. This is not only a modern preoccupation, and in the 1870s he drew up lists of all sorts of things including, as we have seen, the books he was reading aloud and the titles of his own books. Yet there was a more practical purpose: 'All who use libraries know, a catalogue is nothing unless it shew the spot on which every book is to be found ... Only those who have done it know how great is the labour of moving and arranging a few thousand volumes.' This was not his first catalogue: he had had one of his collection at Waltham House printed in 1867 which showed that he had 5,163 books. In drawing up his Montagu Square catalogue he had the help of his teenage niece Florence. Each book had a bluish-grey bookplate about three inches by two inches with a not particularly good engraving of the Trollope family arms showing the three leaping stags surmounted by the crest of one stag, as on his writing-paper. Underneath was the name 'Anthony Trollope'. Each book also had a small paper slip with a capitalised letter in red with a small red circle in which he would write a number showing both the section and the place where the book rested.[27] He could glance at his catalogue and see immediately where any book should be. Only those who have attempted to pick their way round their own unorganised collection can know how much time he saved by this.

Trollope's next step with this catalogue was a strange one. He took it to Virtue, the former publisher of *Saint Pauls*, to be printed. It was not unusual for him to have some private printing done: a few copies of a lecture or his unpublished play based on *The Last Chronicle of Barset*. Yet to have a library catalogue printed makes it difficult to add new items. Trollope then distributed the catalogue to friends and acquaintances. To many this seems a rather pretentious act; yet Henry

Trollope as an old man would tell Michael Sadleir, 'Of all the men I have ever known my father was about the least affected by vanity – the least of a *poseur*.'[28] Likewise Trollope never pretended to a knowledge or an understanding he did not possess: in his tribute to G.H. Lewes he openly said that he knew nothing of philosophy or science and admitted that he simply could not comprehend one book by Emerson. Yet this man distributed an 86-page catalogue of his books.

Fortunately one copy has survived among the papers of Dickens's biographer, John Forster, who on his death bequeathed his own large library to the Victoria and Albert Museum where the catalogue may now be found. On the paper cover is printed 'Anthony Trollope / Catalogue of His Books / 1874.' This copy is inscribed: 'John Forster with kind regards from AT Ap 1874.' The odd thing is that Forster was not a particularly close friend of Trollope's, even though as editor of the *Examiner* he had published his 'Letters' on Ireland. As we have seen, Trollope had written from Australia to tell George Eliot and G.H. Lewes how 'distasteful' he had found Forster's recently published *Life of Charles Dickens*. He had also written: 'Forster himself is too coarse-grained, (though also a very powerful man) to know what is and what is not disgraceful; what is or is not heroic.' Yet here is Trollope, two years later, making sure that Forster has a catalogue of his library. Forster had not only a large but a famous collection, and not just of books but of manuscripts which together amounted to some 18,000 volumes. He owned the copy of the *Dunciad* which Pope gave to Swift, the proof-sheets of Johnson's *Lives of the Poets* with the author's own corrections, and a first folio of Shakespeare. Since Trollope's library was not a specialised collection, a catalogue of its contents would have had little interest in its own right. Could it be that once again Trollope was trying to demonstrate to his friends and acquaintances, including Forster, that he was not only a writer of amusing novels but a serious and well-read student of European literature, the classics and contemporary issues? Is the catalogue yet another indication of that search for seriousness and respect which underlay so much of his life, a search which began when his father warned him against 'idling'?[29]

It is not easy to say how many books were in Trollope's library, because the catalogue sometimes lists books under both the author and the title. For example, it puts the number 38 after Thomas Adolphus Trollope, meaning that there were 38 volumes of his works, but his books are also listed under their titles. When the catalogue was printed the collection amounted to about 5,000 volumes. Some contained early memories: the *Sectionum Conicarum Elementa* was inscribed: 'Left to Arthur William Trollope by his grandfather the Rev'd William Milton. Arthur survived his grandfather only ten days; dying July 22'd 1824'; the 1575 Paris edition of Horace that Trollope had carried to Harrow, with comments in his schoolboy hand; the edition of Burke's *On the Sublime and Beautiful* where he had conducted an argument on aesthetics with the author; *The Remains of the Elegeiakon* with an inscription by his mother dated 13 October 1831, ten weeks after her return from America.*

'The history of man's mind must have in it more of poetry than the history of man's body' wrote Trollope to Lewes, as we have noted, complimenting him on his *Life of Goethe*. A man's books, of course, are a good indication of his mind, but in Trollope's case we are faced with a problem, because of his great kindness. In 1867 his friend Robert Bell, a well-known man of letters whom he had wanted as his assistant on his new magazine, died leaving a widow with scant means. When Trollope heard, he set about raising money for her. It was on this occasion that Dickens wrote to him, 'I had heard with much satisfaction that poor Mrs. Bell had found a friend in you, for I knew she could have no stauncher or truer friend.' When he heard that Bell's library was for sale Trollope bought the lot, almost 4,000 volumes, offering a larger price than the widow would have received if they had been sold individually. 'We all know the difference in value between buying and selling of books,' Trollope told one friend. He probably spent some time deciding what to do with these new additions, and it may have provided an opportunity to tackle that difficult chore of intellectual gardening, weeding out one's shelves. Actually he had slightly fewer books at Montagu Square than at Waltham House and some may have been given to Henry. Fred's luggage for the long trip to Australia may also have contained more books than he expected. The Bell purchase may account for some odd works on Trollope's shelves whose presence we cannot otherwise explain, such as *A Grammar of the Afghan Language*. Yet he did write in an essay about his library in 1880 that one tends to buy books of foreign grammar before learning that 'life was limited and that there are some branches of human knowledge which must be renounced by anyone who values his brain'. Trollope was continually adding to his collection and studied catalogues of second-hand books. From time to time he would ask his

*Trollope's copy of the *Sectionum Conicarum Elementa* belongs to Mr Lance O. Tingay; Trollope's copy of Horace and *The Remains of the Elegeiakon* are in the Parrish Collection, while his copy of Burke's *On the Sublime and Beautiful* is in the Taylor Collection, both at Princeton. It is appropriate that Robert Taylor, the most civilised of book collectors, also owned Trollope's copy of the five-volume edition of Jane Austen.

publishers to obtain certain items for him, presumably because they could get a similar discount as on wine or glassware. His widespread travelling also allowed him to shop abroad: a particularly cherished volume of Cicero was found in Australia.[30]

Many of the books reflect his own writing, particularly his travel books. Once he had written on countries, he liked to read more about them. There are, for example, several histories of Australia, while his interest in America is reflected in many works of American literature, history and politics extending even to Senate reports. There is a large amount of eighteenth-century literature, including a fifty-volume set of 'British Novelists'. There was also a great deal of poetry, including numerous collections edited by Bell. There were books by friends, like Robert and Elizabeth Browning, Oliver Wendell Holmes, Lord Stanhope and George Eliot. The fact that her name is misspelt in the catalogue – George Elliot – implies that Trollope did some of the compiling himself and did not dictate everything to Florence as he habitually misspelt her literary surname. It is hardly surprising to find a great deal on Ireland, including *Gleanings in the West of Ireland* by S.G.O., whose writings had so infuriated Trollope and inspired him to write his *Examiner* articles for Forster. If Forster was one of those whose first act on receiving a volume is to see if their name is included, he should have been pleased, as Trollope had Forster's biographies of Dickens and Goldsmith as well as his *Statesmen of the Commonwealth of England*. As for Carlyle, the author about whom Trollope never made up his mind, there were fifty-four volumes.

The library boasted a large collection of dictionaries, including several for foreign languages. Trollope's favourite dictionary in English was Todd's 1818 edition of Dr Johnson in four volumes, which may help to account for his penchant for archaic words. Some of the other reference works are obviously useful for a novelist: a volume of fictional names, as well as Burke's *Landed Gentry*, with which he could ensure that he was not using real names for his characters. Naturally an inveterate traveller would have a collection of guide books: thus there is one for the Isle of Wight published in 1864, the year the Trollopes visited the island and the occasion when another traveller remembered that 'he asked a great many practical questions about the houses and lands which we drove past'.[31] Guides to the Pyrenees and Egypt marked other and farther travels. There were books that had been used for particular novels such as the *Memoirs of Madame de Rochejaquelin* and the 1847 three-volume Bohn Standard Library edition of Lamartine's *Histoire des Girondins* translated by H.T. Ryde as *History of the Girondists*, both mentioned in *La Vendée*.

There were few rare volumes to stir the envious spirits that lurk in most book collectors, and the catalogue made very few comments about particular volumes. His interest in the stage and famous actors is shown in a few 'association copies', such as *The Chances* by Fletcher in a copy Kemble had cut for acting, and the theatrical prompt copy of Byron's *Marino Faliero*, which had belonged to Macready. One suspects that this may have belonged to that great admirer of Byron, Fanny Trollope, as Macready was a close friend of hers who tried to persuade her not to go to America with Fanny Wright.[32] Trollope eventually acquired another of Macready's prompt copies, this for a production of Congreve's *Love for Love*. (This copy is now among Trollope's theatrical collection in the Folger Library, Washington, D.C.) There are, of course, practical works such as Mayhew's *Illustrated Horse-Doctor* and long runs of periodicals with which Trollope was connected, such as the *Cornhill* and the *Fortnightly Review*.

The 'family literature' was well represented. The catalogue listed fifty-five volumes of his mother's works which were prized possessions: when someone asked for information about her books he said that, while he would lend copies of his own works, he would never allow any of his mother's books out of his possession as it would be impossible to replace them.[33] There were thirty-eight volumes of Tom Trollope's, one volume by his first wife and, already by 1874, six volumes by his second, as well as Cecilia Tilley's *Chollerton* and Henry Milton's *On the Fine Arts*. Oddly, he did not list any copy of the first volume of his father's ecclesiastical dictionary. As for Trollope's own books, by the time he and Florence sat down to compile the catalogue they had reached seventy-one volumes and filled the third, fourth and fifth shelves of Case A. The catalogue does not list all the books in the house, but only those in Trollope's library and book room. There are, for instance, no copies of the Bible or the Prayer Book listed, as these would have been kept elsewhere, probably by Rose, who had her own collection with her own book plate, the intertwined letters R and T. She also had some bound editions of proofs of her husband's novels. In addition he gave her unusual editions of his works such as the New York edition of his 1876 Christmas story for the *Graphic*, 'Christmas at Thompson Hall', which Harpers published as a novel in America.

*

One might easily conclude, from looking at his shelves, that Trollope was a playwright rather than a novelist, as there were more books about the theatre than about any other subject. He had an enormous collection of old plays and spent much time reading them. Fortunately many of his copies of sixteenth- and seventeenth-century dramatists have survived.* From extant copies we know that Trollope annotated some 250 plays with comments on plots and language. In the month of June 1874 – while writing *The Prime Minister* – he read eleven, all but two by Beaumont and Fletcher. Echoes of this reading constantly turn up in the novels, so that in *The Prime Minister* he not only names a character Fletcher but even has him refer to 'what you have read, in the old plays' [XVI]. We have already seen how echoes of *Othello* were present throughout *He Knew He Was Right*. Trollope's marginalia show the great interest he took in his reading: this is what he meant about the 'adequate use' of a book. His was no desultory reading but a serious study of the way other men had used plots and language to achieve what he considered the greatest feat in literature, truly representing human nature in its infinite complexities. He was evidently a restless reader, always ready to make comments in the margin: he must have read pencil in hand. When he finished he would write an assessment at the end, usually in ink and presumably at his desk. He dated his comments, and from the way the occasional digit is cut off it appears that he had the plays bound after reading. Reading plays was not a new habit for in a copy of Marlowe's *Faustus* he writes on 2 December 1867: 'I remember well my reading of this play 30 years since.' At that time – this would take it back to his days as a clerk – he had thought it 'to be full of grand poetry. I now find the fine passages to be few and very short.'[34] Here we have a clue to the motive behind his reading and his marginalia: they provided him with chances not only to study great literary productions but to observe his own changing reactions. That is one reason why he dated his marginalia.

This absorption in his own processes of thought gives a key to his ability to follow his characters' minds. He had a deep reverence for Shakespeare and owned not only numerous editions, concordances and commentaries, but forty-seven volumes of Shakespeare Society publications which he had collected at Waltham. His reverence never precluded criticism of a work like *Henry VI*. His favourite character in Shakespeare was Brutus, although he detested the actual historical figure. Naturally Trollope's comments reflect the view of his era; thus he wrote in his copy of Beaumont and Fletcher's *The Woman's Prize*

---

*The Folger Memorial Shakespeare Library in Washington acquired eighty-six of these volumes, containing 240 plays, not out of any devotion to Trollope but because of its interest in Shakespeare and his successors. One comes closer to Trollope's reading in his extensive marginalia in these volumes than in almost any other of his surviving books, and one does so in Washington, a city he detested.

that Shakespeare was 'definitely beyond his age in discovering the manliness of decency', which is just what Trollope himself endeavoured to present in all his work. His reactions also throw light on what he held important in writing. His marginalia on Marlowe's *The Jew of Malta* mention two qualities he rated highly: 'pathos' and the skilful use of language. 'There is neither pathos nor tenderness in this piece ... But there is a certain power of language which carries the reader on.' Among the earliest works added to his library at Montagu Square was a four-volume edition of the plays of Shakespeare's contemporary Thomas Dekker. Trollope criticised the Victorian editor for praising one play with 'much too loud a mouth'. He found he had little time for the edition itself, which 'is very poor. It is a simple reprint of an early edition, with all its blunders – A list of the persons of the play has not even been added – The editor would say that such was not the purpose. But why not?' Trollope decided that *The Honest Whore* had two bad plots and one good one. A further comment on this play was written in light of Henry's recent escapade: 'the story is graced by so strong a denunciation of prostitution from the lips of the man the whore loves as to make the whole play remarkable for its force.' Trollope obviously believed that studying the language and plot of these old dramas was useful for a writer. When Walter Pollock, his neighbour's son who was himself a writer, was married in 1876 Trollope's wedding present was a collection of Elizabethan plays! 'When you have read them all and thoroughly digested them, so as to be able to answer satisfactorily all questions as to plot, language, character, and customs, I will send some more.'[35]

Yet it was not only the old dramas that attracted his restless mind and waiting pencil. He had a large collection of fiction, almost all of it English, with sets of his great contemporaries, Thackeray and Dickens, and, somewhat surprisingly, some works by Disraeli. He also cherished the novels of one of his closest friends. In his copy of the first edition of *Romola* there is an inscription in his handwriting: 'Given to Anthony Trollope by George Elliot.' Since he thought of the author as 'Mrs Lewes' he misspelt her pen name once again. His reading of other novelists was not merely for amusement or inspiration. He seriously considered writing a history of English fiction. It is unfortunate that he did not do so. In many ways this was just a more reasonable version of his adolescent scheme to write a history of world literature. In a fragment he wrote that the point of the work would be 'to vindicate' both his 'profession' as a novelist and the public taste for novels which had been attacked by such people as Carlyle and the Archbishop of York. His defence of his craft even led him to something he had disliked, and he gave a lecture 'On English Prose Fiction as a Rational Amusement' in various places from Scotland to Australia.[36]

For his projected history Trollope embarked on a course of reading and re-reading novels. He believed, like Scott, that many pre-nineteenth-century novels conveyed an immoral message, and as he said in his lecture they were not books one would want a daughter to read. Believing that it was 'a convincing sign of a good novel that it takes long in the reading', he criticised Scott not because of the length of his novels but because there was so much in his books that could be skipped. When he reread *Emma* he criticised his old favourite Jane Austen for 'timidity in dealing with the most touching scenes', particularly for not 'allowing the final part to be told in dialogue'. His reading and comments were not confined to the great novelists. If we had looked on the first shelf in his library, A1, we would have come across his copy of the first, 1796, edition of *The Monk*, a novel of superstition, murder and magic by M.G. Lewis. Trollope wrote in the third volume: 'This is so bad, that nothing could ever have been worse.'[37]

*

Although Trollope never wrote his history of fiction, he did write a short book on his favourite novelist and cherished friend which he entitled, simply, *Thackeray*. It was for the excellent 'English Men of Letters' series launched in 1878 and edited by John Morley. As with so many books of this period, the series was designed for readers wanting background for their leisure reading. Trollope himself reappeared later in the series, not as a writer but as a subject, when Hugh Walpole published his *Anthony Trollope* in 1928. When speaking of Trollope's book on Thackeray, Walpole wrote, 'one can feel the throb of his affection in every page'. Yet, as he rightly says, the book is more revealing about the author than about the subject: 'for anyone who cares for Trollope the man this book is revealing and deserves reading.' Many of Trollope's comments on his own friendship with Thackeray as well as his views on novel-writing in general have already been discussed. Morley offered Trollope £200 for the book and said it would be helpful if he could finish the 200 pages in two months. In the event Trollope took about seven weeks, finishing it in March 1879. He was hampered by the fact that Thackeray had asked that no biography be written. Fortunately the book was meant to be mainly literary criticism, and so only sixty pages, one chapter, deal with Thackeray's life. For his facts, Trollope sent a questionnaire about his life and finances to Anne Thackeray, whom he had befriended after her father's death.[38]

Trollope was discreet with his 'very few words' about the painful subject of Thackeray's wife who was still alive in a private mental asylum. 'The misery came from God and was in no wise due to human fault.' Trollope's emphasis throughout the book on Thackeray's rather indolent ways – often implicitly contrasted with the author's disciplined energy – annoyed many of the dead novelist's friends and admirers. In an obscure journal called *Cope's Tobacco Plant* the minor poet James Thomson assailed 'little t' for criticising 'big T', particularly as he was 'only a superior postman'. 'Little t' probably never heard of this outburst, but he was pleased with a letter from a former schoolfellow and much admired captain of cricket, Henry Manning, now the Cardinal Archbishop of Westminster. 'When the memories of your readers turn back over your many works,' he wrote, 'they will bear to you the witness you bear to Thackeray. And that is one of signal honour.' The Cardinal wanted to send one of his own works, but admitted they were 'so insufferably clerical'. 'I will however try to find something which Carlyle would not call shovel-hatted.' While pleased with such praise, Trollope was genuinely distressed that Thackeray's daughter disliked his book. She had become a novelist herself, 'a household word to the world of novel readers' Trollope called her in the book. Among the memories they shared was one of a July walk in Kent. In the party were the Trollopes, John Millais and his wife Effie and Anne Thackeray. They saw a painter at work in the woods and Millais went up to him: 'Why,' he said to the amateur, 'you have not got your lights right. Look, *this* is what you want.' He took the brush out of the man's hand, painted a few lines, nodded and walked off. Trollope laughed, Anne Thackeray recalled, and said: 'The man looks bewildered; he ought to know it is Millais.' He then ran back to tell him. Someone else in the party said that the man ought to be told that his informant was none other than Anthony Trollope, so Anne Thackeray now ran back to deliver a second message. When she returned someone else decided that the poor man should be told that his third visitor was Thackeray's daughter, so a third messenger was sent to the now bewildered painter.[39]

Anne Thackeray's upset at the book caused a breach in their friendship, but fortunately in the last year of Trollope's life they met, most appropriately, at George Smith's house. Trollope came up to her by the fireplace 'very big and kind' and, as she wrote in her journal, 'I said I'm so sorry I quarrelled with you. He said so am I my dear.' Trollope wrote to Rose: 'I am very glad because my memory of her father was wounded by the feeling of a quarrel.' A decade later Anne Thackeray Ritchie made the reconciliation public in a graceful tribute: 'Mr Trollope, that kind old friend, who knew him so much, saw him from a very different point of view from mine, but he writes with an affection which never varied and which was constant to my father's children, though not untried I fear by the present writer.'[40]

*

In the 1870s Trollope continued to add to his library, particularly to his third great interest, Classical literature, especially Latin. He acquired the 177 volumes of the 1825-8 *Bibliothèque Latine-Française*, a collection of Latin texts with French translations which he extensively annotated. Many years before his move to Montagu Square his review of Merivale's Roman history led to a fascination with Caesar and while he agreed with Merivale's view that Caesar was 'the greatest name in history' he came to detest Caesarism, the exaltation of one man who was necessarily dishonest. To Trollope, Disraeli or, even more, Napoleon III (himself the author of yet another book on Caesar) were modern examples of Caesarism, as indeed was Melmotte on a fictional scale. In 1868 John Blackwood embarked on a long-cherished series of 'Ancient Classics for English Readers', admitting with admirable frankness that this was intended for people 'like myself who was educated up to the muzzle ... [and] other busy men, and ladies or gentlemen who have not had a thorough education'. The idea was for a series of small books at 2s 6d containing translations of important Latin and Greek authors 'metaphorically boiled down to meet the now universal demand for an ox in a tea-cup' as his daughter, recalling a popular advertisement, put it. Trollope thought such a series a splendid idea and inserted a 'puff' for it in *Saint Pauls* in 1870. Blackwood then suggested that Trollope might wish to do the volume on Caesar's *Commentaries*. This was fortunate for Trollope, not just because it allowed him to write about a long-standing interest but because it introduced him to the editor of the series, the Rev. W. Lucas Collins, who was to become one of his closest friends. Trollope set to work with his usual determination and completed the book within a few months. It was not so much a translation as a retelling of the story. He also sent Blackwood what must surely rank as one of the most unusual as well as one of the most charming letters from an author to a publisher: 'It is a dear little book to me, – and there is one other thing to be said about the little dear. I think the 1st of June is your birthday. At any rate we'll make it so for this year, and you will accept it as a little present.'[41]

This should lay to rest the idea that Trollope had no other motive for writing but money. He believed that a writer should be paid for his work as much as anyone else and he detested the hyprocrisy of both authors and public who affected shock at the commercial side of writing. Yet he knew there were other motives for writing. Caesar's *Commentaries* appealed to him because they gave him a chance to show his ability with Latin and also because they allowed him to fulfil his increasing desire to educate. He told Blackwood, 'It has been a tough bit of work, but I have enjoyed it amazingly ... It has been a change to the spinning of novels, and has enabled me to surround myself with books and almost to think myself a scholar.' No one, least of all Trollope, would claim that this translation is a magnificent piece of erudition. While aware of some contemporary scholarship, Trollope was anxious to assert that the lessons of his schooldays had been 'fairly accurate'. Mrs Oliphant, Blackwood's most constant writer, told her publisher: 'I cannot read [it] without laughing – it is so like Johnny Eames.' Although not meant as a compliment, it was one, for the series was intended for real versions of Johnny Eames to read, sitting in their lodging houses with the tea and other good books that Trollope's anxious relatives had recommended to him as a young clerk. A more scathing response arrived from Charles Merivale, the Dean of Ely, who was praised in the book. Merivale replied, thanking Trollope for sending his 'comic Caesar'. Although the Dean's equally waspish nephew, Herman, later claimed that 'Trollope wept' when this verdict arrived, there is no evidence that young Herman was hiding in the room at the time. Trollope's own comment on this remark (though he avoids giving Merivale's name) is a calm assessment of the pompous snobbery of those who resent anyone else's invading 'their subject':[42]

> I do not suppose he intended to run a dagger into me. Of any suffering from such wounds, I think, while living, I never shewed a sign; but still I have suffered occasionally. There was, however, probably present to my friend's mind ... a feeling that a man who had spent his life writing English novels could not be fit to write about Caesar. It was as when an amateur gets a picture hung on the walls of the Academy.

Such an attitude still thrives today in places far less elegant than the Deanery at Ely!

Trollope's interest in Classical studies did not fade and occupied a large part of his time throughout this decade. One of his basic attitudes in politics was his fear of rule by one 'individual'. Throughout the 1870s – stimulated probably by his detestation of Disraeli and his memory of Napoleon III – he pondered Caesar's influence on Rome.

This drew him increasingly to study Cicero, whom he regarded as the perfect author for anyone seeking consolation [*An Old Man's Love* II]. In 1876 he told a friend: 'I have just completed all Cicero's works from beginning to end. He was nearer to a christian than any unXtian that ever lived.'[43] Although we shall be passing over some of his novels, it is worth examining his *Life of Cicero*, published on 1880, while we are still, as it were, guests in Trollope's library, because this book is one of the two best portrayals of his mature mind produced in this room. Its only rival is the *Autobiography*, written about the same time.

In 1877 he sent two articles on Cicero to the *Fortnightly* which were preliminary studies for the book. Another novelist, George Meredith, wrote: 'Trollope's art. on Cicero shows him to have a feeling for his hero. It reads curiously as though he were addressing a class of good young men.' 'I am conscious of a certain audacity in thus attempting to give a further life of Cicero', Trollope announced at the beginning of his book, adding with all truthfulness that he has no new information. His motive is a simple one, a 'love of the man, and from a heartfelt admiration of his virtues and his conduct as well as his gifts'. In this Trollope was part of an important strain in nineteenth-century thought which felt a need to buttress their own civilisation by reference to the Classics. Gladstone, with his attempt to make Homer an honorary member of the Church of England, is only the best-known example. In his *Cicero* Trollope always draws direct parallels with his own world:

> How popular he would have been at the Carlton ... How supreme he would have sat on the Treasury bench, ... How delighted would have been the middle-aged Countesses of the time to hold with him mild intellectual flirtations ... With the penny post instead of travelling messengers at his command, and pen instead of wax and sticks ... he would have answered all questions and solved all difficulties.

Of course every age attempts to dress the past in its own costume, and Trollope's efforts to slide a frock coat over Cicero's toga are no more ludicrous than modern attempts to festoon the great Victorians with the slogans of a later age. *Punch* expressed this in a gentle cartoon showing Trollope placing a top hat on Cicero's bust. Some of the insertions of Victorian speech have an amusing ring: Mark Antony is 'one of the greatest rascals the world has known', a minor politician is 'this dirty fellow' and the election of Quaestors is full of 'tomfooleries'.

Throughout the book two central preoccupations are clear: the need for honesty in public life and the importance of Christianity. For Trollope the two go hand in hand, and he would almost argue that you cannot have one without the other although he did acknowledge that Cicero had 'the innate honesty which there is in the hearts of men'. Part of Trollope's excessive admiration for the great orator is that he is the least 'Roman' of them all. 'Cicero was almost a Christian, even before the coming of Christ,' he tells his readers. Yet, he asks, 'how near have we approached to the beauty of truth, with all Christ's teaching to guide us.' He concludes the book with a chapter on Cicero's religion so as to leave this message uppermost in his reader's mind.[44]

One minor aspect of his research had fascinated Trollope: how had Cicero's dictation to a secretary affected his work? This reflects his own practice at the time, and the manuscript of this book is in Rose's hand, although there are corrections and additions in his. We get a sudden insight into their life when he speaks of the way to cope with unfair treatment. Here he is almost certainly referring to his loss of the Assistant Secretaryship at the Post Office. 'I hold it to be natural that a man should wail to himself,' announced Trollope. 'A sense of wrong done him by friends will stir him, not by the misery inflicted but because of the injustice. And that which he says to himself he will say to his wife, if his wife be to him a second self.' Can there be any better tribute, made in his characteristically involved manner, to the role Rose played in his life? She, who was acting as secretary on one of his last books, just as she had acted as copyist with his earliest novels, was indeed his 'second self'. Nor did he forget another 'injustice' that still rankled, when he inserted a footnote protesting against Freeman's use of a Ciceronian tag to attack fox-hunting, which Trollope saw 'as an argument against all out of door sports'.[45]

Trollope's *Cicero* made little impact in his day and has been virtually forgotten. Criticism, however, arrived from Rome itself, when one of Trollope's earliest and hardest tutors, his brother, wrote: 'You ought to have let me correct the Latin words in your proof ... diphthongs have been among your worst enemies.' Perhaps the best comment about the book was made by his friend W. Lucas Collins. Trollope had been staying at his rectory when the book appeared, and Collins felt obliged to review it in *Blackwood's*, though he wrote privately to the editor, 'I tried to say all the good for it that I *honestly* could, and in many respects it is a very pleasant book to read, even when one can't quite share Trollope's enthusiastic admiration for St. Cicero.' Whatever its Classical scholarship, the book is interesting for any consideration of Trollope: that a busy writer would take time off from those novels which brought him money to produce a serious work that could bring him little shows a devotion to learning and education that lay at the centre of Anthony Trollope's being. It also shows his pride in the library he had collected: in the midst of his book, when speaking of Cicero's library, he says, 'how impossible it would be for me to repeat this oft-told tale of Cicero's life without a crowd of books within reach of my hand'.[46]

*

According to one acquaintance, his *Life of Cicero* was the work of which Trollope was most proud. Certainly one important impulse behind his research was an attempt to show that the unsuccessful schoolboy had honoured his father's devotion to learning. He was working on his *Autobiography* at about the same time that he was writing *Cicero* and the tragedy of his father was often before him: 'I sometimes look back,' he wrote in that *Autobiography*, 'meditating for hours together, on his adverse fate.' When he wrote those words, the celebrated novelist was almost exactly the same age his father had been when he died in exile. While we are still, at least in spirit, in the library of which he was so proud, we should perhaps consider the other and far more famous product of that room in Montagu Square. That book still gives greater insight into the mind and personality of its creator than anything else he wrote. The first thing that strikes most readers looking at *An Autobiography* is its remarkable simplicity and honesty. It 'moves us more than we care to admit,' says Harold Laski, 'by its humble simplicity.' 'The style shall be simple and familiar: but style is the image of character' are the words used in the first few lines of the *Memoirs of Edward Gibbon*, and the same can be said of Trollope. The style of Trollope's account of his life is simple, often deceptively so, as it is in all his best work. More than a year after finishing the book he wrote to his elder son, 'No doubt many a literary artist so conceals his art that readers do not know that there is much art. But they like the books and read them, – not knowing why.' In an earlier letter Henry had suggested three such examples of writers who had concealed their art: Molière, Macaulay, and his own father. Trollope warned his son, 'I would not have you bracket your third example with such names to other ears than mine lest you be laughed at.'[47] Henry's bracketing, however, was not out of place, and the *Autobiography* has stood the test of time, largely because in its writing Trollope did conceal his art.

One aspect of the *Autobiography* that is seldom taken into account is that it was written when its author was comparatively young. In 1875, Trollope turned sixty and before the end of the year began work on what proved to be his single most revealing book, which he completed on 11 April 1876. He noted that he was 'LXI' years old but then added a faint pencilled correction – 'in 13 days'. Not all of the book was written in the library at Montagu Square: some may have been composed on his fifth voyage from New York while some was written at the ancestral seat of the Trollopes, Casewick. This visit in mid-February may well have been one of his final appearances in the hunting field. His stay was not allowed to interfere with his autobiographical work and he managed to write eight or nine pages a day, including his defence of the hereditary aristocracy as embodied in Plantagenet Palliser. Surely Trollope, like anyone, especially a man who used the family crest to decorate his letters and bookplates, would have been influenced in his writing by staying at the seat of generations of Trollope baronets. Here family history, legends, portraits and memorabilia combined to remind him of the traditions from which he had come and to which so many of his novels were devoted, the world of country gentry and clergy. Although he finished the *Autobiography* by April 1876, he occasionally made a few additions: the most notable was an account of the Royal Commission on Copyright, of which he was a member. This was added in 1877; two years later he added yet another title, *John Caldigate*, to his list of books.

Trollope did not appear to take a strong interest in autobiographical literature although his library had some standard autobiographies, such as Rousseau's. While his novels were the product of a man who had read an enormous number of other novels, his *Autobiography* does not appear to have been much influenced by other writers. Most autobiographies are written when the author's active life is over, but when Trollope finished his he still had almost twenty more books to write. Yet before he settled down to write it, he had his first real sign of physical decay. Since his mysterious illness as a clerk, his various illnesses, such as the occasional problem with his liver, or his numerous bruises from tumbles into Essex ditches, had only kept him in bed for a week or so. In the autumn of 1873, when he and Rose were paying their return visit to the splendours of Killarney, a new problem appeared:[48]

> I fear I have lost the hearing of one ear ... For such troubles a man ought to be prepared as old ... But for a time it frets me, and confuses me. I fancy that I am always going to be run over, and everybody seems to talk to me on the wrong side ... Why should anything go wrong in our bodies? Why should we not be all beautiful? Why should there be decay? – why death? – and, oh, why, damnation? The last we get out of by not believing it.

Trollope, while not certain of his views on eternal damnation, was certain of eternal life, and he also had the traditional belief that one must render an account of one's life. Not long afterwards he told his fellow members of the Copyright Commission: 'an author ... has it upon his conscience to use his life for doing good work for the world around him.' That is what his *Autobiography* is: an 'apology', or, better, 'apologia', in the sense that Newman used the word, a rendering of what he had done with his God-given time. Yet, as with almost all the work of his last two decades there was another serious purpose, an educational one: he hoped that his book would help younger writers in following what he regarded as the finest profession in the world. Therefore he shows how long it took him to achieve success and how his disciplined methods helped him to preserve it. That is one reason why he includes such a detailed account of how he set about his work mechanically. 'I have been constant and constancy in labour will conquer all difficulties.' The other reason he wrote so much about the 'cobbler's wax' as the key to his success was the same reason he talked about it at almost every dinner table: it was a way to preserve the decorum of a gentleman lest it be thought he was too emotionally overwrought in the writing of fiction. This is another meaning behind the concealing of his art.

The *Autobiography*'s deceptive simplicity should never cause the reader to forget that he is dealing with a creative artist and one whose art is always disguised. The book has a simple theme: how a miserable boy became a happy and successful man. Anything that gets in the way of this authorised version is excised: within this format the book is remarkably honest. Naturally there are errors of date and other minor mistakes, but there are hardly any real efforts to mislead the reader. Honesty, however, must not be confused with contrived self-revelation. Trollope makes it perfectly clear that his is no 'confession' in the style of Rousseau: 'That I, or any man, should tell everything of himself, I hold to be impossible.' The way in which he used his literary skills to paint a picture is best seen in the most memorable part of the book: his early years at school. His facts are accurate but he overdoes the misery, as he admitted he had done in *The Way We Live Now*. His earlier references to his schooldays, such as the article on 'Public Schools' written in the 1860s, are nowhere so bleak. Then he preached the conventional sermon: 'There we made our friendships ... there we became men.' Yet to read the *Autobiography* is to hear that he had no successes, no friends and nothing but misery. However, this friendless youth mentions at least three of his school friends while touring round Australia and New Zealand. He was still in this affectionate mood shortly after settling in Montagu Square when he was asked to address some students at the Liverpool Institute. There he spoke of his days as a 'a Charity boy' at Winchester and said 'I still regard the spot on

which my boyhood was passed with a mixture of awe and affection.'[49]
He also made certain Winchester had a signed set of his *Chronicles of Barsetshire* when the set appeared at the end of the 1870s.

He tells us about his life as a postal official and writer. We hear much of Trollope as a son but little of Trollope as a father and even less of Trollope as a husband. He was a Victorian gentleman and such men did not disrobe in public – except when swimming. His private life was his own not because he had some dark secret to hide but because it was his own. We have seen how often he used his novels to send private messages of love or amusement to his wife, but he had no intention of openly discussing his deepest feelings in any book. Rose played her role in the creation of this book, as she had done and would do in so many others. Early in 1876 he asked her to prepare a chronology of their life. She must have kept a diary in order to remember minor events, such as their spending a week in London in July 1854. She wrote seventeen pages of dates with some short descriptions of what they did. Some of her comments, which have already been quoted, give us a brief glimpse of her own personality. There is obvious directness, but the only outspoken emotion is the first entry, that of 11 June 1844: 'Married' and '(Hurrah)'. Most of her entries concern their foreign travels, although she does not mention countries about which he wrote books. Thus for the 1861 trip to America her husband is told: 'See your own journal for 1861.' Several entries convey that bemused air of the devoted wife who has spent decades living with and occasionally curtailing an incarnate gale of wind: 'Row with driver when we start.' 'Conductor takes us for discharged prisoners.' 'You go somewhere in October.' 'You cut your leg with knife in the train.' In addition to this list Rose made what her son calls 'transcripts', presumably of documents, such as Thackeray's letter asking Trollope to write for the *Cornhill*.[50]

If one compares Trollope's *Autobiography* with some other Victorian memoirs, it is obvious that many of them suffer from what he calls in his second sentence 'the garrulity of old age'. Take *Bygone Years*, a fairly typical representative of a minor politician's memoirs written in his eighties by Trollope's friend, the Hon. Frederick Leveson Gower. There is a similar reticence about his private life. He refers to his wife's death after five years of 'uninterrupted happiness'. This happened in 1858 but when writing his book in 1905 he says little about his marriage: 'This is a subject which I am unwilling to dwell upon, and will therefore content myself with this simple reference to it.'[51] The rest of the book has the usual range of anecdotes: how the Duke of Wellington shot my father in the face, how I shook hands with Sir

Walter Scott and what Mr Gladstone thought of gambling (worse than drunkenness). One closes the book with a feeling that while it was jolly nice being a Leveson Gower in Victorian times, one has no sense of having understood another person's life or of having really known that person.

Even a professional writer can be disappointing. Tom Trollope wrote *What I Remember* when he was in his mid-seventies. In many ways these rambling memoirs are entertaining and, of course, they are invaluable for the history of the Trollopes. The main theme throughout is: I am now in my seventies and the world has changed much for the worse and I will tell you how good the coffee and the mutton and the Belgian barges were in the old days. He dwells lovingly on his public school days and discusses the intricacies of flogging, a fairly standard ingredient in most Victorian memoirs; he describes his travels and introduces chapters on his friends as a way to make the book longer and more popular. Some of these are entertaining and useful, notably that on George Eliot. He tells little about his own writing although he shares his brother's detached attitude: 'I wrote well-nigh a score, I think of novels ... The majority of them are on Italian subjects; and these, if I may be allowed to say so, are good ... Those which I wrote on English subjects are unquestionably bad.' The reader closes this book with almost the same feeling as he closed Leveson Gower's: he does not feel he really knows this man. Tom's second wife's letters are far more revealing: she told a friend when the memoirs were published that they were receiving 'all manner of flourishing reviews' which was very nice. 'What Mr. Trollope cares about,' she added, 'is the number of copies sold.'[52]

The difference with Anthony Trollope's *Autobiography* is striking. While there is no sense of striving after literary effect, the reader is always aware of being guided by a skilful writer. The book moves at a pleasant canter. The author is always present but there is no sense of egoism. Everything is seen through his eyes and only events that affected him are told. There are no pleasant but purposeless anecdotes about royalty or celebrities, which do not affect Trollope himself. To take one example, he does not even mention that he had a meeting with the Prime Minister in 1866.[53] He analyses himself and his parents just as he analysed fictional characters: he is detached but respectful. In a revealing phrase he says of his mother, 'I can remember now her books, and can see her at her pursuits.' This is an interesting insight into Trollope's memory: he remembered objects but visualised people. This was the gift he had used to make so many of his characters live. Always present in the *Autobiography* is his pride in his profession as a writer, not a precious parading of artistic vanity, but a justified sense of achievement as he subjects each of his works to analysis and dismisses many as failing to reach his standards: *The Last Chronicle of Barset*, 'the best novel I have written'; *Doctor Thorne*, 'I have been surprised by its success'; *Ralph the Heir*, 'one of the worst novels I have written', and *The West Indies*, 'the best book that has come from my pen'. Posterity has rejected many of his assessments and most would not agree all his verdicts on his fellow novelists, which are inserted in three chapters about the Victorian novel. He never disguises how important the material rewards of writing were to him and he even provides a list of receipts and the total he had earned to date from writing, £68,959 17s 5d. This offended many people when the book was published, but when the reader closes the *Autobiography* he feels he knows the man who wrote it.

When the book was finished he tied up the mansucript with a letter to Henry giving instructions about publishing it. The letter ended: 'need I say how dearly I have loved you? Your most affectionate father, Anthony Trollope.' That was placed in a brown parcel endorsed, 'To be opened after my death. A.T.' About two years later he and Henry were in the library at Montagu Square: he spoke briefly about the manuscript and said, 'Now we'll lock it up and say no more about it.' Yet as he put it in the drawer of the writing desk 'he mentioned a sum of which he thought it might be worth'. This was £1,800.[54] The sealed letter containing a declaration of love, the crested note-paper and the concern that Henry get a just price for the manuscript are all intrinsic parts of his personality. With the manuscript locked away, Trollope could leave his library and walk downstairs and out into the noisy street with its German bands, cabs and sweeps to resume the outward parade of life where few knew of the thoughtful and sensitive man who lived among his books.

*

Trollope still carried on his hectic pace of life although his schedule obviously changed as a result of living in London. Fortunately one friend gave an account of his new timetable: he would wake about six, an hour later than at Waltham, read in bed for about an hour and then go to his book room to work for about four hours. Another sign of his slightly more relaxed ways came about 11.30 when the family met for what his cousin called a 'partly foreign and wholly substantial meal' to which close friends were always welcome. This was what the French called a *déjeuner à la fourchette*. One day an American acquaintance arrived shortly before noon and declined to join them at another breakfast: 'What,' asked Trollope, 'do you mean to say you are not man enough to eat two breakfasts?' If there were time to spare after this mid-day meal, he would return to his library to correct proofs or to read until the horses were brought round to the door. Riding relaxed his body just as reading did his mind and he would have agreed with his hero, Lord Palmerston, that 'the best thing for the inside of a man is the outside of a horse'. Once the horses appeared he would set out for a ride in Hyde Park, usually accompanied by Florence. He normally avoided Rotten Row as no doubt the crowds and the constant bowing and tipping of hats would have interrupted his stride. On a fine afternoon during the Season, as many as a thousand carriages, with elegantly dressed ladies in landaus resplendent with polished harnesses and tall footmen would promenade through the Row. Here was almost everyone 'who mattered' in Victorian London: every day the editor of *The Times* – the real 'Tom Towers' – could be seen riding alongside the Rothschild carriage to learn the latest rumours of financial upsets.[55] 'Not to be taken two or three times round the park would be to Lady Tringle,' wrote Trollope of one wealthy banker's wife, 'to rob her of the best appreciated of all those gifts of fortune' [*Ayala's Angel* XVII]. It may be recalled that it was at this great rendezvous of Society that Lily Dale saw Crosbie for the first time since he jilted her [*The Last Chronicle of Barset* LIII].

It comes as no surprise to those who have followed Trollope so far that he had firm views of what a horse for the Park should be: it must not be 'a prancing, restless, giggling, sideway-going, useless garran' but 'well made, well bitted, with perfect paces'* [*The Prime Minister* I]. Sometimes Trollope and his niece would be accompanied by other people such as a schoolfriend of Florence's, Ada Strickland, who was so anxious for the ride that she suggested they start early, breaking into Trollope's work period: 'Do you want to see me begging my bread?' he asked. When they got to the Park, Ada was so excited that the horse ran away with her and bolted down Rotten Row. Trollope managed to overtake the girl and save her from injury. He could not have known then that he was saving the life of his future daughter-in-law. Mrs Oliphant may well have noticed him riding by: 'The systematic way in which Mr. Trollope grinds out his work is very funny. It must have answered, however, for he seems extremely comfortable; keeps a homely brougham, rides in the Park, etc. I envy and admire.'[56] By

---

*It is interesting that Trollope used an Irish term for a horse even though he had been fifteen years out of Ireland. A garron (the proper spelling) is a small but inferior horse.

having his own brougham in Town, a luxury which would have cost him about £200 a year in upkeep and maintenance of the horses and carriage, the Trollopes were in the ranks of 'carriage folk' and thus at the top of Victorian society. It is no wonder that Mrs Oliphant stared enviously.

After the ride Trollope and Florence would return to Montagu Square and then he would walk to the Athenaeum or Garrick, arriving between five and six. He used his clubs even more after settling in London. Sometimes he entertained at all-male dinners, inviting old friends to meet rising celebrities, like the two American writers Joaquin Miller and Mark Twain. Miller was an exotic character out of the 'Wild West' who had been a horse thief and Pony Express rider before he won acclaim in England through his poetry. He was known as 'The Byron of Oregon'. Trollope teased Kate Field about this party: 'Pity you have not yet established the rights of your sex or you could come ... and be *as jolly as men.*' According to Twain, the host was 'voluble and animated' but spent most of his time speaking to Leveson Gower: 'Trollope talked all the time ... pouring forth a smooth and limpid and sparkling stream of faultless English.'[57] Trollope may well have been interested to gather not only the latest political news but reactions to the visit of the Shah of Persia, as he was then writing in *The Way We Live Now* about the visit of the Emperor of China.

The Garrick had another attraction as Trollope's passion for whist began to equal that for fox-hunting. As so often, he turned a pleasure into an article when he described 'Whist at Our Club' for *Blackwood's*: 'Perhaps a dozen gentlemen, mostly well-stricken in years, who having not much else to do with their afternoons, meet together and kill the hours between lunch and dinner.' With that increasingly half-serious half-mocking tone he adopted about mortality, he saw whist as 'the delight' that 'makes easy the passage to the grave'. As with so many things in Trollope's life, whist was a family inheritance. His father had been a noted player but, as with everything else, his disruptive personality caused problems, as one partner remembered: 'Many men will scold their partners occasionally but Trollope invariably scolds us all round.' His son Anthony had moderated this tradition though he insisted that 'whist without scolding was altogether out of the question'. Whist was an old game, but with the adoption of new rules in 1864 it achieved great status in Victorian clubs, where there were men who devoted most of their lives to it, such as 'Mr. Maule, Senior' who was miserable when 'everyone' was out of London from August to October because 'there was no whist, no society, – it may almost be said no dinner' [*Phineas Redux* XXI]. According to one obituary, Trollope 'was not a whist player of first class'.[58] He had too many pleasures to allow any one to dominate his life but he made sure each contributed to his books.

Trollope used his whist matches to gather information for his political novels – he often played with members of the Liberal Cabinet like W.E. Forster (their mutual scoldings during whist were a Garrick legend), or with Abraham Hayward, the best-informed journalist of Society and political life and the author in 1873 of *Whist and Whist Players*. At the club they never played for vast stakes and were usually content to play for shillings. However, Arthur Sullivan once won £6 from Trollope at a card game after an all-male dinner at Millais's house, where Thomas Hardy was among the guests. This was on 17 May 1881, only three weeks after *Patience* had opened on St George's Day, 23 April. It was in this opera that 'Anthony Trollope' was included as one of the 'remarkable people in history'.[59] Whist frequently occurs in the later novels, as in *The Way We Live Now*, when he refers to five in the afternoon as a time when ladies are drinking tea and 'idle men [are] playing whist at the clubs' [III].

During his first years at Montagu Square Trollope continued to hunt two or three times a week. This entailed more time and expense than when he lived in the country. On hunting mornings a cab would arrive about dawn: to ensure that the man was there, he was invited to have his breakfast before taking Trollope to the train to Essex where his horses were kept. Only a few days after his return from Australia he was exulting:

> We had 2 h. 45 min. after the same fox on Saturday, the biggest bellyful of hunting I ever had in my life ... I never had such a day before. Buff carried me through it all as well as ever. But was *very tired*. He and a second horse I had out were both too tired to be got home. You will be sorry to hear that Banker and another of my small lot are laid up with coughs. I have four in all.

The expense, combined with the added effort of getting to meets, only increased his fervour. As he wrote to the Warden of New College, 'It is my duty to hunt ... as nothing breaks a man's heart so thoroughly as having a lot of horses and giving them nothing to do ... A hunting man is bound to hunt if he can hunt in order that he may in some degree justify the expense.'

In 1876, Trollope decided that he was getting too old to hunt. He finished the season and, indeed, ended his fox-hunting just about the time he completed his *Autobiography*, a decision that no doubt aided the elegiac tone that pervades that book. He paid an emotional farewell to the sport that had excited and sustained him by adapting some lines of Horace:

> I've lived about the covert side,
> I've ridden straight, and ridden fast;
> Now breeches, boots, and scarlet pride
> Are but momentoes of the past.

Perhaps his straightforward prose is better: 'I think I may say with truth that I rode hard to the very end.'[60]

Most of Trollope's readers will probably find it difficult to understand his virtual obsession with hunting: the pleasures of our friends, when carried to a degree beyond which we would choose, are seldom easy to understand. Some, of course, may find his passion offensive. Yet for him it was an essential part of his life. From the moment he discovered its joys in Ireland, he felt himself part of society and no longer an outcast. Trollope's genius was such that it could only function from within his society. He could not be the eccentric and introspective artist who observes life from a virtuous garret. Hunting also was essential to his physical well-being, as one friend saw: 'I believe, however, his health was never the same after he gave up hunting. Hard exercise was a necessary outlet to his energetic temperament, and a counterpoise to his incessant brain-work.'[61] None but the most extreme 'philo-animalists' can really regret that a few Victorian foxes ended their days in an Essex spinney, if that was the price to pay for Trollope's novels.

*

During his London years Trollope devoted many hours each week to helping the Royal Literary Fund, a charitable organisation almost a century old. He was a member of the Fund for eighteen years and for thirteen of these he served as a treasurer. He was also constant in his attendance at meetings when decisions were taken to help worn-out authors or their families. Not only did he give a vast amount of time to this charity but he often set up his own private appeal to provide extra help for someone in distress, often an author's widow. In all of this he was conscious that he had been remarkably lucky, and he felt it his duty to help others who had never known the prosperity that surrounded Waltham House or Montagu Square. It is in no way surprising to find that he spent so much time in helping others, but it is a pleasant surprise to see how remarkably delicate he could be to avoid trespassing on injured pride or recent bereavement. In 1874 Shirley Brooks, the editor of *Punch* and a minor novelist who had been amazed at Trollope's writing regime, died leaving his widow in some need. Because her application to the Fund arrived too late to be considered at the April meeting she would have to wait a month. Not only did Trollope persuade the Fund's secretary to send her £50 immediately but he wrote to the artist Frith whom he knew to be her friend, asking him to assure her that 'this is merely an antedating of the money ... I hope she will not regard it as an interference on my part'.[62] By writing 'some hundreds' of letters as 'beggar-in-chief' Trollope was able to raise about £1,000 for this widow.

Trollope never overrated his abilities to raise money or to use influence to get a literary pension on the Royal Civil List. Thus he advised one lady that if she wanted names on her petition to impress the Prime Minister, Disraeli, she should get literary figures who were also politicians, men like W.H. Smith, as the Prime Minister 'pays little or no attention to the names of merely literary men'. Even so, Trollope's name and his popularity with so many fellow writers carried much weight. A.W. Kinglake, the historian and former MP, agreed to contribute to the Fund because Trollope was involved in it, 'for,' he explained, 'I am always mindful of the un-numbered hours of pleasure that I owe to your delightful books. And, apart from the pleasure, it is so good for one ... to see the play of healthful English life as you with your genius present it.'[63]

*

Kinglake was, of course, just one among hundreds of thousands in England alone who owed 'hours of pleasure' to Trollope in the more than thirty years he had been writing novels. As the *Edinburgh Review* stated in 1877, 'We have little hesitation in asserting that the present generation owes a larger debt of gratitude to Mr. Trollope than to any other writer of fiction, living or lately dead.' Yet by the late 1870s some of the public were clearly looking elsewhere for pleasure. In his history of the English novel Walter Allen, speaking with the joint authority of critic and novelist, sees a great change not only in the novel but in its readers, starting about 1880, a change which led to 'many publics, some of them existing in almost complete isolation from the others' and each of them looking to different types of modern novelists. 'Since Trollope,' he concludes, 'it is unlikely that any single novelist has captured them all.'[64] It is, of course, possible to show that his statement about Trollope is too broad. We tend to forget – rightly to forget – that there were many novelists, or rather tale-spinners, far more popular than Trollope, George Eliot, Thackeray or even Dickens, turning out sugary sentimentality or repetitious sensationalism which could be bought at railway stalls in gaudy covers for sixpence. It is perhaps a comfort that, as every age produces so much rubbish of its own, it has little time for the rubbish of the past. Walter Allen's assertion still has a core of truth. Trollope did stand at the end of a long line, not only of writers, but of creative people in every art, who tried to appeal to all 'sorts and conditions of men'. In the last decade of his life the trend in European civilisation that would divide 'culture' from ordinary life and make it the preserve of the illuminati was steadily gathering pace. The early dogmas of the cult of 'art for art's sake' and the doctrine of the 'sacred office' of the novelist were already being promulgated.

William Frith caught this moment superbly in his painting 'The Private View of the Royal Academy, 1881'. He explained that he constructed his painting so that the eye fell on two symbolic figures: the 'well-known apostle of the beautiful', Oscar Wilde, caught gazing upwards not only at the paintings but towards some artistic Elysium, and, on the other side, 'Anthony Trollope, whose homely figure affords a striking contrast to the eccentric forms near him'. Trollope, elegantly dressed as a Victorian gentleman complete with top hat, is observing both the paintings and the behaviour of those about him. He is caught looking at life with that same penetrating gaze which forty years earlier the Irishwoman had compared to a woman's as she examines dress material. He holds the catalogue and uses it as a notebook to record comments and observations none of which, we may be certain, he would ever have thought to be 'inspired'. The Victorian world stands round the dominating figures of Wilde and Trollope. Even the Prime Minister, Mr Gladstone, is kept firmly in the background, so that Frith's message of the two contrasting worlds is never obscured.[65]

The message in Frith's painting helps to explain why Trollope's popularity had passed its peak by the late 1870s and why he could no longer command the high prices he had obtained in the decade after *Framley Parsonage*. Younger reviewers tended not to treat him as well as those who had been reviewing in the days when the stories from Barsetshire held thousands entranced. Some of the decline was his own fault. He had 'over-crowded' his market with too many novels for too many years. This endless production had become something of a joke between himself and his friends. Inscribing a copy of *Is He Popenjoy?* to John Merivale, he wrote, 'I'll send the shelves to hold them some day.'[66] From the end of the 1860s he had not managed all his relations with publishers to the best advantage. Compared with most authors, he was a relief for publishers, as he was always open in his dealings and prompt with his work. Yet he had had feuds and disagreements enough to close some doors against him. Although he remained a friend of George Smith, he never returned to his firm after the late 1860s. One suspects Smith was not delighted with Trollope's attempts to set up *Saint Pauls* as a rival to the *Cornhill*.

Changes were also occurring both in the public's taste for novels and in the methods of publishing. At the beginning of the decade John Blackwood, a highly experienced publisher, wrote to Mrs Oliphant: 'The days of the three-vol. novels are over for profit, but what is to be the substitute? Trollope was strong that their day is gone by, but equally incapable of suggesting a remedy.' Nor were part issues as popular or as profitable as they had been in their heyday. Actually Trollope had tried to meet the changing taste by writing short novels as well as the traditional 'three-deckers'. In *Nina Balatka* he attempted to break the old mould by writing a short novel set on the continent. He chose to remain anonymous to avoid the charge of writing too many books. It was not a success. He continued to experiment with different forms. After *The Eustace Diamonds* in 1873 none of his novels was a 'three-decker' until *The American Senator* in 1877. The previous year he tried yet another idea with the penultimate novel in the Palliser series, *The Prime Minister*, published in four volumes. Also with that novel he attempted a new type of publishing: it was available in eight monthly divisions at five shillings each.[67] In his last few years he published many short novels, e.g. *Cousin Henry, An Eye For An Eye* and *Dr. Wortle's School*, in all of which the plot centres on a single moral dilemma.

Trollope was aware that he had passed his peak of popularity, and accepted the fact. 'When I am told that I have failed, I never fight the point,' he wrote to John Blackwood who had reported that *John Caldigate* did not seem popular with his magazine's readers. He continued, 'one attains a certain average of moderate success, & thanks the gods that the matter is not worse'. A few years before he had written: 'Fame is a skittish jade, more fickle even than Fortune, and apt to shy, and bolt, and plunge away on very trifling causes' [*Phineas Redux* XXVI]. Neither fame nor fortune deserted Trollope in his last years: there was simply a slow decline. Some individual novels, like *The Eustace Diamonds*, proved remarkably popular, particularly with the circulating libraries. It is virtually impossible to have any real idea how many people read Trollope's novels, but a knowledgeable bookseller and publisher recalled that 'those who in society had not read his last novel were out of the fashion' while the *Athenaeum* in its review of *The American Senator* alluded to 'readers of Mr. Trollope's books (and that means everybody)'.[68]

Whatever decline there was in sales, in the 1870s Trollope was an accepted fixture of Victorian culture, referred to by Gilbert and Sullivan in *Patience*, portrayed in cartoons such as Frederick Waddy's excellent drawing showing him as a puppet master with a bishop in lawn sleeves doing his bidding or in the 1873 'Spy' cartoon in *Vanity Fair* in which Trollope flicks his cigar and glares as if Disraeli had just sauntered into his library. George Goschen, a rising Liberal politician – 'our young Apollo', Trollope had somewhat extravagantly once called him – gave a dinner in 1878 in honour of the Crown Princess of Prussia, Queen Victoria's eldest and cleverest child. The Princess was anxious to meet the literary celebrities of her native land. Naturally Trollope was among the guests, perhaps forgetting how he had had a gentle laugh at the 'Household' of the Princess when she was a few years old [*The Kellys and the O'Kellys* II]. Many Victorians would have agreed with an enthusiastic young writer, Thomas Escott, who interviewed Trollope for an article in *Time* in 1879 and awarded him 'nearly the most conspicuous place in the first rank of novelists of the day'.[69]

At times Trollope could not be sure whether it was his general reputation which was in decline or whether individual novels had simply not proved a great success. He had, after all, had failures during his most popular period – the 1860s. Sometimes he thought the public was preoccupied with some passing topic, such as the lengthy search for the legitimate heir to the Tichborne baronetcy: 'I hope the English-reading public may now return to the reading of fiction,' Trollope wrote to his sister-in-law. 'We poor novelists had not, amongst us, the wit to invent such a grand plot as that!' Of course he knew that he was getting less money for his novels. He regarded the £2,800 he received for *The Claverings* in 1866 as his highest 'rate of pay', which presumably means income per words written. *Phineas Finn* had brought in £3,200, as had *He Knew He Was Right*. Yet as late as the mid-1870s *The Way We Live Now* earned him £3,000 and in the late 1870s he could still command close to £2,000 for a three-volume novel. His was a gentle decline, not a precipitate fall like that experienced by Charles Reade or Wilkie Collins. Nor can one forget that there was a fall in the price of many commodities, while at the same time publishers' costs were rising. To take one example: the average weekly wage of the compositors who set the type of novels and other books had been eighty-three shillings during Trollope's greatest period, but in his

last years it had risen to ninety-six shillings. The compositors earned –
more than earned, as anyone who looks at the manuscripts of Victorian
books can testify – about the highest wage any skilled man could
imagine. Trollope's decline in payments has to be seen in comparison
with that. He wrote that short delightful novel *Dr. Wortle's School* in
three weeks and received £500, which means that for every week he
spent on writing he received a sum equal to that which thirty-five
compositors, the highest-paid skilled men, received for the same period,
and they worked at least a full day while he spent but a few hours in the
morning.[70]

No doubt the more critical attitude, or the condescending dismissal of
his novels in some influential journals, played a part in lowering both
his reputation and his income. Trollope was so shaken by a review of *The
Prime Minister* in the *Spectator* that he unlocked his drawer and added
a footnote to his *Autobiography* that he was 'specially hurt' by what was
said. It was not a vicious review, but it wondered whether 'Mr Trollope's
power itself had declined'. The comment hurt because he thought it had
been written by Richard Hutton, who had always been his favourite
reviewer. Actually it was by Hutton's partner, W.W. Townsend. It is, of
course, always difficult to decide – particularly when one has so little
statistical evidence – whether reviews reflect public taste or simply the
taste of the reviewer. Living critics have a habit of repeating dead ones.
We cannot assume, because some reviewers in London disliked a book,
that it was rejected everywhere. The *Illustrated London News*, for
example, found much to praise in Trollope's 'gallant effort to keep true to
his new love – high politics', although they did think that the book
should have ended with Lopez's dramatic suicide.[71]

Whatever a few London critics thought, Trollope's reputation
remained high in other countries. In Australia, where his recent travel
book had been greatly praised, *Lady Anna* was being serialised in the
Australasian. In America Trollope's tremendous popularity – almost
part of 'our national life' – was shown in one comment in *Harper's* about
The Way We Live Now:

> Mr Anthony Trollope's novels are not only 'among the enjoyments of life,'
> they are also among its instructors; for no modern novelist, and perhaps
> no novelist of any time, has depicted with such scrupulous fidelity to the
> truth the actual facts of society, the phases of our national life and social
> life which almost inevitably escape the historian, and which are rarely
> caught even by the tourist or the essayist.

Another American magazine, the radical *Nation*, took up this point
about tourists and, referring to the 'great international controversy
which has been raging so long between England and the United States

as to which is the worse country of the two', thought that Trollope's description of English society which now included the Melmottes gave Americans new 'justification for ... love of country'.[72]

Trollope's fame was not confined to countries which shared the English literary tradition and language. The Swedes had a translation of *Ralph the Heir* by 1874 and five years later the French had *The Warden* as *Le Gardien*, although Frenchmen could have read *La Petite Maison d'Allington* as early as 1866. Readers of a Swiss newspaper had their own version of *The Warden* in *Legs de John Hiram*. Trollope's book on Thackeray was translated into German the year after its English appearance to join *Das Pfarrhaus Framley* and *Ist er Popenjoy?*. The Danes had *Familien Bertram*, the Norwegians, *Marion Fay* and the Hungarians, the melodramatic *Szemet-szemért* or *An Eye For An Eye*. The Dutch seemed to have the greatest interest in their distant kinsman's books, of which there were numerous translations, which eventually included his last, unfinished novel *De land-ligers*. Trollope was also enjoyed in that other great centre of the nineteenth-century novel, Russia. We have already noted Tolstoy's fondness for Trollope. He especially admired *The Prime Minister* and there is some ground for thinking that he took Lopez's suicide as a model in *Anna Karenina*. After reading *The Prime Minister* Tolstoy wrote, 'Trollope kills me with his excellence.' Of course, Trollope had the same advantage in Russia that Tolstoy was to have in England: he was foreign and therefore intellectually more respectable. An article in 1874 on contemporary English literature in the *St Petersburg News* referred to Trollope's 'remarkable vein of humour' and asserted that 'no novelist has ever depicted the English girls so faithfully and so attractively as Trollope'. It predicted that many of his novels would 'long remain unforgotten' for they were a 'pleasure to read over and over again'. As so often, the perspective afforded by distance is similar to that afforded by time and this analysis has proved more accurate than many of the dismissive comments that clever young critics were beginning to write in new journels like the *Academy*. Trollope was evidently pleased with this Russian view as a translation of it has survived among his papers.[73]

*

By the late 1870s the certainties Englishmen had enjoyed in the 1850s and even 1860s were fraying. To many Trollope was seen as 'early Victorian', even to the normally sympathetic High Church *Guardian* which praised 'the most successful novelist of the day in the delineation of modern society – that is, society of the early part of the nineteenth century'.[74] Throughout the 1870s he had tried and to a degree had succeeded in keeping his books topical even if some of his admirers, like the *Guardian*, wanted to pigeon-hole him in the past. He did this by continuing to deal with current subjects, like scandals in the City, just as twenty years earlier he had dealt with the abuses in charitable foundations in *The Warden*. He also reflected minor changes in fashion in his books. In *The Prime Minister*, when the Duke returns from Windsor with his commission to form a government, he has a 'very simple dinner' of 'a beefsteak and a potato, with a glass of sherry and Apollinaris water'* [VII]. This was even more topical when this part of the novel appeared in November 1875 than when Trollope wrote it. On 3 June *The Times* began carrying large advertisements for Apollinaris, a German bottled water which soon became fashionable in Britain. Trollope would already have known it, as George Smith served it to guests and, finding how much they liked it, made a second fortune by acquiring British distribution rights. Trollope was not Smith's only friend to introduce Apollinaris into a book: Browning did so in his long poem *The Inn Album* of 1875, where he also refers to someone's reading 'Trollope's novels'.

Slowly, but not imperceptibly, the novel itself was changing. Only a month after the publication of *The Prime Minister* the *Publishers' Circular* declared that 'literature is undergoing a sea-change ... when the sins of men and women are to be chronicled with a biblical plainness'. Throughout the late 1870s this was a frequent strain in trade journals representing those with a financial stake in the publication of fiction. 'Now from every quarter, sacred to literature and its professors, one can hear wails for the downfall of the novel.' This version of an oft-expressed anxiety appeared in an article, 'Is the Novel Moribund?', in *Tinsley's Magazine* in the last year of Trollope's life. Fiction was being affected by its very popularity: in the last twenty-five years – almost exactly the span of Trollope's fame – the number of novels published seemed to be increasing faster than the increase in novel readers. Between 1880 and 1881 there had been a 17 per cent increase in the number of novels published. The other factor hurting the traditional three-volume novel was the introduction of the American idea of serialised novels in newspapers. In Britain novels had long been popular in monthly magazines, but newspapers demanded a less leisurely approach. Before the introduction of

---

*If the Duke of Omnium had really gone to Windsor he could have had his Apollinaris water there as it had become the Queen's custom to add it to her own specially blended whisky.

newspaper serialisation the rights of a three-decker, according to the *Tinsley* article, were worth 'about twice as much as they will fetch today'. Trollope was adapting to this new method by having *Cousin Henry* appear in the *Manchester Weekly Examiner*, as well as in a Scottish newspaper. The well-informed author concluded, in laments still heard, 'The cause of the trouble is not far to seek. The English nation ... *borrows* books instead of *buying* them, it supports that vast and useful system the circulating library, not the individual author.'[75]

*

Trollope's 'decline' therefore may be seen as part of this general 'sea-change' in Victorian literature, and even as another indication that Victorian literature itself had passed its peak rather than as a rejection by readers. There is a superb insight into the English literary world of the 1870s in the work of the Royal Commission on Copyright of which Trollope himself was the most active member. This Commission, under the chairmanship of Lord John Manners, began its work in May 1876 and carried on its investigations for about one year. Trollope asked more questions than any other member and evidently did his background work. Characteristically he made no attempt to disguise the fact that he had read the entry on 'copyright' in the *Encylopaedia Britannica*. Well-known writers of all types were examined as well as publishers like Macmillan, Murray and Blackwood. Nor was copyright restricted only to books, for Sir Charles Barry testified about architectural copyright and Arthur Sullivan about music. Trollope asked his friend Sullivan if he could prevent street musicians from making free use of new songs. 'I wish I could,' replied the composer. Among the witnesses were Matthew Arnold, Herbert Spencer and Sir Charles Trevelyan, the 'Sir Gregory Hardlines' of *The Three Clerks*.

Most of the Commission's attention was directed to novels, something made particularly poignant by the oft-cited fact that Dickens's copyrights expired in 1876, six years after his death. Trollope was painfully aware of this because Chapman had written to him the previous year saying that the firm had paid £3,500 for all of Dickens's copyrights even though they had only a year to run. This may be an indication of the bad business practices that characterised that firm! John Blackwood explained how much the circulating libraries hurt sales and kept publishers from paying larger amounts to authors. Blackwood – three years younger than Trollope – said that 'in [his] own time' the circulating libraries had grown twenty-fold. In many ways

Trollope agreed with his friend but wanted to make his own views heard: 'We ... think that on our bench we have good and honest judges, because we pay them well. Do you not think that the same effect would result with regard to authors in England?' His fault as a member of the Commission was his fondness for converting a question into a statement. He was 'rather in the speech making line' was the way John Blackwood put it when describing the Commission to his nephew in Edinburgh.[76] He was courteous to witnesses with one exception: when T.H. Farrar, Permanent Secretary to the Board of Trade, said he would be 'sorry' to hear that men like Dr. Johnson, Scott or Dickens wrote for money, he touched a raw Trollopean nerve, which snapped back: 'Do you not think that an author is in exactly the same category as any other workman, who has it upon his conscience to use his life for doing good work for the world around him and who cannot do that good work unless he is paid for it?'

The twin roadblocks presented by circulating libraries and the lack of international copyright kept novelists from reaping the rewards of their popularity at home and abroad. In his questions Trollope showed particular interest in colonial and American sales. Evidence was produced to show how *The Prime Minister* was sold in the United States for 5s 9d, one-sixth of the British price. This disparity increasingly affected the growing Canadian market where a legal copy of the novel was even more expensive than in England with the inevitable result: Canadians bought smuggled American copies, particularly as there was even a paperback costing less than three shillings. Trollope also showed particular interest in whether or not a novelist had a copyright in his plots or whether someone else could use them. This was another sore point with him. When in Australia he had received a letter from his friend Charles Reade announcing that he had adapted *Ralph the Heir* as a play which would soon appear at the Gaiety Theatre. A furious correspondence ensued and the two friends did not speak for five years, though the play called 'Shilly-Shally' failed and was even accused of being indecent. It is said that the two novelists would play whist at the Garrick without ever exchanging a word. To Trollope 'Shilly-Shally' was yet another example of why the law on copyright needed reform.[77]

The Commission's impressive report may not have led to immediate reforms but it still provides one of the best insights into publishing and authorship at the time. For anyone interested in Trollope it shows, yet again, his fierce determination to get justice and adequate recompense for 'the man who has worked with his brain'.[78]

*

Trollope also occupied a central role in London literary society. Since George Eliot rarely moved in these circles, he was the most famous novelist to be seen at gatherings. Alfred Domett, Browning's close friend and himself a poet, saw Trollope at a 'conversazione' at the Colonial Institute in 1876: he 'certainly looks less like "the man of genius" he certainly is, than most other distinguished men'. Part of the reason was because Trollope's appearance did not meet the approved canon of the pseudo-science of phrenology. He was 'bald, bearded, irongrey, rather ruddy and rough, spectacled, eyes not so full or prominent as "phrenologically" they should be in so ready a writer – nor so wide apart nor forehead so broad, as would betoken so fertile and facile an inventor.' Nevertheless Domett still found him 'free, frank and lively'. Frederick Locker-Lampson, another poet who knew Trollope well – well enough for the novelist to give him the manuscript of *The Small House at Allington* bound in dark morocco – saw that his role in literary society was based on a regard for his genuine kindness: 'Not the worse part of a distinguished man's reputation is the esteem in which he is held by his friends, and in this Trollope was rich. He indulged in no professional jealousies; indeed he had none to indulge in. He only had much nobility of nature.'[79]

It is appropriate that the best portrait of Trollope in society comes from the son of the man who gave the best description of his novels. By 1879, the year in which Trollope paid a tribute to Nathaniel Hawthorne in the *North American Review*, the writer had been dead for fifteen years. It was about the same time that Julian Hawthorne appeared in London, where he was known as the author of some promising novels. He was a frequent guest in 'rooms full of tobacco-smoke and talk, amid which were discernible ... the figures and faces of men more or less renowned in the world of books'. 'Most noticeable among these personages' he continued,

> was a broad-shouldered, sturdy man ... with a ruddy countenance and snow-white tempestuous beard. He wore large, gold-rimmed spectacles ... and looked at his interlocutor with a certain genial fury of inspection. He seemed to be in a state of some excitement; he spoke volubly and almost boisterously, and his voice was full-toned and powerful, though pleasant to the ear. He turned himself, as he spoke with a burly briskness, from one side to another ... Meanwhile he flourished in the air an ebony walking stick, with much vigour ... narrowly missing ... the pates of his listeners. He was clad in evening dress ... an exceedingly fine-looking old gentleman. At the first glance, you would have taken him to be some civilised and modernised Squire Western, nourished with beef and ale, and roughly hewn out of the most robust and least refined variety of human clay.

Hawthorne not only left us a superb picture of Trollope in society but went on to describe the essence of his character, what George Eliot had called his '*Wesen*':

> Looking at him more narrowly, however, you would have reconsidered this judgement ... the lines of his features were delicately cut ... and his face was susceptible of very subtle and sensitive changes of expression ... It might be thought that he was overburdened with self-esteem, and unduly opinionated; but, in fact, he was but over-anxious to secure the good-will and agreement of all ... There was some peculiarity in him – some element or bias in his composition that made him different from other men; but, on the other hand, there was an ardent solicitude to annul or reconcile this difference, and to prove himself to be ... of absolutely the same cut and quality as all the rest of the world.

Hawthorne had indeed penetrated to the heart of Trollope: the boy who had been miserable at school, the frustrated youth in London who had read old plays and modern novels and had determined at some point in his life – probably when he heard the hunting horns call out over County Galway – that he would no longer stand apart from others but join them, portray them, and in so doing, conquer his own fears. Hawthorne concluded that 'after he had shown you all he had in him, you would have seen nothing that was not gentlemanly, honest, and clean'. How Trollope would have relished that remark! Hawthorne concluded: 'It was impossible to help liking such a man at first sight; and I believe that no man in London society was more generally liked than Anthony Trollope.'

In his rounds of that Society young Hawthorne encountered another Trollope. Rose told him that she wished Anthony were not a writer: 'He never leaves off and he always has two packages of manuscript in his desk, besides the one he's working on, and the one that's being published.' Hawthorne, noting that Rose 'was always fashionably dressed' reasoned that the money for such things 'does not come unasked, unsought'. Rose certainly did not really regret her husband's vocation, but she may well have wished, at times, that he would go about it a little more quietly, a little less vigorously and possibly a little later in the morning. Hawthorne, doubly perceptive, discovered the other secret from all these meetings: 'His wife was his books.'[80]

*

None of his work in his library, whether it was reading, annotating old plays, writing his novels and articles or giving advice to young writers, none of his life in the clubs and Society, none of his work in defending the rights of authors at Commissions or in helping their widows at the Royal Literary Fund prevented Trollope from pursuing his love of travel. His European travels were no longer centred on seeing art. Increasingly he and Rose, usually with Florence, spent weeks in the mountains of Switzerland or in the Black Forest, where he liked 'to rove about'. Gradually the weeks grew into months, for Trollope could work wherever he was. He found the mountain air restful, although he disliked 'those stuffy, fluffy, soft, slippery coverings which always fall off a German bed when an Englishman tries to sleep in it'.[81] Sometimes they were joined for part of the holiday by Henry, and usually they were joined by Tom and his wife.

As in the earlier travels in the 1850s, there could be troublesome encounters with continental officials. In 1874 Trollope sent an outraged letter to *The Times* from the Garrick Club describing his difficulties on a recent trip from Switzerland to London. First, the tickets were six francs more than advertised; secondly, while he had been told that each member of the party could have fifty-six pounds of luggage free they were charged for everything they brought, which was no doubt a large amount; thirdly, after a stop at Strasbourg, so hurried that they could not finish their coffee, the guard dropped one of the books of tickets between the window frames. 'His horror at his own deed was so complete and vivid that no traveller could have been angry with him.' Other officials were summoned: ' "So" said the one conductor. "So-o!" exclaimed a second. "So-o-o-o!" ejaculated the oldest and biggest and most authoritative of the lot.' Twice men with hammers attempted to retrieve the lost tickets. At Brussels Trollope saw the stationmaster, 'a gentleman with the manners of a Duke and the urbanity of a Prime Minister'. There seemed nothing to do but pay £3 to replace the tickets lost by the railway. Trollope's anger in this letter was as nothing compared to his second, sent a few days after the *Saturday Review* had accused him of displaying 'more than average ... ignorance and weakness' in his letter to *The Times*. Carping at his novels was one thing but insulting the family tradition of travelling was another. 'Had I possessed the omniscience of a *Saturday Reviewer* and the Jove-like strength of the editor himself, I could have done nothing,' Trollope replied in his second letter. Eventually, after three letters to *The Times*, Trollope forced the railway company to refund his money. It had been many years since he had written so many words for so little money, but justice had at last triumphed.[82]

In spite of such annoyances these long holidays in the Black Forest and in Switzerland allowed Trollope to wander in the woods where he could dream new plots and live with his characters. He loved trees of all types and practised and preached the need to conserve them: 'A man who will plant a poplar, a willow ... how good is he! But the man who will plant an oak will surely feel the greenness of its foliage and the pleasantness of its shade when he is lying down, down beneath the sod!' As much as he loved English oaks, he found the pine forests of Germany a better place to pursue his thoughts. 'There is a scent from them which reaches my brain and soothes it. There is a murmur among their branches, best heard when the moving breath of heaven just stirs the air, which reminds me of my duty without disturbing me ... I walk ... with my stick in my hand and my story half-conceived in my mind.' It was in these woods, as in the book-lined rooms at Montagu Square, that this thoughtful, serious and kindly man gathered the material he needed for his writing and the calm he required to temper his constant activities. He needed this calm and solace as he aged because he had no intention of stopping his activities: as he wrote when describing his devotion to whist, 'Excitement is a great step towards happiness particularly to those who are over sixty.'[83]

Trollope on his trip to Iceland, from *How the 'Mastiffs' Went to Iceland* (Mrs Hugh Blackburn).

CHAPTER FIFTEEN

The Radius of his Circle

Fanny Trollope – the second edition, Tom's wife – was in a nervous state on 4 March 1875. She and her husband were expecting Anthony in Rome, but he had telegraphed that his train had been delayed by snow. Then news arrived that an avalanche had blocked the line outside Florence. Shortly after ten she was sitting writing to her friend Linda Villari when she glanced out of her window to see an omnibus in the Via Santa Susanna. Among the tourists sat the unmistakable forms of the two Trollope brothers. 'Anthony has arrived since I wrote the last words,' she informed her friend, 'he is looking very robust and is in good spirits.'[1] He was stopping in Italy on his way to Australia: for his second round-the-world trip he wanted to try a different route. He carried on to Brindisi, where he took ship for Egypt, and then crossed by land to the Red Sea where he boarded another ship sailing to the Indian Ocean.

Rose, no doubt recalling her adventures in the snow drifts of New Zealand, did not accompany him. She and Florence went to the continent to 'roam about' as she put it. Trollope missed her greatly and wrote from his ship, 'God bless you, dearest love – I do hope you will enjoy your trip … I doubt your liking Hamburg or Danzig, but … you will like Dresden & the Dutch pictures.' As always, he had had a desk fixed up in his cabin where he was attempting some concession to Victorian 'new technology'. In addition to finishing his current novel, *Is He Popenjoy?*, he was writing a series of newspaper articles and had agreed to make two copies in case one got lost. So he had a cumbersome device that made a copy as he wrote but it made his fingers dirty 'in a disgusting manner'. That was nothing to the mess he found when he opened one of his cases in the Gulf of Aden. 'You remember my big bottle of ink?' he asked Rose. 'I found the bottle'[2]

> smashed to pieces inside the case … There were three shirts on top put in to keep things steady. I wish you could see those three shirts. And there

were 100 loose cigars. I have not yet tried how cigars, bathed in ink, smoke; – but I shall try. Some wretch had pitched the desk down like a ball, and all my beautiful white paper! ... God bless you dearest, dearest love. I do so hope you will be happy & enjoy yourself. Tell me every thing of your doings & goings, and of your travelling adventures. Best love to Flo.

He stopped for about two weeks in Ceylon where William Gregory was now Governor. They had been at Harrow together but had only become friends in Trollope's early days in Ireland. The visitor was impressed with 'the gentleness of the present British rule, and the appreciated desire of British rulers to give the natives all the privileges of free men'.[3] Under the benign rule of the British Empire Ceylon was free from racial war and good roads were improving the island's economy. He saw this as an improvement on the days of Portuguese and Dutch rule but attributed it to 'the advance of civilisation rather than the difference of races'. Coffee was then the main crop and it was bringing great riches to the planters. Not only did Trollope investigate all the facts about growing coffee but he even joined the planters and their dogs on an elk hunt. He was frustrated in 'one of my grand desires to see an elephant – a real wild elephant – and perhaps to shoot one'. Such hunting had been banned by the government unless an elephant wandered into someone's garden. Actually, for all his love of fox-hunting, Trollope hardly ever engaged in shooting.

On the journey from Ceylon to Australia he finished *Is He Popenjoy?* Since his long book on Australia and New Zealand, as well as his articles for the *Daily Telegraph*, had been published only two years before, he decided not to write another book about this second trip. It was a sign of the times even more than an indication of his declining reputation that he arranged to write newspaper articles for that new entity, a press agency, which sold his twenty pieces to about a dozen newspapers, of which the main one was the *Liverpool Mercury*. His account of Australia is basically a simpler version of his book, with the statistics left out. The purpose of the trip was not just a strong desire to see Fred again but to find out about his prospects. When he arrived in May, he was not happy with what he discovered at the sheep station. He described to his friend Millais how rough the life still was: no sherry and no one to clean his boots. This did not really bother him, as he had distractions. He began his next novel, *The American Senator*, on 4 June and wrote for four hours every day. For once something or someone was allowed to disturb him:

I play with my grandchildren, – of whom I have two and a third coming. Fred ... is always on horseback and seems to me to have more troubles on his back than any human being I ever came across. I shall be miserable when I leave him because I do not know how I can look forward to seeing him again without making this long journey. I do not dislike the journey, or the seas, or the hardship. But I was 60 the other day, and at that age a man has no right to look forward to making many more voyages round the world.

This was the only time in his life that Trollope would see any of his grandchildren: Frank was about three, while Harry was a year younger. The full state of Fred's desperate financial position only emerged after Trollope had returned home but while he was in Australia a formal document was drawn up whereby Fred acknowledged an indebtedness of £6,000 – an enormous sum – to 'Anthony Trollope at present of Sydney'. When he wrote of this to Henry there was no word of complaint: 'It is the kind of misfortune which I can bear ... Poor dear Fred. Do not suppose ... that I blame him.'4 Fred eventually was forced to give up the sheep station and follow his father's example by becoming a civil servant in Australia. Seldom if ever in literary history have so many sheep absorbed the profits of so many novels!

*

As on his earlier Australian trip, Trollope returned home by way of America. Although the voyage to Hawaii was in excessively hot weather, he was the only passenger who forsook his cabin to sleep on deck. He did not like San Francisco: it was not a city, he decided, for 'an old-fashioned Englishman'. He did, however, enjoy an expedition to see the redwood trees. As a lover of trees he insisted on measuring the diameter of one and found it to be seventy-eight feet. After a week spent in crossing America by train, 'meeting people ... whom I had never seen before and from whom I parted as old friends', he paid a hurried farewell visit to Boston, that city he so deeply loved. For the last time he knocked at 'doors of which the latches were familiar to my hands' and saw 'the faces which I knew so well'. It must have been a rather tired man who settled onto the *Bothnia* as it sailed out of New York in October 1875. He had now completed the last of his five visits to America, and perhaps his farewells had put him in a retrospective mood, for he now began to work on his *Autobiography*. There was another novelist aboard during the ten days of a rough crossing. Henry James, on his way to 'take possession of the old world', had the same initial reaction as some other people to the novelist some thirty years his senior. 'We had also Anthony Trollope, who wrote novels in his state room all the morning (he does it literally every morning of his life, no matter where he may be,) and played cards ... all the evening. He has a gross and repulsive face and manner, but appears *bon enfant* when you talk with him. He is the dullest Briton of them all.' Later, when James had talked with the elder novelist at the Cosmopolitan Club and at a dinner party, he changed his mind and found him 'a very good, genial, ordinary fellow – much better than he seemed on the steamer'. By the time James wrote his tribute to Trollope, a few months after his death, the Atlantic crossing was seen in a new light:[5]

[I have] never forgotten the magnificent example of plain persistence ... The season was unpropitious, the vessel overcrowded, the voyage detestable; but Trollope shut himself up in his cabin every morning for ... communion with the muse. He drove his pen as steadily on the tumbling ocean as in Montague [*sic*] Square ... Trollope has been accused of being deficient in imagination, but ... The power to shut one's eyes, one's ears (to say nothing of another sense), upon the scenery of a pitching Cunarder and open them to the loves and sorrows of Lily Dale or ... Lady Glencora Palliser, is certainly a faculty which could take to itself wings.

This is an excellent insight into how a sensitive person's reactions to Trollope changed after the initial annoyance at his boisterous and energetic ways. Of course, we often forget when reading such reactions that it was not just Trollope's undoubtedly exuberant manner that caused them. Henry James at this time was a young novelist whose first important book, *Roderick Hudson*, was just starting to appear. No one on the ship would have been very impressed by that when the most famous male novelist in the English-speaking world was on board. Furthermore James, like all young artists, had an inflated notion of the 'sacredness' of his calling. Trollope, being perfectly satisfied with the religion into which he had been baptised, had no need to invent another out of his art, but his insistence upon such a point would understandably have upset a dedicated beginner.

*

Trollope was not long home before he was writing to the lady with whom he had played nightly card games on the *Bothnia*: 'Here we are all agog about the Turks and the Russians, and are so hot that every body is ready to cut everybody's throat. I and my brother ... happen to be on altogether different sides. To my thinking Disraeli is the meanest cuss we have ever had in this country.' Tom's wife watched the letters flying back and forth between London and Rome with some bemusement: 'Anthony ... has fully expounded the anti-Turk-down-with-Disraeli cause ... Tom and he disagree on the subject and write each long arguments about it.' The crisis had begun with a rebellion in the Balkans which caused the Turks to massacre Christians with more than their usual barbarity. Many people in England were horrified at the spectacle of thousands of fellow Christians being impaled and murdered by a corrupt Mohammedan Empire. Disraeli, more concerned that Russia would grab the Balkans should Christian intervention unsettle the Ottoman Empire, dismissed the agitation as coffee house babble. Trollope was just one of many thousands who read Gladstone's famous pamphlet *The Bulgarian Horrors and the Question of the East*. Some 200,000 copies of this were sold in one month alone! On his first night back at Montagu Square, Trollope read aloud to Rose and Florence Gladstone's impassioned demand that the Mohammedans clear out 'one and all, bag and baggage' from Christian Europe, and one can imagine the fury with which he read.[6]

On 8 December 1876 a day-long grand protest meeting – what the Victorians called a 'demonstration' – was held at St James's Hall, Piccadilly. It was a remarkable event and was, in many ways, the first time an organised protest representing every conceivable segment of society was assembled, something that was as novel then as it is commonplace now. It was a gathering not only of important national politicians like Gladstone and influential local leaders like John Wild, Mayor of Oldham, but of great intellectual figures like Ruskin, Mark Pattison, T.H. Green and Herbert Spencer, as well as religious leaders from every spectrum of opinion ranging from Dr Pusey to the Birmingham Nonconformist R.W. Dale. Trollope only found his invitations to speak on the morning of the meeting as he had been out of London when it arrived; even on such short notice he was 'glad to speak'. As tickets were severely limited he asked for one for Henry and then sent a servant round to collect it. Hundreds of delegates assembled, reporters sat in the front row using their top hats as temporary desks and files while ladies beamed down from the gallery.[7]

Trollope was one of the first speakers and he went right to the heart of what he saw as a moral question regarding the difference between Christian Englishmen and 'the Turk' who 'does not see the difference between good and evil as we see it. That which is good to us is evil to him, and that which is most evil to us, such as tyranny, cruelty, and oppression, are all absolutely good to him.' As there were so many speakers each was limited to a few minutes – except for Gladstone who spoke for an hour and a half – but Trollope was determined to have his say. Thomas Hardy, sitting in the audience, was amused at what happened. After Trollope had exceeded his time limit the Chairman, the Duke of Westminster, allowed himself several graceful coughs. When these had no effect and Trollope was still speaking after seven minutes he began to ring his bell. Finally in desperation he reached forward and 'tugged at Trollope's coat-tails'. Trollope simply turned round and said 'Please leave my coat alone' and carried on: when in full flight he was intimidated by no one, not even the richest peer in the country! Trollope, writing three days after the meeting, was convinced it had been 'most successful' although he was amused at the 'outrageous anger of the hangers on of the Government'. Their anger was as nothing when compared to that of his Sovereign who denounced these *'disgraceful proceedings'* and told Disraeli that the Attorney-General should prosecute all these 'disloyal' and 'unpatriotic' speakers. In spite of the coat-tugging, Trollope now had a Duke whom he was soon describing as a 'friend'.[8]

*

From the time of his second trip to Australia until his death seven years later Trollope wrote thirteen novels, though the last was never completed. At one time these novels tended to be dismissed whereas there is a danger now of their being over-emphasised. Certainly, from the biographical point of view, they tend to be less interesting than the novels of his early years or those written when he was at the peak of his fame in the 1860s. As we have seen, he completed the absurdly named *Is He Popenjoy?* the day before his ship arrived in Melbourne. It has one similarity with *Lady Anna*, the novel he finished on his first voyage to Australia: it revolves round the question of who is the heir to a wicked nobleman entangled with a dubious Italian woman. The action follows the family of the Marquess's younger brother, Lord George Germain, and his wife, Mary, daughter of the local Dean. When the child of the Italian woman dies, followed by the wicked Marquess, Lord George becomes Marquess of Brotherton and his son becomes the heir, Lord Popenjoy.[9]

Trollope used this novel to mount his fiercest assault upon feminist lecturers, reflecting distant memories of Fanny Wright and the fact that Kate Field was spending much of the 1870s in London. In the novel there are two rival lady lecturers, the German Baroness Banmann with her 'considerable moustache' and her talk of 'De manifest infairiority of de tyrant saix' and 'Miss Doctor Olivia Q. Fleabody from Vermont' in her trousers. At their 'Rights of Women Institute', 'strongly-visaged spinsters and mutinous wives ... were worked up by Dr. Fleabody to a full belief that a glorious era was at hand in which women would be chosen by constituencies, would wag their heads in courts of law ... and have balances at their banker's' [XVII, LX]. Later generations can hardly guess from this satire that the same man was active in a movement to help reduce the hours of work of female shop assistants. On the day of Trollope's birth *The Times* had remarked in one article, 'This is the age of female triumph.' Trollope believed that women were equal 'in intellectual capacity' and had been prepared to accept that a woman was the greatest living novelist; he was more than willing to help to find work for women printers, but he could never accept feminist lectures from any of Fanny Wright's spiritual heirs. 'You cannot by Act of Congress or Parliament,' he wrote to an American correspondent,[10]

> make the woman's arm as strong as the man's or deprive her of her position as the bearer of children. We may trouble ourselves much by debating a question which superior power has settled for us, but we cannot alter the law ... The necessity of the supremacy of man is as certain to me as the eternity of the soul. There are other matters on which one fights as on subjects which are in doubt, – universal suffrage, ballot, public education, and the like – but not, as I think, on these two.

*

In 1876 J.L. Motley, the American diplomat, wrote to his friend Trollope from Dorset, saying that he had 'no visitor but the American Senator whom we are expecting again with much anxiety'. Motley was not referring to some migrating politician but to the novel Trollope had started at his son's sheep station. *The American Senator* is filled with various love affairs and is one of Trollope's best portrayals of country life. In the last chapter he admits he should have called the book 'The Chronicle of a Winter at Dillsborough', and the Dutch, taking his hint, called their translation, which also appeared in 1876, *En vinter i Dillsborough*. Trollope had reached an agreement with George Bentley, of his mother's old publishers, for the novel to appear in their magazine *Temple Bar* for an agreed fee of £600. The most memorable character in the book is Senator Gotobed, who arrives in Dillsborough anxious to study English country life. The Senator is a failure as a character because he is too much a stereotype, a crude and interfering provincial whose only redeeming feature is a genuine love of justice. It is unfortunate that Trollope decided to eliminate the Senator's wife from his story as she may well have added a lighter touch. A crossed-out portion of the mansucript, for example, has Mrs Gotobed preferring Unitarian chapels for one simple but untheological reason: 'because they warmed their churches.'[11] Trollope makes clear that the midwestern Senator is not a 'Yankee', a title that should be used only for New Englanders like Trollope's friend Motley, the type of Americans he particularly liked.

It is virtually impossible for any but the closest student of this novel to see that Trollope actually agrees with much of the Senator's criticism of England. As he wrote to a friend while the story was half-way through its run in *Temple Bar*: 'I do not think that the Senator from Mikewa will be unpopular in the U.S. – rather the reverse, as he is a thoroughly honest man wishing to do good, and is not himself half so absurd as the things which he criticises.' One can only assume, however, that Trollope did not endorse the Senator's tirades against fox-hunting. Where Trollope did agree was when the Senator rudely told the clergymen who were seated at the dinner table with him that the 'big plums find their way so often to sons and sons-in-law and nephews of bishops' [XLII]. Here the Senator was precisely expressing Trollope's views: ten years earlier he had written an article for the *Pall Mall Gazette* denouncing Bishop Wilberforce for giving his son a lovely plum as a living, but Smith refused to publish it.[12] *The American Senator* fails, much as the Senator himself did in his lecture about English 'institutions', because it is never possible to decide whether the author is laughing at the English customs being mocked or at the bumptious American who mocks them.

In 1879 Trollope published three novels – as well as his *Thackeray*. *An Eye For An Eye*, which begins with a woman confined in a private mental asylum, could well be thought to have been connected with the *Thackeray* book but Trollope had written the novel years before. It is a melodramatic tale set in Dorset and Ireland about the conflict between love and duty. The young heir to an earldom loves, in a rather off-hand way, an Irish girl whom he seduces. The young man, now an Earl, is pushed over a cliff in the West of Ireland by the girl's outraged mother, who in her turn loses her mind. The tragedy is the result of the young man's dreamy longing for 'an adventure'. This novel also had a standard Trollope stand-by, the female religious fanatic, in this case a Countess. There is a rather similar woman, Mrs Bolton, in *John Caldigate*, a novel which began serialisation in *Blackwood's* in April 1878.[13] The portrayal of Mrs Bolton's religious mania, mixed with her jealousy of her daughter's love for Caldigate, is fascinating. This is the only novel in which Trollope makes detailed use of his knowledge of postal matters. The question whether or not Caldigate has committed bigamy is determined by a postal clerk's evidence about the validity of a post mark. In novels like *Orley Farm*, written while he was still a Surveyor, Trollope could boast of things like the improved quality of postmarks [XLV], but it was only after he had retired that he felt free to make a story hinge on a postal question. Trollope also made use of his time in Australia, particularly his visits to the gold mines with their exotic names and his meetings with gold miners, like his son's schoolfriend.

The final novel of that year was *Cousin Henry*, which is set in Wales. It is not a very good book because so many of the characters are not developed. It is also almost totally lacking in 'authorial intrusions', and one misses having Trollope at one's side. A canon of Hereford Cathedral is introduced, but nothing is really made of him, which is a pity because he is an example of the late Victorian clergyman who rose from a humble background. *Cousin Henry* shows how Trollope's genius required the leisurely space of three volumes in which to develop its potential. As with so many of the later novels it centres on a question of inheritance, in this case on whether or not Henry Jones is the true heir to his uncle's estate. Most of the local people believe that the old squire made a will leaving the estate to his niece, Isabel, but no one can find the will. Henry actually discovers it in a book of Jeremy Taylor's sermons in the library but he can bring himself neither to reveal its existence nor to destroy it. Trollope's portrayal of this man shows his great skill at handling disturbed minds. Henry Jones is neither mad nor bad, but on this one subject he is incapable of action. His dilemma is made all the worse by the contempt in which he is held by his new neighbours and servants. Trollope well understood that peculiar aspect of human nature which prevents so many people from destroying a document that can ultimately destroy them. 'We are too apt to forget,' says Trollope, 'when we think of the sins and faults of men how keen may be their conscience in spite of their sins' [XVII].

In *Cousin Henry* is also found the answer to a question that had been plaguing Trollope for more than a decade. How was he to provide for his niece, Florence Bland? In the novel the old squire is torn between his devotion to his niece and his belief that an estate must descend to the male heir. It was 'his duty to maintain the old order of things' [I]. In his quandary the old squire compiles many different wills reflecting his varying moods, but in the penultimate one (which is assumed to be valid until the last one is found) he leaves his niece, who happens to be named Florence, £4,000 [I]. Of all the private messages Trollope inserted into his books this is the most revealing. He began the novel on 26 October 1878 and three days later he went to his solicitors to sign his own will in which he left, like the squire, £4,000 to his niece,

Florence Nightingale Bland. When he gave Florence a copy of the two-volume edition of *Cousin Henry* he wrote above the title, 'Florence Bland from Anthony Trollope', but beneath the title he added another message in pencil. Someone, presumably Florence herself, eventually erased this, but a careful examination can just make out all but one word: 'From the Author to the writer. From the uncle to his own —?— niece.' As so often in reconstructing Trollope's family affairs, the one vital word cannot be seen. Rose did not entirely give up her duties to her niece because, as we have seen, soon after this she took Trollope's dictation for *Cicero*. She had also told him, quite rightly and in her usual, forthright manner, that one of his proposed titles for *Cousin Henry*, 'Getting at a Secret', 'sounds claptrap'.[14]

Just as Trollope had used his earlier novels for private messages to his wife, who copied his scrawl for the printers, so now he used *Cousin Henry* for messages to Florence Bland. By the late 1870s she had become his secretary, and the mansucript of this novel – now at Yale – shows that this work was mainly in her hand. Trollope, who celebrated his sixty-fourth birthday in 1879, was beginning to suffer from 'writer's cramp'. The years of writing – and we must remember that his official postal reports and correspondence were also voluminous and mostly written by himself – had begun to take their toll. At times he was able to carry on using his straight pen as he had for decades, but many of the novels of his last four years are in his niece's hand. This was about the time the 'type-writing machine' was coming into use: by the mid-1870s several government departments including the Admiralty and the Post Office had introduced them and, with them, the 'type-writers' who worked them. There were restrictions on their use: for many decades it was considered wrong ever to type the Sovereign's name or title, so the words 'Queen Victoria' or 'The Queen' were written in later by hand. The writer of an article commending the new machines to authors 'who find the work of the desk monotonous and unhealthy' claimed that he could write twenty-five words a minute with a pen but that a 'type-writer' could produce seventy. Mrs Oliphant – who, Trollope admitted, might surpass him in the number of novels she would write – was having her novels typed by the 1880s because her 'writer's cramp' had worn a hole in her hand.[15]

Trollope however became more and more dependent on Florence rather than a typewriter. He told one friend: 'However early the hour, however dull and depressing the dawn, we soon warm to our work and get so excited with those we are writing about, that I don't know whether she or I are most surprised when the time comes to leave off for breakfast.' Faithful to his teaching, Trollope expected her to marry, and yet he feared that, when that happened, 'I shall have a bad time of it'. One cousin described her as 'the tenderest and most devoted of daughters, an untiring and reliable secretary'. Florence Bland thus became the last of that trio to whom those who enjoy Trollope's novels owe gratitude along with her Aunt Rose and Barney the faithful groom and human alarm-clock. Looking at the manuscripts of some of the other novels that she wrote down, one often sees that Trollope's own handwriting suddenly appears, often for a short passage. Perhaps she was called out of the room, or perhaps he may have felt the need to use his pen for a certain passage, as Thackeray had when dictating to his daughter. Trollope insisted that 'Flo' should not interrupt while he was dictating. He described her once as 'clever but not demonstrative', which is just what he needed, particularly as he could be difficult when he was dictating.[16] It is said that he once ripped up a whole chapter when Florence made a suggestion to improve it. Only Rose was allowed that freedom.

It is difficult for anyone to accept that he is no longer capable of doing something he has regarded as essential to his well-being. The fact that Florence was sitting attentively at her writing desk, like the fact that he could no longer hear in one ear, was a sign that mortality was at hand. He may also have heard some version of a rumour picked up by one American magazine, 'that Mr Trollope is beginning to "let out" portions of his novels to less renowned assistants'. His insistence on silence during these early morning writing sessions is a further sign of that bear-like personality that people so often noticed. It became a family joke, and guests at those long, late morning breakfasts often asked Florence if her uncle beat her. She reacted with a smile while 'Uncle Tony' laughed, banged the table and declared that such a remedy was long overdue. Eventually he began to dictate many of his letters, which must have been harder for him to accept as Victorian convention ordained that one gentleman did not use a secretary to write to another. He continued to send what he called, with scarcely any exaggeration, his 'illegible scrawl' to close friends although they often told him they 'could not make out a word'. With business forms, of course, he would have to sign things himself: when Blackwood sent him a payment of £100 for *The Fixed Period* he signed his initials across the penny stamp at the bottom to confirm receipt while Florence wrote the acknowledgment.[17]

To what degree did this change in writing methods affect his final books? The answer is: not as much as it affected Henry James's style after he began to dictate his books. With Trollope it is difficult to decide whether any change in style is due to old age or to the different method of composition. Certainly in *Cousin Henry* there are far fewer 'authorial intrusions': perhaps dictating, as opposed to writing, weakened the confidential bond between writer and reader which these asides presume. Of course, the new method may have had a greater effect in *Cousin Henry* than in later novels. No doubt it was why he showed such interest in the effect of dictation on Cicero's works. We may also wonder what effect it had on Florence. So little is known about her that it is impossible to say. However, her real cousin Henry did tell a publisher after his father's death that, while Florence had written the manuscript of *An Old Man's Love* only a year before, she could no longer remember anything about it![18]

Cousin Henry, Is He Popenjoy? and *The American Senator* all dealt with the role of individuals in an hierarchical society increasingly subject to criticism and change. *The Duke's Children*, as already mentioned, was the sixth and final novel in the Palliser series, and it showed the Duke's final acceptance that his children were not devoted to their aristocratic duty and did not believe they should marry within their own sphere. According to the *Spectator*, it was a 'dramatic essay ... upon the aristocratic principle', while a modern critic finds it 'an essay in the power of parental and filial love'. The disagreement over the message of the 'essay' shows how Trollope can appeal to different centuries and different types of readers.[19] Although his decision to begin the novel with the Duke already a widower at first seems strange, it does mean that he, and not his fascinating wife, occupies centre stage. His bereavement also gives him the isolation from which to reflect on his own marriage by observing the behaviour of his daughter.

If the Duke came to terms with changing society, so did his creator in the publication of the book. The novel was serialised in *All the Year Round*, which had been founded by Dickens and was still edited and owned by his son though it had declined from its great days when it serialised *A Tale of Two Cities, Great Expectations* and *The Woman in White*: few things connected with Victorian fiction, other than Mudie, lasted many decades. Trollope had wanted the final Palliser book, which he originally called 'The Ex-Prime Minister', to be as long as the four volumes of *The Prime Minister*, but the young Dickens insisted that it should be cut. Trollope did more revision on this novel than on any other and even went so far as to deprive the Duke of one of his children. After his disappointment at the *Spectator*'s reception of *The Prime Minister*, the final novel in the series lay in the drawer in Montagu Square for three years, until serialisation began in October 1879. It met with a favourable reception from the critics including the

Spectator, which said that if the author were 'not quite at his best' his book was still 'thoroughly readable'. The American magazine which had recently reported the rumour that others had been hired to write part of his novels now praised Trollope as 'the last of the realists'. 'No one ever, we fancy, read a novel of his without wishing that he might soon write another, and it is only born story-tellers who leave us in this frame of mind.'[20]

Trollope had negotiated with Chapman and Hall to publish *The Duke's Children* as a book. When the serialisation still had about six months to run he became involved with them not as a writer but as a partner: the firm had decided to become a limited company and was raising capital. Trollope now entered the world of business as a director when he was approaching his sixty-fifth birthday, a time when most businessmen are retiring. The new company's venture was judged a 'complete success' by the *Publishers' Circular*. Trollope appears to have had various financial links with Chapman since 1869, when Henry became a partner, and these had survived his leaving in the early 1870s. Trollope had never been involved in its management, but now, as one of the three directors of the new company, he found himself spending about ten hours a week at board meetings. It was work he hated: 'nothing more pernicious and damnable ever occurred,' he wrote. Once again he had a salary: £500 a year. No doubt the fact that many of the Trollopes, including Tom and his wife, as well as Henry and Rose, also had shares in the firm, preyed on his mind, particularly as he never really trusted Chapman. When, however, the firm's accountant showed him that the company had lost £120 on *The Duke's Children*, Trollope wrote, not as a director but as a man of letters and of honour, to Chapman's father-in-law: 'I cannot allow that. It is the first account I have ever seen of one of my own books. I will repay to the Company the amount lost.'[21]

The Spectator, in its review of *The Duke's Children* quoted above, saw that the theme of the book was one of great contemporary interest. 'Mr. Trollope appears to suggest that the religion of caste is hopelessly and helplessly incompatible with the creed of progress, when, nevertheless, caste is the very root of the tree of the political English oak, and can be interfered with only at the risk of destroying the entire organism.' This is a topic that runs throughout the Palliser novels: how exclusive can any group be and yet survive? What is the role of the gentleman and does personal merit, honourable behaviour and the esteem of one's fellows merit a relaxation in the rules of entry? How exclusive, in short, can the 'Ten Thousand' be and yet survive? The problem was that no one, other than the College of Arms, could offer a precise definition of 'gentleman'. In *The Duke's Children* Lady Mary Palliser protests that the man she wishes to marry, although not an aristocrat, 'is a gentleman' and the son of a gentleman and as such is good enough to marry the daughter of the most powerful Duke in England. It is, in short, his personal merits, not his membership of a caste that matters. The Duke is both angered and hurt: 'So is my private secretary. There is not a clerk in one of our public offices who does not consider himself to be a gentleman ... The word is too vague to carry with it any meaning' [VIII]. The Duke might have been amused by a definition given by Gladstone at about this time. When he was told that government should live like a gentleman now that it had so much money from the British taxpayer, he replied that 'living like a gentleman means paying five times the value for every thing you buy'.[22]

For Trollope, however, the word 'gentleman' did carry a meaning, though it was not one about which he could be entirely precise. It was not merely a vague rank that gave privileges – happy though he was to avail himself of them. It carried obligations and duties which Palliser embodied in fiction and Trollope fulfilled, for example, in his dealings with publishers. It was not based, to any great extent, on snobbery. 'Colonials' have ever been the best detectors of English snobbery. Captain Mair who guided Trollope in New Zealand observed: 'he hated snobs and society snobbishness with a deadly hatred.' This is almost exactly what his American friend Glenn had said. In the last passages of *Australia and New Zealand* Trollope denounced the 'hat-touching' and 'servility' in English life as something which was 'hardly compatible with exalted manhood'. He concluded: 'I regard such manhood among the masses of the people as the highest sign of prosperity which a country can give.'[23] A man who tells the wealthiest Duke in England to let go of his coat tails in front of thousands is no snob!

Yet he was not a complete democrat either. In the *Autobiography* – written, as we have seen, immediately before this novel – he discussed his own entry into the Post Office and concluded:[24]

As what I now write will certainly never be read till I am dead, I may dare to say what no one now does dare to say in print, – though some of us whisper it occasionally into our friend's ears. There are places in life which can hardly be well filled except by 'Gentlemen.' The word is one the use of which almost subjects one to ignominy ... It may well be that the son of the butcher in the village shall become as well fitted ... as the son of the parson. Such is often the case. When such is the case, no one has been more prone to give the butcher's son all the welcome he has merited than I myself; but the chances are greatly in favour of the parson's son. The gates of one class should be open to the other; but neither to one class or to the other can good be done by declaring that there are no gates, no barrier, no difference.

Once is left then, as so often with Trollope, with a divided attitude towards a profound question which touches on the deepest feelings regarding human society and behaviour, all of which only make it the more worthwhile to read what he says.

*

Trollope, however, was not content to sit in his library at Montagu Square and dictate novels to a quiet niece. The old restless spirit, the inherited love of travel, asserted itself once again. In April 1877 he had decided to go on a visit to the South African colonies. He had long wished 'to "do" South Africa' and he felt he had to undertake the trip soon as he was 'becoming too old for any more such "doing" '. This would be a different trip for two reasons. First, he was engaged on what the Victorians called 'book-making' – he was visiting a place specifically in order to write a book. Secondly, the colonies he would be visiting would be of a new type. By 'colonies' he usually excluded India and most of the newer, African possessions. He explained his view at the start of his South African book: 'In my own mind I always include the United States, for to my thinking, our Colonies are the lands in which our cousins, the descendants of our forefathers, are living and still speaking our language.' They were places which Englishmen had settled, to which they still went as settlers and which were destined to achieve independence in due course. Just as a war had provided the impetus to realise a long desired goal to write a book about America, so the sudden occupation of the Transvaal by Sir Theophilus Shepstone in April 1877 provided the final reason for his South African book. Accompanied by twenty-five mounted policemen Shepstone rode into Pretoria and added yet another possession to the British Empire. Although Trollope did not support continuous imperial expansion, he came in time, as he wrote to Shepstone, to think that this action had been 'for the advantage of the country, – Dutch, English, and native'. For modern historians the absorption of the Transvaal was 'inspired by thoroughly mid-Victorian schemes for reducing expenditure and devolving authority without sacrificing supremacy'.[25] For Trollope it was 'a typical instance of the beneficent injustice of the British'. In spite of this absorption there was still no 'South Africa' at the time of

Trollope's visit, as the area was still divided between the independent Boer republic and British colonies. The Union of South Africa would not be created until 1910.

Trollope arranged to write a two-volume book for Chapman and Hall, who offered him £850, or £400 less than he had received from them for either *North America* or *Australia and New Zealand*. It probably reflects the lower degree of interest in the subject as much as any decline in Trollope's popularity. He also agreed to supply Trübner's press agency with fifteen travel letters for provincial newspapers for £175. The trip had one happy benefit: Henry, violating family tradition, began to preserve the many letters his father wrote to him, and these give an attractive picture of Anthony's deep love for his son. He describes details of his trip with that slight touch of malice we expect in a traveller's letters. He sends instructions on the care of his horses and on how to deal with publishers about various novels – much as his mother had done with him forty years before – and offers paternal advice on books that Henry was translating or editing. He was not particularly happy on his ship from Dartmouth to Cape Town:

> I dont like anyone on board, but I hate two persons. There is an old man who plays the flute all the afternoon and evening. I think he and I will have to fight. And there is a beastly impudent young man with a voice like a cracked horn, who will talk to me. He is almost unsnubbable but I think I will silence him at last ... I fancy from all I hear and the little I see that I shall find the Cape a most uninteresting place. The people who are going there on board this ship are just the people who would go to an uninteresting Colony.

Back in England, Henry was busy with a life of Bianconi, his father's old friend who had set up his coaches in Ireland and whom Trollope had defended before Parliamentary committees. (In theory the book was by Bianconi's daughter.) The old author was full of advice to the new: 'I hope you are getting on with your biography – I have no doubt you find it very dull work, but it has to be done now.' 'I am glad you are getting on with your biography. I am sure your mother could help you a good deal if you will let her. Do not forget your Corneille.' Henry was also writing a volume for Blackwood's 'Foreign Classics' series, *Corneille and Racine*, although he had difficulties with the series' editor, Mrs Oliphant, who had little regard for Henry. Trollope had a reminder of Henry's work on French literature with him, as he had grabbed one of his son's notebooks when leaving London for South Africa. When he heard that the Bianconi book was finished he rejoiced, though he wondered why Henry was getting £50 rather than the agreed £60 for his stint as ghost-writer. 'Mamma says it is good reading.'[26]

Trollope worked steadily at his own book, but the task of combining difficult travelling and extensive socialising with writing was becoming more of an effort. He started on 23 July and only managed two pages; by the next day he managed three, and the day following, five. However, by September he informed Henry: 'I am working very hard, tasking myself to write 1,300 words, – which as I am travelling all the time is hard enough.' 'I was subject to the privileges and inconveniences of being known as a man who was going to write a book,' he later recalled, though he would never admit, while travelling, that he was gathering material for a book. Although he was not particularly delighted with Cape Town, he said he found a 'keener relish of life than among our steadier and more fastidious folk at home'. Yet he had the same feeling that he had had in Canada: Cape Town was over two centuries old and yet could not equal Melbourne, any more than Quebec could equal Chicago, in population. He made his usual visits to botanical gardens and libraries, where he admired the collection, envied a first folio of Shakespeare and bemoaned the lack of readers. As usual, there was a call to be made on a place still close to his heart:[27]

> Wherever I go I visit the post-office, feeling certain that I may be able to give a little good advice. Having looked after post-offices for thirty years at home I fancy that I could do a very good service among the Colonies ... My advice is always received with attention and respect, and I have generally been able to flatter myself that I have convinced my auditors. But I never knew an instance yet in which any improvement recommended by me was carried out.

Some weeks later the retired Surveyor exerted his old authority, this time in a mail coach from Pietermaritzburg to Newcastle, when he discovered that a large tin box was being sent at the lower book-rate although it was full of bonnets. It was raining when they stopped for breakfast, and the driver attempted to put the suspect box where Trollope's lengthy legs should have gone:

> Trollope: 'It can't come in here.'
> Driver: 'It must.'
> Trollope: 'But it won't' ... I bethought myself a moment and then declared my purpose of not leaving the vehicle though I knew breakfast was prepared ... 'May I trouble you to bring a cup of tea to me here,' I said

[to a fellow passenger]. 'I shall remain and not allow the tin box to
enter the cart.'
Driver: 'Not allow!'
Trollope: 'Certainly not! It is illegal.'

Finally the man asked if Trollope would permit the mail bags inside as
long as the illegal tin box was not put inside to inconvenience the
passengers. He agreed and after breakfast they were happily on their
way with Trollope's comfort undisturbed and his sense of justice
triumphant. Almost fifty years earlier his mother had won a similar
battle in upstate New York when a group of 'whiskey drinkers' tried to
shove a bonnet box under her feet in a stage coach.[28]

Travelling conditions in South Africa in the 1870s were as primitive
as his mother had found in America in the 1830s. When he arrived in
Ceres, a German woman who kept the hotel refused his request for a
separate room for himself and a travelling companion, declaring that
she needed to keep one room for an expected party of twelve. When
Trollope came down in the morning he felt remorse over his angry
disbelief when he saw the poor woman trying to cope with a
drawing-room occupied by seven dozen canaries that another German
had asked her to sell. 'I can safely recommend the hotel at Ceres as the
canaries will no doubt have been all sold before any reader can act on
this recommendation.' Almost every one of his travels had led to
problems with the large amount of luggage that accompanied him.
This time his progress was marked by a trail of abandoned luggage. At
Cape Town he had abandoned one trunk; at Port Elizabeth he was
persuaded to leave his portmanteau and a despatch case and 'to trust
myself to two bags':

> So I tied addresses to the tabooed receptacles ... and started on my way
> with a very limited supply of wearing apparel ... when the bag has been
> stamped full to repletion with shirts, boots, and the blue books which are
> sure to be accumulated for the sake of statistics, the first thing to be
> rejected is one's dress suit. A man can live well without a black coat,
> waistcoat, and trousers ... and I trusted myself to two pair of boots.

On his way from Durban to Pietermaritzburg he escaped from one
crowded stage coach by mounting the driver's box. When a new
passenger tried to place a dead fish weighing forty-five pounds on the
foot-board, Trollope announced that the fish was not coming on *his*
foot-board and the man threatened to pull him off the box. The
coachman, anxious to prevent a fight as well as to avoid another
passenger in the crowded coach, cracked his whip and the coach set off.

'With more than colonial alacrity' the man chased them and grabbed onto the back of the coach with one hand while holding the huge fish by means of his teeth and his free hand. When Trollope looked round the man had got a seat and forced another passenger over so that the fish also had a seat.

As a way to escape crowded coaches and dead fish, Trollope and a companion – he almost always acquired a companion on his colonial rambles – bought a cart and some horses. He had to buy another horse for £23 when one of his original pair died, but he could sell the cart and horses in Kimberley. When the auctioneer had some trouble getting a good price, he announced that the horses had been bred on 'Orley Farm' for the novelist's special use. Trollope described all this in his book, but he did not include the fact that he had to ask the Governor to send the Inspector of Police to the auctioneer to make him hand over the £100 raised by this sale! He particularly hated Kimberley and its diamond fields. Trollope was always suspicious of places made rich by sudden discoveries, be it gold in Australia or diamonds in South Africa. Forgetting his pledge to avoid mines, he was soon busy exploring a diamond mine. 'I have been handling diamonds till I am sick of them,' he wrote to Henry.[29] He recalled this part of his visit in his last completed novel when a character goes to Kimberley to make his fortune. 'I know no spot more odious in every way to a man who has learned to love the ordinary modes of English life. It is foul with dust and flies; it reeks with bad brandy; it is fed upon potted meat; it has not a tree near it' [*An Old Man's Love* VI].

As in Australia, he was interested in the local wine and found some of it 'very good, resembling a fine port that was just beginning to feel its age in the diminution of its body'. He thought 'the Cape wines have hardly yet had a fair chance' in Britain. While he was inspecting the methods of wine-making someone pointed to a cooper who was making the casks and commented that this black man earned £300 a year but never saved a penny. Trollope was anxious to learn what he did with this large sum. 'Hires a carriage on Sundays ... and drives his wife about' was the dismissive answer. Trollope's attitude was different: 'it pleased me to learn that a black man should like to drive his wife about – and that he should have the means.' Once again, his mother had had a similar reaction years before in New York.[30]

In Pietermaritzburg, the town he liked best, Trollope was able to hear the famous Bishop Colenso preach. Trollope had been one of his supporters when he was almost deprived of his see for his unorthodox views. The Bishop's family were excited at the prospect of the novelist's visit, particularly as Colenso himself was a great admirer – as so many colonial bishops have been – of the Barchester books. Nevertheless the Bishop's daughter concluded when *South Africa* was published that Trollope 'looks through a pair of government spectacles'. In South Africa, as in New Zealand, colonial officials were anxious to have the famous writer say kind things about their work. They even arranged for him to meet some twenty native chiefs. Trollope carried on 'my colloquy with the dusky princes' and their spokesman said: 'We were told we must come in and see you, and therefore we put on our trousers. Very uncomfortable they are, and we wish you and the trousers and the magistrates, but above all the prisons would go – away out of the country altogether.' Trollope gave the man all the tobacco he could find and then added half-a-crown, which delighted him. Trollope remembered this encounter in a lecture he would later give in England on the Zulus, when he said that as material prosperity increased, the Zulu 'soon ... will desire to add a pair of trousers'. He had higher hopes for the Zulus than for other native races because of their different attitudes: 'That love of money which we observe so often is the parent of all industry will be so with the Zulu.' Yet he was not a complete materialist as he criticised those white 'colonists [who], like some other people nearer home, have an eye mainly to making money and feel that compelled labour would be very useful'.[31]

Trollope was genuinely perplexed by the racial question in South Africa, for which he saw no easy or simple solution. Since he wrote as he went along, he often used his travel books to argue a difficult point not just with his readers but with himself. This is why extracting the odd sentence on a contentious topic and saying that it represents Trollope's view is so misleading. Never before on his travels had he been so unsure that Britain had a right to take or even to purchase native land, particularly since he could not accept the right of any chief to give away communal property. This had not bothered him in America or Australia and had only mildly worried him in New Zealand, but in South Africa he was troubled. There are few passages in his travel books that show so well his essential fairness:

The difficult question meets one at every corner in South Africa. What is the duty of the white man in reference to the original inhabitant? The Kafir Chief will say that it is the white man's duty to stay away and not to touch what does not belong to him. The Dutch colonist will say that it is the white man's duty to take the best of the thing God has provided for his use ... The Briton has to go between the two, wavering much between the extremes of philanthropy and expansive energy ... He knows that he has to get possession of the land and use it ... but he knows also that it is wrong to take what does not belong to him ... As I am myself a Briton I

am not a fair critic ... but it does seem to me that he is upon the whole
beneficent, though occasionally very unjust.

Here he reached a different conclusion from his other journeys: 'South
Africa is a land not of white but of black men, and that the progress to
be most desired is that which will quickest induce the Kafir to put off
his savagery and live after the manner of his white brethren.' In South
Africa, unlike the other 'colonies' he had visited, he knew that the
majority would always be black. Therefore he thought it essential that
the great message of his own life be accepted: 'Who can doubt but that
work is the great civilizer of the world – work and the growing desire
for those good things which work only will bring.' Yet he did not want a
regime enforced by coercion. 'There can be no good done till the two
[white and black] stand before the law exactly on the same ground.' He
was perplexed when he turned to the question of voting: 'He who would
give the black man a vote ... is to be found in London rather than in
South Africa.' Trollope's view was that while the franchise should
never be based on colour it should be extended only to those who were
qualified and not simply given to all.

As in Australia and New Zealand, his mission was to see if these new
colonies were places for English workmen. He saw that 'an
Englishman in South Africa will not work along side of a coloured man
on equal terms'. In Durban he saw that 'nothing of manual work seems
ever to be done by a European' and warned anyone considering
emigration that they must have above average intelligence and a
determination to abstain from excessive drinking. It is difficult to
think that any Englishman, apart from prospective diamond miners,
would have wished to emigrate after reading *South Africa* or Trollope's
newspaper articles, something which could never have been said about
his other travel books. As he pointed out in his lecture, the existence of
so much native labour made it difficult for newly arrived English
colonists to earn sufficient money to justify emigrating.

*

Although he was delighted to leave South Africa after being away from
home for almost six months, one friend found that he had 'greatly
benefited by his voyage to the Cape'. 'I have got back alive – and well;
and as I have survived the passing of various nights in a Boer's best
bed, I think I may say that I am qualified to undergo any hardship' he
wrote to John Blackwood early in January 1878. His Scottish friend
saw this himself a few weeks later when he enjoyed a 'cheery dinner

with the Trollopes yesterday – Anthony has come back as loud as ever and in great force'.[32]

'I am going to Iceland! Last year it was South Africa. Does it not sound like – "Greenland's rocky mountains and Afric's sultry plains." You'll think I am no better than a hymn.' Thus Trollope informed a friend of his latest travel intentions. For years he had been friendly with John Burns, later Lord Inverclyde, and chairman of Cunard, who had a large yacht at his command. He invited a party of sixteen friends to accompany him and his wife on a three-week cruise to Iceland. That isolated and rugged country had begun to attract attention from an even hardier race, the Victorian traveller. Lord Dufferin's *Letters from High Latitudes* had been published in 1856 and was one of the most popular Victorian travel books. Iceland became a popular spot for Englishmen seeking adventure without the time or money to go too far afield. Some younger writers were also becoming fascinated with the Nordic sagas and William Morris, for example, visited the country twice in the 1870s.[33]

Trollope went neither for sagas nor for adventure but because it was another place to see and a wealthy friend was prepared to take him there in the comfort that wealth brings with it. In one sense he paid for his passage by acting as 'Chronicler' and by writing a short account, *How the 'Mastiffs' Went to Iceland*. Burns had this privately printed and illustrated with delightful drawings by another of the party, Mrs Hugh Blackburn. This was Trollope's last travel book and indeed the end of that long line of Trollopean travel books which had begun with *Domestic Manners of the Americans*. *The Mastiffs* is a pleasant, though slight, *jeu d'esprit*, recounting amusing anecdotes of a tour he clearly enjoyed. Everything was well-organised and there was a mixture of mild adventure with considerable luxury, reassuring to a man increasingly conscious of failing strength. 'The Mastiffs' – being good Victorians they constituted themselves into a club named after the yacht – sailed from Burns's home in Scotland and first paid a short visit to the remote island of St Kilda. The ex-Surveyor watched his host carry the Royal Mail bag with its one letter ashore. Postal matters were still on Trollope's mind when they reached their next stop, the Danish Faroe Islands. The local postmaster, who resembled Gladstone, entertained them: 'I should have liked to have asked this gentleman what was his salary, and what his duties, and whether there ever came an inspector from the head office in Denmark to look after him.'

In Iceland they invited the Governor, the Bishop and other dignitaries to a banquet on board the yacht and Trollope enjoyed a courtly infatuation with the Bishop's daughter, Thora Pjetursson, 'our particular friend'. Sixty-five ponies were provided to carry the party on a tour of the island but one lady insisted on inspecting them to see that they had been well treated.[34] Trollope, for his part, was less concerned with sores on ponies than with his own worries as to which would be given the responsibility of transporting him. He was, he admitted, the oldest and heaviest member of the party – 'something over sixteen stones'. His first mount proved the worst horse he had ever ridden but when he changed to another he was delighted. The daily ride was usually in two segments of four hours each. 'Trotting was our usual pace ... In the East and the West, in Syria and in Central America, I have found it expected that I should never get out of a wretched amble ... In Iceland I was going at a very fair pace for fox hounds.' Burns had sent a party of servants ahead so that when the guests arrived at an agreed spot tents were already pitched and kettles boiling for tea. Their goal was the island's main attraction, the geysers, which Lord Dufferin had made famous. Trollope, who had seen the far more awesome geysers in New Zealand, and yet others in South Africa, was not too impressed. On the way back they slept one night in a church: the ladies lying round the communion table and the men occupying the nave aisle. During the night one woman crept to the bell and began ringing it, whereupon Trollope stood up and made a speech about the 'ladies who were very tired, – ladies who would certainly wish to sleep'.

Trollope enjoyed this last of his far-off travels and took back to Montagu Square a copy of Macbeth in Icelandic that had been printed in Reykjavik. In return he sent a copy of his *Caesar* to a young Icelander he had met on the trip. Burns had Trollope's 'chronicle' privately printed and gave its author twenty-five copies. Trollope also wrote a less personal account, which he called 'Iceland', for the *Fortnightly Review*, which published it on 1 August 1878 and then printed it as a pamphlet. Gladstone, who was beginning to wonder whether Iceland, still linked to the Danish crown, could provide any guidance on Ireland, was among its readers.[35]

Trollope was not long in Montagu Square after his return. Within a few weeks he was in Switzerland, having joined Rose and Florence in the Black Forest. From Felsenegg he wrote to George Eliot: 'Here we are on top of a mountain, where I walk for four hours, eat for two, and sleep out the balance satisfactorily. I am beginning to think that the more a man can sleep the better for him. I can take a nap of nine hours each night without moving, in these latitudes.' Their Swiss holidays had been increasing in length: this time they were there for almost two months. He was, as always, busy on his current novel, *Ayala's Angel*, and he also had some reading on his mountain top: a publisher had asked him to look over a translation of the *Odyssey* and advise on its publication. Rose also enjoyed these holidays, and the following year Trollope wrote to Henry: 'Your mother has been doing wonders in walking – ten miles one day – about three hours 5 days a week – In London she can't walk a mile.'[36]

*

'You say of me; – that I would not choose to write novels unless I were paid. Most certainly I would; much rather than not write them at all' was what Trollope said in a letter to his old friend Tilley. He began *Ayala's Angel* on 25 April 1878 – the day after his sixty-third birthday, took it to Iceland and completed it on 24 September in Switzerland. It is a lighter and happier story than many of his later novels, though in its own way it attacks an old foe, utopian idealism. Ayala has formed an image in her mind of a perfect man – her 'Angel of Light' – and, like Eleanor Bold, she is pursued by three suitors. It is only when she casts her idealised vision aside that she accepts Colonel Stubbs, a rare instance of a serving officer playing a leading role in a Trollope novel. A good deal of the action is centred on the family of Ayala's uncle, a wealthy banker. His son is one of the disappointed suitors rejected by Ayala, and after many troubles he is sent off on a world tour. As a modern novelist observes, the rejected young man would today be 'advised to seek psychiatric help'.[37]

Much of the autumn was occupied with *Cousin Henry*, but a few days before Christmas Trollope started another three-volume novel, *Marion Fay*. He even managed four pages on Christmas Day but he put it aside about a week later and within a month was working on his book about Thackeray. In April 1879 he and Rose went to stay at the rectory in Lowick in Northamptonshire. The rector, W. Lucas Collins, had become a close friend after editing Trollope's *Caesar* for Blackwood. From a former pupil's description it is easy to see why Collins and Trollope got on so well: the rector 'belonged to the old "High and Dry", "Church and Queen" school, but was by no means a ritualist'.[38] He was one of those Victorian clergyman who supplemented his clerical income with literary work. Not only did he edit the 'Classics for English Readers' but he was a frequent contributor to *Blackwood's Magazine* and a general advisor to the firm. He must have used the extra income for his travels as he and his wife liked to spend a large part of the winter in the South of France or Italy. Earlier in the decade he had lent his rectory to Trollope as a hunting base.

By 1879 Trollope no longer rode to hounds except in some wistful chapters of his novels. Nevertheless he and Rose still liked to visit the rectory as they had made friends in the area. Collins also tutored some young men who came to 'read' in the interval between school and university. At Lowick there seem to have been numerous activities other than reading, according to the memoirs of George Leveson Gower, the son of Trollope's friend. Young George spent much of his time there arranging a lawn-tennis court, while Blackwood's son busied himself laying out a golf course. In April 1879, however, there was little opportunity to see either of these memorials to study. When Rose wrote from the rectory asking Blackwood to send the manuscript of *John Caldigate*, so that her husband could correct his proofs, she added, 'We here have much snow! Pleasant in the middle of April.' Perhaps the snow kept Trollope long at his desk, for during this stay he wrote a novel in three weeks! Every day he wrote exactly twelve pages until there was one break of two days before the final day's twelve pages finished the novel. 'I do not know,' as one scholar put it, 'that the history of fiction affords another instance of a novel of real merit, running to 85,000 words, having been written in twenty-two days.' Perhaps Anthony was having a final combat of strength with his brother who wrote a novel in twenty-four days![39] For his three weeks' work Trollope received £500. Dr Johnson, of course, had bettered not only his but Tom's time when he wrote *Rasselas* in a week, though his remuneration was hardly the same.

There are, perhaps, few better introductions to Trollope's fiction than his fortieth novel, *Dr. Wortle's School*. He used the rectory as the setting, changing the name from Lowick to Bowick. It even has a court for lawn-tennis. He took Collins's occasional pupils and converted them into an organised school and perhaps drew on his own time as a pupil at just such a school kept by one of the tribe of ordained Drurys at Sunbury. Dr Wortle, the fictional rector who 'combined two professions', does not seem to be modelled on Collins; indeed, as has often been pointed out, he has many similarities to his creator. This can neither be proved nor disproved; but the unconscious mind, particularly of a castle-builder, can play tricks. Trollope could so easily have become a clergyman himself, and perhaps he imagined what his life would have been had he been the occupant of the rectory rather than the observer of the comfortable life that went on in it. Dr Wortle is faced with a great dilemma when another clergyman, Henry Peacocke, a master at his school, discovers that the marriage he made to an American woman when teaching at a small college in St Louis, Missouri, is bigamous. Here Trollope drew on his own visit to Washington College and his acquaintance with T.S. Eliot's grandfather, the College's president.

While Peacocke goes off to America to discover the truth, thereby allowing Trollope to recall more of his American experiences, Dr Wortle refuses to dismiss him despite pressure from his Bishop and the parents of his pupils. The novel is a fine study of a man who stands up for justice; he is all the more admirable because he does not particularly care for the injured man.

The situation of a clergyman involved in a bigamous marriage, undertaken only because he had assumed the first husband was dead, required delicate handling. When William Blackwood began reading the novel for his magazine he admitted to Trollope, 'I was rather alarmed about the story when I read that Mr. & Mrs. Peacocke were not man & wife but your explanation of the mystery speedily dispels any disgreeable feelings about the tone of the story that might startle sensitive readers.' In general the reviewers liked this novel, though the *Saturday Review* took the opportunity to fire a small dart: the book was 'as happy ... as Mr. Trollope usually is when he does not meddle with things too high for him'.[40]

*

The letter about the serialisation of *Dr. Wortle* had come from William Blackwood because Trollope's old friend John Blackwood, to whom he had presented the copyright of *Caesar* as a birthday gift, had died in 1879. It was one of a series of deaths in these years that shook Trollope. G.H. Lewes had died at the end of 1878, and Trollope prepared a moving tribute in the *Fortnightly*, of which Lewes had become the first editor after much persuasion from Trollope. In December 1880 Trollope was shocked to receive word from Lewes's son that George Eliot had died. 'I had only been saying on the very morning that she died that I would go and see her.'[41] Her death left Trollope the most famous novelist in England, but it also made a void in his life: there was no longer any writer whom he could look up to with admiration and respect.

At the end of 1879 Trollope was involved in something he had described in dozens of novels: arranging the details of a girl's marriage. Tom's daughter Beatrice, or 'Bice', had met Charles Stuart Wortley, a rising young barrister and Tory politician. Did the name stir Rose's memory? Wortley's grandfather, Lord Wharncliffe, had been a prominent client at her father's bank. Wortley's sister recalled that 'Bice' was 'a beautiful little creature, with something Italian in air and colouring, and she had the voice of an angel'. She had been the spoiled darling of a colony of exotic expatriates and romantic dreamers ever since the day when she was not even two, when her grandmother wrote: 'Miss Beatrice ... is (of course) a species of prodigy.' Her voice had made her celebrated in Florentine and Roman society, and recently she had been seen much in the company of the Crown Prince of Sweden – singing duets. Since Tom had been so ill that even his wife could 'scarcely have thought it possible he should recover', the interview with young Wortley fell upon Anthony's shoulders. He reported to Rome that he quite liked the young man. 'The only drawback', he wrote to Bice's step-mother, sounding like a character in one of his novels, 'is that as he has nothing but his profession ... the engagement threatens to be a long one.' Yet it was not long before Anthony and Rose repeated their journey to the British Embassy in Paris, for the wedding in August 1880. Less than a year later Trollope wrote to Henry: 'Do you know that Bice is very ill. Fever after her confinement.' Bice died the next day, and about three weeks later Trollope, who was genuinely distressed, wrote an assessment of her which shows that even grief could not stem his ability to analyse character:[42]

> The fault was that she had been too much spoilt ... allowed to have her own way and to make a society for herself ... Everything was done for her that could be done; – but there were not carriages nor parties. I say this in justice to my brother's wife, who has been very very good. The fault was my brother's in allowing her to have her own way, till her own way ceased to please her. Poor Bice!

*

In 1878 Trollope saw the realisation of something he had desired for more than a decade: the publication of a collected edition of *The Chronicles of Barsetshire* in eight volumes by Chapman and Hall. This had involved intricate negotiations with the various publishers who held rights in the different novels. At one time he did not think either *The Small House at Allington* or *Doctor Thorne* essential to this collected edition. He added a few footnotes about changes that had occurred since he had first discovered the county. Thus, when Mr Harding gives an attendant five shillings and is guided into the Strangers' Gallery at the House of Commons, Trollope, who had done his 'research' for the Pallisers in that same Gallery, now wrote, 'How these pleasant things have been altered since this was written a quarter of a century ago.' For this edition he wrote a short introduction full of quiet pride:

I, the Author, had formed for myself so complete a picture of the locality, had acquired so accurate a knowledge of the cathedral town and the county ... and had become by a long-continued mental dwelling in it, so intimate with sundry of its inhabitants, that to go back to it and write about it again and again have been one of the delights of my life ... But now, when these are all old stories, – not perhaps as yet quite forgotten by the readers of the day, and to my memory fresh as when they were written, – I have a not unnatural desire to see them together, so that my records of a little bit of England which I have myself created may be brought into one set, and that some possible future reader may be enabled to study in a complete form the

CHRONICLES OF BARSETSHIRE.

A few years later an American politician requested information about the Barsetshire books and Trollope, in thanking him, said 'I am now an old man, 66, and shall soon have come to the end of my tether.' He must have been ageing quickly, for six months later he wrote to the same persistent admirer who wanted him to return to Barset, 'I am nearly seventy years of age, and cannot hope to do what you propose ... bringing back our old friends. Though I still go on writing, the new characters are much less troublesome than the old ones; and can be done without the infinite labour of reading back again and again my old works.'[43]

By the time that letter crossed the Atlantic – 288 hours if Trollope's treaty was being adhered to – the *Graphic* was almost ready to print *Marion Fay*. Perhaps nothing better illustrates the mixed nature of Trollope's last books than the fact that he had returned to writing this, one of his worst novels, after completing *Dr. Wortle's School*, one of his best. The manuscript, amounting to 768 pages, is about three-quarters in Trollope's hand with the rest in his niece's. Most of the novel was written in Switzerland in the midst of a two-month holiday. Much of it is a conventional piece of Victorian melodrama: a young Post Office clerk turns out to be an Italian Duke. Trollope drew on his memory of Colonel Maberly, who was still alive – indeed he outlived his former clerk – to create Sir Boreas Bodkin. Yet even many of the postal scenes are rather flat [VII]. Trollope recalls some of the issues and phrases of his youth, such as the reactionary Duke of Newcastle's statement after evicting his tenants for voting against his candidate, that a man could do what he liked with his own [I]. Trollope had quoted this same remark in his second novel, *The Kellys and the O'Kellys*, almost thirty-five years before [XVI]. Marion Fay herself is a young Quaker with whom a radical peer is in love. A Quaker – albeit one who appears to be more or less Anglican – was an odd choice of heroine for

Trollope, who normally disliked the Society of Friends. He manages to get in at least one barb, however, by attacking 'that touch of hypocrisy which seems to permeate the now antiquated speech of Quakers' [XV]. It is difficult to quarrel with Hugh Walpole's assessment: '*Marion Fay* ... is the exact negation of every virtue Trollope possessed.'[44]

*

In 1880 Trollope wrote a series of eleven essays about the world of London tradesmen for the *Pall Mall Gazette*. These provide an evocative picture of how Victorians shopped and obtained services. They range from butchers, plumbers and chemists to coal merchants and horse-dealers. A young relative who accompanied him on his early morning research long remembered how he looked forward to each day's expedition and his voracious appetite for information as he questioned and observed, storming his way through Billingsgate or Smithfield. After these forays they would return 'tired but triumphant' to breakfast. Trollope, who liked to be well but never flashily dressed, announces in the essay on tailors: 'What is there in the world equal to a pair of well-fitting trousers!' He tells us his tailor was 'a very pleasant man with whom to while away a quarter of an hour'. While Trollope listened, the tailor lectured on all his difficulties, particularly how everything was in decline thanks to the greed and incompetence of his suppliers. In the essay on haberdashers it is obvious that Trollope looked askance at the rise of the new 'department stores', though he implies that Rose liked them. He preferred the speciality shops of old. He also encountered an old foe, advertising, which he had denounced in *The Struggles of Brown, Jones, and Robinson*. He met his old enemy in a roundabout way: he noticed that some of the envelopes which Rose rescued and re-used were marked with one word, 'coal'. He investigated and discovered that coal merchants were regularly putting advertisements through letter boxes with this word on their envelopes. They can thus claim the dubious credit for launching that bane of modern life, 'junk mail'. 'We never shall deal with them,' he announced.[45]

Perhaps one motive for these essays was a desire not only to observe life but to gain some extra money to pay for yet another move. In the spring of 1880 the Trollopes decided to leave London. Rose does not seem to have been as delighted with London life as her husband. Perhaps the move also had some financial motivation. Trollope's finances are extremely difficult to disentangle during his last years. His literary earnings were certainly falling, but he had begun to invest heavily in various stocks. As with many fathers, the state of his portfolio became a favourite topic between him and his son. 'We shall have 15 p cent from the Union Bank this half year. The shares have gone up steadily.' He also made some investments in property: 'Buying ... two of those ground rents in Montagu square for £840 – They will give us 7½ per cent for 24 years.'[46]

Trollope had reached the decision to move by April 1880, but he had to finish his work on *Cicero* before his library was packed. The books were indeed a great worry. 'As soon as we are settled,' he wrote to Henry in France, 'I shall expect you to come over and put up the books for me. Oh the books – and oh the wine! I am beginning to tremble at the undertaking.' There was another problem because Henry was one of those sons who encumber their parents' home with books after they have left: 'What are we to do with your books ... There are still here about 700 volumes.' There was obviously a dispute under way between Anthony, who thought that Henry's books should remain in London, and Rose, who thought they should come to the country. Rose won. Anthony, however, saw no reason not to use his defeat to exert a little moral blackmail on his son: 'When I die it will be convenient to have them altogether.' There was also the difficulty of the servants. It seems that Barney, who was about eighty, had returned to Banagher and was living on a pension from Trollope. Their London man-servant drank too much: 'When he does drink,' Trollope grumbled, 'he does not become drunk, but is exactly like an owl.'[47]

Trollope described in another *Pall Mall Gazette* article, 'The Migration of a Library', the unsettling effects of moving thousands of books when the mover sees his own life paraded before him as the volumes come off the shelves recalling the dreams of youth. Did all those tomes on America not reflect the one-time desire to be another Tocqueville? 'Books are live things. Each has, and ... loves its peculiar nook.' Now they, like their owner, were being uprooted. Once he was settled in the country, he informed Henry:

> You may imagine what a trouble the library has been. At present though the bulk of the books are placed; and are placed on their old shelves and with their own numbers, still that which is not the bulk, but which forms a numerous portion, is all in confusion so that sometimes I am almost hopeless. I cannot describe to you the room. It is very much larger than the library in London, but still will not hold as many books.

Part of this was a ploy to get Henry to visit them. For the next two years Trollope would be engaged in a persistent campaign to get Henry to leave Paris, where he was living while translating various books. As

Trollope was thinking of printing another library catalogue, he coaxed Henry (who already knew that he would inherit the books) to help him. 'If however I am in confusion with my books, I have got my wine into fine order.'[48]

*

The Trollopes had found a house at Harting in Sussex, close to the Hampshire border. For once Trollope did not buy the property but took it on a lease, which allowed him to use the money from the sale of the Montagu Square house for investment. 'We have got a little cottage here, just big enough (or nearly so) to hold my books, with five acres and a cow and a dog and a cock and a hen ... I am as busy as would be one thirty years younger, in cutting out dead boughs and putting up a paling here and a little gate there. We go to church and mean to be very good, and have maids to wait upon us.' Although he liked to call it a 'cottage' it was really quite a large house and even sported an Italianate tower that had been the fashion ever since Prince Albert had erected one at Osborne. When he first saw North End House, he exclaimed 'in a very deep voice': 'I don't like that tower.' Nevertheless, after they took possession on 4 July 1880, both Trollopes came to like the house and village. The villagers grew fond of their famous neighbour, and memories of him lingered far into this century. After the BBC broadcast an adaptation of some of the Barset books during the Second World War, someone wandered round the village talking to the oldest inhabitants about the celebrated author who had lived there sixty years before. These previously unknown recollections found their way into the West Sussex Record Office. They give us a pleasing portrait of Trollope in his last years. He had a large conservatory built, which like many Victorian glass houses, was as much for the entertainment of guests as for the propagation of plants, although he often tended to his flowers there. The 'cottage' – a superb example of Trollope's penchant for embroidering words when describing something close to himself – was, in reality, two good-sized farm-houses joined together. The 'five acres', according to Escott, who probably visited the Trollopes there, was closer to seventy and as at Waltham, there were cows to provide milk and cream. Just as Trollope's deep voice was long remembered so was Rose's wit: every time she heard a squeaking pump in the house, she said it was declaring 'I'm Postlethwaite's pump' – J.L. Postlethwaite being the owner of the house. Having a garden, after a decade without one, was a delight to both Trollopes, particularly as they had a gardener to relieve them of the more bothersome chores among the apple trees, asparagus and strawberry beds. The garden became quite celebrated among Trollope's friends and one of them, the poet Alfred Austin, is said to have recalled it in his once-famous book, *The Garden That I Love*.

In spite of increasing breathing problems, due apparently to a return of the asthma from which he had suffered as a youth, Trollope was still active and often walked up the 'Long Walk', shaded by tall trees, to the South Downs. In the 1940s some elderly villagers still recalled that the famous author, normally so friendly, 'would walk for miles without lifting his head, or speaking to passers-by, as though thinking out some position in one of his books'. Recollections of the daily ride, with Trollope mounted on a large black horse and Florence on her bay, also lingered in the area. When he arrived in the village he had two horses; on days when he could not exercise them, his servant Ringwood would do the duty although villagers noted that the man's rides usually ended at the pub! Trollope also had a brougham and pony cart with its own pony, 'a nice little beast but rather old'.[49] One of these could take him to Petersfield, four and half miles away, or to the smaller station at Rogate which was even closer. From there trains could have him in Waterloo Station in not much more than a hour. When he was coming back from town, sometimes carrying coffee or some special fish, he would write to Rose to have the pony cart at the station. Trollope often had friends down from London for a few days. Large dinner parties would be given on Saturday when neighbours like the Frisbys from the Manor House would be invited to meet some celebrated author or painter. Another neighbour's 'partiality for sherry was acquired through his contact with the author', we are told somewhat ambiguously. When he wanted to entertain in London, as when a friend gave him a haunch of venison, he could always arrange for it to be served at the Garrick.

'Man in his rudest state begins in the country, and in his most finished state may retire there' Trollope had written almost two decades before. Of course, he had no intention of retiring when he moved. Harting was – and still is – a pleasant village. The naturalist W.H. Hudson wrote two decades later that 'of all downland villages it is to my mind the most attractive'.[50] Trollope had a vague family connection with the village as one of the many clerical Trollopes had been vicar there for five years in the 1790s. Near the village lies the magnificent late-seventeenth-century mansion of Uppark, the home of the Fetherstonhaughs.* The house had above the average share of

---

*Since this was written, a fire has destroyed most of Uppark although the National Trust have announced plans to rebuild the house.

scandals: Emma Hart, later Lady Hamilton, had lived there with one of her first 'protectors', Sir Harry Fetherstonhaugh. The echo of another of Sir Harry's scandals was just fading when Trollope arrived in the village. His widow had only died in 1875, exactly fifty years after Sir Harry heard a song coming from his dairy. The baronet, then well into his seventies, was attracted by the dairymaid's singing, and soon made her Lady Fetherstonhaugh. Trollope had caught some garbled – or perhaps suppressed – version of the tale when he wrote to give Tom his first impressions of the village: 'The squire is an old game-keeper's daughter, who [*sic*] sister married the late squire.'

'The parson perhaps I shall know,' he also told Tom in the same letter. Fortunately he did come to know the Rev. H.D. Gordon quite well and the rector, who had been in the village since 1864, left an attractive portrait of Trollope as an active villager and churchman in his last years. They obviously enjoyed many talks, and Trollope told him stories of his adventures – of how he had nearly drowned on the ice as a youth, only to be saved by a future Dean of St Paul's, and how on another occasion he had been thrown by his horse while hunting and saw the hooves coming towards his head when the horse suddenly shifted enough to spare his master's life. Trollope, who had long preached the need for better education, became 'the life of our school manager meetings and a generous patron of the education of the poor'. Fortunately some of the records of this Church school, which had been built about fifteen years before, have survived. As a school manager, he took part in approving the 'indenture' of a local girl which would allow her to become a pupil-teacher, and in enquiring into the non-payment of the weekly school fees by four families in the village. (These were normally a penny a week per child.) Trollope sometimes pressed visiting friends like Millais to lecture in order to raise money for the school. Gordon said that Trollope was soon known throughout the village for his kindness: 'The sick poor in particular found in him a staunch benefactor, and he would find a few minutes in his daily ride to visit them and say a few cheery words.' The Church of St Mary and St Gabriel would have met with his approval, for it was becomingly High without being ritualistic. The rector noted of his new parishioner that he 'rarely, even when his health was failing, missed Sunday morning service, always punctual to the minute – an alert and reverent and audible worshipper, and a steady communicant'.

Of course, his old temper could still flare up: one day the gardener came running into the house to say that a man whom Trollope had employed to repair his fences had gathered up some of the fallen apples. The gardener wanted to summon the village constable.

Trollope rushed from his library and found the man seated under a tree munching a purloined apple. 'Who allowed you to take some of my apples?' Trollope roared. 'I had nothing but bread and it's better with an apple,' was the pert reply. Trollope rushed back into the kitchen, cut what Gordon calls some 'Homeric slices' of cheese and ham and hurried back, handed them to the man and commanded: 'Eat and *be better*.' 'It was,' the rector said, 'just what he would have done as a Winchester boy fifty years ago, and a Winchester boy he was at heart to the end of his life.'[51]

In spite of his friendship with Gordon, his kindness to poor neighbours and the beauty of his home and surrounding countryside, the move was not entirely good for Trollope's spirits. He wrote to his elder brother before moving: 'It will sometimes take a man more than 5 years to die. I thought I was going to die in Montagu Square when I came here. But it is not comfortable enough.' He ended with an assertion that could have guaranteed him immortality: 'As soon as I have not a book to finish, I shall go.' At Harting there was not as full a routine to fill the day when the writing was finished as there had been in London, nor was there as much to do. 'I miss you most painfully,' he wrote to Henry after he had been on a visit. 'This is the longest day of the winter and I shall begin now to look for the lengthening days. Ah, me! How I used to look for the shortening days, when I was hunting, and had the first of November as a golden day before me for which my soul could long. I have now to look for the time when the green things in the garden may begin to shew themselves.' Then he brightened:[52]

> I finished on Thursday the novel I was writing, and on Friday I began another. Nothing really frightens me but the idea of enforced idleness. As long as I can write books even though they be not published, I think that I can be happy.

The short work he had finished was *Kept in the Dark*, written for *Good Words*. It is a perfectly adequate, standard Victorian novel, showing how jealousy and secrecy can threaten a marriage. It even has a bad baronet, one whose title was older than the Trollopes'! The novelist drew on some of his recent holidays in Rome and Switzerland, but much of the novel is set in a city he had portrayed before, Exeter. This had been used in his much more memorable picture of marital jealousy, *He Knew He Was Right*. It is difficult to disagree with one review that described this as an enjoyable but 'slight' novel.[53]

The novel which Trollope began before writing to Henry was *The Fixed Period*, which remains his strangest work. It is an oddity among

Trollope's fiction for it is told in the first person and is set in the future on a mythical island near New Zealand. When the new colony of Britannula was formed from 'the *élite* of the selected population of New Zealand', it had one peculiar feature: 'the prearranged ceasing to live of those who would otherwise become old' [1]. At the age of sixty-seven the citizens would be 'deposited' in a 'college', and some time during the next year they would be put to death in a painless way. Trollope took the plot from a seventeenth-century play, *The Old Law*, by Massinger, Middleton and Rowley. This unpleasant novel is often and mistakenly said to show that Trollope supported euthanasia. Far from it: this was his final assault upon the Utopians – 'the *élite*' – against whom he had waged war for four decades. The Utopian scheme falls apart when President Neverbend's closest friend is about to become the first victim and a rebellion occurs. The warship *John Bright* arrives at Gladstonopolis, re-establishes British rule and takes President Neverbend to England. Throughout the book Trollope predicts what the world will be like in the 1980s: the United States will have split into two parts, east and west, as he had forecast in *North America*, and the Americans will have formed an alliance with the Russians against the British and French. Only one prediction has happily come true: Britain in the 1980s is ruled by a Queen. Naturally a love plot is inserted, but the only light relief comes in the form of some amusing names like Sir Kennington Oval and Sir Lords Longstick, introduced when a great cricket match is mentioned.[54]

Trollope finished the book a few weeks before his sixty-sixth birthday, or one year before he would have been 'deposited' if he had lived on Britannula. Certainly he had become increasingly fearful of surviving if his bodily or mental powers failed but by the way in which he handles the question of euthanasia he clearly shows that he rejected the idea. Had he advocated such a radical measure, the book would never have appeared in such a Conservative magazine as *Blackwood's*. As with all their contributions it was anonymous. 'I suppose I recognise the "fine Roman hand" of Anthony in "The Fixed Period", ' wrote his friend Lucas Collins, who had actually entertained the novelist while he was writing the book, though he did not mention it then. He had found Trollope 'very well and vigorous', which makes one wonder if lower spirits were not associated with Harting. The visit also shows that it was not Trollope's habit to discuss his books while writing them with anyone other than Rose, even though a book like *The Fixed Period* raised questions which could so easily be discussed with a priest. Ironically it was to Collins, who found the book 'curious' – which to him meant bad – that Trollope later spoke of it. Collins told William

Blackwood that Trollope had said that the book was 'quite true'. Collins's published version of the statement became 'It's all true – I *mean* every word of it.' Mistakenly, this has often been quoted to show that Trollope supported the 'Utopian' scheme. In fact his aim was to show through the islanders' rebellion that the scheme was not only wrong, because opposed to human nature and Christian teaching, but unworkable.[55]

Shortly after finishing *The Fixed Period* the Trollopes and Florence left for Nice to join Collins and his wife. The enlarged party planned a two-month holiday on the Riviera and in Rome. Trollope did not know the South of France all that well, though he had once taken Henry there when he was about eighteen: as an old man Henry would recall that he slept most of the time. Normally Collins sent lengthy letters to Blackwood describing his winter holidays; this time, unfortunately, he was called back to his rectory before writing even one. The Trollopes, however, carried on and stayed in Rome till after Easter. While there Trollope made his peace with one old enemy, E.A. Freeman. Someone who knew them said that their clash about the morality of fox-hunting had been 'a collision of two rough diamonds'. Yet when they met on 29 March 1881 Freeman recalled, 'I certainly took to Mr Trollope, and I have every reason to think that Mr Trollope took to me.' Trollope told the historian that he had 'hated' him for two reasons: because he had used Cicero to attack fox-hunting, and because a long letter from him had been read out at a meeting about the 'Bulgarian Atrocities' and this had cut into what little time was left for the speakers. The two men went to Tusculum where they climbed the *arx*, and there, as well as reciting poetry, they talked of Cicero. 'One might have thought that his life had been given up to Cicero and nothing else,' Freeman later wrote. Standing there by a Roman tomb, they found the perfect way to end an old enmity and cement a new alliance: 'We cursed a common enemy who shall be nameless.' However, Freeman was more frank in a letter to a young historian: 'He is very full of Cicero and curses Froude becomingly. I don't say A. T. is any great scholar but he knows enough.' Writing a year and a half later, however, Freeman defended his friend against the *Pall Mall Gazette*'s sneer that his books on 'the classics ... are worthless'. He continued:[56]

Now when one hears about 'the classics,' one knows at once what the argument is worth. When a man opposes 'the classics' to something of our own day ... one knows at once that his 'classics' are something apart from the run of real human affairs, scraps perhaps from Horace and Virgil ... Mr. Trollope's interest in Roman history was something much higher than this. He took it as something which was a part of the real course of

human affairs ... It was because Mr. Trollope had seen a good deal of
men and things in England and Ireland and other parts of the world that
he was able to understand men and things at Rome.

Tom and his wife had a large apartment and Florence, 'of whom we
are all very fond' as the younger Fanny Trollope said, stayed with
them. On their return to England the Trollopes broke their journey in
Florence, no doubt allowing Anthony a chance to see his mother's grave
in the city that held so many memories for him. Then they were on
their way towards the Channel, crossing the Alps through the tunnel
rather than on the top of a diligence as in days of old. Henry was
ordered to meet the train in Paris and to bring four Havana cigars –
'the best you can get' – to the station to sustain his father until he
reached his supply in Harting.[57] When he crossed the Channel in early
May, it was almost fifty years since he had made his first trip, escorting
his sister as the family fled to Bruges. He had had his last view of the
continent.

Naturally he had not been idle during those months in Rome. Even
so, the number of pages he was doing every day had fallen and the
work sheets themselves, those semi-sacred governors of his existence
since he started writing *Barchester Towers*, were increasingly written
in an unsteady hand. The novel he was working on, *Mr. Scarborough's
Family*, has a direct link to the last of his many continental jaunts.
Music had been the least important of the arts to Trollope and was
never as important as painting, drama or literature. While he had not
inherited his mother's love for opera, particularly for Mozart, he had
once heard a solo cello, which he had never forgotten and which no
doubt inspired Mr Harding's devotion to that instrument in the
Barchester books. In the 1850s he had lounged in the Volksgarten in
Vienna to hear Strauss, violin in hand, conducting his own waltzes.
Glee-singing and hunting songs he had enjoyed, but in *Mr.
Scarborough's Family* he describes the 'golden splendour' of 'the
magnificent gambling-house at Monte Carlo ... with all its luxuries of
liveried servants, its wealth of newspapers, and every appanage of
costly comfort'. For the gambling he had no use. What he remembered
was the music: 'There are to be heard sounds in a greater perfection of
orchestral melody than ... in the great capitals of Europe ... you walk
in with your wife in her morning costume, and seating yourself
luxuriously in one of those soft stalls you give yourself up with perfect
ease to absolute enjoyment.' All this was free to anyone who cared to
walk in and was suitably dressed. Trollope felt a little ashamed that he
had not flung a few golden coins onto the gambling tables which paid

for this luxury. It had evidently moved him, for he took the fairly unusual step in his fiction of announcing that 'I ... having lately been there ... thoroughly enjoyed myself!' [XI].[58]

Mr. Scarborough's Family appeared in *All the Year Round*. For this, his last completed three-volume novel, Trollope received £1,000, exactly what he had received for *Framley Parsonage*, which launched his great fame twenty years before. Scarborough himself is a rather sinister character – a 'pagan' – who has two sons. He disinherits first one and then the other by declaring them illegitimate. This allows Trollope to descant on a topic that filled so many of his last novels: inheritance. Into the novel he brings places that had played large roles in his life: Hertfordshire, with a story of a Tory squire who tries to disinherit a difficult nephew – exactly what Adolphus Meetkerke did to Thomas Anthony Trollope seventy years before; Brussels, where the young Trollope passed a short time as an usher in Drury's school and, finally, Cheltenham, where he had lived while reorganising the post in the early 1850s. The novel shows very few signs of failing powers, though about half the manuscript is in Florence's hand. Often Trollope would start a chapter and then Florence would take over. The next day, the manuscript indicates, he would go over what she had written and make small revisions. As with *Cousin Henry*, he paid her a small tribute by naming the main female character Florence. The first part appeared on 27 May 1882, and in spite of the difficulties Trollope faced in writing the book anyone who reads it would agree the verdict of a later writer that 'it has a verve worthy of his prime'.[59]

Trollope arranged a final collection of his short stories, the fifth, and used the title of one of those included as the book's title, *Why Frau Frohmann Raised Her Prices*. This collection ranged from a story about an Austrian innkeeper, in which Trollope portrayed one of his favourite plots, the honest Tory who is forced, after a great battle, to adapt to changing times, to another story, 'The Telegraph Girl', which tells of two girls who work for the GPO. On 20 February 1882 he turned to his forty-sixth novel, *An Old Man's Love*. He managed four pages of this short work on his first day, and although he finished twenty pages that week he only wrote on four out of the seven days, perhaps indicating failing strength. Nevertheless the determination and discipline remained, and by 9 May he was able to write seven pages and record, for the last time, 'Finis' at the bottom of a novel's work sheet. He was obviously worried that he was not doing his set number of words per page, so he made a pencilled chart showing whether each chapter was 'over' or 'under'.[60] The novel is the story of an old gentleman who falls in love with his ward; she agrees to marry him, but he eventually releases her from her promise so that she can marry her young man, who is back from those gold mines at Kimberley which Trollope so detested. The young man gets the girl and the elderly gentleman is left to contemplate his Horace in peace only ruffled by the occasional feeling of wistful loneliness. This novel was not published until after Trollope's death.

Within a few days of completing *An Old Man's Love* Trollope turned his hand to a new field, historical writing, and in the space of a few weeks produced a short book about Lord Palmerston for which he received £200. Trollope did not intend this as a 'biography' but as a 'memoir'. Indeed Palmerston is not actually born in the book, but makes his first appearance when he is 'breeched'. Perhaps Trollope thought that Viscounts, unlike Zulu chiefs, should never appear without their trousers. It is a thoroughly bad book and virtually worthless as a study of Palmerston, except to show his appeal to his contemporaries. Trollope did some slight research but took most of his information from published biographies. The book would have been better if he had indulged in more personal recollections. He tells how his uncle showed him the spot where a madman tried to assassinate the statesman, and refers briefly to his own presence in Washington when the Trent affair almost led to war between Britain and America. Yet these references are limited. Even his allusions to Palmerston's Irish estates, which he knew well, are tantalisingly brief.[61]

One motive for turning to 'Pam' was to use him as a means to portray the confidence and beliefs of the mid-Victorian era, the period personified in Palmerston, the period of Trollope's greatest successes. Presumably one motivation for the book was the realisation that what he had lived through was now 'history'. Younger Liberals, like his new friend Freeman, found Palmerston not only outmoded but more than a little reactionary. The book also shows Trollope's growing wariness of contemporary Liberalism. Attitudes towards foreign affairs, because rarely based on detailed knowledge, are almost always the best indication of the prejudices that underlie political views. On domestic questions one can have intimate knowledge, but when the eye, as well as the mind, wanders abroad it usually either reacts or imposes its own preconceptions on situations it does not understand. *Lord Palmerston* provides a good example. In novels like *Nina Balatka* or travel books like *North America* Trollope had adopted the conventional disapproving tones of a Victorian Liberal towards Austria or the American South, sustained by a lack of knowledge about either place. What his *Palmerston* shows is that he was no longer reproducing the accepted

Liberal views he had once adopted: he speaks of the Emperor Franz Joseph not as a 'tyrant', but correctly as one who has 'reigned, through many troubles, with good sense and moderation'.[62]

On domestic issues Trollope's Liberalism was also under strain. Both Tom Trollope and Escott imply that he abandoned the Liberal Party some time before he died; yet they were mistaken in this and were guided by their own later views. It is virtually certain that if Trollope had lived another four years he would have become a Liberal Unionist and followed his friends Forster and Sir Henry James in breaking with Gladstone over his Home Rule policy for Ireland. People writing after 1886 tended to presume that the years before that watershed were the same as those that followed. Gladstone was tending towards Home Rule, but had not as yet had his famous 'conversion'. The growing tendency troubled Trollope because he wished to remain a Liberal. He had always admired Gladstone and was upset in 1880 when he thought that Gladstone had 'shunned' him at a Royal Academy banquet. Trollope was puzzled and wrote to him. He accepted that Gladstone had 'not unnaturally forgotten me', but now he was worried that he had given offence. He recalled a quarrel with a friend of Gladstone, 'an awkward man, [who] altogether misinterpreted me, who am also most awkward'. He ended: 'My sympathies are with you in all things and I want nothing from the Prime Minister.' Gladstone, who replied before he hurried off to Windsor Castle, assured him that no offence had been intended: 'I must have been guilty of a rudeness quite unintentional.' As much as he admired Gladstone's character, Trollope had noted a flaw in him years before in an essay in *Saint Pauls*: 'There is always the danger in Mr. Gladstone's oratory – that he finds it easy to prove anything, and is, therefore, prone to prove too much.' In *Palmerston* he mentioned Gladstone's 'damaging passion' as something that had marked his whole career.[63]

However, Trollope's loyalty to Liberalism remained to the end. In October 1882 Lord Carnarvon exulted that 'three-fourths of the literary power of the country and four-fifths of the intellectual ability' are Tory. This statement incensed 'A Literary Man', who wrote a letter to *The Times* which appeared on 17 October 1882, listing those he knew to be 'Liberal, in the broad, general sense of the the term'. One of the first on the list was Anthony Trollope. A letter in the Gladstone Papers reveals that the author was Abraham Hayward, Trollope's friend and whist partner, with whom he often discussed politics. They had been in touch recently because Trollope had given him an autographed copy of *Palmerston*. While Trollope was not an 'advanced'

Liberal, as the term was being interpreted by the 1880s, he was, however tenuously, still a Liberal. As the *Athenaeum* commented a few months later, the *Palmerston* book was 'a sort of Liberal confession of faith'.[64]

It is unlikely that Trollope knew it, but some important figures in the Liberal party were wondering whether they could fulfil his lifelong desire to sit in Parliament – not in the House of Commons but in the House of Lords. Lord Acton was one of Gladstone's closest advisors in the Lords, where Liberal peers were declining in strength. Writing from his villa in the South of France in February 1881 to Mary Gladstone, who would undoubtedly have discussed it with her father, he said: 'I talked about bringing in outsiders ... and I spoke of Trollope.' It is not clear with whom he had talked. There was, however, one drawback: he had heard that 'Trollope is condemned as noisy'. Trollope was still seen by party leaders as a sound Liberal. His soundness did not necessarily mean that, if he were ever in the Lords, he would automatically do what, in Gilbert and Sullivan's phrase, his leaders 'tell 'em to'. It was about this time that he wrote to Tom about whether or not the Lords ought to accept a controversial measure. His own view was that 'for their own sake, the Lords ought to pass it, – though I, were I a Lord, would not do so'. He probably would have taken the title if it had been offered, for he had written in his *Cicero* that 'a man with us will laugh at the Sir Johns and Sir Thomases who are seated around him, but still, when his time comes will be pleased that his wife shall be called "My Lady" '.[65]

*

In *Palmerston* Trollope had referred to the 'spirit of democratic enmity' that was prevailing in Ireland. This was to be the theme of his last novel, *The Landleaguers*. Three decades before, in one of his *Examiner* articles, he had said that politics were quiet after the Famine but 'when there is another O'Connell in Ireland, we may again expect political agitation'.[66] Now such a man had arisen, although Charles Stewart Parnell had none of O'Connell's desire for compromise. Trollope deeply loved Ireland, but he believed that 'Home Rule' would lead to independence, which in turn would be a political and economic disaster for the Irish. In the mid-1870s, as Parnell was beginning to surplant Trollope's old courtroom opponent, Isaac Butt, he remarked: 'For the moment there was not even a necessity to pretend that Home Rule was anything but an absurdity from beginning to end' [*The Prime Minister* XII]. Trollope expressed his own opposition in the words of his

Irish MP, Phineas Finn, who is asked whether he will accept Home
Rule if the majority insist on it:

> Certainly not; – any more than I would allow a son to ruin himself
> because he asked me. But I would endeavour to teach them that they can
> get nothing by Home Rule, – that their taxes would be heavier, their
> property less secure, their lives less safe, their general position more
> debased, and their chances of national success more remote than ever
> [*The Prime Minister* XII].

Trollope's basic position was a loving paternalism. Since leaving
Ireland in 1859 he had been back a few times and had even set part of
one novel, *An Eye For An Eye*, there despite the unpopularity of Irish
novels.

When Parnell began his campaign urging tenants not only to avoid
paying their rents but to shun anyone who opposed the aims of his
Land League, the name of Captain Boycott, a land agent in County
Mayo, became symbolic of the passions of the time and added a new
verb to the English language. The Land League drew much of its
money from supporters in America; in the vile words of its founder,
Michael Davitt, 'the wolf-dog of Irish vengeance bounds over the
Atlantic'. As early as February Trollope was thinking of visiting
Ireland to gather material for a new novel, but he warned Henry: 'I
have not mentioned this to your mother as yet.'[67] However, on the
evening of Saturday 6 May shocking news arrived in London.
Gladstone was called out of a reception at the Admiralty and when he
and his wife walked into the hall of Number 10, they were told that the
new Chief Secretary for Ireland, Lord Frederick Cavendish, and
Thomas Burke, the highest ranking civil servant, had been hacked to
death by a gang of terrorists while strolling in Phoenix Park. The
Gladstones' first act was to sink to their knees in prayer.

It is almost impossible to exaggerate the wave of horror that swept
over Britain. Lord Frederick was married to Gladstone's niece and her
heroic resignation at the awful news, as well as the dreadful murders
themselves, are mentioned in almost every diary of the time. The
murderers had really wanted to kill W.E. Forster, Trollope's friend,
who had just resigned as Chief Secretary. Lord Frederick had been
sent not only because of his desire to do good for Ireland but because
'the fragrance of Cavendish is essential' to a Liberal government,
particularly one in difficulties [*Phineas Redux* XL]. Ironically the event
had been foreshadowed in *The Prime Minister*: when the Duke of
Omnium is describing his new government to his wife he mentions
that Phineas Finn was being sent as Chief Secretary to Ireland: 'Poor

Phineas!' replied the Duchess, 'I hope they won't murder him, or anything of that kind. They do murder people, you know, sometimes' [VIII]. This was written eight years before the Phoenix Park murders. No doubt it was fortunate that Lady Frederick Cavendish had probably given up the Palliser novels before this, as she was not entirely happy with the second book, which she had read at Chatsworth: 'Finished *Phineas Finn*; it has cleverness and some successful characters, but it is a disagreeable, sham sort of book.'*[68]

It was at this moment of extreme tension that Trollope, accompanied by the faithful 'Flo', left for Ireland. Rose, who remained in Sussex, had good grounds for worry. An attempt to blow up the Mansion House was made while Trollope was passing through London, and the clubs where he dined buzzed with rumours of terrorists stalking the streets, so much so that the Home Secretary's son armed himself with a sword-stick. Trollope suffered no greater problem in London than his oft-repeated loss of his wallet at one of his clubs; when he hurried back it was waiting for him 'in the hands of the faithful waiter'. Although he was clearly failing, he still struggled to gather information for his new novel. Rose was reassured by several letters each week, with Florence no doubt writing in between. Trollope came to feel that this was not the time for yet more conciliation: 'we ought to see the Parnell set put down.' Once again on familiar ground in Cork, he was amazed how quiet everything was and wrote to his wife, recalling how the newspapers had exaggerated the dangers in 1848, something that had so alarmed his mother. Sometimes his thoughts were of past happiness, but often they returned to Harting and his 'dearest love': 'How is the garden, and the cocks & hens, & especially the asparagus bed?' Not all the news from home was encouraging: Henry, who was staying with his mother, had spotted their man-servant dropping 'into the pot [public] house' after leaving him at the station. Rose presumably was complaining about her husband's absence, for he wrote: 'I will give up being Surveyor's clerk as you don't seem to like it, but in that case must take to being guide at Killarney.'[69]

Trollope was back in Harting after about a month in Ireland and was able to start work on *The Landleaguers* in June 1882. He turned aside from the novel to attend to one family question that had long plagued him. As we have seen, when he made his will he left £4,000 to Florence

---

*John Bailey, the editor of Lady Frederick's diary, obviously disagreed with his sister-in-law, as he noted: 'I have heard it described as the truest picture of Parliamentary life in English fiction. He then quoted a Prime Minister who shared his opinion.' That could well have been Lord Rosebery, who had a high opinion of Trollope's political novels.

at the time he was describing a similar will in *Cousin Henry*. She had become even more necessary to him since then and he may have increased her allowance or perhaps even have given her the money she was to inherit. In any event, on 12 July Ada Frisby was summoned from the Manor House to join Rose in witnessing Florence's will by which she agreed to make Henry and Fred Trollope her heirs as 'all the money I possess has been given me by my uncle'. With that settled, Trollope could resume dictating *The Landleaguers* to Florence. For the only time since *Framley Parsonage*, he violated his rule not to allow serialisation to start before he had finished his work, and this worried him. He had reached an agreement for the story to begin in *Life*, as well as for a three-volume edition for Chatto and Windus, a new publisher with which he was forming promising links. *The Landleaguers* is suffused with his detestation of the Land League and their supporters in America who gleefully sent money so that others might die. The basic plot revolves round Philip Jones, a Protestant squire in Galway. His eldest son falls in love with an Irish-American opera singer, whose father has returned to Ireland and become a Home Rule MP. Sometimes echoes of Trollope's old power reappear, as when a character is called 'as limp and dowdy as the elder sister of a Low Church clergyman of forty' [XVIII]. An unusual feature of the book is that a child, the ten-year-old Florian Jones, occupies a central role. In Trollope's novels children are usually of little importance: they may occasionally be seen, as at family gatherings or holding a visitor's horse, but they are seldom heard. Florian becomes a Catholic and is pledged by his priest, Father Brosnan, not to reveal the names of those guilty of violence.

Trollope made an attempt to depict the various strains of opinion among Irish Catholics in his portraits of three priests. Father Giles, an old man of seventy, is the type of priest Trollope knew and remembered, a pious man who devotes his time to his people's spiritual and material welfare but who does not meddle in politics. (His name recalls the short story 'Father Giles of Ballycloran', which described the author's earliest days in Ireland.) His curate, Father Brosnan, is interested in politics – like all curates, says Trollope. He has 'gleams in his mind of a republic' and supports 'Boycotting' and Home Rule. While he disapproves of violence, it is he who forces the young Florian to take an oath to protect those who practise it. Between these two is Father Malachi who wants Home Rule but is opposed to the agitators [III]. It is a pity that Trollope did not concentrate more on this trio than on the opera singer and on a peer in London who serves the basis for one of the sub-plots. In his *Palmerston* Trollope had argued, as had some perceptive politicians, that the best way for the government to gain an important ally in Ireland would be to pay the Catholic clergy from public funds. As so often he saw this as a question of 'human nature'. 'Had we paid the priests, as we paid and still pay, the parsons ... the priests would have worked for the Government. To expect that they should do so under other circumstance is to dream of a Utopia.'[70]

Trollope had not been content with his month's investigation so he returned with Florence in mid-August. For a man as tired as he was, he would have been better to accompany Rose to Switzerland. From County Wicklow he wrote to her in a bit of a rage because someone had taken the rooms he had reserved: 'I grumble fearfully ... The cooking is wretched, – with good tea and coffee. But the sauces! Everything is done with melted butter ... all varnish paste, – which you could paper a room with.' But there were compensations which brought back old shared memories: 'the brook still warbles just beneath our windows!' Fortunately less than a week later he was dining with Sir Charles Booth, the famous gin distiller, who 'gave us the best dinner that I ever ate'. However, the strain of this second trip was telling on him: 'Alas, alas; – I got a terrible attack of asthma ... It comes in the morning and absolutely forces me to sit upright in bed and it is gone.' He wondered whether he could carry a small alcohol stove to make his own tea as 'nothing seems to do me so much good as a cup of hot tea'. This was written from Kingstown, where forty years before he had met Rose Heseltine, and he ended his letter, 'God bless you, Your own A.T.'[71]

By mid-September he was back in Harting and at work on his novel. He felt that the air there was not good for his asthma, and a friend noted: 'he was decidedly moped, for he sadly missed his London friends and his whist and gossip.' He had been told by a local doctor in January before he even thought of going to Ireland that he was suffering from angina. 'I am to eat and drink, and get up and sit down at my peril, and may drop down dead at any moment,' he told one friend. 'They tell me,' he wrote to Tom, 'my heart is worn out having been worked too hard. I cannot, among them, understand anything of it.' He certainly had placed enormous demands on his heart for many years. When someone wrote, at about this time, asking for a summary of his life, he replied: 'I have written above 80 novels and novellettes, have written about almost all English speaking people, have written a life of Cicero, & memoirs of Caesar & Thackeray. I have also been round the world twice, and was for 35 years in the post office ... I have, I think ... answered all your questions.' He went up to London to see a well-known specialist: 'He says I have not a symptom.' To Henry he announced, 'I am disposed to believe him. Therefore I am going at once to walk up all the hills in the country.' This was a vain boast because walking became increasingly difficult, as he was now forced to wear a truss after suffering a rupture. Yet even now he could not restrain his impetuous nature. He would, one cousin recalled, 'still dash out of railway-carriages before the stopping of the train, would hurry in and out of cabs'. Lucas Collins, who came down to Harting for a short visit at about the time of Trollope's sixty-seventh birthday in April, found him 'by no means well'.[72]

His thoughts turned with even greater frequency to smoothing Henry's path after he was gone. Fifteen years before, he had written. 'A grown-up son must be the greatest comfort a man can have, – if he be his father's best friend' [*Phineas Finn* XI]. Now, in his last years Trollope found that 'Harry' in his mid-thirties had indeed become his 'father's best friend'. Henry was not only to inherit the library that meant so much to his father, but another collection that was almost as treasured:[73]

> My dear Harry,
> I wish you to consider the wine lying in the two further binns as your own
> ... They contain Leoville ... and Beycheville ... They are at present 24
> dozen in each ... The Leoville cost 72s. a dozen and the Beycheville 54s. It
> is 1874 wine and will not be fit for use until 1884 ... Should I take a few
> bottles for use I hope you will pardon the intrusion.

As well as seeing to Henry's wine cellar, he arranged for him to be elected to the Athenaeum. Henry was accepted by a vote of 204 with only 4 against. His father awaited the result in the card room but had spent days hurrying round London seeing friends to gather support. He was delighted when the news was brought to him. He knew that the vote, the greatest majority anyone could remember, was a tribute to him and showed how popular he was among his fellow writers and clubmen.

*

In spite of his declining health Trollope still derived pleasure from his books and his garden. Rose hoped they would soon see a bond with Fred there, as he had promised to send seeds of Australian flowers. She in turn sent him some photographs of the house. The garden was in full bloom when Tom and his wife paid a visit in the summer of 1882, and she recalled: 'I have never seen him in more complete possession of his vigorous powers of mind than he was then. Memory as strong, observation as keen, interest as intense, humour as genial as ever.' The two brothers laughed as they watched the dog chase an apple in the orchard and enjoyed various walks, during one of which Anthony repeated the lines from Milton that he had always loved:

> Fame is the spur that the clear spirit doth raise
> (That last infirmity of noble mind)
> To scorn delights, and live laborious days.

Since the sad days they had both known in Harrow each had lived laborious days, because each was his father's son, though neither had scorned delights, because each was his mother's son as well; but it was Anthony who had won fame. He bade farewell to Tom and Fanny at Harting on 9 August. After they left he decided he must see them once again and hurried up to London. He was able to see them the evening before they started for Rome. After their dinner, as Tom's wife remembered, 'I wished him "good bye" that night. But Tom went up to his bedroom at 7 o'clock the next morning to say a farewell word, and that was the last he will ever say in his brother's ear. The two were not only brothers but dear friends throughout a long life, and their affection for each other remained unclouded to the end.'[74]

This scene was probably at Garlant's Hotel in Suffolk Street, off Pall Mall, where Trollope had frequently taken suites of rooms since moving to Harting and where he had stayed in his days as a Surveyor. It was also where Eleanor, Dean Arabin's wife, stayed when she returned from Italy. John Eames, who escorted her, had been surprised to find the hotel 'patronized by bishops and deans of the better sort', and it was there that he had overheard two men in gaiters and shovel hats discussing the recent death of Mrs Proudie [*The Last Chronicle of Barset* LXX]. In recent years Trollope had had to make frequent trips to London for directors' meetings at Chapman and Hall. When in Town he could also visit his clubs to play some rubbers of whist, and when at the Cosmopolitan stand under the vast Watts painting and hear the latest political gossip on Wednesday nights. For some time he had been trying to persuade Henry that the two of them could share a small flat in London, with only one servant, for part of the week, and went so far as to claim that the London air was better for his breathing than that in the country. From Harting in August he had written to his son: '*I certainly cannot live here all winter*.'[75]

His new-found friend Freeman was always complaining that 'nobody comes to see me' at his country home, Somerleaze, near Wells. In the autumn of 1882 he found some hope: 'Anthony Trollope talks of coming down here in October or November.' From Garlant's Hotel Trollope told Freeman that he was coming, but he warned:

> I can, with due time, walk up anything, – only I can't sleep, walking or not walking, I can't write, as you see, because my hand is paralysed I can't sit easily because of a huge truss I wear, and now has come this damnable asthma! But still I am very good to look at; and as I am not afraid to die, I am as happy as other people.

This attitude towards death was the same he had expressed, paraphrasing an old prayer, shortly before, to the rector of Harting: 'I have no fear of death itself, but only the long wait for it. When once a man has made up his mind that God means to do him good, he ceases to fear death.' This attitude was not something he had acquired in his declining months when he was beset with so many ills. He had expressed similar thoughts in the mid-1860s, when his health, like his fame, was at its height. Writing about the Alpine Club in a rather light essay, he suddenly expressed a serious thought: 'We are going ever with our lives in our hands, knowing that death is common to all of us; and knowing also, – for all of us who ever think do know it, – that to him who dies death must be horrible or blessed, not in accordance with an hour or two of final preparation, but as may be the state of the dying man's parting soul as the final result of the life which he has led.' Even before that he had written that a man has three duties on earth: to work, to enjoy life and to pray.[76] He had done all three and was ready to go.

After writing to Freeman, and sending a letter to Fred, he had another bad night, but finally got to sleep after taking some chloral.[77] He took the train to Wells and soon was at Freeman's house. His host regarded *The Warden* and *Barchester Towers* as among his favourite books, and was anxious to get him to admit that Barchester had been modelled on Wells. Two bishops 'of different branches of the vineyard' were also at Somerleaze. On the first day the party set out for a walk over some nearby hills. Freeman noted that his guest 'was clearly not in his full strength, but there was no sign that serious sickness was at all near'. Nevertheless the mud and the stiles were hard going, and it was appropriate for one who had always been so friendly towards Catholicism that it was a Catholic bishop who helped him over the stiles. The next day there was a trip to the monastic ruins at Glastonbury and then the glorious sight of Wells Cathedral with its magnificent West Front dominating the quiet close. Surely, Freeman insisted, Barchester was Wells. No, Trollope replied, Barset was indeed Somerset but Barchester was Winchester 'where he was at school'. It was in this late October sunshine that the creator of Barset, standing on the hills above Wells, took his farewell view of his beloved county which he had described a quarter of a century before:

> There is a county ... very dear to those who know it well. Its green pastures, its waving wheat, its deep and shady and ... dirty lanes, its paths and stiles, its tawny-coloured, well-built rural churches ... and frequent Tudor mansions, its constant county hunt ... [and] country postmen ... a resident bishop, a resident dean, [and] an archdeacon [*Doctor Thorne* I].

By the next day he was seated in the Athenaeum, in that long room where, he always said, Mrs Proudie met her end; he was writing to an even greater ecclesiastical figure. Cardinal Newman had heard that his favourite novelist was suffering from asthma and had asked a mutual friend and former Postmaster General, Lord Emly, to give him the recipe for a remedy of saltpetre inhaled through blotting paper. This had once helped one of the Cardinal's friends. With the remedy he had sent something much more valauble, an expression of his high regard for Trollope's novels. Trollope was evidently much moved by this as he sat in the Athenaeum:

> May I be allowed to take this opportunity also of telling your Eminence how great has been the pleasure which I have received from understanding that you have occasionally read and been amused by some of my novels. It is when I hear that such men as yourself have been gratified that I feel that I have not worked altogether in vain ... I have, the honour to be, My dear Lord Cardinal
>
> > your most obedient Servant
> > Anthony Trollope

Thanks to the splendid service of the Victorian Post Office, which he had done so much to forward, Trollope would have had time to read Newman's reply: 'It is very kind in you to express pleasure at hearing of my admiration of your novels. Many of them I read again and again. I have just been reading one for the third time.'[78]

On 1 November he was back at the Garrick, giving a dinner to Browning, and the next night he was in Tooting at yet another dinner, where his host, appropriately enough, was a publisher, Alexander Macmillan. Freeman was there and noted that, while Trollope was 'not in strong health', he 'talked as well and heartily as usual'. The next day dawned pleasant in the morning but soon turned to gales. Yet into Suffolk Street, outside Garlant's Hotel, came the unmistakable din of a

German band. A decade before, in Montagu Square, Trollope had tried to persuade himself to be understanding of such disturbances. The increasing noise of London had long upset him, and when a lady at one dinner party tried to defend barrel organs he replied that he would take care to send any he heard to her house.[79] On this Friday an old and ill man was struggling to complete his forty-seventh novel and he simply could not tolerate the disturbance to his work with either resignation or humour. He dashed to the window, flung it open and berated the band leader.

That evening he went to John Tilley's – now Sir John Tilley's – house for dinner. Tilley's daughter Edith was there, the girl whom Tilley and Fanny Trollope had taken to Ireland to leave with Rose and Anthony after her mother Cecilia had died. 'Uncle Tony' was especially fond of Edith, particularly after she had memorised all of *Lycidas* to please him and gain five pounds. Tilley and Trollope shared even longer memories: Tilley had been at his desk at St Martin-le-Grand when a new young clerk had taken his seat in November 1834, and together they had fought many battles, mostly against Rowland Hill and one against each other. After dinner Edith picked up a novel to begin that popular Victorian pastime, reading aloud. For almost four decades the words of Anthony Trollope had been read aloud in millions of English-speaking homes. There had been tears at such scenes as the death of Septimus Harding and laughter at episodes like Mrs Proudie's reception in the Bishop's Palace at Barchester when Bertie Stanhope tore her dress: 'Unhand it, sir!' she had cried. Edith Tilley had selected the latest success published by George Smith, Anstey's comic novel *Vice Versa.* 'Uncle Tony roared as usual.' Suddenly the laughter ceased and the two Tilleys saw that he had suffered a seizure. After a while he seemed somewhat better and a carriage took him back to his hotel.

During the night, he had a turn for the worse, and it was obvious that he had had a stroke and had lost control of his right side and the power of speech. That which he had always dreaded had come upon him: he might linger without the power to speak or write. Henry must have been there quickly for he telegraphed to Tom in Rome advising him not to come. At times, when Henry or Rose were by his bed, he seemed able to make sounds which were almost like words, and there were days when they hoped all would be well. He was moved from the hotel to a nursing home in Welbeck Street. Various doctors were summoned, including one of the Queen's physicians, the famous Sir William Jenner. Newspapers published almost daily bulletins recording any improvement or decline in his condition. In the *Illustrated London News* a columnist noted that he had stopped to buy a copy of *Ayala's Angel* when he saw the Tauchnitz edition in a bookshop window in Brussels. Then he expressed the common hope of so many: 'I sincerely trust that dear A.T. is quite well and hearty again.' A month after the stroke his condition worsened, and on 5 December Millais, who had called almost daily to enquire, wrote to another old friend, 'Billy' Russell: 'Dear old Trollope is in a *very critical state* and I believe there is little hope ... He is rarely conscious and has only been able to utter one word ... "No".' He concluded with a tribute the dying man would have loved: ' "Fill up the ranks and march on" as Dickens said when he heard of Thackeray's death.' The next day the *Guardian* alerted the rectories and vicarages of England that their chronicler was 'in a very critical state'.[80] At six p.m. that evening, Wednesday 6 December 1882, Anthony Trollope breathed his last.

Henry telegraphed the news to Rome, where his aunt wrote: 'I grieve for poor Rose who was devoted to him and for Florence ... She adored him, poor girl and will long grieve for him I am sure.' After a few days Tom wrote to Henry: 'Yes! I have no doubt, that he is happy; and I trust to meet him again.'[81] The funeral was at Kensal Green, where twenty years earlier he had followed Thackeray's coffin. The interment was of a 'private and unostentatious character'. There was a hearse, followed by four mourning coaches and three private carriages. As was the custom, only men attended. Henry was there with Tilley, Millais, Browning, one of the Merivales and G.W. Rusden, who had only recently arrived from Australia. The Rev. W. Lucas Collins came to say some prayers over 'dear Trollope'. When Henry had time to examine the manuscript of *The Landleaguers* he found the following passage almost at the end of this, his forty-seventh and last novel [XLIX]:

> From his first coming ... his purport had been to do good, as far as the radius of his circle went, to all whom it included. The necessity of living was no doubt the same with him as with others, – and of living well. He must do something for himself and his children. But together with this was the desire, nearly equally strong of being a benefactor to those around him.

Epilogue

Within a few weeks of her husband's death Rose was attending to some of his wishes, such as giving his bust of Milton to the Athenaeum. She received official resolutions from bodies like the Royal Literary Fund, and many private letters. It was weeks before one of the saddest arrived from Australia. Fred had written to his father on Christmas Day to make arrangements for one of his sons to come to school in England at his grandfather's expense. It was the second half of January before Fred heard the news from his elder brother, and he was able to take some consolation that his father 'did not suffer much pain during his illness'.[1]

'*The Last Chronicle of Barset* is closed for ever,' proclaimed the *Illustrated London News*. Its author had become, said the *Academy*, 'the object of personal interest and good will to his uncounted readers, who feel ... as if they had lost ... an old and trusted friend'. At Harting there must have been a great deal of discussion about the obituaries, particularly such comments as that of *The Times*: 'If he had relaxed a little sooner he might have been spared to us the longer.' Those who had known Trollope, such as the rector of Harting, pointed to his character: 'No one was ever more vigorous in his hatred of what was wrong and mean; he was the perfect type of gentle English manhood and honour.' Others saw him as the embodiment of recent history, as did the *Graphic* and *The Times* by recalling that he was born 'in the famous Waterloo year'. While almost all were highly complimentary about him as a man there was disagreement about his literary reputation. The *Spectator* said in a leader: 'Mr Trollope's name will live in English literature.' Yet some who most lauded his character were dismissive of his lasting influence. *Truth*, despite its reputation for scandal-mongering, offered one of the most informative of all the tributes and had nothing but good to say: 'He was the perfect gentleman in every fibre of his nature.'

The Times, on the other hand, while pointing out his abilities and praising 'his kindly nature', also printed an anonymous article by Mrs Humphry Ward who decided that it would be 'rash' to think that 'his work [would] long be read'. (Forty years later – at about the time of one of the first 'Trollope revivals' – F. Scott Fitzgerald laughingly described a house as being 'as unfashionable as the works of Mrs Humphry Ward'.) The *Pall Mall Gazette*, for which Trollope had written so much, proclaimed it 'very certain' that his novels would 'drop out of memory'. Henry Trollope was so annoyed at this that he wrote to George Smith to complain. The *Illustrated London News* was most accurate in its prophecy that the Barset novels 'will be studied, enjoyed, and believed in ... They will probably outlive the realities which are so vividly delineated ... when our ecclesiastical establishments shall have under-gone a process of modification demanded by the ideas of the age.'

The death of a figure who had occupied such a central role in literature for almost thirty years was noticed almost everywhere. F.E. Trollope said that virtually all the papers in Rome carried articles. In America the *Princeton Review* commented, 'he could be a realist without ceasing to be pure', while the popular *Harper's Weekly* announced: 'The name of no English writer is so honored by American readers.' Eventually a number of considered essays appeared, most notably in the *Spectator* by R.H. Hutton, which contrasted Trollope's portrayal of English life with Jane Austen's, and by Henry James in New York's *Century Magazine*, which remains one of the best assessments, though Henry Trollope found it a 'lumbering piece of criticism'.[2]

There were of course legal details to settle concerning the will; Trollope's estate was proved at £25,892 19s 3d, with Rose as the principal beneficiary. Fred's considerable debts had to be cancelled, while Henry's most important duty as 'eldest son' and 'Literary Trustee' was to arrange publication of the *Autobiography*. By 19 January he was in negotiation with William Blackwood. As his father had suggested, he asked for £1,800, but eventually accepted £1,000. Blackwood's two closest advisors were divided about Henry's role as editor: Joseph Langford felt that 'Harry is ... very straight forward but possibly a little opinionated', while Lucas Collins had 'little confidence in his editorial ability'. Actually Henry did not make many significant changes, but worried over small matters such as whether the frontispiece made his father look too 'corpulent'. He removed a few passages such as a comment about W.H. Russell's indolence that 'would give him pain and might displease others'. Collins was the first outsider to read the *Autobiography*, when Blackwood sent him a proof-copy. His reaction is that felt by many since:

> I read it at once with great interest ... To me it seems at once the most interesting and the most honest auto-biography I ever met with. You have the man himself – I could fancy, all the time, he was telling me the

story himself – as I have heard him tell some parts of it. The story of his school days is very pathetic – too sad, some of it, for publication … if I were given to tears I would have found them often.

To Henry he wrote: 'every word reveals to me the man himself, his warm heart, sterling honesty, abhorrence of meanness and injustice and even his prejudices.'[3]

The book's publication in October 1883 stirred considerable interest: Mudie paid tribute to its most popular novelist by taking 1,000 copies. Rose was pleased with the appearance of the book and delighted when Blackwood sent her a framed copy of the frontispiece – after it had undergone some judicious slimming. As he told Henry, Blackwood hoped that the book would show that 'your father had more genius than the world has yet recognised or than he himself takes credit for in the Autobiography'. With many it did: the *Spectator* said that Trollope 'was not only a man of genius, but a man of energy, ability, and manliness'. They saw much of this as 'an inheritance from his mother' whom the *Daily Telegraph* called 'the brave mother from whom he derived so many of his best qualities'. The *Pall Mall Gazette*, making up for its lukewarm obituary, not only praised the book but printed various selections, including the list of what Trollope had earned from each book. This list, as well as Trollope's pride in his material success, annoyed some fastidious people, particularly those who were horrified that an author should write to make money. Henry, sounding like his father, objected to such criticism: 'Is a man wanting in ideal notions because he wants to give a horse and carriage to his wife?' Yet even a sympathetic critic like the editor of the *Cornhill* wrote: 'He has done his literary reputation as much harm by the revelation of his method of work as by his material views of its results.'[4]

The £1,000 from the *Autobiography* was his father's gift to Henry, and it may have provided the impetus for him to become engaged in Rome, in the Coliseum no less, to Ada Strickland, a friend of Florence's from Jersey. She was the girl whom Trollope had saved when her horse had bolted in Rotten Row. 'I think Mrs Anthony is quite satisfied with the match,' noted Frances Eleanor. Henry attempted to carry on the family business of writing novels with *My Own Love Story* in 1887. If it had really been his 'own love story', which had inspired his father to send him on a visit to Australia, it might have been a success! The novel has the occasional familiar echo: there is one character who is a government clerk with £90 a year. In addition to preparing various translations and articles on French drama, Henry eventually brought out a biography of Molière almost a century after his father and uncles had performed some of the Frenchman's plays for family guests at Harrow. Like his Uncle Tom, Henry spent much time on the continent both in Switzerland and in Florence. Tom himself survived his younger brother by a decade and died in 1892 a few years after settling in Devon. He and his wife chose Budleigh Salterton because it had three postal deliveries every day: a tribute to the way Anthony Trollope had improved the quality of life. It was also in Budleigh Salterton that Trollope had met his first biographer, Thomas Escott, when improving rural deliveries in the 1850s. Appropriately Tom died while on a trip to Bristol, close to his mother's birthplace. He had given his wife instructions: 'Mind, where I fall let me lie. Make no fuss. Give no trouble.' It was also appropriate that his widow compiled a life of Fanny Trollope as a memorial to her husband.[5]

Rose, who became sixty-two four days after her husband's funeral, did not remain long at Harting and the villagers often saw her walking up the Long Walk to the Downs, where her husband had enjoyed his long ramble with his brother. She moved to London and took a house in Cheyne Gardens 'near where the Chelsea lunatic used to live', as Henry, far more hostile to Carlyle than his father, commented. Florence remained with her aunt as companion. Sometimes they would let the house and retire abroad: 'Our object will be to spend as much of our time ... as we can near the Alps,' Anthony had written in the 1850s, and Rose remained faithful to this into the present century. She was particularly fond of the Tyrol, often spending several months there. She and Florence found a quiet hotel where they could stay for 'wonderfully little money'. In Kitzbühel she spent much time at an old castle, which had been turned into a sedate hotel by an English lady. Here they could stay for six shillings a day, including all meals! A young New Zealander met Rose there in the 1890s and found her 'a gentle and kindly lady'. One wonders if she told him of past battles through the snow drifts in his country.[6]

Rose kept up her reading though she disliked the 'new woman' novels. In 1889 she asked *Blackwood's* to consider a story she had written called 'The Legend of Holm Royde'. They were not interested; a few years later she tried to persuade them to publish a translation of a book by a friend of hers in the Tyrol. This shows, once again, Rose's own interest in literature.[7] She had followed her husband's teaching and had not adopted the most extreme forms of Victorian mourning, but her letter to Blackwood in 1899 retained the narrow black band of the widow. 'A woman may thoroughly respect her husband, and mourn him truly, honestly, with her whole heart, and yet enjoy the good things which he has left behind for her use' [*The Eustace Diamonds*

XXI]. Yet by the 1890s there seemed to be less of those 'good things'. Perhaps too much had been invested in Chapman and Hall or in bad investments made since her husband's death.

Motivated presumably by the fact that Frances Eleanor had received a pension on the Civil List, some of Rose's friends decided to apply for one for her. These were granted by the Queen, out of her settled income, on the advice of her government. Alfred Austin, the new Poet Laureate, wrote to Arthur Balfour, who was in effect deputy Prime Minister to his uncle, Lord Salisbury. After much 'anxious consideration' Balfour wondered, as indeed may we, what had happened: 'Trollope, of course *did* make money, – and a good deal of it; and it seems peculiarly unfortunate that not only all that part of his fortune which he left his widow, but also that which he left to his two sons, should have been ... nearly altogether lost.' 'The general rule with regard to Literary Pensions is that they are not given to novelists,' he wrote, because 'a good novelist is certain to make money. This cannot be predicted with confidence of a good poet, or a good historian – still less of those whose work lies in the direction of literary research.' Yet he concluded that 'Anthony Trollope was a man of such mark in his time ... that it would not be creditable to the country that the widow of one who has given such widespread pleasure should be wholly unassisted in her present very straitened circumstances.'

Within a few months the Diamond Jubilee provided an opportunity to celebrate 'Sixty Glorious Years'. The Post Office now decided to extend rural deliveries to the few places that still lacked them. Thus Trollope's goal of bringing the post to every breakfast table was realised. The Jubilee also provided an opportunity to assist the widows of some of the great names of the reign, and a Civil List pension of £100 a year was granted to Rose 'in consideration of the distinguished literary merits of her husband, the late Mr Anthony Trollope'. There is a perplexing footnote to this. A few weeks later Balfour decided to look into Rose's income tax returns and discovered that she had had £538 in dividends from investments. Had she or Henry convinced Austin and others that she was 'in very straitened circumstances'? Perhaps that was the last year in which she would be entitled to such dividends. Certainly Rose died worth very little: £373 4s 8d. We do not know, perhaps we should not know, the full details. So the story of the family finances ends in as much mystery as in the days of Thomas Anthony Trollope.[8]

In August 1904 Tom's widow wrote: 'tomorrow my dear old sister-in-law Mrs Anthony Trollope with her niece Florence Bland begins a visit to me. She will stay two or three weeks I hope. She is a wonderful woman a fine old English gentlewoman turned 83 but as full of spirit and life as a two-year-old. Her bodily powers are not, of course, what they were, but her lameness is the result of a carriage accident in [the] Tyrol some years ago. It has incapacitated her from walking.' Four years later, on 9 June 1908, Florence Bland died at Cheyne Gardens. Faithful to her uncle's wishes, her estate, proved at £4,556 14s 4d, went to Henry and Fred Trollope. Rose kept in touch with her younger son Fred, who had become Chairman of the Land Board in Australia. She also heard from her Australian grandchildren and one wonders what she thought in 1912 when her grandson Gordon Trollope wrote from his house, Clavering, to announce his engagement to the daughter of the engineer under whom he had studied. That after all is just what Harry Clavering did in *The Claverings*: a novel the boy's grandfather had written almost half a century before!

After Florence's death, Rose moved to 'Greylands', Henry's pleasant three-storey house in the centre of Minchinhampton in Gloucestershire. The house, part of which appears to date back to the seventeenth century, also had a rambling garden. Henry's daughter, Muriel, remembered the old lady's devotion to strong tea first thing in the morning and to large piles of books that arrived every week from a circulating library. When Muriel went to work in a Red Cross Hospital in 1915, Rose asked a question recalling the first years of her marriage seventy-one years before: 'Will there be any Irish soldiers there?' Rose Trollope survived until 25 May 1917, when she was ninety-six: the wife of a man who was born at the time of Waterloo died during the First World War and the Russian Revolution. *The Times* saw her as 'a venerable figure, bearing a name which will always be honoured in English literature'. Fred had died in 1910, but eventually one of his sons – whose birth had been expected during his grandfather's second visit to Australia – succeeded to the Trollope baronetcy, which remains in Australia, part of 'the English world' to which Trollope was so devoted. Henry survived his mother by about ten years, dying a few weeks after his eightieth birthday in 1926. His daughter, Muriel Rose Trollope, by translating one novel, was the last of the line involved in the 'family literature'.[9]

The Times in its obituary of Rose had commented: 'Mrs Trollope lived long enough to see his reputation, on the strength of his best work, perhaps even more securely established than at the height of his popularity during his lifetime.' As this shows, far too much has been made of Trollope's 'decline'. Popular editions of his novels had continued to appear, and if critics may have rejected him readers and many other writers still recognised his excellence. When *The Times* in

1909 spoke of 'a fatal, perhaps an irreparable, blow to his reputation' caused by the *Autobiography*, Arnold Bennett not only made fun of the language – 'a blow which in addition to being fatal is perhaps also irreparable is diverting' – but defended his great predecessor's methods of writing: 'people who chatter about the necessity of awaiting inspirational hypersthenia don't know what the business of being an artist is'. During a respite from the trenches in the First World War Siegfried Sassoon wrote: 'Life in a railway carriage is better than a dug-out, and my three comrades ... gamble for pennies and prepare curious meals of bully beef and eggs and tinned coffee over a spirit lamp, while I ponder the European landscape ... [and] read *Barchester Towers*.' During a dinner at the Versailles Peace Conference Austen Chamberlain discussed with Arthur Balfour which novelist to take to a desert island. Chamberlain suggested Trollope: 'I thought that not only the *Barchester Towers* series were perfect of their kind but that the political novels ... were equally good ... Balfour seemed interested: he must look at them again.' Did he recall all the difficulties about Rose Trollope's pension? There was already a large audience for Trollope before Michael Sadleir published his biography in 1927, which greatly helped but did not start the 'Trollope revival'. It was early in that same year that James Barrie wrote: 'I feel that Trollope and I are living here together, for I seem to spend so much of my time with him, especially in the long hours after midnight. We then wander about Barsetshire in a heavy carriage drawn by two slow horses ... the motors whizz by us, but with Anthony on the box we do reach our destination which they perhaps don't.' The vast number of Trollope's novels, which provoked so much criticism in his own day, has aided his popularity in recent times, as more and more readers have come to share the view of Noël Coward who noted in his diary, 'Trollope is fortunately inexhaustible.'[10]

In the Second World War Trollope became even more popular, particularly after the BBC dramatised some of the Barsetshire books. He was the favourite novelist of Field Marshal Montgomery in North Africa, while among the savage horrors of the war in Burma 'Wingate's Raiders' sought relaxation in the quiet lanes of Barset. In embattled Britain itself one writer suggested that uncovering minor inconsistencies in 'the most luminous and restful of Victorian novelists' could provide 'a solace during evenings of black-out and "Blitz" '. By the end of the war Trollope's novels, 'the very perfection of escapist literature', were said to be 'quite unobtainable'. When Somerset Maugham was asked to draw up a list of books to help Americans to understand the national character of their ally, the first novel on his list was *Barchester Towers*. Many must have followed this advice, for in August

1945 – in the issue giving details about the new atomic age – *Time* magazine carried an article about Trollope's popularity in America.

The clergy have long been known as Trollope addicts, and there is the old joke that the 'bishop is in bed with a Trollope'. Yet strangely the novelist who not only has given constant pleasure to the clergy but has provided the most memorable portrait of the Church of England itself has not even been granted a plaque in Westminster Abbey. At the end of his book on Thackeray, Trollope said: 'What is needed by the nation in such a case is simply a lasting memorial there, where such memorials are most often seen and most highly honoured.' The time is long overdue for such an honour to be given to the creator of Barchester.

Politicians throughout the English-speaking world have long relished Trollope's novels. Early this century President Theodore Roosevelt used to request another Trollope novel from the Library of Congress as soon as he had finished one. In the 1950s Sir Winston Churchill commented: 'I am reading another Trollope. I find him very readable.' Harold Macmillan was well known for his love of Trollope – appropriate for a man whose great-uncle had been the host of what was virtually Trollope's last dinner. Not only did Trollope's books solace political upsets, but they helped him when he became Chancellor of Oxford, for he announced that he learned how to distribute patronage from Trollope! It is also appropriate that Garret Fitzgerald – most cultivated of Irish Prime Ministers – should revel in the novels of a man who so loved Ireland.

Trollope's reputation has been helped by an increasing number of academic critics, who have written admirable studies on aspects of his work. At one time it was fashionable to sneer at a novelist who had won the admiration of a Newman and the envy of a Tolstoy and to deny him admission to a 'great tradition'. Possibly some who turned up their noses may have been annoyed by Trollope's comment in a lecture 'On the Higher Education of Women':

> To base your life on the reading of novels, – to make that the chief work of the mind and the intellect which God has given you; – surely that must be very bad! Do you think that such an employment can be compatible with anything worthy of the name of higher education?

Trollope was expressing the view of the nineteenth century; the twentieth century has taken a different view. We have come to see that at its highest the novel can provide a vision, a partial vision, of life. There is nothing more important in that vision than to learn to understand ourselves and to come to some understanding of the personalities of those we encounter. For this there can be no better, certainly no more enjoyable, teacher than Anthony Trollope.

A few years ago a columnist in a New York tabloid newspaper hailed the television dramatisation, the 'Barchester Chronicles':

> Superficially Trollope's people are nothing like you and me ... But you'll know them. Just look at yourself and your neighbors. Their manners, incomes and some of their moralities may seem remote, but their emotions are as real as yours.

This writer also saw how Trollope gained such an understanding of human behaviour, one that has never lost its validity. It was because he 'takes and uses what this century squanders – time ... Thank heaven for Barsetshire, and the workaholic old postal official who put it there for us all.'

George Saintsbury, who as a clever young man had been among the *Academy* reviewers who dismissed Trollope, came in his old age to see that he frees his readers 'from the most degrading of intellectual slaveries – that of the exclusive Present'.[11] George Eliot once said that reading the novels of Anthony Trollope is like a walk in a beautiful garden. Perhaps it is more like 'a walk in a wood', like one of those in which he wandered while building the castles which became his novels. You may enter tired and jaded but after a long ramble down winding but shady paths with your wise old guide, you emerge amused, refreshed and enlivened.

Books by Trollope

These are listed in chronological order, giving the original publisher and price, and details of any serialisation.

Novels

The Macdermots of Ballycloran. 1847. 3 vols Newby. 31s 6d.
The Kellys and the O'Kellys. 1848. 3 vols Colburn. 31s 6d.
La Vendée. 1850. 3 vols Colburn. 31s 6d.
The Warden. 1855. 1 vol. Longman. 10s 6d. *Barset I*
Barchester Towers. 1857. 3 vols Longman. 31s 6d. *Barset II*
The Three Clerks. 1858. 3 vols Bentley. 31s 6d.
Doctor Thorne. 1858. 3 vols Chapman and Hall. 31s 6d. *Barset III*
The Bertrams. 1859. 3 vols Chapman and Hall. 31s 6d.
Castle Richmond. 1860. 3 vols Chapman and Hall. 31s 6d.
Framley Parsonage. 1861. 3 vols Smith, Elder. 21s. (serialised: *Cornhill Magazine*, Jan. 1860 – June 1861) *Barset IV*
Orley Farm. 1862. 2 vols Chapman and Hall 22s. (20 monthly part issues, Mar. 1861 – Oct. 1862, at 1s)
The Struggles of Brown, Jones, and Robinson. 1870. 1 vol. Smith, Elder. 5s. (serialised: *Cornhill Magazine*, Aug. 1861 – Mar. 1862)
Rachel Ray. 1863. 2 vols Chapman and Hall. 21s.
The Small House at Allington. 1864. 2 vols Smith, Elder. 26s. (serialised: *Cornhill Magazine* Sept. 1862 – Apr. 1864) *Barset V*
Can You Forgive Her? 1864-5. 2 vols Chapman and Hall. 22s. (20 monthly part issues, Jan. 1864 – Aug. 1865 at 1s) *Palliser I*
Miss Mackenzie. 1865. 2 vols Chapman and Hall. 21s.
The Belton Estate. 1866. 3 vols Chapman and Hall. 31s 6d. (serialised: *Fortnightly Review*, May 1865 – Jan. 1866)
Nina Balatka. 1867. 2 vols Blackwood. 10s 6d. (serialised: *Blackwood's Magazine* July 1866 – Jan. 1867; serial and book were anonymous)
The Last Chronicle of Barset. 1867. 2 vols Smith, Elder. 20s. (32 weekly part issues, Dec. 1866 – July 1867, at 6d) *Barset VI*
The Claverings. 1867. 2 vols Smith, Elder. 26s. (serialised: *Cornhill Magazine* Feb. 1866 – May 1867)
Linda Tressel. 1868. 2 vols Blackwood. 12s. (serialised: *Blackwood's Magazine* Oct. 1867 – May 1868; serial and book were anonymous)
Phineas Finn. 1869. 2 vols Virtue. 25s. (serialised: *Saint Pauls Magazine* Oct. 1867 – May 1869) *Palliser II*

He Knew He Was Right. 1869. 2 vols Strahan. 21s. (32 weekly part issues, Oct. 1868 – May 1869, at 6d)

The Vicar of Bullhampton. 1870. 1 vol. Bradbury, Evans. 14s. (11 monthly part issues, July 1869 – May 1870 at 1s except final double issue at 2s 6d)

Sir Harry Hotspur of Humblethwaite. 1871. 1 vol. Hurst and Blackett. 10s 6d. (serialised: *Macmillan's Magazine* May – Dec. 1870)

Ralph the Heir. 1871. 3 vols Hurst and Blackett. 31s 6d. (19 monthly part issues, Jan. 1870 – July 1871, at 6d and separately as a supplement to *Saint Pauls Magazine*, Jan. 1870 – July 1871)

The Golden Lion of Granpère. 1872. 1 vol. Tinsley. 12s. (serialised: *Good Words* Jan. – Aug. 1872)

The Eustace Diamonds. 1873. 3 vols Chapman and Hall. 31s 6d. (serialised: *Fortnightly Review* July 1871 – Feb. 1873) *Palliser III*

Phineas Redux. 1874. 2 vols Chapman and Hall. 24s. (serialised: *Graphic* July 1873 – Jan. 1874) *Palliser IV*

Lady Anna. 1874. 2 vols Chapman and Hall. 14s. (serialised: *Fortnightly Review* Apr. 1873 – Apr. 1874)

Harry Heathcote of Gangoil. 1874. 1 vol. Sampson Low. 10s 6d. (*Graphic* Christmas issue, 1873)

The Way We Live Now. 1875. 2 vols Chapman and Hall. 21s. (20 monthly part issues, Feb. 1874 – Sep. 1875 at 1s)

The Prime Minister. 1876. 4 vols Chapman and Hall. 36s. (8 monthly part issues, Nov. 1875 – June 1876 at 5s) *Palliser V*

The American Senator. 1877. 3 vols Chapman and Hall. 31s 6d. (serialised: *Temple Bar* May 1876 – July 1877)

Is He Popenjoy? 1878. 3 vols Chapman and Hall. 31s 6d. (serialised: *All The Year Round* Oct. 1877 – July 1878)

An Eye For An Eye. 1879. 2 vols Chapman and Hall. 12s. (serialised: *Whitehall Review* Aug. 1878 – Feb. 1879)

John Caldigate. 1879. 3 vols Chapman and Hall. 31s 6d. (serialised: *Blackwood's Magazine*, Apr. 1878 – June 1879)

Cousin Henry. 1879. 2 vols Chapman and Hall. 12s. (serialised: *Manchester Weekly Times* Mar. – May 1879, simultaneously in *North British Weekly Mail*)

The Duke's Children. 1880. 3 vols Chapman and Hall. 31s 6d. (serialised: *All The Year Round* Oct. 1879 – July 1880) *Palliser VI*

Dr. Wortle's School. 1881. 2 vols Chapman and Hall. 12s. (serialised: *Blackwood's Magazine* May – Dec. 1880)

Ayala's Angel. 1881. 3 vols Chapman and Hall. 31s 6d.

The Fixed Period. 1882. 2 vols Blackwood. 12s. (serialised: *Blackwood's Magazine* Oct. 1881 – Mar. 1882)

Marion Fay. 1882. 3 vols Chapman and Hall. 31s 6d. (serialised: *Graphic* Dec. 1881 – June 1882)

Kept in the Dark. 1882. 2 vols Chatto and Windus. 12s. (serialised: *Good Words* May – Dec. 1882)

Mr. Scarborough's Family. 1883. 3 vols Chatto and Windus. 31s 6d. (serialised: *All The Year Round* May 1882 – June 1883)

The Landleaguers. 1883. 3 vols [incomplete] Chatto and Windus. 31s 6d. (serialised: *Life*, Nov. 1882 – Oct. 1883)

An Old Man's Love. 1884. 2 vols Blackwood. 12s.

Collections of short stories

Tales of All Countries. 1861. Chapman and Hall. 10s 6d.
Tales of All Countries. Second Series. 1863. Chapman and Hall. 10s 6d.
Lotta Schmidt and Other Stories. 1867. Strahan. 10s 6d.
An Editor's Tales. 1870. Strahan. 12s.
Why Frau Frohmann Raised Her Prices and Other Stories. 1882. Isbister. 12s.

Travels

The West Indies and the Spanish Main. 1859. 1 vol. Chapman and Hall. 15s.
North America. 1862. 2 vols Chapman and Hall. 34s.
Australia and New Zealand. 1873. 2 vols Chapman and Hall. 36s.
South Africa. 1878. 2 vols Chapman and Hall. 30s.
How the 'Mastiffs' Went to Iceland. 1878. 1 vol. Virtue. Privately Printed.

Other books

Hunting Sketches. 1865. 1 vol. Chapman and Hall. 3s 6d.
Travelling Sketches. 1866. 1 vol. Chapman and Hall. 3s 6d.
Clergymen of the Church of England. 1866. 1 vol. Chapman and Hall. 3s 6d.
British Sports and Pastimes, edited by Anthony Trollope. 1868. 1 vol. Virtue.
    10s 6d. (Trollope wrote only the Preface and the Essay 'On Hunting'.)
The Commentaries of Caesar. 1870. 1 vol. Blackwood. 2s 6d.
Thackeray. 1879. 1 vol. Macmillan. 2s 6d.
The Life of Cicero. 1880. 2 vols Chapman and Hall. 24s.
Lord Palmerston. 1882. 1 vol. Isbister. 2s 6d.
An Autobiography. 1883. 2 vols Blackwood. 21s.

Since Trollope's death, three important volumes of his writings have been published as books:

London Tradesmen, edited by Michael Sadleir. 1927. (A collection of Trollope's
    essays first published in the *Pall Mall Gazette* in 1880.)
The Tireless Traveller, edited by Bradford Booth. 1941. (A collection of articles
    Trollope wrote for provincial newspapers describing his second trip to
    Australia in 1875.)
The New Zealander, edited by N. John Hall. 1972. Oxford.

Manuscript Sources

Surviving manuscripts relating to Anthony Trollope and his family are now located in several major collections in Britain and the United States. The two most important are at Princeton University and are named after their creators, Robert Taylor and Morris Parrish. These contain not only letters but MSS. of books and printed volumes. The University of Illinois at Urbana-Champaign holds the Trollope Family Papers which contain material relating not only to Anthony Trollope but to his mother, wife, sons and brother. The Bodleian Library's holdings have been divided into four groups for easier reference. The first is the Sadleir MS. which is the manuscript of Michael Sadleir's biography of Trollope including transcripts he made of letters, many of which were subsequently destroyed in the war. The second is the Trollope Business Papers which contain various business letters, contracts and 'work sheets'. The third is the volume of letters from Trollope to George Smith and the fourth is a collection of letters from Frances Eleanor Trollope to her friend, Linda Villari (née White) which appear never to have been used but which give a first-hand account of Trollope's later years. The University of California at Los Angeles's collection of Trollope Family Papers is mainly centred on MSS. relating to Trollope's mother and brother. The Beinecke Library at Yale has several MSS. of Trollope's novels and some of his earlier writings and letters. The National Library of Scotland holds the Blackwood Papers which contain a large number of letters not only from Trollope to John and William Blackwood but from Rose and Henry Trollope and from various people who knew Trollope. The Archives of John Murray, publisher of works by both of Anthony Trollope's parents, contain many valuable letters which may be divided into two sections. The first contains letters between the Trollope family and John Murray, and the second, between George Smith and Anthony Trollope. The Archives of the Howard family at Castle Howard, York, contain hitherto unpublished correspondence between Trollope and the seventh Earl of Carlisle and others. The final holding, of Trollope's own collection of English plays, is at the Folger Memorial Shakespeare Library in Washington, D.C. Almost all of Trollope's correspondence has now been published by N. John Hall. Since it is unlikely that many would wish to consult in manuscript letters that are now available in his excellent edition, I have not normally given as full citations to those manuscript sources included in that edition as to unpublished letters and documents. Fuller citations are given to letters and documents subsequently discovered.

The following abbreviations have been used to designate the principal collections of Trollope manuscripts:

Blackwood MS.   National Library of Scotland.
Castle Howard MS.   Trollope's letters to Lord Carlisle and others, Castle Howard, York.
F.E. Trollope MS.   Letters from F.E. Trollope to Linda Villari, Bodleian Library.
Folger Library.   Trollope's annotated copies of plays in the Folger Memorial Shakespeare Library, Washington.
Murray MS.   Correspondence between Trollope family and John Murray, John Murray Archives.
Parrish MS.   Morris L. Parrish Collection, Princeton.
*Parrish MS.   Letters acquired by the Parrish Collection in recent years and not included by N. John Hall.
Sadleir MS.   Sadleir Papers, Bodleian Library.
Smith/Murray MS.   Correspondence between George Smith and Anthony Trollope, John Murray Archives.
Taylor MS.   Robert H. Taylor Collection, Princeton.
Trollope Business MS.   Trollope's publishing records, Bodleian Library.
Trollope MS., Ill.   Trollope Family Papers, University of Illinois at Urbana-Champaign.
Trollope MS., U.C.L.A.   Trollope Family Papers, U.C.L.A.
Trollope MS., Yale.   Beinecke Library of Rare Books, Yale.
Trollope/Smith MS.   Trollope's letters to George Smith, Bodleian Library.

Other collections which have proved valuable for this book are:

Dr Henry Allon MS.   Dr Williams's Library, London
Arents Collection   New York Public Library.
Autograph Collection   Bodleian Library, Oxford.
Bentham MS.   British Library.
Bentley Papers, B.L.   British Library.
Bentley Papers, Ill.   University of Illinois Library at Urbana-Champaign.
Berg Collection   New York Public Library.
Bryce MS.   Bodleian Library, Oxford.
Dr Samuel Butler MS.   British Library.
R.W. Chapman MS.   Bodleian Library, Oxford.
Cobden MS.   British Library.
Cushing MS.   Library of Congress, Washington.
Disraeli MS.   Bodleian Library, Oxford.
English Letters
    Collection   Bodleian Library, Oxford.
Escott MS.   British Library.
Kate Field MS.   Boston Public Library.
John Forster Bequest   Victoria and Albert Museum.
Gladstone MS.   British Library.
Mary Gladstone MS.   British Library.
Gloucestershire Deeds   Gloucestershire County Record Office.
Harcourt MS.   Bodleian Library, Oxford.
Hardwick MS.   British Library.
Harting School MS.   West Sussex Record Office.
George Howell MS.   Reform League Papers, Bishopsgate Institute, London.

Ingram MS.	Bodleian Library, Oxford.
Liverpool MS.	British Library.
Lyttelton MS.	Hereford and Worcester County Record Office – since removed.
Lytton MS.	Hertfordshire County Record Office.
Manning MS.	Bodleian Library, Oxford.
Millais MS.	Pierpont Morgan Library, New York.
Mitford MS.	Berkshire County Record Office.
Macvey Napier MS.	British Library.
Northwick MS.	Muniments of Lord Northwick at the Greater London Record Office.
Palmerston/Sulivan Correspondence	British Library.
Peel MS.	British Library.
Garnett-Pertz MS.	Houghton Library, Harvard.
Post Office Archives	Freeling House, London.
Royal Archives	Windsor Castle.
St Georges Bloomsbury/St Giles-in-the-Fields Joint Vestry Records	Local History Department, Holborn Borough Library, London.
Somerset House	Principal Registry of the Family Division, Somerset House.
Weigall MS.	Kent County Record Office.
Wright MS.	Houghton Library, Harvard.

Notes

Abbreviations

A.T.	Anthony Trollope
Auto.	Anthony Trollope, *An Autobiography* (1883) in the edition by Frederick Page, 1950.
B.L.	British Library
Bl.M.	*Blackwood's Magazine*
Booth [ed.], *Letters*	Bradford A. Booth ed., *The Letters of Anthony Trollope* (1951)
C.M.	*Cornhill Magazine*
C.R.	*Contemporary Review*
Escott	T.H.S. Escott, *Anthony Trollope: His Public Services, Private Friends and Literary Originals* (1913)
F.E.T.	Frances Eleanor Trollope
F.M.	Frances Milton (later Trollope)
F.R.	*Fortnightly Review*
F.T.	Frances Trollope
F.W.	Fanny Wright
Fr.T.	Frederic Trollope
Frances Trollope	F.E. Trollope, *Frances Trollope: Her Life and Literary Work from George III to Victoria* (1895, 2 vols)
G.L.R.O.	Greater London Record Office
H.M.T.	Henry Merivale Trollope
Hall [ed.], *Letters*	N. John Hall, with the assistance of Nina Burgis, *The Letters of Anthony Trollope* (Stanford, Calif., 1983, 2 vols)
Hansard	*Hansard's Parliamentary Debates*, Third Series.
I.L.N.	*Illustrated London News*
Ill.	University of Illinois at Urbana-Champaign.
J.B.	John Blackwood
N.Y.P.L.	New York Public Library
N.&Q.	*Notes and Queries*
P.M.G.	Postmaster General
P.O.	Post Office
P.P.	Parliamentary Papers
P.R.O.	Public Record Office, London
Post	Post Office Archives
R.L.F.	Royal Literary Fund
Remember	Thomas Adolphus Trollope, *What I Remember* (New York, 1888, 2 vols)

S.R.	*Saturday Review*
St.P.	*Saint Pauls Magazine*
T.A.T.	Thomas Anthony Trollope
T.T.	Thomas Adolphus Trollope
W.B.	William Blackwood

Unless noted otherwise, the place of publication is London.

Chapter 1

1. T.T., Incomplete MS., Trollope MS., Ill. Earl of Malmesbury, *Memoirs of an Ex-Minister* (1884, 2 vols.), I.234. Sidney Herbert, who was at Harrow, told Malmesbury the story in 1848. For A.T.'s view of Herbert see his 'On Anonymous Literature' in *F.R.* I (July 1865), 492-3. For the family's history see: the Rev. Mark Trollope, *A Memoir of the Family of Trollope* (1897); Edward Trollope, *The Family of Trollope* (Lincoln, 1875), *passim*; C. Holmes, *Seventeenth Century Lincolnshire* (Lincoln, 1980), 67-8.

2. The first baronets were created by James I on 22 May 1611. The Trollope baronetcy was created on 5 Feb. 1642 by Charles I. Obituary of the Rev. Anthony Trollope, who died aged 71, *Gentleman's Magazine* LXXVI (June 1806), 587-8 and J.A. Venn, *Alumni Cantabrigienses* (Cambridge, 1954), Part II, VI.233. W.R. Winterton, 'The Meetkerkes of Rushden', *Hertfordshire Past and Present* IX (1969). For Adolf van Meetkerke (1528-1592), the President of Flanders, see A.J. van der Aa, *Biographisch Woordenboek der Nederlanded* (Haarlem, 1869), XII.527-53.

3. There has been some confusion about the 'trade' of Trollope's great-grandfather: some say he was an apothecary, others a distiller and still others a saddler. He described himself in his will as a 'gentleman, late distiller'; he died aged 92. See *N.&Q.*, 28 May 1949, 240.

4. *Remember* I.13.

5. *Liber Ecclesiasticus* (1835), Table IV under Heckfield.

6. F.T., *Paris and the Parisians in 1835* (1836, 2 vols), II.134.

7. *Frances Trollope* I.12.

8. T.A.T. to F.M., 23 Sep. 1808. Taylor MS. A selection of these letters was published by Michael Sadleir in *Trollope: A Commentary* (1927), 30-41. Hereinafter Sadleir, *Commentary*.

9. T.A.T. to F.M., n.d., Taylor MS.

10. T.A.T. to F.M., 1 Nov. 1808, Taylor MS.

11. The Settlement, an indenture, was dated 23 May 1809. Gloucestershire Record Office, D 341/IX/94.

12. T.A.T. to F.M., 9 Mar. 1809. F.M. to T.A.T., 9 Mar. 1809. T.A.T. to F.M., 4 May 1809. T.A.T. to F.M., 10 Feb. 1809. Taylor MS.

13. T.A.T. to F.M., 11 May 1809. Taylor MS.

14. A copy of A.T.'s baptismal certificate, transcribed on 4 June 1857, is in the Trollope MS., Ill. Donald J. Olsen, *The Growth of Victorian London* (1979 edn), 134. Frances Trollope, *Paris* I.231-2.

15. *Remember* I.3.

16. *Remember* I.34.

17. Anon., 'London in the Days of George IV', *London Society* XLIV (Sep. 1883), *passim*. Spencer Walpole, *A History of England from the Conclusion of*

the Great War in 1815 (1890, 6 vols, rev. edn), I.84. Louis Simond [ed. Christopher Hibbert], *An American in Regency England* (1968, 1st publ. 1815), 33-4.

18. The short story is 'Father Giles of Ballymoy'. There has always been confusion as to when the family moved. Evidence from MS. letters, Vestry Rate Books and memoirs seems to show that while moving to Harrow in 1815 the family continued to use the Keppel St. home until well into the 1820s. T.A.T.'s original plan was to live at Harrow in the summer. As a very small boy A.T. could have attended school in London. For this see R.H. Haddon [ed.], *Reminiscences of William Rogers* (1880), 4 and the Poor Rate Book for Keppel St., 1815-16 Microfilm Reel 118, Holborn Borough Library.

19. Jane Austen, *Sense and Sensibility*, ch. XIX. In novels where there are several editions available, only the chapter is cited.

20. F.T. to Lord Northwick, 21 Feb. 1819, Muniments of Lord Northwick, G.L.R.O., Acc. 76/1578. Anon., 'Middlesex' in *Supplement to the Fourth, Fifth, and Sixth Editions of the Encyclopaedia Britannica* (1824, 6 vols), V.403-5.

21. T.A.T. to Lord Northwick, 12 Feb. 1820 q. in Helen Heineman, *Mrs. Trollope* (Athens, Ohio, 1979), 23.

22. A.T., [Donald Smalley and Bradford Allen Booth, eds], *North America* (New York, 1951 edn), 26. *Remember* I.10-11 (for Farmer), 169-70, 41.

23. A copy of Princess Victoria's time-table of lessons and list of text books can be found in Lord Liverpool's MS., Add. MS. 38303 ff 1-38.

24. *Remember* I.18-19. Dickens also refers to 'Captain Bold of Halifax' in *Martin Chuzzlewit*, ch. IX.

25. *Remember* I.14. In *The Bertrams* A.T. sets Arthur Wilkinson's parish of Hurst Staple in the same area as Heckfield.

26. James Stephens to Macvey Napier, 10 Jan. 1846, Macvey Napier MS, Add. MS. 34626 ff 21-2. Lyttelton was one of the two junior ministers at the War and Colonial Office. In time he took colonial matters very seriously. For reaction to his comments on A.T.'s book, *Australia and New Zealand* see A.T. to Lyttelton, 16 Sep. 1874, Lyttelton MS., Hereford and Worcester Record Office, BA 5806/9 Class 705:104. In 1978 this collection was withdrawn by Viscount Cobham for sale. *The Times*, 6 May 1829.

27. John Anderdon to Henry Manning, 19 Oct. 1822, Manning MS., MS. Eng Lett c 652 ff 72-3. Anderdon was Manning's brother-in-law.

28. These figures were collected by a Commons Select Committee in 1818 and cited by Henry Brougham in the Commons on 8 May 1818. See *Hansard* XXXVIII, 593.

29. A.T., 'Public Schools', in *F.R.* II (Oct. 1865), 486.

30. Henry Manning to John Anderdon, 23 Oct. 1826, Manning MS., MS. Eng Lett c 652 ff 94-5.

31. R. Courtenay Welch [ed.], *The Harrow School Register 1801-1893* (1894), 66. Judith Merivale [ed.], *Autobiography and Letters of Charles Merivale* (Oxford, 1898), 36. *Auto.*, 4.

32. *Remember* I.491. Merivale, *Autobiography*, 33. A.T., *South Africa* (1878, 2 vols), I.137-8.

33. Anon. [J.W. Cunningham], *The Velvet Cushion* (1814), 8. It ran to ten editions by 1816. *Remember* I.10.

34. F.T., 'Salamagundi – aliena – 1834', Trollope MS., Ill. The poem consists of 61 eight-line stanzas. It was edited, with A.T.'s comments, by N. John Hall

as *Salamagundi: Byron, Allegra and the Trollope Family* (Pittsburgh, 1975).

35. Escott, 16.

36. Henry Drury to James Ingram, 12 Dec. 1828, Ingram MS., Dep. c 733 f 60

37. E.S. Purcell, *Life of Cardinal Manning* (1896, 2nd edn, 2 vols), I.20. Ashton Oxenden, *The History of My Life* (1891), 16.

38. Viscount Esher [ed.], *The Girlhood of Queen Victoria* ... (1912, 2 vols), I.280. J.A. Symonds to Charlotte Symonds, 8 Feb. [1857], H.M. Schueller and R.L. Peters [eds], *The Letters of John Addington Symonds* (Detroit, 1967, 3 vols), I.90.

39. Escott, 17.

40. F.T., 'The Righteous Rout', 54 pp. MS in Trollope MS., Ill.

41. Welch [ed.], *Harrow School Register*, 66.

42. Sydney Smith q. in G.W.E. Russell, *Sydney Smith* (1905), 7.

43. Preb. G.F. Nott to F.T., 20 Feb. [1825], Trollope MS., U.C.L.A.

44. F.T. to T.T., 11 Apr. 1827 q. in *Frances Trollope* I.95. In *The Bertrams* A.T. sets part of ch. I at Winchester. *Auto.*, 8.

45. *Auto.*, 18. *Remember* I.80-1.

46. Anon., *Questions for Junior Classes* (Winchester, 2nd edn, corrected, 1828), iv, 28. The book cost 2s 6d. F.T., *Paris*, I.263-4.

47. *Remember* I.94-5. A.T., 'Public School', *F.R.*, 477.

48. James Pycroft, *Oxford Memories* ... (1886, 2 vols), II.87.

49. A.T., 'Public School', *F.R.*, 478. *Remember* I.96.

50. Frederick Bussby, *Winchester Cathedral 1079-1979* (Southampton, 1979), 215. *Remember* I.69-70.

51. *Remember* I.40.

52. F.T. to T.T. and A.T., n.d., q. in *Frances Trollope* I.77. F.T. to T.T. and A.T., May 1825 q. in *Frances Trollope* I.78.

53. *Frances Trollope* I.85, 88. F.T. to T.T. and A.T., [May?] 1827 q. in *Frances Trollope* I.96-7.

54. A.T., *South Africa* I.160-2.

Chapter 2

1. *Auto.*, 21-2. In his memoirs T.T. took exception to this passage which, he said, 'grates upon my mind, and, I think, very signally fails to hit the mark'. For his part Tom, as an old man, was keen to play down his mother's and his own early liberalism (*Remember* I.490-4).

2. [Frances Wright], *Biography, Notes, and Political Letters of Frances Wright D'Arusmont* (Dundee, 1844), 8. Guglielmo Pepe, *Memoirs of General Pepe* (1846, 3 vols), III.236; see also *Frances Trollope* I.43 and Pepe's 1824 pamphlet, 'Relation des événements politiques et militaires ... à Naples en 1820 et 1821...' in Richard Mullen [ed.], *The Pamphleteer 1813-1828: An Introduction and Guide* ... (Dorking, 1978), 91, 166. F.W. (from Paris) to Jeremy Bentham, 12 Aug. 1822, Bentham MS., Add. MS. 33545 f 588.

3. The reference comes from Lord Malmesbury who was describing Napoleon III's 'revolutionary' activities as a young man in Italy to Queen Victoria in 1858. (A.C. Benson & Viscount Esher [eds], *The Letters of Queen Victoria* ... (1907, 3 vols), First Series, III.346-7. Pepe, *Memoirs* III.237.

4. Pepe, *Memoirs* III.270. Stanley T. Williams [ed.], *Journal of Washington Irving* (Cambridge, Mass., 1931) 42.

5. Lafayette q. in F.W. to F.T., 17 Sep. [1823], Trollope MS., U.C.L.A. Lafayette to Genl. Pepe, 1 Aug. 1824 q. in Pepe, *Memoirs* III.272-3. *Journal of a Visit to La Grange*, Trollope MS., Ill.

6. *Remember* I.106. E.H.A. Koch [ed.], *Leaves from the Diary of ... John Herman Merivale 1819-1844* (1911), 40-1. This Merivale, a Commissioner in Bankruptcy, was the host. He was a friend of Byron, Coleridge and Isaac D'Israeli. One of his six sons was John, who later became A.T.'s friend.

7. F.W. to Mary Shelley, 15 Sep. 1827, Wright MS. F.T. to Harriet Garnett, 8 Oct. 1827, Garnett-Pertz MS. See Frances Trollope [Richard Mullen, ed.], *Domestic Manners of the Americans* (Oxford, 1984), esp. pp. xi-xiv. Hereinafter all references will be to this edition unless noted otherwise. See also Heineman, *Mrs. Trollope*. This is the best life of Frances Trollope.

8. F.T. to Harriet Garnett, 7 Dec. 1828, Garnett-Pertz MS.

9. F.T. to Julia Garnett, 17 May 1827, fragment, Garnett-Pertz MS.

10. Robert Dale Owen to ?, 2 Nov. 1827, English Letters MS., Bodleian, MS. Eng. Lett. b 32 f 101. F.W. to Jeremy Bentham, 4 Nov. 1827, Bentham MS., Add. MS. 33546 f 172.

11. Lafayette to Charles Wilkes, 8 Nov. 1827 q. in A.J.G. Perkins and Theresa Wolfson, *Frances Wright ...* (1939), 180-1.

12. F.T. to Miss Mitford, 10 June 1827, Parrish MS. She wrote that Hervieu was 'our' protégé, not 'my'. A.T.'s reference may also have drawn on two equally bizarre ventures by writers whom he knew, Thomas Hughes and Laurence Oliphant.

13. *Domestic Manners*, 24. Lafayette to F.T., 11 Nov. 1828, (copy). Trollope MS., U.C.L.A. F.T. to Miss Mitford, 20 Jan. 1829 q. in A.G. L'Estrange, *The Friendships of Mary Russell Mitford* (1882, 2 vols), I.191-3.

14. Escott, 62.

15. *Domestic Manners*, 75.

16. Escott, 16.

17. [Thomas Hamilton], *Men and Manners in America* (1833, 2 vols), II.169. The manuscript of the *Auto.* in the British Library shows that A.T. originally wrote 'showy', which he then changed to 'a sorry building'.

18. *Remember* I.158.

19. *Remember* I.41, 205.

20. Sir William Gregory [Lady Gregory, ed.], *An Autobiography* (1894), 35.

21. A.T., 'Public Schools', *F.R.*, 483.

22. Gregory, *An Autobiography*, 35. To Gregory, Harrow had been 'a fine, manly place ... a little world in itself' where 'boys were the arbiters of their own unhappiness or happiness', a place with little bullying although he admitted the teaching was dreadful.

23. Frederick Ponsonby q. in Percy M. Thornton, *Harrow School and its Surroundings* (1885), 250. E.D. Laborde, *Harrow School: Yesterday and Today* (Winchester, 1948), 75. *Auto.*, 13. The impression of the fight on schoolboy lore is seen by a chance meeting of A.T.'s son, Fred, with an Old Harrovian in Australia in 1881. This man, who had been A.T.'s 'fag' still remembered the 'great fight' (Fr.T. to A.T., 18 Jan. 1881, Trollope MS., Ill). T.H. Baylis q. in Escott, 16-17. Baylis recalled: 'While a home-boarder ... Anthony Trollope ... used to call for me on his way to the school. I used to sit next to him ... I think he much exaggerated his Harrow sufferings; they were less than other home-boarders ... they were often sadly bullied and pursued with stones on

their way home' (q. in Edmund Howson & G.T. Warner, *Harrow School* (1898), 80).

24. *Domestic Manners*, 147-8. A.T., 'On English Prose Fiction as a Rational Amusement' in Morris L. Parrish [ed.], *Four Lectures* (1938), 104. This was first given as a lecture before the Edinburgh Philosophical Institution on 28 Jan. 1870. See *The Warden*, ch. XV for Mrs Radcliffe's 'twaddle'.

25. *Remember* I.116. W.M. Thackeray, *Vanity Fair*, ch. VI. *Domestic Manners*, 138. The incongruous thought came to her on first approaching a revivalist 'camp meeting'.

26. *Remember* I.156.

27. Cincinnati *Gazette*, 12 Apr. 1828 q. in Donald Smalley [ed.], Frances Trollope, *Domestic Manners of the Americans* (1949), xxvii-xxviii.

28. F.T. to Julia Garnett Pertz, 12 Mar. 1830, Garnett-Pertz MS.

29. F.T. to Mary Mitford, 29 May 1831 q. in L'Estrange, *Friendships of Mary Russell Mitford* I.226-8.

30. F.T. to T.T., n.d., q. in *Frances Trollope* I.131.

31. 'Swing' to Lord Northwick, n.d. [20 Dec. 1830], Northwick MS., Acc. 76/2275. T.A.T. to Lord Northwick, 17 Dec. 1830, Northwick MS., Acc. 76/2273. F.T. to Julia Garnett Pertz, 22 Aug. 1831, Garnett-Pertz MS. F.T. to Charles Wilkes, 18 June 1828, Parrish MS.

32. Mary Mitford to F.T., [18 Sep. 1831], Mitford MS., Berkshire Rec. Off. F.T. to T.T., 17 Feb. 1832 q. in *Frances Trollope* I.150-2. [Basil Hall], *Quarterly Review* XLVII (Mar. 1832), *passim*. F.T. to John Murray, 15 Oct. 1833, Murray MS.

33. F.T. to T.T., n.d. [Mar./Apr. 1832] q. in Frances Trollope, I.161.

34. *Domestic Manners*, 357-8.

35. Anon., *American Criticism of 'Mrs Trollope's Domestic Manners of the Americans'* (1832), *passim*. *Domestic Manners*, xxii.

36. Thomas L. Nichols, *Forty Years of American Life* (1864, 2 vols), II.22. *Domestic Manners*, xxviii, 369. The first comments were suppressed in the first edition of *Life on the Mississippi*; that which follows was in Twain's marginalia in his copy of *Domestic Manners*, in the Arents Collection of the N.Y.P.L.

37. F.T. to Julia Garnett Pertz, 25 Nov. 1831. Garnett-Pertz MS. F.T. to Mary Mitford, 23 Apr. 1832 q. in L'Estrange, *Friendships of Mary Russell Mitford* I.233-5.

38. *Auto.*, 24.

39. *Remember* I.163. Escott, 29.

40. Welch [ed.], *Harrow School Register*, 88. F.T. to Julia Garnett Pertz, 25 Nov. 1831, Garnett-Pertz MS. T.A.T. to James Ingram, 4 July 1824, Ingram MS., Dep. c 732 f 64. According to some marginalia written by A.T.'s contemporary at Winchester, Lord Selborne, in his interleafed copy of Thomas Mozley's *Reminiscences of Oriel ...*, Aristotle's *Ethics* was the most important book at Oxford from 1830 to 1835 (Bodleian Library). Maisie Ward, *Young Mr. Newman* (1952), 39, 43.

41. A.T., *Thackeray* (1906 edn, 1st publ. 1879), 5.

42. Susan L. Humphreys, 'Trollope on the Sublime and Beautiful' in *Nineteenth Century Fiction* XXXIII (Sep. 1978), 201-14.

43. F.T. to Julia Garnett Pertz, n.d. [1834], Garnett-Pertz MS. J.W. Croker to Lord Hertford, 1 June 1833 in Louis J. Jennings [ed.], *The Croker Papers* (1884, 3 vols), II.211. Croker was the supposed model for Disraeli's Rigby in

Coningsby while Hertford was the supposed model for Thackeray's wicked Marquess of Steyne in *Vanity Fair*.

44. One scholar has noted at least 14 references to the Prayer Book and 27 to the Bible in 42 of A.T.'s 47 novels. See John W. Clark, *The Language and Style of Anthony Trollope* (1975), 166, 174.

45. A.T.'s school text of Horace's poems, with his annotations, is now in the Parrish Collection. *Auto.*, 18.

46. Clark, *Language and Style of Anthony Trollope*, 179. A.T., *North America*, has at least four quotes from Horace.

47. A.T., 'Public Schools', 476.

48. Rev Wm. Longley to Northwick, 24 Apr. 1831; Quilton to Northwick, 3 Apr. 1834; T.A.T. to Northwick, 15 Nov. 1833; Quilton to Northwick, 18 Apr. 1834 (Acc. 76/2263, 2372, 2346, 2375); F.T. to Murray, 22 Apr. 1834, Murray MS; Quilton to Northwick, 10 Oct. 1832 (Acc. 76/2325).

49. George Quilton to Lord Northwick, 26 Apr. 1834, Northwick MS., Acc. 76/2377.

Chapter 3

1. F.T., *Belgium and Western Germany in 1833* ... (1834, 2 vols), II.19-28. F.T. to ? [Col. Grant], 3 June 1834 [?], Parrish MS.

2. F.T. to Julia Garnett Pertz, 13 July 1834, Garnett-Pertz MS.

3. *Auto.*, 28. W.M. Thackeray, 'Little Travels and Road-side Sketches: No. II. Ghent-Bruges' in *The Works of William Makepeace Thackeray* (1900, 13 vols), VI.292.

4. Henry Greville's diary, 1 July 1833, Viscountess Enfield [ed.], *Diary of Henry Greville* (1883-1905, 4 vols), I.14. For the terms of entering the Austrian army in the 1830s see P.C. Yorke [ed.], *Letters of Princess Elizabeth of England* ... (1898), 206-7, 210. See also Egerton Castle [ed.], *The Jerningham Letters (1780-1843)* (1896, 2 vols), II.196-7. Several other Englishmen had taken Austrian commissions including F.W. Cartwright, a Fellow of All Souls and later MP (for whom see the memorial plaque in Aynho Church, Northants.) and Fitzgerald Ross, for whom see Ch. 10, n. 18; F.T., *Belgium* I.254; F.T. to John Murray, 22 July 1834, Murray MS.

5. Palmerston to Laurence Sulivan, 15 Nov. 1834 in Kenneth Bourne [ed.], *The Letters of the Third Viscount Palmerston to Laurence and Elizabeth Sulivan 1804-1863* (1979), 257-8. See also Lord William Russell to Lord Palmerston, 10 July 1835 q. in Georgiana Blakiston, *Lord William Russell and his Wife 1815-1846* (1972), 333. George Quilton to Lord Northwick, 27 Aug. 1832, Northwick MS, Acc. 76/2318. Scrope Davies to Francis Hodgson, 1828 q. in T.A.J. Burnett, *The Rise and Fall of a Regency Dandy: The Life and Times of Scrope Berdmore Davies* (1981), 200.

6. F.T. to Wm. Drury, 31 Oct. 1834. Taylor MS.

7. Henry Drury to Dr Samuel Butler, 6 Jan. 1829, Dr Samuel Butler MS., Add. MS. 34587 f 109. Samuel Smiles, in *A Publisher and His Friends: Memoir and Correspondence of the late John Murray* (1891, 2 vols), II.384 is responsible for the legend that A.T. owed his appointment to Murray. However this letter in the Murray MS. of 20 July 1835 from F.T. to Murray clearly shows this was not the case. Perhaps Smiles had seen a letter, also in the Murray MS. of 27 May 1829 from Sir Francis Freeling to Murray, virtually offering the publisher the right to nominate a postal clerk, but this is more than five years before A.T.'s nomination.

8. 'Christmas at Thompson Hall'. Tom recalled that at night his mother kept herself going on green tea and laudanum (*Remember* I.490).

9. Post 58/68: Appointments, Vol. I, No. 558.

10. A.T., 'The Civil Service as a Profession' in Parrish [ed.], *Four Lectures*, 5, 6.

11. F.E. Baines, *On the Track of the Mail-Coach, Being a Volume of Reminiscences* (1895), 13, 16, 45. F.E. Baines, *Forty Years at the Post Office* (1894, 2 vols), I.164-8. N.P. Willis, *Pencillings by the Way* (1942 edn, 1st publ. 1835), 403.

12. *The Times*, 4 May 1847.

13. F.T. to T.T., 27 Sep. 1837, Parrish MS. Rowland Hill to Richard Cobden, 17 May 1838, Cobden MS., Add. MS. 43678 f 1.

14. Earl of Ilchester [ed.], *Chronicles of Holland House 1820-1900* (1937), 269. See also Esher [ed.], *Girlhood of Queen Victoria* II.292-3 where Lord Melbourne complained of titled ladies asking him for franks. *The Standard Library Cyclopaedia* (1848, 4 vols), IV.557. By the mid-1850s Englishmen were receiving an average of 20 letters a year. (P.P., 1857, IV, *Third Report of the P.M.G. on the Post Office*, 8.) It was 7 letters per person in Ireland. By 1860 the number employed by the P.O. had, like the number of letters, soared, in this case to 24,860 with 3,955 on the 'establishments' in London, Edinburgh and Dublin, and 15,137 in the provinces (P.P., 1860, IX, *Report from the Select Committee on Civil Service Appointments*, 122). Elizabeth Gaskell, *Wives and Daughters*, ch. XLI. (This appeared 1864-1866.)

15. See M.J. Daunton, *Royal Mail: The Post Office Since 1840* (1985) which shows that Hill's role has been overrated. Hill's Post Office Journals show how he felt himself to be isolated. Freeling had urged a reduction in postage rates but had been blocked by the Treasury who feared a loss of revenue. A.T., *North America*, 467. The effect of the reforms, especially on the poor, was hotly debated. See Anon., 'The Administration of the Post Office ... ' (1844) where the author argues that the £1.5m lost annually since 1841 did not benefit the poor, who did not write letters, but the 'mercantile firms ... and ... rich generally' (195). A.T., *North America*, 470. See also Ch. XII.

16. Henry Taylor, *The Statesman* (1836), 39. See A.T., 'Henry Taylor's Poems' in *F.R.* (June 1865), I, esp. 146.

17. See *The Royal Kalendar ... for 1834*, 247-9. Each year it listed every member of the Post Office 'establishment' in London, Dublin and Edinburgh.

18. Framley Steelcraft, 'The G.P.O. Museum', *Strand Magazine* XIV (Aug. 1897), 219.

19. Post 35/27: No. 562 CC: English Minutes, 19 Dec. 1838.

20. Post 35/30: No. 301 EE: English Minutes, 16 May 1839. The month before Maberly had complained to the P.M.G. that A.T. had not returned to work until the middle of the day on Tuesday after being given leave of absence for Saturday and Monday. He urged his superior to suspend his pay but the P.M.G. decided he would take no action (Post 35/30: No. 301 EE: English Minutes, 2 Apr. 1839).

21. For this subject see R.H. Super, *Trollope in the Post Office* (Ann Arbor, Michigan, 1981), 5-6. Prof. Super's biography of A.T. appeared too late for me to take it into consideration.

22. For John Tilley see Frederic Boase, *Modern English Biography* (1892-1928), Supplement to Vol. VI, 691. Tilley also became a friend of John Merivale (see Post 101/10, 178-9: Tilley Private Letter Book). Merivale, *Autobiography*, 210. Merivale's mother was a daughter of Joseph Drury, Headmaster of Harrow (1785-1805). J.H. Merivale, Diary, 1 Jan. 1831, Anna W. Merivale [ed.], *Family Memorials* (Exeter, 1884), 302. The paterfamilias wrote an evaluation of each son. John was 'in many respects the oddest' of all he wrote.

23. Algernon West, *Recollections 1832-1886* (n.d., Nelson Lib. edn), 34.

24. Theodore Martin, *Life of ... The Prince Consort* (1877, 5th edn, 5 vols), II.168-9.

25. Mrs C.S. Peel, 'Homes and Habits' in G.M. Young [ed.], *Early Victorian England 1830-1865* (1934, 2 vols), I.129.

26. W.M. Thackeray, *Vanity Fair*, ch. XXXIV.

27. F.T. to Richard Bentley, 24 June 1835, Taylor MS.

28. F.T. to Richard Bentley, 7 Nov. 1835, Taylor MS. *Gentleman's Magazine* V (new ser.) (Apr. 1836), 445.

29. The Taylor Collection has a copy of the death certificate signed by John Smith, Clerk of the Protestant Parish of Bruges and by a Belgian policeman. *Auto.*, 31-2.

30. F.T. to Julia Garnett Pertz, 25 Nov. 1831, Garnett-Pertz MS. *Remember* I.207. A.T. to T.T., 12 Feb. 1836 q. in *Frances Trollope* I.259.

31. E.S. Morgan to Richard Bentley, 21 Sep. 1840, Bentley MS., Ill. L49.

32. F.T. to John Murray, 20 July 1835. Also Apr. 1835, Murray MS. A.T. to Richard Bentley, 24 May 1835, Taylor MS.

33. A.T., *North America*, 501.

34. *The Times*, 29 Nov. 1876.

35. A.T., 1835-1840 Commonplace Book, Trollope MS., Yale, entry for 'Cowley, Johnson's Life of'. This MS. can now be seen in *Nineteenth Century Fiction* XXXI (June 1976) and as Appendix A in Hall [ed.], *Letters* II.1021-8. Samuel Johnson, *The Lives of the Poets* (1816, new edn, 3 vols), I.134. This was another place where A.T. and Thackeray agreed: see *Vanity Fair*, ch. I. Clark has counted 14 references to Milton in A.T.'s novels and 11 are from *Lycidas* (Clark, *Language and Style of Anthony Trollope*, 147).

36. T.T. to H.M.T., 16 Sep. 1892, Trollope MS., Ill.

37. A.T., Commonplace Book, Trollope MS., Yale, under entry for 'Henry IV'. A.T., 'Henry Taylor's Poems', *F.R.*, 146.

38. Escott, 31.

39. A.T., Commonplace Book, Trollope MS., Yale, *passim*.

40. A.T., Outline for a History of Literature, Trollope MS., Ill. This MS. can now be seen in *Nineteenth Century Fiction* XXIX (Sep. 1974) and as Appendix B in Hall [ed.], *Letters* II.1029-32. A.T., Commonplace Book, Trollope MS., Yale, entry for 'Order-Method'.

41. For A.T.'s tribute to Dickens see his essay 'Charles Dickens' in Richard Mullen [ed.], *Malachi's Cove and other Stories and Essays* (Padstow, 1985), 120-7. A.T.'s article was first published in *St.P.*

42. A.T., Commonplace Book, Trollope MS., Yale, entry for 'Bulwer Sir E.G. Pompeii – Pelham. Godolphin &c'. See A.T. to Lord Lytton, 20 Dec. 1865 where he recalls reading Lytton's novel, *Pelham*, first published in 1828, Lytton MS., Hertfordshire Rec. Off., Vol. 5, 24, D/EK C4.

43. A.T., Commonplace Book, Trollope MS., Yale, entry for 'Man – essay on – 1st. Epistle'. A.T. dated these reflections 29 Aug. 1836.

44. A.T., 'The National Gallery' in *St. James's Magazine* II (Sep. 1861), 163-76. The National Gallery, founded in 1824, was first housed at J.J. Angerstein's House, No. 100 Pall Mall; in 1834 it was moved to No. 105. Only in 1838 was it removed to its present site. This is another example of A.T.'s accuracy: 'No 100 it was', he wrote. Edmund Burke, *A Philosophical Inquiry into the Sublime and Beautiful* in the *Works of the Right Honorable Edmund Burke* (Boston, 1866 rev. edn, 12 vols), I.82-3.

45. A.T., Commonplace Book, Trollope MS., Yale, entry for 'Bulwer'.

46. F.T. to T.T., 27 Sept. 1837, Parrish MS. A.T., *Thackeray*, 3. F.T. to T.T., 18 Aug. 1838, Parrish MS.

47. See James Pope Hennessy, *Anthony Trollope* (1971), 66. A.T. to Miss Dancers, 16 Aug. 1838, Parrish MS.

48. F.T. to Julia Garnett Pertz, 26 Jan. 1838, Garnett-Pertz MS. Anna Drury to F.E. Trollope, n.d., q. in *Frances Trollope* II.260-1.

49. F.T. to ?, 23 Dec. 1838, Parrish MS.

50. George Leveson Gower, *Years of Content* (1940), 70. *Remember* I.248.

51. A.T., *North America*, 183. For his view of 'that paternal monarch' see also *The Bertrams*, ch. XXIV.

52. A.T. to T.T., Jan. 1836 q. in *Remember* I.248.

53. A.T., Outline for History of Literature, Trollope MS., Ill. A.T., *North America*, 502. Escott, 35.

54. F.T. to Rosina Bulwer Lytton, n.d. [July 1840] q. in Louisa Devey, *Life of Rosina, Lady Lytton* (1887), 195.

55. *Remember* I.257-60. Tom devoted one chapter of his memoirs to 'Mesmeric Experiences'. F.T. and T.T. to Rosina Bulwer Lytton, 9 Jul. 1840 q. in Devey, *Life of ... Lady Lytton*, 200-1.

56. Col. Maberly to the P.M.G., 13 Oct. 1841 where the Colonel referred to A.T.'s 'carelessness in February last year'. Post 36/12: No. 1002: Ireland Reports and Minutes. The novel was *Charles Chesterfield; or the Adventures of a Youth of Genius* (1841, 3 vols), I.140-1.

57. *Remember* I.323. Post: Minute of 10 Nov. 1840: Secretary's Orders, No. 33.

Chapter 4

1. Sir Robert Peel, 'Letter ... to the Electors for the Borough of Tamworth' (1847), 7.

2. Anon., 'The Novels of Mr. Anthony Trollope', *Dublin Review* LXXI (Oct. 1872) q. in Donald Smalley, *Trollope: The Critical Heritage* (1969), 365.

3. [Gertrude Lyster, ed.], *A Family Chronicle derived from Notes and Letters selected by Barbarina, the Hon. Lady Grey* (1908), 122.

4. q. in Norman Gash, *Sir Robert Peel ...* (1972), 398. See Hardwicke MS., Add. MS. 35804-5: these cover Post Office correspondence just for 1 Nov.-26 Nov. but include some 1053 ff almost all asking for positions in the P.O. F.T., *The Vicar of Wrexhill* (1837, 3 vols), I.5-6.

5. J.G. Lockhart, *The Life of Sir Walter Scott Abridged from the Larger Work* (1879 edn of 1848 abridgement; 1st publ. 7 vols), 576-7. Both Scott and Lockhart were, of course, Tories.

6. A.T. [N. John Hall, ed.], *The New Zealander* (Oxford, 1972), 192.

7. King's County has been renamed County Offaly. Samuel Lewis. *A Topographical Dictionary of Ireland* (1837), I.474. This is a useful guide for the places A.T. mentions in Ireland.

8. Lyster [ed.], *A Family Chronicle*, 122.

9. A.T., *South Africa* I.102. P.P., 1857, IV, *Third Report of the P.M.G. on the Post Office*, 1857, 62. This includes A.T.'s history of the Irish Post Office. See also his testimony before a Commons Select Committee on postal arrangements in his district in P.P., 1854-5, XI, *Report from the Select Committee*, 160-1. P.P., 1857, IV, *Third Report*, 62.

10. 'Anthony Trollope – Travelling Journal' 15 Sep. 1841 to 18 Sep. 1871, 6 vols, Vol. I (15 Sep. 1841-5 Jan. 1845) *passim*, Parrish MS. Post 36/12: No. 1017: Ireland: Reports and Minutes, 11 Oct. 1841.

11. A.T. also complained that one reason for the high cost of Irish post was that Irish innkeepers, unlike their English counterparts, were reluctant to arrange horses and fodder for the Post Office even though such work was highly profitable (P.P., 1857, IV, *Third Report*, 62).

12. W.R. Le Fanu, *Seventy Years of Irish Life* (1893), 190-2. The fictional Father Giles bears some resemblance to the Very Rev. Peter Daly, a well-known Catholic priest in Galway. He was also involved in efforts to improve the postal service to Galway, which must certainly have brought him into contact with A.T. See *Illustrated News of the World*, 8 Mar. 1862.

13. A.T., *North America*, 526.

14. *Remember* I.10, 178-9. F.E. Baines, *On the Track ...*, 211.

15. W.H. Lecky to Lady Amberley, 30 Jan. 1871 in Bertrand and Patricia Russell [eds], *The Amberley Papers ...* (1966 edn, 2 vols), II. 392-5.

16. Escott, 52.

17. The P.M.G. approved A.T.'s request for an extra month's leave on 31 Aug. 1842 (Post 36/13: No. 955: Ireland: Reports and Minutes). F.T. to Julia Garnett Pertz, 26 Sep. 1839, Garnett-Pertz MS. *Remember* I.327.

18. For an assessment of A.T.'s use of this landscape see A.G. Bradley, *Highways and Byways in the Lake District* (1919), 307-8.

19. Cecil Driver, *Tory Radical: The Life of Richard Oastler* (New York, 1946), 403-4. F.T., *Michael Armstrong* (1840), iii; T.T. to Henry Allon, 6. Oct. 1885, Dr. Henry Allon MS. Between March 1835 and September 1840, F.T. received £5,105 from her principal publisher. At the same time, she was receiving £650 for one novel; Dickens received £500 from the same publisher for *Oliver Twist*. Bentley Papers, B.L., Account Book 46676 A.

20. *Remember* I.327-8. Rowland Hill had a low view of Irish Surveyors in the 1840s. See Post 100/10: Rowland Hill's P.O. Journal 1850-1.

21. *Remember* I.328-9.

22. *Remember* I.329.

23. Charles Lever, *Harry Lorrequer*, ch. I. John Cronin, 'Trollope and ... Ireland' in Tony Bareham [ed.], *Anthony Trollope* (1980), 14-15.

24. A.T., Travelling Journal, Oct. 1843, Parrish MS. In October A.T. did his usual calculation of travel expenses and income for the previous 12 months. On the opposite page he started a new list of expenses, for the period 6-30 Oct. 1843 – the visit to Drumsna – and in the one column left blank wrote 'Began my Irish novel'. This would seem to conflict with his later memory that he began writing in September.

25. Janet Egleson Dunleavy, 'Trollope and Ireland' in John Halperin [ed.],

Trollope Centenary Essays (1982), 68 n. 19. The real Fr. Daly mentioned in n. 12 above was a well-known book collector.

26. A.T., *Australia and New Zealand* (1873, 2 vols), I.215. A.T., *North America*, 23.

27. A.T., *Australia and New Zealand*, I.207-10. M.A. Titmarsh [W.M. Thackeray], *The Irish Sketch Book* (1843, 2 vols), I.4. *Black's Picturesque Tourist ... Ireland* (1857), 216. Kingstown is now known as Dun Laoghaire.

28. Henry Garnett, *Reminiscences of Rotherham* ... (1891), 8-9. Baptismal Register of Hollis Chapel, Rotherham, now in the Rotherham Central Library. Edward Heseltine q. in William Lee, *Report ... the Sanitary Conditions of ... Rotherham* (1851), 24-5.

29. Frederick Pollock, *Personal Remembrances* (1887, 2 vols), II.149-51.

30. Michael Sadleir, 'Trollope and Bacon's Essays' in *The Trollopian* I (Summer 1945), 24. The book was given him by his son Henry on 4 Apr. 1879.

31. A.T., *Australia and New Zealand* I.477.

32. *Domestic Manners*, 258.

33. Henry James, 'Anthony Trollope' in Smalley [ed.], *Trollope: The Critical Heritage*, 542. It was first published in New York in July 1883 in the *Century Magazine*, before publication of A.T.'s *Autobiography*.

34. A.T., *North America*, 199. Edmund Burke, *Reflections on the Revolution in France*, in *Works*, III.331.

35. A.T., *Australia and New Zealand* I.477-9.

36. *S.R.*, 26 Mar. 1859. *S.R.*, 14 May 1864.

37. A.T. to Kate Field, 4 Feb. 1862 q. in Sadleir, *Commentary*, 224-5.

38. A.T., *North America*, 260.

39. Mary, Lady Barrett-Lennard to Bodley's Librarian, 22 Jan. 1928, MS. Autograph d 19 f 174, Bodleian Library.

40. Henry Brackenbury, *Some Memories of my Spare Time* (1909), 49.

41. A.T., *North America*, 25. A.T. q. in Gladys Green, 'Trollope on Sidney's *Arcadia* and Lytton's "The Wanderer"' in *Trollopian* I (Sep. 1946), 51.

42. A.T., 'The Telegraph Girl' in *Why Frau Frohmann Raised Her Prices and Other Stories* (1882), 317. *Paterson's Roads* (1824, 17th edn), 364. *Sheffield and Rotherham Independent*, 15 June 1844, 5. The witnesses were Rose's father and sister, Isabella. A.T., Travelling Journals, entry under June 1844. R.T.'s Chronology is now in the Trollope MS., Ill. *The Times*, 30 May 1917.

43. A.T., 'English Prose Fiction' in Morris L. Parrish [ed.], *Four Lectures* (1938), 119. The copy of the lecture which A.T. gave to his wife is now in the Parrish MS.

44. R.T. to F.T. q. in *Frances Trollope* II.39. T.T. to John Murray, 5 July 1844 and another letter of about the same date, Murray MS. re an article on French theology and book on the history of the Stuarts.

45. F.T. to R.T., 7 Aug. 1844, Taylor MS.

46. R.T.'s Chronology, Trollope MS., Ill. F.T. to R.T., 7 Aug. 1844, Taylor MS. Post 36/16: No. 864, 6 Aug. 1844: Ireland: Reports and Minutes. Post 36/16: No. 893, 27 Aug. 1844: Ireland: Reports and Minutes.

47. T.T. to H.M.T., 5 May 1883, Trollope MS, Ill.

48. A.T., *North America*, 142. R.T.'s Chronology (re H.M.T.'s illness), Trollope MS., Ill. A.T., 'The Higher Education of Women' in Parrish [ed.], *Four Lectures*, 79-80.

49. A.T. to George Smith, 10 Nov. 1860, Trollope/Smith MS. A.T. to H.M.T., 7

Oct. 1877, Taylor MS. Julian Hawthorne, *Shapes That Pass: Memories of Old Days* (1928), 134-5.

Chapter 5

1. *Literary Gazette*, 1 May 1858. 'Railroad Bookselling' in *S.R.*, 31 Jan. 1857. A.T., 'English Prose Fiction' in Parrish [ed.], *Four Lectures*, 108. Mr Gladstone, who became Prime Minister for the first time two years before, was a voracious reader. His taste in novels tended towards those of his youth, mainly Scott.

2. Anon. [Elizabeth Eastlake], 'Vanity Fair and Jane Eyre', *Quarterly Review* LXXXIV (Dec. 1848), 153-4. A.T. to J.B., 19 Sep. 1867, Parrish MS.

3. A.T., *Thackeray* (1879), 10. Mrs Oliphant to George Craik, 24 Dec. 1880, Mrs Harry Coghill [ed.], *The Autobiography and Letters of Mrs. M.O.W. Oliphant* (1899), 291.

4. A.T., *Thackeray*, 203.

5. See Bradford A. Booth, *Anthony Trollope: Aspects of His Life and Art* (1958), 143-5.

6. [Sir Walter Scott], 'Emma; a Novel', *Quarterly Review* XIV (Oct. 1815), 188. *Auto.*, 219. R.B. Martin, *The Dust of Combat: A Life of Charles Kingsley* (1959), 101. The friend was the Rev. Charles Mansfield, a Cambridge-educated scientist and colleague of Kingsley in his social work.

7. Esher [ed.], *Girlhood of Queen Victoria* I.260. See Richard Mullen and James Munson, *Victoria: Portrait of a Queen* (1987), 18.

8. Walpole, *History of England* I.252. Mullen and Munson, *Victoria*, 10-11.

9. John W. Dodds, *The Age of Paradox: A Biography of England 1841-1851* (1953), 361-2. Edward Cook, *The Life of Florence Nightingale* (1913, 2 vols), I.41-2.

10. Christabel Coleridge, *Charlotte Mary Yonge* (1903), 189. Laura Troubridge [Jaqueline Hope-Nicholson, ed.], *Life Among the Troubridges* (1966), 113.

11. *Remember* I.155.

12. Edward FitzGerald to Frederick Pollock, June 1873 in A.M. and A.B. Terhune [eds], *The Letters of Edward Fitzgerald* (Princeton, 1980, 4 vols), III.427.

13. J.A. Sutherland, *Victorian Novelists and Publishers* (Chicago, 1976), 25. The standard source for Mudie is Guinevere L. Griest, *Mudie's Circulating Library and the Victorian Novel* (1970). Philippe Daryl [tr. Henry Frith], *Public Life in England* (1884 rev. edn), 5-6. Hawthorne, *Shapes That Pass*, 226-7.

14. J.W. Cross [ed.], *George Eliot's Life* (n.d., new edn), 412. Even so, she still received £5,000 for *Felix Holt* and a further £1,000 for a 10-year copyright of the cheap edition. Cross, *George Eliot's Life*, 500. By the middle of the century 90 per cent of the volume and 75 per cent of the value of all books sold were at the cheap end of the trade, that is under 2s 6d. The vast bulk of books sold cost either 1s or 1s 6d (*S.R.* 31 Jan. 1857). *Athenaeum*, 2 Jan. 1828.

15. *Howitt's Journal*, 19 June 1847.

16. F.T. to R.T., 7 Aug. 1844, Taylor MS. Escott, 113. A.T. to R.T., 2 Feb. 1858, Taylor MS. Such a low fee would imply that the subscription was to a provincial library.

17. *The Times*, 23 May 1859.

18. Mark Lemon [ed.], *The Jest Book* (1864), 103. A.T., *The New Zealander*, 183. Escott, 115.

19. Herbert Paul, *Men & Letters* (1901, 4th edn), 142. Anon. [ed. Jack Simmons], *The Railway Traveller's Handy Book of Hints, Suggestions and Advice* (Bath, 1971 edn, 1st publ. 1862), 61, 65.

20. A.T. to Richard Bentley, 16 Oct. 1847, Taylor MS. Robert H. Taylor, 'The Trollopes Write to Bentley' in Robert H. Taylor, *Certain Small Works* (Princeton, 1980), 121. T.T. to Richard Bentley, 3 Sep. 1876 q. in Taylor, 'The Trollopes Write to Bentley', 138.

21. A.T. to Mrs Anna Steele, 25 Mar. 1876, Parrish MS. Edward Chapman to A.T., 16 June 1858, Trollope Business MS.

22. *S.R.*, 31 Jan. 1857. See Michael Sadleir, *Trollope: A Bibliography* ... (1964 edn, 1st publ. 1928), 268-9.

23. P.P., 1878, XXIV, Minutes of Evidence taken before the Royal Commission on Copyright and the Report of the Commissioners, 40-2.

24. J.B. to Mrs Oliphant, 13 Jan. 1868 q. in Mrs Gerald Porter, *John Blackwood*: Vol. III of Margaret Oliphant, *Annals of a Publishing House* (1897-8, 3 vols), III.175. F.E.T. to Richard Bentley, 21 Dec. 1886, Taylor MS. Arthur Tilley, 'Ivan Turgénieff' in *National Review* V (Aug. 1885), 829-41. Arthur Tilley was a son of John Tilley by his second marriage with Trollope's cousin, Mary Ann Partington, but all the Tilley children looked upon Trollope as 'Uncle Tony'.

25. *S.R.*, 14 July 1894.

26. *Athenaeum*, 5 June 1858. *Nation*, 28 Sep. 1865. The review was of *Can You Forgive Her?*. Cardinal Newman to Emily Bowles, 10 Jan. 1874, [C.S. Dessain, I. Ker & T. Gornall, eds], *The Letters and Diaries of John Henry Newman* (1961-), XXVII.8. *Spectator*, 4 Mar. 1865.

27. F.T. was also fond of letters in her novels, e.g. *Uncle Walter* published in 1852. *Spectator*, 31 Aug. 1878.

28. A.T. q. in Booth, *Anthony Trollope*, 146. A.T. also felt that *Oliver Twist* was the best of Dickens's novels in artistry because it had only one story line! (145). Sutherland, *Victorian Novelists and Publishers*, 12.

29. P.P., *Copyright Commission*, 145.

30. A.T., *Thackeray*, 7.

31. See N. John Hall, *Trollope and His Illustrators* (New York, 1980), 93.

32. P.P., *Copyright Commission*, 241.

33. Viscount Chilston, *W.H. Smith* (1965), 46.

34. A.T. to Baron Tauchnitz [in English], 17 Dec. 1872 in [Freiherr Bernhard von Tauchnitz ?], *Fünfzig Jahre der Verlagshandlung Bernhard Tauchnitz, 1837 bis 1887* [*Fifty Years of Publishing*] (Leipzig, 1887), 150. Tauchnitz began his 'Collection of British and American Authors' in 1841. The negotiations behind the series and the wide range of authors published are discussed in Kurt Otto, *Der Verlag Bernhard Tauchnitz 1837-1912* (Leipzig, 1912), 51-8 and 61-126. H.M.T. recalled that Tauchnitz 'has always been a good friend to my father' (H.M.T. to W.B., 20 Feb. 1883, Blackwood MS., 4452 f 48). P.P., *Copyright Commission*, 245. Ironically the Tauchnitz firm lasted until 1943 when it was destroyed by a bombing raid on Leipzig. There were other German firms apart from Tauchnitz, such as Asher, who reprinted some of A.T.'s works in English with varying success. *Remember* I.171. Douglas Jerrold, *Mrs. Caudle's Curtain Lectures* (1902), 153-4.

35. J.A. Symonds to Charlotte Symonds, 31 Jan. [1861] in Schueller & Peters [eds.], *Letters of John Addington Symonds* I.268-9.

36. The offending words occurred in ch. XLIII of *Is He Popenjoy?*; A.T. restored them when the work was published as a book. The young Dickens perhaps should have recalled that his father had been quite explicit about Mrs Micawber as a nursing mother in *Great Expectations*. T.C.D., 'Victorian Editors and Victorian Delicacy' in *N.&Q.* CLXXXVII (2 Dec. 1944), 251-3. A.T. to W.M. Thackeray, 15 Nov. 1860, Parrish MS.

37. *Athenaeum*, 3 Aug. 1867. A.T., *Thackeray*, 51-7.

38. A.T. to Richard Bentley, 20 Nov. 1869, Parrish MS. [Sir Walter Scott], 'Emma; a Novel', *Quarterly Review*, 193.

39. A.T. q. in R.L.F., *Annual Report* (1867), 28-9.

40. *Auto.*, 126.

41. *Athenaeum*, 9 Dec. 1882. W.G. Elliot, *In My Anecdotage* (1925), 94-5. For A.T.'s lists of principal characters for *Sir Harry Hotspur of Humblethwaite* and *The Way We Live Now* see Sadleir, *Commentary*, Appendix IV. A.T., *Thackeray*, 122-3.

42. A.T. to A.F.A. Woodford, 30 Sep. 1878, Trollope Business MS. Woodford was editor of the *Masonic Magazine*. The story in question was 'Catherine Carmichael' which took A.T. two weeks to write. A.T., 'A Walk in a Wood' in Mullen [ed.], *Malachi's Cove*, 138.

43. For A.T.'s work for the R.L.F. see Ch. XIV.

44. A.T., 'A Walk in a Wood', in Mullen [ed.], *Malachi's Cove*, 128.

45. A.T., 'On English Prose Fiction', in Parrish [ed.], *Four Lectures*, 108. A.T., 'Novel-Reading: The Works of Charles Dickens. The Works of W. Makepeace Thackeray' in *Nineteenth Century* V (Jan. 1879), 27. A.T. to William Longman, 3 Mar. 1857, Trollope Business MS. A.T. to George Smith, 9 Aug. 1860, Smith/Murray MS.

46. See, for example, *The Virginians*, chs XVI and XXVIII.

47. William Glenn's Diary, 1 Jan. 1864, B.E. Marks & M.N. Schatz [eds.], *Between North and South ... The Narrative of William Wilkins Glenn 1861-1869* (1976), 111.

48. A.T., 'Higher Education of Women' in Parrish [ed.], *Four Lectures*, 69. See A.T., 'Formosa' in *St.P.* V (Oct. 1869), 75-80 and Ch. XIII.

49. Sadleir, *Commentary*, Appendix IV.

50. *The Times*, 16 Nov. 1870.

51. Arthur Waugh, *A Hundred Years of Publishing, Being the Story of Chapman and Hall Ltd.* (1930), 86-8.

52. On the use of 'vulgar' see David Skilton, *Anthony Trollope and his Contemporaries* (1972), 90-1.

53. A.T., *Thackeray*, 202.

54. Clark, *Language and Style of Anthony Trollope*, 18. A.T., *The West Indies and the Spanish Main* (4th edn, 1860, 1st publ. 1859), 348-9. A.T., 'Henry Taylor's Poems', *F.R.*, 130.

55. For A.T.'s use of 'but' to create a distinctive cadence in his writing see H.S. Davies, 'Trollope and His Style' in *A Review of English Studies* I (Oct. 1960), 76ff. For the influence of Freeling et al. see Coral Lansbury, *The Reasonable Man: Trollope's Legal Fiction* (Princeton, 1981), 7-24.

56. Robert Taylor, 'The Manuscript of Trollope's *The American Senator* Collated with the First Edition' in *Papers of the Bibliographical Society of America* XLI (Apr. 1947), 133. A.T. to R.T., 2 Feb. 1858, Taylor MS.

57. *Spectator*, 19 May 1860. O.W. Hewett, *Strawberry Fair: A Biography of*

Frances, Countess Waldegrave (1956), 200. A.T. to Lord Lyttelton, 16 Sep. 1874, Lyttelton MS., BA 5806/9 Class 705:104. *Remember* I.101. In *The King's English* (3rd edn, 1934) the brothers Fowler charged A.T. with 13 offences against pure English including distorted idioms, tautologies, 'over-stopping', misuse of nouns of multitude and perfect infinitives; worst of all, had A.T. known it, was an accusation of bad Latin. Many errors were due to faulty type-setting and proof-reading: for these see the papers of R.W. Chapman who edited various Trollope novels in the 1940s and compiled detailed lists not only of errors but of inconsistencies (Chapman MS., MS. Eng. Misc. c 927).

58. F.T., *Travels and Travellers* I.209-10. *He Knew He Was Right*, ch. LXX. A. Tilney Bassett [ed.], *Gladstone to His Wife* (1936), 55. In the parable of the two debtors in St Luke 7:41-3 Jesus is recorded as saying: 'Tell me therefore, which of them will love him most? Simon answered and said, I suppose that he, to whom he forgave most. And he said unto him, Thou hast rightly judged.' The Fowlers' judgment on St Luke and the seventeenth-century translators is not given.

59. *Auto.*, 176, 177-8.

60. Cecilia Meetkerke, 'Last Reminiscences of Anthony Trollope' in *Temple Bar* LXX (Jan. 1884), 129. Mrs Oliphant, *Autobiography*, 43.

61. A.T. to W.H. Bradbury, 16 Aug. 1869 in Hall [ed.], *Letters* I.479. the Oxford World's Classic edn (1st publ. 1931) catches the first but not the second mistake. See Taylor, 'The Manuscript of Trollope's *The American Senator*', 125.

62. Taylor, 'The Manuscript of Trollope's *The American Senator*', 124.

63. A.T. to George Smith, 10 Nov. 1860, Trollope Business MS. Helen, Dowager Countess of Radnor, *From a Great-Grandmother's Armchair* (n.d.), 52.

64. A few years later, in *The Vicar of Bullhampton*, the name 'Crittenden' is used for the village doctor though earlier in the novel he is called Dr Cuttenden.

65. *S.R.*, 4 May 1861. Henry James, 'Anthony Trollope', in Smalley [ed.], *Trollope: The Critical Heritage*, 535-6.

66. A.T., *South Africa* I.78-9. A.T.'s marginalia dated 1 Dec. 1867 in his copy of *Edward II* in A. Dyce [ed.], *The Works of Christopher Marlowe* (1850, 2 vols), II.290, Folger Library. A.T., *Travelling Sketches* (1866), 108. These eight essays were first published in the *Pall Mall Gazette* in Aug. and Sep. 1865. *Spectator*, 15 Apr. 1871. Anon., 'The Novels of Mr. Anthony Trollope', *Dublin Review* q. in Smalley [ed.], *Trollope: The Critical Heritage*, 363.

67. 'Of Old Freedom Sat on the Heights.'

68. Frederick G. Blair [ed.], 'Trollope on Education: An Unpublished Address' in *Trollopian* I (Mar. 1947), 5. The Address was given at the distribution of prizes on 13 Nov. 1873. Frederick Locker-Lampson, *My Confidences* (1896), 334. Blair [ed.], 'Trollope on Education', 3.

Chapter 6

1. In her Chronology R.T. noted simply: '1845. Penrith in July.' However, on 2 June 1845 Augustus Godby, Secretary of the Irish Post Office, recommended that A.T. be allowed one month's leave of absence from the 'later end of next month' which would fix the completion of his first novel at the end of July 1845 (R.T., Chronology, Trollope MS., Ill.; Post: Vol. 17, No. 704: Ireland, Reports and Minutes: Minute of 2 June 1845, 515). *Auto.*, 74.

2. F.T. to R.T., 7 Aug. 1844, Taylor MS.

3. Mrs Gaskell [Clement K. Shorter, ed.], *The Life of Charlotte Brontë* (1900 edn, 1st publ. 1857), 345. Trollope Business MS.

4. F.T. to Cecilia Tilley, ? Aug. 1846, Taylor MS.

5. q. in Lance O. Tingay, 'The Reception of Trollope's First Novel' in *N.&Q.*, CXCV (23 Dec. 1950), 563-4. See his articles in *Nineteenth Century Fiction* VI (1951) and *The Times Literary Supplement*, 30 Mar. 1956.

6. Sutherland, *Victorian Novelists and Publishers*, 47. E.D.H. Johnson, 'Romantic, Victorian, and Edwardian' in *Princeton University Library Chronicle* XXXVIII (Winter-Spring, 1977), 198.

7. *Spectator*, 8 May 1847. Escott, 70.

8. *John Bull*, 22 May 1847. *Critic*, 1 May 1847. *Howitt's Journal*, 19 June 1847. *Athenaeum*, 15 May 1847.

9. Anon., 'The Novels of Mr. Anthony Trollope', *Dublin Review* q. in Smalley [ed.], *Trollope: The Critical Heritage*, 364-5. A.T., Review of E.S. Dallas's 3-vol. abridgement of Samuel Richardson's *Clarissa, St.P.* III (Nov. 1868), 171.

10. Peel to Henry Goulburn, 16 Aug. 1845, Peel MS., Add. MS. 40445ff 136-7. Lord Brougham, House of Lords, 19 Jan. 1847, *Hansard* LXXXIX, 53.

11. T. Wemyss Reid, *Memoirs and Correspondence of Lyon Playfair ...* (1900 edn, 1st publ. 1899), 99.

12. See Desmond Bowen, *The Protestant Crusade in Ireland, 1800-70* (Dublin, 1978), 208-56. A.T., 'What Does Ireland Want?', *St.P.* V (Dec. 1869), 298.

13. A.T. to R.T., 20 May 1882 from Cork, Parrish MS.

14. q. in Cecil Woodham-Smith, *The Great Hunger ...* (1962), 77. A.T., *Thackeray*, 60. Charles Dickens to A.T., 9 May 1867, Taylor MS. Sadleir, *Commentary*, 309.

15. There are also interesting passages regarding absentee landlords in ch. III of *The Kellys* and ch. IX of *The Macdermots*.

16. *Remember* I.249.

17. A.T., *The New Zealander*, 29-30.

18. A.T., 'The Zulus', unpublished 40-page lecture delivered in Nottingham on 23 Oct. 1879, Parrish MS.

19. Boris Ford [ed.], *From Dickens to Hardy*: Vol. 6 of the Pelican Guide to English Literature (1979 edn), 196. The figures were for 1845. J. Fenimore Cooper [Donald A. Ringe and Kenneth W. Staggs, eds], *Gleanings in Europe: England* (Albany, New York, 1982), 203.

20. A.T., 'Irish Distress', *Examiner*, 25 Aug. 1849. The next five letters, published under the title 'The Real State of Ireland', appeared on 30 Mar., 6 Apr., 11 May, 1 June and 18 June 1850. A.T., *The New Zealander*, 29.

21. A.T., *Lord Palmerston* (1882). A.T. wrote that he had 'been told on the spot [County Sligo] nearly forty years ago that that wonderful "Irishman", Lord Palmerston, had for the last ten years spent all his income upon the estate'. His improvements in the 1820s included building a harbour and reclaiming bog-land (12, 23-4, 42) For this 'apathy and deadness' see the Conclusion [ch. XLIV] of *Castle Richmond*.

22. G. Kitson Clark, 'Statesmen in Disguise: Reflexions on the History of the Neutrality of the Civil Service', *Historical Journal* II.1 (1959), 19-39. Emilie I. Barrington, *The Servant of All ... Life of ... James Wilson* (1927, 2 vols), I.91-2: a more than normally pompous Victorian biography by a dutiful daughter.

23. On the other hand, in its obituary of A.T. the *Publishers' Circular* said

that the articles had 'attracted much attention' (18 Dec. 1882).

24. A.T. to Richard Bentley, 16 Oct. 1847, Taylor MS. Henry Colburn to A.T., 30 Mar. 1848, Trollope Business MS.

25. In his Election Address at Beverley in the 1868 General Election A.T. claimed that the Church of Ireland lacked charity towards the poor (*Beverley Recorder*, 31 Oct. 1868).

26. See also A.T.'s comments in *The New Zealander*, 104.

27. See *Domestic Manners*, 13-15, 150-3.

28. Henry Colburn to A.T., 11 Nov. 1848 q. in *Auto.*, 78-9.

29. *Frances Trollope* II.175.

30. A.T., *Australia and New Zealand* II.35. *The Times*, 25 July 1848. A.T., Letter V, *Examiner*, 18 June 1850. A.T. to F.T., [Spring, 1848] q. in *Frances Trollope* II.123-4

31. F.T. to John Murray, 3 Dec. 1836, Murray MS. A.T., *North America*, 183. See *West Indies* (p. 113) for A.T.'s vague reference to 'Mr Smith' at Newhaven.

32. A.T. to G.W. Rusden, 26 Apr. 1879 in Hall [ed.], *Letters* II.826. For an excellent account of Dickens's sources see William Oddie, *Dickens and Carlyle: the Question of Influence* (1972), 61-85. F.T.'s MS. account of her visit to Lafayette (referred to in Ch. II) may have been in A.T.'s possession when he wrote *La Vendée*. T.T., *A Summer in Brittany* (1840, 2 vols), I.351, 142. Cecil Biggane [ed. & tr.], *Memoirs of the Marquise de la Rochejaquelein* (1933), 304 for the story of the captured cannon. The introduction, map and notes are most useful for anyone reading *La Vendée*.

33. Henry Colburn to A.T., 11 Nov. 1848 q. in *Auto.*, 78-9. The contract was signed on 15 Feb. 1850: Trollope Business MS. Hugh Walpole, *Anthony Trollope* (1928), 40. See pp. 39-42 for an interesting discussion on the historical novel. For a contrary view of *La Vendée* see Arthur Pollard, *Anthony Trollope* (1978), 200-1.

34. *Examiner*, 15 June 1850.

35. A.T. to T.T., [May 1851] q. in *Frances Trollope* II.217.

36. George Bartley to A.T., 18 June 1851, Taylor MS. See Robert H. Taylor, 'Trollope as Dramatist' in Taylor, *Certain Small Works*, 157-64.

37. Mona Wilson, 'Holidays and Travel' in Young [ed.], *Early Victorian England* II.309-10. The handbook on Ireland was eventually written by G.P. Bevan who received £226 16s for the copyright and an additional £21 for revisions to the second edition. Information courtesy of Virginia Murray, John Murray Archives.

38. P.P., 1854-5, XI, *Report from the Select Committee on Postal Arrangements (Waterford etc.)*, 128; William Allingham's Diary, 8 Oct. 1864, A.H. Allingham and D. Radford, [eds], *William Allingham: A Diary* (1907), 106. F.T. to R.T., 15 Aug. 1859, Taylor MS.

39. q. in *Frances Trollope* II.161, 162.

40. q. in *Frances Trollope* II.162-3, 161.

41. Post 100/8: Rowland Hill's P.O. Journal, 29 & 30 Sep. 1848. A.T., *Thackeray*, 34-5.

42. F.T. to R.T., 7 Aug. 1844, Taylor MS. F.T. to R.T., 20 Apr. 1849, Taylor MS.

43. A.T. to John Tilley, 7 Apr. 1849, Trollope MS., U.C.L.A.

44. F.T. to T.T., 14 Apr. 1849 q. in *Frances Trollope* II.144. F.T. to R.T., 20 Apr. 1849, Taylor MS.

45. Tom's description of his wife's appearance reads remarkably like one in A.T.'s novels except that he prefers hair and eyes to noses (*Remember* I.382). A.T. was to make use of her maiden name, Garrow, in his story 'The Mistletoe Bough'.

46. P.P., 1868-9, XXXIV, *Post Office (Foreign Mails), passim*. There were two mails a day, each taking 50 hours and 10 minutes to get to Florence; the return journey was 47 hours and 30 minutes.

47. *Frances Trollope* II.203-5. For A.T.'s interest in Joan of Arc see his review of Harriet Parr's *Life and Death of Jeanne d'Arc* in *F.R.* VI (Nov. 1866).

48. A.T., Travelling Journals, *passim*, Parrish MS.

49. Peel to Lord Heytesbury, 25 Oct. 1844 in C.S. Parker, *Sir Robert Peel* (1891-99, 3 vols), III.123. Nicholas Mansergh, *The Irish Question, 1840-1921* (1965, new edn), 63. Isaac Butt, a graduate of Trinity College, Dublin, had won great fame in May 1848 by defending Smith O'Brien at his trial for sedition. (David Thornley, *Isaac Butt and Home Rule* (1964), 15-19.)

50. Escott, 59. Justin McCarthy, *Reminiscences* (1889, 2 vols), I.372. *Tralee Chronicle*, 31 Mar. 1849. *Kerry Evening Post*, 28 July 1849. Post 36/27: Ireland: Reports and Minutes, No. 2061, 208.

51. Post 100/10: Rowland Hill's P.O. Journal, 18 Dec. 1850. Hill was also worried about the 'urgent necessity for regulating' travelling expenses. There was, he claimed, a 'strong temptation to unnecessary travelling' (Post 100/8: Rowland Hill's P.O. Journal, 19 Oct. 1848. See also entries for 15 Aug. 1850, 23 Nov. 1850, 13 Jan. 1851, and 24 Sep. 1851 for references to Irish problems).

52. A.T. to F.T., [Summer, 1850] q. in *Frances Trollope* II.186.

53. A.T. to T.T., March [1851] q. in *Frances Trollope* II.217. Muriel Trollope, 'What I Was Told' in *Trollopian* II (Mar. 1948), 235. R.T.'s Chronology, Trollope MS., Ill.

54. A.T. to F.T., [7 May 1851] q. in *Frances Trollope* II.218-19. *The Times*, 2 May 1851. Omnium's real name was M.J. Higgins, although this particular article appeared under the name 'Pimlicola'. Perhaps A.T.'s change of mind even before his own visit reflected his daily reading of *The Times*. Higgins later became a friend and fellow clubman. (Cf. A.T., *Auto.*, 199.)

55. A.T., *The New Zealander*, 209.

Chapter 7

1. Post 100/7: Rowland Hill's P.O. Journal, 28 Nov. 1847. Hill recorded that the Treasury approved the plan for rural deliveries on 12 Aug. 1850. [R.H. Hutton], 'From Miss Austen to Mr. Trollope', *Spectator*, 16 Dec. 1882.

2. Harold Perkin, *The Age of the Railway* (1970 edn), 220.

3. *The Times*, 31 Oct. 1838. Nathaniel Blaker, *Reminiscences* (Brighton, 1906), 25. Cecil Torr, *Small Talk at Wreyland* (Bath, 1970, 3 vols in 1), I.68-9.

4. T.T. echoed A.T.'s feelings in his memoirs: *Remember* II.317.

5. A.T. to J.B. Blake, 1 Oct. 1858, Parrish MS. T.T. to Henry M. Trollope, 10 Dec. 1882, Trollope MS., Ill.

6. P.P. 1854-5, XI, 1854-5, *Report from Select Committee on Postal Arrangements*, 174, 196. q. in William Lewins, *Her Majesty's Mails* (1864), 237-8. Capern was released from Sunday duties and eventually given a pension from the Royal Bounty Fund.

7. Daniel Briggs, *The Bristol Post Office in the Age of Rowland Hill 1837-1864*

(1983), 14. B.S. Trinder [ed.], *A Victorian M.P. and his Constituents: The Correspondence of H.W. Tancred, 1841-1859* (Banbury, 1967), *passim*. See letters of Sir John Trollope, MP to the P.M.G., Lord Hardwicke, asking for similar favours. These are in the Hardwicke MS., Add. MS. 35790 f 389 and 35792 f 149. When asked his opinion by a Commons' Committee in 1860, A.T. said that it was a 'matter of fact' that MPs 'who support the Government' had influence but, he added, 'we know nothing of that. I mean that, officially, they are made not by the Treasury [i.e. politically], but by the Post Master General. We should be glad to have that done away with, if we could, and these appointments also given to the local officers' (P.P., 1860, IX, *Civil Service Appointments*, ques. 1938).

8. Post: File 49a, England 685K/1814. Philip Stevens, 'Anthony Trollope and the Jersey Postal Service', *Annual Bulletin of the Société Jèrsiaise*, 21-33, reprint in the Post Office Archives. Post: File 3, E706/1859. See P.P., IV, 1857, *Third Report of the P.M.G. on the Post Office, 1857*, 3-4. The oldest pillar box in existence, in St Helier, is still in use. There were, in 1989, 55 rural deliveries instead of 10 rural 'walks' and a postman's starting wage in Jersey has risen from 9s a week to £164.50 (Controller Mails and Operations, St Helier, Jersey to the author, 10 July 1989).

9. *The Times*, 10 Oct. 1968. The standard work on the pillar box is Jean Young Farrugia, *The Letter Box: A History of Post Office Pillar and Wall Boxes* (Fontwell, Sussex, 1969).

10. Piers Brendon, *Hawker of Morwenstow: Portrait of a Victorian Eccentric* (1975), 66.

11. Escott, 113-15. Brendon, *Hawker of Morwenstow*, 66. E.G. Sandford, 'Exeter Memoir, 1869-1885' in E.G. Sandford [ed.], *Memoirs of Archbishop Temple* (1906, 2 vols), I.379n.

12. A.T., *North America*, 5. See A.T. to E.J. Smith, 3 Feb. 1864, Parrish MS.

13. Tom Trollope recalled that in his rounds A.T. was 'very much his own master' without any subordinates. (T.T. to H.M.T., 24 Mar. 1892, Trollope MS., Ill.) J.G. Uren, 'My Early Recollections of the Post Office in the West of England', *Blackfriars* IX (July-Dec. 1889), 157-8. Uren, 'My Early Recollections', 158.

14. A.T. to G.C. Boase, 14 July 1876 in Hall [ed.], *Letters* II.695. See Mullen [ed.], *Malachi's Cove*, xi. The story has been made into a film.

15. Uren, 'My Early Recollections', 158-9. Flora Thompson, *Candleford Green* in *Lark Rise to Candleford* (n.d. [1951], 3 vols in 1), 407.

16. A.T. to F.T., [autumn 1852] q. in *Frances Trollope* II. 241-2. A reference in the letter to the public tributes to the Duke of Wellington shows that it was written between the Duke's death on 14 Sep. and his state funeral on 18 Nov. 1852. A.T. to T.T., 5 Oct. 1852 q. in *Frances Trollope* II.242-3.

17. Bryan Little, *Portrait of Exeter* (1983), 71, 86-8. This shows how well A.T. knew Exeter. Little was still able to identify Miss Stanbury's house even though A.T. was speaking of Exeter before the city got its two stations. In W.G. & J.T Gerould, *A Guide to Trollope* (1948), 142. The Geroulds, in one of their few mistakes, list Littlebath as the pseudonym for Bath.

18. A.T. to Mary Holmes, 27 Dec. 1876, Parrish MS. Here A.T. admits to a 'long-ago-entertained dislike of Dean Close & Cheltenham School [College?]'. *The Times*, 22 Dec. 1882. Anon., *Memorials of Dean Close by One Who Knew Him* (1885), 9.

19. A.T. to Thomas Walton, 27 Nov. 1852, Parrish MS. In *The Last Chronicle of Barset*, ch. XVII, A.T. described Mr Crawley's walk of about 24 miles as a 'practicable distance'. 'A Retired Post Office Official', 'Anthony Trollope as a Post Office Surveyor', *St Martin's-le-Grand* XIV (Oct. 1904), 453.

20. A.T. to Thomas Walton, 27 Nov. 1852, Parrish MS. Walton had succeeded his father as Postmaster of Bristol (Briggs, *The Bristol Post Office*, 11). Charles and Frances Brookfield, *Mrs. Brookfield and Her Circle* (1905, 2nd edn, 2 vols), II.458.

21. Walpole, *Anthony Trollope*, 74-5.

22. A.T., *Australia and New Zealand* I.464-5.

23. A.T., *Clergymen of the Church of England* (1866), 124.

24. A.T., *Hunting Sketches* (1865), 71.

25. A.T. to Lord Lyttelton, 16 Sep. 1874, Lyttelton MS., BA 5806/9 Class 705:104, Hereford and Worcester Record Office. A.T., *North America*, 277. George Eliot to Charles Bray, 16 Apr. 1863 in G.S. Haight [ed.], *The George Eliot Letters* (New Haven, 1954-78, 9 vols), IV.81-2. An example of A.T.'s eschewing 'fine distinctions' is in his *Life of Cicero* (1880, 2 vols), where he argued that belief in the great 'mysteries' of Christianity, by which he meant the doctrines of the Incarnation, Trinity etc., as opposed to belief in God, 'was not essential for forming the conduct of men' (II.397). See A.T., *The New Zealander*, 104.

26. A.T., 'Commonplace Book', under entry for Pope, Trollope MS., Yale. A.T., *Cicero* II.403. A.T. to G.W. Rusden, 8 June 1876 in Hall [ed.], *Letters* II.691-2. 'I can understand that a man should be humble before his brother men the smallness of whose vision requires self-abasement in others; – but ... to my God I can be but true, and if I think myself to have done well I cannot but say so' A.T., *Cicero* I.66. Some writers have come to rather odd conclusions about A.T.'s religious views. James Pope Hennessy decided, for unfathomable reasons, that A.T. rarely referred to God (*Anthony Trollope*, 178). Equally ridiculous is the conclusion arrived at by Lucy and Richard Stebbins that A.T. disliked 'nearly all organized religion' (*The Trollopes* (1947), 25).

27. A.T. to R.S. Oldham, 19 Nov. 1879, Trollope MS., Ill. Henry Drury to Samuel Butler, 24 Oct. 1829, Samuel Butler MS., Add. MS. 34587 f 197.

28. A.T. to Lord Carlisle, 2 Mar. 1861, Castle Howard Archives, J19/1/92/87, Castle Howard, York. By kind permission of the Howard Family. Edwin Hodder, *The Life ... of the Seventh Earl of Shaftesbury* (1886, 3 vols), II.164. A.T., *Cicero* I.66. John Morley and Mrs Humphry Ward, Review of A.T.'s *Autobiography* in *Macmillan's Magazine* XLIX (Nov. 1883), 56. Morley sneered that A.T. 'did not recognise the delicacy of Truth, but handled her as freely and as boldly as a slave-dealer might handle a beautiful Circassian'. In turn Lord Rosebery, who endured Morley's delicacy as a Cabinet Minister when he was Prime Minister, 1894-5, said that he 'was a difficult person to manage but always "a perfect lady" ' (Lord Rosebery q. by Lewis Harcourt in his Journal, 1 Apr. 1895, Harcourt MS., MS. Harcourt dep. 417 f 41).

29. For the controversy over hell see Geoffrey Rowell, *Hell and the Victorians* (1974) and Owen Chadwick, *The Secularization of the European Mind in the Nineteenth Century* (Cambridge, 1977 edn), 104-5. A.T. to G.W. Rusden, 8 June 1876, Hall [ed.], *Letters* II.691-2.

30. A.T., Commonplace Book, entry for 'Order-Method', Trollope MS., Yale. The Rev. H.D. Gordon, *Guardian*, 13 Dec. 1882. This was the basis for the notice of A.T.'s death in the *Publishers' Circular* of 18 Dec. 1882. The *Guardian* was, of course, the weekly High Church paper, not to be confused with the *Manchester Guardian*. A.T., *South Africa* I.104-5.

31. A.T., *Thackeray*, 136. A.T., *Australia and New Zealand* I.226-7. *The Times*, 8 Dec. 1876. A.T. to Mary Holmes, 27 Dec. 1876, Parrish MS. The old proverb of the shorn lamb was one of A.T.'s favourites. It was popularised by Sterne's *Sentimental Journey* (see W.G. Smith [ed.], *Oxford Dictionary of English Proverbs* (Oxford, 1936), 122). A.T. even used it in novels not set in England such as *La Vendée* [chs V, XIV] when Cathelineau is dying, and in his *Life of Cicero*. I do not entirely accept Dr Clark's view (*Language and Style of Anthony Trollope*, 167n.) that A.T. thought the proverb originated in the Bible. A.T. owned the 1793 10-volume edition of Sterne's works as well as a biography of him.

32. A.T. to Mary Holmes, 26 Jan. 1875, Parrish MS.

33. Ralph Waldo Emerson, *English Traits* (Oxford, 1923, World's Classics edn, 1st publ. 1856), 130.

34. Lady Charlotte Guest's diary, 15 Feb.-17 Apr. 1850, Earl of Bessborough [ed.], *Lady Charlotte Guest, Extracts from her Journal* (1950), 234-40.

35. A.T., *The New Zealander*, 91. *Remember* I.10. Escott, 111. Lord John Russell to Lord Lansdowne, 11 Nov. 1847 q. in John Prest, *Lord John Russell* (1972), 277. For a criticism of A.T.'s handling of Evangelicals see Owen Chadwick, *The Victorian Church: Part I* (1970, 2nd edn), 446-52.

36. W.E. Gladstone, *Gleanings of Past Years: Miscellaneous* (1879, 7 vols), VII.219.

37. *Pall Mall Gazette*, 10 May 1865.

38. *The Times*, 2 Oct. 1867. Queen Victoria to Lord John Russell, 9 June 1850 in Benson and Esher [eds], *Letters of Queen Victoria* II.290; Hodder, *Shaftesbury* II.304-7. A.T., *The New Zealander*, 92.

39. Ann Thwaite, *Edmund Gosse: a Literary Landscape 1849-1928* (1984), 26. A.T., 'Novel Reading: the Works of Charles Dickens and W. Makepeace Thackeray' in *Nineteenth Century* V (Jan. 1879), 27. E.E. Kellett, *As I Remember* (1936), 116.

40. F.T., *Vienna and the Austrians* (1838, 2 vols), II.221. For example see A.T.'s letter of 7 Apr. 1849 to his brother-in-law, John Tilley, on Cecilia's death, cited before (Trollope MS., U.C.L.A.); A.T. to his mother, 28 June 1854 (Taylor MS.); A.T. to Kate Field, 30 Sep. 1868 (Sadleir, *Commentary*, 290-1); A.T. to G.W. Rusden, 18 Feb. 1873 (Booth [ed.], *Letters*, 513); A.T. to H.M.T., 24 Sep. 1882 (Taylor MS).

41. Escott, 84. A.T. may have heard Newman while visiting Tom or while in Oxford to sit his scholarship. For an example of A.T.'s sympathetic treatment of Newman see *Barchester Towers*, ch. XXV. Escott, 106-7. The Rev. William Sewell (1804-1874) was a Wykehamist and fellow of Exeter College. A moderate High Churchman, he broke with the Tractarian movement's leaders after the publication of Tract XC in 1841. He was one of the founders of St Columba's College, Dublin where A.T. sent his sons in the 1850s. Escott says that A.T. once called Septimus Harding an 'idealised photograph' of members of the Sewell family whom he knew both at Winchester and at Oxford. The family is also referred to in *The Bertrams* [ch. I]. A.T., *The New Zealander*, 193-4. A.T. to Lady Trollope, 13 Feb. 1877, Hall [ed.], *Letters* II.1016.

42. A.T., *Clergymen of the Church of England*, 25. In 1835 Sydney Smith told Mr Gladstone: 'Whenever you meet a clergyman of my age, you may be sure he is a bad clergyman' (q. in Gladstone, *Gleanings* VII.220). The Warden and Archdeacon Grantly discuss this same topic, although in less assertive terms, in *The Last Chronicle of Barset* [ch. XXII].

43. A.T., *West Indies*, 24. In her novel Cecilia Trollope also referred to 'the lately-revived good taste and right feeling of the age ... to elevate and soothe the heart of the worshipper' (*Chollerton: A Tale of Our Times* (1846), 1).

44. G.F. Nott, *Religious Enthusiasm Considered; in eight sermons, preached before the University of Oxford in the year MDCCCII* (Oxford, 1803). This is a classic exposition of eighteenth-century attitudes towards balance and fear of the effects of 'enthusiasm', better understood today as fanaticism. This was the Bampton Lecture for 1802.

45. A.T., *North America*, 53. Bowen, *Protestant Crusade in Ireland*, 68.

46. A.T., *The New Zealander*, 94. G.O. Trevelyan, *The Life and Letters of Lord Macaulay* (1876, 2 vols), II.287.

47. A.T., *The New Zealander*, 94. A.T. distinguishes between the old High Church party and the new High Church movement which attempts too much that is not essential in *Barchester Towers* [ch. VI]. A.T., *The New Zealander*, 96. D.C. Lathbury [ed.], *Correspondence on Church and Religion of William Ewart Gladstone* (1910, 2 vols), I.375-6. The use of incense was the hall-mark of the extreme Ritualists or Anglo-Catholics. A.T., *South Africa* II.269. Peter Cobb, 'Thomas Chamberlain – a forgotten tractarian' in Derek Baker [ed.], *The Church in Town and Countryside* (Oxford, 1979), 379. Chamberlain was vicar of St Thomas's, Oxford. Stoles in liturgical colours were used here in 1851 and caused a furore. [A.T.], 'My Tour in Holland', *C.M.* VI (Nov. 1862), 616-22.

48. A.T., *The New Zealander*, 88. The quote comes from *Ralph the Heir* [ch. XIV]. A.T. told Escott that 'Dickens gibbeted cant in the person of Dissenters, of whom I never knew anything. I have done so in Mr. Slope ...'. (Escott, 111-12) Again in *North America* A.T. was surprised to see that 'nonconformists' were part of the mainstream of life: 'the meeting-houses prepared for these sects are not, as with us, hideous buildings contrived to inspire disgust by the enormity of their ugliness' (280).

49. A.T. to Mary Holmes, 26 Jan. 1875, Parrish MS.

50. Frederick Waddy, *Cartoon Portraits and Biographical Sketches of Men of the Day* (1873), 68. W.P. Frith, *My Autobiography and Reminiscences* (1887-8, 3 vols), I.357-8. The Rev. Lord Arthur Hervey to W.E. Gladstone, 4 Oct. 1869, 22 Oct. 1881, Gladstone MS., Add. MS. 44207 ff 231-41 & ff 277-8. John Kelly [ed.], *Purple Feaver: Some sayings and alleged sayings of Bishop Douglas Feaver* (Northampton, 1985), 13.

51. G.K. Chesterton, *The Victorian Age in Literature* (1925 edn, 1st publ. 1913), 133-4. Chesterton, a convert to the Roman Catholic Church, was hardly an unbiased critic at the best of times. Colin Haycraft, 'City of a shaming pyre' in *The Times*, 4 Mar. 1989.

52. A.T., *North America*, 281. This strain of the old High Church reticence survived into the twentieth century in the novels of writers like Barbara Pym.

53. Henry Greville's diary, 31 Mar. 1850, where Greville notes that Bishop Phillpotts's *Letter* attacking the Archbishop of Canterbury had gone through ten editions in one week (Enfield [ed.], *Diary* I.352). Newman's Tract XC sold 12,000 copies. The Rev. T. Mozley, *Reminiscences Chiefly of Oriel College and* *the Oxford Movement* (1882, 2 vols), II.93-4. In the 1850s and 60s S.G.O. bit off more than he could chew when he attacked Bishop Wilberforce. See the Bishop's letters to him in R.K. Pugh and J.F.A. Mason [eds], *The Letter-Books of Samuel Wilberforce 1843-68* (Oxford, 1970), 240, 375, 379-80, 383.

54. *The Times*, 10 Dec. 1850. Charles Greville's diary, 11 Dec. 1850, Henry Reeve [ed.], *The Greville Memoirs* (1888, new edn, 8 vols), VI.381. The conversation over proposed changes to approximate the German system suggests that A.T. had not only followed the hearings of the Commission set up to investigate the ancient universities but had closely read the opposition voiced by E.B. Pusey (Ieuan Ellis, 'Pusey and University Reform' in Perry Butler [ed.], *Pusey Rediscovered* (1983), 104-5). P.P., 1852-3, LXXXIX, *Report and Tables for England and Wales, passim*. While the population of England and Wales was 17,928,000 only 6,356,222 people were at the 'best attended service' on 'Census Sunday'. Of these the C. of E. claimed 2,971,258 and Dissent 3,110,782. When expanded to include irregular attenders the figures showed that Nonconformist attenders had shrunk to 70 per cent of the C. of E. total.

55. *The Times*, 16 Apr. 1846. D. Wallace Duthie, *The Church in the Pages of 'Punch'* (1912), 129. At St Cuthbert's, Carlisle, the incumbent received £1,500 but paid his curate £5 16s 8d.

56. A.T. discovered that French archbishops got the equivalent of £600 p.a., bishops, £480 and parish priests, at best, £60. Trollope MS., Ill. Duthie, *The Church in the Pages of 'Punch'*, 73. A.T., *Clergymen of the Church of England*, 27-8 and *passim*.

57. Henry James, 'Anthony Trollope' in Smalley [ed.], *Trollope: The Critical Heritage*, 534. Other writers had also tackled abuses in old charitable foundations. In *The Newcomes* Thackeray has Col. Newcome seek refuge in such an establishment and Dickens had also attacked the abuses in *Household Words* in 1852 (John Carey, *Thackeray: Prodigal Genius* (1977), 164-5). See also G.F.A. Best, 'The Road to Hiram's Hospital' in *Victorian Studies* V (Dec. 1961), 135-50. A.T. thought the Dulwich College collection should go to the National Gallery (*The New Zealander*, 202)

58. Sir Benjamin Hall, House of Commons, 28 May, 8 June and 10 June, 1852, *Hansard* CXXI, 1358-62, CXXII, 314-17 and 466-7. F. Bennett, *The Story of W.J.E. Bennett* (1909), 163-71. For Edward Horsman's performance in the Commons see *Hansard* CXX, 20 Apr. 1852, 895-916. The entire debate is found in cols 895-943 and the story of the thin walls is in col. 902.

59. *The Times*, 13 Nov., 22 Nov., 13 Dec. 1852. Escott, 103. Escott thought the letters that interested A.T. were concerned with clerical absenteeism but it seems that this correspondence on pluralism had a greater effect.Even when choosing names of characters, A.T. seems to have drawn on his reading and clerical gossip. His most notorious pluralist was Canon Vesey Stanhope and Stanhope in Durham was one of the most lucrative livings at £4,848 a year. See *Liber Ecclesiasticus* under Stanhope. At this time the High Churchman, Roundell Palmer, Liberal-Conservative M.P. for Plymouth, who had been at Winchester with A.T., was a leader-writer for *The Times*. A.T., *Catalogue of Books belonging to Anthony Trollope* (1874), John Forster Bequest, 1876. The entry under 'Black's Book of Abuses in Church and State. 1835' on p. 6 is presumably the famous exposé of 'establishment corruption' by the Unitarian controversialist, John Wade, *The Extraordinary Black Book*, which first

appeared as pamphlets in the 1820s and as a book in 1831, 1832 and 1835. Its first chapter was devoted to the Church of England. A.T.'s extensive collection of pamphlets is listed on pp. 53-8 under seven headings: Church Education; Colonization, Emigration, &c.; Corn, Currency, Banking; Domestic Politics; Foreign Questions; Ireland; Miscellaneous. There was also a section devoted to tracts, pp. 79-83. A.T., 'The Irish Church', *F.R.* II (Aug. 1865), 82. A.T., *Clergymen of the Church of England*, 8. A.T., 'Public Schools', *F.R.*, 476.

60. For the background to Septimus Harding see n. 41. George Saintsbury, 'Trollope Revisited' in *Essays and Studies* (Oxford, 1920), VI.64.

61. *Frances Trollope* II.218. A.T., *Catalogue of Books*, John Forster Bequest. Francis Espinasse, *Literary Recollections and Sketches* (1893), 216.

62. Henry Greville's diary, 21 Mar. 1855, Enfield [ed.], *Diary* II.201. Escott, 296 where A.T.'s real friendship with Delane is said to have begun in 1875.

63. Escott states that *The Warden* was published in 1855 (Escott, 312); Sadleir, in *Bibliography*, that it was published on 20 Dec. 1854 (18) although in *Commentary* (158) he says Jan. 1855. In his *Autobiography* (97) A.T. wrote 1855 and Bodley's Catalogue lists 1855, as does the title page.

64. *Spectator*, 6 Jan. 1855 q. in Escott, 110-11.

Chapter 8

1. F.T. to A.T., 24 July 1854 q. Tom's letter. Taylor MS. A.T. to F.T., n.d. [Sep.-Nov. 1852], Taylor MS. A.T. to T.T. q. in *Frances Trollope* II.231-2.

2. A.T. to Hardwicke, 25 Nov. 1852, Hardwicke MS., Add. MS. 35805 ff 321-2. Maberly was pleased with A.T.'s work both in Ireland and in the Western District. John Tilley to Hardwicke, 25 Nov. 1852, Hardwicke MS., Add. MS. 35805 ff 323-4. Sir John Trollope to Hardwicke, 25 Nov. 1852, Hardwicke MS., 35805 ff 325-6. Sir John was A.T.'s first cousin once removed. A.T., *Palmerston*, 145.

3. Ronald Sutherland Gower, *My Reminiscences* (1895, 5th edn), 200. Baines, *Forty Years* I.167-8. Above the clerk's bedroom and near the fireplace a keg of gunpowder had been stored since the Chartist fright of 1848 in case the building was garrisoned by troops. There was also a supply of empty stone ink jars on the roof to be thrown down at potential rioters. Post 100/11: Rowland Hill's P.O. Journals, 3 May and 25 Nov. 1852.

4. A.T. to Frances Trollope, 28 June 1854, Taylor MS. In Oct. Hill recommended to the P.M.G. that A.T. be paid the *per diem* travelling allowance due a Surveyor, to take effect from 6 Sep. 1853. (Post 35/127: No. 6494: English: Hill to P.M.G., 15 Oct. 1853).

5. A.T. to T.T., 28 June 1854, Taylor MS. Post 100/11: Rowland Hill's P.O. Journals, 15, 16 Nov. 1852.

6. R.S. Smyth, 'The Provincial Service Fifty Years Ago' in *St Martin's-le-Grand* XIII (Oct. 1903), 371-7. A.T.'s efforts to help his stationery clerk, J.B. Blake, to get advancement can be seen in his letters of 1 Oct., 11 Nov., and 25 Dec. 1858 and 10 July 1859, Parrish MS. See p. 351 above.

7. Avy Dowlin, *Ballycarry in Olden Days* (Belfast, 1963), 73. Lewins, *Her Majesty's Mails*, 225, 212.

8. R.S. Smyth, 'An Old Time Instruction for an Irish Sub Office' in *St Martin's-le-Grand* XIV (July 1904), 292-6. These orders originated with A.T.'s predecessor, Urquhart, but his would have been of the same kind.

9. Lewins, *Her Majesty's Mails*, 335. Post 36/42: No. 265: Ireland: Reports and Minutes, 15 Mar. 1856.

10. John Tilley q. in A.T. to T.T. 28 June 1854, Taylor MS.

11. F.T. to A.T., 24 July 1854, Taylor MS. Michael Sadleir, 'Trollope and Bacon's Essays' in *Trollopian* I (Summer 1945), 26.

12. R.T.'s Chronology, Trollope MS., Ill.

13. R.T.'s Chronology. The trip in question was that of Apr.-May, 1853. Trollope MS., Ill. q. in Sadleir, *Commentary*, 330-1.

14. R.T.'s Chronology, Trollope MS., Ill. Kate Field, *New York Tribune*, 22 Dec. 1880. Richard Mullen, 'Fanny Trollope in Florence' in *Orient Express Magazine* II.2 (1985), 65-8.

15. *Remember* I.420.

16. W.P. Courtney, *English Whist and English Whist Players* (1894), 98-100. *Remember* I.345.

17. q. in *Frances Trollope* II.244. q. in Sadleir, *Commentary*, 103. Robert Browning to George Barrett, 7 Oct. 1853 in Paul Landis [ed.], *Letters of the Brownings to George Barrett* (Urbana, Illinois, 1958), 201.

18. A.T., Review of Ruskin's *Sesame and Lilies* in *F.R.* I (July, 1865), 635. A.T.'s friendship with Millais, who married Ruskin's wife after the annulment, meant that he could have known details of Ruskin's failed marriage. This would not have enhanced his view of him as a man. For Carlyle's fury at A.T.'s attack on Ruskin see Hall [ed.], *Letters* I.305.

19. F.T., *Petticoat Government: A Novel* (1850, 3 vols), ch. LXV. A.T., 'The National Gallery', *St. James's Magazine*, 163-76. A.T., 'The Art Critic' in *Travelling Sketches*, 58. It was in this essay that A.T. attacked Guercino (62).

20. Lord Malmesbury, Foreign Secretary in 1852 and 1858-9, was annoyed at the 'freaks of travelling Englishmen who get themselves into scrapes abroad, and, being often deservedly punished or arrested, call upon their Government for protection'. The case in hand was of a British tourist who blocked the progress of Austrian troops marching in Florence; he was struck down and slightly wounded by an exasperated Austrian officer (Earl of Malmesbury, *Memoirs*, I.335). The Earl of Clarendon was Foreign Secretary in 1853-5, 1855-8, 1865 and 1868-70.

21. For example, *Auto.*, 113 and *North America*, 5.

22. *Frances Trollope* II.254-5. A.T. to T.T., 28 June 1854, Taylor MS. A.T., 'On English Prose Fiction' in Parrish [ed.], *Four Lectures*, 114.

23. A.T. to Thomas Walton, 23 Nov. 1854, Parrish MS. P.P., 1857, IV: *Third Report of the P.M.G. on the Post Office*, 1857, 48. Post 36/41: No. 1046: Ireland, Reports and Minutes: Hill to P.M.G., 4 Oct. 1855. Hill said he had discussed this with A.T. when in London. The new rate for a 'walk' under 10 miles was 6s and rose to 10s a week for walks 16 miles and over. Hill admitted that this was a 'modified' version [i.e. less of a rise] than A.T. had suggested.

24. R.T.'s Chronology, Trollope MS., Ill. Weston St John Joyce, *The Neighbourhood of Dublin* (1912), 76-9. Charles Greville's diary, 22 Aug 1859, Reeve [ed.], *Greville Memoirs* VIII.270.

25. Anon. [Charles J. Chislett?], 'Mr Trollope's Father In Law' in *Three Banks Review* LXVI (June, 1965), 25-38. One consequence was that Rose's step-mother did not receive her widow's pension. Muriel Trollope, A.T.'s last descendant in England, was apparently unaware of the scandal.

26. A.T., *The New Zealander*, 82-3.

27. A.T. to William Longman, 17 Feb. 1855 q. in Sadleir, *Commentary*, 169-70. Sadleir, *Bibliography*, 262. T.B. Macaulay, 'Review of Ranke's *History of the Popes*' in *Edinburgh Review* CXLV (Oct. 1840), 228. Joseph Cauvin to William Longman, 8 Dec. 1856 in Sadleir, *Commentary*, 169-70. T.T. in a p.s. to F.T. to A.T., 8 July 1856, Taylor MS. Tom had the habit in his letters to A.T. of referring to F.T. as 'my mother'.

28. A.T., *Palmerston*, 165-6. Olive Anderson, *A Liberal State at War* (1967), 27. Nathaniel Hawthorne [Randall Stewart, ed.], *The English Notebooks* (New York, 1941), 99. Alexis de Tocqueville [Roger Boesche, ed.], *Selected Letters* (Berkeley, Calif., 1985), 314.

29. Joseph Cauvin to William Longman, 2 Apr. 1855, Sadleir MS.

30. Post 100/12: Rowland Hill's P.O. Journals, 9 June 1855. When Hill was invited by Lord Hardwicke to dinner to celebrate the Queen's birthday in 1852 he moaned about having to wear Court Dress: 'I am to play the fool'. He probably did not like the fact that Col. Maberly had also been invited.

31. Robert Blake, *Disraeli* (1966), 509-11. A.T. repeats the assertion in *Clergymen of the Church of England*, 8. Here A.T. also made the common mistake of referring to the Sovereign as 'head' of the Church. She is, of course, 'Supreme Governor', a title symbolising the Church's position under the law, not the Queen's ecclesiastical powers.

32. For an insight into the Queen's work during Feb. and Mar. 1855 see Benson and Esher [eds], *Letters of Queen Victoria*, 1st ser., III.106-47 and Mullen and Munson, *Victoria*, 62-4.

33. A.T. incorrectly assumed, as most historians still do, that Lord Derby was controlled by Disraeli. He also incorrectly assumed that Derby entered the Lords on the death of his father; in fact he had been 'called up' in the 1840s. His father did not die until 1851. The only part of the Lords' work A.T. dealt with was the judicial functions. A.T., Commonplace Book, Yale MS.

34. A.T., *The New Zealander*, 26-7. In Wiltshire the American agricultural expert, F.L. Olmstead, found in 1850 that on some farms workers got as little as 6s a week (*Walks and Talks of an American Farmer in England* (Ann Arbor, Michigan, n.d. 1st publ. 1852), 273). A.T., *The New Zealander*, 12.

35. Barchester Towers Work Sheet, Trollope Business MS. In 1958 Booth (*Anthony Trollope*, 237) listed the 12 most popular works by A.T. as published in the Oxford World's Classics series. *Barchester Towers* was the first by a large margin, followed by *Last Chronicle*, *The Warden* and the *Autobiography*. The results were based on an average of years. For example, the Post Office on 8 June 1858 paid his expenses, £13 1s 2d, for trips to Mansfield and Edinburgh (Post: Vol. 179, No. 2563: English: Reports and Minutes, 203). Locker-Lampson, *My Confidences*, 333. *The Railway Traveller's Handy Book* of 1862 did not include writing among recommended ways to pass the time although it did include 'that delightful occupation known as "building castles in the air" ' (62, 67). In *Barchester Towers* both the Proudies sleep on the train during their first trip to Barchester. Escott, 115.

36. The young and highly critical Lady Rose Fane commented that Rose's lovely white hair was set in the latest style although she disliked the rose in her hair (Lady Rose Fane to the Countess of Westmorland, n.d. 1866, Weigall MS., Kent Record Office, U 1371 C17/32).

37. A.T. to William Longman, 10 Jan. 1857 in Sadleir, *Commentary*, 171-2. A.T. to William Longman, 3 Mar. 1857 in Sadleir, *Commentary*, 174.

38. Henry James, 'Anthony Trollope' in Smalley [ed.], *Trollope: The Critical Heritage*, 541.

39. A.T., *Thackeray*, 117.

40. James Jennings [ed.], *The Dialect of the West of England particularly Somersetshire* ... (1869, 2nd rev. edn), 18. A.T. also made use of 'ax' for 'ask', which Chaucer used. For the Barsetshire dialect, see Clark, *Language and Style of Anthony Trollope*, 82-6.

41. A.T. to Mr ?, 8 Mar. 1866, Parrish MS. L.E. Denison [ed.], *Fifty Years at East Brent: The Letters of George Anthony Denison* (1902), 4. A.T., *The New Zealander*, 191.

42. For Dod see p. 477 above. Henry James, 'Anthony Trollope' in Smalley [ed.], *Trollope: The Critical Heritage*, 541. J.A. Symonds to Charlotte Symonds, 2 Sep. [1861] in Schueller and Peters [eds], *Letters of J.A. Symonds* I.309-10. 'Maniery' is based on *maniéré*, meaning affected or unnatural. *Guardian*, 13 Dec. 1882.

43. Escott, 61.

44. [H.F. Chorley?], Review of *Barchester Towers* in the *Athenaeum*, 30 May 1857. [George Meredith], Review of *Barchester Towers* in the *Westminster Review* LXVIII (Oct. 1857), 594-6. For attribution to Meredith see G.S. Haight, 'George Meredith and the Westminster Review' in *Modern Language Review* LIII (Jan. 1958), 1-16. [R.H. Hutton?], 'Mr Trollope's Novels' in the *National Review* VII (Oct. 1858), 425.

45. J.H. Newman to J.H. Pollen, 8 Oct. 1858 in Dessain et al. [eds.], *Letters and Diaries of* ... *Newman* XVIII.482. Thomas Hardy to Mary Hardy, 28 Oct. 1865 q. in F.E. Hardy, *The Life of Thomas Hardy* (1972 edn), 51-2.

46. Queen Victoria to Princess Royal, 11 Dec. 1858, 2 Mar. 1859 in Roger Fulford [ed.], *Dearest Child: Private Correspondence of Queen Victoria and the Princess Royal 1858-1861* (1977 edn), 150-1, 163-4. Princess Royal to Queen Victoria, 28 Feb. 1859, Royal Archives, Z.7/87. Theodore Martin, *The Life of* ... *the Prince Consort* (1877-80, 5th edn, 5 vols), IV.340. The Prince read *Barchester Towers* in Dec. 1858 as 'no unpleasant relief to the perusal of Archbishop Whately's work *On the Mind* and of the *Memoirs of Prince Eugène*, with which it disputed his attention'. The statement by Martin (a friend of Trollope) that 'all novels of character had for him an irresistible charm', while directed at early works by George Eliot, seems also to refer to *Barchester Towers*. Queen Victoria to Princess Royal, 2 Mar. 1859, in Fulford [ed.], *Dearest Child*, 163-4 q. in Mullen and Munson, *Queen Victoria*, 136, cf. 6. A copy of *Barchester Towers* was in the Royal Library which shows that the Queen had bought it and had not ordered it from Mudie (Anon., *The Private Life of the Queen* (1898), 126).

47. Princess Feodora to Queen Victoria, 13 Apr. 1859, Royal Archives, R.A. Y.41/117. Frank Colenso to Frances Colenso, 5 Sep. 1877, in Frances Colenso [Wyn Rees, ed.], *Letters from Natal* (Pietermaritzburg, 1958), 337-8.

48. For the Circumlocution Office see ch. X of *Little Dorrit*. A.T. to Editor of the *Athenaeum* [W.H. Dixon], 5 Feb. 1856, Booth [ed.], *Letters*, 43. See Bradford Booth, 'Trollope and *Little Dorrit*' in the *Trollopian* II (Mar. 1948), 237-40. A.T., 'Charles Dickens' in Mullen [ed.], *Malachi's Cove*, 125.

49. Benjamin Jowett to A.P. Stanley, n.d. q. in Evelyn Abbott and Lewis Campbell, *The Life* ... *of Benjamin Jowett* (1897, 2 vols), I.182n.

50. See *Auto.*, 111-12. It is an example of the working of A.T.'s mind that when he describes Sir Gregory he also refers to Macaulay's style in passing.

51. John Morley, *The Life of William Ewart Gladstone* (1903, 3 vols), I.509. A.T., 'The Civil Service', *F.R.* II (Oct. 1865), 613-26. This is the best discussion by A.T. of his attitude towards the reforms. See also his 1861 lecture, 'The Civil Service as a Profession' in Parrish [ed.], *Four Lectures,* and his testimony before the Commons Select Committee on Civil Service appointments: here A.T. did not oppose examinations altogether but at the lower level, such as letter-carriers, where he thought examinations for general knowledge nonsensical. Here he was at logger-heads with Hill. When asked if the examination now required of rural letter-carriers had improved the service, A.T. replied, 'no improvement, certainly' (P.P., 1860, IX, *Civil Service Appointments,* 122-44). When he was helping G.H. Lewes's son get a place in the Post Office he admitted, 'My belief is that if you took the 12 most popular authors in England they would all be beaten. For myself I should not dream of passing. I sd. break down in figures & spelling too, not to talk of handwriting' (A.T. to G.H. Lewes, 20 July 1860, Trollope MS., Yale).

52. A.T., The Three Clerks Work Sheet, Trollope Business MS. A.T. to William Longman, 21 Aug., 29 Aug. 1857 in Sadleir, *Commentary,* 180-1. *Auto.,* 109.

53. *Auto.,* 110-11. R.T.'s Chronology, Trollope MS., Ill.

54. F.T. to A.T., 8 July 1856, Taylor MS. A.T. to Richard Bentley, 10 Oct. 1857, Booth [ed.], *Letters,* 55. Richard Bentley to A.T., 13 Oct. 1857, Trollope Business MS. The other novel was *The Struggles of Brown, Jones, and Robinson* which he began on 24 Aug. 1857.

55. E.B. Browning to Theodosia Trollope, n.d. [Dec. 1857 – Jan. 1858], q. in *Remember* I.401-2. *Literary Gazette,* 6 Feb. 1858. T.T. was their Italian correspondent. *S.R.,* 5 Dec. 1857.

56. *Auto.,* 107.

57. *Lancet,* 4 Jan. 1851. *The Times,* 16 Jan. 1851.

58. A.T., *The New Zealander,* 194.

59. For a discussion of A.T.'s natural political dichotomy from the perspective of the 1980s see Ronald Butt, *The Times,* 27 Apr. 1989: 'The Duke of Omnium, and Anthony Trollope, had, however, never met Mrs Thatcher with all her driving energy.' See also Richard Mullen, 'A Modern Twist to Trollope', *Daily Telegraph,* 6 Dec. 1982. Gash, *Sir Robert Peel,* 502. For the background to this see my Oxford D.Phil. thesis, 'The House of Lords and the Repeal of the Corn Laws' (August, 1974). By the time A.T. wrote *Lord Palmerston* he had changed his view and called Peel 'a great man' who 'will remain as long as English history is read and understood' (87).

60. Dowager Duchess of Argyll [ed.], *George Douglas Eighth Duke of Argyll ... Autobiography and Memoirs* (1906, 2 vols), II.7. P.P., 1854-5, XI, *Report ... Postal Arrangements,* 127, 214, 174, 184, 196. Irish postmen were now getting 8s a week; in England the wage could be as high as 14s. Where revision of rural post was complete the wage was 12s in England. Sometimes Irish postmen sub-let their work to children because their post bags were so light (174).

61. A.T. to William Longman, 15 July 1857 in Sadleir, *Commentary,* 177. A.T., *The New Zealander,* 74.

62. A.T., Introduction to the collected edition of *The Chronicles of Barsetshire* I, v; for details see pp. 630-1 above. Dr Thorne Work Sheet, Trollope Business MS.

63. Barrington, *The Servant of All* II.53-5.

64. *Auto.*, 117. Richard Bentley to A.T., 25 Jan. 1858, Trollope Business MS. MS. agreement between Chapman and Hall and A.T., 29 Jan. 1858, Trollope Business MS. It is, of course, possible that A.T. only went once to Chapman, on 29 Jan., and was in a rush not because of the royal wedding but because he was leaving the next day for Paris. This is unlikely because of the time needed to draw up the agreement – printed contracts were little used in the 1850s – and because it was very out of character for A.T. to wait from 25 to 29 Jan. to find an acceptable publisher.

65. In his biography of A.T., Pope Hennessy said there had been a rumour in the 'art world' that T.T. had sold works of art. This may originate in his once trying to sell an Orcagna terracotta to what was the South Kensington Museum, later the Victoria and Albert Museum. (T.T. to A.T., 27 July 1860, Trollope MS., Ill. Only part of this letter was reproduced in Hall [ed.], *Letters* I.113.)

66. A.T. to R.T., 2 Feb. 1858, Taylor MS. R.T.'s Chronology, Trollope MS., Ill.

67. *Graphic*, 16 Dec. 1882.

68. See M.A. Titmarsh [W.M. Thackeray], *Notes of a Journey from Cornhill to Grand Cairo* ... (1846), ch. XIV. 'You might be as well impressed with Wapping as with your first step on Egyptian soil,' Thackeray wrote.

69. In 1875 A.T. pointed out that even with the new Suez Canal, 'the quicker traffic which has reached the Mediterranean by Brindisi is still carried from Alexandria to Suez by railway' and not through the canal. This included the post. (A.T. [Bradford Booth, ed.], *Tireless Traveler* (Berkeley, Calif., 1978 edn), 28.

70. Escott, 123-4.

71. A.T.'s report regarding P. & O.'s delaying the mails in Egypt may be found in Post: Pkt. 84.1, Nos. 1012/58, 928/58. For the new postal arrangements to Cairo via Marseilles see *The Times*, 14 May 1859. A post office was set up in Cairo and the cost of a letter became 9d.

72. The Bertrams Work Sheet, Trollope Business MS.

73. J.H. Newman to Ambrose St John, 29 Sep., 2 Oct. 1862 in Dessain et al. [eds.], *Letters and Diaries of ... Newman* XX.281, 284. L.N. Tolstoy Diary, 29 Sep., 2 Oct. 1865, *Polnoe sobranie sochinenii* (Moscow, 1952, 1953), 48-9, 63-4 and 66-8, 71. There were eventually eleven Trollope novels, all in Tauchnitz editions, in Tolstoy's library. Later Tolstoy listed Trollope along with Victor Hugo, George Eliot and Mrs Henry Wood as one of the four modern writers who had most influenced him in the 1860s and 70s.

74. The Bertrams Work Sheet, Trollope Business MS.

Chapter 9

1. *New Monthly Magazine* CXV (July 1859), 500.

2. David Masson, *British Novelists and Their Styles* (1859), 235.

3. *The Times*, 23 May 1859.

4. B.R. Mitchell & Phyllis Deane [eds], *Abstract of British Historical Statistics* (Cambridge, 1971), 313-21. *S.R.*, 8 Jan. 1859. All quotes regarding the West Indies or A.T. during the trip are from his book *The West Indies and the Spanish Main* (1859).

5. Post 101/4: John Tilley's Private Letter Book, 153.

6. Anon., 'Anthony Trollope and the Negro Waiter', *London Society* XLIII

(Jan. 1883), 108. Douglas Woodruff, 'Expansion and Emigration' in Young [ed.] *Early Victorian England* II.396-7.

7. For A.T. and the idea of imperial mission see A.P. Thornton, *The Imperial Idea and Its Enemies: A Study in British Power* (New York, 1968 edn), 42-3.

8. A.T. to Edward Chapman, 11 Jan. 1859, Parrish MS. On 14 July 1859 a second, more formal, agreement was signed by A.T. and Chapman. This contradicts A.T.'s statement in the *Autobiography* that he had proposed the book to Chapman in Nov. 1858 (129). Chapman had paid Thackeray £200 for his travel book on Egypt in 1844. A.T. to F.T., 27 Jan. 1859 q. in *Frances Trollope* II.283-4. Trollope Business MS.

9. Robert W. Johannsen, *Stephen A. Douglas* (New York, 1973), 528-30, 322-7.

10. *Auto*, 129.

11. *Remember* I.179.

12. There is also a reference to the gaol in *Castle Richmond* [ch. XLIII].

13. Harper re-published *The Bertrams* in 1859 and *Barchester Towers* in 1860.

14. *Auto.*, 128. Super, *Trollope in the Post Office*, 38-43. Post 100/8: Rowland Hill's P.O. Journal, 29 Jan. 1849 where in a pencilled note in the margin Hill notes his management of all treaties; Rowland Hill and G.B. Hill, *The Life of Sir Rowland Hill* (1880, 2 vols), II.288; Eleanor C. Smyth, *Sir Rowland Hill* (1907), 277-8, where A.T.'s work in the West Indies is even praised. P.P., 1860, XXIII, *Sixth Report of the P.M.G. on the Post Office*, 1859, 28.

15. A.T. to Lady Pollock [Aug. or Sep. 1873?], Parrish MS. Although there were at least 30 editions by the end of 1852, only one publisher volunteered to give Mrs Stowe any payment and this was well under what she would have made had her copyright been honoured (J.E.B. Munson, 'Uncle Tom in England' in *Civil War Times* XXI (Jan. 1983), 42). A.T., writing 14 years later in *Australia and New Zealand* I.37, launched another attack on Mrs Stowe and her 1853 triumphant tour of Britain and Europe which she recounted in breathtaking detail in *Sunny Memories of Foreign Lands* (1854): 'We remember republican Mrs Beecher Stowe with her sunny memories of duchesses.' G.H. Lewes to T.T., 5 July 1861 in *Auto.*, 9. *Remember* I.476.

16. *The Times*, 6 Jan. 1860. *Auto.*, 130-1. However, on 18 Jan. 1860 *The Times* criticised A.T. regarding his discussion of the convicts.

17. *S.R.*, 26 Nov. 1859. *Spectator*, 12 Nov. 1859. William Scarborough [ed.], *The Diary of Edmund Ruffin* (Baton Rouge, Louisiana, 1972, 2 vols), I.471.

18. A.T. to R.T., 2 Aug. 1859, Taylor MS.

19. Post 100/11: Rowland Hill's P.O. Journal, 25 Nov. 1852.

20. David Piper, *The English Face* (1978 edn), 317. *Auto.*, 9. *Remember* I.15. If A.T.'s short story, 'The O'Conors of Castle Conor, County Mayo' can be read as autobiographical, A.T. also had large feet, not surprising for a man of his height.

21. q. in Piper, *The English Face*, 317. H. Sutherland Edwards, *Personal Recollections* (1900), tells how beards spread from the army to railwaymen (3-4). Malmesbury, *Memoirs* ... I.361-3. Henry W. Lucy, *Memories of Eight Parliaments* (1908), 286.

22. E.B. Browning to George Barrett, 1 Nov. 1860, Landis [ed.], *Letters of the Brownings to George Barrett*, 247-8.

23. Brackenbury, *Some Memories*, 51.

24. A.T. to ?, 15 Aug. 1878, Trollope MS., Yale. Castle Richmond Work Sheet, Trollope Business MS.

25. A.T. to ? [Harper Brothers], 1 Sep. 1859, Taylor MS. Castle Richmond

Work Sheet, Trollope Business MS. Mullen [ed.], *Malachi's Cove*, xvii-xviii. In the event *Harper's* published three stories: 'The Relics of General Chassé, a Tale of Antwerp' (Feb. 1860); 'The O'Conors of Castle Conor, County Mayo' (May 1860); 'The Courtship of Susan Bell' (Aug. 1860).

26. Jasper Ridley, *Lord Palmerston* (1970), 400-1. E.B. Browning to George Barrett, 1 Nov. 1860 in Landis [ed.], *Letters of the Brownings to George Barrett*, 248.

27. *Illustrated News of the World*, 4 Jan. 1862. For an illustration of these see *Auto.*, facing p. 273. A.T. to Lord Stanley of Alderley, 1 Sep. 1862, Castle Howard Archives, J 23/92. This previously unknown letter and a *carte de visite* photograph of A.T. were placed in the Autograph Book of the Countess of Carlisle (Stanley's daughter). I am grateful to Eeyan Hartley, Keeper of the Archives at Castle Howard and to the Howard family for permission to cite it.

28. Griest, *Mudie's Circulating Library*, 29. *S.R.*, 19 May 1860.

29. Even so the *Bookseller* of 26 Oct. 1859 still referred to the depressed state of publishing in a 'magnificent but sadly neglected country': some things never change.

30. A.T. to W.M. Thackeray, 23 Oct. 1859, Trollope Business MS.

31. Returns to the House of Lords re Letter Carriers q. in *The Times*, 3 May 1859. The annual wage, therefore, assuming no holidays, would have been £61 10s 8d.

32. George Smith to A.T., 26 Oct. 1859, Trollope Business MS.

33. Escott, 132. q. in J.W. Robertson Scott, *The Story of the Pall Mall Gazette* (1950), 45. Escott, 132. Mrs Gaskell, *Charlotte Brontë*, 368n.

34. W.M. Thackeray to A.T., 28 Oct. [1859], Taylor MS.

35. A.T., *Thackeray*, 52. Leonard Huxley, *The House of Smith, Elder* (1923), 97. A.T., *Thackeray*, 51n. However, in his Work Sheet for Framley Parsonage, A.T. says that he began writing on 2 Nov. which was a Wednesday, the day before he went to London, and that he wrote 7 pages that day and 38 pages by the end of the week, i.e. by Saturday, 5 Nov. As 3 Nov. 1859 was, indeed, a Thursday we can only assume that A.T. erred either in compiling his work sheet, which seems unlikely, or in recalling the date of his journey to London when writing the *Autobiography*.

36. *Auto.*, 142-3.

37. *Publishers' Circular*, 16 Jan. 1860 and 1 Mar. 1860. W.M. Thackeray, 'Roundabout Papers', *C.M.* I (Jan. 1860), 124-8. Mrs Gaskell to George Smith, 1 Mar. 1860 in J.A.V. Chapple and A. Polland [eds], *The Letters of Mrs. Gaskell* (Manchester, 1966), 602.

38. *S.R.*, 4 May 1861.

39. Mary Chesnut's diary, 25 Feb. 1861, C. Vann Woodward [ed.], *Mary Chesnut's Civil War* (New Haven, 1981), 10. E.D. Forgues, 'Une Thèse sur le mariage en deux romans' in *Revue des Deux Mondes* XXIX (Sep. 1860), 369-98. F.G. Kenyon [ed.], *Letters of Elizabeth Barrett Browning* (1897), II.377.

40. *Critic* q. in *Publishers' Circular*, 1 Feb. 1860. On 6 April, 1860, Tom wrote to A.T. to thank him for sending a copy of *Castle Richmond*. Trollope MS., Ill. *Remember* I.490. F.T. to A.T., n.d., Taylor MS.

41. A.T. to George Smith, 22 Sep. 1860, Smith/Murray MS.

42. Theodosia Trollope, *Social Aspects of the Italian Revolution* (1861), 1, 280-1. The book was first published in the *Athenaeum*; the comment on the Vendée was published on 6 Nov. 1860.

43. A.T., 'The Present Condition of the Northern States of the American Union' in Parrish [ed.], *Four Lectures*, 43. By 1862, however, A.T. had modified his view and in *North America* he cited Garibaldi's uprising in Sep. 1859 as an example of a justified rebellion (185). Thirteen years later A.T. returned to Garibaldi. Writing from Rome he described Garibaldi's continuing importance in Italian politics with approval (see Booth [ed.], *Tireless Traveler*, 19-23). T.T. to A.T., 6 Apr., 27 July, 1860, Trollope MS., Ill. A.T. to George Smith, 1 Oct. 1860 and Smith to A.T., 8 Oct. 1860, Smith/Murray MS.

44. A.T. to Arthur Helps, 26 Jan. 1869, Parrish MS. Laurence Poston, 'Thomas Adolphus Trollope: A Victorian Anglo-Florentine' in *Bulletin of the John Rylands Library* XLIX/1 (Autumn, 1966), 133-64. *Reader*, 3 Dec. 1864 in reviewing Tom's novel, *Lindisfarne Chase*. E.B. Browning to George Barrett, 12 Oct., 1 Nov., 1860, in Landis [ed.], *Letters of the Brownings to George Barrett*, 244, 247-8.

45. Kate Field, *New York Tribune*, 22 Dec. 1880. *Auto.*, 316-17.

46. For A.T. and Sir Charles Taylor see Escott, 145-6. A.T. to George Smith, 12 Apr. 1867, Smith/Murray MS. A.T. to Mary Holmes, 27 May 1876, Parrish MS. La Salle (Corbell) Pickett, *Across My Path: Memories of People I Have Known* (Freeport, New York, 1970 edn, 1st publ. 1916), 79-83. General George Pickett led the famous 'charge' at Gettysburg.

47. Lilian Whiting, *Kate Field: A Record* (Boston, 1899), 123). A.T. to Kate Field, 15 Nov. 1860 q. in Sadleir, *Commentary*, 213-14.

48. *The Times*, 16 Jan. 1878.

49. A.T. to Kate Field, 8 July, 1868 q. in Sadleir, *Commentary*, 279-81.

50. Huxley, *The House of Smith, Elder*, 104. A.T., *Thackeray*, 31, 49-50.

51. A.T., *Thackeray*, 7, 15-16. Thackeray told Lord Stanley in 1863 that 'Esmond, which he thought his best, had brought him only £1,500 for a year's hard work. The publishers did not like *Esmond*: they said, "Don't give us any more old English" ' (Lord Stanley's diary, 19 Feb. 1863, John Vincent [ed.], *Disraeli, Derby and the Conservative Party: Journals and Memoirs of Edward Henry, Lord Stanley 1849-1869* (1978), 196). A.T., *Thackeray*, 20; A.T. to Kate Field, 17 Jan. 1881 q. in Sadleir, *Commentary*, 341-2.

52. *The Virginians*, ch. XXXV. For 'Tom Garbage' see ch. XLIII.

53. Edmund Yates, 'Echoes from the London Clubs' in *New York Times*, 26 May 1860. *S.R.*, 23 June 1860. Gordon N. Ray [ed.], *The Letters and Private Papers of William Makepeace Thackeray* (1945-6, 4 vols), IV.190. George Smith, 'Our Birth and Parentage' in *C.M.* LXXXIII (Jan. 1901), 4-17.

54. G.A. Sala, *Things I Have Seen and People I Have Known* (1894, 2 vols), I. 30-1.

55. A.T. to George Smith, 3 July 1860 q. in Sadleir, *Commentary*, 208-9. W.H. Russell only got £1,200 for his Indian Journals (*Bookseller*, 25 June 1859). In the same letter A.T. proposed a 'short story' in eight parts to be published monthly, each part having 16 pages: for this he asked £75 a number, over three times what he had got from *Harper's* and almost double what he had got from *Cassell's*. T.T. to A.T., 27 July, 1860, Trollope MS., Ill.

56. Saintsbury, 'Trollope Revisited' in *Essays and Reviews*, 49. *Illustrated News of the World*, 4 Jan. 1862. The same issue praised *Orley Farm*. *S.R.*, 11 Oct. 1862.

57. A.T., 'A Walk in a Wood' in Mullen [ed.], *Malachi's Cove*, 128-9. *S.R.*, 11 Oct. 1862. W.E. Gladstone to Catherine Gladstone, 29 Sep. 1863, A. Tilney

Bassett [ed.], *Gladstone to His Wife* (1936), 150.

58. A.T. to George Smith, 12 Feb. 1860, Trollope Business MS. Anon. [Jane Panton], *Leaves From a Life* (1908), 202.

Chapter 10

1. Mary Chesnut's diary, 2 Dec. 1863, 25 Feb. 1861, 11 Apr. 1864, Woodward [ed.], *Mary Chesnut's Civil War*, 10, 595.

2. [A.T.], 'President Johnson's Last Message', *St.P.* III (Mar. 1869), 664.

3. A.T., *The New Zealander*, 37. John Cassell, who had published some of A.T.'s short stories, made the same point. He visited America in 1859-60 and published his travels in *Cassell's Illustrated Family Paper* between 29 Dec. 1860 and 16 Nov. 1861. Article XIV is 'The New York Press'.

4. A.T., *West Indies*, 389.

5. Mary Chesnut's diary, 18 Feb. 1861, C. Vann Woodward [ed.], *The Private Mary Chesnut* (Oxford 1984), 3-4. Many Southerners used the South Carolina flag as it had been the first state to secede, on 20 Dec. 1860. The familiar Confederate Flag came later in the war.

6. Lord Stanley to Lady Stanley, 10 Aug. 1860, Nancy Mitford [ed.], *The Stanleys of Alderley* ... (1968 edn), 243-4. *Catalogue, Bye-Laws and Regulations of the Post Office Library and Literary Association* (1858). The P.M.G., Lord Colchester (in office from 13 Mar. 1858 to 24 June 1859), hoped in time to see a similar body established for letter-carriers and praised the enterprise as a sign of the 'taste for reading, and a desire for mental cultivation and pleasures of a superior kind'. P.P., 1859, VIII, *Fifth Report of the P.M.G. on The Post Office*, 25. A.T., 'The Civil Service' in *Dublin University Magazine* XLVI (Oct. 1855). He returned to the topic in 1865 with an article, 'The Civil Service' in *F.R.* II (Oct. 1865), 613-26.

7. A.T., 'The Civil Service as a Profession' in Parrish [ed.], *Four Lectures*, 24. The lecture was first published in an abridged form in *C.M.*, in March 1861, under the title 'The Civil Service as a Profession'. A.T. then had the complete lecture printed privately: this is the version used here. Post 100/14: Rowland Hill's P.O. Journal, 1 Feb. 1861.

8. Post 35/212: English: 12-13 for correspondence between Hill and Lord Stanley. Hill wrote to Stanley on 9 Apr. 1861. A.T. was helped because Hill was feuding with Stanley. Nine days after Hill wrote to the P.M.G. regarding A.T. they had a row over promotions. According to Hill, Stanley lost his temper but 'fortunately, I was able fully to command my temper – I told him calmly that he was mistaken ... It is quite clear we cannot work together' and Hill once again talked of resigning (Journal, 18 Apr. 1861). The Washington government suspended postal services to the Confederate States on 27 May 1861.

9. Kate Stanley to Maude Stanley, 7 Aug. 1862 from Karlsbad in Mitford [ed.], *The Stanleys*, 284-5.

10. Post 35/212: English: 12-13.

11. Trollope Business MS. The agreement was dated 20 Mar. 1861.

12. Sydney Smith to the editor of the *Morning Chronicle*, 3 Nov. 1843, *The Works of the Rev. Sydney Smith* (1859, 2 vols), II.327. This was the first of two letters. Smith had also petitioned the US Congress on 18 May 1843. A.T., *North America*, 372.

13. Lord Malmesbury's diary, 24 July 1860, Lord Malmesbury, *Memoirs*

II.231. William H. Austin, *'Susanna'* ... *The Songs of Stephen C. Foster* (New York, 1975), 17-19.

14. I have only found one exception among English travellers; she was Sarah Mytton Maury. See her *The Statesmen of America in 1846* (1847), 365-7. She had married into the Maury family of Virginia.

15. Leslie Stephen q. in Anon. [ed.], *The History of The Times* (1935-1952, 4 vols), II.359. Moses Tyler, *Glimpses of England* (1898) q. in H.S. Commager [ed.], *Britain Through American Eyes* (1974), 385. A.T., *West Indies*, 144.

16. Nathaniel Hawthorne to James T. Fields, 11 Feb. 1860, Taylor MS and q. by A.T. in his *Auto.*, 144-5. A.T., 'The Genius of Nathaniel Hawthorne' in *North American Review* (Sep. 1879), *passim*. See especially 204-5. A.T. quotes Hawthorne's comment to Fields but by 1879 obviously did not think it was Fields who had showed it to him (205).

17. *Harper's New Monthly Magazine* XVII (Sep. 1858), 693.

18. Nathaniel Willis, *Loiterings of Travel* (1840, 3 vols), I.xiv-xvi. Willis was specifically referring to Disraeli's popularity in America. Mrs Burton Harrison, *Recollections Grave and Gay* (New York, 1911), 124. Her husband was secretary to President Jefferson Davis. Fitzgerald Ross [R.B. Harwell, ed.], *Cities and Camps of the Confederate States* (Urbana, Ill., 1958), 70-1n quoting *Index* IV,28.

19. Mary Chesnut's diary, 7 June 1861, Woodward [ed.], *The Private Mary Chesnut*, 77.

20. Henry Greville's diary, 21 Aug. 1858, Strafford [ed.], *Diary* III.146-7. On 5 Aug. 1858 news had reached London of the successful laying of the cable, which broke in Oct. 1858.

21. A.T., *North America*, 18. Hereinafter no citations will be given in this chapter for quotes from the book; all unidentified quotes come from it.

22. *Frances Trollope* II.164.

23. See Charles K. Tuckerman, *Personal Recollections of Notable People* ... (New York, 1895, 2 vols), II.8-11 for an account of A.T. as both a presenter and receiver of such letters. An example of such a letter in which F.E.T. introduces A.T., Rose and her niece, Florence to Professor and Signora Villari in Florence in 1881 has survived in the F.E. Trollope MS.

24. See Leon Edel, *Henry James: A Life* (1987), 57-61: this was the time of the young James's mysterious accident.

25. *Domestic Manners*, 134. George Eliot, *Middlemarch*, ch. XVIII. Anon., 'Orley Farm' in *National Review* XVI (Jan. 1863), 28. A.T. q. in *Beverley Recorder*, 14 Nov. 1868.

26. North America Work Sheet, Trollope Business MS.

27. Sidney Lee, *King Edward VII* (1925, 1927, 2 vols), I.105. A.T., Review of Anna Sewell's *Rose of Cheriton* in *F.R.* VII (Feb. 1867), 254.

28. Here we must compare A.T.'s description with his mother's: 'wonder, terror, and delight completely overwhelmed me. I wept with a strange mixture of pleasure and of pain ... How utterly futile must every attempt be to convey an idea of the sensations it produces! ... Yet pleasure it is, and I almost think the greatest I ever enjoyed' (*Domestic Manners*, 337, 343).

29. *Domestic Manners*, 12.

30. Anon., *The Railway Traveller's Handy Book* ..., 92.

31. *Domestic Manners*, 17.

32. Smalley and Booth [eds] in A.T., *North America*, 165, n.7.

33. Charles Tuckerman, *Personal Recollections* II.8-10.

34. F.T., *Paris and the Parisians* II.234. Richard Stoddard, 'The World of Letters', *New York Mail and Express*, 20 June 1893 q. in Edward F. Grier [ed.], *Notebooks and Unpublished Prose Manuscripts* (New York, 1984, 6 vols), II.527 in G.W. Allen and Sculley Bradley [gen. eds], *The Collected Writings of Walt Whitman* (New York, 1961-84, 22 vols). Stoddard was on the staff of the New York Hospital when A.T. visited.

35. A.T., Review of *Rose of Cheriton*, *F.R.*, 254. *Beverley Recorder*, 14 Nov. 1868. In one important sense A.T. was unfair: when he visited America, England had no state system of elementary schools. These were provided by two national systems, the larger by the Church of England, the smaller by a non-denominational body. In addition there were 'free' or 'charity' schools in slum areas. The real comparison was not between a state school and a free school in London but with a school provided by one of the two national networks. Elementary schools charged a very small weekly fee, normally a penny, and did not become free until 1891.

36. James T. Fields to Nathaniel Hawthorne, 18 Sep. 1861 q. in James C. Austin, *Fields of the Atlantic Monthly* (San Marino, California, 1953), 215. J.R. Lowell to ?, 20 Sep. 1861 q. in H.S. Scudder, *James Russell Lowell: A Biography* (1901, 2 vols), II.82-4. A.T., 'Hawthorne' in *North American Review*, 207.

37. North America Work Sheet, Trollope Business MS. J.R. Lowell to ?, 20 Sep. 1861 q. in Scudder, *James Russell Lowell* II.82-4.

38. A.T. to Kate Field, 4 Jan. 1862 q. in Sadleir, *Commentary*, 221-2. A.T. to Kate Field, 4 Feb. 1862 q. in Sadleir, *Commentary*, 224-5.

39. Henry James, 'Anthony Trollope' in Smalley [ed.], *Trollope: The Critical Heritage*, 538.

40. A.T. would have known of the Twisletons through his postal work in Banbury and the nearby Broughton Castle, the home of Lord Saye and Sele, brother of the Hon. Edward Twisleton. He would also have known of them through London literary circles as they were friends of Thackeray, Milnes and Browning. Mrs Twisleton died in May 1862. See E.T. Vaughan [ed.], *Letters of the Hon. Mrs. Edward Twisleton* (1928). A.T. used the name Twisleton for a minor character in *The Bertrams*, ch. XXXIV.

41. A.T. to Kate Field, 4 Jan. 1862 q. in Sadleir, *Commentary*, 221-2.

42. William M. Wallworth and Walter E. Anderton to the author, 23 July 1989. Mr Anderton is Rose Trollope's great-great-great-nephew. North America Work Sheet, Trollope Business MS.

43. A.T. to Kate Field, 12 Jan. 1861 [1862] q. in Sadleir, *Commentary*, 224. A.T. to Kate Field, 17 Dec. 1861 q. in Sadleir, *Commentary*, 219-20.

44. C.F. Adams, Jnr., *The Trent Affair* ... (Boston, 1912) 16 q. in Frank J. Merli, *Great Britain and the Confederate Navy 1861-1865* (Bloomington, Indiana, 1970), 77-8. A.T. to Kate Field, 17 Dec. 1861 q. in Sadleir, *Commentary*, 219-20.

45. A.T., *Palmerston*, 195 q. in R.C. Terry [ed.], *Trollope: Interviews and Recollections* (1987), 81, n.7. Samuel S. Cox, *Three Decades of Federal Legislation* (Freeport, New York, 1970 edn, 1st publ. 1885), 291. Lord Newton, *Lord Lyons* (1913, 2 vols), I.76. Lord Stanley of Alderley to Lady Stanley, 4 Jan. 1862 in Mitford [ed.], *The Stanleys*, 279. This was the date on which the Foreign Office received a telegram from the British Minister in Washington.

Lord Palmerston to Laurence Sulivan, 26 Jan. 1862, Palmerston/Sulivan Correspondence, Add. MS. 59783 f 30 (provisional). A.T. to Frederic Chapman, 1 Jan. 1861 [1862], Parrish MS.

46. A.T. to Kate Field, 4 Jan. 1862 q. in Sadleir, *Commentary*, 221-2. A.T. told Kate Field he had spent four nights in camp, but his itinerary of his American visit listed three (1-3 Jan. inclusive).

47. William Glenn's diary, 1 Jan. 1862, Marks and Schatz [eds.], *Between North and South*, 47.

48. William Glenn's diary, 14 Feb. 1862, Marks and Schatz [eds.], *Between North and South*, 50. Henry Adams, *The Education of Henry Adams: An Autobiography* (Boston, 1961 edn), 131. William Glenn's diary, 14 Feb. 1862, Marks and Schatz [eds.], *Between North and South*, 50.

49. Anon., Review of *North America* in *Frazer's Magazine* LXVI (Aug. 1862), 257.

50. W.M. Thackeray to Mrs Elliott, 24 June 1856, in Ray [ed.], *Letters ... of ... Thackeray* III.591. A.T., *Australia and New Zealand* I.228.

51. *Pall Mall Gazette*, 7 Feb. 1865. *Pall Mall Gazette*, 25 Feb. 1865. A.T., Review of Goldwin Smith's *The Civil War in America* in *F.R.* V (June 1866), 251-4.

52. *Index*, 26 June 1862, 140-2.

53. A.T., 'The Present Condition of the Northern States' in Parrish [ed.], *Four Lectures*, 36. This lecture was first given on 30 Dec. 1862. A.T. asked George Smith to print two dozen copies for him. A.T., Review of Sir [Samuel] Morton Peto's *Resources and Prosperity of America* in *F.R.* V (May 1866), 128.

54. A.T., Review of Peto's *Resources ...*, *F.R.*, 127.

55. North America Work Sheet, Trollope Business MS.

56. North America Work Sheet, Trollope Business MS. A.T. wrote one word at the end: 'Over.' R.H. Dana, Jnr.'s diary, fragment, 1862 q. in Hall [ed.], *Letters* I.170, n.2. For A.T.'s eventual friendship with Dana see William Coyle, 'The Friendship of Anthony Trollope and Richard Henry Dana, Jr.' in *New England Quarterly* XXV (1952), 255-62. Other people who experienced similar reactions when first meeting Trollope but who came in time to see that his gruff exterior and off-hand manner hid an extremely sympathetic nature include: Clara Kellogg, *Memoirs of an American Prima Donna* (New York, 1913), 48 and R.S. Smyth, 'The Provincial Service Fifty Years Ago', *St Martin's-le-Grand* (cited before).

57. *North American Review* XCV (Oct. 1862), 434. Henry Wadsworth Longfellow to A.T., 16 July 1862, Taylor MS.

58. A.T. to Kate Field, 23 Aug. 1862 q. in Sadleir, *Commentary*, 226-8.

59. J.B. Lippincott to A.T., 24 July 1862, Trollope Business MS. A.T. to J.R. Lowell, 2 Sep. 1862 in *Athenaeum*, 6 Sep. 1862. Trollope Business MS. (MS Don. c. 10 f 75). A.T. received £35 from Baron Tauchnitz for reprinting the book. (A.T., Travelling Journal).

60. Post 100/15: Rowland Hill's P.O. Journal, 14 Apr. and 16 Sep. 1862. *New York Herald*, 23 June 1862. There is a cutting of the letter in Hill's Journal. A.T., who disliked the American press in general, detested the *Herald*. See *North America*, 236, 504.

61. *Literary Gazette*, 26 Apr. 1862. Edward Hamley to J.B., 16 July, 17 Aug. 1862, Blackwood MS., 4170 ff 51, 54. *Bl.M.* XCII (Sep. 1862), 372-90. *S.R.*, 31 May 1862. The owner of the *S.R.*, Beresford Hope, became a close friend of the Confederate President, Jefferson Davis. G.H. Lewes to T.T., 2 June 1862, Haight [ed.], *The George Eliot Letters* VIII.302. *C.M.* VI (July 1862), 105-7.

62. *Index*, 26 June 1862.

63. Lord Clarendon to the Duchess of Manchester, 14 Sep. 1862 in A.L. Kennedy [ed.], *'My Dear Duchess'* (1956), 201-3. Sir Howard Elphinstone to Sir John Cowell, 1 Feb. 1870 q. in Mary Howard McClintock, *The Queen Thanks Sir Howard* (1945), 125.

Chapter 11

1. S.M. Ellis [ed.], *A Mid-Victorian Pepys: Letters and Memoirs of Sir William Hardman* (1923), 143-4.

2. A.T. became a life member in Apr. 1867 for which he paid £52 10s 0d. His certificate, signed by Sir Charles Taylor, is now in the Taylor Collection. Scott, *Pall Mall Gazette*, 84.

3. Brian Heeney, *A Different Kind of Gentlemen* (Hamden, Connecticut, 1976), 14.

4. G.S.R. Kitson Clark, *An Expanding Society* (Cambridge, 1967), 34. J.L. Motley to his wife, 28 May 1858, G.W. Curtis [ed.], *Correspondence of John Lothrop Motley* (1889, 2 vols), I.229-30. Algernon West, *Recollections*, 298-9. George Leveson Gower, *Years of Content*, 172-4. The enormous Watts painting eventually came into the possession of the Tate Gallery and now hangs somewhat incongruously in the Hall of Keble College, Oxford, almost completely covering the end wall which the high table faces.

5. J.B. to W.B., n.d. [June 1864] q. in Porter, *John Blackwood* III.126-7. Lord Stanley's journal, 19 Feb. 1863, Vincent [ed.], *Disraeli, Derby and the Conservative Party*, 196. George Eliot was in fact first offered £10,000 by Smith for the right to serialise *Romola* in 16 numbers in the *Cornhill*. She did not want more than 12 numbers and settled for £7,500, not £7,000 as Thackeray believed. As the book did not do as well as Smith had hoped, Eliot gave him another story for the *Cornhill*, free.

6. J.L. Motley to his wife, 28 May 1858, Curtis [ed.], *Correspondence of ... Motley* I.227.

7. Cecilia Meetkerke, 'Last Reminiscences', *Temple Bar*, 130-4.

8. Lee, *King Edward VII* I.176-7. Algernon West, *Recollections*, 298.

9. Richard Hough, *The Ace of Clubs: A History of the Garrick* (1986), 25. Hippolite Taine [W.E. Rae, tr.], *Notes on England* (1873), 229.

10. *Spectator*, 7 June 1862. *Auto.*, 159.

11. A.T. q. in Sadleir, 'Trollope and Bacon's Essays', *The Trollopian*, 27. A.T., *West Indies*, 275-6. A.T., *Thackeray*, 60. W.M. Thackeray to W.W.F. Synge, May 1862, Ray [ed.], *Letters ... Thackeray* IV.262-3. Each novelist lent Synge £900 at 5 per cent. Despite A.T.'s statement in *Thackeray* (60), much of the loan had not been repaid by the time of Thackeray's death. See A.T. to Herman Merivale, 13 Jan. 1864: this letter, edged in mourning for F.T., was inserted into a copy of *The Warden* and is now in the Berg Collection, N.Y.P.L. By Jan. 1864 Synge had repaid A.T. £500. A.T.'s friendship with Synge continued: his cancelled cheques show that he paid the ten guineas contribution to the Thackeray Testimonial for Synge who was Consul in Honolulu at the time. His cheque was drawn on the Union Bank of London (MS. Autograph d 19 f 177, Bodleian Library). He also sent Synge autographed copies of his books: Synge's copy of *The Belton Estate* is in the Taylor Collection.

12. Muriel Trollope, 'What I Was Told', *Trollopian*, 233. For A.T.'s servants see the relevant Enumerator's Book for the Waltham Cross Registration District, 1861 Census, P.R.O. A.T., like his father, had to pay an annual tax of 21s on his man-servant (as he was over 18) plus 10s 6d per horse. Income tax was 6d in the pound (P.P., 1868-9, XXXIV, *Returns of Rates of All Taxes and Imposts, passim*). A.T., Travelling Journal, Parrish MS. P.P., 1874, LXXII, *Accounts and Papers: Return of Owners of Land, England and Wales* ..., under Herts. William Paul is shown with 20 acres, 2 rods and 5 furlongs, but this total may have included other land-holdings in Herts. than Waltham House.

13. Scott, *Pall Mall Gazette*, 84. Bernard Darwin, 'Country Life and Sport' in Young [ed.], *Early Victorian England* I.295. *Truth*, 14 Dec. 1882. Robert Lumsden, 'Trollope Started the Palliser Novels in Hertfordshire' in *Hertfordshire Countryside* XXIX (July 1974), 36-7. Mrs Frederick (later Lady) Pollock to Henry Taylor, 1 July 1869, Edward Dowden [ed.], *Correspondence of Henry Taylor* (1888), 296-8. William Glenn's diary, 22 Sep. 1863, Marks and Schatz [eds.], *Between North and South*, 103.

14. Pollock, *Personal Reminiscences* II.149. Richard H. Grossman and Andrew Wright, 'Anthony Trollope's Library', *Nineteenth Century Fiction* XXXI (June 1976), 48-64. A.T. to G. Smith, 18 July 1864, Smith/Murray MS. A.T. to ?, 18 Nov. 1864 in Hall [ed.], *Letters* II.1008.

15. Copies of A.T.'s correspondence on mourning note-paper have survived in his letters to George Smith, Trollope/Smith MS. The width of the border normally depended on the nearness of the relation and the time elapsed since the death. One moved from full to half and then to quarter mourning. In most cases the borders started at half an inch for full mourning. Trollope appears to have used only a relatively thin band but he never lost a wife or child. A.T. to Mrs Harriet Knower, 18 Feb. 1866, Parrish MS. Henry's purloined envelope survives in the Taylor Collection. The MS. of *Phineas Finn* is now in the N.Y.P.L. A.T., *North America*, 29.

16. Brackenbury, *Some Memories*, 50-1. A.T. to George Smith, 31 Mar. 1865, Smith/Murray MS. A.T. to Messrs. Gibbs, Bright & Co., 6 Aug. 1866, Parrish MS.

17. A.T., *North America*, 250. A.T. to Mrs Harriet Knower, 18 Feb. 1866, Parrish MS., A.T., *North America*, 487. A.T. to George Smith, 10 Feb. 1864, Smith/Murray MS. A.T. asked Smith when in Paris to get 'the biggest bottle you can conveniently do'; they cost about 12 Fr. Rosina Bulwer Lytton to Tom Trollope, 31 May ?, Trollope MS., U.C.L.A., Delta Collection, 712 8x.1 f 16.

18. A.T., *North America*, 25. Eleanor Smyth, *Sir Rowland Hill*, 277-8.

19. Rose later noted that in 1852-3 the boys were in school in Cheltenham. Records show that neither boy was ever at Cheltenham College. In 1854 the boys appeared to be attending school in Ireland where the Trollopes had returned in August 1853: A.T. told his mother that 'Harry came home from Cork today – with such a Cork brogue ... They must both go to some school here in the North after midsummer' (A.T. to F.T., 28 June 1854, Taylor MS.). By 1855, however, Rose noted, 'boys at school near Chester'. In 1856 F.T. sent Harry a sovereign for pocket money 'when he goes to his foreign school' (F.T. to A.T., 8 July 1856, Taylor MS. and R.T.'s Chronology, Trollope MS., Ill).

20. Thomas Stevens to Mr Gwynn, 10 Dec. 1859; Stevens to A.T., 17 Dec.

1859; Stevens to Arthur Powell, 15 Dec., 1859 q. in J.E.H. Blackie, *Bradfield: 1850-1975* (1976), 9. See above, p. 691 n. 41 (One wonders whether Trollope borrowed the Irish headmaster's name for Dr Gwynne, Master of Lazarus College, Oxford in *Barchester Towers*, written when the Trollopes were in Dublin.) George Eliot to François d'Albert-Durade, 6 Dec. 1860, Haight [ed.], *The George Eliot Letters* III.362 and G.H. Lewes to A.T., 15 Dec. 1860, Hall [ed.], *Letters*, I.134. Thomas Mozley, *Reminiscences* I.18-23 and G. Wakeling, *The Oxford Church Movement* (1895), 269 and *passim*. Arthur Leach [ed.], *Bradfield College* (1900), 5 and *passim*. A.T., 'Public Schools' in *F.R.*, 484.

21. T.T. to A.T., 27 July 1860, enclosing stamps for Henry, Trollope MS., Ill. To A.T. collecting stamps was an 'unalluring task' ('The Art Tourist' in *Travelling Sketches*, 67). Leach [ed.], *Bradfield College*, 116; *Bradfield College Register* (1924), 75, Nos. 214, 215 (information courtesy of F.E. Templer, M.A., Archivist of Bradfield College).

22. *Remember* I.490, 518. Can You Forgive Her? Work Sheet, Trollope Business MS. *Auto.*, 33, 25.

23. The Trollope MS. at the University of Illinois has A.T.'s copy of F.T.'s will, given to him some years before her death. Tom inherited almost everything she owned in Italy and some interest in property she held in Lincolnshire.

24. William Glenn's diary, 22 Sep. 1863, Marks and Schatz [eds.], *Between North and South*, 103. Tuckerman, *Personal Recollections* II.10-11.

25. The Enumerator's Book for the 1861 Census for the relevant Registration District of Whiston Grove, Moorgate, Rotherham shows that the Bland household consisted of Joseph and Isabella, aged 32 and 36 respectively. Four children are listed: Catherine, 9; William, 8; Florence Nightingale, 6; and Frederick, 1. (The names, however, are very difficult to read on the microfilm.) There was also one female servant. Rotherham Central Library, Ref. RG/9 3504 ed. 7.

26. A.T.'s autographed copy of 'On the Higher Education of Women' given to Florence Bland is now in the Parrish Collection. 10 Feb. 1882, F.E. Trollope MS.

27. q. in Sadleir, *Commentary*, 192-3. This comes from his short story, 'Christmas at Thompson Hall', published in the Christmas Number of the *Graphic* for 1876. For A.T. and Christmas see Richard Mullen, 'Happy Ghosts of Christmas Past' in *Illustrated London News*, Christmas Number, 1989.

28. A.T. to George Smith, 9 Aug. 1860, Smith/Murray MS. A.T., 'The Butcher' in [Sadleir, ed.], *London Tradesmen* (1927), 25-6.

29. A.T., *North America*, 154-5.

30. A.T., *North America*, 43. A.T. to George Smith, 2 July 1861, Trollope/Smith MS. A.T. to [Frederic] Chapman, 30 Sep. 1863, Parrish MS. A.T. asked Chapman to order and pay for some wine which he wanted to buy in London. Mrs Gaskell to Marianne Gaskell, 31 Aug. 1865, Chapple and Pollard [eds.], *Letters of Mrs Gaskell*, 580. George Smith also advanced her a £1,000 mortgage against future writings. It may be that Smith also helped the Trollopes in purchasing some glasses for Waltham House (A.T. to George Smith, 16 June 1861, Smith/Murray MS.) In the R.W. Chapman MS. someone noted, 'T. and his times ring with the sourness of *Gladstone* (claret).' MS Eng. Misc. c 927 f 47.

31. William Younger, *Gods, Men and Wine* (1966), 419.

32. The correspondence appeared in *The Times* in Jan. 1859 including a letter on 18 Jan. about the problems of entertaining on an income of £1,000 a year. A.T. mentions this correspondence in *The West Indies*, 44. Abraham Hayward, *The Art of Dining* (1852), 91.

33. A.T., *Thackeray*, 85.

34. A.T., 'The Butcher', Sadleir [ed.], *London Tradesmen*, 24. A.T. to Major John Bent, 26 May 1864, Parrish MS. A.T. to W.H. Russell, 29 May 1863, Taylor MS.

35. A.T. to George Smith, 8 Jan. 1861, q. in Sadleir, *Commentary*, 224. *Truth*, 14 Dec. 1882. W.L. Collins, 'The Autobiography of Anthony Trollope' in *Bl.M.* CXXXIV (Nov. 1883), 591.

36. William Banting, *Letter on Corpulence addressed to the Public* (4th edn, 1869), 8-10, 17. George Eliot to Charles Bray, 15 Dec. 1864, Haight [ed.], *The George Eliot Letters*, IV.170. *Truth*, 14 Dec. 1882.

37. [A.T.], 'My Tour in Holland', *C.M.* VI (Nov. 1862), 616-22. For this A.T. was paid £15 (A.T., Travelling Journal, Parrish MS.). For an example of the popular view that Dutchmen were fat see A.T., *The Kellys and the O'Kellys*, ch. XI. Among the reasons A.T. would have disliked the 'Phiz' illustrations for *Can You Forgive Her?* was the scene showing the heavily costumed bathers at Yarmouth.

38. Mrs Reginald Smith and Sir George Leveson Gower, 'They Knew Trollope' in *Trollopian* II (Sep. 1947), 117-18. Anon. [Jane Panton], *Leaves From a Life*, 203. Lady Amberley's diary, 8 Apr. 1867 in Bertrand and Patricia Russell [eds.], *The Amberley Papers* II.27. A.T. had been her guest before, in July 1866. She was the fourth daughter of Lord Stanley of Alderley, P.M.G. from Aug. 1860 to July 1866. Sadleir, *Commentary*, 331.

39. Gay, *Old Falmouth*, 216. Lord Houghton to A.T., 25 Dec. 1865, (Muriel Trollope transcript), Parrish MS. A.T. to Lord Houghton, 26 Dec. 1865, Hall [ed.], *Letters* I.321. Lady Rose Fane to the Countess of Westmorland, 17 Jan. 1866, Weigall MS., U1371 C17/32. Spedding's long devotion to writing about Sir Francis Bacon may well have inspired A.T.'s character, Sir Thomas Underwood in *Ralph the Heir*, who never completes his biography of Bacon. For Bishop Robert Bickersteth of Ripon see Bowen, *Protestant Crusade in Ireland, passim.*

40. *Daily Telegraph*, 12 May 1864. A.T. q. in K.J. Fielding [ed.], *The Speeches of Charles Dickens* (1960), 374. Laura Friswell, *In the Sixties and the Seventies* (1905), 169-70. She was the daughter of James Hain Friswell, a minor novelist 'whose literary output was miscellaneous and largely forgettable'. (John Sutherland, *The Longman Companion to Victorian Fiction* (1988), 235).

41. A.T. to George Smith, 4 Dec. 1862 q. in Sadleir, *Commentary*, 233. A.T. to George Smith, 21 Nov. 1862, Sadleir MS. A.T. to W.W. Glenn, 12 Feb. 1864, Hall [ed.], *Letters* I.253. George Leveson Gower, *Years of Content*, 70. 'Seven horses' may be somewhat of an exaggeration as it was recalled by Leveson Gower in old age and in the midst of the austerities of the Second World War.

42. A.T., *Hunting Sketches* (1865), 18. The 8 essays which make up this volume were first published in the *Pall Mall Gazette* between 9 Feb. and 20 Mar. 1865. Herman Merivale and Frank T. Marzials, *Life of W.M. Thackeray* (1891), 247. The authors must have had the information from A.T. who, curiously, had not used it in his *Thackeray*. Muriel Trollope, 'What I Was Told' in *Trollopian*, 230, gives Barney's surname as FitzPatrick while the

Enumerator's Report for the 1861 Census which included Waltham House listed a Bernard Smith, aged 63. A.T. to Beatrice Trollope, 8 June 1865, Booth [ed.], *Letters*, p. 267. Shirley Brooks q. in Arthur A. Adrian, *Mark Lemon: First Editor of Punch* (1966), 72. *Graphic*, 16 Dec. 1882

43. A.T. to W.W. Glenn, 10 Nov. 1863, Parrish MS. Marks and Schatz [eds], *Between North and South*, 117-18.

44. *Truth*, 14 Dec. 1882. The anonymous writer of this obituary specifically refers to *Can You Forgive Her?* as an example of A.T.'s using his hunting notes. R.F. Ball and Tresham Gilbey, *The Essex Foxhounds* (1896), 154. A.T. to George Smith, 31 Mar. 1865, Trollope/Smith MS. [A.T.], 'Hunting' in *St.P.* I (Mar. 1868), 677. The first half of this article was in the Nov. 1867 issue.

45. Mrs M. Evangeline Bradhurst, 'Anthony Trollope – The Hunting Man' in *Essex Review* XXXVIII (Oct. 1929), 185-9.

46. A.T. to George Smith, 4 Dec. 1862 in Sadleir, *Commentary*, 233. A.T. to Kate Field, 3 Dec. 1862, Kate Field MS., Boston Public Library, Vol. 7, No. 705. Marquess of Huntley, *Milestones* (1926), 270-1.

47. *Guardian*, 13 Dec. 1882. A.T., 'In the Hunting Field' in *Good Words* (Feb. 1879), 98-105. (The reference at the end is probably to Whyte-Melville.)

48. Ball & Gilbey, *The Essex Foxhounds*, 138-9, 146, 152-3. R.F. Ball, 'Hunting' in H.A. Doubleday and William Page et al. [eds], *The Victoria County History of Essex* (1903-1983, 10 vols), II.572. Bishop Wilberforce to the Rev. W. Bell, 9 Jan. 1854 in Pugh and Mason [eds], *Letter-Books of Samuel Wilberforce*, 295. Wilberforce pointed out that under Canon Law priests were forbidden to hunt. In the Bodleian Library there is a copy of the *Bucks. Gazette* of 27 Sep. 1845 in which some contemporary has ticked the name of every clergyman in the list of those licensed 'to destroy game'. There were 18 priests' names. For the debate over clerical fox-hunting see *S.R.*, 22 Oct. 1859. A.T., *Hunting Sketches*, 71.

49. A.T., 'Alice Dugdale' in *Why Frau Frohmann ...*, 391. A.T., *Hunting Sketches*, 30-1. A.T. to George Smith, 4 Dec. 1862 in Sadleir, *Commentary*, 233. A.T., *Australia and New Zealand* I.472.

50. A.T. to Major John Bent, 19 Mar. 1861, Parrish MS.

51. Anon., 'The Novels of Anthony Trollope', *Dublin Review* IX (Apr. 1883), 324. Skilton, *Anthony Trollope*, 20, 34. There is also a town called Lily Dale in upstate New York but I have been unable to ascertain if it is named after the fictional character. As it is the 'world's largest spiritualist center' and a hub of 'Thought Exchange' we should perhaps hope not.

52. *Athenaeum*, 26 Mar. 1864. Only part of this review is q. in Smalley [ed.], *Trollope: The Critical Heritage*, 194. *Reader*, 2 Apr. 1864. *Spectator*, 9 Apr. 1864. Italics are the magazine's. This episode occurs in ch. XIV.

53. Ernest Baker, *The History of the English Novel* (1937, 8 vols), VIII.141. The words occur in the Collect for All Conditions of Men in the Prayer Book's Prayers and Thanksgivings Upon Several Occasions. In his *Autobiography* (273-4) A.T. stated incorrectly that *The Last Chronicle* appeared monthly whereas it appeared weekly.

54. A.T. to G.H. Lewes and George Eliot, 27 Feb. 1872, writing from Melbourne, in Haight [ed.], *The George Eliot Letters* IX.42. *Academy*, 27 Oct. 1883, review of A.T., *Auto*.

55. *Auto.*, 275.

56. Cecilia Meetkerke, 'Anthony Trollope' in *Bl.M.* CXXXIII (Feb. 1883), 317.

Other recorded versions of the story occur in: A.T., 'A Walk in a Wood' in Mullen [ed.], *Malachi's Cove*, 128-9, written after the *Autobiography*; Augustus Hare, *The Story of My Life* (1896-1900, 6 vols), V.300: on 11 Jan. 1881 Hare heard the story from Mrs Duncan Stewart to whom A.T. had told it; Anon. [Jane Panton], *Leaves From a Life*, 203 where the two critics wish Mrs Proudie were dead; Walter Pollock, 'Anthony Trollope' in *Harper's New Monthly Magazine* LXVI (May 1883), 907-12. Last Chronicle of Barset Work Sheet, Trollope/Smith MS. The Sheet in the Trollope Business MS. (MS. Don. c 9 ff 161-2) is a copy of the original which for some reason is found in the letters to George Smith and his family. It may have been a gift.

57. A.T. to George Smith, 12 Aug. 1866, Trollope/Smith MS. The original title was 'The Story of a Cheque for £20, and of the Mischief Which It Did' (A.T. to George Smith, 24 June 1866, Sadleir MS.). By 21 Sep. 1866 the title had been changed to 'The Last of the Chronicles of Barset' and, probably on Smith's suggestion, it was then shortened to the final form. By this date proofs of the first six numbers had already been sent to A.T. who was returning them to Smith (A.T. to George Smith, 21 Sep. 1866, Trollope/Smith MS.). A.T. to ?, 15 June 1867, Ogden MS., No. 103.

58. Mrs Oliphant, 'Novels' in *Bl.M.* CII (Sep. 1867), 277. A.T., 'A Walk in a Wood' in Mullen [ed.], *Malachi's Cove*, 128-9. A.T. was criticised for 're-using' old characters in the *Dublin University Magazine* (XXXV, May 1850, 647-62), in two issues of the *S.R.* (Nos 44 and 75) and in the *London Review* (No. 97). Augustus Hare, *The Story of My Life* V.300.

59. Last Chronicle of Barset Work Sheet, Trollope/Smith MS. The distinction A.T. made is still not understood by some critics, even some of the best. Professor Sutherland, for example, says that 'for Trollope, clergymen tended to be Civil Servants in dog collars' (Sutherland, *The Longman Companion to Victorian Fiction*, 477).

60. *Spectator*, 13 July 1867. *Athenaeum*, 3 Aug. 1867.

61. A.T. to ?, 5 Apr. 1866, *Parrish MS. There was, in addition, a third writer named Frank Trollope who also wrote several three-deckers.

62. Norman Macleod to A.T., n.d. [Apr.? 1862], Trollope Business MS. On 5 Dec. 1862 new terms were agreed: six monthly parts to appear from 1 July 1863 to 1 Dec. 1863. Trollope Business MS. Rachel Ray Work Sheet, Trollope Business MS.

63. *Record*, 13 Apr. 1863. See also 20 Apr. 1863. This was the oldest Church newspaper, having been established in 1828 by, among others, J.H. Newman, then in his Evangelical phase.

64. A.T. to Alexander Strahan, 10 June 1863, Trollope Business MS. A.T. had already agreed with Chapman to print 1,500 copies of the book after serialisation; for this they would have paid him £500. On 10 June they agreed to pay £1,000 for 3,000 copies. Donald Macleod, 'Anthony Trollope', *Good Words* XXV (Apr. 1884), 252.

65. Miss Mackenzie Work Sheet, Trollope Business MS. Sir Edward Bulwer Lytton to A.T., 12 Dec. 1865, Parrish MS. This is a copy of the letter in Muriel Trollope's hand; the original MS is in the Taylor Collection. A.T. to E.R. Bulwer Lytton, 20 Dec. 1885, Hertfordshire Record Office. Lytton was A.T.'s M.P. at the time.

66. Mrs E.M. Ward [Isabel G. McAllister, ed.], *Memories of Ninety Years* (2nd ed., n.d.), 147.

67. F.O. Matthiessen and Kenneth B. Murdoch [eds], *The Notebooks of Henry James* (New York, 1961 edn), 10, 93.

68. Nina Balatka Work Sheet, Trollope Business MS. C.A. Macartney, *The Habsburg Empire 1790-1918* (1969), 516-18 for Jews in the Empire and especially, Prague. W.E.H. Lecky, *Democracy and Liberty* (1896, 2 vols), I.437-8 and II.155-7 for the condition of the Jews and relevant marriage laws.

69. *London Review*, 2 Mar. 1867.

70. J.B. to Joseph Langford, 10 Apr. 1866: Langford then sent the letter on to A.T., Trollope Business MS.

71. Laurence Oliphant q. in J.B. to Joseph Langford, 3 Apr. 1867 q. in Porter, *John Blackwood* III.361-2. Pollock, 'Anthony Trollope', *Harper's New Monthly Magazine*, 907-12. Escott, 232. 'The Great Unknown' had been the term used to describe Sir Walter Scott's anonymity (*Spectator*, 23 Mar. 1867). Mrs Oliphant to J.B., 25 May 1867, Blackwood MS., 4225 f 48. George Eliot had also used the famous bridge as a scene in *The Lifted Veil* which was also first published in *Bl.M.* In his work sheet for *Nina Balatka* A.T. had made a small sketch map apparently to show the relation of the bridge from which she attempted suicide to public buildings and her house (Trollope Business MS.).

72. J.B. to A.T., 14 Apr. 1866, Trollope Business MS. R.T. to J.B., 8 Sep. 1868 (from Inverness), Blackwood MS., 4241 ff 45-6. The ballad seems to have disappeared. Rose also wrote to Blackwood about her reaction to stories he published in his magazine. See her letter of 4 Dec. 1868, Blackwood MS., 4241 ff 47-8 q. in Porter, *John Blackwood* III.197-8.

73. George Eliot's journal, 28 Nov. 1860, Haight [ed.], *The George Eliot Letters* III.360. A.T. to Kate Field, 17 Jan. 1881, Hall [ed.], *Letters* II.892.

74. A.T., 'George H. Lewes' in *F.R.* XXV (n.s.) (Jan. 1879), 23.

75. *The Times*, 8 June 1989. The letter was part of a MS. auction noticed in the paper. *Auto.*, 109. George Eliot to A.T., 23 Oct. 1863, Parrish MS., AM 15542.

76. Frederic Harrison, *Studies in Early Victorian Literature* (1895), 325-6.

77. A.T. to G.H. Lewes, 7 Apr. 1861, Haight [ed.], *The George Eliot Letters* VIII.279. A.T., *North America*, 379.

Chapter 12

1. A.T., 'Public Schools', *F.R.*, 476. Collins, 'Autobiography of Anthony Trollope', *Bl.M.*, 591-2. A.T., *Clergymen of the Church of England*, 124-5.

2. A.T., *Palmerston*, 44. The phrase occurs in *The Prime Minister*, ch. LVI. Thornley, *Isaac Butt*, 19. Chilston, *W.H. Smith*, 48. Lord Stanley's journal, 16 Apr. 1853 in Vincent [ed.], *Disraeli, Derby and the Conservative Party*, 106.

3. *Auto.*, 291; A.T. to T.A.T., *Frances Trollope* I.248. A.T., *Palmerston*, 81. A.T. had praised Russell in his *Examiner* letters on Ireland. Lord Melbourne had frustrated A.T.'s father's hope for a London stipendiary magistracy.

4. *Auto.*, 291-5. This has the best summary.

5. See Managers' Minute Book, Harting School, for 1881 and 1882 and the Harting School Log Book, West Sussex Record Office, E98/1/1 and E98/12/1. See Ch. XV. A.T., Review of Mrs Sewell's *Rose of Cheriton*, *F.R.*, 254. A.T., *Tireless Traveler*, 96. A.T., Review of Peto's *Resources and Prosperity*, *F.R.*, 128.

6. Lord Moran's diary, 13 July 1953, Lord Moran, *Winston Churchill: The Struggle for Survival* (1966), 455-6. See also 470. Robert Tracy, *Trollope's Later*

Novels (Berkeley, 1978), 18. This is a particularly good summary of the series.

7. Lord Randolph Churchill to the Duke of Marlborough, 20 Aug. 1873 q. in Winston Spencer Churchill, *Lord Randolph Churchill* (1907, one-vol. edn), 33-4. See also 31-46 for the story of Lord Randolph's courtship and election.

8. John Halperin, 'The *Eustace Diamonds* and Politics' in Bareham [ed.], *Anthony Trollope*, 138-58.

9. *Truth*, 14 Dec. 1882. Charles Lever to J.B., 16 Sep. 1868, Blackwood MS. 4235 f 187. Bishop Magee of Peterborough to J.C. MacDonnell, 12 Mar. 1874, J.C. MacDonnell, *Life ... of William Connor Magee* (1896, 2 vols), II.2-3. Lord Robert Cecil to J.A. Shaw-Stewart, 17 Apr. 1867, Lady Gwendolen Cecil, *Life of Robert Marquis of Salisbury* (1921-32, 4 vols), I.262-4.

10. q. in Blake, *Disraeli*, 206. This, Lord Blake concludes, is the 'best statement for the prosecution' against Disraeli's novels. A.T. to ?, 17 Feb. 1877, Parrish MS.

11. Blake, *Disraeli*, 753.

12. Escott, 259, 264. Pope Hennessy, *Anthony Trollope*, 280. The real Pope Hennessy was described, unflatteringly, by Lord Kimberley in his Journal of 6 Sep. 1873 in Earl of Kimberley, [Ethel Drus, ed.], *A Journal of Events during the Gladstone Ministry 1868-1874* (1958), 42. If one must have an 'original' for Phineas Finn, Chichester Fortesque is a better candidate; this is what his wife thought. See Hewett, *Strawberry Fair*, 1. A.T.s friend and fellow Wykehamist, William Monsell, Irish MP 1847-74, PMG, eventually Lord Emly, also has some similarities to Finn.

13. *Daily Telegraph*, 4 Apr. 1869. A.T. anonymously praised Bright in 'The New Cabinet and What it Will Do for Us', *St.P.* III (Feb. 1869), 547-7. Some confusion derives from A.T.'s badly worded letter of 15 June 1876 to Mary Holmes (Parrish MS.) where he says that 'in former novels' Disraeli and Gladstone were 'models' for characters like Daubeny but adds that this only applied to their 'political tenets', not to their 'personal characteristics'. Characters like Palliser and Lady Glencora were 'pure creations'.

14. His elections at Bodmin in Cornwall may also have given A.T. some background for the Cornish election in *The Duke's Children* [ch. LV]. See Frederick Leveson Gower, *Bygone Years ...* (1905, 3rd edn.), 244-54 for Bodmin. This shows how accurately A.T. has captured local flavour. For A.T.'s praise of Forster see 'The New Cabinet', *St.P.*, 547-8. Hayward to Gladstone, 17 Oct. 1882, Gladstone MS., Add. MS. 44207 ff 206-8.

15. Strictly speaking, proxies were not abolished, but discontinued. See Mullen, 'The House of Lords', D. Phil. Thesis, 30-2. By this time not only was Baron Stockmar dead but when the Queen telegraphed to her eldest daughter in Germany she sent -- she did not ask for – advice. A.T. was friendly with two officials of the Privy Council, Sir Arthur Helps and Roden Noel. Helps assisted Queen Victoria in her literary projects. Both men would have been extremely discreet in anything they said about her.

16. *Remember* I.41, 9.

17. Trollope could not vote under 22 George III c. 41. See *The Standard Library Cyclopaedia* II.594. Maberly was appointed a Commissioner of Customs in 1834. Two years later he moved to the Post Office. A.T., 'The Civil Service', *F.R.*, 626. A.T., 'The Civil Service' in Parrish [ed.], *Four Lectures*, 24-5.

18. A.T. to the Rev. Charles Merivale, n.d. [Dec. 1860], Taylor MS. A.T. had

himself arranged the postal routes in the Diocese of St Davids and was presumably having a joke at its Bishop, Connop Thirlwall, the most liberal of the bishops and a Classical historian.

19. A.T., Travelling Journal, 1864-1869, Parrish MS. A.T.'s investments had grown enormously: whereas he was getting £605 10s in dividends in 1868, in 1864 he had only received £152 1s 6d. His annual income between 1864 and 1869 had more than doubled, from £3,169 2s 2d to £6,994 18s 1d. Of course his annual income from writing varied. A.T. to William Gay, 29 May 1863, Parrish MS.

20. Baines, *Forty Years* I.134-5. Edmund Yates, *Recollections and Experiences* (1884, 2 vols), II.223. Post 100/17: Rowland Hill's P.O. Journal, 30 Dec. 1864. After A.T.'s *Autobiography* had been published with its criticisms of Hill, his family published A.T.'s letter in *The Times* of 1 Dec. 1883 to imply that A.T. was, at best, inconsistent and, at worst, hypocritical for earlier praising Hill. He was neither. His letter was a courteous farewell to someone for whom he had a genuine if not total respect. His *Autobiography* simply showed that he had not liked Hill and that he did not think him quite as perfect as did his admirers.

21. A.T., 'The Civil Service' in Parrish [ed.], *Four Lectures*, 22.

22. ? to ? n.d. [ca. 1860], Parrish MS., AM 21646.

23. W.L. Collins to W.B., 30 Aug. 1883, Blackwood MS., 4443 ff 46-7. *Auto.*, 279. Lord Kimberley's diary, 26 July 1873 in Drus [ed.], *A Journal of Events*, 40. *The Annual Register* for 1873 has an account of the scandal (80) as does the *Spectator*, 26 July, 2 Aug. 1873. Kimberley was an acquaintance of A.T. Edmund Yates was Scudamore's assistant throughout this period. In turn Scudamore was a frequent contributor to the magazine, *Time*, edited by Yates (Blake, *Disraeli*, 495). In 1881 Sir William Harcourt told Gladstone he had acted for the submarine telegraph companies several years later when the G.P.O. took them over. He studied Scudamore's earlier deal and demanded the same generous treatment by the G.P.O. or else he 'threatened to show up Scudamore ... This so alarmed Scudamore that he immediately gave in, and so one bad bargain unintentionally let him in for another' (Lewis Harcourt's diary, 3 Nov. 1881, MS. Harcourt dep. 349 f 450).

24. [A.T.], 'The New Cabinet', *St.P.*, 544.

25. Post: England: 3174/68, A.T. to John Tilley, 8 July 1864. Post 101/6, John Tilley's Private Letter Book, 184: John Tilley to Lord Stanley, 9 July 1864. Post 30/185, E3174/1868, John Tilley to A.T. [13 July 1874]. Post 30/185, E3174/1868, A.T. to Lord Stanley, 18 July 1864.

26. Post 100/17: Rowland Hill's P.O. Journal, Nov. 1864. R.W.J., 'Early Post Office Days', *St. Martin's-Le-Grand* VI (July 1896), 295. Using a handkerchief to absorb excess energy seems to have been a trait of A.T. Seven years later someone else watched him gnaw at a silk pocket-handerchief, 'often biting it into holes' (Anon. q. in Mabel E. Wotton [ed.], *Word Portraits of Famous Writers* (1887), 313).

27. A.T. to Christopher Hodgson, 21 Oct. 1867, Hall [ed.], *Letters* I.396. *Auto.*, 277-8. Post: England: 3908/1870, 10 Oct. 1867. *Auto.*, 281. Tilley's official letter of 9 Oct. 1867 is on 280-1.

28. *Spectator*, 2 Nov. 1867. *The Times*, 2 Nov. 1867. Ironically, immediately above this article was one on the death of a Post Office official aboard the *Attrato* from yellow fever. This was the same ship that A.T. had sailed in for his

West Indian mission in 1858. For minstrels see A.M.W. Stirling, *The Richmond Papers* (1926), 184-5 and W.F. Monypenny and G.E. Buckle, *The Life of Benjamin Disraeli* (1929, rev. edn, 2 vols), II.286. *The Times*, 7 Feb. 1868.

29. A.T., 'George Henry Lewes', *F.R.*, 17. The Editor [A.T.], Introduction to *Saint Pauls*, *St.P.* I (Oct. 1867), 1-7. John Henry Newman, *The Scope and Nature of University Education* (1965 edn, 1st publ. 1873), xxxix. The lectures were delivered in 1852.

30. Lord Edmond Fitzmaurice, *The Life of ... Second Earl Granville* (1905, 2nd edn., 2 vols), I.487. *Pall Mall Gazette*, 19 Oct. 1865.

31. G.F. Browne, *The Recollections of a Bishop* (1915), 110-12. A.T., Travelling Journals, 1865, 1868, Parrish MS.

32. A.T., *Clergymen of the Church of England*, 42. Chadwick, *The Victorian Church* II.372. Henry Alford, 'Mr Trollope and the English Clergy', *C.R.* II (June 1866), 240-62. The Dean, editor of the *Contemporary*, did praise A.T.'s final essay, 'The Clergyman who Subscribes for Colenso'. A.T. did not mention Alford by name. H.L. Mencken, *The American Language* (4th edn., 1947), 27. A.T. had one of G.W. Moon's other books in his library.

33. *Guardian*, 6 June, 18 July, 25 July 1866. A.T. to George Smith, 21 July 1866, Smith/Murray MS. *Pall Mall Gazette*, 20, 24 July 1866. See Ruth ap Roberts's introduction to her edition of *Clergymen of the Church of England* (Leicester, 1974), 38-49 and Chadwick, *The Victorian Church* I.522.

34. A.T., 'On Anonymous Literature', *F.R.*, 497. *S.R.*, 25 Mar. 1865. See my forthcoming article in the *Contemporary Review* on 'Anthony Trollope and the *Fortnightly*'. The *Contemporary Review* now incorporates the *F.R.*

35. Espinasse, *Literary Recollections*, 294-5. Espinasse was editor of the *Bookman* in the 1890s. Escott, 173-81.

36. E.A. Freeman to James Bryce, 5 Nov. 1869, Bryce MS., MS. Bryce 5 ff 226-7. A.T., Travelling Journal, 1869, Parrish MS. Frederic Harrison, *Studies in Early Victorian Literature*, 222-3.

37. I completely disagree with Prof. Sutherland's view that Trollope 'was prepared to take advantage of Virtue's inexperience' (John Sutherland, 'Trollope and *St. Paul's* 1866-70' in Bareham [ed.], *Anthony Trollope*, 126). He asserts that A.T.'s warnings to Virtue were not sincere, but they were completely in character. Trollope was scrupulously honest in his business dealings. In 1869, when Edmund Routledge asked him to write a short story for *Routledge's Christmas Annual*, A.T. told him that he charged six guineas a page and that the story would cost £100. He ended, 'But I am sure it could not be worth that sum to you.' In the end Routledge accepted the fee and 'Christmas Day at Kirkby Cottage' was published in the 1870 *Annual* (A.T. to Edmund Routledge, 22 Apr. 1869, Hall [ed.] *Letters*, II.1010). In 1878 he told John Blackwood over negotiations about the timing of a serialised novel that he would accept a reduction in the number of serialised parts and in payment from £600 to £450 in order to get the novel started at an earlier date, to ensure republication as a three-volume novel as planned. Blackwood rejected his offer (A.T. to J.B., 14 Jan. 1878, Taylor MS.). There are numerous other examples of his honesty.

It was not unusual to name a periodical after its famous editor – John Cassell, William Tinsley, Eliza Cook and William Howitt – but none of these was of the level of the *Cornhill* which was Virtue's goal. The other choice for names, beside London place-names, was that of the publisher, such as *Macmillan's, Blackwood's* and so on.

38. [A.T.], Introduction to *St.P.*, 1-7. *Spectator*, 5 Oct. 1867. *I.L.N.*, 7 Nov. 1868.

39. *Auto*, 288. A.T., *Thackeray*, 54. Dobson recalled some of this in an interview with the *Morning Post* (17 Jan. 1914). Unfortunately his facts are rather unreliable. Stewart Ellis quoted a large portion of this interview in *Mainly Victorian* (n.d.), 213-14.

40. Jehoida Rhodes, 'A Sheffield Workman's Excursion to Paris and Back for Seventy Shillings' in *St.P.* I (Nov. 1867), 195, 200. This is the type of article one would normally have expected to see in papers like *Cassell's Illustrated Family Paper*. The identification of the author and the payment come from the Trollope Business MS. A.T. to Austin Dobson, 12 Jan. 1870, Hall [ed.], *Letters* I.492-3.

41. Edward Bradley, 'Some Recollections of Mr. Anthony Trollope' in the *Graphic*, 23 Dec. 1882. Joseph Langford to J.B., 8 Oct. 1868, Blackwood MS. 4235 f 89. A.T.'s view of Tupper is found in *North America*, 275, 495.

42. A.T. to James Virtue, 14 Dec. 1868, Parrish MS. The agreement of 13 Apr. 1869 is in the Trollope Business MS. James Virtue to A.T., 25 Jan. 1870, Trollope Business MS. A.T. contributed articles until June 1870. *Auto.*, 288.

43. Post: 101/10, John Tilley's Private Letter Book, 178-9, John Tilley to John Merivale, 8 Sep. 1868.

44. A.T., 'On the Best Means of Extending and Securing an International law of Copyright' in George W. Hastings [ed.], *Transactions of the National Association for the Promotion of Social Science*, 1866 (1867), 119-25. For the discussions see W.L. Clay [ed.], *Social Science, ... Journal and Sessional Proceedings ... for the Year 1866-7* (n.d.), 6. The Official Report refers to 'the valuable paper of Mr. Anthony Trollope'.

45. *The Times*, 7, 9, 31 Dec. 1867, 31 Jan. 1868 for the controversy over which shipping line to use. Post: 101/10, John Tilley's Private Letter Book, 8, John Tilley to Duke of Montrose, 12 Dec. 1867. Duke of Montrose to A.W. Randall, 24 Jan. 1868 in P.P., 1868-9, XXXIV, *Accounts and Papers: Postal Conventions (England and America), passim.*

46. [A.T.], 'On Sovereignty' in *St.P.* I (Oct. 1867), 88, 89.

47. Lee, *King Edward VII* I.197-8. Sir George Leveson Gower, *Mixed Grill* (1948), 14. *The Times*, 19 Mar. 1868. Benjamin Disraeli to Queen Victoria, 17 Mar. 1868 in G.E. Buckle [ed.], *The Letters of Queen Victoria Second Series ... 1862-1878* (1926, 2 vols), I.516.

48. George Dolby, *Charles Dickens as I Knew Him* (1885), 325. A.T., 'Charles Dickens' in Mullen [ed.], *Malachi's Cove*, 121.

49. See the Commons debate on 1 June 1869 in *Hansard* CXCVI, 1127-59, particularly the speech of Charles Seely, Liberal M.P. for Lincoln (cols 1135-6). *Dictionary of American Biography* IV.344-5. *Pall Mall Gazette*, 11 July 1868, from 'a well-known English author, now on a visit to the United States'.

50. A.T. to Kate Field, 18 June 1868, Sadleir, *Commentary*, 278-9. (The letter was incorrectly dated by Sadleir as 10 June.) *Boston Daily Evening Transcript*, 16 June 1868 q. in Booth [ed.], *Letters*, 380. The pointed 'minnie balls' were the most widely used ammunition during the war.

51. Post: 101/10, John Tilley's Private Letter Book, 124, 134, John Tilley to A.T., 1 July 1868. P.P., 1868-9, XXXIV, *Mail Contract (U.S.).* Winter was 1

Nov. to 31 Mar.; summer was 1 Apr. to 31 Oct. The treaty was signed by the Duke of Montrose on 18 June 1867 and in Washington by the President, the Postmaster General and the Secretary of State. (*The Statutes at Large and the Proclamations of the United States of America from December 1867 to March 1869* (Boston, 1869).) A.T. to Bulwer Lytton, 1 [?] Aug. 1868, Herts. Record Office, Lytton MS. DE/KC 35/54.

52. A.T. received £582 15s at five guineas a day; in addition the Post Office paid the cost of travel and his expenses. He stayed a total of 111 days, leaving England on 11 Apr. and returning on 26 July (A.T., Travelling Journals, Apr.-July, 1868, Parrish MS.) A.T. may have had some interest in the raiders as his library contained the *Memoirs* of Raphael Semmes, the greatest of their captains. [A.T.], 'The New Cabinet', *St.P.*, 546-7.

53. Charles Dickens to T.T., ? Dec. 1868 q. in *Remember* I.362. Escott, 35. J.A. Thomas, *The House of Commons* (Cardiff, 1939), 14. 'Men of Letters' at this time included academics (Walter Bagehot, 'The Advantages and Disadvantages of Becoming a Member of Parliament' in the *Economist*, 7 Feb. 1874 q. in Norman St John Stevas, *Walter Bagehot* (1959), 457). Cornelius O'Leary, *The Elimination of Corrupt Practices in British Elections, 1868-1911* (Oxford, 1962), 54.

54. H.B.W. Brand to Gladstone, 18 Aug. 1868, Gladstone MS., Add. MS. 44194 ff 97-8. *The Pall Mall Gazette* recalled the handwriting anecdote on 31 Oct. 1883. Thomas Sanders, *Report of Beverley*, Howell MS., Bishopsgate Institute, London. The Institute developed from the work of, among others, Trollope's friend, the Rev. William Rogers. See A.T. to William Frith, 10 Nov. 1876 q. in W.P. Frith, *My Autobiography and Reminiscences* III.386-7. For the way in which these Reports were compiled see H.J. Hanham, *Elections and Party Management* ... (1969 edn), 330-9. H.B.W. Brand, one of the Liberal whips, was standing in the Hertfordshire constituency which included Waltham Cross. In the event there were not 2,114 names on the new Register but 2,672.

55. [A.T.], 'The New Cabinet' in *St.P.*, 538. *Beverley Recorder*, 31 Oct. 1868.

56. *Auto.*, 299-300. It is not clear who said this. A.T. referred to 'my agent' which has led some, including Lance Tingay, in his excellent article on the election, to assume that A.T. meant his agent in Beverley, a local solicitor named W.S. Hind. This cannot be the case as A.T. says the man was an MP and very knowledgeable about Yorkshire. This would point to his friend W.E. Forster, MP for Bradford and a frequenter of the Cosmopolitan Club. His re-election for Bradford also led to a petition, but he kept his seat (Lance O. Tingay, 'Trollope and the Beverley Election', *Nineteenth Century Fiction* V (June 1950), 23-37). P.P., 1868-9, L, *Accounts and Papers: Elections* ..., 58-60. The official cost of the campaign to A.T., excluding money paid to local party officials, came to £244 1s 1½d which included £38 0s 11d, his half of the Returning Officer's expenses for the Liberals. The total cost for the two Liberal candidates was £488 2s 3d. For the Tories it was £483 5s 8d. The Returning Officer's costs were £152 3s 9d which included £5 for 'refreshments at poll booths'.

57. A.T., *Life of Cicero*, I.24. Henry Edwards to Benjamin Disraeli, 19 Feb. 1969, Disraeli MS., B/XXI/E/74.

58. For A.T.'s earlier attack on the Church of Ireland see his article, 'The Irish Church', *F.R.*, 15 Aug. 1865. *Beverley Recorder*, 31 Oct. 1868; *The Times*, 30 Oct. 1868. *The Times*, 3 Nov. 1868.

59. Anon., *The Stranger's Hand-Book to Beverley* (Beverley, n.d., 2nd rev. edn), 70. Escott, 250.

60. *Manchester Guardian*, 7 Nov. 1868. Henry Edwards to Benjamin Disraeli, 15 Dec. 1868, Disraeli MS., BX/XXI/E/73. Escott, 249-50.

61. *Beverley Recorder*, 14 Nov. 1868. G. Philip Brown, *Minster Life: Some Historical Themes of Beverley* (Beverley, n.d.), n.p. Escott claimed (250) that a group of local Tories told him that Trollope's appearance in hunting costume one day gave him additional support; this seems unlikely as A.T. clearly says in a letter of 21 Nov. 1868 to Mrs Anna Steele, 'I was out [hunting] today and yesterday for the first time [since the start of electioneering]' (Bradhurst, 'Anthony Trollope', *Essex Review*, 188-9. Mrs Bradhurst mis-dated this as 21 Nov. 1869). A.T.'s Travelling Journals do show he had one day of hunting in the first week on November when he was back at Waltham House after his initial speech in Beverley. *Beverley Guardian*, 14 Nov. 1868.

62. Arthur Pollard, *Trollope's Political Novels* (Hull, 1968), 8-9. This gives a good account of the feuding over bribery. John Markham, *The Beverley Arms: The Story of a Hotel* (Beverley, 1986), 12.

63. *The Times*, 11 Dec. 1868, which gives the notice of the Beverley petition. P.P., 1868-9, XLVIII, *Election Petitions*, 2-6. The evidence taken is found on 415-508; the index is on 511-23. O'Leary, *The Elimination of Corrupt Practices*, 50-2. Sir Harry claimed that Martin was influenced by his friend, George Leeman, a former Liberal MP for York, and also that the Beverley Town Clerk had done all he could for the Liberals (Sir Harry Edwards to Benjamin Disraeli, 19 Feb. 1869, Disraeli MS., B/XXI/E/74). P.P., 1868-9, VIII, *Report from the Select Committee on Parliamentary and Municipal Elections*, Appendix I … Beverley, 560-3. The judge held that over 800 electors were bribed by the Tories who had argued in self-defence that the Liberals were already doing it. *Hansard* CXCV, 9 Apr. 1869, 559-65.

64. *Auto.*, 305-6. A.T. q. in Escott, 250-1. q. in Brown, *Minster Life*, n.p.

Chapter 13

1. George Eliot to J.B., 18 Oct. 1867, Haight [ed.], *The George Eliot Letters* IV.392.

2. Ralph the Heir Work Sheet, Trollope Business MS.

3. *I.L.N.*, 7 Nov. 1868. Strahan also sold each month's instalments separately.

4. David Skilton, *Anthony Trollope* (42-5) is particularly illuminating on the critical response to Bozzle. *The Times*, 26 Aug. 1869. Mrs Oliphant to A.T., [? 7 March 1869], Hall [ed.] *Letters* I.470. Edward FitzGerald to W.F. Pollock, Mar. 1873, Terhune [eds], *The Letters of Edward FitzGerald* II.403.

5. *I.L.N.* wrote of Miss Stanbury as 'one of the finest pieces he has ever wrought … true to the very life' (7 Nov. 1868). For his part Tom hated the tunnel because 'those accursed enemies of the human race, the French' had taken off express trains once it was open thereby making the journey longer, not shorter (T.T. to Richard Bentley, 5 Nov. 1871 q. in Taylor, 'The Trollopes Write to Bentley' in Taylor, *Certain Small Works*, 132-3).

6. A.T. to Kate Field, 15 Apr. 1870, Booth [ed.], *Letters*, 447-9. Another American girl whom A.T. met in Washington, Constance Beale, was delighted when he promised to portray her in this novel. See Lansbury, *The Reasonable Man*, 43.

7. Henry James, 'Anthony Trollope' in Smalley [ed.], *Anthony Trollope: The Critical Heritage*, 543.

8. *The Times*, 26 Aug. 1869. [A.T.], 'The Uncontrolled Ruffianism of London', *St.P.* I (Jan. 1868), 424.

9. The Contagious Diseases Acts of 1869 allowed the police in 14 military and naval districts to force women suspected of being prostitutes to undergo medical inspections. Innocent women were sometimes detained and one such later killed herself. The Acts were repealed in 1886. A.T. to Mrs Anna Steele, 25 May 1870 q. in Bradhurst, 'Anthony Trollope – The Hunting Man' in *Essex Review*, 190. A.T., 'Formosa', *St.P.*, 75-80.

10. E.S. Dallas to A.T., 22 Mar. [1869], Trollope Business MS. *Auto.*, 326-8.

11. R.T.'s Chronology, Trollope MS., Ill.

12. H.M.T., 'son of Anthony surveyor of the G.P.O., and of Waltham Cross, Herts'. was admitted to Lincoln's Inn on 19 Nov. 1866, aged 20. Henry was called to the Bar on 7 June 1869 (*The Records of the Hon. Society of Lincoln's Inn, Admissions and Chapel Registers, 1800-1893* (1893, 3 vols), II.323 and Joseph Foster, *Men-at-the-Bar* (1885), 472). Matthiessen and Murdoch [eds], *The Notebooks of Henry James*, 10, 93. James seems to have confused Harry with Fred in this story.

13. Joseph Langford to John Blackwood, 30 Aug. 1869, Blackwood MS. 4248 f 141.

14. A.T. to Edward Chapman, 11 Jan. 1859, Parrish MS. Edward Chapman to A.T., 8 Feb. 1859, Trollope Business MS. For H.M.T.'s correspondence with *Blackwood's* see Blackwood MS. vols 4446 and 4452. Also see the Epilogue.

15. George Eliot to Sara Sophia Hennell, 2 Jan. 1871, Haight [ed.], *George Eliot Letters* V.132.

16. A.T. to Ivan Turgenev, 24 Apr. 1871, q. in Patrick Waddington, 'Turgenev and Trollope: Brief Crossings of Paths' in *Journal of the Australasian Universities Language and Literature Association* XLII (Nov. 1974), 200. George Leveson Gower thought the two men, who had met at a dinner party given by George Eliot on 23 April, resembled one another in appearance (*Years of Content*, 105). A.T. to James R. Fields, 22 Apr. 1871, Berg MS. Actually the terms for *North America* had been better as Trollope was offered a further £750 if the publishers wished to purchase his share of the copyright after two years. According to A.T.'s records he actually made £1,300 on his Australia book, only £50 more than on the American. *Truth*, 14 Dec. 1882.

17. Lady Anna Work Sheet, Trollope Business MS.

18. William Pollock, *Personal Remembrances* II.151. Golden Lion of Granpère Work Sheet: the book was written between 1 Sep. and 22 Oct. 1867 but not published till 1872. Trollope Business MS.

19. A.T. to Lady Wood, 21 June 1873, Parrish MS.

20. A.T. to Mrs Anna Steele, 25 May 1870 q. in Bradhurst, 'Anthony Trollope – The Hunting Man' in *Essex Review*, 190.

21. George Eliot, *Middlemarch*, 'Finale' [ch. LXXXVI]. Sadleir wrote: 'George Eliot herself told Mrs Lynn Linton that, but for Trollope, she could hardly have persevered with the extensive, patient study necessary to the completion of *Middlemarch* (*Commentary*, 367n).

22. *Spectator*, 10 May 1873. *The Times, The Annual Summaries for a Quarter of a Century* (1876), 363. The quote comes from the Summary for 1868. T.E. Kebbel [ed.], *Selected Speeches of ... the Earl of Beaconsfield* (1882, 2 vols), II.527-8.

23. Oscar Wilde, *Lady Windermere's Fan*, Act II, scene I. A.T., *The New Zealander*, 29. A.T., *The New Zealander*, 177.

24. A.T., *Australia and New Zealand*. Given the number of references to this book in the remainder of this chapter, all references to Australia and New Zealand and to the Trollopes' trip there may be assumed – unless otherwise noted – to come from this work. Oscar Wilde, *Lady Windermere's Fan*, Act I, scene I. A.T., 'The Present Condition of the Northern States' in Parrish [ed.], Four Lectures, 54-5. A.T., Review of *The Rose of Cheriton*, *F.R.*, 255.

25. A.T., *The West Indies*, 85. Chapman's Critique of Sadleir's *Commentary* (with reference to p. 169), Chapman MS., MS. Eng. Misc. c 927 f 221.

26. q. in *Australian Dictionary of Biography* VI.72-3. A.T. to G.W. Rusden, 29 Oct. 1871, Booth [ed.], *Letters*, 487. Lord Kimberley's diary, 2 Mar. 1872 in Drus [ed.], *A Journal of Events*, 29. Ethel Drus notes that Kimberley shared 'the widespread pessimism about the retention of the colonies' at the time (xvii). A.T. referred to Lord Kimberley in his letter of 29 Oct. as a man 'whom I like and respect'.

27. A.T., *The West Indies*, 110. A.T. to W.H. Archer, 27 July 1872, Hall [ed.], *Letters* II.567. Archer was Registrar of Titles for Victoria from 1868 to 1874. Asa Briggs, 'Trollope the Traveller' in Halperin [ed.], *Trollope Centenary Essays*, 25. *Australia and New Zealand* comes to 1,049 pages while *North America* comes to 962 including appendices.

28. Only seven cities in Britain outside London had a larger population: Birmingham, Edinburgh, Glasgow, Leeds, Liverpool, Manchester and Sheffield.

29. P.P., 1878, XXIV, *Minutes of Evidence taken before the Royal Commission on Copyright*, 54.

30. q. in 'Anthony Trollope', *Australian Dictionary of Biography* VI. 303-4. *Sydney Punch*, Oct. 1871 q. in Marcie Muir, *Anthony Trollope in Australia* (Adelaide, 1949), 27.

31. A.T. to G.W. Rusden, 29 Oct. 1871, Booth [ed.], *Letters*, 487.

32. Gordon Trollope, 'Trollope in Australia', *Sydney Bulletin*, 2 Apr. 1930. Gordon may well have been personally aware of Rose's attitude as he visited her in her widowhood (Gordon Trollope to R.T., 8 Mar. 1912, Trollope MS., Ill.).

33. R.H. Horne, 'Australia and New Zealand', *C.R.* XXII, (Oct. 1873), 705, 729. A.T. later paid great tribute to Horne's once famous poem, 'Orion', in his article on Longfellow (p. 395). A.T. to Henry Parkes, 2 July 1872, Booth [ed.], *Letters*, 498.

34. A.T. to George Eliot and G.H. Lewes, 27 Feb. 1872, Haight [ed.], *The George Eliot Letters* IX.42. A.T. to George Smith, 20 May 1872, Parrish MS. *Spectator*, 10 May 1873. Nevertheless the magazine felt the book to be important enough to give it a two-part review; the second part appeared on 17 May. The reviewer concluded that A.T. could have become the Tocqueville of Australia.

35. Trollope MS. Diary for July-Aug., 1872, Trollope MS., Ill. Lord Kilbracken, *Reminiscences* (1931), 2-9. Kilbracken was Godley's son.

36. A.H. Reed [ed.], *With Anthony Trollope in New Zealand* (Wellington, New Zealand, 1969), 47. Reed is quoting from E.M. Lovell-Smith, *Old Coaching Days* (Christ Church, New Zealand, 1931) who is assumed to have heard the story from Tommy Pope, A.T.'s coachman on this journey.

37. Miss Edith Hodgkinson q. in A.H. Reed [ed.], *With Anthony Trollope*, 43. She saw A.T. the day after his arrival in New Zealand.

38. *New Zealand Herald*, 19 Sep. 1872 q. in Reed [ed.], *With Anthony Trollope*, 140. *Southern Cross*, 3 Oct. 1872 q. in Reed [ed.], *With Anthony Trollope*, 145-8. A.T. was 'repeatedly and warmly cheered while he was speaking upon his colonial experiences'. This story was written for the *Masonic Magazine Christmas Number*, 1878 but was not republished in any of the collected editions of A.T.'s stories in his lifetime. A.T. q. in Alfred Domett's diary, 30 Sep. 1873, E.A. Horsman [ed.], *The Diary of Alfred Domett*, 1872-85 (1953), 107.

39. A.T. to J.E. Taylor, 24 Sep. 1868, Parrish MS. As Editor of *Saint Pauls* A.T. was refusing to consider an article on Darwin: 'I am afraid of the subject of Darwin. I am myself so ignorant on it, that I should fear to be in the position of editing a paper on the subject.' Re the lecture see A.T. to J.A. Pond q. in *Daily Southern Cross*, 17 Sep. 1872 q. in Reed [ed.], *With Anthony Trollope*, 141. Pond was the Hon. Secretary of the Auckland Mechanics' Institute. This letter to Pond is not included in either Booth's or Hall's edition of A.T.'s correspondence.

40. q. in *N.&Q.* CLXXXIX (14 July 1945), 14. The story does not mention that A.T. was being guided by a government official and accompanied by the two orderlies.

41. Gilbert Mair, *Reminiscences* q. in Reed [ed.], *With Anthony Trollope*, 149.

Chapter 14

1. A.T., Travelling Journals, Parrish MS. John Bateman, *The Great Landowners of Great Britain and Ireland* (Leicester, 1971 edn, 1st publ. 1883), xxiv-xxv. This is a most valuable source for anyone concerned with the quality of A.T. and other novelists' portrayal of Victorian upper-class and rural society. Vincent [ed.], *Disraeli, Derby and the Conservative Party*, xvii. Vincent shows how like Plantaganet Palliser Lord Stanley (later the 15th Earl of Derby) was. A.T. knew Stanley when he was Chairman of the R.L.F. Bateman, *The Great Landowners*, 499-500. *Spectator*, 30 Nov. 1872.

2. A.T. to ?, 20 Dec. 1872, Parrish MS. A.T. to Henry Irving, 24 Apr. 1873 q. in Laurence Irving, *Henry Irving: The Actor and His World* (1951), 232-3. This letter was sent from Montagu Square. Although A.T. had never met Irving he wrote to say how sorry he was that Irving had not been elected to the Garrick Club. He added, 'I am a member of the Committee, and should you consent to be put up again for nomination I will make it my business to give your candidature what little support may be in my power.' Irving did get in the next year. R.T. to J.B., 26 Mar. 1874, Blackwood MS., 4326 f 35.

3. A.T. to Mary Holmes, 3 Jan. 1873, Parrish MS.

4. The Way We Live Now Work Sheet, Trollope Business MS.

5. A.T. to G.W. Rusden, 3 Feb.1873, Hall [ed.], *Letters* II.580-1. For details of Tom's sale, said to be one of the most important art sales of the decade in Europe, and the problems relating to it, see F.E.T. to Isa Blagden, 19 May 1872, Charlotte Cushing MS., Box 14, Library of Congress, Washington, D.C. The sale catalogue was distributed in America as well as Europe.

6. Joseph Langford to J.B., 24 Dec. 1872, Blackwood MS., 4292 ff 155, 162-3. Langford and A.T. were both dinner guests of a fellow Garrick Club member, the artist Henry O'Neil, on 17 Dec. On that occasion he had found A.T. in 'great force'. O'Neil painted the portrait of A.T. that hangs in the Garrick Club. A.T. visited him in the Highlands in 1873 (Joseph Langford to J.B., Blackwood MS., 25 July 1873, Blackwood MS., 4306 f 56). G.H. Lewes's Diary, 1 Jan. 1873 in

Haight [ed.], *The George Eliot Letters* V.357. A.T. was very close to Sir Charles Taylor; a copy of *Australia and New Zealand* which A.T. inscribed to him is in the Taylor Collection at Princeton.

7. An Eye For An Eye Work Sheet, Trollope Business MS. The novel was not published until 1878 when it was serialised in the *Whitehall Review* between 24 Aug. and 1 Feb. 1879. It appeared as a two-volume novel in Jan. 1879.

8. Queen Victoria q. in Mullen and Munson, *Victoria*, 95. Lord Kimberley's Journal, 4 Mar. 1871, Drus [ed.], *Journal of Events*, 21. W.E. Gladstone q. in H.C.G. Matthew, *Gladstone* (Oxford, 1986), 210.

9. *The Times*, 11 Mar. 1873. It quoted the New York *Journal of Commerce* that the Senate had become 'the radiant centre of corruption'. Lady St. Helier, *Memories of Fifty Years* (1909), 127-35. Ralph Nevill [ed.], *Leaves from the Note-books of Lady Dorothy Nevill* (1910 edn), 28. Joseph Langford to J.B., 30 Aug. 1869, Blackwood MS., 4248 f 141. Langford was greatly involved in the publication of this novel and would almost certainly have mentioned it to A.T. when they met. For Langford's work with Lytton see Blackwood MS., vols 4292 and 4306.

10. MS. Don. c. 10 ff 13-21, Trollope Business MS. Sadleir prints some of these notes in Appendix IV of *Commentary*, 422-4. In the Notes, Madame Melmotte is a 'fat Jewess' whereas Melmotte is only described as the father of Marie and a 'great French swindler'. G.M. Young [G. Kitson Clark, ed.], *Portrait of An Age* (1977 annotated edn), 148, 336-7. A.T. also drew on other, current scandals such as the sale of the Pacific Railway in Canada to 'an American ring' (Earl of Dufferin to Queen Victoria, ? Nov. 1873 in Buckle [ed.], *Letters of Queen Victoria Second Series* II.287- 9).

11. In *The Prime Minister* [ch. I] the speculator, Ferdinand Lopez, who is also assumed but never stated to be a Jew, keeps a horse at Leighton Buzzard, then the site of a Rothschild home. James Pope Hennessy [ed.], *Baron Ferdinand de Rothschild's Livre d'Or* (Cambridge, The Roxburghe Club, 1957, priv. printed), 5. Mrs James de Rothschild, *The Rothschilds at Waddesdon Manor* (1979), 16-17. A.T. was never at Waddesdon as the land was only bought in 1874.

12. Escott, 280. Tracy, *Trollope's Later Novels*, 174. In *Sir Harry Hotspur of Humblethwaite* the Christian money-lender is far worse than his Jewish equivalent.

13. Trollope Business MS. A.T. to Mary Holmes, 26 Jan. 1875, Parrish MS. A.T. to Mary Holmes, 6 July 1874, Parrish MS. Only a few years before, in *Phineas Finn*, A.T. has Phineas say that, while as a Roman Catholic layman he never attacks Protestantism, he expects Roman Catholic priests to do so as a duty [ch. VI]. This was perfectly in character for the religious climate of the last third of the nineteenth century when the warfare between the Church of England and the Roman Catholics was very bitter. It was due to the strength of the converts in the R.C. church and the growing influence of the Oxford Movement, especially the Anglo-Catholics, in the C. of E.

14. Trollope Business MS. See Bampfield's obituary in *The Tablet*, 27 Jan. 1900. A.T. to Mary Holmes, 26 Jan. 1875, Parrish MS.

15. A.T., *Auto.*, 355. T.T. to Richard Bentley, 21 Dec. 1875, q. in Taylor, 'The Trollopes Write to Bentley' in Taylor, *Certain Small Works*, 138. A.T. to Mary Holmes, 6 July 1874, Parrish MS.

16. *Spectator*, 26 June 1875. *S.R.*, 17 July 1875. *Examiner*, 28 Aug. 1875. *The Times*, 24 Aug. 1875.

17. George Clinch, 'Marylebone and St. Pancras' in *Knight's Cyclopaedia of London* (1890), 65-6.

18. A.T. to G.W. Rusden, 3 Feb. 1873, Booth [ed.], *Letters*, 511. Frederick Pollock, *Personal Remembrances* II.139. *I.L.N.* 1 July 1882. A.T., 'A Walk in a Wood' in Mullen [ed.], *Malachi's Cove*, 130.

19. Tuckerman, *Personal Recollections* II.10-11.

20. Julia Cartwright's diary, 28 Jan. 1902, Angela Emanuel [ed.], *A Bright Remembrance: The Diaries of Julia Cartwright* (1989), 260. Escott, 306-7. Cecilia Meetkerke, 'Last Reminiscences', *Temple Bar*, 131. Mullen and Munson, *Victoria*, 113. *The Times*, 29 Jan. 1873. Tobacco consumption had been 13¾ oz in 1841; in 1871 it stood at 1 lb 5½ oz, an increase of 7¾ oz.

21. q. in R.P. Ashley, *Wilkie Collins* (1952), 105-6. Cecilia Meetkerke, 'Last Reminiscences', *Temple Bar*, 130-1.

22. Austin Dobson, *Morning Post*, 17 Jan. 1914 q. in Ellis [ed.], *Mainly Victorian*, 213-14. A photograph of the National Portrait Gallery's copy of the statuette may be found in Philip Collins, *Thackeray: Interviews and Recollections* (1983, 2 vols), in Vol. II between pp. 264 and 265. A.T., 'The Migration of a Library', *Pall Mall Gazette*, 17 Sep. 1880. A.T. to H.M.T., 23 July 1880, Taylor MS. George Smalley, 'English Men of Letters' q. in Terry [ed.], *Trollope: Interviews and Recollections*, 153. The article was first published in *McClure's Magazine* XX (Jan. 1903), 298-9.

23. *I.L.N.*, 16 Dec. 1882. *The Times*, 4 Mar. 1876.

24. *Auto.*, 158. A.T. to T.H.S. Escott, 14 Mar. 1880, Escott MS., Add. MS. 58749 ff 150-1. A.T. to H.M.T., 24 Apr. 1880, Taylor MS. A.T. did not specify which Renan book he was reading: it could have been his famous 'Life' of Jesus, or one of his other books: on the Christian church, on St Paul, on the Apostles or on the Evangelists: for a man who believed so little he wrote a great deal. A.T. agreed he was 'well informed' but too intent on 'teaching the world'.

25. Trollope MS., Ill. The list is now available as Appendix C in Hall [ed.], *Letters* II.1033-4.

26. *Remember* II.192-5. 14 Mar. 1874, F.E. Trollope MS. F.E.T. to R. Bentley, 26 Jan. 1873, Taylor MS. T.T. to H.M.T., *passim*, Trollope MS., Ill.

27. A list of his own books survives in the Trollope MS., Ill. *Auto.*, 353.

28. H.M.T. to Michael Sadleir, 24 Sep. 1925 q. in Sadleir, 'Trollope and Bacon's Essays', *Trollopian*, 22.

29. A.T. to G.H. Lewes and George Eliot, 27 Feb. 1872, Haight [ed.], *The George Eliot Letters* IX.42. C.E. Norton to J.R. Lowell, 22 Feb. 1869, M. Howe [ed.], *Letters of Charles Eliot Norton* (1913, 2 vols), I.321. A.T., *Catalogue of Books*, John Forster Bequest. Lance O. Tingay, 'Trollope's Library', *N.&Q.*, 28 Oct. 1950, 476-8.

30. A.T. to G.H. Lewes, 26 June 1864, Haight [ed.], *The Letters of George Eliot* VIII.319. Charles Dickens to A.T., 9 May 1867, Taylor MS. It was Bell who had proposed A.T. for the Garrick. A.T.'s tribute to him appears in the *Pall Mall Gazette* on 13 Apr. 1867. A.T. may not have known that Bell probably wrote the hostile notice on the 'constitutional coarseness' of Mrs Trollope's novels as he wrote some of the essays in the 1844 publication edited by R.H. Horne, *A New Spirit of the Age*, criticising her. Horne added a footnote signed 'H', objecting to some of the comments and insisting that 'Mrs. Trollope is clever', which strengthens the view that the critical essay was by Bell (R.H. Horne [ed.], *A New Spirit of the Age* (1907 edn), 169). Escott, 306-7. A.T. to

Frederic Chapman, 13 June 1867, Parrish MS. A.T., *Life of Cicero* II.376.

31. A.T. to Alfred Austin, 1 Nov. 1874, Parrish MS. William Allingham's diary, 8 Oct. 1864, Allingham and Radford [eds], *William Allingham: A Diary*, 106.

32. Anon., *N.&Q.*, 24 May 1941, 372-3. Cecilia Eckhardt, *Fanny Wright* (Cambridge, Mass., 1984), 67.

33. A.T. to ?, 15 Aug. 1878, Trollope MS., Yale.

34. Elizabeth Epperly, 'Trollope's Notes on Drama', *N.&Q.* XXXI/4 (n.s.) (Dec. 1984), 491-7. For a discussion of how A.T. made use of these plots see Geoffrey Harvey, *The Art of Anthony Trollope* (1980).

35. A.T. noted his ownership of the Shakespeare Society publications in his copy of J.O. Halliwell's *Dictionary of Old English Plays* (*N.&Q.*, 24 May 1941, 327-3). Booth, *Anthony Trollope*, 150-5: this is an excellent discussion of A.T. and his interest in plays. For A.T. and 'pathos' see Booth, *Anthony Trollope*, 212-16. A.T. to Walter Pollock, 10 Jan. 1876, Parrish MS.

36. A.T.'s copy of *Romola* is now in the Parrish Collection. Trollope Business MS. (MS. Don. c 10 ff 96-8). The fragment of A.T.'s projected history was published by Sadleir in *Commentary*, Appendix III, 420-1. For lectures A.T. only asked a fee of £15 (A.T. to W.H. Chamberlain, 28 Dec. 1869, *Parrish MS.).

37. Booth, 'Trollope on *Emma*: an Unpublished Note', *Nineteenth Century Fiction* IV (Dec. 1949), 245-7 and Booth, *Anthony Trollope*, 146-7. A.T.'s copy of *The Monk* is now in the Taylor Collection.

38. A.T., *Thackeray*, 156-7. John Morley to A.T., 27 Jan. 1879, Trollope Business MS. The questionnaire which A.T. sent to Anne Thackeray Ritchie is in the Trollope Business MS.

39. H.E. Manning to A.T., 3 June 1879, Parrish MS. A.T., *Thackeray*, 20-1. Skilton, *Anthony Trollope*, 34-5. David Skilton discovered this amusing source which was in the house organ of a Liverpool tobacco importer. A.T., *Thackeray*, 20. Hester Ritchie [ed.], *Letters of Anne Thackeray Ritchie* (1924), 233-4.

40. Winifred Gérin, *Anne Thackeray Ritchie: A Biography* (Oxford, 1981), 193. A.T. to R.T., [? Feb. 1882], Taylor MS. Anne Thackeray Ritchie, 'Thackeray and His Biographers', *I.L.N.*, 20 June 1891. The article was written on the occasion of the publication of the Merivale and Marzials biography. For his part Herman Merivale, who disliked A.T., was furious at his charges of idleness against Thackeray. See his *Life of Thackeray*, 25-7. See Robert A. Colby, 'Trollope as Thackerayan', *Dickens Studies Annual: Essays on Victorian Fiction* XI (1983), 262-73.

41. A.T.'s copy of the *Bibliothèque Latine-Française*, published 1825-8, was sold in March 1987 at the Bloomsbury Book Auction for £5,280 although it had been forecast to sell for £100 to £150. The higher price was due to the Trollope provenance and annotations. It is not listed in his 1874 catalogue (*The Times*, 27 Mar. 1987). A.T., *The Commentaries of Caesar* (1870), 5 (Vol. IV in the 'Ancient Classics for English Readers'). J.B. to John Delane, 21 Dec. 1869 in Porter, *John Blackwood* III.401-2. A.T. to J.B., 7 May 1870, Taylor MS.

42. A.T., *Commentaries of Caesar*, 4-5. A.T. to J.B., 16 Apr. 1870 in Porter, *John Blackwood* III.363. Mrs Oliphant to Miss Blackwood, 19 Oct. 1874, Blackwood MS., 4323 ff 177-8. Herman Merivale, *Bar, Stage, and Platform* (1902), 96. For his dislike of A.T. see 60. *Auto.*, 339.

43. A.T. to Mary Holmes, 27 Dec. 1876, Parrish MS.

44. A.T.'s 'Cicero as a Politician' appeared in the *F.R.* on 1 Apr. 1877; his 'Cicero as a Man of Letters' appeared on 1 Sep. 1877. George Meredith to John Morley, 31 Mar. 1877, W.M. Meredith [ed.], *Letters of George Meredith* (1912, 2 vols), I.272-3. A.T., *Life of Cicero* I.1-2, 38; II.216, 108, 205, 332, 77, 397, 299, 403.

45. A.T., *Life of Cicero* I.364; II.48. The MS. is in the Parrish Collection.

46. Escott, 290-1. W.L. Collins to W.B., 31 Jan. 1881, Blackwood MS., 4417 f 192. Collins may have had two copies of the book as the Taylor Collection has a copy inscribed 'From his affectionate friend, The Author'. Collins' review appeared in *Bl.M.* CXXIX (Feb. 1881), 211-28. A.T., *Life of Cicero* I.401.

47. *Guardian*, 13 Dec. 1882. Harold Laski [ed.], Introduction to *The Autobiography of John Stuart Mill* (1924, World's Classics edn), ix. A.T. to H.M.T., 19 Nov. 1877, Taylor MS.

48. The MS. of *An Autobiography* (Add. MS. Autogr. 42856) shows that A.T. spent time going over the text, correcting and inserting material. The manuscript is normally on display in the British Museum, next to the MS. of George Eliot's *Middlemarch*. The dating of *An Autobiography* is rather complex and I shall be dealing with that in my forthcoming edition of the book. A.T. to ?, 9 Oct. 1873, Parrish MS. A reference to the recipient's living in 'the square' implies it could be Sir Frederick or, more likely, Lady Pollock. The following day A.T. wrote to Joseph Langford that he was now 'permanently deaf in one ear' (Joseph Langford to J.B., 10 Oct. 1873, Blackwood MS., 4306 f 108).

49. A.T., 'Public Schools, *F.R.*, 479 q. in F.G. Blair, 'Trollope on Education: An Unpublished Address, 13 November 1873' in *Trollopian* I (Mar. 1947), 7.

50. R.T.'s reference to 'your own journal' meant his Travelling Journals, which contains a day-by-day account of where he went during his American visit of 1861-2. See H.M.T.'s correspondence with Blackwood regarding the publication of *An Autobiography* in 1883 in Blackwood MS., Vol. 4452 regarding Rose's 'transcripts'.

51. Frederick Leveson Gower, *Bygone Years*, 261.

52. *Remember* I.419. 22 Nov. 1887, F.E. Trollope MS.

53. On 21 Feb. 1866, George Ellerton, Lord John Russell's secretary, writes to A.T. giving him an appointment to see the Prime Minister (Parrish MS.). It is not clear why A.T. asked for the meeting: it could have been regarding an article for the *Pall Mall Gazette*, or A.T.'s crusade to abolish the restriction on civil servants' voting, or some other issue.

54. Part of the wrapper is bound with the MS. in the British Library. H.M.T. to W.B., 19 Jan. 1883, Blackwood MS., 4452 ff 30-3. H.M.T.'s draft of this letter is in the Parrish MS.

55. A.T.'s daily routine at Montagu Square comes from the *Guardian*, 13 Dec. 1882 and *Truth*, 14 Dec. 1882. Cecilia Meetkerke, 'Last Reminiscences of Anthony Trollope', *Temple Bar*, 30. See H.M.T. [?] in Charles Dickens Jnr. [ed.], *Dickens's Dictionary of Paris, 1882: An Unconventional Handbook*, 215. George Smalley, 'English Men of Letters' q. in Terry [ed.], *Trollope Interviews and Recollections*, 153.

56. Muriel Trollope, 'What I Was Told', *Trollopian*, 224. Mrs Oliphant to Frank Wilson, 5 May 1876, Coghill [ed.], *Autobiography and Letters of Mrs ... Oliphant*, 258.

57. A.T. to Kate Field, 5 July 1873, Hall [ed.], *Letters* II.591. Bernard de Voto [ed.], *Mark Twain in Eruption* (1940), 332-3.

58. [A.T.], 'Whist at our Club', *Bl.M.* CXXI (May 1877), 597-604. Courtney, *English Whist and English Whist Players*, 262. *The Times*, 10 Sep. 1880. *The Times*, 14 Dec. 1882.

59. [A.T.], 'Whist at our Club', *Bl.M., passim.* A.T. was particularly concerned that his authorship be kept secret when the article was included in *Blackwood's* next edition of their series, *Tales From Blackwood's* (Vol. XII) (A.T. to W.B., 24 Oct. 1879, Blackwood MS.) Arthur Jacobs, *Arthur Sullivan* (Oxford, 1986), 157.

60. A.T. to Mrs Anne Steele, 24 Dec. 1872 q. in Bradhurst, 'Anthony Trollope – The Hunting Man', *Essex Review*, 191. A.T. to the Rev. J.E. Sewell, 4 Dec. 1875, *Parrish MS. Part of this letter was included in Hall [ed.], *Letters* II.673 based on a sale catalogue as the letter was not then in the Parrish Collection. q. in *Auto.*, 352. A MS. copy of this adaptation of Horace, perhaps the original, written on Garrick Club note-paper is now in the Trollope MS., Ill.

61. *Truth*, 14 Dec. 1882.

62. R.L.F., Resolution of Sympathy of 14 Dec. 1882 sent to R.T. A large selection of correspondence showing A.T.'s work and concern for fellow authors through the R.L.F. may be found in Hall [ed.], *Letters* I.494ff; II.707ff. A.T. to W.P. Frith, 9 Apr. 74, *Parrish MS. For A.T.'s other work for Mrs Brooks see Hall [ed.], *Letters* II.610-29.

63. A.T. to ?, 22 July 1878, *Parrish. The lady was presumably applying for a Civil List pension on her father's merits as a writer. Disraeli did help the R.L.F.: see Disraeli MS., A/IV/M/79-104. A.W. Kinglake to A.T., 31 Mar. 1878, Parrish MS.

64. Anon., 'Mr. Anthony Trollope's Novels', *Edinburgh Review* CLXVI (Oct. 1877), 455-8. Allen, *The English Novel*, 261.

65. Escott, 52. Frith, *My Autobiography* I.441. A.T. had long been in the custom of attending Royal Academy exhibits. He would tell Millais that such visits were among the things he most missed on his second visit to Australia (A.T. to J.E. Millais, 30 June 1875, Millais MS. MA 1485).

66. This inscribed copy is now in the Parrish Collection.

67. q. in Porter, *John Blackwood* III.175. George Eliot attempted the same with her novel *Daniel Deronda*. See *Publishers' Circular*, 1 Feb. 1876. A.T. found that book 'trying', 'all wrong in art'; Eliot was 'striving for effects which she does not produce' (A.T. to Mary Holmes, 27 May 1876, Parrish MS.).

68. A.T. to J.B., 9 Sep. 1879, Taylor MS. Sadleir, *Bibliography*, 301. William Tinsley, *Random Recollections of an Old Publisher* (1900, 2 vols), I.136. *Athenaeum*, 16 June 1877.

69. Frederick Waddy, *Cartoon Portraits*, 68-70. Waddy wrote that A.T.'s 'one fault' was that 'he has, perhaps, too much to parsons given up what was meant for mankind'. The next caricature after A.T. was Mudie. *Vanity Fair's* comment which implied that A.T. wrote too much was 'amusing' to the biographer of the man who wrote it as he, Thomas Bowles, was a writer who 'turned out' an enormous amount of words (Leonard Naylor, *The Irrepressible Victorian: The Story of Thomas Gibson Bowles* (1965), 22). [A.T.], 'The New Cabinet', *St.P.*, 550. A.T.'s Travelling Journals for 1868 show he had an appointment with Goschen in March. The year before A.T. had asked him to write an article on the 1867 Reform Bill, 'The Leap in the Dark', for the first issues of *St.P.* 'Young Apollo' wound up a Tory and the Chancellor of Oxford.

I am grateful to Mr Oliver Everett of the Royal Archives, Windsor for his help in trying to track down an account of this dinner by the Princess Royal, but none survives in the Royal Archives, Windsor. T.H.S. Escott, 'A Novelist of the Day', *Time* I (Aug. 1879), 632. Ironically the new magazine was edited by A.T.'s old rival, Yates.

70. A.T. q. on 14 Mar. 1874, F.E. Trollope MS. The original letter from A.T. to F.E. Trollope seems to have disappeared. Sutherland, *Victorian Novelists and Publishers*, 189. Mitchell and Deane, *Abstract of British Historical Statistics*, 350.

71. For Richard Hutton's importance as a reviewer of A.T. see Skilton, *Anthony Trollope*, 100-25. *I.L.N.*, 8 July 1876.

72. Anon., *Harper's* LI (Oct. 1875), 754 and Anon., *The Nation* XX-XXI (Sep. 1875), 153-4 in Smalley [ed.], *Trollope: The Critical Heritage*, 413-14. *The Way We Live Now* had been published serially in the US in the traditionally Unitarian magazine *Old and New*, but it ceased publication before the series had ended. The idea of Trollope as 'historian' has also been made by the great Walpole scholar W.H. Lewis, when he compared A.T. to Horace Walpole (Wilmarth Lewis, *Collector's Progress* (1952), 26).

73. See the Rev. Charles Berthoud to A.T., 28 Dec. 1878, Trollope MS., Ill. Berthoud was the translator. A.T. was annoyed at the change of title. (A.T. to the Rev. Charles Berthoud, 8 Jan. 1879, Trollope MS., Ill.) A.T. later mellowed and allowed Berthoud to translate *The Vicar of Bullhampton*. John Hiram's legacy of 1434 had established 'Hiram's Hospital' in Barchester. A.N. Wilson, *Tolstoy* (1988), 274. The article is dated 15/27 Jan. 1874. The translation is in the Trollope MS., Ill. Of A.T.'s novels, 31 were available in nineteenth-century Russian translations. See Bradford Booth and K. Harper, 'Russian Translations of Nineteenth Century Fiction', *Nineteenth Century Fiction* VIII (Dec. 1953), 188-97. For the *Academy* see Skilton, *Anthony Trollope*, 33-4.

74. *Guardian*, 13 Dec. 1882.

75. *Publishers' Circular*, 16 June 1876. On 15 Apr. 1876 it had attacked Thomas Hardy and other, newer writers, on this same score. [Anon.], 'Is the Novel Moribund?', *Tinsley's Magazine* XXX (1882), 389-90. The author could well have been Tinsley himself as the views accord with those in his *Random Recollections* and in a letter to *The Times* of 4 Dec. 1871.

76. J.B. to W.B., 22 May 1876, Blackwood MS., 4341 f 214. The letter was written four days before J.B.'s own appearance before the Commission.

77. An extract of a letter from A.T. to John Hollingshead, who had been involved in the production of *Shilly Shally*, was presented as evidence to the Commission. P.P., *Royal Commission on Copyright*, 347.

78. P.P., *Royal Commission on Copyright, passim*. There were a total of 5,898 questions put to witnesses.

79. Alfred Domett's diary, 28 June 1876, Horsman [ed.], *The Diary of Alfred Domett*, 172-3. The Colonial Institute was a centre of imperialist views. Locker-Lampson, *My Confidences*, 332-6.

80. Julian Hawthorne, *Confessions and Criticisms* (Boston, Mass., 1887), 140-3. Hawthorne, *Shapes That Pass*, 226-7.

81. 17 July 1874, F.E. Trollope MS. A.T., *How the 'Mastiffs' Went to Iceland*, ch. V.

82. A.T. to *The Times*, 24 Sep. 1874. *S.R.*, 26 Sep. 1874. A.T. to *The Times*, 28 Sep., 27 Nov., 10 Dec. 1874.

83. A.T., *South Africa* I.103. A.T., 'A Walk in a Wood' in Mullen [ed.], *Malachi's Cove*, 137. [A.T.], 'Whist at our club', *Bl.M.*, 598.

Chapter 15

1. F.E. Trollope MS., 4 Mar. 1875.

2. R.T.'s Chronology, Trollope MS., Ill. A.T. to R.T., 10 Mar. 1875, Parrish MS. According to her sister-in-law, Rose disliked Berlin: see F.E. Trollope MS., 14 Oct. 1883. A.T. to R.T., 17 Mar. 1875, Parrish MS.

3. A.T., *The Tireless Traveler*, 49. Hereafter all quotations relating to his 1875 articles are from this edition.

4. A.T. to J.E. Millais, 30 June 1875, Millais MS., MA 1485. Trollope MS., Ill. A.T. also agreed to guarantee an overdraft facility for Fred the following year. A.T. to H.M.T., n.d. [1876], Trollope MS., Ill.

5. Carleton Green, 'Trollope in Hawaii', *Trollopian* III (Mar. 1949), 301. To Mr Green, A.T.'s comments on Hawaii are 'notable for their ineptitude'. Henry James to his family, 31 Oct. 1875 and to his mother, 31 Jan. 1877, Leon Edel [ed.], *Henry James Letters* (1974-84, 4 vols), I. 486 and II.94. Henry James, 'Anthony Trollope' in Smalley [ed.], *Anthony Trollope: The Critical Heritage*, 526.

6. A.T. to Mrs Katherine Bronson, 12 Dec. 1876, B.L. photocopy, RP 1368. (The MS. of the letter is in the Parrish MS. I am not sure whether A.T. wrote the American 'cuss' or the standard 'curse'. Hall opts for 'curse' (*Letters* II.699).) F.E. Trollope MS., 19 Dec. 1876. List of Readings Aloud, Trollope MS., Ill. It is unlikely that A.T. could have reached London in time to read it before 31 Oct.

7. *The Times*, 8 Dec. 1876 said it had never known a gathering that had such wide support. The intellectual world was divided: George Eliot, for instance, did not share the passion of 'prophetic souls'. R.T. Shannon, *Gladstone and the Bulgarian Agitation of 1876* (1963), 216-26. *I.L.N.*, 16 Dec. 1876. A.T. to J.W. Probyn, 8 Dec. 1876, Castle Howard Archives, J22/92.

8. *Report of Proceedings of the National Conference at St James's Hall* (1876), 19-21. Florence Hardy, *Life of Thomas Hardy*, 112-13. A.T. to J.W. Probyn [?], 11 Dec. 1876, Castle Howard Archives, J22/92. Queen Victoria to Lord Beaconsfield, 18 Dec. 1876, Buckle [ed.], *Letters of Queen Victoria Second Series* II.504. Disraeli to Lady Bradfield, 16 Dec. 1876, Marquess of Zetland [ed.], *The Letters of Disraeli to Lady Bradford and Lady Chesterfield* (1929, 2 vols), II.93. A.T. to Octavian Blewitt, 24 Feb. 1880, Hall [ed.], *Letters* II.858.

9. Some claim that A.T. drew on the strange marriage of the heir to Lord Stanley of Alderley (the former PMG) to a Mohammedan. I think there is a greater resemblance to the case of the Marquess Townsend in the 1840s. Mullen, 'House of Lords', Oxford D. Phil. Thesis, 314

10. *The Times*, 24 Apr. 1815. A.T. [Sadleir, ed.], *London Tradesmen*, 96. A.T. to ?, 4 Apr. 1879, Adrian H. Joline, *Meditations of an Autograph Collector* (New York, 1902), 224.

11. J.L. Motley to A.T., 29 June 1876, Parrish MS. Motley had met A.T. in 1867 and had liked him 'very much; he was excessively friendly' (J.L. Motley to his wife, 17 July 1867, Curtis [ed.], *Correspondence of ... Motley* II.265). Memorandum of Agreement, 10 Feb. 1875, Bentley MS., 46618 ff 330-1. Taylor, 'The Manuscript of Trollope's *The American Senator*', *Bibliographical Society of America*, 126.

12. A.T. to Mary Holmes, 27 Dec. 1876, Parrish MS. For similar sentiments see fragment of letter, A.T. to T.T., n.d. [1876?], Parrish MS. A.T. to George Smith, 24 June 1866 (fragment of letter), Sadleir MS.

13. H.M.T. to J.B., 13 Nov. 1877, passing on A.T.'s wish to call the novel Mrs. John Caldigate, Blackwood MS. 4367.

14. A.T.'s Will, Somerset House, 2. The Will was dated 29 Oct. 1878. Probate was granted 23 Jan. 1883. Florence's copy of *Cousin Henry* is now in the Taylor Collection. I am grateful to Mrs Nancy Coffin for her help in deciphering the erased message. A.T. to Alexander Ireland, 10 Dec. 1878, Parrish MS. R.T.'s bound set of proofs of *Cousin Henry* is now in the Taylor Collection.

15. *Publishers' Circular*, 15 Apr. 1876. Locker-Lampson, *My Confidences*, 333. The B.L. Catalogue lists 95 works of fiction by Mrs Oliphant.

16. Escott, 300. A.T. to Sir Charles Trollope, 25 Aug. 1881, Hall [ed.], *Letters* II.920. Cecilia Meetkerke, 'Last Reminiscences', *Temple Bar*, 130. A.T. to Alfred Austin, 17 Jan. 1875, Taylor MS.

17. Review of *The American Senator*, *The Nation*, 23 Aug. 1877 in Smalley [ed.], *Trollope: The Critical Heritage*, 433. The MS. of this novel was all in A.T.'s hand. Cecilia Meetkerke, 'Last Reminiscences', *Temple Bar*, 129-30. A.T. to W.B., 30 Sep. 1881, Blackwood MS. 4427 f 69. I cannot be positive the initials are A.T.'s but they appear to be so.

18. H.M.T. to W.B., 1883, Blackwood MS. 4452. Perhaps the excessively cautious Henry did not want Blackwood to think that others had seen the novel; he may also have wanted to explain why it was not in A.T.'s hand.

19. *Spectator*, 12 June 1880. John H. Hagan, 'The Duke's Children: Trollope's Psychological Masterpiece', *Nineteenth Century Fiction* XIII (June 1958), 9.

20. See Andrew Wright, 'Trollope Revises Trollope' in Halperin [ed.], *Trollope Centenary Essays*, 121-9. *Spectator*, 12 June 1880. *Nation*, 19 Aug. 1880 in Smalley [ed.], *Trollope: The Critical Heritage*, 473.

21. *Publishers' Circular*, 2 Feb. 1880. In his correspondence with H.M.T., T.T. often refers to the Chapman and Hall shares as does H.M.T. in his letters well into the 1920s. Trollope MS., Ill., and Trollope MS., U.C.L.A. A.T. to R.P. Harding, 13 Aug. 1880 (copy), Trollope Business MS.

22. Lewis Harcourt diary, 4 Nov. 1881, MS. Harcourt dep. 349 f 153.

23. Gilbert Mair q. in Reed, *Anthony Trollope in New Zealand*, 149. For Glenn see p. 407 above. A.T., *Australia and New Zealand* II.499-500.

24. A.T., *Auto.*, 39-40.

25. A.T. to Sir Theophilus Shepstone, 30 Sep. 1877 q. in J.H. Davidson [ed.], *South Africa* (Cape Town, 1973), 473. Robert Robinson and John Gallagher, *Africa and the Victorians* (1961), 56.

26. A.T. to H.M.T., 2 July 1877, Taylor MS. W.L. Collins to W.B., 5 June and 30 Aug. 1883, Blackwood MS. 4443 ff 41-2, 46-7. H.M.T. received £60 for this book but had to wait two years for payment. H.M.T. to W.B., 3 Feb. 1881, Blackwood MS. 4427 f 79. W.L. Collins clearly sided with Mrs Oliphant and had little regard for H.M.T.'s abilities. Henry's notebook is now in the Parrish Collection. Likewise Fanny Trollope had used one of her son's – Henry's – notebooks to work on her American book. A.T. to H.M.T., 24 Oct. 1877, Taylor MS.

27. South Africa Work Sheet, Trollope Business MS. A.T. to H.M.T., 3 Sep. 1877, Taylor MS.

28. *Domestic Manners*, 348-9.

29. A.T. to H.M.T., 15 Oct. 1877, Taylor MS.

30. *Domestic Manners*, 309-10.

31. Mrs Frances Colenso to Mrs Katherine Lyell, 15 July 1878, Rees [ed.], *Letters from Natal*, 337. A.T., Lecture on the Zulus, Parrish MS. In *Australia and New Zealand* A.T. makes the same point: 'The desire for accumulating property, combined with the industry necessary for doing so, is perhaps of all qualifications for civilization the most essential' (II.419).

32. *Truth*, 14 Dec. 1882. A.T. to J.B., 9 Jan. 1878, Blackwood MS. J.B. to W.B., 25 Feb. 1878, Blackwood MS. 4369 f 14.

33. A.T. to Mrs Ellen Robinson, 6 June 1878, Parrish MS. The two lines A.T. misquoted come from the first stanza of Bishop Heber's famous hymn: 'From Greenland's icy mountains/ From India's coral strand/ Where Afric's sunny fountains/ Roll down their golden sand/ From many an ancient river/ From many a palmy plain ...' J.W. Mackail, *The Life of William Morris* (1950 edn), 247-82, 303-8. A.T. had read Lord Dufferin's book.

34. Mrs Blackburn, 'To Iceland', *Good Words*, June-Sep. 1879, 559.

35. Gladstone read A.T.'s article in the *F.R.* on 7 Sep. 1878. He returned to the question of Iceland in 1886. See Gladstone to James Bryce, 29 May 1886, MS. Bryce 10 ff 60-1.

36. A.T. to George Eliot, 13 Aug. 1878, Parrish MS. A.T. to H.M.T., 7 Sep. 1879, Taylor MS.

37. A.T. to John Tilley, 18 Apr. 1878, Trollope MS., U.C.L.A. Alice Thomas Ellis, Introduction to *Ayala's Angel* (The Trollope Society edn, 1989), x.

38. Marion Fay Work Sheet, Trollope Business MS. This includes a small sketch map which A.T. drew of a street with the 'Duke of Edinburgh' public house on the corner. George Leveson Gower, *Years of Content*, 64-7.

39. R.T. to [?] B., 13 Apr. 1879, Blackwood MS. 4400 ff 41-2. Booth, *Anthony Trollope*, 239. *Remember* I.248.

40. W.B. to A.T., 7 Apr. 1880, copy, Blackwood MS. *I.L.N.*, 9 Oct. 1880. *S.R.*, 22 Jan. 1881.

41. A.T. to Charles Lewes, 24 Dec. 1880, Trollope MS., Yale.

42. Caroline Grosvenor and Lord Stuart of Wortley, *The First Lady Wharncliffe* ... (1927, 2 vols), I.xiii. F.T. to A.T., 17 Dec. 1854, Taylor MS. Walpurga, Lady Paget, *The Linings of Life* (n.d., 2 vols), I.267. 15 Oct. 1879, F.E. Trollope MS. A.T. to H.M.T., 25 July 1881, Taylor MS. A.T. to Lady Pollock, 14 Aug. 1881, Parrish MS.

43. For details of this see Sadleir, *Bibliography*, 245-8. The Bodleian has a bound proof-copy of *Small House at Allington* that H.M.T. gave to Lady Barrett-Lennard showing minor changes in punctuation and running heads. This comment was made regarding *The Warden*, ch. XVI. A.T. also noted 'the changes which years have made' at the hurried chanting at Westminster Abbey that had so distressed Mr Harding. A.T., Introduction to *The Chronicles of Barsetshire* (1878, 8 vols), I.v-vi. A.T. to Henry Howard, 26 Feb. 1881, Taylor MS. A.T. to Henry Howard, 29 Aug. 1881, Booth [ed.], *Letters*, 836. Howard was the former Governor of Rhode Island.

44. Sadleir, *Bibliography*, 314. This was the 4th Duke of Newcastle, not to be confused with the 5th whom A.T. praised in the 1850s. Walpole, *Anthony Trollope*, 122.

45. A.T. [Sadleir, ed.], *London Tradesmen*, 83.

46. A.T. to H.M.T., 27 June 1880, Taylor MS. A.T. had inherited at least some of these shares from his mother; in the late 1860s he was getting £150 in dividends from this bank where he also had his current account. A.T., Travelling Journals for 1860s and Fanny Trollope's Will, Trollope MS., Ill. A.T. to H.M.T., 29 Aug. 1879, Taylor MS.

47. A.T. to H.M.T., 9 May 1880, Taylor MS. A.T. to H.M.T., 13 June 1880, Taylor MS. A.T. to H.M.T., 14 June 1880, Taylor MS.

48. A.T., 'The Migration of a Library', *Pall Mall Gazette*. A.T. to H.M.T., 23 July 1880, Taylor MS.

49. Cecilia Meetkerke, 'Last Reminiscences', *Temple Bar*, 133. Escott, 299-300. A.T.'s reference to 'five acres and a cow' is based on the famous programme of land reform advocated by Jesse Collings, Liberal M.P. Anon., 'Anthony Trollope and Harting', Sussex Record Office, M.P. 2698. A.T. to H.M.T., 23 July 1880, Taylor MS.

50. A.T., *North America*, 50. W.H. Hudson q. in D.C.R. Francombe, *The Parish Church of St. Mary & St. Gabriel, Harting: A Guide & History* (n.d. [1983]). A.T. to T.T., n.d. [late spring, 1880], fragment, Parrish MS.

51. A.T. to T.T., n.d. [late spring, 1880), fragment, Parrish MS. The Managers Minute Book for Harting School, p. 121, E98/1/1 and the School Log Book E98/12/1, West Sussex Record Office. I am grateful to the County Archivist, Mrs. Patricia Gill, for her help with this. H.D. Gordon, *Guardian*, 11 Dec. 1882.

52. A.T. to T.T., n.d. [?May-June, 1880], fragment, Parrish MS. A.T. to H.M.T., 21 Dec. 1880, Taylor MS.

53. *Pall Mall Gazette*, 9 Dec. 1882.

54. Tracy, *Trollope's Later Novels*, 285-94, is particularly valuable on this; see also David Skilton, 'The Fixed Period: Anthony Trollope's Novel of 1980', *Studies in the Literary Imagination* VI (1973), 39-50.

55. W. Lucas Collins to W.B., 30 Sep. 1881, Blackwood MS., 4417 f 209. W. Lucas Collins to W.B., 6 Jan. 1881, Blackwood MS., 4417 f 184. W.L. Collins to W.B., 9 Jan. 1882, Blackwood MS., 4430 f 119. Collins, 'The Autobiography of Anthony Trollope', *Bl.M.*, 594.

56. W. Lucas Collins to W.B., 19 Feb. 1881, Blackwood MS., 4417 f 200. H.M.T. to W.B., 8 Mar. 1881, Blackwood MS. 4427 ff 83-4. For H.M.T.'s later recollection see H.M.T. to Geoffrey Robinson, 10 Mar. 1921, Trollope MS., U.C.L.A. James Bryce, *Studies in Contemporary Biography* (1903), 120. E.A. Freeman to James Bryce, 10 Apr. 1881, MS. Bryce 7 ff 11-12. A.T. and Freeman both disliked J.A. Froude's writing on Roman history. A.T.'s copy of Froude's *Caesar* (1879), now in the Houghton Library at Harvard, is heavily annotated with comments attacking Froude's conclusions. See 'Trollope on Froude's Caesar by Bradford Booth in *Trollopian* I (Mar. 1946), 33-47. Froude had been annoyed with A.T.'s writing on South Africa about which he was also writing. To Freeman Froude was 'a queer creature' (E.A. Freeman to James Bryce, 9 May 1879, MS Bryce 6 ff 200-2). E.A. Freeman, 'Anthony Trollope', *Macmillan's Magazine* XLVII (Jan. 1883), 236-40.

57. Easter Monday, 1881, F.E. Trollope MS. A.T. to H.M.T., [Apr. 1881], Taylor MS.

58. Mr Scarborough's Family Work Sheet, Trollope Business MS.

59. Andrew Wright, 'Trollope Revises Trollope' in Halperin [ed.], *Trollope Centenary Essays*, 129-32. The MS. is in the Taylor Collection. Oliver Edwards,

'Trollope's Singletons', *The Times*, 25 Mar. 1965.

60. An Old Man's Love Work Sheet, Trollope Business MS.

61. The Taylor Collection has the MS. of *Palmerston* and a copy with corrections by A.T. although none was incorporated in the published edn.

62. A.T., *North America*, 182-3

63. A.T. to Gladstone, 2 May 1880 and Gladstone's instructions to his secretary for a reply written on the back of A.T.'s letter on 3 May 1880, Gladstone MS., Add. MS. 44464 ff 34-5. W.E. Gladstone's diary, 3 May 1880 shows that he replied to A.T. between an interview with Lord Monson and his departure for Windsor, M.R.D. Foot and H.C.G. Matthew [eds], *The Gladstone Diaries* (1968–, 9 vols), IX.513. A.T., 'Mr Gladstone's Irish Land Bill' *St.P.* VI (Mar. 1870), 622. A.T., *Palmerston*, 123.

64. Abraham Hayward to Gladstone, 17 Oct. 1882, Gladstone MS. 44207 ff 206-8. The copy of *Palmerston* which A.T. gave Hayward is in the Parrish Collection. *Athenaeum*, 9 Dec. 1882. The rector of Harting also definitely described A.T. as 'a Liberal' (*Guardian*, 11 Dec. 1882).

65. Lord Acton to Mary Gladstone, 2 Feb. 1881, Mary Gladstone MS., Add. MS. 46239 ff 67-8. A.T. to T.T., [Aug. 1880?], fragment, Parrish MS. A.T., *Life of Cicero* II.105n.

66. A.T., *Palmerston*, 104. A.T., 'The Real State of Ireland', *Examiner*, 18 June 1850.

67. Davitt q. in A.G. Gardiner, *The Life of Sir William Harcourt* (1923, 2 vols), I.425. A.T. to H.M.T., 19 Feb. 1882, Taylor MS.

68. Lady Frederick Cavendish's diary, 18 May 1869, John Bailey [ed.], *The Diary of Lady Frederick Cavendish* (1927, 2 vols), II.71.

69. Lewis Harcourt's diary, 13, 18 May 1882, MS. Harcourt dep. 351 ff 27-32, f54. A.T. to R.T., 16 May [1882], Parrish. A.T. to R.T., 23 May 1882, Parrish MS. A.T. to R.T., 20 May 1882, Parrish MS. A.T. to R.T., 1 June 1882, Parrish MS. A.T. to R.T., 4 June 1882, Parrish MS.

70. Florence Bland's will at Somerset House. A.T., *Palmerston*, 97-8.

71. A.T. to R.T., 14 Aug. 1882, Parrish MS. A.T. to R.T., 18 Aug. 1882, Parrish MS. A.T. to R.T., 18 Aug. 1882, Parrish MS. A.T. to R.T., 28 Aug. 1882, Parrish MS.

72. *Truth*, 14 Dec. 1882. Cecilia Meetkerke, 'Last Reminiscences', *Temple Bar*, 134. A.T. to T.T. [before July, 1881], Parrish MS. A.T. to ?, 29 Nov. 1881, Parrish MS. By 'novellettes' A.T. meant 'tales' or short stories. A.T. to H.M.T., 15 Jan. 1882, Taylor MS. Cecilia Meetkerke, 'Last Reminiscences', *Temple Bar*, 134. W.L. Collins to W.B., 19 June 1882, Blackwood MS., 4430 f 138.

73. A.T. to H.M.T., 4 Jan. 1882, Taylor MS.

74. Fr.T. to R.T., 8 Sep. 1882, Trollope MS., Ill. 10 Dec. 1882, F.E. Trollope MS.

75. A.T. to H.M.T., 9 Aug. 1882, Taylor MS.

76. E.A. Freeman to James Bryce, 1 Oct. 1882, Bryce MS., Vol. 7, f 50. A.T. to E.A. Freeman, [Oct. 1882], Parrish MS. *Guardian*, 11 Dec. 1882. A.T., *Travelling Sketches*, 108. A.T., *The New Zealander*, 151.

77. A.T. to R.T., 24 Oct. 1882, Parrish MS.

78. A.T. to Newman, 27 Oct. 1882 (Muriel Trollope's copy), Parrish MS. Newman to A.T., 28 Oct. 1882, Dessain et al. [eds], *Letters ... of John Henry Newman* XXXI.97-8.

79. E.A. Freeman, 'Anthony Trollope', *Macmillan's Magazine*, 240. E.S.P.

Haynes, *The Lawyer: A Conversation Piece* (1951), 57. The lady in question was Haynes's mother. For the weather see the *Graphic*, 11 Nov. 1882.

80. *I.L.N.*, 1 Dec. 1882. J.E. Millais to W.H. Russell, 5 Dec. 1882 q. in J.B. Atkins, *The Life of Sir William Howard Russell* (1911, 2 vols), II.316-17. *Guardian*, 6 Dec. 1882.

81. 10 Dec. 1882, F.E. Trollope MS. T.T. to H.M.T., 12 Dec. 1882. A.T.'s grave, No. 28529, may be found in Square 138.

Epilogue

1. J.E. Millais to R.T., 25 Dec. 1882. Secretary of the Athenaeum to R.T., 22 Jan. 1883. Lord John Manners on behalf of R.L.F. to R.T., 22 Dec. 1882. Fr.T. to R.T. 18 Jan. 1883. All in Trollope MS., Ill.

2. *I.L.N.* 16 Dec. 1882. *Academy*, 16 Dec. 1882. *Guardian*, 13 Dec. 1882. *Graphic*, 9 Dec. 1882. *The Times*, 7 Dec. 1882. *Spectator*, 9 Dec. 1882. *Truth*, 14 Dec. 1882. For A.T.'s detestation of the magazine see Hall [ed.], *Letters* II.706. *Pall Mall Gazette*, 7 Dec. 1882. *I.L.N.*, 16 Dec. 1882. F. Scott Fitzgerald, 'Dice, Brassknuckles and Guitar' in Matthew J. Bruccoli [ed.] *The Last Uncollected Stories of F. Scott Fitzgerald* (1979, 2 vols), I.64. *Princeton Review* XII (July 1883). *Harper's Weekly*, 16 Dec. 1882. R.H. Hutton, *Spectator*, 16 Dec. 1882. Henry James, 'Anthony Trollope', Smalley [ed.], *Trollope: The Critical Heritage*, 525-45. H.M.T. to W.B., 1883, Blackwood MS., 4452 ff 106-7.

3. A.T.'s will is at Somerset House. This is based on a large correspondence in the Blackwood MS. between H.M.T. and W.B. and between Joseph Langford, W.L. Collins and W.B. (Vols 4452, 4446, 4443) and on correspondence between H.M.T. and W.B. at Princeton, especially the letter from W.B. to H.M.T. of 3 May 1883.

4. W.B. to H.M.T., 3 May 1883 (see above). *Spectator*, 20 Oct. 1883; this same issue has the advertisement on p. 1360 quoting the *Daily Telegraph* comment. *Pall Mall Gazette*, 15 Oct. 1883. H.M.T. to W.B., 27 Nov., 1883, Blackwood MS. 4452 f 121-2. H.M.T. was particularly objecting to a comment in the *Christian World*. [James Payn], 'Some Literary Recollections', *Cornhill* XLIV (Jan. 1884), 53.

5. 15 Oct. 1883, 23 Nov. 1892, F.E. Trollope MS. *Athenaeum*, 19 Nov. 1892. Even as a man in his late 70s, Tom told one editor he still had the 'will for work'. T.A.T. to Henry Allon, 2 Mar. 1886, Allon MS., no fol., Dr Williams's Library, London.

6. Anon., 'Anthony Trollope and Harting', Sussex Record Office. H.M.T. to W.B., 16 Nov 1884, Blackwood MS., 4465 f 93. A.T. to T.T., 28 June 1854, Taylor MS. 28 June 1884, F.E. Trollope MS. R.T.'s hotel was almost certainly Schloss Lebenberg where the *pension* rate was 7 krone, 20 heller or 6s a day (Karl Baedeker, *Austria-Hungary* (1905), 122). John Macmillan Brown, *Memoirs* (Christchurch, N.Z. 1974), 190. This was before 1893. R.T. wrote from Kitzbühel to Bentley giving permision for F.E. Trollope to reproduce a painting of F.T. in her biography (R.T. to Richard Bentley, 9 Aug. 1895, Bentley MS., B.L., Add. MS. 46626 f 37).

7. R.T. to W.B., 18 Aug 1889, 20 Nov. 1889, Blackwood MS., 4553 f 142, 4624 ff 184-5.

8. A.J. Balfour to Alfred Austin, 2 Dec. 1896, 4 Aug. 1897 (almost certainly

dictated to his secretary Jack Sandars), Trollope MS., Yale. (There is no reference to this correspondence in the relevant section of the Sandars MS. in the Bodleian Library.) *Annual Register for 1897* (1898), 37. Elizabeth Dickens, Dickens's daughter-in-law, received the same amount. R.T.'s Will, Somerset House. All was left to H.M.T. Henry's estate was proved at £6,734 18s 2d, Somerset House.

9. 14 Aug. 1904, F.E. Trollope MS. [Sir] Gordon Trollope to R.T., 8 Mar. 1912, Trollope MS., Ill. Muriel Trollope, 'What I Was Told', *Trollopian, passim. The Times*, 30 May 1917, 26 Mar. 1926. Rose Trollope is buried in Minchinhampton churchyard under a large beech. Her grave, which is also that of Henry, is marked by a Celtic cross.

10. *The Times*, 30 May 1917. Arnold Bennett, 'Trollope's Methods', in *Books and Persons*, 109 (originally published on 23 Sep. 1909). Siegfried Sassoon to Sir Hamo Thornycroft, 19 Feb. 1918 q. in Elfrida Manning, *Marble & Bronze* (1982), 177. Austen Chamberlain, *Down the Years* (1935), 245. J.M. Barrie to ? Pixton, 26 Feb. 1927, Viola Meynell [ed.], *The Letters of J.M. Barrie* (1942), 211. Noël Coward's diary, 13 Feb. 1966, Graham Payne and Sheridan Morley [eds.], *The Noël Coward Diaries* (1982), 624. Trollope seems to have a particular appeal to insomniacs, e.g. A.E. Housman. See Henry Maas [ed.], *The Letters of A.E. Housman* (1971), 436.

11. *The Times Literary Supplement*, 22 Mar. 1941. *The Times Literary Supplement*, 22 Oct. 1944. W. Somerset Maugham, 'Reading and Writing and You' and Appendix II [Reading List Accompanying 'Reading ...'], John Whitehead [ed.], *A Traveller in Romance: Uncollected Writings of W. Somerset Maugham, 1901-64* (1984 edn), 203, 272. *Time Magazine* 20 Aug. 1945. Lord Moran's diary, 19 Aug. 1953, Moran, *Churchill*, 482. Beth Fallon, 'Barchester ... Now, that's my cup of Chronicles' in *New York Daily News*, 26 Oct. 1984. George Saintsbury, 'Trollope Revisited', *Essays and Studies*, 66.

Index

The Index is divided in two parts. The first lists references to Trollope's works and fictional characters. For his books significant references have been divided into three categories: I references to the writing, publishing and immediate reactions to that work; II other references to that book; III quotations. In the list of fictional characters, people are cited by the name or title normally used for them. In the second part, the General Index, dates are given for Trollope's family, friends, business associates and some important contemporaries. The dates of office of Postmasters General and Secretaries of the Post Office are also given. For abbreviations see page 670.

WORKS

Novels

736

Travel Books

Collected Essays, Lectures and Other Works

Short Stories

Fictional Characters

GENERAL